C.S.E. PHYSICS

By the same Author

HART-DAVIS EDUCATIONAL

Principles of Physics (O-level)

Introductory Physics Books 1 and 2 (*with M. V. Detheridge*)

Fundamentals of Physics

Exercises in Ordinary Level Physics

SI Units: An Introduction for A-level

Revising Basic Physics

* * *

Advanced Level Physics (SI) (*with P. Parker*)

Advanced Level Practical Physics (SI) (*with J. Ogborn*)

Scholarship Physics (SI)

Principles of Atomic Physics and Electronics (SI)

Optics, Sound, Waves (SI)

Mechanics and Properties of Matter (SI)

An Introduction to the Mathematics of Physics (SI) (*with J. H. Avery*)

Graded Exercises in A-Level Physics (SI)

Test Papers in A-Level Physics (SI)

Revision Notes in A-Level Physics (SI)

Book 1. Mechanics, Electricity, Atomic Physics

Book 2. Optics, Waves, Sound, Heat, Properties of Matter

Electronics and Radio (*with H. I. Humphreys*)

Elementary Physics, Books 1 and 2 (*with A. F. Abbott*)

Elementary Physics

(complete edition)

Revision Book in O-Level Physics (SI)

Solutions to O-Level Physics Questions (SI)

Solutions to A-Level Physics Questions (SI)

Heinemann Educational

Electricity (*Advanced Level Course–SI*)

Edward Arnold

Heat (SI)

(for A-level students)

Blackie

The cover photograph shows the refraction of light through a cut diamond. The light has been broken up to show many of the different colours of the spectrum. (Courtesy of De Beers.)

C.S.E. PHYSICS

M. NELKON
M.Sc., F.Inst.P., A.K.C.
Formerly Head of the Science Department,
William Ellis School, London

HART-DAVIS EDUCATIONAL

Granada Publishing Limited
Hart-Davis Educational Limited
First published in Great Britain 1969 by Chatto & Windus Educational Limited
Second edition 1971
Reprinted 1972
Third edition published 1975 by Hart-Davis Educational Limited
Frogmore, St. Albans, Hertfordshire
Reprinted 1976, 1977, 1978

ISBN 0 247 12843 0

Printed in Great Britain by
Fletcher & Son Ltd, Norwich

THIRD EDITION

In this edition an introduction to static electricity has been added in a new chapter in response to requests by teachers, and a new section containing shorter revision questions has now been included before the revision papers at the end of the book. The opportunity has also been taken to revise further the units used in the mechanics, fluids and heat sections of the book, to revise parts of the text and to add recent examination questions to the exercises.

The author is indebted to many teachers for helpful comments, particularly B. Brierley, Hewarth Grange Comprehensive School, Gateshead, and J. Watson, University College School, London. He is also grateful to the examining boards listed overleaf for continued use of past examination questions.

PREFACE TO FIRST EDITION

FOLLOWING the wide acceptance of *Fundamentals of Physics* for G.C.E. O level, I have made an adaptation of the book for C.S.E. pupils, to cover the C.S.E. examinations of the various boards. The main part of the text deals with the basic principles to this standard of mechanics, fluids, heat, optics and electricity. Some applied physics, to a C.S.E. level, has also been included in the text and comprises electronics, optical instruments, heat engines and sound recording and reproduction.

To assist in co-ordinating theory and practical, a number of suggested class experiments have been given at the end of most chapters. They cover basic principles. Brief instructions only have been listed, and supplementary details are necessary depending on the apparatus or supplies available. I am indebted to pupils of the Somerset School, Tottenham, London, for checking many experiments. Experienced teachers will no doubt have many other experiments for class use.

It is not possible to comment on more than a few points borne in mind in the presentation. Modern ideas, and modern apparatus, have been introduced where possible. Molecules and simple experiments concerning molecules have been discussed first, for example, and molecular explanations of common phenomena in heat have been given. In electricity, electrical carriers such as electrons and ions have been introduced at the outset. The ripple tank has been used to show the effects of waves, and waves have been discussed before optics and sound. Electromagnetic waves have been given prominence in view of their importance. In dynamics, ticker-timers and ticker-tapes can provide a practical introduction to motion. Numerous applications are discussed, such as electrical supply in the home, heat insulation, the transistor receiver and the camera. Finally, in view of their scientific importance and their future use in industry, metric and S.I. units have been introduced in some of the essential numerical work.

I am very much indebted to the following for their generous assistance at various stages in compiling the work: S. S. Alexander, senior science master, Woodhouse School, London; R. Yarrow, senior physics master, and A. L. Mann, Somerset School, London; Mrs R. Mann, head of the science department, Creighton School, London; F. L. Hodgkins, senior science master, Edgware School, London; A. C. Covell, senior science master, and M. W. Poole, Forest Hill School, London; R. P. T. Hills, St John's College, Cambridge; T. E. Walton, William Ellis School, London; R. Pollard, Electrical Development Association; Mrs M. E. Pickford, Electrical Association for Women.

I am also indebted to the following C.S.E. Examining Boards for permission to reproduce questions set in past examinations: Metropolitan Regional (*M*); Middlesex Regional (*Mx*); East Anglian (*E.A.*); South-Eastern Regional (*S.E.*); North-Western Secondary Schools (*N.W.*); Associated Lancashire Schools (*L*); West Midland (*W.Md.*); Southern Regional (*S*).

ACKNOWLEDGEMENTS

THE author and publishers are also indebted to the following firms and organizations, whose names are given alphabetically for convenience, for supplying photographs and information in connection with the following plates:

Air Ministry, 19A; Associated Press Ltd, 3B; AVO Ltd, 30B; Barr and Stroud Ltd, 18B; British Gypsum Ltd, 10B; Central Electricity Generating Board, 31A, B, 33H; Central Office of Information, 21D; Chloride Storage Co., 25B, C; Dunlop Ltd, 7D, E; Elliott-Automation, 30A, 32C; English Electric Ltd, 32F; Ferranti Ltd, 27A; Fibreglass Ltd, 10A; Frigidaire, 12A; Goodman's Loudspeakers Ltd, 23C; Griffin and George Ltd, 14A, B, C, D; Hovercraft Development Ltd, 7C; Iliffe Books Ltd, *Autocar* Handbook (Singham), 13.12; Leybold-Heraeus GMB & Co. (Photo: Dr H. W. Franke), 32B; Mallory Batteries, 25A; Mullard Ltd, 23B, 32A, D, E, G, I; 3M Company, 23A; National Physical Laboratory, 3A, 7F, G; Negretti and Zambra Ltd, 6B; W. B. Nicolson (Glasgow) Ltd, 7A, 33A; P. and O. Orient Lines, 21A; Panax Equipment Ltd, 33C; Plessey Ltd, 23D, 29A, B, C; Polaroid Ltd, 21B; Royal Festival Hall, 22C; Royal Free Hospital (Photo: Walter Nurnberg), 33B; Science Museum (P. M. S. Blackett), 33F; Scientific Teaching Apparatus, Ltd (Leybold), 2A; G. Severn, Esq., 7B; Shell Co., 22A, B; Smiths Industries Ltd, 10C, D; I. D. B. Taylor, Esq., 9A, B; U.K. Atomic Energy Authority, 18A, 33D, G, I; Unilever Ltd, 2B; U.S. Information Services, 7H, 32H; Vauxhall Ltd, 6A, 13A, B, 33E.

CONTENTS

SI UNITS

The following is a list of some quantities and their units used in the book.

Quantity	*Definition or Formula*	*Unit*
mass		kilogramme (kg)
length		metre (m)
time		second (s)

MECHANICS, FLUIDS

velocity	displacement/time	metre/second (m/s)
acceleration[1]	velocity change/time	m/s^2
force	mass × acceleration	newton (N)
work[2]	force × distance	joule (J)
power	work per second	watt (W)
moment	force × perp. distance	newton metre (N m)
density[3]	mass per unit volume	kg/m^3
pressure[4]	force per unit area	N/m^2

HEAT

quantity		joule (J)
heat capacity	heat per unit temperature rise	J/K [5] (J/°C)
specific heat capacity	heat capacity per unit mass	J/kg K (J/kg °C)
specific latent heat	heat to change state per unit mass	J/kg (J/g)

ELECTRICITY

current		ampere (A)
potential difference	energy per coulomb	volt (V)
resistance	p.d./current	ohm (Ω)
quantity		coulomb (C)
energy		joule (J)
power		watt (W)

Notes.

1. Acceleration due to gravity = $9{\cdot}8\ m/s^2$ or $10\ m/s^2$ (approx.)
2. The joule (J) is the unit of mechanical, heat and electrical energy.
3. Density of water = $1000\ kg/m^3 = 1\ g/cm^3$
   Density of air (s.t.p.) = $1{\cdot}2\ kg/m^3$
   = 1·2 g/litre
4. Atmospheric pressure = $100\ 000\ N/m^2$ (approx.)
   = $0{\cdot}1\ N/mm^2$
5. The kelvin (absolute) scale is the SI temperature scale. 1 K = 1°C.

Book One

MATTER, MECHANICS, FLUIDS, HEAT

I

INTRODUCTION

SCIENTIFIC METHOD · FORMS OF ENERGY · UNITS · MEASUREMENTS

PHYSICS is a science concerned with the behaviour of matter. Some of its branches are electricity, optics, heat, sound, properties of matter and atomic theory.

Scientists of many different nationalities, such as British, American, Russian, French, Italian, Japanese and Chinese, are today engaged in researches in physics. As a result, many useful inventions and machines have been produced. Radar control at London and other large airports; computers in banks; colour television transmission by British and other national radio corporations; high-power microscopes for use in laboratories; and anti-skid tyres for cars, have all developed from researches in physics.

Scientific Method

In ancient times people believed something simply because a famous person said it. A good example occurred in the case of falling objects. A famous Greek philosopher called Aristotle said that heavy objects always fell to the ground faster than light objects. This was believed for nearly 2000 years.

In the 17th century, however, someone performed a simple *experiment*. He dropped a heavy and a light object from the top of a tall building. (Legend says that the building was the Leaning Tower of Pisa in Italy, which still exists.) He observed that, contrary to what Aristotle thought, the heavy and the light object *both* reached the ground at the same time. Aristotle's theory was therefore wrong.

Today, scientists will not accept a theory unless there is experimental evidence to support it. If an experiment gives results which are contrary to the theory, the theory is abandoned or modified. Sometimes the result of an experiment suggests a theory. About 1910, for example, Lord Rutherford examined the results of an experiment by two of his research students at Cambridge. They were firing tiny particles at atoms. Some of the particles bounced off at large angles on making collisions. Some even bounced back. He came to the conclusion that the atom contained a very tiny concentrated mass in the middle which repelled the particles violently. He called it the *nucleus* of the atom. And this led years later to the discovery of nuclear energy and then to the development of the large nuclear power stations throughout Britain today.

Forms of Energy

'Work' and 'Energy' are two ideas which are widely used in all branches of physics.

A boy pulling a sledge or a girl pushing a pram are said to do *work*. Any object which produces movement is said to do work. Thus on climbing the stairs, we do work in moving our bodies upward. If an object has the capacity for doing work, it is said to have *energy*. The spring of a watch when wound up has energy because it moves gear wheels as it slowly unwinds. A cricket ball thrown at the wicket has energy because it can knock down the stumps.

The wound spring and the fast-moving cricket ball are examples of objects having *mechanical energy*. Over the past centuries, scientists gradually realized that there are many different forms of energy. An electric motor uses *electrical energy* to drive an electric train. *Light energy*, falling on a light meter used in photography, causes a pointer to move across a scale. *Sound energy* causes a microphone diaphragm or thin plate to vibrate. *Chemical energy* is the source of energy in our food which makes us grow and also provides us with muscular energy to move objects. *Nuclear energy*, the energy in the nucleus of atoms, produces heat energy, which in turn is used to generate electrical power in nuclear power stations.

Energy Conversions · Principle of Conservation of Energy

By means of suitable machines or apparatus, energy can be changed from one form to another. This is illustrated in Fig. 1.1. Thus a steam engine converts heat energy to mechanical energy. Mechanical energy is converted to heat energy when a match is struck. A light meter or photoelectric cell converts light energy to electrical energy. An electric lamp converts electrical energy to light energy. A solar cell converts the heat of the sun to electrical energy to power space ships. An electric fire converts electrical energy to heat energy. A microphone converts sound energy to electrical energy. A telephone earpiece converts electrical energy to sound energy. A battery converts chemical to electrical energy; a reverse change occurs in electroplating. The energy from the sun produces chemical changes which make plants and trees grow, and the energy is stored underground in coal centuries later, after the wood is absorbed by the soil and sinks.

An electric plant at a power station illustrates how energy can be changed from one form to another until a desired form of energy is produced. Coal is first burned, so that heat energy is produced from chemical energy. By means of a steam engine or turbine, the heat energy is converted into mechanical energy, which turns the coils of an electric generator. Electrical energy is then produced. Electric

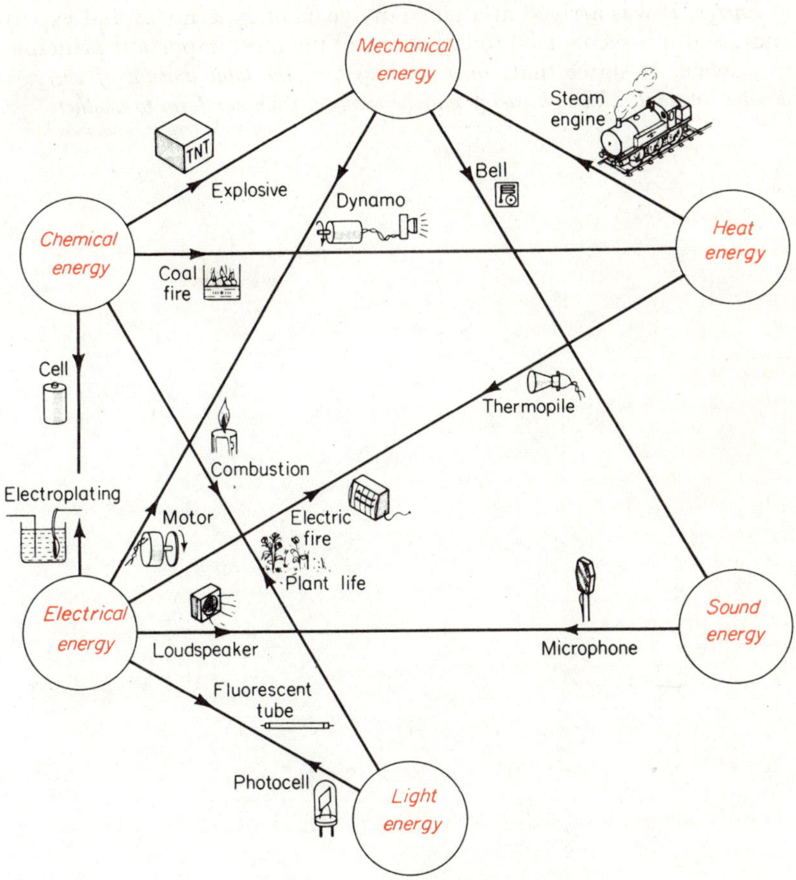

Fig. 1.1 Energy and transformations

lamps and heaters in homes and buildings now convert electrical energy to light and heat energy. Finally, the light energy collected by the eye falls on nerves in the retina, which stimulates the sensation of vision.

The heat energy received by the steam turbine is not all converted into mechanical energy. Some of the energy is wasted in overcoming the frictional forces in the wheels of the turbine. Sound energy is also produced by the spinning wheels owing to air disturbance. However, if the whole generating plant receives 100 units of energy, initially in the form of heat from the coal used, the total energy produced, calculated by adding together all the different forms of energy, will still be 100 units.

This leads to a generalization known as the *Principle of the Conservation of Energy*. It was arrived at after many years of experiment and experience, and it is recognized today as one of the most important principles in science. It states that, *in a given system, the total amount of energy is always constant, although energy may be changed from one form to another.*

2

MOLECULES AND MATTER

Solid, Liquid, Gaseous States

WATER is one of the most common substances on our planet, the Earth. As we travel all over the world, it is found in the form of *solid*, *liquid* and *gaseous* states or phases. In polar regions on the top of high mountains, it is found as ice, the solid state. Rainwater is an example of the liquid state. Water vapour or gas exists in the air. Pools of water on the ground after rain gradually disappear. They evaporate slowly. Water vapour or 'steam' is produced when a kettle boils.

We can see a solid or a liquid. We cannot see a gas such as air. But we recognize its presence when leaves on trees are seen moving. Some gases are coloured—chlorine gas, for example, is greenish-yellow.

All matter, that is, anything which has weight, is found in the solid, liquid or gaseous state. Some differences between the states are illustrated in Fig. 2.1. Thus:

1. *Solids* always have the same volume. They cannot be poured. They have the same shape.

2. *Liquids* have the same volume. They can be poured. They take the same shape as the containing vessel.

3. *Gases* have the same volume as their container. They can be poured. They have no shape.

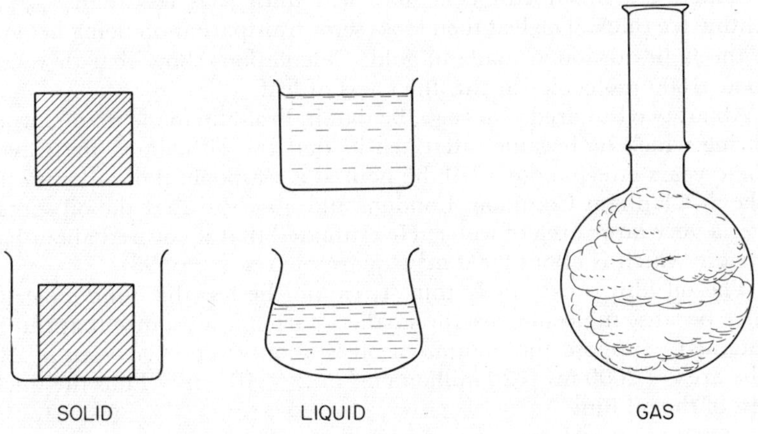

Fig. 2.1 Solid, liquid, gas

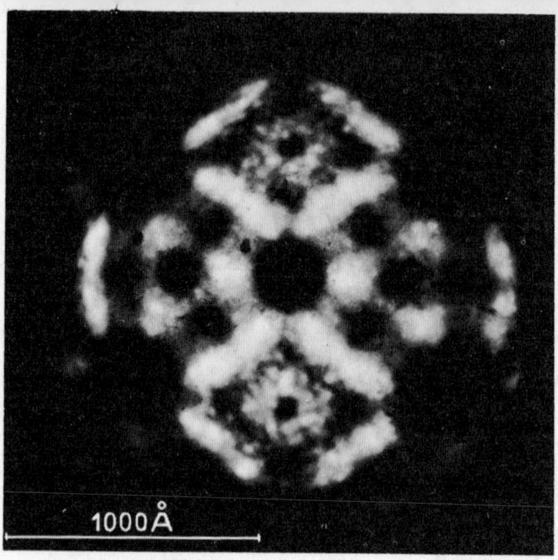

Plate 2(A) Visible atoms. Barium atoms, deposited on the tungsten point, are recognizable as coarse grains. On heating the point the thermal vibrations of the atoms can be seen.

Molecules

If you look at the corner of the page of this book it looks very smooth. Touch it with your finger and test the smoothness. Using a microscope, however, we can see that the paper actually has a 'grain'. The surface is *not* perfectly smooth. Thus matter may be quite different from what we can see with the naked eye or feel by the sense of touch.

If you scrape the surface of a piece of chalk, millions of very tiny chalk particles flake off and can be seen floating through the air. There is a limit to the size of particles which the eye can see. Dalton suggested the existence of *molecules* in matter. These were minute particles from which the whole of a solid or a liquid or a gas is made up. The tip of a needle has many millions of molecules of metal.

Molecules themselves are made up of *atoms*. See Plate 2A. As we discuss later in the book, gifted scientists with imagination, such as Sir J. J. Thomson and Lord Rutherford, were able to make an inspired guess or theory about the particles inside atoms after experiments, although these particles can never be seen.

Size of molecules · Oil films

Skilled craftsmen can beat gold leaf until it is less than $\frac{1}{100\,000}$ centimetre thick. The leaf then looks semi-transparent on being held up to the light, although made of gold. Calculations show that there are about 1000 molecules in this thickness of leaf.

About two hundred years ago, Benjamin Franklin made a sea journey during which he became interested in the way oil calmed the waves. Some years later, about 1770, he poured a teaspoonful of oil on to the lake at Clapham Common, London, and observed that the oil spread over a very large area of water. He estimated that it covered about half an acre which is about 2000 m^2 (square metres, see p. 23).

The oil film is extremely thin. It cannot be less than one molecule thick because molecules are the smallest part of a substance that can be obtained. Suppose the volume of oil is about 5 cm^3 (cc—see p. 23). The area of 2000 m^2 is 20 million cm^2 or 2×10^7 cm^2. Thus the thickness of the oil film

$$= \frac{\text{volume}}{\text{area}} = \frac{5\ \text{cm}^3}{2 \times 10^7\ \text{cm}^2} = 2{\cdot}5 \times 10^{-7}\ \text{cm}.$$

Thus the diameter of a molecule must be of the order of 10^{-7} or one ten-millionth cm, or less.

Estimate of Molecular Size

About a hundred years after Franklin's experiment, Lord Rayleigh suggested that certain oils spread over water in a film one molecule thick. An experiment to estimate roughly the diameter of an oil molecule is shown in Fig. 2.2.

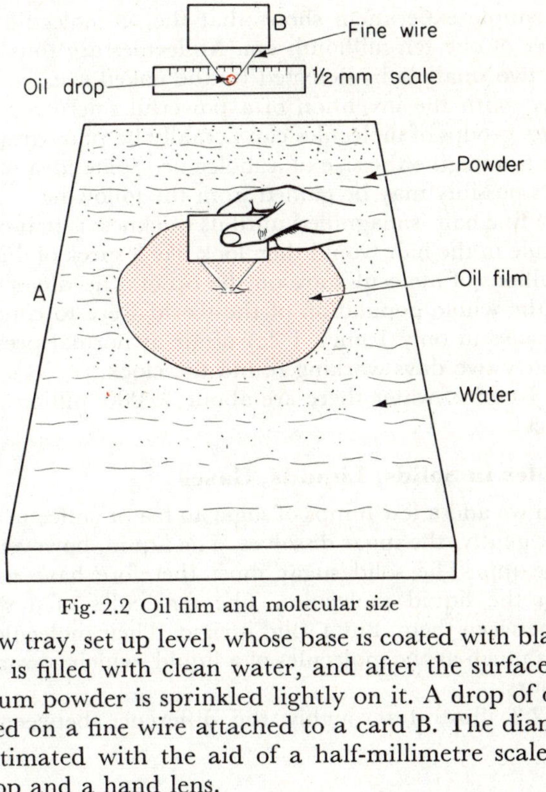

Fig. 2.2 Oil film and molecular size

A is a shallow tray, set up level, whose base is coated with blackened wax. The tray is filled with clean water, and after the surface is still, some lycopodium powder is sprinkled lightly on it. A drop of olive oil is then collected on a fine wire attached to a card B. The diameter of the drop is estimated with the aid of a half-millimetre scale placed behind the drop and a hand lens.

The drop is now placed gently in contact with the water surface. The drop immediately spreads across the water into a circular film. As it spreads, the powder moves back. The clear space on the surface is the oil film, as shown. Its diameter is now quickly measured with a ruler.

Calculation. Suppose the diameter of the film is 20 cm, so that the radius is 10 cm. The area of the circular film is then πr^2 or $\pi \times 10^2$ cm^2. Assume that, roughly, π is 3 instead of 3·14. Then the area is 300 cm^2.

The volume of the drop is that of a sphere. This is $4\pi r^3/3$, where r is the radius. Assume π is 3, so that the volume is then $4r^3$. If the diameter of the drop is 0·5 mm, the radius is 0·25 mm or 0·025 cm. Hence

$$\text{volume} = 4 \times 0{\cdot}025^3 = 0{\cdot}000\ 06\ \text{cm}^3\ \text{(approx.)}$$

$$\therefore\ \text{thickness of film} = \frac{\text{volume}}{\text{area}} = \frac{0{\cdot}000\ 06\ \text{cm}^3}{300\ \text{cm}^2}$$

$$= 0{\cdot}000\ 000\ 2 \text{ or } 2 \times 10^{-7}\ \text{cm}.$$

Numbers of Molecules

This simple experiment shows that the oil-molecule diameter is of the order of one ten-millionth cm. Molecules are thus extremely tiny and far two small to be detected by the naked eye.

Today, with the invention of a powerful microscope called an *ion microscope*, groups of molecules can actually be photographed. It is very difficult to imagine the size of a molecule. Some idea of their size and numbers possibly may be gained from the following:

1. If a fine hair is magnified until its thickness is that of a wide street, a molecule in the hair would then look like a speck of dust in the street.
2. Millions of molecules are on the tip of a needle or pin.
3. If the whole population of the world were to count the number of molecules in only 1 cm³ (1 cc) of air at normal pressure, it would take nearly two days working round the clock.
4. In 1 cm³ of water there are about 30 000 million million million molecules!

Molecules in Solids, Liquids, Gases

When we add a few lumps of sugar to tea or coffee in a full cup, and then stir gently, the sugar dissolves. The liquid, however, does not spill over the top. The solid sugar must therefore have gone into *spaces* between the liquid molecules. The molecules of a solid also have spaces between them. But a solid is rigid. Their molecules do not move about as much as the molecules of a liquid, which constantly exchange neighbours.

Fig. 2.3 illustrates roughly the difference between molecules in

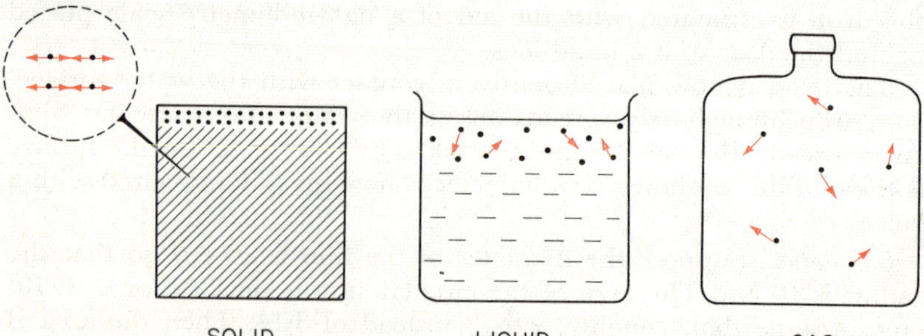

Fig. 2.3 Molecular motion in solids, liquids, gases

solids, liquids and gases. In *solids*, the molecules vibrate about an 'anchored' or mean position. In *liquids* the molecules move about and constantly exchange neighbours and they also vibrate. In *gases*, at normal pressures, the molecules move about in all directions and are practically independent of each other.

Movement of Molecules · Solids

Solids such as moth-balls (naphthalene) and camphor have pungent smells. Their molecules evaporate from, or leave, the solid and spread into the air where their presence is detected. If some camphor or naphthalene is weighed and left for a period of a week or more, subsequent weighing will thus show a loss in weight. Due to their motion, then, some molecules have sufficient energy to leave the solid.

Molecules in Liquids

The motion of molecules in liquids can be shown by running three layers of liquid carefully into a large test-tube T with the aid of a pipette Fig. 2.4. S is a layer of colourless sugar solution, on top of

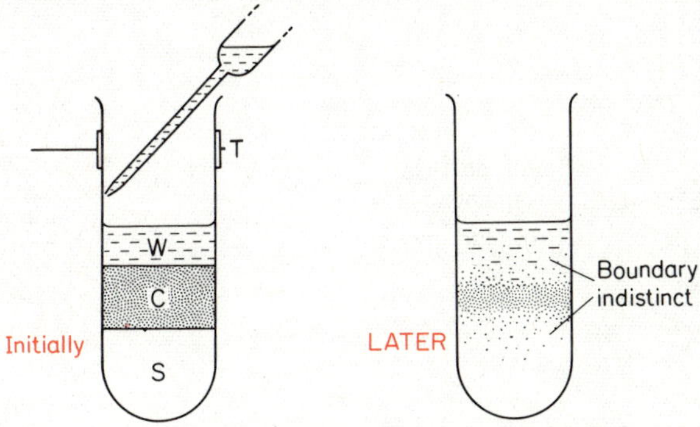

Fig. 2.4 Molecular motion in liquids—diffusion

it is a layer C of blue copper sulphate solution and the layer W is water. Two distinct boundaries are seen. But after a time, the boundaries become indistinct. The blue colour of the copper sulphate solution has extended a little way into the colourless layers above and below it. The blue colour is also less intense. As time goes on, no boundaries can be detected and the liquids all mix. This shows that the molecules of the liquids are constantly in motion in all directions.

Molecules in Gases

Perfume, or flowers such as roses, can be detected in different parts of a small room. This shows that the molecules of a gas are in constant motion.

The movement of molecules can also be seen by collecting a gas-jar of brown nitrogen dioxide sealed with a cover-slip. This gas is denser than air. After inverting a gas-jar of air above it and removing the cover slip between the gases, a brown colour is also soon observed in the upper jar. The nitrogen dioxide gas molecules had thus mixed with the air, showing that its molecules are in constant motion.

Bromine capsules in a sealed glass apparatus can be obtained from most manufacturers to demonstrate the movement of gas molecules. These capsules can be broken and brown bromine vapour is then seen to spread quickly throughout the apparatus.

Evidence for Existence of Molecules · Brownian Motion

When we look at a glass of still water on the table, it seems incredible that millions of molecules are moving about restlessly inside it. A British botanist called Brown, however, discovered evidence of this movement over 200 years ago. He was observing through a microscope some very tiny particles of pollen in suspension in water. To his surprise, he saw that some of the smaller particles were moving about continually in a haphazard way. Like a drunken man, they staggered about in different directions, as illustrated by Fig. 2.5 (i). This 'Brownian motion', as it is now called, is due to the bombardment of a tiny particle by the liquid molecules all round it. The particle is so tiny, that any difference between the magnitudes of the forces due to molecular impacts on both sides makes it move in the direction of the resultant force. This is shown by small arrows in Fig. 2.5 (i). The direction of the resultant force is constantly changing. Hence the motion of the particle is completely random.

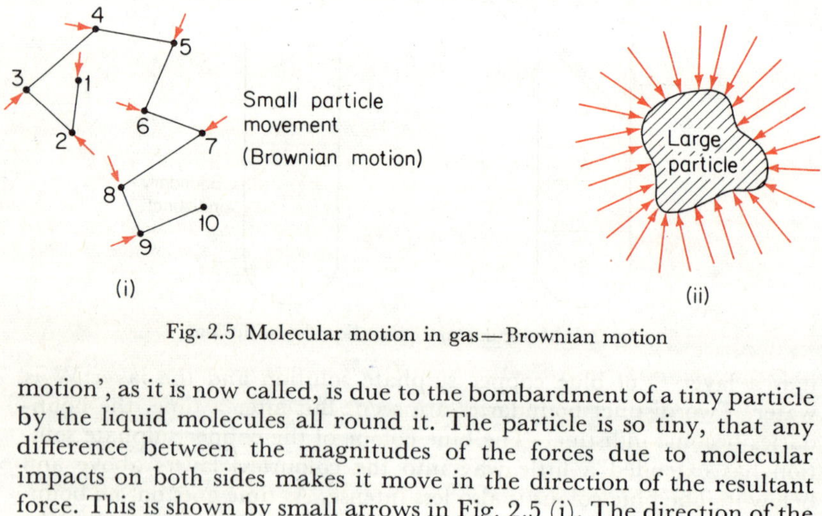

Fig. 2.5 Molecular motion in gas—Brownian motion

Nowadays, 'Brownian motion' can be demonstrated simply by releasing some smoke particles from burning cord into a small glass container. When the tiny particles are illuminated and observed through a microscope, their random motion can be seen.

With a large particle, the difference in the magnitudes of the forces on either side has now practically no effect, Fig. 2.5 (ii). The particle thus appears unaffected. In air, your body is subjected to impacts on either side by millions of molecules. The resultant force is now negligible.

Density

From the microscopic world of molecules we now turn to matter in bulk. All matter is made up of molecules, which have mass and size.

A length of balsa wood, used in making model aircraft, is surprisingly light compared to a length of iron of the same volume. A block of iron is lighter than a block of lead of the same volume. Fig. 2.6 shows the masses of six metals each having the same volume. It is a 'unit volume', 1 cm^3 (see p. 23) in this case. Aluminium is the lightest metal here and gold is the heaviest.

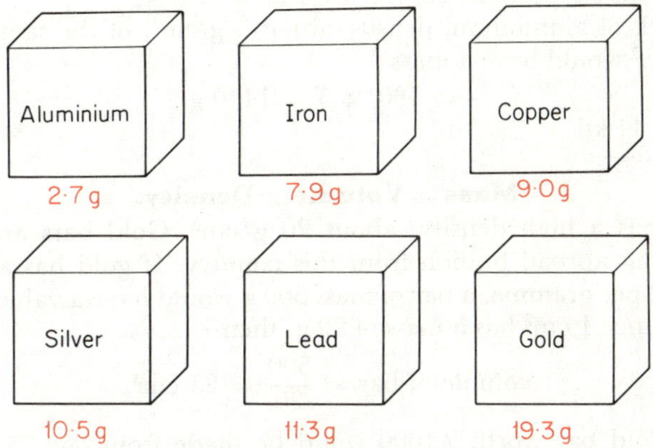

Fig. 2.6 Masses of metals of volume 1 cm^3

The *mass per unit volume* of any substance is called its *density*. The SI unit of density is 'kilogramme per metre^3', kg/m^3. It is often more convenient to use 'gramme per cm^3', g/cm^3. The density of aluminium is about 2·7 g/cm^3 (2700 kg/m^3). The density of gold is 19·3 g/cm^3 (19 300 kg/m^3).

If the mass of a substance and its volume can be measured, the density can be simply calculated. Thus suppose a block of wood has a mass of 60 g (0·06 kg) and a volume of 100 cm^3 (0·0001 m^3). Then its density

$$= \frac{60\text{ g}}{100\text{ cm}^3} = 0{\cdot}6\text{ g/cm}^3\ (600\text{ kg/m}^3)$$

A lump of aluminium of volume 100 cm^3 has a much greater mass, about 270 g, than the same volume of wood. The density of aluminium

$$= \frac{270\text{ g}}{100\text{ cm}^3} = 2{\cdot}7\text{ g/cm}^3\ (2700\text{ kg/m}^3)$$

Remember:

$$\textbf{Density} = \frac{\textbf{mass}}{\textbf{volume}}.$$

All the elements have characteristic densities. If you were a mineral prospector, you could identify an element by measuring its density.

Density Calculations

Lead, used on roofs for weather protection, is very heavy. It has the high density of over 11 g/cm³. Let us calculate the mass of a solid piece of lead whose dimensions are those of a book, say 20 cm × 12 cm × 2 cm. The volume of lead is then 480 cm³. Since the mass per cm³ is about 11 g, then approximate mass

$$= 480 \times 11 = 5280 \text{ g}.$$

This is 5·28 kilogramme (kg), since 1000 g = 1 kg

A block of aluminium, density about 3 g/cm³, of the same volume of 480 cm³ would have a mass

$$= 480 \times 3 = 1440 \text{ g}.$$

This is 1·44 kg.

Note:

$$\textbf{Mass} = \textbf{Volume} \times \textbf{Density}.$$

Gold has a high density, about 20 g/cm³. Gold bars are used in transferring abroad bullion from this country. If gold has a value of about £2 per gramme, a bar of mass 500 g would have a value of about £1000. Since 1 cm³ has a mass of 20 g, then

$$\text{volume of bar} = \frac{500}{20} = 25 \text{ cm}^3.$$

Thus a gold bar worth £1000 could be made from one 25 cm long and cross-section 1 cm × 1 cm assuming its value per gramme is that given.

Note:

$$\textbf{Volume} = \frac{\textbf{mass}}{\textbf{density}}.$$

Example

An alloy is made by mixing 180 g of copper, density about 9 g/cm³, with 240 g of iron, density about 8 g/cm³. Find the approximate density of the alloy, assuming the volume of metal used does not change.

First, we find the volume of copper and the volume of iron.

$$\text{Volume of copper} = \frac{180}{9} = 20 \text{ cm}^3$$

$$\text{Volume of iron} = \frac{240}{8} = 30 \text{ cm}^3$$

$$\therefore \text{Total volume} = 20 + 30 = 50 \text{ cm}^3.$$

Now

$$\text{Total mass} = 180 \text{ g} + 240 \text{ g} = 420 \text{ g}.$$

$$\therefore \text{Density of alloy} = \frac{\text{mass}}{\text{volume}} = \frac{420 \text{ g}}{50 \text{ cm}^3} = 8{\cdot}4 \text{ g/cm}^3.$$

Densities of Liquids

Water is the most common liquid. Years ago, the mass of 1 kilogramme, or 1000 g, was defined as the mass of 1 litre, or 1000 cm³, of water at 4°C—it is necessary to add the temperature values as the densities of liquids are sensitive to temperature changes (p. 174). For practical purposes,

density of water = 1 g/cm³.

We have no need to weigh 50 cm³ of water to find its mass. This is 50 g.

When the cubic metre (m³) is used as the unit of volume, the density of water is 1000 kilogramme per cubic metre.

Density of water = 1000 kg/m³

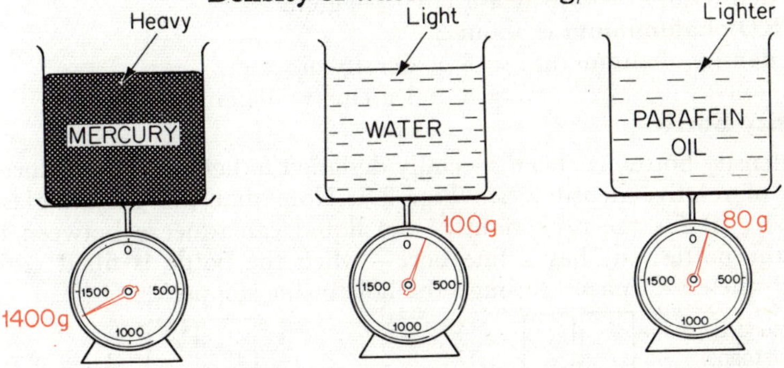

Fig. 2.7 Dense and less dense liquids

Mercury is a liquid widely used in scientific work for making high-grade or standard barometers and for making mercury-in-glass thermometers. A small jar of mercury is quite heavy. Mercury has a density of about 14 g/cm³ (14 000 kg/m³). Conversely, a can of paraffin oil is very light to lift. The oil has a density less than water, about 0·8 g/cm³ (800 kg/m³). A test-tube of volume 10 cm³ will contain a mass of $0{\cdot}8 \times 10$ or 8 g if filled with oil. If it is filled with mercury, the mass will be about 14×10 or 140 g. See Fig. 2.7.

Relative density

Water, the most common liquid, is a useful standard for comparing densities.

As an illustration, the mass of 20 cm³ of copper is 180 g. The mass of an *equal volume*, 20 cm³, of water is 20 g. Thus comparing equal volumes, copper has 9 times the mass of water. We say that:

relative density (RD) of copper = 9.

This means that because a volume of 100 cm³ of water has a mass of 100 g, a volume of 100 cm³ of copper has a mass of 9×100 or 900 g. Again, since a volume of 200 cm³ of water has a mass of 200 g, a volume of 200 cm^3 of copper has a mass of 9 × 200 or 1800 g. Note carefully that we must take *equal* volumes of the water and metal when using the relative density figure.

Another meaning can now be given to relative density. The density of copper is say 9 g/cm^3, or 9 g is the mass of 1 cm^3. The density of water is 1 g/cm^3, or 1 g is the mass of 1 cm^3. The ratio 9 g/1 g or 9, is the relative density of copper. Hence in general

$$\textbf{Relative density, RD} = \frac{\textbf{Density of substance}}{\textbf{Density of water}}.$$

This also means that:

Density of substance = RD × Density of water.

For example, the RD of iron is 8.

$\therefore$ density of iron $= 8 \times 1\ g/cm^3 = 8\ g/cm^3$.

The RD of aluminium is about 3.

$\therefore$ density of aluminium $= 3 \times$ density of water.

$= 3 \times 1\ g/cm^3 = 3\ g/cm^3$.

Density Bottle

A density bottle has been specially designed to help in the measurement of relative density. See Fig. 2.8. Note that the ground-glass stopper: (i) fits the neck tightly—no liquid can squeeze between it and the bottle; (ii) has a fine bore—when the bottle is filled with liquid, the excess passes through the hole in the stopper.

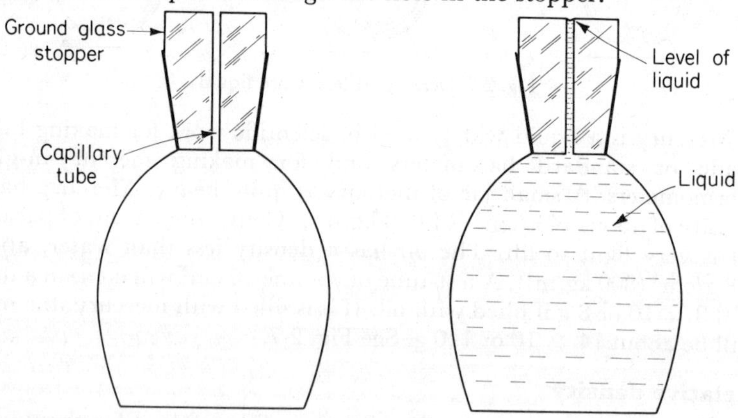

Fig. 2.8 Density bottle

Wipe the bottle dry with a cloth—do *not* use a filter or blotting paper, which may draw up some liquid through the stopper.

If the mass of liquid filling the bottle is determined, and then after drying it is filled again with water and this mass is determined, then

$$\textbf{RD} = \frac{\textbf{mass of liquid}}{\textbf{mass of water}}.$$

Density of Air

Gases are very much lighter than solids and liquids of the same volume. Thus 1 litre of air at normal pressure weighs a little over 1 g, whereas 1 litre of water weighs 1000 g. 1 litre of copper weighs about 9000 g. The density of a gas is usually given as the density at '0° C and 760 mm mercury pressure' called 's.t.p.' (standard temperature and pressure). The volumes of gases are very sensitive to changes of temperature and pressure, so this information is needed when the density is stated.

The density of air can be found by the method described on p. 33.

It is interesting to note that very accurate measurements of the density of air led to the discovery of the rare gases in the atmosphere. One is argon, used for filling electric lamps; two others are helium and neon. Lord Rayleigh and Sir William Ramsay found that nitrogen gas obtained from the atmosphere was very slightly denser than nitrogen gas obtained from a chemical reaction. They came to the conclusion that there was an impurity in the 'atmospheric' nitrogen, and after further investigations they discovered argon and other rare gases.

Molecular forces in Solids · Elasticity

Density and specific gravity concern the masses of molecules and their 'packing'. We now consider phenomena which concern the *forces between molecules.*

A thin vertical wire, fixed at the upper end, will extend slightly when a small load is attached at the bottom. If the load is removed, the wire returns to its original length. The metal of the wire is therefore said to be 'elastic'.

A metal under load increases in length. Its molecules are thus slightly further apart than before. Since the metal returns to its original length on removal of the load, powerful forces of attraction must have existed between the displaced molecules. Further, solids (and liquids) cannot be compressed indefinitely. Thus molecules have strong repulsive forces when closer together than normal.

Extension of Spring

The extension in length of a coiled spring demonstrates elastic forces. In Fig. 2.9 (i), S is a spring with a pointer L attached. The position of L is first observed on a vertical metre ruler R alongside. A scale-pan P is then attached to the spring and a mass such as 50 g is placed on P. The pulling force on the spring is the weight of this mass, 0·5 newton (0·5 N), together with the scale-pan weight. The new reading on the ruler R, and hence the extension of the spring, is then noted. When the load on the end is removed, the spring returns to its original length. The spring is thus elastic.

If more weights are added in equal steps, the extension can be measured for increasing loads. The elasticity can be examined each time by removing the load.

Spring balance · Elastic limit

Fig. 2.9 (ii) shows the results when a graph is plotted of the *extension* v. *load* with zero as origin on each axis.

(i) The first part OA of the graph is a straight line passing through the origin. Along OA the spring was elastic. Thus up to a particular load OX, *the extension of the spring was directly proportional to the load* (Hooke's law). This is utilized in the *spring balance* (see p. 25). The spring in the balance is calibrated as in this experiment. On account of the fact that the extension is directly proportional to the load, equally spaced divisions on the scale represent equal changes in load or weight. We say that the scale is 'uniform'.

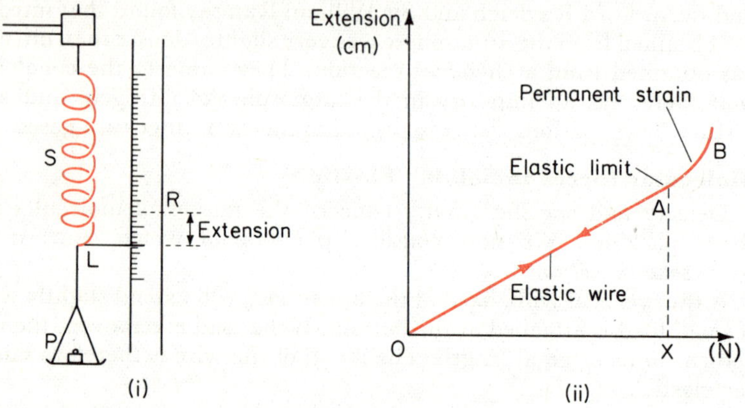

Fig. 2.9 Elasticity of spring

(ii) Beyond the point A, however, the graph curves upward along AB. The extension is thus no longer proportional to the load. Further, beyond A the spring does not return to its original length when the load is removed. The spring is permanently strained. The load OX corresponding to A is thus called the *elastic limit*. A spring balance must not be loaded beyond the elastic limit otherwise the spring will become permanently strained and useless.

Surface tension

If you have observed a drop of water forming slowly on a tap, you will have noticed that the liquid surface appears to act like a 'bag'; it supports the weight of the liquid before the drop falls, Fig. 2.10 (i). Mercury spilled on a clean glass plate gathers into small spherical droplets. Fig. 2.10 (ii). The surfaces of water and mercury thus appear to act like an elastic 'skin' covering the liquid.

Other observations lead to a similar conclusion. An insect called a 'pond skater' can walk across the surface of water without falling in,

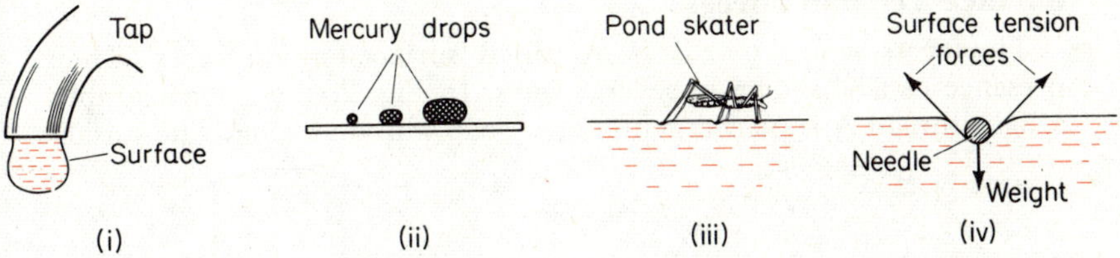

Fig. 2.10 Effects of surface tension

Fig. 2.10 (iii). A slight depression of the surface is produced by the legs, showing that the surface acts like an elastic 'skin'. Further, with care a dry needle can be floated on the surface of water, Fig. 2.10 (iv). The weight of the light needle is supported by forces in the surface which together act upwards.

Molecular forces

The existence of the surface 'skin' is due to the forces of attraction between liquid molecules. Below the surface, a liquid such as A is attracted by molecules all round it. The most powerful forces come from those inside a tiny sphere of molecular dimensions, Fig. 2.11. Other

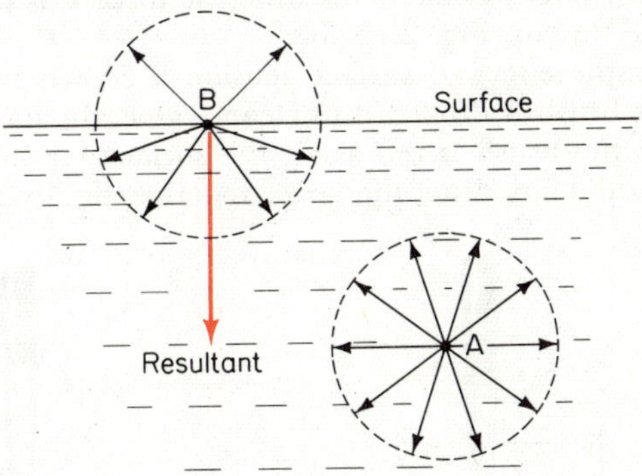

Fig. 2.11 Molecular attraction in liquids

molecules outside the sphere have negligible attraction and can be ignored. In any direction, there are as many pulling forces on A one way as there are the opposite way. Thus the resultant force is zero.

This is not the case for a molecule such as B in the surface. There are far more molecules of the liquid below the surface than there are above in the vapour. Consequently there is a resultant pull on B into the liquid. This is the case for all molecules which happen to be in the surface. The pull into the liquid interior has the effect of making the surface area as small as possible. Thus the surface is under 'tension', and acts like a 'skin' covering the liquid.

Surface Tension Forces

The forces *in the surface itself* are called 'surface tension forces'. Their presence can be shown in several ways. In Fig. 2.12 (i), for example, a light thread A is placed gently on a soap film on a ring. The surface

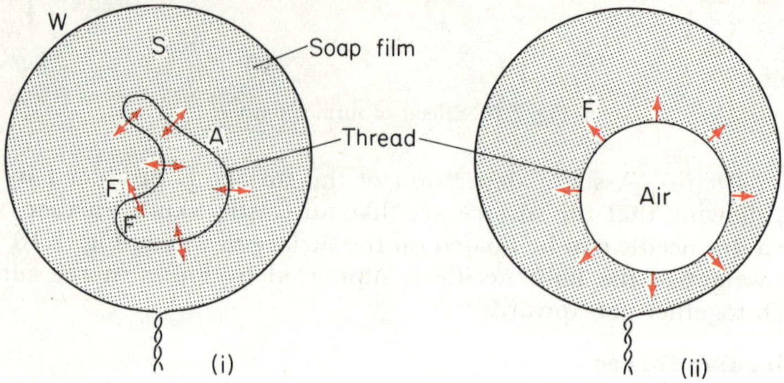

Fig. 2.12 Surface tension of soap film

tension forces F act across both sides of A at every part of it and counterbalance. When the film inside the thread is pierced, however, the thread is pulled into a circle. This time the force F is present only on one side of the thread, Fig. 2.12 (ii).

Another simple effect of surface tension is shown in Fig. 2.13 (i). When a paint brush is dipped into clean water, the hairs splay out as shown. When the brush is removed, the surface tension forces in the film between the hairs draw the latter together tightly, Fig. 2.13 (ii).

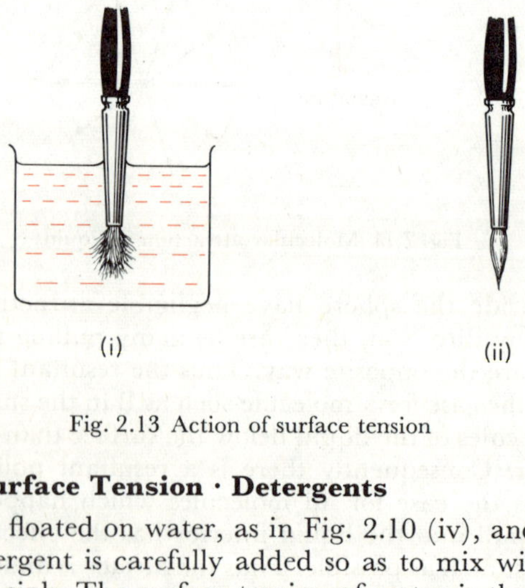

Fig. 2.13 Action of surface tension

Changes in Surface Tension · Detergents

If a needle is floated on water, as in Fig. 2.10 (iv), and a little soap solution or detergent is carefully added so as to mix with the water, the needle will sink. The surface tension of water is thus reduced by soap or detergent. The reduction of surface tension also accounts for the movement of a toy duck across water when a piece of camphor is attached below it. The camphor dissolves and lowers the surface tension of the water below it. The resultant force across the camphor boundary with the clean water drags the light duck along.

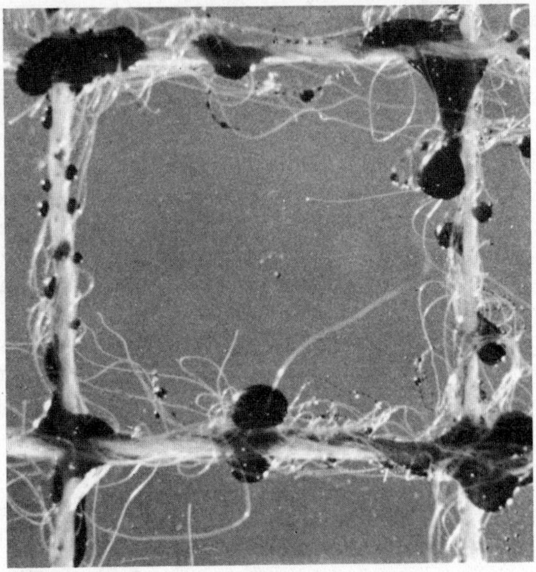

Plate 2(B) Forces between liquid molecules—detergent action. A detergent in solution removing oil from fibres. Observe the spherical shapes of the drops, especially those which are small.

Detergents are chemicals which are mixed with water to increase its cleaning power. They lower the surface tension of water. This increases the 'wetting' power of the water or its ability to float small dirt particles away from the articles being washed. Plate 2B. Detergents also contain special chemicals to combine with oils and fats and thus to make them soluble in water. They can then be 'wetted' and removed from the material. In areas with hard water, the detergent first combines with the 'hard' chemicals and forms a scum in the water. When all these chemicals are removed in this way, the detergent then acts in the normal way on the dirt to be removed.

Capillarity

The attraction between molecules is also shown when a tube with a fine bore or *capillary tube* is dipped into a beaker of water so that the inside is wetted and then slightly withdrawn. The water is then observed to have risen up the tube, Fig. 2.14 (i). This is called 'capillarity'. The narrower the tube, the higher is the rise of water inside. The reverse effect is observed when capillary tubes are dipped

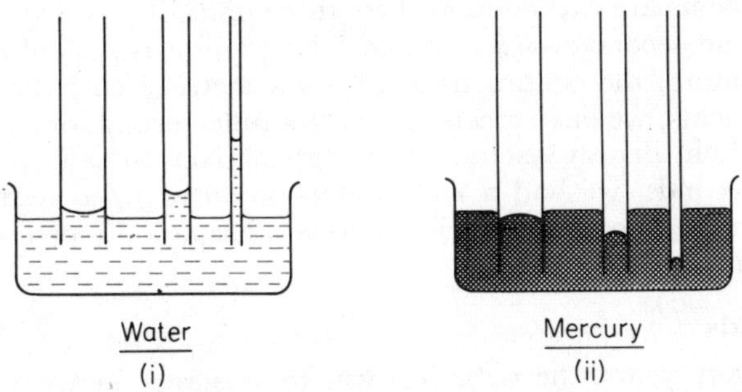

Fig. 2.14 Capillary rise and fall

into mercury, Fig. 2.14 (ii). This time the liquid is depressed below the outside level.

Blotting paper has many fine pores, which act as tiny capillary tubes. The ink rises into the blotting paper through the fine pores. The fibres of a candle wick act like capillary tubes of fine bore. The melted wax is drawn up into the wick by capillary action. Bricks are porous—water can seep up them from the ground by capillary action. *Damp courses*, a layer of non-porous material such as slate, are therefore necessary at the base of houses to protect them from damp.

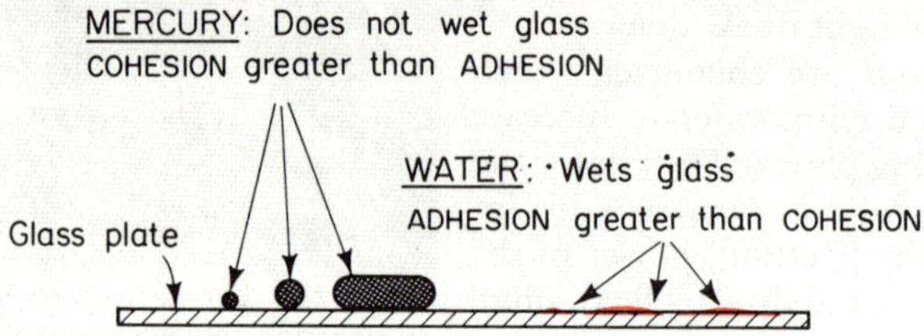

Fig. 2.15 Cohesion and adhesion

Fig. 2.15 shows the non-wetting of a glass plate by mercury and the wetting by water. This is due to the fact that the 'cohesion' between two mercury molecules is greater than the 'adhesion' between a mercury molecule and a water molecule. The reverse is the case for water and glass molecules.

UNITS · MEASUREMENT OF VOLUME AND MASS

Mass, Length, Time · SI (Système International) Units

If a scientist measures the mass of a bottle or the length of a wire, for example, he usually uses the metric system. This is because results are more easily set out and compared in this system.

In the metric system, the unit of length is the *metre* (m); the unit of mass is the *kilogramme* (kg); the unit of time is the *second* (s). If all measurements are expressed in these three units, it is called the metre–kilogramme–second or *m.k.s.* system. The gramme is $\frac{1}{1000}$ of the mass of a kilogramme; the centimetre is $\frac{1}{100}$ of a metre. Using these units in measurements, we have a centimetre–gramme–second, or *c.g.s.* system. Using the old British system, with length in feet, mass in pounds and time in seconds, we had a foot-pound-second or *f.p.s.* system. Great Britain and most other countries, however, has now adopted the metric or SI units.

Standards

For many years, the *metre* (m) was the distance between two fixed marks on a particular long rod made of platinum–iridium alloy. This

	SI	c.g.s.
Length	METRE (m)	centimetre (cm)
Mass	KILOGRAMME (kg)	gramme (g)
Time	SECOND (s)	second

1 metre is about 3 in more than 1 yard.
1 cm is less than $\frac{1}{2}$ in (about $\frac{3}{8}$ in)
1 kilogramme is about $2\frac{1}{5}$ lb, or 1000 kg is about 1 ton.

was kept in an air-conditioned vault in Paris. The metre is now defined in atomic units. It is the length of a number of wavelengths of a radiation from a krypton atom. The wavelengths of the atomic radiation are constant, whereas the distance between the marks on the metal rod may change slightly with time.

The *kilogramme* (kg) is the mass of a particular solid cylinder made of platinum–iridium alloy. It is known as the International Prototype Kilogramme and is kept in Paris. Copies are available for laboratories in countries all over the world.

The *second* was defined for many years as $\frac{1}{86\,400}$ part of the 'mean solar day', which was based on the time of rotation of the earth. Like the metre, the second is now defined by reference to an atomic standard because the rate of rotation of the earth varies slightly with time. It is the time for a definite number of vibrations originating from a caesium atom. *Atomic clocks* are now used as standards of time.

Volumes

The volume of a liquid was formerly measured in litres or cubic centimetres (cc) in scientific work. Nowadays, a volume is measured in 'cm^3' rather than 'cc'. The 'cm^3' is a volume of a cube whose side is 1 cm long. Similarly, area is measured in 'cm^2' rather than 'sq cm'.

Three instruments for measuring volumes of liquids are shown in Fig. 2.16 (i), (ii), (iii).

A *burette* B, allows a known volume of liquid to be transferred to a vessel, for example; it is usually graduated in cm^3 (cc or ml).

A *measuring cylinder* C, is also graduated in cm^3.

A *pipette* P, provides an accurate fixed volume, such as 10 cm^3 for example. Unlike the other two vessels, it has only one graduation on it to mark the fixed volume.

In measuring volumes of liquids, always measure from the *bottom* of the meniscus (surface) of the liquid. This corresponds to the level A shown inset in Fig. 2.16.

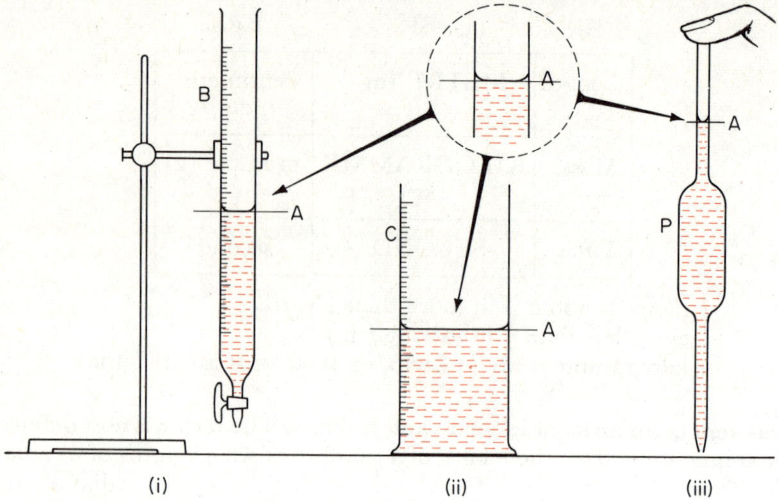

Fig. 2.16 Vessels for measuring volume

Balances

A mass can be measured by various types of balances.

1. *Chemical (common) balance*, Fig. 2.17. When raised for weighing, the beam B of the balance should swing freely about its fulcrum or axis. This is the lower edge of a small wedge-shaped hard crystal K of agate in the middle of the beam.

The two scale-pans hang from the upper edges of similar small wedge-shaped agate crystals P and Q. If the arms of the balance are equal, then, when the beam balances, the masses on the scale-pans are

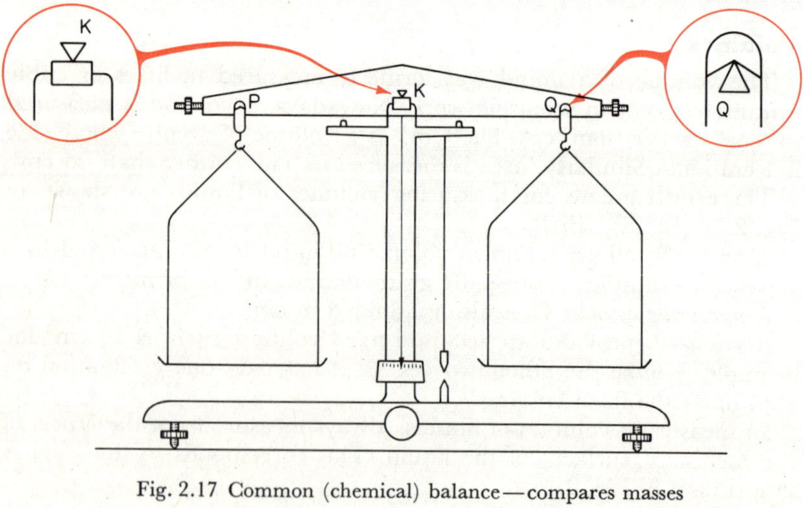

Fig. 2.17 Common (chemical) balance—compares masses

equal. Thus an unknown mass can be measured by using known or standard masses, obtained from a weight-box, for example.

Lower the beam *gently* when weighing. It then rests on supports which take the load off the delicate agate wedges. The scale-pans rest on the wooden base.

If the two equal masses in the scale-pans were taken from England to Canada and weighed again on the balance, they would be found equal once more. This is because the effect due to gravity on the mass on one scale-pan, which pulls the beam down on this side, is exactly counterbalanced by its effect on the other mass. Hence the masses of objects can be compared by a chemical balance.

2. *Lever* (*Butchart*) *balance*, Fig. 2.18. This balance provides a quick method of measuring masses—it is not as accurate as a common balance, but in many experiments it is accurate enough for the purpose.

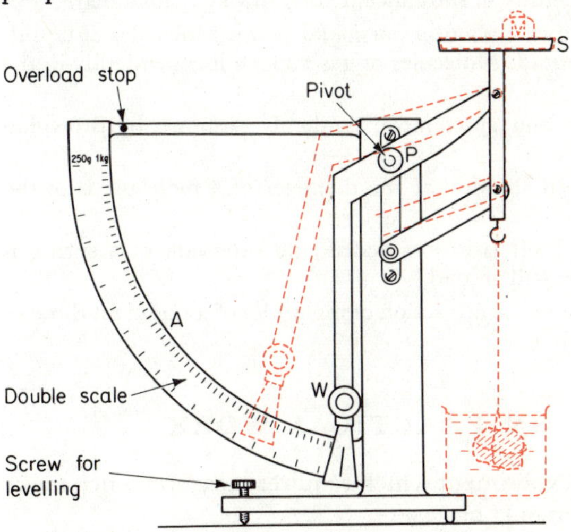

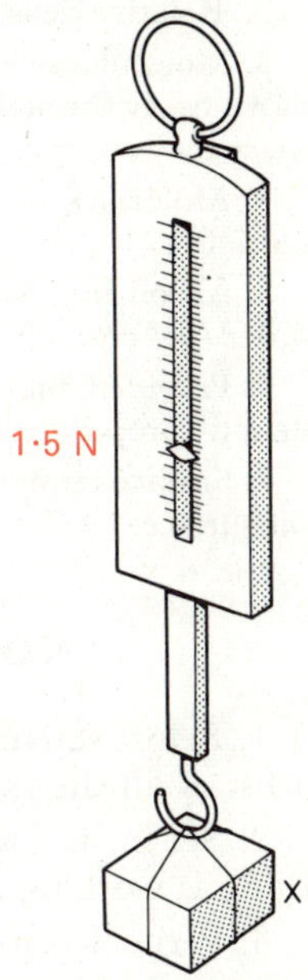

Fig. 2.18 Lever (Butchart) balance *Right:* 2.19 Spring balance—measures weights (forces)

The pointer is first arranged to be at the 'zero' of the scale by levelling the balance with the screw provided at the base. The levelling can be checked by placing a 100 g, for example, in the scale-pan S, and seeing if the reading on the scale is exactly this value. The mass M to be measured is then placed on the scale-pan. Its mass is read directly from a graduated scale A. By moving a weight W, one of the two scales may be used, for high or low values of mass respectively.

3. *Spring balance*. Fig. 2.19. This balance provides a quick method of measuring weight. The object X is suspended from the hook and the

spring is then pulled out by a length proportional to the weight of X in newtons, N. The spring balance is calibrated already. Its scale is 'uniform', that is, equal divisions represent equal changes in weight in newtons along the whole scale.

Unlike the chemical or lever balance, the reading on the spring balance will vary slightly if the same mass is taken to different parts of the world. At the north pole for example, it will weigh slightly more than at the equator. This is on account of the difference in gravitational pull, or weight, which affects the extension of the spring. See p. 139.

SUMMARY

1. Density = mass/volume. Units: g/cm^3 or kg/m^3.
   Density of water = 1 g/cm^3 or 1000 kg/m^3.

2. Relative density = density of substance/density of water (no units).

3. Molecules of solids vibrate about a particular point. Molecules of liquids move freely through the liquid. Molecules of gases move independently in the space they occupy.

4. Molecules of liquids and gases move randomly — shown by Brownian motion.

5. An oil film experiment shows that the diameter of a molecule is of the order 10^{-8} cm.

6. Provided the elastic limit is not exceeded, the extension of a spring is directly proportional to the pull or load.

7. Surface tension is due to the attraction of molecules of a liquid on those in the surface.

NOTES ON PRACTICAL WORK

1. Before starting an experiment which requires measurements, make a list of all the measurements necessary.

2. Set up the apparatus following the instructions and test if everything is working satisfactorily.

3. Write down every measurement you make — do not subtract two measurements, for example, and write down only the result. You can then check back later if anything is wrong.

4. Write up the account of your experiment under headings: *Title, Diagram, Method, Measurements, Calculation, Graph* (if any), *Conclusion* or *Result.*

5. Neat labelled diagrams are essential — use a pencil with a sharp point and a ruler.

6. In your Method, write an account of the way you carried out the experiment referring to the diagram. Mention particularly anything you did to overcome difficulties and to obtain accurate results.

7. Set out the Measurements neatly and clearly, either in a ruled table or in columns (see p. 29 and p. 33 for some examples).

8. Units are essential, that is, whether you have measured a certain length in centimetres or metres, for example. Always give the units in the measurements section, on the axes of the graphs if these are plotted, and in your final result for the quantity you set out to find.

9. The final result of an experiment must always be given to a sensible 'order of accuracy'. This means that if your final result is calculated from 17·8/15·3, for example, do *not* go on working out decimals and give your answer as 1·1634. . . . The answer should probably be given to one decimal place as 1·2.

Always give your result of an experiment to the degree of accuracy in keeping with the measurements taken.

PRACTICAL

In measuring mass, a lever (Butchart) balance or spring balance of a suitable range will be found useful for rapid weighing.

1. Area · Volume · Thickness

Find the area of the cover of this book to the nearest cm^2. Then find the volume of the book to the nearest cm^3.

Estimate the thickness of one page of the book.

Measurements.

Length = .. cm
Width = .. cm
∴ *Area* = .. cm^2
Thickness = .. cm
∴ *Volume* = .. cm^3.

2. Volume-time measurement

Apparatus. Burette; beaker; stop-watch or stop-clock.

Method. (i) Fill a burette B with water and place a beaker C below it. Fig. 2.20.

(ii) Open the burette tap so that a *slow* water flow is obtained. Using a stop-watch, observe the water-level in the burette after regular intervals of time, such as 5 or 10 seconds.

(iii) Before all the water flows away, fill up the burette again and repeat your measurements.

Measurements.

Burette reading	t (s)	Volume V (cm^3)
..	0	0
..	..	..

Calculate the volume of water V flowing away after times t recorded.

Graph your results, with V on the vertical (y) axis and t on the horizontal (x) axis. Start from a zero on each axis—when $t = 0$, $V = 0$, so mark the zero with

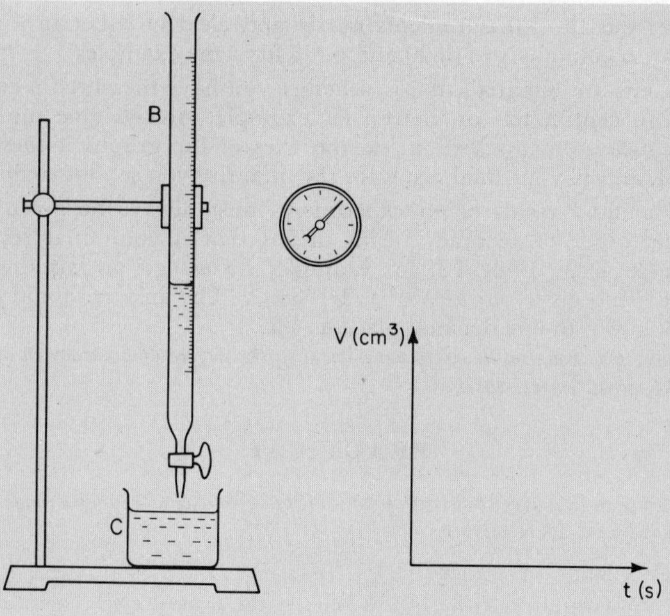

Fig. 2.20 Volume-time

a cross and draw your graph to pass through the zero. After plotting all the points, draw a smooth curve through them. Does the graph show that equal volumes flowed away in equal times?

3. Spring balance principle

Apparatus. Coil spring; scale-pan; weights ruler; stand and clamp.

Method (i) Suspend a coil spring S from a clamp—make sure the suspension is rigid. Fig. 2.21.

(ii) Attach a piece of wire P near the end of S to act as a pointer, and note the position A of P on a metre rule R fixed vertically beside it in a clamp.

(iii) Measure the weight of a scale-pan M. Attach it to the end of S. Add a small known weight to M. Record the reading B of P on R. Add more known weights in small equal steps (consult your teacher to make sure you will not 'overload' the spring) and each time record the reading on R. Now remove the weights from M and check your readings—they should be close to the first set of readings, otherwise you have overloaded the spring.

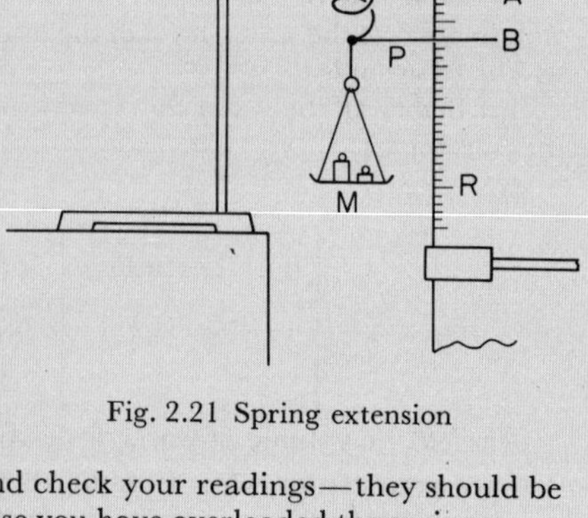

Fig. 2.21 Spring extension

Measurements. (If required, use weight of 1 g mass = 0·01 N.)
Weight of scale-pan M = .. N

Weight added to S (N)	Reading on R (cm)	Force pulling S (N)	Extension of S (cm)
0	..	0	0
..	..	..	..

Calculate the force F pulling the spring (= weight of scale-pan + weight added) and the extension of the spring (e).

Graph F (N) v. e (cm)—use 'zero' as an origin on each axis. Since $e = 0$ when $F = 0$, the graph will pass through the zero (origin). Draw the most suitable line through all the points plotted. Does the extension double when the pulling force is doubled?

Using graph. Attach an unknown weight to the spring and measure the extension produced. From your graph, read off the unknown weight. Compare the value you obtain with the weight recorded on a balance.

4. Extension of spring and elastic limit (p. 18)

Apparatus. Coil spring—Nuffield type (Griffin & George, No. 2A); ruler; scale-pan; clamp and stand; masses 100 to 1000 g.

Method. Suspend the spring with a ruler beside it, as in Experiment 3, Fig. 2.21. Note the reading on R. Weigh the scale-pan, attach it to the spring and add equal weights in steps of 100 g to the scale-pan. Each time a weight is added, note the reading on R. At one stage the spring extends more than previously—the elastic limit has been passed. Continue adding more masses until about 900 –1000 g is added, and note the readings on R each time.

Measurements. As in Experiment 3.

Graph. Plot the force F on the spring v. the extension e, using a zero on each axis. From the graph, read off the force where the straight line part finishes and a curve begins. This is the elastic limit.

Conclusion. The elastic limit is . . . N. If the elastic limit is not exceeded, the extension of the spring is .. to the force applied.

5. Amplitude of swings

Apparatus. Small weight, card of sides about 8 cm; metre rule; thread; clamp and stand.

Method (i) With the aid of a clamp, fix a metre rule R horizontally at the edge of the bench. Fig. 2.22.

(ii) Attach the weight B to a length of thread about a metre long. Suspend B firmly from a clamp—two pennies or two blocks of wood with the thread between them will produce a firm support at O.

(iii) Arrange B so that the thread is at the middle (50·0 cm mark) of the ruler. Pull B to C, the 90·0 cm division. Release B. As it oscillates or swings note (a) the readings r on the same side M of the ruler when B returns to this side after 3 swings, for example (b) the number n of the swings, 3, 6, 9, for example. Do this for many swings—if you miss the reading at the first swing, start again and be ready to take the reading at the place expected.

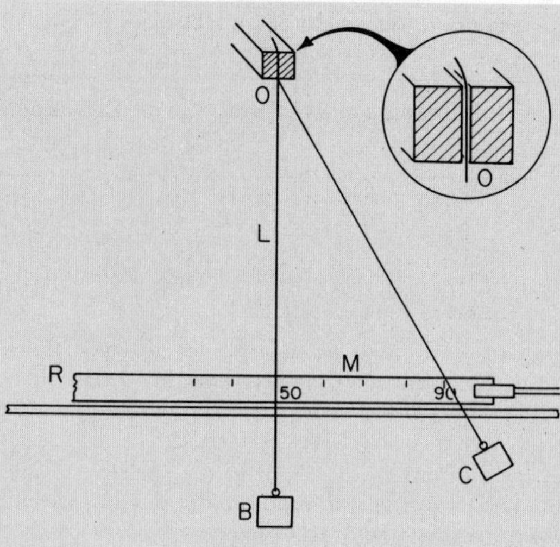

Fig. 2.22 Amplitude of swings

(iv) Now attach the card to the weight by Sellotape. Repeat the experiment, noting the reading *r* and number *n* of swing.

Measurements.

No. of swing (*n*)	Reading (*r*)
0	90·0 cm
..	..

Graph. Reading (*r*), v. number of swing (*n*).

Draw a smooth curve through the points for: (i) weight only; (ii) weight plus card. Why are the curves different? If you have time, repeat the experiment with a bigger card.

6. Making a micro-balance

Method (i) Cut a scoop D from one end of a plastic straw with a razor-blade and insert a small screw C of the same diameter into the other end as far as possible. Fig. 22.3.

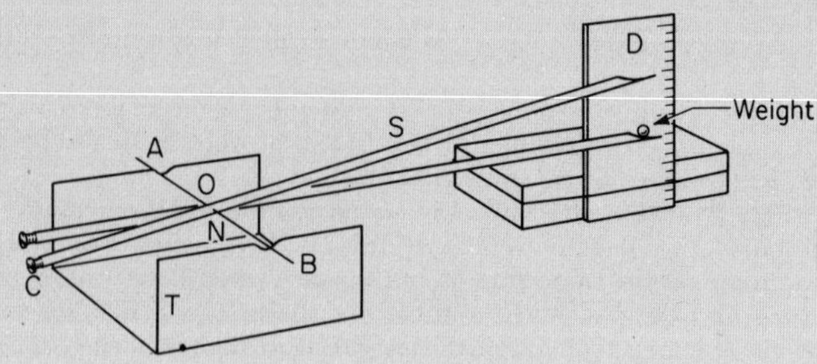

Fig. 2.23 Micro-balance

(ii) Cut two grooves A and B into an aluminium support T so that a sewing-needle can rest on A and B.

(iii) Balance the straw on the sewing-needle to find the approximate position of its centre of gravity. Then push the needle N through the straw at a point O slightly nearer the scoop end of the straw from this position and just *above* the central axis of the straw. Rest N on A and B. It should be slightly inclined, as illustrated by CSD. If necessary, adjust the position of the screw C. Finally, fix a vertical small millimetre scale D just behind the scoop end of the straw—or mark one on a plane piece of wood—and fix it by a rubber-band to a wooden block.

Calibration. (i) 'Weights' may be made from graph paper. Weigh a packet or a larger number of sheets on a balance. The weight of one sheet is then found by division. Then cut one sheet into say ten small squares. By division, the weight of one square is known.

(ii) Note the initial reading of the scoop on the scale D. Roll up one small square of paper, place it in the scoop and note the new reading. Take another reading with a second small square. Calculate the weight which produces a deflection of 1 division on D.

Experiment

Use your balance to find: (i) the weight of a human hair; (ii) the thickness of some aluminium foil. In the latter case, cut off an area of say 5 cm × 5 cm or 25 cm^2, screw it into a small ball, place it in the scoop. From the number of divisions, estimate the mass of the aluminium. Since about 3 g of aluminium has a volume of 1 cm^3, calculate the approximate volume of the aluminium. Then estimate the thickness by *volume/area* (one decimal place).

Measurements. Mass of .. sheets = .. g Reading on scale initially = ..
Mass of 1 sheet = .. g Reading with 1 square = ..
Mass of 1 square = .. g Reading with 2 squares = ..
Mass producing 1 division deflection = ..

Hair. No. of divisions deflection = ..
∴ Mass of hair = .. g.

Aluminium foil. Area = .. cm^2
No. of divisions deflection = ..
∴ Mass = .. g

$$\therefore \text{ Volume} = \frac{\text{mass}}{3\text{g}} = \ldots \text{cm}^3$$

$$\therefore \text{ Thickness} = \frac{\text{volume}}{\text{area}} = \ldots \text{cm.}$$

7. Density of solid (p. 13)

Apparatus. Lever balance or spring balance; lump of metal; measuring cylinder or Eureka can.

Method. (i) Find the mass of a lump of metal S (or large glass stopper).

(ii) To find its volume, immerse it fully inside a measuring cylinder L half full of water and read the difference in levels. Fig. 2.24 (i). Make sure that no bubbles are trapped under the object. If S is too large for a measuring cylinder, use a Eureka can E and catch the water displaced in a measuring cylinder M. Fig. 2.24 (ii).

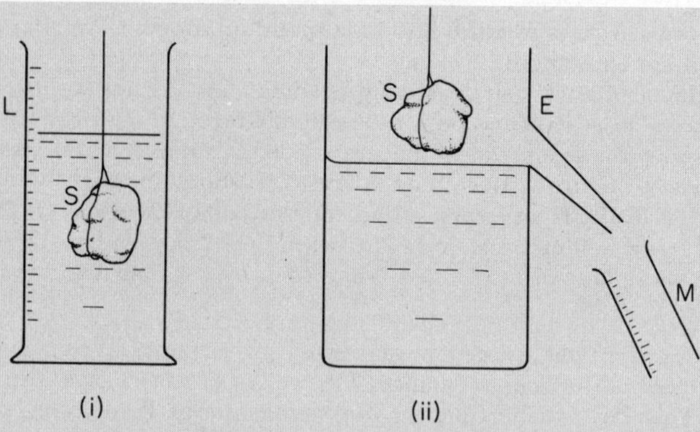

Fig. 2.24 Density of solid

Measurements. Mass of object = .. g/cm³.

Initial reading on L	Final reading	Volume
.. cm³	.. cm³	.. cm³

$$\text{Density} = \frac{\text{mass}}{\text{volume}} = \text{..}\ \text{g/cm}^3.$$

(iii) Calculate the density = mass/volume. (Do not forget the units.) Repeat the experiment.

8. Density of Liquid (p. 15)

Apparatus. Burette; oil; beaker; lever balance.

Method. (i) Fill a burette B with liquid such as oil. Fig. 2.25.

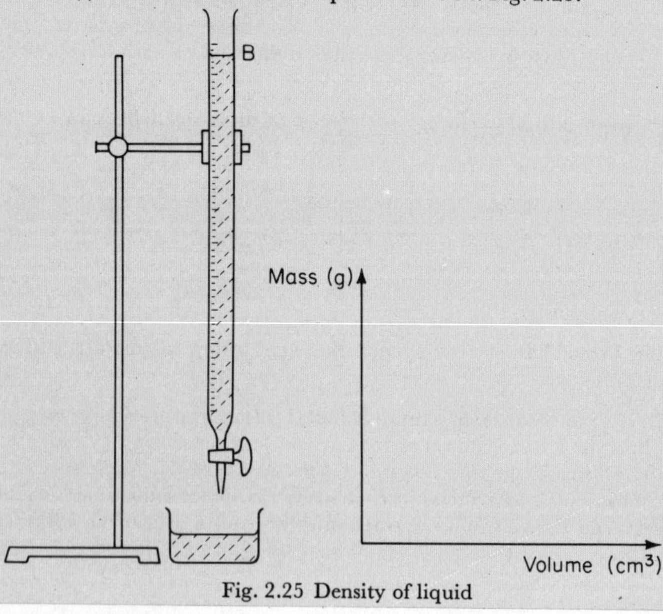

Fig. 2.25 Density of liquid

(ii) Weigh an empty beaker. Then run in 10 cm^3 (10 cc) of liquid. Reweigh the beaker.

(iii) Now run in another 10 cm^3, making 20 cm^3, and reweigh.

Repeat with two more volumes of 10 cm^3, making a total of 40 cm^3.

Measurements.

Volume (cm^3)	Mass (g)
10 ..	..
20 ..	..

Then plot a graph of *mass* v. *volume*, using a zero on each axis. Draw the best straight line from the zero passing through all the points. From the graph, take several values of mass and volume and work out the density from mass/volume.

9. Relative density of liquid (p. 15)

Apparatus. Density bottle; paraffin or other oil; two beakers.

Method. (i) Weigh a clean dry density bottle with the stopper.

(ii) Then fill it with water and reweigh.

(iii) Empty the bottle, dry it and fill it with paraffin oil or other suitable liquid, and reweigh.

(iv) Calculate the RD of the liquid from mass of liquid/mass of water.

Measurements. Mass of bottle empty = .. g
Mass of bottle + water = .. g
Mass of bottle + oil = .. g
Mass of oil filling bottle = .. g
Mass of water filling bottle = .. g

$$\therefore \quad \text{RD} = \frac{..\text{g}}{..\text{g}} = \; .. \text{ (no units).}$$

10. Density of air

This can be found roughly as follows, using apparatus obtainable from leading manufacturers such as Griffin & George Ltd, Wembley, London.

1. Weigh a large plastic container A by suspending it from a spring balance, leaving the tap open. Fig. 2.26.

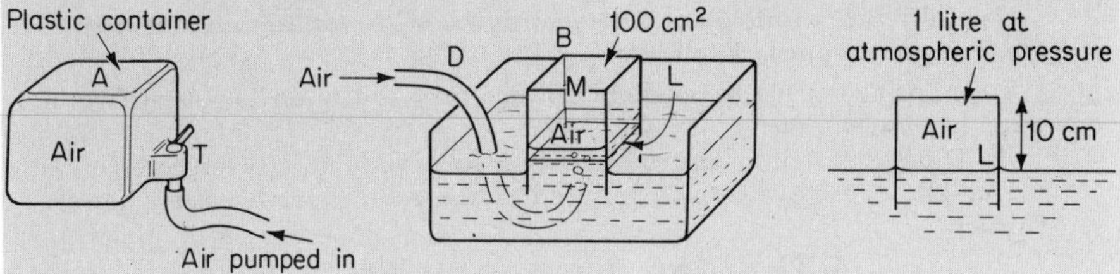

Fig. 2.26 Density of air

2. Using a bicycle pump or foot pump with a *one-way* valve, pump in air to A. Do this until A is about 7 or 8 g heavier, closing the tap firmly and removing the pump.

3. Take an open semi-transparent box B which has a line L drawn on it which gives a volume of exactly 1 litre from the closed end M. Fill B *completely* with water and then invert it over a trough of water ready for the collection of gas—air in this case.

4. Pass the rubber tubing D from A under the open end of M in the trough. Open the tap T so that air slowly bubbles through and pushes the water-level down inside B. Move B up or down until the water-level inside B is at the 1 litre mark *and is level with the water in the trough outside*. At this point, turn the tap to stop the air flow. You have now collected exactly 1 litre of air at atmospheric pressure.

5. Remove the box B from the water. Refill, and as before, collect another 1 litre of air at atmospheric pressure. Repeat this procedure until you have collected from A a whole number of litres and an estimated fraction at atmospheric pressure.

6. Now reweigh A. Find the mass of air from its loss in weight.

7. Work out, to one decimal place, the density of air at atmospheric pressure and room temperature from density $= \frac{\text{mass of air}}{\text{volume of air}}$.

11. Surface tension (p. 18)

1. Dip three capillary tubes of different internal bore well into water in a beaker so that the inside is wetted. Raise the tubes. Observe the difference in levels of the water inside. Draw a sketch of the water-levels.

2. Drop some very small pieces of camphor into a large beaker of water or trough. Observe the movement of the camphor. Explain.

3. (i) Bend some bare copper wire into a circular or rectangular frame and twist the ends together, leaving part of the wire as a 'handle'.

(ii) Make a strong soap solution, dip the wire in and remove it so that a soap film fills the frame. Hold the frame horizontal. Place a light closed thread in the middle of the film. Now pierce the middle of the film inside the thread with a sharp point. Observe the effect on the thread. Repeat with different shapes of closed thread.

4. Fill a glass beaker to the brim with water. Place a dry clean needle on a small piece of filter paper and push the paper gently on to the water surface. After a short time the paper sinks, leaving the needle floating.

Carefully add a little oil or detergent to the water surface near the needle. Observe what happens. Explain.

5. (i) Sprinkle some lycopodium powder very lightly on to the surface of water in a large beaker.

(ii) Dip one end of a glass rod into some soap solution or detergent. Touch the middle of the water with this end of the rod. Observe what happens. Explain.

EXERCISE 2 · ANSWERS, p. 257

1. The mass of a block of steel is 200 g and its volume is 8 cm³. What is its density?

2. The density of gold is 19 g/cm³ (19 000 kg/m³). What does this mean? What is the mass of a gold ring which has a volume of 2 cm³? What volume has a mass of 1900 kg?

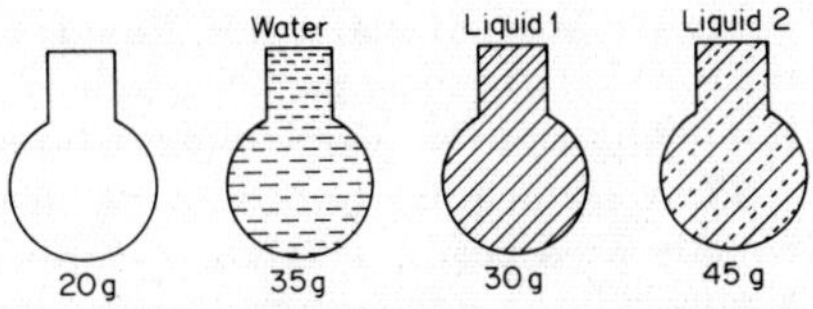

Fig. 2A

3. Calculate the relative densities of liquids 1 and 2, Fig 2A. *Mx.*

4. The mass of a wooden cube is 75 g. Its density is 0·6 g/cm³. Find: (i) the volume of the cube; (ii) the length of one side.

5. 'The relative density of copper is 9.' What does this mean? Write down: (i) the density of copper in g/cm³; (ii) the mass in kg of 4 m³ of copper if the density of water is 1000 kg/m³.

6. What is the density of water? What is the density of mercury if its relative density is 13·6?

7. The dimensions of a steel block are 4 m by 0·5 m by 0·5 m. Calculate its mass if the density of steel is 8000 kg/m³.

8. What is meant by (i) 'mass', (ii) 'weight'? How are they different?
In an expedition on the moon a specimen is 'weighed' twice, once on a spring balance graduated on earth and once on a beam balance The spring balance reads 20 gf and the beam balance gives a figure of 100 g. Explain this. What is the correct mass of the specimen? (*S.E.*)

9. Complete the following table on your answer paper to show which type of balance would be best used for each purpose, Fig. 2B. (Use ticks.)

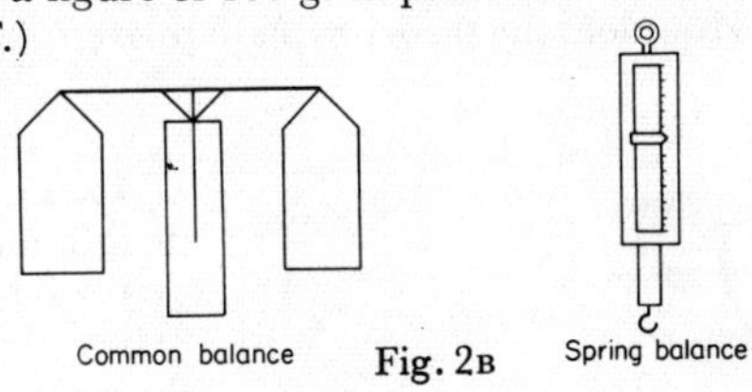

Fig. 2B

	Spring Balance	*Common Balance*
Measurement of horizontal forces		
Measurement of the Force of Gravity acting upon a body		
Comparing the weights of objects		

If you weigh an object with both these instruments: (i) at the North Pole; (ii) at the Equator; (iii) at the top of a mountain; (iv) down a mine; what results would you obtain compared with those you would obtain in your present location? (*W.Md.*)

10. Name the *three* states of matter: (i) . . ; (ii) . . ; (iii) . . (*Mx.*)

11. Explain why: (i) solids have a fixed shape whereas liquids flow; (ii) liquids have a fixed volume whereas gases fill any container in which they are placed. (*S.E.*)

12. We are told that solids, liquids and gases are all made up of small particles. What are these particles called? Describe an experiment which suggests this might be so for *either* a solid *or* a liquid *or* a gas. (*S.E.*)

13. A rectangular box, 5 cm × 20 cm × 30 cm, is completely filled with equally sized beads. The box is emptied out on to a large tray and the beads arranged into a single, closely packed layer in the shape of a rectangle 150 cm × 40 cm. Estimate the diameter of the beads. Explain your calculation. (*S.E.*)

14. Describe an experiment you could perform to estimate the diameter of an atom. Mention all the precautions you would take and all the measurements you would make but there is no need to explain how the result is calculated. (*S.E.*)

15. In the kinetic theory of matter, solids, liquids and gases are all considered to be made up of small, hard particles of fixed size.

(*a*) With this theory, how do we imagine the particles in a solid to be arranged?

(*b*) Solids expand when heated. How does the theory explain this?

(*c*) What happens to the particles when a solid changes into a liquid?

(*d*) What happens to the particles when a liquid changes into a gas?

(*e*) When a gas is heated in a limited space the pressure it exerts increases. How does the theory explain this. (*E.A.*)

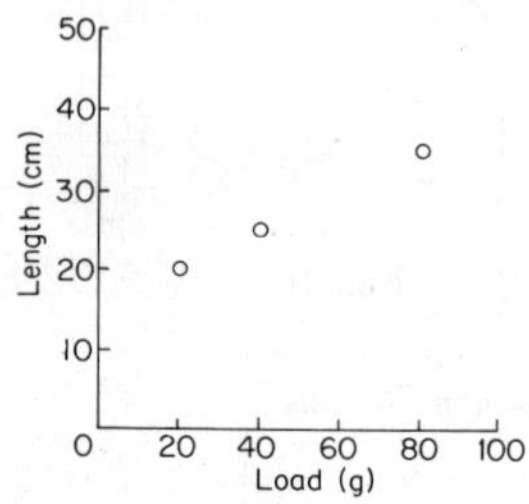

Fig. 2c

16. Fig. 2c shows three points on a graph of length plotted against load for a spiral spring.

(*a*) By completing the graph find: (i) the load when the spring is 30 cm long; (ii) the natural length of the spring.

(*b*) Show how the graph would continue if the load were considerably increased. (*E.A.*)

17. A spring is loaded by stages and its length noted each time. The results are shown in the table.

Load in N	0·5	1·0	1·5	2·0	2·5
Length of spring in cm	36·0	41·5	48·5	54·0	60·0

Draw a graph of these results, plotting 'load' across the page and 'length of spring' up the page. From the graph:

(i) What will be the length of the spring when a load of 1·1 N is applied to it?

(ii) What is the length of the unstretched spring?

(iii) What load will produce an extension of 20 cm? (*S.E.*)

18. (*a*) State *Hooke's law.*

(*b*) Describe in full an experiment to verify this law.

(*c*) Explain how the spacing of the 'marks' on the scale of a spring balance depends upon the law. (*Mx.*)

19. Surface tension can explain all of the following **except** the: (*a*) formation of drops of a liquid; (*b*) floating of a needle on water; (*c*) floating of a cork on water; (*d*) rise of water in narrow tubes; (*e*) soaking up effect of a sponge. (*M.*)

20. A needle will float if carefully placed on the surface of water. This is due to . . . A drop of washing-up liquid added to the water causes the needle to . . (*W.Md.*)

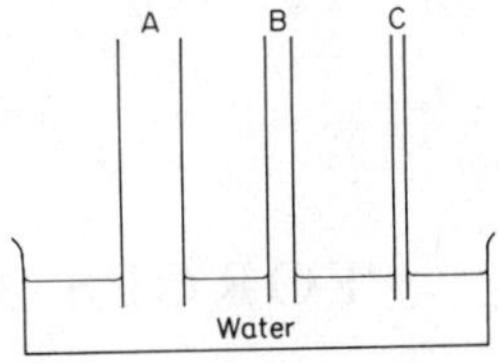

Fig 2D

21. Show the water-levels inside the tubes marked A, B and C. Fig. 2D. The apparatus shows the phenomenon (process) of . . (*W.Md.*)

22. Water is said to 'wet' a glass surface whereas mercury does not. What does this mean?

If a narrow capillary tube were to be placed vertically in troughs of both mercury and water, show with the aid of diagrams what would take place. (*W.Md.*)

23. Fig. 2E shows a piece of very narrow bore capillary tubing partly immersed in water.

(*a*) Explain why the water rises up inside the tube.

(*b*) By referring to your answer to (*a*) explain how: (i) hoeing ground in dry weather helps to keep soil damp; (ii) rolling a cricket pitch brings moisture to the surface. (*L.*)

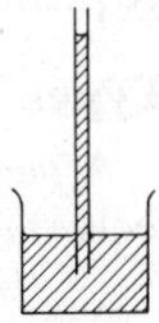
Fig. 2E

24. (*a*) Give an example of the principle of capillarity. Explain the relationship between the dampness on the inside wall of a house and capillarity.

(*b*) What is meant by the surface tension of a liquid?

(*c*) What is the difference in the removal of grease from a dirty plate: (i) with boiling water; (ii) with a detergent and warm water? (*W.Md.*)

25. The diameter of the oil drop in Fig. 2F is measured and is found to be 0·5 mm. When the drop is dipped in water in a tray it spreads out to form a circular patch with a diameter of 20 cm.

(i) What is the volume of the drop?

(ii) If the patch is t mm thick write down the volume of the patch in terms of 't'.

(iii) What is the relationship between the volume of the drop and the volume of the patch?

(iv) How thick will the patch be if a drop of diameter 0·5 mm makes a patch with a diameter of 20 cm?

(v) What does your value of the thickness of the oil film tell you about the size of a molecule of oil? (*S.E.*)

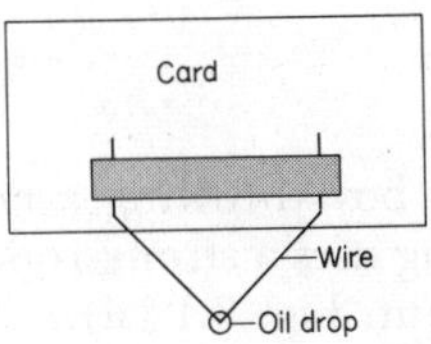

Fig. 2F

3

FORCES AND MOMENTS · CENTRE OF GRAVITY

In this chapter we discuss *forces* and their turning-effects. Many machines have been designed to exert large forces. Cranes and pulleys, seen at building sites, can lift heavy girders, for example. Heavy rollers at printing presses or textile mills are driven by powerful motors.

Types of Forces

A *push* and a *pull* are examples of forces. If a girl pushes a pram she feels the force exerted by her muscles, which become taut, Fig. 3.1 (i).

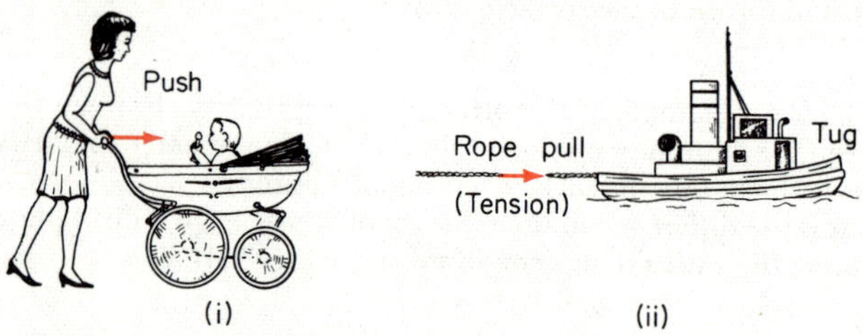

Fig. 3.1 Force may be (i) push or (ii) pull

A boy throwing a cricket ball feels a force in the same way. When a tug uses a strong rope to pull a boat from a sandbank the rope becomes taut. Fig. 3.1 (ii).

Forces are described by different names. Some forces are shown in Fig. 3.2. A *tension* is the force in a rope or chain, Fig. 3.2 (i). A *weight* is the pulling force due to gravity—note that it always acts vertically downwards. A *reaction* is the force of a surface on an object resting against it. In Fig. 3.2 (ii), if the ladder rests against a part of the wall which is smooth, the total reaction is perpendicular (normal) to the wall, as shown. But to prevent the ladder from slipping, a *frictional force* must act at the ground.

It is very important to note that a force has direction as well as magnitude (size). A force is an example of a class of quantities in physics called 'vectors'—these all have direction as well as magnitude. *In diagrams, always draw a line with an arrow on it to mark the direction of the force or vector.*

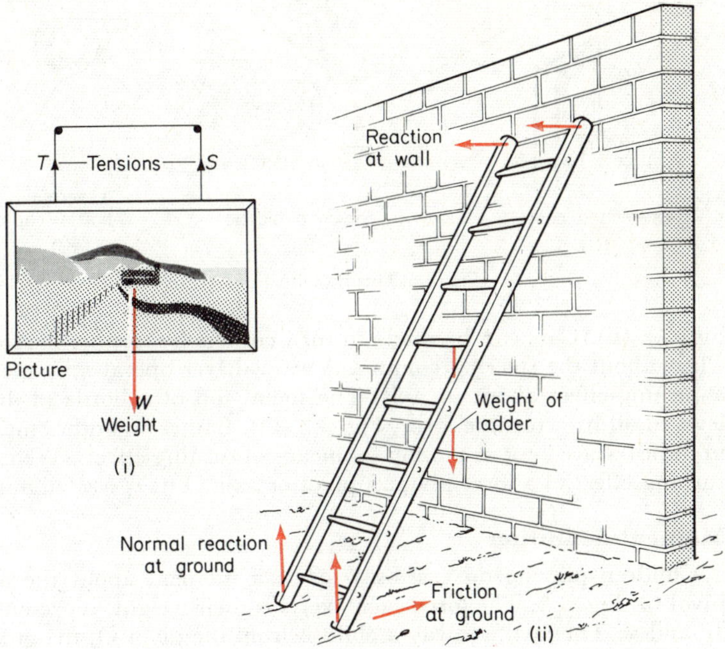

Fig. 3.2 Types of forces

Units of Force

The most common force is 'weight', the force due to gravity. Gravity acts on all objects, large or tiny.

In SI units, force is measured in *newtons*, symbol N. The newton is defined on p. 138. The force of gravity on a 1 kg mass (its weight) is about 10 N. The weight of a cricket ball is about 1·5 N. The weight of a girl may be 500 N.

On the Moon, where the force of gravity is one-sixth of that on the Earth, the weights of all objects would be one-sixth of their weights on the Earth.

Moments of forces

The *turning-effect* of a force is widely used in everyday life and in machines. When a door is opened, for example, the force at the handle exerts a turning-effect on the hinges, Fig. 3.3 (i). The force on the pedals of a bicycle exerts a turning-effect about the wheel axle.

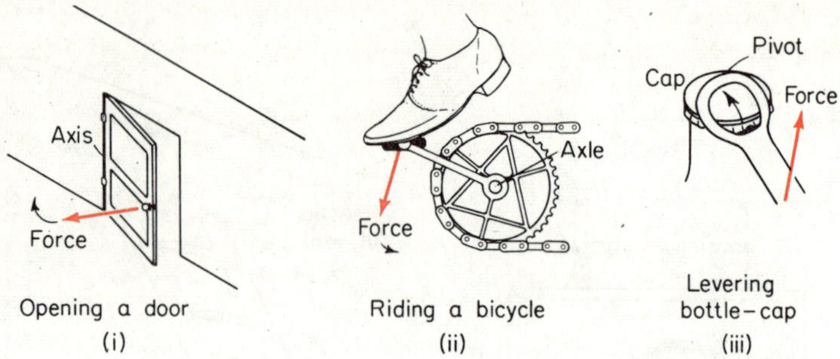

Fig. 3.3 Turning-effect of forces

Fig. 3.3 (ii). Cars can be made to turn corners by turning the steering wheel about the steering column. A screwdriver operates by means of a turning-effect about its axis. The metal top of a bottle of drink is levered off by a turning force, Fig. 3.3 (iii). Lathes and other machines in industry are kept in motion by means of turning effects. We call the turning effect of a force about a pivot or axle O its *moment* about O.

Moment definition

Children playing on a see-saw exert a moment about the axis or pivot O, Fig. 3.4. The force each exerts is their weight, represented by W and w. The farther away a child is from the pivot O, the greater is

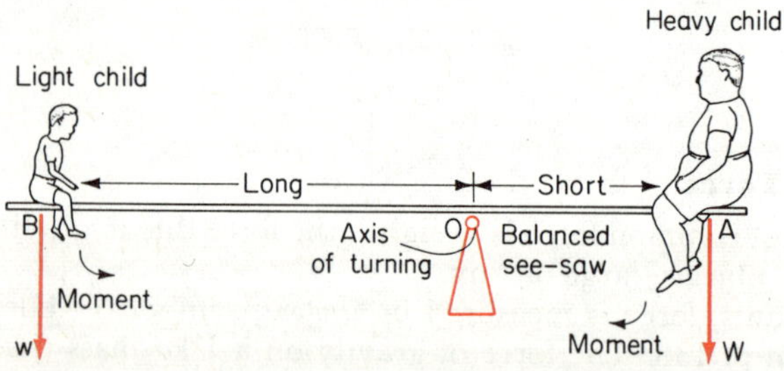

Fig. 3.4 Moment depends on distance and force

the moment about O. Thus the moment increases when the distance of the weight from O increases. Also, a heavy child at the same place has a greater moment than a light child. Thus the moment increases when the weight or force increases.

Both force and distance are taken into account in the definition of moment. This states:

Moment about point or axis O = Force × perpendicular distance from O to line of action of force

Moment can be clockwise or anticlockwise. In Fig. 3.4, the heavy child at A has a moment about O which is clockwise. The light child at B has a moment about O which is anticlockwise. If the clockwise moment is 20 units and the anticlockwise moment is 15 units, the total or resultant moment is 20 − 15 or 5 units and is clockwise. The beam turns, with the heavy child going down. The rule is:

Subtract moments which are clockwise from those which are anticlockwise to find their resultant, or vice versa.

Add moments which are all clockwise, or all anticlockwise.

Calculating moments

In calculating moments, one has to be careful about the 'perpendicular distance' or 'arm' of the force about the point or axis concerned. Here are some examples:

1. In Fig. 3.5 (i) a rope attached to the upper edge X of a heavy box exerts a force P of 10 N. The force acts horizontally. Thus its moment about the edge O on the ground = 10 × perpendicular distance from O = 10 × OX = 10 × 3 = 30 N m (newton metre), clockwise. The moment of the weight, 20 N, about O = 20 × 1 = 20 N m, anticlockwise.

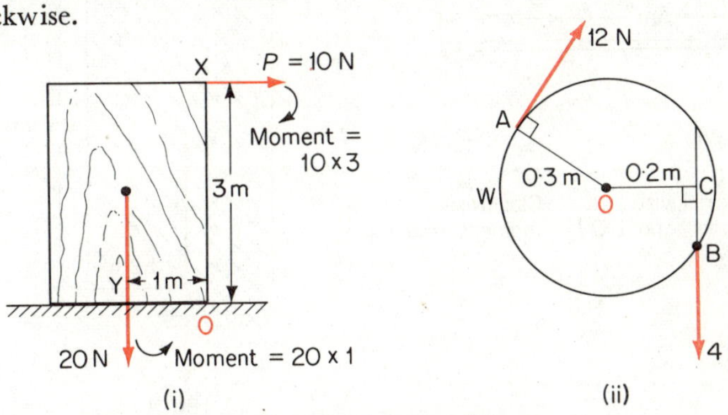

Fig. 3.5 Moments of forces

2. In Fig. 3.5 (ii) a rope attached to A on a wheel W of centre O exerts a force of 12 N along the tangent to W at A. The radius OA, say 0·3 metre, is then the perpendicular distance from O to the force. Thus moment = 12 × 0·3 = 3·6 N m, clockwise.

Another rope at B exerts a 4 N force which is not tangential to the wheel. Suppose the perpendicular distance OC from O is 0·2 metre. Then moment = 4 × 0·2 = 0·8 N m, clockwise.

The units of the moment are always those of the force and distance concerned; the force unit is always given first. Thus moments may be expressed in 'newton metre'.

Equilibrium and Moments

When a see-saw is just balanced by two children on opposite sides of the pivot, it is said to be in equilibrium. The clockwise moment of one weight about the pivot must now be exactly *equal* to the anticlockwise moment of the other weight about the pivot. The same *principle of moments*, as it is known, is true when there are several forces on one side of the pivot. We can say that, generally:

If a pivoted object is in equilibrium under several forces, the total clockwise moment of the forces about the pivot = the total anticlockwise moments of the forces about the pivot.

1. As a simple illustration of what this means, consider a light beam pivoted at O in equilibrium under forces of 40 and 100 N at either end. Fig. 3.6. Taking moments about O:

$$\text{Total clockwise moment} = \text{Total anticlockwise moment}$$
$$\therefore \quad 100 \times x = 40 \times 3$$
$$\therefore x = \frac{120}{100} = 1{\cdot}2 \text{ m}$$

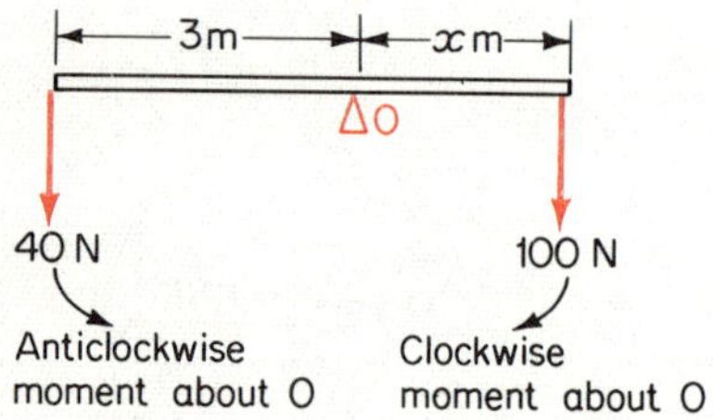

Fig. 3.6 Clockwise and anticlockwise moments

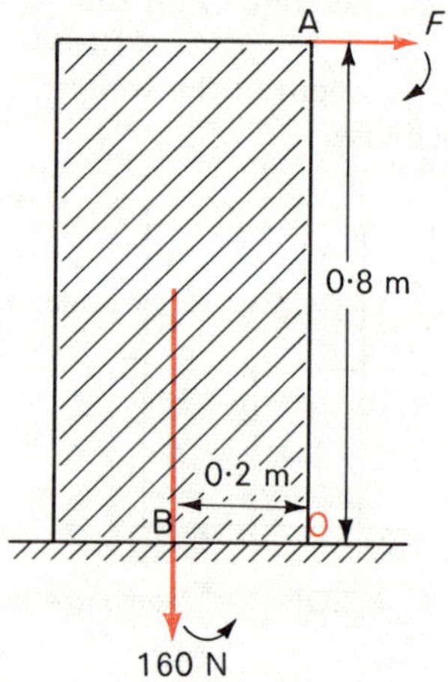

Fig. 3.7 Calculation in moments

2. Fig. 3.7 shows a heavy solid block with a rope tied to its upper edge A. The weight of the block is 160 N acting vertically, OB is 0·2 m and OA is 0·8 m. To find the force *F* which will just tilt the block about O, take moments about O.

Then:

$$\text{Total clockwise moment about O} = \text{total anticlockwise moment about O}$$
$$\therefore F \times 0{\cdot}8 = 160 \times 0{\cdot}2$$
$$\therefore \quad F = \frac{160 \times 0{\cdot}2}{0{\cdot}8} = 40 \text{ N.}$$

3. Fig. 3.8 shows a beam AB of weight 80 N acting at its centre G. It is pivoted at O and is in equilibrium under a force of 200 N at B and an unknown weight *W* at A. To find *W*, we have:

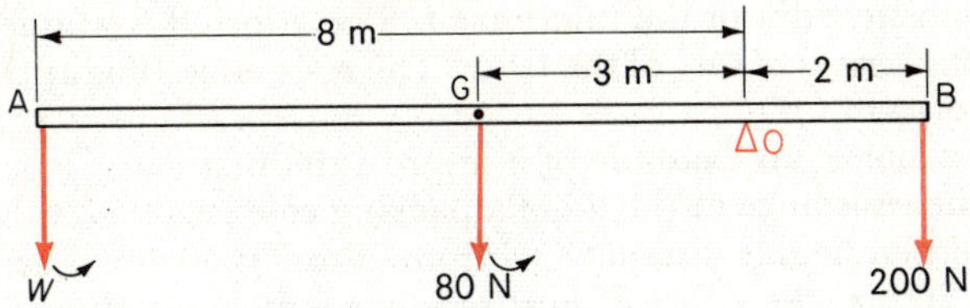

Fig. 3.8 Beam calculation

Total clockwise moment about O = total anticlockwise moment about O

$$\therefore 200 \times 2 = W \times 8 + 80 \times 3$$
$$\therefore 400 = 8\,W + 240$$
$$\therefore 400 - 240 = 8\,W$$
$$\therefore 160 = 8\,W$$
$$\therefore 20\text{ N} = W.$$

Levers

A *lever* is a class of machine which uses the turning-effect or moment of a small force to overcome a large weight or resistance or load. All levers have a pivot or axis called the *fulcrum*, about which the leverage takes place.

Levers are divided into three classes. The *first class* is shown diagrammatically in Fig. 3.9 (i). Here the force or effort P, and the resistance W

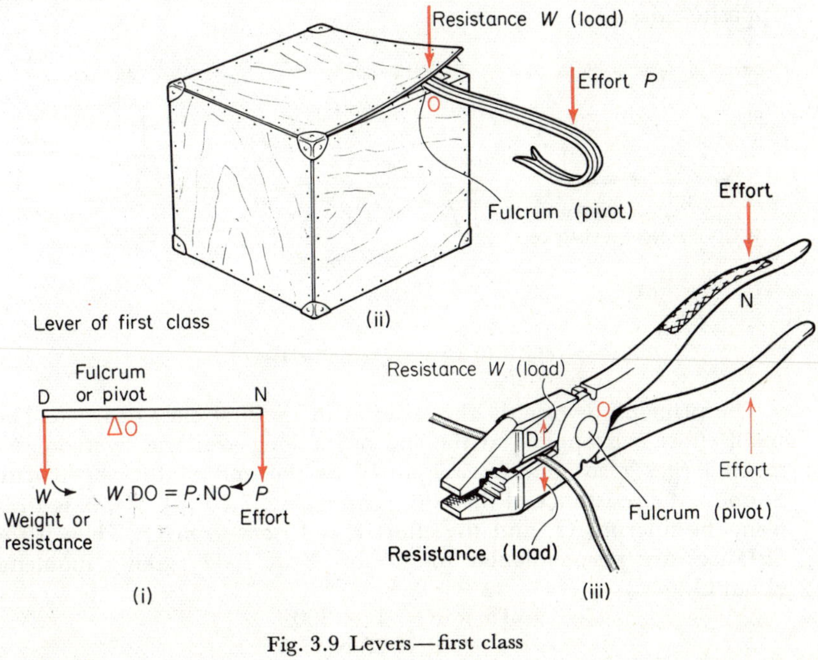

Fig. 3.9 Levers—first class

are on opposite sides of the fulcrum O. The effort P is applied at the end N of the *long* arm ON of the lever. The resistance W is at the end D of the short arm OD.

The crowbar is an example of a lever of the first class. Fig. 3.9 (ii). Suppose the resistance at the lid of a packing case is 200 N, OD is 5 cm and the perpendicular distance ON from O to P is 50 cm. Then, to just overcome 200 N, the effort P must produce a moment about O which is very slightly greater than the moment of the 200 N force about O. Thus, practically,

$$P \times 50 = 200 \times 5$$
$$\therefore 50P = 1000$$
$$\therefore P = \frac{1000}{50} = 20 \text{ N}.$$

Thus a force P of 20 N can overcome a force 10 times as great.

Pliers, used for cutting wire, are another example of the first class of levers. Fig. 3.9 (iii). A small force or effort overcomes the large resistance of the wire. A pair of scissors is another example of a lever of the first class.

Second Class of Levers

A *bottle-top opener* and a *nut-cracker* are examples of levers of the second class. Fig. 3.10 (i), (ii), (iii). Here the resistance W is on the *same* side of the fulcrum O as the effort P. In the first class of levers they are on opposite sides.

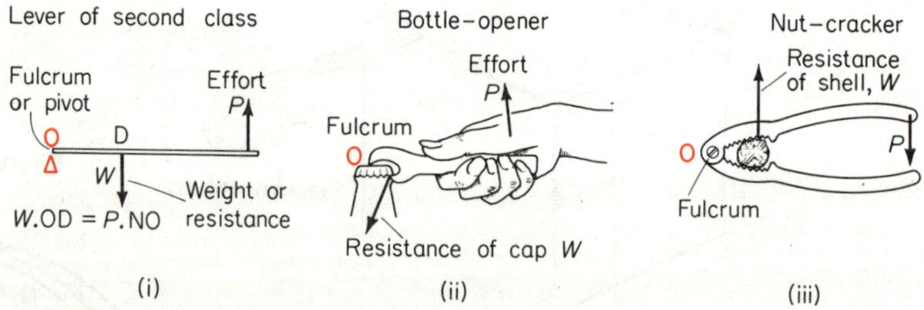

Fig. 3.10 Levers—second class

The principle is exactly the same as in the first class of lever. The small effort P is applied at the end of the long arm and overcomes a much larger resistance or weight W at the end of the short arm. Suppose the resistance of the bottle cap in Fig. 3.10 (ii), 300 N is 1 cm from the fulcrum O, and the effort P is 15 cm from O. Then if the distances are perpendicular to the forces we have, taking moments about O,

$$15 \times P = 1 \times 300$$
$$\therefore P = 20 \text{ N}.$$

Third Class of Levers

If sugar tongs or coal tongs are used however the effort P is *nearer* the fulcrum O than the resistance of weight W. Fig. 3.11 (i), (ii). This is the characteristic of the third class of levers.

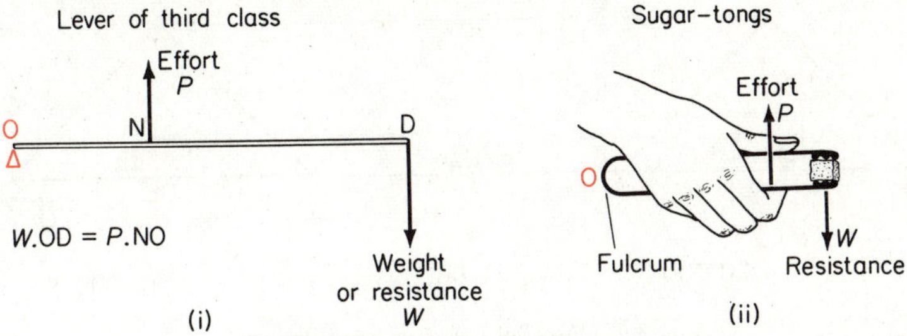

Fig. 3.11 Levers—third class

To find P when a lump of coal has a resistance W of 1 N and the perpendicular distances to the hinge or fulcrum O are 20 cm and 30 cm respectively, take moments about O. Then:

$$P \times 20 = 1 \times 30, \text{ or } P = 1{\cdot}5 \text{ N}.$$

An effort larger than the resistance is now required.

The *forearm*, used for picking up objects using the elbow O as a fulcrum, is an example of the third class of levers. The muscular force P of the biceps is nearer O than the weight W. Fig. 3.12 (i). The *lever*

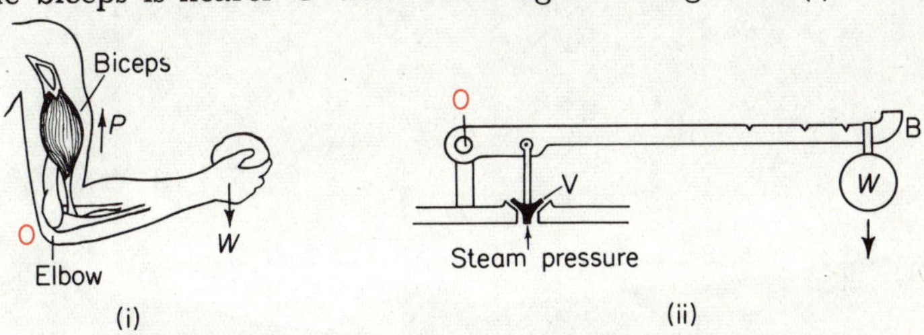

Fig. 3.12 Levers in use. (i) arm (ii) boiler safety-valve

safety valve, used on boilers, has a valve V fitting into the boiler, and a lever OB carrying a weight W. Fig. 3.12 (ii). When the steam pressure exceeds a dangerous value, fixed by the position of W, the valve V rises and allows the steam to escape until the pressure falls. This is another example of a third class of levers

PARALLEL FORCES

Equilibrium of Parallel Forces

In mechanics there are a number of cases where an object is kept in equilibrium by parallel forces. Consider the case of part of a bridge with traffic stationary on it at some instant. Fig. 3.13. The weights of the individual vehicles shown are 20 000, 5000 and 10 000 N respectively. The reaction forces on the bridge at the supports are P and Q. If the weight of the bridge is omitted from consideration for convenience, then the bridge is under the equilibrium of five parallel forces.

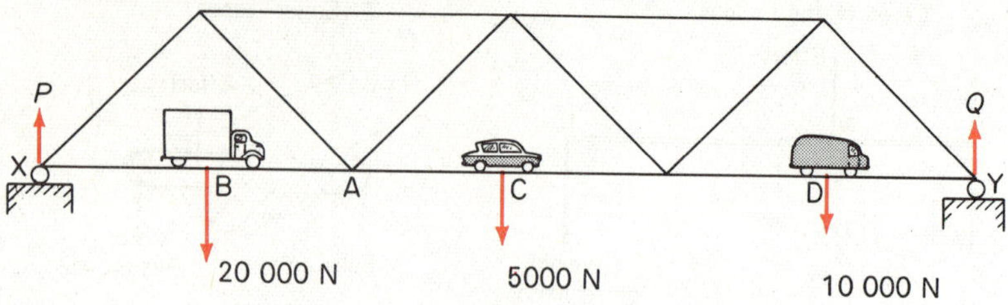

Fig. 3.13 Parallel forces in equilibrium

The total upward force on the bridge is $(P + Q)$. The total downward force is 35 000 N. Thus, for equilibrium, $P + Q = 35\,000$ N.

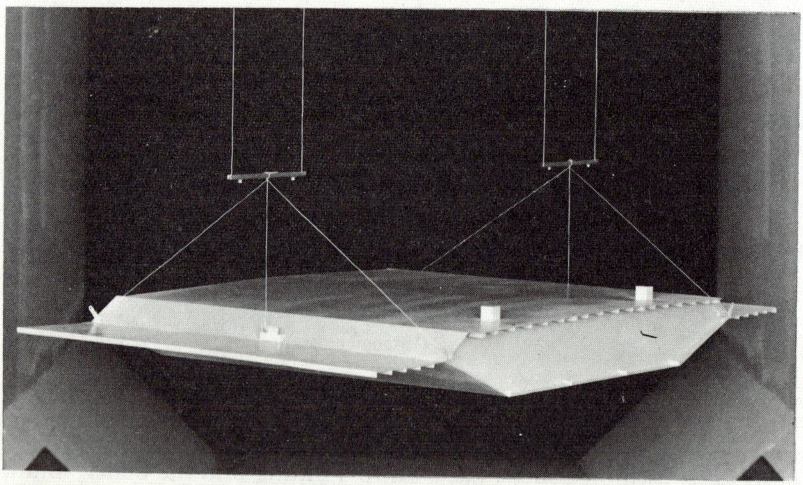

Plate 3(A) Model cross-section of the Severn Bridge, tested in a wind tunnel at the National Physical Laboratory for behaviour in high winds.

Moments

If a bridge is in equilibrium, the total clockwise moments of the forces *about any point or axis* must equal the total anticlockwise moments of the forces about the same point. Otherwise, the forces will produce a resultant moment, either clockwise or anticlockwise, about that point, and the bridge will then *not* be in equilibrium. Suppose we choose to take moments about the point A in Fig. 3.13. Then:

total clockwise moments about $A = (P \times XA) + (5000\ N \times CA) + (10\ 000\ N \times DA)$; and total anticlockwise moments about $A = (20\ 000\ N \times BA) + (Q \times YA)$.

These two moments are equal.

Again, suppose we choose now to take moments about the point Y. *Q has no moment about Y*. Taking moments for the remaining four forces,

total clockwise moment about $Y = P \times XY$

and total anticlockwise moment about $Y = (20\ 000\ N \times BY) + (5000\ N \times CY) + (10\ 000\ N \times DY)$

These two moments are equal.

Summarizing: When an object is in equilibrium under the action of parallel forces:

Plate 3(B) A new suspension bridge, spanning the Danube at Budapest, is tested before opening by loading with vehicles.

(i) *Total forces in one direction = total forces in opposite direction.*

(ii) *The total clockwise moment about any point or axis = the total anticlockwise moment about the same point.*

Calculations with Parallel Forces

We can now apply these two principles to calculate unknown parallel forces.

(1) In Fig. 3.14, AD is a rod of negligible weight with a load of 400 N at O. It is supported at B and C on the respective shoulders of two men. The distances in metres are shown.

To find the forces of reaction P and Q at B and C respectively, we first use the principle that the total upward force = the total downward force.

$$\therefore P + Q = 400 \quad . \quad . \quad . \quad . \quad . \quad . \quad (1)$$

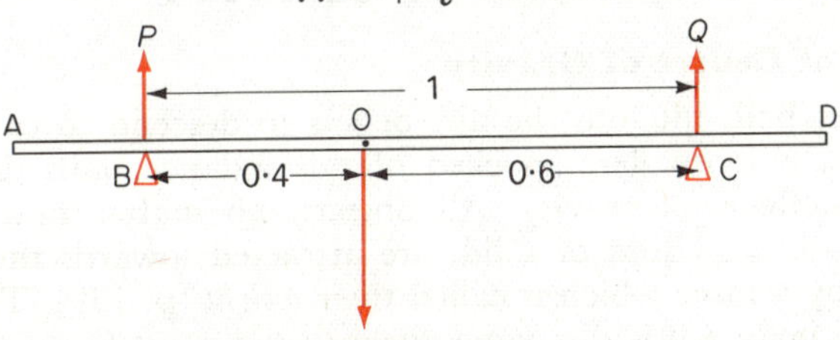

Fig. 3.14 Beam calculation

Next, use the principle that the total clockwise moment about any point equals the total anticlockwise moment about the same point. We can take moments about any point on the beam. But to eliminate the force Q, for example, take moments about C, where Q acts, *because the moment of Q about a point on its line of action is zero.*

Then Moment of P about C $= P \times BC = P \times 1$, clockwise

Moment of 400 N about C $= 400 \times OC = 400 \times 0{\cdot}6$, anticlockwise

Moment of Q about C $= 0$

$\therefore P \times 1 = 400 \times 0{\cdot}6$, or $P = 240$ N. . . . (2)

Hence, from (1), $Q = 400 - P = 400 - 240 = 160$ N.

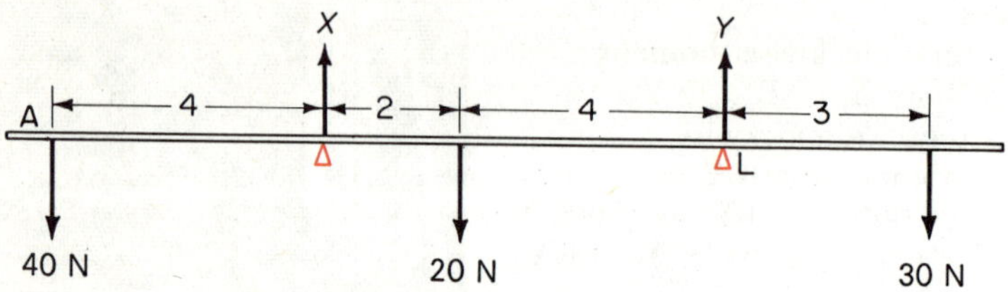

Fig. 3.15 Beam calculation

(2) Another example is shown in Fig. 3.15; forces are in N, distances in metres. To find X and Y, the reactions at the supports, we have:

(i) Total upward force $= X + Y =$ Total downward force $= 40 + 20 + 30 = 90$ N.

(ii) Moments about left-hand support,

Total anticlockwise moment $= 40 \times 4 + Y \times (2 + 4)$
$= 20 \times 2 + 30 \times 9$
$=$ total clockwise moment

$\therefore 160 + 6Y = 40 + 270 = 310$

$\therefore Y = 25$ N

From above, $\therefore X = 90 - Y = 65$ N.

CENTRE OF GRAVITY

Meaning of Centre of Gravity

A cricket ball, hit into the air, begins to descend to earth after a short time; a footballer, knocked off his balance, falls downwards. These are effects of gravity. All objects, no matter how small, or whether gaseous, liquid or solid, are attracted towards the centre of the earth by a force which is called their *weight* (p. 139). The *centre of gravity* of a body AB is the name given to the point G through which its total weight appears to act, Fig. 3.16.

If you balance your ruler on a horizontal pencil P, you are supporting

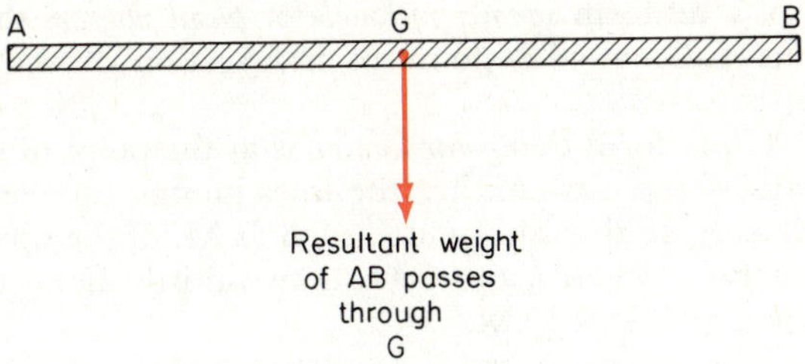

Fig. 3.16 Centre of gravity (C.G.)

the whole weight of the ruler, Fig. 3.17 (i). Its centre of gravity G must then be somewhere directly above the line of the pencil. If the ruler is now balanced on the end B of the pencil, G is somewhere directly above B, Fig. 3.17 (ii).

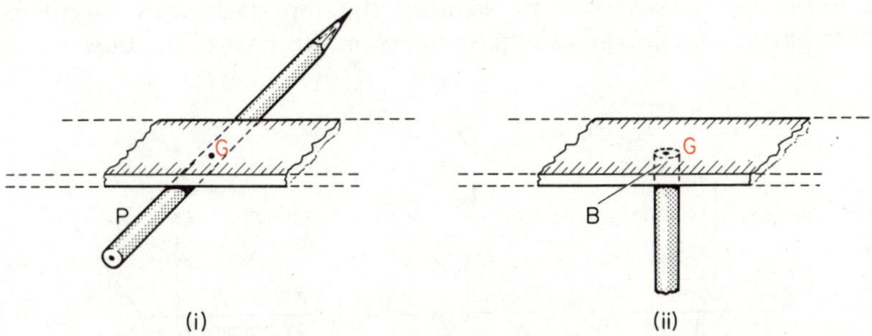

Fig. 3.17 Finding C.G.

C.G. Positions

The centre of gravity (C.G.) of a *uniform rod* is at its mid-point. The C.G. of a uniform *circular disc* is at the centre of the circle, Fig. 3.18 (i). The C.G. of a uniform *ring* is at the centre, Fig. 3.18 (ii). Here we can divide the whole ring into equal small pieces at the end of the diameter. Although there is no material at the centre of a ring, this is the point where the resultant or total weight of the ring appears to act.

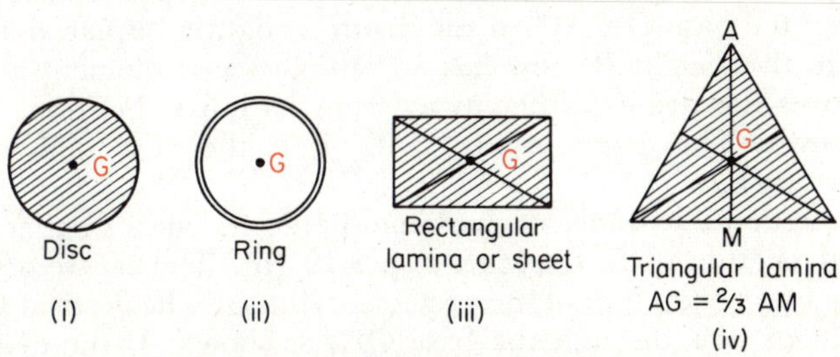

Fig. 3.18 C.G. positions

The C.G. of a uniform *square*, *rectangle* or *parallelogram* thin sheet or lamina has its C.G. at the point of intersection of the diagonals, Fig. 3.18 (iii).

The C.G. of a uniform *triangular lamina* is at the point of intersection of the 'medians'—the medians are the lines joining the vertices of the triangle, such as A, to the mid-points, such as M, of the opposite sides, Fig. 3.18 (iv). By geometry, the C.G. is two-thirds along the median from any vertex, or AG = $\frac{2}{3}$AM.

Stability and Centre of Gravity

In designing a car or a ship, the engineer must take into account its *stability*. A car turning a corner fast or going round a sharp bend in the road at high speed has a tendency to overturn. Ships, which are liable to considerable rolling and lurching in heavy seas, must be designed to be in stable equilibrium even in rough weather. Tests for stability of buses are carried out by loading the top deck with sandbags, representing an equivalent of passengers on this part of the bus.

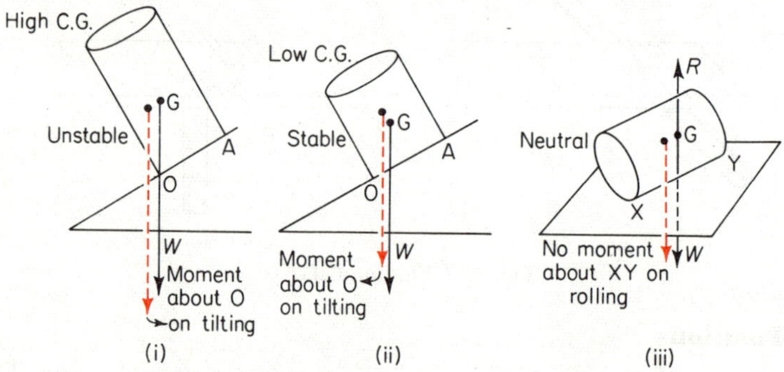

Fig. 3.19 Stable, unstable and neutral equilibrium

The stability of an object depends on the position of its centre of gravity and the moment its weight exerts. As a simple example, consider an oil-drum held on an inclined plane as shown in Fig. 3.19 (i). The vertical through its centre of gravity G just passes through the edge O of the base OA. When the drum is slightly displaced about O as shown, the weight *W* now has an anticlockwise moment about O. This moves the drum farther away from its initial position. Thus it topples over. The drum in Fig. 3.19 (i) is therefore said to be in *unstable equilibrium*.

Suppose that a cylinder of the same diameter, but a smaller height, is placed on the inclined plane, Fig. 3.19 (ii). The centre of gravity G is now lower than that of the previous cylinder. The vertical through G may then pass through the base OA, as shown. If the cylinder is slightly tilted about O and then released, the weight *W* now exerts a clockwise movement about O. This restores the cylinder to its original position. Consequently, the cylinder is said to be in *stable equilibrium* in Fig. 3.19 (ii).

Summarizing: (i) If the vertical line through the centre of gravity of an object passes through its base when the object is slightly displaced the object is in stable equilibrium; (ii) if it passes outside the base when the object is slightly displaced the object is in unstable equilibrium.

If the cylinder is taken and placed with its curved surface XY on a horizontal plane, it will be in equilibrium no matter what position it assumes on rolling, Fig. 3.19 (iii). This is due to the fact that in a displaced position, unlike the previous cases the weight W has no moment about the axis XY. The cylinder is therefore said to be in *neutral equilibrium*. Here the upward reaction R of the plane always passes through G and is always equal and opposite to W.

Stable and Unstable Objects

From what has been said, it can be seen that the risk of unstable equilibrium is increased as the height of the centre of gravity of an object is increased. The vertical through the C.G. is then more liable to fall outside the base when the object is slightly tilted. The nearer the centre of gravity is to the ground, the more stable is the equilibrium likely to be.

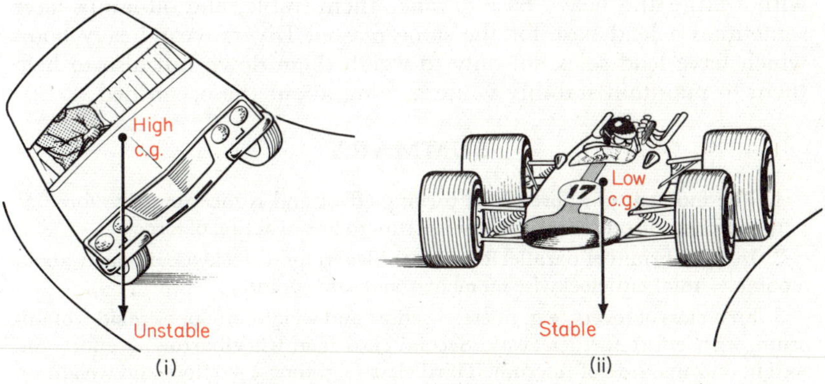

Fig. 3.20 Unstable and stable cars

For this reason, extra passengers are allowed on the lower deck of a crowded bus, but not on the upper deck; the centre of gravity G of bus and passengers must be low, so that the vertical through G falls between the wheels even when the bus is rounding a corner. A car turning a sharp corner at a too high speed may become unstable if its centre of gravity is high, Fig. 3.20 (i). For the same reason racing cars are built low, Fig. 3.20 (ii).

The base of the stand of a punchball is a very heavy piece of metal; the C.G. of the whole arrangement is then so low that it is in stable equilibrium, and the ball returns to the boxer however powerfully it is struck. Toys which spring up to the vertical, no matter how they are laid on the table, have a rounded heavy lead base, so that the vertical through the C.G. of the toy always passes through the base, Fig. 3.21.

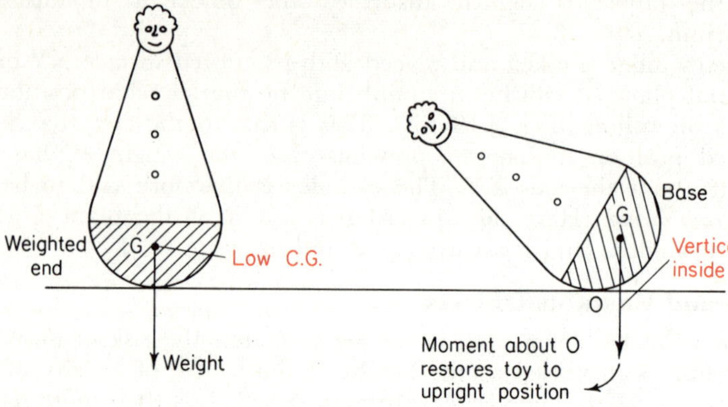

Fig. 3.21 A low C.G. helps stability

Articles such as bunsen burners and electric lamp-stands are designed with a large and heavy base to make them stable, and oil-lamps have sometimes a lead base for the same reason. Divers wear heavy boots which have lead soles not only to weigh them down but also to help them to maintain stability while moving about the ocean-bed.

SUMMARY

1. The moment of a force is its turning-effect and is measured by 'force × perpendicular distance from axis or fulcrum to line of action of force'.

2. In equilibrium of parallel forces or the lever, total clockwise moment about a point = total anticlockwise moment about same point.

3. First class of levers (e.g. pliers) — effort and weight on opposite sides of fulcrum, with effort further away. Second class (e.g. wheelbarrow)—effort and weight on same side of fulcrum. Third class (e.g. tongs)—effort and weight on same side with effort nearer fulcrum.

4. Centre of gravity is the point where the total weight of object acts. Found by a balancing or plumbline method.

5. If an object returns to its original position on being slightly displaced, its equilibrium was stable. If it moves further away, it was unstable. If it remains in its displaced position, it was in neutral equilibrium.

PRACTICAL (Notes for guidance, p. 26)

1. Moments

Apparatus. Light rod or ruler; weights such as 100 or 50 g; thread: clamp and stand.

Suspend a ruler R by string at its mid-point O so that it balances—a small piece of plasticene at one end may be needed to produce a balance, Fig. 3.22 (i).

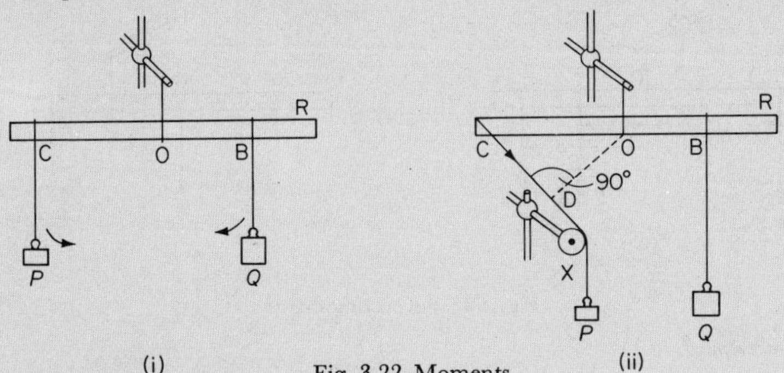

Fig. 3.22 Moments

Attach a 100 g weight Q by a loop of thread on one side at B and a smaller weight P such as 50 g on the other side at C.

Move the larger weight until R balances. Measure OC and OB. Move P twice more, counterbalance each time by moving Q, and again record the values of OC and OB.

Measurements.

Q (N) P (N)	OB (m)	OC (m)	$Q \times$ OB (N m)	$P \times$ OC (N m)

Calculate the moments $P \times$ OC and $Q \times$ OB for each of the measurements.

Conclusion. State the conclusion.

2. Moment and perpendicular (p. 40)

Apparatus. Light rod or ruler; two different weights; pulley wheel; thread; two clamps and stands.

To investigate the moment when one force acts at an angle to a balance beam, place a grooved or pulley wheel X as shown in Fig. 3·22 (ii). Attach the weight P by thread to C and pass the thread round X as shown. The force at C now acts at an angle to the ruler which is not 90°. Restore the balance by moving Q.

Using a large protractor or two rulers, measure the perpendicular distance OD from O to XC.

Measurements.

Q (N)	P (N)	OB (m)	OD (m)	$Q \times$ OB (N m)	$P \times$ OD (N m)

Calculate the moments $P \times$ OD and $Q \times$ OB. Compare the results. Vary the position of X and repeat the measurements of the moments.

Conclusion. State the conclusion.

3. Several moments (p. 48)

Apparatus. Light rod or ruler; three different weights; thread; clamp and stand.

Balance a ruler R at its middle O, Fig. 3·23 (i). Attach two different weights P and Q on one side of O and move a larger weight W on the other side until the ruler is balanced again.

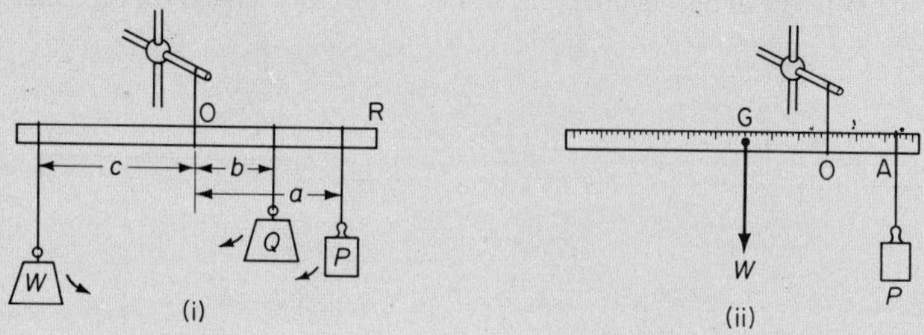

Fig. 3.23 Several moments

Measurements.

P (N)	Q (N)	W (N)	a (m)	b (m)	c (m)

Total clockwise moment $= P \times a + Q \times b = ..$ N m.
Total anticlockwise moment $= W \times c = ..$ N m.

Calculate the total clockwise moment about O of the forces P and Q; and the clockwise moment about O of the force W. Compare the results.

Repeat the experiment by moving the positions of P and Q on the ruler.

4. To find weight of a ruler

Apparatus. Light rod or ruler; weights.

Method. (i) Balance a metre ruler lengthwise on a pencil, and hence find roughly the position of its centre of gravity G.

(ii) Suspend the ruler at a whole number division O such as '75 cm', Fig. 3.23.

(ii) Attach a suitable weight P to A on the opposite side to G, and move A until the ruler balances.

(iii) Measure OA and OG.

Measurements.

P (N)	OA (m)	OG (m)

$$W \times \text{OG} = P \times \text{OA}$$
$$\therefore W \times .. = .. \times ..$$
$$\therefore W = \quad .. \text{N}.$$

Calculate the weight W of the ruler from $W \times \text{OG} = P \times \text{OA}$. Repeat the experiment with a different weight to P or with a different position for O. Find the unknown weights of other suitable objects in this way, for example, an umbrella or bat or racket.

5. Parallel forces in equilibrium (p. 45)

Apparatus. Metre rule or light rod; two spring balances; heavy weight; rod, clamps and stands as support for spring balances.

Method. (i) Suspend two spring balances P and Q from a rod BC supported in two clamps, Fig. 3·24.

(ii) Place a light beam or ruler A between the hooks of P and Q.

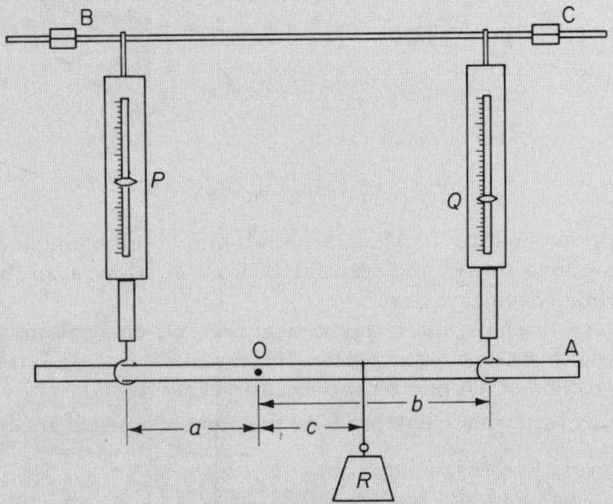

Fig. 3.24 Parallel forces

(iii) Attach a known heavy weight R between P and Q, and record the readings on P and Q. Does $P + Q = R$? How do you account for any difference between $(P + Q)$ and R?

(iv) Take *any* point O on the beam. Measure the respective distances a, b and c of the three forces P, Q and R from O.

Measurements.

P (N)	Q (N)	R (N)	a (m)	b (m)	c (m)

(i) $P + Q =$ .. N. $R =$ .. N.
(ii) Total clockwise moment about O = .. N m.
Total anticlockwise moment about O = .. N m.

Calculate the total anticlockwise moment about O, $Qb + Rc$, and the clockwise moment about O, $P.a$. Compare the two results.

Repeat for another position of R. Repeat by attaching another weight W near R so that there are two downward forces on A.

6. Centre of gravity by plumb-line (p. 48)

Apparatus. Irregular-shaped cardboard or other flat sheet; long pin; thread attached to small weight as plumb-line.

Method. Take a thick piece of cardboard or hardboard L of irregular shape, Fig. 3·25 (i). Bore a hole A in it. Pass a smooth nail or pin P through A so that L swings freely about P—if necessary, enlarge the hole. Now suspend L by P,

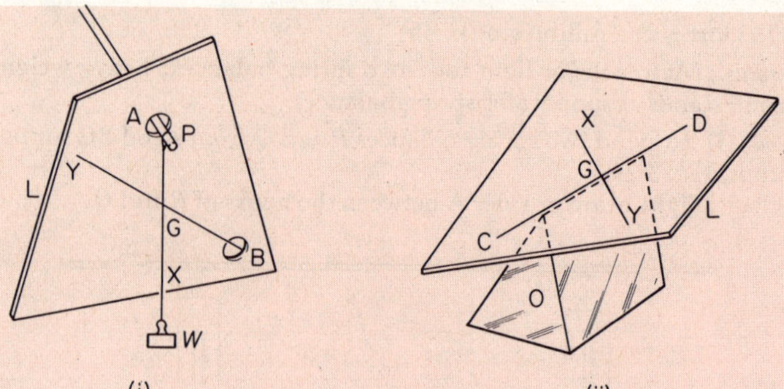

Fig. 3.25 Centre of Gravity

using a clamp for holding P. Make a plumb-line by attaching a small heavy weight *W* to a long thread and suspend *W* from P. Move L so that it swings about P and finally comes to rest.

With a pencil or chalk, mark the vertical line AX on L. Remove L, bore a hole B near another corner, and repeat. If the vertical line on L is now BY the point of intersection of AX and BY is the centre of gravity G.

Check roughly by trying to balance L on the point of a pencil at G.

7. Centre of gravity by balancing

As shown in Fig. 3·25 (ii), balance the cardboard on the edge of a triangular prism O—a glass prism may be suitable. Mark the line CD of the edge. Then turn L round and re-balance. Mark the new line XY. The centre of gravity G is then the point of intersection of CD and XY.

8. Centre of gravity of a stool

Suspend the stool from some point such as the place where a crossbeam meets a leg. As in 6, proceed to use a plumb-line. Mark its direction with thread and Sellotape. Repeat by suspending the stool from another point and find where the two threads meet.

EXERCISE 3 · ANSWERS, p. 257

1. A uniform beam AB is balanced at P. Fig. 3A. Calculate the distance from P to the 200 N weight when weights are hung as shown. (*Mx.*)

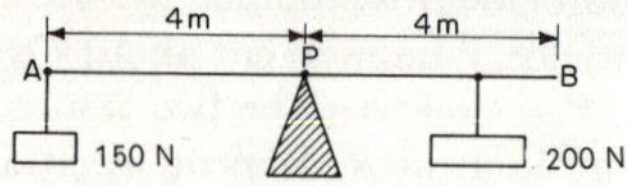

Fig. 3A

2. The wheelbarrow is an example of a . . Order Lever. Its fulcrum is at . . How many joules of work must be undertaken to move the barrow and load (total weight 56 N) up a plank to the top of the 10 m high wall? (*W.Md.*) (See also p. 60.)

3. A motor vehicle will have stability if its centre of gravity is . . or if it has a . . distance between its near and offside wheels. (*W.Md.*)

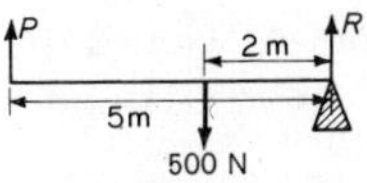

Fig. 3B

4. The diagram shows a beam in equilibrium. Fig. 3B.

(*a*) What force P is necessary to keep the rod in equilibrium?

(*b*) What is the reaction R? (*L.*)

5. (*a*) Using any apparatus with which you are familiar, how could you show what is meant by: (i) stable equilibrium; (ii) unstable equilibrium?

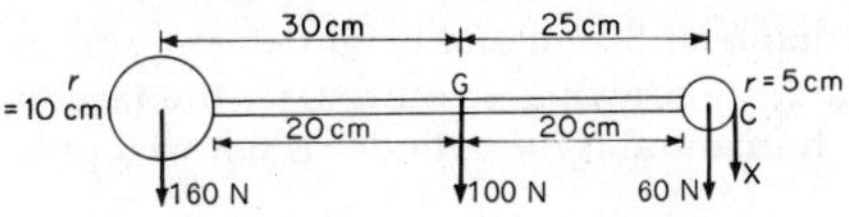

Fig. 3C

(*b*) An error is made in the delivery of dumb-bell parts, and the man assembles the final parts to give one the shape in Fig. 3C. The uniform rod is 40 cm long and weighs 100 N with two spheres of radii 10 cm and 5 cm and weights 160 N and 60 N respectively attached at either end as shown in the diagram. What weight, X, must be attached at C so that the centre of gravity is at the mid-point of the rod G? (*W.Md.*)

6. Racing cars are always low built because: (*a*) the drivers may want to get out in a hurry; (*b*) the cars are more stable; (*c*) the wheels can be made smaller; (*d*) it is easier to service the cars at the pits; (*e*) the cars use petrol and oil. (*M.*)

7. The stick shown is horizontal and its centre of gravity is at the mid-point. Fig. 3D. Calculate its mass. (*Mx.*)

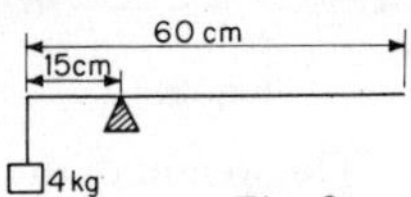

Fig. 3D

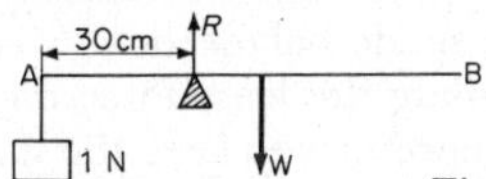

Fig. 3E

8. If AB is a uniform metre rule which is balanced as shown in the diagram, Fig. 3E, (*a*) what is the weight (W) of the rule; (*b*) what is the reaction R? (*L.*)

9. What is meant by *centre of gravity*? A, B and C are three thin sheets of metal (Fig. 3F). Indicate by a cross where the centre of gravity is. (*Mx.*)

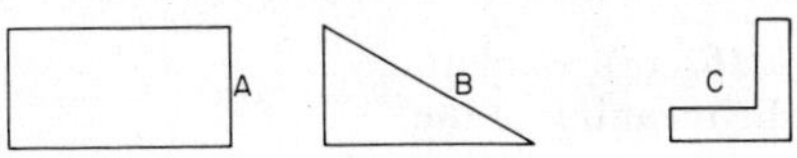

Fig. 3F

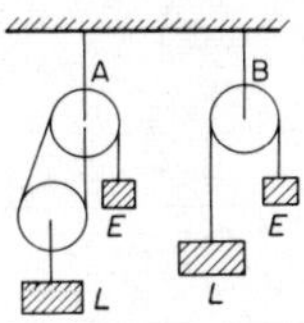

Fig. 3G

10. Delete the statements which are incorrect, Fig. 3G:

(*a*) In machine A the load *L* will be greater than/same as/less than the effort *E*.

(*b*) In machine B the load *L* will be greater than/same as/less than the effort *E*. Give reasons why machine A is likely to be less efficient than machine B. (*Mx.*)

11. (*a*) The figures represent thin sheets of cardboard Fig. 3H. Mark with a cross, X, the position of the centre of gravity of each.

(*b*) There are **three** types of equilibrium. Name the type for which the centre of gravity: (*i*) is raised on tilting (.. equilibrium); (*ii*) remains at the same height when the body is displaced (.. equilibrium). (*E.A.*)

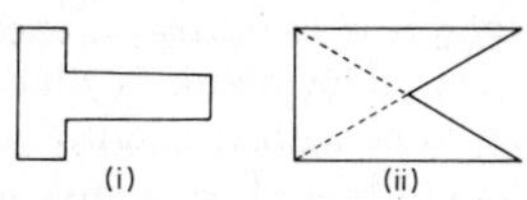

Fig. 3H

12. (*a*) State the *principle of moments*.

(*b*) A bridge over a stream is made from a uniform wooden beam which weighs 4500 N and is 16 m long. Its end A and B are supported on boulders.

If a man weighing 800 N is standing on the bridge 4 m from A, what is the reaction at the boulder: (i) under A; (ii) under B? (Credit will be given for a diagram of the forces.) (*Mx.*)

13. (*a*) Explain what is meant by the 'centre of gravity' of a body.

(*b*) How would you find the centre of gravity of a bicycle by experiment?

(*c*) Why is it desirable that the centre of gravity of a motor-car is as near the ground as possible?

(*d*) A solid iron cylinder, with base diameter 30 cm and height 40 cm, stands with its base on an inclined plane. Find, by drawing or otherwise, the largest possible inclination of the plane to the horizontal if the cylinder is not to topple over. (*S.E.*)

14. (a) (i) Define *moment of a force*; (ii) state the *principle of moments*.

(b) With the aid of diagrams, explain how levers are used in everyday life with the pivot position: (i) between load and effort; (ii) at one end of the lever with the load just inside it; (iii) at one end of the lever with the load at the other end. (*Mx.*)

15. Fig. 3I shows a spade. It is being used to lift soil weighing 15 N from the ground.

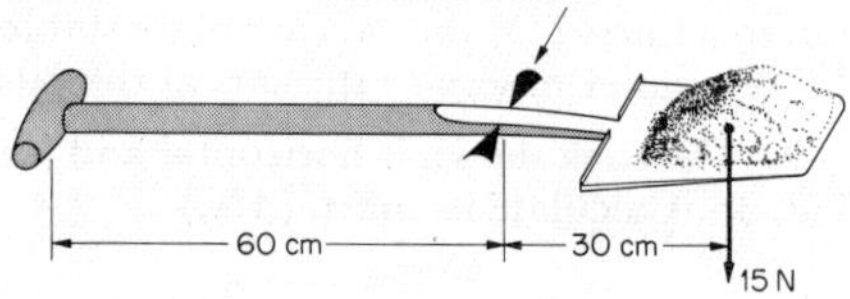

Fig. 3I

(i) Mark the direction of the least force on the handle necessary to keep the spade balanced.

(ii) Calculate the least force on the handle necessary to keep the spade balanced. (The weight of the spade may be neglected.)

(iii) If the left hand was moved towards the soil on the spade, would the force on the handle necessary to keep the soil balanced be greater or less? Give a reason for your answer. (*M.*)

16. (*a*) Explain the meaning of the term *centre of mass* (centre of gravity).

(*b*) A uniform plank of wood has the dimensions 100 cm × 6 cm × 1 cm as indicated in Fig. 3J (i).

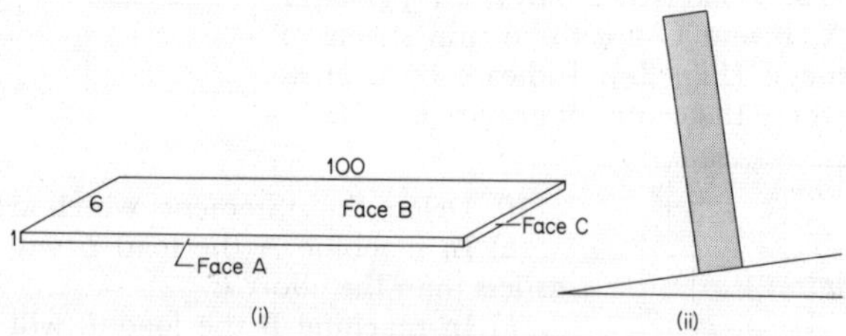

Fig. 3J

(i) State, with reasons, the position of the centre of mass.

(ii) The plank can be made to stand on a horizontal surface on each of the three faces A, B, C. Explain and contrast the stability of the plank of wood when it is standing on each of the faces.

(iii) The plank is placed on an inclined plane as shown in Fig. 3J (ii). Explain, with the aid of a diagram, the angle of inclination of the plane and the position of the plank when it is on the point of toppling. (*E.A.*)

4

WORK AND ENERGY · MACHINES

A HEAVY roller or barrel can best be raised up a step by rolling it up an inclined plank of wood, with one end resting on the step. The inclined plank, or inclined plane, is an example of a *machine*; it enables a large weight or resistance to be overcome by a small effort. A lever, such as a bottle-top or can opener, is also an example of a machine (p. 43).

We shall deal shortly with the principles of machines. First, however, we must discuss the meaning of 'work' and 'energy', which are concerned in all machines.

Work

A boy pulling a sledge along steadily is said to be doing *work* while moving the sledge, Fig. 4.1. If the force he exerts in the direction of the sledge is say 40 N and the sledge moves 10 metres, the amount of work done is defined as:

Work = *force* × *distance moved in direction of force*
= 40 newtons × 10 metres
= 400 joules,

since 1 newton × 1 metre = 1 joule (J). See pages 138 and 144 for units and work.

Note that the 'joule' is a metric unit of work. The work done by an engine in pulling a train steadily is calculated in the same way, namely, work = force exerted by engine × distance moved by train. As the result in joules is very large, the work done is measured in megajoules (MJ). 1 megajoule = 1 million joules.

Energy

Any object which has the ability to do work is said to have *energy*. The boy pulling the sledge or the engine pulling the train are said to have energy. The various forms of energy were discussed on p. 4. If any work is done, it must come from a store of energy. When a boy pulls a sledge, he expends an equivalent amount of energy from the store of chemical energy in his body. The food he eats should restore energy used up as work. In the case of an engine pulling a train, the the energy to do work comes from the electrical power if it is an electric train, or from the heat energy produced by burning oil if it is a diesel engine.

Work is done, and energy is expended, when objects are moved against *opposing* forces. A sledge is pulled against the opposing force of friction at the ground, Fig. 4.1. A train is pulled against the friction

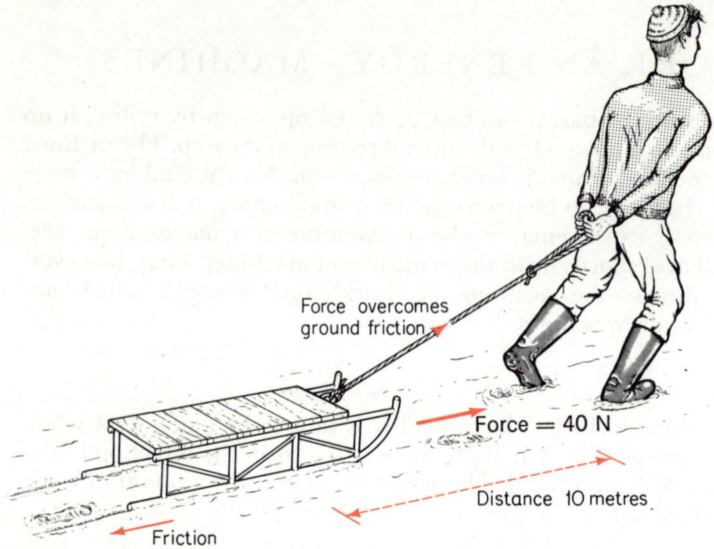

Fig. 4.1 Work done pulling sledge

between the metal wheels and rails and against air friction. In machines, discussed shortly, friction is always present. One metal moves over another in bearings, for example. The work done in overcoming friction produces an equivalent amount of heat energy, and this is energy wasted in the machine.

Work done in raising Loads

If a load is raised by a machine, work is done against the opposing force of the *weight* of the load, which acts downwards towards the earth. A girl climbing stairs also does work in moving against the opposing force of her weight. The work done in lifting an average-size apple, about 1 newton weight, from the floor to a table 1 metre high is 1 joule roughly.

Suppose a crane raises a girder of weight 10 000 N steadily through a distance of 60 m, Fig. 4.2. Then, since the force exerted by the crane to just overcome the weight is 10 000 newtons,

$$\text{Work done } W = \text{force} \times \text{distance}$$
$$= 10\,000 \text{ N} \times 60 \text{ m} = 600\,000 \text{ J.}$$

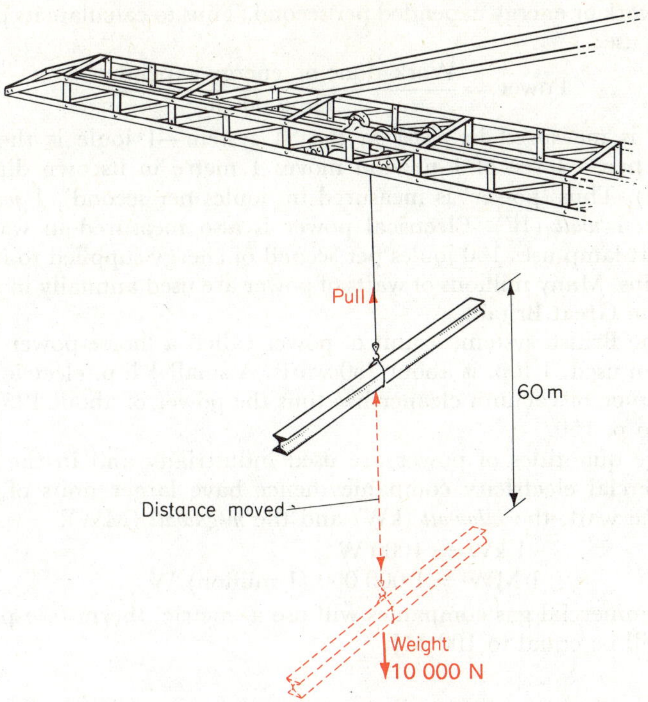

Fig. 4.2 Work done raising girder

Conservation of Energy

Each year, the Patent Office in England has to turn down a few applications by inventors. They want to patent a machine which produces more work or energy than the total given to it. This would be contrary to an important law in science which no one has yet disproved. It is the *Principle of the Conservation of Energy*. This principle means that if 100 joules of energy or work is expended on any machine, then we can get no more than a maximum of 100 joules of energy or work out of the machine (p. 6).

If a machine were perfect, no energy would be wasted when it was used. In this case 100 joules of energy would be obtained from it. In practice, however, some energy is wasted in overcoming friction. If this is 10 joules, the useful energy would be 90 joules. The machine is then said to be '90% efficient' (p. 64).

Power

Large car engines are more powerful than small engines—they can work faster than a small engine. The *power* of any engine may be defined as the work or energy expended per second. Thus to calculate its power, we can use:

$$\text{Power} = \frac{\text{Work done or energy expended}}{\text{Time taken}}.$$

'Work' is measured in *joules* in the SI system—1 joule is the work done when a force of 1 newton moves 1 metre in its own direction (p. 144). Thus 'power' is measured in 'joules per second'. 1 *joule per second* = 1 *watt* (*W*). Electrical power is also measured in watts. A 100 watt lamp uses 100 joules per second of energy supplied to it from the mains. Many millions of watts of power are used annually in all the homes in Great Britain.

In the British system, a unit of power called a 'horse-power (h.p.)' has been used. 1 h.p. is about 750 watts. A small $\frac{1}{6}$ h.p. electric motor in one type of vacuum cleaner has thus the power of about 125 watts. See also p. 150.

Large quantities of power are used industrially and in the home. Commercial electricity companies hence have larger units of power than the watt, the *kilowatt* (kW) and the *megawatt* (MW).

$$1 \text{ kW} = 1000 \text{ W}$$
$$1 \text{ MW} = 1\,000\,000 \text{ (1 million) W}$$

The commercial gas companies will use a 'metric' therm (see p. 206). This will be equal to 100 MJ.

Calculation of Power

Suppose a machine raises a load of 1000 newtons steadily through a height of 20 metres in 5 seconds.

$$\therefore \text{Work done} = 1000 \text{ newtons} \times 20 \text{ metres} = 20\,000 \text{ joules}$$
$$\therefore \text{Power} = \frac{\text{work done}}{\text{time}} = \frac{20\,000}{5} \text{ joules per second}$$
$$= 4000 \text{ watts} = 4 \text{ kilowatts.}$$

Machines · Mechanical Advantage

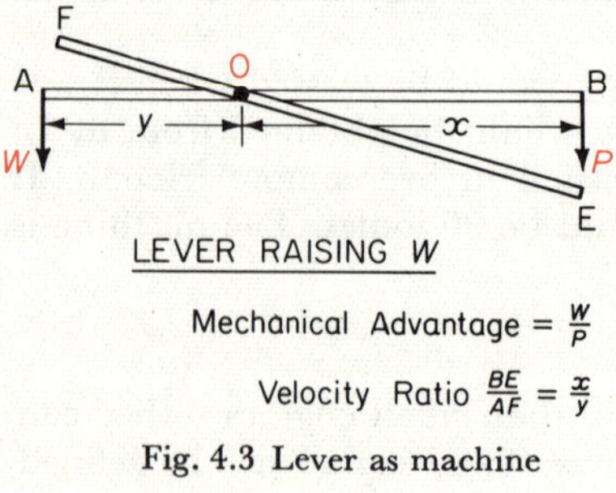

Fig. 4.3 Lever as machine

We now consider details of *machines*. Generally, a machine is used to overcome a large resistance or load by applying a small force.

Levers, discussed on p. 43, are very useful machines. Suppose a lever AOB, with a pivot at O, is used to raise a load *W* steadily at A, Fig. 4.3. If the least effort needed is P, the *mechanical advantage* of the machine is defined as the ratio W/P, or

$$\textit{Mechanical Advantage} = \frac{\textit{Load }(W)}{\textit{Effort }(P)}.$$

If a load of 100 N is raised steadily by an effort of 20 N, the mechanical advantage = 100 N/20 N = 5. Using a different machine, suppose a load of 40 N is raised steadily by an effort of 4 N. In this case, then, mechanical advantage = 40 N/4 N = 10. If an effort of 5 N is applied to a machine with a mechanical advantage of 12, the load just overcome = 12 × 5 N = 60 N. Of course, a machine with a high mechanical advantage is a very useful one because it will enable a heavy load to be raised by applying a small effort.

All machines have a certain amount of friction, for example, at a pivot or a bearing. The effort applied must overcome the frictional force, in addition to raising the load. In practice, therefore, *the mechanical advantage depends on the friction present* in the machine, Fig. 4.4. The greater the friction, the smaller is the mechanical advantage.

Velocity ratio

As we can see from the lever in Fig. 4.3, the small effort P moves through a large distance BE.

The large resistance or load W moves through a small distance AF in the same time. The relative distances per second moved steadily by an applied effort and the load overcome is called the *velocity ratio*. Thus:

$$\text{Velocity ratio (V.R.)} = \frac{\text{distance moved by effort}}{\text{distance moved by load in same time}}$$

Hence in the lever shown in Fig. 4.3,

$$\text{Velocity ratio} = \frac{\text{BE}}{\text{AF}} = \frac{x}{y}.$$

Thus if the arm of length x is 10 times as long as that y of the shorter arm, then the velocity ratio of the lever is 10. This means that when the lever is used to raise a load W steadily by applying an effort P, P moves 10 times the distance per second moved by W. The effort in a machine usually moves through a much greater distance than the heavy load

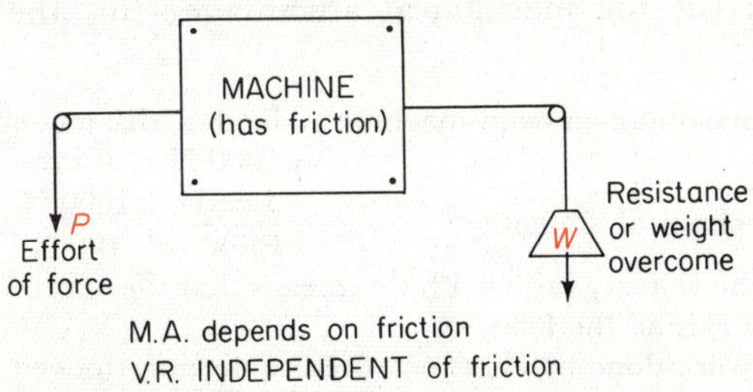

Fig. 4.4 Mechanical advantage and velocity ratio

overcome, from the law of conservation of energy. It should therefore be remembered that the velocity ratio is usually much greater than one.

Although there may be considerable friction at the pivot of the lever in Fig. 4.3, the *ratio* of the distance moved by the effort to the distance moved by the load in the same time is unaffected. The ratio is always x/y. Thus the velocity ratio is *not* affected by friction. The mechanical advantage, however, depends on the friction, Fig. 4.4.

Efficiency

If 1000 joules of work is spent on or supplied to a machine, and 200 joules is used to overcome the friction in the machine, then (1000 − 200) or 800 joules is obtained from the machine. The *efficiency* of any machine is defined by:

$$\textit{Efficiency} = \frac{\textit{Work or energy obtained}}{\textit{Work or energy supplied}} \times 100\%.$$

In this case, therefore,

$$\text{efficiency} = \frac{800 \text{ joules}}{1000 \text{ joules}} \times 100\% = \frac{8}{10} \times 100\% = 80\%.$$

A machine with a low efficiency has a lot of friction and a good deal of work or energy is wasted. A machine with a high efficiency wastes very little energy (p. 61).

From above,

$$\text{efficiency} = \frac{\text{Load} \times \text{distance moved by load}}{\text{Effort} \times \text{distance moved by effort}} \times 100\%,$$

where the two distances are moved in the same time. Now the ratio Load/Effort = Mechanical advantage. The ratio 'distance moved by effort/distance moved by load' in the same time = Velocity ratio.

$$\therefore \text{efficiency} = \frac{\text{Mechanical advantage (M.A.)}}{\text{Velocity ratio (V.R.)}} \times 100\%.$$

EXAMPLE

A machine has a velocity ratio of 12. A load of 1000 N is raised 6 m steadily by an effort of 100 N. Find: (i) the work obtained from the machine; (ii) the mechanical advantage; (iii) the efficiency of the machine.

(i) Work obtained from machine = load × distance moved

$= 1000 \text{ N} \times 6 \text{ m} = 6000 \text{ J}$

(ii) Mechanical advantage $= \dfrac{\text{Load}}{\text{Effort}} = \dfrac{1000 \text{ N}}{100 \text{ N}} = 10.$

(iii) If the velocity ratio is 12, this means that the effort has moved 12 × 6 m or 72 m in raising the load.

$\therefore$ work done by effort = effort × distance moved

$= 100 \text{ N} \times 72 \text{ m} = 7200 \text{ J}$

$$\therefore \text{ efficiency} = \frac{\text{work obtained by raising load}}{\text{work supplied by effort}} \times 100\%$$
$$= \frac{6000\text{ J}}{7200\text{ J}} \times 100\% = \frac{60}{72} \times 100\%$$
$$= 83\tfrac{1}{3}\%.$$

Wheel and Axle

A *wheel and axle* machine can be used to raise heavy loads such as the anchor of a ship.

Fig. 4.5 illustrates the principle. The effort P turns a large wheel of radius R. The heavy load or weight W is attached to a rope round the axle of the wheel of much smaller radius r. Fig. 4.5 (i) shows a model

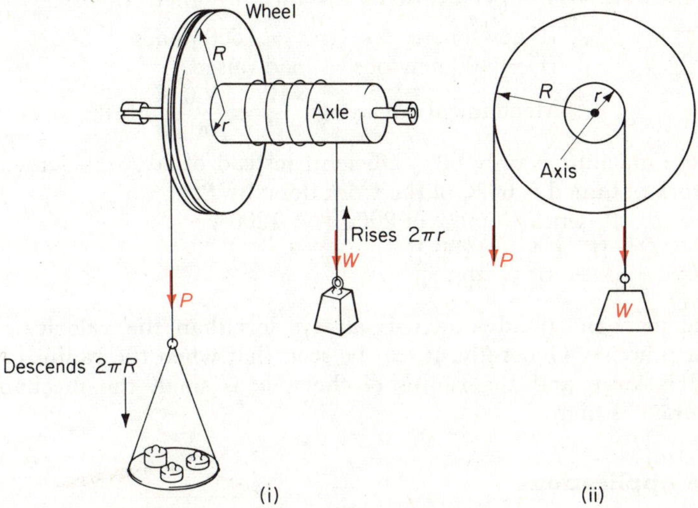

Fig. 4.5 Wheel and axle

wheel and axle. When supported with its axis horizontal, the force P, pulling on a string round the wheel, raises the load W attached to the other string round the axle. Note that the two strings are wound in *opposite* directions, otherwise the load will not be raised. Fig. 4.5 (ii) is an end-on view.

To find the velocity ratio, V.R., suppose the wheel is turned exactly one revolution by a constant force P. The effort P then moves through a distance $2\pi R$, the circumference of the wheel. In the same time, the load W rises through a distance corresponding to one revolution of the *axle*. This is $2\pi r$. Hence

$$\text{velocity ratio V.R.} = \frac{2\pi R}{2\pi r} = \frac{R}{r}.$$

Thus a wheel of radius 50 cm and an axle of radius 5 cm has a velocity ratio 50/5 or 10.

Mechanical Advantage

Suppose a constant effort P of 50 N is used to raise steadily the load W through a height of 4 metres. If the velocity ratio is 10, this means that P moves through a distance 10×4 or 40 metres, from the definition on page 63.

The work done by P = force $\times$ distance.

So:

$$\text{work done} = 50 \text{ newtons} \times 40 \text{ metres} = 2000 \text{ joules.}$$

This is the work put in to the machine. Suppose it is 80% efficient. Then the work obtained = 80% (4/5) of 2000 joules = 1600 joules. Now the load W has been raised a distance of 4 metres.

$$\therefore W \text{ newtons} \times 4 \text{ metres} = 1600 \text{ joules}$$

$$\therefore W = 400 \text{ newtons} = \text{load raised.}$$

$$\therefore \text{Mechanical advantage, } \frac{W}{P} = \frac{400 \text{ N}}{50 \text{ N}} = 8.$$

If the machine is only 60% efficient, instead of 80% efficient, then the work obtained is 60% of the work done by P.

$$\therefore \text{work} = 60\% \text{ of } 2000 \text{ J} = 1200 \text{ J}$$

$$\therefore W \times 4 = 1200 \text{ J}$$

$$\therefore W = 300 \text{ N}$$

The mechanical advantage is always less than the velocity ratio R/r in practice. Generally, it can be seen that when the radius of the wheel is large and the radius of the axle is small the mechanical advantage is high.

Some Applications

Fig. 4.6 shows a bucket of water raised from a well by a form of wheel and axle machine.

Fig. 4.7 shows a wheelbrace, used for unscrewing the wheelnuts of a car. This may be considered a form of wheel and axle machine. Note that the force turns through a circle of large radius R.

Inclined Plane

Loads such as heavy lawn mowers or barrels can be raised with the aid of an *inclined plane*. The Pyramids in Egypt are thought to have been built by slaves hauling loads to heights by means of inclined planes. The stone pillars at Stonehenge, England, are considered to have been raised by the same method, after which the earth was scooped away.

Suppose that a load X of weight W at the bottom A of the incline is rolled steadily to the top C by an effort P, Fig. 4.8.

Part of the weight is supported by the plane AC. The rest of it, which is less than W and acts down the plane, must be overcome by

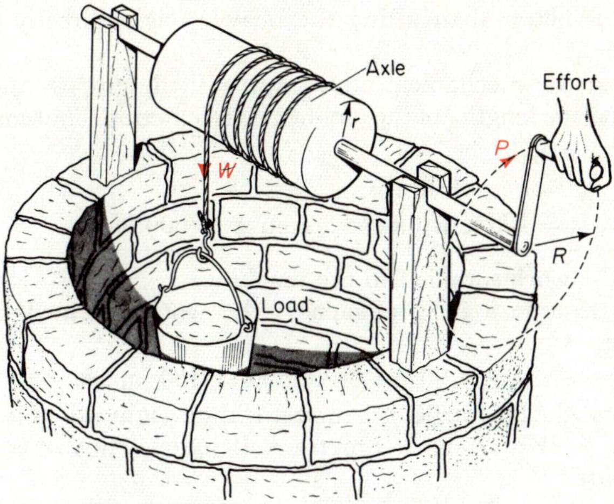

Fig. 4.6 Application of wheel and axle

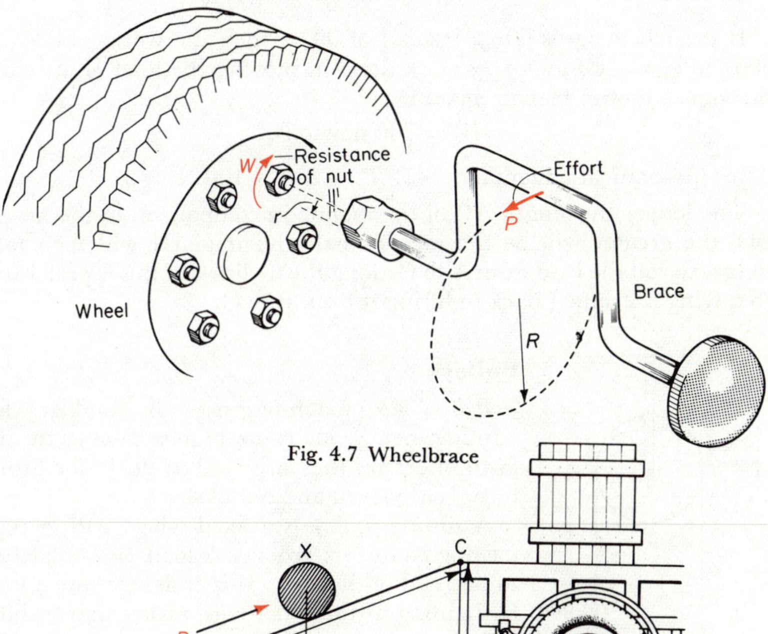

Fig. 4.7 Wheelbrace

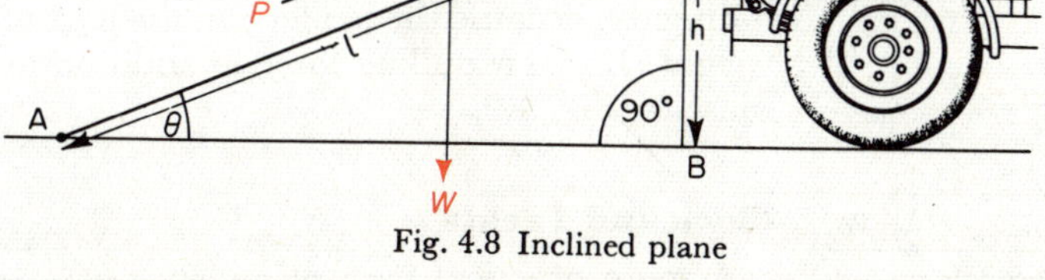

Fig. 4.8 Inclined plane

P. This is better than lifting the heavy weight directly through the height BC.

To find the mechanical advantage gained, suppose the effort P is 100 N and the length l of the incline AC is 5 metres. The work is done by P:

$$= P \times \text{distance}$$
$$= 100 \text{ newtons} \times 5 \text{ metres} = 500 \text{ joules.}$$

This is the work supplied to the machine.

If we assume a 90% efficiency, the work obtained by using the machine

$$= 90\% \ (\tfrac{9}{10}) \text{ of } 500 = 450 \text{ joules.}$$

Suppose the height BC is 1 metre. If the weight raised is W, the work obtained $= W$ newtons $\times$ 1 metre $= W$ joules. Thus $W = 450$ newton, in this case.

Thus $$\text{mechanical advantage} = \frac{W}{P} = \frac{450 \text{ N}}{100 \text{ N}} = 4{\cdot}5.$$

If the efficiency is 60%, instead of 90%, then the work = 60% of 500 joules = 300 joules = work done in moving the load W newtons through 1 metre. Hence this time,

$$W = 300 \text{ newtons.}$$

Thus mechanical advantage $= W/P = 300 \text{ N}/100 \text{ N} = 3$.

The longer the length AC of the incline in comparison to the height BC, the greater will be the mechanical advantage. It will then take longer to roll the load from A to C along the incline but this is preferable to having a strained back in lifting it from B to C.

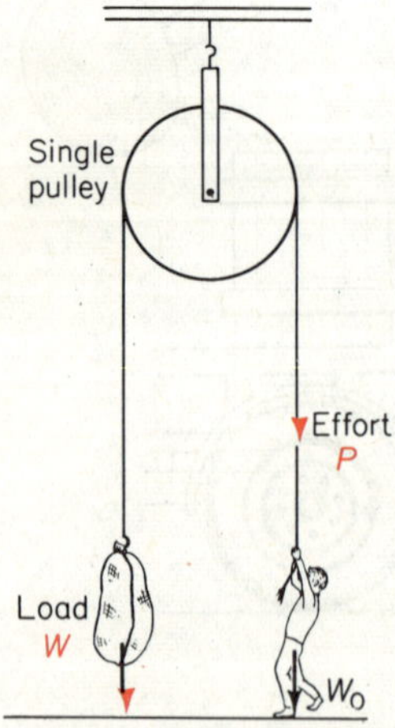

Fig. 4.9 Single pulley

Pulleys

Pulleys are machines used by builders for hauling heavy loads to higher floors. In the form of cranes they are used at docks for lifting heavy cargoes in and out of ships.

A simple pulley is a fixed wheel with a rope passing round its groove. A load W is attached to one end of the rope. It is easier to raise a load by hauling at the other end, rather than raising it directly, because the hauler can use part of his weight, W_0, as a pulling force in addition to his muscles, Fig. 4.9.

Block and Tackle

A more practical form of pulley system is to

use a number of pulleys and to pass a continuous rope round them. Fig. 4.10 (i) shows a system of four pulleys. The upper two are fixed, and the lower two are movable. The load W to be raised is attached to the lower pulleys, and the effort P is applied to the end of the rope passing round the top pulley. Fig. 4.11 shows a system of five pulleys.

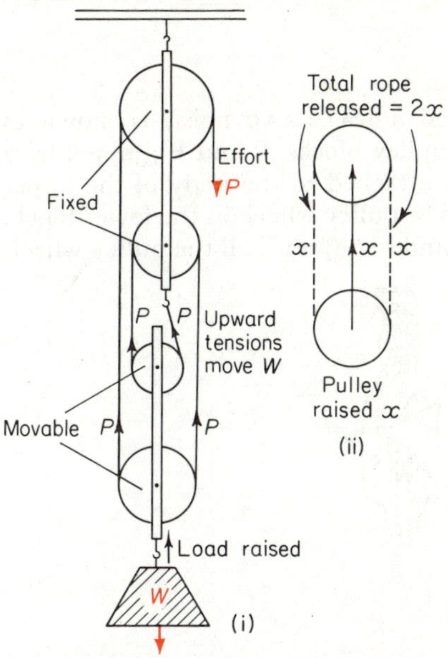

Fig. 4.10 Action of four pulleys

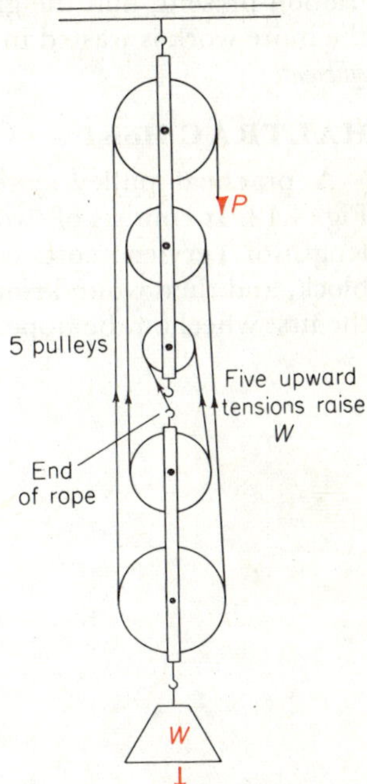

Fig. 4.11 Five pulleys

Suppose the rope is pulled down with a vertical force P of 500 newtons. The tension everywhere in the rope is then 500 N if frictional forces are neglected. Now there are four pieces of rope pulling upward on the load, two round each of the lower two pulleys. Hence the total upward pull is 4×500 or 2000 N. Thus the load W raised is 2000 N when the effort P is 500 N.

In practice, owing to the weight of the lower block and the friction at the pulley wheels, the force P needed to raise a load of 2000 N is more than 500 N, say 600 N. In this case,

$$\text{Mechanical advantage M.A.} = \frac{\text{Load}}{\text{Effort}} = \frac{2000}{600} = 3{\cdot}3.$$

Fig. 4.10 (ii) illustrates what happens when the load W in Fig. 4.10 (i) is raised a distance x. Each of the lower pulleys then 'releases' a length of rope $2x$. Thus the effort P moves through a total distance $4x$.

The velocity ratio = distance moved by P/distance moved by W in the same time $= 4x/x = 4$. In Fig. 4.11, an additional length x of string is released when W moves up x, making a total length of $5x$. The velocity ratio is 5. Generally, *the velocity ratio = the total number of pulleys*.

The velocity ratio is independent of friction. The mechanical advantage depends on friction, as we have stated. The greater the friction present, and the greater the weight of the lower set of pulleys, the more work is wasted in raising a load. The pulley system is then less *efficient*.

HALTRAC Hoist

A practical pulley system, called a HALTRAC hoist, is shown in Fig. 4.12. It consists of two 4-way pulley blocks, P and P′, joined by a length of Terylene cord C. This is attached to the body of the upper block, and then wound round the first pulley wheel on the lower block, the first wheel on the upper block, and so on, until all the pulley wheels

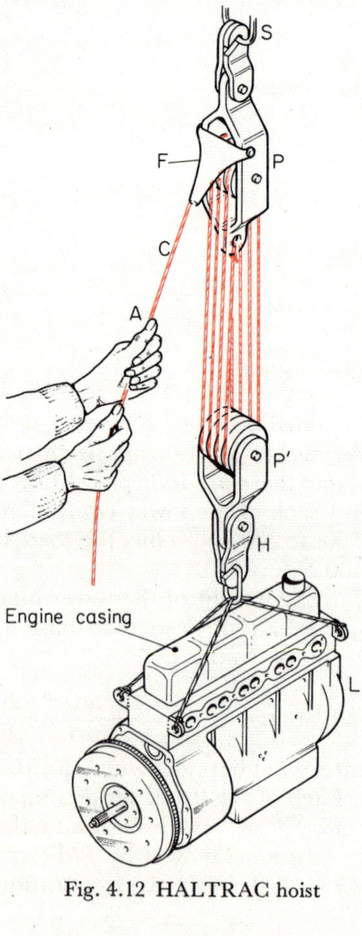

Fig. 4.12 HALTRAC hoist

are in use. The cord emerges at the fourth pulley wheel of the upper block and passes through a *friction-brake* F. This allows the cord to pass through when F is raised, but grips the cord firmly when F is lowered, as when pulling is stopped.

PARALLELOGRAM AND TRIANGLE OF FORCES

In this section we consider forces which are not parallel and which keep objects in equilibrium. In girders, such forces maintain the stability of bridges, for example, and engineers must know how the forces are added together.

Resultant of Two Forces

If two boys pull a sledge in the same direction by ropes, and the tensions P and Q in each rope are 150 and 100 N respectively, the total or *resultant force* is $(150 + 100)$ or 250 N, Fig. 4.13 (i). If the forces act

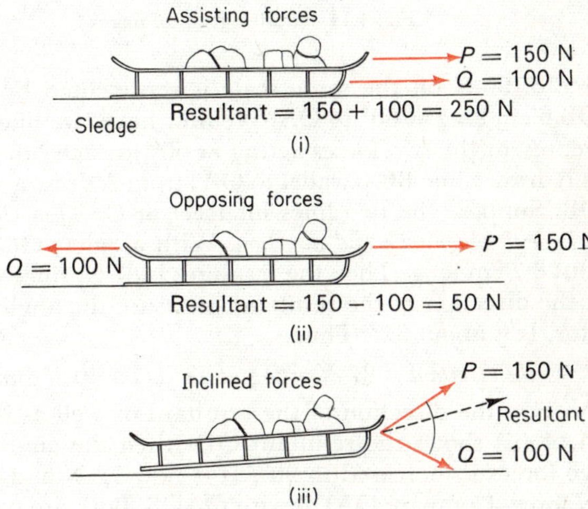

Fig. 4.13 Resultant of forces

in opposite directions the resultant force is $(150 - 100)$ or 50 N in the direction of the larger or 150 N force, Fig. 4.13 (ii).

Suppose now that the ropes are inclined at 60° to each other and that the tensions are again 150 and 100 N, Fig. 4.13 (iii). Experience shows that the sledge moves forward more in the direction of the 150 N than the 100 N force, as one might expect, and that the total or resultant force on the sledge is now less than $(150 + 100)$ or 250 N.

Parallelogram of Forces

The resultant force of two inclined forces can be found by drawing a particular *parallelogram*.

As an illustration, suppose we need the resultant of two forces of 40 N and 60 N which act at an angle of 60° to each other, Fig. 4.14 (i). Choose a suitable scale to represent the forces, say 10 N = 1 cm. The force of 40 N is then represented by a line 4 cm long. Draw the line OA to represent 40 N.

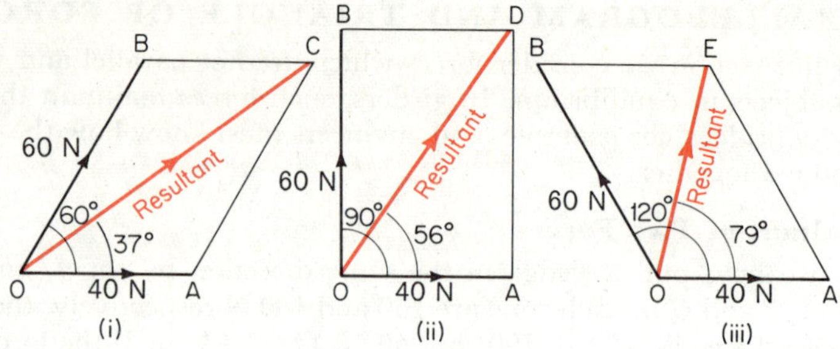

Fig. 4.14 Parallelogram of forces

A force of 60 N on the same scale is represented by a line 6 cm. Draw OB 6 cm long at 60° to OA. We now have two lines OA and OB which represent the two forces acting at 60° to each other.

From B draw a line BC parallel to OA; from A draw a line AC parallel to OB. Suppose the two lines intersect at C. *Then OC represents the resultant in both magnitude and direction.* With a ruler, OC is measured. It is about 8·7 cm long. Then the resultant is 87 N, since 1 cm = 10 N. To find the direction of the resultant, measure the angle COA with a protractor. It is about 37°. Thus:

the resultant is 87 *N acting at* 37° *to the* 40 *N force.*

Always give the direction of the resultant as well as its magnitude.

Fig. 4.14 (ii) shows the resultant OD when the angle between the same two forces is increased to 90°. It is now 72 N and acts at 56° to the 40 N force. Compare OADB with OACB. Both are parallelograms, but OADB is a rectangle since angle AOB is 90°.

Fig. 4.14 (iii) shows the resultant OE when the angle between the two forces of 40 and 60 N is increased to 120°. It is now 52 N and acts at 79° to the 40 N force. The angle between two forces has a considerable influence on the resultant, as shown by Fig. 4.14.

The parallelogram drawing method is usually stated as a law called the *Principle of the Parallelogram of Forces*:

If two inclined forces are represented in magnitude and direction by the adjacent sides of a parallelogram, their resultant is represented in magnitude and direction by the diagonal of the parallelogram passing through the point of intersection of the two sides.

An experiment to investigate the parallelogram of forces is described on p. 78.

Equilibrium of Three Forces Acting at a Point

There are many cases in engineering practice and in everyday life in which an object is kept in equilibrium by three forces acting at a point. Fig. 4.15 (i) illustrates the hinge O of the corner of a bridge resting on a support. The equilibrium of O is maintained by the forces P and Q, in the girders CO and OD, and the reaction R of the support. In Fig. 4.15 (ii) an object is held on a smooth inclined plane by a string along the plane. The forces maintaining the equilibrium are the weight W of the object, the tension T in the string and the reaction R of the plane. *When the plane is smooth the reaction R acts normally to the surface*, a point to be remembered by the student (p. 38).

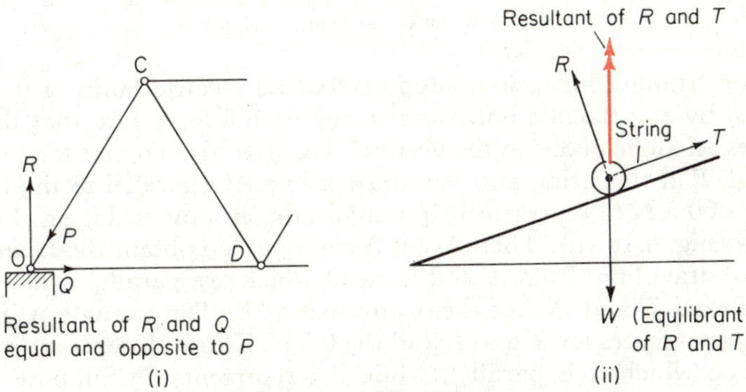

Fig. 4.15 Triangle of forces

Suppose the object resting on the inclined plane in Fig. 4.15 (ii) has a weight W of 100 N. Since it is in equilibrium, the sum (resultant) of the two forces R and T must also be 100 N and must act in an opposite direction to W; if either of these two conditions is not obeyed the object cannot be in equilibrium. For the same reason, the resultant of the forces R and Q in Fig. 4.15 (i) must equal P. The name *equilibrant* is given to the single force such as P which maintains the two forces in equilibrium.

Triangle of Forces

If two of the three forces such as R and T are known, Fig. 4.15 (ii), the third force W can easily be found. We simply draw the parallelogram of forces for R and T, and measure their resultant. Then W is equal in magnitude to the resultant and exactly opposite in direction.

If only one force of the three is known, we adopt a different method. It is based on the *Principle of the Triangle of Forces*. This states:

If three forces acting on an object are in equilibrium a triangle can be drawn whose sides, taken in order, represent the forces in magnitude and direction.

The words, 'taken in order' mean that the sides are followed the same way round the triangle.

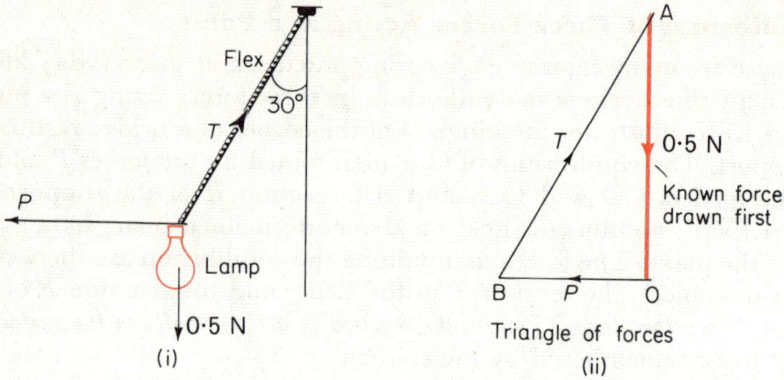

Fig. 4.16 Drawing triangle of forces

As a simple illustration, suppose that an electric lamp of 0·5 N is pulled by an attached horizontal string with a force P so that the flex makes an angle of 30° to the vertical, Fig. 4.16 (i). To find the tensions P and T in the string and flex draw a line AO parallel to the known force of 0·5 N to represent it in magnitude on some scale, e.g. 1 cm = 0·1 N, Fig. 4.16 (ii). Then AO is 5 cm long. To obtain the triangle of forces, draw lines from A and from O which are parallel to the other two forces T and P. Let them intersect at B. The triangle AOB is a triangle of forces for T and P and the 0·5 N. Thus OB represents P, the force to which it is parallel, while BA represents T. Suppose OB is 2·9 cm long and BA is 5·8 cm long by measurement. Then, since 0·1 N is represented by 1 cm, $P = 0{\cdot}29$ N and $T = 0{\cdot}58$ N. Remember to start the triangle by drawing first the side representing the *known* force.

Another example is shown in Fig. 4.17 (ii). Here a small object X rests on a smooth plane inclined at 60° to the horizontal and is prevented by a string XA from slipping down. The tension in the string

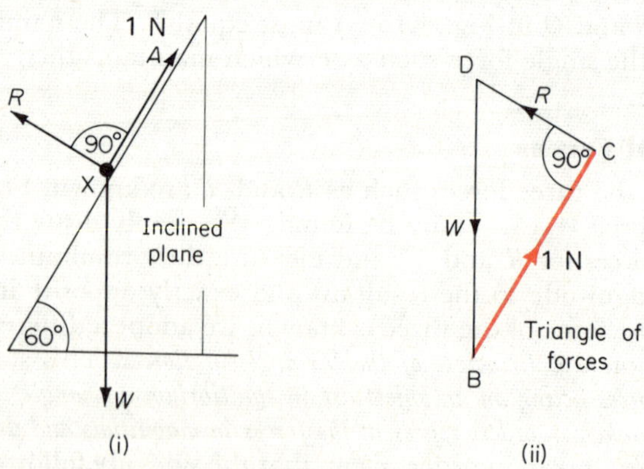

Fig. 4.17 Drawing triangle of forces

is 1 N and the weight W and the reaction R of the plane are both required.

The weight W acts vertically downwards. The reaction R acts normal (perpendicular) to the plane since it is smooth (p. 73). Start by drawing a line BC parallel to the known force 1 N to represent it completely, Fig. 4.17 (ii). For example, with a scale of 1 cm = 0·1 N, draw BC 10 cm long. We then draw a line CD from C parallel to the force R (note that, from the direction of the arrows, CD follows 'in order' from BC). Finally, the line BD is drawn parallel to the force W to intersect CD at D. The triangle BCD is the triangle of forces. Measurement of BD shows it is about 12 cm long. Hence, since 1 cm = 0·1 N, W = 1·2 N. Measurement of CD shows it is about 6 cm long. Hence, since 1 cm = 0·1 N, R = 0·6 N.

An experiment to investigate the triangle of forces is described on p. 78.

SUMMARY

1. Work = force × distance moved in direction of force. Unit: joule (newton × metre), symbol J. 1 MJ (megajoule) = 10^6 J.

2. Power = work done per second. Unit: watt (joule per second), symbol W. 1 kW = 1000 W. 1 MW = 10^6 W. 1 h.p. 750 W (approx.).

3. Mechanical advantage = load/effort (depends on friction). Velocity ratio = distance per sec moved by effort/distance per second moved by load (independent of friction). Efficiency = work obtained/work supplied to machine = M.A./V.R.

4. Velocity ratio of wheel and axle = R/r; of block-and-tackle pulley = number of pulleys; of inclined plane = sloping length/vertical height.

5. Resultant of two forces may be found by drawing the parallelogram of forces—the diagonal represents the resultant.

6. If three forces are in equilibrium, and one is known, the others may be found by drawing a triangle of forces—start with the known force.

PRACTICAL (Notes for guidance, p. 26)

1. Lever (p. 43)

Bore a hole O in a long rod about one-sixth of its length from one end A. Fig. 4·18 (i). Push a long nail or knitting-needle N through O to act as a pivot or fulcrum for a 'lever'—the rod should turn freely about O; if not, increase the size of the hole.

Support N from a clamp. Attach a heavy known weight or load W to A. Weigh a scale-pan and attach it to the end B.

(i) Add weights until W is seen to just rise steadily. Record the total weight on the scale-pan. This weight plus the weight of the scale-pan is equal to the effort P. *Calculate* the mechanical advantage W/P to one decimal place.

(ii) Arrange two metre rulers C and D vertically beside W and P. Move P down slowly until W rises a distance y equal to an exact number of centimetres, say 4 cm. Measure the distance x then moved by P. *Calculate* the velocity ratio, x/y (to one decimal place). Compare this with the calculated ratio BO/AO. Can you account for any difference in the two values?

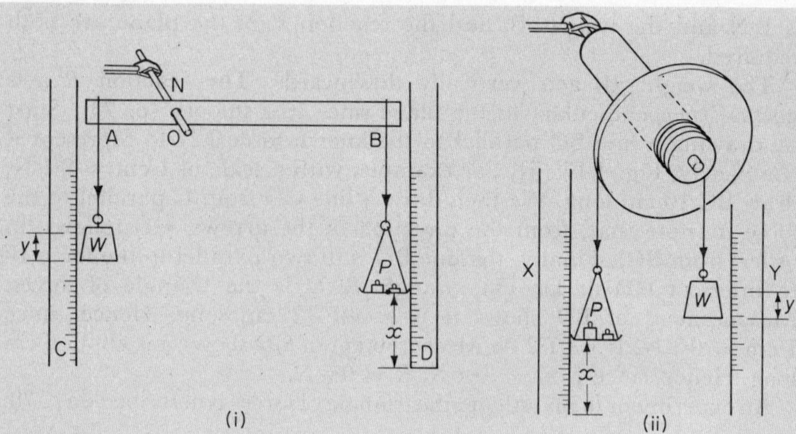

Fig. 4.18 (i) Lever (ii) Wheel and axle

(iii) *Calculate* the efficiency $(W \times y)/(P \times x) \times 100\%$

(iv) Repeat the experiment using another pivot or fulcrum F; bore a hole F about one-quarter along the rod from A.

Weight of scale-pan = .. N

Measurements.

1. Mechanical advantage:

Weight added to S (N)	W N (load)	P N (effort)	M.A. = W/P

2. Velocity ratio:

y (cm)	x (cm)	V.R. = x/y

Ratio of arms = BO/AO = ..

3. Efficiency: Work obtained = $W \times y$ = ..

Work supplied = $P \times x$ = ..

Efficiency $= \dfrac{W \times y}{P \times x} \times 100\%$ = ..

2. Wheel and axle (p. 65)

Support a model wheel and axle in clamps. Use a known weight W as a load, Fig. 4·18 (ii). Use a scale-pan and increasing weights to find the effort P needed to just raise W steadily. Use rulers, X and Y, to find the relative distances moved by P and W. From measurements, as previously described, find (i) the mechanical advantage; (ii) the velocity ratio—compare this with the ratio R/r after measuring the radii of the wheel and axle, (iii) the efficiency.

Measurements. Set out in table as for the Lever experiment but add R/r.

3. Pulleys (p. 68)

(i) Support a pulley system A. Fig. 4.19 (i). Add a heavy known weight W to the lower block. Attach a scale-pan S, previously weighed, to the end of the string—if the scale-pan is likely to become entangled in the string, pass the string round a separate grooved wheel or pulley B as shown.

(ii) Add increasing weights to S until the weight W just rises steadily. Note the total weight on S. The effort P is the total weight plus the weight of the scale-pan.

(iii) Set up two vertical rulers X and Y in clamps near W and S respectively. Move S down until W rises through a whole number of centimetres, a distance y. Note the larger distance x moved by P.

(iv) Obtain the efficiency from $(W \times y)/(P \times x) \times 100\%$.

Repeat with a heavier load W. Compare your results for mechanical advantage, velocity ratio and efficiency, with the previous result. Which are different and which are the same?

Measurements. Set out in table as for the Lever experiment but add number of pulleys.

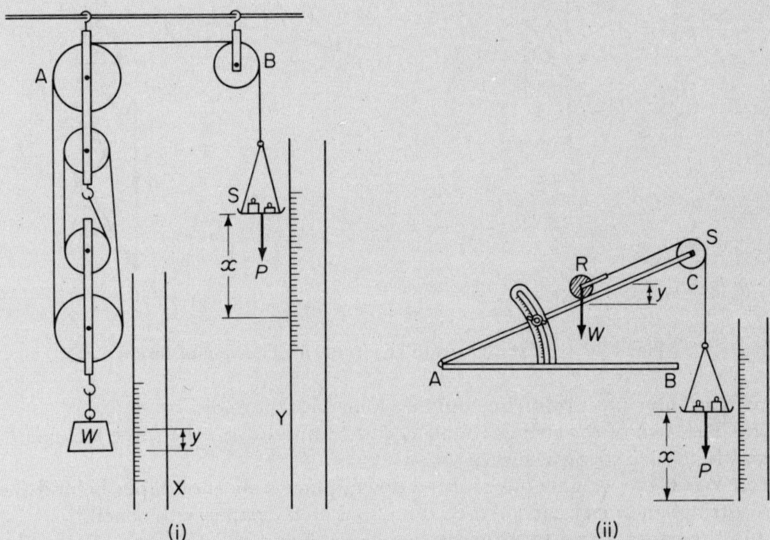

Fig. 4.19 (i) Pulley (ii) inclined plane

4. Inclined plane (p. 66)

Arrange a wooden plane AC at a definite angle to another piece of wood AB on the table. 4·19 (ii). (A suitable apparatus is obtainable from manufacturers, with an inclined plane whose angle can be varied, an attached grooved wheel, and a smooth roller R as a load.) A smooth roller R of a weight W may be used as a load—obtain its weight from a lever or spring balance. Attach a length of string to R, pass the string round a grooved wheel S at the top of the plane, and attach a scale-pan, previously weighed, to the end of the string, so that it hangs freely, as shown.

(i) Add weights to the scale-pan until W rises steadily—it may be necessary to give the scale-pan a slight push. The effort P is the sum of all the weights and the weight of the scale-pan. *Calculate* the mechanical advantage W/P.

(ii) Using a ruler, measure the distance x moved down by P and the corresponding *vertical* distance y moved up by W. *Calculate* the velocity ratio from x/y.

(iii) *Calculate* the efficiency from the ratio $(W \times y)/(P \times x) \times 100\%$.

Measurements. Set out in table as for the Lever experiment.

5. Verification of parallelogram of forces (p. 71)

Apparatus. Two pulley wheels; clamps and stands; three different known weights; rod for pulley supports.

Method. (i) Support the two pulleys L and M from the rod S held in two clamps, Fig. 4.20 (i).

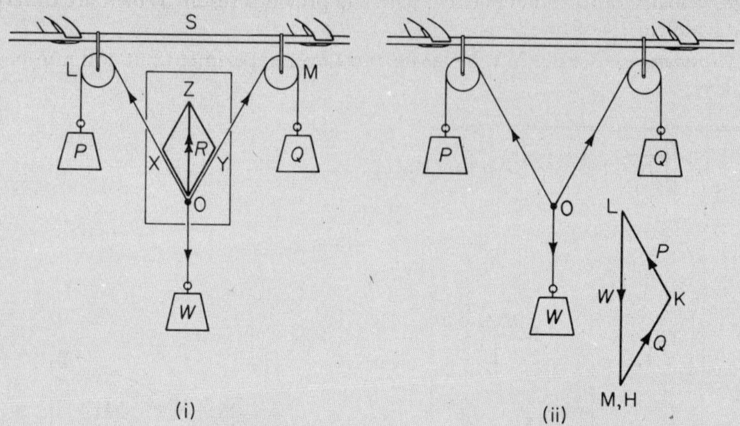

Fig. 4.20 (i) Parallelogram of forces (ii) Triangle of forces

(ii) Cut three pieces of string and tie a knot with the ends.

(iii) Pass two of the strings round L and M and attach the three weights P, Q and W to each string as shown.

(iv) When the weights have settled down, place a sheet of paper behind the three strings and mark each of their directions on the paper with pencil.

On the paper, draw to scale the two forces P and Q—OX and OY, in Fig. 4·20 (i). Complete the parallelogram OXZY and find the resultant R from the length of the diagonal OZ. See if the magnitude of R is the same as W. By taking the paper back to the strings and aligning OX and OY along OL and OM, as in Fig. 4·20 (i), see if R is exactly opposite in direction to W. Since W must be exactly equal and opposite to counterbalance R, state the *conclusion* of the experiment.

Repeat the experiment by moving L and M closer together or wider apart, or by changing the weights.

6. Verification of triangle of forces (p. 73)

Use the same apparatus shown in Fig. 4·20 (i). This time, after the weight has settled down, *there are three forces in equilibrium at O.* They are P, Q and W. Fig. 4·20 (ii).

Record the values of P, Q and W. Obtain their directions at O by placing paper behind the strings and marking the three lines of the string on it. To see whether a triangle can be drawn, choose a suitable scale and draw a line HK to represent Q say. From K draw the line KL which represents P in magnitude and direction. From L draw a line LM which represents *W* in magnitude and direction. *See if M practically coincides with H.* If so, a *triangle* can be drawn to represent the three forces in equilibrium.

Repeat by moving L and M closer together or changing the weights.

EXERCISE 4 . ANSWERS, p. 257

1. Fig. 4A represents a partly completed diagram of a single string pulley system. Complete this diagram and indicate where the effort must be applied to lift the load. Then answer the following questions:

(*a*) What is the velocity ratio of the system?

(*b*) If the pulley system is 75% efficient and the load is 600 newtons: (i) what effort must be applied to lift the load; (ii) what work must be done in lifting the load through a distance of 2 m, using this machine? (*M.*)

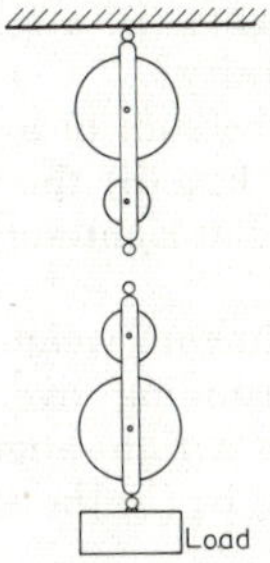

Fig. 4A

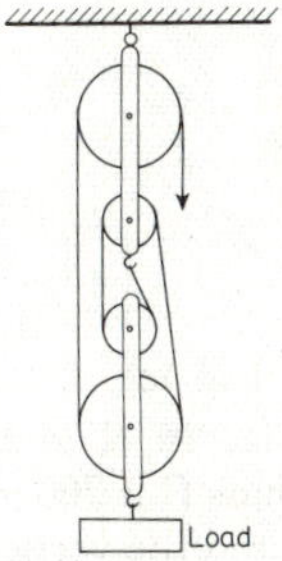

Fig. 4B

2. (*a*) What is the velocity ratio of the pulley system shown in the diagram Fig. 4B.

(*b*) If an effort of 30 newtons is needed to lift a load of 90 newtons, what is the mechanical advantage?

(*c*) What is the efficiency? (*L.*)

3. (*a*) Give **one** everyday example of the action of (i) the force of friction; (ii) the force of gravity; (iii) the tension in a rope or string.

(*b*) (i) Define *efficiency* of a machine; (ii) calculate the efficiency of a machine in which an effort of 20 newtons moving through 5 m raises a load of 83 newtons through 1 m.

(*c*) Explain why the efficiency of a machine is always less than 100%.

(*d*) (i) Draw a diagram of a pulley system of velocity ratio 2; (ii) if your pulley system is 75% efficient, what effort would you have to apply in order to lift a 300 N load? (*Mx.*)

4. What is meant by the *efficiency* of a machine? Say what factors could make a pulley system inefficient and how it would be possible to improve it.

If a boy is capable of exerting a force of 50 newtons, describe and illustrate *two* ways in which it would be possible to raise a load of 150 newtons a distance of 10 m. (*Mx.*)

5. Draw a diagram of a block and tackle system with a velocity ratio of 5. This system is used to raise a load of 1500 N with an effort of 500 N. Calculate: (i) the efficiency of this machine; (ii) the distance moved by the effort when the load has been moved through 12 m. (*W.Md.*)

6. (*a*) Draw a diagram of a pulley system with a velocity ratio of 3.

(*b*) If the efficiency of the system is 80% what effort would be needed to lift a load of 240 N? (*L.*)

7. Describe experiments you have performed to measure the mechanical advantage and velocity ratio of a pulley system.

Give a diagram of a pulley system of velocity ratio 6. If this pulley system is 70% efficient, what effort will be needed to raise a load of 8400 N? (*Mx.*)

8. A man wants to raise an outboard motor from his boat on to the pier and uses a block and tackle with a velocity ratio of 4. Draw a diagram of the system he is using, and label it clearly.

If the mechanical advantage is 3, calculate the efficiency of this system. (*W.Md.*)

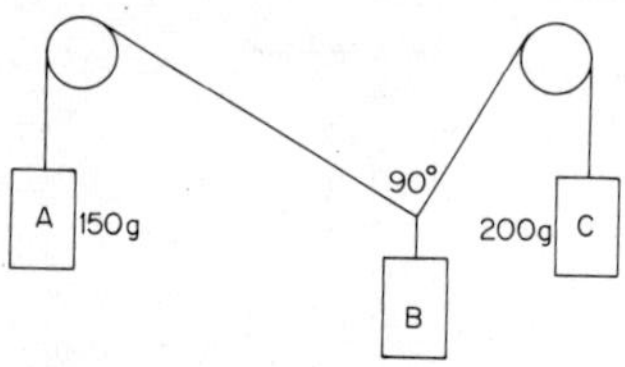

Fig. 4c

9. (*a*) What is the difference between: (i) mass and weight; (ii) a scalar quantity and a vector quantity?

(*b*) Find: (i) the sum of a mass of 9 kg and a mass of 12 kg; (ii) the resultant of a force of 9 N acting at right-angles to a force of 12 N.

(*c*) In an experiment a weight is supported by two strings running over pulleys, as shown in Fig. 4c. The angle between the strings is a right-angle, mass A is 150 g and mass C is 200 g. Find: (i) the value of mass B; (ii) the angle between each string and the vertical. (*E.A.*)

10. (*a*) Draw a simple but clear diagram of any simple machine you care to choose.

(*b*) Describe how you would find by experiment the mechanical advantage and velocity ratio of this machine.

(*c*) Suppose a machine with a velocity ratio of 6:1 is 50% efficient. What effort would be needed to lift a load of 3000 N with it?

(*d*) If the 3000 N load was lifted 1·25 metres in 50 seconds, what was the rate at which work was done on the load? (*S.E.*)

11. (*a*) Draw a diagram of a pulley system of *velocity ratio* 4.

(*b*) Describe an experiment to find the *mechanical advantage* of this pulley system.

(*c*) If the system is 80% efficient, calculate the effort required to lift a load of 640 N. (*Mx.*)

12. A trolley of total weight 5000 N is pulled up a sloping ramp as shown in Fig. 4D. The trolley is moved from position X to position Y.

(*a*) What work is done on the trolley in raising it from X to Y?

(*b*) What work is done by the persons pulling on the rope?

(*c*) Find the values of the mechanical advantage, velocity ratio and efficiency of the system. Show all your working. (*M.*)

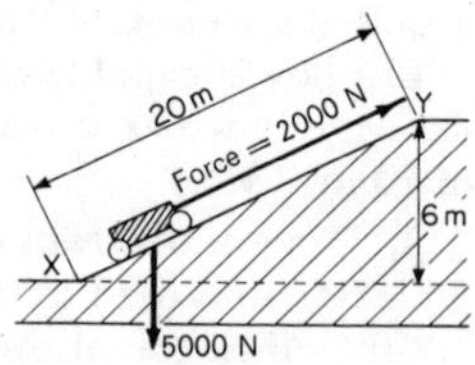

Fig. 4D

5

FORCES DUE TO FLUIDS

Upthrust of Fluid

IF a cork is held below the surface of a liquid and then released it immediately rises to the surface. The cork has thus experienced an upward force or *upthrust* due to the liquid. An upthrust is always exerted on any object immersed in a liquid, whether wholly or partially submerged. Thus ships and submarines would sink if it were not for the upthrust of the sea. We are able to float on water or swim because of the upthrust on our bodies by the liquid.

Water and other liquids are examples of *fluids*. A gas is a fluid. Liquids and gases transmit pressure and both exert pressure. A floating balloon has an upthrust on it due to the greater pressure of air below it, which counterbalances the weight of the balloon. A liquid usually exerts a greater pressure than a gas because it is more dense (p. 100), and hence it exerts a much greater upthrust.

Measurement of Upthrust

The upthrust of a liquid on an object can easily be measured on a small scale. Suppose, for example, that a solid brass object A is attached to a spring balance, which then registers 1·5 N. This is the natural weight W of A, Fig. 5.1. If A is now completely immersed in a liquid, the reading may diminish to 1·2 N, Fig. 5.2. This is due to the upward

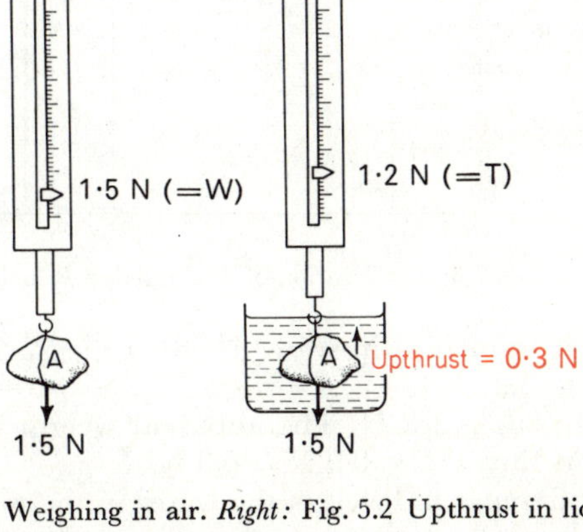

Fig. 5.1 Weighing in air. *Right:* Fig. 5.2 Upthrust in liquid

force or upthrust of the liquid on A. The magnitude of the upthrust = 1·5 − 1·2 = 0·3 N.

The reading of the spring balance when A is immersed in a liquid is sometimes called the 'apparent weight' of A in the liquid. The difference between the natural and 'apparent' weight of A is known as the 'apparent loss in weight'. As we have seen, the apparent loss in weight is the upthrust due to the liquid.

If a swimmer is lifted into a boat, the pulling force needed at first is less than the weight of the swimmer owing to the upthrust of the water. Thus if his weight is 700 N and the upthrust at first is 200 N, the lifting force needed is 500 N. As more of his body leaves the water the upthrust diminishes. After he is clear of the water his weight of 700 N must be overcome. Thus a greater lifting force is now needed. On account of the upthrust of the water, therefore, it is easier at first to lift a person out of the sea into a boat.

Magnitude of Upthrust

We can investigate the magnitude of the upthrust due to a liquid by: (i) weighing an object A in air with a spring-balance; and then

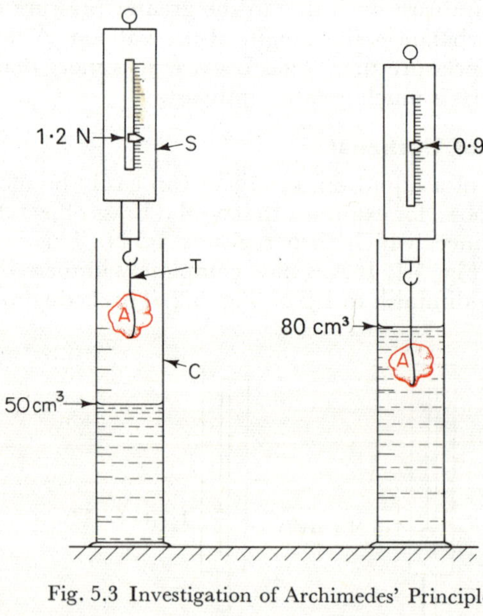

Fig. 5.3 Investigation of Archimedes' Principle

(ii) weighing it immersed in water inside a measuring cylinder. This is shown in Fig. 5.3.

The weight of A is 1·2 N. The apparent weight in water is 0·9 N. The upthrust is thus 1·2 − 0·9 N = 0·3 N.

From the difference in levels of the water in the measuring cylinder, the volume displaced by A = 80 − 50 = 30 cm^3. Since 1 cm^3 of water has a mass of 1 g or weight 0·01 N (p. 139), the *weight of water displaced* is 0·30 N. This is the same as the upthrust. The experiment therefore shows that the upthrust on an object immersed in water is equal to the weight of water displaced by the object.

Similar results are obtained with other liquids.

Archimedes' Principle

Liquids and gases are known as 'fluids'. Objects experience an upthrust in fluids, that is, in gases such as air as well as in liquids such as water.

More than 2000 years ago, Archimedes stated the principle or law giving always the magnitude of the upthrust in a fluid. This states:

When a body is totally or partially immersed in a fluid, the upthrust on it is equal to the weight of fluid displaced.

As examples of Archimedes' Principle, consider the following:

1. An iron cube of volume 800 cm^3 is totally immersed in: (i) water; (ii) oil of density 0·8 g/cm^3; (iii) oxygen gas of density 0·0015 g/cm^3. Calculate the upthrust in each case

$$\text{Upthrust} = \text{Weight of fluid displaced.}$$

(i) $\therefore \text{Upthrust} = \text{weight of } 800 \text{ cm}^3 \text{ of water} = 800 \times 1 \times 0{\cdot}01 \text{ N} = 8 \text{ N}$

(ii) $\therefore \text{Upthrust} = \text{weight of } 800 \text{ cm}^3 \text{ of oil} = 800 \times 0{\cdot}8 \times 0{\cdot}01 \text{ N} = 6{\cdot}4 \text{ N}$

(iii) $\therefore \text{Upthrust} = \text{weight of } 800 \text{ cm}^3 \text{ of oxygen} = 800 \times 0{\cdot}0015 \times 0{\cdot}01 \text{ N} = 0{\cdot}012 \text{ N}.$

Note the smaller upthrust in fluids of smaller density.

2. A metal cube weighs 10 N in air (mass 1 kg) and 8 N when totally immersed in water. Calculate its volume and density.

We have,

$$\text{Upthrust} = 10 \text{ N} - 8 \text{ N} = 2 \text{ N}$$
$$\therefore 2 \text{ N} = \text{weight of water displaced}$$
$$\therefore \text{Mass of water displaced} = 2/0{\cdot}01 = 200 \text{ g}$$
$$\therefore \text{Volume of water displaced} = 200 \text{ cm}^3 = \text{Volume of cube}$$
$$\therefore \text{Density} = \frac{\text{Mass}}{\text{Volume}} = \frac{1000 \text{ g}}{200 \text{ cm}^3} = 5 \text{ g/cm}^3.$$

Observe that this is a method for finding the unknown density of a solid.

3. An iron cube, mass 480 g and density 8 g/cm^3, is suspended half-immersed in an oil of density of 0·9 g/cm^3. Find the tension in the suspension.

$$\text{Volume of cube} = \frac{\text{Mass}}{\text{Density}} = \frac{480}{8} = 60 \text{ cm}^3$$

$$\therefore \text{Upthrust} = \text{Weight of } 30 \text{ cm}^3 \text{ of oil} = 30 \times 0{\cdot}9 \times 0{\cdot}01 = 0{\cdot}27 \text{ N}$$
$$\therefore \text{Tension in string (apparent weight)} = 4{\cdot}8 - 0{\cdot}27 = 4{\cdot}53 \text{ N}.$$

Density Measurement

Solid

Archimedes' Principle enables the relative density or density of solids to be measured. As an illustration, suppose that a brass object weighs 1·6 N in air, and that 1·4 N is the 'apparent weight' when A is completely immersed in water, Fig. 5.4. The upthrust of the water is

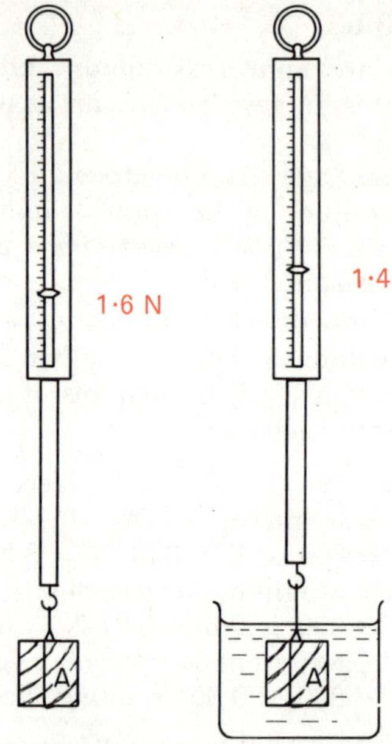

Fig. 5.4 Measuring density of solid

then 0·2 N. By Archimedes' Principle, this is the weight of water *displaced by* A. This mass of water = 0·2/0·01 = 20 g. Since the density of water is 1 g/cm³, the volume of A is 20 cm³. So

$$\text{Density of brass} = \frac{\text{Mass of A}}{\text{Volume of A}} = \frac{160\ \text{g}}{20\ \text{cm}^3} = 8\ \text{g/cm}^3.$$

The weight of water displaced by A is simply the weight of water which has the same volume as A.

$$\therefore \textit{relative density} \text{ of brass} = \frac{\text{Weight of A}}{\text{Weight of equal volume of water}}$$

$$= \frac{1{\cdot}6\ \text{N}}{0{\cdot}2\ \text{N}} = 8.$$

Liquid.

To find the relative density of a liquid such as oil, three weighings are carried out: (i) Weight of any solid B in air; (ii) Apparent weight of B totally immersed in water; (iii) Apparent weight of B totally immersed in oil, Fig. 5.5. Of course, B is a solid such as a metal which is unaffected by the liquids.

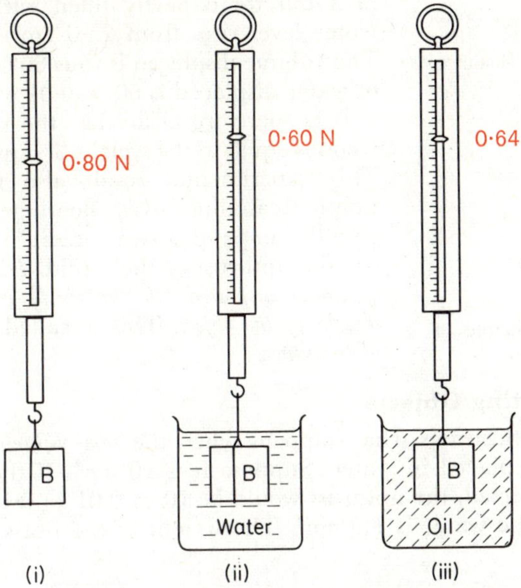

Fig. 5.5 Measuring density of liquid

As an illustration, suppose the object B weighs 0·80 N in air, 0·60 N totally immersed in water and 0·64 N totally immersed in oil. Then

$$\text{Upthrust in water} = 0{\cdot}80 - 0{\cdot}60 = 0{\cdot}2\text{ N}$$
$$= \text{Weight of water displaced.}$$

and

$$\text{Upthrust in oil} = 0{\cdot}80 - 0{\cdot}64 = 0{\cdot}16\text{ N}$$
$$= \text{Weight of oil displaced.}$$

But the volume of the water and the oil are both equal to the volume of B. Hence, comparing the *same* volumes of oil and water,

$$\text{Relative density of oil} = \frac{0{\cdot}16\text{ N}}{0{\cdot}2\text{ N}} = 0{\cdot}8.$$

Since the *volume* of the oil of weight 0·16 N (mass 16 g) is 20 cm^3, the density of the oil = 16 g/20 cm^3 = 0·8 g/cm^3.

Floating Objects

So far we have discussed the upthrust on objects totally immersed in liquids; *floating* objects, such as ships, are also subject to an upthrust.

We can investigate the upthrust on a floating object by weighing a

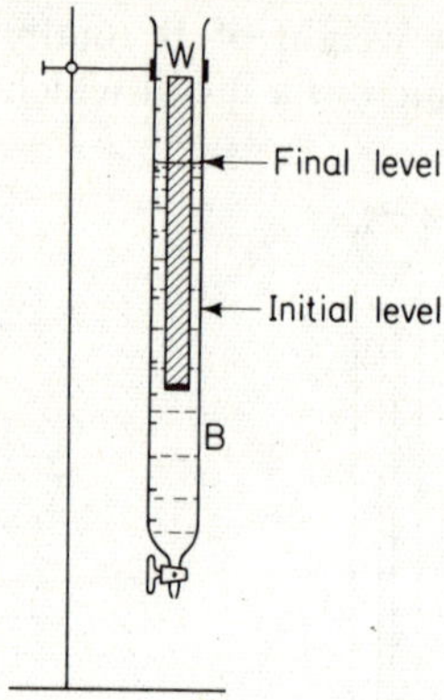

Fig. 5.6 Principle of flotation

narrow wooden rod W slightly weighted at one end and so as to float upright, Fig. 5.6. Suppose the weight is 0·6 N. If it is then placed in a burette B partly filled with water, the water level rises from 25·0 cm^3 to 85·0 cm^3. The volume displaced is thus 60 cm^3. So *weight* of water displaced is $60 \times 0{\cdot}01 = 0{\cdot}6$ N.

It is therefore clear that the weight of the wood is equal to the weight of liquid displaced. This experimental result also follows from simple reasoning. Any floating object is in equilibrium under two forces: (i) its weight; (ii) the upthrust of the liquid. *Hence the weight of liquid displaced (the upthrust) is equal to the weight of the object.* This is called the *Principle of Flotation.*

Some Floating Objects

Fig. 5.7 illustrates what happens when the *same volume* of different materials is placed in water. Suppose it is 10 cm^3. If the brass were totally immersed, the upthrust would be $10 \times 0{\cdot}01 = 0{\cdot}1$ N, since the density of the water is 1 g/cm^3. The weight of the brass, however, is

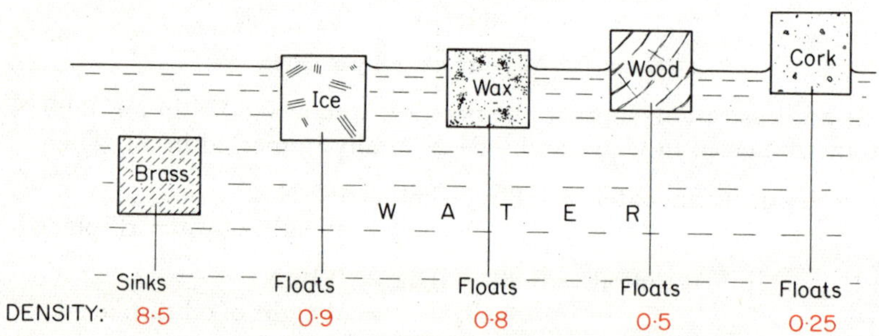

Fig. 5.7 Floating solids (density in g/cm^3)

$10 \times 8{\cdot}5 \times 0{\cdot}01 = 0{\cdot}85$ N. Thus the brass sinks. Ice, however, has a density less than 1 g/cm^3. Assuming a value of 0·9 g/cm^3, the weight of the ice $= 10 \times 0{\cdot}9 \times 0{\cdot}01 = 0{\cdot}09$ N. It therefore sinks with 9 cm^3 immersed, that is, with about $\frac{9}{10}$ immersed. Paraffin wax, wood and cork, which have densities of 0·8, 0·5, 0·25 g/cm^3 respectively, have less and less of their volume immersed since their weights diminish, as shown. Generally, all objects which have a density less than 1 g/cm^3 will float in water. Objects which have a density greater than 1 g/cm^3 will sink if released in water.

A swimmer is able to float more easily in dense water such as sea-water as this provides a greater upthrust, Fig. 5.8 (i). A ship is made of steel and other material whose density is greater than 1, and at first sight one might expect them to sink in water. This would be the case if all the metal and other materials were melted down completely, in which case they occupy a small compact volume and the upthrust is small. But if all the material is spread around so that the volume enclosed is large, as in the ship, the upthrust is large. Thus ships float, Fig. 5.8 (ii).

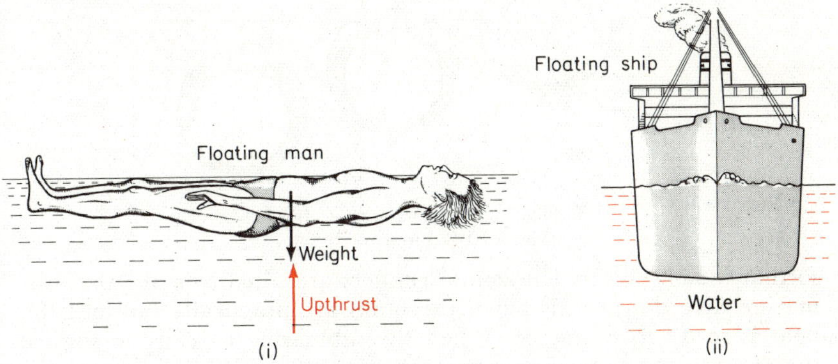

Fig. 5.8 Floating objects

The weight of water displaced by a ship is equal to the ship's weight. It is therefore common to refer to the size of a ship as '8000 tonnes wt displacement' for example, which means that this is the weight of water displaced. Without a cargo, a ship stands more out of the water, since the weight of water displaced is less.

Plimsoll Line

A ship sinks in water until its weight is equal to the upthrust on it, which is the weight of water displaced. Now the density (or specific gravity) of sea-water varies in different parts of the world, according to whether the climate is hot or cold. Hence a ship sinks to different levels if its journey takes it to different regions. When a ship sinks too low in water it is unsafe in heavy seas, and the danger increases if the cargo carried is very heavy. Accordingly, in the 19th century, Plimsoll agitated for a safety line to be drawn clearly on the side of a ship. It is now illegal for a ship to be loaded so that the Plimsoll line, as it is called, is below the water level. Fig. 5.9 illustrates markings of the Plimsoll line; the letters LR stand for Lloyd's Register of Shipping, TF for tropical fresh water, F for fresh water, T for tropics, S for summer, W for winter, WNA for winter in the North Atlantic.

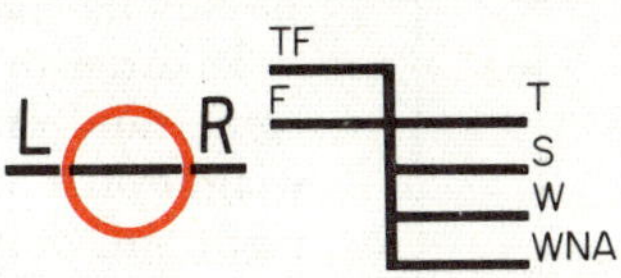

Fig. 5.9 Plimsoll line

Submarine

The submarine is another application of Archimedes' Principle. In surface trim (Fig. 5.10) the submarine floats with its conning tower and most of the deck clear of the water. The boat is provided with large ballast tanks which may be filled with water, thus increasing the weight

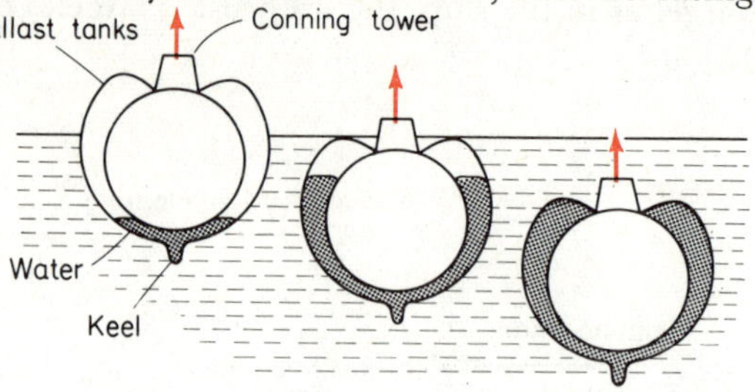

Fig. 5.10 Submarine diving

so that it sinks lower. Horizontal rudders are tilted to make the submarine dive downwards when the tanks are practically full and the boat is ready to submerge. When the submarine is ready to surface the rudders are moved to drive the boat upwards, and compressed air is forced into the ballast tanks to drive the water out so that the submarine can rise again.

The Hydrometer

Hydrometers are instruments which measure directly the density or relative density of a liquid. They are used, for instance, by inspectors to test the richness, or otherwise, of milk. This is related to its relative density; the instrument is then called a *lactometer*. The strength of spirits must also conform to a certain standard. This is checked by inspectors with the aid of a hydrometer. The instrument is also used to test the relative density of the acid in accumulators, as this gives an excellent guide to the general condition of the accumulator (see p. 444). The relative density of the water in a ship's dock must be entered in the log book by the captain.

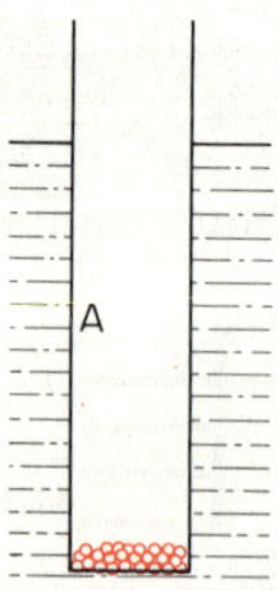

Fig. 5.11 Model hydrometer

A *simple hydrometer* can be made from a test-tube A having its end flattened, Fig. 5.11.

In order to keep it upright when it is placed in a liquid, some sand or lead shot is placed inside A. Suppose the weight of A and its contents is 0·1 N and it is placed upright in water, density 1 g/cm³. Then, from the Principle of Flotation, it sinks to such a depth that its weight is equal to the upthrust of the liquid, which is equal to the weight of liquid displaced. Hence the weight of water displaced is 0·1 N. The volume of water displaced is thus 10 cm^3. Suppose the uniform cross-sectional area of A is 1 cm^2. Then the depth to which it is submerged is 10 cm.

Now suppose A is transferred to a liquid of much greater density, say 2 g/cm^3. The upthrust when A floats = weight of A = 0·1 N. Hence the volume submerged is now only 5 cm^3. A thus stands more out of the liquid than when in water.

Generally then, A will sink more in lighter liquids and less in denser liquids. A *model hydrometer* can be made, therefore, by placing A in liquids of known density, and marking on a paper scale inside it the values of the density on a level with the liquid surface outside. From what has been said, the density values increase in a downward direction on the paper scale. This is also shown in the practical hydrometers in Figs. 5.12 and 5.13.

Practical Hydrometer

One form of practical hydrometer is shown in Fig. 5.12. It consists of: (i) a hollow narrow glass tube or stem T; (ii) a paper scale inside T graduated in densities; (iii) a wide bulb B; (iv) a loaded end S containing lead shot, for example, to keep it upright in liquids (p. 52).

A *battery hydrometer* is shown in Fig. 5.13. The tube at the bottom is

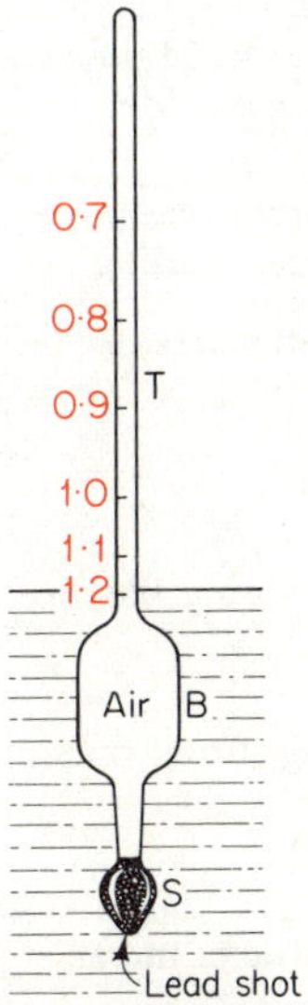

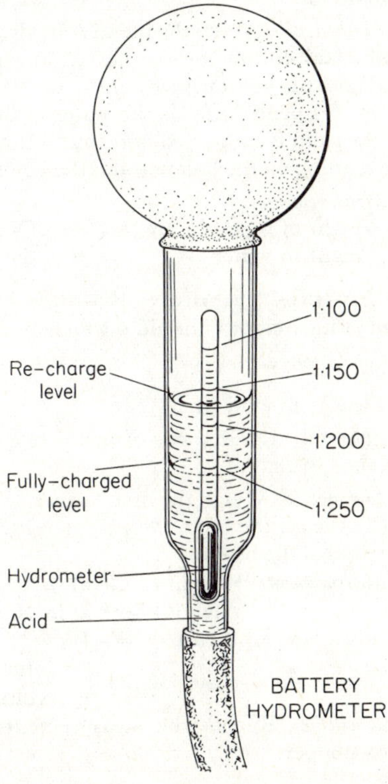

Fig. 5.12 Practical hydrometer
Right: Fig. 5.13 Battery hydrometer

immersed in the battery acid and the bulb at the top is squeezed to expel air. Some acid then enters the tube below the bulb. The hydrometer now floats in the acid as shown. The acid density is read from the markings on the hydrometer scale. The density of the acid is a good indication of the condition of the battery.

SUMMARY

1. Archimedes principle states: The upthrust on an object immersed in a fluid (liquid or gas) is equal to the weight of fluid displaced.

2. If an object is totally immersed in water, measurement of the upthrust enables the volume of the object to be found. Thus the density of the object may be calculated.

3. Floating objects: upthrust = weight of object.

4. Hydrometers have a narrow stem, wide bulb, weighted end. The density values on the graduations increase downwards.

PRACTICAL (Notes for guidance, p. 26)

1. Investigation of Archimedes' Principle (p. 82)

Apparatus. Large piece of metal; spring or lever balance; measuring cylinder; thin thread.

Method. (i) Weigh the metal A in air.

(ii) Half-fill the measuring cylinder with water to a convenient graduation and note the volume reading.

(iii) Suspend A inside the water in the measuring cylinder, making sure that all the solid is immersed and that it does not touch the sides of the vessel. Note the reading on the balance and the volume reading on the cylinder.

Measurements.

Weight of metal in air, W_1 = .. N.	Initial cylinder reading = .. cm^3.
Weight in water, W_2 = .. N.	Final cylinder reading = .. cm^3.

Calculation. Upthrust = $W_1 - W_2$ = .. N. Volume of water displaced = .. cm^3; thus weight of liquid displaced = .. N.

Conclusion

2. Density of solid (p. 84)

Apparatus. Large piece of metal (e.g. brass weight); spring balance or lever balance; beaker.

Method. (i) Weigh the metal in air.

(ii) Weigh the metal *fully* immersed in water, making sure it does not touch the sides of the beaker.

Measurements Weight of metal in air, W_1 = .. N.
Weight of metal in water, W_2 = .. N.

Calculation. Upthrust = $W_1 - W_2$ = .. N. Hence volume of metal = .. cm^3.

$$\therefore \text{ Density of metal} = \frac{\text{mass of metal}}{\text{volume of metal}} = \text{.. g/cm}^3.$$

Conclusion. Repeat the measurements with other materials such as a large glass stopper.

3. Density of liquid (p. 84)

Apparatus. Large piece of metal or other solid; spring or lever balance; beaker of liquid such as oil; beaker of water.

Method. Weigh the solid.

(i) In air, W.

(ii) Fully immersed in the liquid, W_1.

(iii) Fully immersed in water, W_2, after drying the solid. Take care the solid does not touch the sides of the beaker.

Calculation. Upthrust in liquid $= W - W_1 =$ .. N = weight of liquid displaced.
Upthrust in water $= W - W_2 =$ .. N. Hence volume displaced = .. cm^3.

$$\therefore \text{Density of liquid} = \frac{\text{mass of liquid displaced}}{\text{volume of liquid displaced}}.$$
$$= \frac{W-W_1}{W-W_2} = \text{.. g/cm}^3.$$

Conclusion. Repeat for a dense solution of copper sulphate or a dense salt solution.

4. Investigation of principle of flotation (p. 86)

Apparatus. Test-tube; measuring cylinder; lead shot; spring balance or Butchart balance.

Method. (i) Tie thread round the neck of the test-tube A and leave a loop so that it can be hung from a spring balance or Butchart balance hook.

(ii) Half fill a measuring cylinder B with water to a level corresponding to one of the graduations on the cylinder. Record the reading. Place the test-tube inside and then add sufficient lead shot to make it float upright and away from the sides. Fig. 5.14. (i) Take the volume reading again.

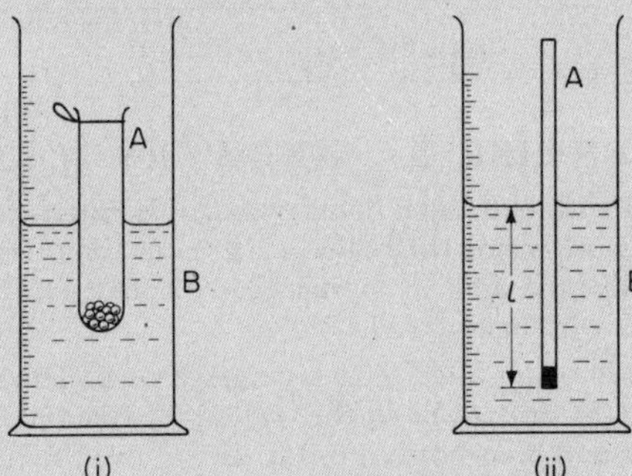

Fig. 5.14 (i) Flotation (ii) Model hydrometer

(iii) Hook the test-tube and lead shot on to the spring balance or Butchart balance, dry the test-tube and record the weight.

Measurements.

Initial reading on cylinder = .. cm^3

Final reading (cm^3)	Weight of tube+shot (N)	Weight of liquid displaced (N)

Calculate the volume displaced in cm^3 from the two readings. Since the density of water is 1 g/cm^3, the weight of water displaced is now known.

Compare this with the measured weight of test-tube and lead shot. What is your conclusion?

Replace the test-tube and lead shot, add more lead shot to sink the tube to about half its length. Record the new measurements. Add more lead shot to sink the tube to about three-quarters of its length and record the measurements again.

5. Model hydrometer (p. 88)

Apparatus. Plastic drinking straw A; measuring cylinder B; four liquids of increasing density such as paraffin oil or meths, water, concentrated salt solution and glycerine or other very dense liquid. Measure the density of your salt solution, or of any other liquid whose density cannot be found from tables of density values, by Method 3 above.

Method. (i) Plug one end of the straw with plasticene. See if it floats upright in water with about half its length immersed. If not, alter the weight at the end by adding lead shot or other small solids. Fig. 5·14 (ii).

(ii) Record the length of straw immersed from the corresponding number of divisions on the measuring cylinder. Record the density of the liquid. Do this for the four liquids.

(iii) *Graph* the density (d) values and the length (l) of straw immersed. Draw a smooth curve through the points. This is a 'density chart' for your model hydrometer.

(iv) Take a different liquid, such as turps or castor oil or vinegar. Immerse the hydrometer. Read the length immersed. Then find its density from your 'density chart'.

Measurements.

Length immersed	Density of liquid
.. divisions	.. g/cm^3

EXERCISE 5 . ANSWERS, p. 257

1. A balloon filled with hydrogen floats upwards because: (a) hydrogen is an element; (b) the pressure inside the balloon is greater than that outside; (c) hydrogen is colourless like the air; (d) air has been displaced by the hydrogen; (e) air pressure decreases with height. (*M.*)

2. A ship's holds are being filled with a cargo of cork. The ship will: (a) rise higher in the water; (b) sink lower in the water; (c) remain at the same level; (d) tend to turn over and float bottom upwards; (e) need to have heavy ballast added to the cargo. (*M.*)

3. Of the following, the substance which has the greatest density is: (a) cork; (b) ice; (c) lubricating oil; (d) water; (e) soft wood. (*E.A.*)

4. Select the **best** answer in the following cases:

(a) It is not easy to swim under water in the Dead Sea, which is very salty, because: (i) the salt gets in your eyes and makes them sting; (ii) the salt makes you too buoyant; (iii) the salt makes you sink; (iv) the salt is an electrolyte; (v) the density of the water is too low.

(b) Archimedes' principle states that when a substance is totally or partly immersed in a fluid the upthrust is equal to: (i) the amount of fluid displaced;

(ii) the volume of fluid displaced; (iii) the weight of fluid displaced; (iv) the volume of the substance; (v) the volume of the substance in the fluid.

(*c*) The efficiency of a machine is **defined** as: (i) Work got out/Work put in; (ii) Load lifted/Effort required to lift it; (iii) Velocity ratio/Mechanical advantage; (iv) Distance moved by load/Distance moved by effort; (v) Work put in/Work got out.

(*d*) A hydrometer is used to measure: (i) atmospheric pressure; (ii) water in the atmosphere; (iii) hydraulic pressure of a fluid; (iv) density; (c) water pressure. (*E.A.*)

5. A piece of iron weighs 1·4 N in air and 1·2 N when completely immersed in water. Find its density. Why would it weigh less when suspended in a solution of salt water? (*Mx.*)

6. You cannot swim easily under water in the Dead Sea, which is very salty, because: (*a*) the salt in the water will make you sink; (*b*) the salt in the water makes you too buoyant; (*c*) the salt in the water gives it too much resistance; (*d*) you will generate electricity as you move through the salty water; (*e*) the salt crystallizes and injures your skin. (*W.M.*)

7. Lead has a density of 11·3 g/cm³. Mercury has a density of 13·6 g/cm³. Lead will .. when placed in water. Lead will .. when placed in mercury. Linseed oil will float when placed in water so its density must be .. than 1·0 g/cm³. (*L.*)

8. Three cubes of the same size are painted to look identical and lettered A, B and C. Fig. 5A. It is known that one is made of wood, one of aluminium and one of lead. The following experiments are performed using these cubes: Fig. 5A (*a*), (*b*), (*c*), (*d*), (*e*).

(*a*) What material do you think C is made of?

(*b*) What material do you think cube A is made of?

(*c*) What is the relative density of the material of cube B?

(*d*) How does the density of the blue liquid compare with that of water? Give a reason.

(*e*) Will the second reading of the spring balance be greater or less than the first? Give a reason. (*M.*)

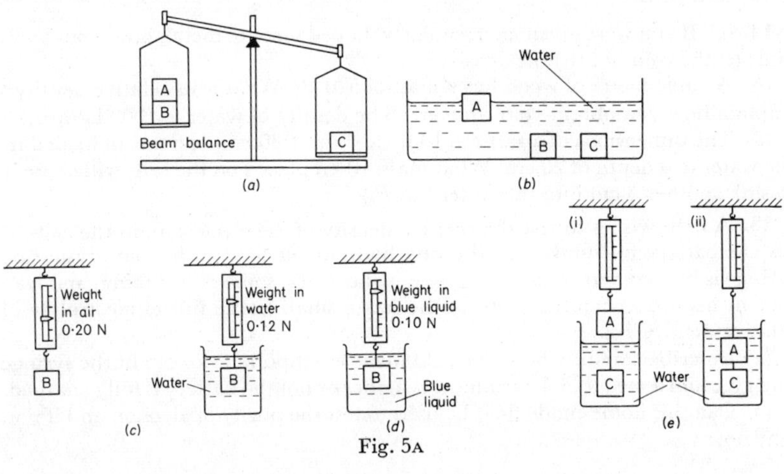

Fig. 5A

9. (*a*) State the law of flotation.

(*b*) Give a diagram of the loading (Plimsoll) lines on a ship's side, and explain their importance.

(*c*) A 20 million-kg ship floats in sea-water of relative density 1·02. Find: (i) the weight of displaced sea-water; (ii) the volume of this sea-water. (Pure water has a density of 100 kg/m³.) (*Mx.*)

10. Explain fully how you would construct a home-made hydrometer given a flat-based glass test-tube, and any other apparatus you consider necessary. Describe how you would graduate the instrument for measuring the relative density of liquids between 0·8 and 1·2. If you wished to have an hydrometer which covered a wider range, what differences would there have to be in the glass test-tube supplied? (*E.A.*)

11. (*a*) Define *density* of a substance.

(*b*) Describe carefully how you would find the density of stone, if you were given an irregular stone about as big as your fist. Show how you result is calculated.

(*c*) Consider these three steps of procedure: *Step* 1—A nail, a cork and some water are placed in a beaker. *Step* 2—Some mercury is now poured in. *Step* 3—Some oil is added. Draw a diagram for *each* of the steps, showing the beaker and its contents.

Densities: cork, 0·2 g/cm³; iron, 7·0 g/cm³; mercury, 13·6 g/cm³; oil, 0·8 g/cm³.

12. State *Archimedes' principle*. Describe, with the aid of diagrams, an experiment you could perform to show the truth of this principle.

What are *loading lines* on ships? Why should the loading lines on ships vary according to time of year and location of the sea (*Mx.*)

13. (*a*) If a balloon is filled with hydrogen is the total weight greater than, the same as, or less than the weight of the empty balloon? If it is released in air will it rise or fall? Explain your answers.

(*b*) A raft is made of 400 kg of wood and floats half immersed in water. What weight of metal must be attached to the top of the raft so that it will just sink? Explain what difference there would be if the metal were attached to the bottom of the raft. (*E.A.*)

14. (*a*) If you were given an irregularly shaped piece of metal, how would you find: (i) the volume; (ii) the density?

(*b*) A cubic metre of wood has a mass of 520 kg. What is its relative density? Explain how you obtain your answer. (The density of water is 1000 kg/m³.)

(*c*) The dimensions of a raft are 10 m × 6 m × 30 cm. It floats unloaded in the water to a depth of 20 cm. What mass, when placed on the raft, will cause it to sink another 5 cm into the water? (*S.E.*)

15. A man wishes to test the relative density of the electrolyte in the cells of his car battery but finds that the tiny hydrometer float in his battery-testing syringe is broken and unusable. There is, however, some glass tubing, and lead shot in his son's chemistry set and he has a small bottle full of electrolyte of relative density 1·2.

(*a*) Describe carefully how he could make a temporary float to fit the syringe and give him a means of determining whether or not the battery is fully charged.

(*b*) Can this home-made float be used to test the purity of alcohol, and if not, why not?

(*c*) How is such a float used to test whether milk has been illegally 'watered' or not? (*W.Md.*)

16. (*a*) State: (i) *Archimedes' principle*; (ii) the law of flotation.

(*b*) Describe, with the aid of diagrams, an experiment you could perform to show the truth of *Archimedes' principle*.

(*c*) A hydrometer which has a scale reading from 0·5 to 1·5, in steps of 0·1, is placed first in water, then in paraffin and then in brine. Draw *three* diagrams showing the hydrometer floating in these liquids. Include the scale each time. Density of paraffin = 0·8 g/cm³. Density of brine = 1·1 g/cm³. (*Mx.*)

17. (*a*) An object was weighed on a spring balance, first of all in air and then in water. The results are shown in Fig. 5B.

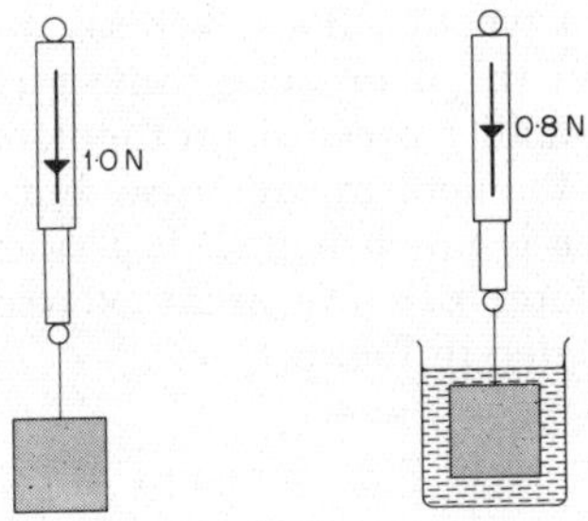

Fig. 5B

(i) What is the upthrust on the object when it is placed in water?

(ii) What is the downward force on the object when in the water?

(iii) What upward force, other than upthrust, acts on the object when in the water?

(iv) Explain why the object would sink in water if it were released from the spring balance.

(v) What would the upthrust be if the object were placed in a liquid of twice the density of water? What would then be the reading in the spring balance? (*M.*)

18. (i) Why does a piece of wood float and a piece of lead sink in water?

(ii) A wooden block, whose volume is 16 cm³, has a hole of 1 cm³ drilled in it. The hole is filled with lead. Will the block sink or float in water? (Give reasons for your answer and show any calculations you make.) Density of lead 11 g/cm³. Density of wood 0·5 g/cm³. Density of water = 1 g/cm³.

(iii) Which is denser, milk or cream? (Give your reason for your answer.) (*S.E.*)

6

PRESSURE IN FLUIDS

LIQUID PRESSURE

Pressure

A GIRL wearing very narrow or 'stiletto' heels can produce an impression of the heels on a wooden floor. We say this effect is due to the *pressure* of the heel on the floor. The same girl wearing wide-heeled shoes exerts a much smaller pressure on the floor. The same force, her weight, is exerted on the floor in each case, but the area of the heel in contact with the floor is much less with a stiletto heel. In the latter case, therefore, the 'force per unit area' exerted by the heel is much greater. This is calculated in Fig. 6.1.

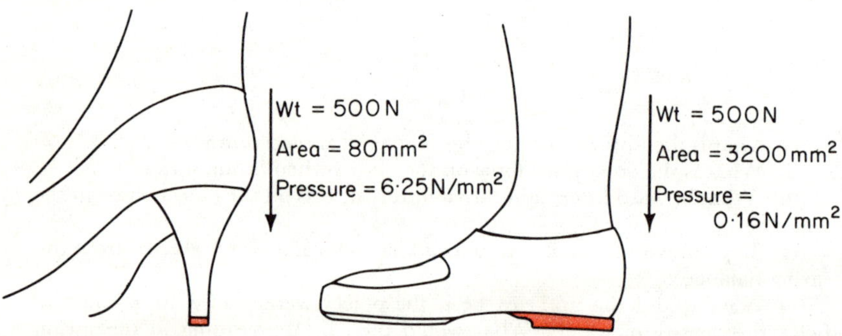

Fig. 6.1 High and moderate pressure

Scientists define **pressure** as *force per unit area.* Thus the pressure on the head of a diver at work on a sea-bed is the weight of water per unit area of the surface of his head. The unit of pressure may be given as 'newton per metre^2, N/m^2', or 'N/mm^2'. If the average pressure on a diver's head-gear of surface area 60 000 mm^2 is 0·3 N/mm^2, the *force* on the head-gear is $60\ 000 \times 0{\cdot}3$ or 18 000 N, the product of the area and the pressure. If the total force due to the pressure of water on a plate in the side of a ship is 15 000 N and the area of the plate is 5000 mm^2 the average pressure on the plate is 3 N/mm^2. Thus the average pressure p over a surface is given by

$$p = \frac{\text{Total force on surface } (F)}{\text{Area of surface } (A)} \quad \ldots \ldots \quad (1)$$

Note that *'pressure' is not the same as 'force'*. The force F on a surface of area A can be calculated, if the average pressure p is known, by the relation

$$F = p \times A \quad . \quad . \quad . \quad . \quad . \quad . \quad . \quad . \quad (2)$$

Examples of Pressure

A standing boy exerts a force equal to his weight on the ground below his feet. If the weight is 500 N, and the area of his shoes is 0·01 m², then the average pressure on the ground, p, is given by

$$p = \frac{\text{Force}}{\text{Area}} = \frac{500 \text{ N}}{0{\cdot}01 \text{ m}^2}$$
$$= 50\,000 \text{ N/m}^2.$$

If the boy lies flat on the ground his area in contact with the ground increases considerably. Suppose it is now 0·20 m², which is twenty times the original area. The new average pressure p is then 500 N/0·20 m² or 2500 N/m², which is twenty times *less* than before. A person who goes to the rescue of someone who has fallen through ice into a pond would therefore be well advised to crawl over the ice rather than walk.

If a heavy parcel is carried by thin string the small area of string in contact with the flesh produces a large pressure and the string tends to cut into the flesh. Thick string or thick luggage handles produce much less pressure on the hand. A ballet dancer pirouetting on her toes produces a high pressure on the floor. Great pressure is encouraged in the design of ice-skates. The blade makes such a small area of contact with the ice that the pressure below it is very high and ice melts. The skate thus moves through a thin film of water (see p. 222).

Pressure in Liquid

We can investigate the pressure in a liquid by using the apparatus shown in Fig. 6.2.

Thin plastic membranes or covers are tied firmly over the tops of several thistle funnels, each bent at different angles as shown. One of them is connected by rubber tubing to a U-tube containing light oil. If the plastic is pressed lightly with the finger the air inside is compressed and the liquid levels alter. The greater the pressure on the plastic, the greater is the difference in levels. Thus the U-tube acts as a convenient pressure gauge or *manometer*.

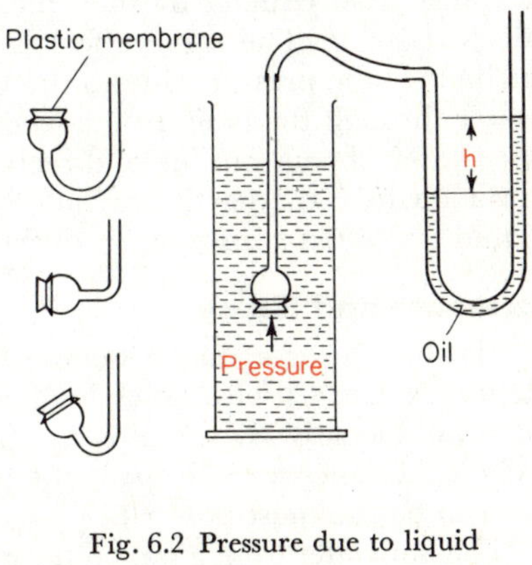

Fig. 6.2 Pressure due to liquid

1. Lower the funnel into a glass vessel, filled with water. Notice that, the deeper it goes, the greater is the difference in levels of the liquid in the U-tube. Thus the *pressure of water in the vessel increases with depth.*

2. Replace the funnel by others in turn, whose mouths are pointing in different directions. You will observe that the results obtained at a particular depth are the same as those in the first case. Thus the *pressure in a liquid is the same in all different directions.*

3. Lower a thistle funnel to the same depth in a number of different liquids in turn, such as paraffin and dense copper sulphate solution. Notice that *the greater the density of the liquid, the greater is the pressure at the same depth.*

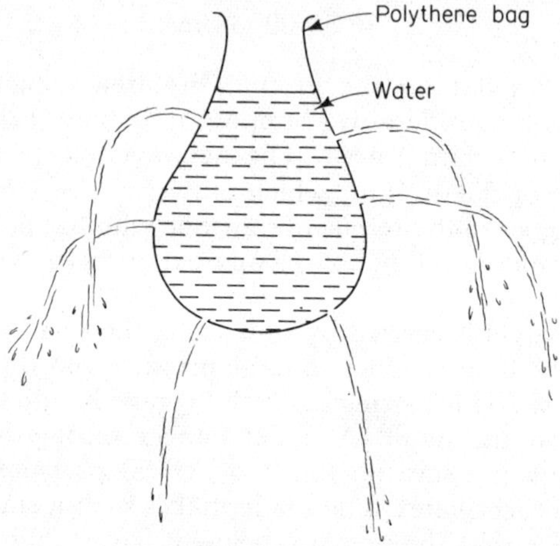

Fig. 6.3 Pressure acts normally to surface

A rubber ball or a polythene can, punctured by many fine holes and filled with water, sprays water in all directions when squeezed, Fig. 6.3. The pressure on the liquid, although applied in one direction outside, is transmitted equally by movement of the molecules of the liquid to all parts of it. The same effect is produced when a watering-can is inclined—the pressure due to the weight of water behind it forces out water through the holes in the rose of the can. It should be noted that the water shoots out in a direction normal (perpendicular) to the surface where the particular hole is situated. Thus the pressure of the liquid is exerted *at right-angles* to the surface with which it is in contact.

Pressure and Depth

Fig. 6.4 shows a simple demonstration that pressure increases with depth. A can, C, with holes H of equal size perforated in it, is placed on a tall block B. By stopping up the holes, C can be filled with water. When the holes are all open, the jet of water from the lowest hole is seen to be the most powerful.

The hot water from a tap on the ground floor of a building issues with a greater speed than the water from a tap on the third floor, for the same reason. The bottom of a dam is made much thicker than the top because the pressure of water increases with the depth.

In a comparatively small depth of water, a diver needs no special protective clothing. The increase in pressure on diving is small, Fig. 6.5 (i). A deep-sea diver, however, who may investigate wrecks at the bottom of the ocean, requires protective hand-gear and clothing to counteract the great pressure of these depths, Fig. 6.5 (ii).

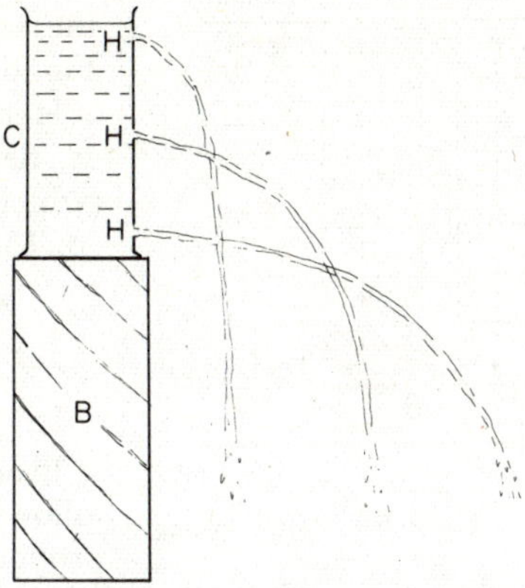

Fig. 6.4 Pressure increases with depth

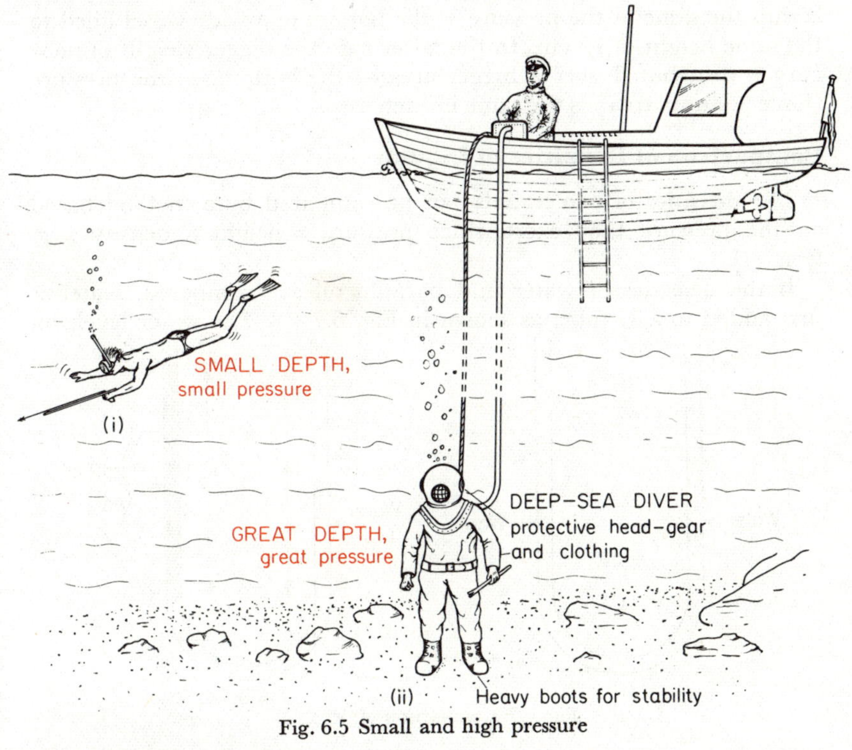

Fig. 6.5 Small and high pressure

Pressure Formula

We can now obtain a general formula for the pressure at a place below the surface of a liquid of density ρ kg/m^3. Suppose a horizontal area B of 1 m^2 is placed h m below the surface. The pressure on B is

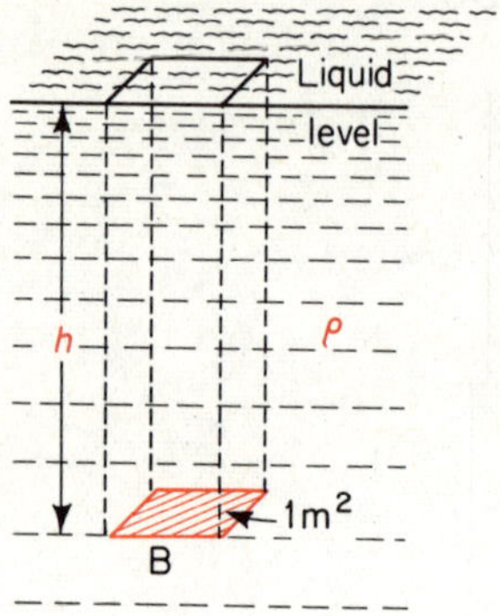

Fig. 6.6 Pressure = $h\rho g$

due to the weight of liquid acting on it. Now the volume of this liquid $= 1 \times h = h$ m³, Fig. 6.6.

Hence the mass of the liquid = volume × density = $h\rho$ kg. Its *weight* in newtons (which is a force) = $h\rho g$, where $g = 10$ (p. 138).

$$\therefore \text{ pressure on B} = \frac{\text{force on B}}{\text{area of B}} = \frac{h\rho g}{1}$$
$$= h\rho g.$$

In general, **Pressure = hρg** . . . (1)

From the formulae for the pressure in (1), it follows that the pressure in a liquid increases proportionally with the depth h of the place below the surface, and with the density d of the liquid. The pressure at the bottom of a narrow vessel filled to a height of 10 cm with mercury is thus the same as the pressure at the bottom of a wide vessel filled to the same height of 10 cm. In the latter case the bigger weight of mercury is distributed over a bigger area at the bottom, so the pressure (force per unit area) is the same in each case.

Comparison of Densities of Liquids

The densities of two liquids can be compared by a method based on the pressure they exert, since pressure = height × density × g, from (1).

If the densities of water and paraffin oil are compared, water is first added to a U-tube, as shown in Fig. 6.7 (i). The water levels on

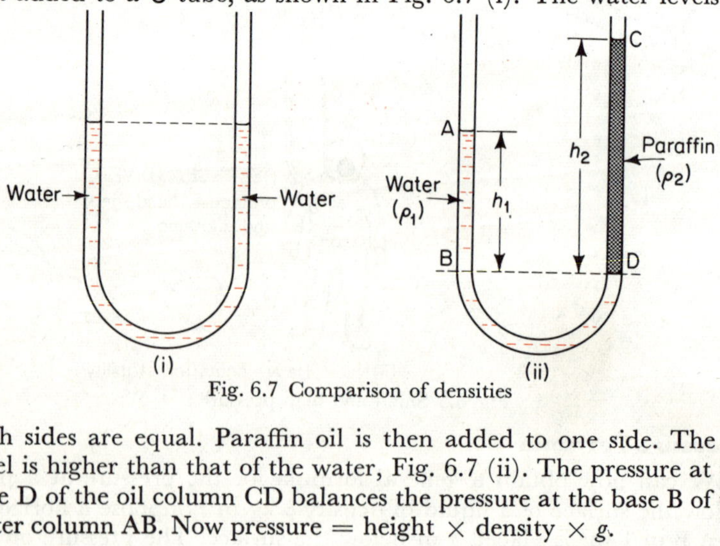

Fig. 6.7 Comparison of densities

both sides are equal. Paraffin oil is then added to one side. The oil level is higher than that of the water, Fig. 6.7 (ii). The pressure at the base D of the oil column CD balances the pressure at the base B of the water column AB. Now pressure = height × density × g.

Thus

$$\text{oil density} \times \text{oil height} \times g = \text{water density} \times \text{water height} \times g$$

$$\therefore \frac{\text{oil density, } \rho_2}{\text{water density, } \rho_1} = \frac{\text{water height, } h_1}{\text{oil height, } h_2}.$$

Suppose $h_1 = 7$ cm and $h_2 = 10$ cm. Then

$$\frac{\text{oil density}}{\text{water density}} = \frac{7}{10} = 0{\cdot}7.$$

Since the density of water is 1 g/cm^3, the density of the oil is 0·7 g/cm^3.

The same method can be used for comparing or measuring the densities of *any two liquids which do not mix*. If they mix, another form of balancing column method can be adopted, as explained in *Practical*, p. 113.

Transmission of Fluid Pressure · Hydraulic Press

When a pressure is exerted on a liquid it is transmitted equally in all directions (p. 98). Depth charges, exploding at some point below the water, can give rise to enormous forces at least 50 m from the place of the actual explosion. The transmission of pressure through a liquid is utilized in the *hydraulic press*, a machine whose principle is illustrated in Fig. 6.8.

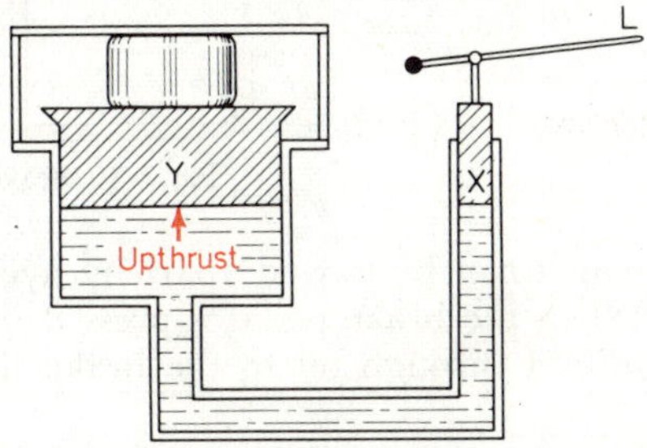

Fig. 6.8 Hydraulic press

By means of a lever L a small force, 20 N for example, is applied directly to a piston X of cross-sectional area 30 cm^2, say. The *pressure* on the liquid due to the movement of X is then $\frac{20}{30}$, or $\frac{2}{3}$ N/cm^2. This is transmitted through the water filling the vessel to a tight-fitting piston Y of an area of 1200 cm^2, the *upward force* F exerted on it is given by F = pressure × area = $\frac{2}{3} \times 1200 = 800$ N. Thus a large force is obtained by the application of the comparatively small force of 20 N.

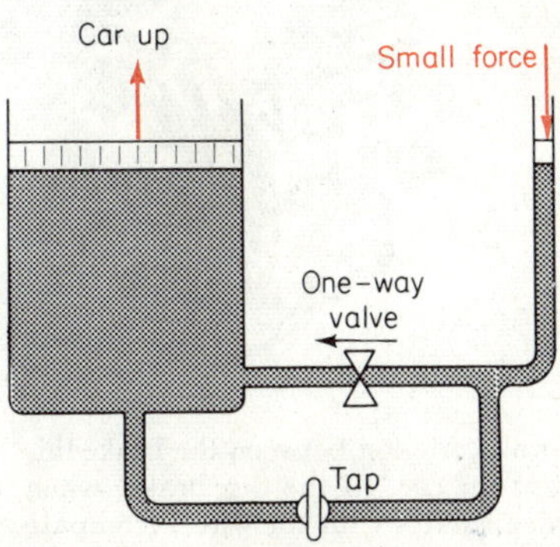

Fig. 6.9 Hydraulic jack

Hydraulic Devices · Car Brakes

The general principle of the hydraulic press, that pressure is transmitted equally to all parts of a liquid, is used in many appliances. Some car jacks, for example, consist of an oil-filled press used for lifting, Fig. 6.9. Most mechanical diggers and bulldozers now use hydraulic principles to power the shovel or blade. Large hydraulic hammers are used to forge red-hot steel into various shapes, and automatic pit props in coal mines are hydraulically operated and moved.

The modern car requires a braking system which retards each wheel equally to minimize the dangers of skidding or locking the wheels when the brakes are applied. The best way is to operate the brakes hydraulically, Fig. 6.10. Each brake consists of two brake shoes,

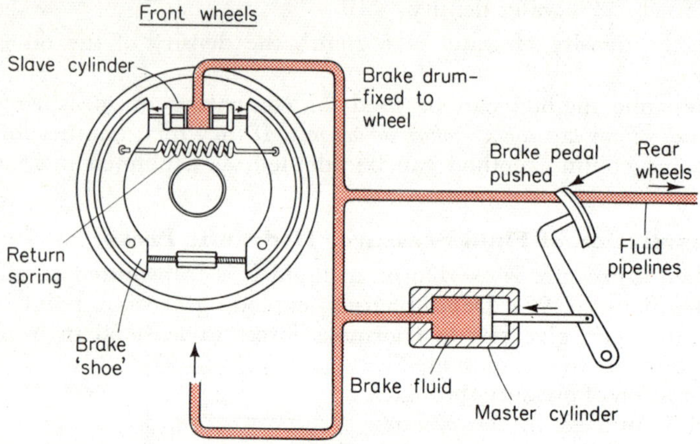

Fig. 6.10 Brake system in car

which can be moved apart by hydraulic pressure in a slave cylinder. When the brake pedal is pressed the increased pressure on it is transmitted through oil to the brake shoes, which are then forced apart.

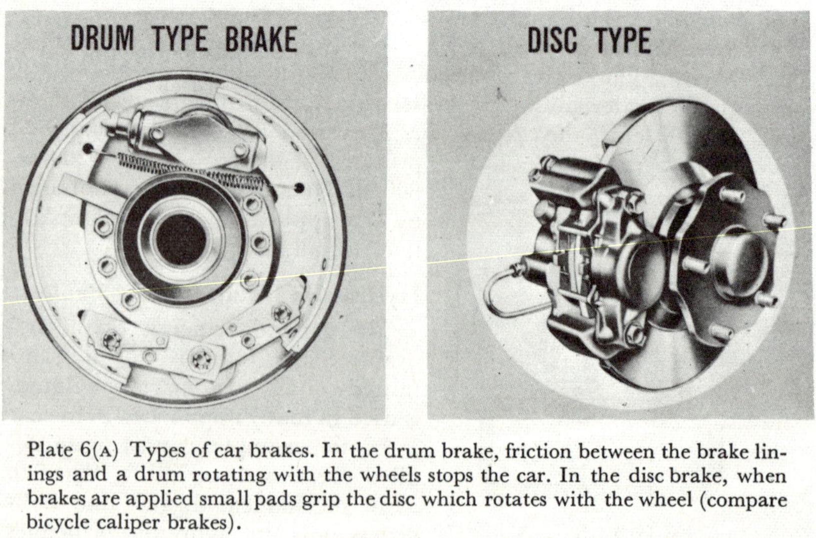

Plate 6(A) Types of car brakes. In the drum brake, friction between the brake linings and a drum rotating with the wheels stops the car. In the disc brake, when brakes are applied small pads grip the disc which rotates with the wheel (compare bicycle caliper brakes).

They now bear on a revolving brake drum to which the wheel is bolted, so that the wheel is made to stop. When the pressure on the brake pedal is released a spring connected between the two brake shoes contracts and pulls them together again. The drum is then released and the wheel is free to turn.

The slave cylinders on all four wheels are connected together by oil-filled pipes and are operated by a master cylinder connected by levers to the brake pedal. The amount of braking applied to each wheel is exactly equal, since the same pressure is transmitted through the oil or brake fluid. See Plate 6A.

ATMOSPHERIC AND GAS PRESSURE

Earth's Atmosphere

The earth's surface is surrounded by a thick layer of air called the atmosphere. Air is a mixture of gases, containing about four-fifths by volume of nitrogen, about one-fifth oxygen and a small percentage of carbon dioxide, together with very small quantities of neon, argon, krypton, xenon, helium, hydrogen, ozone and water vapour. At considerable heights traces of ozone are formed by the action on oxygen of the sun's radiation. This ozone layer plays a vital part in shielding the earth from excessive ultra-violet radiation, which in high dosage is harmful to life.

The atmosphere is most dense at ground- or sea-level, estimated at about 1·2 g/litre, and extends to a height of about eighty to several hundred kilometres, an approximate figure. The higher one goes the less dense is the air, since there is then less weight of air above to compress it. At an altitude of 2000 m (2 kilometres) the density falls to about 1 g/litre; at 10 000 m (10 kilometres) the density is about 0·4 g/litre. Above the earth's atmosphere in interstellar space there is practically a vacuum—only a very small number of molecules, estimated at about a thousand per litre, exist here, whereas at ground-level the number per litre of air molecules is of the order of 10^{22}.

Evidence of Air Pressure

We cannot see the air because it is so 'thin', but the winds are practical evidence of its existence. Sailing boats are driven by air pressure, windmills rotate owing to winds and an aeroplane is kept in flight by air pressure. In the laboratory two convincing demonstrations of air pressure are as follows:

(1) *Collapsing Tin*

Obtain a can with a narrow neck, such as an empty paraffin can. Place a *little* water in the can, and boil for a few minutes, Fig. 6.11 (i). Then remove the can from the tripod and knock in the rubber bung very tightly. Pour cold water over the can to cool it. Notice that the can collapses, Fig. 6.11 (ii). When the can is removed from the tripod it is filled with steam. After inserting the stopper the can cools down

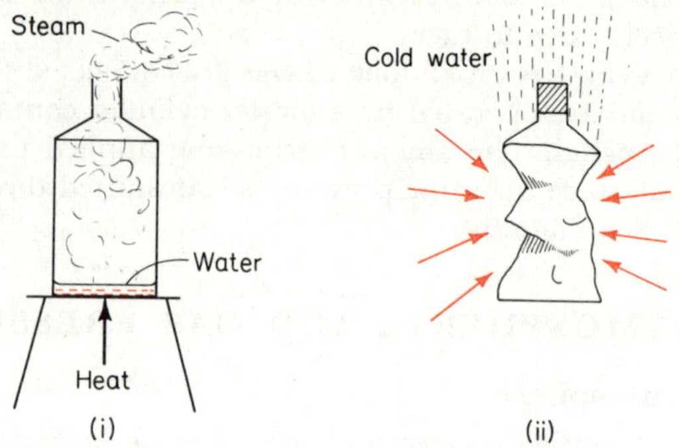

Fig. 6.11 Effect of air pressure

and the steam condenses to give water, of negligible volume compared with the steam. There is therefore practically no air inside the can, and no steam, and the external air pressure on the can now causes the sides to collapse.

Alternatively, the air can be pumped out by connecting the can to a vacuum pump.

(2) *Magdeburg Hemispheres*

If air is pumped out of two strong metal hemispheres in contact, with grease round their joint to make it air-tight, two boys are unable to pull them apart tugging in opposite directions. The pressure of the

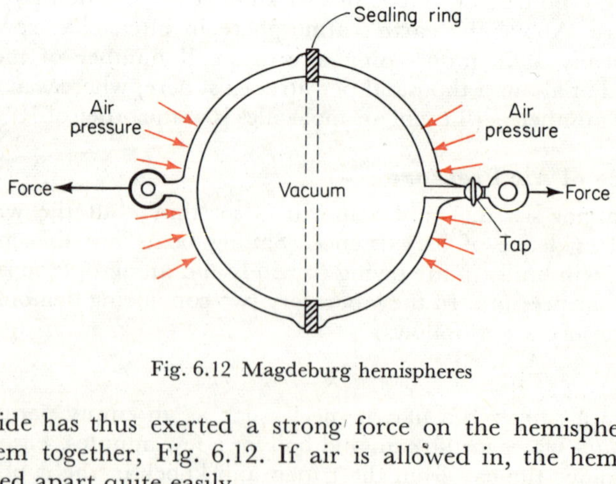

Fig. 6.12 Magdeburg hemispheres

air outside has thus exerted a strong force on the hemispheres and kept them together, Fig. 6.12. If air is allowed in, the hemispheres are pulled apart quite easily.

The experiment was first performed in Magdeburg in 1640. Two large hemispheres, about 55 cm in diameter, could not be pulled apart by two teams of eight horses each, pulling in opposite directions! Atmospheric pressure can thus create very powerful forces.

Counterbalancing Atmospheric Pressure

If a tumbler is filled to the brim with water and a card placed over the top, then no air is between the card and the water. When the tumbler is turned over the water does not fall out, Fig. 6.13 (i). The upward air pressure on the card is thus greater than the downward pressure due to the short height of water in the tumbler.

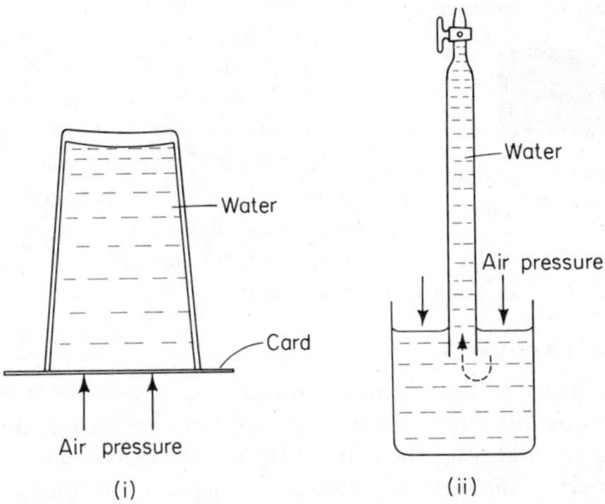

Fig. 6.13 Air pressure effect

We can repeat the experiment by filling a long burette with water to the brim, then placing a finger over the top so that air is excluded, and inverting the burette in water. The air pressure outside the burette, which is transmitted through the water to the base of the burette and acts upward there, easily supports the water column, Fig. 6.13 (ii).

A much denser column of liquid is therefore needed to counterbalance the atmospheric pressure at its base. This was first obtained over 300 years ago by Torricelli. He used mercury to make the first *barometer*, which measures atmospheric pressure.

Making a Simple Barometer

Take a clean dry thick-walled glass tube about 1 m long. Using clean mercury, fill the tube nearly to the top, then place a finger over the top and invert the tube, so that a large air-bubble runs up and collects all the tiny air-bubbles which may be trapped in the mercury. The tube is turned round again and the finger is removed, and the top is now completely filled with mercury to exclude all air.

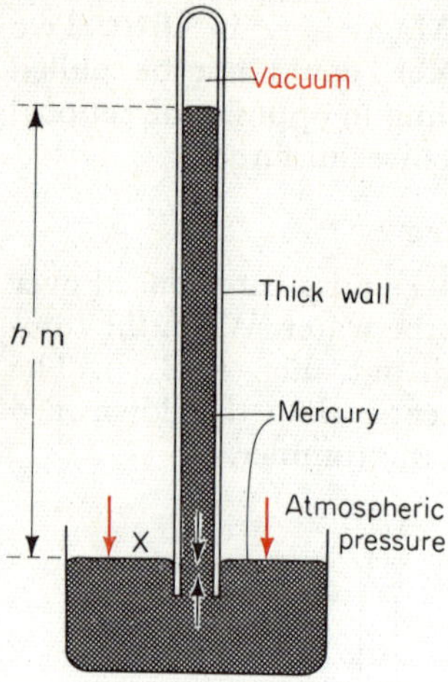

Fig. 6.14 Simple mercury barometer

Place a finger over the top end of the tube. Invert it, place the end under the surface of mercury in a dish or reservoir and remove the finger. The instant the finger is removed, notice that the mercury drops in the tube to the height *h* shown in Fig. 6.14. Since air was completely excluded, the space now at the top of the tube is a *vacuum*; it is often called a 'torricellian vacuum'. It can now be seen that the atmospheric pressure is numerically equal to the pressure at the base of a column of mercury of height *h*, about 76 cm or 30 in. Observe carefully that *h* is the *vertical height above the outside free level* X *of the mercury surface in the trough.* In making a simple barometer, then, a metre rule should be placed (i) vertically, (ii) a little away from the glass tube where surface tension has no effect, so that the zero end just touches the free mercury surface.

Testing the Vacuum

If the vacuum is faulty and contains air and water-vapour the barometer reads less than the true atmospheric pressure. The vacuum can be tested by inclining the tube. The horizontal level of the mercury should then be constant as shown, indicating a constant vertical height above the mercury surface in the trough, Fig. 6.15. When the tube is inclined so that the vertical height of its closed end is less than 70 cm, for example, the whole of the mercury should fill the tube. If the vacuum is faulty an air-bubble is seen at the top.

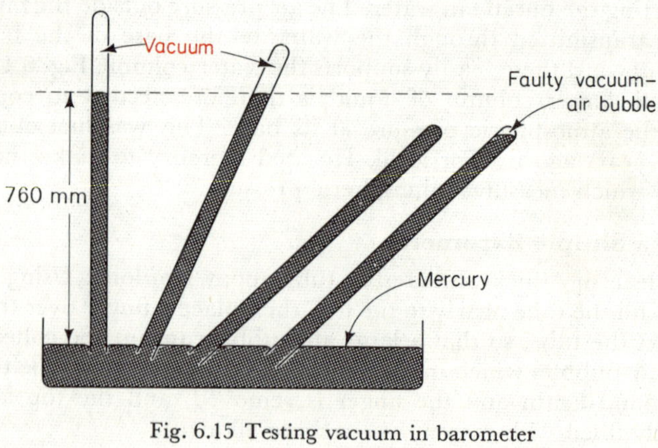

Fig. 6.15 Testing vacuum in barometer

Water and Air Pressure

The height of *water* supported by one atmosphere of pressure must be 13·6 times the height of mercury supported, since water is 13·6 times *less* dense than mercury. One atmosphere is the pressure due to a column of mercury 760 mm high.

$\therefore$ height of water $= 13{\cdot}6 \times 760$ mm $= 10\,340$ mm $= 10$ m (approx.)

A water barometer would hence not be practical. It would also suffer from the defect of having water vapour above the liquid. This exerts a pressure which pushes the liquid column down, thus reducing the height. Further, the vapour pressure would change as the air temperature changed, leading to errors.

At sea-level, the density of air is about 1000 times less than that of water. Consequently, the height of *air* of this density which would have a pressure of 1 atmosphere at its base is about 1000×10 m or 10 000 m. This is about 10 kilometres. Actually, the air extends very much higher above the earth than this height. The higher one goes, the less is the weight of air above the place concerned. Consequently the air at this place is under less pressure than at a place lower down. Thus the density of the air decreases with height—it is extremely 'thin' at heights of more than 30 kilometres, for example.

Airmen and Divers

Our head and body support a pressure of about 100 000 N/m^2 due to the atmosphere; for an area of 0·5 m^2 the total force is hence about 50 000 N. We suffer no discomfort, however, as the pressure of the blood and its dissolved gases counteracts the atmospheric pressure; but airmen ascending to great heights need special apparatus on account of the reduced air-pressure, which results in bleeding through the nose and other parts where the tissues are thin, owing to the greater pressure of the blood. Divers working at great depths in water on salvage work, and men engaged in tunnelling operations in compressed air (situations where the pressure is much greater than atmospheric pressure) have to ascend by degrees to the surface. A sudden decrease in pressure is harmful to the body.

Aneroid Barometer

The aneroid barometer is a form of domestic barometer which contains no liquid. This barometer consists essentially of a steel corrugated cylinder B partially evacuated of air, and the top face C is supported by a strong spring S to prevent B from collapsing under the atmospheric pressure, Fig. 6.16. When the pressure increases, the upper face of B is slightly depressed. The reverse occurs when the atmospheric pressure decreases. The slight movements of B are magnified by means of an attached rod R with a system of small jointed levers, which operate a pointer P controlled by a spring. P moves over a circular dial, as shown,

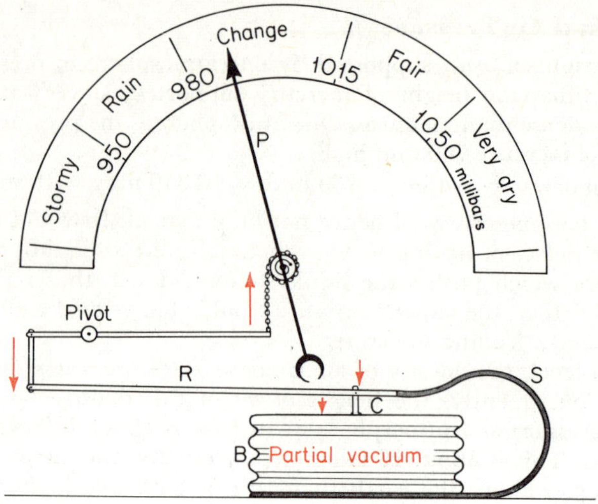

Fig. 6.16 Aneroid barometer

which is graduated in inches of mercury by comparison with a mercury barometer. The words *stormy*, *rain*, *change*, *fair*, *very dry*, are printed on the dial, but are only a very approximate guide to the weather. Plate 6B shows details of an aneroid barometer.

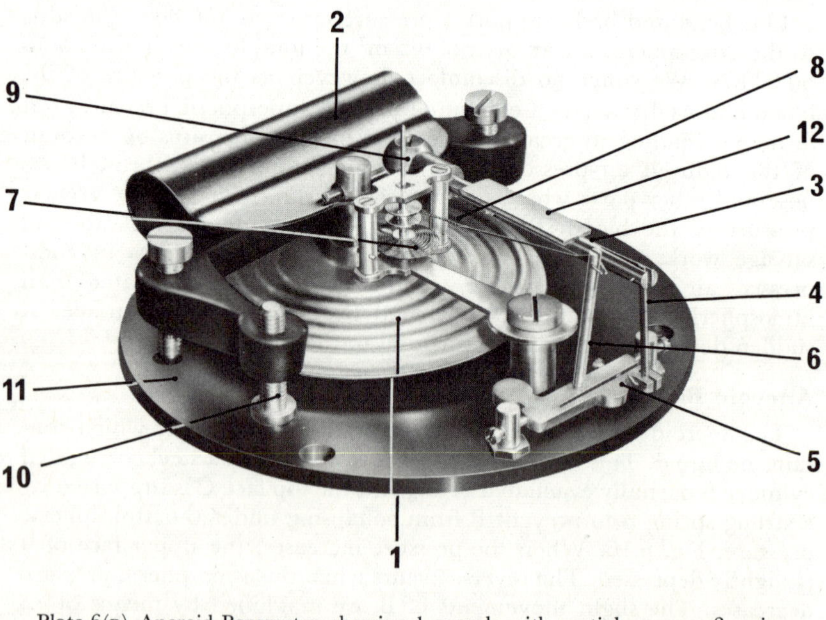

Plate 6(B) Aneroid Barometer, showing 1 capsule with partial vacuum, 2 spring, 3 arm, 4 link, 5 rocking bar, 6 arm of bar, 7 hair spring, 8 fine chain, 9 spindle, 10 zero adjustment screw, 11 base plate, 12 bimetal for temperature compensation.

Altimeter

As already discussed, the pressure of the air decreases with height. At 600, 1200, 2400 and 48 000 m the pressure is respectively about 940, 875, 750 and 550 millibar (mb); one millibar is a pressure equal to about 100 N/m^2. The dial of an aneroid barometer can thus be calibrated to read altitudes in metres in place of the pressure. The instrument is used in aeroplanes as *altimeters*, and mountaineers, and cars in mountainous countries, carry altimeters which indicate the height reached.

Radio Sonde

Nowadays regular observations are taken of the temperature, pressure and humidity high above the earth. Small balloons, which carry instruments, are released from meteorological stations, and may rise as high as 20–30 km above the earth before they burst owing to the considerably reduced air pressure at this height. The instruments are brought safely to the ground by an automatic parachute. The whole apparatus is known as a 'radio sonde'.

The radio sonde contains a small radio transmitter, which automatically sends out signals at short intervals. These signals are derived from: (i) a small aneroid box, which enables the pressure (and hence the height) to be determined; (ii) a humidity element; and (iii) a thermometer element.

Vacuum Brakes

On trains and locomotives, *vacuum brakes* are used to bring the heavy loads to rest. Fig. 6.17 illustrates the principle.

A piston P, operated by the driver, is linked to the wheel brakes. A partial vacuum is present on one side A. This counterbalances the pressure on the other side, B, which is maintained by a pump P and

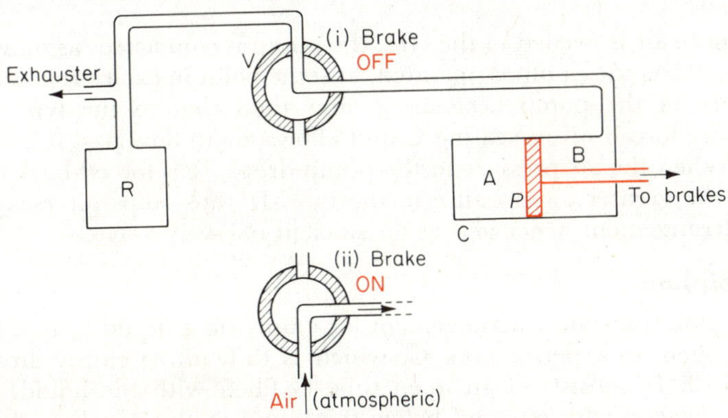

Fig. 6.17 Train brake

exhauster R when the brakes are off, Fig. 6.17 (i). When the brakes are applied, the valve V is turned round, Fig. 6.17 (ii). Air at atmospheric pressure is now introduced to the side B and the piston is forced to the left. The brakes are now on. When the brakes are released, the valve V returns to the position shown in Fig. 6.17 (i).

Bicycle Tyre Valve

A modern type of cycle tyre valve is shown in Fig. 6.18. It consists essentially of a cylindrical piece of rubber R which fits into the seating C of the valve. When the tyre is used, R is held firmly against C because the air pressure inside the tyre is greater than the atmospheric pressure. A good air-seal is thus provided.

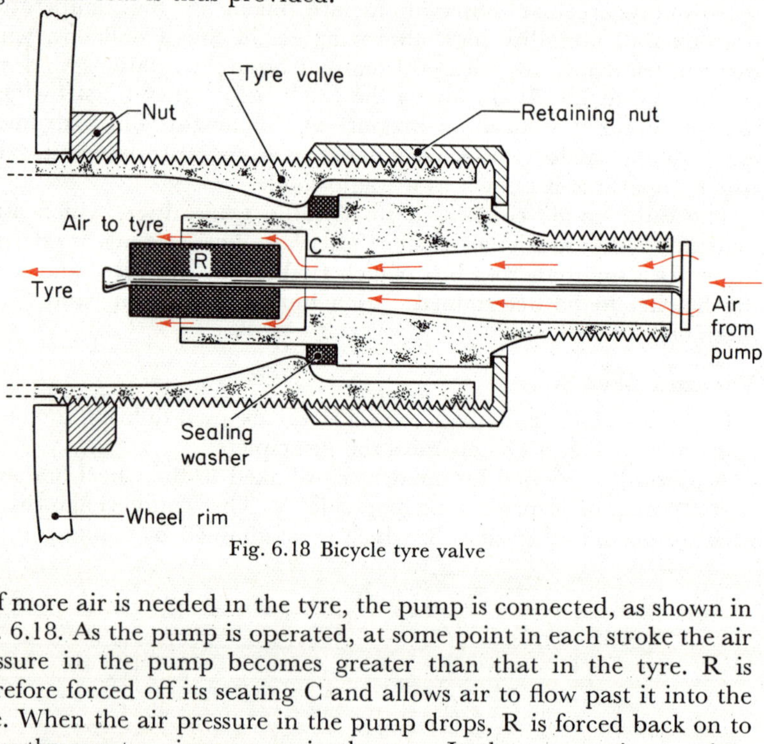

Fig. 6.18 Bicycle tyre valve

If more air is needed in the tyre, the pump is connected, as shown in Fig. 6.18. As the pump is operated, at some point in each stroke the air pressure in the pump becomes greater than that in the tyre. R is therefore forced off its seating C and allows air to flow past it into the tyre. When the air pressure in the pump drops, R is forced back on to C by the greater air pressure in the tyre. It thus stops air escaping. The arrangement hence acts as an efficient one-way valve.

The Siphon

A *siphon* is a simple arrangement for emptying a liquid from a fixed vessel such as a petrol tank C, which is difficult to empty directly, Fig. 6.19. It consists of an open tube G filled with the liquid. This is then placed with one end below the liquid in the vessel, as shown. The liquid in C is then observed to run out of the vessel through A, as long as the other end of G is dipping below the surface of the liquid and A is kept below the level BL.

The explanation of the siphon action is as follows. The pressure at points in the same horizontal level of a liquid is the same. Thus the pressure inside the liquid at B is equal to the pressure at L, which is the atmospheric pressure. The pressure of the liquid A is therefore greater than the atmospheric pressure by the amount *hd*, where *d* is the density of the liquid and *h* is the height of AB. But the pressure of air at A is atmospheric, and is therefore unable to support the liquid. It therefore runs out at A. If G is *empty* and is placed with one end below the liquid in C the siphon does not work; there is now no net force on the liquid, as the pressure on it at L, which is atmospheric pressure, is also equal to the air pressure inside the tube G.

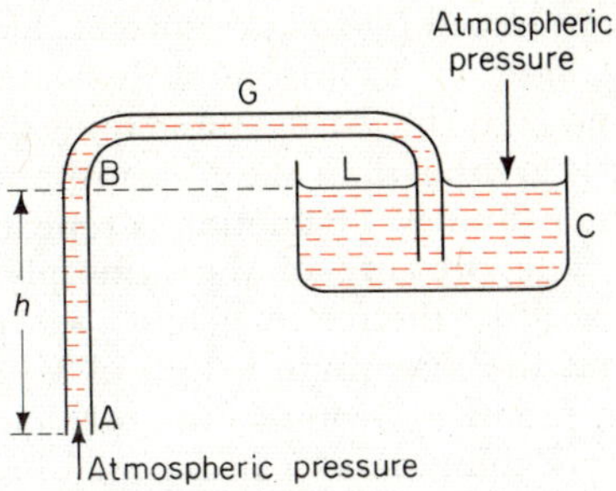

Fig. 6.19 Siphon principle

Pumps · Lift-pump

A *lift-pump* raises water from a well. As shown in Fig. 6.20, it has a one-way valve V_2 in the piston inside the barrel or cylinder and a one-way valve V_1 at the bottom which leads to the pipe entering the well.

On the *downstroke*, V_2 opens and the water pours through. V_1 is

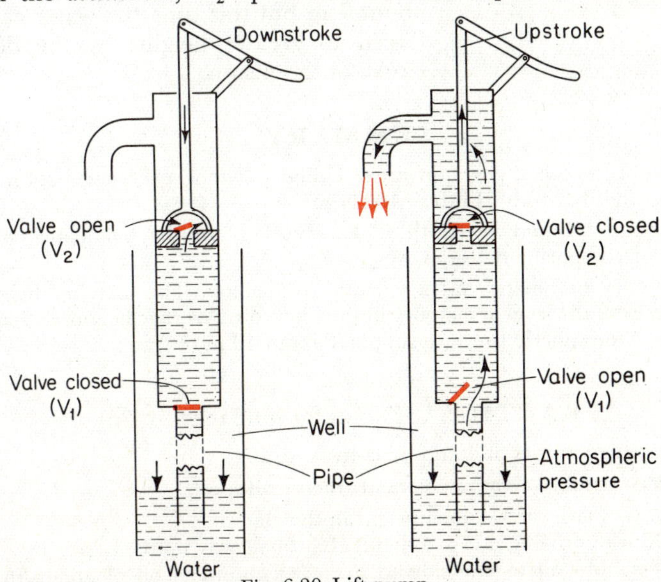

Fig. 6.20 Lift pump

kept closed by the pressure of the water above it, Fig. 6.20 (i). On the *upstroke*, V_2 is closed and the water is raised and pours from the outlet, Fig. 6.20 (ii). At the same time V_1 opens as the pressure of water below it is greater than the pressure above. Thus more water is drawn into the cylinder. The action is repeated.

The pressure of the atmosphere can support a column of water about 10 metres in height. See p. 107. It should therefore be noted that the maximum height of V_1 above the well is theoretically 10 m. In practice, owing to the inefficiency of the pump, this should not be more than about 7 m for useful operation.

Force-pump

A *force-pump* is shown in Fig. 6.21. This has no valve in the piston, unlike the lift pump. Instead, another one-way valve is fitted into the side of the cylinder, as shown. On the downstroke, the side valve is forced open and water in the cylinder is forced out of the pump. On the upstroke, the side valve is closed and water is drawn into the cylinder through the lower valve, which is now open. By using an air dome, as shown, water continues to flow from the outlet on the up-stroke—the water is forced out by the pressure of air in the dome.

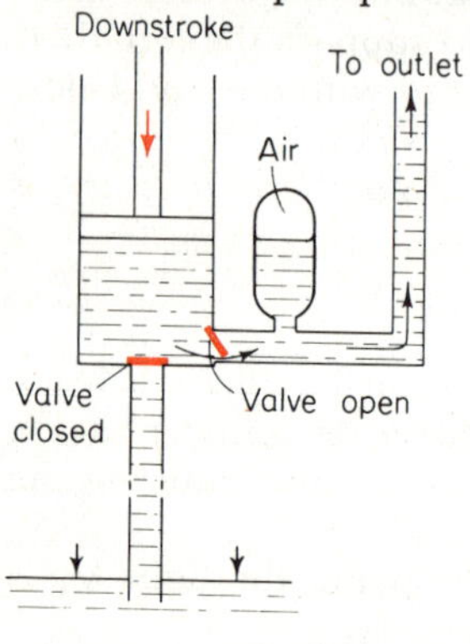

Fig. 6.21 Force pump principle

The maximum height of the lower valve above the water in the well is still about 7 m but this time the water can be forced to greater heights by the downstroke of the piston.

SUMMARY

1. Pressure = force per unit area. Units: newtons per metre² (N/m^2) or N/mm^2 or millibar (mb). 1 mb = 100 N/m^2.

2. Pressure in liquid = depth × density × g. In the balancing column method for comparing densities, $h_1\rho_1 = h_2\rho_2$.

3. Mercury barometer has a vacuum at the top. The mercury height is measured from the level of mercury in the reservoir. Average height = 760 mm (0·76 m). Atmospheric pressure supports about 10 m of water.

PRACTICAL (Notes for guidance, p. 26)

1. Comparing densities of liquid by U-tube (p. 100)

Apparatus. U-tube; clamp and stand; metre rule; oil.

Method. (i) Place the U-tube upright in the clamp.

(ii) Add water to one side to a depth about half-way up the tube.

(iii) Then add oil to one side to make a column of oil of about 10 cm.

Measure the height h_2 of the oil column and the height h_1 of the balancing column of water on the other side.

(iv) By adding more oil, obtain another set of values.

From each pair of values, calculate ρ_2/ρ_1 (give your answer to one decimal place).

Assuming the density of water is 1 g/cm³, obtain the density of the oil.

Measurements.

h_2 cm (oil)	h_1 cm (water)	$\rho_2/\rho_1 = h_1/h_2$

Calculation. $\rho_2 = \dfrac{h_1}{h_2} \times \rho_1 = \,..$

2. Comparing densities of liquids which mix

Make a Hare's apparatus by joining a T-piece to two long glass tubes X and Y with rubber tubing. Fig. 6.22. Place the end X in a beaker A of water.

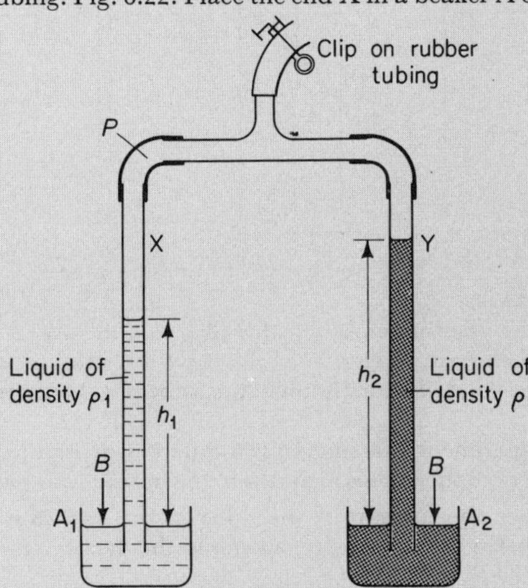

Fig. 6.22 Comparison of densities

Method. (i) Place the end of Y in a beaker B containing a solution of copper sulphate.

(ii) By sucking carefully at the top, draw up a column of the two liquids in X and Y respectively and quickly close the clip.

(iii) Measure the two heights h_1 and h_2 above the outside levels in the beaker. Draw up two more columns of greater height, and each time measure h_1 and h_2.

Measurements.

h_2 (solution)	h_1 (water)

Calculation. Since the pressure due to a column of liquid plus the reduced air pressure above it balances the atmospheric pressure, then $h_2\rho_2 = h_1\rho_1$. Thus $\rho_2/\rho_1 = h_1/h_2$.

(i) For each pair of values of h_1 and h_2, calculate the ratio ρ_2/ρ_1 (give your answer to one decimal place).

(ii) Assuming the density of water is 1 g/cm^3, find the density of the copper sulphate solution.

3. Comparing densities by pressure gauge (p. 97)

Apparatus. Thistle funnel A with plastic cover and attached oil manometer M; two wide cylinders, three-quarters full of water and paraffin (or other oil) respectively. Fig. 6.23.

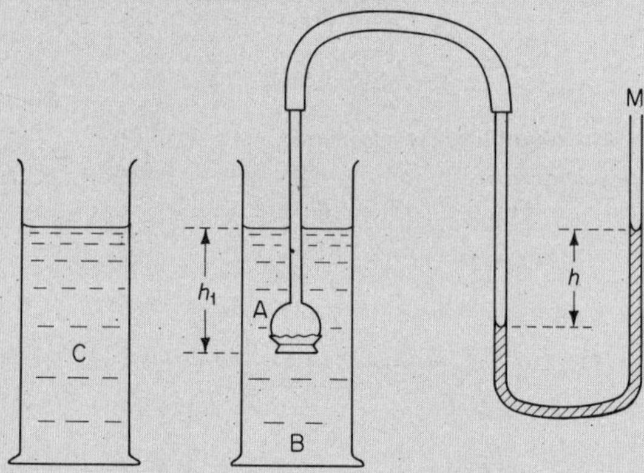

Fig. 6.23 Comparison by pressure gauge

Method. (i) Push the funnel A into the oil B to a measured depth of 20 cm. Observe the difference in levels h in M. Now push A into the water C until the difference in levels in M is exactly the same as before. Measure the depth h_2 of A in C.

Repeat the experiment, starting with a different depth of the funnel in the oil B. Each time, note the depths h_1 and h_2 in the oil and water respectively.

Calculation. Since the pressure is the same in the two cases, $h_1\rho_1 = h_2\rho_2$ or $\rho_2/\rho_1 = h_1/h_2$. Obtain the oil density, assuming the density of water is 1 g/cm^3.

Measurements.

h_1 cm (oil)	h_2 cm (water)

Calculation.

$$\rho_2 = \frac{h_1}{h_2} \times \rho_1 = \,..$$

4. Grading liquid densities by flotation.

Apparatus. Five test-tubes; beakers with some glycerine A, coloured water B, olive oil C, turps D, paraffin oil E.

Method. (i) Pour a little of A and B *gently* in turn into a test-tube. Note which liquid floats on the other—this gives the less dense liquid.

(ii) Take a clean test-tube. Pour a little of the less dense liquid into it. Then pour a little of C gently into the tube. Note which liquid is less dense.

(iii) Repeat in turn with liquids D and E. *Results.* The order of densities is . .

(iv) After you have graded all the liquids in order of density, pour a little at a time into a clean test-tube. Starting with the most dense liquid, and see if all the layers float one on the other.

5. Measuring gas pressure

Use a water manometer (pressure gauge) similar to that on p. 97, and find the gas pressure for: (i) a small turn of the gas-tap; (ii) a larger turn of the gas-tap. Each time measure the constant difference in levels *h very quickly,* so as to avoid using too much gas which could be dangerous. *Turn off the tap as soon as you have finished taking measurements.*

Calculate the actual gas pressure in cm of mercury (add the existing atmospheric pressure as below).

Measurements. Atmospheric pressure ($A =$ . . cm mercury).

1. Moderate gas pressure, $h =$ . . cm water $= \frac{..}{14}$ cm mercury (approx.)

∴ Actual gas pressure $= A + h =$ . . cm mercury.

2. Higher gas pressure—proceed as above.

(*Note.* The density of mercury is about 13·6 g/cm³—the value of 14 g/cm³ has been used above, which is an error of 4 in 136 or 3% error.)

6. Boyle's law

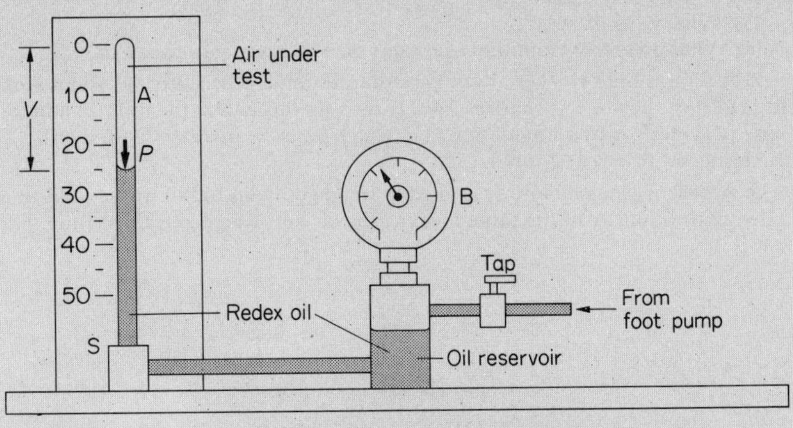

Fig. 6.24 Boyle's law

Apparatus. Boyle's law apparatus with Bourdon gauge, foot pump and adaptor. Fig. 6.24. The volume V of the air trapped above the oil in A is read from the scale S beside the tube. The pressure p of the air is read directly in N/m² from the Bourdon gauge.

Method. The tap is opened and air is pumped in from the foot pump. This increases the pressure on the oil in the reservoir and this is transmitted to the air in A which is compressed. The tap is then closed.

When the oil surface in A becomes steady, the pressure p and volume V are both read and the results entered in the table below.

The process is repeated four times, increasing the pressure each time to a suitable value. The pressure p and volume V are recorded each time.

Measurements.

p	V	$p \times V$	$\frac{1}{V}$

Calculation. (i) Work out the product $p \times V$ for each pair of readings and enter the results in the table.

Do your results agree with 'Boyle's law' which states: For a fixed mass of gas at constant temperature, *pressure* $\times$ *volume* is a constant value?

(ii) Find the values of $1/V$, the reciprocal of V, and enter the results in the table. Plot a graph of p against the corresponding values of $1/V$, starting from zero for each axis.

What kind of graph do you obtain? Does it show that the pressure, p, is proportional to $1/V$?

EXERCISE 6 · ANSWERS, p. 257

1. A 2 cm cube is made of metal of density 8 g/cm³. (*a*) What is its volume? (*b*) What is its mass?
(*c*) What pressure would the cube exert on a horizontal surface? (*E.A.*)

2. A dam is built thicker at the base than at the top because: (*a*) water seeks its level; (*b*) there is less chance of water seeping through at the top; (*c*) a broad base provides a firmer foundation; (*d*) water pressure increases with depth; (*e*) Archimedes' principle applies. (*M.*)

3. A flask is weighed empty and then weighed again full of water; and then filled with liquid A to the same level as shown and weighed a third time. Fig. 6A (i).

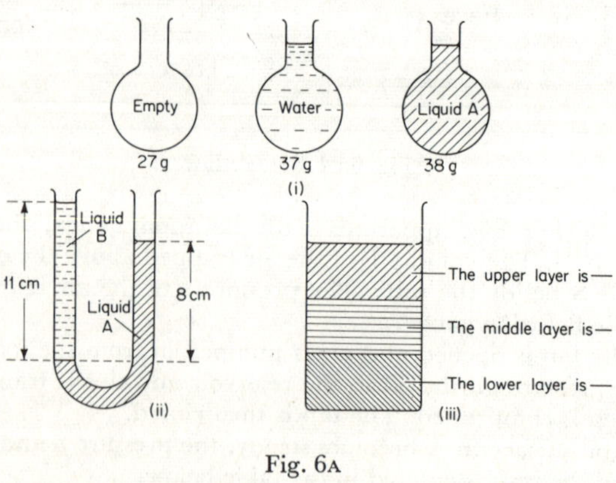

Fig. 6A

(*a*) Find the relative density of liquid A. Show your working for your answer.

(*b*) The same liquid A and another liquid B are then poured into a U-tube as shown. Fig. 6A (ii). Which is more dense, liquid A or liquid B?

(*c*) Calculate the density of liquid B. You will need to use your answer to part (*a*) to do this. Show your working.

(*d*) Liquids A and B and water are then all three poured into a large beaker. It is found that the liquids do not mix, and appear as shown. Fig. 6A (iii). Use your previous answers to identify Liquid A, Liquid B and the water from the positions they occupy in the beaker. (*M.*)

4. (i) What is meant by *pressure* on a surface?

(ii) What pressure is exerted on the ground by a crate of weight 3600 N whose base measures 60 cm × 50 cm?

(iii) In the fruit juice extractor illustrated in Fig. 6B, the crushing plunger has a cross section of 25 cm². What *pressure* is exerted on the fruit in B when a downward force of 400 N is applied at A? (*Mx.*)

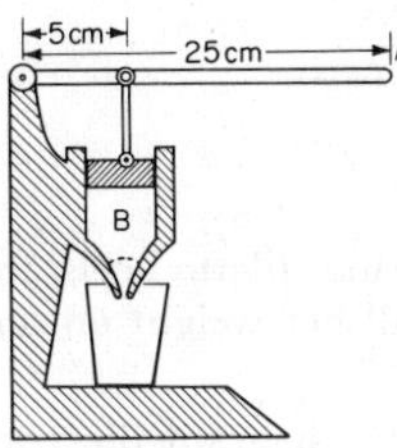

Fig. 6B

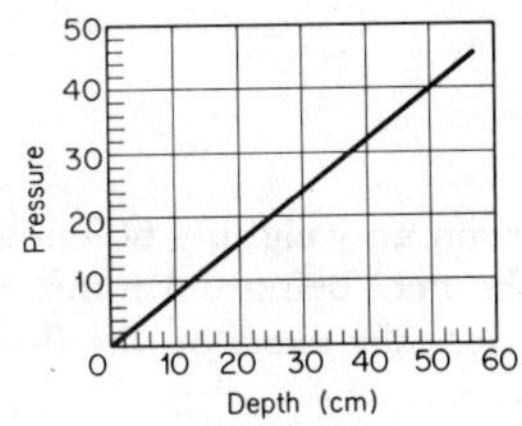

Fig. 6C

5. The graph shows the relationship between pressure and depth for a liquid. Fig. 6C. On the pressure scale, 1 unit = 100 N/m².

(*a*) What relationship may we deduce between pressure and depth?

(*b*) What is the pressure at a depth of 50 cm?

(*c*) What is the density of the liquid? (*L.*)

6. Draw and label a diagram of a hydraulic press or a hydraulic jack. Indicate in your labelling the rather special care which goes into its construction. What is the maximum mechanical advantage that could be obtained from a hydraulic press fitted with cylinders of 5 cm and 60 cm diameters? Calculate the force exerted by the ram when a force of 30 N is applied to the smaller plunger. (Ignore friction and weight of moving parts.) (*Mx.*)

7. (*a*) Explain, with the aid of a diagram, how a hydraulic press works and the principle upon which it is based. Show how this theory of hydraulic pressure can be used in the braking system of a car, illustrating your answer with a diagram.

(*b*) If a hydraulic press is provided with cylinders of diameters of 5 cm and 60 cm respectively, what is the velocity ratio? Why, in practice, would the mechanical advantage be less than this value? (*W.Md.*)

8. A woman has a mass of 50 kg. Each of her shoes has an area of 50 cm² in contact with the ground.

(*a*) What is the force exerted by the woman on the ground? (Weight of 1 kg mass = 10 newtons.)

(*b*) What is the force on 1 cm² if she is standing with both feet on the ground? (*E.A.*)

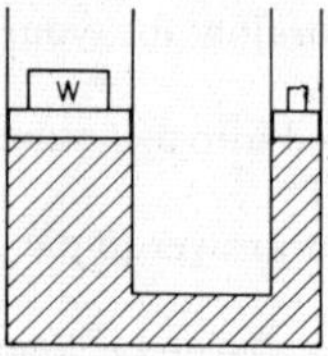

Fig. 6D

9. (*a*) Define pressure and state the units in which it can be measured. Fig. 6D shows a U-tube with unequal sides that demonstrates the principle of the hydraulic press. The frictionless pistons have areas of 10 and 2 cm². The small weight is 0·4 N.

(*b*) What is the pressure in the liquid just under the small piston?

(*c*) What is the value of the large weight, W? (*E.A.*)

10. (*a*) From Fig. 6E, what is the relative density of methylated spirit? (*b*) What is the purpose of the mercury? (*L.*)

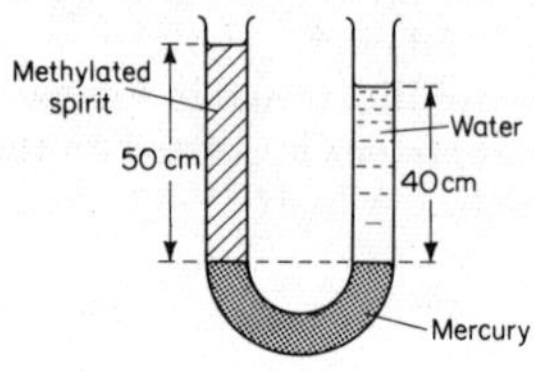

Fig. 6E

11. A woman weighing 600 newtons is wearing stiletto heels, the area of the base of the heel being 0·3 mm². If she puts all her weight on one heel, what pressure does she exert on the floor? (*Mx.*)

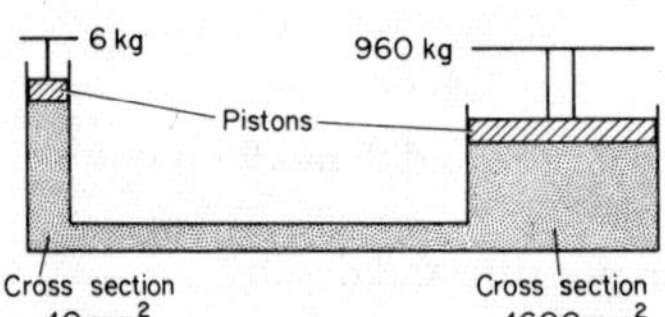

Fig. 6F

12. The diagram illustrates the principle of the hydraulic weigh bridge. Fig. 6F. A 6 kg bag of potatoes on the small piston just balances twenty 48 kg sacks of potatoes on the large piston. An extra 6 kg bag would cause the twenty sacks to rise. Has the law of conservation of energy broken down? Is a small amount of work done by the extra 6 kg bag causing a large amount of work to be done on the twenty sacks? Explain your answer. (*N.W.*)

13. On a day when a mercury barometer reads 76 cm, a water barometer would read approximately: (*a*) the same; (*b*) 1·5 m; (*c*) 7·5 m; (*d*) 10 m; (*e*) 12 m (mercury is 13·5 times as heavy as water). (*M.*)

14. All the following make use of air pressure *except* a: (*a*) self-filling fountain-pen; (*b*) domestic flushing cistern; (*c*) house water system; (*d*) rubber sucker; (*e*) cycle pump. (*M.*)

15. Normal atmospheric pressure at sea-level is . . per . . In what way would it differ at the top of a high mountain? (*S.E.*)

16. A form of barometer is used inside an aircraft as an indicator of . . This instrument must be adjusted every day because . . constantly varies. (*W.Md.*)

17. If a barometer were filled with water instead of mercury, what would be the height of the water column at normal atmospheric pressure? Give *three* advantages of filling a barometer with mercury rather than water. (*S.E.*)

18. An ideal lift-pump cannot raise water more than a height of 10 m because: (*a*) a lift-pipe of any greater length could not be made strong enough; (*b*) the density of water is 1 g/cm³; (*c*) the pressure of the atmosphere is only about 0·1 N/mm²; (*d*) it is only worked by hand; (*e*) the pump handle has no mechanical advantage. (*W.Md.*)

19. Fig. 6G shows part of an aneroid barometer.

(*a*) What is the purpose of a barometer?

(*b*) Name and state the use of the labelled parts: 1 . .; 2 . . (*E.A.*)

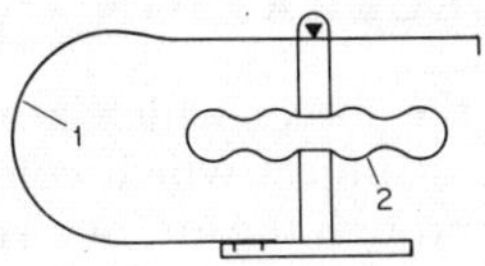

Fig. 6G

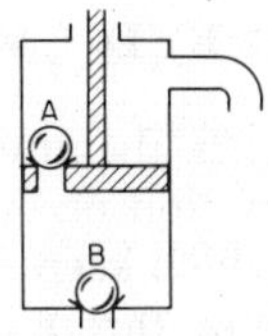

Fig. 6H

20. In this lift-pump (Fig 6H) the: (*a*) valve A should be open on the upstroke of the piston; (*b*) valve A should be open all the time; (*c*) valve A should be open when valve B is closed; (*d*) design is faulty and the pump could not work. (*M.*)

21. (*a*) State what is meant by pressure.

(*b*) Describe any experiment which shows that air exerts pressure.

(*c*) If atmospheric pressure is 0·1 N/mm² (i.e. 100 000 N/m²) and the density of water is 1000 kg/m³, what is the total pressure 3 m below the surface of a lake? (*L.*)

22. (*a*) Fig. 6I shows a simple barometer. What is present in the glass tube at (A) above the liquid? What is the name of the liquid (B)? If the liquid (B) were replaced by a less dense liquid, how would this affect the height? Give a reason.

(*b*) The original barometer is tilted as shown. How would the barometric height x in 6I shown compare with the original value of 76 cm? Give a reason.

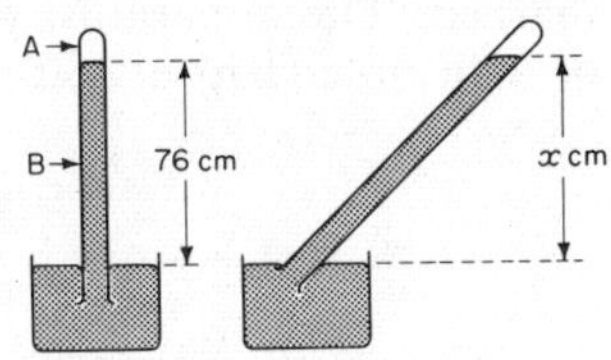

Fig. 6I

(*c*) What is an aneroid barometer? Describe briefly why such a barometer is sensitive to changes in atmospheric pressure.

(*d*) Why can an aneroid barometer be used as an altimeter in an aeroplane? (*M.*)

23. (*a*) Describe two experiments you would perform to demonstrate that the atmosphere exerts a pressure.

(*b*) A syringe is simply a cylindrical tube containing a tight-fitting piston. When it is placed with the open end in a liquid and the piston is drawn up, liquid rises in the tube. Explain why this happens.

(*c*) A small balloon filled with hydrogen and released in the atmosphere usually bursts when it reaches a great height. Explain why this is so.

(*d*) A man in a balloon which is descending and about to land, trails a very long rope. One end is firmly attached to the basket of the balloon. As more and more of the rope comes in contact with the ground the rate of descent is checked. Explain why this happens. (*S.E.*)

7

DYNAMICS

SPEED · VELOCITY · ACCELERATION

DYNAMICS is the study of motion and of the forces which keep an object in motion or oppose its motion. It is a subject which concerns the forces which keep an aeroplane in flight through the air, or a speed-boat in motion through water, or a racing car or train in motion along a road or track. All these machines have reached their present development through the skill of scientists and engineers, who have studied and understood the principles of dynamics. The founder of mechanics is generally recognised to be Sir Isaac Newton, who published a work called *Principia* in 1687 in which 'Laws of Motion' were clearly stated for the first time (see p. 137).

Ticker-timer

The simple motion of a moving object can be studied in a laboratory with the aid of a ticker-tape, on which equal intervals of time can be marked. The apparatus, which we shall call a 'ticker-timer', consists of a flexible strip of soft-iron A clamped at one end B and passing

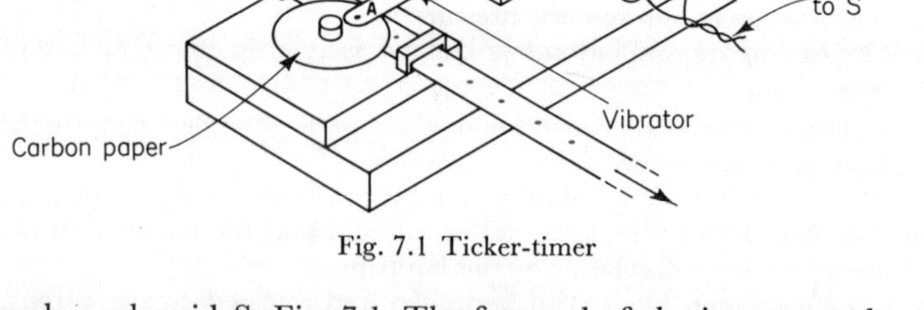

Fig. 7.1 Ticker-timer

through a solenoid S, Fig. 7.1. The free end of the iron passes between the poles of a strong magnet M, placed at the end of S. When a low alternating voltage from the 50 cycle per second mains is joined to the solenoid terminals the iron strip vibrates at this frequency. A stud beneath the iron at A strikes a carbon paper disc below it. A moving

Plate 7(A) Ticker-timer and tape, with trolley.

tape C, running past A, is then marked with a series of dots or ticks spaced at equal intervals of $\frac{1}{50}$ s. See Plate 7A.

Motion

A simple illustration of the information the ticker-timer can provide is shown in Fig. 7.2. In this case one end of the tape was held by a pupil, who then moved away through the room and collided with other pupils at intervals.

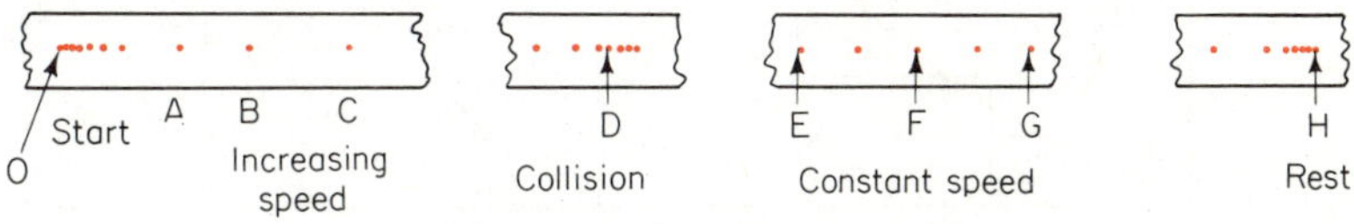

Fig. 7.2 Ticker-tape studies of motion

The tape shows clearly that the pupil started his or her movement at a time corresponding to O, and then began to walk faster, since the distances travelled in equal times increase, as shown by the increasing gaps between A, B and C. A collision with another pupil occurred at D, after which the walk continued. It was a steady walk for a short period as the same distances EF and FG were travelled in successive equal times. Finally, the pupil came to rest at a time corresponding to H.

Fig. 7.3 (i) shows part of the tape after a particular period. To see how the distance s travelled varied with time t, successive strips such as 1, 2, 3 and 4 are cut off the tape. Their respective lengths are the distances travelled in equal intervals of time, 'five-tick' intervals of $\frac{5}{50}$ ($\frac{1}{10}$) s in this

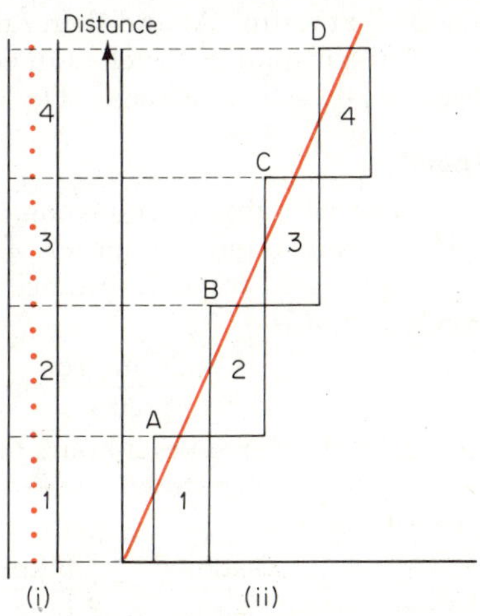

Fig. 7.3 Ticker-tape motion graph

case. We can therefore paste the strips A, B, C, D vertically one above the other on paper as shown in Fig. 7.3 (ii); the equal widths of the paper now represent the equal intervals of time, $\frac{1}{10}$ s. Choosing the middle of the tops of the strips for convenience, we find they join up in a straight line. Thus equal distances are travelled in successive equal times. The motion of the pupil was therefore regular.

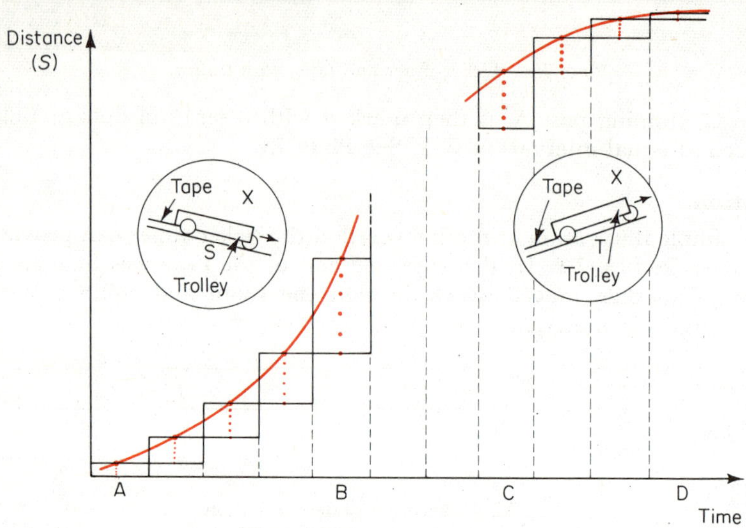

Fig. 7.4 Velocity rise and fall

In contrast, the distance–time variation in Fig. 7.4 shows an irregular motion. It is the motion of a trolley X which started off quickly down a slope S at a time A, and then ran up an incline T from B to C. From A to B the distances travelled in equal times increase; from C to D the distances travelled decrease. The trolley's motion is thus irregular.

Speed

We can now discuss some common terms used in motion.

If you run round the corner of a street from A to B to see a friend, Fig. 7.5 (i), and travel a distance of 24 metre in 20 seconds, then your average *speed* is

$$\frac{24 \text{ metre}}{20 \text{ s}} \text{ or } 1{\cdot}2 \text{ m/s}.$$

Similarly, if a car takes 2 hours to travel along a winding road from a town C to another town D 96 km away, Fig. 7.5 (ii), the average speed of the car.

$$= \frac{\text{Distance}}{\text{Time}} = \frac{96 \text{ km}}{2 \text{ hours}} = 48 \text{ km/h}.$$

The term 'speed' is always used when the motion of an object changes direction. Thus if a satellite such as *Early Bird*, used for world television communication, takes 24 hours to move round the earth in a circular path 60 000 km long, Fig. 7.5 (iii), then

$$\text{Average speed} = \frac{60\,000 \text{ km}}{24 \text{ hours}} = 2500 \text{ km/h}.$$

If the satellite moves through equal distances in equal times, no matter how small the times may be, then the satellite is said to have a constant or *uniform* speed.

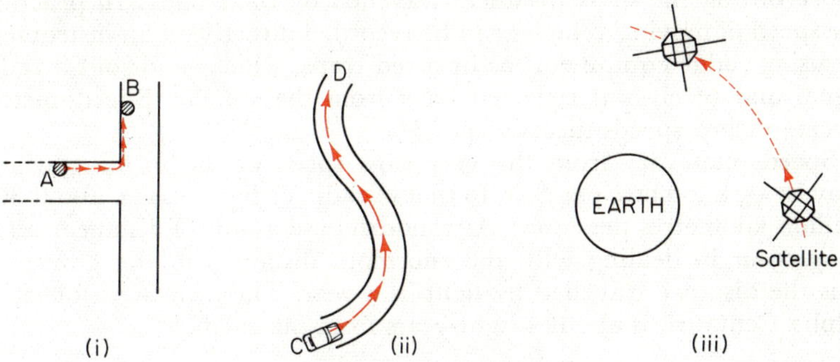

Fig. 7.5 Speed of objects

In calculations it is sometimes necessary to change 'kilometre (km) per hour' to 'metre per second'. Note that:

$$36 \text{ km/h} = 10 \text{ m/s}.$$

Speed calculations from Ticker-tapes

The ticker-tape enables us to find the average speed of objects to which it is attached. As an illustration, Fig. 7.6. (i) shows part of the tape A attached to a small trolley moving along a horizontal rough board. In a time of 5 ticks or $\frac{5}{50}$, $\frac{1}{10}$ s, a distance of 4·0 cm has been travelled. Hence

$$\text{Average speed} = \frac{4{\cdot}0 \text{ cm}}{\frac{1}{10} \text{ s}} = 40 \text{ cm/s}.$$

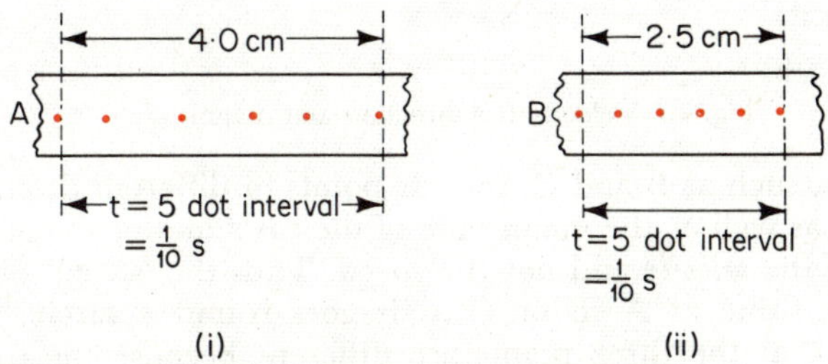

Fig. 7.6 Calculation from ticker-tape

Fig. 7.6 (ii) shows that the distances between the dots or ticks at another part B of the tape are now equal, so that the speed is uniform over the time of $\frac{5}{50}$ or $\frac{1}{10}$ s. In this case,

$$\text{speed} = \frac{2 \cdot 5 \text{ cm}}{\frac{1}{10} \text{ s}} = 25 \text{ cm/s}.$$

We could say that the speed was uniform from one tick to the next, that is, over a very small time-interval of $\frac{1}{50}$ second, if we had a clock which could measure extremely short intervals of time and a mechanism for recording the short distances travelled by the trolley. In practice, the speed of moving vehicles can be recorded directly on an instrument by using radar equipment, as in speed traps, which sends out a radio signal and receives it reflected back from the vehicle. Speedometers in cars record speeds directly (p. 534).

Speeds can vary from the very slow speed of the tortoise, which may be $\frac{1}{10}$ kilometre per *hour*, to that of radio or light waves, about 300 million kilometres per *second*. Astronomers use a unit of distance called a *light-year* in dealing with the enormous distances in the Universe; it is the distance travelled by light in a year. The nearest visible star, Alpha Centauri, is about 4 light-years from the earth.

Velocity

Consider a car moving round a circular track ABC with a uniform speed, Fig. 7.7 (i). At the instant it reaches A the car points along the direction of the arrow shown, which is the tangent to the circle. At

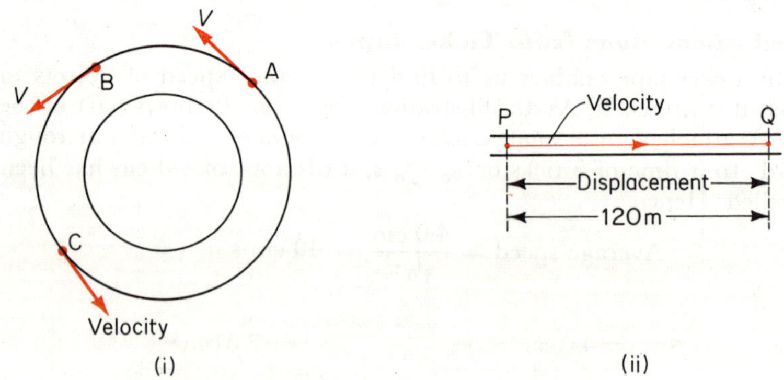

Fig. 7.7 Velocity has direction and magnitude

other places, such as B and C, the car points in different directions. If the *direction* as well as the magnitude of the car's motion is considered, we speak of the *velocity* and not the speed. Thus the 'speed' of the car may be the same at A, B or C as it goes round a circle. But the 'velocities' v, at the three points are different because the directions are different. Velocity, then, has direction and magnitude. Speed has magnitude only, and we therefore speak of the average speed of a car along a winding road.

If a car moves in a constant direction we use the word 'displacement' rather than 'distance'. Thus along a perfectly straight road PQ 120 m long, Fig. 7.7 (ii), which takes a car 8 s to travel,

$$\text{Average velocity} = \frac{\text{Displacement}}{\text{Time}} = \frac{120\text{ m}}{8\text{ s}}$$
$$= 15\text{ m/s}.$$

If the displacement along the road in equal times is constant no matter how small the times may be, the velocity is said to be *uniform*.

A train with a uniform velocity of 96 km/h travels 192 km in 2 h. Generally, it can be seen that, if the velocity is uniform,

$$\text{Velocity} = \frac{\text{Displacement}}{\text{Time}}$$

$$\text{Displacement} = \text{Velocity} \times \text{Time}$$

$$\text{Time} = \frac{\text{Displacement.}}{\text{Velocity}}$$

EXAMPLES

1. A car has a velocity of 72 km/h. How far does it travel in $\frac{1}{2}$ minute?

We must *always* use the same kinds of units in calculations. Thus 72 km/h = 20 m/s and $\frac{1}{2}$ min = 30 s.

$$\therefore \text{Displacement} = 20 \times 30 = 600\text{ m}.$$

2. A car moving round a circular racing track takes 120 s to do a lap of 8 km. What is the speed in km/h?

$$\text{Time} = 120\text{ s} = 2\text{ min} = \frac{1}{30}\text{ hour}$$

$$\text{Speed} = \frac{\text{Distance}}{\text{Time}} = \frac{8\text{ km}}{\frac{1}{30}\text{ h}} = 240\text{ km/h}.$$

Displacement–Time Graphs

Displacement–time graphs provide useful information about the motion of an object. If the graph is a straight line such as OA the velocity is uniform, since equal distances are then travelled in equal times, Fig. 7.8 (i). Further, considering a time OP,

$$\text{Velocity} = \frac{\text{Displacement (distance).}}{\text{Time}} = \frac{QP}{OP}.$$

The ratio QP/OP is called the *gradient* of the line OA. Hence

$$\text{Velocity} = \text{Gradient of OA}.$$

The gradient is constant everywhere along OA, since it is a straight line.

Fig. 7.8 (ii), however, shows the displacement–time curve OLM for the motion of a ball thrown vertically in the air. It reaches a maximum height at L, and then descends again to the ground at a time M. This

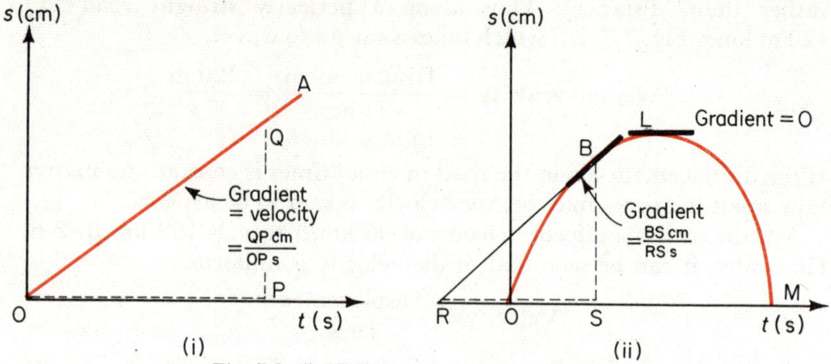

Fig. 7.8 (i) Uniform (ii) variable velocity

is an example of non-uniform velocity. The velocity at any height such as B is now the gradient of the *tangent* to the curve at B, which is BS/RS. At the highest point L the velocity is similarly the gradient of the tangent here, which is zero; momentarily the ball is at rest.

Velocity–Time Variation with Ticker-tape

Fig. 7.9 shows successive tape strips pasted beside each other after a run by a trolley down an incline AB, then along the horizontal BC and

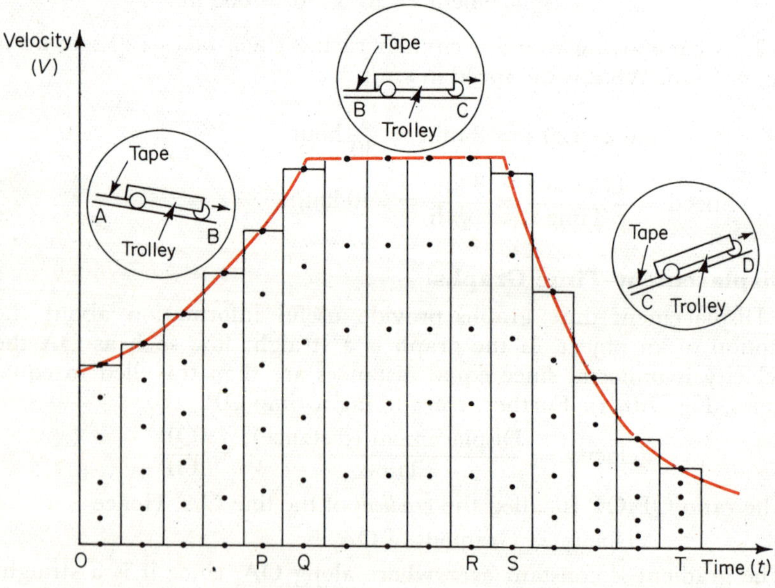

Fig. 7.9 Velocity-time graph

then up an incline CD, as shown inset in Fig. 7.9. Each strip represents the actual distance travelled in successive $\frac{5}{50}$ or $\frac{1}{10}$ s, and thus if the tops are joined the variation in the velocity at the end of equal time-intervals can be seen from the line obtained. Observe carefully that here the strips are pasted beside each other on the time-axis; whereas in Fig. 7.3 they were pasted above each other to show distance–time variation.

Fig. 7.9 shows clearly that the velocity increased with time from time O to time P, then became constant between times Q and R, and decreased in velocity between times S and T.

Velocity–Time Graphs

Instead of using strips whose lengths represent the distance travelled in $\frac{1}{10}$, it is better to plot the distance of displacement in 1 second, because this is the *actual velocity* of the moving object, Fig. 7.10. A

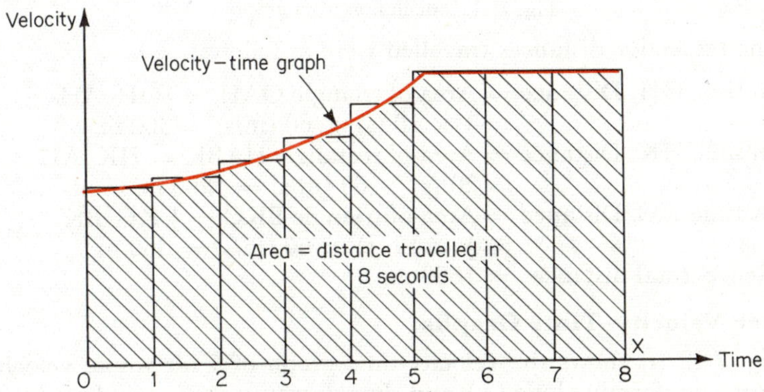

Fig. 7.10 Velocity-time graph

velocity-time graph is then obtained. The *area* of each strip is now a measure of the distance travelled in each second of the motion. Thus the total area beneath the velocity–time graph is a measure of the total distance travelled from time O to time X or 8 seconds.

The speedometer of a car measures velocity directly. Along a straight road suppose the variation of velocity with time is recorded as follows in a short run:

Time (s)	0	2	4	6	8	10	12	18	24	30	32	34	36	38	40	42
Velocity (m/s)	0	12	24	36	48	60	60	60	60	60	50	40	30	20	10	0

Fig. 7.11 shows the velocity–time graph of the motion. We can see from it that the velocity increased uniformly along the part OA, then became constant over the part AB and came to rest along the part BC when its velocity decreased uniformly to zero.

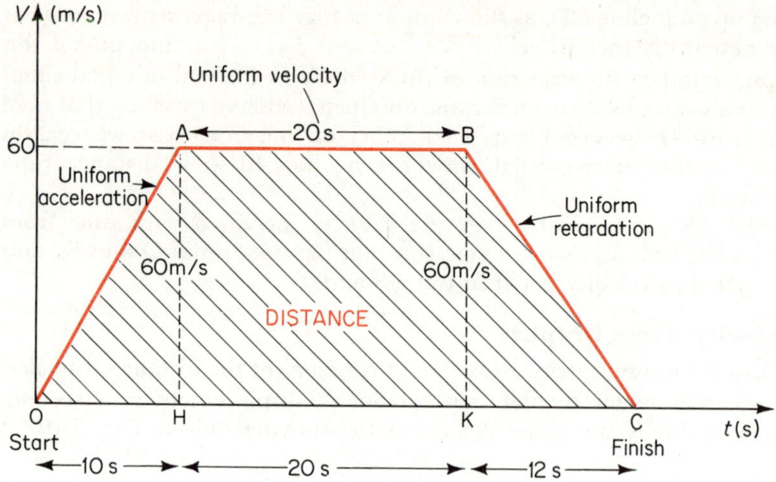

Fig. 7.11 Calculation from graph

The respective distances travelled were as follows:

In time OH, Distance $= \text{Area of triangle OAH} \times \frac{1}{2}\text{OH.AH}$
$= \frac{1}{2} \times 10\ (\text{s}) \times 60\ (\text{m/s}) = 300\ \text{m}.$

In time HK, Distance $= \text{Area of rectangle HABK} = \text{HK.AH}$
$= 20\ (\text{s}) \times 60\ (\text{m/s}) = 1200\ \text{m}.$

In time KC, Distance $= \text{Area of triangle BKC} = \frac{1}{2}\ \text{KC.BK}$
$= \frac{1}{2} \times 12\ (\text{s}) \times 60\ (\text{m/s}) = 360\ \text{m}.$

Hence, total distance $= 1860\ \text{m}.$

Other Velocity–Time Graphs

Fig. 7.12 (i) shows the velocity-time graph of a lift whose velocity increases uniformly along OA and then decreases uniformly in velocity to rest along AB. The distance travelled is the area of the triangle OAB.

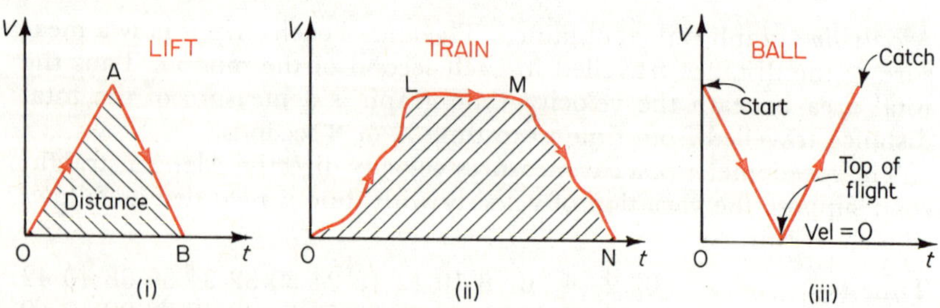

Fig. 7.12 Velocity-time graphs

Fig. 7.12 (ii) shows the velocity–time graph of a train between two stations. The train's velocity increased along OL as it pulled away from the station, it travelled with fairly uniform velocity for a time along

LM, and finally decreased in velocity to rest at N. The distance travelled is the area below the curve OLMN. Similar graphs are obtained in speed tests on railway engines by British Railways.

Fig. 7.12 (iii) shows the velocity–time graph of a cricket ball thrown vertically upwards. The velocity decreases uniformly to zero at the top of its flight and then increases in velocity uniformly as it returns to the hand of the thrower.

Acceleration

When an object increases its velocity it is said to 'accelerate'. A saloon car starting from rest may accelerate to a velocity of 48 km/h in 10 s; a sports car may accelerate from rest to 48 km/h in 3 s, a much greater acceleration. Acceleration can be defined by:

$$\text{Acceleration} = \frac{\text{Velocity change}}{\text{Time taken to make the change}}.$$

In the case of the saloon car, therefore,

$$\text{Average acceleration} = \frac{(48 - 0)\text{ km/h}}{10\text{ s}}$$
$$= 4{\cdot}8\text{ km/h/second}$$

In the case of the sports car,

$$\text{Average acceleration} = \frac{(48 - 0)\text{ km/h}}{3\text{ s}}$$
$$= 16\text{ km/h/second.}$$

The 'zero' in the numerator of the acceleration value has been deliberately inserted. It emphasises that acceleration always refers to a velocity *change*, not to the actual velocity. Thus a car travelling with a uniform velocity of 48 km/h has no acceleration. A car accelerating from 48 to 80 km/h in 4 s has an average acceleration given by

$$\frac{\text{Velocity change}}{\text{Time}} = \frac{(80 - 48)\text{ km/h}}{4\text{ s}}$$
$$= \frac{32\text{ km/h}}{4\text{ s}}$$
$$= 8\text{ km/h/second.}$$

This means that the velocity increases by 8 km/h every second. Thus if the acceleration remains constant after 80 km/h is reached the velocity increases 2 s later by 2 × 8 or 16 km/h. The velocity reached is thus 16 km/h more than 80 km/h, or 96 km/h.

Non-uniform and Uniform Acceleration

Fig. 7.13 (i) shows lengths of successive tape strips when a heavy block of wood first moves down a rough inclined plane. Successive lengths are the distances travelled in equal times of 5 ticks or dots, and hence it can be seen from joining the tops of the strips that the velocity increases in an irregular way with time. This is an example of *non-uniform* acceleration. By contrast, if tape is attached to a trolley on a smooth inclined board, and the trolley is released so that it runs down the board, the tape has the appearance of Fig. 7.13 (ii) after the run.

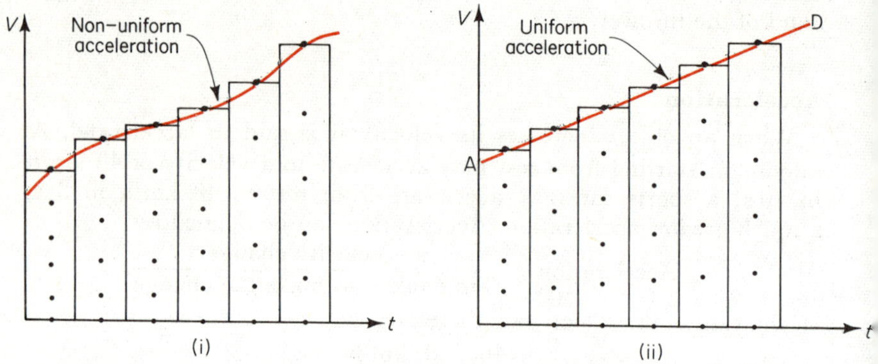

Fig. 7.13 Acceleration by ticker-tape

On cutting the tape after successive equal time intervals and pasting the strips beside each other, the tapes now lie on a fairly straight line AD. The acceleration of the object is therefore *uniform*.

Uniform acceleration is defined as *the motion of an object whose velocity increases by equal amounts in equal times, no matter how small the time intervals may be.*

Acceleration from Velocity–Time Graphs

We can now see how acceleration can be measured generally from a velocity–time graph. From Fig. 7.14, for example,

$$\text{Uniform acceleration along OA} = \frac{\text{Velocity change}}{\text{Time}}$$

$$= \frac{\text{LA}}{\text{OL}}, \text{ if the time is OL.}$$

The ratio LA/OL is the *gradient* of the line OA. Hence

Acceleration = Gradient of velocity–time graph.

Along OA the gradient is constant. In calculating the acceleration from the gradient, we read LA from the velocity-axis and OL from the time-axis.

In Fig. 7.14, AB represents uniform or constant velocity and the gradient or acceleration is zero. The velocity–time graph represented by BC is a line with steeper gradient than OA, and hence the acceleration here is greater. When the graph shows an irregular velocity variations as along CD, the acceleration at a time corresponding to X, for example,

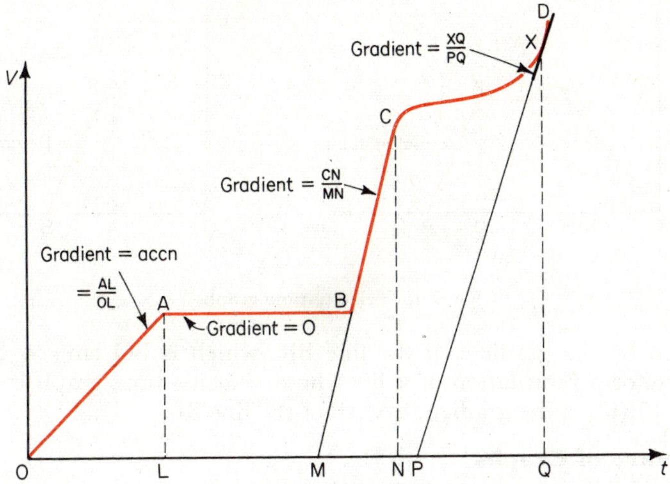

Fig. 7.14 Acceleration from velocity-time graph

is the gradient of the *tangent* to the graph at this point, as shown (compare p. 125).

Retardation or Deceleration

If the brakes of a bicycle or car are pressed the velocity decreases. The bicycle or car is then said to undergo 'retardation' or 'deceleration'. 'Uniform retardation' means that the velocity decreases by equal amounts in equal times, no matter how small the times may be. Like acceleration,

$$\text{Retardation} = \frac{\text{Velocity change}}{\text{Time taken}},$$

but as the velocity decreases with time it can be considered as 'negative acceleration'.

Suppose a train slows uniformly from 96 to 48 km/h in 10 s. Then

$$\text{Retardation} = \frac{(96 - 48)\ \text{km/h}}{10\ \text{s}}$$
$$= 4{\cdot}8\ \text{km/h/s}.$$

2 s after the velocity of 48 km/h is reached, therefore, the velocity decreases by $4{\cdot}8 \times 2$ or 9·6 km/h. The velocity is then $48 - 9{\cdot}6$ km/h or 38·4 km/h. It can be seen that 10 s after 48 km/h is reached the train comes to rest.

Fig. 7.15 (i) illustrates the velocity–time curve OABR of a train which departs from a station with uniform acceleration at a time O to a time P, then moves with a uniform velocity from P to Q, and is uniformly retarded from Q to R at the next station. The retardation

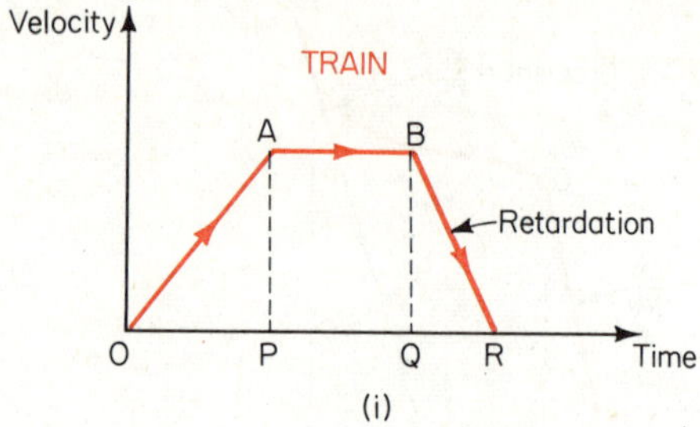

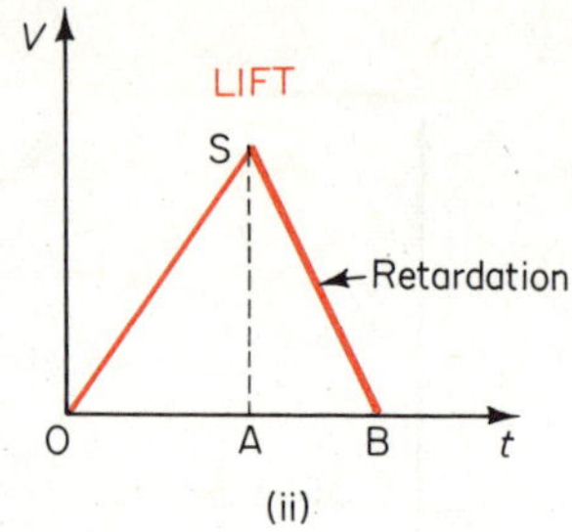

Fig. 7.15 Velocity-time graphs

is given by the gradient of the line BR, which is BQ cm/s ÷ QR s. The uniform retardation of a lift whose velocity–time graph is OSB, Fig. 7.15 (ii), is the gradient SA/AB of the line SB.

Summary of Graphs

We can summarize the information obtainable from graphs as follows:

1. *Displacement* (s)*–time* (t). The *gradient* at a place represents velocity.
2. *Velocity* (v)*–time* (t). (i) The *area* between the graph and the time-axis represents displacement or distance.

(ii) The *gradient* at a point represents acceleration or retardation.

Plate 7(B) Parabolic path of ball projected horizontally with uniform velocity and rebounding from floor after falling. Observe the acceleration and retardation (deceleration).

Acceleration Due to Gravity

A cricket or tennis ball, hit straight up into the air, slows down as it reaches the top of its flight. This is due to the attraction of the earth on the ball, or *gravitational attraction*. At its maximum height the ball momentarily stops. It then falls with increasing velocity to the ground owing to gravitational attraction. This is discussed more fully later. Here we may note that the ball undergoes a retardation as it moves up, and an acceleration while it falls. See Plate 7B.

One method of measuring g, the acceleration due to gravity, is to time a free fall by an electric clock capable of measuring one-hundredths of a second or centiseconds.

The apparatus consists of an electromagnet M which is energized by a switch (not shown) incorporated with the electrical supply to the clock, Fig. 7.16. A steel ball, with a piece of thin paper between itself

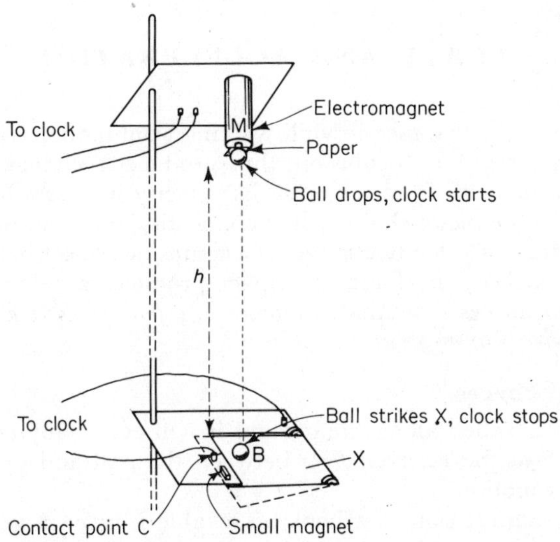

Fig. 7.16 Measuring g by free fall

and the iron core, is held by M. When the switch is pressed, the current in M is cut off and the ball begins to fall. Simultaneously, the clock is switched on. After falling a height h the ball strikes a hinged plate X at B. X then breaks contact with C, and the clock automatically stops.

The time t of fall can be read to $\frac{1}{100}$ s. The height h of fall is the distance from the bottom of the ball when held at M to the plate X. On repeating the experiment with magnetic materials of different mass in place of the ball, practically the same time of fall is obtained. Thus all objects, no matter what their mass may be, fall under gravity with the same acceleration.

Calculation. In one measurement the height h was 120·0 cm and the average time of fall was 0·50 s. Thus the *average* velocity during fall = 120·0/0·50 = 240 cm/s.

Since the ball fell from rest, it had no velocity at the start. The velocity reached after 0·50 s must therefore be 480 cm/s, since the average of zero and 480 cm/s is 240 cm/s.

The ball thus gains a velocity of 480 cm/s from rest in 0·5 s. Hence

$$\text{acceleration due to gravity } g = \text{increase in velocity per second} = \frac{480}{0{\cdot}5} = 960 \text{ cm/s/s.}$$

Accurate experiments show that the acceleration due to gravity, g, in Great Britain is about 980 cm/s/s, or about 10 metres per second per second. Since the term 'second' occurs twice, this is often written as '10 m/s^2'.

FORCE AND ACCELERATION

Force

If you collide with someone while walking, your motion is immediately checked. A *force*, due to collision, thus produces a change in velocity. When a train starts from a station its velocity increases from zero. A force, due to the metal chain or link connecting the train to the engine, again produces a velocity change. If a tennis or cricket ball is hit, or a football is kicked, the force at impact produces a velocity increase. All these examples show that, in general, *a force produces a change in the motion or velocity of an object.*

Frictional Forces

If a ball is rolled along the ground it will eventually come to rest. This is due to the *frictional force* between the ball and ground which opposes the motion.

For the same reason, if a book on a table is given a gentle push it travels a short distance and then comes to rest, Fig. 7.17 (i). Suppose,

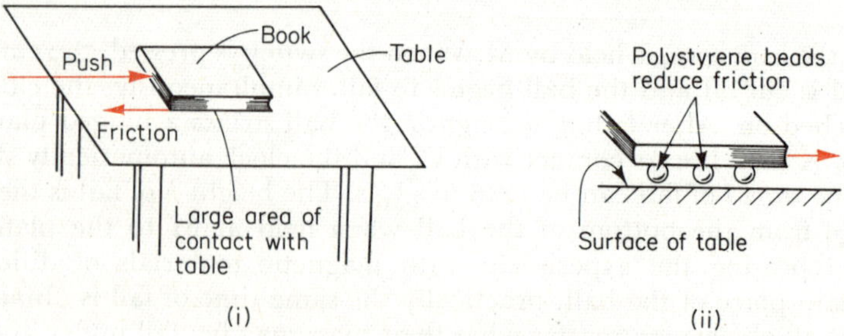

Fig. 7.17 Reduction of friction

however, that polystyrene beads are sprinkled liberally on the table and the book is pushed gently as before. This time the book slides easily along the table across the beads. The frictional force between the book and the table has thus been considerably reduced. As illustrated in Fig. 7.17 (ii), the tiny beads act like millions of small 'rollers', separating the physical contact between the surface of the book and that of the table.

In the same way a metal *puck* P, which has dry ice (solid carbon dioxide) packed beneath its base, glides smoothly along a plane sheet of glass carefully levelled if it is given a gentle push. Gaseous carbon dioxide, released between the dry ice and the glass, forms a cushion of gas on which the puck moves. Friction is thus reduced to an extremely small value. The motion of the puck continues for a very long time, rebounding continually from the surrounding sides after collision. The *Hovercraft*, now crossing the English Channel with passengers, is a vessel which directs a curtain of jets of air downwards below it so that it floats on a cushion of air while moving, Fig. 7.18. It travels at much

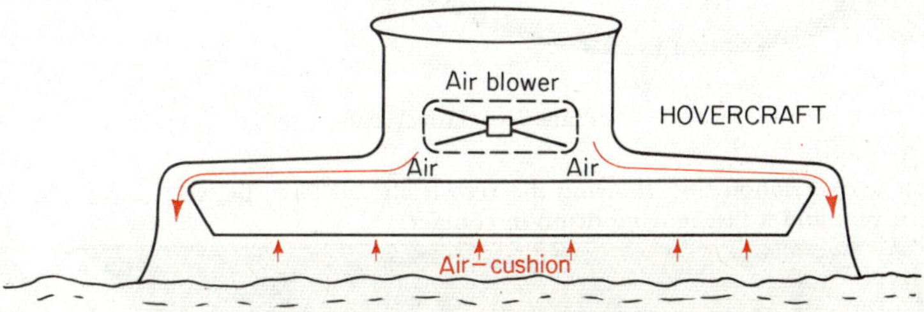

Fig. 7.18 *Hovercraft* principle

faster speeds than a steamer ploughing through water because of the reduction in friction. See Plate 7c. Conversely, car tyres are specially designed to increase friction between the ground and the tyre. See Plates 7D, 7E. *Air friction* is important in aerodynamics. See Plates 7F, 7G.

Newton's First Law

By using a rotating stroboscope in front of its lens, or by using regular flashes of light in a darkened room from an electronic stroboscope, a camera can take successive photographs after equal intervals of time of a puck gliding on its own across glass. The photographs show that the puck with dry ice underneath it, which has practically no frictional force acting on it to affect its motion, moves with a constant velocity, Fig. 7.19 (i). A similar result is obtained by photographing a perspex model moving freely along a linear air-track, like a Hovercraft moving on air. Thus in the absence of any force acting on it, an object continues to move with a uniform velocity. Of course, if the

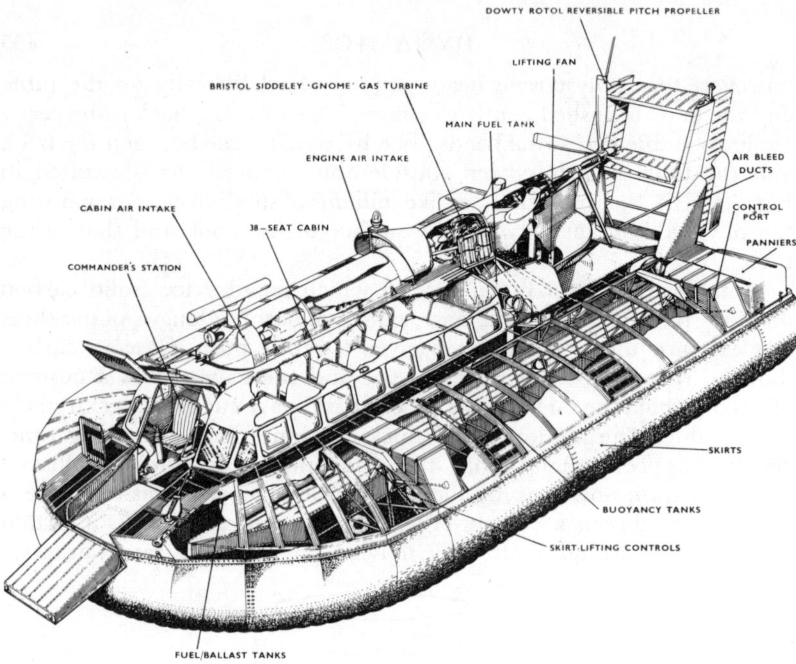

Plate 7(C) Hovercraft.

Plate 7(D) Friction test, showing the zero frictional force between a completely-worn tyre and a fast moving drum in contact.

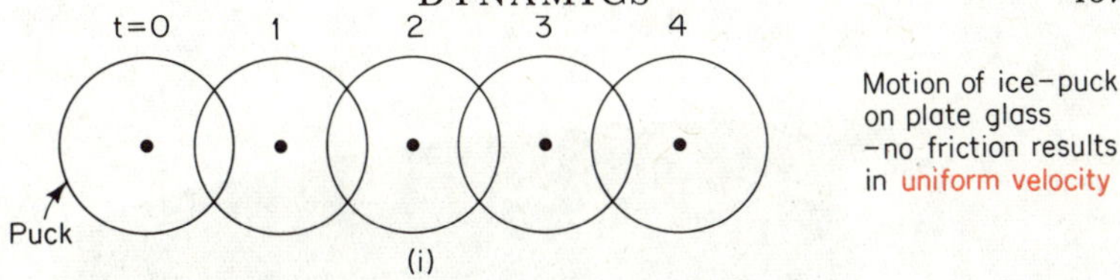

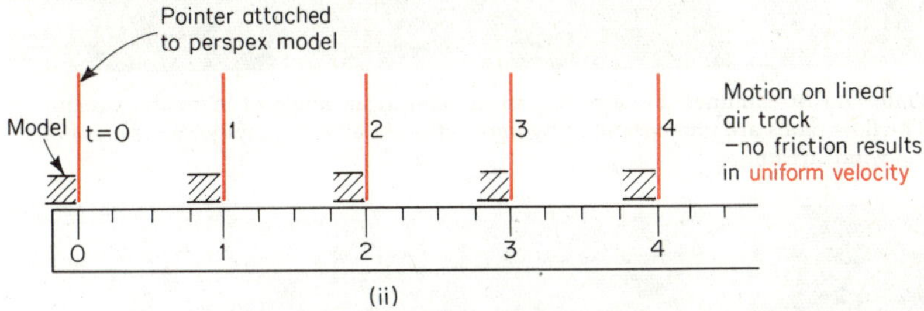

Fig. 7.19 No force—uniform motion

object is initially at rest, then, in the absence of any force, it continues to remain at rest.

Newton's first law summarizes experience. It may be stated:

Every object continues in its state of rest or uniform motion in a straight line unless impressed forces act on it.

Thus a rocket, fired from the earth to reach the moon, eventually reaches outer space, where the gravitational attraction of the earth is very small. If no other force acts on it at this point the rocket continues to move in a straight course with uniform velocity. When it comes within the gravitational field of the moon, however, its path is influenced by the moon's gravitational attraction. On December 24, 1968, astronauts Borman, Anders and Lovell orbited the moon in Apollo 8.

Passengers in a fast-moving car which suddenly comes to rest continue to move forward, since there is little restraining force on them. Safety-straps oppose the forward motion.

Plate 7(E)
Motor tyre tread.

Inertial Mass

Newton's first law recognized that objects have a reluctance to move when they are at rest. They also have a reluctance to stop when they are moving. Objects thus have a certain amount of *inertia*.

Plate 7(F) Streamlines. Flow round an aerofoil at an angle of 9° to the stream. The flow paths are photographed by light reflected by tiny polystyrene spheres in the wind stream.

Plate 7(G) Flow when the aerofoil is stalled at an angle of 14° to the stream.

A large block of stone can hardly be pushed along the ground. The *mass* of the stone is a measure of its inertia. The mass of the stone is therefore large. Conversely, a football can easily be kicked along the ground. The mass of the football is relatively small. Newton said that the mass of an object was a measure of the 'quantity of matter' in it, without stating the nature of matter. Masses are measured accurately in terms of a *standard mass*. The standard 'kilogramme' and 'pound' are certain lumps of metal kept in the National Bureau of Weights and Measures of France and England respectively (p. 23). All masses can be measured accurately with a chemical balance as so many kilogrammes or grammes, or as so many pounds.

Units of Force

The magnitude of a force is defined by the acceleration it produces in standard masses.

The *newton* (N), used by many scientists, is a metre-kilogramme-second or SI unit. It is defined as the force which gives a mass of 1 kg an acceleration of 1 m/s^2. Approximately, it is the weight of an average-size apple, which has a mass of 100 g.

Suppose a car of mass 1000 kg accelerates at 2 m/s^2. From the definition of the newton, the force on the car $= 1000 \times 2 = 2000$ newtons. We can see that always

$$F = m \times a,$$

where F is the force, m is the mass, and a is the acceleration.

Gravity exerts a force on all objects. The force due to gravity on a mass of 1 kilogramme, the *weight* of 1 kg mass, is 10 N in round figures. So the weight of 1 g mass is 0·01 N. 'Weight' varies all over the world, being greatest at the poles and smallest at the equator. 'Mass' is constant all over the world.

Circular Motion

A car moving along a straight road will change its velocity when the accelerator pedal is pressed and greater engine force is exerted, Fig. 7.20 (i). It should be carefully noted that a velocity has direction as well as magnitude (see p. 124). If either alters, the velocity alters. In the case of the car, the magnitude altered and the direction remained unchanged.

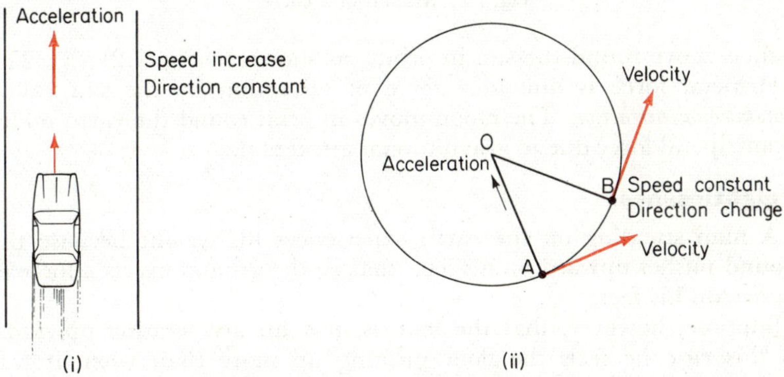

Fig. 7.20 Acceleration of objects

When a stone is tied to the end of a string and whirled round in a horizontal circle at a constant speed, the magnitude of the velocity is unchanged *but the direction alters continuously.* If the string were cut at any instant the stone would fly off along a tangent to the circle. Thus the velocity is always in the direction of the tangent at the point concerned. This is illustrated in Fig. 7.20 (ii). Since the velocity changes from A to B, objects which move in a circle with constant speed have an *acceleration.*

Centripetal forces

Objects accelerate when a force acts on them (p. 134). In the case of a stone whirled round in a circle, the force is due to the tension in the string—we can feel the force on the hand as the stone is whirled round. It is called a *centripetal force* because it acts towards the centre of the circle in which the stone is moving. This must also be the direction of the acceleration it produces. Thus the acceleration of an object moving in a circle is toward the centre.

In the case of a racing car moving round a circular track, the centripetal force is provided by the frictional force at the ground on the wheels. This acts towards the centre of the track, Fig. 7.21 (i).

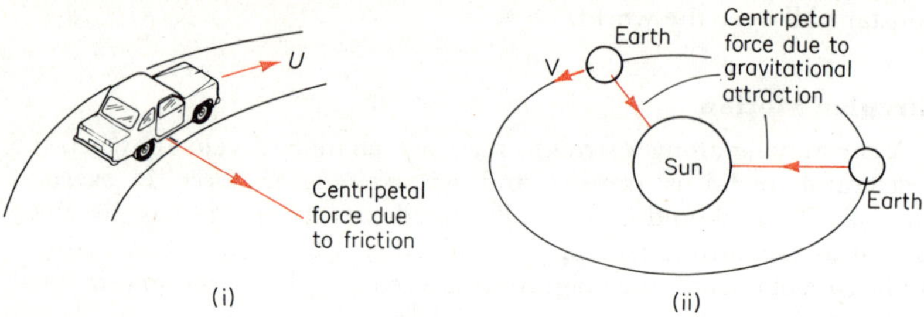

Fig. 7.21 Motion in a curve

Planets move round the sun in orbits, as shown in Fig. 7.21 (ii). The centripetal force is due to a force of attraction by the sun called *gravitational attraction*. The moon moves in orbit round the earth under a centripetal force due to gravitational attraction.

Weightlessness

A man standing on the earth experiences his weight because the ground pushes upward on his feet, that is, the ground exerts a force of *reaction* on his feet.

Suppose, however, that the man is in a lift accelerating upwards. In this case he feels the floor pushing up more than when it was stationary. His weight is apparently increased. This is the case for all objects which may be in the lift.

If the lift accelerates downwards, however, the man experiences a smaller reaction at the floor. His weight is apparently reduced. If the lift were to fall *freely*, that is, the man and the lift have now the same acceleration as that of gravity outside the lift, there is no contact between the man and the floor. The man is now apparently *weightless*. All objects in the lift are likewise 'weightless'.

Pictures of astronauts orbiting the earth in satellites show that they appear to be weightless inside. In orbit, the acceleration of the astronaut and the satellite are both the same as that of gravity outside the satellite at the height of its orbit. Thus the astronaut and the satellite can be considered to be falling 'freely' at that height. The astronaut hence experiences no reaction of the floor of the satellite if he moves

Plate 7(H) Astronauts are subjected on a centrifuge to about 16*g* acceleration, corresponding to the highest force to be encountered in an actual space mission.

around. He appears weightless and 'floats' about. For the same reason, instruments must be firmly fixed to the satellite so that they cannot move about. See Plate 7H.

Rockets

Satellites, or missiles, require very high launching speeds to rise to great heights. The motor in the rocket used for launching provides the necessary high force or thrust. It is completely self-contained and carries its own fuel, since there is very little oxygen or atmosphere at great heights.

A rocket engine is described on p. 244. The direction or path of the rocket is set by a guidance system and steered by it. Fig. 7.22 shows roughly the various stages in rocket flight. The *payload*, such as a space capsule, is usually carried in the nose of the rocket.

Action and Reaction

If you lean on a table with an elbow, the downward force on the table is called an 'action' force. The upward force due to the table on the elbow is called the 'reaction' force. One of Newton's Laws of Motion states:

Action and Reaction are equal and opposite.

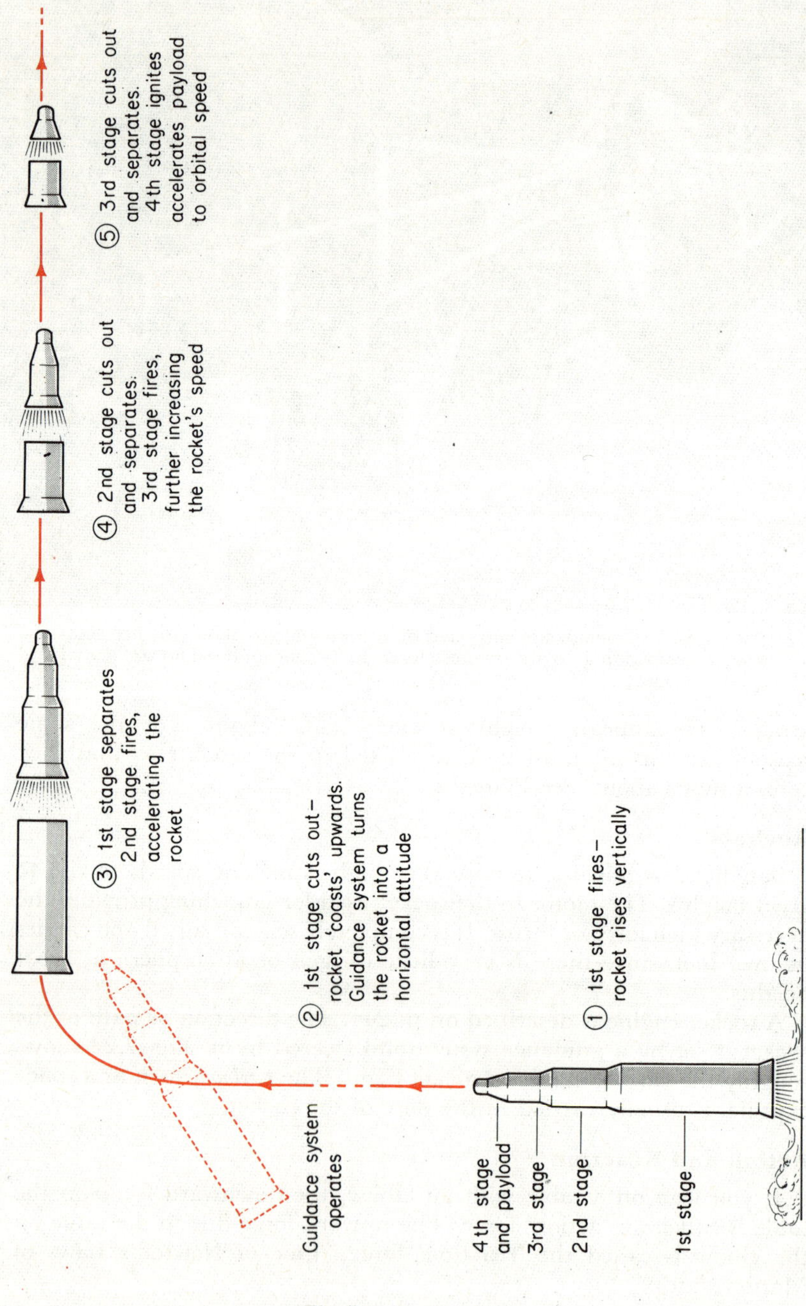

Fig. 7.22 Rocket flight

Thus if you strike a wall with your fist, the force on the wall from your fist will equal the force on your fist from the wall. The 'action' on the wall will have little effect on it. The 'reaction' force on your fist will have appreciable effect on you. The force of reaction can be seen on stepping on shore from a small boat—it moves backwards as you step off.

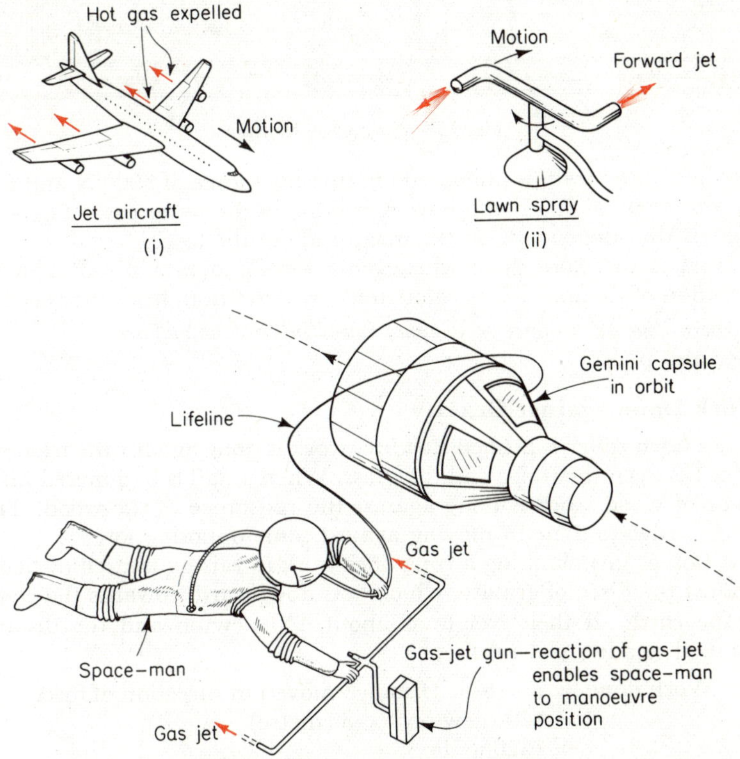

Fig. 7.23 Uses of reaction forces

Forces of reaction can be very useful. In the jet aeroplane, for example, very hot gases issue in jets from the rear with great force, Fig. 7.23 (i). The reaction drives the aeroplane forward. The same principle is used in firing a rocket. When a jet of water issues from a lawn spray, the reaction makes the spray turn and water is scattered, Fig. 7.23 (ii). A gas-jet gun was used by astronauts to manoeuvre in space, Fig. 7.23 (iii).

WORK · ENERGY · POWER

Work

In mechanics we usually associate the term 'work' with movement. Thus an engine which pulls a train along a track is said to do *work*,

Fig. 7.24. If the train is pulled 100 m by a force of 5000 N, and then a further 200 m by the same force, more work is done in the latter case. The work done thus depends on the distance moved by the force.

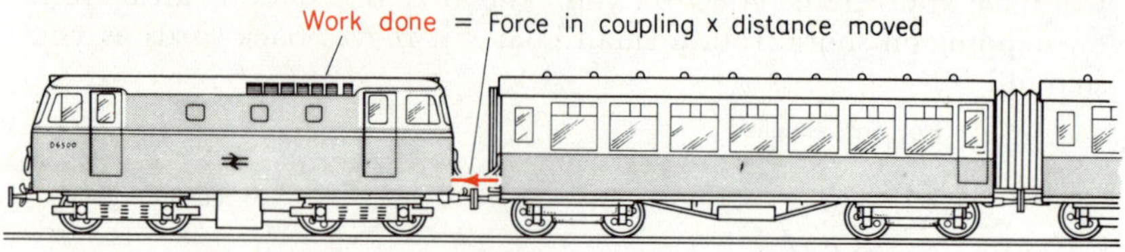

Fig. 7.24 Work done by train

Further, if the train is pulled 100 m first by a force of 5000 N and then by a force of 10 000 N more work is done in the latter case. The work done is thus dependent on the magnitude of the force.

Work is therefore done whenever a force moves a distance in the direction of the force. It is calculated, by definition, from the relation:

Work done W = force × distance moved in direction of force . . . (1)

(See also p. 59.)

Work Done against Gravity

If a lawn roller is pushed steadily, work is done against the frictional force between the roller and the grass. When a nail is hammered into a piece of wood work is done against the resistance of the wood. Thus work is always done in moving against some opposing force.

A boy or girl climbing a rope does work in raising himself or herself against the force of gravity, which acts downwards towards the centre of the earth. If their weight is about 440 newton and the distance climbed steadily is 3 m, then

$$\begin{aligned}\text{Work done} &= \text{Force} \times \text{Distance moved in direction of force}\\ &= 440\ (\text{newton}) \times 3\ (\text{metre})\\ &= 1320\ \text{joule}.\end{aligned}$$

Climbing stairs, or climbing a mountain, likewise requires work to be done against gravity. If the climb is high a person out of condition will be very conscious that he or she has done work by the end of the climb!

Energy

A *pile-driver* is a heavy concrete weight used to drive a thick stake or pile of timber into the sea-bed when constructing, for example, foundations for a pier or bridge, Fig. 7.25. By means of an engine, the pile-driver is first raised high above the pile. Here, the poised pile-driver is stationary. But when it falls and crashes into the pile it drives it into the sea-bed. The pile-driver thus does work against the resistance of the sea-bed. Consequently, the pile-driver had *energy* when it was poised stationary above the pile, that is, *it was capable of doing work.* If it was raised higher it was capable of driving the pile farther into the sea-bed; and hence, in its new position, it had more energy than before. *Energy is defined as the capacity for doing work.*

Of course, the energy of the stationary pile-driver high above the pile comes from the energy spent by the connected engine in raising it to this height. We shall discuss the relation between different kinds of

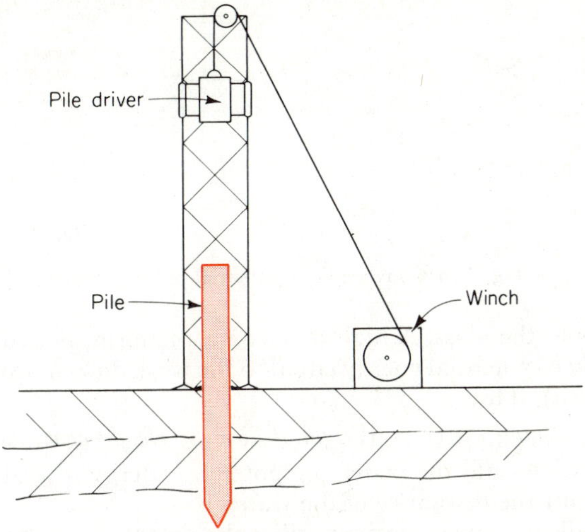

Fig. 7.25 Pile-driver

energy later (p. 238). Here we must carefully note that *the energy of an object is always equated to the work done in bringing it to its position.* In this case, therefore, if the pile-driver has a weight of 660 newton and is raised steadily 20 m, then

$$\begin{aligned}\text{Energy of stationary pile} &= \text{Work done} = \text{Force} \times \text{Distance}\\ &= \text{Weight of pile} \times \text{Distance}\\ &= 660\ (\text{newton}) \times 20\ (\text{m})\\ &= 13\,200\ \text{joule.}\end{aligned}$$

Potential Energy · Hydroelectric Energy

A stationary object above the ground, such as a poised pile-driver, is said to have *potential energy*. Potential energy is defined as 'energy possessed by reason of level or position'.

There are many examples of potential energy. A stationary brick on a shelf above the ground has potential energy; if it is pushed off the shelf and crashes into a sheet of glass near the floor it will splinter the glass into many pieces, Fig. 7.26 (i). The moving glass splinters, some of which may be hurled through big distances, show that the stationary brick on the shelf had potential or stored energy which it

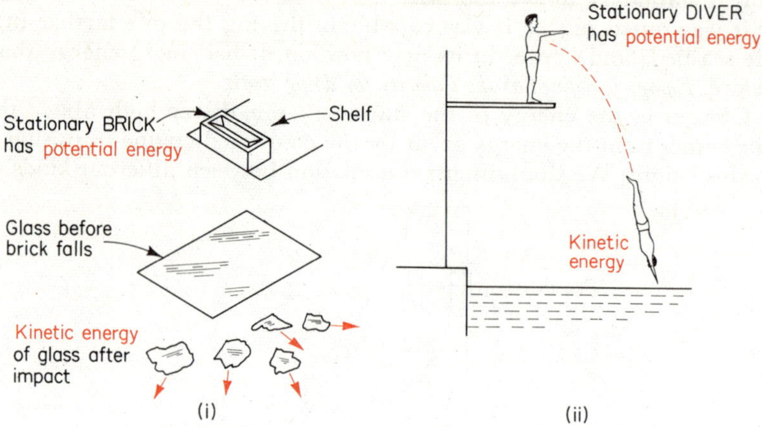

Fig. 7.26 Conversion of potential to kinetic energy

now gives to the glass. A high-diver on a platform, poised to dive, has an amount of potential energy equal to the work done in raising himself, Fig. 7.26 (ii). Thus

Potential energy = Weight of diver × Height above water.

When he dives into the water the potential energy is used up in doing work against the resistance of the water.

Hydroelectric power stations utilize the potential energy of water as it falls to a lower level under gravity. Here it moves with considerable kinetic energy and pushes against blades attached to a large wheel, which is therefore set into motion. The wheel is attached to a generator, which then produces an electrical voltage.

Other Potential Energies

These are examples of potential energy due to work done in moving against the force of gravity. A different example of potential energy is that of a wound spring. Unwound, the spring has a certain amount of potential energy. When it is coiled it has a greater amount of potential energy, Fig. 7.27 (i). As the spring gradually unwinds, the wheels of a clockwork car, for example, move, Fig. 7.27 (ii), so that work is done as the potential energy is used up. Where does the potential energy of the spring come from in this case? It comes from the work done in compressing the spring against the elastic forces in the metal, which are due to forces between molecules (p. 17).

If a piece of elastic is stretched slightly work is done against the forces of attraction between the molecules of the elastic, which opposes the movement. The stretched elastic thus has potential energy equal to the work done against these forces. If the elastic is released it flies back to its original length under the action of the attractive forces. A

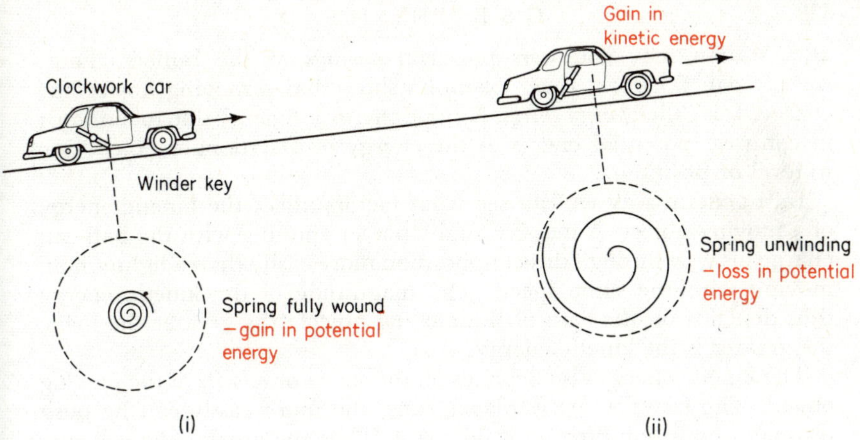

Fig. 7.27 Energy in wound spring

stretched catapult first gives a missile potential energy, so that, when released, the latter flies through the air with considerable speed. The bow of an archer gives energy to an arrow in a similar way, Fig. 7.28.

Kinetic Energy

A fast-moving cricket ball which crashes into a window pane hurls splinters of glass through big distances. A moving train coming to rest

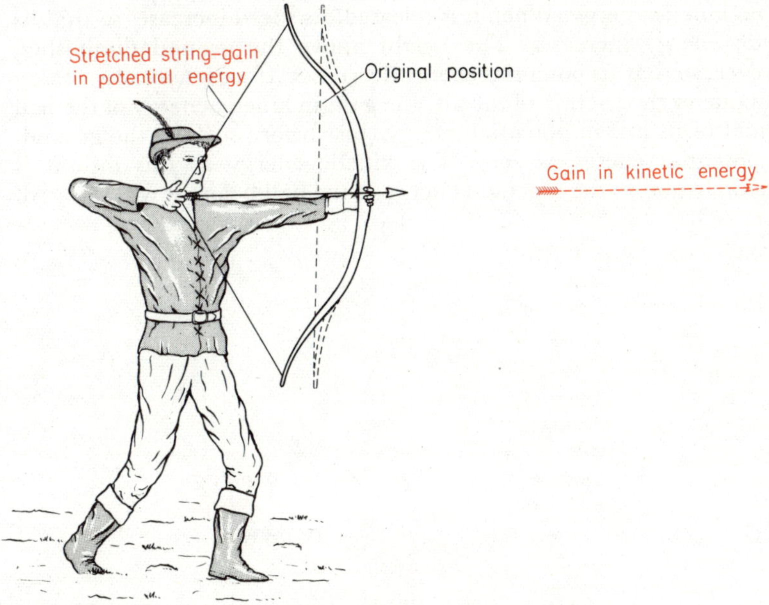

Fig. 7.28 Energy of stretched string

at a station may compress powerful springs at the buffers. Thus, since it can do work, these examples show that a moving object has energy. It is called *kinetic energy*. Kinetic energy is 'energy due to motion'; in contrast, potential energy is the energy of a stationary object due to level or position.

In a general way we can see what factors affect the kinetic energy of a moving object. A massive rugby player running with the ball can charge his way through direct opposition more easily than a lighter man moving with the same speed. The magnitude of the kinetic energy thus depends on the *mass* of the moving object; the greater the mass, the greater is the kinetic energy.

The kinetic energy also depends on the speed or *velocity* of the moving object. The faster a rugby player runs, the more easily can he push through opposition directly in his path. Thus the greater the velocity, the greater is the kinetic energy of a moving object.

A bullet is a very light object. But because it moves with very high speed it has a considerable amount of kinetic energy and penetrates deeply into the flesh. A cricket ball is much heavier, and moving with far less speed than a bullet, it can knock a stump out of the ground. Similarly, a heavy mallet moving with slow speed can make a peg penetrate deeply into the ground.

Energy changes

A stationary ball, held high above the ground, has potential energy but no kinetic energy. When it is released, its speed increases so that its kinetic energy increases. The height above the ground diminishes, however, so that its potential energy decreases. If we ignore any energy losses due to the friction of the air, the gain in kinetic energy of the ball is equal to its loss in potential energy. Just before striking the ground, the potential energy is zero. The kinetic energy at this instant is therefore equal to the potential energy of the ball before it was released.

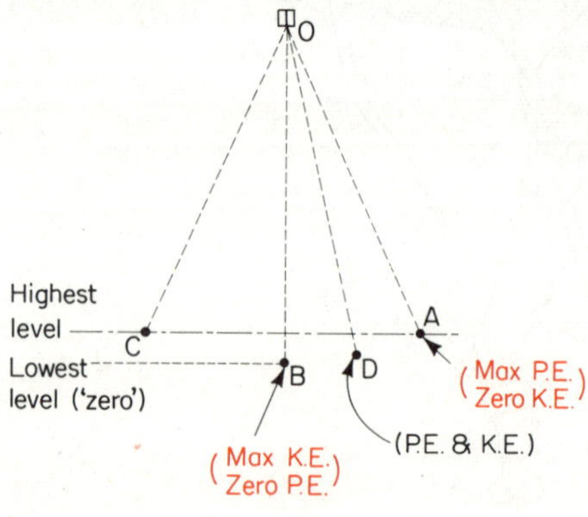

Fig. 7.29 Energy changes

A heavy bob, swinging to and fro at the end of a pendulum, shows similar changes in potential and kinetic energy. If the horizontal through the lowest point B of the swing is taken as a reference 'zero' of potential energy, then at the top of the swing A the bob has maximum potential energy (P.E.) but zero kinetic energy (K.E.), Fig. 7.29. At the middle B, the kinetic energy becomes a maximum and the potential energy is correspondingly zero.

Power

Two boys of the same weight each set out from the bottom of a hill to reach the top walking at a steady speed. One, X, is athletic and strong. The other, Y, is the opposite type, not athletic and weak. X can reach the top in a much shorter time than Y. Walking steadily,

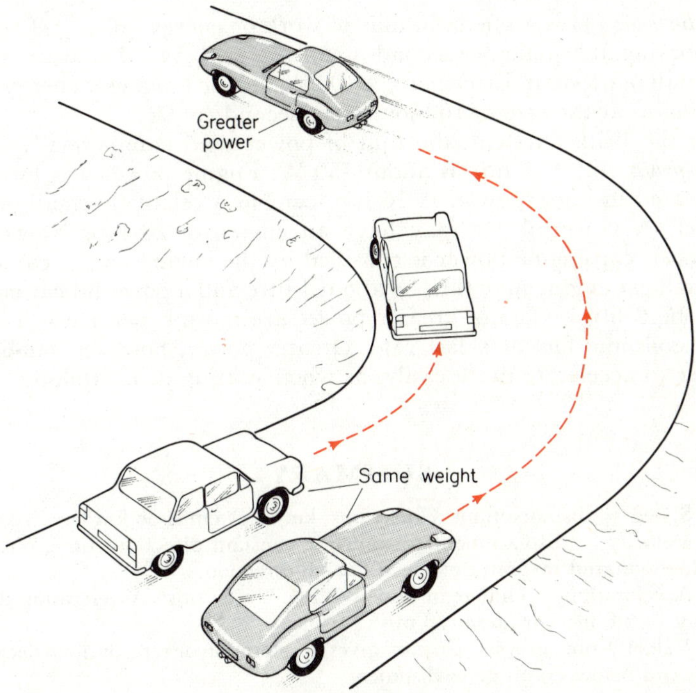

Fig. 7.30 Power

each has overcome the same frictional forces at the ground, and each has raised the same weight through the same height. Consequently each has done the same amount of work. X, however, has done it in a shorter time than Y. We say that X has a greater *power* than Y. In the same way, a large engine can work faster than a small engine of the same kind and is said to have a greater power. In Fig. 7.30, for example, the dark car is climbing a hill at a faster steady speed than the light car, which has the same weight. Its engine has greater power than that of the light car because it does more work per second.

Power is defined as the rate of doing work or expending energy, or as the work done or energy expended per second. Thus:

$$\text{Power} = \frac{\text{Work done or energy expended}}{\text{Time taken}}$$

For a car engine, for example, the power is the force on the car × the distance moved per second. Since the distance moved per second is the speed, then at constant speed,

$$\textit{Power} = \textit{Force} \times \textit{Speed of Car}.$$

Units of Power

The *joule* (J) is a scientific unit of work or energy (p. 62). The rate of working at 1 joule per second is called a *watt* (W). The watt is used as a unit of power in Electricity. A 100 W electric lamp uses energy from the mains at the rate of 100 joules per second (p. 62).

In the British system, the unit of power used commercially is the *horse-power* (h.p.). 1 h.p. is about 750 W. Engine power was formerly estimated in horse-power. A 10 h.p. car has a relatively small engine power. A powerful car may have an engine of 20 h.p. Nowadays, however, car engine power is classified by the engine size or capacity. A small car engine may thus be about 1 litre and a powerful car engine may be 3 litres. Cars of greater power are more expensive to run as they consume fuel at a fast rate. Greater power, however, enables a driver to accelerate more easily, as when starting or overtaking.

SUMMARY

1. Speed = distance/time. Units: m/s, km/h, or cm/s. 36 km/h = 10 m/s.
2. Velocity = displacement (distance in constant direction)/time. Velocity has direction and magnitude; speed has no direction.
3. Acceleration = change in velocity/time. Units: m/s^2. Acceleration due to gravity = 9·8 m/s^2 or about 10 m/s^2.
4. Velocity-time graphs: *Gradient* gives acceleration or retardation (deceleration); *area* below graph gives distance.
5. Force = mass × acceleration. Units of force: newton. Note weight of mass of 1 kg = 10 N (approx.) and weight of mass of 1 g = 0·01 N.
6. An object moving in a circle with a constant speed has an acceleration towards the centre. The force towards the centre is called the 'centripetal force'.
7. Action and reaction are equal and opposite.
8. Work = force × distance moved in direction of force. Unit: joule, J (= 1 newton × 1 metre). Power = work done/time or the rate of doing work. Unit: watt, W (= 1 J/s).

PRACTICAL

Velocity, acceleration, and the effect of a force can all be investigated in a simple way by using a ticker-timer and a trolley. This apparatus can be purchased from leading manufacturers.

1. Velocity

Apparatus. Ticker-timer; tape; trolley.

Method. (i) Attach a tape A to the trolley B. Fig. 7.31. Switch on the ticker-timer. Try and pull the trolley along a horizontal bench with a steady velocity.

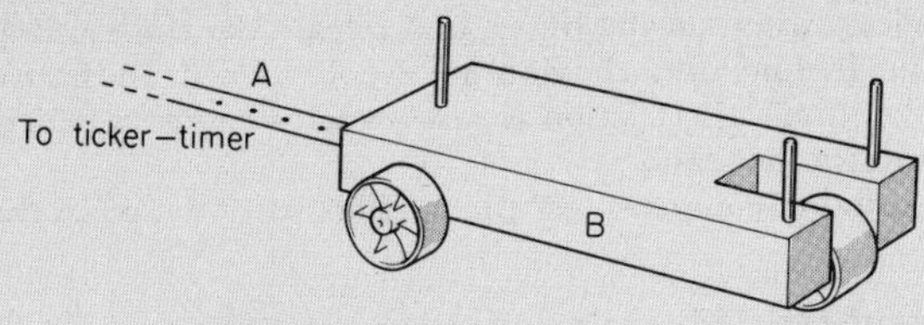

Fig. 7.31 Ticker-tape and trolley experiment

(ii) Switch off the timer. Remove the tape. Cut it into strips of 10-tick lengths. As shown on p. 130, to which you should refer, paste the strips beside each other to obtain a velocity-time graph.

(iii) Draw a line through the middle of the tops of the strips. Note the appearance of the line or graph for uniform or constant velocity.

2. Acceleration

Apparatus and Method as in **1**, but this time try and pull the trolley along with increasing speed so that the trolley has an acceleration. Cut the tape into strips and proceed as in **1**. Note the appearance of the line or graph when an acceleration is obtained.

3. Falling under gravity

Apparatus. Ticker-timer; tape; trolley; heavy object such as a wooden ball.

Method. (i) Fix the timer well above the ground by clamps and turn it round so that the tape can run freely vertically downwards.

(ii) Attach the tape to the heavy object, place a soft material on the ground directly below to break its fall. Start the timer and allow the object to fall.

(iii) Switch off the timer. Remove the tape. Cut it into 10-tick lengths. Paste them beside each other and draw a line through the middle of the tops of the strips. From the graph, what kind of motion did the falling object have?

4. Deceleration (Retardation)

Apparatus. Ticker-timer; tape; rough wooden block.

Method. (i) Attach a tape to the wood.

(ii) Switch on the timer.

(iii) Give the block a short sharp push so that it slides across the bench. As soon as the block comes to rest, switch off the timer.

(iv) Remove the tape. Cut it into 10-tick lengths and paste them beside each other. Draw a line through the middle of the tops. From the graph, what kind of motion did the moving block have?

5. Forces. Friction-compensated plane

Apparatus. Ticker-timer; tape; trolley; smooth board.

Method. (i) Attach a tape to the trolley.

(ii) Tilt the board by placing one end on a block of wood. Place the trolley on the upper end of the board and release it.

(iii) After it has reached the bottom, switch off the timer and examine the tape. If the spacing of the ticks or dots increased along the tape, the trolley was accelerating—the weight of the trolley down the plane was greater than the frictional forces at the wheels.

(iv) Reduce the inclination of the board to reduce the acceleration. Attach a new tape to the trolley, switch on the timer, and release the trolley. Repeat if necessary, altering the incline, until the dots are evenly spaced. In this case the trolley has no acceleration—the friction is now exactly counteracted by the weight of the trolley down the plane.

You now have a 'friction-compensated' plane. This will be used in the next experiment.

6. Force and acceleration (p. 134)

Apparatus. Ticker-timer; tape; trolley, friction-compensated plane; three lengths of similar elastic with eyelets at each end.

Method. (i) Place the trolley on the friction-compensated plane B. Fig. 7.32. Place the eyelet E of an elastic on the peg P of the trolley. Pull out the elastic until the other end is at a fixed reference point on the trolley such as the axle of a wheel or the pegs R and S, as shown.

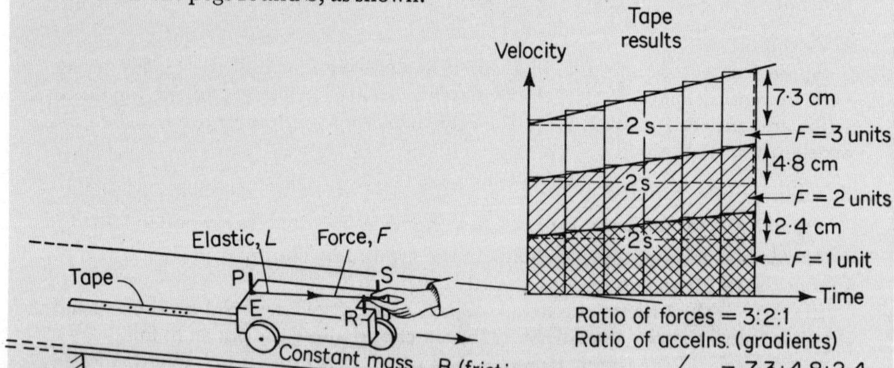

Fig. 7.32 Force and acceleration

(ii) Pull the trolley by the elastic. Try and keep the pull or force constant by keeping the elastic extended to the same length while the trolley is pulled. Practice this several times, so that you can pull the trolley by a constant force.

(iii) Attach a tape to the trolley. Pull out of the elastic as described previously. Switch on the ticker-timer. Keeping a constant force, pull the trolley along the board for a few seconds.

(iv) Switch off the timer, cut the tape into 10-tick lengths, paste beside each other and draw the best straight line through the middle of the tops of the strips, as shown.

(v) Repeat using two pieces of elastic, pulling them both out to the same length as before. This produces a force twice as great as previous, or a force of 2 'units'. Draw the best straight line through the tops of the strips.

Repeat with three pieces of elastic, each pulled out to the same length as before, and draw the best straight line through the tops of the strips.

Measurements. The acceleration of the trolley is proportional to the gradient of the graph obtained. As in Fig. 7.32, measure the vertical distances corresponding to 2·4, 4·8 and 7·3 cm. These lengths are proportional to the gradients of the three lines. Hence they give a measure of the acceleration on each occasion.

Force	Acceleration	Force / Acceleration
1 unit	. .	
2 units	. .	
3 units	. .	

Calculation. Work out the ratio 'force/acceleration' for the three forces.

Conclusion. . . .

7. Measuring power

(i) Measure the height of flights of stairs about 6 metres high.

(ii) With a friend to time you, run up the flights steadily and quickly. Repeat several times and take an average value.

Calculation. Suppose the time taken is 4 s and your weight is 500 N. Then work done per second

$$= \frac{6 \times 500\ \text{J}}{4\ \text{s}} = 750\ \text{W}.$$

$$\therefore \text{Power in horse-power} = \frac{750}{750} = 1{\cdot}0.$$

Repeat, this time walking steadily up the stairs. Calculate the new value of the power.

EXERCISE 7 · ANSWERS, p. 257

1. Three balls, A, B and C are placed near the edge of a cliff. All the balls are identical in size, but one is made of lead and two are made of aluminium. One of these balls is kicked forcibly while the other two are rolled gently so that all three go over the edge of the cliff at the same instant. There is no air resistance.

(*a*) Which ball follows path A, Fig. 7A (i)?

(*b*) Which ball follows path C?

(*c*) Tick the *one* of these statements which is correct: balls A and B hit the ground first; ball C hits the ground first; all balls hit the ground at the same time.

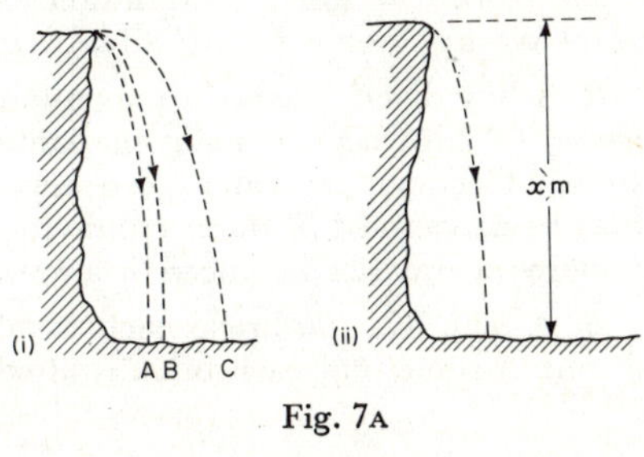

Fig. 7A

(*d*) Give a reason for your choice of answer in part (*c*) above.

(*e*) Ball B falls through a distance of *x* metre and takes exactly 1 second to do so, Fig. 7A (ii). If the acceleration due to gravity is 10 m/s², find the distance *x*.

(*f*) If all three balls were made of the same material, how would this affect the result of the experiment. Give a reason for your answer. (*M*).

2. Fig. 7B represents graphically the velocity of a car moving along a straight level road over a period of twenty minutes. Use the letters on the graph to answer the following questions:

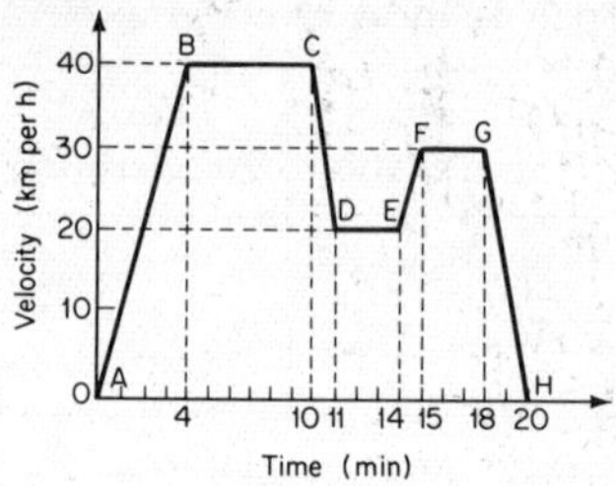

Fig. 7B

(*a*) Explain what the car is doing between A and B.

(*b*) Explain what the car is doing between D and E.

(*c*) How far has the car travelled between B and D.

(*d*) Calculate the retardation of the car between G and H. (*M*.)

3. A car travels along a level road. A number of lines are marked across the road 15 m apart and a man starts a watch as the car crosses the first of the lines. His watch reads 3·7 s as the car passes the second line, 6·0 s at the third line, 8·9 s at the fifth line and 9·7 s at the sixth line.

(*a*) Devise a table which will enable you to present this information clearly.

(*b*) Draw a graph of the motion of the car plotting 'distance of the car from first line' up the page and 'time' across the page.

(*c*) Would the motion of the car be correctly described as: (i) uniform velocity; (ii) acceleration; (iii) deceleration; or (iv) motion under gravity?

(*d*) How far from the first line is the car after 5 s?

(*e*) At what time does the car pass the fourth line?

(*f*) What is the average velocity between the second and fifth lines?

(*g*) What is the velocity of the car *as it crosses* the fifth line? (*S.E.*)

4. State units suitable for the following relationships:

(*a*) Force . . = mass . . × acceleration . .

(*b*) Work . . = force . . × distance . .

(*c*) Work . . = power . . × time . .(*E.A.*)

5. A 'sky diver' reaches a maximum speed after a few seconds free fall because; (*a*) his weight remains the same during the rest of the fall; (*b*) he may suffer a black-out at greater speed; (*c*) too long a delay in opening his parachute may be dangerous; (*d*) force of gravity decreases with distance from the earth; (*e*) force of gravity is balanced by air resistance. (*M*.)

6. A man lifts 100 bricks each of mass 5 kg from the floor on to a lorry in 2 min. Assume that each brick is lifted through a vertical height of 2 m.

(*a*) How much work does the man do? (Assume weight of 1 kg mass = 10 N.)
(*b*) At what horse-power is he working? (1 h.p. = 750 W, approx.) (*L.*)

7. A motor working a lift raises a load of 3000 N to the top of a building 30 m high in 1 min. What is the horse-power of the motor? (Assume 1 h.p. = 750 W.) (*Mx.*)

8. A small object is allowed to slide from rest down an inclined plane which is smooth. Complete the following table to show whether the velocity, acceleration and mechanical energy of the body; (*a*) remain the same; (*b*) increase; or (*c*) decrease as the body slides down.

Velocity	
Acceleration	
Mechanical energy	

9. If you weighed yourself when standing on a spring-type balance on the moon, would you appear to have lost or gained weight compared with your weight on the earth? Why is this so? (*S.E.*)

10. The graph in Fig. 7c shows the relationship between velocity and time for a moving body. What kind of motion is represented by (*a*) AB; (*b*) BC; (*c*) CD? (*L.*)

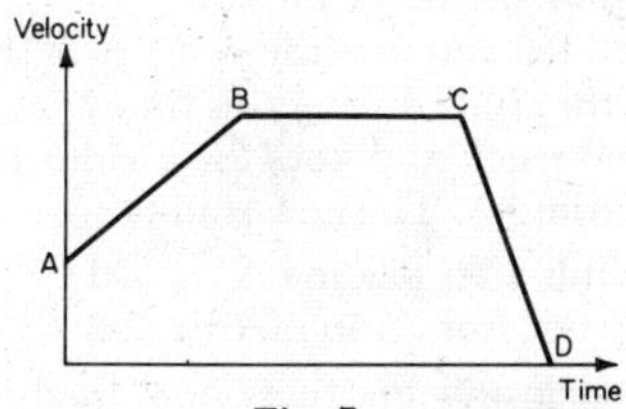

Fig. 7c

11. A boy who weighs 450 N carries 150 N of bricks 3 m up a vertical ladder in 30 s:

(*a*) How much work does the boy do?
(*b*) At what horse-power is he working? (1 horse-power = 750 W.)
(*c*) How much useful work does he do?
(*d*) What is the efficiency of this operation? (*L.*)

12. (*a*) Explain what you mean by uniform acceleration and give **one** example of a uniformly accelerated body.

(*d*) Describe an experiment to determine the acceleration due to gravity. Divide your answer into four parts: (i) labelled diagram; (ii) method; (iii) results; (iv) calculation (from graph if appropriate). (*N.W.*)

13. (*a*) Explain the terms potential energy and kinetic energy.

(*b*) Describe the energy changes that takes place in: (i) a stone falling from rest; (ii) a swinging pendulum.

(*c*) State a practical example of each of the following energy changes: (i) potential energy into electrical energy; (ii) electrical energy into heat energy; (iii) kinetic energy into heat energy. (*E.A.*)

14. Trace back to its source the mechanical energy needed to drive a railway train. (*S.E.*)

15. By means of a 'chain' diagram, show how the energy you use for running originates from the sun. (*S.E.*)

16. Briefly explain the meanings of the terms 'kinetic energy' and 'potential energy'. A cyclist starts from rest on a level road, accelerates and then continues at constant speed until he reaches a downward slope. He applies the brakes lightly so that he free-wheels downhill at constant speed, coming to rest on the horizontal at the foot of the hill. Give an account of the energy changes during the ride. (*E.A.*)

17. What do you understand by (*a*) velocity; (*b*) acceleration? How would you find by experiment a value for the acceleration due to gravity? (*L.*)

18. A section of a miniature railway has a long, straight, regular, downhill slope. A boy experiments with a railway truck on this slope. He gives the truck a starting push and finds that the distances it covers in the first 4 s after passing a marking post A as shown in the following table:

Time in seconds after passing A	1	2	3	4
Distance of truck from A in metres	1·5	3·0	4·5	6·0

(*a*) On a sheet of the graph paper provided draw axes showing distances from 0 to 25 m (scale to be given according to the size of paper to be used) vertically and times from 0 to 5 s (scale again given) horizontally. On this plot a distance/time graph of the motion of the truck for 4 s.

(*b*) How does this graph tell you that the velocity of the truck is uniform?

(*c*) What forces act on the truck during this time?

The boy jumps into the truck and goes for a ride. He again takes time and distance readings after passing A. The new results are:

Time in seconds after passing A	1	2	3	4
Distance of truck from A in metres	2·5	7·0	13·5	22·0

(*d*) Plot a distance/time graph for these new readings on the same axes as for (*a*).

(*e*) Find from your graph the distance now covered between 1·5 and 3 s.

(*f*) From the second graph find the velocity of the truck 3 s after passing A. (*S.E.*)

19. (*a*) Name four different forms of energy.

(*b*) Explain what is meant by the 'conservation of energy' by referring to what happens to the chemical energy in the petrol used by a car. (List the various stages involved.)

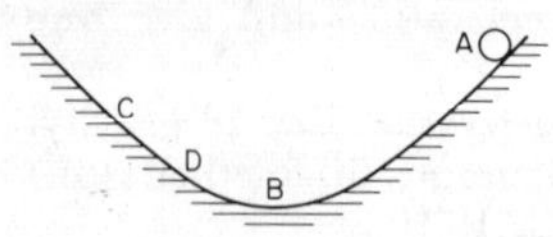

Fig. 7D

(*c*) Fig. 7D shows a solid copper ball on a slope. The ball, initially at rest at A, is allowed to run down the slope to B and then runs up the other side until it momentarily comes to rest at C.

(i) What will happen after this?

(ii) Why is the ball able to climb from B to C in this way?

(iii) Why will C be lower than A?

(iv) A horse-shoe magnet is placed across the path of the ball at B, in such a way that the ball will pass between the poles of the magnet without touching them. The ball is released from A, passes through the magnet and up the other side as far as point D before coming to rest. Suggest why the ball only reaches this height. (*S.E.*)

20. (*a*) A railway truck is given a push to set it rolling and eventually comes to rest. Which factors decide how quickly this happens?

(*b*) (i) A cart weighs 5000 N and is loaded with coke which weighs 7500 N. If a horizontal force of 2500 N is required to pull the loaded cart 2 km along a level track, calculate the work done; (ii) had the truck been pulled the same distance up an incline of 1 in 100, how much work would have been done against gravity?

(*c*) If the force is changing during the motion and you plot 'force' against 'distance travelled', how could you obtain from the graph the work that has been done? (*S.E.*)

21. In Fig. 7E, all distances are marked in metres and show the successive positions of a block at 1 second intervals.

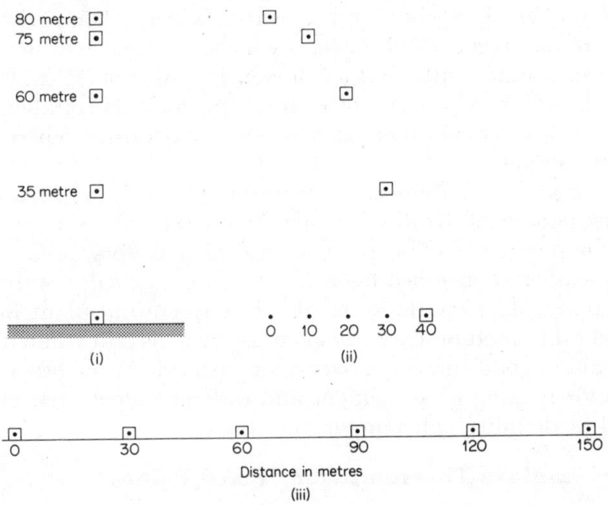

Fig. 7E

(*a*) Fig. 7E (i) shows the block released from rest 80 m above the ground. Explain why the distance travelled by this block increases every second.

(*b*) Fig. 7E (ii) shows the block pushed off a ledge 80 m above the ground. (i) Explain why the path of the block is curved. (ii) What is the horizontal velocity of the block?

(*c*) Fig. 7E (iii) shows the block pushed along a smooth surface. What is the velocity of the block? Sketch a diagram showing the block moving across a rough surface instead of a smooth surface. (*M.*)

22. (*a*) A body accelerates from rest at 3 m/s² for 7 s.

Find (i) the speed at the end of 7 s, (ii) the average speed during the 7 s, (iii) the total distance covered during the 7 s.

(*b*) A ball is thrown vertically upwards with a speed of 30 m/s and returns to its starting point. Sketch a speed time graph of the motion. State how the graph may be used to find the maximum height which the ball reaches. (*E.A.*)

8

TEMPERATURE AND THERMOMETERS

Temperature

IF a thimbleful of hot water is poured into a cup of warm water the latter becomes slightly warmly. *Heat* thus passes from the hot to the warm water, although the volume of hot water is considerably smaller than that of the warm water. We say that the *temperature* of the hot water is higher than that of the warm water. 'Temperature' is a property of an object which decides which way heat will flow when it is placed in contact with another object. It must not be confused with heat itself, which is a form of energy (p. 206). Heat always passes from one object to another at a lower temperature when they are placed in contact.

Temperature measurement is important in everyday life. Thus one of the first actions of the doctor when he is called to a sick patient is to take his temperature. The temperature of a factory or a mill must conform to a value specified by law, otherwise the health of the workers may be upset. The temperature of the refrigerating plant for storing meat and other food on cargo boats must be a certain value if the food is to remain in good condition over a long period. At the other extreme, furnaces for making glass, cement and different types of steel must be operated at definite high temperatures.

Mercury-in-glass Thermometer · Fixed Points

The sense of touch is not very reliable for estimating or measuring temperature. Thus warm water feels cool if a finger is transferred to it from hot water. The *thermometer* is a much more reliable instrument for measuring temperature. Unlike a human being, it has no 'feelings' to influence its response to temperature change. The thermometer uses some physical property of a substance which changes when the temperature is altered. In the *mercury-in-glass* thermometer for example, which is a common one in everyday use in school laboratories, the volume of mercury changes when its temperature alters.

In making any thermometer, two constant temperatures or *fixed points* must first be marked on it. The 'lower fixed point' is choosen as the *melting point of ice*. The higher or 'upper fixed point' is the *temperature of steam in contact with water boiling at normal atmospheric pressure*, 76 *cm mercury* (p. 227).

Over two hundred years ago Celsius suggested: (i) that the temperature of the melting-point of ice should be given the number '0' and the temperature of steam at 76 cm mercury pressure should be given the number '100'; (ii) that there should be 100 equal parts or *degrees* between the two fixed points. Thus temperature was called the Centigrade scale on account of the 100 degrees. It is now called the *Celsius scale*. Thus, on the Celsius scale:

$$\text{Melting-point of ice} = 0^\circ \text{ C.}$$
$$\text{Steam temperature at 760 mm mercury} = 100^\circ \text{ C.}$$

A room at a temperature of 16° C should not feel cold. In good health, the temperature of a human being is about 37° C.

The fixed points are marked on ungraduated thermometers with the aid of apparatus shown in Fig. 8.1. To obtain the lower fixed point,

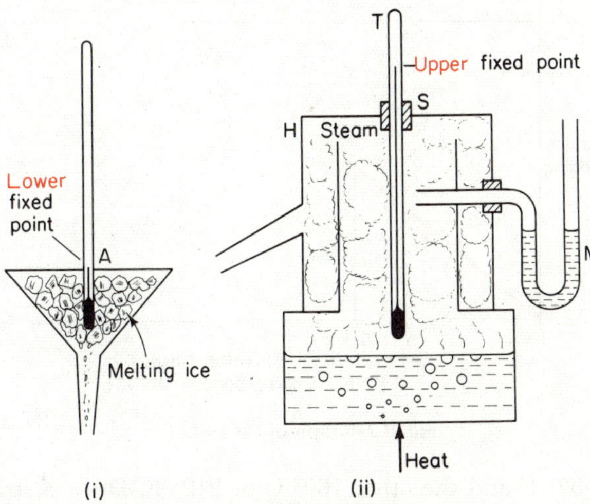

Fig. 8.1 Lower and upper fixed points

the thermometer is placed upright in pure melting ice, Fig. 8.1 (i). When the mercury level is constant, a mark is made opposite on the glass. To obtain the upper fixed point, a *hypsometer* is used, Fig. 8.1 (ii). The thermometer T is placed in the steam (*not* in the boiling water, because this temperature is affected by dissolved impurities in the water). A water manometer M is used to measure the pressure of the steam—if not 760 mm mercury, an adjustment is made to the upper fixed point. The latter is marked at the top of the mercury thread when the level is constant.

Temperature Scales

The *Celsius scale* has been recommended for general use as well as for scientific use. The *Fahrenheit scale* was an earlier scale. The lower fixed point is 32° F and the upper fixed point is 212° F on the scale, so that the interval between the two temperatures is divided into 180 degrees, Fig. 8.3.

Conversion from one scale to another of a particular temperature can be done in several ways. One is a graphical method.

On a piece of paper, mark Celsius on the horizontal axis and Fahrenheit on the vertical axis, Fig. 8.2. Plot two points, one corresponding

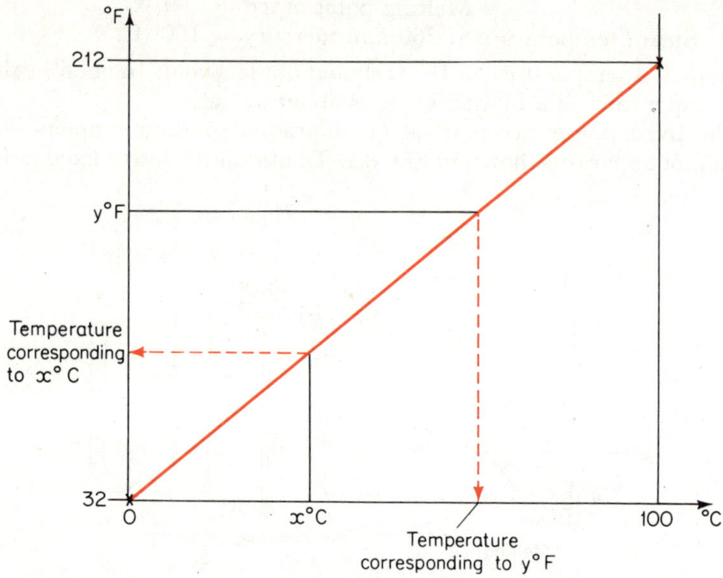

Fig. 8.2 Graph of °C and °F

to 0° C or 32° F and the other 100° C or 212° F. Draw a straight line between the two points. You can now read off the Fahrenheit temperature corresponding to any value on the Celsius scale, and vice versa.

Fig. 8.3 illustrates that the one degree change on the Celsius scale is a greater change of temperature than one degree change on the Fahrenheit scale. In fact, 100° C change (0° C to 100° C) = 180° F change (32° F to 212° F). Thus

$$1^\circ \text{ C change} = \frac{180}{100} \text{ or } \frac{9}{5} \text{ F change} = 2^\circ \text{ F change approximately.}$$

The temperature of a human body in normal health is 98·4° F. On the Celsius scale this is 36·9° C, or in round figures, 37° C.

Temperature Conversion

Temperatures can be converted from °C to °F and vice versa by calculation.

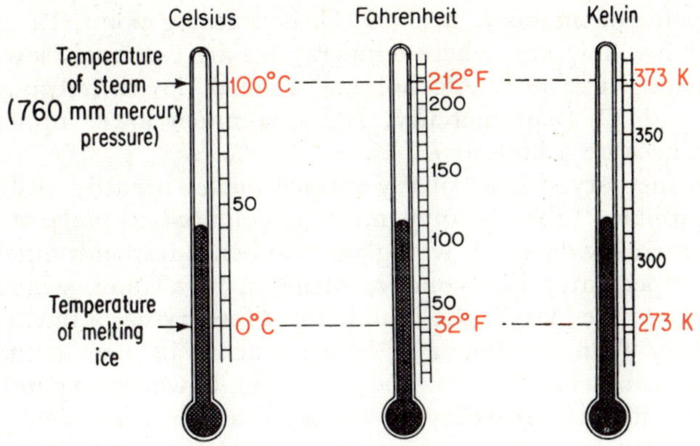

Fig. 8.3 Temperature scales

As an illustration suppose we wish to convert 15° C to °F. Always work in degrees above the lower fixed point. Thus

$$15^\circ\ C = 15 \text{ deg above the lower fixed point, } 0^\circ\ C$$

Now 100 degrees change on the Celsius scale = 180 degrees change on the Fahrenheit scale.

$$\therefore 15^\circ C = \frac{15}{100} \times 180^\circ F = 27^\circ F$$

But lower fixed point on Fahrenheit scale is called 32° F.

$$\therefore \text{Temperature} = 32 + 27 = 59^\circ\ F.$$

Suppose we wish to convert the high temperature of 257° F to °C. Again find the number of degrees from the lower fixed point. This is 32°F, so the number of degrees above the lower fixed point = 257 − 32 = 225°F. Now 180° on the Fahrenheit scale = 100° on the Celsius scale.

$$\therefore 225^\circ F = \frac{225}{180} \times 100^\circ C = \frac{225 \times 5}{9}\,^\circ C$$
$$= 125^\circ C.$$

But the lower fixed point on the Celsius scale is 0°C. Thus 125° above this number = 125°C.

Fig. 8.3 shows three temperature scales. The kelvin or absolute scale is used in the SI system of units. As explained on p. 178, 0 K = −273°C (approx.). Thus 273 K = 0°C and 373 K = 100°C. Note that a temperature change of 1°C = 1 K change, so that a heat quantity '50 J per °C' can also be written '50 J per K' or 50 J/K.

Alcohol Thermometer

The mercury-in-glass thermometer is widely used in chemical laboratories for temperature measurements in the range 360° C, the boiling point of mercury, to $-39°$ C, its freezing point. In arctic or polar regions, however, where temperatures are extremely low, *alcohol* thermometers are used. Alcohol has a much lower freezing point, about $-112°$ C, than mercury. It has a much lower upper limit, however, because it boils at 78° C.

Unlike mercury, whose silvery surface makes it easily visible even in fine capillary tubes, alcohol must be coloured to make it visible. Further, mercury does not 'wet' glass, and hence responds quickly to a falling temperature. The concave meniscus of alcohol, which 'wets' glass, sticks to the glass as the liquid falls. Mercury has a much greater conductivity than alcohol, and hence reaches its new temperature quickly on contact with a hot body. Alcohol, however, expands about six times as much as mercury for the same temperature rise.

The Clinical Thermometer

The clinical thermometer is used by doctors for determining the temperature of the human body. It consists of a mercury thermometer with: (i) a short range of about 35–43° C; (ii) a constriction at A in the capillary tubing, Fig. 8.4. When the temperature of a patient is

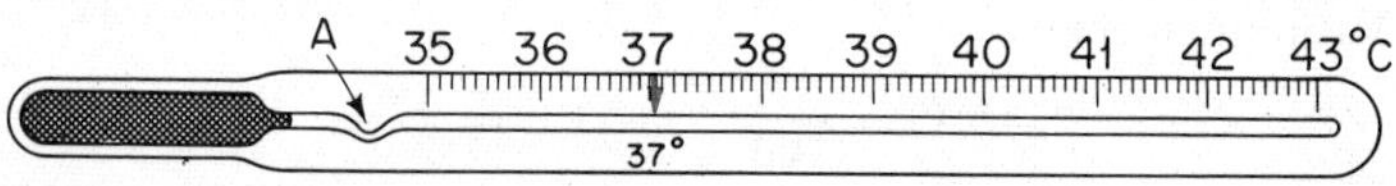

Fig. 8.4 Clinical thermometer

taken with the thermometer the mercury thread easily passes A owing to the large force exerted in expansion. When the thermometer is removed from the patient the mercury thread to the left of A recedes, but the column to the right remains in position owing to the constriction; by this means, the thermometer can still be read. It is afterwards reset by jerking it sharply, when the thread beyond A rejoins the mercury in the bulb.

Maximum and Minimum Thermometers

It is often necessary to record the maximum and minimum temperatures during each day in studies of the weather.

A *maximum thermometer* utilizes the convex meniscus of mercury, which pushes along a small steel index when the temperature rises and the mercury expands, Fig. 8.5 (i). When the temperature falls, the index stays in position. At the end of the day, therefore, the maximum temperature corresponds to the lower end of the index. The index can be reset by tilting the thermometer or by using a small magnet.

A *minimum thermometer* utilizes the concave meniscus of alcohol. This time the index is *below* the meniscus, Fig. 8.5 (ii). Thus when the temperature falls, the index is pulled down by the meniscus. When the

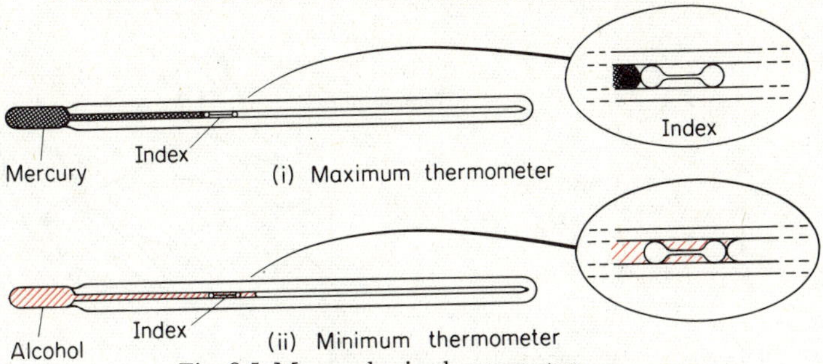

Fig. 8.5 Max and min thermometers

temperature rises, the alcohol expands past the index, which stays in position. At the end of the day the minimum temperature corresponds to the upper end of the index (compare the case of the maximum thermometer index). The index is reset in the same way as described above.

Fig. 8.6 shows a *combined maximum and minimum thermometer*. When the temperature rises, the expansion of the alcohol in A makes the mercury thread push the index X. Thus the lower end of X indicates the maximum temperature. When the temperature falls, X remains in position and the index N is pushed up. Thus the lower end of N indicates the minimum temperature.

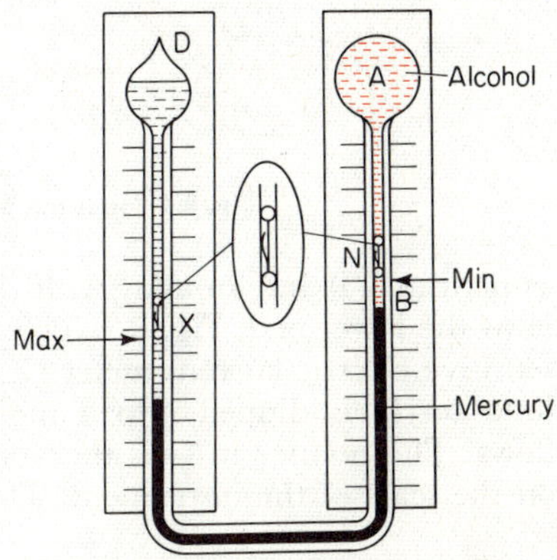

Fig. 8.6 Combined max and min thermometer

Gas Thermometer · Pyrometers

Mercury-in-glass thermometers are not used for very accurate measurement of temperature. Apart from the disadvantage of a relative small range of temperature—the freezing point of mercury is −39° C and its boiling point is 360° C—the glass also expands and its expansion is irregular.

Gas thermometers are used for very accurate temperature measurement at the National Physical Laboratory, for example. A large volume change of gas occurs when its temperature is altered, so that the glass expansion of the containing bulb is negligible. Gases also expand much more regularly with temperature change than mercury. The range of temperature is very large, from about −260° C to 1500° C.

In industry, the high temperatures of furnaces or molten metals need to be measured. Sometimes a *thermoelectric thermometer* or *pyrometer* is used. This consists simply of two metals of high melting point such

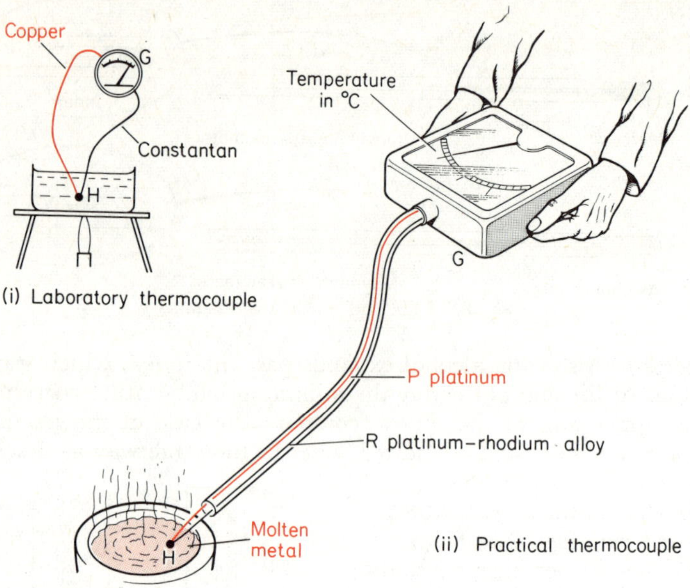

Fig. 8.7 High temperature measurement

as platinum P and an alloy with rhodium R, with a common junction H at the lower end, Fig. 8.7. The free ends of P and R are joined to a sensitive electric current meter G, already calibrated in °C. When the junction H is dipped into a molten metal, for example, a current flows. The pointer in G is then deflected to a particular temperature on the scale of the instrument. Thus the temperature is read directly.

SUMMARY

1. Lower fixed point = melting-point of ice = 0°C or 32°F.

Upper fixed point = temperature of steam in contact with water boiling at 760 mm atmospheric pressure = 100°C or 212°F.

2. 100°C = 180°F (temperature changes).

3. Alcohol has a lower freezing-point than mercury—hence used in arctic countries.

4. Clinical thermometer has constriction in capillary tube and short range.

Maximum thermometer—index pushed by mercury meniscus.

Minimum thermometer—index pulled down by alcohol meniscus.

PRACTICAL

1. Comparison of °C and °F (p. 160)

Method. (i) Fill a beaker half full with water.

(ii) Place inside a °C and a °F thermometer. Record the temperature in °C and °F when the readings are steady.

(iii) Heat the water with a moderate flame. As the temperature rises, record the values at suitable intervals on both the °C and the °F scales. Make sure the liquid is stirred continuously so that its temperature is the same everywhere, and stop at about 90°C.

Measurements.

°C	°F

Graph. Make a graph of the results by plotting °C v. °F. Draw the best straight line BA through all the points. Fig. 8.8.

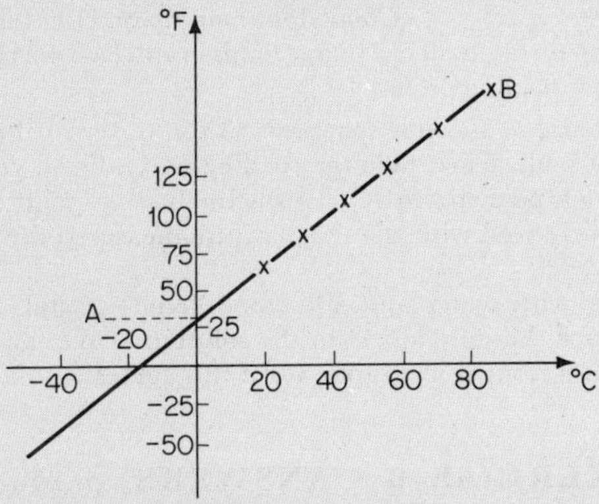

Fig. 8.8 °C and °F graph

(i) Extend the straight line to A—does this read 32°F?

(ii) From your graph, read off the temperature: (*a*) in °F corresponding to 100°C; (*b*) in °C corresponding to − 40°F. Check your results by calculation.

2. Checking fixed points (p. 158)

Method. (i) Place a thermometer bulb well inside melting ice in a beaker. Observe the steady temperature on the thermometer.

(ii) Heat the ice until it all melts, add tap water, and heat until boiling occurs. Note the steady reading on the thermometer—is it exactly 100·0°C?

(iii) Add common salt to the water, stir to make a concentrated solution, and see if this has any effect on the boiling-point.

(iv) Pour the salt-water into a flask. Insert the thermometer through one hole of a two-hole cork. Fit the cork into the flask and arrange the bulb of the thermometer to be *well above* the water. Boil and observe the reading in the thermometer. Compare this with the boiling-point in (iii) when the bulb was *inside* the salt-water.

3. Thermoelectric thermometer (p. 163)

Apparatus. About a metre length of copper and Constantan (or Eureka) wire, A and B; beaker; microammeter or sensitive galvanometer G and series resistance; thermometer 0–100° C; tripod; gauze; burner.

Method. (i) Twist the wires together at one end to make a common junction H. Fig. 8.9.

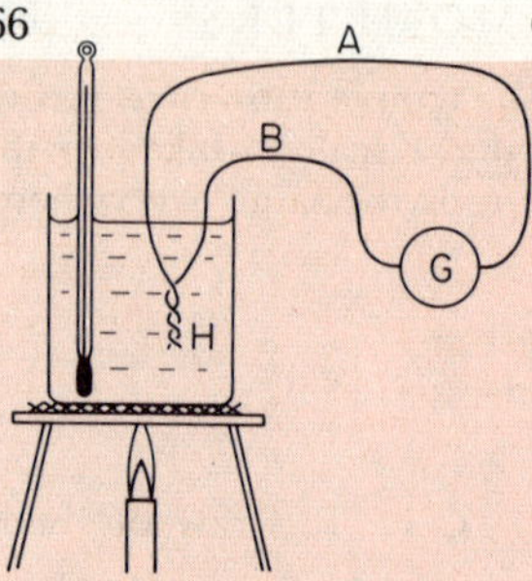

Fig. 8.9 Thermoelectric thermometer

(ii) Join the free ends of A and B to the microammeter G and place H inside water in the beaker.

(iii) Note the reading on G and the temperature of the water t°C. Warm the water about 10°C at a time until about 90°C and each time record the reading in G.

Measurements.

Temperature of H, t°C	Reading on G

Graph. Plot reading on G v. temperature t°C. Draw the best line through all the points. This graph enables the temperature to be found from the reading on G.

Temperature measurement. (i) Add some salt to the water in the beaker. Heat the solution until it boils. Then take the reading on G. From your graph, find the corresponding temperature in °C. This is the boiling-point of the solution. See if this agrees fairly well with the temperature measured directly by a mercury thermometer.

(ii) Fill a beaker with water and add some 'hypo' crystals or ammonium nitrate crystals. Place the junction H in the solution. Take the reading on G. Find the temperature from your graph. See if this agrees with a mercury thermometer reading.

EXERCISE 8 · ANSWERS, p. 258

1. The boiling-point of water is . . °C, . . °F.

The freezing-point of water is . . °C, . . °F. (*Mx.*)

2. (*a*) *Calculate* the temperature on the Fahrenheit scale which is the same as 25°C.

(*b*) *Calculate* the temperature on the Celsius (centigrade) scale which is the same as 221°F.

(*c*) On a very cold and frosty day a Fahrenheit thermometer registers 14°. What temperature would be registered on a Celsius (centigrade) thermometer? (*M.*)

3. A clinical thermometer has: (i) a range of temperature from . . to . .; (ii) a . . between bulb and stem; (iii) a well-defined mark at a temperature of . . (*Mx.*)

4. State two advantages and one disadvantage of using mercury as the liquid in a thermometer. Advantages (*a*) . . (*b*) . . Disadvantage . . (*L.*)

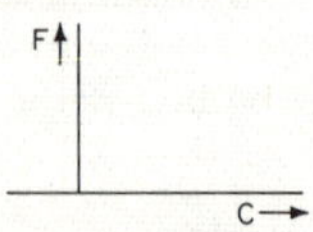

Fig. 8A

5. (*a*) On the axes shown in Fig. 8A draw a line which can be used for the conversion of the Fahrenheit and Celsius scales.

(*b*) Use the graph to convert: (i) 160°F to the Celsius scale; (ii) 20°C to the Fahrenheit scale; (iii) 0°F to the Celsius scale. (*E.A.*)

6. (*a*) Draw a diagram of a thermometer suitable for recording the maximum temperature during a given time. Show clearly where the maximum temperature is read.

(*b*) How may the instrument be reset? (*L.*)

7. The average, normal temperature of the human body is . . °F. Pure water at normal atmospheric pressure boils at . . How does increasing the pressure alter the boiling point? (*S.E.*)

8. (*a*) Draw a labelled diagram of a clinical thermometer.

(*b*) Describe any special features of this thermometer.

(*c*) Explain how a clinical thermometer is more sensitive than an ordinary laboratory thermometer. (*E.A.*)

9. Make a sketch of any thermometer which does not employ a liquid, such as a resistance or thermoelectric thermometer. Label fully the various parts of this and explain how the thermometer is used to read a particular temperature. What are the advantages and disadvantges of the thermometer you have described compared with a mercury-in-glass thermometer? (*M.*)

10. (*a*) What temperature on the Kelvin scale is the same as 0°C?

(*b*) What temperature on the Celsius scale is the same as 373 K?

(*c*) If a temperature increases by 40 degrees on the Celsius scale, what is the increase on the Kelvin scale? (*E.A.*)

11. (*a*) Give the meanings of the terms (i) heat, (ii) temperature, making clear the distinction between them.

(*b*) Draw a simple sketch of a clinical thermometer to show the mercury a short time after the thermometer has been removed from the patient's mouth and has cooled. Explain why the mercury is in this position. Other details of the thermometer are not required.

(*c*) Explain, with the aid of a diagram, one method of measuring temperature which does not involve the expansion of a liquid. Give the principles of the method but details of the structure of the apparatus are not required.

(*d*) Explain why there is a limit to the temperature to which a substance can be cooled. (*E.A.*)

9

EXPANSION OF SOLIDS, LIQUIDS AND GASES

Expansion of Solids

If telegraph wires are observed in winter and in summer it will be noted that the wires sag more in summer. This shows that the length of the wires has increased as the temperature has risen. Observations show that *most materials expand when their temperature increases*, and contract when their temperature decreases.

A simple laboratory experiment to demonstrate the linear expansion of a solid is shown in Fig. 9.1. A long metal pipe B, with rubber tubing

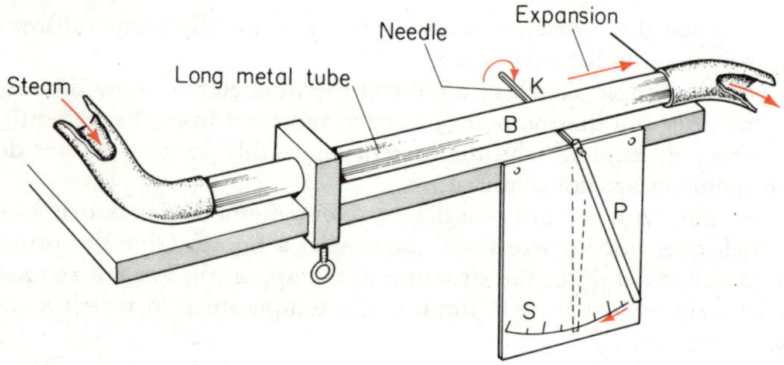

Fig. 9.1 Linear expansion demonstration

at one end, is gripped in a vice at this end. The other end passes over a steel knitting needle K. A long drinking straw P, or a long thin piece of balsa wood, is attached to the end of K. On blowing down B, the pointer P is seen to move over a graduated scale S on a card fixed to the bench. Hot breath has warmed up the tube B which has then expanded slightly. The expansion turns the needle and hence P moves.

When steam is passed through tube B, the pointer P turns round considerably. On allowing B to cool, or pouring cold water over it, P returns to its original reading, showing contraction.

Force due to Expansion

When metals are prevented from expanding or contracting, very large forces are exerted.

This is demonstrated by a 'bar-breaker' experiment Fig. 9.2. A thick steel bar B has a cast-iron pin P at one end and is tightened by a large nut K against a metal frame. The bar is heated by a bunsen burner for a time. As B expands, the nut is continually tightened so that the pin

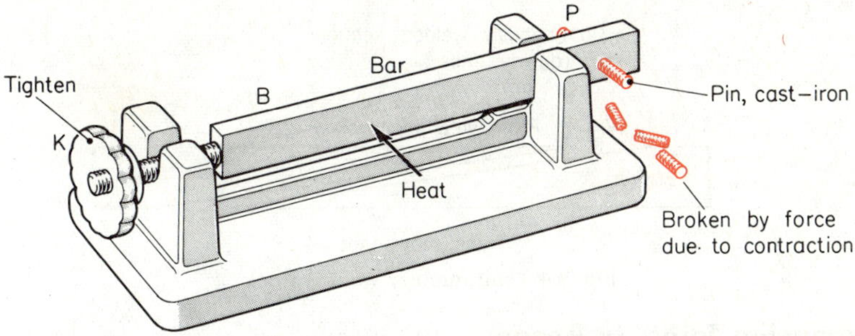

Fig. 9.2 Force due to contraction

P is still tightly held against the frame at the other end. The flame is then removed and B cools. At one stage the cast-iron pin breaks. Thus a large force is exerted when a metal is prevented from contracting. A large force is also exerted when a metal is prevented from expanding.

Continuously Welded Track

Railway tracks have gaps to make allowance for expansion due to temperature rise, otherwise the rails would buckle. In the past years, many miles of conventional railway track have been replaced with long sections of *continuously welded track*. The old track had fish-plate junctions F at short intervals, Fig. 9.3. A 'clickety-click' effect was experienced as the train passed over the jointed parts. The newer and safer track has long rail lengths joined by rigid welds. These are flush with the rail surfaces so that a much smoother train ride is obtained.

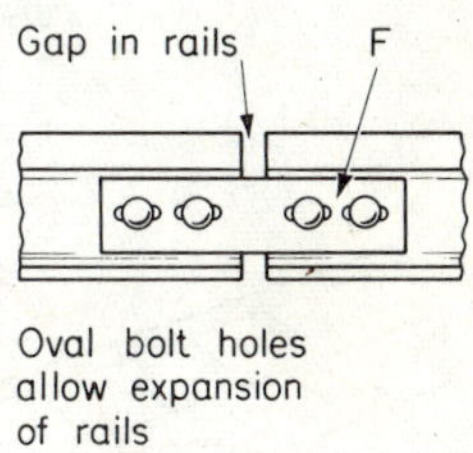

Fig. 9.3 Fish-plate in rail

The expansion of metal which can be expected from a long length of track is correspondingly long. An expansion of up to one foot or 30 cm may be expected. Special expansion joints are therefore used, Fig. 9.4. These joints are made by tapering the ends of the adjacent rail lengths, as shown, and placing them in line. The actual gap w is small and only of the order of half-an-inch or a centimetre. But the total expansion d allowed in the direction of the rails is much larger than w, owing to the long slope. If a conventional fish-plate were used, this could allow only for expansions up to about one inch or two centimetres. A typical continuously-welded expansion joint, however, is about 1–2 m long. It can allow for expansion of about 30 cm of the rail.

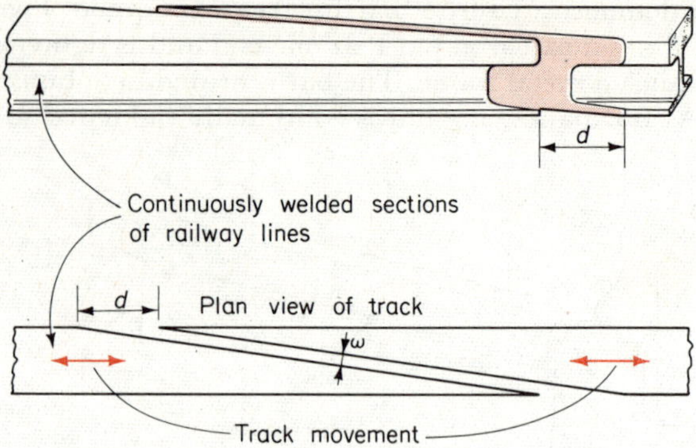

Fig. 9.4 Continuously welded track

Expansion Joints in Roads

Roads are often constructed as a series of reinforced concrete slabs. Since the slabs expand when they get hot, the joints between them are not made rigid. Instead, they are designed to allow for expansion or contraction on temperature changes. A gap of about an inch or a few centimetres is left between the slabs and this is filled with a rubber-tar compound known as *bitumen*. An expansion joint, normally extending at right angles to the direction of traffic, is thus formed, as shown in Fig. 9.5.

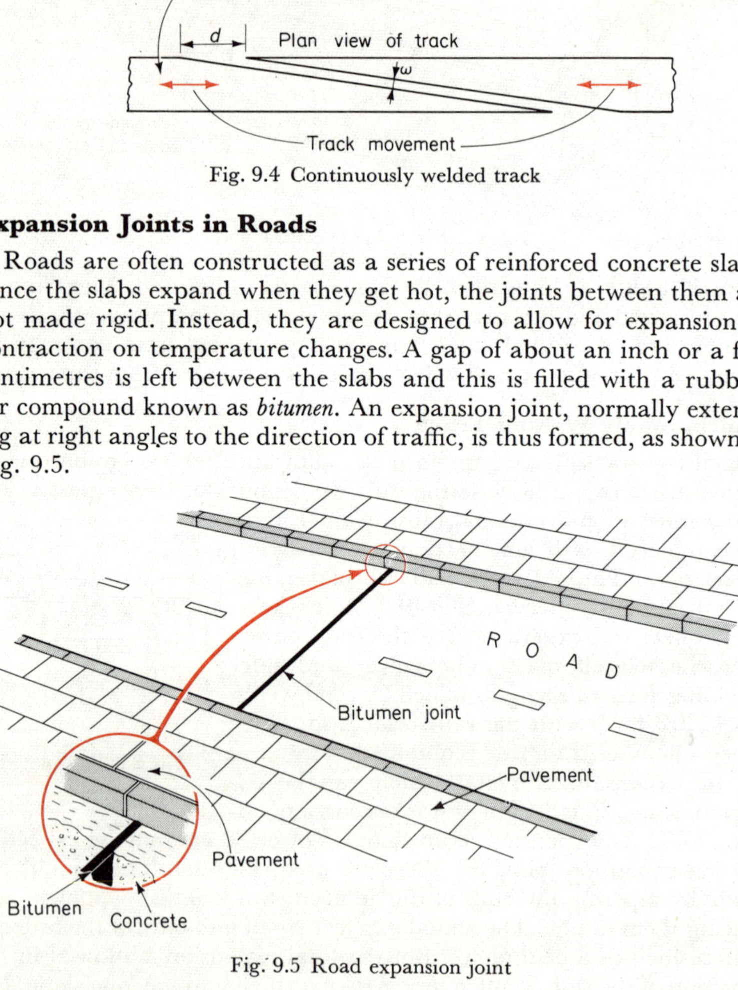

Fig. 9.5 Road expansion joint

When the slabs expand, the bitumen is squeezed out of the gap and the ends of the slabs move closer together. The ridges of bitumen formed can sometimes be felt as a succession of 'bumps' when travelling in a car on a hot day. When the temperature decreases the bitumen returns to the gap as the slabs contract. This keeps the joint sound and waterproof.

Central Heating Expansion Joints

The water pipes in a central heating system undergo considerable changes in temperature when they become hot or when they become cold. Consequently they expand and contract considerably. Special expansion joints are necessary. They allow a pipe to move relative to the connection during expansion or contraction.

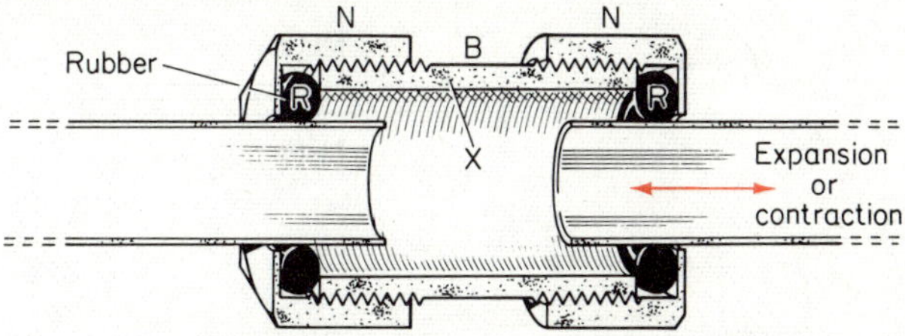

Fig. 9.6 Central heating expansion joint

A typical connection or union X is shown in Fig. 9.6. The pipe P is inserted into the union, and a rubber ring R is slid along the pipe to the union. A specially flanged nut N is then screwed on to the threaded end of the body B of the union. The flange compresses the rubber ring between itself, the pipe and B. This now provides a firm but flexible seal. It allows the pipe to expand or contract without breaking the seal.

Rivets

Steel plates such as those used in shipbuilding or in large boilers are usually riveted together using red-hot rivets. Holes are made in the overlapping plates, A, C, a red-hot rivet is pushed through and its

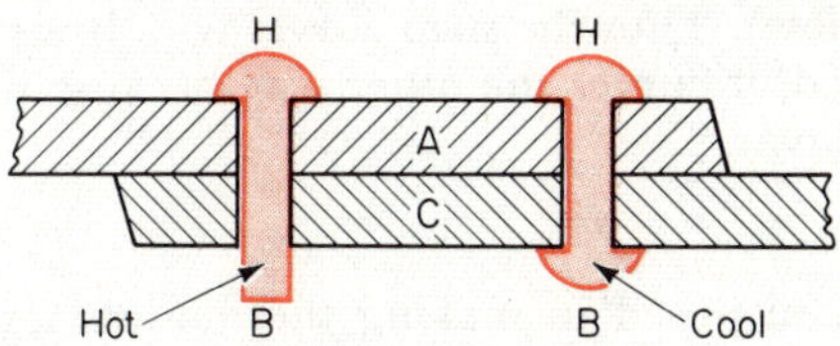

Fig. 9.7 Rivets

head H held tightly against one plate A, Fig. 9.7. The other end B of the rivet is hammered tight against the plate. On cooling, the rivet contracts and holds the plates tightly together. This provides a good seal against the sea for ship plates and against steam in large boilers.

In contrast to riveting, in some engine casings nuts and bolts are secured very tightly by first cooling the bolt in liquid air, until the nut just fits on. When the bolt reaches air temperature, the large force due to expansion of the bolt makes a very tight fit with the nut.

Bimetal Strips

Bimetal strips are widely used in appliances.

A *bimetal strip* can be made by placing two strips of different metals (e.g. brass and iron) side by side and welding them together along their entire length. One end of the bimetal may then be inserted into a wooden handle, Fig. 9.8.

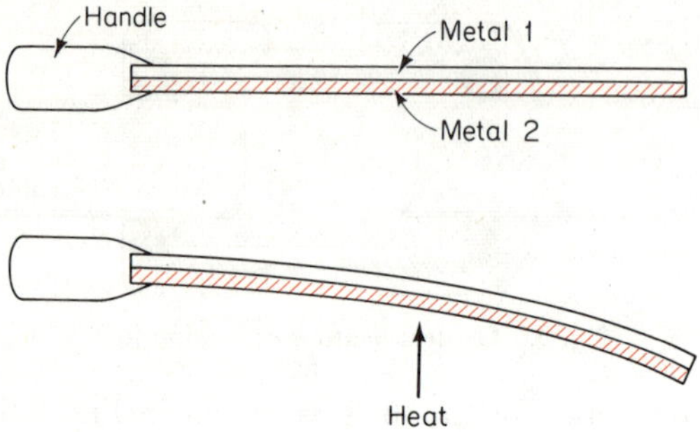

Fig. 9.8 Bimetal demonstration

If the bimetal strip is heated, it curves as shown. Hence *brass expands more than iron* for the same temperature rise.

The bimetal strip straightens when it cools to room temperature. If it were cooled below room temperature the brass would contract more than the iron. The strip would thus curve with the iron on the outside of the curve.

A straight length of thin bimetal, made of brass–invar, is very sensitive to temperature changes. It curves when one end is warmed by a match. Invar is an alloy with an extremely small expansion when warmed (see below). Thus the strip curves with brass on the outside. If the strip is cooled, it curves the other way because the brass contracts more than the invar.

Thermostats

Bimetal strips are used in making thermostats for gas cookers and electric blankets. In a modern gas cooker the temperature is controlled using the very low coefficient of expansion of invar (steel containing 36% nickel). This expands only a millionth of its length per degree C rise in temperature.

Fig. 9.9 illustrates the principle of a gas thermostat. A brass tube Y projecting into the oven, encloses an invar rod X attached to it at one end. A valve is attached at the other end of X and allows gas from the mains to flow through to the burners, as shown. When the oven

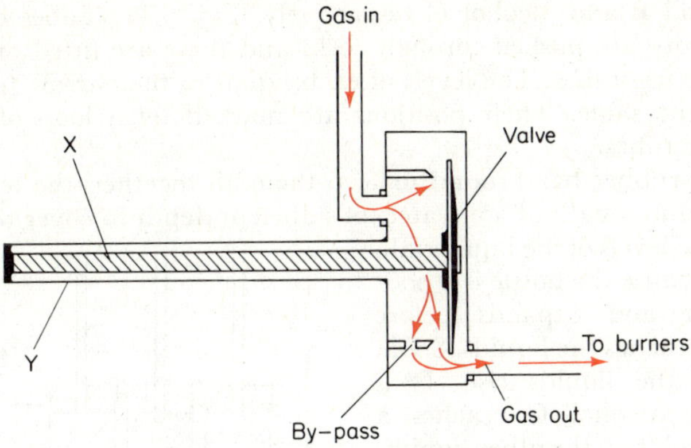

Fig. 9.9 Gas thermostat uses bimetal

temperature rises, the brass tube Y expands and moves to the left, but the invar rod X is practically unaffected. Hence the valve moves to the left nearer its seating and partially closes. The gas flow is then reduced. If the oven temperature decreases, the brass tube Y contracts a little and the valve moves farther away from its seating. The gas flow is then increased. A required oven temperature is set by turning a knob on the regulator. This adjusts the valve opening so that the gas supply is shut off at the required temperature.

Fig. 9.10 shows the principle of an electric thermostat of the type used in electric blankets for maintaining a steady temperature. The blanket contains a length of insulated resistance wire sewn between two

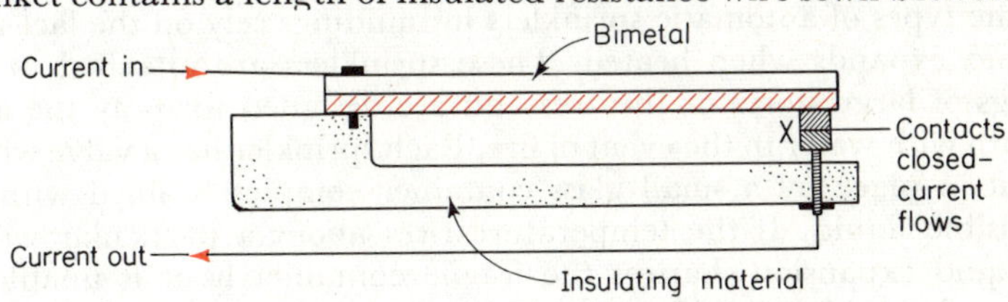

Fig. 9.10 Temperature control by bimetal

layers of blanket material. When the blanket is first switched on the current flows through a bimetal strip to a fixed metal block *via* contacts between them. As the temperature rises the bimetal strip curves away from the block, and at one stage the contacts are broken. The current is then cut off. When the bimetal strip cools down contact is again made at one stage. Current then flows once more to warm up the blanket again as shown.

Expansion of Liquids

The expansion of *liquids* can be demonstrated by filling three large test-tubes (or small flasks) of exactly the same volume with water A, paraffin oil B and alcohol C respectively, Fig. 9.11. Tubes of equal narrow bore are pushed through corks and these are fitted on to the respective test-tubes. The levels of each liquid in the narrow tubes are roughly the same. Their positions are marked by a loop of thread round the tubes.

With a rubber band round to keep them all together, the test tubes are placed in a bath of hot water, of sufficient depth to cover them all. At first the levels of the liquids fall. This is because the bottle is a poor conductor and expands before the heat reaches the liquids. Soon, however, the liquids rise. It is seen that alcohol C reaches a higher level than the other liquids. Thus 1 litre of alcohol, for example, will expand much more than 1 litre of water for the same temperature rise.

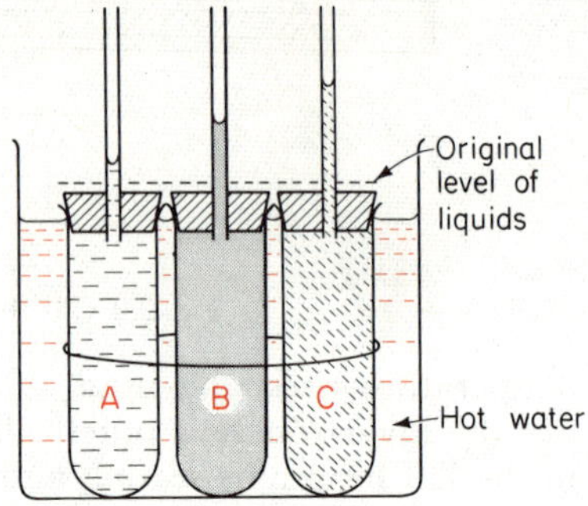

Fig. 9.11 Expansion of liquid

For equal volumes and the same temperature rise, accurate measurements show that paraffin oil B expands about twice as much as water A and alcohol expands about three times as much as water. The expansion of alcohol and of mercury with temperature rise is used in common thermometers (p. 161).

Sprinklers

Some types of automatic sprinklers in buildings rely on the fact that a liquid expands when heated. These sprinklers are attached to the ceilings of large stores or theatres and are designed to spray the area beneath with water in the event of fire. Each sprinkler has a valve which is kept in place by a small glass container completely filled with an expansible liquid. If the temperature rises about a particular value, the liquid expansion shatters the fragile container as it is unable to withstand the high liquid pressure. The valve then opens and allows water to flow out and spray the area affected.

Density of Liquids and Gases

If a beaker of a liquid is heated by a bunsen burner, the liquid at the bottom becomes warm first and expands. Since density = mass/volume, the density of the liquid at the bottom *decreases*. The liquid above is denser. Thus the liquid at the bottom rises. Its place is taken by the colder liquid. This in turn becomes warmed and rises. In this way all the liquid becomes heated, with the warmest or least dense liquid on top.

In the same way, the warmest air in a room is at the top since it is the least dense. The cooler air is at the bottom.

Expansion of Water

Most solids and liquids expand when their temperature rises. Water is unusual in this respect over a small temperature range. From 0° C to about 4° C, when its temperature rises, water actually *contracts* in volume. A liquid such as mercury will expand as its temperature rises from 0° C to 4° C and higher, Fig. 9.12 (i). After about 4° C, water behaves normally. It expands as its temperature rises.

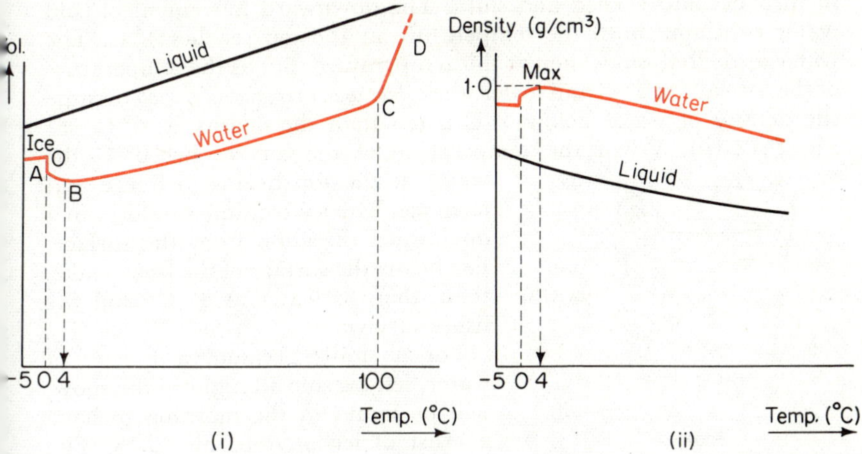

Fig. 9.12 Volume and density change

Fig. 9.12 (i) shows roughly what happens if we start with a block of ice. Ice floats on water—it has a density of about 0·9 g/cm³. This means that 1 g of ice has a volume about $\frac{1}{9}$ more than 1 cm³ or about 1·1 cm³. Water, however, has a density of 1 g/cm³. Thus when 1 g of ice changes to water on melting, 1·1 cm³ of ice changes to 1 cm³ of water, that is, the *volume contracts*. This is shown by the line OA in Fig. 9.12 (i). The point O represents the solid state, ice, and the point A represents the liquid state, or water, after all the ice has melted. From 0° C to 4° C the water contracts. After B the volume increases until the boiling point C is reached at 100° C. The vapour state, or steam, is now formed. About 1600 cm³ of steam is formed from 1 cm³ of water at normal pressure.

Density of Water

The mass of a given quantity of water does not alter when its temperature changes. But if the volume shrinks, *its density* (mass/volume) *increases*. Thus from 0° C to 4° C, the density of water increases. Above 4° C the density decreases. Hence *water has a maximum density at about 4° C*, Fig. 9.12 (ii). Unlike water, the densities of most liquids such as mercury decrease continuously as their temperature rises, since their volume then increases.

The exceptional expansion of water makes it possible for fish to survive in winter-time in Arctic and other cold regions. Consider the air outside a lake, for example, when the temperature begins to fall from say 10° C. The water at the top of the lake then increases in density. It falls to the bottom of the lake, where the water is less dense. Other water takes the place of the water which sinks to the bottom, and this in turn becomes cooled and sinks. The downward movement of cold water continues until the temperature at the top reaches 4° C. The water at the bottom is then at this temperature. But as the temperature of the top falls to 3° C and lower, the *colder water remains at the top* because the density of water below 4° C is *less* than the density at 4° C, see Fig. 9.12 (ii). When the temperature of the air reaches 0° C the water at the top begins to freeze and form ice. The ice continues to form in a downward direction from the surface. Far below the surface of the frozen lake, then, there is water at 4° C; and the fishes survive.

For a similar reason, a bucket of water, left outside all night in the snow, will be found in the morning to have a crust of ice on top, Fig. 9.13. The ice thickens downwards. Below the ice, water at the bottom is at 4° C.

Fig. 9.13 Maximum density of water

Expansion of Gases

The expansion of a *gas* such as air can be observed by using an inverted flask F with a narrow tube T through its cork, dipping into coloured water in a beaker B. Fig. 9.14.

When a warm hand is placed on F, bubbles of air can be seen passing out from T through the water. Some air has expanded and has escaped from the flask F. When the hand is removed, the air left in F cools. This time the liquid rises up the tube T to a height such as A. When the warm hand is placed on F again, the level of A falls rapidly. On cooling F by placing a moist cloth on it, the level of A rises.

The experiment shows that the volume of a gas is very sensitive to temperature change. Charles found a law relating volume and temperature (p. 181).

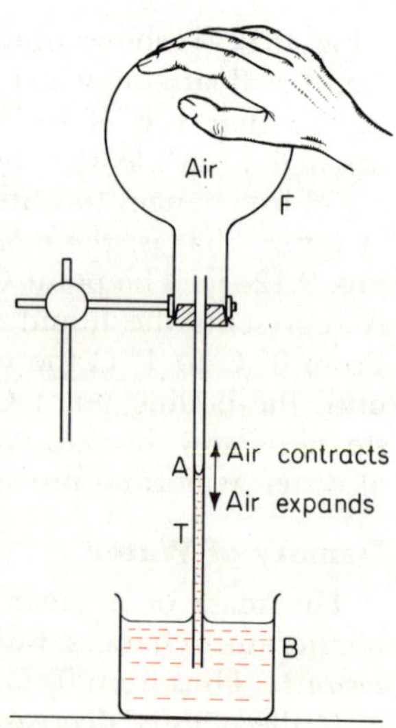

Fig. 9.14 Expansion of air

Molecular Theory of Expansion

On p. 10, we explained that the molecules of *solids* are 'anchored' to particular positions and vibrate about these positions, Fig. 9.15 (i). The maximum displacement of a molecule is called *the amplitude* of the motion. It is represented by the length of the arrow drawn either side of the average position in Fig. 9.15 (i).

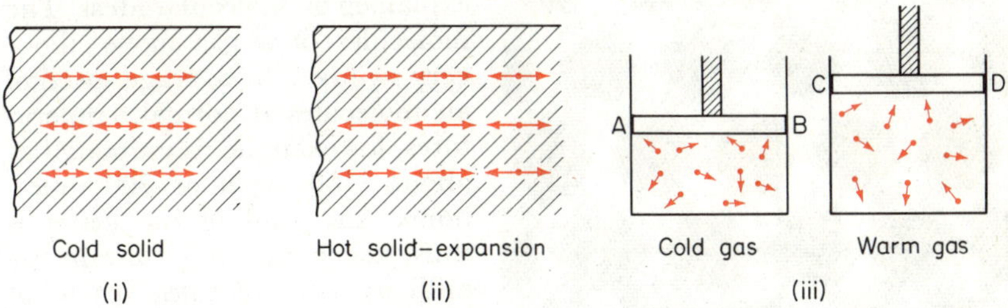

Fig. 9.15 Molecules in heated solid and gas

When the solid is heated, the molecules gain more energy. They now vibrate through a greater amplitude than before. This is represented in Fig. 9.15 (ii) by the longer arrows. As the molecules occupy a greater length than before, the solid has expanded, see Plates 9A, 9B.

The molecules of a *liquid* are mobile. They move about and constantly exchange neighbours. At the same time they vibrate. If we could 'freeze' the movement of the molecules at an instant, their average distance apart would be about the same as that of solids. When the liquid is heated their amplitude of vibration increases. Consequently these molecules occupy a larger volume than before and hence the liquid has expanded.

The molecules of a *gas* are relatively free. At normal pressure, they move about fairly independently of any attraction by neighbours, unlike molecules in solids and liquids, Fig. 9.15 (iii). When the gas is heated, the energy, and hence the speed, of the molecules increases. If they are confined by a piston AB exerting a constant pressure, the molecules now strike the piston with greater momentum than before and push it back to CD, for example. Thus the gas expands.

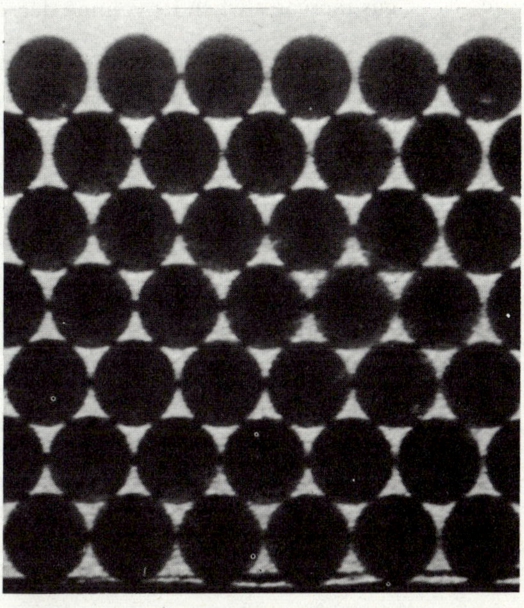

Plate 9(A) Layers of molecules.

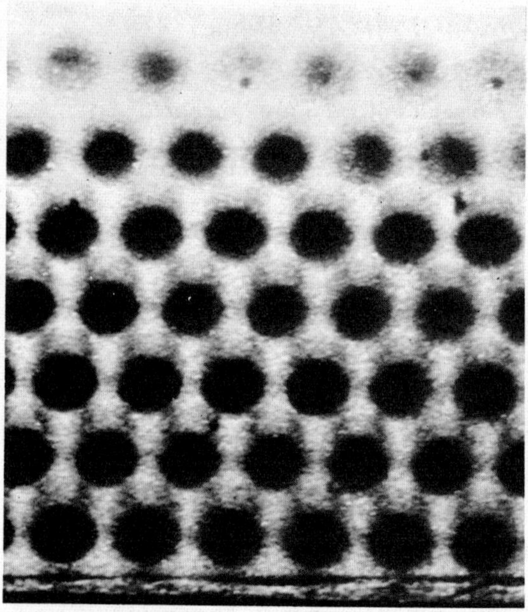

Plate 9(B) Increasing the amplitude of vibration of the molecules, simulating temperature rise, leads to thermal expansion.

Molecular Explanation of Gas Pressure

The pressure of the air or any other gas in a closed vessel can be explained on molecular ideas. The molecules of a gas move about very swiftly. The average speed of air molecules at normal temperatures, for example, is estimated at about 1100 km/h or 700 miles/hour. Any wall of the vessel is thus struck at every instant by millions of molecules, each of which has a tiny mass but very high speed. Since the molecules move about and strike the walls repeatedly, there is an enormous number of impacts per second at the wall. This bombardment produces at the wall a *pressure*. It is the gas pressure. Suppose the gas is kept in a vessel by a piston. If the piston is moved so as to decrease the volume of the gas, the molecules take a shorter time than before to reach a wall as they move about. The number of impacts per second at a wall is hence greater than before. The pressure therefore increases. Thus the pressure of a given mass of gas increases when its volume decreases (see *Boyle's law*, p. 115).

Absolute Zero · Absolute Temperature

The same molecular ideas explain heat and temperature. Heat is a form of energy (p. 206). If a gas is heated, the kinetic energy of the molecules increase, that is, the molecules have an average greater speed than before. If the gas is cooled, the average speed is lowered. Theoretically, the molecules would have zero speed at an extremely low temperature called the *absolute zero*. The gas pressure would then be zero theoretically. In practice, however, a gas liquefies before reaching the absolute zero.

A scale of temperature with the absolute zero as '0 degrees' is widely used by scientists. It is called the *Kelvin* or *absolute scale*, after Lord Kelvin who proposed it. The absolute zero is denoted by 0 K. Experiment shows that 0 K = −273° C (approx). The melting point of ice is 0° C on the Celsius scale. It is thus 273° higher than 0 K on the Kelvin scale, or 273 K. The temperature of steam at normal temperature and pressure, 100° C, is 100° more than 0° C, or 373 K.

SUMMARY

1. Large forces are exerted in expansion or contraction. This is overcome by continuously welded track and expansion joints.

2. Bimetal strip has two metals welded together. When warmed it curves—the metal with greater relative expansion is on the outside. Used in thermostats.

3. When liquids are heated, their density usually decreases. Water is exceptional—it contracts from 0°C to 4°C and then expands; maximum density is about 4°C.

4. Roughly, gases expand relatively about ten times as much as liquids, which expand about ten times as much as solids.

PRACTICAL

1. 'Bimetal' demonstration

Method. (i) Cut a strip of aluminium foil and a strip of writing paper of dimensions about 15 cm by 1 cm (or 6 in by $\frac{1}{2}$ in).

(ii) Paste the two strips together so that they form a composite strip. *Press this strip flat* and allow it to dry thoroughly.

(iii) Warm the strip over a radiator—or on a gauze on a tripod with a very low flame below. Note how the strip curls. Which material is on the outside—aluminium or paper? Which expands more?

(iv) Allow the strip to cool and note that happens. (Be careful not to overheat the strip, otherwise the aluminium will break away from the paper and a 'bimetal' effect is not obtained).

Also, apply a little paste all along a paper strip. Allow to dry. Place the strip on a radiator—or on a gauze on a tripod with a very low flame below. Observe and account for what happens.

2. Linear expansion

Join a metre length of thin Constantan wire, 24–32 s.w.g. to two rods A and B in clamps. Fig. 9.16. Place A and B apart so that the wire is reasonably

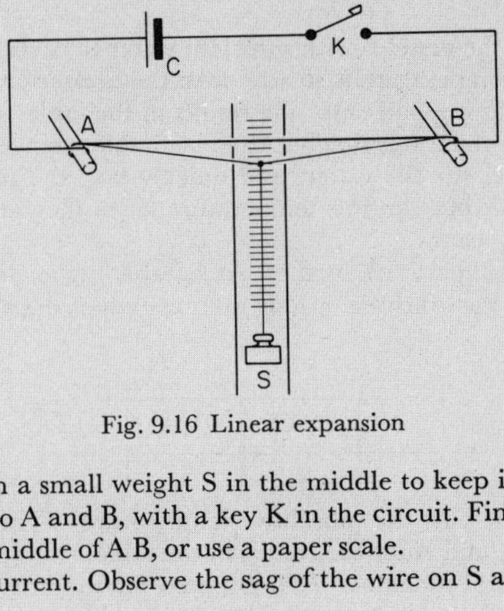

Fig. 9.16 Linear expansion

straight and attach a small weight S in the middle to keep it taut. Connect an accummulator C to A and B, with a key K in the circuit. Finally, place a metre rule S behind the middle of A B, or use a paper scale.

Switch on the current. Observe the sag of the wire on S as the wire becomes hot. Switch off the current, allow the wire to cool, and observe the contraction on S.

Can you suggest a way to magnify the sag by a lever method?

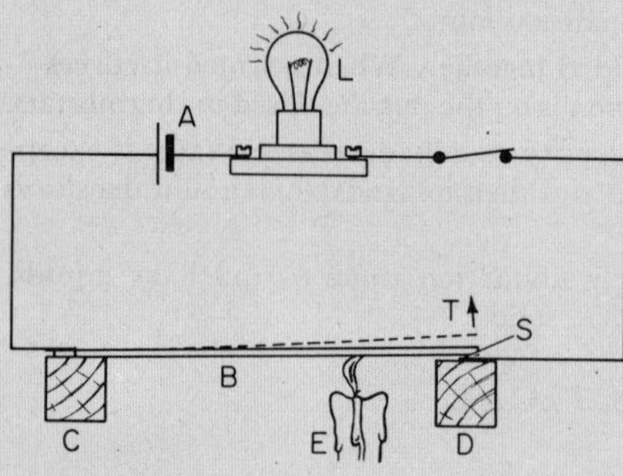

Fig. 9.17 Bimetal flashing unit

3. Bimetal flashing unit

Attach a thin flexible length of bimetal (brass-invar) strip B to a block of wood C by a nail. Fig. 9.17. The more expansible material of B should be underneath so that the bimetal curves upwards from S to T on warming—this can be found by using a match or taper first below B before fixing it to C. Place another block of wood D with a nail S protruding at the other end of B so that B makes contact with S.

Join one pole of an accumulator A to the nail at C. Join a bulb B of suitable voltage between the nail S and the other pole of A. The bulb L should then light—if not, clean the contacts. Place a lighted candle E below the bimetal so that B becomes warm. Observe what happens and explain.

4. Volume expansion of liquids.

As explained on p. 174, compare the expansion of different liquids such as water, paraffin oil or olive oil and alcohol.

5. Expansion of gas

Pull the neck of a balloon over the top of an empty flask. Warm the flask with the hands and observe what happens. Warm the flask gently with a low flame and observe what happens.

6. Pressure change of gas at constant volume with temperature change.

Apparatus. Round bottomed flask A, large beaker B, thermometer C, Bourdon gauge G connected to the sealed flask by rubber tubing, bunsen burner. Fig. 9.18.

Method. (i) Fill the vessel B with sufficient water to cover nearly all the flask.

(ii) When the temperature is steady, take the pressure reading of the air in A and the temperature, and enter the results in the table.

(iii) Now warm the water slowly. After a suitable temperature such as 30°C, remove the burner, stir the water, and quickly take the readings of both the pressure p of the air in A and its temperature when they are steady. Enter the results in the table below.

(iv) Raise the temperature further. At suitable higher temperatures, say in steps of 15°–20°C, record three or four more values of the air temperature and pressure.

Measurements.

p	t (°C)	T (K)	p/T

Calculation. Work out the absolute temperature T in kelvin (K) from $T = 273 + t$ (°C), and enter the results in the table.

(i) Plot a graph of p against T, using zero for the origin of both axes. Is your graph consistent with the gas law which states: For a fixed mass of gas at constant volume, *the pressure is proportional to the absolute temperature*?

(ii) Work out the ratio p/T for each result. Enter your values in the table. From your values, can you say that $p \propto T$?

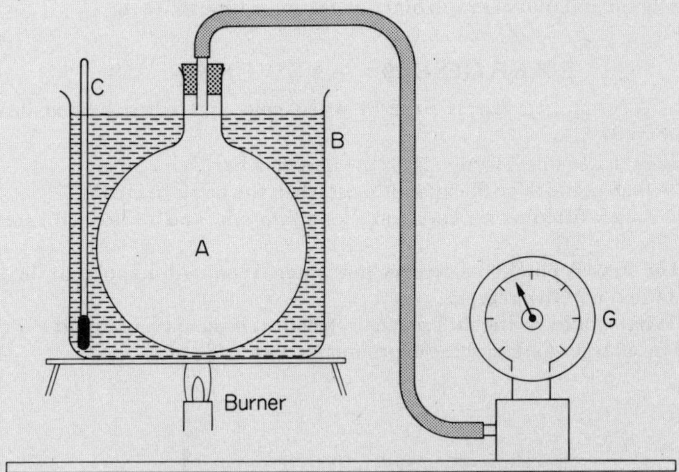

Fig. 9.18 Pressure—temperature change of gas

7. Maximum density of water (p. 175)

Apparatus. Beaker, two thermometers; two clamps and stands; ice.

Method. (i) Fill the beaker C with water nearly to the top.

(ii) Clamp one thermometer B with its bulb near the surface and the other A with its bulb near the bottom of the water. Fig. 9.19.

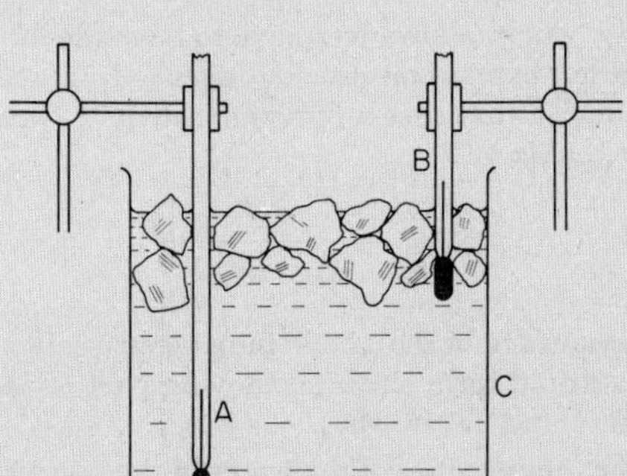

Fig. 9.19 Maximum density of water

(iii) Add a large quantity of crushed ice to the water. Observe the fall in temperature on A and on B. After a considerable time such as half an hour, record the temperatures on A and on B (see also *Additional* p. 182).

Measurements. Temperature on A = . . °C
Temperature on B = . . °C.

Conclusion. From the experiment an approximate value for the temperature of maximum density of water is . . °C.

Additional. Take the temperatures of A and B after equal intervals of time such as 2 min and plot of graph of temperature v. time for each.

EXERCISE 9 · ANSWERS p. 258

1. (*a*) A compound bar is straight when cold and when heated bends as shown Fig. 9A (i).

(i) Suggest *two* suitable metals for use in such a bar. A is . . B is . .

(ii) Which metal A or B, expands most when the bar is heated?

(*b*) A flask is fitted with a cork and a long thin tube and is filled with coloured water. Fig. 9A (ii).

(i) The flask is plunged into very hot water. What will happen to the liquid level marked L? Give reasons.

(ii) What would be the difference in the effect if the flask of liquid F were replaced by a larger flask and the experiment repeated? (*M.*)

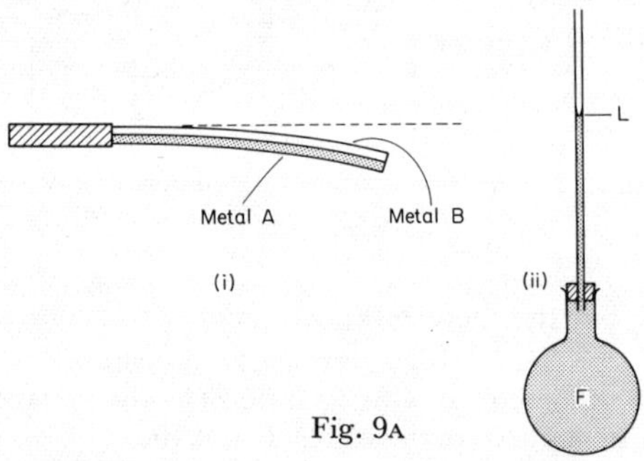

Fig. 9A

2. Name one case where allowances have to be made for expansion . . Name one solid that does not expand on heating (over normal temperature range) . . Name one useful device that uses a bimetallic strip . . Name one metal with a low melting-point . . (*Mx.*)

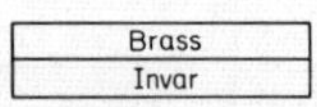

Fig. 9B

3. Draw the appearance of the above bimetal strip after it has been heated. Fig. 9B. This strip would form the vital moving part of an apparatus called a thermostat used in . . and . . (*W.Md.*)

4. (i) What is the temperature of the water in the pond Fig. 9C: (*a*) at X; (*b*) at Y?

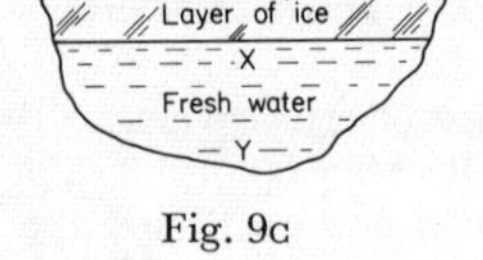

Fig. 9C

(ii) What property of the ice slows down the complete freezing of the water in the pond? (*E.A.*)

5. When equal volumes of a gas, a liquid and a solid at 15°C are heated to 25°C: (*a*) the gas expands less than the liquid; (*b*) the gas expands more than the liquid; (*c*) the liquid expands more than the gas; (*d*) the solid expands more than the gas; (*e*) the solid expands more than the liquid. (*E.A.*)

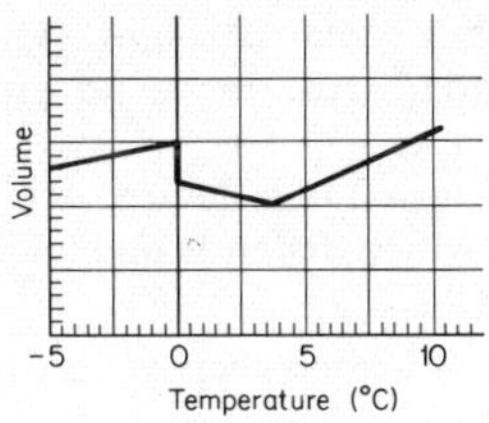

Fig. 9D

6. The graph shows how the volume of a fixed mass of water changes with temperature between −5°C and 10°C. Fig. 9D. Complete the table below to show how the density of the water changes over the various temperature ranges.

	−5°C to 0°C	0°C to 4°C	4°C to 10°C
Density			

7. Fig. 9E shows a simplified diagram of a compensated balance wheel of a watch.

(*a*) Why is the balance wheel compensated?
(*b*) Which metal expands the more? (*E.A.*)

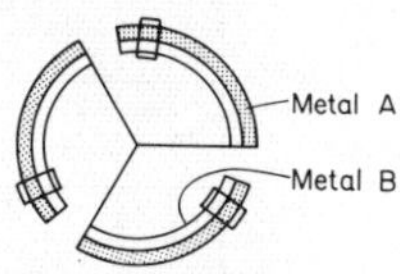

Fig. 9E

8. (*a*) Give a detailed account of an experiment which shows that a metal contracts with great force when it is cooled.

(*b*) Explain how rivets hold the plates of a boiler together so well that the joints are watertight.

(*c*) Explain, with the aid of a diagram, the action of any one kind of thermostat. (*M.*)

9. Describe in detail all the changes that take place when ice at −10°C is heated to become water at 10°C. If you now place a large cube of metal cooled to—60°C into this water, what would occur? (*W.Md.*)

10. (*a*) Under normal conditions the temperature of pure water cannot be raised above a certain maximum. What is this temperature, and what change in conditions would enable the temperature to be raised still further?

(*b*) (i) Mercury and alcohol are commonly used in thermometers. State the advantages and disadvantages of each liquid; (ii) describe briefly how you would check the fixed points of a thermometer.

(*c*) A mass of ice which is initially below melting temperature is steadily and slowly heated. The temperature is read at half-minute intervals until boiling water is obtained. The results are plotted on a graph. Sketch the type of graph you would expect, and comment on the curve you obtain (*S.E.*)

11. (*a*) When two strips of identical dimensions, one of brass and the other iron, are heated separately they remain straight. When they are riveted together to form a bimetallic strip, and heated, they bend with the brass on the outside of the curve. Explain why this is so.

(*b*) Draw a good, clear diagram of a device such as a thermostat, fire alarm, winking electric lights, etc., which depends upon a bimetallic strip for its operation. Explain how it works. (*S.E.*)

12. (*a*) A fixed mass of gas is heated keeping its pressure constant. The following set of readings was taken:

Volumes	cm³	19·40	20·65	21·95	23·05	24·85	25·95
Temperatures	°C	0	17	35	50	75	90

Plot a volume-temperature graph for these results.

(i) At what temperature does the volume of the gas become 22 cm³?

(ii) What is the volume of the gas at 80°C?

(iii) At what temperature (according to graphs of this type) does the volume of the gas become zero? What name is given to this temperature?

(*b*) How does the molecular theory of matter account for the fact that most solids expand when they are heated? (*S.E.*)

13. It is possible to use the apparatus shown in Fig. 9F (i) as a thermometer to measure air temperature.

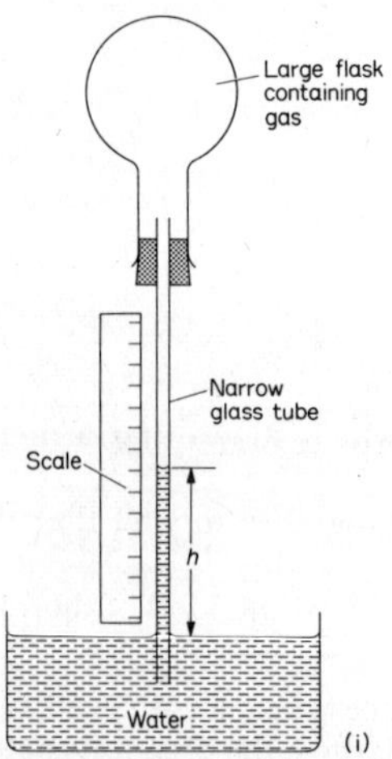

(i)

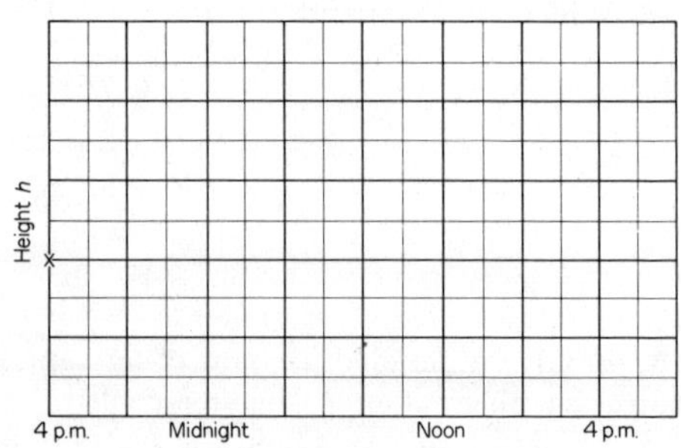

(ii)

Fig. 9F

(i) Explain how it works.

(ii) Plot the graph you would expect if the thermometer was placed out of doors at 4 p.m. on a summer's day and readings taken say every few hours for a period of 24 hours. (The first reading has been marked in Fig. 9F (ii).)

(iii) State any disadvantage that this thermometer might have. (*M.*)

10

CONDUCTION · CONVECTION RADIATION

Conduction

THE end of a spoon dipping into hot tea, and the handle of a poker in a fire, both become hot in a short time. This is an example of *conduction* of heat along metals.

If two rods of similar dimensions, one of iron and the other of glass, are held in a bunsen flame the end of the iron soon feels warm, but the end of the glass does not. Some solids thus conduct heat well; others are poor conductors. This can also be shown by the following experiment.

Conductivities of Copper and Wood

Take a long wooden rod, wind some copper foil tightly round the middle and nail the foil to the rod, Fig. 10.1. Then wind a piece of paper round the rod so that it overlaps the wood and copper, and stick

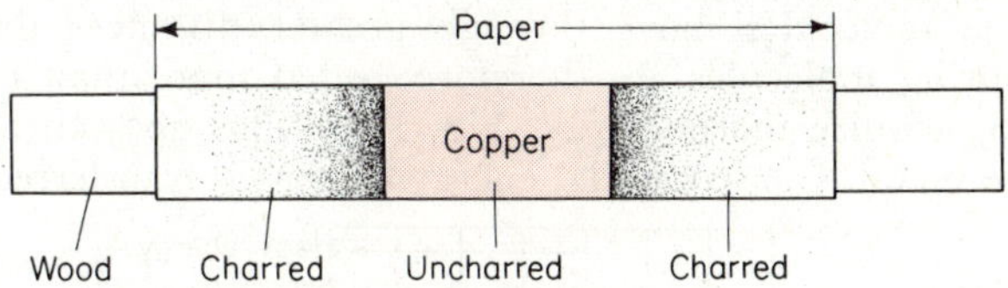

Fig. 10.1 Good and bad conductor

it so that it makes firm contact with them, excluding the air. Hold one end of the rod and move it to and fro so that the paper passes repeatedly through the flame of a bunsen burner. Observe that the paper is unaffected where it covers the copper, but is charred where it covers the wood.

Conclusion. Since the temperature of the paper round the copper stays below the burning point, the heat of the flame is conducted away quickly by the copper. Conversely, heat is conducted away slowly by the wood because the paper becomes charred. Thus copper is a good conductor, wood is a bad conductor.

Experiment to Compare Roughly Conductivities of Metals

The apparatus is set up as shown in Fig. 10.2. Essentially it consists of a watertight container filled with some water which can be heated

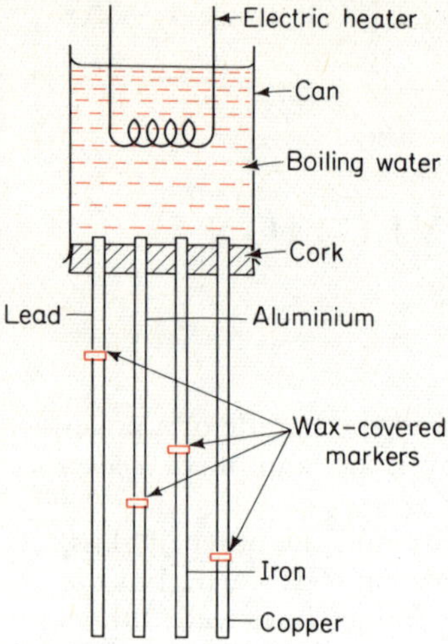

Fig. 10.2 Metals have different conductivities

electrically. Rods of metal of equal size, such as copper, lead, aluminium and iron, project vertically from the base, so that the ends are heated by the hot water. Small rings, which just slide on the rods, are coated with paraffin wax and slid to the top. The rods are also coated with wax.

The heater is switched on, and soon the top of the rods reach a high temperature. As heat is conducted along the rods the wax inside the ring melts and the ring now moves farther down. After a while it can be seen that the ring has travelled farthest down the copper rod and least down the lead rod, showing that copper is a much better conductor than any of the four metals and that lead is the worst conductor.

Molecular Explanation. In conduction, heat is transferred from particle to particle throughout a body without any visible signs of movement. Our theory of solids on p. 177, however, tells us that their molecules are vibrating, and when one end of a metal is heated the energy supplied makes the molecules move through greater distances than before. Neighbouring molecules are therefore jostled more than before, and they, too, acquire more energy, Fig. 10.3. This goes on all the way along the metal. Consequently, energy or heat is transferred along the

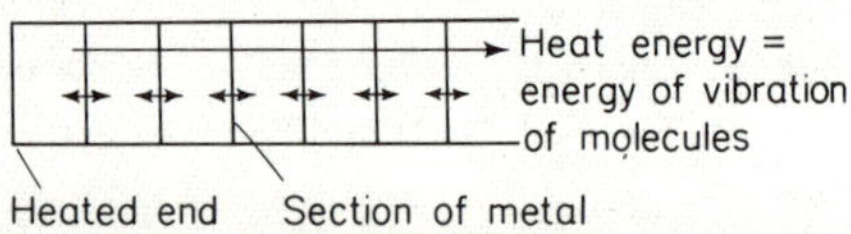

Fig. 10.3 Molecular explanation of conduction

metal, without any alteration in the *average* position of each molecule.

Manufacturers can provide heat-sensitive paper for comparing roughly the thermal conductivities of metals. The passage of heat along a metal is shown by a colour change in the paper.

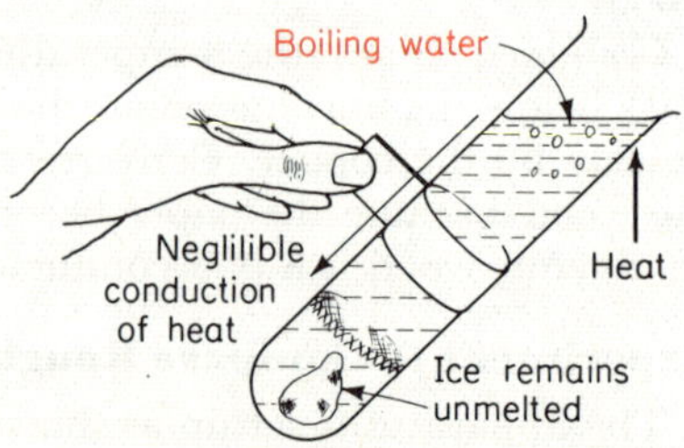

Fig. 10.4 Water is a poor conductor

Conductivity of Liquids

We can investigate the conductivity of water by the following experiment:

By using a piece of metal gauze

above or round it, keep a lump of ice at the bottom of a test-tube filled with water, Fig. 10.4. Hold the tube inclined with a paper grip and bring the top to a bunsen flame as shown. After a time the water at the top is seen to boil, but the ice below remains unaffected. Thus little heat is conducted from the top to the bottom of the water.

Conclusion. Water is a poor conductor.

Generally, substances which are liquids at ordinary temperatures are poor conductors, with the exception of mercury.

Ignition Point of Gas

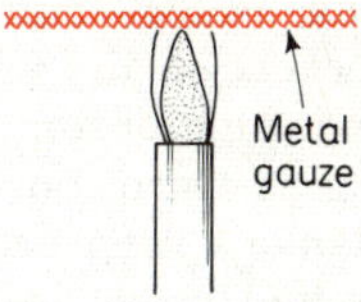

Fig. 10.5 Ignition point of gas

Gases burn when their ignition point or temperature is reached, but if a metal, a good conductor, is placed in the gas it can affect the ignition point.

Place a metal gauze a short distance above a bunsen burner. Turn on the gas and apply a light *below* the gauze. The gas is seen to burn here, but no flame is obtained above the gauze, Fig. 10.5.

Repeat the experiment with a cool gauze, but this time light the gas *above* the gauze. A flame is obtained above the gauze but not below.

Explanation. The metal gauze is a good conductor. It therefore conducts the heat of the flame away rapidly from the gas on the unlighted side, so that the gas here never reaches its ignition point. When the gauze becomes red-hot this gas may be ignited.

Davy Safety Lamp

At the beginning of the 19th century Sir Humphry Davy, an eminent scientist of the day, was urged to invent a device to protect miners from gas explosions, mainly due to methane, caused by naked flames used for lighting at that time. The result was the Davy safety lamp, in which a gauze metal cylinder surrounds a burning wick 'fed' by oil from the base, Fig. 10.6. Holes at the top of the cover let the air in and the combustion products out. As in the demonstration with the metal gauze in Fig. 10.5, the heat of the flame is conducted away from any dangerous gas outside. It is thus kept below its ignition point. When there is inflammable gas in the mine it enters through the gauze and burns with a blue flame outside the white flame of the oil, indicating its presence.

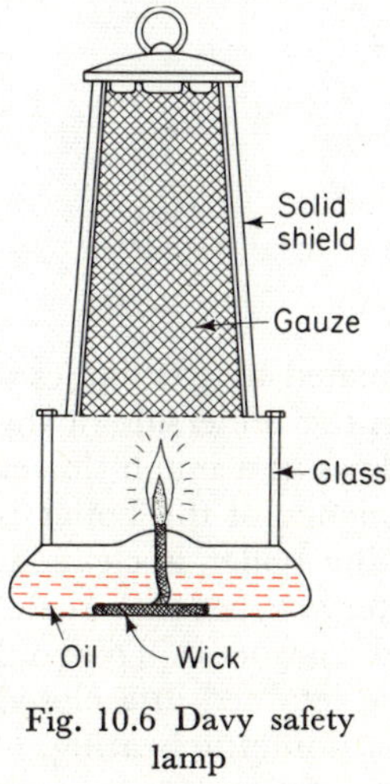

Fig. 10.6 Davy safety lamp

Good and Bad Conductors

In the kitchen, saucepans are made of metal such as aluminium, which is light and a good heat conductor. Thus heat passes quickly from the gas burner, or electric-cooker filament, to the food inside. The handles of the saucepans, however, must be made of insulators, such as plastic or wood materials, so that the utensils can be handled when hot. The handles of kettles and oven doors must likewise be made of insulators.

Air, like all gases, conducts heat extremely slowly, and is therefore a very good insulator. Pockets of air account for the insulation properties of many materials, of which wool is one example. In winter birds look 'fatter' than in summer. They fluff their feathers more to trap pockets of air, which help to keep them warm. If you examine the underside of some car bonnets you will find a felting which keeps the engine warm on account of the many pockets of air in the material. Blankets keep people warm by trapping pockets of air, Fig. 10.7. A quilted cover insulates the hot-water tank in the domestic heating system for the same reason, Fig. 10.8.

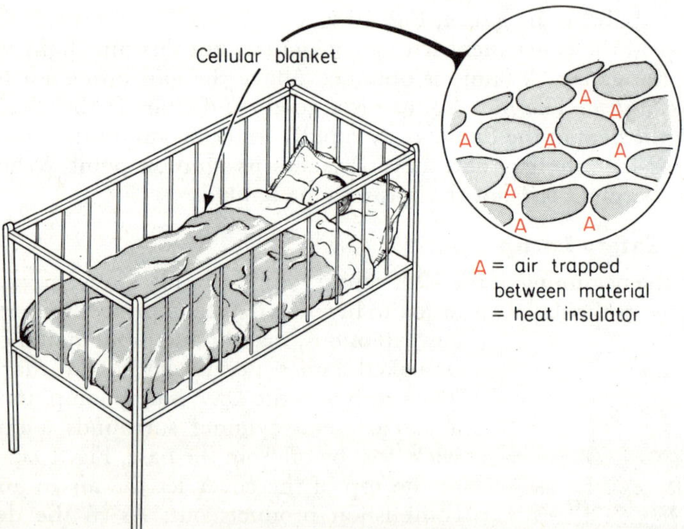

Fig. 10.7 Heat insulation

When large steel boilers used in industry are heated by gas flames a thin layer of gas may be permanently present on the underside of the boiler. As the gas is an insulator, the heat now flows at a much slower rate to water inside, and hence the thermal efficiency of the boiler is lower. Periodically, therefore, the underside of the boiler is cleaned. The inside of the boiler is also cleaned at intervals because scale, deposited from the minerals in the water, is a bad conductor. To avoid further deposit of scale, the same water should be retained in a closed hot-water system such as that used in the home for domestic heating.

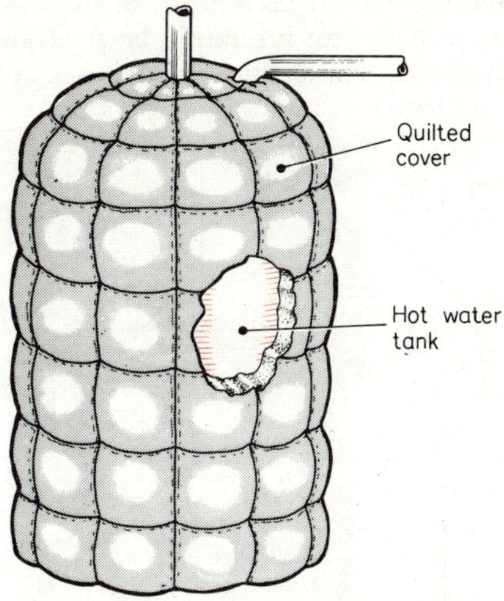

Fig. 10.8 Tank insulation

Heat Insulation in the Home

Any heat which is allowed to escape from a house in winter will add to the bills for fuel. Heat losses may occur through the ceiling, the loft, the chimneys and the walls, doors and windows. Fibre glass or felt can be used to insulate the loft, Fig. 10.9. Expanded polystyrene, a light material full of pockets of air, is an excellent insulator. Floors can be insulated by having a thick layer of felt under the carpet. Double

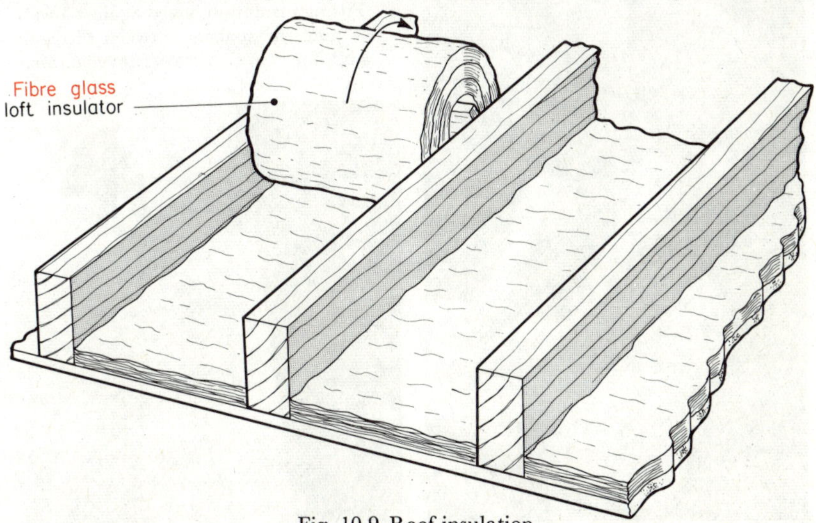

Fig. 10.9 Roof insulation

glazing of windows, widely used in the Scandinavian countries and the Soviet Union, provides an insulating layer of air between the outside and inside windows. This reduces heat losses appreciably, Fig. 10.10. See Plates 10A, 10B.

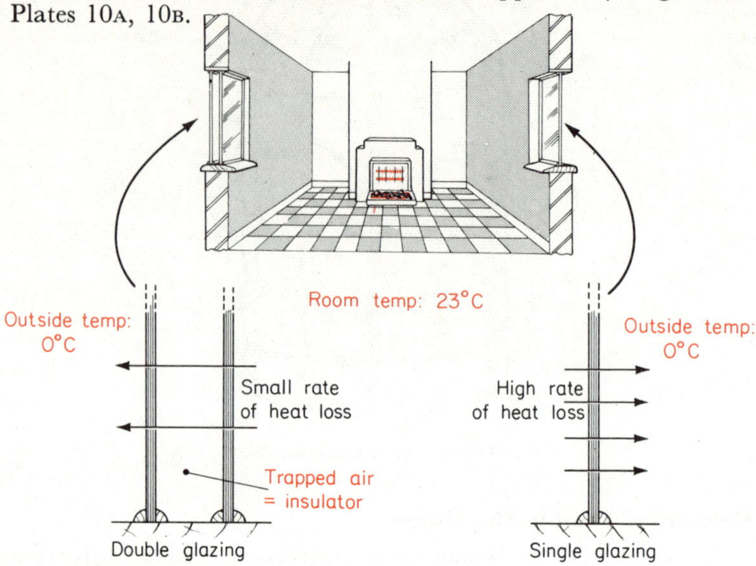

Fig. 10.10 Double glazing

Plate 10(A) Laying fibreglass in a loft to provide heat insulation.
Plate 10(B) Domestic heat insulation. Fitting insulation board against a wall—note the spacers between the wall and board which trap a layer of air.

Convection Currents in Liquids

By using a long glass tube, drop a tiny crystal of potassium permanganate through it to the bottom of a flask filled with water, Fig. 10.11. Now gently heat the bottom of the flask just below the crystal. Observe the upward movements of the coloured liquid from the region of the crystal, which dissolves slowly and helps to show the liquid movement.

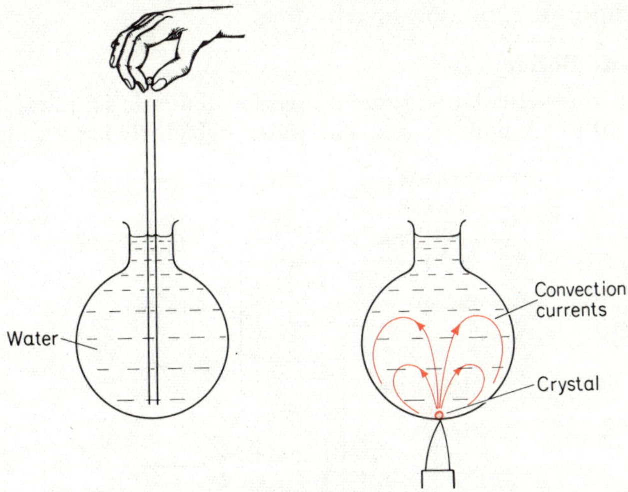

Fig. 10.11 Convection currents in liquid

The upward movement of the coloured liquid is due to *convection* and the circulation of liquid is called a *convection current*. It is due to the effect of heat at the bottom of the liquid. Heat causes a fluid (liquid or gas) to expand. This makes the warm fluid less dense than the cold fluid above it, and it therefore rises. The cold and denser fluid takes its place by moving down. The phenomenon is called *convection*. Unlike the case of conduction, where the average position of the molecules remain the same, the heat is carried to other parts of the liquid by

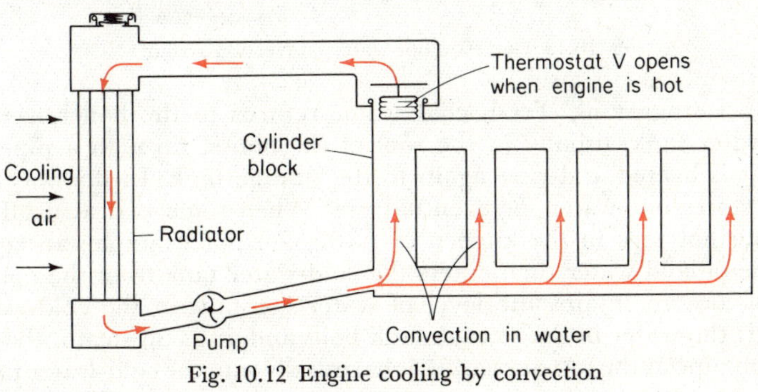

Fig. 10.12 Engine cooling by convection

movement of the warm liquid itself. In boiling water in a kettle, then, convection currents circulate continually, keeping the water stirred up as it is heated.

As shown in Fig. 10.12, water circulates by convection currents round the engine of a car and keeps it cool. Air round the radiator provides the initial cooling of the water, and a pump helps the circulation. A thermostat, which opens when the engine rises to a suitable high temperature, prevents overheating.

Domestic Boiler

A hot-water circulation system, used for domestic supplies, is shown in Fig. 10.13. A boiler heats cold water, which then rises up a pipe

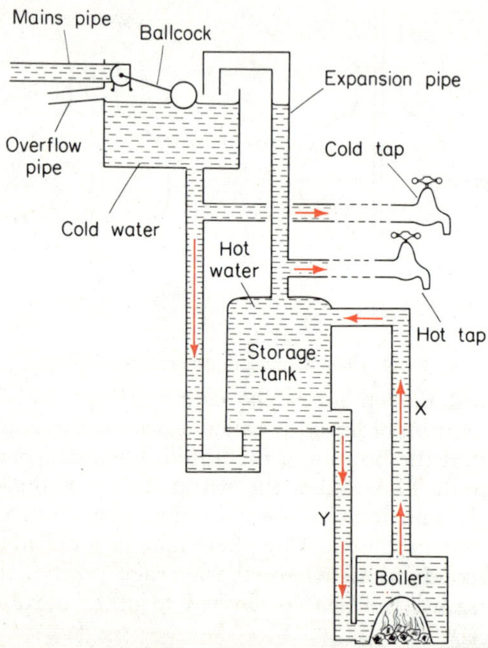

Fig. 10.13 Domestic hot-water convection system

X to a storage tank. Fresh cold water returns to the boiler from a cold-water tank, usually in the roof of the house, through a pipe Y. Here it is heated and rises again to the storage tank. In this way the latter stores hot water for eventual use. When some is drawn off by opening hot taps in the kitchen or bathroom, for example, an equal volume of cold water then enters the cold-water tank from the mains. A ball-cock maintains the level of water constant in the cold-water tank. If the water in the storage tank boils and gives off steam, the expansion pipe at the top discharges it harmlessly into the cold-water tank.

Convection in Gases

Convection of heat occurs much more readily in gases than in liquids because they expand very considerably when their temperature rises (p. 176).

A simple demonstration of convection currents in air can be given with the apparatus in Fig. 10.14. It consists of a closed rectangular box (such as a shoe box) with a plane glass front so that the interior is visible. Two wide glass tubes are fixed in holes at the top of the box as 'chimneys'. A candle is now lit below one tube X and a smouldering taper is held above the other tube Y. The smoke movement shows that an air convection current passes down through Y and up through X.

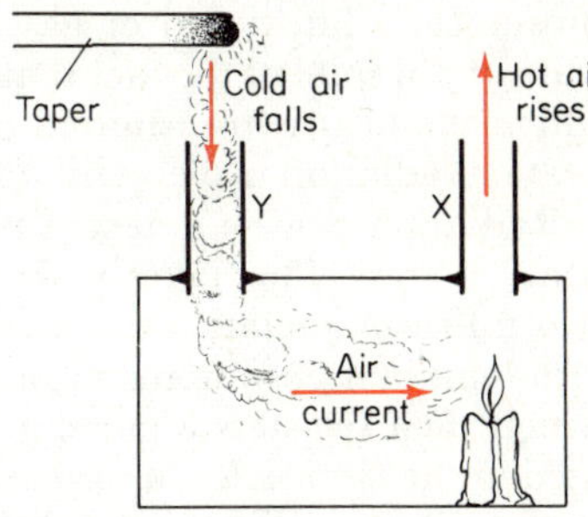

Fig. 10.14 Convection air currents

Explanation. The air above the candle flame becomes hot and less dense and rises up X. Colder air then flows down Y and takes its place, giving rise to a circulating convection current.

Chimneys help to circulate fresh air in rooms in this way.

Land and Sea Breezes

Land and sea breezes on the coast are natural convection currents. In summer in daytime the sun warms the land to a higher temperature than the sea, as it has a lower specific heat than sea-water and the sea is in continual motion. The air above the land is heated and rises, and

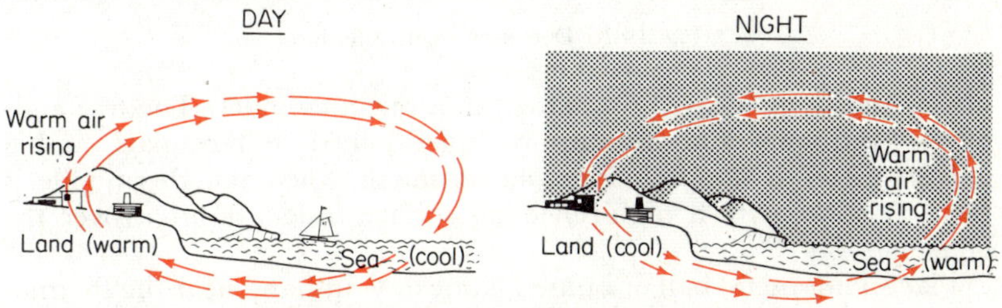

Fig. 10.15 Natural convection currents

its place is taken by cooler air above the sea moving inland, Fig. 10.15. Air higher in the atmosphere completes the circulation, and hence a *sea-breeze* is obtained.

At night the sea temperature drops only slightly, since it is warmed to a considerable depth during the day. On the other hand, the land temperature drops considerably at night. This time, therefore, a convection current is obtained in the opposite direction to daytime, and this is a *land-breeze*. Fig. 10.15.

Radiation

When the sun rises over the horizon in the early morning one can immediately feel its heat. The heat of the sun reaches us by *radiation*. In the transfer of heat by conduction and convection, some material substance, solid, liquid or gas, must be present. But we feel the sun's warmth, in spite of the fact that the space high above the earth through which the heat is transmitted contains practically no matter. Radiant heat or radiation travels with the speed of light (p. 272).

Radiation can be detected by converting the heat energy into electrical energy. This takes place when the heat falls on the junction of two different metals, the other end of the metals being joined to the terminals of a galvanometer, a sensitive current-measuring instrument, which then registers a current. Bismuth and antimony are two metals used in the *thermopile*, an instrument for detecting radiant heat. In order to magnify the effect, many bismuth–antimony junctions are joined in series. The radiation then falls on a set of junctions at one end, as shown in Fig. 10.16. The metal bars are carefully insulated from each

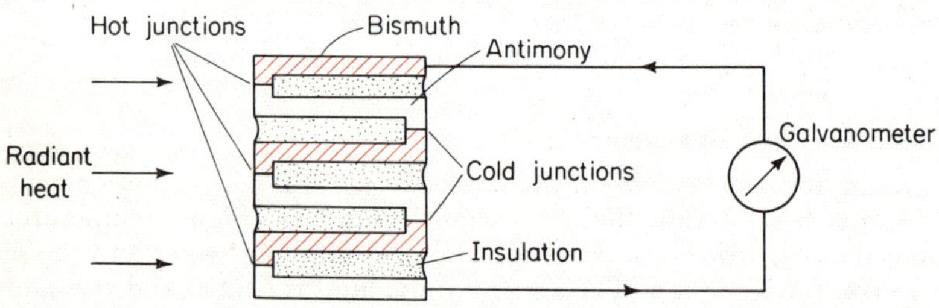

Fig. 10.16 Detecting heat radiation

other, and then encased, insulated, in a metal cylinder. The free ends of the antimony and bismuth bars are joined to terminals, and a galvanometer is connected to the terminals when the thermopile is used. A cone, with a high-reflecting surface inside, is fitted over the end.

Place a hot metal ball or bunsen flame or your hand near the thermopile cone and observe the galvanometer deflection.

Radiation from Different Surfaces

The magnitude of the radiation from different surfaces kept at the same temperature can be investigated with the aid of a hollow cube of metal, called a *Leslie cube* after the inventor, Sir John Leslie, Fig. 10.17. One vertical side is coated dull black (a candle flame can be used for this purpose), another side is highly polished silvery-bright, and the remaining two sides painted with different colours such as grey and white.

Fill the cube with hot water. Place the thermopile close to the cube, so that the cone would intersect the vertical face of the cube if it is imagined to be produced to the cube. Turn the cube round so that each

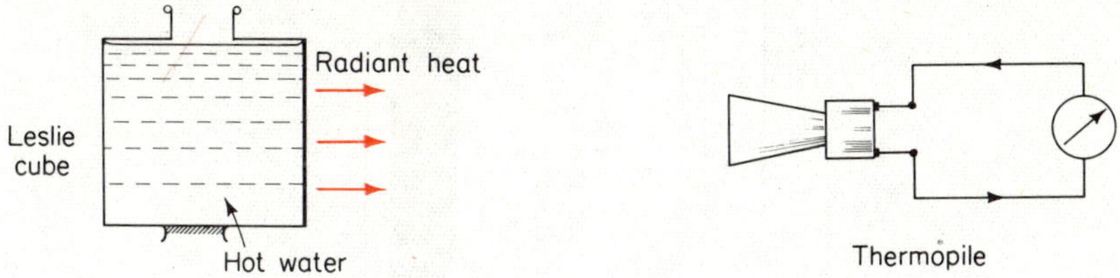

Fig. 10.17 Radiation from different surfaces

face in turn is presented to the cone, which collects the radiation. Record the steady deflection each time. Repeat the experiment with hotter water and compare your results.

Results. The dull black surface produces the greatest deflection and the polished surface the least. The roughened surface lies second and the white surface third.

We therefore conclude that the radiation from a body depends on the nature of its surface and on its temperature. It also depends on its area—the larger the area, the greater is the radiation. *For a given temperature, a body radiates most heat when its surface is dull black and least when its surface is silvered and highly polished.*

Emission and Absorption

Are good emitters of heat also good absorbers? We can investigate this by using the apparatus shown in Fig. 10.18.

(*a*) A and B are two air-filled bulbs connected to a U-tube C, which is partially filled with a light oil. This is called a *differential-air thermometer*, because a temperature rise of one bulb such as A causes the oil level X on this side to drop owing to the expansion of the air.

A is painted matt black. B is painted gloss white or a colour different from black. A small electric lamp L, placed exactly midway between A and B, is switched on. It is then observed that the oil level falls on the side of A. We therefore conclude that a blackened surface, which is a good emitter as previously seen, is also a good absorber of radiation. Conversely, a white or highly polished surface is a poor absorber as well as a poor emitter of radiation.

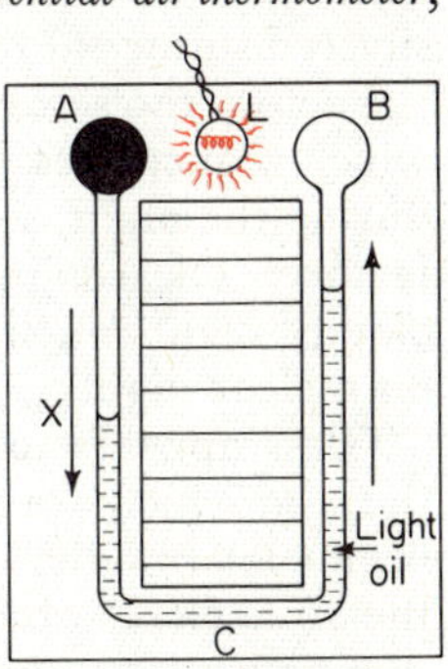

Fig. 10.18 Absorption of heat

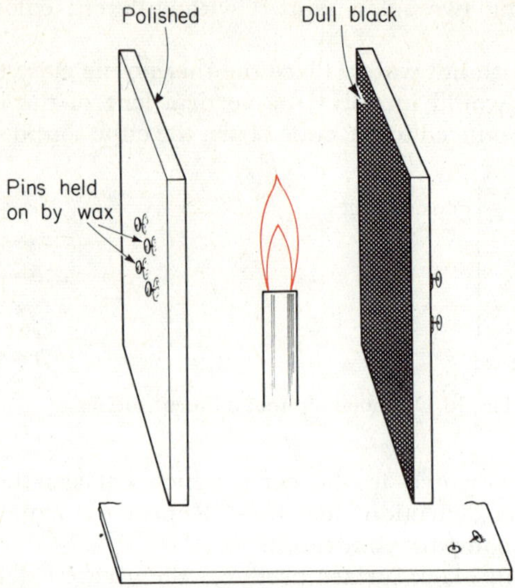

Fig. 10.19 Blackened and silvered surfaces

(*b*) We may also use two sheets of tinplate, one blackened and the other polished brightly, Fig. 10.19. Fix drawing pins on to the reverse side of each sheet using paraffin wax. Place a bunsen burner mid-way between the sheets, fixed vertically a short distance apart. Light the burner and record what happens. Explain your observations.

Applications of Radiation

Our experiments have shown that *a dull matt surface is a good radiator and a good absorber, especially when black, whereas a light polished or silvery surface is a poor radiator and poor absorber.* You should now be able to explain the disadvantage of a black-painted car in hot weather, the advantage of a tea-pot with a silvery surface and the purpose of a silvered surface at the base of an electric iron.

Factory roofs are sometimes coated with an aluminium (light) paint, which reduces absorption of heat during the day and reduces radiation during the night, so that a fairly steady temperature is obtained in the factory. The cooling of the earth at night is due to radiation; on a cloudy night much heat is reflected back, so that it is not so cold as on a clear night.

Glass appears to be transparent to radiation from bodies, such as the sun, which are hotter than about 500° C, and opaque to radiation from cooler bodies. A greenhouse thus acts as a 'trap' for the heat from the sun. Good absorption of radiation by dark bodies causes ice or snow on a mountain to melt where a stone 'hides' it from the sun, while remaining frozen in full sunlight.

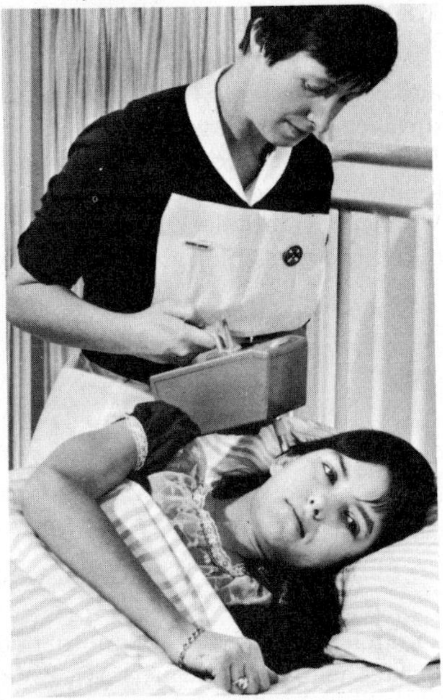

Plate 10(D) Infra-red thermometer. It detects infra-red radiation from the human body and records the temperature instantly.

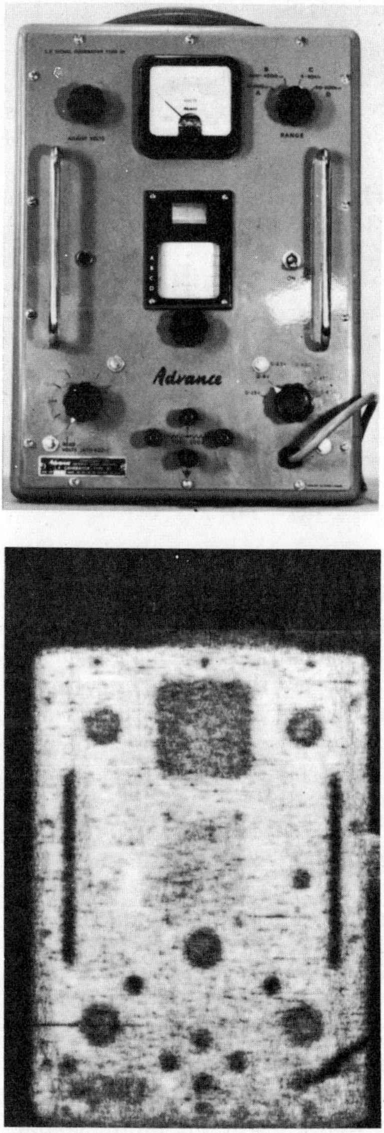

Plate 10(C) Photographs of electrical instruments taken by ordinary light (top) and by infra-red light (bottom). Taken in the dark, the bright parts in the infra-red photograph are due to warm components inside the instrument. The dark parts are due to the cooler portions of the instrument; in particular, the dark vertical lines are due to the highly polished chrome handles which are poor emitters of radiation.

Infra-red Radiation

Radiant heat, like visible light, consists of *electromagnetic waves*. They have much longer wavelengths than the longest wavelengths in visible light, which is red, and they are therefore called *infra-red rays* (p. 271). Infra-red rays are thus not visible to the eye. Plate 10C shows a photograph taken by infra-red rays and Plate 10D an infra-red thermometer.

When infra-red rays fall on an opaque object, part of it is absorbed and converted into heat, and part is reflected. A highly-polished silvered surface, as we have seen, is an excellent reflector of infra-red rays. Infra-red rays obey the same laws of reflection as light (p. 286), as the following demonstration shows.

Place a small electric radiator S, which emits heat rays, at the focus of a large concave reflector M_1, Fig. 10.20. Some distance away, place

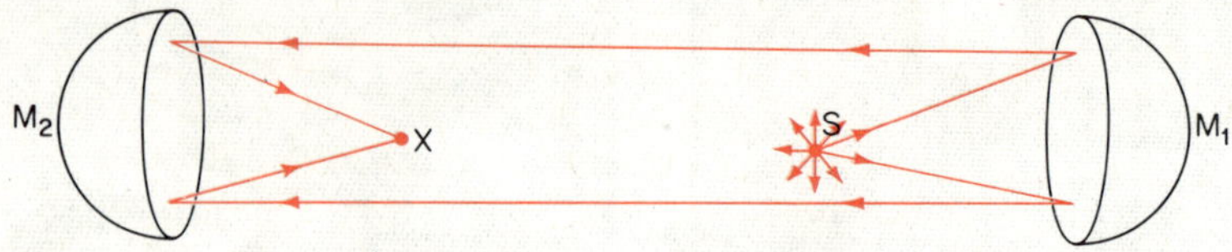

Fig. 10.20 Reflection of infra-red rays

a match at the focus X of another concave reflector M_2, whose reflecting surface is turned towards M_1. Shield the match from direct heat from the radiator. After a time the match will burst into flame.

Replace the electric radiator by a candle and the match by a shielded thermopile joined to a galvanometer. Observe the change in deflection in the galvanometer used when the candle is lit and when extinguished.

Replace the thermopile by a phototransistor Mullard OCP71, which is sensitive to infra-red rays. Observe the change in current when the candle is lit and when extinguished.

Conclusion. The heat or infra-red rays are reflected by M_1 so that they are brought to a focus by M_2. The rays therefore obey the same laws of reflection as light rays.

Infra-red electric heaters, used in bathrooms, for example, have a filament embedded in a rod of silica. When it is hot the silica emits infra-red rays. These are reflected into the room by a concave reflector positioned behind the rod.

Radiation and Convection in Heating Rooms

Metal radiators, used in a central-heating system for heating rooms, or electrically heated panels on the walls, warm the air in contact with them. The warm air rises and its place is taken by cooler air, and the process is repeated. In this way *convection currents* circulate in the room. Some heat is radiated directly into the room, of course, from the radiators. But since they warm the room mainly by convection, they are more correctly termed 'convectors'. Thus radiators may be painted in light colours without seriously affecting their heating efficiency.

A coal or log fire warms a room partly by radiation. Some of the heat, however, warms the air above it, part of which then rises up the chimney. Cooler air from open windows, or through openings in doors, then flows into the room and takes its place. Thus fires with an open chimney not only helps to heat a room but also to circulate fresh air in it. If a chimney fireplace is sealed, air heated by radiators or electric fires in the room does not escape. The air is then not as fresh as before.

Vacuum or Dewar Flask

About 1890 Sir James Dewar was engaged in researches on liquid air. He designed a vessel to keep the very cold liquid air at its low temperature once it had been made. Equally, as a *thermos flask*, it can keep a liquid hot.

The vacuum (thermos) flask consists of a double-walled glass container with a vacuum between the walls, A B, Fig. 10.21. The sides of A, B in the vacuum are silvered, and cork supports C are placed between the glass and the outside M of the flask. If a hot liquid is placed inside the flask it cannot lose heat by conduction or convection, as the space between the walls A, B is a vacuum. The small amount of heat lost from the liquid by radiation is diminished by the silvering on the wall A, and any radiation striking the wall B is reflected, as the latter is also silvered. A thermos flask should always be handled carefully. If the glass seal is broken by accident the vacuum becomes filled with air and the flask is ruined.

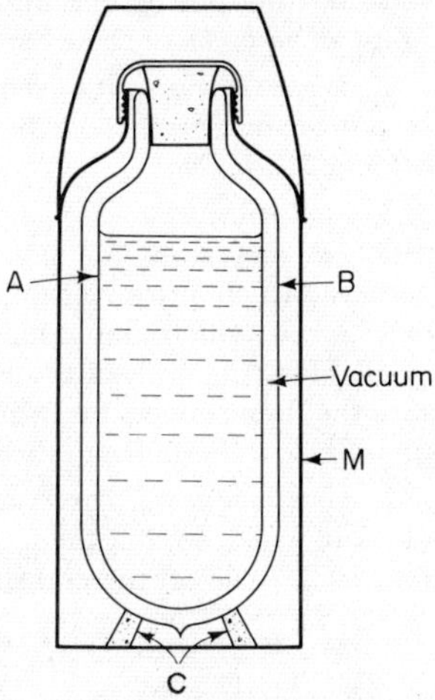

Fig. 10.21 Thermos (vacuum) flask

SUMMARY

1. Conduction—heat transferred without change of average position oı molecules. Convection—heat carried to other places by molecules themselves. Radiation—heat transfer without medium playing any part.

2. Metals are good conductors. Water is a poor conductor. Air is a very poor conductor—trapped air as in double-glazing or woollen materials is good insulator.

3. Dull-black surfaces are good emitters of radiation and good absorbers. Highly polished silvered surfaces are poor emitters and absorbers.

4. A miner's lamp works on the principle that a metal gauze is a good *conductor*. A hot-water circulation system transfers heat by *convection*. Land and sea breezes are due to natural *convection*. A vacuum-flask has a double-walled vessel with a vacuum between the walls and silvering on the inside.

PRACTICAL

Conduction: 1. *Solids.* Use a long metal rod and glass rod of the same dimensions.

(i) Grip the end of each rod in your hands. Which feels warmer? Why?

(ii) Hold the ends of the rods and place their other ends in a bunsen flame. (*Take care* with the glass rod.) Which rod feels warmer first?

(iii) When the rods have cooled down, attach a drawing-pin or small ball-bearing to the ends of the rod with paraffin-wax. Place the rods on a tripod with their other ends together and heat both ends with a burner. From which rod does the pin or bearing fall first? Draw sketches to illustrate the results. State a *Conclusion* of these experiments.

2. *Water.* As on p. 186, keep some ice at the bottom of a test-tube full of water by a piece of metal. Heat the water at the top until it boils and observe the ice. State a *Conclusion.*

3. *Comparison of conductivities.* (i) Support on a tripod two or more rods of different metal but the same dimensions. Put one end of each rod close together. Attach a drawing-pin or ball-bearing by paraffin-wax to the other end of each rod, which should be well separated from each other.

(ii) Heat the ends of the rods which are close together by a burner—make sure the flame covers the whole of the ends. Observe which pin or bearing falls first. State a *Conclusion* to the experiment.

4. *Metal and wood.* Insert a few screws a short-distance from each other in a block of wood, so that their ends just project from the wood in the other side B. Fig. 10.22. File off the end so that they are flush with the wood and make sure

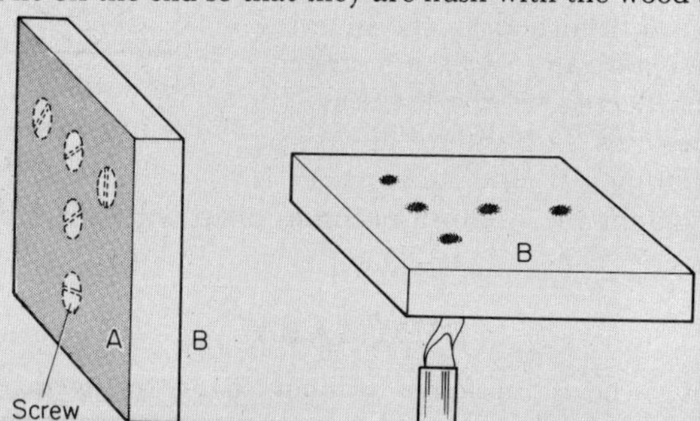

Fig. 10.22 Metal and wood as conductors

the screw heads are also flush with the wood on the other side. Now stick some heat-sensitive paper A firmly over the back and front B so that it makes contact with the wood everywhere.

Wave the side with the screw heads to and fro near a low flame. After a time, observe the effect on the paper, especially near the screw heads. Observe also if any colour change has occurred on the other side of the block. Explain the observations. Draw sketches of the colour effects on both sides.

Convection: 1. *Liquids.* (i) Drop a coloured crystal of potassium permanganate through a tube to the bottom of a water-filled flask. See Fig. 10.11, p. 191. Warm the bottom of the flask gently. Observe what happens. Explain the observations.

(ii) Fill a small flask F completely full of hot water previously coloured. Fig. 10.23. Seal F with a two-hole tight-fitting bung having two glass tubes M and N as shown—N has a slight constriction or nozzle at the top. Place the flask gently at the bottom of a deep vessel T filled with cold water. Observe what happens to the coloured water and explain.

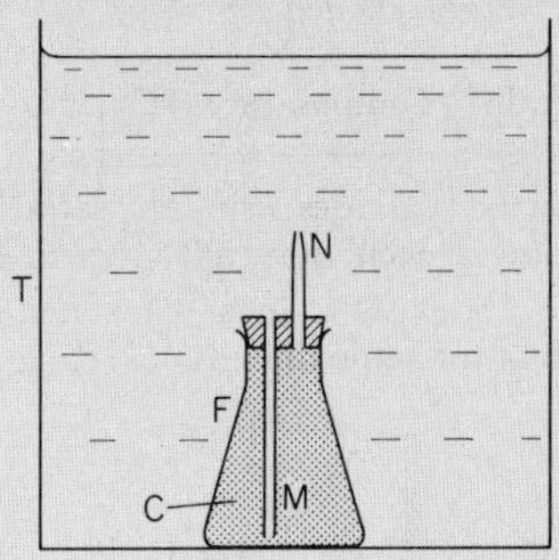

Fig. 10.23 Liquid convection

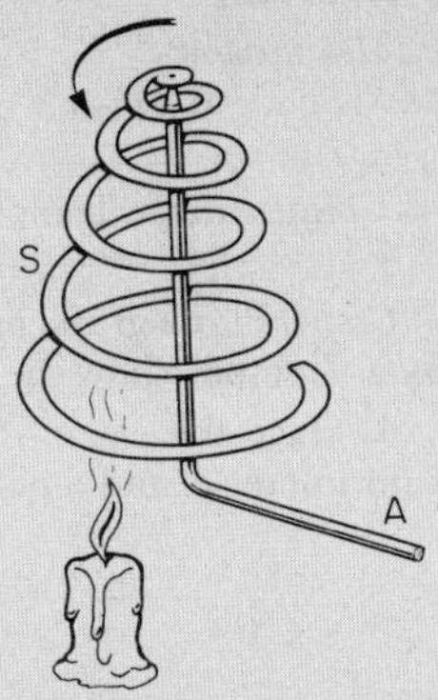

Fig. 10.24 Air convection currents

2. *Gases.* Make a paper spiral S by cutting a piece of paper, and balance the end on a bent piece of wire A. Fig. 10.24. Place a candle or low flame below the spiral and observe its movement due to convection currents in air.

Radiation: 1. Place a thermometer A, whose bulb has been blackened with soot from a taper, for example, and a normal thermometer B *equidistant* from a radiant heater or low flame. Observe if one thermometer rises in temperature faster. State a *Conclusion.*

2. Set up the apparatus in Fig. 10.25. Use large test-tubes A and B, with a light bulb C equidistant from each. A is blackened. Observe what happens to the difference in levels in the oil manometer M. State a *Conclusion.*

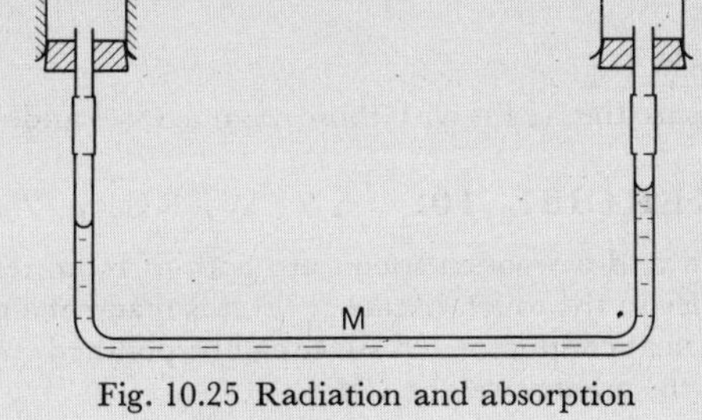

Fig. 10.25 Radiation and absorption

3. Blacken the bulb of a thermometer and support it in a clamp. Place a radiant heater near the bulb and remove it when the thermometer reads about 60°C. Using a stop-clock, take the temperature after every half-minute until the thermometer reads 20°C. Remove the black coating from the bulb. Repeat the experiment.

Measurements.

Blackened bulb

Time (min)	Temperature (°C)

Unblackened

Time (min)	Temperature (°C)

Graph. Plot a graph of Temperature v. Time for the two cases, using the same axes. Compare how the temperature drops with time in each. State a *Conclusion.*

4. Place the same volume of water heated to about 70°C in a blackened calorimeter A and a polished shiny calorimeter B of the same dimensions, each

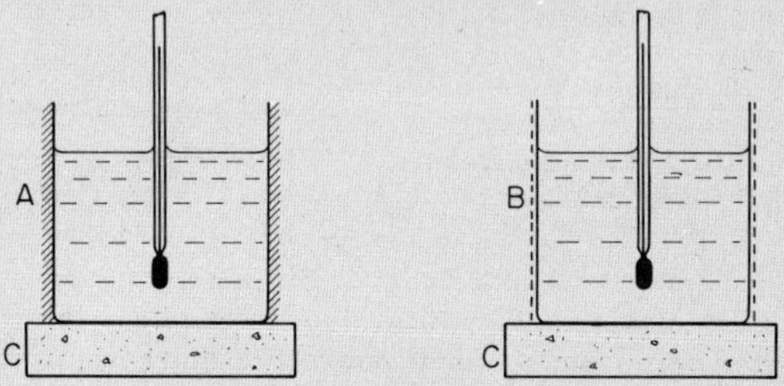

Fig. 10.26 Radiation losses of heat

on cork C. Fig. 10.26. Time how long the temperature of each liquid takes to fall from 60°C to 55°C, 55°C to 50°C, and 50°C to 45°C.

Measurements.

Blackened calorimeter

Temperature range	Time (min)

Unblackened

Temperature range	Time (min)

State a *Conclusion.*

5. *Effect of lagging.* Surround the blackened calorimeter in 4 above by an outer metal can, and pack paper and cotton waste between the two vessels. Use the same volume of water as in 4, heated to about 70°C inside the calorimeter, and again find the time for the liquid to cool from 60 to 55°C, 55 to 50°C and 50 to 45°C.

Measurements. As in 4.

Conclusion. Compare the results with those obtained in 4 and state a *Conclusion.*

EXERCISE 10 · ANSWERS, p. 258

1. A silver spoon and a wooden spoon are both at room temperature. The silver spoon is colder to the touch because: (*a*) it is made of a denser material; (*b*) silver is a good heat conductor; (*c*) silver can be polished; (*d*) wood is a dull material; (*e*) it has the greater weight. (*M.*)

2. One end of a poker is placed in the fire. A short time later the other end becomes hot. Explain how the heat travels along the poker. What is the correct name for transference of heat in this way? (*S.E.*)

3. In the winter time, birds perching on the branches of trees are often seen to 'fluff' up their feathers. How does this help to keep them warmer? (*S.E.*)

4. We place fibre glass around a hot-water tank to keep it hot because the fibre glass . .

A stainless-steel pan sometimes has a copper bottom because . .

'Double glazing' (two panes of glass with a space between) is often used for large windows to stop heat loss because . . (*W.Md.*)

5. Label the parts indicated in the diagram of a Thermos flask (Fig. 10A). Now complete the following sentences:

(i) The Thermos flask was invented by . .
(ii) The purpose of (*d*) is . .
(iii) The glass in (*c*) is silvered on both sides in order to . . (*Mx.*)

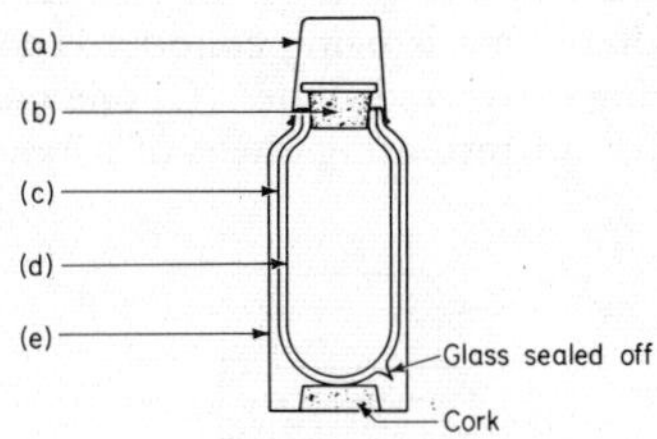

Fig. 10A

6. Heat travels by . . in solids.
Heat travels mainly by . . in liquids and gases.
Heat travels mainly by . . in space. (*Mx.*)

7. When a liquid is heated it . . and becomes less . . The less . . liquid then rises and the . . liquid takes the place of the hot liquid. This course of action sets up a . . current. (Choose the words you require from the following list: contracts, expands, dense, heavier, cold, convection, conduction.) (*Mx.*)

8. If you were launched into space wearing ordinary clothes, the liquids in your body would boil. Why is this so? How does a space suit prevent this? (*S.E.*)

9. Add the necessary pipes to make the diagram (Fig. 10B) into a suitable hot-water system and insert arrows to indicate direction of water flow. (*Mx.*)

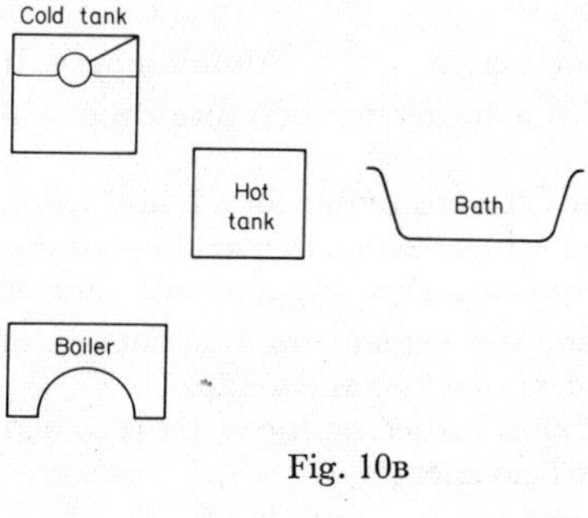

Fig. 10B

10. Label the diagram of a vacuum-flask (Fig. 10c). Which features are responsible for the reduction in heat transfer by (*a*) convection; (*b*) radiation? (*L.*)

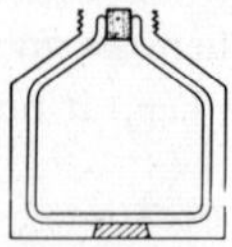

Fig. 10c

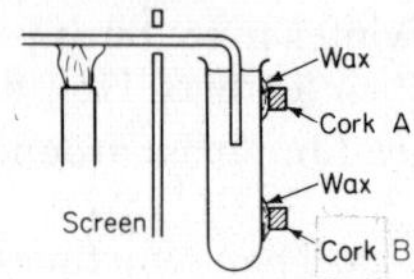

Fig. 10D

11. Fig. 10D illustrates a simple demonstration where a bent copper rod is heated at one end, with the other end dipping into a test-tube of water. Cork A falls off after a short time. Cork B remains in position despite prolonged heating: (*a*) what does this demonstration illustrate? (*b*) what would be the effect if the water were replaced with mercury? (*E.A.*)

12. Fig. 10E shows water being heated on an electric hot-plate. Label with the letter (A) one part where heat is being conducted to the water; letter (B) one part where heat is being convected; letter (C) one part where heat is being radiated; letter (D) where an insulating sheet of asbestos should be placed. (*W.Md.*)

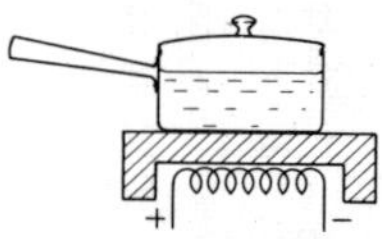

Fig. 10E

13. (*a*) Starting with the chemical energy of the petrol fuel, state the energy changes that take place in producing light energy in a car headlight.

(*b*) Describe how a car engine is cooled using water. (*W.Md.*)

14. Show by diagrams clearly what happens in the following systems: (i) a hot water system containing at least a boiler and two radiators; (ii) a sea breeze on a hot summer's day; (iii) a vacuum-flask. (*W.M.*)

15. The following test results were taken from three central heating water radiators:

	A	B	C
Temperature of water entering radiator	80°	80°	80°
Temperature of water leaving radiator	62°	70°	56°
Surface area of radiator	2 m^2	2 m^2	2·5 m^2
Material used in construction	Aluminium	Iron	Iron

(*a*) Explain why there is a bigger temperature drop with radiator A than radiator B.

(*b*) Why would radiator C be unsuitable for a house system of five radiators?

(*c*) What steps would have to be taken, in carrying out the tests, to make sure that all three tests could be accurately compared with each other? (*W.Md.*)

16. (*a*) Draw a diagram, and explain the functioning, of a household hot-water system which provides hot water at two taps.

(*b*) When a hot-water tap is turned on the water is cool at first. Why is this? What has happened to the heat energy?

(*c*) How may the heat losses from the system be reduced? (*E.A.*)

17. (*a*) Explain why a cool jam-jar may crack if boiling water is poured into it.

(*b*) Explain the common feature which results in wool, fur and feathers being poor conductors of heat. Give *one* method of heat insulation in houses which use this feature. (*c*) Why does a piece of metal feel colder to the touch than a piece of wood, although both are at the same temperature? (*E.A.*)

18. Carefully explain how the following substances are kept cool in a warm climate: (*a*) water, kept in a porous pot; (*b*) ice-cream, kept in a vacuum-flask; (*c*) meat, kept in a compression-type refrigerator. (*W.Md.*)

19. (*a*) Name and give a brief explanation of each of the three ways that heat can be transferred from place to place.

(*b*) A person sitting in the middle of an upstairs room is heated indirectly by a gas-fired boiler in the basement of the house. Show on a labelled diagram how the heat is transferred from the gas flame to the person. (*E.A.*)

20. (*a*) Describe, with the aid of a diagram, an experiment which you could perform to determine which of two metals was the better conductor of heat.

(*b*) Describe the action of a greenhouse. Explain clearly why the temperature inside the greenhouse is greater than that outside. (*L.*)

21. What are *conductors* and *insulators* of heat? You wish to lag your hot-water tank and advertisements show three possible materials you could use. Devise an experiment by which you could test the heat-insulating properties of these materials and how you would compare them. (*Mx.*)

22. (*a*) Describe experiments you have performed (one in each case) to show: (i) that some materials are better conductors of heat than others; (ii) how a convection current can be started in water.

(*b*) Draw a clearly labelled diagram of a vacuum-flask (Thermos flask). Describe it and explain how it minimizes loss of heat from the interior by: (i) conduction; (ii) convection; (iii) radiation. (*Mx.*)

23. (i) The apparatus is set up as shown in Fig. 10F. After a short while, it is noticed that the temperature of the water in vessel A rises while the temperature of the water in vessel B remains almost unchanged. Explain the observation.

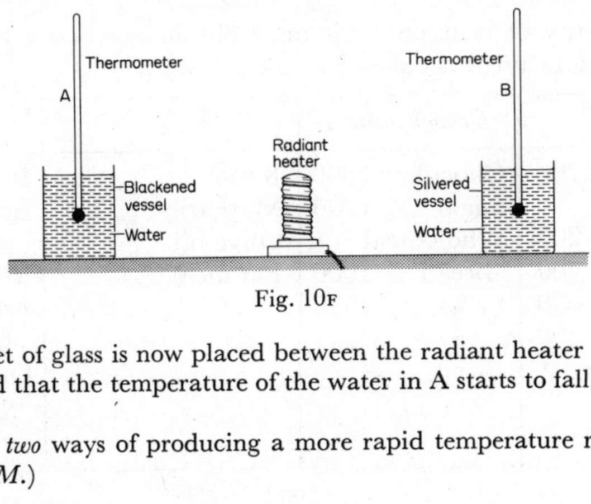

Fig. 10F

(ii) A sheet of glass is now placed between the radiant heater and vessel A. It is observed that the temperature of the water in A starts to fall. Explain this observation.

(iii) State *two* ways of producing a more rapid temperature rise using this apparatus. (*M.*)

11

QUANTITY OF HEAT · HEAT ENERGY

In the home, heat for cooking is obtained by burning gas or by using electricity. Steam engines burn coal, diesel engines burn oil; and, in general, the greater the amount of fuel, the greater is the quantity of heat obtainable from it.

Units of Quantity of Heat

The scientist and the engineer have defined *units* of quantity of heat. The unit in scientific work for many years was the *calorie*, which is defined as *the quantity of heat which raises the temperature of* 1 g *of water by* 1° *C*. For convenience, we often use 1 large calorie, or 1 kilocalorie, to represent 1000 calories.

Since heat is a form of energy, it has been decided to measure quantities of heat in *joules* and heat per second in joules per second or *watts* (see p. 150). Approximately, 4·2 J (joules) = 1 calorie. Thus 4·2 J (1 calorie) is the heat required to raise the temperature of 1 g of water by 1° C. *Any values in calories can be changed into joules, by multiplying them by* 4·2.

In this country, commercial gas companies use a unit of heat known as the *therm*. The metric therm, based on the joule as the unit of heat, is defined as 100 MJ, where 1 MJ = 1 megajoule = 1 million joules.

Calorific Values

The quantity of heat per unit mass obtained when a fuel is burnt or a food is consumed is called its *calorific value*.

Proteins		*Carbohydrates*		*Fats*		*Others*	
Cheese	1700	Chocolate	2300	Butter	3000	Peas	400
Lean meat	1200	Sugar	1600	Margarine	3000	Boiled potatoes	350
Eggs	700	Wholemeal bread	1000	Olive oil	3000	Milk	300
Liver	600			Fat meat	3000	Fresh fruit	200
White fish	300					Green vegetables	150

The calorific value of one grade of coal is approximately 30 million joule per kg. The calorific value of one grade of petrol is about 50 million joule per kg. The human body is a 'machine'. It needs food as fuel to keep working efficiently. Some approximate calorific values, in kilojoules per 100 g, of a variety of foods are given on p. 206. Diets which discourage overweight exclude chocolate and sugar, for example, and include lean meat, and green vegetables.

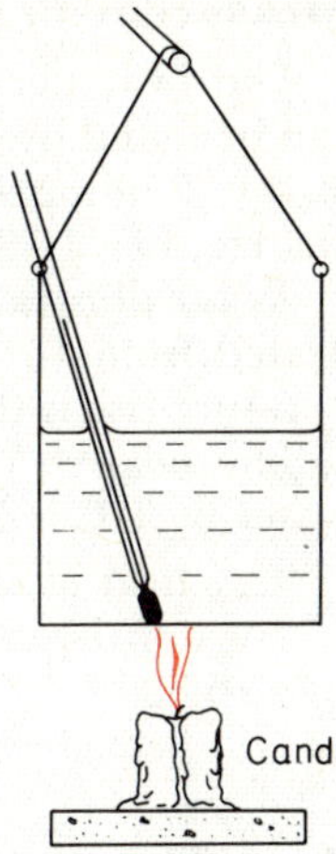

Fig. 11.1 Calorific value

Calorific Value of Candle

The calorific value of a candle, the heat per unit mass when it is burnt, can be found very roughly by weighing it before and after it is used to heat some water, Fig. 11.1. (Why does this give a low value?)

As an illustration, suppose 100 g of water rises in temperature from 12°C to 32°C. Then since 1 g of water rises by 1°C when 4·2 joules is received, 100 g of water rising (32 − 12) or 20°C must have received $100 \times 20 \times 4{\cdot}2 = 8400$ J.

Suppose the loss in weight of the candle is 0·5 g. Then

$$\text{calorific value} = \frac{8400\ \text{J}}{0{\cdot}5\ \text{g}} = 16\,800\ \text{J/g} = 16{\cdot}8\ \text{MJ/kg}.$$

Gas Bills

Calorific values in gas bills in Great Britain will be given in MJ/m³ (cubic metre) of gas consumed. In one region, the calorific value was 18·6 MJ/m³. The bill may be as follows for a period of 6 weeks when the change was 12p per metric Therm:

Meter reading		Gas consumed		Amount
Present	Previous	Cubic metres	Therms	£
6300	6100	200	37·2	4·46

To check the bill, subtract the two meter readings. This gives 200 cubic metres of gas used. From the calorific value, 18·6 MJ/m³,

$$\text{number of MJ used} = 200 \times 18{\cdot}6 = 3720$$

Since 100 MJ = 1 Therm

$$\therefore \text{heat supplied} = \frac{3720}{100} = 37{\cdot}2\ \text{Therms}$$

$$\therefore \text{cost} = 37{\cdot}2 \times 12\text{p} = £4{\cdot}46.$$

Measurement of Heat Supplied

The heat per minute supplied by a burner can be found by heating some water for a period of say 5 minutes, and noting the temperature change, Fig. 11.2.

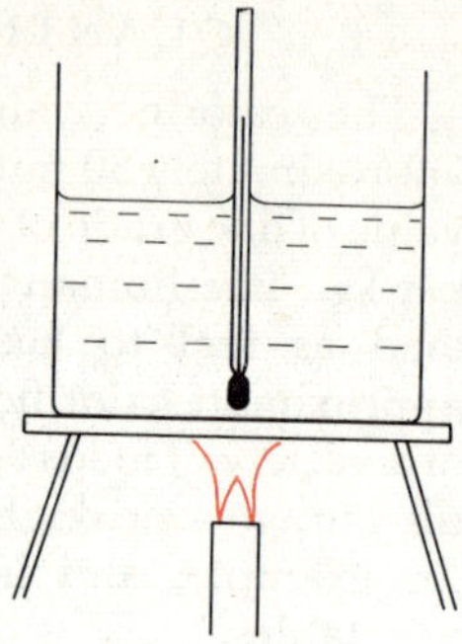

Fig. 11.2 Burner supply of heat

As an illustration, suppose 200 g of water is heated from 15° C to 35° C in 5 min. The temperature rise is then (35 − 15) or 20°C.

The heat to raise the temperature of 1 g of water by 1°C is 4·2 J

∴ heat to raise the temperature of 200 g of water by 20°C = 200 × 20 × 4·2 = 16 800 J

∴ heat supplied per minute $= \frac{16\,800 \text{ J}}{5 \text{ min}} = 3360$ J/min.

Heat (Thermal) Capacity

The burner we have just used will produce a temperature rise of 1°C in 800 g of water when it is supplied with 3360 J of heat. We say that the *heat capacity* of this mass of water is 3360 J/°C. A similar mass of oil may only need 2000 J for a temperature rise of 1°C. The heat capacity of the oil is 2000 J/°C. A similar mass of iron may have a heat capacity of 360 J/°C.

The heat capacity of a body is defined as:

the heat required to raise its temperature by 1°C.

The heat capacity depends on the mass of the particular object—it may be a small bolt in a motor car or a large tank in the loft of a house—and on its nature—it may be made of iron or brass or it may be a liquid. The sea-water in oceans has a high heat capacity, both on account of its huge mass and its nature. Thus sea-water does not get unbearably hot even in the tropics. A metal coin has a low heat capacity. Thus if it is rubbed vigorously on the sleeve, the small amount of heat generated by friction is sufficient to make the temperature of the metal rise appreciably.

Calorimeter

Measurements in heat are often made using a metal container or vessel called a *calorimeter*, Fig. 11.3. In many cases a hot solid or hot liquid is placed inside the calorimeter. The temperature of the calorimeter then rises; it has gained heat from the hot object. At the same time, the temperature of the hot object decreases; it has lost heat to the calorimeter.

If no precautions were taken, some heat would be lost by the calorimeter to the surrounding air as its temperature rose. On this account a calorimeter is: (i) lagged by insulating material round it; (ii) often

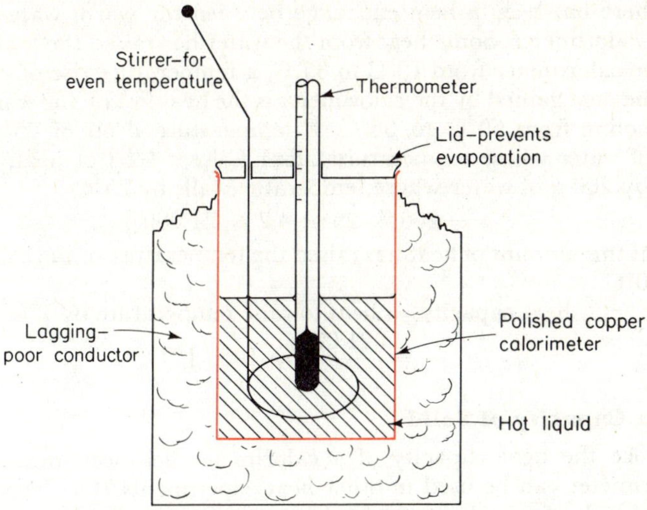

Fig. 11.3 A calorimeter

covered with a lid to prevent heat lost by convection from its surface; (iii) highly polished to prevent radiation to the air.

Heat Capacity of Calorimeter

Suppose the heat capacity of a large thick-walled calorimeter is required. 200 cm^3 (200 g) of water is placed in a beaker using a measuring cylinder, Fig. 11.4. The water is then warmed and maintained at about 60° C. The temperature of the calorimeter is now taken, say 15° C, and the warm water in the beaker then quickly poured into the calorimeter. The water is stirred and its *final steady* temperature taken. Suppose it is 35° C.

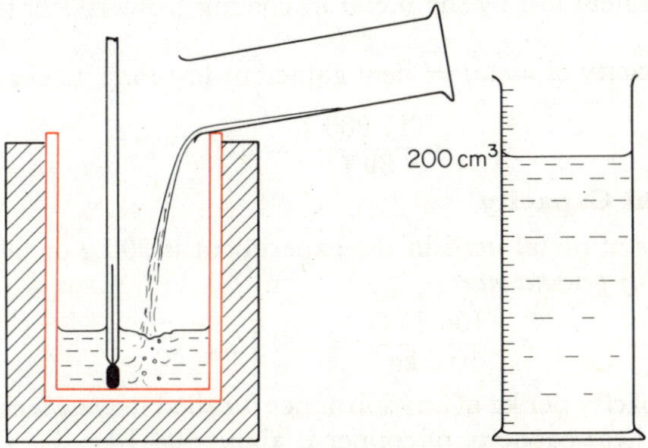

Fig. 11.4 Heat capacity of calorimeter

There has been a heat exchange between the warm water and the cold calorimeter. Some heat from the water has raised the temperature of the calorimeter from 15°C to 35°C, a temperature rise of 20°C.

The heat gained by the calorimeter is the heat lost by the warm water in cooling from 60°C to 35°C, a temperature drop of 25°C. Since 1 g of water whose temperature falls 1°C loses 4·2 J of heat, the heat lost by 200 g of water whose temperature falls by 25°C

$$= 200 \times 25 \times 4{\cdot}2 = 21\,000 \text{ J}$$

But this amount of heat has raised the temperature of the calorimeter by 20°C.

$$\therefore \text{ heat capacity} = \text{heat to raise temperature by } 1^\circ\text{C}.$$

$$= \frac{21\,000}{20} = 1050 \text{ J/}^\circ\text{C}.$$

Heat Capacity of Solid

Once the heat capacity of a calorimeter has been measured, the calorimeter can be used in other heat experiments. The heat capacity of a block of metal, for example, can be measured. To do this, the metal is heated in boiling water for a few minutes so that its temperature reaches 100° C. Meanwhile, the calorimeter is filled about one-third full of water, say 300 g, which has a heat capacity of 300 × 4·2 = 1260 J/°C, and its temperature is noted. Suppose this is 15°C.

The metal at 100°C is quickly transferred to the cold water, and after stirring, the final steady temperature is taken. Let this be 20°C.

Using a calorimeter of 1100 J/°C, the total heat capacity of the water and calorimeter = 1260 + 1100 = 2360 J/°C. The temperature rise = 20 — 15 = 5°C.

Hence heat gained by water and calorimeter

$$= \text{total heat capacity} \times \text{temperature rise}$$

$$= 2360 \times 5 = 11\,800 \text{ J}.$$

But this is the heat lost by the metal in cooling from 100°C to 20°C or 80°C. Thus

$$\text{heat capacity of metal} = \text{heat gained or lost for } 1^\circ\text{C change}$$

$$= \frac{11\,800 \text{ J}}{80^\circ\text{C}} = 150 \text{ J/}^\circ\text{C}.$$

Specific Heat Capacity

If the mass of metal used in the experiment is 300 g or 0·3 kg, then the *heat capacity per unit mass*

$$= \frac{150 \text{ J/}^\circ\text{C}}{0{\cdot}3 \text{ kg}} = 500 \text{ J/kg }^\circ\text{C}.$$

The heat capacity per kg of any substance is called its *specific heat capacity*. The specific heat capacity of copper is about 400 J/kg °C. Thus 400 J is required to raise the temperature of 1 kg of copper by 1°C. The specific heat capacity of aluminium is about 1000 J/kg °C. The specific heat capacity of one type of motor oil is about 2500 J/kg °C. Water has a high specific heat capacity, 4200 J/kg°C.

Tables of specific heat capacities have been compiled. These are more useful than heat capacities. The heat capacity value depends on the particular mass of the object as well as its material. The specific heat capacity, however, is a property of the material itself; it does not depend on the mass.

Measuring Specific Heat Capacity

The specific heat capacity of a metal can be measured by using a thick-walled calorimeter made of the metal.

As explained on p. 209, the heat capacity can be found by pouring a known mass of hot water into the calorimeter and measuring the final temperature of the water. Suppose the heat capacity was found to be 600 J/°C. Then, if the mass of the calorimeter is 0·5 kg,

$$\text{specific heat capacity of metal} = \text{heat capacity per kg} = \frac{600\ \text{J/°C}}{0{\cdot}5\ \text{kg}} = 1200\ \text{J/kg °C}.$$

If the specific heat capacity of copper is 400 J/kg °C, the heat capacity of a copper tank of mass 2 kg

$$= 400 \times 2 = 800\ \text{J/°C}.$$

Generally, then,

heat capacity of object = mass of object × specific heat capacity.

Calculation on Heat Exchange

A hot object always loses heat to a cold object when they are placed in contact.

In such cases, we can always make a 'heat equation'. As an example, suppose 8 kg of hot water at 90°C is mixed with 12 kg of cold water at 10°C and the final steady temperature is required. Suppose this is x°C. Then the hot water has dropped in temperature by $(90 - x)$°C.

$$\therefore \text{heat lost by hot water} = 8 \times (90 - x) \times 4200\ \text{J}$$

The cold water has risen in temperature by $(x - 10)$ °C.

$$\therefore \text{heat gained by cold water} = 12 \times (x - 10) \times 4200\ \text{J}$$

$$\therefore 8 \times (90 - x) \times 4200 = 12 \times (x - 10) \times 4200$$

Dividing by 4 × 4200, $2 \times (90 - x) = 3 \times (x - 10)$

$$\therefore 180 - 2x = 3x - 30$$

$$\therefore 5x = 210$$

$$\therefore x = \frac{210}{5} = 42$$

$\therefore$ Final temperature = 42° C.

Check:
Heat lost by hot water = 8 × (90 − 42) × 4200 = 1 612 800 J
Heat gained by cold water = 12 × (42 − 10) × 4200 = 1 612 800 J.

Heat and Energy

Early scientists considered that heat was a material substance. They called this *caloric*. Thus a body gaining heat increased its caloric content, and one losing heat diminished its caloric content. This conception of heat was generally accepted up to about 1800. Experimental results were then obtained which could not be explained by the caloric theory of heat.

One of the first experiments which disproved the caloric theory was performed by Benjamin Thompson, or Count Rumford, as he was later called. Rumford was an American engaged in 1798 in supervising the boring of cannon in a munitions factory in Bavaria. He noted that the borer, the metal bored and the metal chips all became hot. Further, heat continued to be produced as long as the boring took place. It seemed highly unlikely to Rumford that the small amount of metal bored could contain such an enormous amount of caloric. He also realized that the heat produced was related to the mechanical energy used in boring the cannon. To confirm his view he surrounded a gun-barrel and a borer in a container of water and, to the astonishment of the onlookers, who knew that no flame was being used, the water was made to boil. These demonstrations implied that *heat was a form of energy*. It is not a material substance. Today, it is known that molecules in solids, liquids or gases gain kinetic energy when heated—they move faster than before—that is, heat is a form of energy.

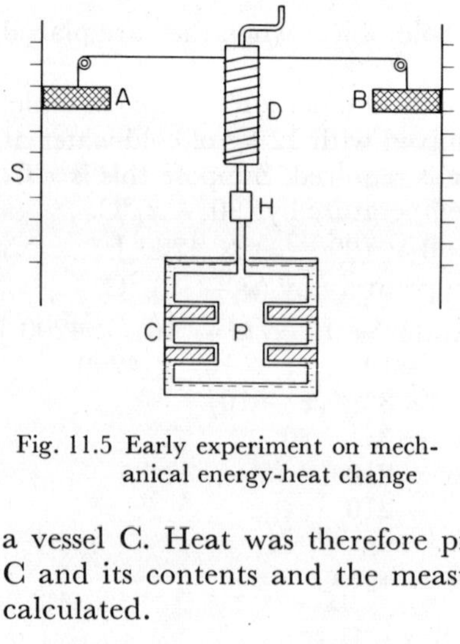

Fig. 11.5 Early experiment on mechanical energy-heat change

Mechanical Energy to Heat · Joule as Heat Unit

J. P. Joule was born near Manchester in 1818 and is famous for his researches on heat and energy, Fig. 11.5 illustrates the essential features of Joule's most famous experiment performed in 1842. He allowed two equal weights A and B to fall through a known height, so that the mechanical energy spent on reaching the ground was known. As the weights fell, a paddle P was automatically turned and churned water inside a vessel C. Heat was therefore produced. From the heat capacity of C and its contents and the measured temperature rise, the heat was calculated.

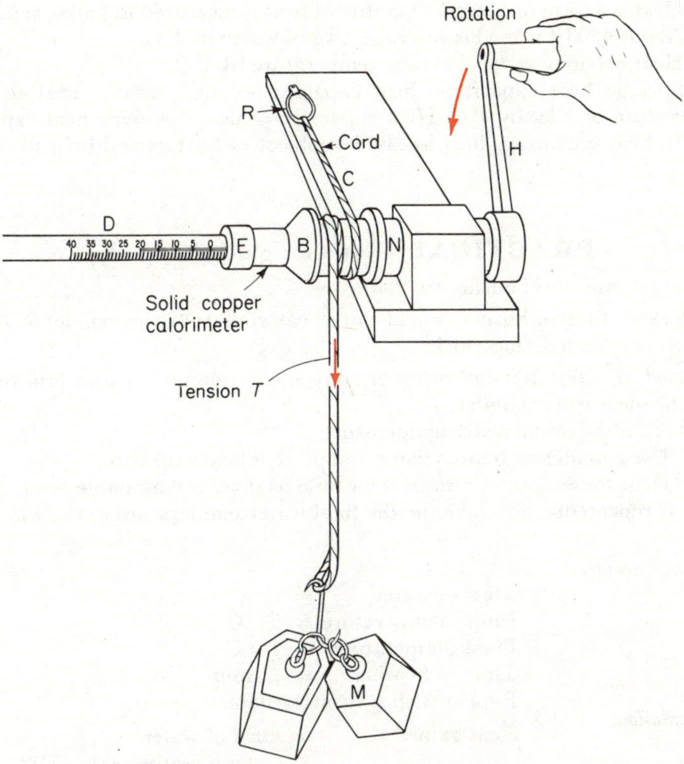

Fig. 11.6 Transferring mechanical energy to heat energy

Fig. 11.6 shows a present-day laboratory apparatus for converting mechanical energy directly into heat. When the handle H is turned a metal drum or calorimeter rubs against a nylon cord C. Friction produces heat, which is measured with the aid of a thermometer D.

Joule performed his experiment many times, with different weights and heights. He found that about 4200 joules of mechanical energy were always required to raise the temperature of 1 kg of water by 1 °C. Joule therefore showed that mechanical energy can be completely transferred to heat energy.

In view of Joule's experiments, it is possible to measure mechanical energy and heat energy in the same unit, the joule. The joule is also the unit of all other forms of energy, such as electrical energy. A larger unit of energy is the kilojoule, kJ. 1 kJ = 1000 J. Commercial units of heat will be expressed in megajoules, MJ. See p. 206.

SUMMARY

1. Heat is a form of energy. Quantity of heat is measured in joules, symbol J.
2. About 4200 J is the heat to raise 1 kg of water by 1°C.
3. Heat capacity = heat to raise temperature by 1°C.
4. Specific heat capacity = heat capacity per unit mass = heat to raise temperature of 1 kg by 1°C. Heat capacity = mass × specific heat capacity.
5. In heat exchanges, heat lost by hot object = heat gained by cold object.

PRACTICAL (Notes for guidance, p. 26)

1. Heat per minute of burner (p. 208)

Apparatus. Bunsen burner; metal can or calorimeter; thermometer 0–100°C; measuring cylinder; stop-clock.

Method. (i) Pour 200 cm^3 or other convenient volume of water into the can from the measuring cylinder.

(ii) Take the initial water temperature.

(iii) Use a moderate bunsen flame and place it below the can.

(iv) Heat for exactly 5 min or such time as gives a reasonable temperature rise, stir repeatedly, and take the the final water temperature at the end of the time.

Measurements.

Mass of water = .. g
Initial temperature = .. °C
Final temperature = .. °C
Time of heating = .. min
Repeat with a stronger flame.

Calculation.

Heat gained = mass of water × temperature rise × 4·2 = .. J

$$\therefore \text{Heat per min} = \frac{..\,\text{J}}{..\,\text{min}} = ..\ \text{J/min}.$$

2. Calorific value of candle (p. 207)

Apparatus. Candle and cork base; metal can or calorimeter; lever balance or spring balance; measuring cylinder; thermometer 0–100°C.

Method (i) Weigh the candle and base.

(ii) Fill the can with 100 cm^3 or 100 g of water and take its initial temperature.

(iii) Support the can from a clamp with thread, place the candle below it, and light the candle.

(iv) When the temperature rise is 30°C or other convenient value, remove the candle, stir the water, and note its final temperature.

(v) Reweigh the candle and base.

Measurements.

Initial mass of candle + base = .. g
Final mass of candle + base = .. g
Mass of water used = .. g
Initial temperature = .. °C
Final temperature = .. °C

Calculation.

Mass of candle used = .. g
Heat supplied = mass of water × temperature rise × 4·2 = .. J
∴ Heat per g of candle = .. J/g

If a small spirit lamp is available, this may also be used. Note that this is not a very accurate method, since a lot of heat is lost to the atmosphere.

3. Heat capacity of calorimeter

Measure the heat capacity (heat/°C) of a large metal calorimeter by the method on p. 209.

Measurements.

Mass of water = .. g
Initial hot temperature = .. °C
Final temperature = .. °C
Initial calorimeter temperature = .. °C

Calculation.

Heat gained by calorimeter = heat lost by hot water = .. J.
Temperature rise of calorimeter = .. °C
∴ Heat capacity = .. J/°C

(i) Repeat the experiment using water at an initial higher temperature than before.

(ii) Weigh the calorimeter. Divide the mass in grammes into the heat capacity value found, and thus obtain the *specific heat capacity* of the metal of the calorimeter (see p. 211). Compare your result with that given in tables of specific heat capacities of metals.

4. Heat capacity of solid

Measure the heat capacity of a large piece of metal by the method on p. 210.

Measurements.

Mass of water = .. kg
Initial temperature = .. °C
Final temperature = .. °C
Initial hot temperature of solid = .. °C
Heat capacity of calorimeter = .. J/°C
(known from a previous experiment).

Calculation.

Heat lost by solid = heat gained by water and calorimeter
= total heat capacity × temperature rise × 4200
= .. J
Temperature drop of solid = .. °C
∴ Heat capacity = heat/°C = .. J/°C

Specific heat capacity. From your result for heat capacity, find the specific heat capacity of the particular metal by dividing the heat capacity by the mass of the metal in grammes. (See p. 210.)

EXERCISE 11 · ANSWERS, p. 258

(Where necessary, assume specific heat capacity of water = 4200 J/kg °C.)

1. What amount of heat would be needed to raise the temperature of 250 g of water from 25°C to 65°C? (*Mx.*)

2. A quantity of water is heated in a modern gas-fired boiler rated at 60 million joules per hour. You can assume that the boiler is 75% efficient. The water enters the boiler at a temperature of 10°C and leaves it at 60°C. Calculate, showing your method of working:

(*a*) How many megajoules (MJ) of heat energy are produced by the boiler in 2 hours.

(*b*) What quantity of heat is actually transferred to the water in this time.

(*c*) What mass of water will pass through the boiler in this time.

(*d*) The cost of heating 1 kg mass of water if the charge made by the Gas Board is 10p per 100 MJ. (*M.*)

3. Two separate amounts of water, (*a*) weighing 5 g and (*b*) weighing 8 g are heated from temperatures of 10°C to 30°C. How much heat does each require for this? (*W.Md.*)

4. (*a*) A spark from a gas-lighter flint may be at a temperature of 1000°C. Why does it not cause a burn when it falls on the skin?

(*b*) Calculate the amount of heat in megajoules (MJ) required to raise the temperature of: (i) 10 kg of water from 20°C to 100°C; (ii) 10 kg of copper, of specific heat capacity 400 J/kg °C, from 20°C to 100°C. (*E.A.*)

5. When some warm water was poured into a calorimeter the following results were obtained:

Mass of the calorimeter	50 g (0·05 kg)
Initial temperature of the calorimeter	20°C
Initial temperature of the warm water	35°C
Final temperature of the mixture	30°C
Mass of the calorimeter plus the water	60 g (0·06 kg)

Complete the following table:

Mass of the warm water	
Fall in temperature of the water	
Rise in temperature of the calorimeter	
Heat given out by the warm water	
Heat taken in by the calorimeter	
Heat capacity of the calorimeter	

(*L.*)

6. (*a*) What is a joule?

(*b*) In an experiment to find the temperature of a Bunsen burner flame a brass weight of 0·2 kg is heated in it. The specific heat capacity of brass is 400 J/kg °C. The hot weight is put into a beaker containing 0·2 kg of water and raises the temperature of the water from 20°C to 80°C.

(i) What is the rise in temperature of the water?

(ii) What is the heat gained by the water?

(iii) Assuming the unknown temperature of the weight is T°C, what is the fall in temperature of the weight?

(iv) What is the heat lost by the weight?

(v) Assume that the heat gained in (ii) is equal to the heat lost in (iv), find the temperature T°C.

(vi) Do you think that this is a good method for finding the temperature of the flame? Give reasons. (*E.A.*)

7. The left-hand column contains a list of quantities and the right-hand column a list of definitions. Decide which quantity belongs with which definition, e.g. I Linear expansivity (Coefficient of linear expansion) corresponds with H Increase in length per unit length per degree rise in temperature.

Select *four* and write the *letters* in the corresponding boxes below.

1 Linear expansivity (Coefficient of linear expansion)	A Amount of heat required to raise the temperature of a body 1°C
2 Specific latent heat of fusion	B Number of joules given out when 1 kg of a substance is completely burnt
3 Heat capacity	C Amount of heat required to change 1 kg of a solid substance at its melting-point into a liquid at the same temperature
4 4200 joules	D Amount of heat required to raise temperature of 1 kg of water 1°C
5 Therm	E 100 megajoules
6 Specific heat capacity	F Amount of heat required to change 1 kg of liquid at boiling point to vapour at same temperature
7 Calorific value	G Amount of heat required to raise the temperature of 1 kg of a substance 1°C
	H Increase in length per unit length per degree rise in temperature
	J Mass of water whose temperature could be raised through 1°C by the heat required to raise the temperature of a body through 1°C

1	2	3	4	5	6	7
H						

(*N.W.*)

8. Either: 70 g of oil cools from 100° to 60°C in 10 min. How much heat has the oil lost to its surroundings in this time? (The specific heat capacity of the oil is 2000 J/kg °C.)

Comment on the time the oil would take: (i) to cool from 60° to 20°C under the same conditions; (ii) to cool from 100° to 60°C under the same conditions if the specific heat capacity of the oil were 4000 instead of 2000 J/kg °C.

Or: 2 kg of oil cools from 90° to 50°C in 10 min. How much heat has the oil lost to its surroundings in this time? (The specific heat capacity of the oil is 2000 J/kg °C.)

Comment on the time the oil would take: (i) to cool from 50° to 10°C under the same conditions; (ii) to cool from 90° to 50°C under the same conditions if the specific heat capacity of the oil were 4000 instead of 2000 J/kg °C. (*S.E.*)

9. (*a*) Define a heat unit.

(*b*) Find the total cost of the gas used in the first quarter of the year by a consumer whose meter readings were: on 31 December—9400 m³; on 31 March—9754m³. The gas yields 20 MJ/m³ and the charge is 12 pence per metric Therm. (1 metric Therm = 100 MJ.)

(*c*) Describe an experiment to find how many joules are given each minute by a small electric immersion heater of the kind that can be used in a jug of water. State the precautions necessary to ensure accuracy. (*Mx.*)

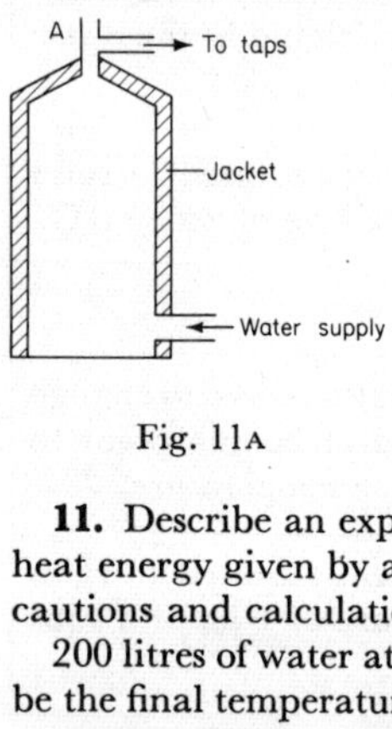

Fig. 11A

10. Fig. 11A shows a hot-water cylinder.

(*a*) For what purpose is the pipe A?

(*b*) For what purpose is the jacket?

(*c*) What would be a suitable material for the jacket?

(*d*) Why is this material suitable?

(*e*) If the water is heated by a 3 kW immersion heater, and all the heat produced is taken in by water, what rise in temperature could be expected in 42 min? Assume that the tank holds 100 kg of water and that 4200 J/kg °C = sp. ht. capacity of water. (*L.*)

11. Describe an experiment you have performed to calculate the amount of heat energy given by a burner or immersion heater in 1 min. Indicate the precautions and calculations you would make.

200 litres of water at 80°C are added to 100 litres of water at 10°C. What will be the final temperature? Assume that no heat is lost. (*Mx.*)

12. (*a*) Define a heat unit.

(*b*) A householder is charged for gas at the rate of 12 pence per metric therm (100 MJ). Calculate the cost of the gas used by him in one quarter if the meter readings at the beginning and end of that quarter were 13 080 and 13 555 m³ respectively. (The calorific value of the gas was 20 MJ/m³.)

(*c*) Explain the meaning of the following statement: 'The diet for a moderately active 60 kg man should provide about 12 000 kilojoules per day.' (*Mx.*)

12

CHANGE OF STATE · LATENT HEAT · EVAPORATION

Fusion

WHEN a solid is heated continuously, eventually it all melts and forms a liquid. This is called *fusion*. The change from solid to liquid is an example of a 'change of state'.

A common case of fusion is the change from ice to water. Suppose a large piece of ice B is placed in a beaker, Fig. 12.1 (i). The temperature of the ice is 0° C. If heat is now applied gently some of the ice begins to

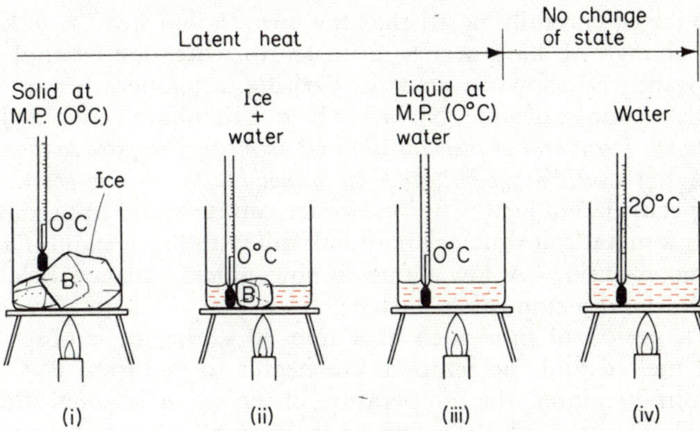

Fig. 12.1 Latent heat of fusion

melt and water is formed, Fig. 12.1(ii). The thermometer continues to register 0° C, however, although heat is supplied to the ice. As more heat is supplied more of the ice melts and the thermometer still continues to read 0° C. Eventually all the ice melts and only water at 0° C is present, Fig. 12.1 (iii). As further heat is supplied, the water temperature *rises*, Fig. 12.1 (iv).

Latent Heat · Molecular Explanation

The temperature remained constant at 0° C while the ice changed to water. Thus there was no visible indication, so far as the temperature was concerned, where the heat had gone. In the 18th century Black therefore gave the name of *latent heat* ('hidden heat') to the heat supplied when a solid changes to a liquid state without temperature change.

Today, we can explain latent heat by reference to molecular theory. A solid is kept in its rigid state by powerful forces of attraction between its molecules. The molecules are not static in position; they *vibrate* about some average or mean position (p. 177). The maximum distance of vibration or displacement is called the 'amplitude' of vibration. As more heat is given to a solid its kinetic energy increases and thus the amplitude increases. The molecules thus move farther and farther away from each other while the solid is heated—this is expansion. At one stage the attraction between the molecules is insufficient to keep the individual molecules in a fixed mean position. The molecules now slide about and constantly exchange partners. A *liquid* is formed.

Thus the latent heat of fusion is a measure of the energy needed to overcome the forces of attraction between the molecules of a solid, which keeps the solid in a rigid structure.

Specific Latent Heat of Fusion

It should be carefully noted that the term 'latent heat' is only used when a change of state occurs, from ice to water for example. Fig. 12.1 (iii) and (iv) shows water at 0° C rising in temperature to 10° C. This is *not* a change of state. No latent heat is therefore concerned here.

The specific latent heat of fusion is defined as *the heat required to change unit mass (1 kg) of a solid at the melting point to liquid at the melting-point.*

The specific latent heat of fusion l for ice can be found approximately by filling a metal calorimeter about half full with dry ice and placing a thermometer inside. A low flame is now quickly placed below the calorimeter and a stopwatch started.

After a period of time such as 4 min 30 s, the ice is observed to have all melted and the temperature begins to rise from 0° C. In a time 4 min 30 s later, the temperature of the water is noted. Suppose it is 65° C. The mass of water formed is the same as that of the ice, say 20 g.

Then, as the rate of supply of heat by the burner was unchanged,

heat given to 20 g water in raising its temperature from 0° C to 65° C
= heat given to 20 g of ice to melt it at 0° C

Now

$$\text{heat given to water} = 20 \times (65 - 0) \times 4{\cdot}2\ \text{J}$$

$$\therefore \text{heat given to ice} = 20 \times 65 \times 4{\cdot}2\ \text{J}$$

$$\therefore \text{heat per g} = \frac{20 \times 65 \times 4{\cdot}2}{20} = 273\ \text{J/g} = 273\ 000\ \text{J/kg}$$

= specific latent heat of fusion of ice.

Note that since the mass of ice (20 g) cancels, its actual mass is not needed in the experiment.

Accurate experiments show that the specific latent heat of fusion of ice is about 340 000 J/kg, that is, 340 000 J supplied to 1 kg of ice at 0°C will just melt it to water at 0°C. The specific latent heat of fusion of aluminium is about 400 000 J/kg, that is 400 000 J supplied to 1 kg of aluminium at 658°C (its melting point) will just melt it to liquid at 658°C.

Calculation of Latent Heat

When ice is heated, the water formed usually reaches a temperature above 0° C. As an illustration of how to calculate the quantity of heat concerned, suppose 3 g of ice at 0° C melts and forms water at 8° C.

This change occurs in two stages, Fig. 12.2:

Stage 1. The 3 g of ice at 0°C melts to 3 g of water at 0°C. This is a latent heat change. The specific latent heat of ice is 340 000 J/kg or 340 J/g,

$\therefore$ heat needed $= 3 \times 340 = 1020$ J.

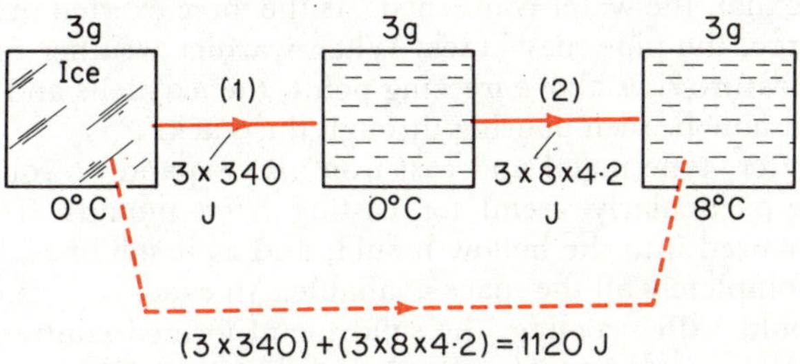

Fig. 12.2 Calculation of latent heat

Stage 2. Once all the water has been formed, its temperature rises to 8° C from 0° C. This is *not* a latent heat change. Since 1 g of water whose temperature rises by 1° C needs 4·2 J

$\therefore$ 3 g of water whose temperature rises by 8° C needs $3 \times 8 \times 4{\cdot}2 = 100$ J (approx.)

Adding 100 J to the 1020 J needed for latent heat,

$\therefore$ total heat $= 1120$ J.

Likewise, 5 g of ice at 0° C melting to form water at 12° C requires

$5 \times 340 + 5 \times (12 - 0) \times 4{\cdot}2 = 1700 + 252 = 1952$ J

(latent heat)

Heat Exchange Method for l

A value for the specific latent heat of fusion l of ice can be found by adding dry ice to water in a calorimeter of expanded polystyrene and finding the final water temperature after all the ice has melted. The heat capacity of the calorimeter can be ignored, and as it is a bad conductor of heat, little heat is lost in the experiment to the air.

Suppose the mass of dry ice melted was 5 g and that 40 g of water at

16° C temperature initially decreased to 6° C after all the ice melted and changed to water. Then

heat gained by ice in changing to water at 6° C $= 5l + 5 \times (6 - 0) \times 4{\cdot}2$ J and

heat lost by water = mass × temperature fall $\times 4{\cdot}2 = 40 \times (16 - 6) \times 4{\cdot}2$ J

$$\therefore 5l + 126 = 1680$$

Solving, $\therefore \quad l = 310$ J/g = 310 000 J/kg.

Change of Volume in Fusion

Many substances shrink when they change from the liquid to the solid state, that is, when they freeze. Water, however, expands when it changes to ice. This can be seen when water in a sectioned container is placed inside a refrigerator to form ice cubes. A little 'hump' is formed on the ice cube owing to the expansion which took place.

In very cold weather, when the temperature is below freezing point, the water in household pipes may freeze. The ice formed is greater in volume than the water concerned. As the force exerted in expansion is very large, the pipe may crack. When warmer weather returns and the temperature rises above freezing point, the ice melts and contracts. Water can now be seen pouring through the crack.

Like water, type metal and cast iron also expand on solidification. They are particularly useful for casting from moulds. The molten metal is poured into the hollow mould, and as it solidifies, it expands and fills completely all the space available. An exact copy is thus made of the mould. After cooling, the solid metal formed contracts slightly due to the drop in temperature to that of the surroundings.

Effect of Pressure on Melting Point

When ice is subjected to a large pressure its volume tends to decrease. Now when ice changes to water its volume becomes smaller. Hence increased pressure on ice helps it to change to water. It follows that ice can be melted if sufficient pressure is applied to it. Thus, in general, *the melting point of ice is lowered when it is subjected to increased pressure.*

Ice-skaters are able to move freely on account of the decrease of the melting-point of ice under increased pressure. The knife-edge bottom of the skate has a very small cross-sectional area, and hence the pressure under the knife-edge $\left(\frac{\text{Weight of skater}}{\text{Area of knife-edge}}\right)$ is very large. Together with the heat produced by friction, the net effect is the melting of ice under the skate, and the skater moves easily through a thin film of water on top of the ice, Fig. 12.3. If it is too cold, the ice does not melt, and the skate moves with difficulty over the ice.

Two small pieces of ice, pressed one against the other, stick together after releasing them. The increased pressure lowers the melting point, and those parts of the ice under high pressure therefore melt. The water formed flows away to a place where the pressure is less. Here it refreezes, thus binding the two pieces of ice together.

Snowballs are made by compressing the snow very strongly, when some of it melts under the increased pressure. When the pressure is

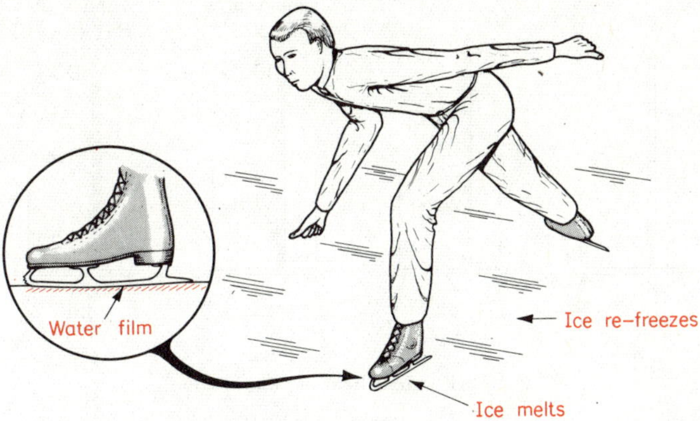

Fig. 12.3 Ice melts under pressure

released the water that was formed freezes, thus making a hard ball. If it is too cold the snow does not melt under increased pressure, and it is difficult to make a snowball.

Many substances *expand* when they change from the solid to the liquid state, unlike ice. Tin and paraffin-wax are two examples of these substances. Since increased pressure is unfavourable to a change from the solid to the liquid state in this case, increased pressure *raises* the melting point.

VAPORIZATION

We now consider the change of state from a *liquid to a gas or vapour*. This is called 'vaporization' or 'evaporation'. As will be seen, many features of vaporization are analogous to fusion.

Vaporization · Molecular Explanation

As a common example of vaporization, suppose a beaker is half-filled with water A and its temperature is 15° C, Fig. 12.4 (i). When the water is heated, its temperature rises and reaches 75° C at one stage, Fig. 12.4 (ii). There is no change of state yet. At about 100° C, however, bubbles of vapour or steam burst open continuously at the water surface having risen from the bottom of the water. A change of state from liquid to gas or vapour now occurs. While steam (vapour) is formed, the thermometer continues to record about 100° C—this is the boiling point of water. The heat needed to change a liquid at its boiling point to vapour at the same temperature is called its 'latent heat of vaporization or evaporation'.

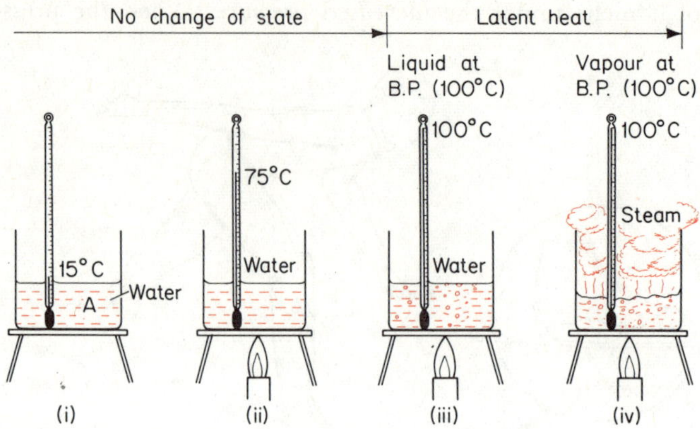

Fig. 12.4 Latent heat of vaporization

Eventually all the water evaporates. If the vapour or gas were collected and heated further, its temperature would rise. There is no change of state in this case.

Molecular Explanation

When a liquid is heated, its molecules gain energy. This enables them to overcome more the force of attraction with neighbouring molecules and to move faster inside the liquid. When the boiling point is reached, the forces of attraction between the molecules in the liquid state are then completely overcome. The molecules now have sufficient energy to escape from the liquid and form a gas or vapour.

The latent heat of vaporization thus provides the energy needed to overcome completely the force of attraction between molecules in the liquid state.

Approximate Measurement of *l*

The specific latent heat of vaporization of a liquid is defined as *the heat to change unit mass of liquid at the boiling-point to vapour to the boiling point.*

An approximate value for the specific latent heat of vaporization of water can be obtained by pouring 100 cm^3 (100 g) of water into a suitable metal can. Suppose the water temperature is 14° C. It is now warmed by a steady flame, and the time taken to reach 100° C, the boiling-point, is noted. Suppose this is 3 min 20 s.

The water is then heated for another 3 min 20 s. During this time vapour is formed. At the end of the time the burner is removed and after cooling, the volume of water remaining is measured. Suppose this is 80 cm³. Then 20 cm³ or 20 g of water has evaporated. Now the heat supplied during this period

$$= \text{heat to raise temperature of 100 g of water from } 14^\circ\text{ C to } 100^\circ\text{ C or } 86^\circ\text{ C}$$

$$= 100 \times 86 \times 4{\cdot}2 = 36\,000\text{ J (approx.)}$$

$$\therefore \text{ specific latent heat} = \frac{36\,000\text{ J}}{20\text{ g}} = 1800\text{ J/g} = 1\,800\,000\text{ J/kg}.$$

The experiment gives only very approximate results for the latent heat. It does show, however, that the specific latent heat of vaporization of water is high compared with the specific latent heat of fusion of ice. Conversely, if steam at 100° C condenses to water at 100° C, the heat given up is high. This is why scalds are painful and dangerous. The condensation of steam does the main damage.

Specific Latent Heat of Vaporization by Thick-walled Calorimeter

The specific latent heat of vaporization of water can be found by a method of mixtures. One form of apparatus is shown in Fig. 12.5.

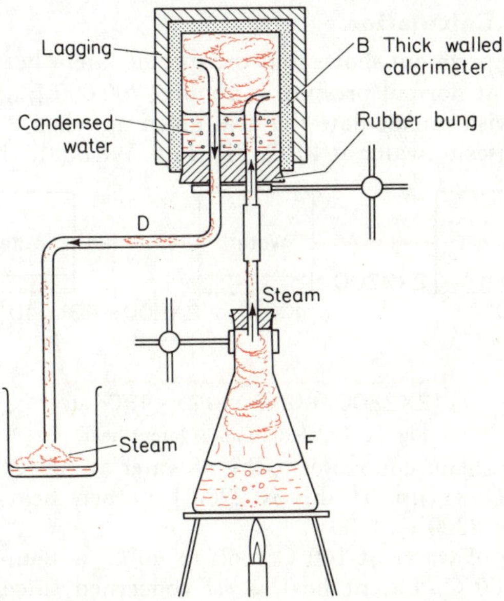

Fig. 12.5 Measurement of specific latent heat

B is an inverted thick-walled calorimeter. It is sealed at the bottom and lagged after its mass and temperature are measured. It is connected to the outlet from a flask F containing water and when steam is produced it passes into B.

At first, the steam condenses in B and water is formed which collects at the bottom. The heat given up by the condensed steam raises the temperature of B. Eventually B is raised to the temperature of the steam, 100° C say, after which the steam no longer condenses and passes out through D.

Calculation

Suppose that 35 g of water condensed in B. Then the heat given up by 35 g of steam in condensing to water at 100° C has raised the temperature of the calorimeter from its initial value, 15° C say, to 100° C. This is a temperature rise of 85° C. Suppose the mass of the calorimeter is 1000 g and its specific heat capacity is 800 J/kg °C or 0·8 J/g °C. The heat gained by the calorimeter is thus

$$1000 \times 0{\cdot}8 \times 85 = 68\,000 \text{ J}$$

The heat per g of steam given out on condensation is therefore

$$\frac{68\,000 \text{ J}}{35 \text{ g}} = 2000 \text{ J/g (approx. } 2\,000\,000 \text{ J/kg)}.$$

This is the value of the specific latent heat of vaporization, since the steam condensed to water at 100° C in the experiment.

Latent Heat Calculation

Accurate experiment shows that the specific latent heat of vaporization of water at normal pressure is about 2 200 000 J/kg or 2200 J/g. Suppose we wish to calculate the heat given up when 2 g of steam at 100°C condenses to water at 40°C, Fig. 12.6. We do this in two stages:

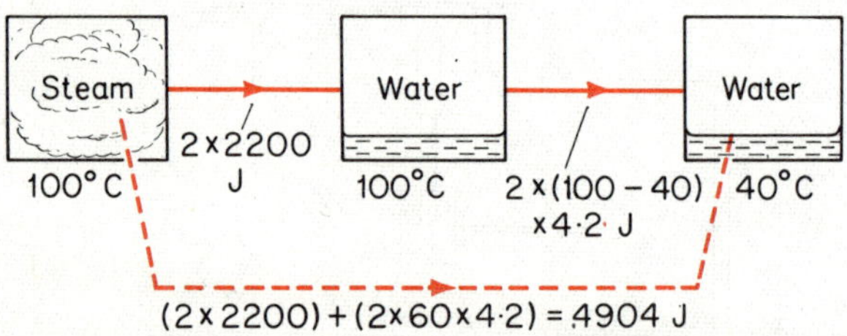

Fig. 12.6 Calculation on latent heat

Stage 1. 2 g steam condenses to 2 g of water at 100°C. Latent heat is given up. If this is 2200 J/g, then heat given up = 2 × 2200 = 4400 J.

Stage 2. 2 g of water at 100°C cools to 40°C, a temperature drop of 60°C. Latent heat is *not* concerned since there is no change of state. The heat given up = 2 × 60 × 4·2 = 504 J.

$$\therefore \text{ total heat given up} = 4400 + 504 = 4904 \text{ J}.$$

Boiling Point and Pressure

As we have seen, when a liquid boils, molecules leave the liquid and form a vapour outside. The energy given to the molecules must not only overcome the force of attraction between the molecules in the liquid state. Some energy is also needed to overcome the *external pressure* on the molecules in the liquid. The external pressure at the surface is the atmospheric pressure. If it is 760 mm mercury, the energy needed for vaporization of water molecules corresponds to a liquid temperature of 100° C. But if the external pressure is reduced, the energy needed for vaporization is reduced. Thus the water now boils at a temperature *lower* than 100° C.

Boiling under Reduced Pressure

The striking effect of a large reduction in external pressure can easily be demonstrated. A round-bottomed flask is filled with a little water, and a tube in the tight-fitting rubber cork is connected to a vacuum pump, Fig. 12.7. When the pump is switched on the air and water-vapour above the water is quickly removed and the external pressure falls to a low value. In a short time bubbles are seen rising through the water and bursting open at the surface. Thus the water has boiled at room temperature! No flame has been necessary to boil the water.

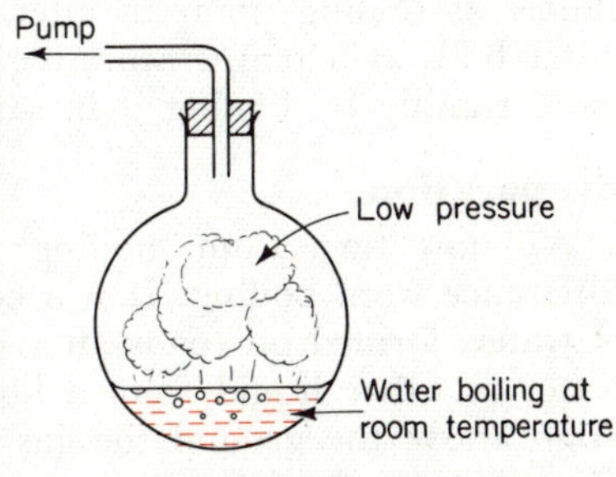

Fig. 12.7 Boiling point depends on pressure

As one climbs higher, the atmospheric pressure decreases. At about 3000 m above sea-level water boils at 90° C, and at 4000 m it boils at 85° C. Certain foods, such as beans, cannot be properly cooked in the open in very hilly regions, as the boiling point of water in these places is too low. The decrease of the boiling-point of water with decreasing pressure is put to practical use at stages in the manufacture of sugar, when the latter is boiled in 'vacuum pans'. These are containers in which the pressure is low, so that the sugar is prevented from charring. It is of interest to note that the hypsometer, the apparatus for determining the boiling point of a liquid (see p. 159), was formerly used by mountaineers to determine the height they climbed, as the boiling point of water depends on the height. The hypsometer has been superseded by the altimeter (p. 109).

Pressure Rise and Boiling Point

Conversely, it follows that water boils at a temperature above 100° C when the external pressure is greater than 760 mm mercury. At a pressure of two atmospheres, for example, the boiling point is raised to about 120°C.

In a *pressure cooker*, used by the housewife for rapid cooking and by the bacteriologist for sterilizing culture media, water is boiled under an

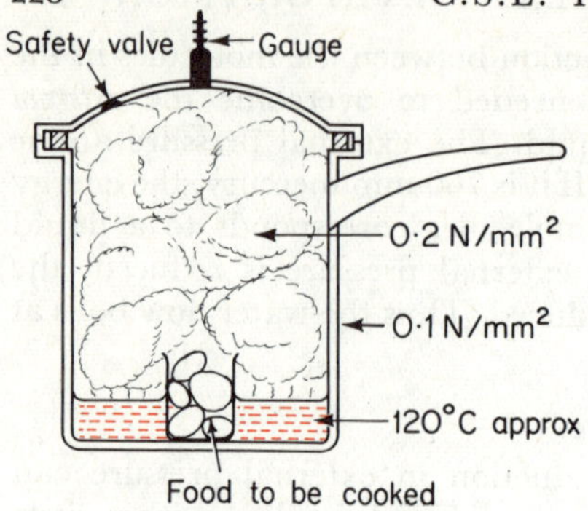

Fig. 12.8 Pressure cooker

increased pressure. If the gauge is set for 0·1 N/mm² or about 1 atmosphere above the external atmospheric pressure, the pressure inside the cooker is then increased to about 0·2 N/mm² or two atmospheres. Now the water boils at 120° C. Food cooked in water boiling at higher temperatures than 100° C takes less time to prepare. Fig. 12.8 illustrates the pressure cooker principle.

An impurity in a liquid also causes its boiling point to alter. When salt is added to water, the latter boils at a temperature higher than 100° C. You can cook food more rapidly by boiling it in salt water than by using pure water.

Evaporation

We now turn from 'boiling' and consider 'evaporation' and its difference from boiling. It is a common observation that small pools of water, formed on roads after rain, soon disappear. This change of water or other liquid from a liquid to a gaseous state is *evaporation.* High above the ground the gas or vapour may condense again and form tiny droplets of water in a *cloud.*

Liquids vary in the ease with which they change into vapour.

Pour a few drops of methylated spirit, then olive oil and finally water on your hand. Each time observe if evaporation occurs and whether your hand feels cold. Note that only the spirit evaporates easily and that your hand feels cold at the same time.

Liquids, such as methylated spirit and ether, which evaporate very easily have low boiling points. They are called *volatile liquids.* Latent heat is needed to change a liquid to vapour at the same temperature (p. 224) and this heat is absorbed from the hand when a few drops of a volatile liquid are placed on it. Consequently, one feels colder. We shall see later that volatile liquids are used in refrigerators.

Demonstration of Cooling by Evaporation

Another demonstration of the cooling produced by evaporation is shown in Fig. 12.9. A beaker is placed on top of a little water on a wooden block, and some liquid ether is then poured into the beaker. Air is now blown through the ether with the aid of a bellows or foot-pump. The ether eva-

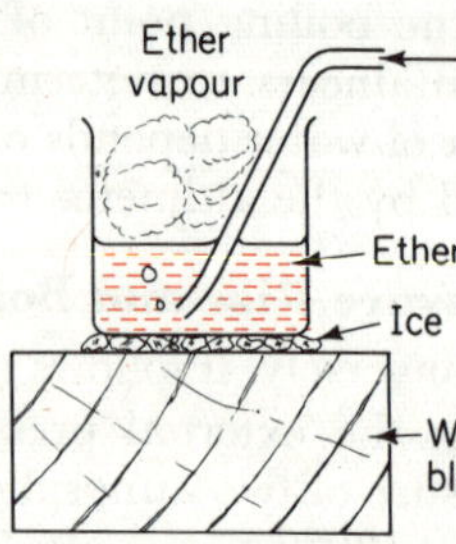

Fig. 12.9 Evaporation produces cooling

porates rapidly, and after a time it is found that the beaker is stuck to the wooden block. A thin layer of ice is formed between them, showing that the latent heat of evaporation for the ether was taken from the water, which then turned into ice.

Factors Affecting Evaporation

For a given liquid, evaporation is affected by the following factors:

(i) *Temperature of the Liquid.* Wet clothes on a clothes line dry more rapidly on a warm day. Thus the higher the temperature, the greater the rate of evaporation.

(ii) *Area of Exposed Surface.* A wet sheet on a line dries more quickly when opened than when left folded. Thus the evaporation increases as the area increases, Fig. 12.10.

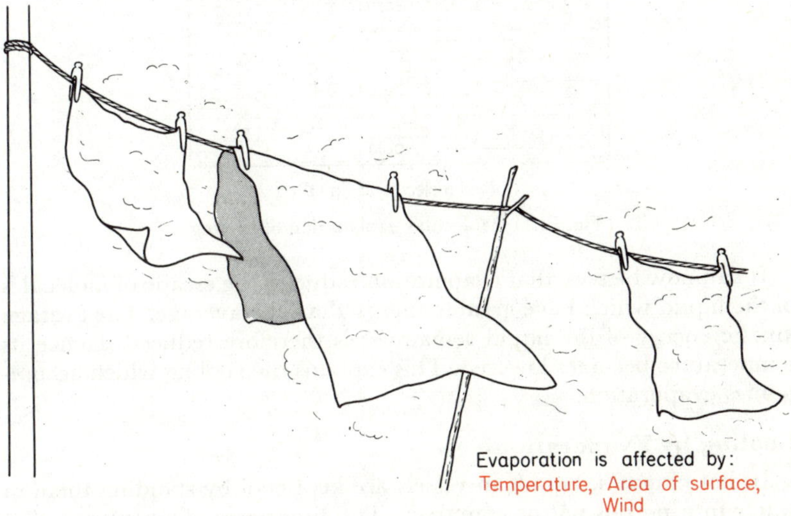

Fig. 12.10 Evaporation

(iii) *Rate of Removal of Vapour.* Wet clothes dry quicker on a windy, cold day than on a calm, cold day. This can also be felt when the finger is moistened and is then moved rapidly about in the air.

The difference between evaporation and boiling should be noted. Evaporation occurs at all temperatures, whereas boiling occurs at one particular temperature. Evaporation occurs by molecules leaving the surface (see p. 230); boiling occurs throughout the whole volume of the liquid. Evaporation depends on the area of the surface exposed; boiling is independent of the area and depends only on the external pressure.

Molecular Explanation

On the kinetic theory, evaporation is explained by the random motion of molecules in a liquid. They all have different velocities, and at any instant they are moving in many different directions. Near the surface, some molecules with high velocities in an upward direction may have sufficient kinetic energy to break through the surface and exist outside as molecules of vapour, Fig. 12.11. Others which escape may encounter molecules of air or vapour and return through the liquid after collision. A wind which removes molecules of air and vapour, thus assists evaporation.

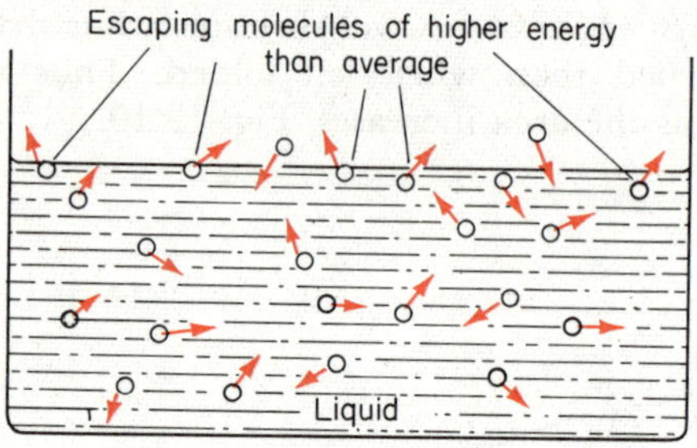

Fig. 12.11 Molecular explanation of cooling

It can now be seen that evaporation is due to the escape of molecules of the liquid which have greater energy than the average. The average kinetic energy of the liquid remaining is therefore reduced. Hence its temperature becomes lowered. This explains the cooling which accompanies evaporation.

Cooling by Evaporation

In hot climates, liquids in vessels are kept cool by standing them in water in a porous pot or container. The tiny pores allow evaporation from an appreciable area of the water. The latent heat for evaporation taken from the water cools the water and hence the vessel and liquid inside it. Milk bottles may be kept cool in summer by wrapping a wet cloth round them. The evaporation from the cloth cools the milk.

The body has a natural cooling system. Through the pores of the skin we sweat continuously. The latent heat of evaporation of the water is taken from the skin, which thus becomes cooled. On a hot day, we sweat more and are therefore cooled more. In this way the body is kept at a constant normal temperature of about 98·4° F or 36·9° C. When we are uncomfortably hot, evaporation does not take place so readily and beads of sweat then form on the skin. In very cold weather the skin contracts and if evaporation does not take place readily it wrinkles. 'Beauty oils', which are hygroscopic or take moisture from the air, may be used for the skin in such cases.

Dew-point

An opposite effect occurs when a glass of cold water is brought into a warm room. The outside of the glass becomes misty. The water-vapour in the air round the cold glass surface condenses to water on the glass. In a bath-room full of steam, the cold tap is misty for the same reason. The hot tap remains unaffected.

When a bright metal surface is cooled, the water-vapour in the air in contact with the surface condenses at one temperature and the surface becomes misty. The *dew-point* is the name given to the temperature when dew first forms as the air temperature is lowered. At night, the earth radiates heat and becomes colder than the air above it. Moisture then forms on metal objects on the ground. Dew forms on blades of grass at night on account of radiation from the grass. This cools it below the dew-point of the air and water-vapour in the air then condenses.

Refrigerator

Fig. 12.12 shows the principle of the action of a domestic refrigerator. A volatile liquid is contained in the pipes surrounding the freezing

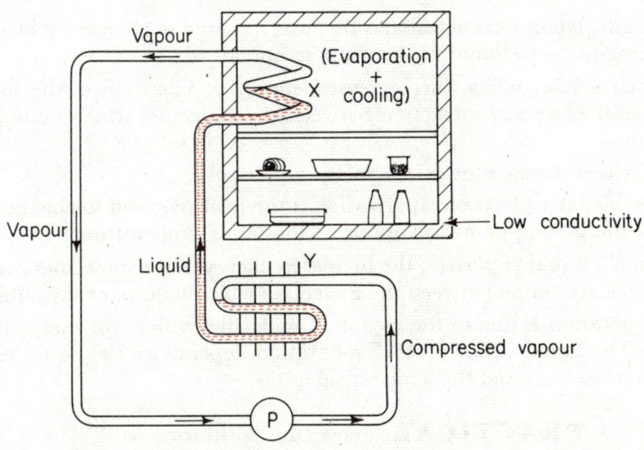

Fig. 12.12 Refrigeration unit

chamber where food is stored. The liquid evaporates, thus cooling the pipes and surrounding air, from which it extracts the necessary latent heat. The vapour formed is removed by a pump P, which compresses it into a condenser Y mounted outside the refrigerator. Here it condenses and gives out latent heat. This is passed to the surrounding

Plate 12(A) *Frigidaire* compressor unit. Cutaway section of interior shows an electric motor (magnetic field provided by coils and rotor in centre) which drives a compressor mounted at the base. The regrigerant vapour is compressed inside and then passes out into a condenser where it changes slowly to liquid.

air by means of metal cooling fins fixed round Y. From Y the liquid is forced into X, where it again evaporates. Thus continuous cooling of the refrigerator chamber takes place. A valve (not shown) between X and Y maintains X at a lower pressure than Y to ensure steady evaporation of the volatile liquid. See Plate 12A.

SUMMARY

1. Specific latent heat of fusion is the heat required to change 1 g of a solid at the melting-point to liquid at the same temperature.

2. When a solid melts, the increased energy of vibration of the molecules overcomes the forces of attraction between the molecules which maintains the solid form.

3. Increased pressure lowers the melting-point of ice.

4. Specific latent heat of vaporization is the heat required to change 1 g of a liquid at the boiling-point to vapour at the same temperature.

5. When a liquid vaporizes, the increased energy of the molecules overcomes the forces of attraction between the molecules which maintains the liquid form.

6. Evaporation is due to the escape of molecules with more energy than the average. The liquid hence cools. Evaporation depends on the liquid temperature, its surface area and the wind outside.

PRACTICAL (Notes for guidance, p. 26)

1. Specific latent heat of fusion of ice

Measure the specific latent heat of fusion of ice by the method on p. 220. Use small lumps of ice, dry them with blotting-paper before putting them into the metal can and then quickly place the flame beneath the can. Repeat the experiment with more ice and compare your results.

Measurements.

Time to melt all the ice = .. min .. s
Temperature of water after .. min .. s = °C.

Calculation.

Heat to raise temperature of water from 0°C to .. °C
= mass × .. °C × 4·2 J
= heat to melt same mass of ice to water at 0°C

$$\therefore \text{Specific latent heat (per g)} = \frac{\text{mass} \times \ldots\ ^\circ\text{C} \times 4{\cdot}2}{\text{mass}} = \ldots$$

(mass cancels).

2. Melting-point of naphthalene

Method. (i) Fill a large test-tube T with naphthalene (moth-balls).

(ii) Support the test-tube in a clamp and stand and heat it in a large beaker B of water until *all* the solid has melted. Fig. 12.13 (i).

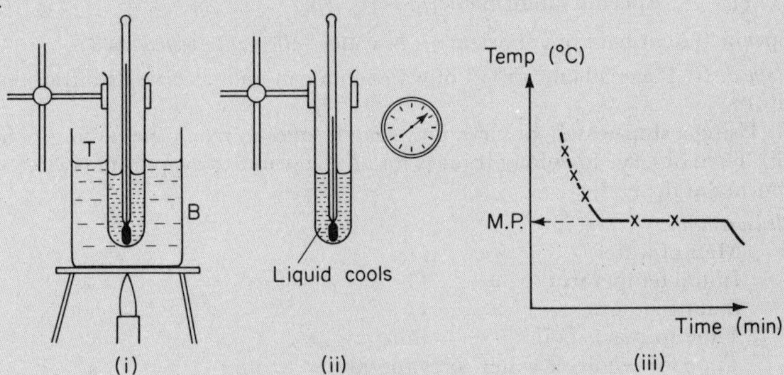

Fig. 12.13 Melting point of solid

(iii) Place a thermometer inside the liquid obtained.

(iv) Remove the test-tube from the water by raising it out with the stand, and then leave the liquid cool in the air on its own. Fig. 12.13 (ii).

Observe the temperature as it falls every 30 s. At some time the temperature will become constant and then it will fall again. Stop timing shortly after the temperature falls again.

Measurements.

Time (s)	Temperature (°C)
0	..

Graph. Plot temperature v. time. Fig. 12.13 (iii).

Melting-point. The melting-point, M.P., of the naphthalene is the temperature corresponding to the flat part of the graph (the latent heat given out on freezing compensates for the heat lost to the surroundings, so the temperature remains constant).

Record your result for the melting-point. Note also the shape of the surface of the solid naphthalene.

3. Specific latent heat of vaporization of water

Measure the specific latent heat of steam by the method outlined on p. 224. Repeat the experiment using a different mass of water.

Measurements.

Mass of water = .. g
Initial temperature = .. °C
Boiling temperature = .. °C
Time to reach boiling = .. min .. s
Mass of water left after .. min .. s = .. g

Calculation.

Heat to raise temperature of .. g of water from .. °C to .. °C (boiling point) = .. J

Mass of water evaporated by this quantity of heat = .. g

∴ Specific latent heat J/g = .. J/kg.

4. Specific latent heat of vaporization of water (*alternative method to* **3**)

Method. (i) Place 50 cm^3 (50 g) of water in a can and observe its initial temperature.

(ii) Using a stop-watch, observe how long it takes to reach the boiling-point.

(iii) Then observe how long it takes for *all* the water to evaporate (switch off the burner at the end).

Measurements.

Mass of water = .. g
Initial temperature = .. °C
Boiling-point = .. °C
Time to reach boiling = .. min .. s = .. s
Time for whole of water to evaporate = .. min .. s = .. s.

Calculation.

Heat gained by water from .. °C (initial) to .. °C (boiling-point)
= mass of water × temperature rise × 4·2 = .. J

Heat needed to evaporate all this water at boiling-point

$$= \frac{\text{Time to evaporate}}{\text{Time to reach boiling}} \times \text{heat gained in reaching boiling-point}$$

= .. J

$$\therefore \text{Specific latent heat} = \frac{..\text{ J}}{\text{mass in g}} = ..\text{ J/g} = ..\text{ J/kg}$$

Note. Since the mass of water cancels in the above arithmetic, the mass of water is actually not needed to find the latent heat.

5. Specific latent heat of vaporization by mixtures

Apparatus. Thick-walled calorimeter; cork to seal top with two holes in it for inlet and outlet; flask; tripod; gauze; burner, 0–100°C thermometer.

Method. Assemble the apparatus as shown on p. 225, *after* weighing the calorimeter. Then follow the method outlined. Remove the burner shortly after steam begins to emerge from the outlet. When cooled, measure the volume of water collected in the calorimeter by a small measuring cylinder.

Measurements.

Mass of calorimeter = .. g, specific heat capacity of metal = ..
Mass of water (condensed steam) = .. g
Initial calorimeter temperature = .. °C
Final temperature = .. °C.

Calculation.
Mass of water × l = mass of calorimeter × sp. heat capacity × temperature rise $\therefore l = \,..\, \text{J/g} = \,..\, \text{J/kg}$.

Repeat the experiment without any lagging round the calorimeter. Compare your result for l with the result when lagging was used.

6. Evaporation

Method (i) Place a thermometer in a test-tube to keep the bulb dry. Immerse the test-tube in a beaker of water and heat the water until the thermometer reads about 80°C. Remove the thermometer, place it in a clamp and allow it to cool in air. Observe the temperature after equal intervals of time such as 30 s.

(ii) Tie some blotting-paper firmly but carefully round the thermometer bulb. Place the thermometer in a beaker of water and heat until the thermometer reads about 80°C. Remove the thermometer, place it in a clamp and allow it to cool in the same place as before. Observe the temperature after the same equal intervals of time as previously.

Measurements.

Dry bulb

Time (s)	Temperature (°C)
0	. .

Wet bulb

Time (s)	Temperature (°C)
0	. .

Graph. Plot a graph on the same axes of temperature (°C) v. time (s).

(i) What 'conclusion' can you draw about the rate of cooling of the bulb in the two cases? Why are the rates different?

(ii) Using fresh blotting-paper round the thermometer bulb, dip this into a 'volatile liquid' such as alcohol or ether. Observe the temperature after equal intervals of time and plot it. What is your 'conclusion', and why?

7. Specific latent heat of fusion of ice by mixtures (p. 221)

Apparatus. Ice; polystyrene calorimeter and lid; thermometer 0–100C°; blotting-paper; beaker; balance weighing to $\frac{1}{10}$ g.

Method. (i) Weigh the calorimeter (to $\frac{1}{10}$ g).

(ii) Fill it about one-third full with water and reweigh.

(iii) Note the water temperature.

(iv) *Dry* small pieces of ice with blotting-paper and add them to the water a little at a time. Stir the ice until it is all melted and stop adding ice when the temperature is about 8° C below room temperature. Note the final temperature of the water.

(v) Weigh the calorimeter and water and melted ice.

Measurements.

Mass of calorimeter = . . g
Mass of calorimeter + water = . . g
Mass of calorimeter + water + ice = . . g.

Initial temperature =°C
Final temperature = . .°C

Calculation.

Mass of ice = . . g. Mass of water = . . g
Follow the calculation on p. 222.

Conclusion. . . .

EXERCISE 12 · ANSWERS, p. 258

1. Latent heat is the: (*a*) residual heat left in an electric oven when the current is switched off; (*b*) heat required to maintain an even temperature; (*c*) heat required to make a metal expand; (*d*) heat required to change the state of a substance; (*e*) heating value of a given volume of coal gas. (*M.*)

2. Steam causes a worse scald than boiling water. Show why this is so by *calculating* the heat given out in the following cases. *No explanation is required.* (Sp. ht. capacity of water = 4200 J/kg °C or 4·2 J/g °C. Sp. latent heat of steam = 2 200 000 J/kg or 2200 J/g.)

(*a*) 10 g of water at 100°C cool to 20°C; (*b*) 10 g of steam at 100°C cool to 20°C. (*E.A.*)

3. Calculate the heat required to change 1 g of ice at 0°C to steam at 100°C. (Specific latent heat of fusion of ice = 340 J/g. Specific latent heat of evaporation of water = 2200 J/g. Specific heat capacity of water = 4·2 J/g °C.) (*E.A.*)

4. Some crushed ice is heated until it changes into steam. Temperatures are taken at regular intervals, the initial temperature being −5°C

(*a*) At which temperature does the ice change into water?

(*b*) At which temperature does the water have its least volume?

(*c*) If the latent heat of fusion of ice is 340 000 J/kg and 0·1 kg of ice are being used, how much heat will have been supplied during the time when the thermometer reads 0°C?

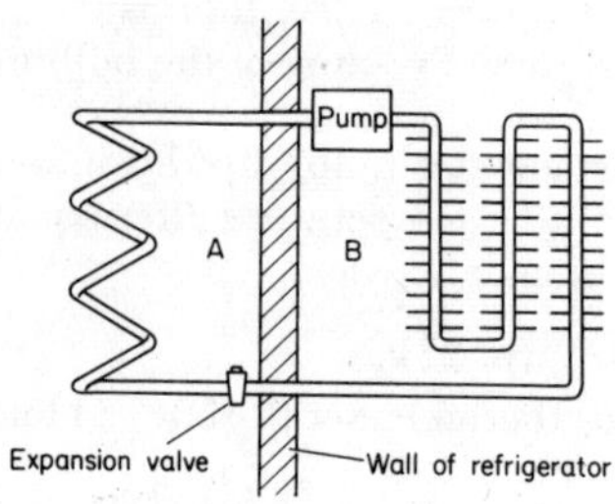

Fig. 12A

(*d*) Which temperature does the thermometer register for the greatest length of time?

(*e*) If salt is added to the ice before heating how does this affect: (i) the original temperature of the ice? (ii) the boiling-point of the water? (*S.*)

Fig. 12A represents the cooling system of a refrigerator. Which is the inside of the refrigerator compartment, A or B?

Show by arrows on the drawing, the direction of flow of the refrigerant (i.e. the fluid in the pipes). Shade in the parts of the pipes where the refrigerant is liquid. Name one substance which is used as a refrigerant in refrigerators of this type. (*S.*)

5. The mistiness that forms on the sides of a glass holding an ice-cold drink is due to the: (*a*) heat of the air around it; (*b*) warming of the glass by the air; (*c*) the liquid passing through the glass from the inside; (*d*) condensation of water vapour on the sides; (*e*) glass being warm when the drink was poured in. (*M.*)

6. (*a*) Explain the difference between evaporation and boiling. (*b*) State the factors which affect the rate of evaporation of a liquid. (*W.Md.*)

7. What effect, if any, is produced on the boiling-point of water by: (*a*) increasing the pressure on it; (*b*) adding salt to the water? (*L.*)

8. Explain, in terms of molecules and heat energy: (*a*) the process of evaporation; (*b*) the method of finding the wind direction by holding up a moistened finger; (*c*) the cooling action of a refrigerator which depends upon rapid expansion of the working substance; (*d*) the fact that a substance gives out heat but stays at the same temperature when changing from liquid to solid. (*M.*)

9. Explain the effect which rapid compression has on the temperature of a gas. What other effect is produced by compressing a gaseous substance such as ammonia? Explain how these principles are made use of in a pump-operated domestic refrigerator. (*M*).

10. (*a*) Why are the *fixed points* on a mercury-in-glass thermometer called: (i) the melting-point of pure ice and *not* the freezing-point of water; (ii) the temperature of stream at normal atmospheric pressure and *not* the boiling-point of water?

(*b*) Show, with the aid of a diagram, the principles of the domestic refrigerator. (*W.M.*)

11. Day and night temperatures of the land and sea were taken on the coast and found to be as follows:

	Land	*Sea*
Day	23°C	16°C
Night	12°C	15°C

Why is there a large variation in the land temperatures and not those of the sea? (*S.*)

12. Calculate the cost of heating the water in a swimming pool from 20°C to 25°C, using gas heating. The pool contains 360 000 litres of water. (Gas heating costs 10p per therm; 1 therm = 100 million joules; specific heat capacity of water = 4200 J/kg °C.)

Explain carefully, referring to the molecular theory, why there is a considerable loss of water through evaporation in an open-air pool, especially in hot or windy weather, whereas in an indoor pool little evaporation occurs.

What effect will evaporation in windy weather have upon the temperature of the water in a swimming pool, and why? (*S.*)

13. A person peels an orange in a large room. After a short while the smell of the orange is all through the room.

(i) Explain how the liquid in the orange evaporates.

(ii) Explain how the smell spreads round the room. (*M.*)

13

HEAT ENGINES AND TRANSMISSION SYSTEM

HEAT energy is converted into mechanical energy in a *heat engine*. The steam engine, the petrol engine, the diesel engine, the diesel engine and the jet engine use different sources of fuel. All use heat energy to provide movement. In the case of the petrol engine, this eventually leads to rotary motion of wheels of cars, for example, and in the case of the jet engine, to linear forward motion of aeroplanes.

It is important to realize that, in practice, machines are less than 100% efficient, that is, the energy obtained is always less than that supplied. In a steam engine some energy is wasted in the exhaust gases; in the jet engine some energy is wasted in the hot gases of the jet as they expand.

Petrol Engine

The petrol engine, commonly used in motor cars, obtains its energy from an exploded mixture of air and the vapour of very volatile petrol. See p. 240. It is sometimes called the 'four-stroke cycle' engine because four piston strokes or movements inside the cylinder repeat themselves continuously. The piston strokes are in the order *intake*, *compression*, *explosion*, *exhaust*. The valve positions controlling the cylinder openings, the directions of the piston movements and the state of gases during each stroke are shown in Fig. 13.1.

Plate 13(A) Cutaway section of typical spark plug.

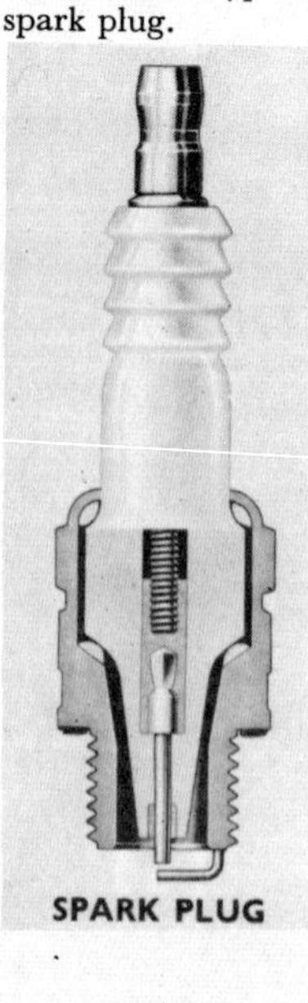

Intake

As the piston moves down the cylinder the inlet valve opens and a mixture of air and vapour is drawn into the cylinder.

Compression

The piston moves up and compresses the mixture to about one-seventh of its volume. At the top of the stroke the mixture is exploded by a spark which passes between the electrodes of a sparking-plug. Plate 13A.

Explosion

The expanding gases force the piston down.

Exhaust

As the piston moves up, the exhaust valve is

opened and the burnt or exhaust gases are expelled from the cylinder. The cycle is then repeated. See Plate 13B, p. 240.

In the four-stroke engine a power stroke is obtained once every four strokes, which corresponds to two revolutions of the crankshaft. A *two-stroke* engine provides a power stroke once every revolution by combining two strokes of the four-stroke cycle into one. As we soon shall see, the valves of the four-stroke engine are replaced by openings or ports in the two-stroke engine cylinder, and these are covered and uncovered by the moving piston.

The petrol engine is an example of an *internal combustion engine* (I.C.E.) because the combustion of fuel takes place inside the engine. The diesel engine (p. 242) is an internal combustion engine. On the other hand, the steam engine, described on p. 243, is not an internal combustion engine. The fuel is burnt in the boiler outside the engine.

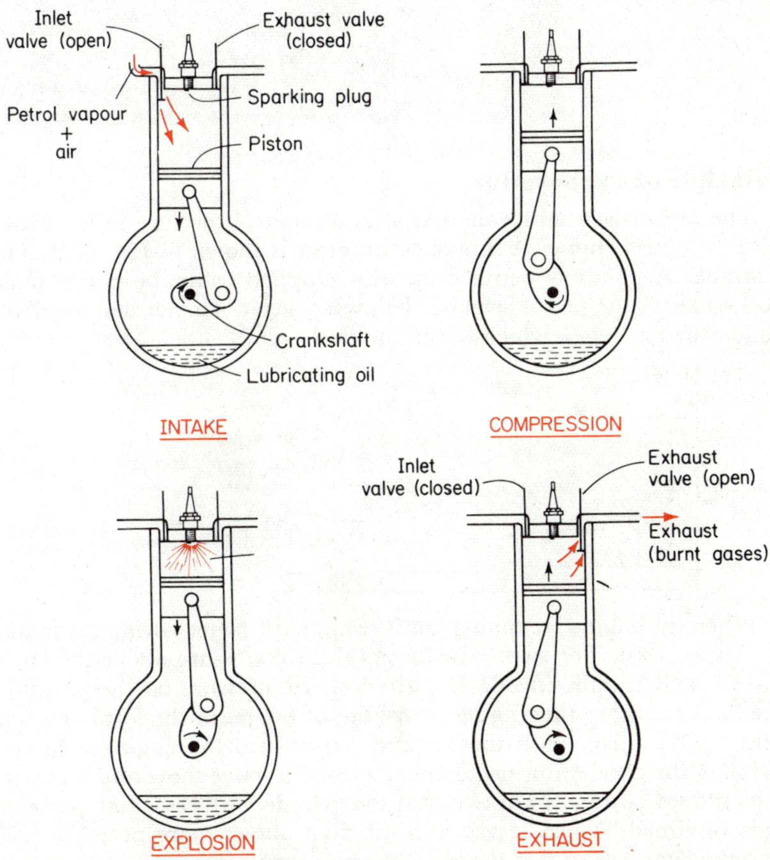

Fig. 13.1 Internal combustion engine—four-stroke cycle

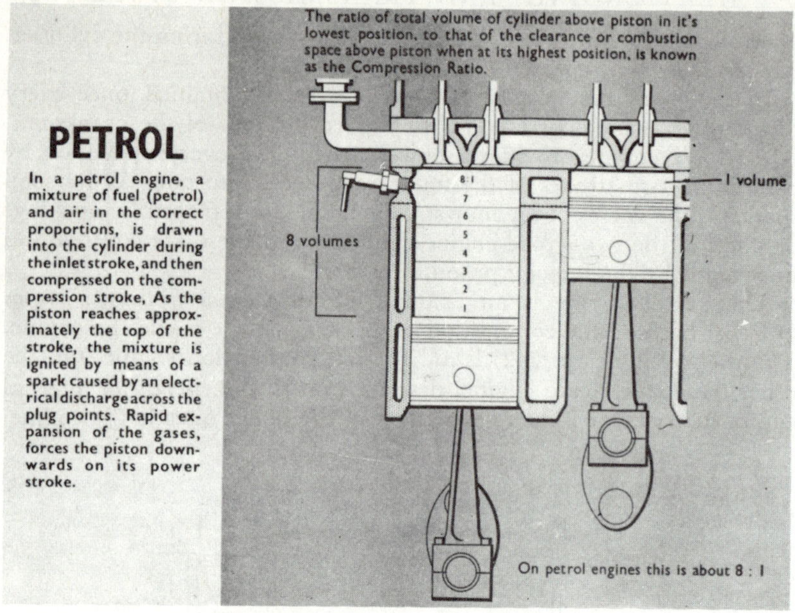

Plate 13(B) Petrol engine

Principle of Carburettor

The *carburettor* enables the required air–petrol mixture to be drawn into the petrol engine. A simple carburettor is shown in Fig. 13.2. The chamber A contains petrol originally supplied from the petrol tank. A float keeps the petrol level just below a fine jet. The jet is in a narrow tube called a *venturi*, which widens on both sides.

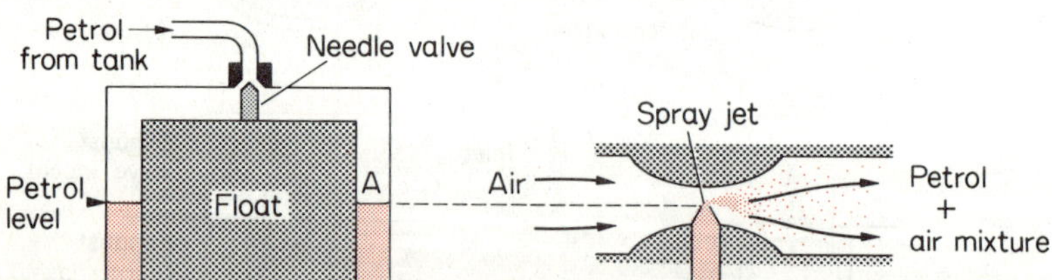

Fig. 13.2

When the engine is running, air is swept past the jet during the intake stroke (p. 238). The swift flow lowers the air pressure above the jet, a so-called 'Bernoulli effect'. The atmospheric pressure on the petrol in the float chamber then forces petrol out of the jet in the form of a fine spray. This mixes with the air and passes into the engine cylinder. Pressing the accelerator pedal opens a throttle valve more and increases the amount of mixture drawn into the cylinder. More engine power is then obtained. A needle valve in the float allows more petrol to pass into the chamber so that the petrol level is kept constant.

Two-stroke Engine

The two-stroke engine is a simplified form of internal-combustion engine. Unlike the four-stroke engine it has no separate valves. And in it the complete cycle of operations—induction, compression, ignition, exhaust—occurs in *two* strokes of the piston.

The piston itself acts as its own valve by uncovering two small holes or ports E and I in the cylinder wall as it slides up and down, Fig. 13.3. These ports are arranged so that the exhaust port E is highest.

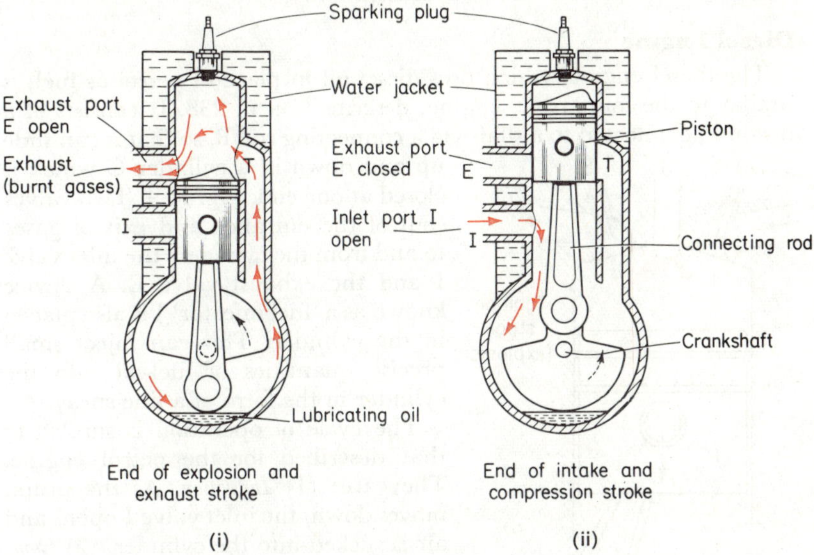

Fig. 13.3 Two-stroke engine

The transfer port T, which enables gases to be transferred from the crankcase to the space above the piston, is almost level with E on the opposite side of the cylinder. Beneath the exhaust port E is the inlet port I.

The cycle of operation is as follows. Assume that a mixture of vapour and air, or 'charge', was originally drawn in. When the piston moves up, it covers the exhaust and transfer ports, as shown in Fig. 13.3 (ii). The mixture is then compressed to the top of the cylinder. The inlet port I is uncovered at the same time. A petrol–air mixture is then drawn into the gas-tight crankcase for later use, as shown by the arrows in Fig. 13.3 (ii).

After the charge has been compressed, it is ignited by the spark from the sparking plug. The hot gases expand and force the piston down, thus covering the inlet port. On moving lower, the exhaust port is uncovered and the burnt gases escape, Fig. 13.3 (i). At the same time, the charge in the crankcase is compressed. The transfer port T is then uncovered and the charge compressed in the crankcase is now forced through T to the cylinder. A specially designed deflector on top of the piston ensures that the fresh charge does not mix with the exhaust gases leaving the cylinder. As the crank rotates the piston rises and the cycle repeats.

The efficiency of the two-stroke engine is low in practice. It is therefore used to drive relatively small machines, such as lawn mowers and mopeds, for example. Here the light motor is an advantage and fuel consumption is not the main consideration.

Diesel Engine

The diesel engine, which uses diesel oil in place of petrol as fuel, is similar to the four-stroke engine, described on p. 238. It consists of a piston P, connected to a shaft via a connecting rod B, so that it can slide up and down in a cylinder C which is closed at one end, Fig. 13.4. Two valves control the entrance and exit of gases to and from the cylinder; the inlet valve I and the exhaust valve E. A device known as a 'fuel injector' J is also placed in the cylinder. This can inject small precise quantities of fuel-oil into the cylinder in the form of a fine spray.

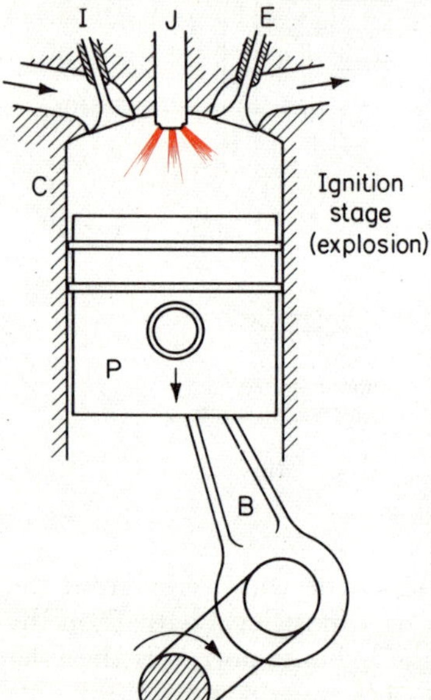

Fig. 13.4 Diesel engine

The cycle of operation is similar to that described for the petrol engine. They are: (1) *Induction.* As the piston moves down, the inlet valve I opens and air is sucked into the cylinder. (2) *Compression.* The inlet valve shuts, and the piston moves up, compressing the air and thereby heating it. (3) *Ignition.* When the air is fully compressed, a small precise quantity of fuel is injected in the form of a spray. This vaporizes, and is ignited spontaneously as shown in Fig. 13.4. The hot burning gases expand and force the piston down. (4) *Exhaust.* When the piston starts moving up again, the exhaust valve E opens and the burnt gases are pushed out of the cylinder. When all the gases have been expelled, the exhaust valve shuts, and the cycle repeats.

As in the petrol engine (p. 238), this is a four-stroke cycle. The main difference is (1) on the induction only air is sucked in and not a petrol–air mixture, (2) the method of ignition is different. In the petrol engine this is done by a sparking plug. In the diesel engine, this is done by compressing the air to a much higher degree than in the petrol engine and then injecting the diesel fuel in the form of a spray just before the piston reaches the top of its motion. The resulting temperature rise causes ignition.

Diesel engines are very efficient with heavy loads. They are robust and need no electrical equipment such as sparking plugs and induction coils. The fuel used is much cheaper than petrol. On this account diesel engines are used in commercial vehicles, for example, buses, lorries, trains and taxicabs, and in civil engineering plant and marine engines.

Steam Engine

The idea of the steam engine is due to Watt. History records that he was led to the invention after observing how steam pressure in a kettle was able to force the lid open.

A steam engine changes some of the heat energy stored in steam into mechanical energy. Fig. 13.5 shows the principle of one form of steam

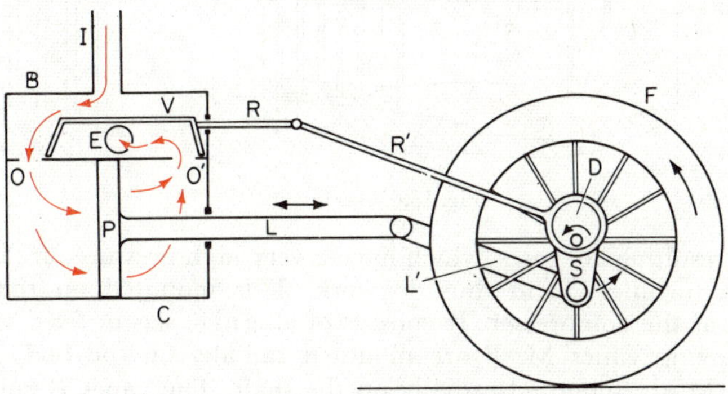

Fig. 13.5 Steam engine

engine. It has a piston P which can slide in a cylinder C, with a connected rod L. C has two openings or 'ports', O and O′, which allow steam to flow into C or out of C respectively As we shall see, a sliding valve, represented by V, controls the direction of flow of the steam into C or out of C. V slides in a valve box B and has a rod R connected to it.

With V in the position shown, the steam entering I passes through O into C. The piston P is then forced to the right by the pressure. Gases or steam on the right of P are now pushed out of the cylinder through O′ and then through the exhaust outlet E. As P nears its right-hand limit of movement, an eccentric cam D, attached to the flywheel F, moves V to the left through rods R and R′. This reverses the flow of steam. It now enters C through O′ and leaves through O. The piston therefore starts to move in the opposite direction, until the cam reverses the position of V again.

The cycle then repeats. Thus a to-and-fro motion of the piston L results. This is called an oscillatory or *reciprocating* motion. It is converted into *rotary* motion (of the flywheel) by the crank S and connecting rod L′.

Gas Turbine

The gas turbine engine contains a fan-like air compressor C, mounted on a shaft S, Fig. 13.6. When the shaft revolves at high speed, air is sucked in as shown and is compressed by C. This air then flows into a series of combustion chambers A, A′, where it is first mixed with a fine spray of oil such as paraffin (kerosene) and then burnt continuously.

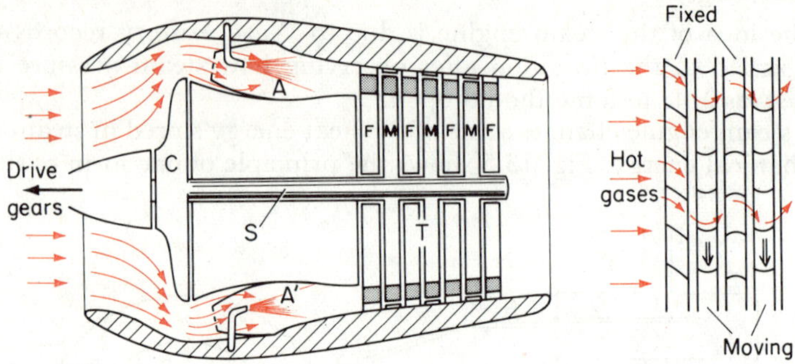

Fig. 13.6 Gas turbine

The resulting hot gases, which have a very high pressure, are used to drive a turbine T and thus do work. T is mounted on the same shaft S as the compressor. It consists of alternate sets of fixed vanes F and moving vanes M. F are mounted radially on the body of the motor. M are mounted radially on the shaft. The vanes F guide the hot gases on to M, as shown in Fig. 13.6, and hence M are forced to turn. The turbine thus drives the compressor, and the process is continuous and self-supporting. Power can be taken from S via a suitable coupling.

Jet Engines · Rocket Engines

Jet engines, invented by Sir Frank Whittle in 1940, derive their thrust from the hot gases expelled continuously at their rear with high velocity. From Newton's law of Action and Reaction, the thrust on the engine is equal and opposite to that on the gas molecules, and this can drive an aeroplane forward at very high speeds.

In a turbo-jet engine, air is drawn in at the front and compressed, and then, after mixing with fuel, it is burnt in a combustion chamber and ejected with very high velocity through an exhaust nozzle at the rear, Fig. 13.7. Jet aeroplanes can fly at very high altitudes, where the efficient engine takes in the very large volumes per second of thin air required.

Rocket engines are used for launching satellites in orbits round the earth. Unlike jet engines, which need air as fuel, a rocket engine

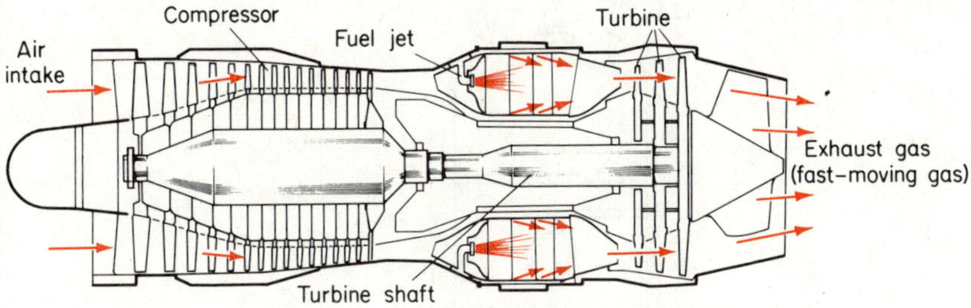

Fig. 13.7 Jet engine

carries its own fuel and oxidizer, and can therefore function at great heights where very little air is present, Fig. 13.8. Liquid or solid fuel may be used, and very hot gases are expelled from the rear with very

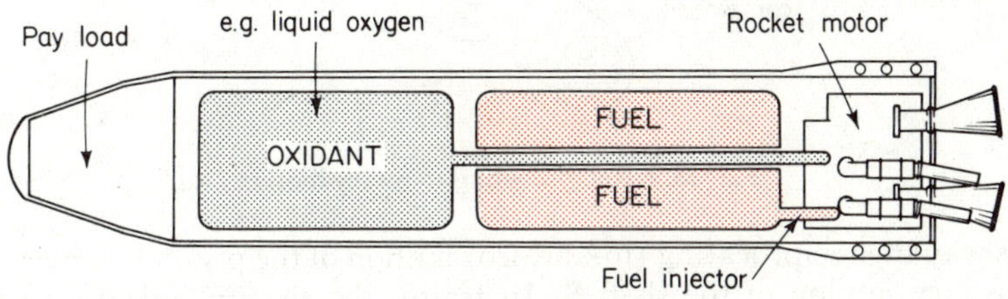

Fig. 13.8 Rocket engine

high velocity. Like the jet engine, the upward thrust on the rocket and load carried is equal and opposite to the downward thrust on the burnt gases. The rocket stops working in outer space as soon as the fuel is used up. See page 142.

Conversion of Motion

The to-and-fro sliding motion of the piston of a petrol engine is called *reciprocating motion* and the engine is an example of a *reciprocating engine*. Diesel and steam engines are reciprocating engines. The gas turbine is not a reciprocating engine—its motion is entirely *rotary*.

To turn the wheels of a car, for example, an arrangement is needed for changing the reciprocating motion of the engine piston to rotary motion. This is done by a mechanism called a *crank*. Fig. 13.9 shows basically how the motion is converted. The piston P slides to-and-fro in the cylinder C. A rod R is fixed to the underside of P. The other end of R is connected to a pin B called the *crankpin*. This is mounted on a radial arm D fixed to a shaft S, shown in section. S is called the *crankshaft*.

When P moves up-and-down, B moves round the axis of S in a clockwise direction. The shaft S is thus made to rotate. S revolves once for a complete cycle of movement (back and forth) of the piston P. In

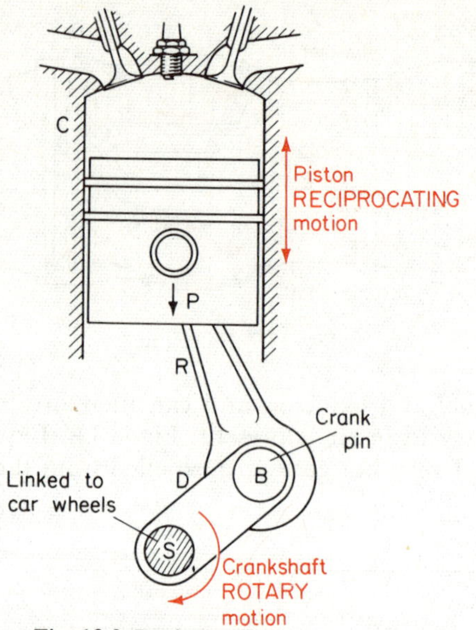

Fig. 13.9 Reciprocating to rotary motion

this way the reciprocating (to-and-fro) motion of the piston is converted to rotary motion of the shaft S. In trains, the shaft is linked directly to the wheels. In the motor car, however, other shafts and gears are needed between the crankshaft and the wheels (p. 251).

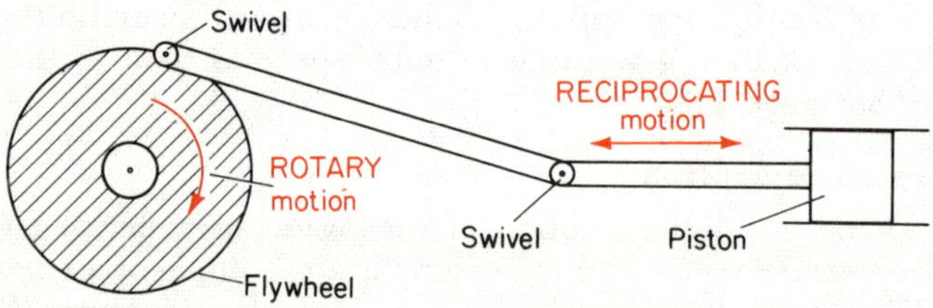

Fig. 13.10 Rotary to reciprocating motion

Fig. 13.10 illustrates how rotary motion can be changed to reciprocating motion. Here the rotary motion of a flywheel is changed to the reciprocating motion of a piston, as for use in a press or forging machine.

Engine Power and Speed

We now consider some general points in connection with car engines. Fig. 13.11 shows a *power output* v. *speed* curve for a typical petrol engine. The power output is expressed in brake horse-power, b.h.p., that is, the power was measured by making the engine work against a brake mechanism. The speed is expressed as the 'number of revolutions per

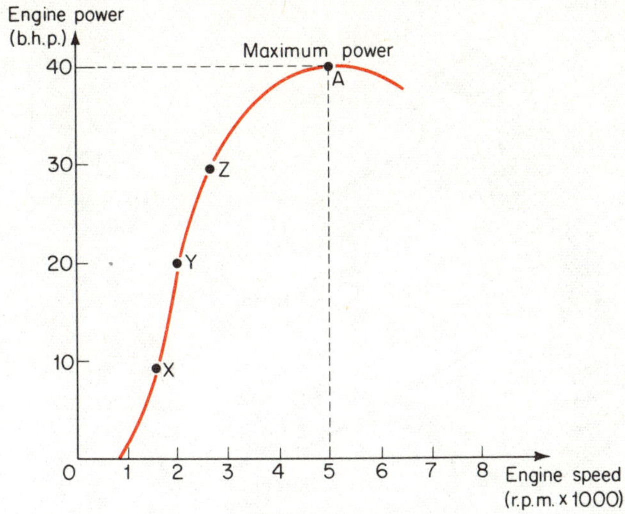

Fig. 13.11 Engine power and speed

minute (r.p.m.)' of the crankshaft, which is directly driven by the engine (p. 251). It shows that a power source such as an engine has a maximum available power at a particular speed. Thus it may produce 40 b.h.p. at 5000 r.p.m., as indicated by A on the curve.

Engine and Road Speeds

The speed of rotation of the wheels at say 70 miles/hour (112 km/h) is about 1000 r.p.m. The speed of the engine, however, is much higher during its normal running. Its maximum speed, for example, may be about 4000 to 5000 r.p.m. Its maximum torque or 'pulling force' may be obtained at about 2500 r.p.m. Some method is therefore needed to couple the engine to the wheels so that the wheels turn at a slower speed than the engine. Further, during its ordinary run the speed of the wheels, or road speed, will vary. Thus an arrangement must also be made for a variable road speed. *Gears* enable this to be done.

Gear Wheels

Intermeshing toothed wheels, known as *gear wheels*, are one of the most efficient and commonly used form of gearing. They are more efficient and more reliable than belts for transmitting power from engines, because belts are liable to slip.

A simple gear arrangement is shown in Fig. 13.12. It consists of two parallel shafts A and B, each having a gear wheel, A′ and B′ respectively, fixed on them. The two gear wheels are intermeshed as shown. As shaft A revolves, the gear wheel A′ revolves with it. Since

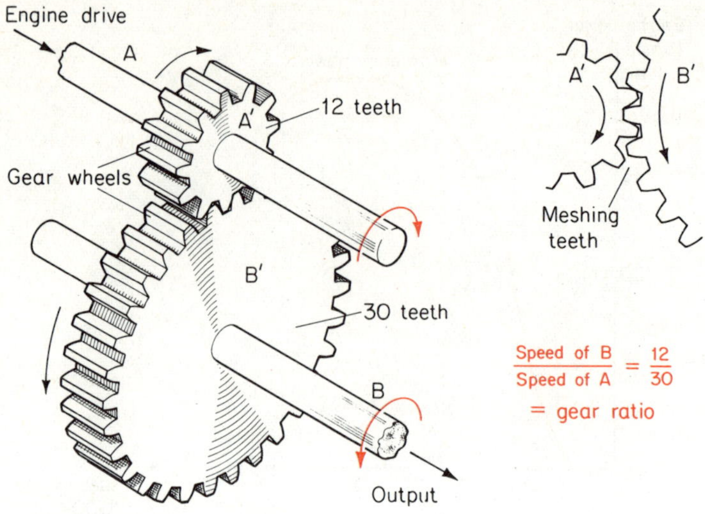

Fig. 13.12 Gear wheels

B′ is meshed with A′, B′ revolves but in an opposite sense to A′. Shaft B is fixed to B′. It therefore turns with B′ at the same speed.

If A′ and B′ are identical, B revolves at the same speed as A. But if the gear wheels have different diameters, that is, they have different numbers of teeth on them, the speed of B is *not* the same as that of A.

Gear Ratios

Suppose there are 12 teeth on A′ and 30 teeth on B′. When A revolves once, a total of 12 teeth on B′ have meshed with A′ and have therefore turned. Thus B will have turned through 12/30 of one revolution. Hence if A is turning at 10 r.p.s., B will turn at a slower speed given by

$$\frac{12}{30} \times 10 \text{ or } 4 \text{ r.p.s.}$$

Generally,

$$\frac{\text{speed of shaft B}}{\text{speed of shaft A}} = \frac{\text{number of teeth in gear A}}{\text{number of teeth in gear B}} = \frac{\text{diameter of gear A}}{\text{diameter of gear B}}.$$

Fig. 13.12 illustrates a *gear ratio* of 12/30 or 1/2·5. It is a 'step-down' gear ratio, that is, the speed of the shaft B is 2·5 times *smaller* than the speed of shaft A. The use of gears does not change the *power* from the engine shaft A transmitted to the shaft B. Power is calculated from:

Torque or 'turning force' of shaft × Speed of rotation of shaft.

Thus if the power transmitted is constant, a reduction in speed of shaft B is accompanied by increased torque delivered by B. This is used in the car gear-box (p. 249).

Car Gear-box

The gear-box in a car contains a variable set of gears. Fig. 13.13 illustrates a simple two-speed gear-box. When in use, the gears connect the crankshaft from the engine to the rear-wheel axle shaft. Typical gear-box ratios provided on a family saloon car are as follows:

(1) *Bottom* (*Lowest*) *Gear*. A step-down ratio of 3·6 : 1, i.e. a gear ratio of 1/3·6. This is provided by two intermeshing gear wheels having 10 and 36 teeth respectively.

(2) *Second Gear*. A step-down ratio of 2·2 : 1, provided by two gear wheels having 12 and 26 teeth respectively. Observe this is a higher gear than the previous gear, since the ratio 1/2·2 is greater than the ratio 1/3·6.

(3) *Third Gear*. A step-down ratio of 1/1·3, provided by two gear wheels having 20 and 26 teeth respectively.

(4) *Top gear*. This is the highest gear. It is a direct drive, that is, a gear ratio of 1.

A further reduction of about 1 : 4 is provided by the pinion (p. 251) in the rear axle. Thus in the above case the overall gear ratios are about 14·4 : 1 (lowest gear) to 4 : 1 (top gear).

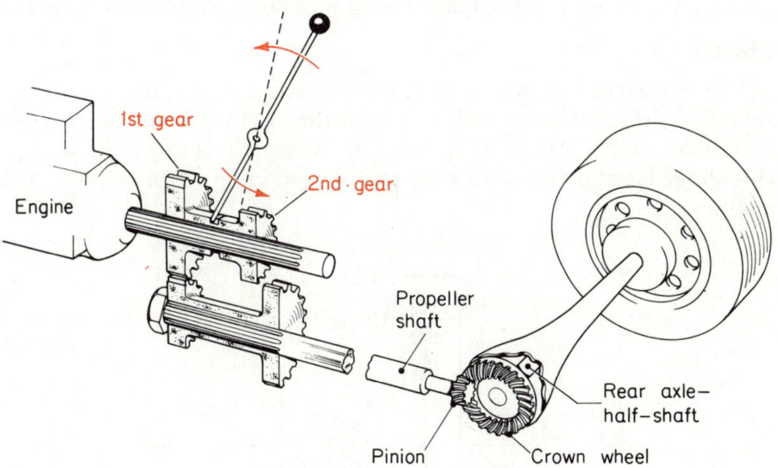

Fig. 13.13 Simple two-speed gear-box

How Gears Work

Suppose a car is travelling steadily at 50 km/h in top gear on a flat road. The torque or pulling force at the wheels is then just sufficient to overcome the frictional forces on the car due to the ground and the wind resistance. If the wheels are turning at 1000 r.p.m., the engine speed due to direct coupling in this gear is 1000 $\times$ 4 or 4000 r.p.m., taking into account the rear axle ratio of 1 : 4.

When the car reaches a hill or up-gradient, the pulling force is now insufficient to overcome the downward force due to the car's weight in addition to the frictional forces. The road speed then decreases. This would decrease the engine speed and hence the engine output power, see Fig. 13.11. In turn, the road speed would decrease further. Thus the engine would soon stop or stall.

To climb the hill, the driver changes down to a lower gear. The road speed now decreases, but by pressing on the accelerator, the engine speed can be increased to provide extra power to maintain the same road speed.

Starting from Rest

Gears are also used when a car starts from rest. To start the wheels turning, a high initial pulling force or torque is needed. The car is thus started by engaging first or lowest gear. As the speed of the wheels and car increases, second gear is engaged. This increases further the speed of the wheels and car. The engine speed is now also increased and from Fig. 13.11 (p. 247), the engine power increases, say from X to Y. As higher gears are engaged to reach higher speeds, the engine power increases more. Eventually, in top gear, the engine develops the power needed to keep the car cruising at a comfortable speed, as at Z.

Clutch

The motor-car clutch is a device which enables the driver of a vehicle to 'disconnect' the drive (from the engine) from the gear-box, and hence from the driving wheels. A clutch is essential for gear changing, for starting from rest, and for stopping without stalling the engine.

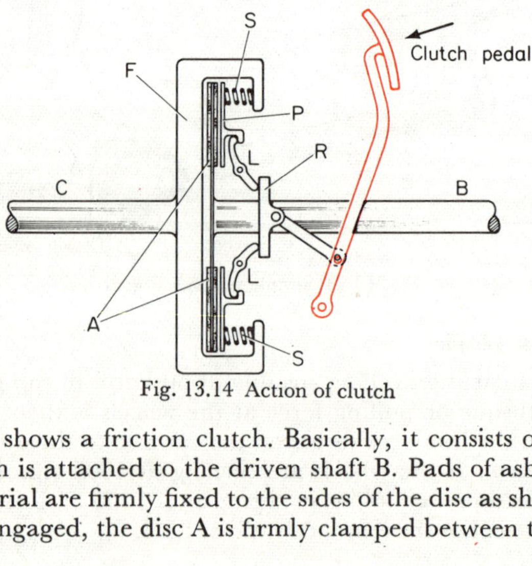

Fig. 13.14 Action of clutch

Fig. 13.14 shows a friction clutch. Basically, it consists of a circular disc A, which is attached to the driven shaft B. Pads of asbestos-based friction material are firmly fixed to the sides of the disc as shown. When the drive is engaged, the disc A is firmly clamped between the flywheel

F and the pressure plate P by strong springs S, placed round the circumference at P. The drive shaft C is then directly connected to B and both turn at the same speed.

To disconnect the drive, the driver presses the clutch pedal, as shown. By hydraulic means, or by a system of levers, a release bearing R is then depressed. This bears against a set of levers L. The plate P is then pulled back against the springs S, thus releasing the pressure on A. Since A is no longer pressed tightly against the flywheel F, there is no friction between them. Hence the drive is disconnected. When the clutch pedal is released, the drive is engaged once more.

Transmission System in Car

When an engine such as a steam turbine is arranged to drive the alternators at power stations, the shaft from the engine is coupled directly to the alternator shaft. In the case of a car engine, however, many mechanical arrangements are necessary before the drive from the engine can be transmitted efficiently to the wheels.

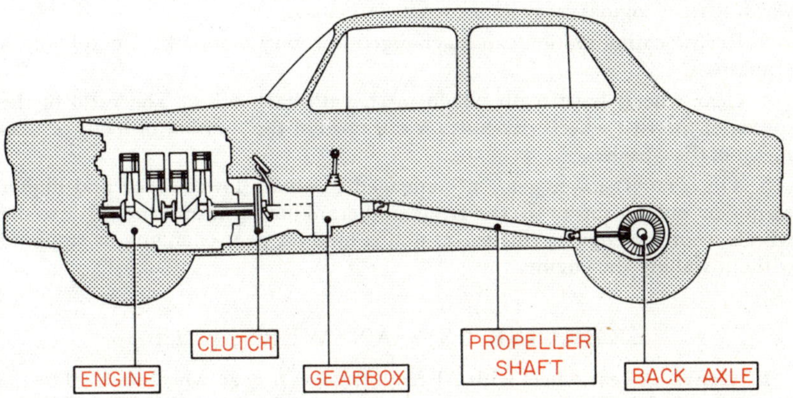

Fig. 13.15 Car transmission system

Some of the transmission system is shown diagrammatically in Fig. 13.15. The function of the *gear-box* has already been explained. The *propeller shaft* from the gear-box transmits the drive from the engine to the rear wheels. This is linked to the gear-box output shafts and the rear axle by *universal joints*. These joints allow the propeller shaft to have some angular movement at the same time as it turns. The joints thus accommodate any up and down movements of the rear axle due to bumps in the road surface and transmit the drive. The *crown wheel and pinion* is used on the rear axle: (i) to turn the drive from the propeller shaft so that the wheels turn at a convenient speed for road conditions; 48 teeth in the crown wheel and 12 in the pinion, for example, will reduce the speed to one-quarter (p. 248).

When the car is travelling in a straight line, both rear wheels travel at the same road speed. On turning a corner, however, the outer wheel travels faster than the inner wheel. This would not be possible if the half-shaft from each wheel was rigidly coupled to the crown wheel. The *rear axle differential* is a set of gears inside the crown wheel which enables the outer wheel to turn faster than the inner wheel on rounding a corner.

SUMMARY

1. Heat engines convert heat energy to mechanical energy. The petrol internal-combustion engine explodes a mixture of air and petrol vapour by means of a spark. For a four-stroke engine the order is intake, compression, explosion, exhaust.

2. Diesel engines use diesel oil as a fuel. The hot gases are ignited by compression—no sparking-plug is needed. Gas turbines have a shaft revolving at high speed and draw air to mix with oil. The burning gases produce a high pressure and may be used to drive a turbine. Jet engines obtain thrust from the hot gases expelled at the rear—the force of reaction pushes the machine forward. Rocket engines carry their own fuel oxidizer.

3. Reciprocating motion can be changed to rotary motion by a crank and a crankshaft.

4. Gear wheels have teeth which mesh with each other. The ratio of the speeds of the two wheels depends on the ratio of the number of teeth or diameter of the wheels.

5. On cars: (i) lower gears are engaged to obtain lower speed and higher torque or pulling force; (ii) the crank and crankshaft transmit the drive to the wheels from the engine; (iii) the clutch is used for gear-changing or stopping without stalling the engine.

EXERCISE 13 · ANSWERS, p. 258

1. Gears. A gear wheel with 20 teeth engages a gear wheel with 40 teeth. Is the speed of the larger wheel greater or smaller than the other wheel? If the small wheel is driven at 1000 r.p.m., what is the speed of the larger wheel?

2. An electric motor drives a shaft at a speed of 500 r.p.m. What gear ratio is needed to drive another shaft at 1500 r.p.m.?

3. In Question 2 the gear wheel from the motor shaft has 120 teeth. How many teeth has the wheel driving the other shaft?

4. A shaft X is geared to a motor shaft Y driven at 360 r.p.m. If the gear ratio from Y to X is $\frac{1}{6}$ at what speed does X turn? If the number of teeth of the gear wheel at Y is 15, how many teeth has the wheel at X?

5. A drum has a circumference of 2 m and raises a cable wound round it steadily at 4 m/s. How many r.p.s. does the drum turn? If the drum is powered by a wheel whose speed is 40 r.p.s. what gear ratio is used?

6. A cyclist travelling up a hill pedals at the rate of $1\frac{1}{2}$ r.p.s. The rear wheel has a circumference of 2 m and the bicycle moves at 6 m/s.

(i) How many r.p.s. does the rear wheel turn?

(ii) What gear ratio is required?

(iii) If the chain wheel has 48 teeth, how many teeth are on the sprocket of the back wheel in this case?

7. The power from an engine is calculated by: *torque (pulling force)* × *turning speed.* A particular engine produces a torque of 500 units and a speed of 1000 r.p.m. Assuming negligible losses in power, what torque is produced at a turning speed of 250 r.p.m. if the engine power remains constant?

8. A car is travelling at top (fourth) gear on a flat road and reaches an up-gradient. What gear is now engaged? How does the gear-change affect: (i) the speed of the wheels, and (ii) the pulling force on the car?

9. (*a*) What gear ratio must be used to enable an electric motor which has a fixed speed of 500 r.p.m. to drive a machine at 300 r.p.m.?

(*b*) A bicycle has a gear ratio of 3. If the chain wheel has 48 teeth, how many teeth are there on the sprocket on the back wheel? (*E.A.*)

Engines. *What are the missing words in the statements* 10–23?

10. In a four-stroke petrol engine the four strokes are *induction (suction)*, *compression*, . ., and *exhaust.*

11. The fuel is a mixture of . .

12. The mixture is ignited by a . .

13. Ignition occurs near the end of the . . stroke.

14. The drive from the piston is transmitted at the end of the . . stroke.

15. The engine has . . valves; the gases pass in through the . . valve.

16. When the exhaust valve opens, the rising piston expels . . gases from the cylinder.

17. The power obtained from the engine depends on the . . consumed per second.

18. For a complete cycle of four strokes, the crankshaft has turned through . . revs.

19. The spark from a sparking-plug is produced by using an . .

20. In a two-stroke petrol-engine there are no valves but . .

21. The mixture is ignited on the . . stroke.

22. After two strokes of the engine, the crankshaft turns through . . revs.

23. The fuel consumption during running is comparatively . . than the four-stroke engine.

24. The internal-combustion engine is a device which converts . . energy, in the form of fuel, into . . energy. The expanding gases move the . . within the cylinder and this stroke is called the . . stroke. (*Mx.*)

25. Explain fully with the aid of *simple* diagram(s) the action of the four-stroke petrol engine, naming all the strokes and clearly showing all the relevant valve positions.

What purpose has the sparking-plug in this engine?

How many revolutions does the crankshaft make in one cycle of four strokes? (*W.Md.*)

26. (*a*) Describe the cylinder and piston of a two-stroke petrol engine and explain what happens during a cycle of operations.

(*b*) State *four* ways in which a spark ignition engine differs from a diesel engine. (*E.A.*)

27. Fig. 13A shows the essential parts of a two-stroke petrol engine. Label this diagram and explain clearly what takes place during one complete turn of the crankshaft when the engine is running. (*M.*)

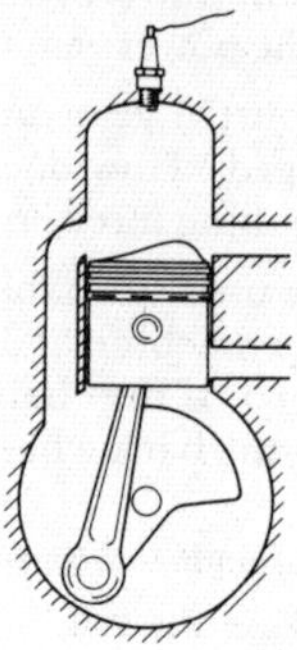

Fig. 13A

28. Explain briefly the principles of any two practical devices which convert heat energy to mechanical energy.

What are the differences between a petrol engine and a diesel engine?

Describe briefly the action of the *carburettor* in a petrol engine.

29. (*a*) Name the parts of the transmission of a motor-car in order, from the engine onwards.

(*b*) What is the purpose of the rear-axle differential?

(*c*) Draw a clearly labelled diagram of a sparking-plug (*W.Md.*)

30. (*a*) Make a simple diagram of one cylinder of a four-stroke internal-combustion engine showing the position of the piston and valves at the beginning of of the firing stroke.

(*b*) In transmitting the power from the engine to the driving wheels of the car what are the purposes of: (i) the gear-box? (ii) the crown wheel and pinion in the back axle?

(*c*) The efficiencies of a petrol and a steam engine are 35% and 7% respectively: (i) what does efficiency mean? (ii) why is the petrol engine more efficient than the steam engine? (*S*)

31. The petrol and diesel engines are examples of *reciprocating engines*. What do you understand by this term? Draw a diagram in your explanation.

32. In the car, the transmission must change from a 'reciprocating' to a 'rotary' motion.

(i) What are the meanings of 'reciprocating and 'rotary'?

(ii) Why is this change necessary?

(iii) Draw a sketch or sketches showing how a crank enables the change to be made.

33. The effects listed A to H are each produced by one of the items numbered 1 to 8. Pair the lists correctly:

A. Sparks the mixture of gases
B. Allows outer and inner rear wheels to turn at different speeds when cornering
C. Links gear-box to rear wheels
D. Disconnects engine from gear-box
E. Produces power for car
F. Produces variation in pulling force
G. Produces right-angle drive and speed reduction
H. Flexible coupling

1. Engine
2. Crown wheel and pinion
3. Rear-axle differential
4. Propeller-shaft
5. Gear-box
6. Universal joint
7. Ignition coil
8. Clutch

34. Draw a diagram showing the four stages in a four-stroke petrol engine cycle. Show clearly in your diagrams: (i) the position of the two valves in each stage—open or closed; (ii) the way the piston is moving—up or down; (iii) when the spark is produced to ignite the mixture; (iv) the stroke of the piston which transmits power to the wheels.

35. Why are diesel engines preferred to steam engines in railways? Describe with diagrams *either* a diesel engine *or* a steam engine.

36. A rocket engine and a jet engine: (i) use the same principle to obtain thrust, but (ii) the rocket engine carries an oxygen supply which is not needed in the jet engine. Explain the statements in (i) and (ii), drawing diagrams in illustration.

Miscellaneous Heat Questions · ANSWERS, p. 258

1. (*a*) Explain why, when heat is supplied to melting ice the temperature of the mixture does not rise until all the ice has melted. What name is given to the heat that is supplied and give a clear definition of it?

(*b*) Explain clearly the principles in the following situations: (i) water in a test-tube can be heated at the top without melting a lump of ice at the bottom; (ii) it is warmer in a greenhouse at the end of a day (without central heating) no matter what the outside temperature is.

(*c*) A block of copper, mass 0·1 kg is cooled to a temperature of −160°C and then completely immersed in water at 0°C. Calculate the mass of ice formed. (Specific latent heat of fusion over ice = 340 000 J/kg; specific heat capacity of copper = 400 J/kg °C.) (*W.Md.*)

2. A pupil is using a power lathe to 'turn' a piece of metal in the school workshop. At the same time coal is being burned in a 'boiler' at the electricity generating station. Make a list of the various changes in forms of energy connecting these two events. Describe briefly the practical detail of bringing about one of these energy changes and a possible method of estimating the power loss involved in the change. (*M.*)

3. Describe and explain an experiment to show that some materials are better conductors of heat than others.

Materials may lose heat to their surroundings by conduction. Name two other ways in which heat losses can occur.

Draw a labelled diagram of a 'Thermos' flask, and explain the various features incorporated in it to minimize heat losses. (*S.E.*)

4. (*a*) Describe with the aid of a diagram how the different expansion of two metals can be used in the construction of a fire-alarm.

(*b*) What are the 'fixed points' on a thermometer and what do they represent on both the centigrade and Fahrenheit scales? What is the 'Absolute Zero' of temperature and how was it deduced? (*W.Md.*)

5. Show by diagrams clearly what happens in the following systems: (i) a hot-water system containing at least a boiler and two radiators; (ii) a sea breeze on a hot summer's day; (iii) a vacuum-flask. (*W.Md.*)

6. Fig. 13B is of a thermometer and is graduated in °F. The bimetallic strip is in the form of a spiral.

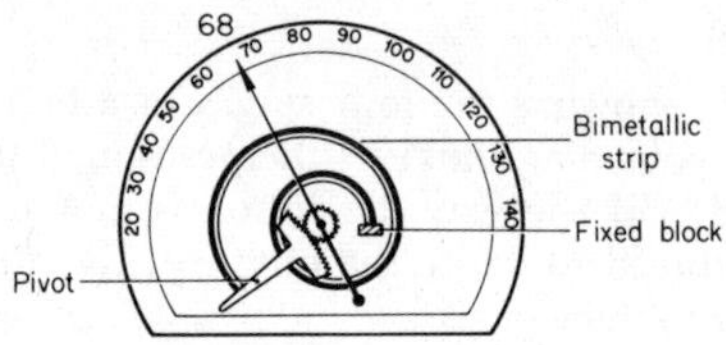

Fig. 13B

(*a*) Explain how the thermometer works.

(*b*) Make a table listing its advantages and disadvantages when compared with a mercury-in-glass thermometer.

(*c*) For what temperature measurements would this thermometer most likely be used?

(*d*) If the scale had been calibrated in °C what would it now be reading? (*S.*)

7. 1 kg of lead shot is put into a 1 metre long cardboard tube which is stoppered at each end. The temperature of the shot is noted. The tube is held vertically and then quickly inverted so that the shot is carried to the top and then falls through a distance of 1 metre to the bottom. This is repeated rapidly 130 times. The temperature is again noted.

(i) How much potential energy has been given to the shot by moving it to the top?

(ii) When the shot rests on the bottom of the tube all its mechanical energy has been lost. What has happened to this lost energy?

(iii) How much energy has been lost in this way during the experiment?

(iv) If the temperature of the lead shot at the beginning of the experiment was 15°C, what will it be at the end?

(v) If the experiment were repeated with copper in place of lead, would the temperature of the copper at the end of the experiment be the same, less or more than the temperature of the lead? Specific heat capacity of lead = 130 J/kg °C, of copper = 420 J/kg °C. (*S.E.*)

ANSWERS TO NUMERICAL EXERCISES

EXERCISE 2 (p. 34)

1. 25 g/cm³ **2.** 38 g, 0·1 m³ **3.** $\frac{2}{3}$, $1\frac{2}{3}$ **4.** (i) 125 cm³ (ii) 5 cm
5. (i) 9 g/cm³ (ii) 4000 kg **6.** 1 g/cm³, 13·6 g/cm³ **7.** 8000 kg **8.** 100 g
9. common balance: same always; spring balance: (i) higher (ii) less (iii) less (iv) less
10. (i) solid (ii) liquid (iii) gas **13.** 0·5 **16.** (i) 60 g (ii) 15 cm
17. (i) 43·0 cm (ii) 30·0 cm (iii) 1·65 N (approx.) **19.** *c*
20. surface tension, sink **21.** surface tension
25. (i) 0·52 mm³ (ii) 10 000 πt mm³ (iv) 0·000 017 mm

EXERCISE 3 (p. 56)

1. 3 m **2.** second, wheel axis, 560 J **3.** low, large
4. (*a*) 200 N (*b*) 300 N **5.** (*b*) 11 kg
6. *b* **7.** 4 kg **8.** (*a*) 1·5 N (*b*) 2·5 N **10.** (*a*) greater (*b*) same
11. (*b*) (i) stable (ii) neutral **12.** (i) 2850 N (ii) 2450 N **13.** (*b*) 37°
15. (ii) 7·5 N

EXERCISE 4 (p. 79)

1. (*a*) 4 (*b*) (i) 200 N (ii) 1600 J **2.** (*a*) 4 (*b*) 3 (*c*) 75%
3. (*b*) 83% (*d*) 200 N **5.** (i) 60% (ii) 60 m **6.** 100 N **7.** 2000 N
8. 75% **9.** (*b*) (i) 21 kg (ii) 15 N (*c*) (i) 250 g (ii) 53°, 37°
10. (*c*) 1000 N (*d*) 75 W **11.** 200 N
12. (*a*) 30 000 (*b*) 40 000 J (*c*) M.A. = $2\frac{1}{2}$, V.R. = $3\frac{1}{8}$, efficiency = 75%

EXERCISE 5 (p. 92)

1. *d* **2.** *b* **3.** *d* **4.** (*a*) ii (*b*) iii (*c*) i (*d*) iv **5.** 7 g/cm³ **6.** *b*
7. sink, float, less **8.** (*a*) lead (*b*) wood (*c*) 2·5 (*d*) 1·25 (*e*) less
9. (i) 200 million N (ii) 19 600 m³ **13.** 4000 N
14. (*b*) 0·52 (*c*) 3000 kg
17. (i) 0·2 N (ii) 1·0 N weight (iii) 0·8 N tension (v) 0·4 N, 0·6 N

EXERCISE 6 (p. 116)

1. (*a*) 8 cm³ (*b*) 64 g (*c*) 1600 N/m² (0·16 N/cm²) **2.** *d*
3. (*a*) 1·1 (*b*) *A* (*c*) 0·8 g/cm³ (*d*) upper-B, middle-water, lower-A
4. (ii) 12 000 N/m² (iii) 800 000 N/m²
5. (*a*) pressure $\propto$ depth (*b*) 400 N/m² (*c*) 0·8 g/cm³ or 800 kg/m³
6. 144; 4320 N **7.** 144 **8.** (*a*) 500 N (*b*) 5 N **9.** (b) 2000 N/m² (*c*) 2 N
10. 0·8 **11.** 2000 N/mm² **12.** No, no. **13.** *d* **14.** *c* **15.** 100 000 N/m²
16. height, air-pressure **18.** *c* **19.** 1 = spring, 2 = 'bellows' **20.** *c*
21. 130 000 N/m² **22.** (*b*) same

EXERCISE 7 (p. 153)

1. (*a*) rolled (*b*) kicked (*c*) all hit at same time (*e*) 5 m
2. (*a*) uniform accn. (*b*) uniform speed (*c*) $4\frac{1}{2}$ km (*d*) 15 km/h/min
3. (*c*) ii (*d*) 22·5 m (*e*) 7·7 s (*f*) 8·7 m/s (*g*) 15 m/s (approx) **5.** *e*

6. (*a*) 10 000 J (*b*) 0·1 h.p. **7.** 2 h.p.
8. velocity = b, accn = *a*, mech. energy = *a* **9.** lost
10. (*a*) uniform accn. (*b*) uniform vel. (*c*) uniform retardn.
11. (*a*) 1800 J (*b*) 0·08 h.p. (*c*) 450 J (*d*) 25%
18. (*e*) 9 m (*f*) 7·5 m/s **20.** (i) 5×10^6 J (ii) $2{\cdot}5 \times 10^6$ J
21. (*b*) (ii) 10 m/s (*c*) 30 m/s

EXERCISE 8 (p. 166)

1. 100°C, 212°F; 0°C, 32°F **2.** (*a*) 77°F (*b*) 105°C (*c*) −10°C
3. (i) 35–43°C (approx) (ii) constriction (iii) 37°C
5. (*b*) (i) 71°C (ii) 68°F (iii) −18°C **7.** 98·4°F, 100°C, b.p.
10. (*a*) 273 K (*b*) 100°C (*c*) 40 K

EXERCISE 9 (p. 182)

1. (i) brass, invar/iron (ii) A **3.** cooker, iron **4.** (*a*) 0°C (*b*) 4°C **5.** *b*
6. decreases, increases, decreases **7.** A
12. (i) 36°C (ii) 25·22 cm³ (iii) −273°C

EXERCISE 10 (p. 202)

1. *b* **2.** conduction **4.** insulates, good conductor, air is insulator
5. (i) Dewar (ii) minimize, conduction, convection (iii) minimize radiation losses
6. conduction, convection, radiation
7. expands, dense; dense, cold, convection

EXERCISE 11 (p. 215)

1. 42 000 J **2.** (*a*) 120 MJ (*b*) 90 MJ (*c*) 430 kg (*d*) 0·02p
3. (*a*) 420 J (*b*) 672 J **4.** (i) 3·36 MJ (ii) 0·32 MJ
5. 10 g, 5°C, 10°C, 210 J, 210 J, 21 J/°C
6. (i) 60°C (ii) 50 400 J (iii) (T–80) (iv) 50 400 J (v) 710°C
7. 2–C, 3–A, 4–D, 5–E, 6–G, 7–B **8.** 5600 J; 160 000 J **9.** (*b*) £8·50
10. (*a*) expansion (*b*) insulation (*c*) fibre glass/quilt (*e*) 18°C **11.** 57°C
12. (*b*) £11·40

EXERCISE 12 (p. 236)

1. *d* **2.** (*a*) 3360 J (*b*) 25 360 J **3.** 2960 J
4. (*a*) 0°C (*b*) 4°C (*c*) 34 000 J (*d*) 100°C (*e*) (i) decreases (ii) increases. Inside = A
5. *d* **7.** (*a*) increases (*b*) increases **12.** £7·56

EXERCISE 13 (p. 252)

1. smaller, 500 r.p.m. **2.** 3 **3.** 40 **4.** 60 r.p.m., 90 **5.** 2 r.p.s., 1/20
6. (i) 3 r.p.s. (ii) 2 (iii) 24 **7.** 2000 units **8.** 3rd gear (i) lowers (ii) raises
9. (*a*) 3/5 (*b*) 16 **10.** ignition **11.** petrol vapour and air **12.** spark
13. compression **14.** ignition **15.** 2, inlet **16.** burnt **17.** fuel **18.** 2
19. induction coil **20.** ports **21.** compression **22.** one **23.** more
24. heat, mechanical, piston, ignition **25.** ignites the fuel, 2
33. A–7, B–3, C–4, D–8, E–1, F–5, G–2, H–6

MISCELLANEOUS HEAT QUESTIONS (p. 255)

1. 20 g **6.** 20°C **7.** (i) 10 J each time (iii) 1300 J (iv) 25°C

Book Two

WAVES, OPTICS, SOUND

14

WAVE PROPAGATION · WAVE EFFECTS

Sun's Radiation

THE sun is the source of most of the energy falling on the earth. It is our natural light source, that is, it sends out a particular kind of energy called *luminous energy* which stimulates the sensation of vision. The sun also radiates energy which does not stimulate vision but produces warmth or heat—we say this is due to *infra-red* radiation from the sun. Another type of invisible radiation from the sun, called *ultra-violet* radiation, produces 'sun-tan' and makes certain minerals fluoresce (see p. 271).

Waves by Ripple Tank

Energy reaches us across millions of miles of empty space from the sun and other stars. It is difficult to see how energy travels from one place to another in its journey. We can gain an understanding of how

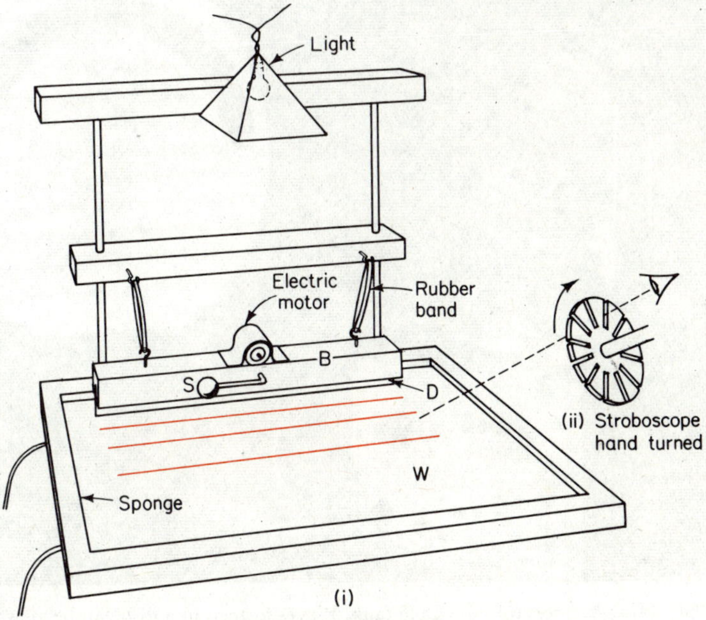

Fig. 14.1 Ripple tank

this may happen, however, by studying the way energy travels or spreads across water from one place to another.

This can be done with the aid of a *ripple tank*, Fig. 14.1 (i). Basically, the tank consists of: (1) a pool of water W in a shallow rectangular dish with a clear glass base and with the edges lined with sponge; (2) a *dipper* for producing water waves—this may be either a vertical long plane metal strip D or one of the small spheres S beneath a bar B; (3) a *vibrator* in the form of an off-centre weight on the rotating armature of a small electric motor rigidly attached to B; (4) a *lamp* with a small filament which illuminates the water surface from below or above, so that the ripples of the wave can be seen and also projected on a screen.

When the height of the metal strip is adjusted so that it just dips into the water and the electric motor is switched on, the strip or vibrator produces ripples or waves. They spread across the water surface and are absorbed at the edge by the sponge. If the lamp is placed above the water the waves can be seen and viewed from above.

A *stroboscope* is used to make the waves appear stationary. A simple form of hand stroboscope consists of a circular wooden disc with evenly spaced slits round it and an axle in the centre, Fig. 14.1 (ii). It is held by the axle in one hand by an observer and spun round with the other.

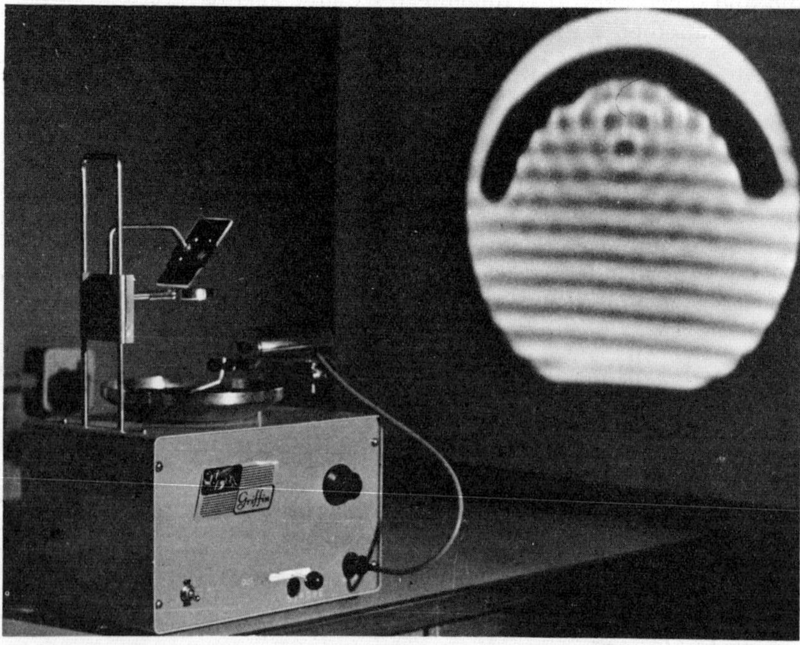

Plate 14(A) Demonstration ripple tank. Waves formed in a dish can be viewed by projection on a screen. Here waves are shown focused by reflection.

The waves can be seen moving in quick succession on looking at the water surface through the revolving slits. As the stroboscope speed is increased from zero, the waves appear stationary at one stage. They can then be studied closely. See Plate 14A.

Plane and Spherical Waves

With the straight edge of the metal strip M dipping into the water, parallel *plane waves* can be seen spreading along the surface, Fig. 14.2 (i). With one sphere S dipping into the water, *spherical* or *circular waves* spread out having S as their centre, Fig. 14.2 (ii).

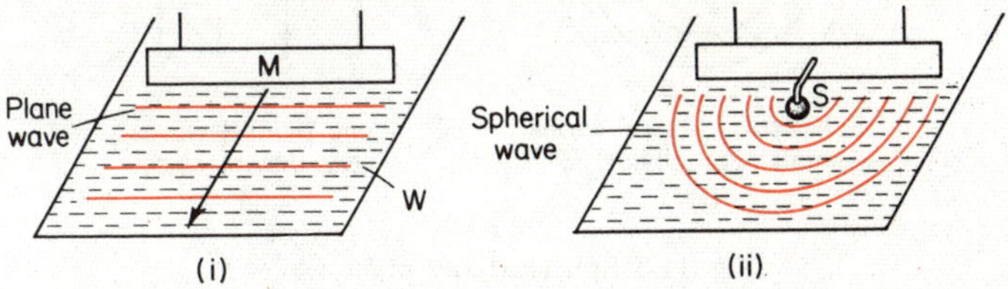

Fig. 14.2 Producing plane and spherical waves

In both cases small pieces of cork on the water will bob up and down, or vibrate, as the wave passes. But they remain at the same place. This shows that the water itself does not move bodily from place to place along the surface as the wave travels. Only *energy*, the energy of movement, travels along the surface. Water is the material or 'medium' in which the energy travels.

A similar wave effect is obtained with a long rope tied at one end to a wall. When a number of white ribbons are attached at intervals to the rope and the free end is jerked up and down, a wave or 'pulse' travels along the rope from one end to the other. The ribbons move up and down, showing the energy of movement of the wave. But they remain at the same place while vibrating. The wave travelling along the rope is now carried by the rope material or medium. It is also instructive to watch waves spreading along a long horizontal flexible coil of wire such as the 'Slinky' type, when one end of the coil is moved rapidly up and down. The waves can be seen travelling along the metal while the average position of one of the coil turns remains the same.

In every wave, then, we distinguish between:

(1) the vibrations, which produce the wave;

(2) the wave itself, which is the energy travelling along the medium.

Wave Theory of Light

Having seen how energy can spread from place to place along water by means of waves, it is reasonable to ask whether light or energy can travel in a similar way. The 'wave theory' of light was first suggested about 1660 by Huygens, a famous Dutch scientist, and it has proved very fruitful in explaining light phenomena, as we shall see.

For a small visible object S, such as a small electric-lamp filament, we imagine *spherical* or *circular waves* spreading out with the speed of light so that the energy reaches our eyes, Fig. 14.3 (i). The sensation

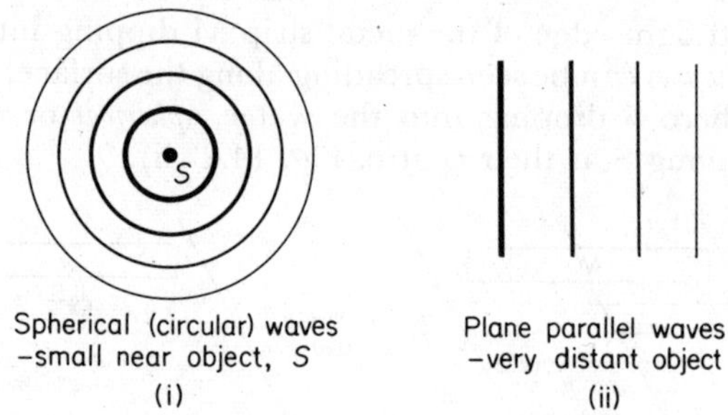

Fig. 14.3 Spherical and plane waves

of vision is then produced. The source S continues to be seen as long as it radiates luminous energy. The flame of a lighted match is visible until its luminous energy disappears.

A long way from the lamp the circular waves have a very large radius. They are then effectively *plane parallel waves*, Fig. 14.3 (ii). The sun is so far away from the earth that waves arriving here are effectively plane parallel waves. As we see later, plane parallel light waves can be obtained from a lamp by placing a suitable lens in front of it (p. 324).

Light Waves

Light waves differ from water waves in two important respects. Water waves are due to vibrations of particles of water, whereas evidence beyond the scope of this book shows that light waves are set up by electric and magnetic vibrations of very high frequencies. These are exactly the same kind of vibrations which produce radio waves. Light waves and radio waves are therefore both examples of *electromagnetic waves* (see p. 271).

Further, water waves are carried by water, which is a material medium. Light waves which reach us from the sun travel through large regions of empty space, and hence no material medium is needed.

Medium for Sound Waves

When a gong or electric bell is placed in an air-tight vessel, and the air is pumped out gradually from the vessel, the sound of the bell also gradually dies away (see p. 368). The clapper of the bell, however, can still be seen striking the gong, although no sound is heard. Thus sound cannot pass through a vacuum. A material medium is necessary to carry the sound, whereas light or electromagnetic waves can pass through a vacuum. We usually hear sounds carried by an air medium, but the sound of horses hooves can sometimes be detected through the earth by placing an ear to the ground. Tapping at one end of a long pipe circulating a building can be heard in other parts of the building, the sound being carried through the metal. A submarine's propellers moving below the sea give rise to sound waves in the water, which can be detected by a special form of microphone.

Frequency, Wavelength, Velocity

We can understand more about wave ideas by studying again the water wave in a ripple tank.

When the electric motor of the ripple tank is speeded up the vibrations of the dipper increase. The plane waves in the water are now generated at a greater rate, and more are seen travelling across the water in the tank, Fig. 14.4 (i), (ii). Thus the *frequency* f of the wave has been increased.

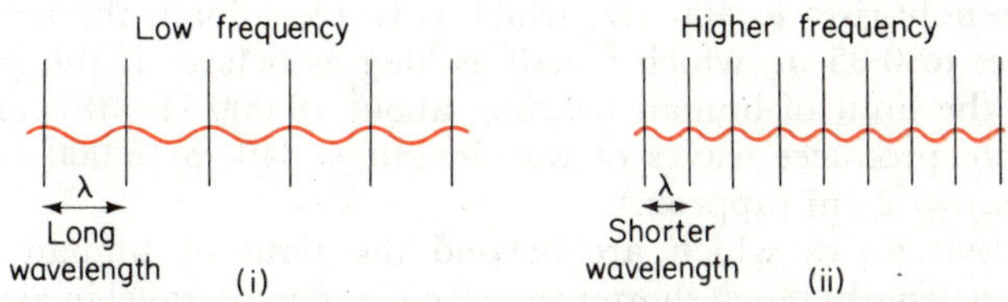

Fig. 14.4 Frequency and wavelength changes

The frequency of a wave is defined as the number of waves passing a given place in 1 sec. This is the same as the number of vibrations per sec of the dipper which produces the waves. The name *cycle* is given to a complete (to-and-fro) vibration because the motion begins all over again after it. Frequency is thus measured in *cycles per second* or *hertz* (Hz), after the discoverer of radio waves. A frequency of 500 Hz means one of 500 cycles per second (c/s).

The *wavelength* λ of the wave is the distance between successive crests, or successive troughs of the wave. At a higher frequency it should be carefully observed that the wavelength becomes shorter, Fig. 14.4 (ii).

The wavelength of a water wave can be measured by placing a transparent glass rule on the base of the dish along the direction of travel of the wave. The water surface is then viewed through a stroboscope. When the speed is increased from zero the waves are seen stationary at one speed.

If the length occupied by 6 successive crests or 5 wavelengths is 10 cm, then the wavelength is 2 cm.

Suppose the dipper or wave has a frequency of 10 Hz (cycles per second). In 1 s, 10 waves pass a given place. Each wave occupies a distance of 2 cm, since this is the wavelength. The distance travelled per second by the wave is thus 10 × 2 or 20 cm. Hence the speed or *velocity* of the wave is 20 cm/s.

The simple calculation shows that whatever kind of wave we deal with, water wave or light wave or sound wave for example, its velocity is always given by:

$$velocity = frequency \times wavelength.$$

Wavelength and Frequency Values · Sound Waves

In air at normal temperatures, sound waves have a velocity of about 340 m per s or 1100 km per hour. A person with a deep voice singing a note of frequency 200 Hz is sending out sound waves whose wavelength is given, from above, by

$$\text{Wavelength} = \frac{\text{Velocity}}{\text{Frequency}}$$
$$= \frac{340\ \text{m/s}}{200\ \text{Hz}} = 1{\cdot}7\ \text{m}.$$

If the note rises to 400 Hz, which is twice as high, the wavelength decreases to 0·85 m, which is half as long as before. If the frequency rises to the limit of human hearing, about 16 000 Hz, this extremely high note produces waves of wavelength = 340 m/16 000 = 0·02 m (approx.) = 2 cm (approx.).

Ultrasonic waves, which are beyond the limit of human hearing, have wavelengths much shorter than 2 cm and may travel in air or other media. Generally, then, the higher the frequency, the smaller is the wavelength.

Reflection of Waves

The effect produced when waves meet a plane surface can be observed with the ripple tank. A vibrator C generates plane waves, which travel a short distance and are then incident on a plane metal strip AB in the water, Fig. 14.5 (i). The plane waves are seen to be reflected

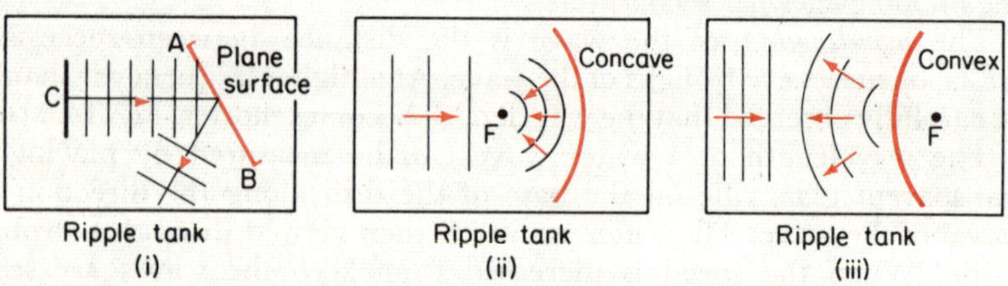

Fig. 14.5 Reflection by plane and curved surfaces

from AB in a definite direction, which varies with the position of AB. See also Plate 14B. In one special case the waves are reflected straight back along their original course. This happens when the waves are incident *normally* on AB, that is, at 90° to AB.

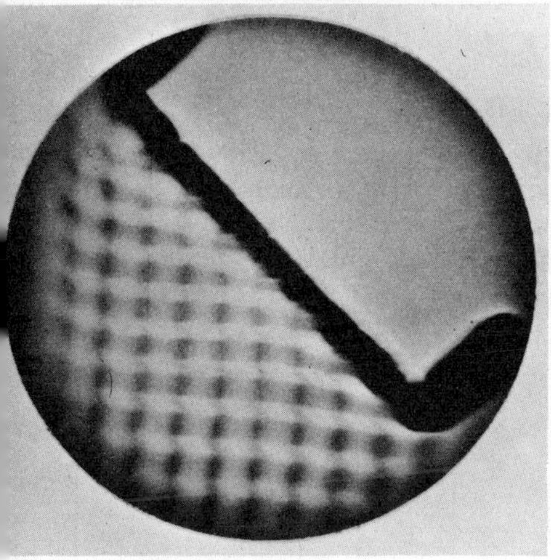

Plate 14(B) Reflection of plane waves, coming from below, at plane surface.

Plate 14(C) Plane waves, coming from the left, reflected to a point by a parabolic reflector.

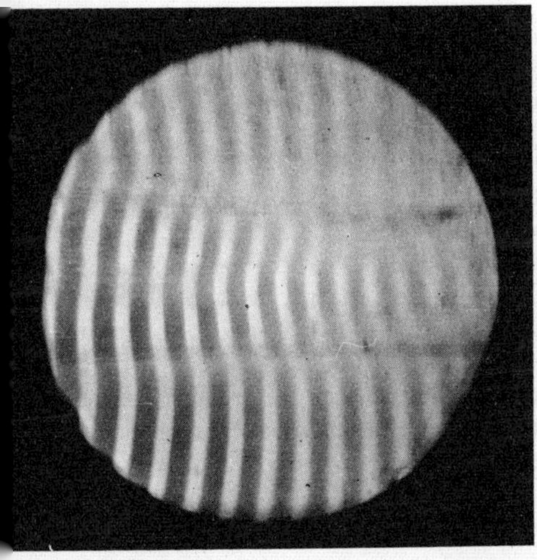

Plate 14(D) Plane waves, coming from the left, slowed down in shallow water by a submerged glass slide (refraction of plane waves).

The regular reflection of waves from a plane surface occurs with all types of waves. Light waves, for example, are reflected by a plane mirror to the eyes of a person using it as a looking-glass (p. 288). Radio waves may be reflected from the plane surface of a metal tank on the roof near an aerial and produce 'interference' in a television receiver. Sound waves are reflected by walls and produce echoes (p. 369).

Plane waves incident on a *concave* surface are reflected as *spherical* waves converging towards a point or focus F in front of it, 14.5 (ii). See also Plate 14C. If they are incident on a *convex* surface, they are reflected as spherical waves diverging from a focus F behind it, Fig. 14.5 (iii). We see the same effect when light is reflected by curved mirrors (p. 295).

Refraction of Waves

The behaviour of waves moving from one medium to another can be observed with a ripple tank. A transparent plate G is fixed inside the tank by means of plasticene, applied to its corners *a*, *b*, *c* and *d*, so that it is level and just below (about 1 mm) the surface of the water,

Fig. 14.6 (i). The best effect is produced by waves of low frequency. The region of shallow water above the plate increases the frictional resistance to the oncoming wave, so that it behaves as a different medium. As the incident waves pass AB and enter the 'new medium' at Y over G it is observed that *they travel more slowly*. It can be seen that, effectively, the wavelength is decreased.

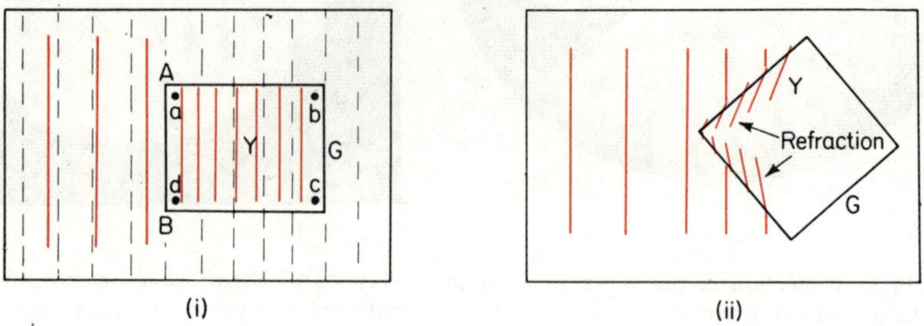

Fig. 14.6 Refraction of water waves

When the plate G is turned round at an angle to the incident waves, it is seen that the waves travel in a different direction in the new medium, Fig. 14.6 (ii). See Plate 14D. This is called *refraction* of waves.

Refraction is due to the *change in speed* of waves on entering a new medium, It occurs with all types of waves. Thus refraction of light waves occurs when glass lenses are used (p. 324). Refraction of radio waves occurs high above the earth when they enter a 'belt' of electrical particles called the *ionosphere*. One layer of these particles, occupying several miles, is called the *Appleton layer*, after their discoverer. At night, radio waves from England sent skyward change their direction on entering the Appleton layer. As they emerge from the layer on the other side of the world, radio messages can hence reach countries such as Australia.

Diffraction of Waves

We now investigate what happens when waves pass through large and small apertures. The results obtained by using water waves in a ripple tank are illustrated in Fig. 14.7 (i). In the case of a wide aperture AB between two metal strips, plane waves incident from X pass through the aperture as plane waves to Y, Fig. 14.7 (i). The boundaries or edges of the plane waves emerging correspond to the edges A and B of the aperture.

But when the gap C between the two metal strips A and B is made very narrow, and plane waves are incident to it, the waves emerge as *spherical* (*circular*) waves, Fig. 14.7 (ii). Thus waves spread round C—they no longer travel in a straight line. Their effect is hence experienced not only in the straight-through direction Y, but also round the

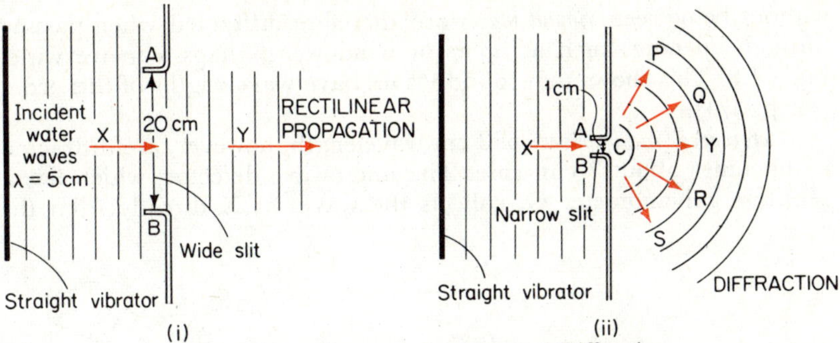

Fig. 14.7 Rectilinear propagation and Diffraction

edges of the aperture C at P, Q, R and S. The waves are said to be *diffracted* at C. Huygens, who suggested a wave theory of light, stated that every point *on a wavefront itself* acts like a source emitting wavelets. We can therefore imagine that when the wavefront reaches the gap C, each point in the gap sends out spherical wavelets. These spread round the gap at the edges, but they are not noticeable here until the gap becomes very small and comparable to the wavelength, as we have seen.

Generally, then, straight-line or *rectilinear propagation* of waves occurs when the opening is very wide compared to the wavelength. Diffraction always occurs when waves are incident on openings, but it becomes noticeable when the width of the opening is comparable to the wavelength.

Effect of Wavelength

Diffraction is a phenomenon obtained with all waves, whatever their nature.

A person speaking loudly in a room can be heard round a corner

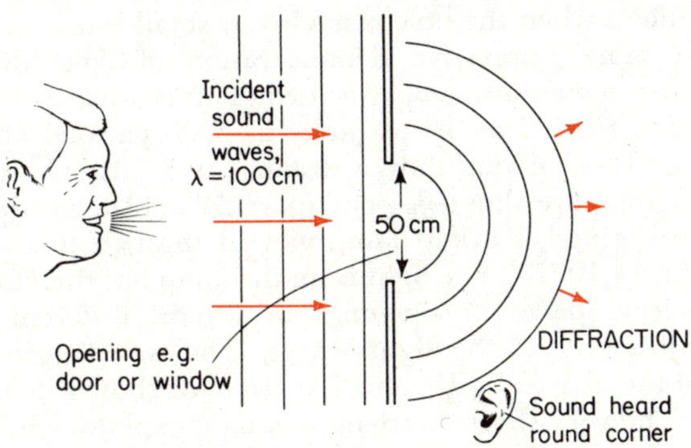

Fig. 14.8 Diffraction of sound waves

without being seen. *Sound waves* are therefore diffracted when passing through openings such as doors or windows, perhaps a metre wide, Fig. 14.8. This shows that sound waves have wavelengths of this order (see p. 374).

Microwaves (*radio waves*) of 3 cm wavelength, however, are diffracted by openings about 1 cm wide. The microwave detector, which has a sensitive galvanometer G, collects the waves at X directly from the

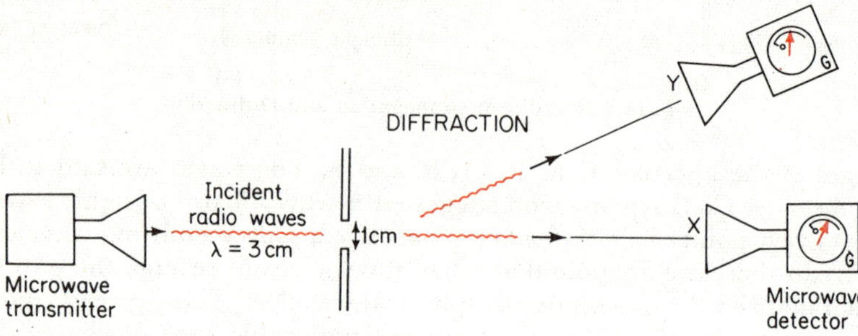

Fig. 14.9 Diffraction of radio waves

transmitter, Fig. 14.9. At Y, at an angle to the incident direction, a large deflection is also obtained on G. The waves are hence diffracted.

Light passing through a wide opening like a window or letter-box into a darkened place has a sharp boundary where the shadow begins. No diffraction is seen. A narrower opening, such as a slit in a ray-box comb a few millimetres wide, still allows light to pass through in a straight-line path. If, however, an adjustable slit is placed about a metre from a bright over-run ray-box or motor headlamp bulb, the patch of light on a screen beyond the slit is seen to broaden as the slit is narrowed. Some light has spread round the edges, as shown in the exaggerated sketch in Fig. 14. 10 (i). The blurred image obtained in a pin-hole camera when the hole is made *very* small is due to diffraction.

An even more impressive demonstration of light diffraction is obtained when a *diffraction grating* is used. This is a piece of transparent film on which there may be as many as 5000 parallel opaque lines, equally spaced, occupying only a distance of 1 cm. The clear spaces between the lines are thus $\frac{1}{5000}$ cm apart. When the grating is placed close to the eye and a bright lamp viewed through it several images are seen, Fig. 14.10 (ii). The light from the lamp has therefore emerged from the clear spaces or openings in several different directions, showing diffraction of the light waves. The wavelength of light is therefore of the order of $\frac{1}{5000}$ cm. Experiments show it is more nearly $\frac{1}{16\,000}$ cm. The very short wavelength of light explains why light passes through most openings without diffraction and produces sharp shadows.

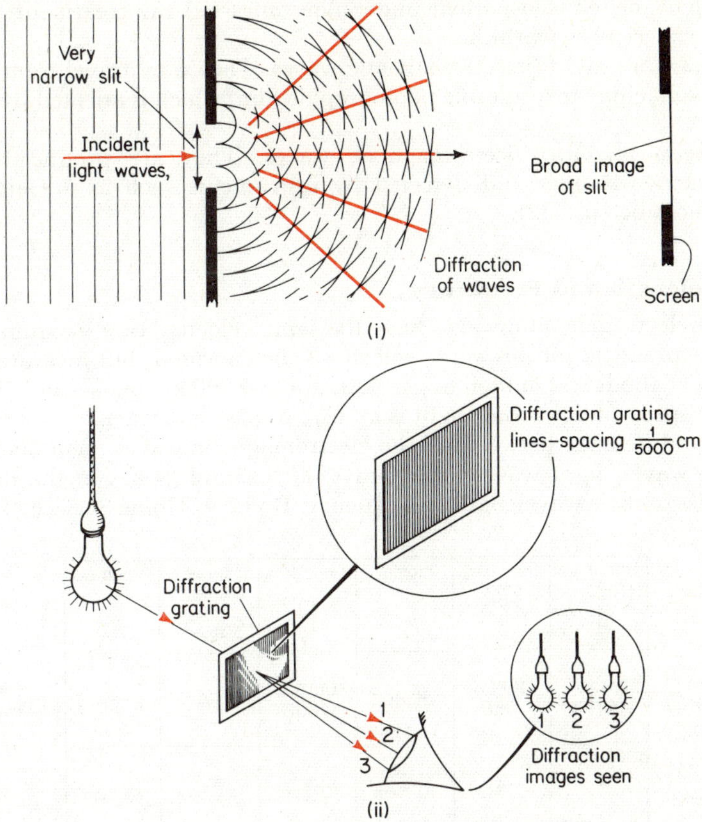

Fig. 14.10 Diffraction of light waves

ELECTROMAGNETIC WAVES

Electromagnetic waves, that is, waves due to electric and magnetic vibrations, are familiar to us in many different forms. The *light* from an electric lamp or the white page of this book is due to electromagnetic waves. They travel from the lamp or page, the source, to your eye, the detector.

Radio waves are electromagnetic waves. They travel from the radiating aerial at a transmitting station, the source, to the receiving aerial attached to your radio or television receiver, the detector. *Ultra-violet rays* are due to electromagnetic waves. These invisible rays may travel from an ultra-violet lamp to a detector such as luminous paint, which then glows, or to a photographic plate which is then affected.

Infra-red rays are also due to electromagnetic waves. These invisible rays may travel from an infra-red filament to a particular transistor, the detector, or to a patient undergoing infra-red ray treatment who then experiences warmth.

X-rays are due to electromagnetic waves. They may travel from the X-ray machine to a suitable photographic film, which is affected by the rays.

Gamma rays are electromagnetic waves. They are produced by radioactive sources and detected by instruments such as a Geiger–Müller tube (p. 582).

Wavelength and Frequency

All electromagnetic waves have the same velocity. In a vacuum, or air for practical purposes, the velocity is the enormous but measurable value of about 300 million m per *second*, or 300 000 km per second. This is the speed of light since light is an electromagnetic wave.

The difference between all the electromagnetic waves mentioned—radio waves, light waves and X-rays, for example—lies in the magnitudes of their wavelength or frequency. Radio 4, Home Service of the

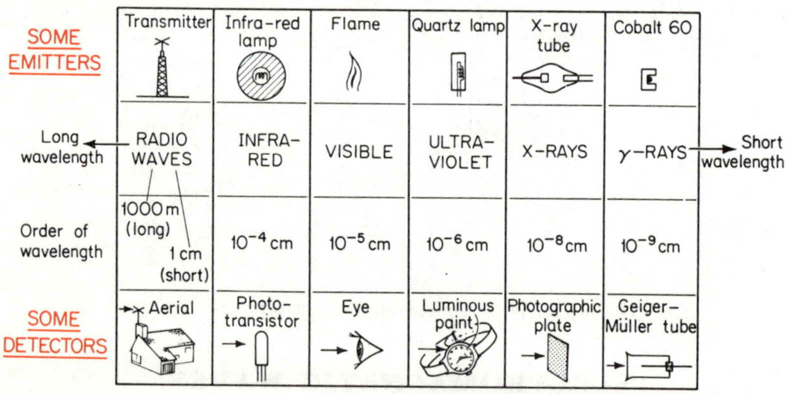

Fig. 14.11 Electromagnetic waves

British Broadcasting Corporation, is radiated on a wavelength of 330 m. The frequency of the radio wave is hence = velocity/wavelength $= 300 \times 10^6$ m per s/330 m $= 10^6$ or 1 million Hz (approx.). Short radio waves called 'microwaves' have wavelengths such as 3 cm. The frequency of the waves is thus: $300 \times 10^6/0{\cdot}03 = 10^{10}$ (ten thousand million) Hz.

As we go lower than 1 cm in wavelength we reach infra-red waves. These with a wavelength of say $\frac{3}{1000}$ cm, have a frequency 10^{13} (ten million million) Hz. At shorter wavelengths we reach visible waves. They occupy only a very short range or band of wavelengths. Red has a wavelength of about 7×10^{-5} ($\frac{1}{14\,000}$) cm and violet has a relatively shorter wavelength of about $4{\cdot}5 \times 10^{-5}$ ($\frac{1}{20\,000}$) cm. The corresponding frequencies are of the order of 10^{15} Hz. Ultra-violet rays have wavelengths of the order of 10^{-6} cm, X-rays of the order of 10^{-8} cm and γ-rays of the order of 10^{-10} cm. The frequencies are respectively of the order of 10^{16}, 10^{18} and 10^{20} Hz. Note again how the frequency rises as the wavelength decreases. The product is always the same, the velocity of electromagnetic waves. Fig. 14.11 illustrates the 'family' of electromagnetic waves. There is no boundary between them and overlapping occurs.

SUMMARY

1. Water waves are due to vibrations of water particles. Sound waves are due to vibrations of particles in the medium concerned. Light waves are electromagnetic waves.

2. For all waves, *velocity* = *frequency* × *wavelength.*

3. All waves can be reflected, refracted and diffracted. Diffraction occurs when the width of an opening is of the same order as the wavelength as the incident waves.

4. Electromagnetic waves = radio, infra-red, visible, ultra-violet, X-rays and gamma-rays. Velocity of electromagnetic waves = velocity of radio and light waves = 300 million metres per second.

PRACTICAL

Apparatus. Ripple tank; hand stroboscope; suitable metal strips for reflection and diffraction experiments.

1. Wavelength and frequency (p. 265)

Using a straight vibrator, obtain a plane wave (see p. 263). Vary the frequency of the vibrator and note the change in wavelength of the waves. Use the hand stroboscope to 'freeze' the waves and hence to examine them more closely.

Using a single small sphere as a vibrator, produce a spherical wave. Note the change when the frequency is varied.

2. Reflection at plane surfaces (p. 266)

Use a plane wave. Set up a plane metal strip in the path of the waves. First observe the effect of normal incidence on the strip. Then turn the strip at an angle to the waves and observe the reflected waves. Repeat for different angles of incidence. Does the angle of incidence equal the angle of reflection always?

3. Reflection at curved spherical surfaces (p. 266)

Use a plane wave. Observe the reflection at a concave metal strip in the path of the waves. Do the waves appear to converge to a focus? Turn the strip round so that a convex surface is presented to the plane waves. Do the waves diverge after reflection as if they are spreading out from a point *behind* the strip?

Repeat the experiment with spherical waves obtained from a single sphere as a vibrator. Vary the position of the sphere or 'point' object.

4. Refraction

Use plane waves. As described on p. 267, set up a flat glass plate to produce a shallow region in the water where the speed of the wave is reduced. Observe the change in wavelength for normal incidence of the wave. Then turn the plate round so that its boundary is now inclined to the oncoming waves and observe any change in direction. See Fig. 14.6, p. 268.

5. Diffraction.

Use two metal strips close together to provide an opening. See Fig. 14.7, p. 269. Observe how a plane wave passes through the opening when: (i) it is wide; (ii) it is narrow and of the order of the wavelength in width. What difference do you observe in the two cases. Vary the opening and observe the effect on the waves after they pass through.

EXERCISE 14 · ANSWERS, p. 402

What are the missing words in the following statements 1–8?

1. Water is the medium of water waves. When we hear a friend speaking, the medium of the sound waves is . .

2. . . waves can travel through a vacuum.

3. The wavelength of a wave is the distance between successive . . or . .

4. Velocity of a wave = wavelength × . .

5. The speed of sound in air is 34 000 cm/s. If the frequency of a note is 1000 Hz, the wavelength is . .

6. One B.B.C. transmitter uses a wavelength of 1500 metres. If the speed of radio waves is 300 million metres per second, the frequency of the radio wave is . . Hz.

7. Light rays and X-rays are both . . waves.

8. The only difference between X-rays and light rays is that X-rays have a much shorter . .

Choose the letter, A, B, C, D, or E, which you think gives the correct answer in the following statements 9–14:

9. A vibrator produces a plane wave on water. When the frequency is increased, the wavelength is: (A) unaffected; (B) increased; (C) decreased; (D) increased twice as much; (E) decreased half as much.

10. When a plane wave is incident on a plane surface, it is reflected: (A) as a spherical wave to a focus; (B) as a spherical wave normal to the surface; (C) as a plane wave always normal to the surface; (D) as a plane wave obeying the law of reflection; (E) as a parabolic wave.

11. When a plane wave is incident on a concave spherical surface, it is reflected as: (A) a spherical wave towards a focus; (B) a plane wave at right-angles to its original direction; (C) a plane wave parallel to its original direction (D) a parabolic wave; (E) a spherical wave whose centre is on the surface.

12. When a wave is incident on an opening small compared with its wavelength, the wave: (A) passes straight through unaffected; (B) is reflected back; (C) is absorbed at the opening; (D) spreads out round the corners; (E) is changed in wavelength.

13. Sound waves are different from light waves because: (A) sound waves need no medium; (B) light waves need a medium; (C) sound waves need a medium; (D) light waves travel through glass; (E) sound waves are not refracted.

14. Light waves and X-rays are both: (A) similar to water waves; (B) similar to radio waves; (C) very long waves; (D) unable to pass through metal; (E) similar to sound waves in glass.

15. (*a*) Fill in the gaps in the list below, which shows the electromagnetic spectrum.

Radio waves	Infra-red		Ultra-violet		Gamma rays

(*b*) Which of the waves listed above do we usually associate with heat?
(*c*) Which waves have the shortest wavelength?
(*d*) Name *two* properties common to all electromagnetic waves.
(*e*) Radio 2 programmes are broadcast on a wavelength of 1500 metres. Calculate the wave velocity if the frequency were 200 000 Hz. (*Mx.*)

16. Water waves are produced in the ripple tank as in Fig. 14A (a), (b), (c).

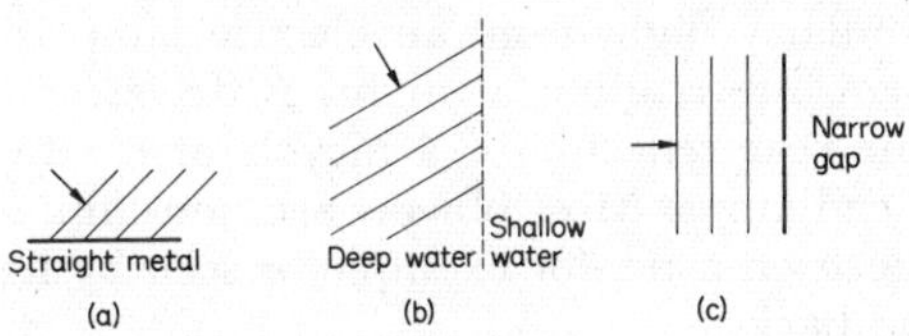

Fig. 14A

Show in diagrams what happens to the waves in each case. On the right of each wave write the appropriate word from the following: interference, diffraction, refraction, reflection, longitudinal. (*Mx.*)

15

RECTILINEAR PROPAGATION OF LIGHT

Luminous and Non-luminous Objects

IN the subject of optics or light we are concerned with luminous energy, that is, energy which causes the sensation of vision. The sun is a *self-luminous* object. So are the stars. Some living creatures such as the glow-worm or fire-fly are self-luminous. Examples of artificial or man-made luminous sources are the electric lamp and the candle.

By contrast, the pages of this book are *non-luminous*. If you are reading it in daylight, then light from the sun falls on the page concerned and some of it is scattered or reflected back to your eyes by the white page. The black print absorbs the light. Consequently, the print stands out on the page. Similarly, light from an electric lamp is scattered back to your eyes if you are reading at night. A driver at night can see a 'Halt' sign or the rear reflector of a bicycle or car by light reflected back from his headlamps. Most objects are non-luminous. A person's face, or the pattern on a tie, for example, is seen by light falling on it which is reflected back.

Rays of Light · Ray-box

The direction or path along which light energy travels is called a light *ray*. The line OABC is a ray from a point source O, Fig. 15.1 (i)

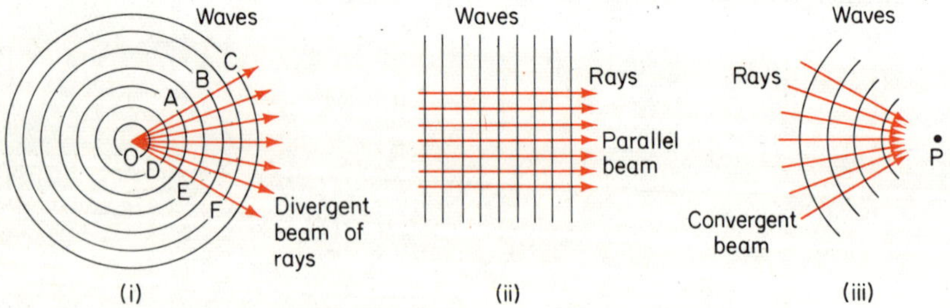

Fig. 15.1 Diverging, parallel and converging beams

ODEF is another ray from O in a different direction. It should be noted that rays are always perpendicular to the waves which spread out from the source O.

A collection or beam of rays which spreads out from O as shown in

Fig. 15.1 (i) is called a *divergent beam*. A *parallel beam* is shown in Fig. 15.1 (ii)—here the waves are parallel. A *convergent beam* is shown in Fig. 15.1 (iii)—here the waves converge to a point P. For demonstration purposes, rays of light are conveniently obtained from a ray-box B, Fig. 15.2. This has a small filament lamp L in an enclosed box,

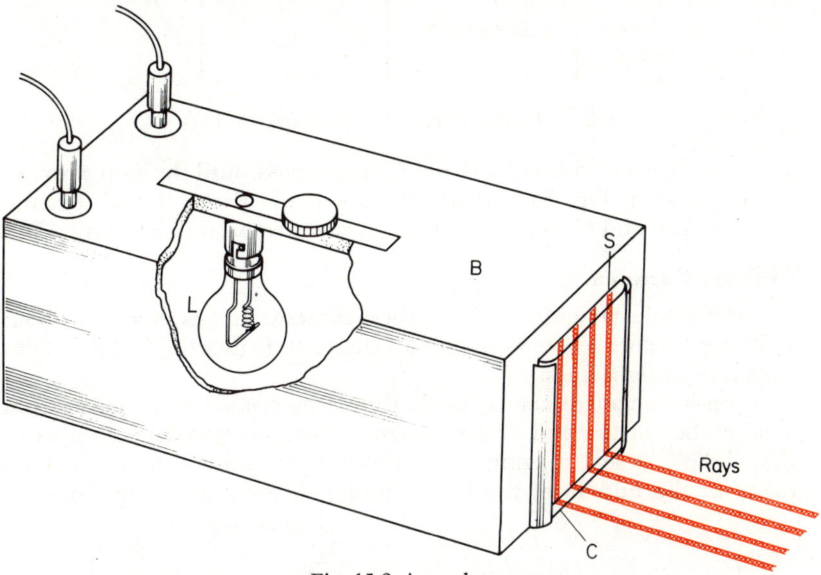

Fig. 15.2 A ray-box

with a cylindrical convex lens C and a 'comb' S containing parallel slits in front of it. 'Rays' of light then emerge from C. By moving the lamp L, a diverging or converging or parallel beam of rays can easily be obtained.

Light Rays and Wide Apertures

If a ray-box is placed on a sheet of white paper and switched on, a thick ray is obtained through each of the rectangular slits of the 'comb'. This may be several millimetres wide, see Fig. 15.2. This so-called ray is actually a very narrow beam of light.

The edges of the ray are well defined. We can therefore say that *light travels in straight lines in this case*. We call this the 'rectilinear propagation of light' (see p. 269). With a much wider aperture, such as an open letter-box or a window, sunlight can be seen streaming through by light scattered from dust particles. The edges of the wide beam are again straight, showing that light travels in straight lines through wide openings.

The rectilinear propagation of light can be demonstrated by placing an illuminated lamp L in front of a hole A in a cardboard. Two other

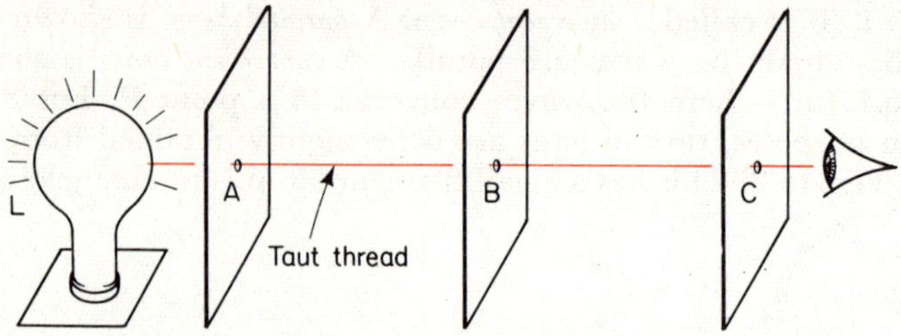

Fig. 15.3 Light usually travels in straight lines

cardboards, each with holes B and C, are moved until the light through A can be seen, Fig. 15.3. It will then be found that a thread, passing through A, B and C and pulled tightly, is perfectly straight along ABC.

Pinhole Camera

The pinhole camera was the earliest camera. It was invented about 1550, well before lenses were used in cameras. It uses the fact that light travels in straight lines.

A pin-hole camera can be made simply by removing the cover from a closed box or tin, and then replacing it by semi-transparent paper so that the box is sealed again from outside light. A small hole H is then made in the middle of the box opposite to the paper, Fig. 15.4 (i).

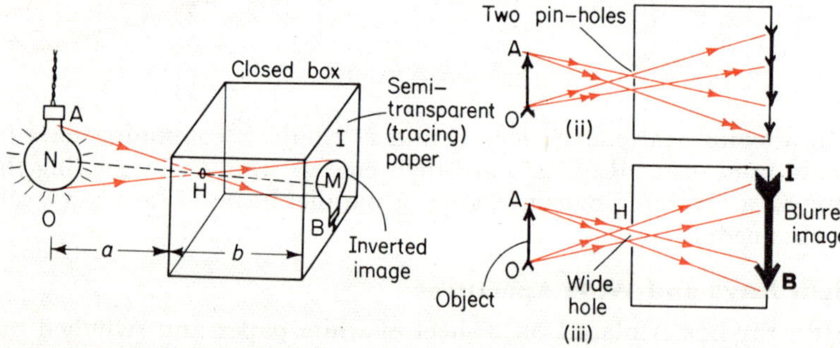

Fig. 15.4 Pin-hole camera and image

When the hole is held up to a bright lamp in a darkened room an inverted small image of the lamp can be seen on the paper. Moving the box towards the lamp increases the size of the image. If the box moves away from the lamp the size of the image diminishes.

An image is always formed by rays of light coming *from* the object. A ray OH from a point O on the lamp, for example, passes through the hole H and strikes the paper screen at I, Fig. 15.4 (i). A ray AH from A produces an image B. If the hole H is small every point on the object produces a corresponding point image. The image is then fairly sharp. Note that the image is inverted.

The pinhole camera has been used by surveyors. It is preferred to the lens camera, as the lens produces distortion. Its disadvantage is the long exposure required for an image to be developed on the photographic plate, because the amount of light passing through the hole is small.

Blurring of Image

If two pinholes are made in a model pinhole camera (see *Experiment*, p. 282), overlapping images are obtained, as shown, Fig. 15.4 (ii). The image is thus indistinct. If a wide hole is made, a blurred image is produced, Fig. 15.4 (iii). Rays from a single point such as A now illuminate an appreciable area round B.

It is instructive to place a suitable converging (convex) lens in front of the many pinholes, or the wide hole H, and in contact with the box. A *sharp* image can now be obtained on the screen. The lens thus brings all the rays from a point on an object to *one* point on the screen. This is why a lens is used in photography (p. 349).

Shadows due to Small and Large Sources

Shadows are due to light travelling in straight lines. When light rays arrive at an opaque obstacle, that is, one which absorbs light, those which strike it are stopped. Those rays which just graze the edges of the obstacle thus produce the outline of a shadow, Fig. 15.5.

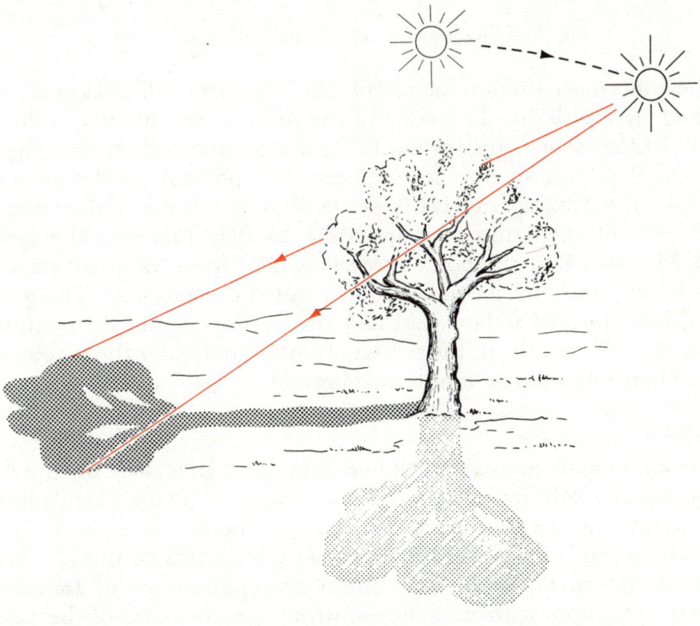

Fig. 15.5 Shadows

The kind of shadow obtained depends on the size of the luminous object sending out the rays. Thus in Fig. 15.6 (i) a ray-box with a small filament, or *point source* of light, produces a sharp shadow of an opaque solid ball B on a screen placed behind B. The shadow is uniformly dark. On the other hand, when the lamp is replaced by a *large source* of light such as a pearl lamp P the shadow is no longer uniformly dark, Fig. 15.6 (ii).

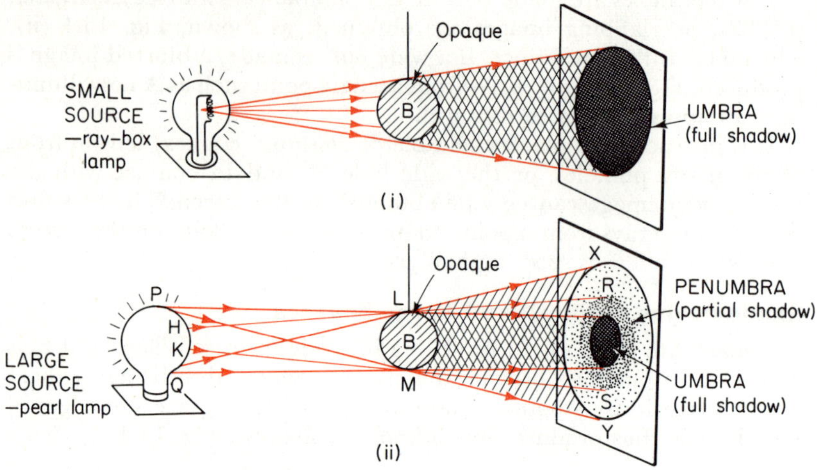

Fig. 15.6 Shadows due to (i) small (ii) large source

The innermost shadow or *umbra*, the region of full darkness, is not reached by any light. The edge of the umbra corresponds to the rays PL and QM, which just graze B. As we go away from the edge the darkness slowly diminishes in intensity. At a point R on the screen, for example, the grazing ray HLR shows that R receives light from that small part of the lamp corresponding to PH. Likewise the grazing ray KM shows that the point S receives light from the small part QK. Thus R and S are in 'partial shadow', called the *penumbra*. The grazing rays QLX and PMY show that X Y are on the edge of the penumbra. Above X or Y, points on the screen are illuminated by the whole of the lamp. Hence no shadow is obtained here.

Eclipses

The moon and earth are both non-luminous. In a clear sky the moon can be seen by light from the sun. This is scattered by the moon's surface. The eclipse of the sun occurs when the moon, an opaque object, comes between the sun and the earth. This is illustrated in Fig. 15.7 (i). Parts of the earth lie in the umbra and penumbra of the moon's shadow. The appearance of the sun from various parts of the earth is illustrated in Fig. 15.7 (ii). A person at *a* sees a *total eclipse*. Another

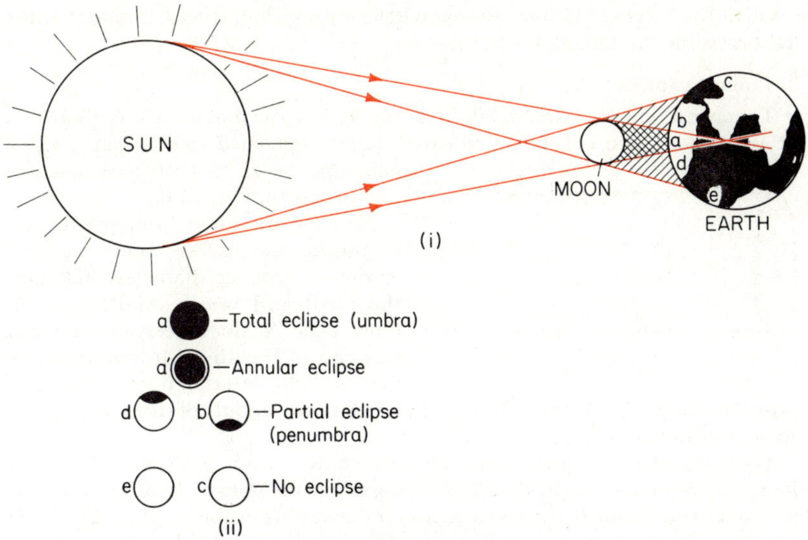

Fig. 15.7 Eclipse of sun

person at *b* or *d* sees a *partial eclipse.* Another person at *c* or *e* sees no eclipse. On another occasion, different from that shown in Fig. 15.7 (i), the earth and moon may be in positions when the extreme rays intersect before they reach the earth. An observer in a position corresponding to *a′* in Fig. 15.7 (i) then sees an *annular eclipse.* This is a ring of light round the shadow of the moon.

An eclipse of the moon occurs when the earth comes between the sun and the moon. The earth is an opaque body, and prevents some of the light from the sun reaching the moon. This time the moon lies partly in the umbra and partly in the penumbra of the earth's shadow.

SUMMARY

1. Luminous objects radiate light; non-luminous objects are seen by diffusely reflected light.
2. Beams of light may be parallel, convergent or divergent.
3. Shadows and eclipses are due to the rectilinear propagation of light. The *umbra* is the region of full shadow (total eclipse); the *penumbra* is the region of partial shadow (partial eclipse).
4. In the pinhole camera the image is inverted. The size of the hole must not be too large, otherwise the image becomes blurred—a point on the image is now illuminated by several points on the object.

PRACTICAL

1. Light travels in straight lines

As explained on p. 277, (i) make a hole at the same height in three cards, (ii) place a source of light such as a lamp behind one hole, and (iii) use a thread to see if all the holes are in line, after you have arranged all three cards so that the light is visible through all the holes.

2. Pinhole camera

To make a pinhole camera, take a short length of cardboard tube A about 4 in or 10 cm long and cover one end with tightly stretched tracing paper using Sellotape, so as to form a semi-transparent screen, Fig. 15.8.

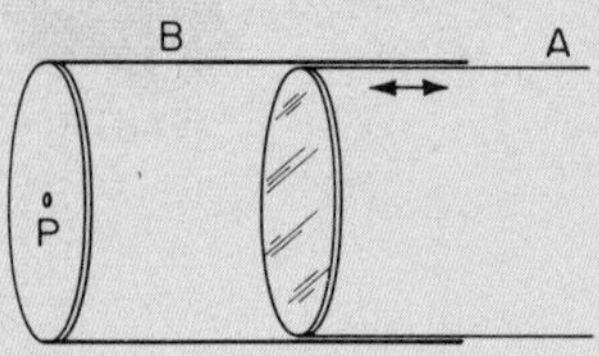

Fig. 15.8 Pinhole camera

Now wrap some thin cardboard round the tube to form another tube B of slightly greater diameter. Sellotape the cardboard firmly. Make sure the inner tube A slides freely. Now cover one end of B with a cardboard disc so that no light enters B here—use Sellotape for attaching the disc. Make a pinhole P in the middle of the disc—do not make this hole too large (see p. 278).

Look at a lamp or other bright object such as a window. Observe: (i) if the image is upside down; (ii) the effect on the size of the image when A is moved in and out, and when B is moved nearer or away from the object. (iii) Make another pinhole close to the first one. Observe the image. Is there a double image? (iv) Make two more pinholes and observe the image. Finally, make an appreciable hole and observe the image. Using a converging (convex) lens whose focal length is about the distance from the hole to the screen of the camera, place the lens in front of the hole. Observe the image.

Results. Make a table of your observations. Draw a ray diagram in illustration of each.

	Image—clear or blurred
1 pinhole	. .
2 pinholes	. .
4 pinholes	. .
Wide hole	. .
Lens used	. .

3. Umbra and penumbra

Method. (i) Use a motor headlamp (ray-box) lamp as a small source and a pearl lamp as a larger source (p. 280).

(ii) With the aid of a white screen, or white paper on a sheet of glass viewed from behind, project shadows of objects such as a key, a ball, a book and your hand—use first the small lamp and then the large lamp. Observe the umbra and penumbra. Alter the positions of the lamps to see if the umbra and penumbra change. Draw sketches to illustrate the results.

EXERCISE 15 · ANSWERS, p. 402

What are the missing words in the following statements 1–11?

1. A region of full shadow is called a . .

2. The penumbra is the region of . . shadow.

3. A small source of light produces a . . shadow of a large opaque object in front.

4. A very small or 'point' source of light sends out a . . beam from the point.

5. Partial shadows may be demonstrated by using a . . source of light in front of a large opaque object.

6. Eclipses are produced on account of the . . propagation of light.

7. Eclipses of the sun are due to the shadow cast by the . .

8. To explain how partial or total eclipses of the sun are produced, lines (rays) should be drawn in the diagram which touch the . . of the sun and moon.

9. In a pinhole camera, the image is . . if the hole is too large.

10. In a pinhole camera, the image produced is always . . and . .

11. Since the hole in the pinhole camera is small, only a small amount of . . passes through.

12. The shadow of a ping-pong ball on a screen is uniformly dark when the: (*a*) shadow is caused by a fluorescent lamp; (*b*) light source is very small; (*c*) screen is very near the ball; (*d*) light source is very large; (*e*) light source is very bright. (*M.*)

13. If the hole of a pinhole camera is made larger, the images become: (*a*) more blurred and less bright; (*b*) brighter but more blurred; (*c*) clearer but less bright; (*d*) clearer and brighter; (*e*) larger and less bright. (*M.*)

14. Fig. 15A shows an eclipse of the sun. State the light conditions in the regions indicated: 1 . . 2 . 3 . . 4 . . (*E.A.*)

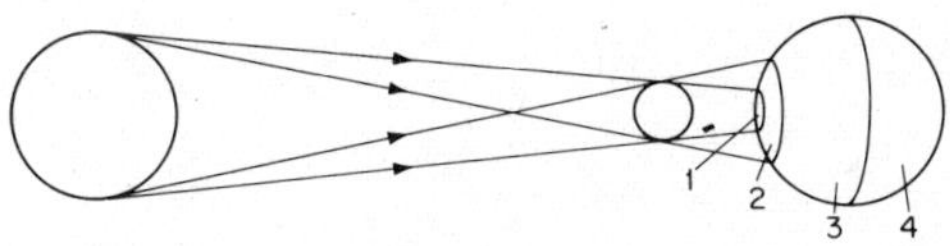

Fig. 15A

15. Fig. 15B shows a pinhole camera

(*a*) Complete the diagram showing the image formed. No rays need be shown.

(*b*) Why would the image become more blurred if the pinhole were larger? (*E.A.*)

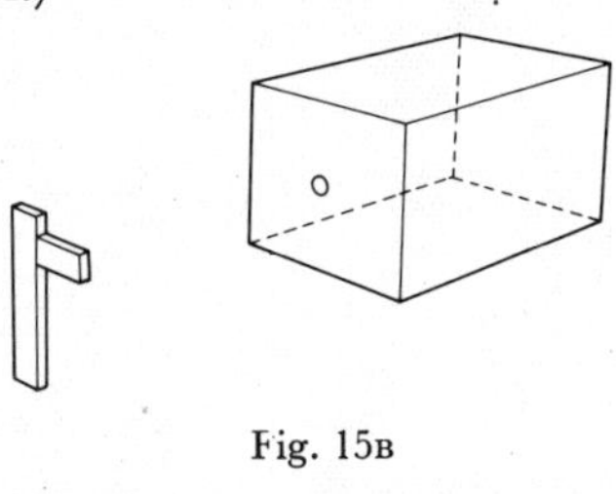

Fig. 15B

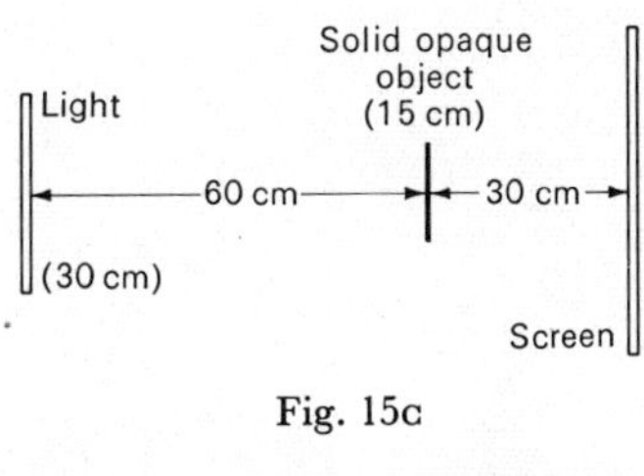

Fig. 15C

16. Study the diagram Fig. 15C and then draw a similar diagram on your answer paper, adding the paths of rays of light to show how two different types of shadow are formed on the screen. Label and describe these shadows.

How can such a diagram be used to explain :(*a*) a total eclipse, and (*b*) partial eclipse of the sun? (*W.Md.*)

17. Make a diagram to show how an eclipse of the moon occurs. Label all parts of your diagram, including the regions known as *umbra* and *penumbra*. (*S.E.*)

18. Draw a diagram of a pinhole camera showing the positions of: (*a*) the object; (*b*) the image with two rays travelling from the object to the image; (*c*) how is the size of the image affected by moving the object nearer to the camera? (*L.*)

16

REFLECTION AT PLANE SURFACES

PLANE mirrors are made by silvering a flat piece of glass. Practically all the light which falls on the front surface of the mirror is reflected back. Plane mirrors are hence used as looking-glasses and as inside mirrors in cars for observing traffic directly behind. They are also used in some scientific instruments. In the sextant, for example, the angle of elevation of the sun is measured with the aid of two plane mirrors.

Reflection of Rays

The reflection of light rays can be investigated with a *ray-box* R and a plane mirror PQ on a sheet of white paper, Fig. 16.1 (i). A parallel

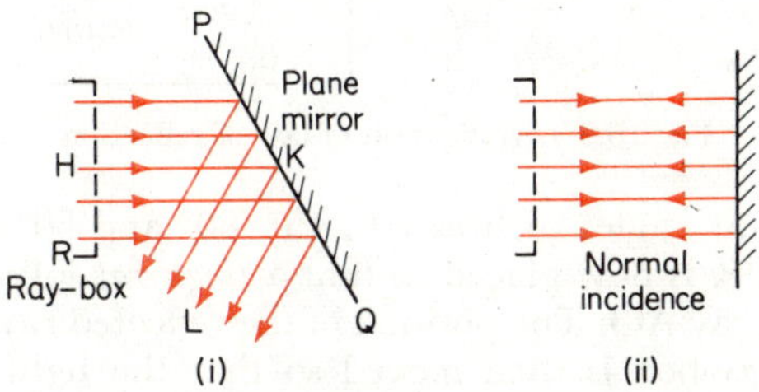

Fig. 16.1 Reflection by plane mirror

beam of light HK is seen reflected by the mirror in the direction KL. When the mirror is turned the direction of the reflected rays changes. When the light rays are incident normally on the mirror they are reflected straight back, Fig. 16.1 (ii). On p. 267 we saw how water waves are similarly reflected by a plane surface.

Diffusion of Light

A plane mirror thus reflects a parallel beam of light in a definite direction. This is due to the high smoothness and polish of the reflecting surface. But most objects do not reflect light with such regularity. Paper and clothing materials are examples. This is on account of the lack of smoothness or 'grain' of the surface, which is readily seen under a high-power microscope. Rays of light incident on such surfaces are

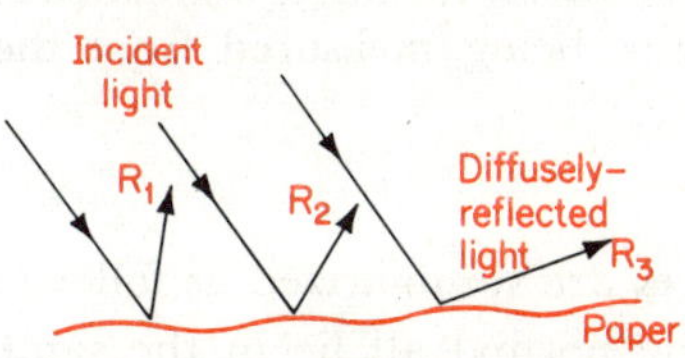

Fig. 16.2 Diffuse reflection

reflected in different directions, R_1, R_2 and R_3. The rays are said to be *scattered* or *diffusely reflected*, Fig. 16.2. The pages of a book, or a person's face, are seen by diffusely-reflected light.

Experiment on Reflection

The reflection of light from a plane mirror can be investigated by supporting it vertically on a white sheet of paper. A line ON, which is normal or perpendicular to the mirror is first drawn from O, a point near the middle of the mirror, Fig. 16.3 (i). Further lines are then

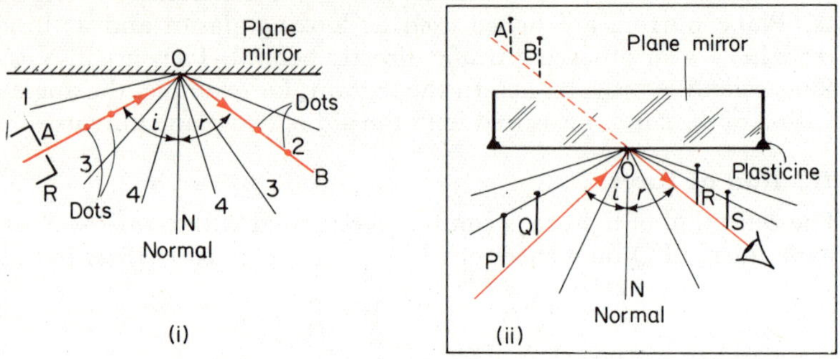

Fig. 16.3 Investigation of law of reflection

drawn inclined at angles such as 20°, 45°, 60° and 80° respectively to ON. A ray-box R is now placed so that a *single ray* follows the path of one of the lines, say AO. The position of the reflected ray OB is marked by dots. The ray-box is then moved so that the light is incident in directions corresponding to the other drawn lines. The positions of the reflected rays are marked again. The different angles of incidence i and reflection r, which are the angles made with the *normal*, ON can now be measured.

Alternatively, the direction of the incident ray can be defined by two pins, P and Q, which are placed along one of the drawn lines, Fig. 16.3 (ii). Their images A and B are lined up by eye with two more pins R and S. The line PQO is an incident ray reflected along ORS, which is then drawn. The experiment is repeated by moving P and Q to other incident lines, and the different angles of incidence i and reflection r are measured.

Results. The experiment shows that, in all cases, the angle of incidence $i =$ the angle of reflection r, both angles being measured from the normal ON, Fig. 16.4 (i).

Laws of Reflection

The laws of reflection at plane surfaces are summarized as follows:

1. The incident, reflected ray and the normal all lie in the same plane.

2. The angle of incidence = the angle of reflection.

The first law is illustrated in Fig. 16.4 (ii). A ray AO is incident on a plane mirror at O. Many lines, such as OC, can be drawn round the

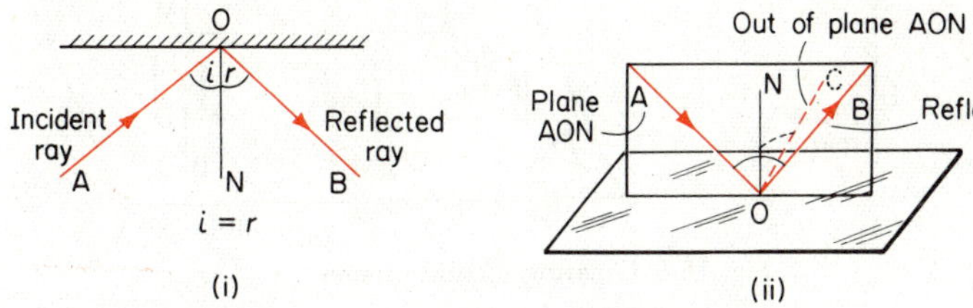

Fig. 16.4 Laws of reflection

normal ON as axis so that they are inclined to it at an angle equal to the angle of incidence AON. But the first law restricts the position of the reflected ray; it must lie in the plane of AO and ON. Therefore the reflected ray can only be OB, which is in this plane.

Simple Periscope

A simple periscope uses plane mirrors to reflect light in suitable directions, Fig. 16.5. Two parallel plane mirrors, A and B are fixed at 45° to the opposite ends of a long tube with two openings X and Y. A ray OL from an object O falls on mirror A at L. Its angle of incidence is 45°. Hence it is reflected along LM at 45° to the normal at L, i.e. at right angles to the incident ray. It is then reflected by mirror B on which it is incident at 45°. The reflected ray MS is therefore at right angles to LM. It passes through the hole Y and is seen by the eye at P. By this device it is possible to view objects obscured by the heads of a crowd. Note that the periscope will not function efficiently if the mirrors are not in their correct positions, that is, they should be parallel and at 45° to the horizontal.

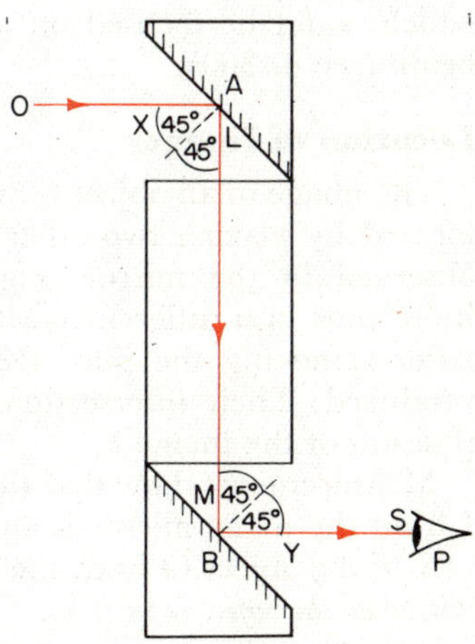

Fig. 16.5 Simple periscope

Formation of Images · Virtual Images

When a small object O is viewed by reflection in a plane mirror, the apparent position of the image I is determined by the direction in which the reflected light enters the eye. An observer at E, for example, looking into the mirror, sees the rays AX BY reflected *as if they come*

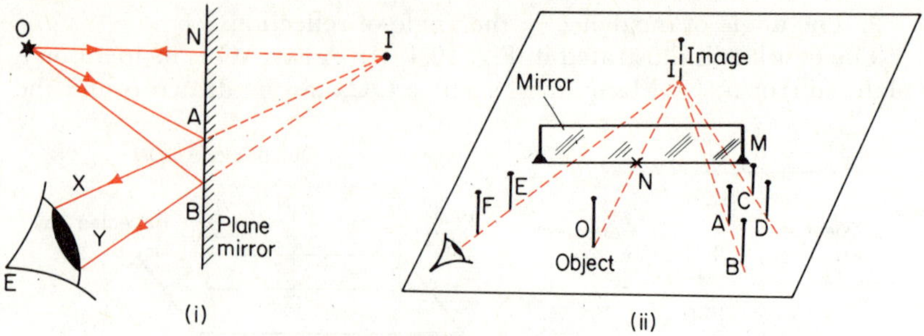

Fig. 16.6 Locating virtual images

from I, which is the point of intersection of these rays produced backwards, Fig. 16.6 (i). He or she is not conscious of the fact that the rays started initially from O. Any other ray from O which enters the eye after reflection also appears to come from I. The *image* of O is therefore at I.

It should be noted that: (1) a normal ray ON is reflected back along NO, so that I lies on ON produced; (2) no rays actually pass through I because a *divergent* beam is obtained by reflection. The image I is therefore described as a *virtual image*; it would not be formed on a screen placed in front of the mirror. In contrast, a *real image* is one which could be focused on a screen and is formed by a convergent beam (see p. 300).

Location of Image

The image of an object O, such as a pin, in a plane mirror M can be located by placing two other pins, A and B, in line with the image I observed in the mirror, Fig. 16.6 (ii). This is repeated with two more pins in a different position, such as at C and D or at E and F. After removing the pins, the lines AB and CD or AB and EF are produced. Their intersection, which is behind the mirror, gives the position of the image I.

Measurements show that the perpendicular distance IN of the image I from the plane mirror is always equal to the perpendicular distance ON of the object O from the mirror. Thus *the image is as far behind the mirror as the object is in front.*

Large Object Experiment

The image of a large object in a plane mirror can be investigated by a class with the aid of a plane glass surface. This may be obtained, for example, by removing the front glass cover of a chemical balance. The glass G is supported vertically, and the fingers of the left hand L are spread horizontally on the bench on one side near G, Fig. 16.7 (i). By moving the *right* hand R behind G, and looking through G at the same time, the image I can be just covered by the right hand.

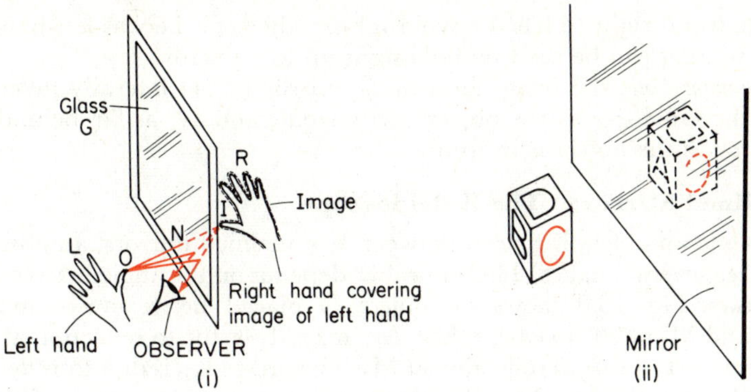

Fig. 16.7 (i) Locating virtual image (ii) lateral inversion

Measurement of the perpendicular distance ON from the top O of the left thumb to G, and of the perpendicular distance IN from the top I of the right thumb to G, shows that IN = ON. Thus the image is as far behind G as the object is in front.

Lateral Inversion

Since the image of the left hand looks exactly like the right hand to an observer, the image of a large object in a plane mirror is said to be *laterally inverted*. The inversion is also seen by placing a lettered cube in front of a plane mirror, Fig. 16.7 (ii). A right-handed batsman or tennis player will therefore appear left-handed if his or her stance is observed in a mirror, Fig. 16.8. Words on a blotting-paper can be seen as they were originally written by holding the blotting-paper to a mirror. The famous artist and inventor Leonardo da Vinci used to

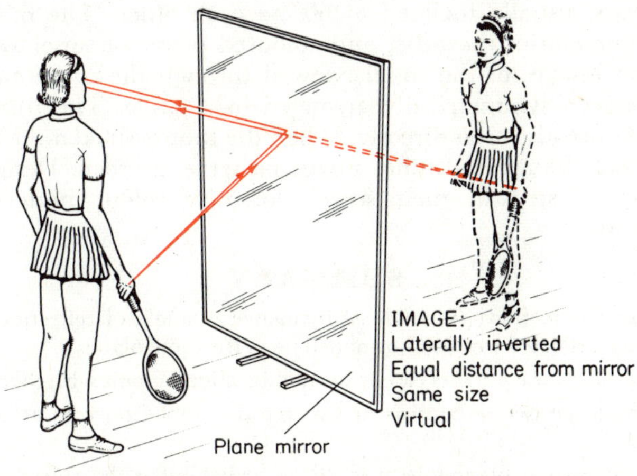

Fig. 16.8 Lateral inversion by mirror

write from 'right to left' to avoid ink-smudges, for he was left-handed. His writing can be read by holding it up to a mirror.

Summarizing, the image in a plane mirror is: (1) laterally inverted; (2) the same size as the object; (3) virtual; and (4) as far behind the mirror as the object is in front.

Inclined Mirrors · The Kaleidoscope

When an object is placed between two inclined mirrors, an observer can see several images. Their number depends on the angle between the mirrors. Fig. 16.8 shows an object O placed between two mirrors M_1 and M_2 at 90° to each other. An image I_1 is due to reflection at M_1. An image I_2 is due to reflection at M_2. The image $I_{1,2}$ is due to reflection at M_1 and then at M_2. Fig. 16.9 shows how rays starting from O reach the observer E by repeated reflection.

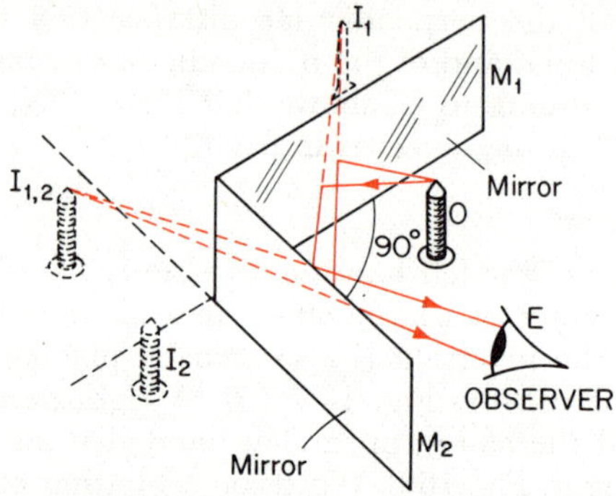

Fig. 16.9 Reflection at two mirrors

The *kaleidoscope* is a toy in which multiple images are formed by two mirrors, usually inclined at 60° to each other. The mirrors are fixed at one end of the tube, and coloured pieces of tinsel are placed here. Five images of the tinsel, viewed through the other end of the tube, are seen symmetrically arranged in a circle. The tinsel pieces themselves are also seen directly. When the tube is shaken the positions of the tinsel change and other image patterns are seen. Designers are sometimes assisted in their search for new colour patterns by a kaleidoscope.

SUMMARY

1. Laws of reflection: (i) angle of incidence = angle of reflection; (ii) the incident ray, reflected ray and normal all lie in the same plane.

2. Images in plane mirrors can be located by aligning pins with them.

3. A simple periscope consists of two parallel plane mirrors at 45° to the horizontal.

4. The image in a plane mirror is: (i) as far behind as the object is in front; (ii) laterally inverted; (iii) the same size as the object; (iv) virtual.

PRACTICAL

1. Law of reflection

Method. As explained on p. 286, use *either* a ray-box *or* pins to obtain five different values of angle of incidence i and angle of reflection r with a plane mirror.

Measurements. Enter all your results in a table:

i	r

Conclusion. State your conclusion.

2. Reflection from two mirrors

Method. (i) Stand a mirror M vertically on a sheet of white paper—use plasticene for keeping it upright, Fig. 16.10 (i). Shine a single ray AO from a ray-box on to M. Alter the direction of AO until the reflected ray OB is 90° to AO measured by a protractor. Then draw the normal OB and measure the angle of incidence i of AO. Record your result.

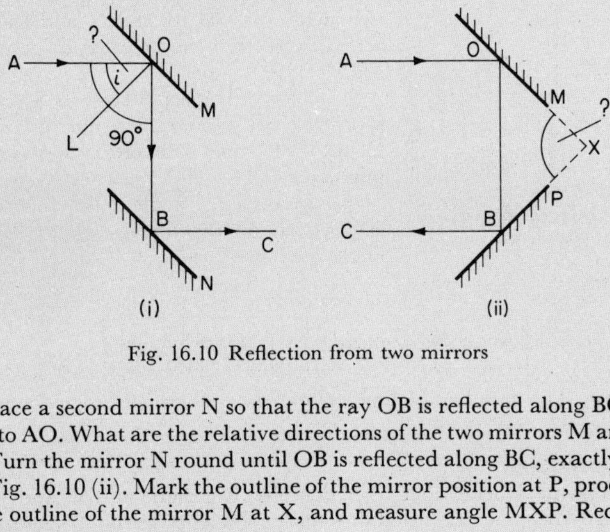

Fig. 16.10 Reflection from two mirrors

(ii) Place a second mirror N so that the ray OB is reflected along BC exactly parallel to AO. What are the relative directions of the two mirrors M and N?

(iii) Turn the mirror N round until OB is reflected along BC, exactly parallel to OA, Fig. 16.10 (ii). Mark the outline of the mirror position at P, produce it to meet the outline of the mirror M at X, and measure angle MXP. Record your results.

Measurements.

(i)	Angle AOB = 90°	Angle i =
(ii)	BC parallel to AO	Mirrors M and N are . .
(iii)	BC parallel to OA	Mirrors M and N are . .

Can you explain your results from the law of reflection?

3. Lateral inversion

Method. (i) Place a sheet of paper on top of the *carbon* side of carbon paper. Write a few words on the sheet of paper. On raising the paper, the words appear laterally inverted on the side originally in contact with the carbon. Hold the words in front of a plane mirror to read them.

(ii) Dry the ink with blotting-paper after writing some words on paper. Hold the blotting-paper in front of a mirror to read them.

4. Image in plane mirror

Method. As explained on p. 288, use a vertical plane sheet of glass on a table as a reflector and your hand as a large object. Locate the image as explained. Measure the perpendicular distance of the thumb (object) from the glass and the distance of its image from the glass. Repeat for the other fingers. Enter all your results in a table.

Measurements.

Object distance	Image distance

Conclusion. State your conclusion.

5. Images in two mirrors

Method. (i) Sellotape together the edges of two plane mirrors M and N and stand them vertically so that they enclose an angle of 60° Fig. 16.11.

(ii) Place an object S such as a screw or a piece of chalk between the mirrors, as shown. Count the number of images you can see in both mirrors.

(iii) Increase the angle between M and N to 90°. Count all the images again. Repeat for angles such as 75° and 30°.

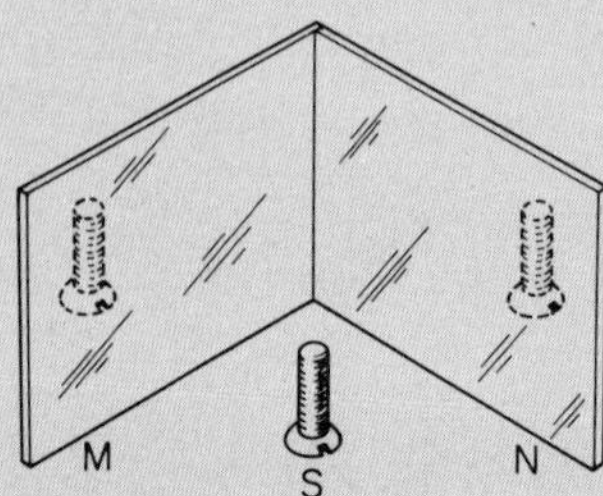

Fig. 16.11 Images in two inclined mirrors

Measurements.

Angle between mirrors	No. of images

Conclusion. The number of images increases when the angle between the mirrors . .

6. Kaleidoscope

Make a simple kaleidoscope by Sellotaping two plane mirrors and a piece of cardboard of the same size so that they form together a long 60° triangular prism. If you look down the prism at coloured pieces of chalk or paper, a kaleidoscope pattern can be seen.

EXERCISE 16 · ANSWERS, p. 402

What are the missing words in the following statements 1–4?

1. The angles of incidence and reflection are the angles made with the . .

2. The angles of incidence and reflection are . .

3. When a ray is reflected at right-angles to its original direction from a plane mirror, the angle of incidence is . .

4. The image in a plane mirror is situated . . the mirror.

Choose the letter, A, B, C, D or E, which you think gives the correct answer in the following statements 5, 6.

5. The image in a plane mirror is: (A) real and the same size as the object; (B) virtual and nearly the same size; (C) virtual and exactly the same size; (D) real and nearly the same size; (E) virtual and half the size.

6. A point object is situated in front of a plane mirror. The incident rays on the mirror are: (A) a convergent beam and are reflected as a divergent beam; (B) a divergent beam and reflected as a convergent beam; (C) a divergent beam and reflected as a divergent beam; (D) a parallel beam and reflected as a parallel beam; (E) a parallel beam and reflected as a convergent beam.

7. A small or point object O is placed in front of a plane mirror. Take two rays from O incident on the mirror and show where the image is formed in your diagram. (*Note.* In drawing ray diagrams, actual rays are shown by lines with arrows on them. Lines which are *not* actual rays may be drawn as broken lines with no arrows on them.)

8. Draw a diagram with a large 'R' 5 cm in front of a plane mirror. Then draw accurately the image of 'R' in the mirror.

9. In a diagram, draw mirrors which together act as a simple periscope. Show how the periscope works, using rays of light.

10. Draw a ray diagram showing how a single plane mirror can reflect light back along its original direction. Show by a diagram how two inclined plane mirrors can be arranged to reflect the light back parallel to its original direction.

11. A plane mirror can be used as a driving mirror. Draw a ray diagram showing its action.

12. Fig. 16A shows a narrow beam of light being reflected from a plane mirror, AB. Give the *names* of the following: ON, PO, OQ, angle PON, angle QON. State how angle PON is related to the angle QON. (*Mx.*)

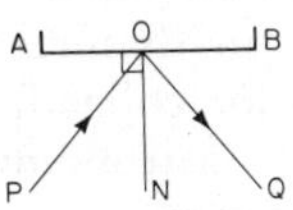

Fig. 16A

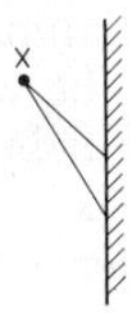

Fig. 16B

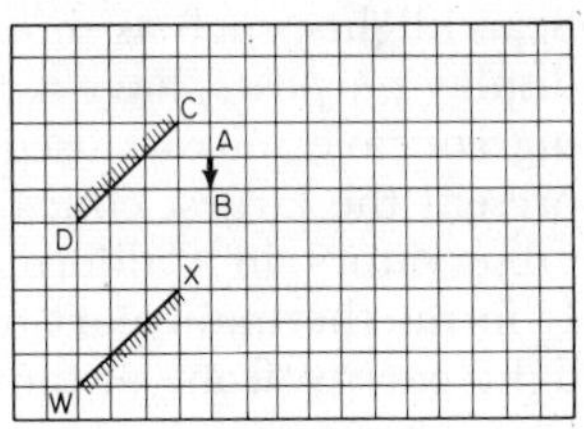

Fig. 16C

13. State the laws of reflection. (*N.W.*)

14. Complete the ray diagram Fig. 16B, to show the position of the image of object X as it would be seen in a plane mirror. (*W.Md.*)

15. (*a*) Draw a position of the image of AB in mirror CD and call it EF, Fig. 16C; (*b*) now draw the image of EF in mirror WX and call it YZ. (*E.A.*)

16. Draw a diagram of a simple periscope which uses two mirrors. Show the path of the light through the periscope; (*b*) what could be used instead of mirrors? (*L.*)

17

CURVED SPHERICAL MIRRORS

CURVED mirrors are widely used. Motor vehicles often have curved mirrors on their wings so that drivers are able to see traffic behind. These mirrors curve outwards towards the observer. They are called *convex mirrors*, Fig. 17.1 (i). Shaving mirrors, however, curve inwards

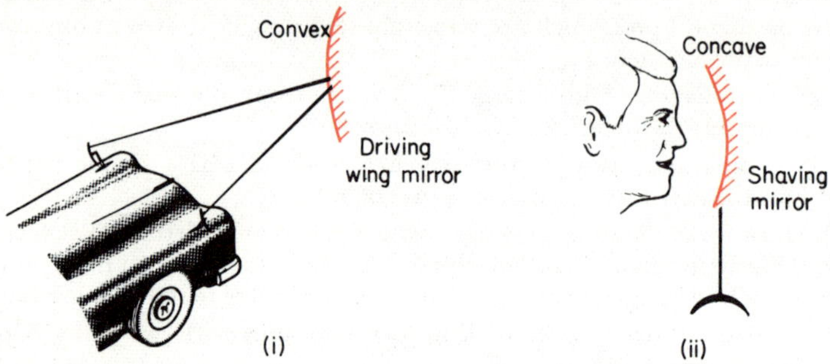

Fig. 17.1 (i) Convex (driving) (ii) concave (shaving) mirrors

away from the observer, Fig. 17.1 (ii). They are called *concave mirrors*. Searchlights, such as those used to illuminate the front of buildings for display purposes, have a concave mirror of a special shape. The reflecting concave mirrors used in car headlamps have a similar shape. At present the largest concave mirror in the world is at Mount Palomar Observatory in California. It is 200 inches (5 metres) in diameter. It forms the main part of an enormous telescope, used for collecting light energy from distant stars and for investigations in astronomy. Curved mirrors are thus of considerable practical importance.

Common Terms

Concave and convex mirrors are made by depositing vaporized aluminium on a glass surface which is part of a sphere, like a watch-glass. The width AB of the mirror is called the *aperture*; the centre P of the mirror is called the *pole*; the centre C of the sphere of which the mirror is part is called the *centre of curvature*; the line PC is called the *principal* (chief) *axis of the mirror*. The *radius of curvature r* is the distance PC; the *focal length f* is the distance PF, Fig. 17.2. As we shall see later, the action of a mirror depends considerably on the magnitude of the radius of curvature r or focal length f. Measurement and theory show that $r = 2f$.

Reflection of Rays

With a *concave* mirror, rays parallel and close to the principal axis CP *converge* to a point F on the principal axis. Fig. 17.2 (i). The point F is called the *principal focus* of the mirror.

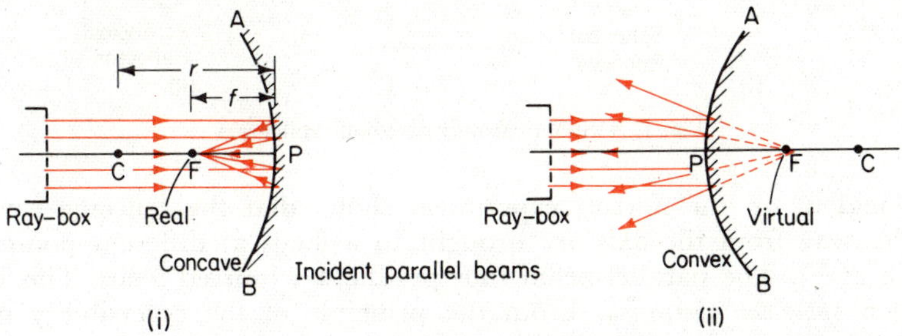

Fig. 17.2 Concave and convex mirrors

By contrast, rays parallel and close to the principal axis *diverge* from the reflecting surface of a *convex* mirror, Fig. 17.2 (ii). They appear to diverge from a point F on the principal axis behind the mirror. The principal focus of a concave mirror is a *real* focus, that is, reflected rays actually pass through it. The principal focus of a convex mirror is a *virtual* focus—reflected rays do not actually pass through it.

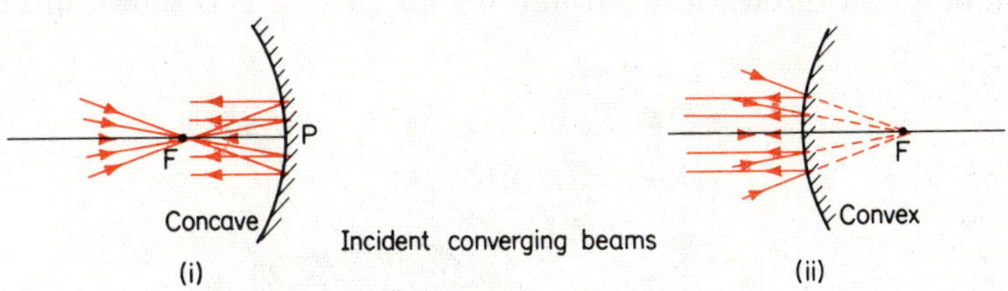

Fig. 17.3 Reflection of parallel beams

If the ray-box is made to produce a beam converging to the principal focus F, then, for both the concave and convex surfaces, a *parallel* beam is reflected back, Fig. 17.3. Figs. 17.2 and 17.3 should be compared with each other. They show that the paths of the light rays are the same, although they travel in opposite directions. This is an illustration of a general law called the *Principle of Reversibility of Light.*

Parabolic Mirrors

If a narrow beam is incident on a concave mirror, all the reflected rays pass through one definite point, the principal focus F, Fig. 17.4 (i). If, however, a *wide* parallel beam covering the whole of the aperture

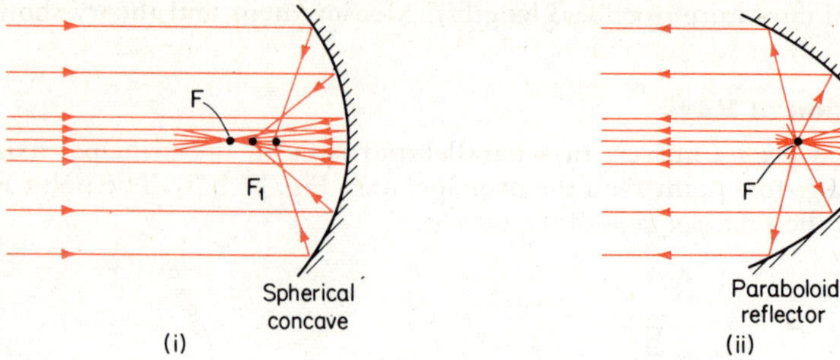

Fig. 17.4 Spherical and parabolic reflectors

is incident on the mirror, experiment shows that the reflected rays well away from the axis are brought to a focus at different points, such as F_1. The parallel beam thus produces a blurred focus. This is called *spherical aberration.* From the principle of the reversibility of light, it follows that if a small lamp is placed at the principal focus F, the rays will be reflected not as a parallel beam from the *outer* parts of the mirror but as a divergent beam. Since the reflected light energy here spreads out from the mirror, it becomes weaker as the distance increases.

On this account the concave spherical mirror is not used in searchlights, Fig. 17.5 (i), or the headlamps of cars, Fig. 17.5 (ii). *Parabolic mirrors* are used—a 'parabola' is a curve similar in shape to the curved path of a ball thrown forward into the air (p. 132). As shown in Fig.

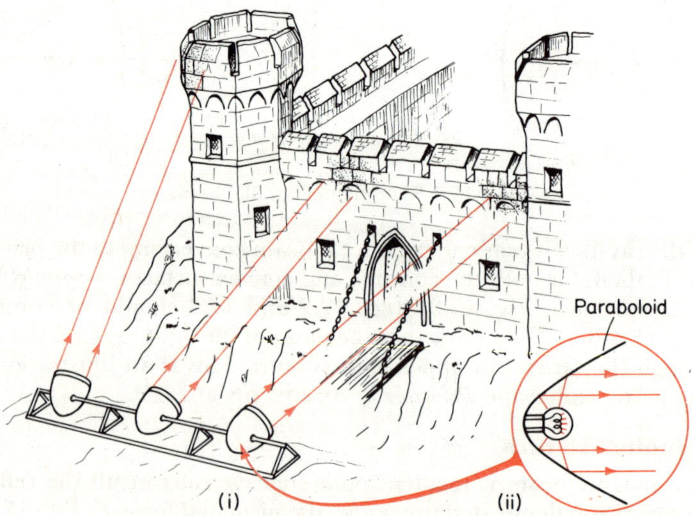

Fig. 17.5 Searchlight and car headlamp reflectors

17.4 (ii), a parabolic mirror reflects all rays parallel to the principal axis when a small lamp is placed at its focus. It does not matter where the rays are incident on the mirror. A bright parallel reflected beam of constant light intensity is therefore obtained. Parabolic mirrors are also used behind the straight filaments in electric fires. The filaments are placed at the focus of the mirror and heat or infra-red rays are reflected back into the room as a parallel beam, Fig. 17.6.

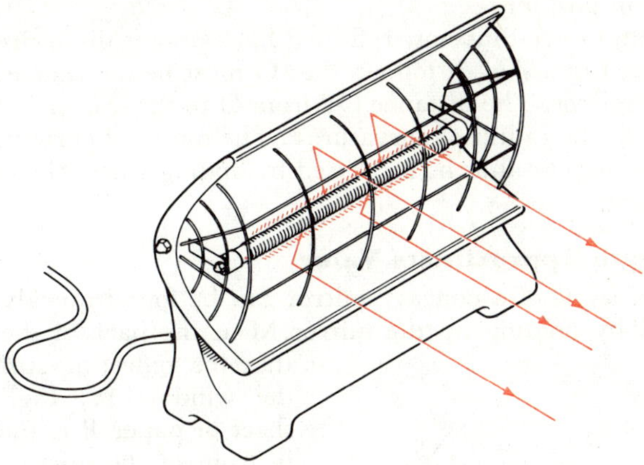

Fig. 17.6 Radiant heat reflector

Centre and Radius of Curvature

By using a single ray from a ray-box and a concave mirror strip, a point C can soon be found on the principal axis such that a ray ACR is reflected back along the same path RCA, Fig. 17.7 (i). Any other ray

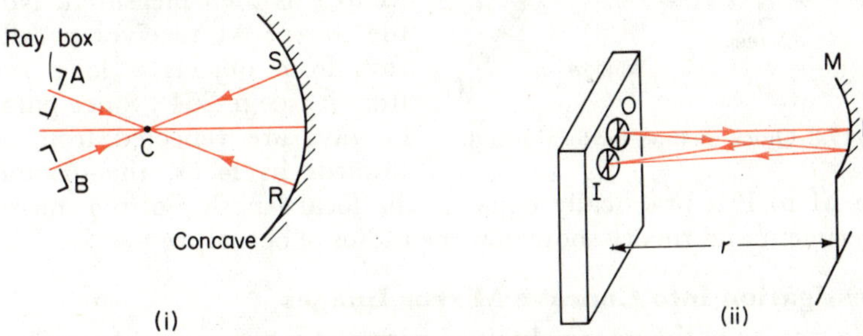

Fig. 17.7 Radius of curvature measurement

through C, such as BCS, is also reflected back along the same path SCB. Now this happens only if the ray CR strikes the mirror *normally* at R and the ray CS strikes the mirror normally at S. Hence CR and CS are normals (perpendiculars) to the mirror at R and S respectively. Consequently, the point C must be the *centre of curvature* of the mirror.

The position of the centre of curvature of a concave spherical mirror can be found by a simple experiment. An illuminated object O, for example, two cross-wires in the centre of a white screen with a lamp behind, is placed in front of the mirror M and in line with its middle or pole P, Fig. 17.7 (ii). When the mirror is moved towards or away from M a blurred image is seen near O. But at some point the image of the cross-wires becomes clear, and the sharpest image I is obtained near O, as shown. The object O and image I are now practically coincident in position.

Rays from O are thus now reflected back practically to itself. From our previous discussion, it follows that O must be the centre of curvature of the mirror. The distance OP from O to the mirror is now measured. This is the radius of curvature *r*. The radius of curvature of any concave surface can thus be measured by finding where the object and image coincide.

Focal Length Approximate Value

The *focal length* of a concave mirror can be found quickly, but not accurately, by holding up the mirror M at the back of the room so that the reflecting surface faces the window W, Fig. 17.8. A sheet of paper P is then moved in front of the mirror until the clearest image of the window-frames is seen or, better, the image of any object such as a tree outside the window. It will be noted that the images are upside down. The distance from M to P is then measured. Now the mirror M receives parallel rays from objects a long way from it (see p. 264). Since parallel rays are reflected from M towards its focus, the distance from M to P is practically equal to the focal length *f* of the mirror. Experiment and theory show that the radius of curvature $r = 2f$.

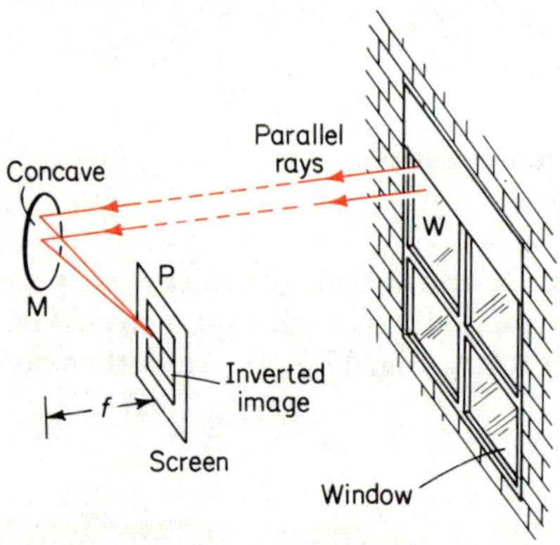

Fig. 17.8 Quick method for focal length

Investigation into Concave Mirror Images

The nature of the image obtained with a concave mirror depends on how far or how close the object is to the mirror. An investigation can be carried out in the laboratory by using illuminated cross-wires as the object O, a concave mirror M on a stand, a white screen S and a ruler for measuring distances see, Fig. 17.9.

We then notice that when the object O is a long way from the mirror as at X, the image S_1 is small, inverted and real. It is formed practically at a distance *f* from the mirror. As the object O is moved towards the mirror M from position I, the image moves back. This is shown by S_1, S_2, S_3 and S_4. The size of the image also grows. At a distance $2f$ from the mirror, which is the distance of C, the centre of curvature, the size of the image is the same as the object. Beyond $2f$ from the mirror the image size is less than that of the object. When the object is nearer than $2f$ the image size is greater than that of the object.

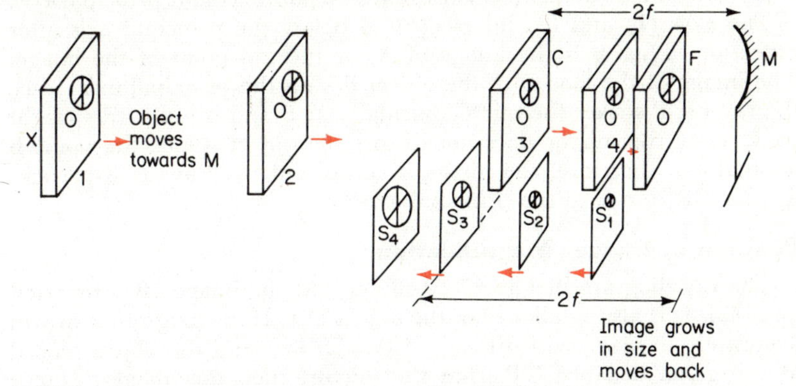

Fig. 17.9 Changes in images as object moves

If the object O is moved nearer to the mirror than f, no image can be received on a screen. But if a concave mirror is held close to the face, a *magnified erect* image is seen. A *virtual* image is hence obtained when O is nearer than f.

Summarizing. When the object is *farther* from the mirror M than f the image is upside down and real; when the object is beyond $2f$ the image is smaller than the object. When the object is *nearer* than f the image is larger, erect and virtual. At the centre of curvature C, at a distance of $2f$ from the mirror, the inverted real image has the same size as the object.

Ray-Diagrams · Drawings of Images

The images obtained in mirrors can always be drawn to scale by means of a *ray-diagram*. As a small central part of the mirror is used, the reflecting surface is represented by a straight line. The object is drawn as a straight line perpendicular to the principal axis, with an arrow to represent its head and its foot O placed on the axis, Fig. 17.10. The image of A, the top of the object, is then found by drawing two rays from it.

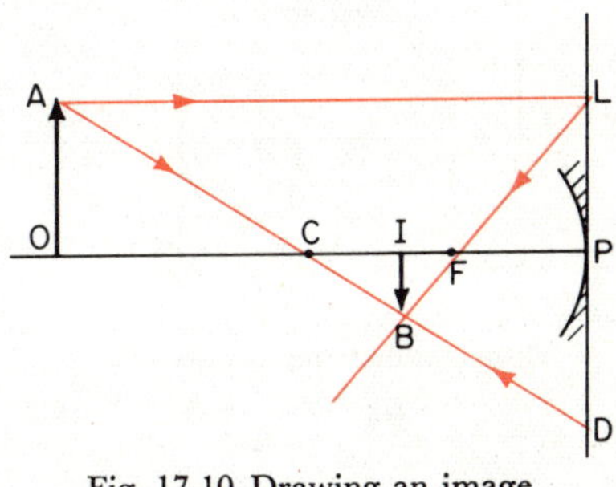

Fig. 17.10 Drawing an image

They may be:

(1) a ray AL parallel to the principal axis, which passes through the principal focus F after reflection;

(2) a ray AC through the centre of curvature C, which is reflected back along the same path ACD after striking the mirror at D (see p. 297); or

(3) a ray AF through F, which is reflected parallel to the principal axis.

The rays (1) and (2) intersect at B below the principal axis after reflection. Thus B is the image of A, or the top point of the image. The image of the foot O of the object lies on the principal axis, since the ray OCP strikes the mirror normally at P and is reflected straight back. Now the mirror does not distort the object. Once the point B is obtained, therefore, the image is completed by drawing a perpendicular BI from B to the principal axis.

Position of Image · Magnification

The ray diagram in Fig. 17.10 shows that the image IB is inverted and real. It is also smaller than the object OA. If the diagram is drawn accurately to scale, with FP $= f$, CP $= 2f = r$ and the object placed at the given distance OP from the mirror, then the image distance IP can be measured accurately.

The *linear* or *transverse magnification m* produced by the mirror can also be found from the drawing. This is defined as:

$$m = \frac{\textit{Height of image}}{\textit{Height of object}} = \frac{\text{IB}}{\text{OA}}.$$

Thus by representing the height of the object OA by some convenient length, and measuring the height IB of the image obtained from a ray-diagram, the magnification can be calculated.

Ray-Diagrams of Images

The following ray-diagrams of images, Fig. 17.11, should be drawn

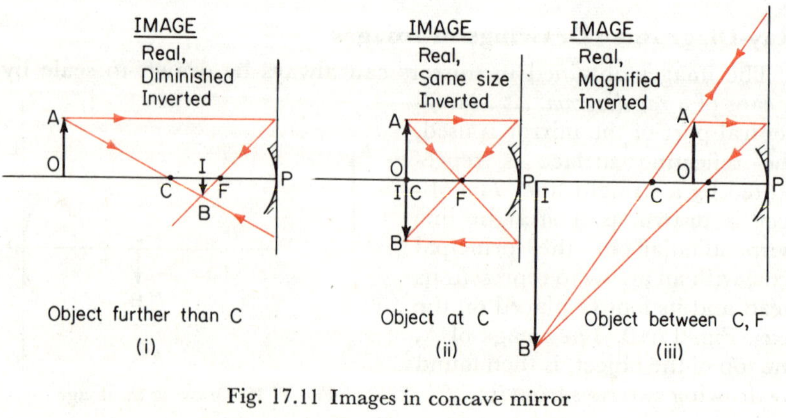

Fig. 17.11 Images in concave mirror

by the reader and the results compared with those obtained by experiment, described on p. 298.

Virtual Erect Image

Between F and the mirror, a large erect image is seen (p. 299). In this case a ray AL parallel to the principal axis is reflected along LF to pass through F, Fig. 17.12. A ray AD, drawn in the direction CAD

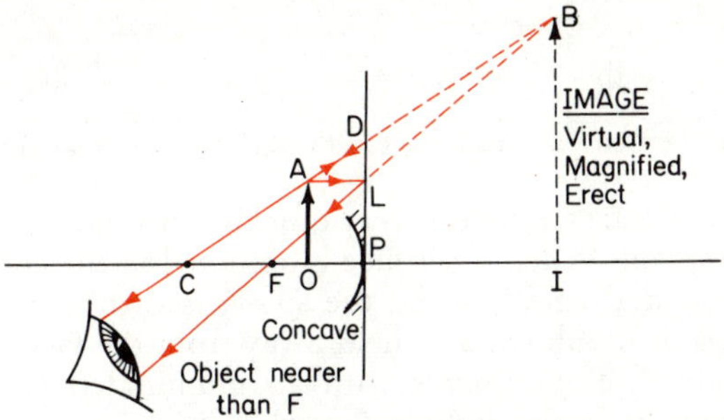

Fig. 17.12 Magnified image

from the centre of curvature C, is reflected back along the same path DA. Since DA and LF intersect at B *behind* the mirror, the image is virtual. It is also magnified and erect. On this account, the concave mirror can be used as a shaving mirror, Fig. 17.13.

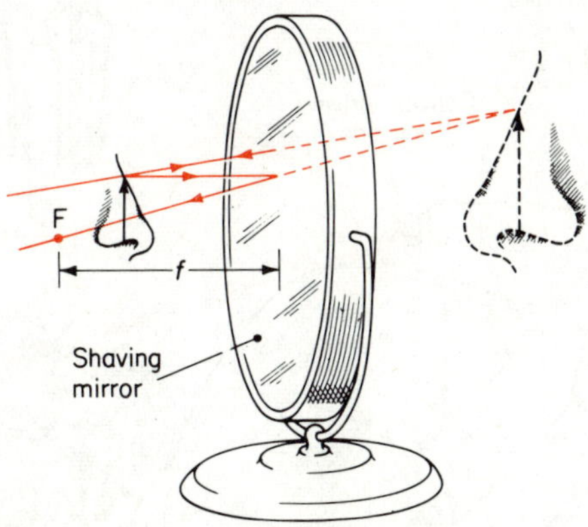

Fig. 17.13 Shaving mirror

Convex Mirror

If a convex mirror is held up and objects reflected in it are observed, the images all appear to be the same way up, or *erect*. They are also *smaller* than the object. This is the case for all object distances from the mirror. The difference between the images produced by a concave

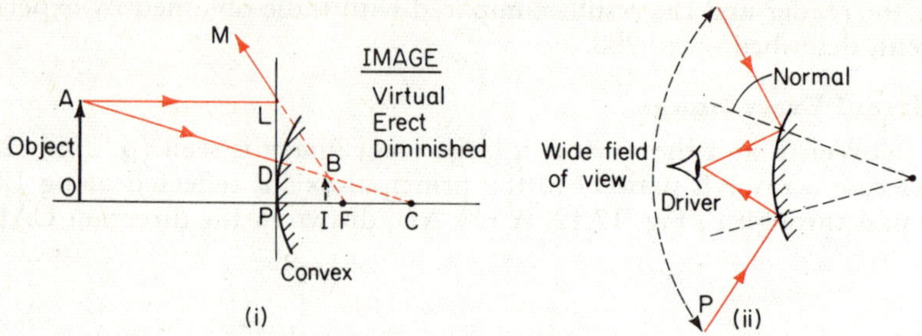

Fig. 17.14 Convex mirror: (i) erect image (ii) wide field of view

and a convex surface can be seen very quickly with the aid of a brightly polished tablespoon. When one's face is observed in the convex surface it appears erect and small; when the spoon is turned over so that a concave surface is obtained, and held away from the face, an inverted image is obtained. Experiments with an illuminated object such as cross-wires show that the light reflected from a convex mirror can never be focused on to a screen. The image seen in such a mirror is therefore *virtual*.

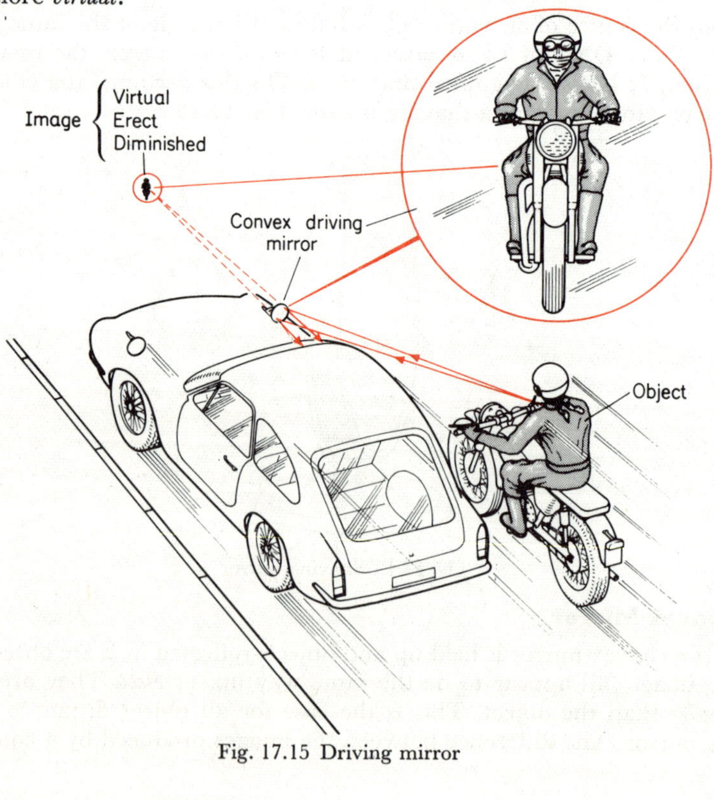

Fig. 17.15 Driving mirror

Fig. 17.14 (i) shows a ray diagram of a typical image produced by a convex mirror. A ray AL parallel to the principal axis is reflected along LM as if it diverged from F, the principal focus, which is behind the mirror (see p. 295). A ray AD, which would pass through the centre of curvature C if produced, is reflected back along the same path DA. Since ML and AD intersect at B behind the mirror, the image IB is virtual. If the object OA is moved nearer the mirror and the image is redrawn it will still be found virtual, erect and smaller than the object.

As the image is always erect, the convex mirror is used as a driving mirror. Objects such as P at a wide angle round the mirror can be observed, Fig. 17.14 (ii). Thus the convex mirror also has the advantage of a wide field of view. Overtaking traffic can be seen, Fig. 17.15. A plane mirror is usually used to observe objects directly behind a car. It has a limited field of view.

SUMMARY

1. Concave mirrors reflect parallel rays to a focus in front of it (real focus). Convex mirrors reflect parallel rays so that they appear to diverge from a focus behind the mirror (virtual focus).

2. The focal length is the distance from the principal focus to the mirror. Focal length = half radius of curvature.

3. A ray parallel to the principal axis is reflected so that it passes through the principal focus. A ray through the centre of curvature is reflected back along the same path. A ray through the principal focus is reflected parallel to the principal axis.

4. Concave mirror images—real and inverted when object farther than f. Same size at $2f$, the centre of curvature. Erect and magnified (dentist's mirror) when object nearer than f.

5. Convex mirror—image erect, diminished and virtual always (driving mirror).

PRACTICAL (Notes for guidance, p. 26)

1. Determination of f

Method. (i) As explained on p. 298, take a concave mirror to the back of the room.

(ii) Hold it up so that light reflected from the window is incident on a sheet of white paper.

(iii) Move the mirror until a sharp image of the window frame, or an object outside such as a tree, is clearly focused.

(iv) Measure the distance of the paper from the mirror—this is roughly f. Repeat twice more. Take the average of your three results if they are close together. Note this is a quick but not accurate method for f.

Measurements.

= .., .., .. cm. Average, f = .. cm.

2. Accurate method for f

Method. (i) As explained on p. 298, set up an illuminated object such as cross wires in front of a concave mirror in a stand. See Fig. 17.7(ii).

(ii) Move the mirror until a sharp image is obtained beside the object O.

(iii) Measure the distance from the mirror to O—this is the radius of curvature r and $f = r/2$.

(iv) Repeat twice more. Take the average of the three results.

Measurements.

$r =$ . ., . ., . . cm.   Average $r =$ . . cm.

$$\therefore f = \frac{r}{2} = \text{. . cm.}$$

3. Images in concave mirrors

Method. (i) By the quick method of **1** above, find the focal length of a concave mirror.

(ii) Then set up an illuminated object in front of the mirror. (If cross wires are not available, place a short length of perspex ruler in a clamp and illuminate it from behind with a lamp—the graduations of the ruler are seen clearly when its image in the mirror is focused.) For different distances of the object, observe if the image is: (*a*) real or virtual; (*b*) magnified or diminished; (*c*) inverted or erect. Enter your results in a table, as follows:

Results.

Image

Object distance from mirror	Real or virtual	Magnified or diminished	Inverted or erect
Further than $2f$ (r)	. . . .	. . . .	. . . .
At $2f$ (r)	. .	. .	. .
Between $2f$ and f	. .	. .	. .
Nearer than f	. .	. .	. .

Draw ray diagrams to illustrate each of the above four cases.

EXERCISE 17 · ANSWERS, p. 402

What are the missing words in the following statements 1–9?

1. The principal focus is in front of a . . mirror.

2. A convex mirror has a principal focus . . the mirror.

3. A shaving mirror is a . . mirror.

4. A car wing mirror is a . . mirror.

5. A ray parallel to the principal axis of a concave mirror is reflected towards the . .

6. A ray passing through the centre of curvature of a spherical mirror is reflected . .

7. The image of an object 25 cm in front of a concave mirror of focal length 20 cm is formed . . the mirror.

8. The image of an object 10 cm in front of a concave mirror of focal length 8 cm: (i) is formed . . the mirror, and (ii) appears . . than the object.

9. The image of an object 10 cm in front of a convex mirror of focal length 8 cm: (i) is formed . . the mirror, and (ii) appears . . than the object.

What is the best answer, A, B, C, D or E, in the following statements 10, 11?

10. A searchlight is a concave parabola-shaped reflector because: (A) the lamp is placed at the centre of curvature; (B) the lamp is placed near the principal focus; (C) the rays are all reflected as a divergent beam; (D) the rays are all reflected as a parallel beam; (E) the image is produced in front of the mirror.

11. A convex mirror is used as a driving mirror because the image is always: (A) erect, magnified and virtual; (B) erect, diminished and virtual; (C) inverted magnified and real; (D) inverted, diminished and virtual; (E) erect, diminished and real.

12. An object 5 cm tall is placed 20 cm in front of a concave mirror of focal length 15 cm. Draw to scale the image formed, and from your drawing, find: (i) its position from the mirror; (ii) its magnification.

13. Repeat Question 12 if the concave mirror has a focal length of 10 cm.

14. Repeat Question 12 if the mirror is a convex mirror of focal length 10 cm.

15. Which of the following is: (i) a motor headlamp mirror; (ii) a dentist's mirror; (iii) a driving mirror; (iv) a shaving mirror; (v) a searchlight mirror?

Concave spherical mirror, plane mirror, parabola-shaped mirror, convex mirror.

16. Car rear-view mirrors can be either plane or convex because: (*a*) in both, the images seen are as far behind the mirror as the objects are in front; (*b*) both give an equally wide field of view; (*c*) both give an equally magnified view of the road behind; (*d*) in both, the images are erect; (*e*) the mirrors can be made quite small. (*M.*)

17. Complete this table to show the particulars of the image formed by a concave mirror of focal length 10 cm.

Distance between object and mirror	Real or virtual	Upright or inverted	Magnified or diminished
3 cm			
13 cm			

(*Mx.*)

18. A large concave mirror gives an . . image of yourself when you stand close to it but an . . image when you stand a long way off. If you stand at the 'focal point' of the mirror, your image will be . . (*W.Md.*)

19. State *two* reasons why a convex mirror is suitable for use as a driving mirror. (*L.*)

20. Explain carefully, how a shop-window of this peculiar shape, Fig. 17A, prevents irritating reflections interfering with your view of displayed goods. (*W.Md.*)

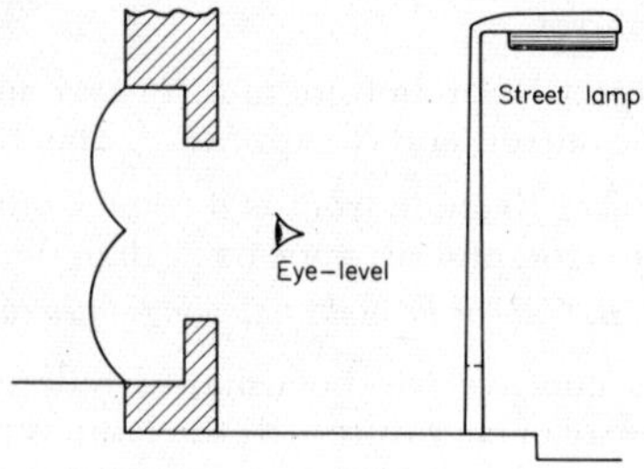

Fig. 17A

21. (*a*) A driver has a plane mirror inside his car and a curved mirror on the offside wing. Compare and contrast the images and the fields of view of the two mirrors.

(*b*) Draw a ray diagram for the curved mirror, showing the formation of the image and the path of the light to the eye. (*E.A.*)

22. Draw a diagram of a concave mirror being used as a shaving mirror. Show clearly the positions of the focus, the object and the image. Draw two rays of light from one point on the object to the mirror, and trace their paths after reflection. (*L.*)

23. (*a*) Draw ray diagrams to show how: (i) a parabolic reflector in a torch produces a parallel beam of light; (ii) a convex driving mirror gives a reduced image of a distant car.

(*b*) A concave shaving mirror has a focal length of 15 cm. By drawing a scale diagram find out how many times bigger your face appears to be when you hold the mirror 10 cm in front of your face? (*S.*)

24. (*a*) A shaving mirror is doubled sided, one side being a plane mirror and the other side a curved mirror.

(i) Describe the image formed by the plane mirror.

(ii) Is the curved mirror convex or concave? Describe the image formed by this curved mirror and state the advantages of using it.

(iii) State, and briefly explain, another use of a similarly curved mirror. (*E.A.*)

18

REFRACTION AT PLANE SURFACES

It is well known that the bottom of a swimming pool appears to be nearer the surface than it really is, Fig. 18.1 (i). Also, the letters in print seem to be nearer when a thick block of glass is placed over them,

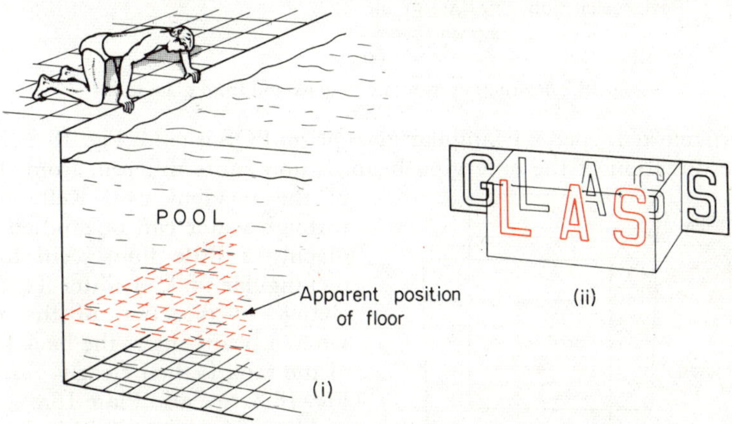

Fig. 18.1 Refraction effects in (i) water, (ii) glass

Fig. 18.1 (ii). As we shall see shortly, this is due to a change in direction, which occurs when light travels from water or glass into air. The phenomenon is called *refraction*. Refraction occurs when light travels from air into glass lenses. A scientific study of refraction has helped to provide very efficient microscopes and telescopes.

Refraction and Ray-box

The refraction of rays of light from air to glass or from glass to air can be investigated with a ray-box. A parallel beam of light from the box R is incident on a rectangular glass block ABCD, Fig. 18.2 (i). When the rays are normal, i.e. 90° to the side AB, they pass straight through the glass and emerge without change of direction. In this case we can see no refraction. But when the ray-box is turned so that the light rays meet the glass surface at an acute angle, say 60°, there is a noticeable change. The beam inside the glass now travels in a different direction, Fig. 18.2 (ii). Refraction has taken place. The light emerges into the air at Z in the same direction as the incident beam at X, but it is displaced sideways. This refraction, or change in direction, is even

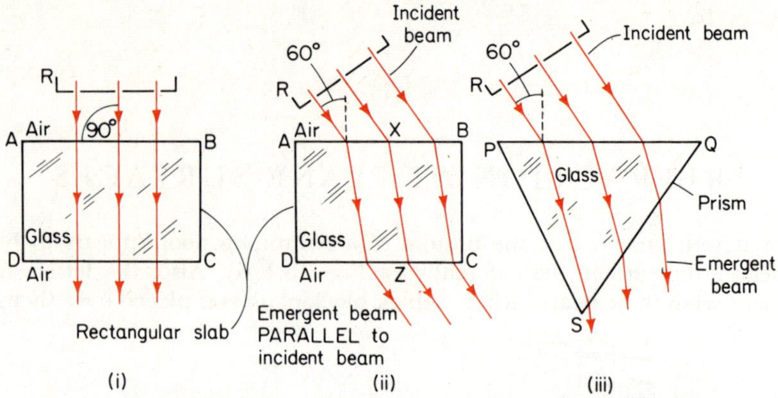

Fig. 18.2 Refraction from air to glass and from glass to air

more marked when a triangular glass prism PQS is used, Fig. 18.2 (iii). The direction of the emerging beam is now quite different from that of the incident ray. Refraction through water can be studied by placing a little fluorescein in a rectangular tank of water T. The change of direction of the ray when a beam enters the back face of the tank is then clearly visible, Fig. 18.3. See also Plate 18A.

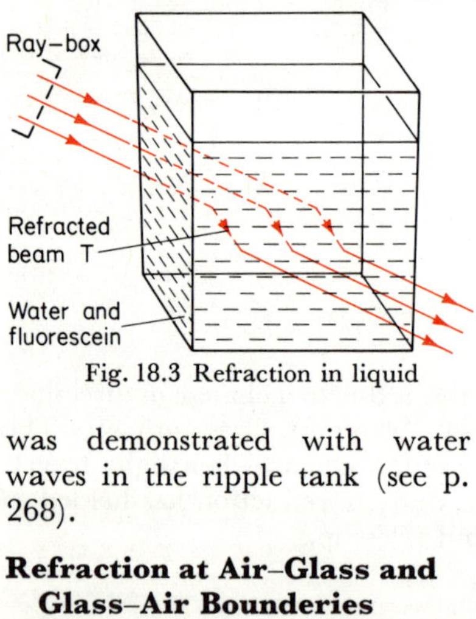

Fig. 18.3 Refraction in liquid

The refraction of light is due to the change in the speed of light waves on travelling from air to glass or from air to water. This was demonstrated with water waves in the ripple tank (see p. 268).

Refraction at Air–Glass and Glass–Air Bounderies

By means of a single ray PA from a ray-box, incident on a rectangular block of glass at A, the following can be observed, using the normal (perpendicular) line NAM to the boundary as a reference line, Fig. 18.4:

(i) The incident ray PA in air is refracted along AB *towards* the normal NAM after it enters the glass.

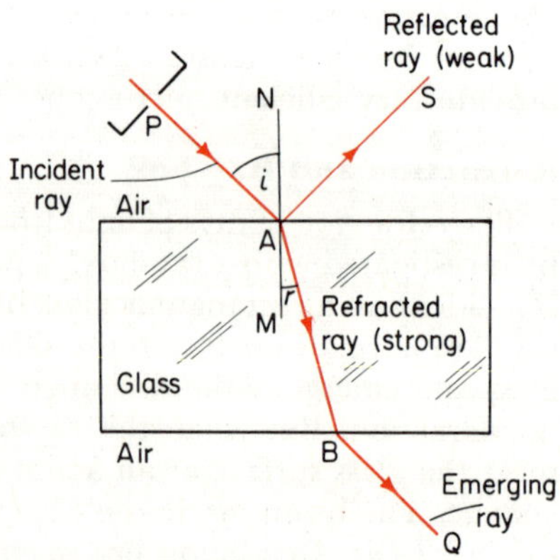

Fig. 18.4 Refraction through glass rectangular block

Plate 18(A) Refraction through glass. A technician at Harwell, England, standing behind a very thick block of glass (about 36 in or 100 cm thick) of a protective window about to be fitted in front of a dangerously radio-active chamber.

(ii) The ray AB, incident on the glass at B, is refracted *away* from the normal at B along BQ on emerging into the air.

Note also that some of the incident light at A is weakly reflected along AS, at the air–glass boundary. The direction of AS follows the law of reflection at plane surfaces. Similar results are obtained for air–water and water–air media, such as Fig. 18.3.

Summarizing. Light travelling from one medium such as air to an optically denser medium such as glass or water is refracted *towards* the normal. When travelling from glass or water to a *less dense* medium such as air, the light is refracted *away* from the normal.

Apparent Depth

We can now explain why a swimming pool appears shallower when looking down into it than is actually the case. Consider an object O at the bottom of a pool in the very exaggerated sketch of Fig. 18.5 (i).

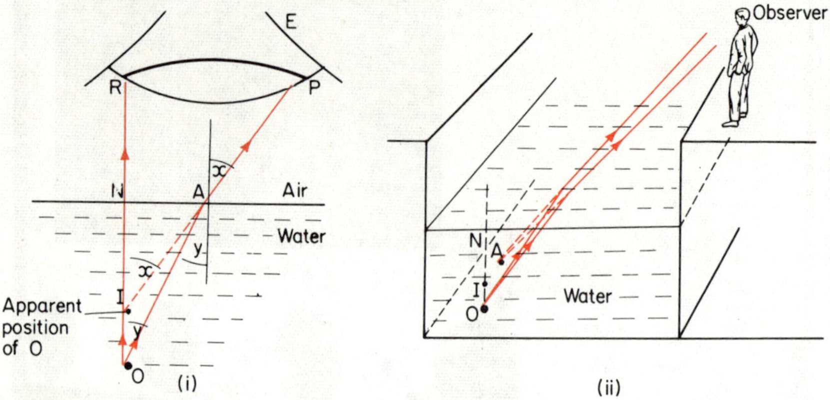

Fig. 18.5 Apparent depth

To find the image, we take *two* rays from O. A ray ON normal to the water surface passes into the air along NR in the same direction. A ray OA, slightly inclined to ON, is refracted into the air along AP away from the normal at A. To the eye E, the emerging rays NR and AP appear to come from a point I, their point of intersection. The point I is nearer the surface than O. Thus an object on the bottom of a pool appears nearer the surface (see also p. 307).

We have just discussed the case of an observer looking at an object directly below him. If an object O in water is viewed from the side, it now appears to be at A, Fig. 18.5 (ii). It is a little higher than I and to the right of the normal ON, as shown.

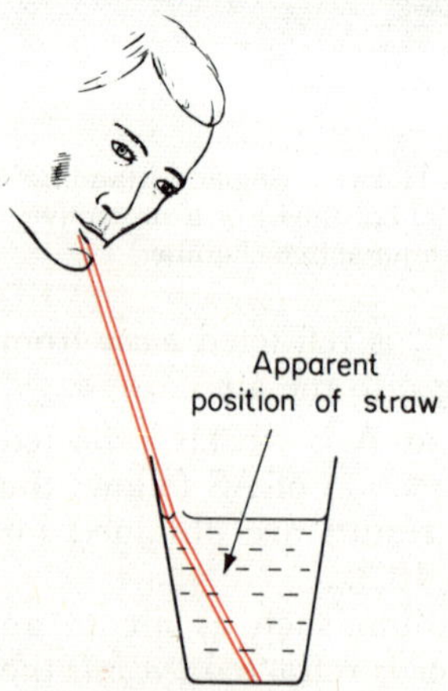

Fig. 18.6 Appearance of straw due to refraction

Part-immersion in Water

A drinking straw, partly immersed in a liquid, appears bent at the surface, Fig. 18.6. A stick partly immersed in water also appears bent at the surface, Fig. 18.7. This is due to refraction. If PO is the stick and MO that part of it below water, the end O appears to be at I, a point nearer the surface, as explained above in Fig. 18.5 (i).

Similarly, another point B on the stick appears to be higher up at C. And so on for all points between O and M. The image of OM is therefore IM. It is not in the same straight line as PM. The stick therefore appears bent, as shown in Fig. 18.7.

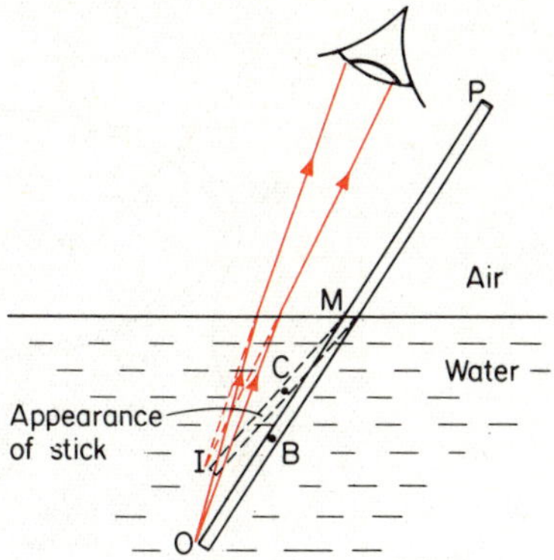

Fig. 18.7 Effect of refraction

Bringing Objects into View

If an object O is placed in a vessel C so that it is just hidden from an observer at E it can be brought into view by pouring sufficient water into the vessel, Fig. 18.8. In Fig. 18.8 (i) rays from O just pass below the edge of C, so that it cannot be seen by E. When water is poured in to a sufficient depth refraction occurs as shown, Fig. 18.8 (ii). The rays from O, refracted away from the normal, now enter the observer's eye and the object is seen at I.

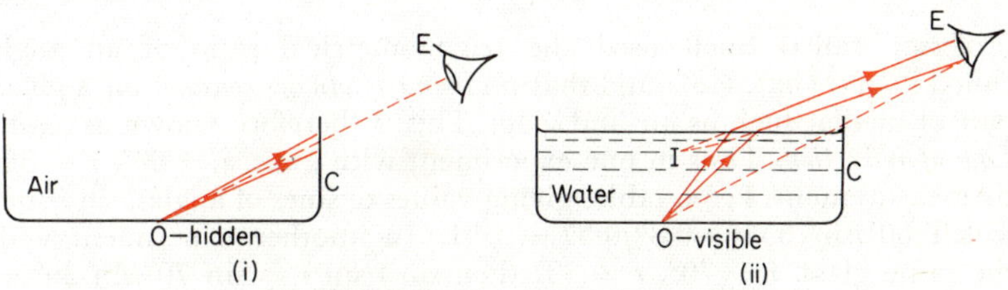

Fig. 18.8 Refraction from water to air

Field of View under Water

A fish E under water, or a man swimming under water on his back, will see rays of light such as BC which are refracted from air along CE in the water, Fig. 18.9. The extreme or limiting rays from the outside reaching E correspond to those like LO which just graze the air–water boundary. The angle of incidence in air is then 90°. If the angle of refraction in the water in this case is $r°$, about 48°, it follows that light from everywhere outside the water is concentrated into a cone whose half-angle is $r°$.

Laws of Refraction · Refractive Index

The refraction of light was known more than two thousand years ago. Many scientists had tried to discover the laws governing refraction. It is recorded for example, that in A.D. 100 Ptolemy made hundreds of measurements of angles of incidence and refraction without being able to discover the relation between them. But in 1621, a Dutch

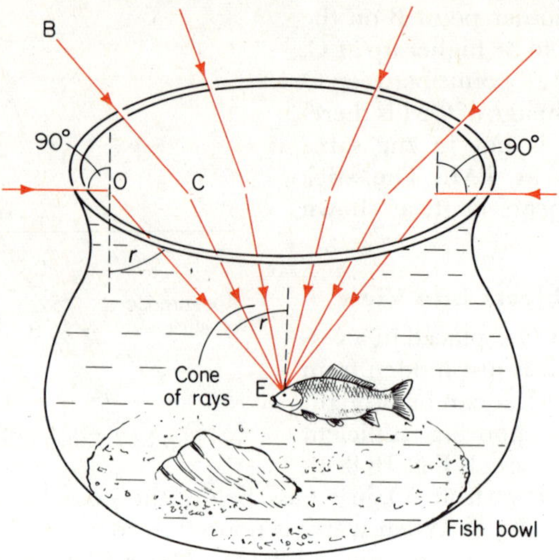

Fig. 18.9 Fishes' view

professor called Snell used the trigonometrical ratio of an angle called its *sine* (*sin*). He found that *sin i/sin r is always constant* for a given pair of media, such as air and glass. This is therefore known as *Snell's Law of refraction.* Thus in one experiment with glass, $i = 60°$, $r = 35°$ by measurement. From tables giving values of sines of angles, $\sin i/\sin r = \sin 60°/\sin 35° = 0{\cdot}87/0{\cdot}57 = 1{\cdot}51$. In another experiment with the same glass, $i = 70°$, $r = 39°$ then $\sin i/\sin r = \sin 70°/\sin 39° = 0{\cdot}94/0{\cdot}63 = 1{\cdot}51$ (approx).

The ratio $\sin i/\sin r$ is called the *refractive index* from air to glass. It is a number which gives a measure of the refraction or 'bending' of light when it travels from one medium to another. If we denote the refractive index by the symbol μ then $\mu = \sin i/\sin r$. Scientists have measured the refractive index of many different kinds of glass and liquids. The construction of the lenses needed for optical instruments depends on an accurate knowledge of the refractive indices of the glass used.

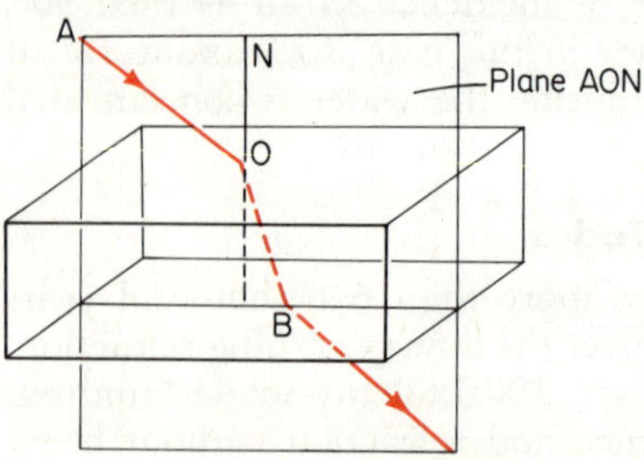

Fig. 18.10 Law of Refraction

A second law of refraction fixes the *plane* in which the refracted ray travels. This states:

The incident ray, the normal, and the refracted ray all lie in the same plane.

Thus, in Fig. 18.10, the incident ray AO, the normal ON

and the refracted ray OB in the glass all lie in the plane AON shown in outline (compare *Law of reflection*, p. 286).

Total Internal Reflection

When a ray of light HK is incident in air on a rectangular glass block most of the light is refracted along KL into the block, Fig. 18.11. A *weak reflected* ray KT is also obtained at the boundary, and from the law of reflection this makes an equal angle *i* with the normal. When the angle of incidence HKN is increased a strong refracted ray and a weak

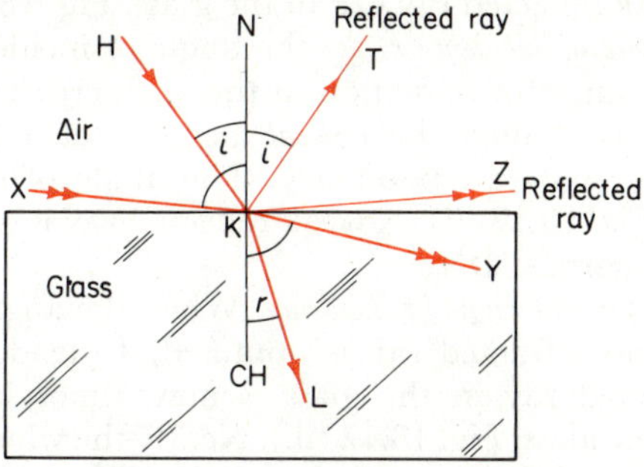

Fig. 18.11 Refraction and reflection

reflected ray are always obtained. This is the case with XK, incident on the glass at nearly 90°. A strong refracted ray KY and a weak reflected ray KZ result.

A striking change occurs when the situation is reversed optically, so that light passes from *glass to air*. This is best investigated with a semicircular glass block G and a ray-box R with a single ray, Fig. 18.12.

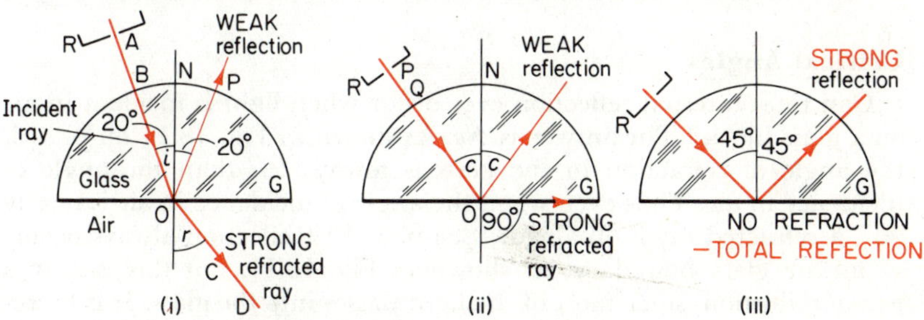

Fig. 18.12 Investigating total internal reflection

G is placed on a sheet of white paper and the centre O of its plane side is marked. Since any line from O is a radius, and therefore normal to the semicircle, a ray such as AB *directed towards* O will pass into the glass without any change in direction. As we are interested in what happens when light is refracted from glass to air, we must think of BO as the incident ray *in the glass*, angle BON as the angle of incidence and OD as the refracted ray in air. The angle BON is now increased from zero by moving the ray-box round from the normal position, and the effects at the glass–air boundary at O can then be seen.

Results

When the angle of incidence in the glass is increased the results obtained are as follows:

(1) *Small angle of incidence, e.g.* 20°. There is a strong refracted ray OCD and a weak reflected ray OP in the glass, Fig. 18.12 (i).

(2) *Critical angle of incidence c.* As the angle of incidence in the glass is increased, the angle of refraction in the air increases. At one special angle of incidence, called the *critical angle c*, the refracted ray OG travels along the glass–air boundary. The angle of refraction in the air is then 90°, Fig. 18.12 (ii). A weak reflected ray is obtained, making an angle *c* with normal ON.

(3) *Beyond the critical angle of incidence.* When the angle of incidence is greater than *c* no refracted ray is obtained. Instead, a new effect is seen. The reflected ray in the glass is now almost as bright as the incident ray in the glass, Fig. 18.12 (iii). Nearly the whole of the incident light energy appears in the reflected light. The glass–air boundary thus behaves as a 'mirror' reflecting light strongly.

This phenomenon takes place sharply as the critical angle of incidence is exceeded. For example, if the critical angle is 42° a ray incident in the glass at 41° will produce a strong refracted ray and a weak reflected ray. But if the angle of incidence is 43° the reflected ray is intense and there is no refracted ray. Since almost all the light incident on the boundary is reflected back into the glass for angles greater than the critical angle, the effect is known as the *total internal reflection of light.*

Critical Angles

Can total internal reflection ever occur when light is incident in air on a glass block? The answer is *No*. As shown in Fig. 18.11 on p. 313, the angle of refraction in the glass is always *less* than the angle of incidence in air. Thus even when the angle of incidence in air is nearly 90°, a refracted ray is obtained. (See p. 313.) Reflection always occurs at an air–glass boundary, as shown in Fig. 18.11, but this is only a *partial* reflection, since most of the light passes into the glass. It is therefore important to note that when the angle of incidence is increased, *total internal* reflection occurs only when light passes from one medium to an optically *less* dense medium. For example, from glass to air or from water to air. The critical angle from water to air is about 49°. The critical angle from glass to air depends on the type of glass. The most common type of glass is crown glass and the critical angle is then about 42°.

Multiple Images

When the image of an object in plane mirrors is observed closely, several faint images can be seen besides a prominent one. The presence of multiple images is due to partial refraction at the non-silvered glass surface of the mirror, as illustrated in Fig. 18.13.

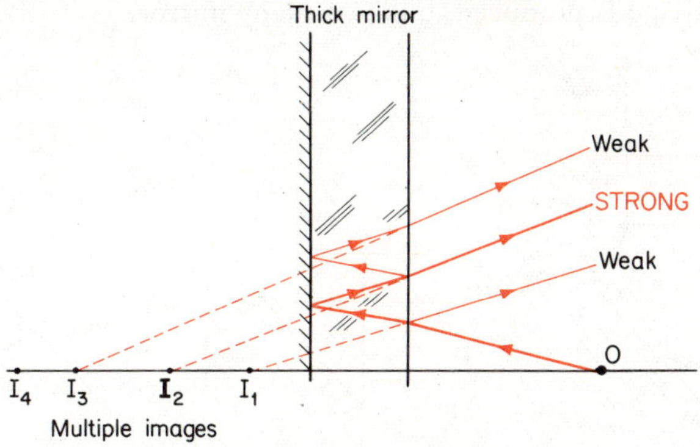

Fig. 18.13 Multiple ('ghost') images

A weak image I_1 is formed by reflection from the glass surface of part of the incident light at O. Most of the light, however, passes through the glass. It is then reflected at the silvered surface and refracted again at the glass into the air to form the main image seen I_2. This is a bright image. A small part of the light reflected from the silvered surface is also reflected at the glass. Further weak images, I_3 and I_4, due to reflection and refraction, are thus obtained. The images are more widely separated if the glass is thicker. Multiple images can be seen when a candle flame is placed in front of a thick mirror.

Total Reflecting Prisms

On account of multiple images, plane mirrors are not used for high-quality periscopes, such as those employed in submarines, where accurate sighting of other ships is required. A special glass prism, producing total internal reflection, is used in this case. It has a great advantage that only one image is produced. As in prism binoculars, which are short telescopes, *right-angled isosceles prisms*, ones with angles of 90°, 45°, 45°, are used as reflectors because they produce one image.

Fig. 18.14 (i) illustrates the optical action of a totally reflecting prism. Consider a ray OP from an object O, incident normally on one of the sides AC containing the right angle C of the prism. The ray passes straight through AC and falls on the hypotenuse face AB at S at an angle of 45°. Since this angle of incidence in glass is greater than the critical angle (42°) for glass of refractive index 1·5, no light passes into the air from S. Instead, total internal reflection takes place at S. A bright reflected ray ST is thus obtained. It makes an angle of 45° with the normal at S in accordance with the law of reflection. ST is therefore at right angles to PS, and is almost as bright as PS. ST is consequently incident on BC normally and emerges into the air. It it now perpendicular to its original direction OS. The emergent light is almost as bright as the incident light from O. Moreover, only one reflected image is produced, unlike a plane mirror.

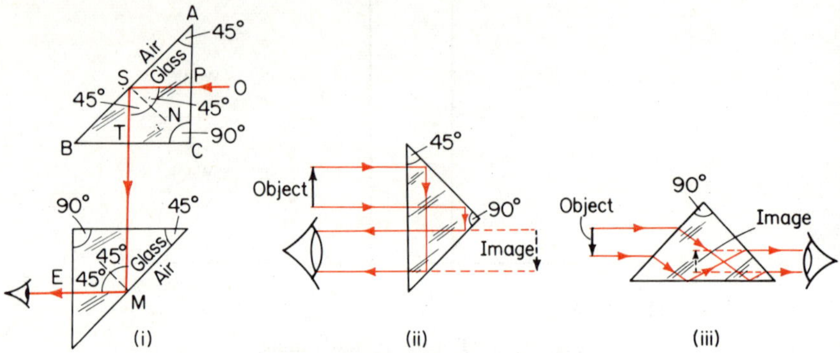

Fig. 18.14 Total reflecting prisms

A periscope is completed by placing a second right-angled isosceles prism below the first. Light falling on this prism behaves in exactly the same way as described above. Total internal reflection thus takes place in the glass at M. The emergent ray ME enters the eye in a direction parallel to OP, and the object O is seen. Right-angled prisms with angles 90°, 30°, 60° do not act as totally reflecting prisms, as the reader should verify.

Fig. 18.14 (ii), (iii) illustrate two other cases of total reflection by the use of right-angled 45° prisms. Fig. 18.14 (ii) shows how an object is inverted, as in prism binoculars (p. 359). Total internal reflection accounts for the observed brilliance of diamonds. The refractive index of a diamond is high, so that its critical angle is correspondingly low. Much of the light entering the diamond is therefore totally reflected to the observer.

Optical Fibres

Nowadays total internal reflection is used in a very useful device known as *optical fibres*. This follows an idea due originally to Baird, the founder of television. Optical fibres consist of many tens of thousands of long fine strands of high-quality glass coated with glass of lower refractive index. The strands may be $\frac{1}{2000}$ cm in diameter and the refractive indices of the respective glasses about 1·7 and 1·5.

When light is incident on one end of the fibre at an angle less than about 60° it passes inside, where it undergoes repeated total internal reflection at the walls, Fig. 18.15. The angle of incidence here is greater than the critical angle between the high- and low-refractive index glass. The trapped light thus travels along the fibre, no matter how it may be curved, and emerges with high intensity at the other end. A bundle of flexible fibres thus enables an image of an object at one end to be seen at the other end. If the fibres are tapered a magnified image can be produced.

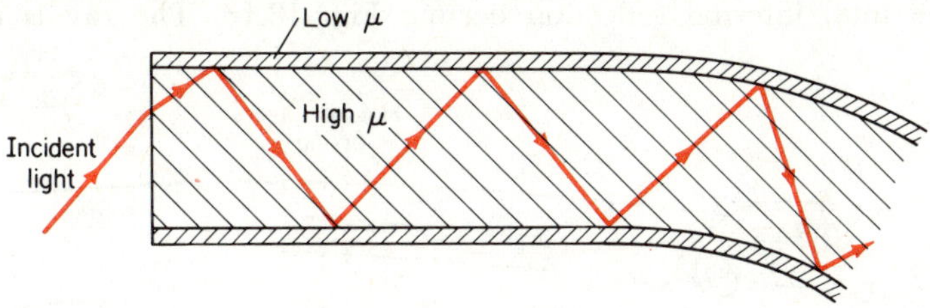

Fig. 18.15 Optical fibre action

Optical fibres are thus flexible guides which can 'pipe' light to the other end. They are used medically, for example, to examine the inside of the throat and in engineering. See Plate 18B.

Mirages

Total internal reflection can occur in gases such as air, as well as in solid media such as glass. An essential condition again is that the light must be travelling from a denser to a less-dense medium.

In hot weather the layers of air close to the ground are hotter than

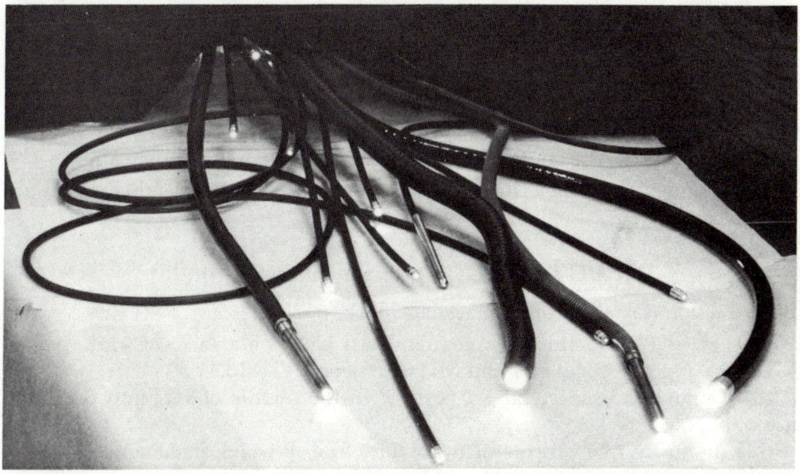

Plate 18(B) Flexible light guides of various shapes. A common light source (hidden) is used at one end for all the guides.

the layers higher up, because they are heated by the hot ground. A ray from part of the sky, passing from a colder to a warmer air layer (i.e. from a denser to a rarer medium) will therefore bend away gradually from the incident direction. At one stage it enters a layer of air *h* where total internal reflection occurs, Fig. 18.16. The ray is then

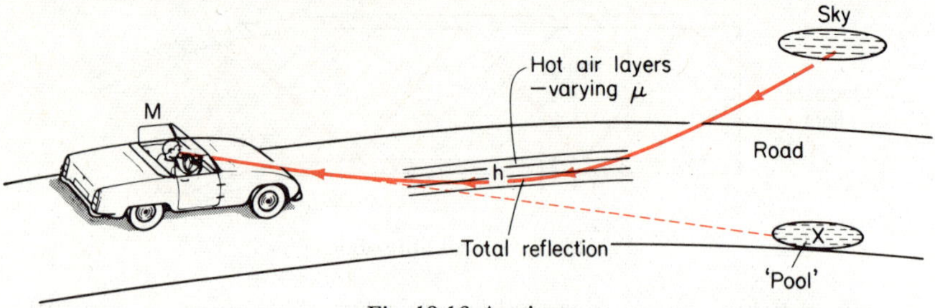

Fig. 18.16 A mirage

reflected upwards into the denser air. After undergoing refraction in an upward direction the ray may finally enter the eye of an observer, M. To him, the ray seems to come from a place X, the image of part of the sky. It gives the illusion of a reflecting pool of water in the road some distance away. In hot deserts an illusion may be created of an inverted image of a tree in a pool of water, standing below the actual tree position.

SUMMARY

1. From less dense to denser medium (e.g. air to glass), rays are refracted *towards* the normal; from dense to less-dense medium (e.g. glass to air) rays refracted *away* from the normal.

2. Objects below water appear nearer the surface as the rays diverge more after refraction from water to air. For the same reason, a stick appears partly 'bent' if partly-immersed.

3. Total internal reflection occurs when: (i) rays pass from a dense to a less-dense medium; (ii) the angle of incidence is greater than the critical angle.

4. For crown glass, the critical angle is about 42°. Total reflecting prisms are 45°, 45° and 90°.

PRACTICAL (Notes for guidance, p. 26)

1. Refraction through rectangular glass block (p. 307)

Method. (i) Place a thick rectangular glass block on a sheet of white paper. Mark the opposite edges HK and ML with pencil. Fig. 18.17 (i).

(ii) Remove the block, take a point P in the middle of HK and draw the normal PN to HK.

(iii) By means of a protractor draw lines from P which make angles of incidence *i* of 30°, 40°, 50°, 60°, 70° respectively.

(iv) Replace the block, and shine a ray from a ray-box along AP which makes 30° with the normal. Mark two dots E and F on the emerging ray QD.

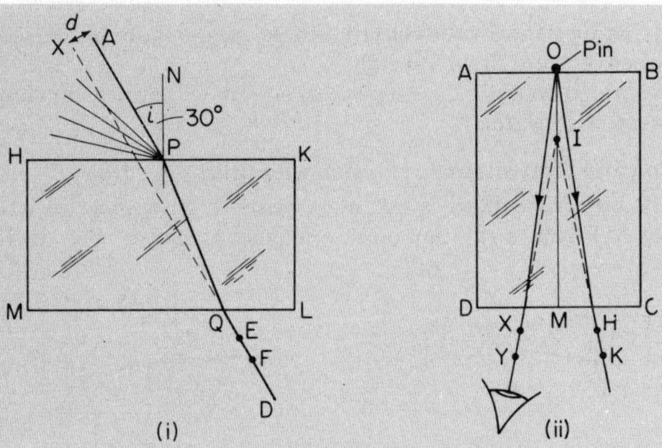

Fig. 18.17 (i) Refraction through glass block (ii) apparent depth

(v) Remove the block. Join E and F and produce the line to X.

Measure the perpendicular distance *d* between the direction of the incident ray AP and the emerging ray QD. This is the distance or shift of the ray AP due to refraction. Record the value of *d* in millimetres and the angle of incidence *i*.

Repeat for the other values of *i* and note the corresponding values of *d*.

Measurements.

i (degrees)	*d* (mm)

Graph. Plot *d* v. *i*. Join the points by a smooth curve.

From your graph read off the displacement due to an angle of incidence of 45°. See if your result agrees with actual measurement of the displacement when a ray at 45° to the normal is shone on P.

2. Apparent depth (p. 310)

Method. (i) Place a rectangular block ABCD on a sheet of white paper with its long sides AD, BC as in Fig. 18.17 (ii) and draw with a pencil the outline of AB and DC.

(ii) Place a pin O in contact with the glass AB roughly in the middle of AB.

(iii) Arrange two pins X and Y in line with the image I of O seen in the glass. On the other side of the normal OM, arrange another two pins H and K in line with I.

(iv) Remove the block and the four pins, and produce the lines YX and KH, joining the pinholes, to meet at I. This is the image of O.

Measure OM, the true depth of O from the surface DC. Measure IM, the apparent depth of I from DC. Calculate the ratio *true depth/apparent depth*, or OM/IM.

Measurements.

OM (mm)	IM (mm)	OM/IM

3. Refraction in liquids (p. 310)

Method. (i) Take a glass beaker, fill it nearly to the brim with water and place inside it a drinking straw or rod S so that these are partially immersed. Observe the appearance of S and draw a sketch.

(ii) As explained on p. 311, see if a metal or coin will appear in view on filling a shallow vessel with water.

4. Refraction and total internal reflection with prisms (p. 315)

Method. (i) 60° *prism.* Place a 60° glass prism P on a sheet of white paper. Direct a ray AO from a ray-box on to one face, as shown. Fig. 18.18 (i). Observe the refraction of the ray inside the glass and then out into the air on the other side. Note the slight colouring of the emerging ray. Draw a sketch of the prism and ray path.

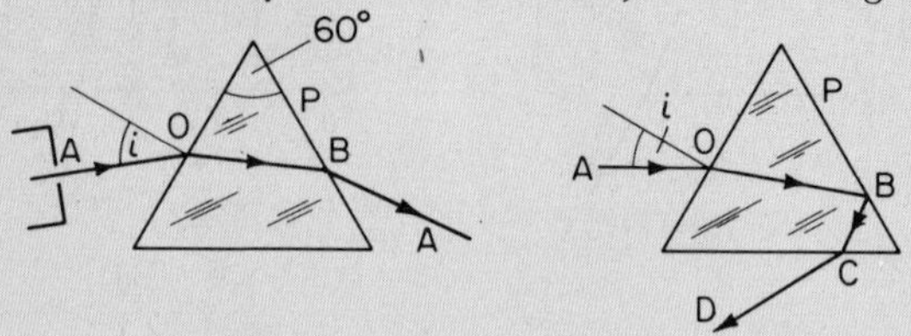

(i) (ii)
Fig. 18.18 Refraction by glass prism

Now decrease the angle of incidence *i* at O by moving the ray-box round. Observe the 'total internal reflection' which occurs at B at one stage and the emergence of the ray CD, Fig. 18.18 (ii).

(ii) 45°, 45°, 90° *prism.* Place the isosceles right-angle prism on a sheet of white paper. Using a ray-box R, direct a ray AO normal (perpendicular) to one face. Fig. 18.19 (i). Observe the total internal reflection at B and the emergence of the ray along BD.

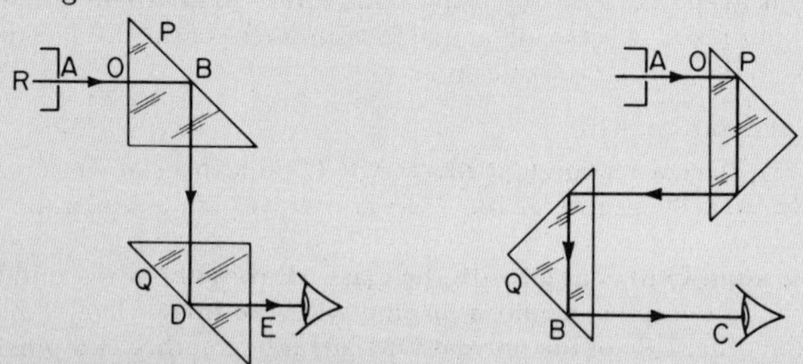

(i) (ii)
Fig. 18.19 Total internal reflection

Place a second prism so that the ray incident on it is reflected along DE. Place the eye at E. What can be seen?

(iii) *Reversing the light path.* Arrange two 45° right-angle prisms P and Q so that a ray AO incident on P finally emerges in a parallel direction along BC. Fig. 18.19 (ii). Place the eye at C. What can be seen?

EXERCISE 18 · ANSWERS, p. 402

What are the missing words in the statements 1–6?

1. A ray of light incident at 30° from air to water is partly: (i) *refracted* . . the normal on entering the water; (ii) *reflected* at the water surface at an angle of . . to the normal.

2. A ray of light incident in glass at 30° to the normal is refracted . . the normal on entering the air.

3. A swimming-pool looks shallower than it actually is because light from the bottom is refracted . . the normal on passing into the air.

4. A thick mirror has several faint images in addition to the main image because . . and . . occurs at the glass.

5. Light can be totally reflected by a right-angle prism of crown glass if one other angle of the prism is . .

6. Light is totally reflected by a glass prism if the angle of incidence in the . . is greater than the . . angle.

7. A ray of light is incident at 45° on the face of: (i) a rectangular block of glass; (ii) a 60° glass prism. Draw a sketch showing how the ray passes through glass in each case.

8. With the aid of a diagram, explain how the face of a right-angle prism may totally reflect light incident on it.

9. A thick plane mirror produces several faint images in addition to a prominent one. Draw a ray-diagram showing how reflection and refraction produces all these images.

10. A fish in water sees everything outside the water by rays of light entering its eye in a small cone of light. Draw a diagram and explain how this happens.

11. Complete the ray diagrams in Fig. 18A. (*M.*)

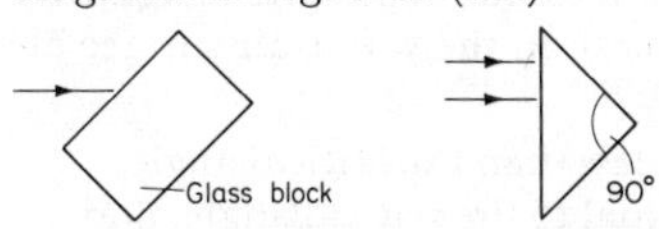

Fig. 18A

12. Viewed from above the depth of a pond appears . . than it actually is. This is due to the . . of the rays of light at the surface of the water. (*W.Md.*)

13. Fig. 18B represents a stone S at the bottom of a pond of water. Using the two rays, as shown, complete the ray-diagram to show where the image of the stone appears when viewed from E. (*Mx.*)

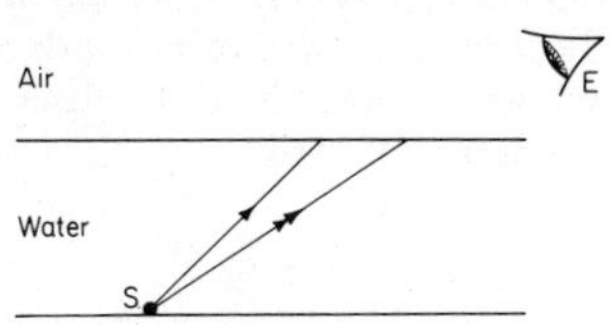

Fig. 18B

14. (*a*) Draw the diagram of a beam of light striking a glass surface at 45° with some of the light reflected and some refracted.

(*b*) A man 1·8 m tall stands 1·2 m in front of a large plane mirror. Draw the man, the mirror and his image in the mirror. Next draw in the rays of light that enter his eye from his feet and top of his head.

What is the minimum height of the mirror for him to see both his head and his feet at the same time? Will the mirror have to be bigger, smaller or the same size if the man stands nearer to it? (*E.A.*)

15. (*a*) When a beam of light passes from air in to a rectangular glass block, the beam is . . and the emergent beam is . . to the incident beam.

(*b*) Show by two rays on the diagram Fig. 18C, where the object appears to be. (*Mx.*)

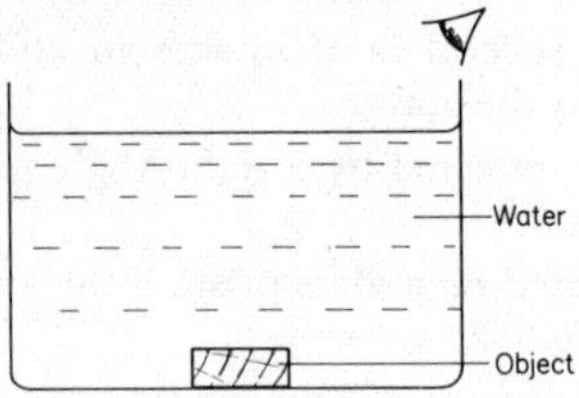

Fig. 18C

16. (*a*) Complete the path of the ray of light through the prism Fig. 18D.

(*b*) State one practical purpose for which light is passed through a prism in this way (*L.*)

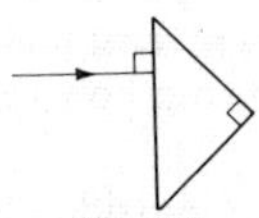

Fig. 18D

17. (*a*) Draw a diagram to show *three* rays of light AN, BN and CN, travelling in water towards a point N on the water-air surface above, their angles of incidence being respectively

less than the critical angle,
equal to the critical angle, and
greater than the critical angle.

Show clearly the paths of these rays after they reach the surface and label them NP, NQ, NR respectively.

(*b*) With the aid of a sketch explain the formation of *either* (i) a mirage in a desert; *or* (ii) the field of view of a pond-fish looking towards the surface. (*Mx.*)

18. (*a*) Draw diagrams to illustrate: (i) the angle of reflection; (ii) the angle of refraction; (iii) the critical angle. When does total internal reflection occur?

(*b*) A brick lies on the bottom of a swimming-bath and you are going to dive and collect it. Make drawings to show the difficulties you will have in judging exactly where it lies in the water. (*W. Md.*)

19

REFRACTION THROUGH LENSES

LENSES consist of pieces of glass varying in thickness from the middle to the edges. They have a spherical surface on one or both sides. They are used in spectacles to correct defects of vision, and in optical microscopes for looking at objects too small to be seen by the naked eye. They are also used in telescopes and prism binoculars for seeing distant objects, and in cameras and film projectors.

Lenses have been used to concentrate light since ancient times. They were then called burning glasses. The first sunshine recorder, made in 1857, used a glass sphere or globe to char a paper graduated in fractions of an hour, Plate 19A. They are still used at the Air Ministry and seaside resorts to record the hours of sunshine.

Types of Lenses

Fig. 19.1 illustrates six common types of lenses. A lens thicker in the middle than at the edges, as in Fig. 19.1 (i), is known as a *converging* or *convex* lenses. A lens thinner in the middle than at the edges is known as a *diverging* or *concave* lens, Fig. 19.1 (ii). Lenses which are biconvex or biconcave are commonly used in the laboratory. Plano-convex and plano-concave lenses have only one curved surface and are used in optical instruments. Converging and diverging meniscus lenses are used as 'contact lenses' to fit the curvature of the eyeball.

The eye has a natural converging or convex lens. A camera has a convex lens. Some spectacles may contain diverging lenses, others may contain converging lenses. One type of telescope has both a converging (convex) and a diverging (concave) lens inside it.

Plate 19(A) Sunshine recorder. A glass globe focuses the sun's rays on to a paper strip graduated in hours, which becomes charred.

Light Rays and Spherical Surfaces

The effect of lenses on light

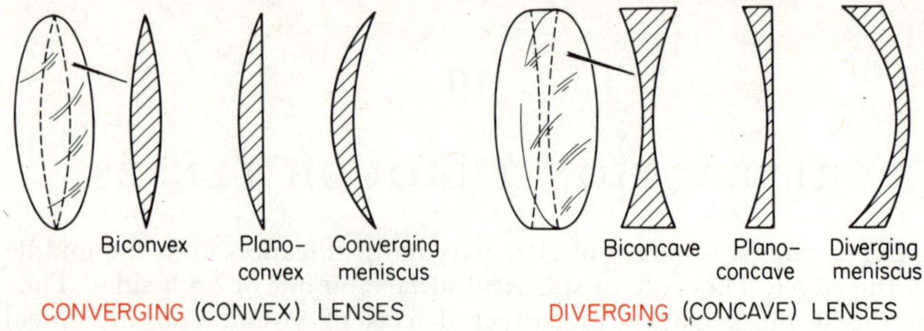

Fig. 19.1 Converging (convex) and diverging (concave) lenses

rays can be seen by using a ray-box R. The lens used could be a model flat glass or plastic convex lens L, Fig. 19.2 (i), or better, an actual convex lens X, pushed halfway through a board, so that rays are incident on the central part of the lens, Fig. 19.2 (ii).

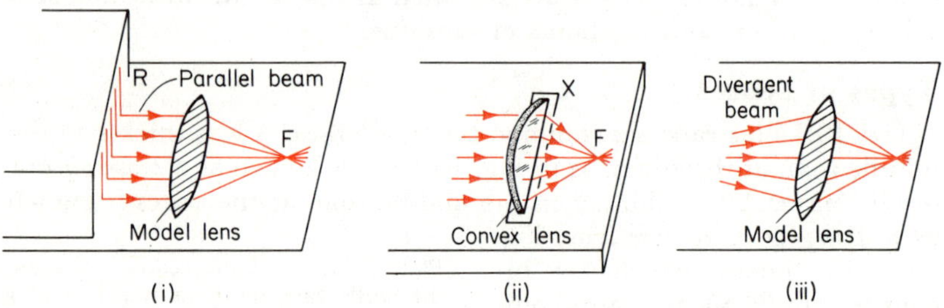

Fig. 19.2 Action of converging (convex) lens

A parallel beam of light is seen to converge to a focus at a point F after refraction through the lens, Fig. 19.2 (i), (ii). Using a diverging beam from R, a converging beam can again be obtained after refraction, as shown in Fig. 19.2 (iii).

Fig. 19.3 shows the action of a diverging or concave lens on a parallel beam. After refraction through the lens a diverging beam of light is obtained. This would pass through a point F *behind* the lens if produced back. The effect of this type of lens is therefore opposite to that of the converging or convex lens.

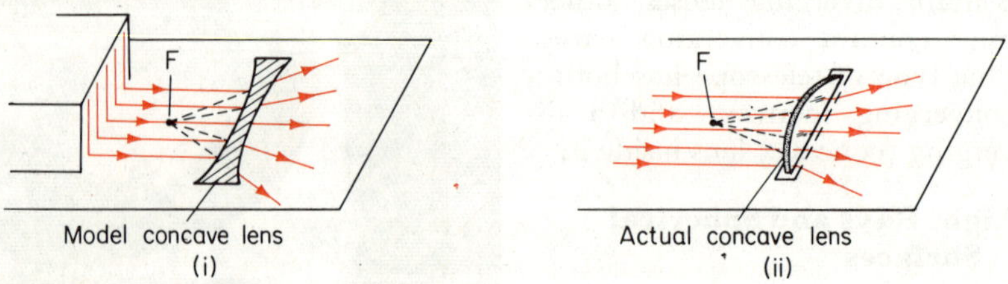

Fig. 19.3 Diverging (concave) lens

Refraction of Single Rays · Focal length

A ray-box R with a single ray shows very strikingly how different parts of a lens have different effects on rays incident on their surfaces, Fig. 19.4 (i).

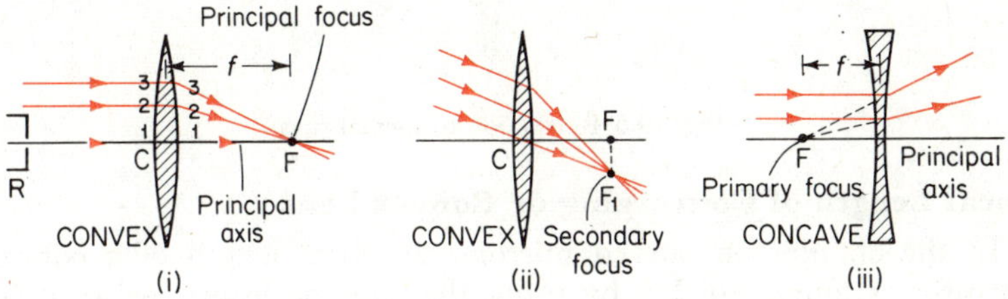

Fig. 19.4 Refraction of parallel rays

When ray 1 strikes the centre part C normally it passes straight through undeviated. The whole ray now lies along the *principal axis* of the lens. This is the line joining the mid-points of the two opposite faces of the lens. When another ray 2 is a small distance above and parallel to the principal axis, it converges to a point F on the principal axis. Another ray 3, parallel to the principal axis but a little higher than 2, also converges to F after refraction. This ray is deviated more from its original path than 2. The *principal focus* F is the point on the principal axis to which rays parallel and close to the principal axis converge after refraction through the lens. A parallel beam of light, travelling in a direction inclined to the principal axis, is brought to a focus at a point F_1, *below F*, called a 'secondary focus', Fig. 19.4 (ii).

The action of a concave or diverging lens on rays parallel to the principal axis is shown in Fig. 19.4 (iii). The rays appear to diverge from a point F on the principal axis, which is called the *principal focus* of the concave lens. Comparing Fig. 19.4 (i) and (iii), it can be seen that:

1. *The principal focus of a convex (converging) lens is real.*
2. *The principal focus of a concave (diverging) lens is virtual.*

The distance from the principal focus to the lens is called its focal length *f*. Lenses of long focal length such as 100 cm are used in telescopes. Lenses of short focal such as 1 or 2 cm are used in microscopes.

By using a single ray from a ray-box, the following rays can be directed on to a convex (converging) lens and the results of refraction noted:

1. *A ray* 1 *parallel to the principal axis*—this is refracted through the principal focus F, Fig. 19.5.

2. *A ray* 2 *incident on the centre C*—this passes straight through. The central part of the lens is a parallel-sided piece of glass; this only slightly displaces the ray but does not change its direction (p. 308).

3. *A ray* 3 *through the principal focus F*—this is refracted parallel to the principal axis.

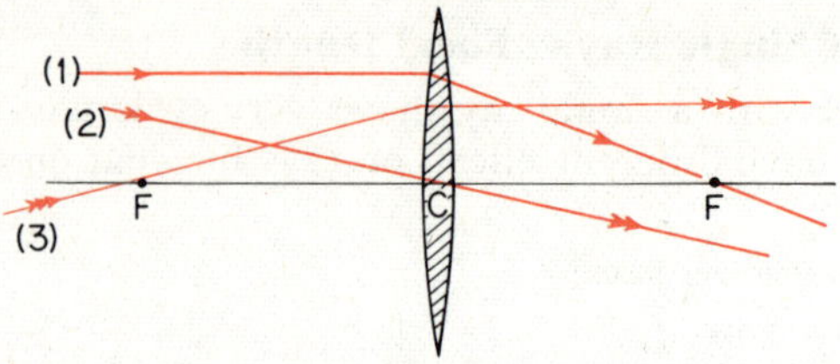

Fig. 19.5 Refraction of special rays

Focal Length of Converging or Convex Lens

In the chapter on curved mirrors, the focal length of a concave mirror was found quickly by using the window frame, or an object outside it, as a distant object. In this case parallel rays arrive at the mirror (p. 298). A similar experiment can be carried out with a convex lens L by holding it as far away from the window W as possible, and moving a paper screen S until a sharp clear image is obtained, Fig. 19.6 (i). Since parallel rays are brought to a focus, the distance LS is equal to the focal length f and is measured. It is an approximate and quick method for f. It is not accurate because the incident rays are not perfectly parallel.

Accurate Method

The focal length of a convex lens L can be measured with good accuracy by placing a plane strip mirror M behind it and an illuminated object O in front, Fig. 19.6 (ii). When O is moved a clear image I is obtained near it at one stage by reflection from the mirror M. The distance LO is then measured. This is the focal length f.

Explanation. Light which passes from O through L is reflected by M, and passes back through L towards O. When a sharp image I is obtained back near O the beam of light striking M must now return from M practically along its original path. This means that the beam is incident *normally* on M, as shown in Fig. 19.6 (ii). The beam incident on L from

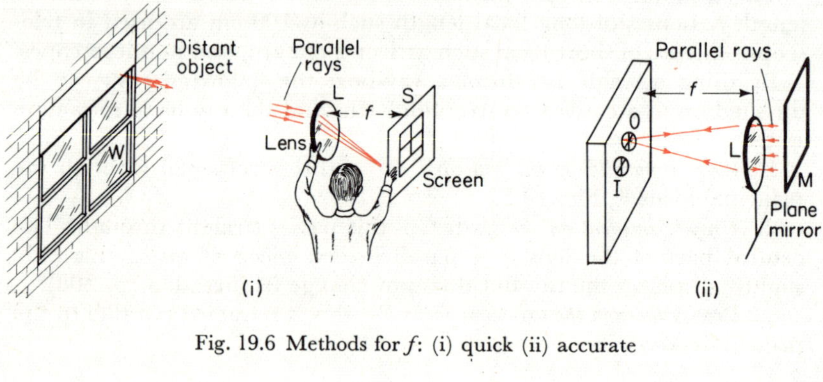

Fig. 19.6 Methods for f: (i) quick (ii) accurate

M is therefore a parallel beam. It is therefore refracted to the focus, which is at O.

Images in Converging or Convex Lens

The nature of the images produced by a converging (convex) lens can be investigated by using illuminated cross-wires as an object and moving it slowly towards the lens from some distance away. Typical distances from the lens at which the image may be observed on a screen are: (1) a long way off; (2) farther than $2f$, where f is the focal length; (3) at $2f$; (4) between $2f$ and f.

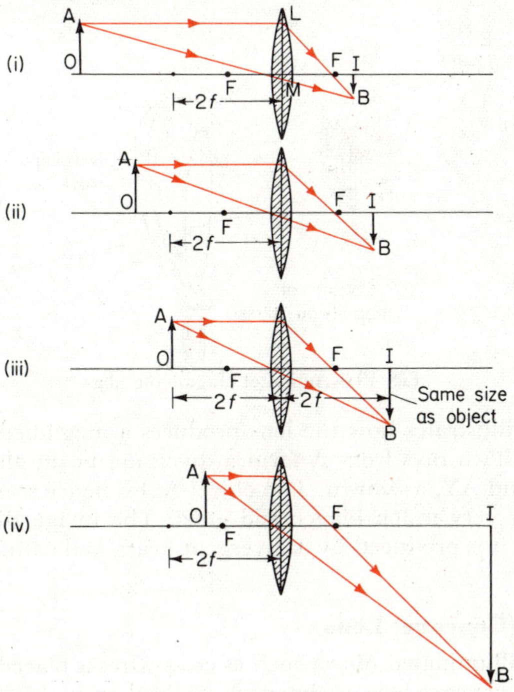

Fig. 19.7 Real images in converging (convex) lens

Results. The results are shown in Fig. 19.7. Generally, as the object moves nearer the lens the image increases in size and remains real and inverted. At a distance of $2f$ the image is the same size as the object (compare the *concave mirror*, p. 299). The image becomes larger as it is moved nearer to the focus. At the focus, however, no image is received on the screen; the rays emerging from the lens are parallel and the image is said to be formed 'at infinity'.

Magnifying Glass or Simple Microscope

If the illuminated object is moved *nearer* the lens than its focal length no image is received on the screen. But if the lens is placed close to a finger-nail, for example, the eye sees a *magnified and erect image.* A convex lens can thus be used as a magnifying glass or simple microscope. To look closely at small print or a map the magnifying glass must be held nearer to the object than its focal length. Otherwise, the image is seen upside down and not particularly large.

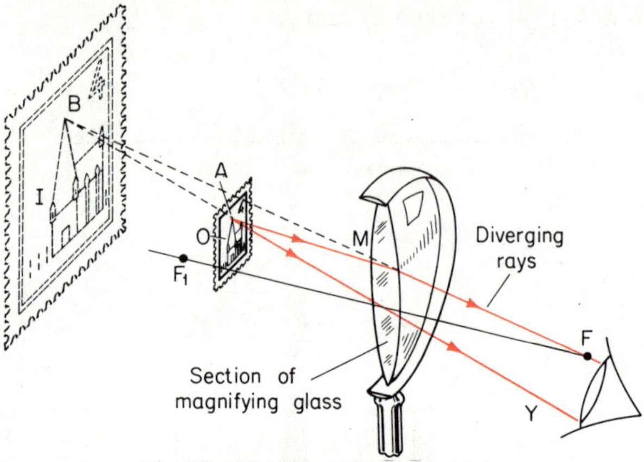

Fig. 19.8 Action of magnifying glass

Fig. 19.8 illustrates how the lens produces a magnified erect image of a stamp. Two rays from A form a diverging beam after refraction along MF and AY, as shown. The object AO is hence seen by E at BI, now looking very much bigger and erect. The image BI is a virtual one because it is produced by a divergent beam and cannot be formed on a screen.

Diverging (Concave) Lens

When an illuminated object such as cross-wires is placed in front of a diverging or concave lens, no image is received on a screen. On looking

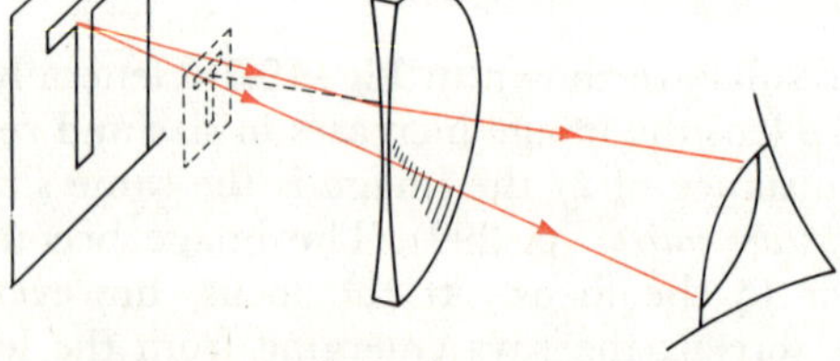

Fig. 19.9 Diverging (concave) lens image

through the lens, however, at a finger-nail or at print, the virtual image is seen to be *diminished* and *erect*, Fig. 19.9. This is always the case wherever the object is positioned, whereas the images in a convex lens are sometimes upside down and on other occasions erect, depending on the object position.

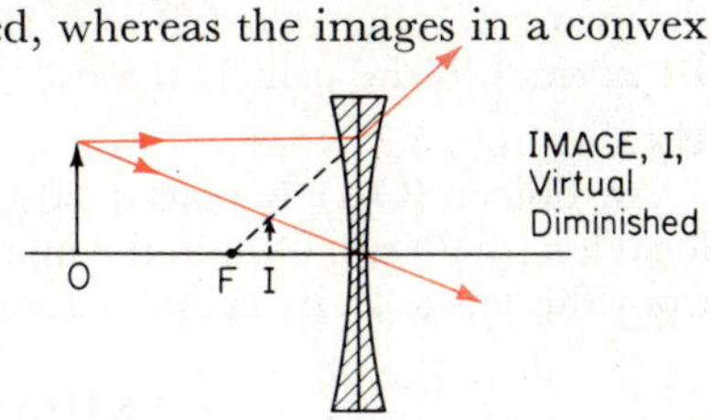

Fig. 19.10 Image drawing in diverging lens

Fig. 19.10 illustrates by a ray-diagram why the image I in a concave lens is always diminished and erect. A ray from the top point of the object O parallel to the principal axis appears to pass through the principal focus F after refraction: Another ray from O through the centre of the lens goes straight through. The diverging rays emerging from the lens appear to come from *behind* the lens above I. The image is therefore virtual, as shown.

Drawing Images

The image in a lens can be drawn as follows:

1. Represent the lens by a straight line XY and mark the position of the principal focus F from the centre C of the lens to some scale, that is, CF represents the focal length. See Fig. 19.11.

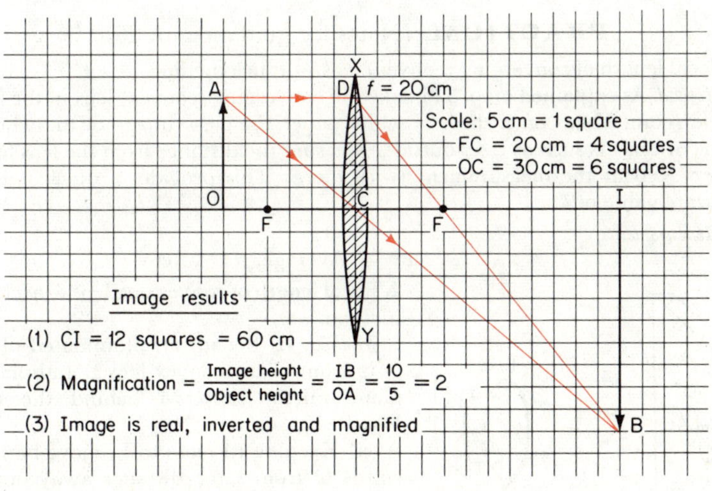

Fig. 19.11 Drawing image to scale

2. Place the object OA at the distance CO from the lens, on the same scale.

3. From the top point A of the object, draw: (i) a ray AD parallel to the principal axis—this is refracted to pass through F; (ii) a ray

through the centre C—this passes straight through without changing direction. The top point B of the image is the point of intersection of the two emerging rays CB and DB. Complete the image by drawing BI normal to the principal axis.

EXAMPLE

An object (OA) is placed 30 cm in front of a converging lens of focal length 20 cm. Obtain the image by drawing. State: (1) its distance from the lens; (2) its magnification; (3) its description. See Fig. 19.11.

SUMMARY

1. Converging lens—parallel rays converge to (real) focus after refraction. Diverging lens—parallel rays appear to diverge from (virtual) focus behind lens after refraction.

2. Focal length = distance from principal focus to lens.

3. A ray parallel to principal axis passes through the principal focus after refraction (converging lens) or passes through the principal focus produced back (diverging lens). A ray passing through the optical centre emerges in the same direction.

3. Converging (convex) lens—produces inverted real images when the object is farther than the focal length. Image the same size as object at $2f$. Nearer than f, image is magnified, erect and virtual (magnifying glass).

4. Diverging (concave) lens—image always diminished, erect, virtual.

PRACTICAL (Notes for guidance, p. 26)

1. Focal length of converging (convex) lens,—quick method

Method. As explained on p. 326, take the converging (convex) lens to the back of the room. Focus on a sheet of white paper the clear image of the window frame or objects such as trees outside. Measure the distance from the lens to the paper. Repeat the measurement twice more. This provides a quick but not accurate value of f.

Measurements.

$f =$ .., .., ..cm Average, $f =$ .. cm

2. Focal length of converging lens—accurate method.

Method. (i) Set up an illuminated object O in front of the convex lens L and place a plane mirror strip M behind the lens. Fig. 19.12.

(ii) Keeping M close to L, move both towards O from same distance away until a clear image I is obtained beside O.

(iii) Measure the distance from O to the lens L—this is the focal length (p. 326). Repeat the procedure and measurement twice more.

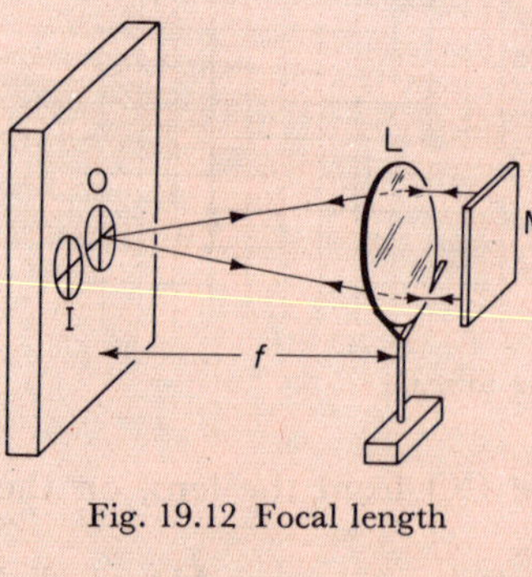

Fig. 19.12 Focal length

Measurements.

$f =$ .., .., ..cm Average, $f =$ .. cm

3. Images in converging lens.

Method. (i) Find the focal length *f* of the lens L by the quick method in **1** above.

(ii) Set up an illuminated object O in front of L and a white screen behind L (a small perspex ruler with a lamp behind it will provide a suitable object).

(iii) Starting with O some distance from L, much farther than 2*f*, obtain a clear image on the screen. Observe the image and enter the results in the table below. Repeat for other object distances as shown in the table.

Results Image

Distance of O from lens	Real or Virtual	Inverted or erect	Magnified or diminished
1. Farther than 2*f*	..	..	..
2. At 2*f*			
3. Between *f* and 2*f*			
4. At *f*			
5. Nearer than *f*			

4. Magnification by Lenses

Apparatus. A converging (convex) lens of short focal length, one of longer focal length, and a diverging (concave) lens.

Method. (i) Hold each lens in turn well away from the words on this page (or a diagram) and move the lens slowly towards the object. Observe what happens to the image. Try the effect of keeping your eye fairly close to the lens. Enter your results in a table.

Object distance from lens	Erect or inverted	Magnified or dimished	Real or virtual
1. Long distance 2. Close to lens			

(ii) By the quick method in 1, find the focal length of the two converging (convex) lenses. Then find their magnifying power by holding each in turn over some inked lines drawn over those on graph paper so that they are clearly seen. In Fig. 19.13, the magnifying power is 3. Enter the results in a table. Which lens has the greater magnifying power?

Focal length (cm)	Magnifying power

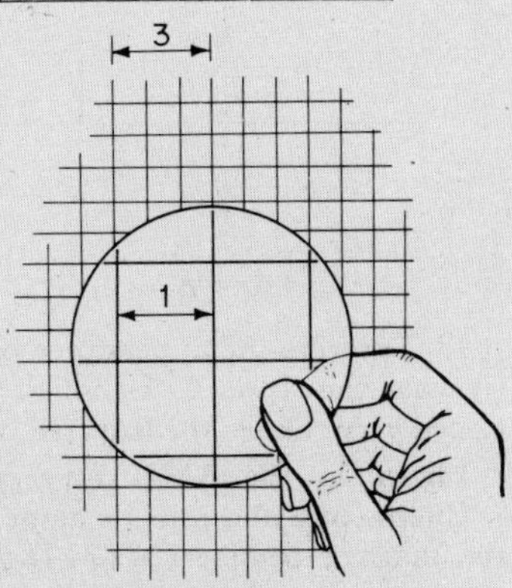

Fig. 19.13 Magnification

EXERCISE 19 · ANSWERS, p. 402

What are the missing words in the statements 1–6?

1. A converging (convex) lens brings parallel rays to a focus . . the lens.

2. A diverging (concave) lens brings parallel rays to a focus . . the lens.

3. A magnifying lens is a . . lens.

4. If an object is farther from a converging lens than its focal length, its image is formed . . the lens and is always . .

5. If the image of print in a lens is always seen to be smaller and erect, the lens is a . . lens.

6. A ray parallel to the principal axis of a converging lens passes through the . . after refraction.

What is the best answer, A, B, C, D or E in the statements 7–10?

7. A ray through the optical centre of a lens passes: (A) through the principal focus after refraction, (B) straight through the lens in the same direction; (C) straight back along the same path; (D) along the principal axis; (E) at right angles to its original direction.

8. In drawing the image of an object in a lens, two rays are usually taken from: (A) the foot of the object; (B) the foot and top of the object; (C) the middle and top of the object; (D) the top of the object; (E) the top of the image.

9. The image of an object nearer to a converging lens than its focal length is: (A) smaller and virtual; (B) magnified and real; (C) magnified and erect; (D) smaller and inverted; (E) magnified and formed very close to the lens.

10. A converging lens can be used to burn a hole in paper by using the sun's rays in summer because: (A) this lens produces a diverging beam; (B) it brings parallel rays to a focus in front of the lens; (C) it brings the rays to a parallel beam on the paper; (D) it increases the power of the sun; (E) it forms a magnified image on the paper.

11. (*a*) If a convex lens is held in front of a wall and moved towards or away from the wall, a position may be found where a clear image of a distant object is formed on the wall. What does the distance from the lens to the wall represent?
(*b*) Why could we not do this with a concave lens? (*L.*)

12. Complete the ray-diagram, Fig. 19A, and describe the image. (*Mx.*)

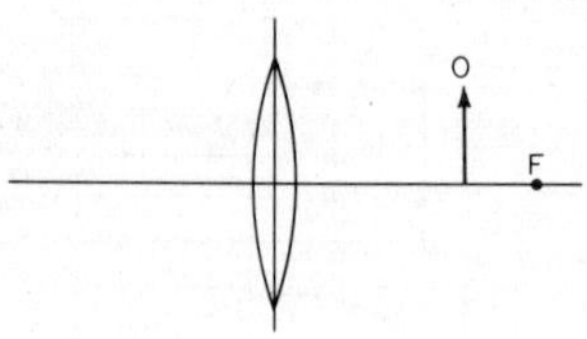

Fig. 19A

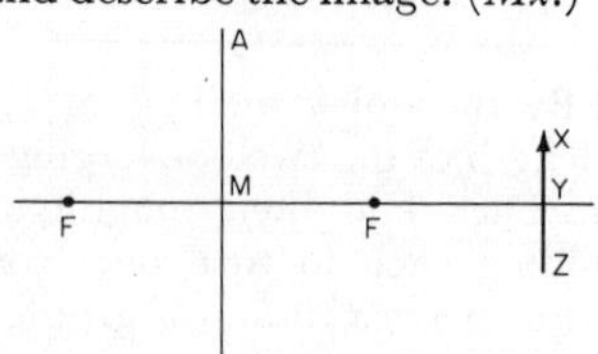

Fig. 19B

13. Describe the appearance of an object seen through a large convex lens: (i) when the object is positioned a long way away; (ii) when the object is positioned very close to the lens. (*W.Md.*)

14. In Fig. 19B, AMK can represent **either** a concave lens **or** a convex lens. Choose **one** and puts its name below K. Draw 4 rays to find the position of the image of the object XYZ. Draw in the image. (*E.A.*)

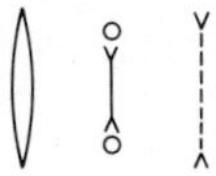

Fig. 19C

15. Complete the paths of two rays of light from the object O—O, Fig. 19C, and hence show how the magnified image shown is formed by the lens. (*W.Md.*)

16. Fig. 19D represents an illuminated object placed 45 cm in front of a converging (convex) lens of focal length 20 cm. By means of a scale drawing or a sheet of graph paper, find the position and size of the image formed by the lens. Describe the image. (*M.*)

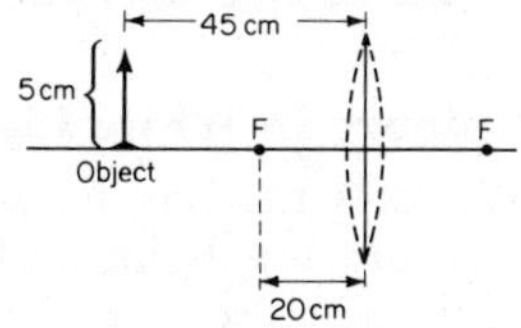

Fig. 19D

17. (i) Draw a sketch to show how a lens is able to produce an image of the sun on a paper screen.

(ii) Would you regard the rays from the sun as being (*a*) divergent, (*b*) parallel, (*c*) convergent?

(iii) What is the name given to the point where such rays meet after they have passed through the lens?

(iv) Why will the image of the sun sometimes burn the paper screen? (*S.E.*)

18. (*a*) What type of lens can be used as a magnifying glass?

(*b*) Show by a ray-diagram the formation of an image by a simple magnifier. Show two rays from each of two points on the object. State the position of the object and describe the image.

(*c*) How may a lens be used to obtain a parallel beam of light? (*E.A.*)

19. An object AB 1 cm high is placed at right angles to the axis of a convex lens, with the end B on the axis. The object is 3 cm from the lens and the focal length of the lens is 5 cm.

(*a*) Using graph paper, draw a full scale diagram of this arrangement.

(*b*) Complete the diagram to find the position and length of the image.

(*c*) State one practical use of a lens used in this way.

(*d*) Describe how you would find an approximate value for the focal length of a convex lens. (*L.*)

20. (*a*) Make scale drawings to show the position of the image of an object placed (i) in front of a convex mirror; (ii) between the pole and the focal point of a concave mirror.

(*b*) Draw a ray-diagram, scale 1 cm to 6 cm, to show how the image is formed in the following case:

A vertical object 6 cm tall is photographed by a camera whose lens is vertical and 18 cm away from the object. The image is formed 4·5 cm behind the camera lens.

21. Make an accurate *scale* drawing of the ray-diagram to show the formation of the image in each of the following cases: (*a*) a vertical, luminous object, 15 cm tall, standing 45 cm in front of a pinhole camera which is 15 cm long; (*b*) a vertical object, 20 cm tall, standing on, and perpendicular to, the principal axis of a convex lens, at a distance of 30 cm from the centre of the lens which has a focal length of 10 cm. (*Mx.*)

20

COLOURS OF LIGHT · THE SPECTRUM

Colours in White Light

WHEN a ray-box R, with a single slit O emitting a narrow beam or 'ray' of white light, is placed opposite a white screen S, a white image I of the slit is seen on S, Fig. 20.1. If a 60° glass prism X is now placed to intercept the white beam, refraction occurs. When the screen S is moved round so that the light emerging from the prism falls on it, a *coloured image* is now observed on S. The edges are red and violet respectively. Further, the coloured image is appreciably wider than the narrow white beam of light seen originally on S.

The prism experiment outlined here was first performed by Sir Isaac Newton in Cambridge in 1666. He made a small circular opening in a shutter in a darkened room and placed a prism near the hole, so that the light was refracted on to the opposite wall, Fig. 20.2. The spectrum produced in this way, although impure, was composed of the following colours, in order from the apex side A of the prism:

Red, Orange, Yellow, Green, Blue, Indigo, Violet (ROYGBIV).

Dispersion and Recombination with Prism

Newton experimented further to find out whether the colouring was imposed on the white light by the prism, or whether the colouring was already in the white light *before* it passed through the prism. We can follow his experiment by placing another 60° glass prism Y, similar to X, to intercept the colours further, Fig. 20.3 (i). On moving S round, the colours are now seen to be more widely separated than before, but are still respectively red, orange, yellow, green, blue, indigo and violet. The prism Y does not therefore create colours.

The prism Y is now turned round so that the angle enclosing the refracting sides point the other way to that of the prism X and the sides of the prisms are parallel, Fig. 20.3 (ii). When the screen S is moved it is seen that the image on S is *white*. The prism Y has now neutralized the colour effect produced by X.

Newton therefore concluded that the colours were present in white light. The glass prisms simply serve to separate them; they travel in different directions in glass. We say that a prism produces *dispersion* of the colours in white light.

Dispersion is due to the different speeds of all the colours in glass. Each colour in a ray of white light is then refracted in a slightly different

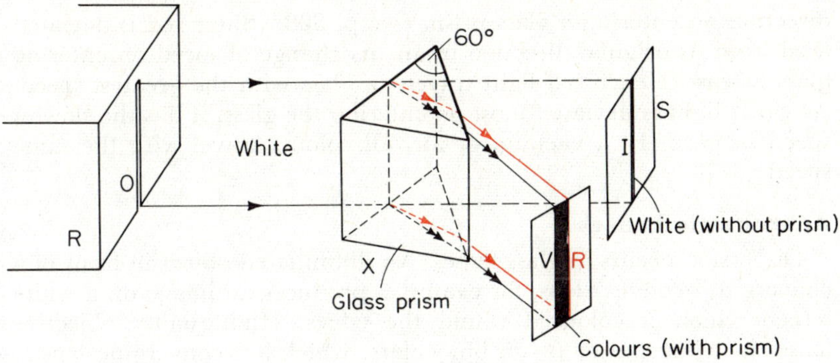

Fig. 20.1 Dispersion by glass prism

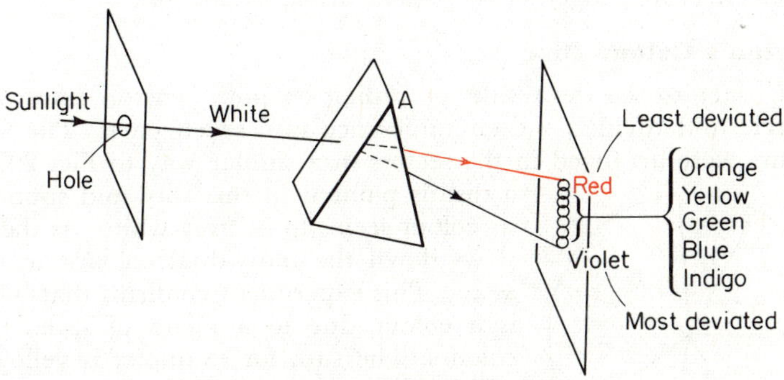

Fig. 20.2 Newton's prism experiment

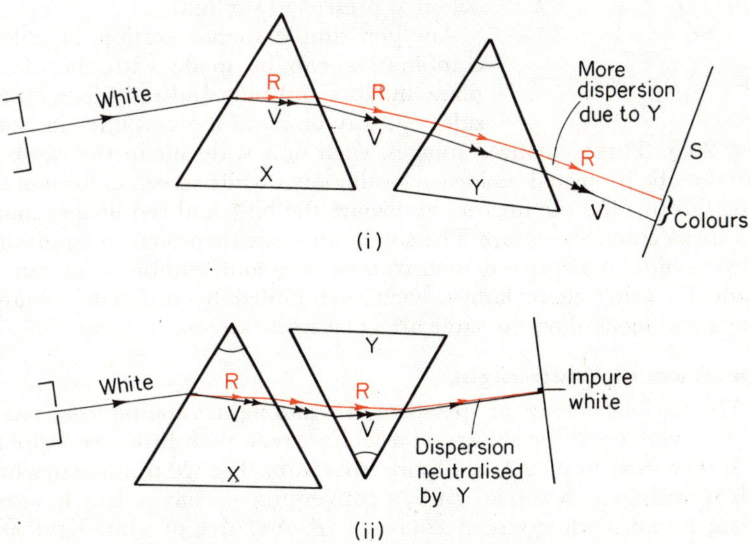

Fig. 20.3 Two prisms—(i) dispersion (ii) no dispersion

direction on entering a glass prism (see p. 308). Since red is deviated least from its original direction in air, its change of speed on entering glass is least. Hence red light travels in glass with the greatest speed. As violet light is deviated most on entering the glass, it has the slowest speed in glass. In a vacuum or air, all colours travel with the same speed.

Achromatic Lenses

Dispersion occurs in glass lenses. An illuminated object in front of a converging (convex) lens, for example, produces an image on a white screen which is coloured round the edges. High-quality objective lenses in telescopes or prism binoculars, which are converging lenses, are built up of a number of lenses. These are designed to reduce the colour effect and together they make an *achromatic lens*.

Newton's Colour Disc

In order to see the results of adding colours, Newton constructed a circle and divided the circumference into seven parts. The seven colours were arranged in the sectors in a similar way to Fig. 20.4. If a disc is painted in this way and spun fast, its colour seems to be grey-white. As the disc slows down the individual colours are seen again. This experiment confirms that 'white' is a colour due to a blend of seven main colours. The sun, for example, is yellowish-white, so that more yellow than any other colour is present in sunlight.

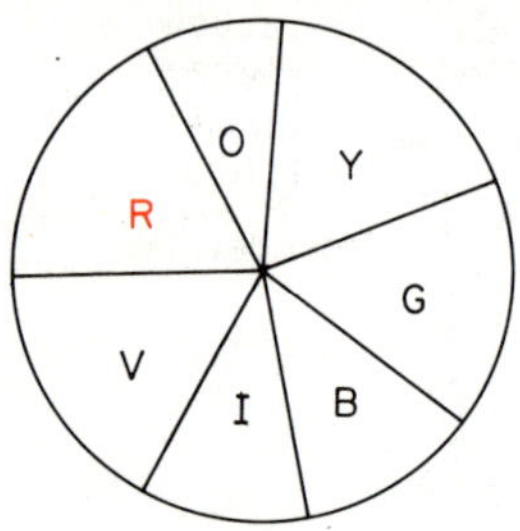

Fig. 20.4 Newton colour disc

Another simple demonstration of colour combination can be made with the aid of plane mirrors and blue and red filters on the sides of a ray-box and a green filter in front, Fig. 20.5. Three coloured images, each of a wide slit in the ray-box, can then be projected beside each other on a white screen in front of the box. On turning the mirrors to deviate the blue and red images more, the three colours overlap. The single image is then seen to be an 'impure' white. A similar demonstration of colour combination can be made by using three lamps, each surrounded by different coloured filters and focused on the same area of a white screen.

Spectrum of White Light

The various colours or spectrum of white light, ranging from red to blue or violet, can be shown on a white screen with little overlapping. It is then said to be a fairly 'pure' spectrum. Fig. 20.6 illustrates how this is arranged. A *narrow* slit S, a converging or convex lens L, at 60° prism P and a white screen are required. A source of white light such as a filament lamp is placed in front of the slit. The lens L is then

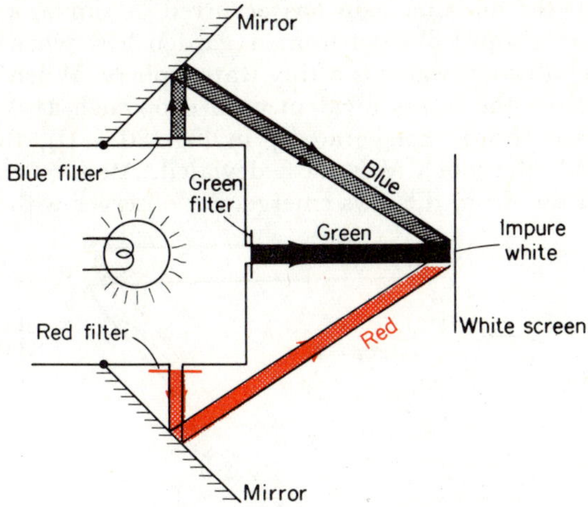

Fig. 20.5 Combining coloured lights

arranged to produce a clear image I of the slit on the screen, and the beam of white light converging to I is then intercepted by P. A fairly pure spectrum is then observed on the screen, moved round if necessary. The prism can then be adjusted to produce the best spectrum. The converging lens helps to bring the different colours to a slightly different focus after they emerge from the prism, so they are then seen apart from each other and then form a fairly pure spectrum.

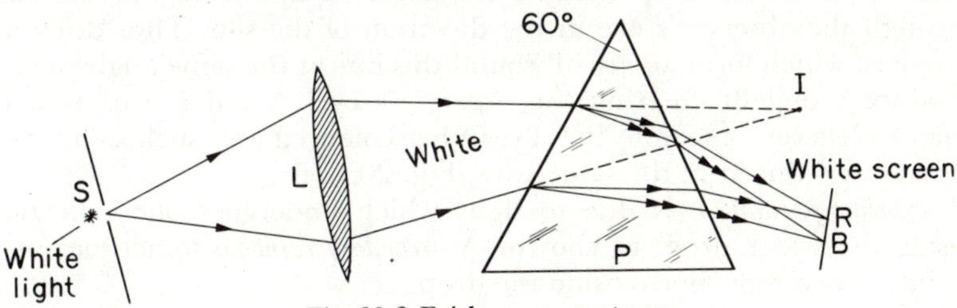

Fig. 20.6 Fairly pure spectrum

A red *filter* absorbs all the colours except red, which it allows to pass through. Thus if a red filter is placed in front of the slit in Fig. 20.6, only a red image of the slit is seen on the white screen. This is because a white screen reflects *all* colours and hence reflects red light. For a similar reason, a blue filter in front of the slit produces only a blue image on the white screen.

Rainbow

Our natural white light is due to the sun. The beautiful colours in the rainbow are due to dispersion of sunlight by water droplets suspended in the air after rain has occurred. A similar colour effect is produced by drops of water from a garden hose when sunlight is present. Each drop of water is a tiny water sphere. When a ray W of white light from the sun is incident on a drop such as A, dispersion occurs. This is shown exaggeratedly in Fig. 20.7. (i), the red R is least deviated; the violet V is most deviated. After reflection at the other side of the drop, the rays emerge. An observer with his back to

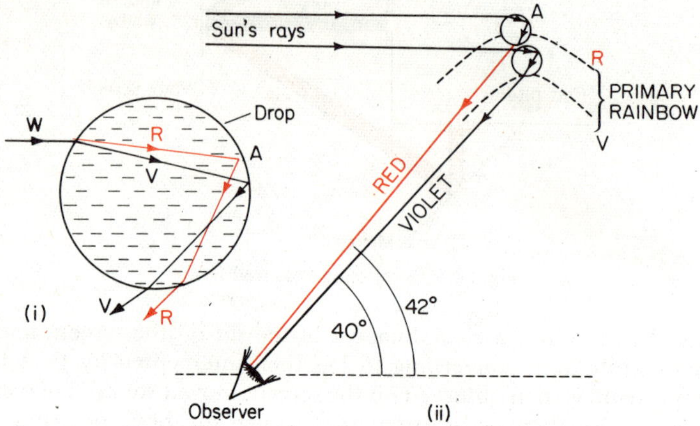

Fig. 20.7 Rainbow—refraction by water drops

the sun may thus see the colours of the spectrum. Most red rays emerge from a particular drop making an angle of about 42° to the line through the observer's eye in the direction of the sun. Thus different droplets, which form an arc all round this line at the same angle of 42°, produce red light entering the observer's eye. A red arc or bow of colour is therefore seen in the sky. Other coloured arcs such as a violet bow are produced in the same way, Fig. 20.7 (ii).

A *primary rainbow* is due to light which undergoes one reflection inside the water drop, as shown. A *secondary rainbow* sometimes seen is due to two reflections inside the drop.

Colour of Objects

An object such as paper, which is white in daylight, reflects all the colours of the spectrum, red, orange, yellow, green, blue, indigo, violet. When it is illuminated in the dark room by blue light, therefore, the paper appears blue. If illuminated by red light it appears red. An object which is black in daylight absorbs all the colours. Thus, if it is illuminated by blue light only it appears black. A red rose has this colour because it absorbs all the colours of white light except red. Consequently, the rose appears black if illuminated in a dark room by blue light. Similarly, a blue tie absorbs all the colours in white light except blue; it looks black if illuminated by yellow light.

Colour and Brightness Sensitivity of Eye

Objects are seen when light from them is focused by the eye lens on to the retina at the back of the eye-pupil (p. 345). The retina is a layer containing a great number of light-sensitive cells. These pass 'messages' along nerves to the brain. This interprets the light detected as the 'image' of the object viewed.

Close examination of the construction and working of the retina shows that there are two basic types of light-sensitive cells. One type consists of *rods*—they produce brightness sensations, that is, we would see objects only as black and white with these cells alone. The other type consists of *cones*—they are sensitive to colour. There are many millions of both types of cells in the retina, although there are many more rods than cones. In daylight, when a large quantity of light is incident on the eye, the cones move forward and the rods withdraw into the retina. Thus the colour of objects is seen sharply in daylight. At night, the reverse happens. Consequently, colours are difficult to distinguish at night. In the dark, objects appear to be grey whatever their colour for this reason.

Primary Colours · Adding Coloured Lights

It has been found that the cones, which are sensitive to colour, can be divided into three groups. One sensitive mainly to red light, another to green light and the third to blue light. The eye 'sees' colour by detecting its red, green and blue components. These three colours are known as *primary colours*. Thus by combining red, green and blue lights in suitable proportions, almost any colour, including white, can be produced. This is used in colour television (p. 570).

The adding of primary colours to produce other colours is known as *additive* colour mixing. Thus red and blue lights on a white paper screen together give a purple colour known as *magenta;* blue and green give a turquoise or blue-green colour called *cyan*; and green and red give *yellow*. The colours which add together to produce white light are called *complementary colours*. Thus magenta is complementary to green; yellow is complementary to blue; and cyan is complementary to red.

Colour Triangle

The colours produced by additive mixing of primary colours can be illustrated by a *colour triangle*, RGB, Fig. 20.8 (i). Each primary colour is placed at the corner of an equilateral triangle. As one moves along an edge or side of the triangle, such as RB, the colours gradually change from one primary, red in this case, to the other, which is blue. Midway between the two primaries will be the colour obtained by mixing or adding equal quantities of the primaries, cyan, yellow or magenta. White is the centre O of the triangle because this is the point which represents the addition of equal quantities of the three primary colours. Any primary colour, when added to the colour directly opposite to it in the triangle will produce white, as these are complementary colours (p. 339). Thus:

$$\text{Blue} + \text{yellow} \longrightarrow \text{white.}$$
$$\text{Red} + \text{cyan} \longrightarrow \text{white.}$$
$$\text{Green} + \text{magenta} \longrightarrow \text{white.}$$

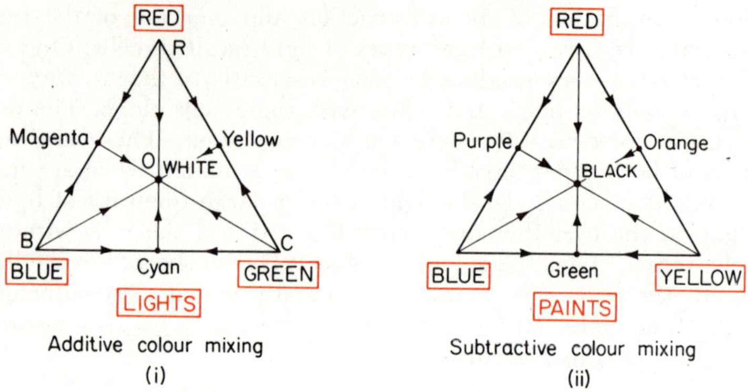

Fig. 20.8 Colour triangle: (i) lights (ii) pigments

In high-fidelity reproduction of sound, engineers aim at reproducing accurately three main qualities of the original sound; frequency (pitch), amplitude (loudness or intensity) and tone (or timbre). In accurate reproduction of colour for colour television, engineers aim at reproducing accurately analogous qualities, for example, the shade or 'hue' of a colour and its intensity and brightness (see p. 570).

Subtractive Colour Mixing

Although the mixing of blue and yellow lights creates whiteness, the mixture of blue and yellow *pigments* (*paints*) produces a green. This is because the results of paint mixing are due to a *subtractive* process. Blue paint absorbs all light except blue and green. Yellow paint absorbs all light except yellow, orange and green. The only light reflected by both yellow and blue pigments is green, and this is the resulting colour seen. Fig. 20.8 (ii) shows a 'colour triangle' for subtractive colour mixing.

SUMMARY

1. Spectrum of white light—red, orange, yellow, green, blue, indigo, violet.

2. A prism produces dispersion of colours because the colours travel at different speeds in glass.

3. Colours in white light can be recombined by using a second prism pointing the opposite way to the first prism, or by spinning a Newton colour disc.

4. A red flower looks red when exposed to red light because it absorbs all colours except red. Thus it looks black when exposed to blue light.

5. Primary colours are red, blue, green, Coloured lights of red and green add to produce yellow.

6. Pigments (paints) produce colours by a subtractive process. Blue and yellow paints mixed together produce green—blue paint absorbs all colours except blue and green, yellow paint absorbs all colours except yellow, orange, green, so green is the only colour not absorbed.

PRACTICAL

(Do the experiments in a darkened room)

1. Spectrum

Apparatus. Ray-box, two 60° glass prisms, white paper, white screen.

Method. Place the ray-box and glass prism on the paper and arrange them so that a ray of white light is incident on the prism as shown in Fig. 20·1 on p. 335. Observe the coloured beam on the paper and place the screen to receive it. Turn the prism and move the screen to obtain the best spectrum. Note the order of colours. Which colour has been deviated most and which has been deviated least?

As shown in Fig. 20·3 (i), p. 335, place the second prism so as to obtain greater dispersion (separation) of colours. Now proceed to 2.

2. Recombining colours.

Method. Place the second prism to *neutralize* the dispersion produced by the first prism, as shown in Fig. 20·3 (ii). Observe: (*a*) the colour of the image on the screen, (*b*) its width compared to that of the spectrum previously obtained. Remove both prisms—does the colour of the image on the screen change?

3. Filters

Apparatus. As in **1**, with gelatine filters red, blue, green, yellow.

Method. Obtain a spectrum as in **1**. Observe the effect on the spectrum produced by interposing each filter in turn in front of the white light from the ray-box.

4. Colours of objects

Apparatus. Ray-box with wide opening; white screen; red and blue gelatine filters.

Method. (i) Direct the white beam from the ray-box on to the screen. Place a red filter in front of the beam and obtain a red image on the screen. Observe the colour of a red object such as a red book or red chalk placed in front of the red light. Repeat with a blue object such as a tie or cloth.

(ii) Replace the red filter by a blue filter. Examine the colours of red and blue objects in blue light.

(iii) Using a red and a blue coloured pencil, draw an object such as a face or house, with parts coloured differently. Observe the object when illuminated by red and then by blue light from the filters.

(iv) Observe the colours of objects in the room and outside the window through the red and blue filters respectively.

5. Combining coloured lights.

Apparatus. Three ray-boxes each producing a wide beam, or three lamps; red, blue and green filters; white screen.

Method. Using the filters to obtain red, blue and green lights, observe the effect on the screen of adding coloured lights as follows: (i) red and blue; (ii) blue and green; (iii) green and red; (iv) red, green and blue. Make a table of your results. Placing 'red', 'green', 'blue' at the corners of a triangle, complete the 'colour triangle' from your results. What are the complementary colours of red, green and blue respectively?

6. Coloured shadows. Subtractive colours.

Apparatus. Three ray-boxes or lamps; opaque object C such as a thick pencil; red, blue and green filters; white screen. (Do the experiment in a dark room.)

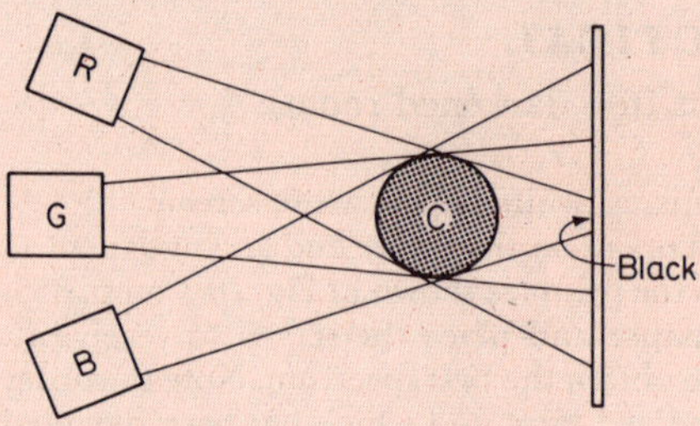

Fig. 20.9 Subtractive colours

Method. (i) Place the object C in front of the screen and illuminate by red light, Fig. 20.9. Observe the black shadow of C on the red surrounding screen.

(ii) Switch on the blue light. Observe the magenta colour of the screen surrounding the shadows. Adjusting the lamps or C if necessary, observe the blue, red and black shadows obtained. (The black shadow produced by the red light is illuminated by blue light and hence the colour here is blue. The red shadow is explained in the same way.)

(iii) Switch on the green light. Observe (*a*) the black shadow in the centre—no light from any of the three lamps reach here; (*b*) the red, blue and green shadows round it; (c) the surrounds coloured yellow, magenta and cyan respectively. (The black shadow of blue light is illuminated by red and green and hence appears . .)

EXERCISE 20 · ANSWERS, p. 402

1. When seen through a piece of red glass the green leaves of a plant: (*a*) appear almost black; (*b*) become nearly invisible; (*c*) are seen in their natural colour; (*d*) take on a bluish hue; (*e*) look purple. (*M.*)

2. What colour would a sheet of green paper appear to be if placed in: (*a*) red light? (*b*) in green light? (*S.E.*)

3. A school badge has a yellow cross on a blue background. State the colour each part would appear when viewed in :(*a*) yellow light; and (*b*) blue light. (*Mx.*)

	Cross	Background
Yellow light		
Blue light		

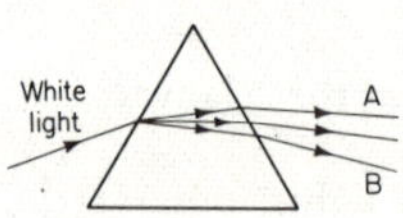

Fig. 20A

4. Fig. 20A shows a ray of white light dispersed in passing through a prism.

(*a*) What colour would you see at: (i) A; (ii) B?

(*b*) What may you detect: (i) above; (ii) below B? (*L.*)

5. In Fig. 20B, the lines with arrows represent rays of light. The letters at the end of the rays refer to the colours of the rainbow and white.

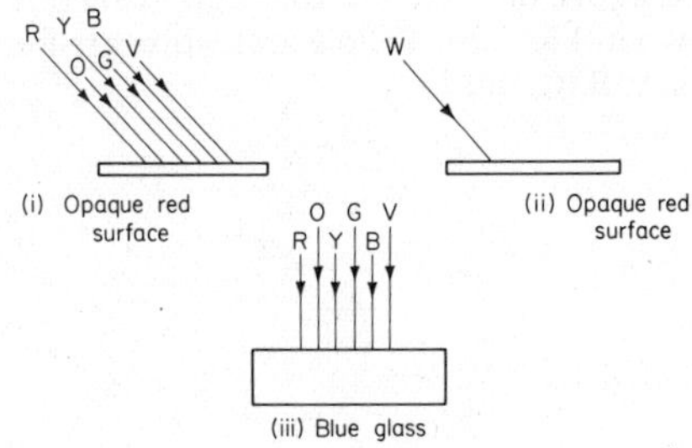

Fig. 20B

(*a*) Draw and label the rays which are reflected or transmitted.

(*b*) What do you see if you look through a piece of red glass at the rays passing through the blue glass in (iii)? (*E.A.*)

6. Describe and explain the appearance of a coloured picture of a red, white and blue flag when projected on to a wall painted with matt dark-blue paint. (*S.E.*)

7. (*a*) Draw a diagram showing how a spectrum may be produced by allowing a narrow beam of white light to fall on a prism. Label the red and blue rays.

(*b*) Describe briefly why an object sometimes appears to be a different colour in daylight than in artificial light. (*L.*)

8. Explain why a mixture of yellow and blue paints appears green. (*E.A.*)

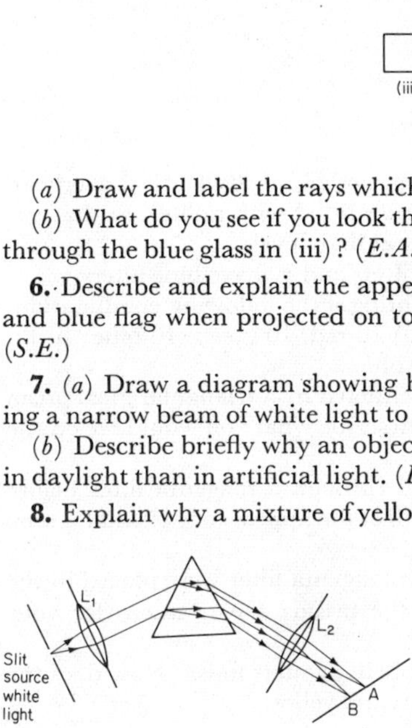

Fig. 20C

9. Fig. 20C is a diagram of how pure spectrum can be produced on a screen from a slit source of white light.

Name the order of colours on the screen from A to B.

Explain exactly each step in the above process, the position of each piece of apparatus and what purpose each serves. (*W.Md.*)

10. Read the following passage carefully and explain the meaning of each of the five items in italics:

'White light can be produced by adding together any three separate *monochromatic lights* in the *right proportions*. This shows that although white light may contain all *wavelengths* in the *visible spectrum* these do not all need to be present for the eye to see white light. This gives us the idea that the human eye contains three different types of *colour receptors*.' (*M.*)

11. (*a*) Given the following apparatus and the use of the laboratory equipment and black-out would you produce a pure spectrum?

White screen, tungsten filament lamp, large card with a vertical 1 in slit at its centre convex lens, triangular glass prism.

Draw a ray-diagram of the arrangement and show where the red and violet ends of the spectrum would appear on your screen.

(*b*) A football shirt, seen in daylight, has a green body, red sleeves and white collar. Describe the appearance of the shirt in a dark room with only a red light glowing. Explain carefully how these *colours* appear. (*Mx.*)

12. Three coloured lights, one red and the others called A and B, overlap on a white screen as shown in Fig. 20D. Yellow and white are formed where shown. What are the colours A, B, C and D?

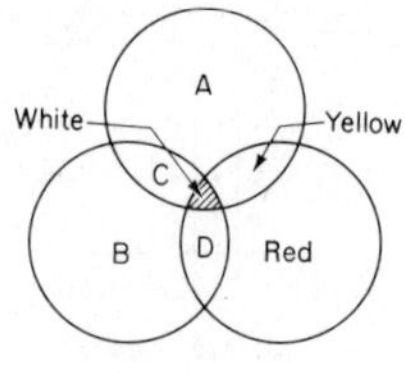

Fig. 20D

13. (*a*) The lighting on a theatre stage is provided by 30 identical overhead lamps, each lamp being housed in a metal case fitted with a filter, so that the light shines downwards, spreading out widely at floor level.

Ten lamps have red filters, 10 have green filters and 10 have blue filters.

What would be the colour of the stage lighting if the following combinations of lamps were used? (i) 10 red, 10 green; (ii) 10 red, 10 green, 10 blue; (iii) 5 red, 10 green, 10 blue; (iv) 5 red, 5 green, 10 blue.

(*b*) A very narrow beam of white light is refracted by a triangular glass prism and then falls on a white screen. Name and describe what you would see on the screen.

If the narrow beam of white light passed through a magenta filter before passing through the prism, how would this affect the appearance of what is seen on the screen?

Would it make any difference whether the magenta filter were placed in the beam of light *after* it had passed through the prism? Give reasons for your answer.

(*c*) A door is painted yellow with an 'eggshell' or matt finish. How does the paint reflect sunlight so that it looks both matt and yellow? (*S.*)

14. (*a*) Draw two lines five millimetres apart and approximately parallel to represent a beam of white light. Complete a diagram which would show how to obtain a spectrum and label the colours on your drawing.

(*b*) Name three forms of electromagnetic radiation other than light.

(*c*) A poster consists of printed letters, some red and some green on a white background. Describe and explain the effect of illuminating it with two lights at once, one red and one green.

(*d*) Explain why uncurtained window panes viewed from a distance generally appear black. (*S.*)

21

OPTICAL INSTRUMENTS

THE EYE AND VISION

The Eye

THE eye is one of the most intricate and sensitive instruments devised by nature, Fig. 21.1. Its chief optical features are:

(1) the *eye-lens*, which focuses light entering the eye;

(2) *ciliary muscles*, which are attached to the eye-lens surfaces and alter the focal length;

(3) the *retina*, the light sensitive area of cells at the back of the eye;

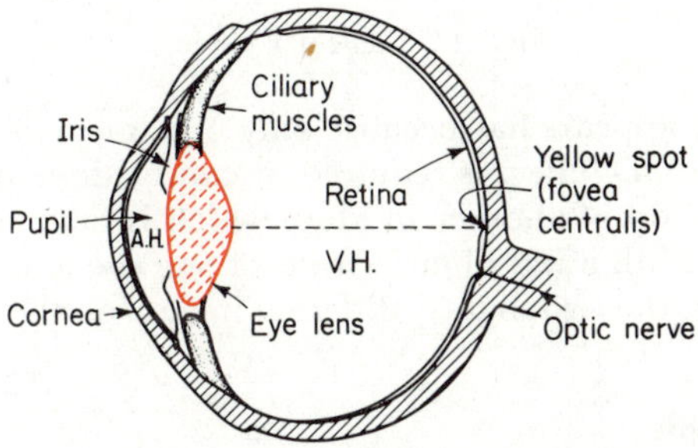

Fig. 21.1 Optical features of eye

(4) the *yellow spot* (*fovea centralis*), the most light sensitive spot on the retina;

(5) the *iris*, the coloured circle round the eye-lens, which controls the amount of light entering the eye;

(6) the *pupil*, the circular opening or diaphragm in the iris through which light passes;

(7) the *cornea*, the thick protective covering of transparent material in front of the eye-lens;

(8) the *aqueous humour* (A.H.) and *vitreous humour* (V.H.), which are respectively liquids in front of and behind the eye-lens in which the eye-lens floats.

Binocular Vision

If you close one eye and attempt to pick up a pen or other object at the corner of the table you will not find it easy. A sense of distance is lacking compared with using two eyes. *Binocular vision* provides two images of the same object which are slightly different in perspective.

The brain combines the two images and gives an impression of depth or solidity. This is missing if only one eye is used. In Fig. 21.2 (i), for example, a view of a pyramid P is seen slightly different by the left eye L and the right eye R, as indicated in (ii). Two retinal images of slightly differing perspective are always necessary to provide depth or a stereoscopic (3D) effect.

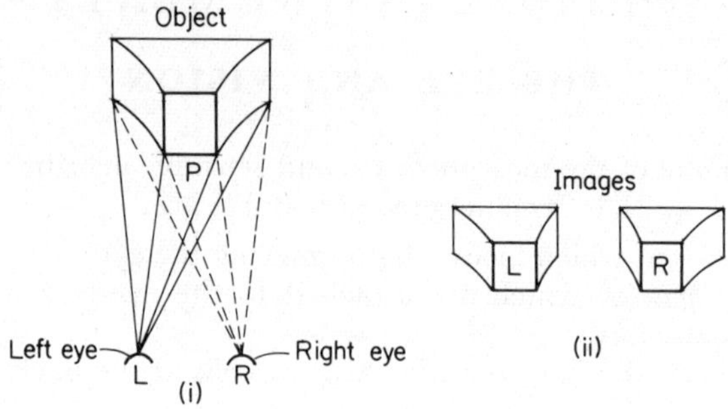

Fig. 21.2 Binocular vision

A photograph appears flat because only one image is formed by the camera lens. If a '3D' effect is required, it can be done by printing one image in red on top of another in blue, which is taken from a slightly different angle. With a red filter in front of one eye and a blue filter in front of the other, the two slightly different images on the retina produce a 3D effect.

Accommodation

The ability of the eye lens to focus points at different distances on to the retina is called its *power of accommodation*. Accommodation is produced by the action of the ciliary muscles. When a person with normal vision looks at a very distant object, at 'infinity', the eye lens focuses parallel rays on the retina. The ciliary muscles are then fully relaxed, so that the accommodation is least. When a near object is viewed, the muscles increase the curvature of the lens surfaces, so that a 'fatter' lens, one with a shorter focal length, is produced. The diverging rays are then focused on the retina. At the nearest point for distinct vision, the ciliary muscles are at maximum strain and accommodation is greatest.

With defective vision, discussed shortly, the normal accommodation of the eye is exceeded in trying to focus an object. In old age, the eye lens tends to become inelastic and unable to accommodate, and spectacles are necessary.

Normal Vision

People with normal vision are able to focus near objects such as reading books when they are about 25 cm or 10 in from the eye. This is the closest point at which the object can be seen clearly, and it is called the *near point* of the eye, Fig. 21.3 (i).

People with normal vision are able to see clearly objects which are a long distance away, or at 'infinity'. The farthest point from the eye which can be seen distinctly is called the *far point* of the eye. For normal vision, then, the far point is at infinity, Fig. 21.3 (ii).

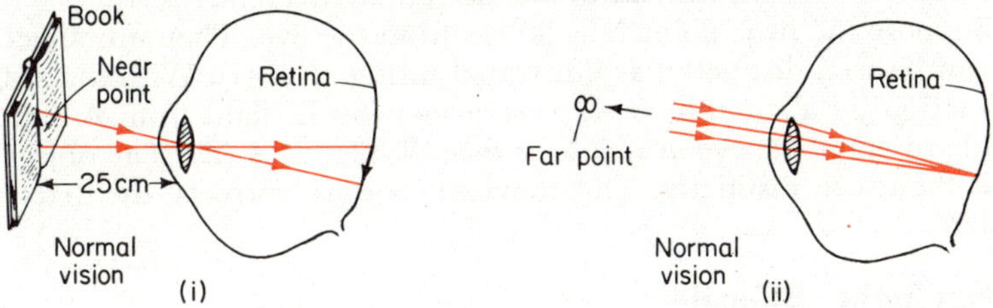

Fig. 21.3 Normal vision—(i) near (ii) far point

If the object in Fig. 21.3 (i) is moved farther back from the eye, the image on the retina becomes smaller and so *the object looks smaller*. This can be shown by drawing rays from the object to the eye-lens after it is moved back. The object also appears *less bright*. This is because the light energy from the object falling on 1 cm^2 of the eye lens diminishes the farther back we move the object. Since the energy is spread more 'thinly' at greater distances, the amount entering the pupil of the eye becomes smaller.

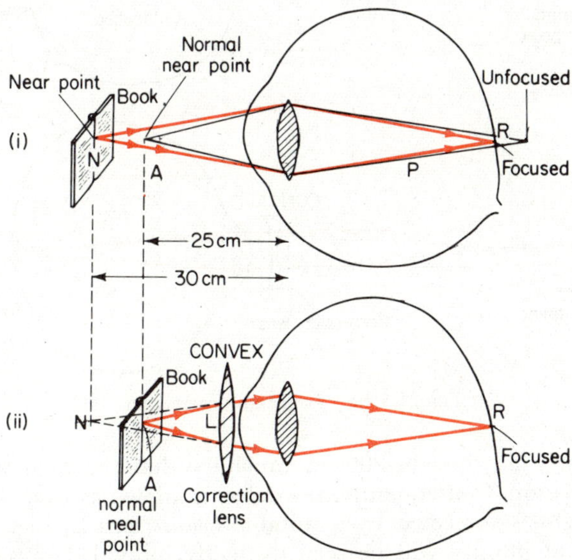

Fig. 21.4 Long sight and correction

Defects of Vision · Long Sight

If you wear spectacles for reading, your near point N is usually farther than 25 cm from the eye. This defect of vision is therefore called *long sight*. It may be due to an eyeball which is too short. Rays from a point A 25 cm from the eye are then brought to a focus at P beyond the eyeball, instead of on the retina R, Fig. 21.4 (i).

Suppose the near point N is 30 cm from the eye. Then an object at N can be seen distinctly, as illustrated in Fig. 21.4 (i). With the aid of refraction by a suitable *convex* (*converging*) *lens* L, light from A can be made to enter the eye *as if it came from N*, Fig. 21.4 (ii). The object at A is then seen distinctly. The convex lens thus 'corrects' the defect of vision.

Short Sight · Bifocals

Some spectators are unable to see cricketers or footballers clearly unless they wear spectacles, and people with such a defect of vision must wear spectacles while driving. In these cases the eyeball is too long. Parallel rays from objects a long way off, at infinity, are then brought to a focus in front of the retina, Fig. 21.5 (i). The farthest point

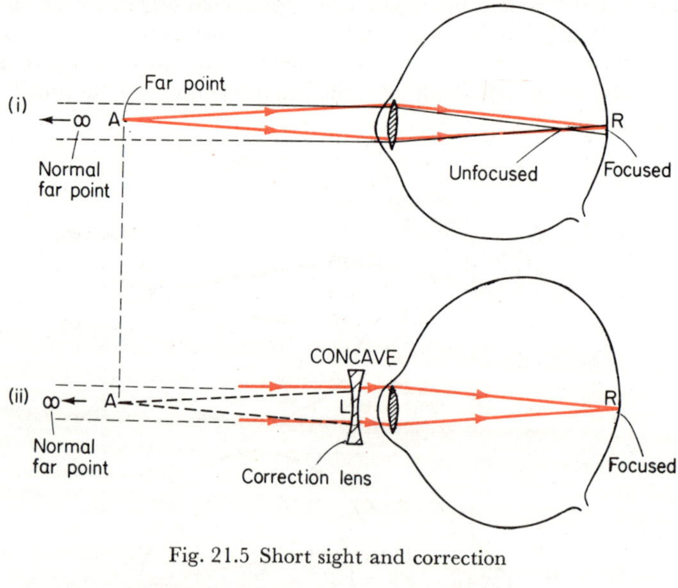

Fig. 21.5 Short sight and correction

A seen clearly may now be 200 cm, much less than the farthest distance of normal vision. Consequently, the defect is known as *short sight*.

Short sight is corrected by a suitable *concave* lens L, Fig. 21.5 (ii). An object at infinity will be seen distinctly, provided rays refracted through the lens enter the eye *as if they came from A*, the person's far point. With the lens close to the eye, this means that parallel rays appear to diverge from A after refraction, as shown. Thus A is the focus of the lens, and AL is hence the focal length. A concave or diverging lens of focal length 200 cm is therefore required to see distant objects clearly. If another person's far point is 150 cm from his or her eye a concave or diverging lens of focal length 150 cm is required.

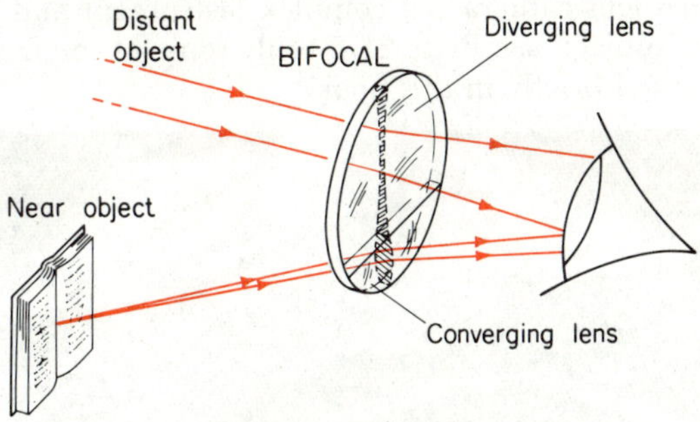

Fig. 21.6 Bifocals

With age, when the eye lens becomes inelastic and unable to accommodate, two pairs of spectacles may be necessary. *Bifocal lenses* have an upper portion for long-distance viewing and a lower portion used for reading, Fig. 21.6.

LENS CAMERA

The lens camera is a man-made 'copy' of the eye. For example, it has an opening or aperture similar to the pupil to allow light to enter, and

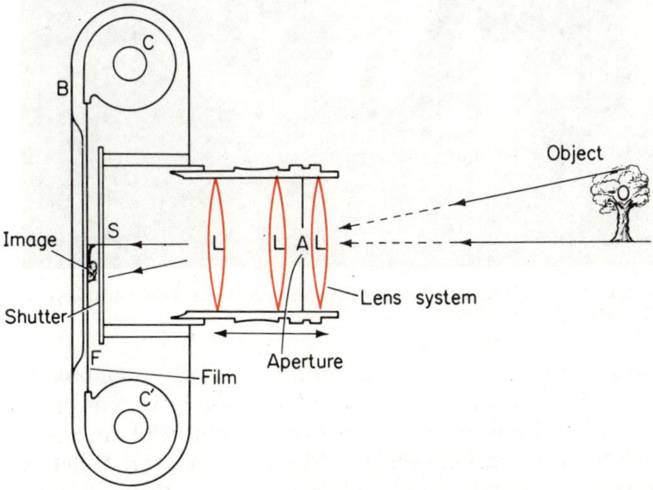

Fig. 21.7 Lens camera

a light-sensitive film at the back similar to the light-sensitive retina of the eye. There are differences, however, in the lens system. In the eye, the focal length of the lens is varied by ciliary muscles. This enables the eye to see clearly objects at different distances. In the lens camera, however, the focal length of the lens is constant. Objects at different distances are focused on the film by moving the lens.

The modern lens camera is a complex instrument and photography is a specialist subject, see Plate 21A. Only some of the main points are listed and treated briefly in this book.

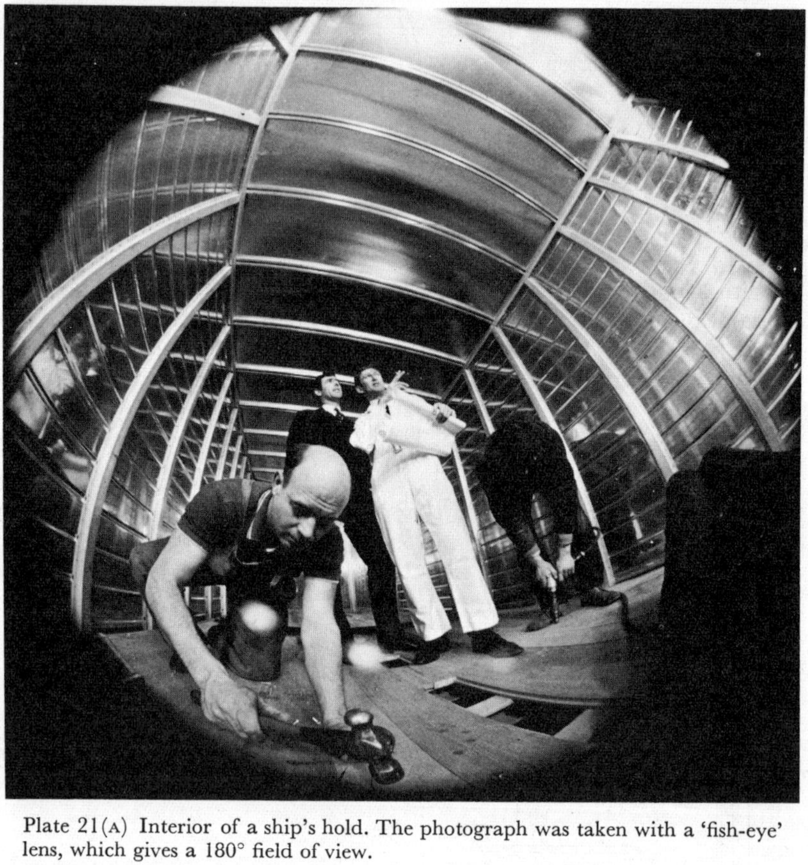

Plate 21(A) Interior of a ship's hold. The photograph was taken with a 'fish-eye' lens, which gives a 180° field of view.

1. **Lens Action.** Basically, the camera consists of a light-proof box B, with a lens system L in front, Fig. 21.7. This acts effectively as a converging or convex lens. It is used to focus light from an object O on to the film F. A shutter S is placed between the lens and the film. When a photograph is taken, the shutter opens and closes rapidly, thus exposing the film for a short time to light entering the camera through the lenses.

By coupling the lens to a rangefinder, mentioned shortly, the lens system can be moved in or out in the direction of the arrows shown. After taking a photograph the film is wound between two spools, C and C′, until it is all used up.

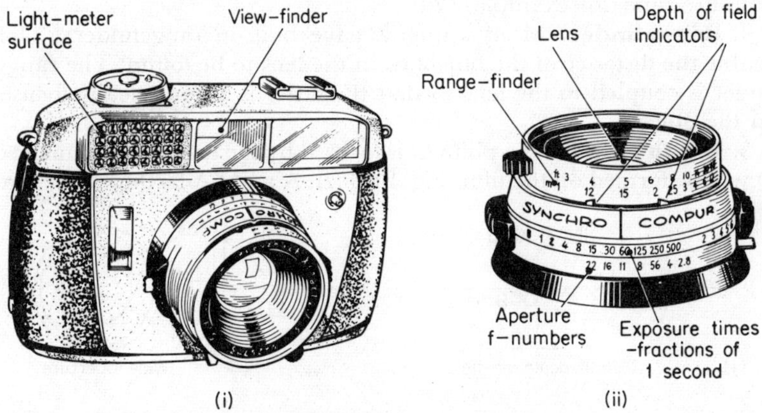

Fig. 21.8 Settings on lens camera

Fig. 21.8 (i) shows the exterior of one type of camera, with some details in Fig. 21.8 (ii).

2. **f-numbers.** The images produced by the lens system have to be bright enough to 'expose' the film sufficiently in the short time the shutter is open. The main factors controlling the brightness are: (i) the *diameter*, d, *of the aperture* or circular opening through which the light passes—this controls the amount of light collected; (ii) the *focal length*, f, *of the lens*—this controls the size or area of the image on the film; (iii) the *exposure time*, discussed shortly.

Since it is linked with the brightness, the diameter d of the aperture is expressed as a fraction of f in 'f-numbers' Fig. 21.9. An aperture of 'f-4' means one whose diameter d is $f/4$. An aperture 'f-16' is one of diameter $f/16$. This is an aperture one-quarter the diameter of f-4. As shown in Fig. 21.8 (ii), some f-numbers used in cameras are $f2{\cdot}8$, 4, 5·6, 8, 11, 16, 22. The smallest aperture here is $f22$; the largest is $f2{\cdot}8$.

The diameter of the aperture is varied by the camera *iris*. This consists of a number of overlapping sections which can move in or out, thus producing a circular hole or aperture of variable size, Fig. 21.9.

3. **Exposure Time.** For best results in using the camera normally, the shutter should open and close very fast so that the film is exposed for a short fixed time. When taking photographs in bright sunlight the brightness of the image will be high, and only a short exposure time, such as $\frac{1}{250}$ s, is needed. If it is a dull day and the same aperture is

used, a longer exposure time, such as $\frac{1}{50}$ s, is needed. Thus the exposure time needed increases as the brightness decreases.

If a photograph is taken of a fast-moving car, a short exposure time, such as $\frac{1}{250}$ s, is needed, otherwise the image will be blurred. A wide aperture is required to collect more light owing to the short exposure time, for example, f2·8.

4. **Rangefinder.** Many cameras have built-in rangefinders. They enable the distance of the object from the lens to be found. The rangefinder is coupled to the lens so that the latter is automatically focused on the object.

5. **Depth of field.** If a point O is focused by the lens, a point image of O will be formed on the film, Fig. 21.9 (i). A point A farther away than

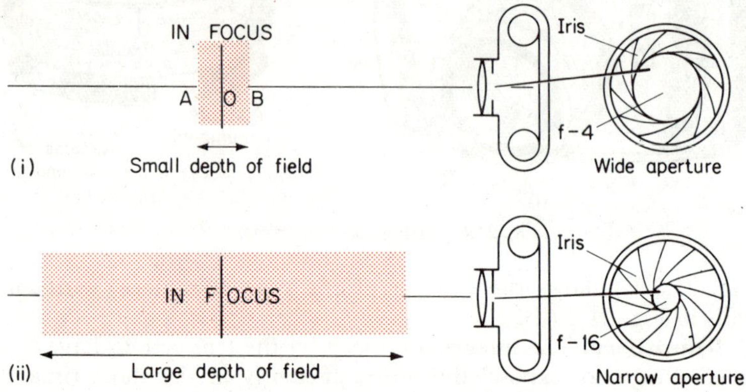

Fig. 21.9 Depth of field and aperture

O will be slightly out of focus and forms a small circular area on the film. So will a point B nearer than O. Now the eye cannot detect any difference between a point and a tiny circular area up to a maximum of about $\frac{1}{100}$ in or $\frac{1}{40}$ cm diameter. Thus if A and B form circular images of this size on the film, objects between A and B appear in focus when the photograph is developed and viewed. This is why a clear photograph can be taken of three rows behind each other of a team of players.

The distance AB in Fig. 21.9 (i) is called the 'depth of field' because objects inside AB are all in focus on the film. A wide aperture produces a small depth of field. A smaller aperture produces a greater depth of field, Fig. 21.9 (ii). The depth of field at various apertures is indicated on the scale adjacent to the focusing ring in Fig. 21.8 (ii).

6. **Film speed.** One of the most important properties of photographic film is its 'speed'. The film speed is a measure of how quickly the film will become correctly exposed when in use, that is how long some of the light-sensitive chemicals on it will take to change suitably (p. 353). A 'fast' film needs a relatively short exposure time for correct

exposure. A 'slow' film needs a much longer exposure time. Fast films are thus used in conditions of poor lighting. Here, the relatively long time needed with a slow film would be inconvenient. Slow films can be used in taking photographs of portraits or still objects, or in very good lighting conditions such as bright sunlight.

Commercially, the speed of a film is measured in units either in the DIN or ASA system. DIN units are continental units and are indicated with a degree (°) sign. For comparison, some values are compared in the table below:

DIN	12°,	15°,	18°,	21°,	24°,	27°
ASA	12,	25,	50,	100,	200,	400,

A speed of 21° DIN corresponds to 100 ASA. High figures are films with high speeds.

7. **Exposure Meter.** A professional photographer measures the brightness of the subject photographed with a separate exposure or light meter. Many cameras for the general use have a built-in light meter. This has a light-sensitive surface, as shown in Fig. 21.8 (i). When the surface is illuminated an electric current flows in the meter whose strength is proportional to the brightness.

8. **Black and White film.** Normal, or black and white, film consists of a thin layer of emulsion consisting of finely divided silver bromide, or other silver halide salt, suspended in gelatine. The composition of the emulsion can be varied to suit different photographic uses, for example, when photographing at night or during the day, and it is coated on to a flexible celluloid base. The silver salt is very sensitive to light, which reduces it to minute particles of metallic silver.

When a film is exposed, the brightest parts of the scene or object photographed affect the film most. The darkest parts affect the film least. Thus an image of the scene or object is 'engraved' on the film.

Developing a Film

The film can be developed with a chemical solution which reduces the parts of the film affected to minute silver particles which are black. Those parts unaffected by the light remain unchanged. The film now carries a *negative* image of the scene photographed. This image can be *fixed* by treating it with another chemical solution. This removes the undeveloped silver halide, so that the film is no longer affected by further exposure to light. A 'positive' image can be obtained by a similar process.

The whole procedure is shown in Fig. 21.10. Practical details of developing a film are shown in Fig. 21.12, p. 355.

Polaroid Camera

The Polaroid camera can produce black and white prints only 10 seconds after the film is exposed.

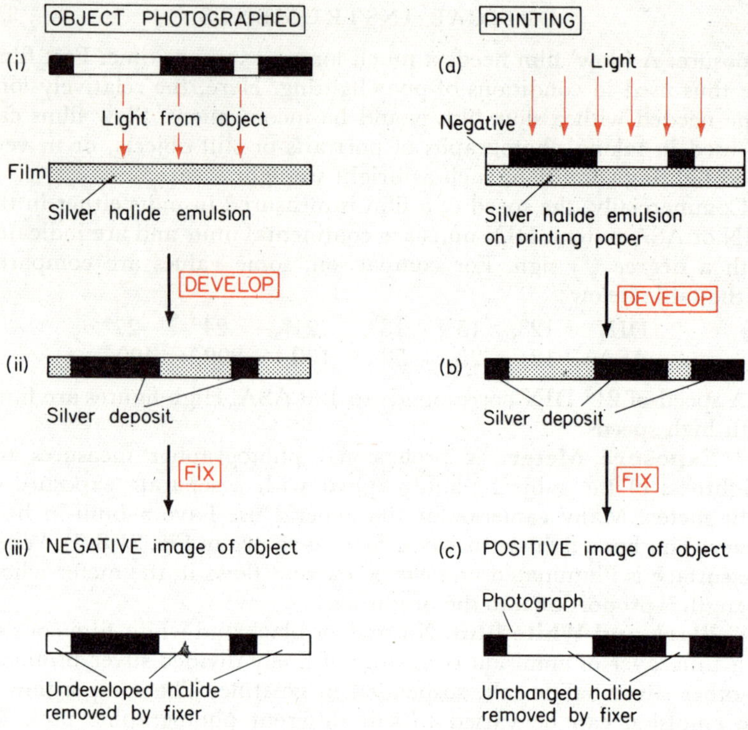

Fig. 21.10 Chemical action on film

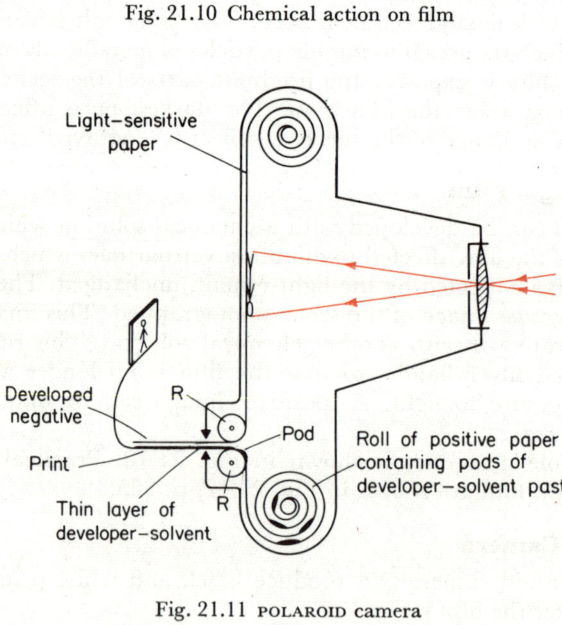

Fig. 21.11 POLAROID camera

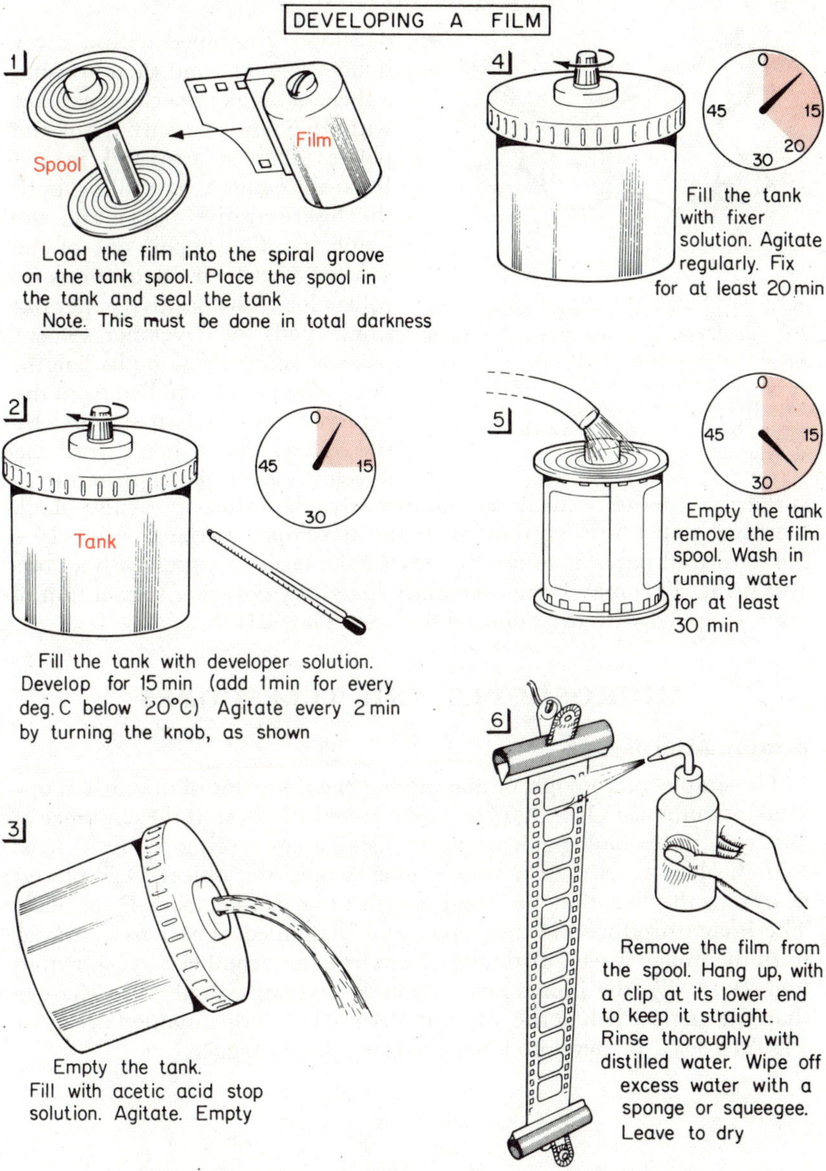

Fig. 21.12 Developing (*times depend on film and chemicals used*)

Fig. 21.11 shows the principle of this type of camera. As in the normal camera, a sharp image is formed by the lens on the surface of a light-sensitive paper by opening the shutter for a brief period. A positive print is obtained by covering the surface of the paper with a layer of

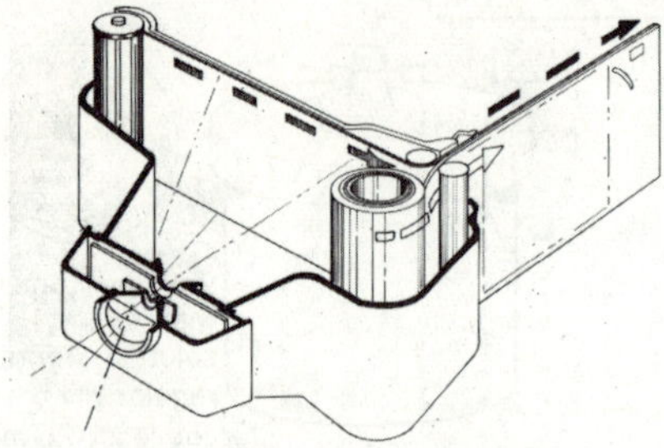

Plate 21(B) *Polaroid* camera action. The left spool contains the film, the right spool contains the developer paste in pods. On pulling the film out of the camera the two rollers shown squeeze a layer of paste over the film, which is then developed.

developer combined with a silver halide 'solvent', and then pressing a sheet of blank paper into contact with the sensitive surface of the paper. This is arranged in the Polaroid camera by pulling both the light-sensitive paper and the blank 'positive paper' out of the camera between two pressure rollers RR. The positive paper has small 'pods' of developer solvent paste at intervals along its length. When the paper is pulled from the camera, the pod is first burst by the rollers, which then spread the developer over the light-sensitive surface in contact with it. Simultaneously, the rollers press the blank 'positive' paper into contact with the developed surface. After 10 s the sensitized paper is removed, leaving the positive paper with a positive print. This may be permanently 'fixed' by covering with a film of fixer, supplied with the Polaroid film. See Plate 21B.

MICROSCOPES AND TELESCOPES

Simple Microscope

The simple microscope, or magnifying glass, was one of the earliest optical instruments. Over 300 years ago, Hooke discovered the existence of the 'cell' in his biological studies by using a converging (convex) lens.

If the lens is used as a simple microscope, the object O is placed nearer to the lens than its focal length or principal focus F (p. 328). The image produced is then erect and magnified. The lens is moved until the image is seen distinctly 25 cm from a normal eye. As shown in Fig. 21.13 (ii), the image now subtends a greater angle $y°$ at the eye than the angle $x°$ when the object is observed with the unaided eye as in Fig. 21.13 (i). It therefore looks correspondingly bigger.

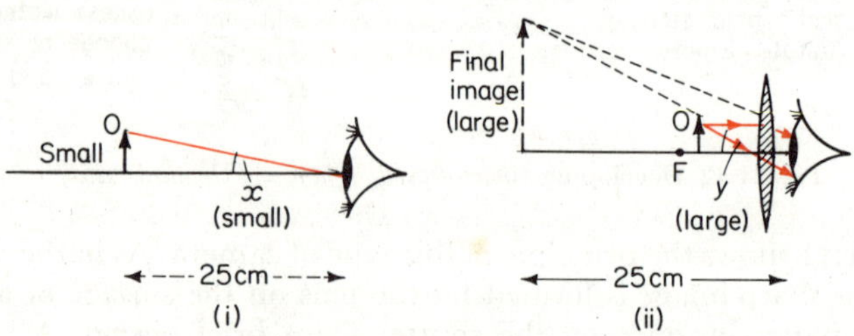

Fig. 21.13 Action of magnifying glass

If a box of convex lenses of different focal lengths is taken, and the lenses in it are held close to the eye and used as magnifying glasses, experiment shows that the greatest magnifying power is obtained from the more 'bulging' lenses, or those which have *short* focal lengths. It is left to the reader to show by drawing that the largest visual angles such as y are obtained in these cases.

Compound Microscope

There is a limit to the angular magnification or magnifying power produced by a single lens, as it is difficult to make lenses of very short focal length. A *compound microscope*, which produces high magnification, is made with two convex lenses. It is used extensively in biological researches and in some researches in physics. Under the microscope, objects as small as bacteria and other carriers of disease have been magnified sufficiently for detailed examination.

Formation of Image

Fig. 21.14 illustrates the basic principle of the compound microscope. It has two converging (convex) lenses. The lens O nearer the object A is called the *objective lens*, and it is positioned so that A is just *farther* from it than F_O, the principal focus. A real, inverted and magnified image I_1 is thus obtained. The lens E through which I_1 is viewed is called the *eyepiece lens*. This is moved until I_1 is nearer to it than its principal focus F_E. The lens then acts as a magnifying glass, and a magnified image of I_1 is hence obtained at I_2. The observer automatically adjusts the eyepiece so that I_2 is at his or her near point, 25 cm from the eye for normal vision, when it is seen most distinctly.

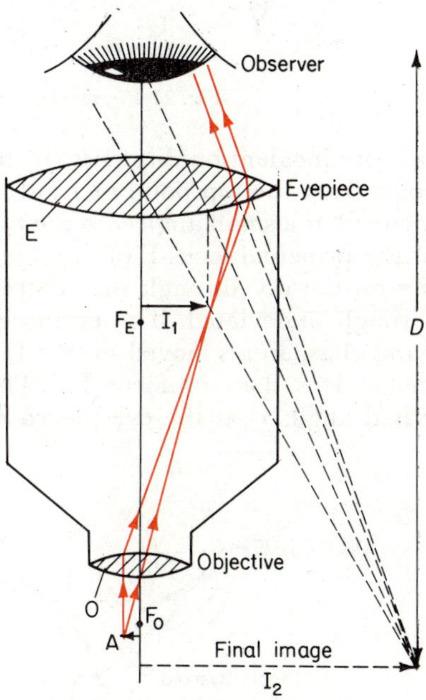

Fig. 21.14 Action of compound microscope

It can be seen from the diagram that the visual angle due to I_2 is much larger than the visual angle obtained if the tiny object A were placed 25 cm from the unaided eye in normal vision. By using convex lenses of short focal length for both O and E, high magnifying power such as $\times 500$ can be obtained. It should be noted that the final image I_2 is inverted compared with the object A. This is no handicap in microscopes. The object A must be strongly illuminated, as it is non-luminous.

Astronomical Telescope

Unlike the microscope, which is used for viewing near objects, the *telescope* is used for viewing distant objects.

A simple astronomical telescope is made by using two converging (convex) lenses of long and short focal length respectively.

The ray diagram of the image formed by an astronomical telescope is shown in Fig. 21.15. The front lens, the objective O, collects light from the distant object. It should be carefully noted: (i) that parallel

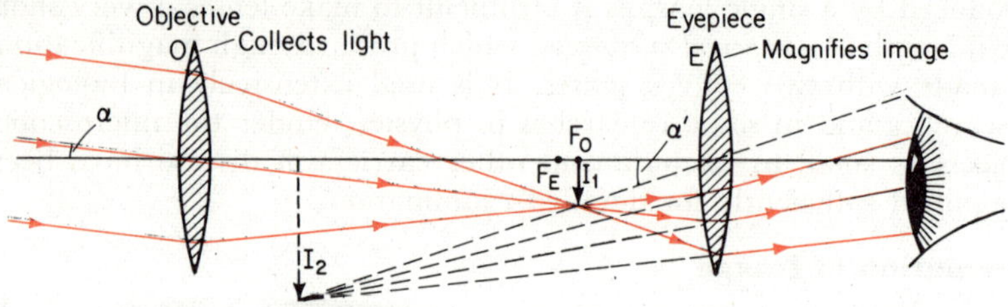

Fig. 21.15 Action of astronomical telescope

rays are incident on this lens; (ii) that the parallel rays are intended to come from the top point or head of the district object, and are hence inclined at a small angle α to the principal axis. The image I_1 is formed at the principal focus F of the objective. To draw I_1, note that its head lies on the ray through the centre of the objective lens, which passes through undeviated. The eyepiece E is once more used as a magnifying glass, and is moved so that I_1 lies inside its focal length, or nearer to the lens than its focus F_E. The final image I_2 subtends a large visual angle α' at the eye placed close to E, so that a large image is

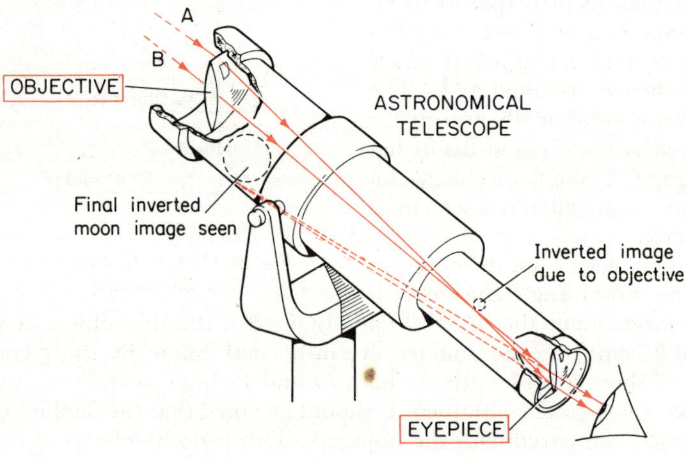

Fig. 21.16 Astronomical telescope

seen. High magnifying power occurs when the objective has a long focal length and the eyepiece a short focal length, as the reader can verify by drawing.

Fig. 21.16 illustrates the inverted final image of the moon viewed through an astronomical telescope. Half of the lenses are shown.

Prism Binoculars

Prism binoculars are short telescopes consisting of a converging (convex) objective and a converging (convex) eyepiece, together with two total reflecting prisms of 90°, 45°, 45°. The edges P, Q of the prisms are perpendicular to each other, and light which passes through the objective is reflected in turn from one prism to the other and then emerges through the eyepiece. This is shown in Fig. 21.17. In the

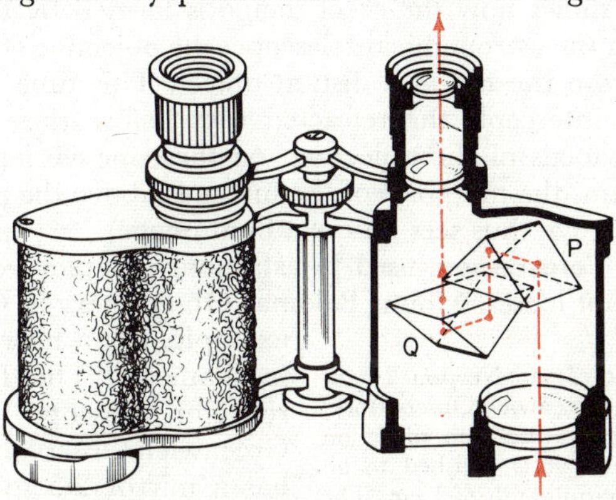

Fig. 21.17 Prism binoculars

absence of the prisms the image would be upside down and laterally inverted. One prism turns the image round and corrects for lateral inversion; the second prism inverts the image the right way up. Thus the final image is seen erect and magnified.

Galilean Telescope

In the astronomical telescope, described on p. 358, the image is inverted. The earliest telescope, however, produced erect images. In 1609 Galileo heard reports that a Dutchman had invented an optical device for bringing distant objects closer, and he set out to discover how this could be achieved. He soon found that objects could be brought over thirty times closer through a combination of a *diverging* or *concave* eyepiece and a *converging* or *convex* objective. He turned the new instrument to the heavens, and so discovered the mountains and craters of the moon and the satellites of Jupiter. The *Galilean telescope*, as it is known, is used today in opera glasses.

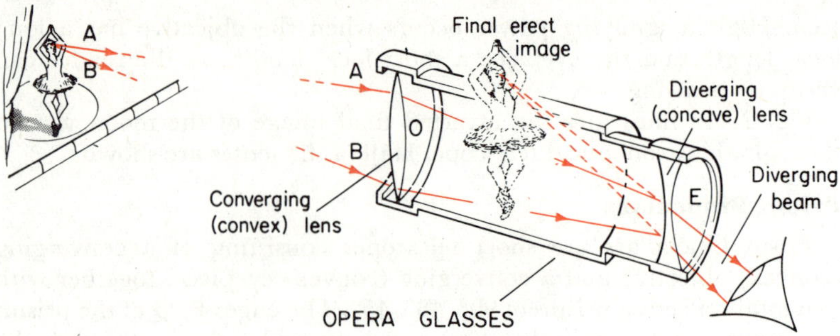

Fig. 21.18 Opera glasses

Fig. 21.18 shows how the erect image is formed by the two lenses O, E. As with the astronomical telescope, the objective collects parallel rays, A, B, from the top of a distant object. This time, however, the concave lens intercepts the refracted rays before they can form an image at the focus of the objective. As the concave lens produces a diverging beam, the top point of the image is above the principal axis, as shown. The eye thus sees an erect final image.

Reflector Telescopes, used in astronomy, employ very large concave *mirrors*, not lenses. Mount Palomar Observatory in California, for example, has a mirror about 5 m in diameter. The Isaac Newton reflector telescope for the Royal Greenwich Observatory, England, has a mirror 2·5 m in diameter. Plate 21c.

Plate 21(c) Manufacture of Isaac Newton 2·5 m reflector telescope for Royal Greenwich Observatory, England. Lowering the Pyrex disc into place on the polishing machine, where it is polished to an accuracy of the order of one-millionth of 1 cm. The concave front surface has a depth of 5 cm and a reflecting coating of aluminium.

The mirror is made large in order to collect as much light as possible from the stars and planets to be observed. The absence of lenses eliminates colour and other defects of images due to the use of lenses. The glass of a lens also reflects and absorbs light. Plate 21D shows a **radio-telescope.**

Projection Lantern

The projection lantern is used for showing audiences large images of slides or other objects on a white screen. The essential features are:

(1) a very powerful small source of light S;

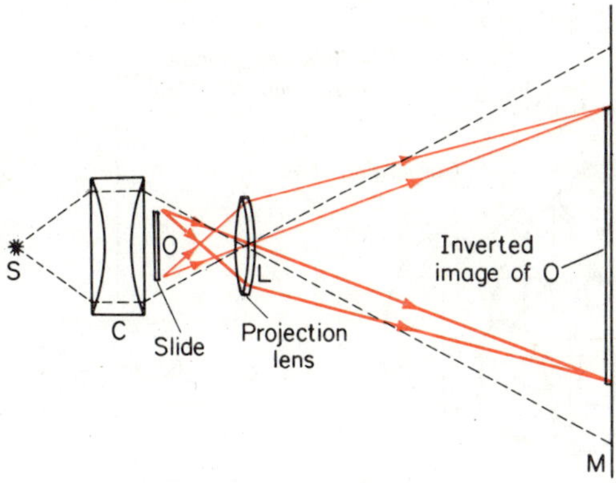

Fig. 21.19 Projection lantern

(2) a condenser C of two convex lenses—this collects the light and beams it towards the slide O, which is therefore strongly illuminated;

(3) a projection lens L near the slide, which produces an enlarged inverted image of O on a distant screen M, Fig. 21.19.

Without the condensing lenses C, the slide would be weakly illuminated. The condenser collects light and sends it through O. A strong source of light is essential as O is non-luminous. The lens L is slightly farther from O than its focal length, so that an enlarged image is obtained on the screen M. The image is inverted. Consequently the slide must be inserted upside down into the projector to see a picture on the screen the right way up. Note that the image of the lamp filament S is produced at L itself, and so the projection lens does not produce an image of the filament on the screen, which would spoil the picture.

Plate 21(D) Jodrell Bank radio-telescope. The large parabolic reflector focuses weak radio signals from distant sources on to the central sensitive receiver which passes the signal to equipment for automatic recording. This telescope received the first television pictures of the moon's surface.

Epidiascope

The *epidiascope*, a convenient form of projector, consists essentially of a light-proof container B, with arrangements for inserting at the back, A, a picture or diagram

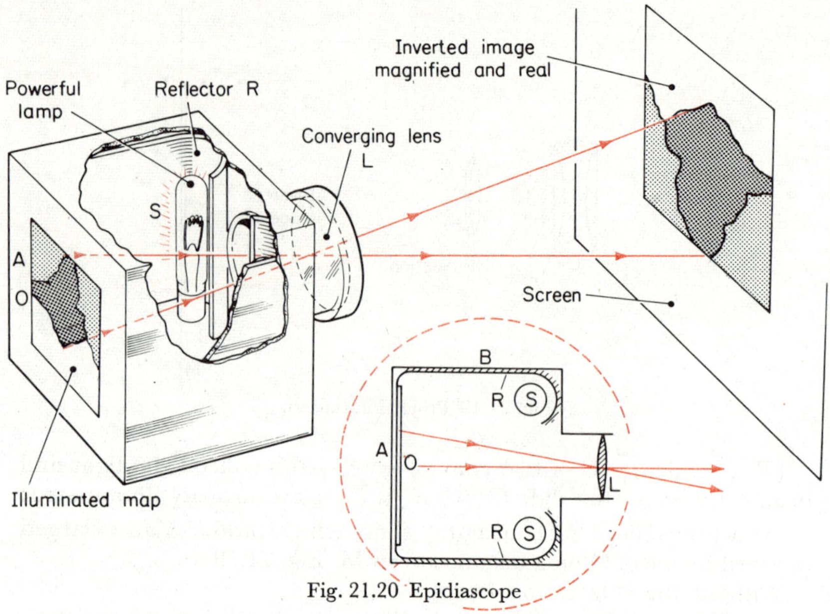

Fig. 21.20 Epidiascope

O to be projected on a screen, Fig. 21.20. The object O is illuminated by light from two or more powerful lamps S with the aid of specially-shaped reflectors R. The position of the converging (convex) lens L may be adjusted to bring the image in focus.

SUMMARY

1. The eye has an eye-lens, a pupil to allow light to enter, and a retina or light-sensitive screen. Ciliary muscles alter the focal length of the lens and thus enables the eye to see objects clearly at different distances.

2. Short sight—one cannot see clearly a long way. Correction by a suitable diverging lens. Long sight—one can see clearly near objects at a distance farther than 25 cm (or 10 in). Correction by a suitable converging lens.

3. Compound microscope has an objective and eyepiece of two short converging (convex) lenses.

4. Telescopes:

(i) *Astronomical*. Objective is converging lens of long focal length and eyepiece is converging lens of short focal length.

(ii) *Galilean*. Eyepiece is diverging (concave) lens of short focal length and unlike astronomical telescope, produces an erect final image.

(iii) *Reflecting*. Has a very large curved mirror to collect light.

5. Projection lantern has powerful source of light, a condenser to collect light and illuminate slide, and projection lens. Slide slightly farther than *f*, thus producing large inverted image on screen.

6. Lens camera. Brightness of image obtained depends on: (i) *f*-number;

(ii) exposure time; (iii) speed of film. Developing, stop and fixing solutions are needed to develop a film.

7. Polaroid camera develops prints quickly by means of 'pods' of developing solvent paste. These burst when light-sensitive and 'positive' papers are pulled from the camera, and develop the image.

PRACTICAL

1. Compound microscope (p. 357)

Apparatus. Two converging (convex) lenses of short focal length; illuminated object; semi-transparent screen; supporting lens stands.

Method. (i) Place an illuminated object such as a perspex ruler or crosswires in front of the lens of smaller focal length, Fig. 21·21. Obtain a clear inverted large image on the semi-transparent screen.

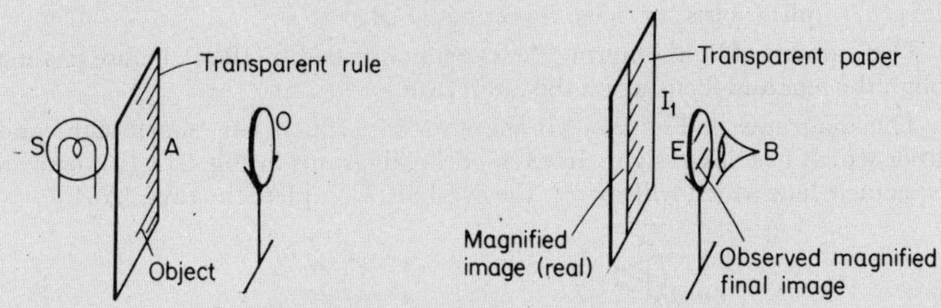

Fig. 21.21 Forming compound microscope

(ii) View this image through the second converging lens or eyepiece close to the eye and move it until a magnified image is seen.

(iii) Remove the screen, Look through both lenses at a book or print or graduations on a ruler. Adjust the eyepiece to obtain the clearest image.

Repeat with other lenses and compare the magnifications obtained.

2. Astronomical telescope (p. 358)

Apparatus. Converging (convex) lens of long focal length and converging lens of short focal length; semi-transparent screen; supporting lens stands.

Method. (i) Set up the lens of long focal length at the back of the room. Obtain an inverted image of the window, or objects outside, on the screen.

(ii) Keeping the eye close to the second lens of short focal length, move this lens towards the image. At one stage, the image comes magnified.

(iii) Remove the screen and observe distant objects through both lenses. Adjust the eyepiece to obtain the clearest image.

Repeat with lenses of other focal length. What focal lengths would you use for an objective and eyepiece to obtain a telescope with a high magnifying power?

3. Galilean telescope (p. 359)

Apparatus. As in **2**, but a diverging (concave) lens of short focal length in place of the converging lens of short focal length.

Method. (i) As in **2**, set up the converging lens in front of the window and obtain an inverted image of the window or distant object on the screen.

(ii) Place the diverging lens or eyepiece a short distance in front of the screen, between the screen and the objective, and then remove the screen.

(iii) Keeping the eye close to the diverging lens, observe distant objects through both lenses. How does the image seen differ from that seen through the astronomical telescope? Adjust the eyepiece to obtain the clearest image.

EXERCISE 21 · ANSWERS, p. 403

1. In the normal human eye the light rays are brought to a focus on the . . (*M.*)

2. Underline the *best* answer to the following. A human eye is very like a good camera in action, *except* for: (*a*) giving an inverted image on the screen; (*b*) having a lens which changes its thickness; (*c*) having an iris to adjust the amount of light entering it; (*d*) being able to focus on objects both near and far away; (*e*) being dark inside. (*W.Md.*)

3. The part of the eye which compares with the aperture of a camera is: (*a*) eyelid; (*b*) pupil; (*c*) iris; (*d*) lens; (*e*) retina. (*E.A.*)

4. The amount of light entering the eye is controlled by the . . before passing through the lens and focusing on the . . (*W.Md.*)

5. The diagrams in Fig. 21A (i) show an eye which has 'short' sight and another which has 'long' sight. In each of the diagrams in Fig. 21A (ii) draw in the spectacle lens which will correct the eyesight. Complete the rays. (*E.A.*)

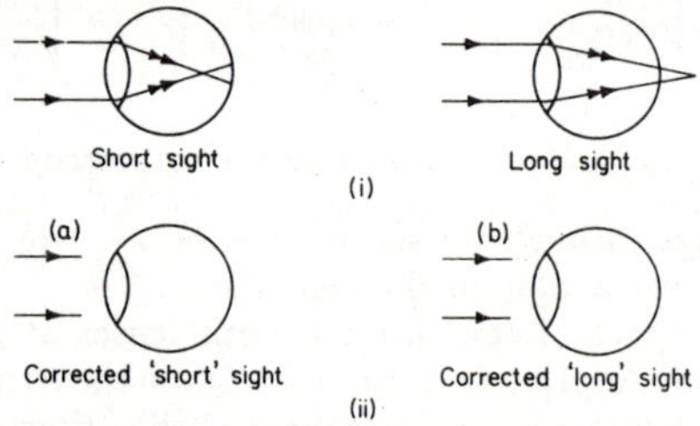

Fig. 21A

6. If a person is short-sighted: (*a*) what type of lenses would he have in his spectacles; (*b*) would he need spectacles to help him see far or near objects? (*L.*)

7. Fig. 21B represents a human eye receiving in turn light from a distant source, from a point 35 cm from the eye and from a point 25 cm from the eye. Explain what is wrong with this person's vision; what type of lenses would be required in spectacles to correct his defect of vision; and when the person would use these spectacles. (*M.*)

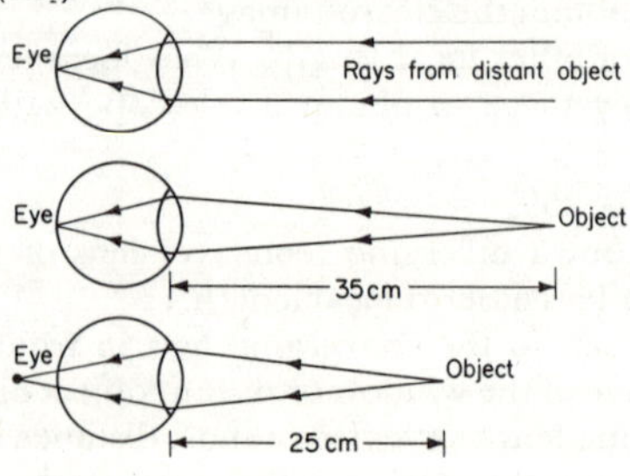

Fig. 21B

8. A certain camera is made so that *three* adjustments can be made. The *shutter setting ring* is marked 1/30th and 1/60th; the *aperture control* is marked *f*8, *f*11 and *f*16; and the *focusing ring* is marked from 1 m up to infinity. Explain briefly but clearly what purpose is served by each of these three adjustments. (*M.*)

9. Fig. 21c represents the essential parts in one half of a pair of prismatic binoculars. Explain clearly and fully the purpose of each of the four parts labelled in the diagram. (*M.*)

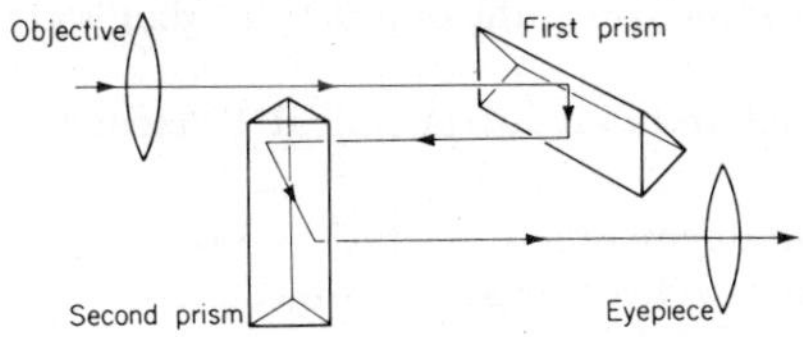

Fig. 21c

10. 'The eye is a camera.' Give reasons why you would agree or disagree with this statement. Describe how the eye can be corrected for the following faults: (i) short-sight; (ii) long-sight. (*Mx.*)

11. (*a*) Draw labelled ray-diagrams to show: (i) the formation of umbra and penumbra when a small ball is hung between a screen and a large globe of light; (ii) the formation of the image of a distant tree on the screen of a pinhole camera; (iii) the formation of a large real image of a slide on a screen by a projector. (Omit the light source, but be sure to label the slide, the projection lens and its focal points, and the screen.)

(*b*) A ship 60 m long is 300 m away from the front of a pinhole camera. The camera measures 25 cm from pinhole to screen. Calculate the length of the image of the ship on the screen. (*Mx.*)

12. (*a*) With the aid of diagrams, explain what is wrong with the eyes of a person suffering from: (i) short sight, (ii) long sight. Describe how the faults can be corrected.

(*b*) A convex lens, of focal length 20 cm, is set up vertically in a room, so that an image of the window can be focused on a screen. The distance from the lens to the window is 60 cm, and a sharp image is formed when the screen is properly positioned.

Make a scale drawing which will enable you to find the position and size of the image if the window is 90 cm tall. State your results. *Horizontal scale*: 1 cm = 5 cm; *Vertical scale*: 1 cm = 30 cm. (*Mx.*)

13. Give two reasons why large telescopes are of the reflecting rather than the refracting type. (*L.*)

14. Any good modern camera has the following features in addition to a lens: (*a*) a variable speed shutter; (*b*) a variable aperture (or stop); (*c*) a focusing adjustment. What is the purpose of each of these three devices.

The lens of a camera has a focal length of 5 cm. The camera is used to take a photograph of a flower which is placed 30 cm in front of the lens. Use a construction to find the correct distance from the lens to the film. (*S.*)

15. (*a*) 'Light travels more slowly in glass than in air.' Using this information, explain why a beam of light is refracted when entering glass obliquely from the air.

(*b*) Draw ray-diagrams to show the effect of placing: (i) a convex mirror; (ii) a concave lens; across the path of a parallel beam of light. In each case label the principal focus and say whether it is real or virtual.

(*c*) (i) If you were given two convex lenses, one of long focal length and one of short focal length, how would you arrange them to form a telescope?; (ii) give a ray-diagram to show the formation of the image of a distant object by this telescope. (*Mx.*)

16. (*a*) Where must the object be placed in front of a convex lens to obtain an image; (i) that is the same size as the object?; (ii) that is at infinity?; (iii) that is virtual?

(*b*) Describe the action of an Astronomical Telescope in normal adjustment (*W.Md.*)

17. A projector produces a picture which is 60 cm high when the projector is 1·8 m from the screen. Where must the projector be placed to produce a picture which is 90 cm high? How must the position of the projection lens be adjusted to refocus the picture in this new position? Explain briefly why this is necessary. (*S.E.*)

18. (*a*) Draw a large, clearly labelled diagram of the human eye.

(*b*) With the aid of ray-diagrams, explain what is meant by: (i) long sight; (ii) short sight.

(*c*) Give a ray-diagram to show how *short* sight can be corrected by means of a lens. Explain how the lens achieves this correction. (*Mx.*)

19. (i) Give *one* advantage of reflecting telescopes over refracting telescopes.

(ii) Some reflecting telescopes are radio telescopes. How do these instruments differ from optical reflecting telescopes?

(iii) What advantages do radio telescopes have over optical telescopes?

(iv) Why are radio telescopes so large? (*W.Md.*)

20. Fig. 21D is a simple representation of a camera.

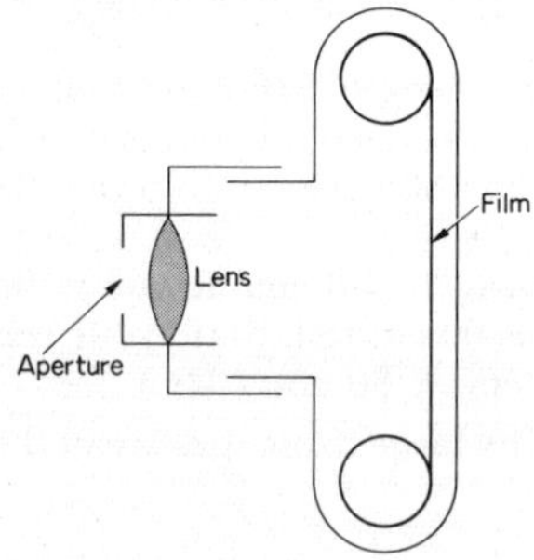

Fig. 21D

(*a*) Explain how the brightness of the light falling on the film depends on (i) the size of the aperture; (ii) the distance of the film from the lens.

(*b*) Explain why it is necessary to change both the shutter speed and the size of the aperture before taking a picture of a moving object.

(*c*) How would the focusing of a near and then a distant object be achieved using this camera? (*M.*)

22

PRINCIPLES OF SOUND AND INSTRUMENTS

Sounding Objects

IF you place your fingers lightly on a bicycle bell immediately after it is rung, you will experience a tingling sensation, Fig. 22.1. You will have detected that the bell is *vibrating* while it sends out a ringing sound,

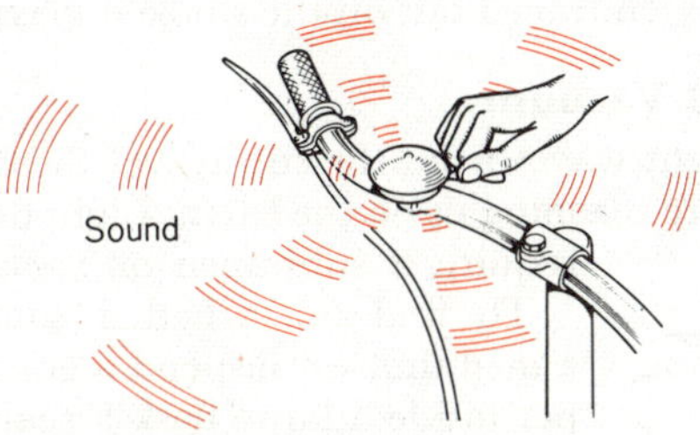

Fig. 22.1 Vibrating bell produces sound waves

that is, it is moving to and fro rapidly. All sounds, whether due to your friend speaking or singing, or a piano, guitar or violin playing, or your loudspeaker working on a radio or television set, are due to vibrating objects. In the case of your friend, this is his or her vocal chords; in the case of the piano, guitar and violin, this is the strings concerned; in the case of the loudspeaker, this is a paper cone.

It is difficult to see the vibrations of a sounding object. But we can obtain evidence of them by the following experiments:

1. *Energy of vibrating tuning-fork*. A tuning-fork is used by musicians who require a 'pure' note. Strike a tuning-fork F on a pad. Listen to the note produced. Then hold one prong near to a piece of cork, or other light material, so that it *just* touches, Fig. 22.2 (i). The cork flies off. This shows that the prong is vibrating with considerable energy while sounding.

2. *Vibrations of tuning-fork*. Attach a small bristle B firmly to one prong of a tuning-fork F with Sellotape so that it projects beyond the prong, Fig. 22.2 (ii). Fix the fork in a clamp. Suspend a smoked glass plate G vertically by thread, and arrange the bristle so that it presses lightly against the plate and vibrates horizontally when the prongs are made

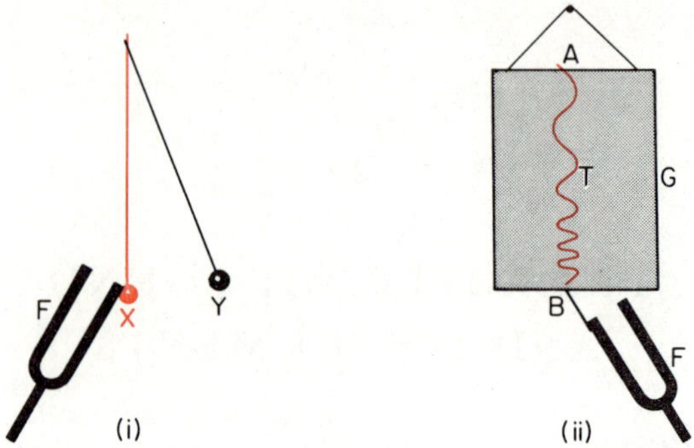

Fig. 22.2 Vibrations of tuning fork

to vibrate. Burn the thread. The plate falls past the vibrating prong. A vibration can be seen traced out on the smoked glass, as shown.

Sound Waves and Vacuum

We know that light waves from the sun travel through vast regions of empty space before reaching us on the earth. Light does not therefore require a substance or *medium* to travel in.

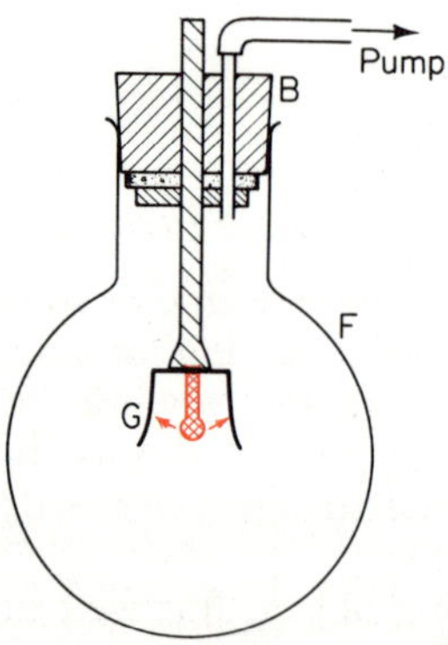

Fig. 22.3 Sound requires a medium

To find out whether sound waves need a medium, we suspend a gong G with a clapper inside a large flask F sealed at the top by a tight-fitting bung B, Fig. 22.3. The air inside the flask can be pumped out by connecting a vacuum pump to a tube passing through B. When the flask is shaken, the gong can be heard ringing. The pump is then started. The sound gradually dies down and soon cannot be heard—a good vacuum is now present round the bell. Although the clapper of the bell can be seen hitting the gong, practically no sound is heard. Thus although light waves can travel through the vacuum, *sound waves cannot pass through a vacuum.*

Sound Media

This demonstration shows that a medium or substance is necessary to carry sound waves. *Air* is the medium when people talk to each other directly, or when listening to sound from a radio receiver or tape-recorder. Years ago, Red Indians listened for horse-riders by placing their ear close to the ground—the sound from the hooves travelled through the *earth.* You can hear sound which travels through *wood* by placing your ear on top of a table and gently scratching the table underneath some distance away. In measuring ocean depths, instruments send out a form of sound waves which travel through the *water* to the bottom and are reflected back. See Fig. 22.5. Sound waves, then travel through gases, liquids and solids.

Speed of Sound · Echoes

If you have watched a football kicked in the distance, or a cricket bat striking a ball, you will have noticed that the sound is heard a fraction of a second after the ball has left the foot or bat. Sound thus

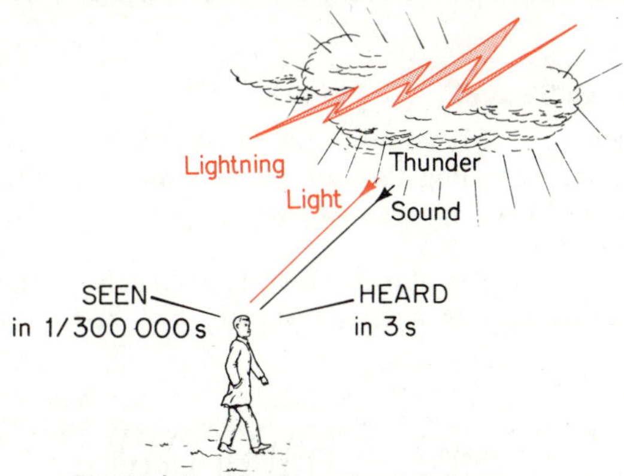

Fig. 22.4 Speeds of sound and light

takes a longer time to reach you than light. The speed of sound in air at normal temperatures is about 1200 kilometres per hour, which is about 340 metres per second, or $\frac{1}{3}$ km per second. The speed of light in air is the enormous one of about 300 000 kilometres per second. Thus whereas sound would take about 3 seconds to travel 1 km, light would take about $\frac{1}{300\,000}$ second, which is negligible compared to 3 seconds. This also explains why the thunder from a storm centre is heard after the lightning takes place. If you wish to make a rough estimate of the distance of the storm centre, count the number of seconds between seeing the lightning and hearing the thunder, Fig. 22.4. Each second interval corresponds to a distance of about $\frac{1}{5}$ mile or $\frac{1}{3}$ km.

Echoes are due to sound heard again a fraction of a second later by reflection from walls for example.

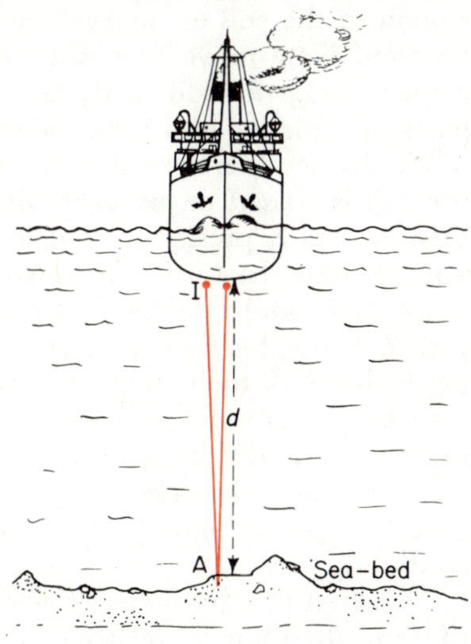

Fig. 22.5 Echo-sounding

Echoes are used in underwater exploration for gas and oil. Plate 22A. They are also used to map the depths of the sea-bed. Plate 22B.

In water, sound travels at a speed of about 1450 metres per second or 5200 kilometres per hour. Thus if sound waves travelled from a ship to the bottom of the ocean and back in $\frac{1}{2}$-s, the total distance travelled would be 725 m, Fig. 22.5. The bottom of the ocean would hence be about 360 m down. The speed of sound in oak is about 4 km/s and in iron about 5 km/s.

How Waves Travel

As stated on p. 367, sound is due to vibrating objects. We cannot see the vibrations travelling through air as a medium. But if a long loose coil called a 'Slinky' coil is used, we can see how a disturbance passes along the metal turns.

Spread the coil AB along a very long bench or along the floor, so that the turns occupy a long distance, Fig. 22.6. Attach a piece of

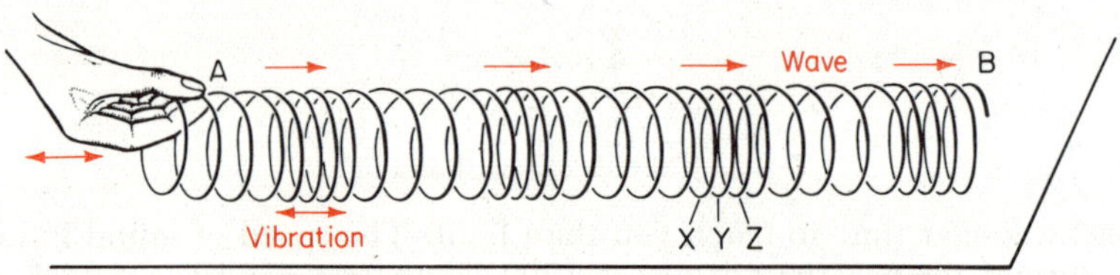

Fig. 22.6 Compression and rarefaction in wave

ribbon to the coil at intervals so that any disturbance of the coil can be seen. Now move end A to and fro. Observe that: (1) the wave ripples along the coil to B; (2) the ribbons move to and fro at their particular places, and their movement is out of step.

We deduce therefore that the disturbance or wave travelling along the coil is passed on by each vibrating turn of the coil. A particular turn such as X presses on or disturbs a neighbouring turn such as Y at some instant. In turn, Y disturbs the neighbouring turn Z. When X moves back and relieves the pressure on Y, then Y moves back. Likewise Z moves back. This is the way the wave or energy of movement passes from A to B along the coil. On the average, each vibrating turn keeps the same position while the wave travels. You should distinguish carefully between the vibrations producing the wave (these have the same average positions at particular places) and the wave itself (this is the energy of the disturbance which travels along the medium).

This kind of wave, where the vibrations of the turns of the coil are in the same direction as the wave, is called a *longitudinal wave*. When a wave spreads horizontally on water, however, the vibrations of the water

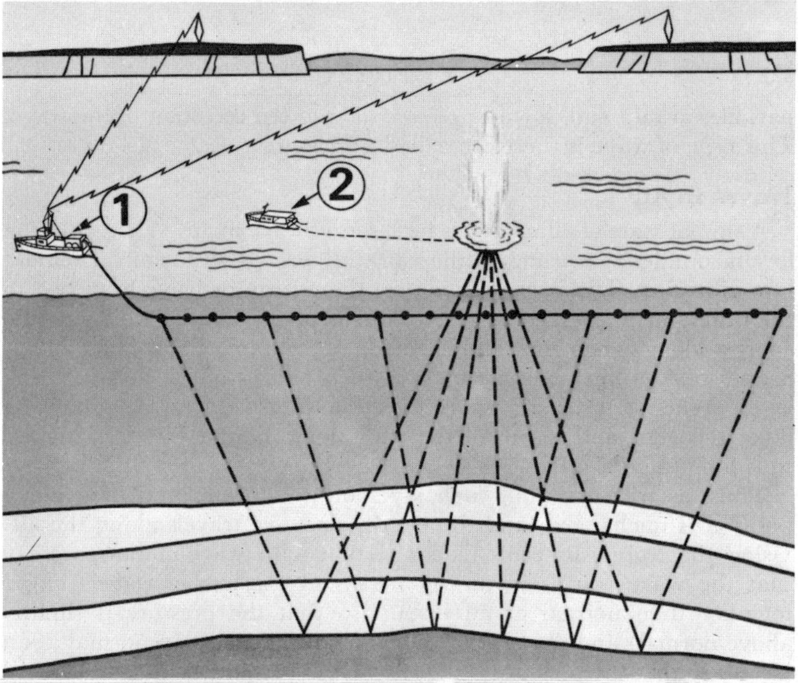

Plate 22(A) Underwater oil and gas exploration. Shock waves, produced by an explosion due to boat 2, are reflected by the various layers of rock and are detected by microphones trailed behind boat 1.

Plate 22(B) Profile of the sea-bed by echo-sounder.

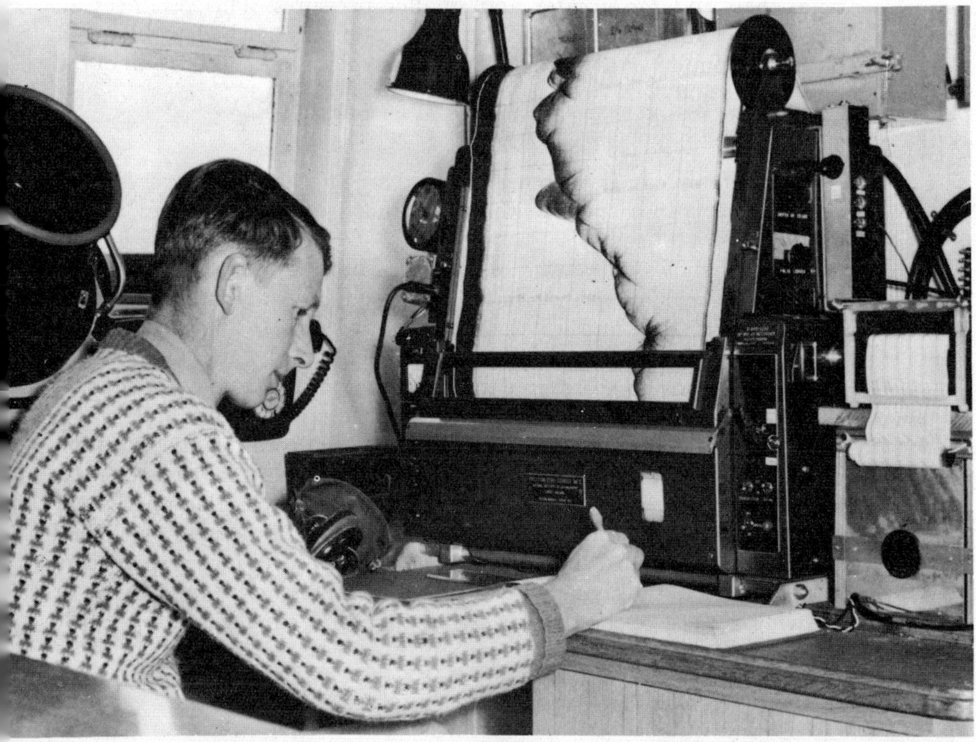

particles are up and down or *perpendicular* to the direction of the wave. This type of wave is therefore called a *transverse wave.*

Waves in Air

A similar state of affairs exists for a sound wave in air. When a tuning fork is sounded, for example, the vibrating prongs set the air in contact into vibration. The layers of air pass the energy or wave from one to the other, in the same way as the turns of the 'Slinky' coil pass the energy along when one end is made to vibrate. Each layer of air presses on the next layer, which in turn presses on its neighbouring layer. When a layer of air recovers in pressure, the neighbouring layer recovers, and so on all the way along. Sound waves in air are thus longitudinal waves.

Thus, as with the coil, each layer of air vibrates and its average position is unchanged, and the energy or wave travels along the air. Using the technical terms in connection with wave-motion, we say that the wave travels in air by means of *compressions* (layers closer together than normal at an instant so that the pressure is slightly above normal) and *rarefactions* (layers further apart than normal at an instant so that the pressure is slightly below normal). This is illustrated in Fig. 22.6. The air at the ear-drums undergoes these changes of pressure when a sound wave arrives, and this produces vibrations of the eardrum and hence the sound we hear. A similar effect takes place when we speak into the microphone inside a telephone. Carbon particles then undergo greater and smaller pressures. This produces an electric current 'wave' along the telephone wires, which is changed back into sound waves by the telephone earpiece at the other end of the line (see p. 508).

The Ear

The human ear is extremely sensitive. It can detect very small pressure variations such as those produced by sound waves in the air.

Fig. 22.7 shows a diagram of the ear. Mainly it has three parts:

(i) *Outer ear*. This consists of the exterior lobe A and a short tube T which directs the sound waves on to the eardrum D. The eardrum is a small membrane sealing the end of T. When sound waves are incident on D, it is made to vibrate at the frequency of the note concerned.

(ii) *Middle ear*. This is the air-filled space on the other side of the eardrum. Three small bones act as a bridge and transmit the vibration of the eardrum through the middle ear. They are called respectively the *hammer*, the *anvil* and the *stirrup* from their shape. The middle ear is connected to the atmosphere through passages in the nose by a small canal or tube E called the *Eustacian tube*. This ensures that the eardrum is not affected by changes in atmospheric pressure. Swallowing, or chewing sweets, opens the Eustacian tube and equalizes the pressure

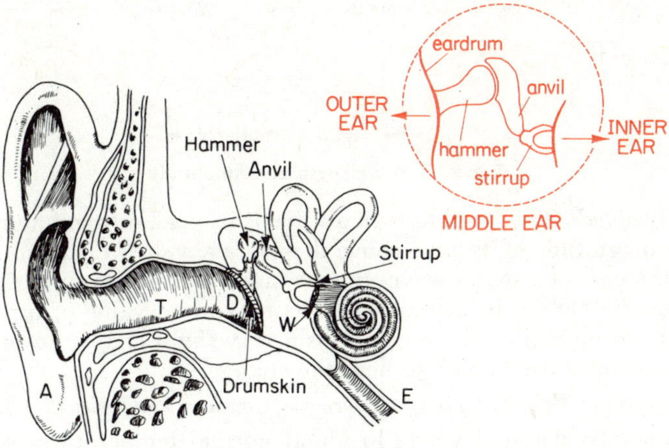

Fig. 22.7 The ear

on both sides of the eardrum. This relieves painful pressure on the eardrum in climbing and descending aeroplanes.

(iii) *Inner ear*. The stirrup presses on a membrane called the *oval window* W, which transmits the vibration to the inner ear. This compartment contains a spiral canal called the *cochlea* filled with fluid. The cochlea communicates to the brain by sensitive nerves, which produce the sensation of sound.

Frequency, Wavelength, Amplitude

Boys and girls may be classified by their height and weight and colour of hair for example. Waves are classified by the following:

1. *Frequency*. The frequency of a wave is the number of complete vibrations or *cycles per second*. (A 'cycle' is a complete to and fro movement of a layer for the case of a sound wave in air, so that at the end of a cycle the layer begins its movement all over again). 1 cycle per second (c/s) is called 1 hertz (Hz), after the discoverer of radio waves. Frequencies range from relatively low ones of sound waves such as 100 Hz to enormously high ones of light waves and X-rays such as 500 million million (5×10^{14}) Hz or higher (p. 273). The lowest frequency which can be heard is about 20 Hz and the highest about 20 000 Hz but the actual value depends on the observer. Cats can hear higher notes than human beings can hear.

2. *Wavelength*. The wavelength of a wave is the distance between successive peaks or crests of the wave, Fig. 22.8.

The waves which spread out from a stone dropped into water may have a wavelength of several centimetres. Sound waves may have a relatively long wavelength such as 100 cm of 1 m. Light waves have a relatively very short wavelength such as $\frac{1}{16\,000}$ cm.

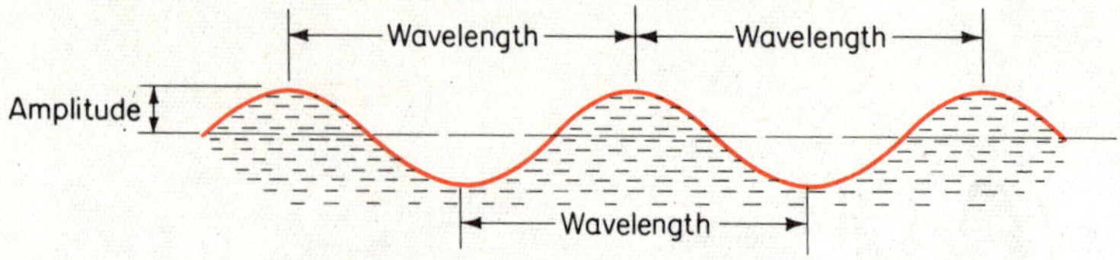

Fig. 22.8 Wavelength and amplitude

3. *Amplitude.* The amplitude of a wave is its peak or maximum value or the magnitude of its crest above the average value, Fig. 22.8.

In the case of a sound wave, the average value of pressure in the air may be 76·000 cm in mercury and its maximum value or amplitude 76·001 cm mercury. Although this is a very slight change in pressure, the ear is sensitive enough to hear the change.

Generally: *Velocity (speed) of wave = frequency × wavelength* (p. 266). The velocity of sound waves in air at normal temperatures is about 340 m/s. A sound wave with a frequency of 1000 Hz thus has a wavelength of 0·34 m or 34 cm; a sound wave with a frequency ten times lower at 100 Hz has a wavelength ten times higher, or 340 cm.

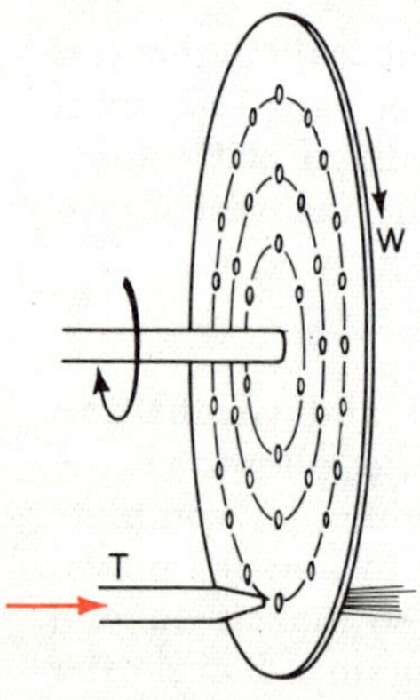

Fig. 22.9 Pitch varies with frequency

Sound Characteristics · Pitch

The sounds of encouragement from boys or girls at sporting events can be distinguished from those of older spectators by their relatively high pitched voices.

Pitch depends on frequency. This can be investigated by using a metal circular plate W with different numbers of holes equally spaced round its axle, which is a form of siren, Fig. 22.9. When W is turned fast by a motor, air from a tube T 'puffs' through the holes and a note is heard. Although the air may be blown harder, the pitch remains the same. As the wheel is turned faster and the frequency of the puffs or note increases, the pitch is heard to increase.

From these experiments, it follows that the pitch of a note depends only on its frequency. A note of high pitch such as that from a baby crying, has a high frequency—a whistle may have a frequency of about 1000 Hz. A note of low pitch such as that from a gruff voice has a low frequency—a low hum may have a frequency of about 100 Hz, Fig. 22.10. Dogs and cats are capable of hearing notes beyond the upper limit of a human being, which is about 20 000 Hz.

Observe the different number of waves per second produced by tuning forks, whistles or speech, using a microphone joined to a cathode-ray oscilloscope (C.R.O.), Fig. 22.10.

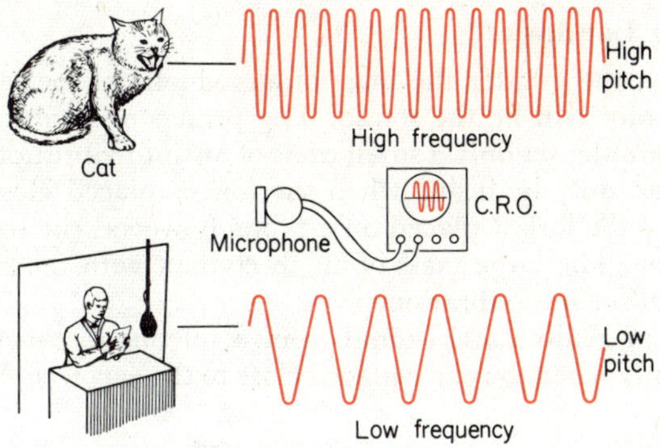

Fig. 22.10 Pitch depends on frequency

Loudness and Intensity

If the volume control of a radio receiver is accidentally turned up so that the sound suddenly becomes very loud, light articles on or near it begin to 'jump'. The *energy* from the receiver is much more than before, and this disturbs the air layers more. We say that the *intensity* of the

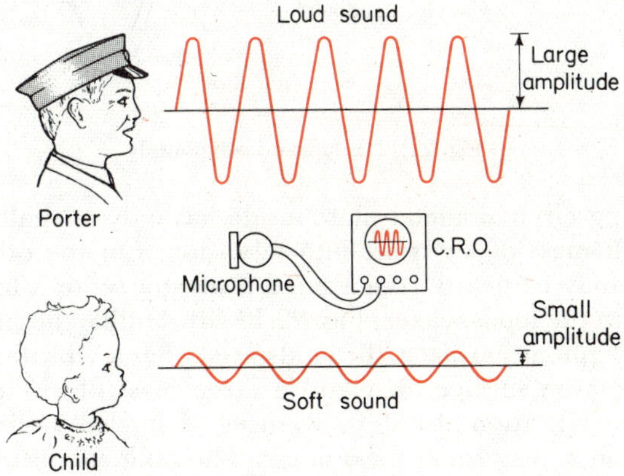

Fig. 22.11 Loudness depends on amplitude

sound has increased. 'Loudness' increases as the sound intensity increases, or when the amplitude of the wave increases. A porter and a child may both shout the same note, that is, the frequency may be the same. But as illustrated in Fig. 22.11, the amplitude of the sound wave from the shouting porter is larger.

Observe the different amplitudes produced by a soft and loud whistle in front of a microphone joined to a cathode ray oscilloscope, Fig. 22.11.

Increasing Loudness

Generally, the greater the mass of air which can be set into vibration the louder will be the sound. The prongs of a vibrating tuning-fork, for example, set only a small mass of air into vibration. The sound is soft; it can only be heard when the fork is placed close to the ear. If the end of the fork is placed on a table, however, the sound is heard much louder. The large mass of air in contact with the surface of the table is then set into vibration.

For similar reasons, the sound from a telephone earpiece is heard distinctly only when the ear is placed close to the earpiece, Fig. 22.12 (i).

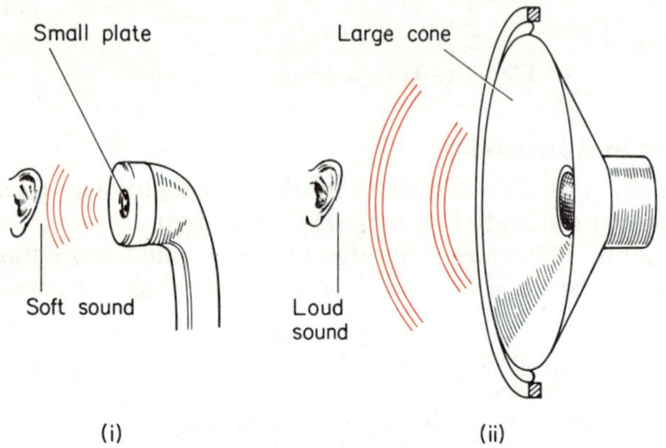

Fig. 22.12 Loud and soft sounds

The vibrating circular metal plate inside has only a small area. Thus only a small mass of air is set into vibration. On the other hand, a loud sound may be heard from a small transistor set or a television set. This is due to the loudspeaker, Fig. 22.12 (ii). Unlike the small circular plate in a telephone earpiece, the loudspeaker has a vibrating cone with a relatively large surface area and a large mass of air in contact is thus set into vibration (p. 399). By itself, a bowed violin string sets into vibration a very small mass of air. The hollow box to which it is attached has a comparatively large surface area and sets into vibration a large mass of air.

Quality or Tone (Timbre)

If the same note is sounded on a piano, an organ or a violin the source of the sound can immediately be recognized by ear. In technical language, we say that the 'quality' or 'tone' (*timbre*) of the note is different when it is sounded on different instruments.

In practice, it is very difficult to get a pure note, or one which contains only one frequency. The note from a tuning fork is a near approach to a pure note. The note from a piano, however, contains a 'background' of other notes, of higher frequency than the one heard. For example, if a note of 256 Hz is sounded, notes of 512, 768 and 1024 Hz are also present; but the latter have a much smaller amplitude than the note of 256 Hz, so that their intensity, or loudness, is much lower. Similarly, an organ pipe emitting a note of 256 Hz also produces notes of 768 and 1280 Hz at a much lower intensity. Notes which provide a 'background' to the note heard are called *overtones*. They are registered subconsciously by the mind. The overtones of the same note vary with different instruments. *The quality or tone of a note is due to the overtones which accompany it*, and this is linked with the *waveform* of the note.

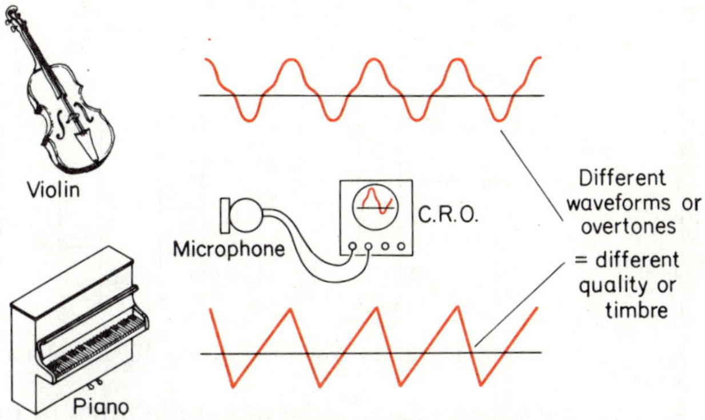

Fig. 22.13 Quality (or tone or timbre) depends on waveform

Thus, as illustrated in Fig. 22.13, although the frequency (number of cycles per second) of the same note sounded on a violin or piano may be the same, the waveforms of the two notes are different. Observe the different waveforms produced by tuning forks, strings and speech, using a microphone and cathode-ray oscilloscope, Fig. 22.13.

Harmonics are frequencies which are multiples of the fundamental frequency from a musical instrument. Thus if the fundamental frequency of a plucked string is 400 Hz, harmonics have frequencies which are two, three, four times as high, and so on. Harmonics are hence 800, 1200, 1600 Hz. Some harmonics may not be present among the overtones from a sounding instrument.

PIPES AND STRINGED INSTRUMENTS

All musical instruments produce sounds by setting a certain material or 'medium' into vibration. In sounding a flute or an organ pipe, the air inside vibrates. When a drum is banged, a taut membrane or skin vibrates. When a violin or cello or banjo is played, a stretched string vibrates. The sound produced by each instrument does not consist only of the *fundamental note* one hears. It also contains other notes of higher pitch. These are *overtones*. They are simply related in frequency to that of the fundamental notes. As explained on p. 377, different instruments have different overtones and hence have different 'quality' or 'tone'.

Vibrations of Air

Flutes, organ pipes, trombones and other wind instruments all produce their characteristic notes when the air inside is made to vibrate by blowing at one end. A simple set of 'pipes' can be made as follows:

Take a number of test-tubes and fill them with different levels of water so that the air columns inside have different lengths, Fig. 22.14.

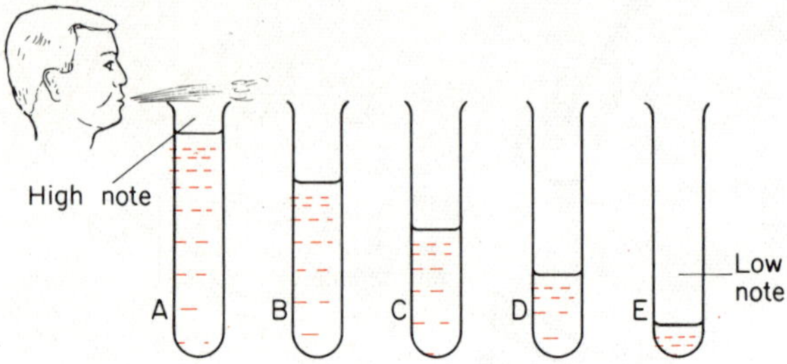

Fig. 22.14 Notes from vibrating air-columns

Fig. 22.15 A flute

Blow gently across the top of the tubes in turn, starting with A and finishing with E. Observe the pitch of the notes produced. You may be able to play a simple tune if you try.

Conclusion. The pitch is higher for a short column of air, so that the frequency increases as the length of the air column decreases.

In wind instruments such as the flute or recorder, air is blown over a hole at one end of the tube, Fig. 22.15. This sets the air column inside vibrating. The length of the air column, and hence the pitch or frequency of the note is varied by opening or closing holes in the tube. These are covered by finger-operated valves. Plate 22c shows organ pipes.

Stationary Waves

The waves which travel out in the air when we speak, or the waves which travel out along the surface of water when a stone is dropped in, are called *progressive waves*, Fig. 22.16 (i). The type of wave in the air inside sounding pipes or in the strings of sounding string instruments is shown in Fig. 22.16 (ii). It is known as a *stationary wave*, because it stays in one place and does not travel outwards like a progressive wave.

Unlike a progressive wave, some points N in a stationary wave are always at rest. They are called *nodes*. Other points between the nodes

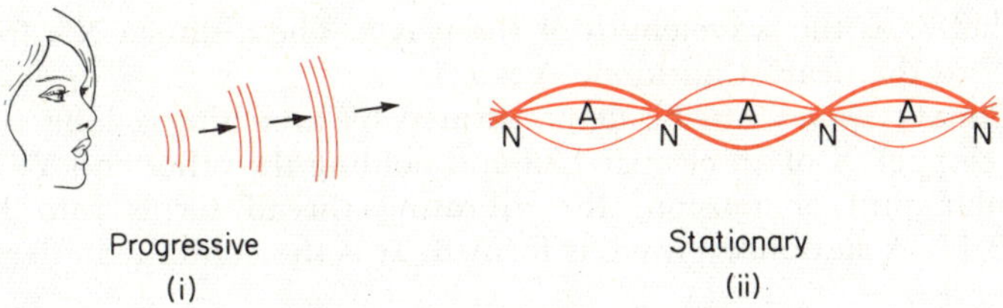

Fig. 22.16 Progressive and stationary waves

are vibrating with increasing amplitude. The points A of maximum amplitude are midway between the nodes. They are called *antinodes*. Note that the distance between two consecutive nodes or antinodes is

Plate 22(c) Chamber organ in Queen Elizabeth Hall, Royal Festival Hall, London, opened in 1967.

$\lambda/2$, where λ is the wavelength of the wave. The distance NA from a node N to the nearest antinode A is $\lambda/4$.

Stationary waves can be demonstrated by attaching a long thread to the clapper X of an electric bell and holding the other end Y. For a particular pull or tension, the vibrating thread forms into loops, Fig. 22.17. A stationary wave is formed. It is the combined effect due

Fig. 22.17 Demonstrating stationary waves

to the reflected wave from the fixed end Y and the incident wave from X, which travel in opposite directions. We say that the stationary wave is due to *interference* between the two waves.

Stringed Instruments and Pipes

In a stringed instrument, the two fixed ends of the plucked string are nodes of a stationary wave because they cannot move. The simplest stationary wave, which produces the lowest or fundamental note, is shown in Fig. 22.18 (i). The length of the string l is $\lambda/2$, or $\lambda = 2l$.

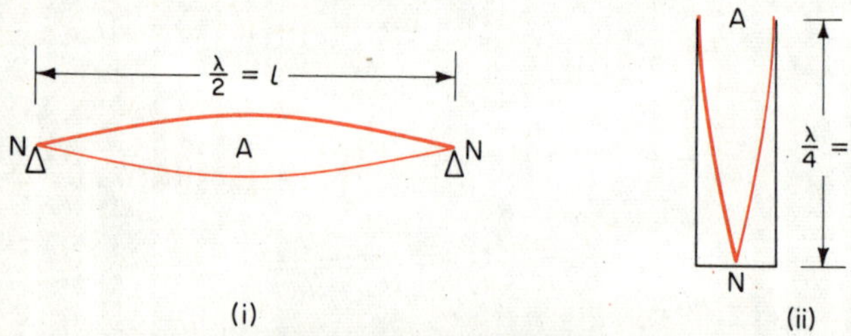

Fig. 22.18 Stationary waves in string and pipe

The simplest stationary wave in the air inside a sounding pipe, which produces the fundamental note, is shown in Fig. 22.18 (ii). The closed end of the pipe is a node N because the air cannot move here. The open end is an antinode A because the air is free to move here. Thus if l is the length of the pipe, $l = \lambda/4$ or $\lambda = 4l$.

Resonance

When we blow gently at one end of a pipe, the air inside is stimulated and it vibrates at its natural frequency. We say that the air has been set into *resonance* by the blower. A high-diver jumps up and down at the end of a spring board. He tries to set the board into resonance or large vibrations and thus gain lift for his dive. The board has a natural frequency of vibration, which depends on its length and material for example. It is set into resonance when the frequency of the jumps at one end is exactly the same as its natural frequency.

Resonance Tube Experiment

An investigation into the variation of the frequency f of the note obtained with the length l of an air column can be carried out with the apparatus shown in Fig. 22.19 (i). Here, by moving a side reservoir R up or down, the water level in T is varied, thus altering the length l of the air column in T. Four or five tuning forks from 512 Hz downwards are required. The forks are used to set the air column into resonance.

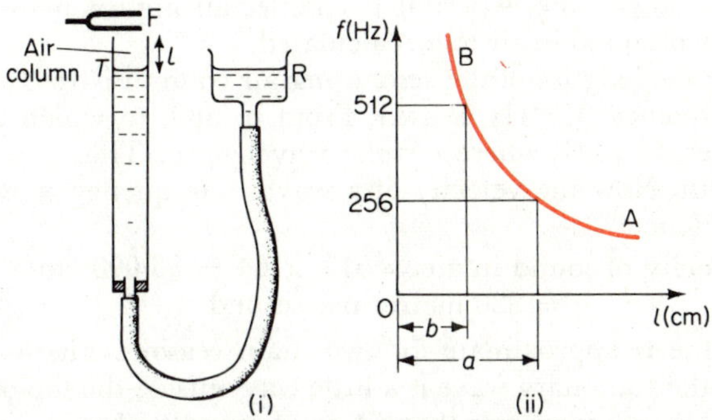

Fig. 22.19 Resonance tube experiment

Raise R so that the water level is near the top of T. Start with the fork F of highest frequency, 512 Hz. Sound it gently and hold the vibrating prongs over the air column as shown. Lower the reservoir R slowly, so that the water level in T drops and the level of air column increases. At first a low sound is heard, but as the level falls a louder sound is heard, rising to a maximum loudness at one stage. The air in the pipe has now been set into resonance by the sounding tuning-fork prongs, that is, the frequency of the fork is exactly equal to the natural frequency of the air column. By moving equal to the natural frequency of the air column. By moving R slightly up or down, find the position when the sound is loudest, and then measure the length l of the air column. Record l and the frequency f in a table of measurements. Repeat with the next fork of lower frequency, and then with the remaining forks.

Measurements.

f (Hz)	l (cm)	$f \times l$

Calculation. (1) Work out the product $f \times l$ and enter the results in your table; (2) Plot a graph of f v. l and draw a smooth curve through the points plotted, Fig. 22.19 (ii).

Conclusions. From your results, $f \times l$ is fairly constant or, approximately, f is *inversely-proportional* to l.

This means that if the length of the air-column is halved, the frequency is doubled. From your graph, see if the length a of the air-column when $f = 512$ Hz is about half the length b when $f = 256$ Hz. Repeat for other ratios of pairs of frequencies such as $f = 480$ Hz and 320 Hz. The ratio here is 3 : 2. See if the lengths of the air-columns are 2 : 3 by using your graph.

Velocity of Sound in Air

The resonance tube experiment enables an approximate value for the velocity of sound in air to be calculated.

Suppose the length l of the resonating air column is 16·0 cm when a fork of frequency 512 Hz is used. From p. 380, to which the reader should refer, $l = \lambda/4$, where λ is the wavelength. Thus $\lambda = 4l = 4 \times 16 = 64$ cm. Now the velocity of a wave = frequency × wavelength (p. 374). Hence

$$\text{velocity of sound in air} = 512 \times 64 = 33\,000 \text{ cm/s}$$
$$= 330 \text{ metres per second.}$$

This value is approximate for two main reasons. Firstly, the antinode A of the stationary wave is a little way outside the top of the pipe, so the wavelength is greater than 64 cm. Secondly, the sides of the tube 'damp' the air vibrations—the air is not 'free' air.

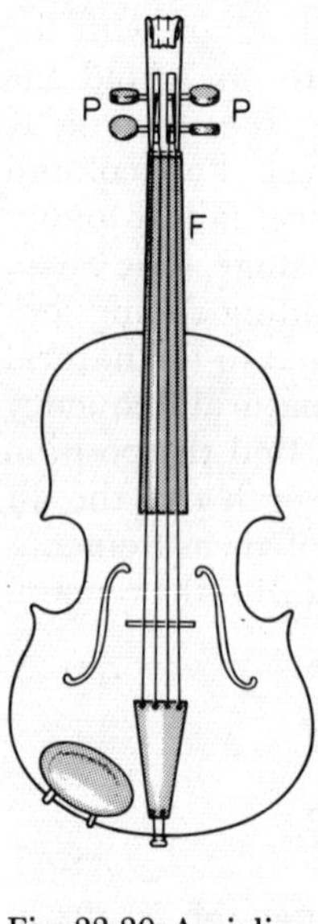

Fig. 22.20 A violin

Vibrations of Strings

Stringed instruments, such as the violin or cello, consist of a set of stretched strings, mounted across bridges on a hollow box of a particular shape, Fig. 22.20. A string is set into vibration by 'bowing' or by plucking. The vibrations are transferred to the box, which is also set into vibration. As explained on p. 376, a loud sound is heard.

Each string on the violin is previously tuned to a set note by adjusting its tension. This is done by tightening (or slackening) the string by means of a peg P at the neck of the instrument, round which the string F is wound, Fig. 22.30. Strings which provide lower notes are thicker and heavier than those providing higher notes. Additional notes are obtained by 'stopping' a string, that is, placing a finger firmly on the string so that it is 'clamped' on to the board of the violin. Effectively this shortens the length of the string. A different note is obtained from different lengths.

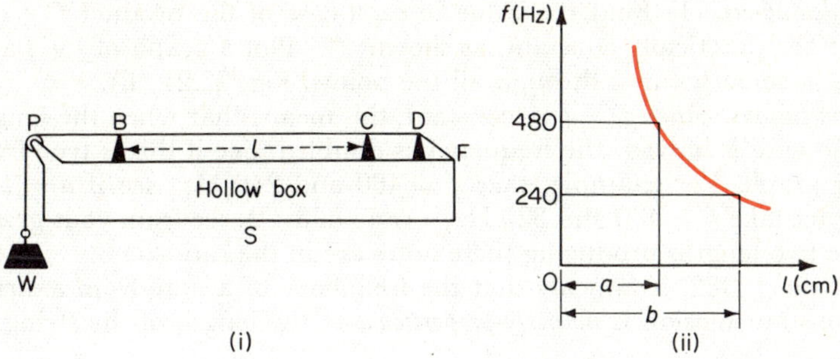

Fig. 22.21 Sonometer experiment

Sonometer

The frequency of the notes obtained from a stringed instrument can be studied with the aid of a *sonometer*. This consists of a hollow box S, with a wire FDP attached to it at F, Fig. 22.21. The wire passes over movable bridges at C and B and then over a fixed pulley P. A weight *W*, such as 5 kg, is attached at the end to keep the wire at constant tension. With C kept fixed, the length of the string BC is altered simply by moving the position of the bridge B.

If the length BC is made 20 cm the note obtained by plucking the wire gently in the middle is a high one. If the bridge is moved so that BC is increased to 30 cm, for example, a lower note is produced. At a length of 40 cm a note is obtained which is recognized as one octave lower in pitch than at 20 cm, or exactly half the latter frequency. Increasing the length of a vibrating wire at constant tension thus lowers the frequency.

Variation of Frequency with Length

The exact relation between the frequency f and the length l of the string can be investigated by using six tuning forks of known frequency, between 256 and 512 Hz, for example.

Keep the tension in the string constant by using a fixed weight *W*. Sound the tuning fork of 256 Hz, and with C kept fixed, move the bridge B until the note obtained by plucking the mid-point of BC is exactly the same as that of the tuning fork. Record the length of BC. Repeat with the other tuning forks, and enter the values of f and the length l in a table of measurements, as below.

Measurements. The following results were obtained in an experiment:

f (Hz)	l (cm)	$f \times l$	f (Hz)	l (cm)	$f \times l$
256	35·0	8960	384	23·6	9060
288	31·5	9070	426	21·2	9030
320	28·0	8960	512	17·5	8960

Calculations. (1) Find the value in each case of the product $f \times l$—these are practically constant, as shown; (2) Plot a graph of f v. l and draw a smooth curve through all the points, Fig. 22.21 (ii).

Conclusions. Since $f \times l =$ constant, this means that when the length of the wire is halved, the frequency is doubled. See if this is true from your graph. For example, take $f = 480$ and 240 Hz; see if $a = b/2$. Further take $f = 480$ and 320 Hz, a ratio of 3 : 2; see from your graph if the two lengths producing these notes are in the ratio 2 : 3.

As on p. 382, it appears that the frequency of a note from a string at constant tension is *inversely-proportional* to the length of the string.

Tension and String

Using a constant length of the wire, the tension in the wire can be increased by adding more weight W. Fig. 22.22 (i). On plucking the

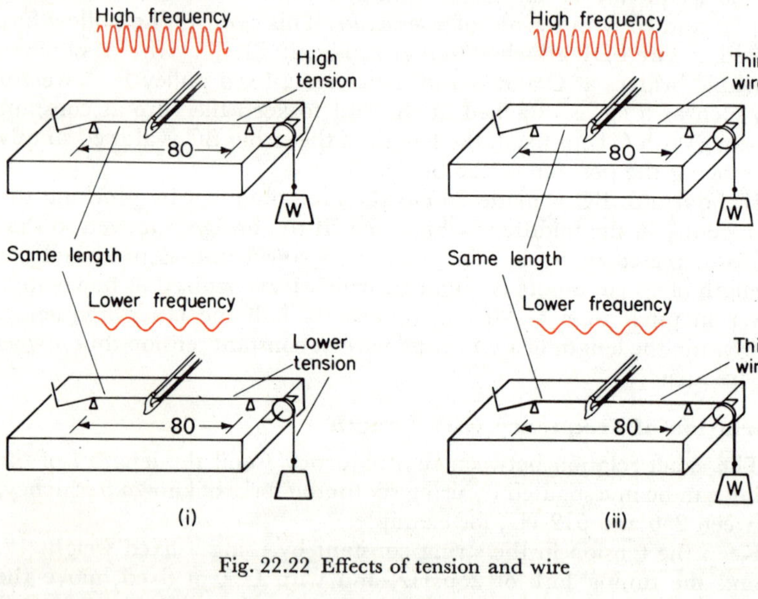

Fig. 22.22 Effects of tension and wire

wire, a note of higher pitch or frequency is heard. Thus tightening a violin string raises its pitch. If the sonometer wire is wound with wire to make it relatively heavier and then plucked, a note of lower pitch is heard, Fig. 22.22 (ii). Thicker wire of the same material also gives a note of lower pitch. A double-bass, which produces very low notes, has much thicker strings than a violin.

Piano

The piano is a stringed instrument which has a keyboard. Basically, it consists of a frame F, which has many strings S stretched across it, shown in simplified form in Fig. 22.23. Each string is originally tuned to a particular note by the piano-tuner.

When a key such as K is depressed, it operates a small felt-tipped hammer H. This then strikes a string or group of strings tuned to the

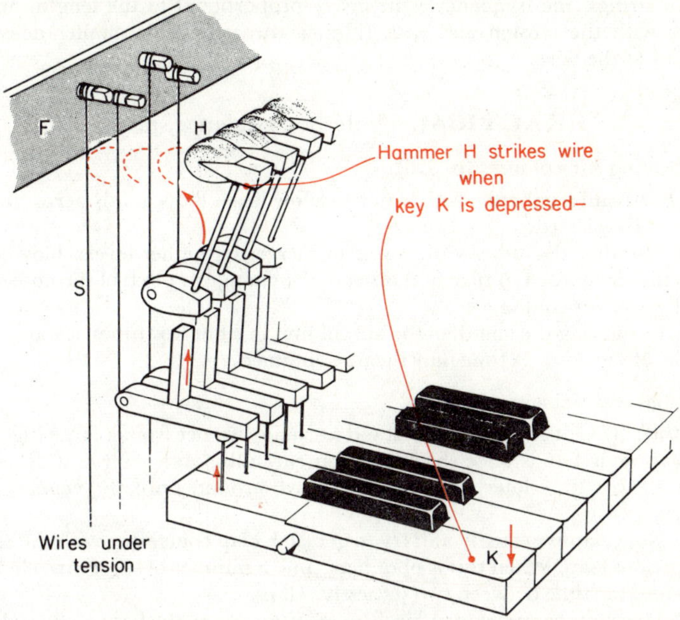

Fig. 22.23 A pianoforte

same note, thus setting them into vibration and producing the sound. Each note is produced by a separate key. No 'stopping' or 'fingering' is needed as in the violin.

When the key is released, a felt 'damper' is made to touch the strings. This stops them vibrating. Thus a note can only sound as long as the key is depressed. Most pianos are fitted with two pedals. One raises all the dampers from their individual strings when it is depressed—this allows the sound from the vibrating strings to die away slowly. The other pedal produces a softer quicker sound—it displaces members of the group of strings tuned to the same note, so that only one note is set vibrating by the hammer.

SUMMARY

1. Sound needs a material medium—it does not pass through a vacuum.

2. The ear comprises an outer, middle and inner ear.

3. Pitch depends on frequency. Loudness depends on amplitude. Tone (quality or timbre) depends on the overtones.

Pipes and Strings

4. In the resonance tube experiment, wavelength $= 4l$ approximately, where l is the length of resonating air column at the first position of resonance. Velocity of sound in air $= 4l \times f$ approximately.

5. In strings, the frequency is inversely-proportional to the length, and increases with the tension and with thinner wire and with smaller density of material of the wire.

PRACTICAL (Notes for guidance, p. 26)

1. Vibrating Air-columns (p. 378)

(i) Partly fill a test-tube with water to a low level. Blow gently across the top. A note will be heard.

(ii) Fill other test-tubes with water to increasing higher levels. Blow gently across the top of each in turn and observe the change in pitch of the note due to the vibrating air columns.

(iii) By varying the length of the air-column in eight test-tubes, try and make a 'scale' of the notes. A tune may then be obtained.

2. Echoes and Velocity of sound

Method. (i) Outside the school, stand at some distance from a large high wall. (ii) Clap your hands once sharply, listen carefully, and observe if an echo is heard a short time later. If necessary, move around until the echo is heard loudest.

(iii) Now clap repeatedly and try to get each clap coinciding with the echo of the previous clap. When this is obtained, time a number of successive claps and hence find the time between two successive claps.

(iv) Measure the perpendicular distance from you to the base of the wall.

Calculation. The sound travels to the wall in a time which is half that between successive claps. Find the speed of sound from *Distance of wall/Time*.

3. Stationary waves (p. 380)

Apparatus. Electric bell and battery supply; long thread; pulley wheel; scale-pan; box of weights.

Method. (i) Remove the gong from the bell. Attach one end of the thread to the clapper. Pass the thread over a pulley some distance away and attach a scale-pan S so that it hangs freely.

(ii) Start the bell so that the clapper and thread vibrate. Add increasing weights to S. At one stage, the thread forms into stationary 'loops'. This is a *stationary wave* pattern. Draw a sketch of the wave. Observe some points are not vibrating and others between are vibrating with increasing amplitude to a maximum in the middle.

(iii) Add more weights to S and see if the number of vibrating loops can be made to change.

Finally, remove the scale-pan, hold the thread at this end, and pull it gently. Try and produce a stationary wave by varying the tension or pull.

4. Resonance tube experiment (p. 381)

Apparatus. Resonance tube apparatus; five tuning forks from 512 Hz downwards; metre ruler. (Otherwise, use the resonance tube apparatus in Fig. 22.24.

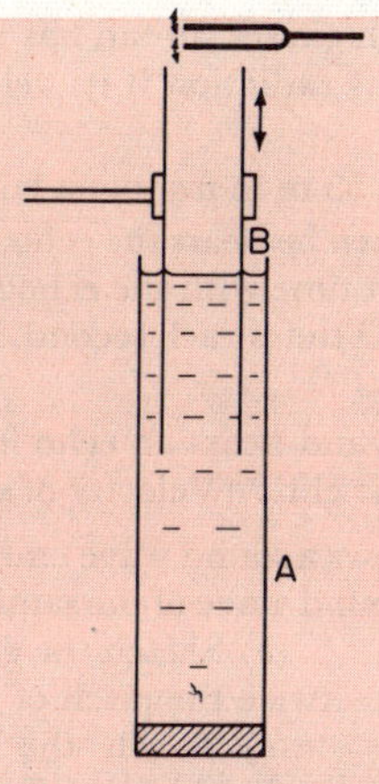

Fig. 22.24 Resonance tube experiment

It consists of a vertical tube A of large diameter and a smaller tube B which can be moved in or out of A. The length of the air column in B is thus varied.)

Method. (i) As described on p. 381, investigate the relation between the frequency of the note obtained from a resonating air-column and its length l.

(ii) Calculate an approximate value for the velocity of sound in air at the temperature of the room from *velocity* $= f \times 4l$. Do this for various forks and take an average value.

5. Sonometer

Apparatus. Sonometer apparatus and weights; five tuning forks.

Method. As described on p. 383, investigate the relation between the length l of a wire under constant tension and the frequency f of the note obtained. If you have a musical ear, a tune can be played on a sonometer wire.

EXERCISE 22 · ANSWERS, p. 403

1. The velocity of sound in air is 330 m/s. If there is an interval of 5 seconds between seeing a lightning flash and hearing a thunderclap, how far away from you is the source of thunder? (*L.*)

2. Indicate in Fig. 22A what represents; (*a*) the amplitude of the wave; (*b*) the wavelength of the wave. (*L.*)

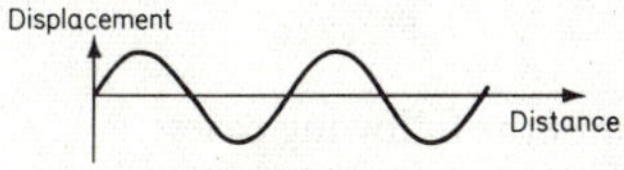

Fig. 22A

3. When the frequency of a note is increased the pitch of the note is . . (*M.*)

4. (*a*) Describe with a diagram, an experiment that shows that sound needs a material medium such as air through which to travel, but light does not.

(*b*) How do you know that sound travels much slower than light? (*E.A.*)

5. (*a*) On axes, draw a diagram of a transverse wave and mark the wavelength.

(*b*) Ultra-violet light which causes suntan has a wavelength of 0·000 03 cm. Calculate the frequency of this radiation if its velocity is 30 000 000 000 cm/s. (*E.A.*)

6. An experimenter stands 55 m in front of a large, flat stone wall, and bangs two metal tubes together. When he hears the echo, he bangs the tubes again. He keeps on banging the tubes in time with the echoes. A friend with a stop-watch finds that he bangs the tubes 3 times each second. What is the speed of sound in air in this case? (*N.W.*)

7. An observer fires a gun and hears an echo from a distant cliff after 1·1 s. How far away from him is the cliff? (Velocity of sound = 340 m/s.) (*Mx.*)

8. The graph, Fig. 22B, shows a sound wave emitted by a tuning fork.

(*a*) Sketch the graph of a sound wave of the same pitch but louder.

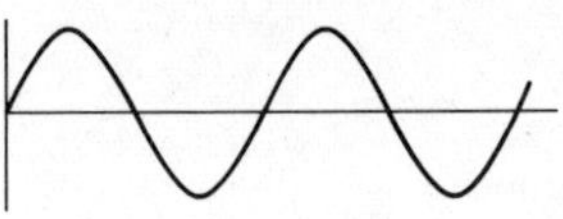

Fig. 22B

(*b*) Sketch the graph of a sound wave having twice the pitch of the original note.

(*c*) Sketch the graph of the sound wave emitted by a different instrument sounding the same note as the original, but of a different quality. (*L.*)

9. How is an echo made? Describe how echoes may be used to measure the depth of the sea bed.

During a storm it was observed that the thunder was heard 5 seconds after the lightning flash. If sound travels 1200 km/h, calculate how far away from the observer the lightning struck.

Discuss briefly the similarities between sound-ranging and radar. (*Mx.*)

10. Complete: The frequency of the lowest note the average human can hear is approximately . . cycles per second; the highest audible frequency is . . cycles per second. (*E.A.*)

11. Fig. 22C shows a diagram of the human ear. State the function of the parts indicated. 1 . . 2 . . 3 . . 4 . .(*E.A.*)

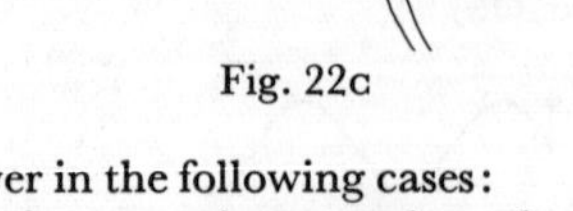

Fig. 22C

12. Select the *best* answer in the following cases:

(*a*) A stretched wire emits a certain note when plucked. Which of the following does *not* affect the pitch of the note?: (i) plucking the wire more strongly; (ii) shortening the wire; (iii) lengthening the wire; (iv) tightening the wire; (v) using a thicker wire of the same material.

(*b*) Which of the following substances is a poor absorber of sound?: (i) glass wool; (ii) concrete; (iii) thick cardboard; (iv) fibre board; (v) curtains.

(*c*) A sound wave, in air is: (i) lateral wave; (ii) long wave; (iii) slinky wave; (iv) transverse wave; (v) longitudinal wave.

(*d*) Which of the following wave forms Fig. 22D, represents the sound wave produced by a gently-struck tuning fork? (*E.A.*)

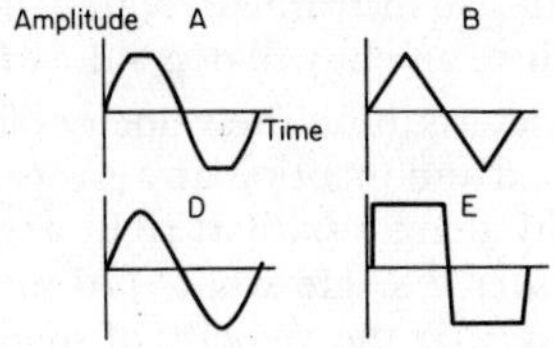

Fig. 22D

13. Read the following passage and explain the physical meaning of the four terms in italics:

'A violin and a piano are both made to sound a note of the same pitch and *loudness* at the same time. The violin note is easily distinguished from the piano note because of the presence of a greater range of *harmonics* in one case. If the two notes are not of exactly the same *frequency*, it may be possible to hear *beats*.' (*M.*)

14. What are echoes, and how are they produced? (*S.E.*)

15. Fig. 22E shows a continuously vibrating tuning fork held above a tube originally full of water. The tap is open and the water level is slowly falling. Describe and explain what happens. (*N.W.*)

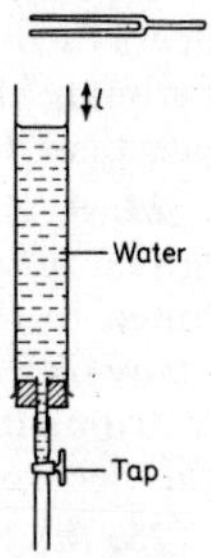

Fig. 22E

16. When a stationary (standing) wave pattern is obtained some points are always at rest:

(*a*) What are these points called.

(*b*) What is the distance between these points? (*L.*)

17. When a stretched wire on an instrument is plucked it . . with a frequency which can be increased by either: . . the effective length of wire; or: . . the tension of the wire. (*Mx.*)

18. With strings of the same material, the note of highest pitch on a string instrument would be produced by the string which is:

(*a*) thin, slack and short; (*b*) thick, slack and short; (*c*) thin, tight and long; (*d*) thick, tight and long; (*e*) thin, tight and short. (*E.A.*)

19. A vibrating tuning fork is held over a long tube with water at the bottom as shown in Fig. 22F. As the water level is caused to rise two levels are reached at which the sound heard is much louder than when the water is at other levels.

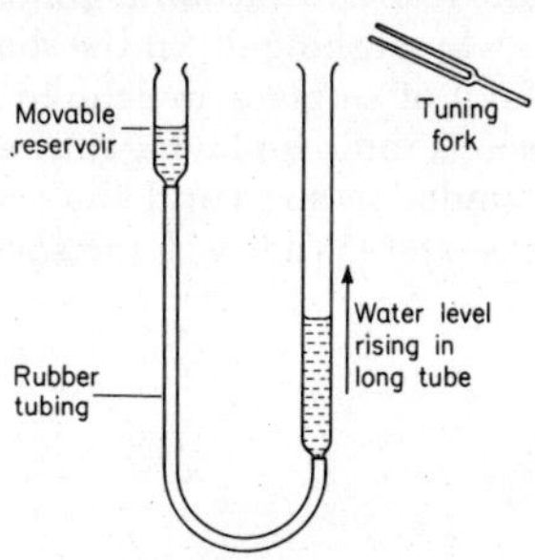

Fig. 22F

Explain why this happens. Briefly describe any musical instrument which uses the physical principle involved. (*M.*)

20. You are given a stringed musical instrument. Name the three factors upon which the note emitted from the instrument will depend. (*Mx.*)

21. (*a*) Describe a method of determining the velocity of sound in air. Show clearly how the results are obtained and mention any errors likely to be present.

(*b*) A boy is approaching a cliff along a path at right angles to the cliff face. He shouts and hears the echo after 2 s. He walks 170 m and now hears the echo 1 s after his shout. Calculate: (i) the velocity of sound; (ii) the distance the boy now is from the cliff. (*E.A.*)

22. What is the relationship between the velocity, V, the wavelength λ, and the frequency n of a wave?

How would you attempt to measure the velocity of sound in air? If the velocity of sound in air is 340 m what is the wavelength of a note whose frequency is 55 Hz? (*L.*)

23. An observer is situated 5 kilometres from the firing location of a rocket being tested. He sees a flash as the rocket is fired, and fifteen seconds later he hears the first burst of noise. What is the cause of this delay in hearing the noise? Estimate the speed of sound in air from this information. Explain briefly any practical device which uses the fact that sound also travels in water. (*M.*)

24. A violin has four strings which produce musical notes when a bow is drawn across them. Explain, giving *scientific reasons*, how: (i) The strings are tuned to the right notes before the violin is played; (ii) the player produces many different notes from each string during his playing; (iii) larger stringed instruments, such as a double-bass, have thicker strings than a violin. Why is this necessary? (*M.*)

25. (*a*) Define the *frequency* of a sound vibration.

(*b*) A loudspeaker is driven by an oscillator the frequency of which can be varied from zero upwards. What changes would you notice in the speaker output as the frequency was increased over the whole range?

(*c*) Explain briefly how a standing wave is set up on a stretched string, one end of which is fixed while the other end is kept vibrating at a constant frequency.

(*d*) Draw a diagram to show *two* complete standing waves on a stretched string and label any one node, N, and any one antinode, A. (*Mx.*)

26. (*a*) Explain each of the following: (i) why sound does not travel through a vacuum?; (ii) that although the strings on a guitar are the same length they sound different notes; (iii) why pushing down the slide of a trombone produces a low note?; (iv) why a shout often gives an echo in hilly country?; (v) why a vase which is in a room where a radio is playing may emit a musical note?

(*b*) A stationary ship sounded its siren and an echo from a cliff 1500 metres distant was heard 8 seconds later. What was the speed of the sound? (*S.*)

23

SOUND RECORDING AND REPRODUCTION

THERE are many ways of recording sound and reproducing the sound. Music and speech are recorded in studios on *tape-recorders* and later released on *gramophone records* for play-back. In broadcasting, the recording and play-back are made by tape-recorders. Sound is recorded on *film* for use in the cinema and played-back from the film. In all these cases high-quality *microphones* are necessary for minimum distortion of the sound and high-quality *loudspeakers* are essential for reproducing it faithfully.

Sound recording and reproduction is a specialized subject and many books have been written about it. Here we can only describe briefly some of the principles of the above instruments. As most of them use techniques concerning electricity, the chapter should be read after the subject of electricity has been studied. References to the appropriate parts of the later text have been given.

Principle of Tape Recorder

In 1898 Poulsen, a Danish scientist, invented an instrument called a *Telegraphone*, in which he succeeded in recording sound magnetically. The instrument used spools of steel wire to record the sound, but the invention lapsed as the machine was cumbersome and not easy to operate.

The modern magnetic tape-recorder developed from about 1940, with the production of a new magnetic oxide. The oxide is made in finely powdered form, mixed with an adhesive or binder and then coated on to a very thin plastic-base smooth tape, which forms a backing for the oxide. Once magnetized, the oxide retains its magnetism.

The principle of the recording-process is shown in Fig. 23.1 (i), (ii). The tape moves at a constant speed past a very narrow gap in a ring of soft-iron, which can be magnetized by current passing into a coil wound round it (p. 506). The ring magnet and coil constitute the *recording head*.

Speech or music is converted by a microphone into a varying or alternating current of exactly the same frequency (p. 509), and this flows in the coil. On one half of a current cycle the oxide arriving at the gap becomes a small magnet by induction (p. 489). On the other

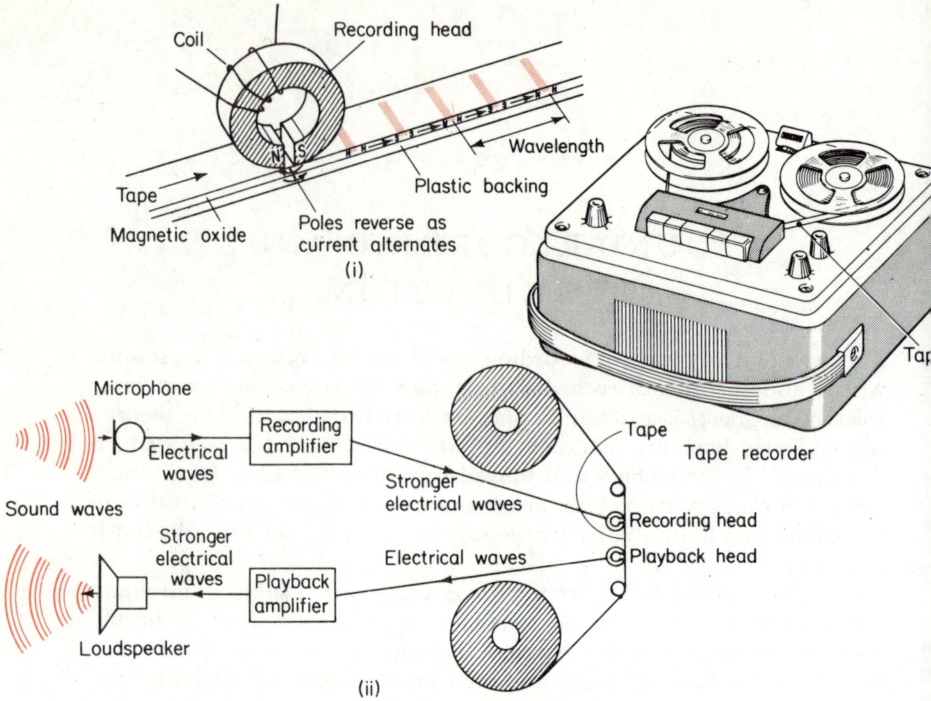

Fig. 23.1 Magnetic tape recording

half of the same cycle the current reverses, and as the tape has moved on, the next small section of oxide arriving at the gap is now magnetized in an opposite direction. As the tape moves along, therefore, a series of small magnets are obtained, pointing opposite ways. The strength of the magnets depends on the current strength, which in turn varies with the loudness of the sound. The number of pairs of magnets obtained per second on the tape is equal to the frequency of the sound. Thus the oxide records the sound magnetically. See Plate 23A.

In play-back the magnetized tape is run at the same constant speed past the same or another soft-iron ring, each magnet closing the gap between the poles as before, Fig. 23.2 (ii). This time, however, the introduction of the magnets into the gap induces a

Plate 23(A) Magnetic field round tape used on tape-recorder, showing regions of small magnets.

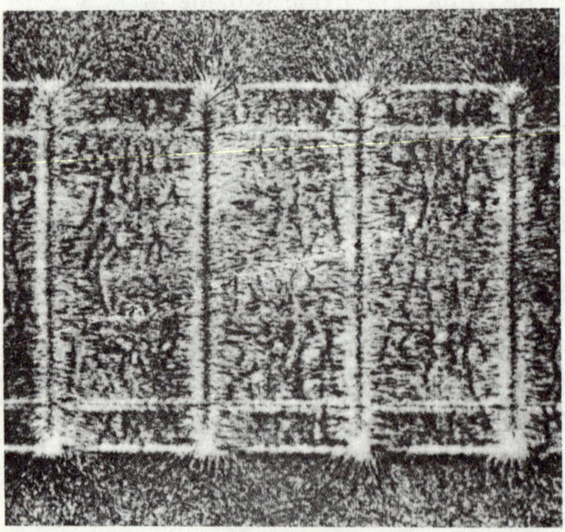

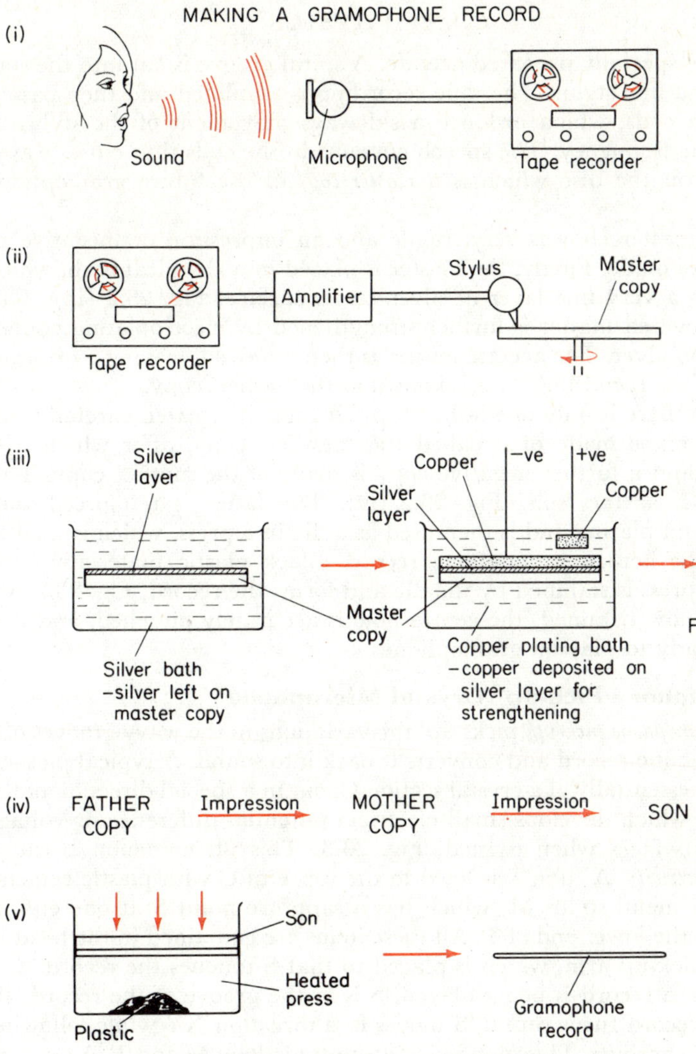

Fig. 23.2 Stages in gramophone record manufacture

current of the same frequency as before in a coil round the ring (p. 530). The current is amplified and passed to a loudspeaker (p. 398), which reproduces the sound.

Making a Gramophone Record

For recording sound on a gramophone record, the complete original performance is first recorded for convenience on tape by a tape-recorder, Fig. 23.2 (i). A master copy of the recording is then made on a disc of specially prepared acetate. A spiral groove is cut into the surface by a fine stylus. The tape recording is amplified and then passed through coils, which produce a sideways movement of the stylus at the same frequency. The speech currents in the coils thus cut a 'wavy' groove on the disc which is a *master copy* of the future gramophone record.

The master copy is very fragile and an impression or 'negative' is therefore made. Firstly, the master is placed in a chemical bath, which deposits a very fine layer of silver on its surface, Fig. 23.2 (iii). This silver-covered master is further strengthened by electroplating copper on to the silver. The acetate master is then removed, leaving a negative copy of the recording. This is known as the 'father' copy.

Since there is only one father copy, it must be treated carefully. An impression is made of it called the 'mother' copy, after which it is stored, and a further negative copy is made of the mother copy. This is known as the 'son', Fig. 23.2 (iv). The latter is reinforced with chromium plating and is then used as a die in a press, which is used to make the actual gramophone record. Black plastic material in the heated press is stamped by the die and forms the record, Fig. 23.2 (v). This is now trimmed, the centre hole is accurately punched, and it is then ready to play on gramophones.

Gramophone Pick-up · Crystal Microphone

A *gramophone pick-up* 'picks up' the variations in the wavy grooves of a gramophone record and converts it back into sound. A typical pick-up consists essentially of a crystal section C, cut in a special direction of the crystal, which develops small electrical potential difference or voltage across its faces when twisted, Fig. 23.3. This phenomenon is called *piezo-electricity*. A tube T is fixed to the top P of C with plastic cement. A small metal stylus M, which has a sapphire point S at one end, is fixed in the lower end of T. All these items are contained in the head H of the pick-up arm, which is placed so that S touches the record.

When a record is being played, S is in the groove of the record, R. As the record turns round, S moves in a direction XY while following the wavy grooves. This motion is transmitted along M and T. A twisting motion, shown by DE, is thus obtained at the top of T. The crystal C is therefore twisted relative to its base B, which remains fixed in the head. A small electrical voltage is then generated across the faces of the crystal which has the same frequency as the variations of the wavy grooves. The voltage is passed to an amplifier system inside the gramophone by the leads L and the sound is heard through the loudspeaker.

A *crystal microphone* uses the same principle as the gramophone pick-up. A crystal unit C is mechanically connected to a flexible diaphragm D by means of a rod R, Fig. 23.4 (iii). When sound waves are incident on D it moves to and fro and this motion is transmitted by

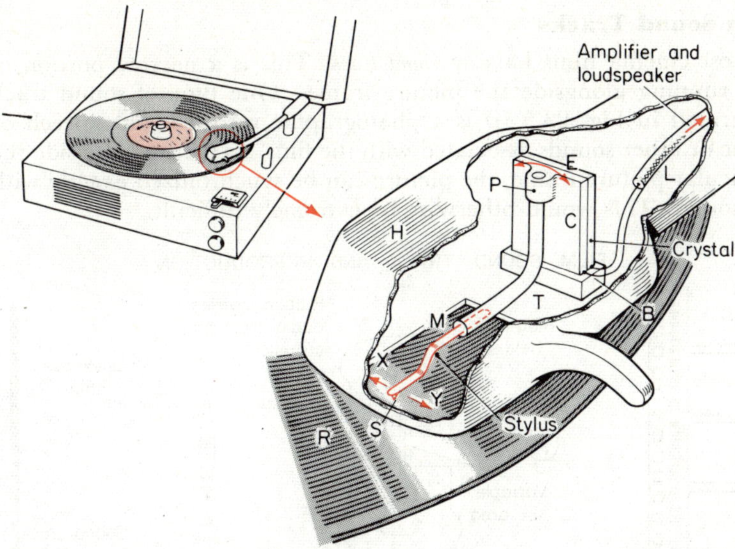

Fig. 23.3 Gramophone pick-up

R to the crystal unit. An electrical potential difference or voltage is therefore produced which varies at the same frequency as the sound. An enlarged section of the crystal unit is shown in Fig. 23.4 (i). Two crystal wafers, A, B, are connected together. If the faces are strained by a force F as shown, the potential difference V is developed across the faces RS and XY. This is connected to the amplifier by leads L and the sound is reproduced by a loudspeaker.

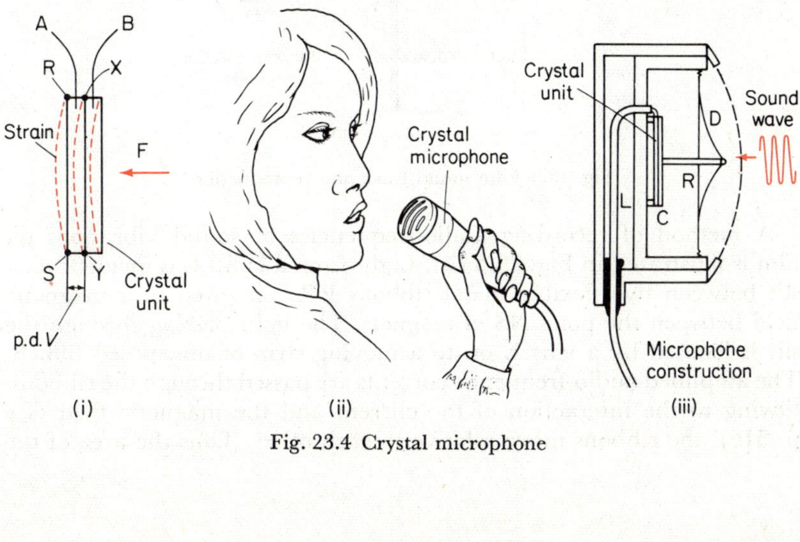

Fig. 23.4 Crystal microphone

Film Sound Tracks

Most cinema films have a *sound track*. This is a narrow portion of film running alongside the picture frames. One type of sound track illustrated in Fig. 23.5 (i) is a photographic record of the speech or music or other sounds associated with the film. As it runs alongside the particular picture frame, the picture can be synchronized exactly with the sound. This would otherwise be extremely difficult.

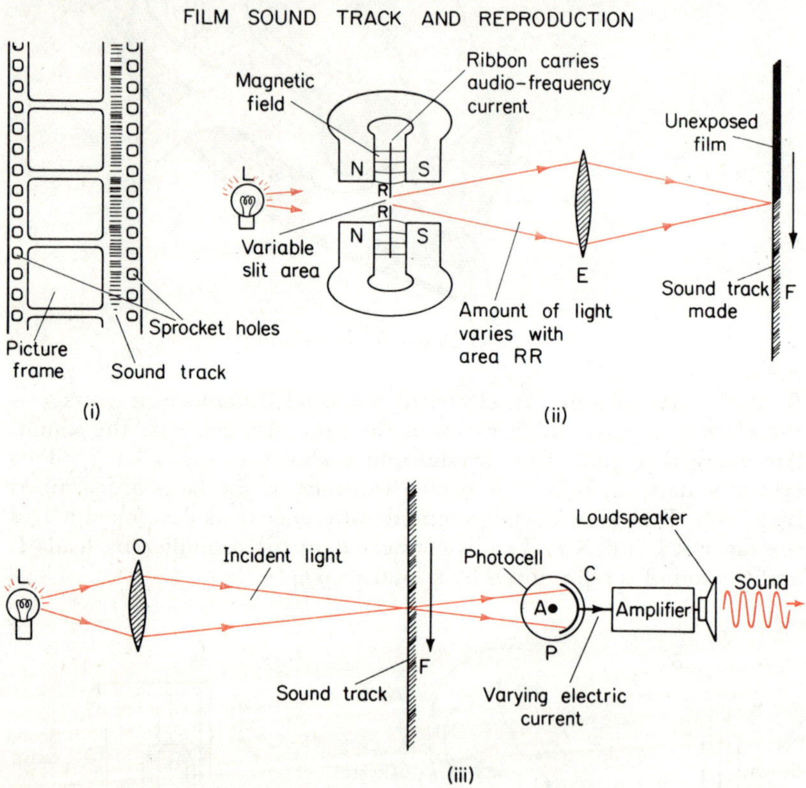

Fig. 23.5 Film sound track and reproduction

A method of recording audio-frequencies or sound vibrations on film is illustrated in Fig. 23.5 (ii). Light from a lamp L is incident on a slit between two flexible metal ribbons RR, mounted in a magnetic field between the poles NS of magnets. The light passing through the slit is focused by a lens E on to a moving strip of unexposed film F. The amplified audio-frequency currents are passed through the ribbons. Owing to the interaction of the current and the magnetic field (see p. 516), the ribbons move relative to each other. Thus the area of the slit between RR varies at the audio-frequency. Consequently the amount of light incident on the film varies at the audio-frequency, and hence when the film is developed the sound track appears as a series of bands of *varying density*, Fig. 23.5 (i). Different sound frequencies cause these bands to change at a different rate. On distribution, copies of the film are made 'positives', that is, exactly opposite to the negative obtained in recording.

Sound Reproduction

To reproduce the sound in a cinema, light from a small lamp L is focused by a lens O on to the sound track of the moving film F, Fig. 23.5 (iii). The light passing through O is then incident on the cathode C of a *photo-electric cell* P. The photocell is a device which has a light-sensitive metal of large area as C and a rod-shaped anode A—both are contained in an evacuated glass bulb. See Plate 23B. When light falls on C it emits electrons in proportion to the light intensity. Thus when the film is almost transparent (corresponding to a dark band on the original negative, or high audio current) the cathode C is well illuminated. A high current is then obtained. When the film is almost black, a small current flows. Thus variations of current flow from the photo-cell with exactly the same variation as the sound frequency. The currents are amplified and passed through a loudspeaker, thus reproducing the original sound from which the sound track was made.

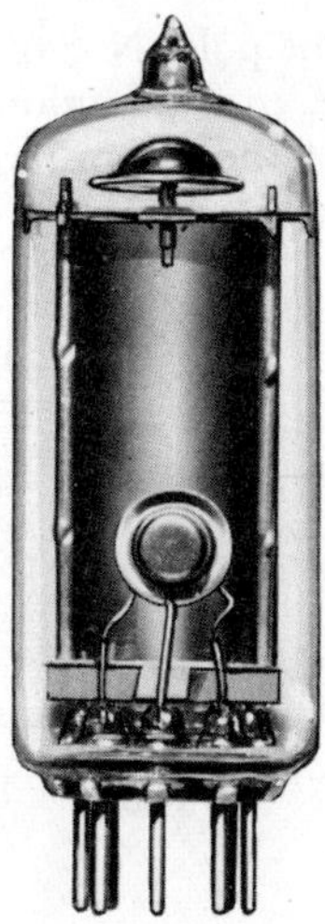

Plate 23(B) Photoelectric cell. The large metal surface is a caesium-antimony cathode, which is particularly sensitive to daylight and to light predominantly blue. The small disc shown is the anode, and the two metals are in a vacuum.

Moving-coil Microphone

Two microphones widely used in the entertainment industry are the *moving-coil* and *ribbon microphones*. Both operate on the principle of electromagnetic induction (p. 530).

When a moving-coil microphone is used, sound waves pass through G and make the cone D vibrate, Fig. 23.6. This makes the coil vibrate at the same frequency as the sound. The movement of the coil in the gap between the poles N–S of the magnet (shown in section) induces a voltage in the coil which varies at exactly the same frequency (see p. 534). This is passed to an amplifier by leads L joined to the terminals TT′.

The ribbon microphone has a metallic ribbon R situated between

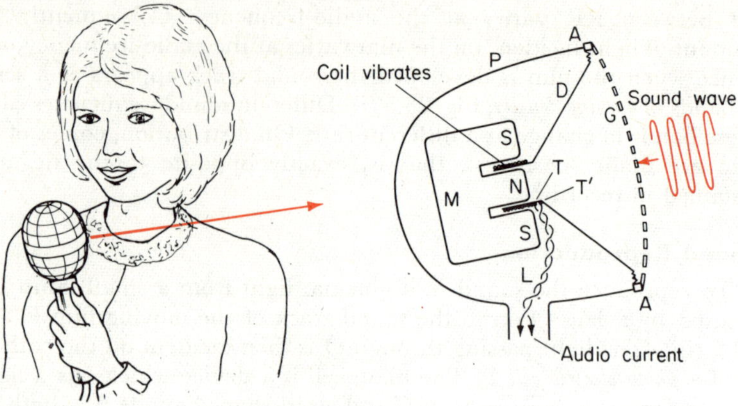

Fig. 23.6 Moving-coil microphone

the poles N–S of a powerful magnet, Fig. 23.7. Sound waves incident on R in a direction MM′ make the ribbon vibrate. An induced voltage of the same frequency is then obtained between the ends P,Q of the ribbon and this is amplified for reproduction in a loudspeaker.

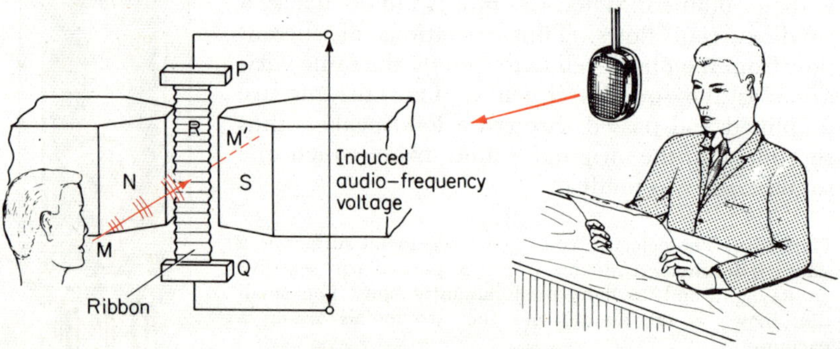

Fig. 23.7 Ribbon microphone

Moving-coil Loudspeaker

The moving-coil loudspeaker is used in radio receivers and in tape-recorders and gramophones. It has the opposite effect to the microphone—it converts sound- or audio-frequency electric currents to sound.

The loudspeaker contains a permanent magnet, with circular concentric north N and south S poles, Fig. 23.8 (i). These poles create a radial magnetic field, so called because the lines of force between the poles spread out along the radii of a circle, Fig. 23.8 (ii). A coil of wire D, known as the *speech coil*, is wound round a small cylindrical 'former', and is placed between the circular poles of the magnet. A large paper

Plate 23(c) Testing the performance of a loudspeaker with a microphone inside a special room which eliminates echoes.

cone is rigidly attached to the former. It is loosely connected to a circular board known as a baffle board, which surrounds the cone. See Plate 23c.

When a radio receiver, for example, is working, electric currents varying at audio-frequencies flow through the speech coil. Then, from Fleming's left-hand rule (see p. 517), an axial force acts on every part

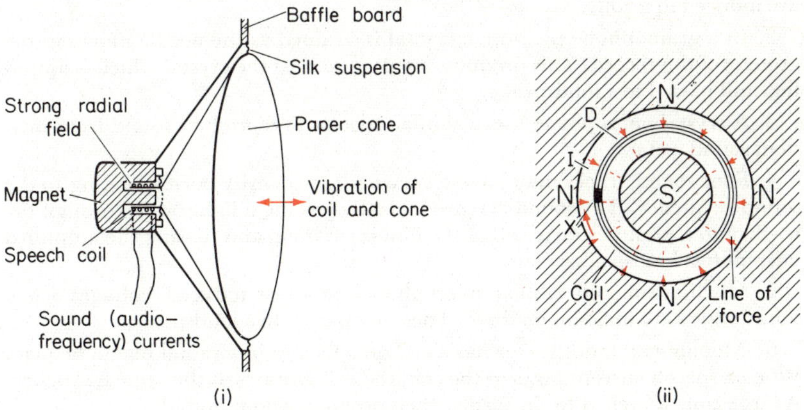

Fig. 23.8 Moving-coil loudspeaker

such as X of the coil, Fig. 23.8 (ii). The force on the coil varies at the same frequency as the current frequency.

The coil is wound tightly round the former to which the cone is attached. Thus the cone vibrates at exactly the same frequency as

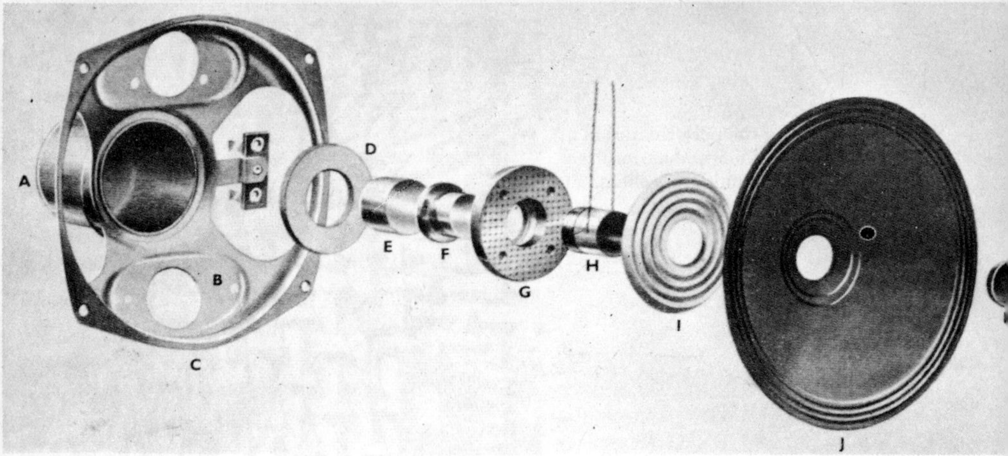

Plate 23(D) Loudspeaker parts. A, steel casing; B, transformer support; C, chassis; D, magnet ring; E, manent magnet; F, G, pole-pieces for radial field; H, speech coil on former; I, centring plate; J, c K, dust cap.

the current in the speech coil. The large mass of air in contact with the cone is set into vibration and a loud sound is produced. The baffle board stops the sound wave behind the cone interfering with that in front.

SUMMARY

1. Tape-recorders use magnetic tape running past a soft-iron ring at constant speed. The ring is magnetized by speech currents and the sound is recorded magnetically. At play-back the process is reversed and sound currents are induced in a coil.

2. In a gramophone pick-up, a crystal is strained as the needle moves in the grooves of the record. This produces a voltage across the crystal which is amplified and passed to a loudspeaker.

3. A crystal microphone uses a similar process to reproduce sound from incident sound waves.

4. Film sound tracks may have a varying light density corresponding to the sound frequency. The sound is reproduced by passing a light beam through the track onto a photo-electric cell as the film is running, and passing the amplified current to a loudspeaker.

5. Moving-coil and ribbon microphones produce induced voltages when sound waves are incident on them. These are passed to a loudspeaker.

6. Moving-coil loudspeaker has a coil on a former in a radial magnetic field. When a speech current flows in the coil, the coil vibrates at the same frequency. A large cone attached to the former then produces a loud sound.

EXERCISE 23 · ANSWERS, p. 403

What are the missing words in the following statements 1–11?

In a tape-recorder:

1. The recording head has a coil which carries the . . electric current.

2. This coil is wound round a . . ring.

3. The tape is covered with a . . powder.

4. During recording the tape becomes . .

5. In play-back, the tape passes a soft-iron ring with a . . round it. Induced . . are then obtained.

6. To record or reproduce faithfully, the tape must have a constant . .

When a gramophone record is made:-

7. The stylus or cutting edge is moved by . . from the tape-recording.

8. The master copy is strengthened in an . . bath.

In play-back from the record:

9. The needle moves round . . grooves on the record.

10. A voltage is then obtained from a . .

11. The phenomenon producing the voltage is called . . electricity.

12. In a moving-coil loudspeaker: (i) the cone has a large surface area; and (ii) a special type of magnetic field is used. What is the purpose of these two arrangements?

13. In one form of sound track, the film has shades of light and dark patches across it. To what is the variation in shade due? How is it produced?

14. A photo-electric cell produces electric current when illuminated by light. Explain how this is used in reproducing the sound from a sound track. Draw a diagram in illustration.

15. Explain the meanings of the following in connection with the tape-recorder: *magnetic tape*, *recording head*, *playback*. Briefly describe how a tape-recorder works. Draw diagrams in your answer.

16. In a moving-coil loudspeaker, explain: (i) why the cone vibrates at the audio-frequency; (ii) why a baffle board is used round the cone.

17. What are the principles involved and how are these applied in producing sound from:

(*a*) an optical sound track on film, as in your school sound-projector, and

(*b*) a magnetic tape as used in a tape recorder? (*M.*)

18. (*a*) Describe a simple demonstration to show that a force acts on a conductor in a magnetic field. Show the field, the direction of the current and the direction of motion.

(*b*) Describe the moving-coil loudspeaker and show how it uses the above effect to change electrical energy to sound energy. (*E.A.*)

19. (*a*) Draw a simple sectioned diagram of a moving-coil loudspeaker and label the parts. Explain what happens in the loudspeaker to make it give out a sound.

(*b*) Three notes from a loudspeaker have frequencies of 200 cycles per second, 400 cycles per second, and 800 cycles per second. What can you say about the pitch of these three notes?

(*c*) A spectator in a football stadium hears sound from two loudspeakers. The first is 100 metres from him and the second is 150 metres from him. What time interval will occur between sound from the nearer speaker reaching the man's ear, and that from the further speaker? (The speed of sound in air is 340 m per second.) (*S.*)

ANSWERS TO NUMERICAL EXERCISES

EXERCISE 14 (p. 274)

1. air **2.** electromagnetic **3.** crests/troughs **4.** frequency **5.** 34 cm
6. 200 000 **7.** electromagnetic **8.** wavelength **9.** C **10.** D **11.** A
12. D **13.** C **14.** B **15.** (*e*) 300 million m/s

EXERCISE 15 (p. 282)

1. umbra **2.** partial **3.** sharp **4.** divergent **5.** large **6.** rectilinear
7. moon **8.** edges **9.** blurred **10.** diminished, inverted **11.** light
12. *b* **13.** *b*
14. 1. total darkness, 2. partial light, 3. full light, 4. total darkness
18. (*c*) image larger

EXERCISE 16 (p. 292)

1. normal **2.** equal **3.** 45° **4.** behind **5.** C **6.** C
12. normal, incident ray, reflected ray, angle of incidence, angle of reflection

EXERCISE 17 (p. 304)

1. concave **2.** behind **3.** concave **4.** convex **5.** principal focus
6. straight back **7.** behind **8.** (i) behind (ii) larger
9. (i) behind (ii) smaller **10.** D **11.** B **12.** (i) 60 cm (ii) 3
13. (i) 20 cm (ii) 1 **14.** (i) $6\frac{2}{3}$ cm (ii) 1/3
15. (i) parabola (ii) concave (iii) convex (iv) concave (v) parabola **16.** *d*
17. 3 cm-virtual, upright, magnified; 13 cm-real, inverted, magnified
18. upright, inverted, at infinity **23.** 3

EXERCISE 18 (p. 320)

1. (i) towards (ii) 30° **2.** away from **3.** away from **4.** reflection, refraction
5. 45° **6.** glass, critical **12.** shallower, refraction **14.** 0·9 m, same
15. refracted, parallel

EXERCISE 19 (p. 332)

1. in front of **2.** behind **3.** converging (convex) **4.** in front of, real
5. diverging (concave) **6.** principal focus **7.** B **8.** D **9.** C **10.** B
16. 36 cm from lens; size–4 cm **19.** (*b*) 7·5 cm from lens, length = 2·5 cm
20. 1·5 cm, $f = 3{\cdot}6$ cm.

EXERCISE 20 (p. 342)

1. *a* **2.** (*a*) black (*b*) green **3.** (*a*) yellow, black (*b*) black, blue
4. (*a*) (i) red (ii) blue (*b*) (i) infra-red (ii) ultra-violet
12. A = green, B = blue, C = turquoise, D = magenta
13. (i) yellow (ii) white (iii) greeny-blue (iv) pale blue

EXERCISE 21 (p. 364)

1. retina **2.** *b* **3.** *b* **4.** iris, retina **6.** (*a*) diverging (concave) (*b*) far
7. long sight; converging (convex), reading **11.** 5 cm
12. 30 cm from lens, 45 cm **14.** 6 cm **16.** (i) $2f$ (ii) f (iii) nearer than f
17. 2·7 m

EXERCISE 22 (p. 387)

1. 1650 m **3.** increased **5.** 10^{15} Hz **6.** 330 m/s **7.** 187 m
9. $1\frac{2}{3}$ km **10.** 20; 20 000 (approx)
11. 1. Outer ear, 2. Eardrum, 3 Cochlea, 4. Eustachian tube
12. (*a*) i (*b*) ii (*c*) v (*d*) D **16.** (*a*) nodes (*b*) $\lambda/2$
17. vibrates, shortening, increasing **18.** *e* **21.** (i) 340 m/s (ii) 170 m
22. $V = n\lambda$, 6·2 m **23.** 333 m/s **26.** 375 m/s

EXERCISE 23 (p. 400)

1. audio-frequency **2.** soft-iron ring **3.** magnetic **4.** magnetized
5. coil, currents **6.** speed **7.** currents **8.** acid **9.** wavy **10.** pick-up
11. piezo **19.** 5/34 s.

Book Three

ELECTRICITY, ELECTRONICS, ATOMIC STRUCTURE

24

PRINCIPLES OF CURRENT, P.D., RESISTANCE

In this modern age, the science of Electricity holds one of the key positions. Electrical devices of one kind or another are needed in television, computers, satellites, telephony and commercial lighting, to name a few examples.

The Battery · Electric Current

Electrical phenomena had been known for thousands of years. But few useful effects were obtained, because it was static or stationary electricity. About 1800, however, an Italian scientist called Volta discovered that suitable chemicals were able to form a simple *cell*, which could keep electricity moving for some time in wires. A group of cells is called a *battery*. Later, the *accumulator* was invented. This is a very efficient cell; it keeps an electric current flowing for a long time (p. 443). To distinguish between the poles or terminals of a cell, battery or accumulator, one is called the *positive* (+) *pole* P and the other the *negative* (−) *pole* N, Fig. 24.1.

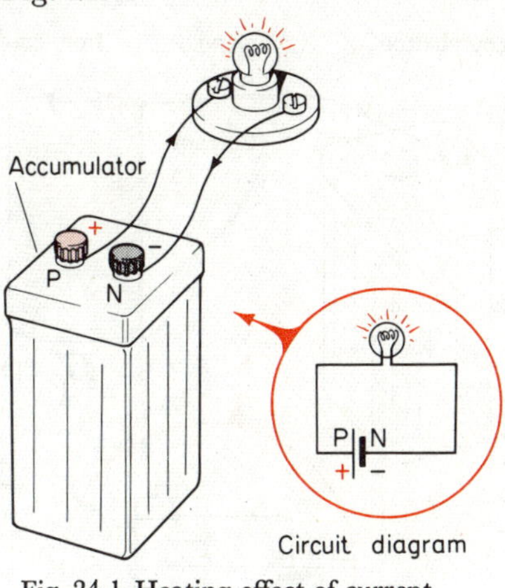

Fig. 24.1 Heating effect of current

Effects of Current

A small bulb glows when an accumulator is connected to it, Fig. 24.1. An electric current thus produces a *heating effect*. When a current

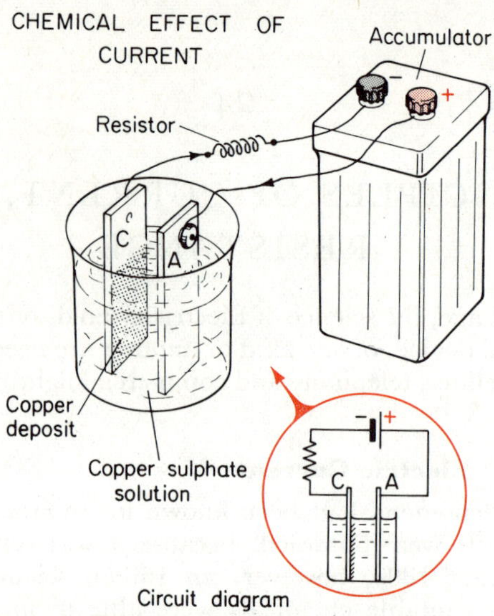

Fig. 24.2 Chemical effect of current

flows through copper sulphate solution with two copper plates A and C dipping into it, some copper is seen deposited on one plate C after a time, Fig. 24.2. An electric current thus produces a *chemical effect*. When a current flows through a long coil of insulated wire, called a 'solenoid',

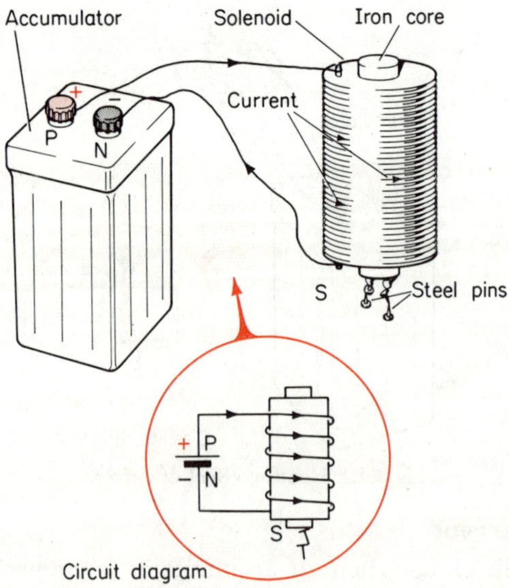

Fig. 24.3 Magnetic effect of current

which is wound round a bar of soft iron, steel pins are attracted to the bar as long as the current flows, Fig. 24.3. An electric current thus produces a *magnetic effect*.

Summarizing. An electric current or flow of electricity can produce a heating, chemical or magnetic effect.

Conductors, Insulators

As we have seen, a small bulb lights up when an accumulator is connected to it, Fig. 24.1. An electric current is now flowing in the circuit. If the circuit is broken at A and B the light disappears, Fig. 24.4. Air, between A and B, does not therefore allow electricity to

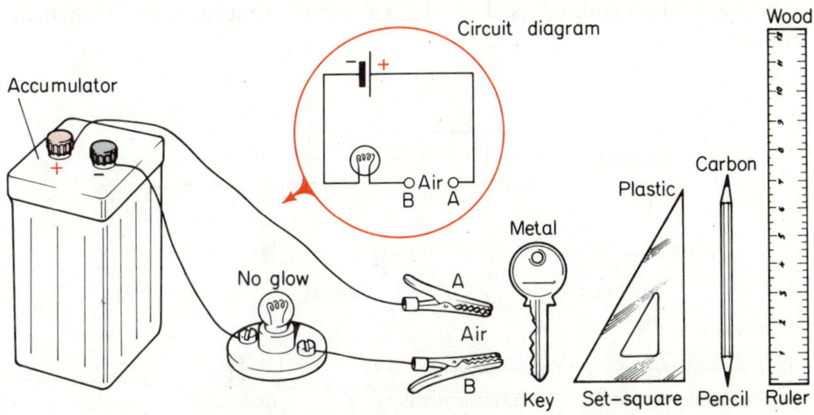

Fig. 24.4 Testing conductors and insulators

flow along it, and is called an *insulator*. When the wires at A and B are connected by any metal, or dipped into a salt solution, the bulb lights up again. These substances are called *conductors*. In this way, experiment shows that under normal conditions materials divide into one or other of these classes, with notable exceptions as we see shortly. Thus

Conductors: Metals, salt and inorganic acid solutions.

Insulators: Air, plastic materials, rubber, wood, paper, ebonite, pure water, organic acid solutions.

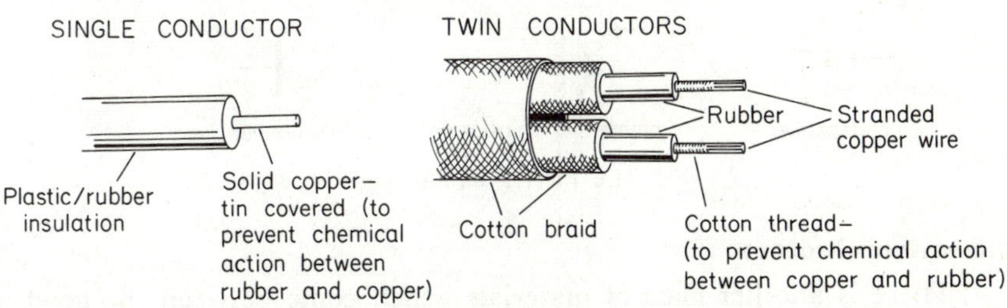

Fig. 24.5 Cables

Silver is the best electrical metal conductor, copper is the next best. Pure copper is widely used for connecting wire, inside flex and plastic materials for domestic and commercial electrical supplies, Fig. 24.5. When any impurities, however small, are mixed with pure copper an alloy is produced of much lower conductivity or, to put it the other way, of much higher electrical resistance. Nichrome and manganin are two copper alloys used in circuits as *resistance wire* (see p. 421). It should be noted that the insulating properties of materials, air or paper, for example, may break down under extreme conditions, and they then become conductors. Flashes of lightning show the conducting path of the air during electrical storms.

Some of the symbols used in electric circuit diagrams are shown in Fig. 24.6.

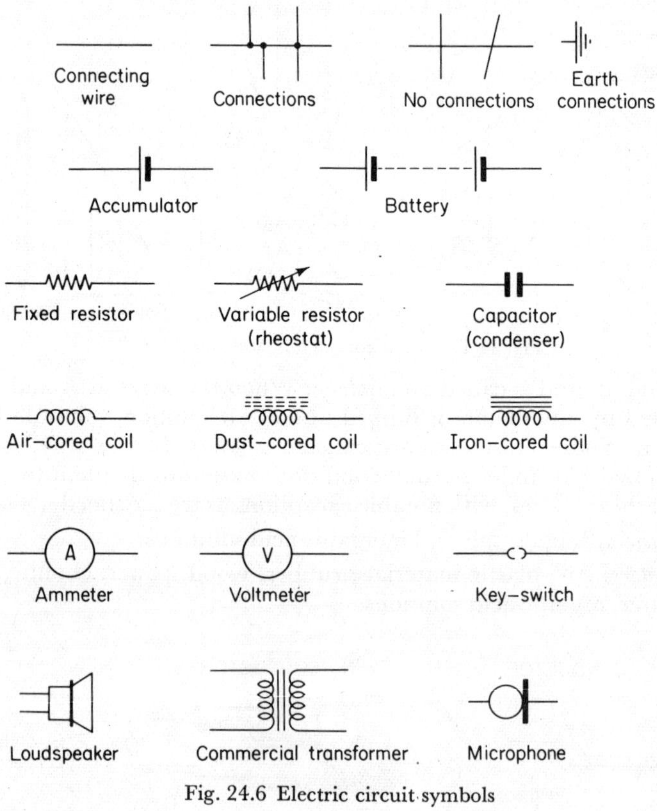

Fig. 24.6 Electric circuit symbols

Semiconductors

There is another class of materials which come between the good conductor and the insulator. They conduct very slightly compared with copper, for example, and are known as *semiconductors*. Germanium and silicon are examples of semiconductors.

Semiconductors were neglected as useful materials for a long time. In 1946, however, Shockley, Bardeen and Brattain in America began an important study of germanium and silicon in an attempt to produce a solid substitute for a glass radio valve, which is a costly item to manufacture and easy to break. Using specially treated germanium, or impure semiconductors, they invented the *transistor* in 1948, Fig. 24.7. This solid material can act like a radio valve, and has many advantages over the valve (p. 562). In due course the transistor should displace radio valves in many electrical applications. A vast field of research into the properties of semiconductors is now under way, and many useful applications will follow.

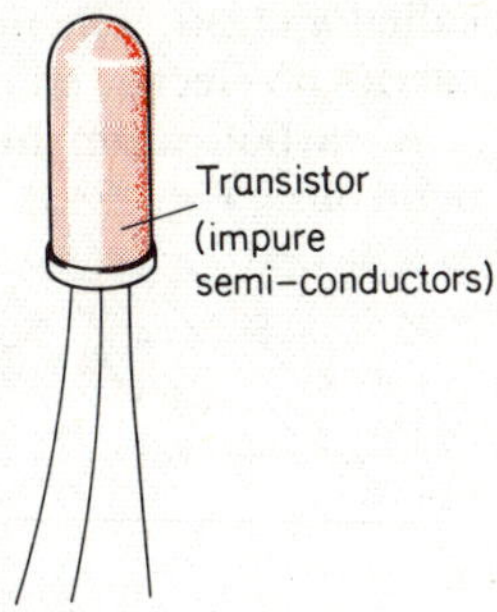

Fig. 24.7 Transistor

Electrons

Researches by Sir J. J. Thomson in 1897 showed that a minute particle existed inside the atom. It was called the *electron*. The electron is about one-two-thousandth of the mass of a hydrogen atom and carries a tiny quantity of *negative* electricity or 'charge'. Electrons are present in all atoms. We do not get any electrical shocks by handling everyday objects, so that normal atoms are electrically neutral. Normal atoms therefore contain a quantity of *positive* electricity equal in amount to the total negative electricity on all the electrons inside them.

The Nucleus

Researches by Lord Rutherford showed that the positive electricity is concentrated in a very tiny core or *nucleus* in the heart of the atom. This is discussed later (p. 584). The electrons move in orbits round the nucleus, creating a 'cloud' of negative electricity. The electrons are so

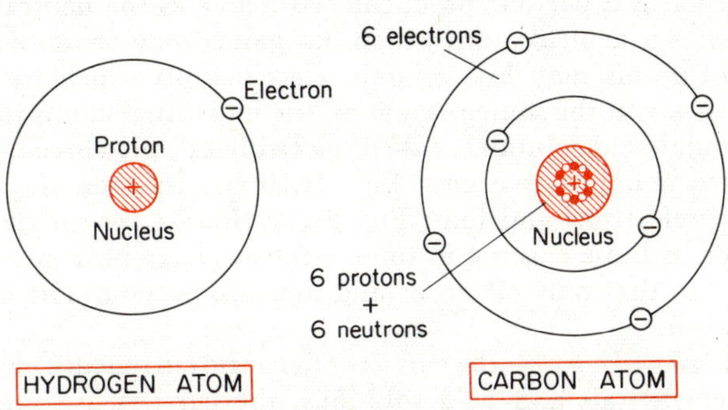

Fig. 24.8 Particles in hydrogen and carbon atoms

light that *practically the whole mass of the atom is concentrated in the nucleus.* The lightest nucleus is that of the hydrogen atom. It is called a *proton*, Fig. 24.8.

With atoms heavier than hydrogen, experiment shows that the nucleus is built up of particles which are protons and others which are called *neutrons*. The neutron has about the same mass as the proton but carries no electric charge.

A carbon atom has 12 particles in its nucleus—6 protons and 6 neutrons, Fig. 24.8. Outside the nucleus are 6 electrons. Natural uranium, one of the heaviest elements, has a nucleus which contains 92 protons and 146 neutrons. This is surrounded by 92 electrons.

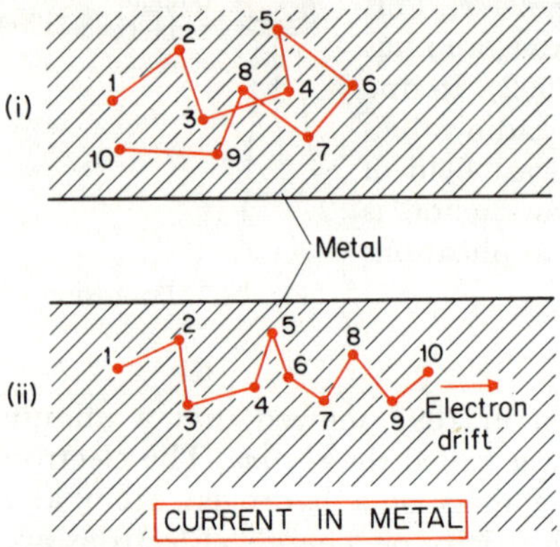

Fig. 24.9 Current carriers in metal

Metals are a special class of materials from an electrical point of view. The electrons in the outermost part of their atoms are relatively 'free'. They wander haphazardly through the metal. There is no external evidence of this random movement, because as many electrons are moving one way at any instant as are moving the opposite way, Fig. 24.9 (i). But when a battery is connected to the metal the electrons are driven one way, Fig. 24.9 (ii). They now drift in one direction along the metal, in addition to moving randomly. *The electron drift is the electric current in the metal.*

Ions

When an electron (negative electricity) leaves an atom completely, the atom is left with excess positive electricity equal in amount to that on the electron. It is now called a *positive ion*. Since the electron is so light, the ion is a particle practically as heavy as the neutral atom. A *negative ion* is a neutral atom which has gained one or more electrons. Groups of atoms may lose or gain electrons, in which case the ion formed has about the same mass as all the individual atoms together.

In salt and acid solutions, called 'electrolytes', the current is carried by positive and negative ions, Fig. 24.10 (i). In gases the current is carried by electrons and ions, Fig. 24.10 (ii). At very high temperatures, such as those existing in stars, electrons have been stripped from the atoms so that only electrons and ions are present. The gas is now called *plasma*.

Summarizing: In *metals* the carriers of electric current are electrons; in *liquids* such as salt and acid solutions, the carriers are positive and negative ions; and in *gases*, the carriers are electrons and ions.

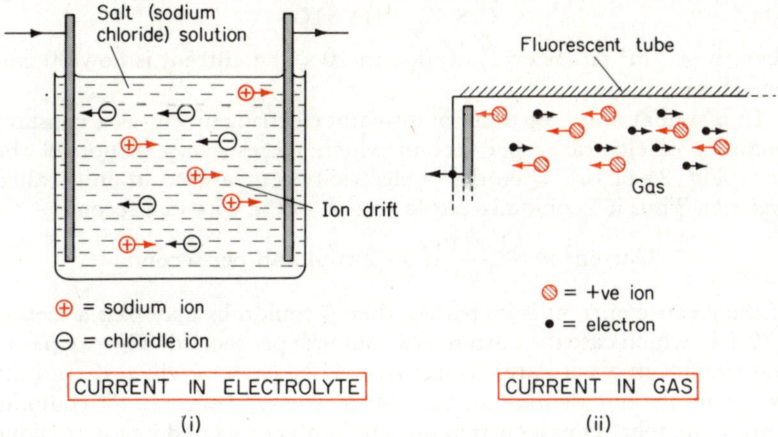

Fig. 24.10 Current carriers in (i) electrolyte (ii) gas

Electric Current

We now consider how an electric current is measured. The magnitude of an electric current is determined in a similar way to a water current. A water current can be measured by collecting the water running out at one end of a pipe in 10 s, for example, and measuring the volume. Suppose it is 60 cm^3. The water current is then a flow of 60 cm^3 per 10 s or 6 cm^3/s. Note that if the current is steady everywhere along the pipe, then 6 cm^3/s is the rate at which the volume passes every section of the pipe, Fig. 24.11 (i). If the water flows faster.

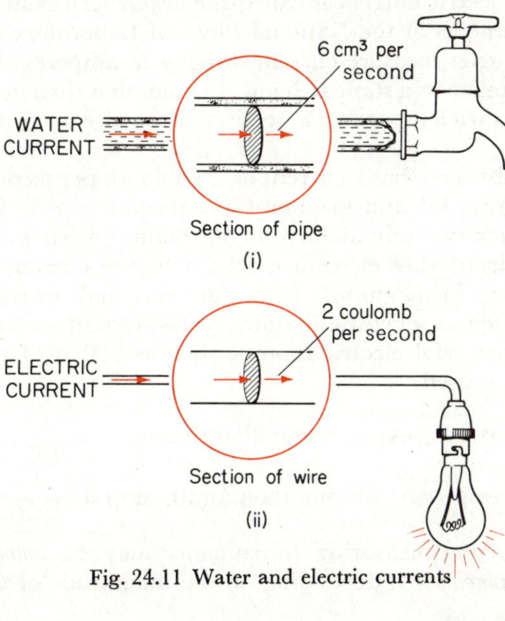

Fig. 24.11 Water and electric currents

then, if 90 cm^3 passes every section in 10 s, the current is now 90 cm^3 per 10 seconds or 9 cm^3/s.

In a similar way, we think of a steady electric current as a constant quantity of electricity per second which passes every section of the wire, Fig. 24.11 (ii). Quantity of electricity is measured in units called *coulombs*. Thus if 4 coulombs pass a section of the wire in 2 seconds,

$$\text{Current} = \frac{\text{Quantity}}{\text{Time}} = 2 \text{ coulomb per second}$$

If the electric current is increased, then 6 coulombs may pass a section in 2 s, in which case the current is 3 coulomb per second. The carriers of the current in a wire are electrons (p. 412), each of which carries the very minute but definite amount of electricity, $1{\cdot}6 \times 10^{-19}$ coulomb approximately. Thus a current of 1 coulomb per second in a wire is due to a flow of about 6×10^{18} electrons per second past any section of it.

All electrical quantities are denoted by an agreed set of symbols. Quantity of electricity is denoted by Q and electric current by I. Thus is Q coulombs flow past a section of a wire in t s, then

$$I = \frac{Q}{t}$$

Hence $$Q = I \,.\, t.$$

This means that if the current I is 4 coulomb per second and the time t is 10 s the quantity Q passing in that time $= 4 \times 10 = 40$ coulombs.

Ampere · Current Instruments

The unit of electric current is called the *ampere* (A). Nowadays, very accurate instruments at the National Physical Laboratory in England and other countries measure current directly in amperes (see p. 524). The ampere is taken as a standard unit. 1 coulomb is then defined as the quantity of electricity passing a section of a wire in 1 s when the current is 1 A.

It can hence be seen that a current of '2 coulomb per second' is a current of '2 amperes (A)', and 4 coulomb per second = 4 A. The current in a 100-watt electric-lamp filament in our mains system is about 0·4 A. A 1-kilowatt electric-fire element carries a higher current of about 4 A. Currents vary in magnitude from the very small in transistor sets or radio sets, such as several millionths or thousandths ampere, to the very large in powerful electric motors, such as 500 A. The following smaller units are used:

$$1 \text{ microamp } (\mu A) = \text{one-millionth amp} = \frac{1}{10^6} \text{ A.}$$

$$1 \text{ milliamp } (mA) = \text{one-thousandth amp} = \frac{1}{1000} \text{ A.}$$

Electrical current-measuring instruments may be *ammeters*, *milliammeters* or *microammeters*, depending on the magnitude of the current.

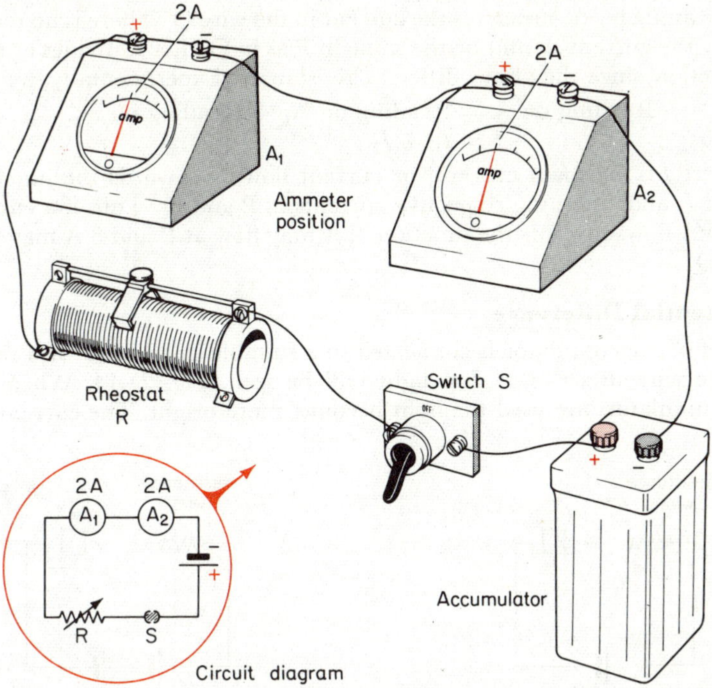

Fig. 24.12 Current in series circuit

A more sensitive instrument than the milliammeter is the *galvanometer*, which may measure or detect currents thousands of times smaller than the microammeter.

Position of Ammeters

The construction of instruments is discussed later (p. 521). Here we should note that an ammeter must always be placed in a circuit so that the current to be measured flows directly through it. In Fig. 24.12, for example, the current flows through the ammeter A_1 and through the ammeter A_2. Both measure the current in the circuit; and as the current does not flow faster at different points, the readings on the instruments are the same. An ammeter is said to be placed *in series* in the circuit. In Fig. 24.13 the ammeter A measures the current through the battery B or 'main' current. The ammeter A_1 measures the current in the wire P.

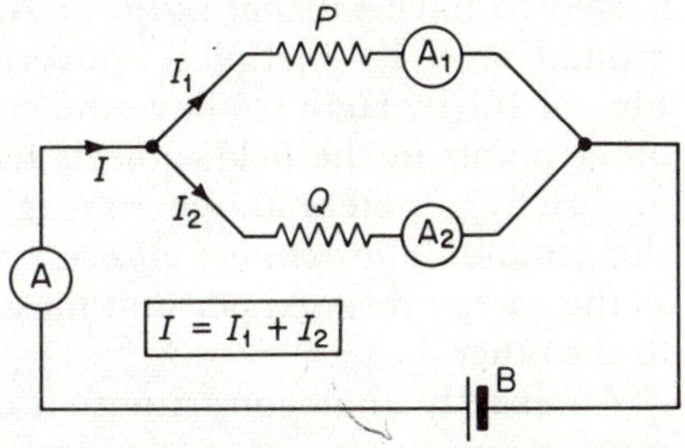

Fig. 24.13 Current in parallel circuit

The ammeter A_2 measures the current in the wire Q. There is no reason why the current should be the same in P as in Q after it divides at their junction, since they have different resistances. Experimentally, we find

$$\text{Reading on A} = \text{Reading on } A_1 + \text{Reading on } A_2.$$

Thus $$I = I_1 + I_2,$$

where I is the main current, or current flowing towards the junction, and I_1 and I_2 are the respective currents in P and Q. Thus if a current of 5 A flows towards the junction, 2 A may flow at P and 3 A may flow at Q.

Potential Difference

If one accumulator is connected to a suitable small bulb with resistance wire in series, a dim light will be seen, Fig. 24.14. When two accumulators are used the light becomes more bright. The current has

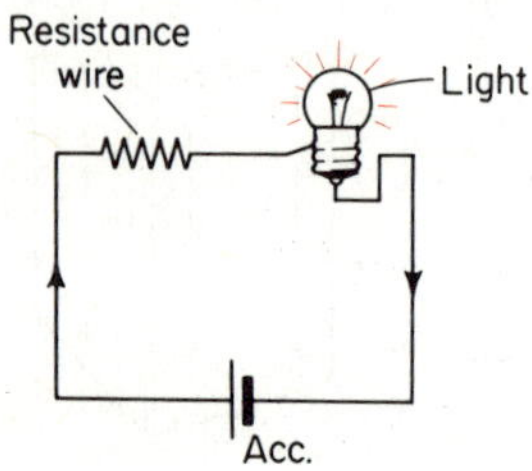

Fig. 24.14 One accumulator—dim light

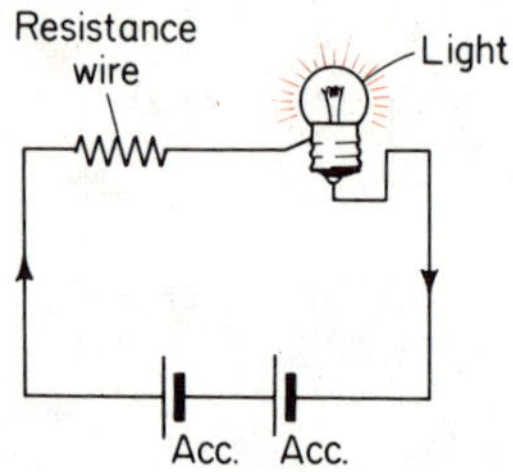

Fig. 24.15 Two accumulators—brighter light

increased, Fig. 24.15. Now heat is a form of energy, and the energy must have its origin in the movement of electricity through the bulb filament. The carriers of the current, the electrons (p. 412), must hence release energy when they move from one end of the filament to the other.

We have already met a case of movement from one position to another where change of position produces energy. This is the case of movement under gravity. An object held at a point A above the ground is said to have *potential energy* at A. When it is released and moves to ground level its energy is converted mainly to heat at the ground, Fig. 24.16 (i). Here we have the earth's 'gravitational field'. At A and other points in the field, objects have an amount of potential energy, or, briefly, a potential, whose magnitude depends on their level above the ground. The *potential difference* between two points may be defined as the energy released per unit mass when an object falls from one point to the other.

An exactly analogous situation occurs in electricity, except that we must imagine movement of quantity of electricity, carried by electrons, for example, instead of movement of masses, Fig. 24.16 (ii). Due to electrical exchanges between the atoms inside its chemicals, with which we are not concerned, the terminals of a battery or accumulator have an *electrical potential difference* (p.d.). One terminal, called the positive (+) terminal, is at a higher electrical potential than the other terminal, called the negative (−) terminal. If it could move, positive

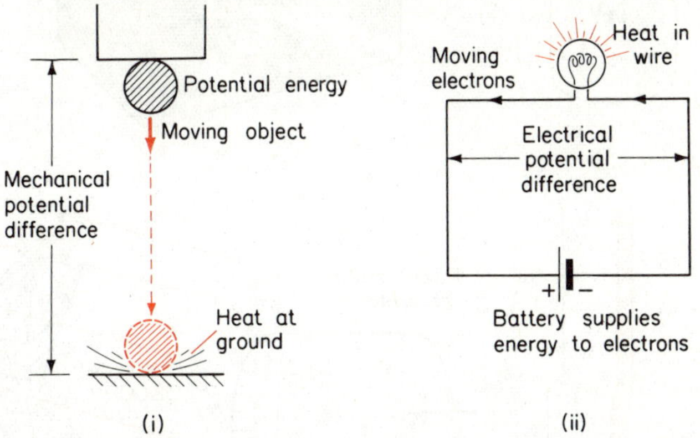

Fig. 24.16 Heat production by (i) mechanical (ii) electrical energy

electricity would move along a conductor joined to the terminals from the positive to the negative terminal. Or, what amounts to the same thing, negative electricity would move along the conductor from the negative to the positive terminal. When, therefore, a wire such as a bulb filament is joined to the terminals, electrons move along the metal from one end to the other. Energy is then released in the wire in the form of heat.

The Volt · Electrical Energy

The *volt* is the practical unit of potential difference. It is defined by reference to the joule, the practical unit of energy, as follows:

1 *volt is the potential difference between two points if* 1 *joule of energy is obtained when* 1 *coulomb moves between the points.*

A small torch battery has a p.d. at its terminals of about $1\frac{1}{2}$ V, Fig. 24.17. Car batteries usually have a p.d. of 12 V. The mains voltage in Great Britain is about 240 V. At power stations the generators have a p.d. of about 11 000 V. This is stepped-up nowadays to nearly 400 000 V for use in the Grid system, which distributes electricity throughout the country (p. 540). A generator built specially for nuclear-energy experiments has the enormously high p.d. of 7000 million V. Units of p.d. other than volts are:

1 microvolt (μV) = one-millionth volt
1 millivolt (mV) = one-thousandth volt
1 kilovolt (kV) = 1000 volts.

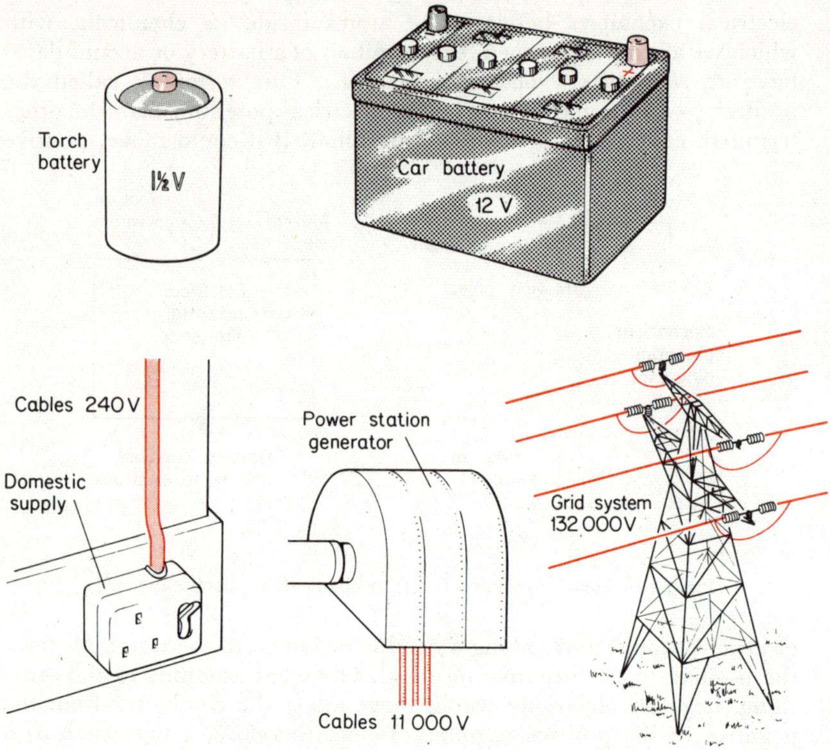

Fig. 24.17 Low and high p.d.s

From the definition of the volt, it follows that when 5 coulombs move between two points having a p.d. of 1 V, 5 J of energy are released. If 5 coulombs move through a p.d. of 2 V, then 10 J are released.

A 2 V accumulator releases this energy in 5 s when it maintains a current of 1 A in a lamp connected to it, since 5 coulombs then flow between the terminals. The 10 J of energy comes from the store of chemical energy in the accumulator. Electrical energy is discussed further on p. 461.

Voltmeter

A *voltmeter* is an instrument for measuring potential difference (p.d.). Since it has to measure the p.d. between two points, its terminals must be connected to those two points. In Fig. 24.18, for example, the voltmeter V_1 measures the p.d. between the ends A and B of the wire P, 0·5 V. The voltmeter V_2 measures the p.d. between

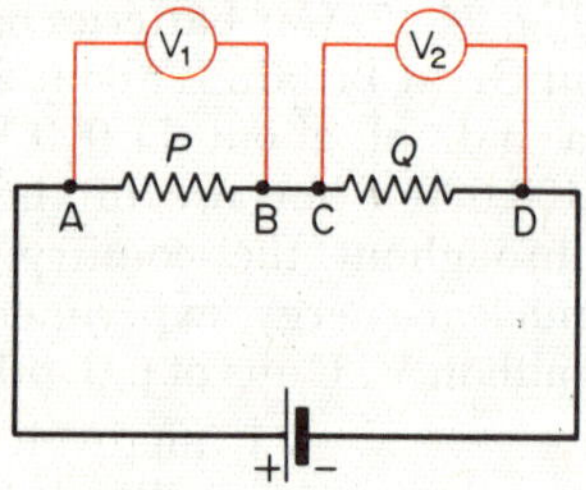

Fig. 24.18 P.d. in series circuit

the ends C and D of the wire Q, 1·5 V. Note that, in distinction from an ammeter, a *voltmeter is always connected 'outside', or in parallel with, a circuit.* Further, since some of the current may be diverted from P, for example, through the voltmeter itself, the voltmeter chosen must have a large electrical resistance compared with that of P. In this case only a very small amount of current flows through the voltmeter, leaving P practically unaffected when the voltmeter is joined across it.

P.d. Across Resistances

A voltmeter provides useful information on the distribution of p.d. in electrical circuits. In Fig. 24.19, for example, the voltmeter V_1 may read 2 V and V_2 may read 4 V. A voltmeter across *both* resistances then

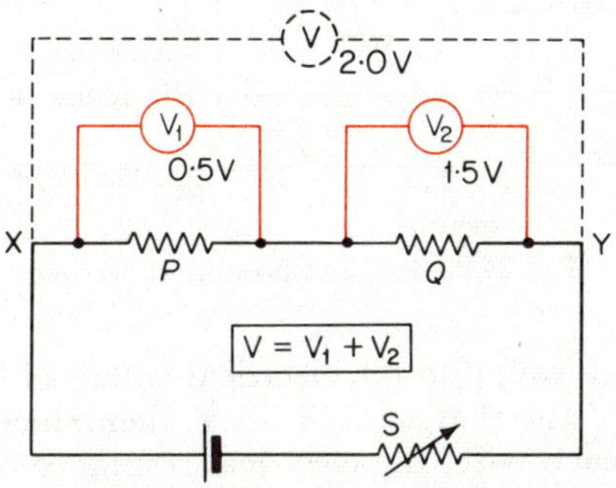

Fig. 24.19 Total p.d. in series circuit

reads 6 V. If the current is altered by the rheostat S, V_1 may now read 0·5 V and V_2 read 1·5 V, and the p.d. across X and Y is then 2·0 V, Fig. 24.19. Generally, then, for *resistance in series*, such as P and Q,

Total p.d. across resistances = Sum of individual p.d.s.

This result is explained from our energy definition of potential difference. The total energy released when electricity moves through P and then through Q must be equal to the sum of the separate amounts of energy in P and Q individually.

Hydrostatic Analogy

Another popular (but not accurate) way of describing potential difference is by means of an analogy with flow of water through pipes. A water current can be obtained only if a pressure difference exists between the ends of the pipe concerned. In the same way, an electric current can flow in a wire only if a potential difference exists between its ends. If two pipes A and B of different internal diameter are joined together, and a steady water current flows along them, the total difference of pressure, XZ, between the extreme ends must be the sum of the pressure differences, XY and YZ, across A and B separately, Fig.

24.20 (i). Further, if B is narrower than A, a greater pressure difference is required to drive the same current through B as through A. We say that the 'resistance' of B is greater than that of A to water flow.

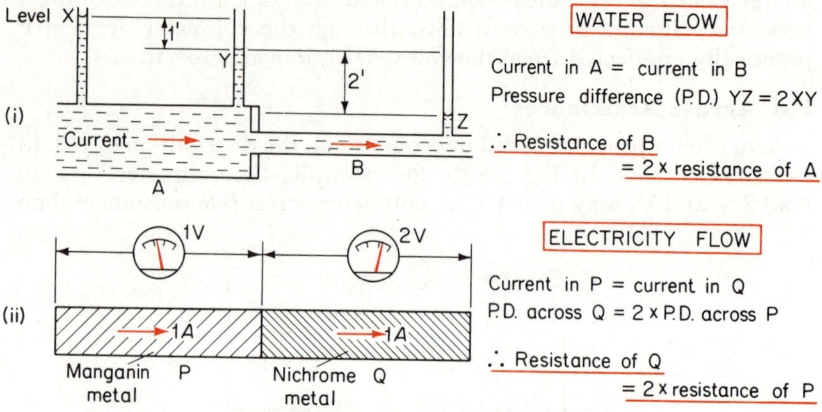

Fig. 24.20 P.d. and pressure difference

In an analogous way, if in the electrical circuit of Fig. 24.20 (ii) the p.d. across Q is 2 V and that across P is 1 V, then, since the same electric current flows in each wire, the electrical resistance of Q is more than that of P.

Resistance · Ohm's Law

In 1826 Ohm found by experiment that:

The electric current in a given conductor is directly proportional to the potential difference applied, provided that the temperature of the conductor and its other physical factors remain constant.

This is known as *Ohm's law*. It means that when the temperature of a given wire is constant, and a p.d. of 1 V, 2 V and 3 V is connected in turn across the wire, the currents flowing on each occasion may be respectively $\frac{1}{2}$ A, 1 A and $1\frac{1}{2}$ A. The ratio

$$\frac{\text{Potential difference}}{\text{Current}}$$

is then constant and equal to 2 units. A thinner wire of the same material and length may carry currents of $\frac{1}{8}$, $\frac{1}{4}$ and $\frac{3}{8}$ A respectively, when a p.d. of 1 V, 2 V and 3 V is connected in turn. The constant ratio for this wire is then 8 units. Although good conductors such as metals and alloys obey Ohm's law, many circuit components widely used in industry do not obey the law. Metal rectifiers, diode radio valves, and voltage-dependent resistors are examples of components which do not obey Ohm's law (see p. 358).

Ohm defined electrical *resistance* by the ratio

$$\frac{\text{P.d. applied}}{\text{Current}}$$

We can see this ratio represents a 'resistance', because the larger the resistance, the greater is the p.d. required to maintain a given current. The symbol used for resistance is R. Its unit is the *ohm* (Ω, Greek letter 'omega' = ohm). *One ohm is therefore the resistance of a wire when a p.d. of* 1 *volt across it maintains a current of* 1 *ampere.*

The magnitude of resistance ranges from very small values, such as $\frac{1}{100}\ \Omega$ for a piece of copper wire, to the very large values used in radio and television sets, such as a million ohms, Fig. 24.21. A small rheostat

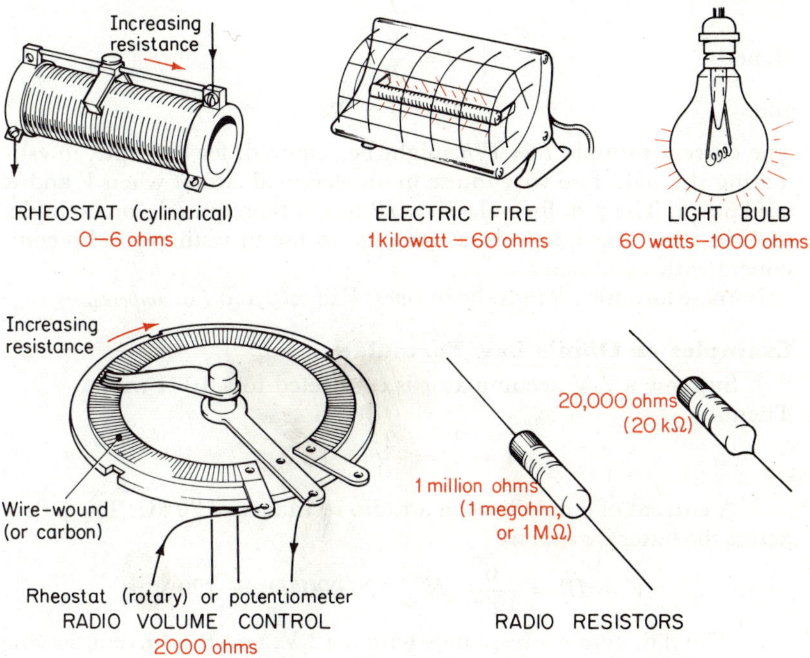

Fig. 24.21 Electrical resistors

in the laboratory may have a total resistance of a few ohms. A rotary rheostat or 'potentiometer' used in radio may have a total resistance of two thousand ohms. Many radio resistors, small in size but having very high values such as a million ohms, for example, are made by mixing a powder of carbon and ceramic. The carbon resistor is moulded and baked. Its value is painted on the outside according to a colour code. The 1-kW element of an electric fire made of Nichrome has a resistance of about 60 Ω. The tungsten filament of a 60 W electric lamp has a resistance of nearly 1000 Ω, Fig. 24.21.

Units of resistance other than the ohm are:

1 microhm ($\mu\Omega$) = one-millionth ohm
1 kilohm ($k\Omega$) = 1000 ohms
1 megohm ($M\Omega$) = one million (10^6) ohms.

Fundamental Formulae

Electrical and radio engineers have particular need of formulae for calculating current, potential difference and resistance. We have seen that, by definition, resistance = p.d./current. Thus if R, V and I represent the magnitude of the three quantities,

$$\boldsymbol{R = \frac{V}{I}}.$$

Hence $$\boldsymbol{I = \frac{V}{R}}$$

and $$\boldsymbol{V = I \times R}.$$

The current formula $I = V/R$ might be required, for example, in estimating the right fuse wire to use in an electrical circuit when V and R are known. The p.d. formula $V = IR$ might be required, for example, in estimating the right voltmeter range to use in testing a radio component with a voltmeter.

In these formulae R must be in *ohms*, V in *volts* and I in *amperes*.

Examples on Ohm's Law Formulae

1. Suppose a 2 V accumulator is connected to a 10 Ω wire. Then

$$I = \frac{V}{R} = \frac{2}{10} = 0{\cdot}2 \text{ A}.$$

2. A current of 6 mA flows in a radio resistance of 20 kΩ. The p.d. V across the latter is given by

$$V = IR = \frac{6}{1000} \text{ (A)} \times 20\,000 \text{ } (\Omega) = 120 \text{ V}.$$

3. The p.d. across a resistance wire is 12 V, and the current flowing is 2 A. Thus the resistance is

$$R = \frac{V}{I} = \frac{12}{2} = 6\ \Omega.$$

Measurement of Resistance · Voltmeter-Ammeter Method

The resistance R of a coil of wire can be found by direct application of the definition $R = V/I$. An accumulator B is connected to the wire, with a rheostat T and an ammeter A in series, Fig. 24.22. A voltmeter V is connected across the wire. When the current is switched on and the rheostat T adjusted for convenient current and p.d. values, the readings on the ammeter and voltmeter are observed.

Suppose $V = 0{\cdot}4$ V, $I = 0{\cdot}3$ A. Then

$$R = \frac{V}{I} = \frac{0{\cdot}4}{0{\cdot}3} = 1\tfrac{1}{3}\,\Omega.$$

By varying the rheostat, other values of V and I may be obtained. The average value of the resistance can then be found either by calculation, or from the gradient of the straight-line graph obtained by plotting V v. I. High currents are unsuitable in the experiment, as the

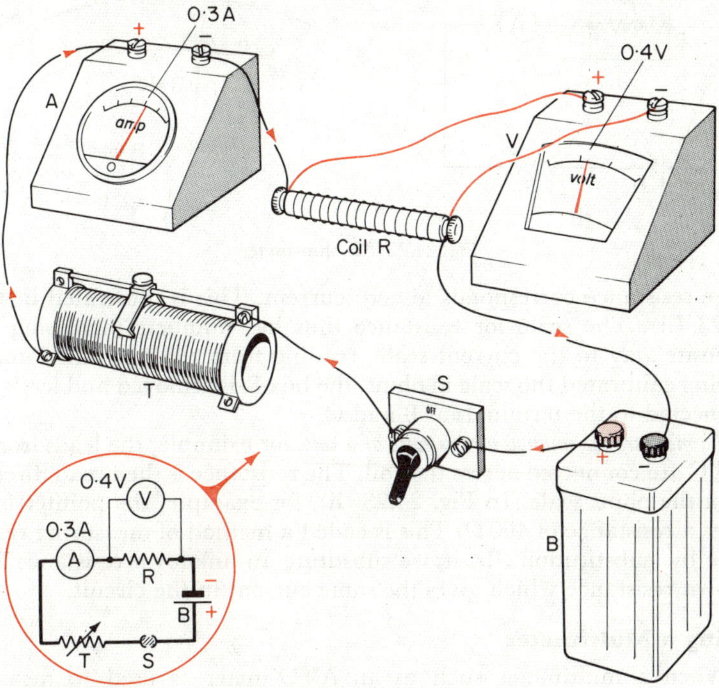

Fig. 24.22 Measurement of resistance

wire may get too hot and its temperature vary, in which case its resistance may change appreciably.

Resistance by Substitution

A *multimeter* is a commercial instrument widely used for measuring directly current ('amps' A), p.d. ('volts' V) and resistance ('ohms' Ω). As explained later on p. 523, switches on the instrument enable different ranges of current and p.d. to be obtained.

The principle of measuring resistance in this way can be understood by using a box of known resistances R in series with a current measuring instrument A such as a milliammeter, a rheostat S and an accumulator D, Fig. 24.23 (i).

Firstly, R is made zero. S is then varied until the maximum reading, say 15 mA, is obtained on the instrument. The figure '0' is then marked on the scale beneath '15'. Fig. 24.23 (ii). This is the zero of the *ohms scale*, since $R = 0$. A resistance of 10 Ω, for example, is then used in R. The current diminishes and the figure '10' is marked on the ohms scale at the new pointer position, since $R = 10$ Ω. In this way, taking more resistance from R, the scale can be calibrated in ohms. An infinitely

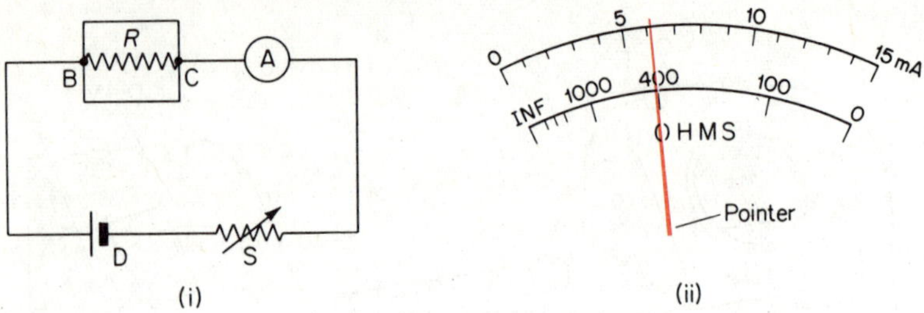

Fig. 24.23 An ohm-meter

large resistance corresponds to zero current. This is illustrated in Fig. 24.23 (ii). The scale for resistance thus has numbers increasing the opposite way to the current scale, reading from right to left. Finally, having calibrated the scale in ohms, the box R is removed and leads are connected to the terminals at B and C.

To measure the unknown resistance of a coil, for example, the leads from B and C are connected across the coil. The resistance is then read directly from the ohms scale. In Fig. 24.23 (ii), for example, the pointer indicates a resistance of 400 Ω. This is called a method of measuring resistance by 'substitution'. In it, we substitute an unknown resistance by a known resistance which gives the same current in the circuit.

Using a Multimeter

When a multimeter such as an AVO-meter is used to measure resistance, the switch is first turned to 'resistance'. This connects a battery at the back to the instrument. Thus when the metal ends of the leads touch, a current flows and the needle is deflected. A rheostat inside the meter is then turned until the needle reaches the end of the current scale. This is the 'zero' on the *ohms* scale. The contact between the leads is now broken, and they are placed across the ends of an unknown resistance R. The magnitude of R is read from the ohms scale directly. In using the ohm-meter, always be sure to connect the ends of the leads together *first* and then set the reading on the ohms scale to zero by means of the rheostat. Otherwise the reading on the ohms scale for an unknown resistance will be in error.

Resistance of Lamp

Electric lamp filaments, which are usually made of tungsten, are designed to work at a particular voltage. Their temperature is then high and a glow is obtained.

Fig. 24.24 shows a circuit for investigating the variation of the resistance of a filament of a 12 V ray-box lamp L with applied voltage. A 12 V battery is joined to the two outer terminals, C, B, of a rheostat. The slider terminal D, and the terminal C, are joined to L. A voltmeter, V, joined to C and D, measures the p.d. applied.

When the slider is moved to D, contact with B is made. The whole p.d. 12 V is then connected to L, which now glows brightly. When the slider is moved to the position shown in Fig. 24.24 (i), contact is made

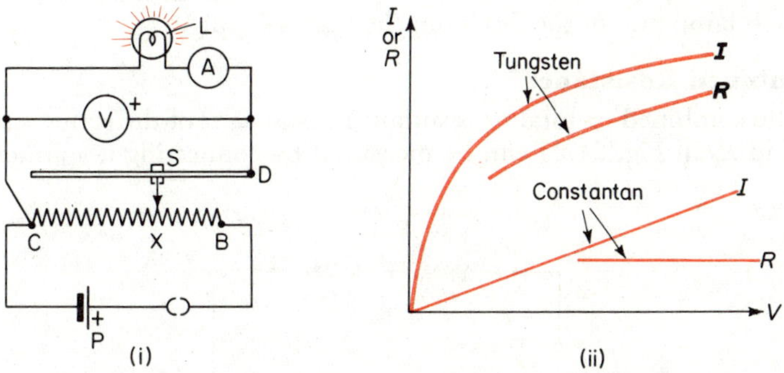

Fig. 24.24 Variation of current and resistance with p.d.

with X on the wire. Only the p.d. across the length CX is connected to L this time. The p.d. is thus less than before. As S is moved farther to C, the p.d. diminishes more. The filament glow thus becomes weaker. When S makes contact with C no p.d. is applied to L.

Measurement of the p.d. V and the current I enables the filament resistance R to be found at different voltages V, using $R = V/I$.

A graph of the results is shown in Fig. 24.24 (ii). It shows that: (i) the current is not proportional to the p.d., (ii) from the graph it follows that the resistance R of the filament increases with the p.d. V, and hence with temperature rise. The filament is made of tungsten, a material which alters in resistance when its temperature changes.

For comparison, Fig. 24.24 (ii) also shows the directly proportional variation of I with V by a coil of wire made of the alloy Constantan. In contrast to the tungsten coil, its resistance R depends very slightly on the p.d. V or temperature, as shown.

Resistances in Series

In electrical circuits such as those in radio receivers several resistances, such as R_1 and R_2 in Fig. 24.25, may be in *series*.

Wherever the ammeter A is positioned, between R_1 and R_2, or to the left of R_1, or as shown, the current registered is always the same. The flow of electricity or current is thus the same in R_1 as in R_2.

If R_1 and R_2 are different, measurement of the p.d. across R_1 may be 3 V and across R_2 it may be 5 V. A smaller p.d. is thus needed across R_1 to maintain the same current as in R_2. This is because the resistance of R_1 is less than the resistance of R_2. The *total* p.d. across R_1 and R_2 is 8 V, the sum of the individual p.ds. of 3 V and 5 V.

Thus: (i) *the current is the same in resistors in series;* (ii) *the sum of the p.ds. across the individual resistors is equal to the p.d. across all of them.* As an illustration, a set of twelve identical lights can be obtained to decorate a Christmas tree. Each is a 20 V lamp designed to carry a current of 0·3 A. When connected to the 240 V mains, the twelve series lamps each have a p.d. of 240 V/12 or 20 V. The same current, 0·3 A, flows in each lamp and in the flex from the mains supply.

Combined Resistance

The combined or total or resultant resistance R of the series resistors R_1 and R_2 in Fig. 24.25 can be measured by connecting a voltmeter V

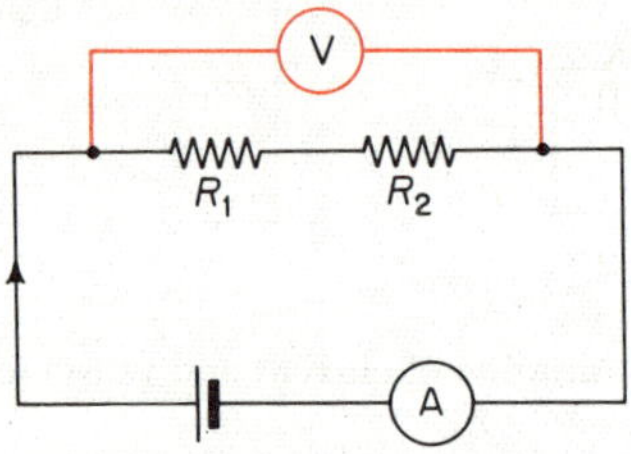

Fig. 24.25 Resistances in series

across both, as shown, and observing the readings on V and the ammeter A. In one case,

$$V = 2{\cdot}4 \text{ V}, \quad I = 0{\cdot}2 \text{ A}.$$

$$\therefore \text{Combined resistance } R_1 = \frac{V}{I} = \frac{2{\cdot}4}{0{\cdot}2} = 12\ \Omega.$$

R_1 and R_2 can each be measured separately, as explained on p. 422. Results were obtained as follows:

$$R_1\colon V = 3{\cdot}2 \text{ V}, I = 0{\cdot}4 \text{ A, so that } R_1 = \frac{V}{I} = 8\ \Omega$$

$$R_2\colon V = 2{\cdot}0 \text{ V}, I = 0{\cdot}5 \text{ A, so that } R_2 = \frac{V}{I} = 4\Omega$$

The experiment thus shows that

$$R = R_1 + R_2$$

when two resistances are in series. The total resistance of 4, 6 and 8 Ω in series is similarly 18 Ω.

Two-way Switch

In most domestic wiring arrangements there is a need for a light which can be switched on when entering one end of a hall or passage and switched off at the other end when leaving or arriving upstairs. A *two-way* switching circuit is used in this case.

Fig. 24.26 shows the necessary circuit. It consists of two double-pole switches A and B in series, connected by a twin-core cable C. These switches are so constructed that terminal *c* on switch A, for example, can be connected either to terminal *a* or to terminal *b*.

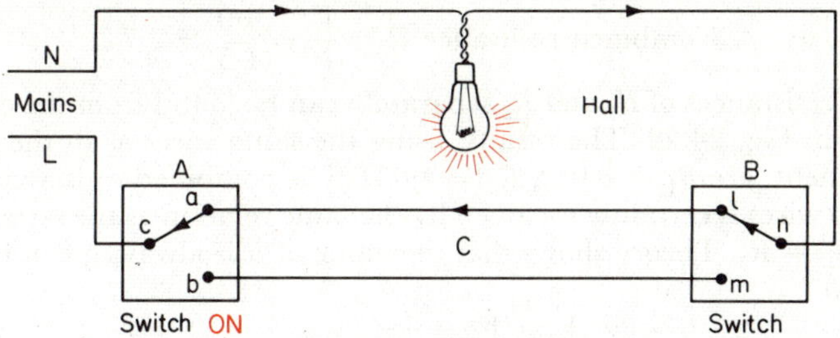

Fig. 24.26 Two-way switch

Consider what happens when switch A is in such a position that terminal *c* is joined to terminal *a*. If switch B is now pressed on entering a hall so as to connect terminals *l* and *n*, the circuit is completed and the lamp lights up. If switch A is pressed on leaving the other end of the hall, the circuit is broken and the lamp is extinguished. Another person switching on A or B at either end of the hall will make the lamp light up again. A two-way switching circuit can therefore control a lamp (or other electrical appliance) by operating either switch.

Resistances in Parallel

In commercial lighting and other circuits resistances are connected to the same two points. They are then said to be *in parallel*. In Fig. 24.27 (i), for example, some lamps L are each connected to the mains, so that switching one lamp on or off in a room has no effect on the p.d. applied to the other lamps in the same building. The lamps are in parallel across the mains. Thus unlike the case of resistance in series, *the p.d. is the same across conductors in parallel.*

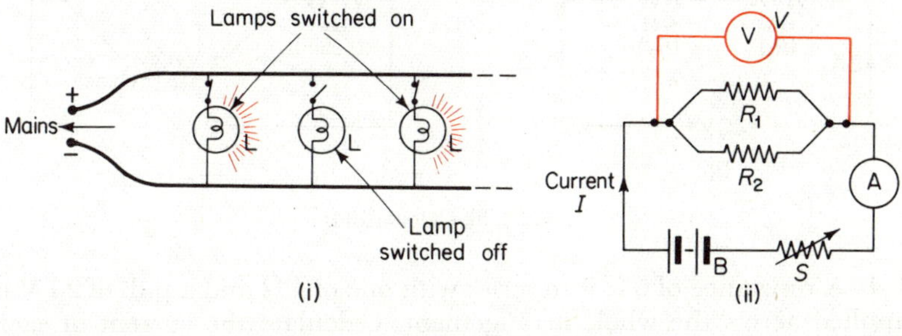

Fig. 24.27 Resistances in parallel

Combining Parallel Resistances

Fig. 24.27 (ii) shows two resistances R_1 and R_2 in parallel in a circuit, with a rheostat S, an ammeter A and a battery B. The p.d. V across the two resistances can be measured by a voltmeter V and the current I flowing towards them is measured by A. In one case, $V = 4{\cdot}0$ V, $I = 1{\cdot}5$ A.

$$\therefore \text{ Combined resistance } R = \frac{V}{I} = \frac{4{\cdot}0}{1{\cdot}5} = 2{\cdot}7\ \Omega \quad . \quad (1)$$

The resistances of R_1 and R_2 separately can be found from the circuit shown in Fig. 24.22. The results, using the same wires as in the series experiment, are $R_1 = 8{\cdot}0\ \Omega$, $R_2 = 4{\cdot}0\ \Omega$. The combined resistance R of the two wires is certainly *not* given by the same relation as the series one, $R = R_1 + R_2$. Theory shows that the value of R is always given by the relation

$$\frac{1}{R} = \frac{1}{R_1} + \frac{1}{R_2}.$$

Thus

$$\frac{1}{R} = \frac{1}{8{\cdot}0} + \frac{1}{4{\cdot}0} = \frac{3}{8}$$

$$\therefore\ R = \frac{8}{3} = 2{\cdot}7\ \Omega.$$

This calculation for R agrees with the experimental result obtained previously in (1). Similarly, the combined resistance of 3 and 6 Ω in parallel is given by:

$$\frac{1}{R} = \frac{1}{3} + \frac{1}{6} = \frac{3}{6}, \text{ or } R = \frac{6}{3} = 2\ \Omega.$$

Examples on Series and Parallel Circuits

The following examples illustrate how currents and p.d.s. are calculated in series and parallel circuits, and should be studied carefully.

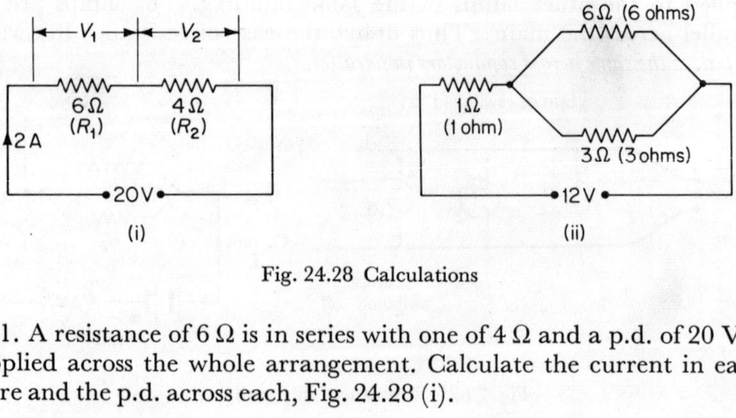

Fig. 24.28 Calculations

1. A resistance of 6 Ω is in series with one of 4 Ω and a p.d. of 20 V is applied across the whole arrangement. Calculate the current in each wire and the p.d. across each, Fig. 24.28 (i).

20 V is the p.d. across *both* wires together.

The combined resistances = 6 + 4 = 10 Ω.

$$\therefore \text{ current } I = \frac{V}{R} = \frac{20}{10} = 2 \text{ A}.$$

Across the 6 Ω wire alone $V_1 = IR_1 = 2 \times 6 = 12$ V.
Across the 4 Ω wire alone $V_2 = IR_2 = 2 \times 4 = 8$ V.

NOTE

A common error is to state that the current in the 6 Ω wire is $\frac{20}{6}$ A. This is *not* the case, because 20 V is not the p.d. across the 6 Ω wire but across both wires.

2. A circuit consists of a 1 Ω wire in series with a parallel arrangement of 6 and 3 Ω, and a p.d. of 12 V is connected across the whole circuit, Fig. 24.28 (ii). Calculate the currents in each of the three wires and the p.d. across each.

Since 12 V is the p.d. across the whole circuit, we must first find the combined resistance S of the 6 and 3 Ω in parallel and add the result to 1 Ω.

We have $$\frac{1}{S} = \frac{1}{6} + \frac{1}{3} = \frac{3}{6}, \quad \text{or} \quad S = \frac{6}{3} = 2 \, \Omega.$$

$$\therefore \text{ Total circuit resistance } R = 2 + 1 = 3 \, \Omega.$$

$$\therefore \text{ Current flowing } I = \frac{V}{R} = \frac{12}{3} = 4 \text{ A}.$$

This is the current in the 3 Ω wire.

To find the current I_1 in the 6 Ω wire, we need to know the p.d. V_1 across the 6 and 3 Ω in parallel. Now the current I, or 4 A in the 1 Ω wire, is also the current flowing through the single wire which could replace the parallel wires in the circuit. This is the wire of resistance S of 2 Ω already calculated.

$$\therefore \; V_1 = I \times 2 = 4 \times 2 = 8 \text{ V}$$

$$\therefore \text{ Current in 6 Ω wire, } I_1 = \frac{V_1}{6} = \frac{8}{6} = 1\tfrac{1}{3} \text{ A}.$$

Similarly,

$$\text{Current in 3-Ω wire, } I_2 = \frac{V_1}{3} = \frac{8}{3} = 2\tfrac{2}{3} \text{ A}.$$

As a check, note that $1\frac{1}{3} + 2\frac{2}{3} = 4$ A = Current in 1 Ω wire. Thus:

(*a*) the currents are respectively 4 A, $1\frac{1}{3}$ A, $2\frac{1}{3}$ A;
(*b*) the p.ds. are respectively 4 V, 8 V, 8 V.

SUMMARY

1. Current carriers in metals are *electrons* (light particles carrying negative electrical charges); carriers in salt and acid solutions are *ions* (particles as heavy as atoms and carrying positive or negative charges).

2. Current, I, is measured in amperes (A). Quantity of electricity is measured in coulombs. Current is 'quantity per second' passing a section of wire.

3. Potential difference, p.d., is measured in volts (V).

4. An ammeter measures current—it is always placed in series with the circuit. A voltmeter measures p.d.—it is always placed in parallel. A voltmeter has a high resistance; an ammeter has a low resistance.

5. $R = V/I$, $I = V/R$, $V = IR$.

6. Resistance may be measured by a voltmeter-ammeter method.

7. Combined resistance. In series—$R = R_1 + R_2$.
In parallel, $1/R = 1/R_1 + 1/R_2$.

PRACTICAL (Notes for guidance, p. 26)

1. Conductors and Insulators

Apparatus. A small electric light bulb L, 2·5 V, 0·3 A, and holder with a 2 V accumulator B (or 1·25 V, 0·3 A bulb and $1\frac{1}{2}$ V dry battery); crocodile clips X and Y if available; connecting wire, Fig. 24.29.

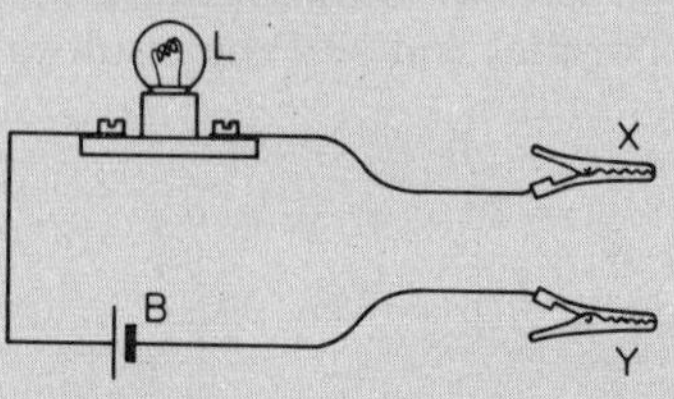

Fig. 24.29 Conductor and insulator

Method. (i) Arrange the circuit shown—start from the positive pole of the battery and work round to the negative pole.

(ii) Place X and Y in contact—the bulb should light. If not, re-check the circuit for faulty connection.

(iii) Connect X and Y across various materials. If the bulb L glows brightly, this is a good conductor; if the glow is faint, it is a poor conductor; and if there is no light, it is an insulator. Some suggestions are: a pen-knife, a key, coins, a nail, copper wire, constantan or eureka wire, carbon in a pencil sharpened at both ends, a pair of pliers, wood, paper, glass, plastic, thread, brine solution, copper sulphate solution, dilute acid solution. Tabulate the results:

Material	Result

Are all metals good conductors? Is air normally a conductor or an insulator?

2. More Investigations

Apparatus. Glass such as microscope slide. Copper plate. Bunsen burner. Candle or taper. About $\frac{1}{2}$-metre twin plastic covered domestic flex. Apparatus with battery, bulb and X and Y as in previous experimental.

Method. (i) Connect X and Y across the glass plate. Observe if the bulb lights. Moisten some blotting paper and wet the glass between X and Y. Observe if the bulb lights.

(ii) Oxidize one surface of a copper plate by placing it in a clamp and playing a low bunsen flame on the surface. Investigate if the oxide has changed the electrical resistance of the surface.

(iii) Expose the copper wires from the plastic covered flex and connect the battery to the bulb by them. (*a*) Test the insulation of the flex by immersing part of it in cold water and then hot water, and observing if this has any effect on the light; (*b*) remove the flex from the liquid, cut the plastic near the bulb so that the two copper wires in each plastic strip actually touch one another, and observe the effect on the light.

3. Series Circuit (p. 425)

Apparatus. Three small bulbs L, M and N, each 2·5 V 0·3 A; 4½ V dry battery or 2–2 V accummulators B; rheostat R of a few ohms; switch S, Fig. 24.30.

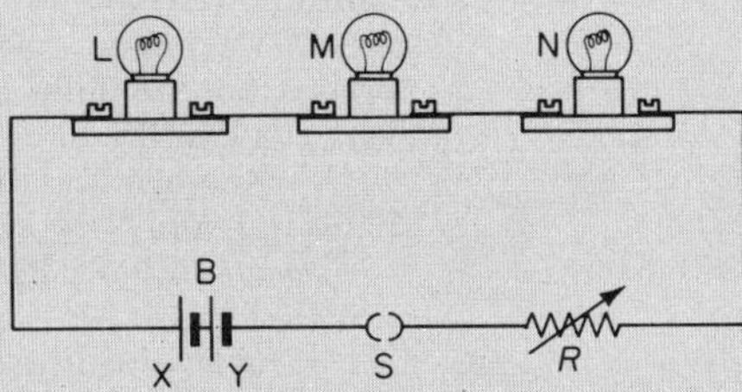

Fig. 24.30 Series circuit

Method. (i) Connect the batteries or accummulators in series, B, that is, join the negative pole of one to the positive pole of the next battery, and so on, leaving one positive pole X and one negative pole Y free.

(ii) Join the three lamps L, M and N in series with the rheostat R and the switch S—start with the positive pole X and work round to the negative pole Y.

(iii) Switch on—if the lamps do not light up, re-check for faulty connection. Check that the rheostat R is working by moving the variable contact, when the lights should change—if not, you have not connected to the variable contact terminal on the rheostat.

Observe the effect on the bulbs in the following cases and enter the results in a table:

Procedure	Effect on bulbs	Deduction
Vary R	(Is light different or same in each bulb?)	Current in L, M, N is (*same or different*?)
Short out M	(*a*) (Is light different or same as before?)	(*a*) Current (*increases or decreases*?)
Then short out L	(*b*) (Is light different or same in two bulbs left?)	(*b*) Current in two bulbs (*same or different*?)
Interchange rheostat R position with M, and then with N	(Is light different or same in L, M and N?)	Current is (*same or different*) in a series circuit when components are interchanged

4. Currents in Parallel Circuit

Apparatus. Three bulbs L, M and N, each 2·5 V, 0·3 A; two 1½ V dry batteries or 2 V accumulator A; rheostat R of a few ohms; switch S.

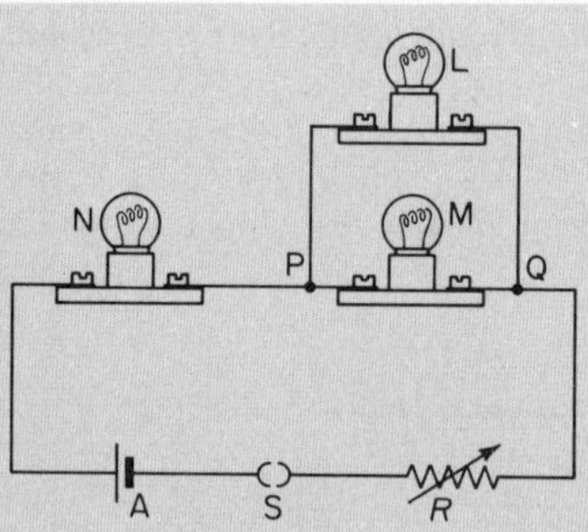

Fig. 24.31 Currents in circuit

Method. (i) Starting from the positive pole of A, connect the circuit as shown in Fig. 24.31. Note that L and M are in parallel—they have common terminals P and Q.

(ii) Switch on. The bulbs should all light up, otherwise re-check connections.

(iii) Vary R so that the light in N is bright. Are the bulbs L and M as bright as N? Is L as bright as M?

(iv) Remove the bulb M. Are the lights in L and N as bright as each other?

Tabulate your results, as in the previous experiment.

Explain the results by considering the current flowing in each bulb.

5. Series circuit—Current and P.D.

Apparatus. Two resistance coils P and Q of a few ohms each: 2 V accummulator B; two suitable ammeters A_1 and A_2 each 0–2 A; suitable voltmeter, 0–3 V; rheostat R of a few ohms; switch S.

Method. (i) *Current.* Starting with the positive pole of B, complete the circuit shown in Fig. 24.32 (i). Make sure the positive terminals of A_1 and A_2 are on the positive side of B, so that their pointers deflect the right way.

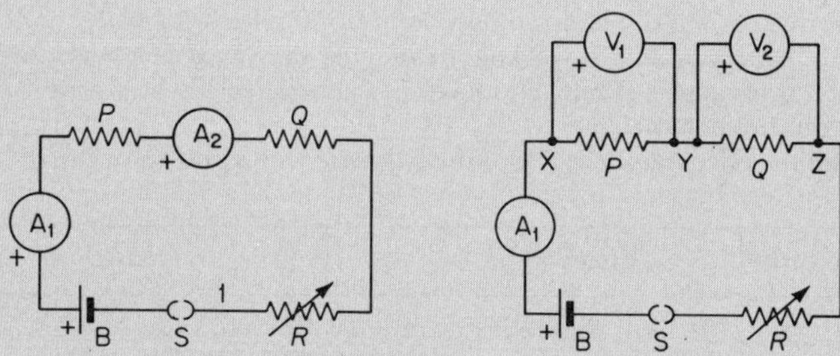

Fig. 24.32 Series circuit

(*a*) Switch on. Note the readings on A_1 and A_2. Vary R so that the readings change. Note the readings on A_1 and A_2 again. Repeat once more by varying R.

(*b*) Switch off. Move A_1 to position 1 between the switch S and R. Repeat for three readings on A_1 and A_2 by varying R.

Measurements.

(*a*)

	Reading on A_1	Reading on A_2
1st position of R		
2nd ,, ,, R		
3rd ,, ,, R		

(*b*)

Reading on A_1	Reading on A_2

(ii) *P.d.* Switch off. Remove one ammeter so that the circuit appears as in Fig. 24.32 (ii). Connect one voltmeter V_1 across the wire *P* and the other voltmeter V_2 across the wire *Q*. (Voltmeters are always joined in *parallel* across a wire, p. 423). Make sure that the positive terminals of the voltmeters are on the positive side of the battery B, so that their pointers deflect the right way.

(*a*) Switch on. Alter *R* so that appreciable readings on V_1 and V_2 are obtained. Record the two values.

(*b*) Switch off. Remove V_2 completely. Move the V_1 connection from Y to Z. Now note the p.d. *V* across X, Z—this is the p.d. across both coils *P* and *Q*.

(*c*) Alter *R* so that the p.d. readings across the coils change. Again note V_1, V_2 and *V*, the total p.d. across the coils, as previously. Repeat once more for a new position of *R*.

Measurements.

	V_1 (across *P*)	V_2 (across *Q*)	*V* (across *P* and *Q*)
1st value of *R*			
2nd ,, ,, *R*			
3rd ,, ,, *R*			

Conclusion. State your conclusion.

6. Variation of p.d.

Method. (i) Cut off a metre length of resistance wire such as Constantan.

(ii) By using crocodile clips or another method, stretch it tightly across the scale of a metre rule so that you can read any length of the wire, HL, from the scale, Fig. 24.33.

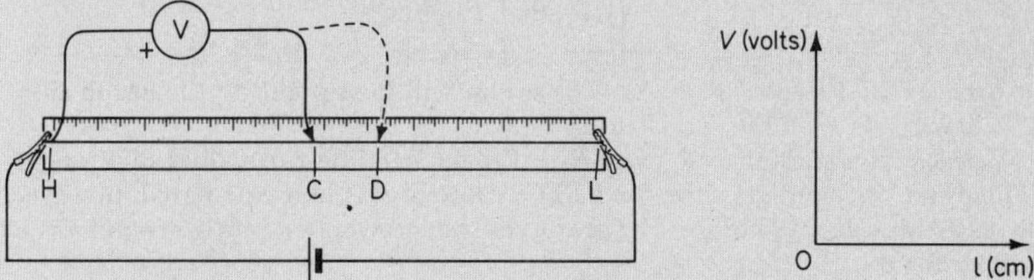

Fig. 24.33 Variation of p.d.

(iii) Connect a 1·5 V dry battery or a 2 V accumulator to the ends H and L. Join one terminal of a 0–2 V voltmeter to the end H. Connect a long wire to the other terminal and attach a crocodile clip to the free end.

(iv) By pressing the clip on the wire at C or D, for example, measure the p.d. *V* across increasing lengths *l* measured from the end H. For example, $l = 10, 20, 30, 40$ .. cm. Enter the results in a table.

Measurements.

l (cm)	*V* (volts)

Graph. Plot V (volts) v. l (cm). Join the points; the graph passes through the origin since $V = 0$ when $l = 0$.

Conclusion. From the graph obtained, how does V vary with l?

7. Measurement of Resistance (p. 423)

Apparatus. 2 V accumulator B, a length of resistance wire PQ of a few ohms,; rheostat R of a few ohms; Switch S; ammeter A, 0–2 A, voltmeter V, 0–3 V, connecting wire, Fig. 24.34 (i).

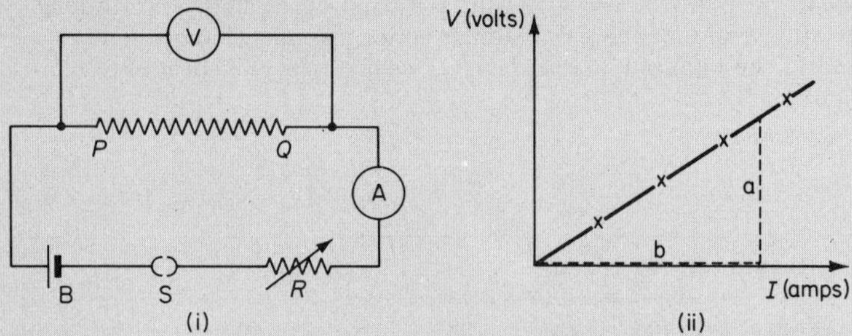

Fig. 24.34 Measurement of resistance

Method. Starting from the positive pole of the battery B, complete the circuit shown. Last of all, connect the voltmeter V across the resistance PQ. The positive terminal of A and the positive terminal of V, are on the positive side of the battery B.

Adjust the rheostat to obtain 5 widely varying readings of V and the corresponding values of I. Enter the results.

Measurements.

V (volts	I (A)

Graph. Plot V (volts) v. I (A). The origin will be a point on the graph since $I = 0$ when $V = 0$, Fig. 24.34 (ii).

Calculate the resistance R from $R = V/I$ for each pair of values of V and I. Then find the average value for R. The value of R is best calculated, however, from the gradient a/b of the V–I graph, as shown, where a is in volts and b is in amperes.

8. Resistance of Lamp Filament

Apparatus. 12 V–24 W motor headlamp or ray-box lamp; 12 V supply, B; 0—3A ammeter, A; 0—12 V voltmeter, V; switch S. (Otherwise, 6 V—24 W or 6 V—12 W bulb, and 6 V supply, and suitable meters.)

Method. If the battery supply B permits, connect 2 V to the lamp with the ammeter A and switch S in series. Connect the voltmeter across the lamp, Fig. 24.35. Switch on. If the pointers of the instruments deflect wrongly, switch off immediately and reverse the connections to them.

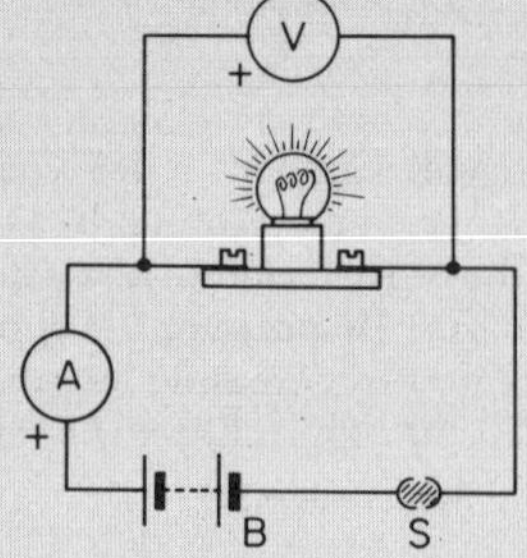

Fig. 24.35 Resistance of filament

Read the p.d. V and current I. Repeat for p.d.s. respectively of 4 V, 6 V, 8 V, 10 V, 12 V.

(*Otherwise*, connect the 12 V supply direct to a rheostat which can carry a current of at least 2 A, as shown in Fig. 24.24 (i), p. 425.

Use the two extreme terminals B and C for the supply first. Vary the rheostat so that readings of 2 V, 4 V, 6 V, 8 V, 10 V and 12 V are obtained on the voltmeter and read the current I each time.)

Measurements.

V (volt)	I (amp)	$R = V/I$ (ohm)

Calculation. Find the resistance R of the tungsten filament at each p.d. V.

Graph. Plot R v. V.

Conclusion. The resistance of tungsten (*decreases or increases or remains constant*) when the p.d. increases.

Remove the lamp and replace it by a length of Constantan (resistance) wire of a few ohms resistance. Repeat the measurements. Plot its resistance R v. V. Does the graph show any difference between tungsten and Constantan?

9. Series and Parallel Resistors

Obtain two lengths, P and Q, of resistance wire, each of a few ohms, for example, 3 and 6 Ω respectively or 4 and 8 Ω. Using the circuit with a voltmeter and ammeter in Fig. 24.22 obtain three values of V and I for P. Repeat for Q. Enter the results and take the average value for P and for Q.

P:

V (volt)	I (amp)	$R = V/I$ (ohm)

Average, $P =$ . . ohms

Q:

V (volt)	I (amp)	$R = V/I$ (ohm)

Average, $Q =$ . . ohm

(i) Using the circuit in Fig. 24.25, p. 426, measure the combined resistance R of P and Q in series. See if $R = P + Q$.

(ii) Using the circuit in Fig. 24.27 (ii), p. 427, measure the combined resistance of P and Q in parallel. Calculate R from $1/R = 1/P + 1/Q$ and compare the result with your measurement of R.

10. Ohm-meter

Apparatus. $1\frac{1}{2}$ V dry battery B; milliammeter 0–1 m A; six known radio resistors between 1500 (1·5 kΩ) and 10 000 ohms. (10 kΩ).

Method. (i) Connect the 10 kΩ (10 000Ω) resistor in series with the battery B and milliammeter. Note the meter reading. (ii) Repeat with the other 5 resistors, as indicated in Fig. 24.36 (i).

Measurements.

R (kΩ)	I (mA)

Graph. Plot R (kΩ) v. I (mA). Draw a smooth curve through the points obtained.

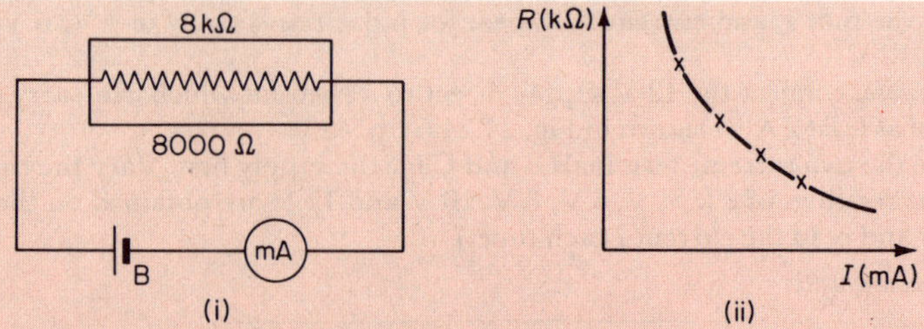

Fig. 24.36 Ohm-meter

This is a calibration curve between R and the meter reading, Fig. 24.36 (ii). *Using calibration curve.* Take an *unknown* resistor of the order of a few thousand ohms. Join it in series with the battery B and meter and note the current reading. Then read off from the calibration curve the resistance corresponding to this current. Repeat with other unknown resistors. Tabulate the results:

Unknown resistor	Current I	Resistance (from curve)

EXERCISE 24 · ANSWERS, p. 616

1. Telephone wires are made of copper because it: (*a*) is cheap; (*b*) is less dense than other metals; (*c*) will not rust; (*d*) is a good conductor of electricity; (*e*) is very strong. (*M.*)

2. Underline the conductors in the following group of materials: copper, lead, rubber, cotton, copper sulphate, P.V.C., sulphuric acid, oil, mica, bakelite. (*Mx.*)

3. The *three* effects of an electric current on matter are heating, magnetic and . . (*E.A.*)

4. (*a*) Find the resistance R of the wire shown in Fig. 24A.

(*b*) What would the current become if the resistance was doubled? (*Mx.*)

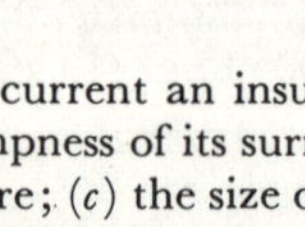

Fig. 24A

5. Choose two good insulators and the two best conductors of electricity from the following list: *lead; paper; tin; iron; cotton; rubber; silver; aluminium; polythene; copper.* (*W.M.*)

6. The amount of electrical current an insulated conductor-wire can safely carry, depends on: (*a*) the dampness of its surroundings; (*b*) the thickness and type of insulator around the wire; (*c*) the size of connectors used; (*d*) how close to the ground the wire is; (*e*) the thickness and type of metal in the wire. (*W.Md.*)

7. Draw a simple electric circuit to show how two 4-volt bulbs can be fully lit from 2-volt electric cells. (*W.Md.*)

8. Give *two* reasons why a lightning conductor is made of copper rather than iron. (*S.E.*)

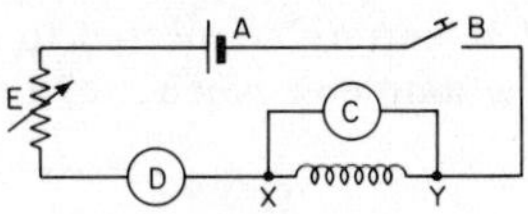

Fig. 24B

9. Fig. 24B shows a circuit which could be used for measuring the resistance of the wire XY. Fill the table with the names of the components.

A	B	C	D	E

(*Mx.*)

10. Fig. 24C shows a 16-volt supply joined in series with resistances of 3 and 5Ω.

(*a*) What is the total resistance in the circuit?

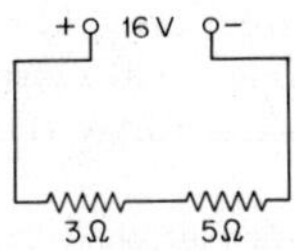

Fig. 24C

(*b*) What current flows in the circuit shown in the diagram? Show on the diagram where you would connect an ammeter (A) to measure this current.

(*c*) What is the voltage across the 5Ω coil? Show on the diagram where you would connect a voltmeter (V) to measure this voltage. (*W.Md.*)

11. (*a*) Calculate the resistance of the resistor AF in the Fig. 24D. *Ignore* the resistance of the ammeter and the internal resistance of the battery.

(*b*) What would be the effect on the current of connecting a voltmeter: (i) in a break in the circuit between A and B; (ii) outside the circuit between A and F? (*N.W.*)

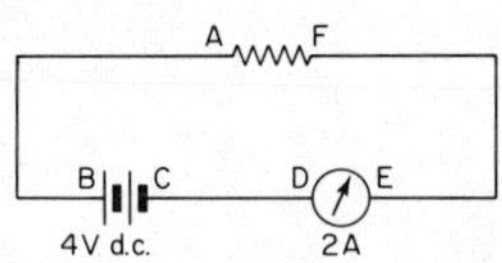

Fig. 24D

12. You are asked to find the resistance of a coil of wire C. Employing the usual symbols, make a large drawing of the circuit you would use, including a three-cell accumulator, an ammeter, a voltmeter, a switch and a variable resistance.

Describe how you would proceed to take several sets of readings.

If your results are as given in the table below what is the average value of the resistance of C?

Reading of ammeter/amps	Reading of voltmeter/volts	Resistance of C
0·9	4·5	
0·6	3·1	
1·0	5·0	
1·1	5·4	
0·8	4·0	

(*Mx.*)

13. Fig. 24E shows a 12 V battery connected to resistors through a switch. What is the reading on the ammeter when: (*a*) the switch is open?; (*b*) the switch is closed? (*E.A.*)

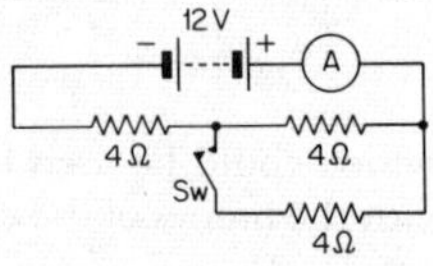

Fig. 24E

14. (*a*) Why are some solid materials good conductors of electricity while others are insulators? Describe how a current is passed along a solid conductor.

(*b*) Calculate the total effective resistance of two 18 Ω resistors arranged: (i) in series; (ii) in parallel.

Draw a diagram illustrating these two combinations.

(*c*) You have the following resistors; one $\frac{1}{2}$ Ω resistor, one 5 Ω resistor, one 10 Ω resistor, two 50 Ω resistors and one 1000 Ω resistor. Which of these resistors would you use and how would you arrange them to produce a combined resistance of 35 Ω?

You may use any of the resistors you wish but you do not necessarily have to use them all. Individual resistors may not be altered in any way. (*S.E.*)

15. (*a*) State Ohm's law.

(*b*) A resistance of 20 Ω has a potential difference of 2 volts across it. What current passes through it?

(*c*) In the circuit in Fig. 24F determine: (i) the effective resistance of the two

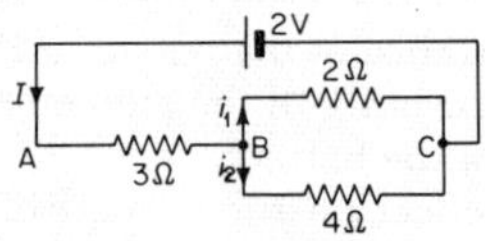

Fig. 24F

resistors in parallel; (ii) the total resistance of the circuit; (iii) the value of the current I; (iv) the potential drop across AB, (v) the potential drop across BC, (vi) the values of the currents i_1 and i_2. (*E.A.*)

16. You are given six 2 V cells, a switch and a 12 V lamp bulb in a holder.

(i) Draw a diagram of the circuit you would arrange in order to light the bulb.

(ii) Draw another diagram showing how you would include a voltmeter and an ammeter in the circuit, to find the resistance of the lamp bulb filament under these conditions.

(iii) What would be the effect on the value of the resistance if only one cell were used in the circuit? Give a reason for your answer. (*S.E.*)

17. (*a*) Draw a circuit diagram showing two lamps in parallel connected to a cell.

(*b*) A switch, an ammeter of resistance $1\frac{1}{2}$ Ω, a resistor X of unknown value, and a parallel combination of a 3 Ω and a 6 Ω resistor, are connected in series. The circuit is connected to the terminals of a battery consisting of four 2 V cells, also connected in series. When the switch is closed the ammeter reads 2 amp.

(i) Draw a circuit diagram of the whole arrangement, using recognized symbols for the various items.

(ii) What is the effective e.m.f. of the battery?

(iii) What is the effective resistance of the combined 3 Ω and 6 Ω resistors?

(iv) Calculate the current flowing in the 3 Ω resistor.

(v) Calculate the value of resistor X.

(vi) What quantity of electric charge will pass through the ammeter in a period of 5 minutes?

(vii) At what rate does the circuit use electrical energy? (*S.E.*)

18. (*a*) State Ohm's law

(*b*) Give a large, clearly-labelled diagram of the circuit you would use and describe the experiment to find the resistance of a coil of wire, using an ammeter and voltmeter and any other apparatus needed to enable you to obtain several sets of readings.

(*c*) In such an experiment, these readings were obtained: ammeter: 0·3 A, voltmeter: 1·5 V. What result does this give for the resistance under test? (*Mx.*)

19. Two 4 ohm resistors are connected to a 2 V cell and an ammeter as

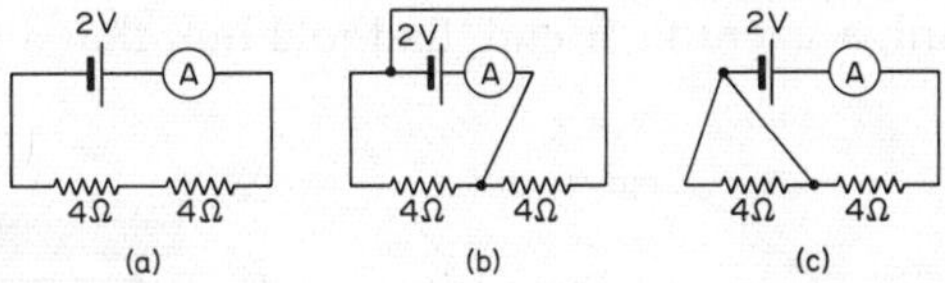

Fig. 24G

shown in Fig. 24G (*a*), (*b*) and (*c*). Find the reading on the ammeter in each case. The resistance of the connecting wires, the meter and the cell may be neglected. (*E.A.*)

25

BATTERIES

Voltaic Cell

MILLIONS of *batteries* are manufactured annually for use in transistor radio sets, bicycle lamps and torches. They maintain an electric current in a circuit. *Accumulators* are made differently from batteries and have advantages over them, as we shall see later. They are used in cars for starting the engine and for lighting, in light trolleys to provide electric power for motors, and in ships as a spare electrical supply if the main generator fails.

Batteries owe their origin to Volta's invention at the end of the 18th century. Galvani, a scientific friend, had told him that a dead frog's leg

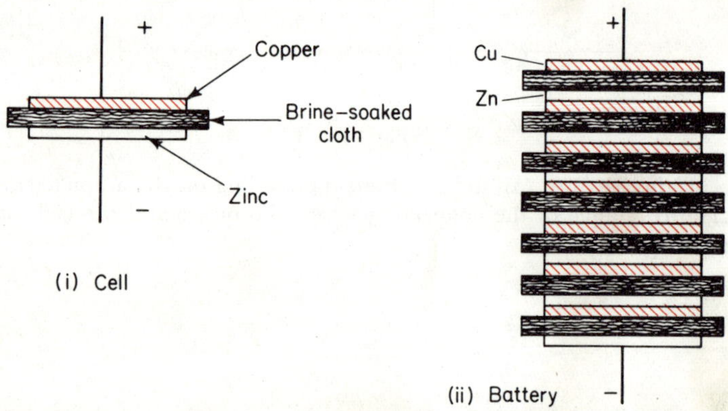

Fig. 25.1 Early voltaic cell and battery

twitched when a knife was lightly placed in contact with it while the frog lay on a zinc plate. Volta came to the conclusion that this was an electrical phenomenon, due to the presence of two unlike metals with chemical material in the frog's leg between them.

After some experiments he placed cloth soaked in brine alternately between a number of discs of zinc and copper (or silver), Fig. 25.1. One unit, zinc and copper with brine between them, is called a *cell*, Fig. 25.1 (i). The whole arrangement, consisting of a series arrangement of cells to produce a greater effect, is called a pile or *battery* of cells, Fig. 25.1 (ii). It was soon found that a wire became warm when connected to the ends of the battery, so that an electric current flowed in the wire.

Basically, the cell or battery converts chemical energy to electrical energy, that is, the chemical materials are gradually used up when the cell is in action. Usually, the cell has two unlike metal plates or *poles*, with chemicals between them. One pole, called the *positive* (+ve) *pole*, is at a higher electrical potential than the other, called the *negative* (−ve) *pole*. The *electromotive force* (*e.m.f.*) of a cell is the p.d. between the poles on 'open circuit', that is, no current flows.

Simple Cell

One of the earliest cells to be constructed, known as the *simple cell*, consists of a copper and zinc plate in dilute sulphuric acid, Fig. 25.2.

When a voltmeter is connected between the plates, the instrument shows that copper is at a higher potential than zinc, that is, copper is the positive and zinc is the negative pole. A suitable small electric bulb

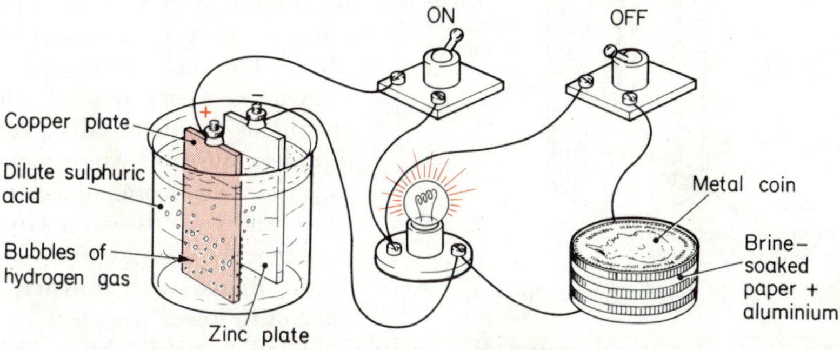

Fig. 25.2 Simple cells

joined to the plates lights up, showing the flow of current from one pole to the other. At the same time observation of the plates inside the cell, made by projection through a plane-glass container on to a white screen, shows that a gas collects at the *copper* plate after movement from the zinc plate. It proves to be hydrogen. The light in the bulb goes out after a short time, and *polarisation* of the cell is said to occur. A few crystals of potassium dichromate dropped in helps to revive the cell.

An aluminium milk-bottle top and a penny as the two metals, with some blotting paper between soaked in brine solution will form a simple cell, Fig. 25.2.

Dry Cell

The reason why the simple cell stops working was traced to the *hydrogen* which forms. This has a high electrical resistance since it is a gas. It also produces a p.d. in opposition to the battery p.d. We therefore need to get rid of the hydrogen. Many different cells containing various chemicals were invented from 1800 to eliminate hydrogen. The only type to survive is the type of cell suggested by Leclanché. The chemicals used are cheap and efficient enough. Many millions of Leclanché cells are manufactured annually for batteries needed for transistor sets, torches and electric bell circuits, for example. These circuits require only small currents of the order of some thousandths of amperes or milliamperes, which the cell can maintain for an appreciable time.

Fig. 25.3 shows a section of the cell. The zinc container or casing is the negative (−) pole. A rod of carbon in the centre, brought out to a terminal at the top, is the positive (+) pole. The active chemical, which reacts with the zinc, is moist ammonium chloride (sal-ammoniac). This is made into a paste or jelly by mixing it with flour and gum, so that it is relatively 'dry'. The cell is therefore known as a *dry cell.* If the chemicals were not dry, the liquid would spill when moving the cell from place to place and ruin the apparatus concerned. Manganese dioxide, mixed with powdered carbon to lower the electrical resistance, is packed round the carbon pole in a muslin bag. This eliminates the hydrogen formed when the zinc reacts with the ammonium chloride. A cardboard separator at the base prevents the carbon (+) rod from coming into contact with the zinc (−) casing. This would stop the cell working if it happened. Fig. 25.4 shows how a round battery is connected inside a torch battery.

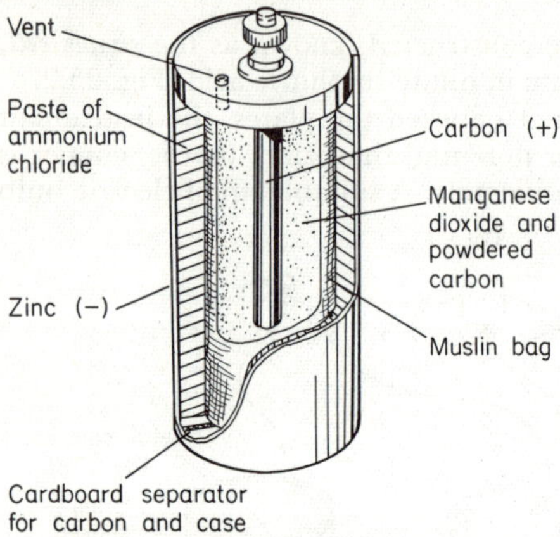

Fig. 25.3 Dry (Leclanché) cell

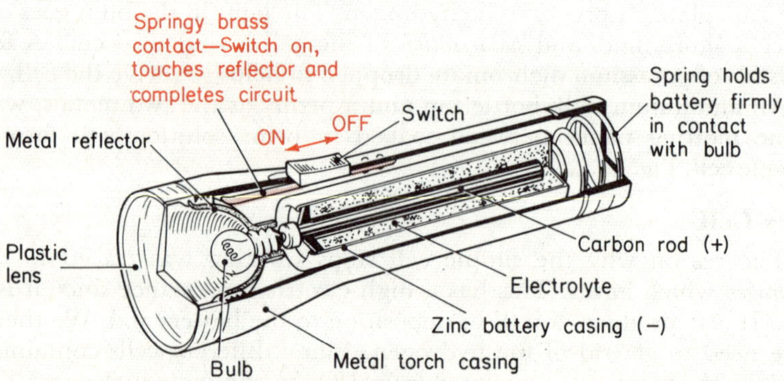

Fig. 25.4 Torch and battery

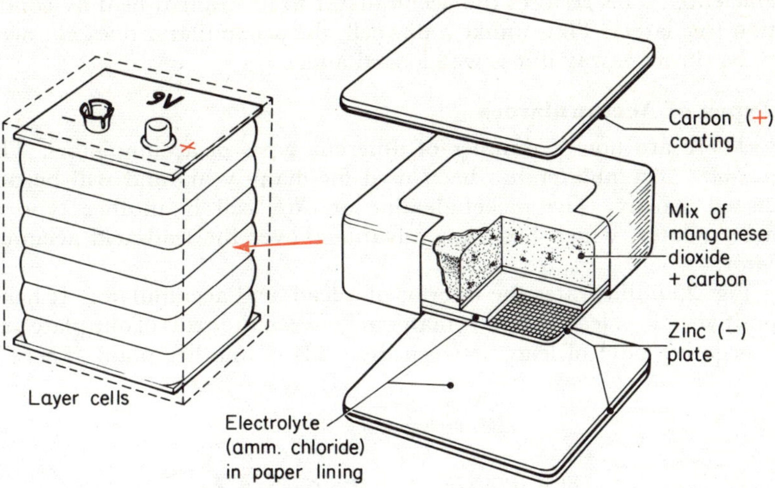

Fig. 25.5 Layer dry cell

The e.m.f. of one dry cell is 1·5 V. Fig. 25.5 shows cells of the *layer* type, which form a 9 V battery. *Layer cells*, made with more pure manganese dioxide and with the electrolyte in a paper lining, provides greater current for a longer time than the round cell. See also Plate 25A.

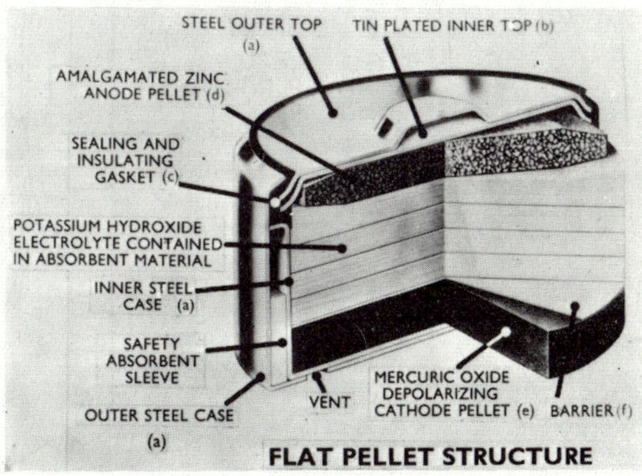

Plate 25(A) *Mallory* mercury cell, a miniature cell used in hearing aids and wrist watches, for example.

Accumulators

A dry Leclanché-type battery can only supply small currents of the order of tenths of amps. Further, the chemicals gradually become used up, after which the battery is thrown away.

Accumulators are cells which can supply large currents of the order of several amperes of more. They are therefore used as the battery supply for light motors on electric trucks at railway goods stations, for motor car sparking coils and the lighting, and on board ship for the lighting if the main generators fail. Batteries of accumulators are stored at Post Office exchanges—they provide the current required in telephone cables when a call is made.

Apart from maintaining a large current, accumulators have the great advantage that they can be re-charged once they cease to function efficiently. This restores the accumulator to its original healthy condition (see later). Thus unlike a dry cell, the accumulator does not need to be thrown away if it is well looked after.

Types of Accumulators

There are now a number of different types of accumulators. The *lead-acid* accumulator has been used for many years and will be discussed shortly. The nickel-alkaline or *Nife* cell is another type of accumulator, which has some advantage over the lead-acid accumulator.

Fig. 25.6 illustrates the interior of a lead-acid accumulator. It has a positive pole of lead peroxide material between the grids of one plate and a negative pole of lead between the grids of another plate. There is

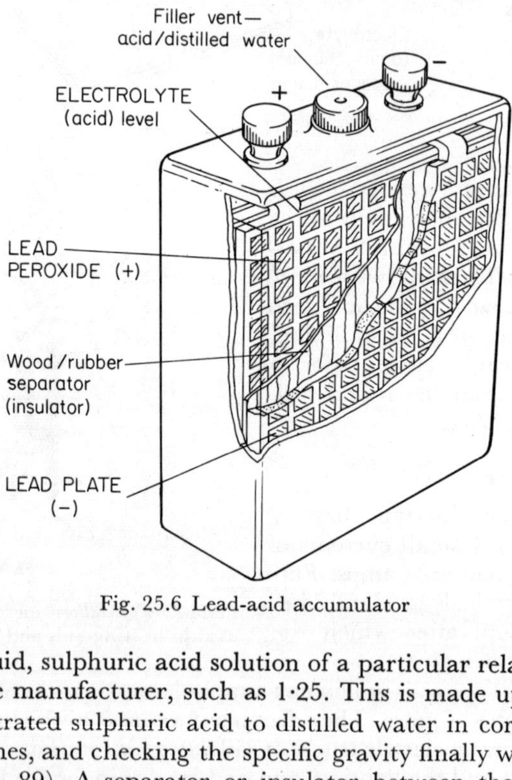

Fig. 25.6 Lead-acid accumulator

only one liquid, sulphuric acid solution of a particular relative density stated by the manufacturer, such as 1·25. This is made up by adding pure concentrated sulphuric acid to distilled water in correct proportion of volumes, and checking the specific gravity finally with a hydrometer (see p. 89). A separator or insulator between the plates prevents them from touching. There are several positive plates and several negative plates, connected respectively to red (+) and black (−) terminals at the top. See Plate 25B.

When the accumulator is freshly-made:

(i) it has an e.m.f. of about 2 V;

(ii) the acid has a relative density of about 1·25, depending on the manufacturer's specification.

The *capacity* of an accumulator is classified in 'ampere-hours'. An accumulator of 30 amp-hours could maintain a current of 1 A for 30 h, or a current of 2 A for 15 h, before recharging is necessary. As higher currents are drawn, however, the time before recharging becomes less than the calculated theoretical figure.

Plate 25(B) Lead-acid accumulator parts—note that the plates are interleaved.

Using (Discharging) the Accumulator

When the accumulator is used a little fresh chemical, lead sulphate, is formed at both plates and the e.m.f. and relative density of the acid slowly diminish. The e.m.f. and relative density should not be allowed to fall below the figures recommended by the manufacturer, for example, 1·9 V may be the minimum for the e.m.f. and 1·18 may be the minimum for the relative density. If this is not observed, excessive lead sulphate, a hard white substance, is formed on the plates. The accumulator may then be permanently damaged, as it is now difficult to recharge.

Accumulators thus require care and maintenance if they are to last for some time. They should be 'topped-up' regularly with distilled water, for example. The accumulator is said to be *discharging* when it is used, and after a time recharging is necessary.

Recharging Accumulators

To restore the materials of a discharged accumulator to their original condition, a current is passed through the accumulator in the *opposite* direction to that obtained when using it, Fig. 25.7. A current in one direction, or direct current (d.c.) is needed.

A *battery charger*, for use with the a.c. or alternating current mains, contains two special pieces of apparatus. One is a *step-down transformer*. This produces a step-down in a.c. voltage from the 240 a.c. of the mains to a lower and more convenient value such as 20 V a.c., as explained on p. 539. The second is a *rectifier*. As explained on p. 358, it changes the alternating voltage of 20 V a.c. to a d.c. or direct voltage.

This is a voltage which acts in one direction, like the voltage from a dry battery. It then provides a steady current through the accumulator while charging, and this restores the chemicals on the plates.

Care must always be taken to connect the positive terminal of the battery charger to the *positive* (red terminal) side of the accumulator and the negative terminal to the *negative* (black or blue terminal) side of the accumulator, Fig. 25.7. The current then passes into the accumulator in the opposite way to when the latter was used, and recharges it.

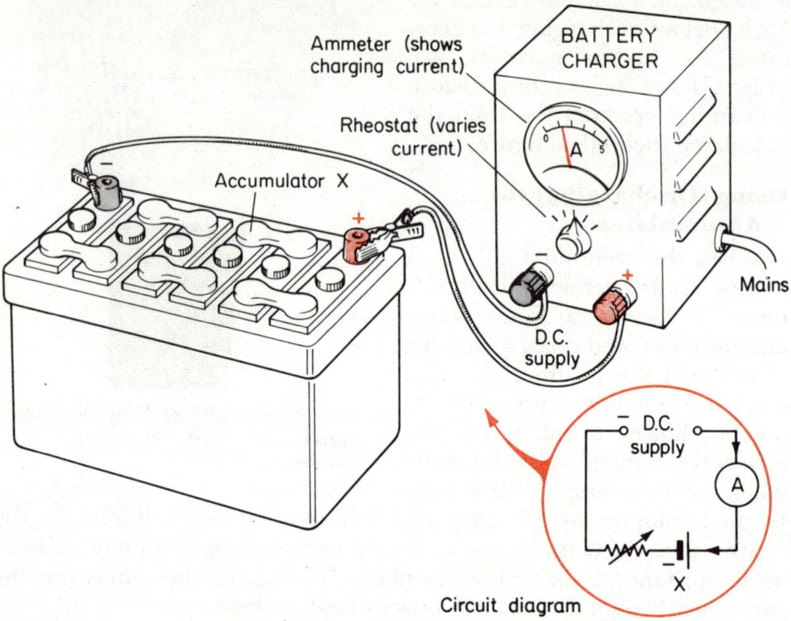

Fig. 25.7 Battery charger

If a mistake is made, and the positive terminal is joined to the negative pole side of the accumulator, the accumulator would be used up even more, which is harmful to the accumulator. A suitable rheostat R is essential in the charging circuit, as the sulphuric acid has a very low resistance such as $\frac{1}{50}\,\Omega$. An ammeter A is also included so that the charging current is always known. The manufacturer's recommended charging current should be used.

As the accumulator is charged and restored to a healthy condition, the ammeter reading is observed to fall. This is due to the rise in e.m.f. of the accumulator. It occurs when the lead sulphate, which was formed on the plates while discharging, is changed back to lead peroxide and lead respectively. The acid relative density also rises. The charging is near the end of its process when 'gassing' occurs inside the accumulator, as the current begins also to decompose the water present. When the

Plate 25(c) A Fuel Cell. Unlike the dry cell and accumulator, these cells obtain electrical energy from fuel fed into it continuously, such as hydrogen and oxygen. They are very efficient, deliver high power, and are likely to be used in the future to power cars and other vehicles.

relative density reaches the recommended value such as 1·25, which is checked by a hydrometer, the accumulator is fully recharged. The e.m.f. is then above 2 V, but soon falls to this figure after short use.

Car Battery or Accumulator

Some cars have an ammeter as one of the panel instruments, which is in series with the car battery, usually 12 V. The ammeter has a maximum range of 30 A on either side of the zero. When a car is started, the starter motor draws a very large current from the battery for a short time. Frequent short journeys by car thus tend to 'drain' the battery, because a very large current flows each time on starting. A home battery-charger is therefore advisable if a car is used in this way.

When the car is in motion a dynamo, driven by the fan-belt, recharges the battery. On a long journey in daylight, when lights are not used, the battery thus becomes fully charged, as shown by the ammeter reading. When the engine is idling the ammeter indicates a discharge. The dynamo is now automatically disconnected from the battery, which is then providing the energy to produce sparks at the electrodes of the sparking plugs.

Short-circuiting

If the two poles of a lead-acid accumulator are accidentally touched by connecting wire, that is, short-circuited, a large current flows through the cell because the internal resistance is very low. The excessive heat produced is liable to damage the accumulator seriously. Thus a short-circuit should always be avoided.

The nickel-alkaline or '*Nife*' cell suffers less from accidental discharge than the lead-acid accumulator. It contains an alkaline liquid which has a higher electrical resistance than acid of the same volume. This cell is also more robust than the acid-type—it can be moved from place to place more easily without fear of damage, as on an electric truck. These are advantages of the '*Nife*' cell. A disadvantage is the relatively low e.m.f. of about 1·3 V compared with 2·0 V of the lead-acid cell.

Fuel cells are a new form of cell which has advantages over the accumulator. One type is shown in Plate 25c, p. 447.

SUMMARY

1. Simple cell has copper (+), zinc (−), and dilute sulphuric acid. Stops working after short time owing to hydrogen produced (polarisation).

2. Dry cell has carbon (+), zinc case (−), paste of sal-ammoniac. Hydrogen eliminated by manganese dioxide.

3. Lead-acid accumulator has lead peroxide (+), lead (−), dilute sulphuric acid. Relative density of acid important—checked by hydrometer. Accumulator re-charged when specific gravity falls to minimum value.

PRACTICAL

1. Making cells

Method. (i) Use an aluminium bottle top, blotting paper soaked in brine solution, and a coin. Connect a voltmeter across the aluminium and coin, and observe the e.m.f.

(ii) Make a battery of three such cells. Measure the total e.m.f. by a voltmeter. See if a small bulb such as 1·25 V, 0·3 A, lights up when the battery is connected to it.

2. Copper, zinc, acid

Method. (*a*) Push a piece of copper and a piece of zinc through the skin of a lemon. Connect the metals to a voltmeter and then to a small bulb, 1·25 V, 0·3 A.

(*b*) Place the copper and zinc inside a beaker of dilute sulphuric acid. Join a small bulb to the plates and see if it lights. If it goes out, add a few crystals of potassium dichromate and observe the effect.

(*c*) Empty the acid solution. Replace it by a concentrated brine solution and repeat.

3. Carbon, zinc, salt solutions

Method. Place a rod of carbon and zinc in a beaker containing sal-ammoniac (ammonium chloride) solution. Connect the rods to a voltmeter and then to a small light bulb.

Repeat using concentrated brine solution in place of sal-ammoniac solution.

4. Dry battery

Method. Break up an old dry battery such as a torch battery. Observe the construction of the cells used and make a sketch of the way they are connected. Cut through the zinc casing in one cell and observe the chemicals inside. Draw a sketch of the section.

5. Lead accumulator principle

Method. Place two lead strips A, B inside a solution of sulphuric acid of relative density about 1·20, Fig. 25.8, Connect a small bulb to the two metals and see if it lights.

Remove the bulb, connect accumulators so that a current flows from one lead strip A to the other B through the acid solution, as shown. After several minutes, disconnect the accumulator. Then connect A and B to the bulb and observe if it lights. Connect A and B to a voltmeter and measure its e.m.f.

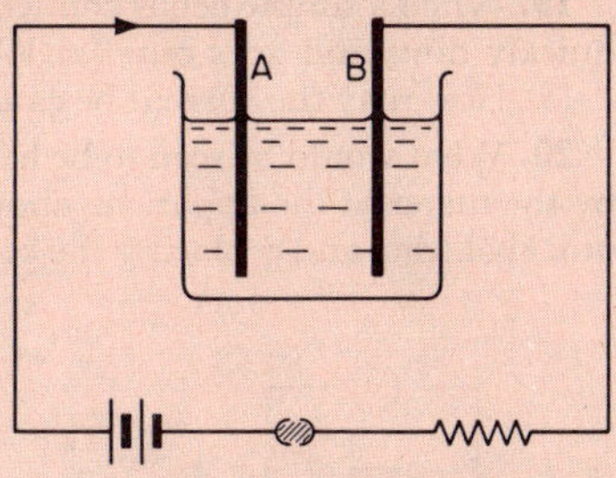

Fig. 25.8 Lead accumulator principle

EXERCISE 25 · ANSWERS, p. 616

What are the missing words in the following statements 1–16?

1. A simple cell has a positive pole of . . and a negative pole of . .

2. The simple cell stops working in a short time on account of the . . produced.

3. When the simple cell is working, hydrogen is produced at the . . pole.

4. 'Polarisation' in the simple cell is due to . .

5. The dry cell has a positive pole of . . and a negative pole of . .

6. In the dry cell, the hydrogen is removed by the action of . .

7. In the dry cell, carbon powder is mixed with manganese dioxide to make a better . .

8. The electrolyte in a dry cell is . .; the depolariser is . .

9. The dry cell is a primary cell; the . . is a secondary cell.

10. Unlike a dry cell, the . . can be re-charged.

11. The lead-acid accumulator has a positive pole of . . and a negative pole of . .

12. The electrolyte in a lead-acid accumulator is . .

13. The condition of an accumulator can be judged from the . . of the acid; this requires the use of a . .

14. An accumulator is re-charged by joining the positive pole of the charging supply to the . . pole of the accumulator in the circuit; on no account should the positive pole of the supply be joined to the . . pole of the accumulator.

15. To test if the accumulator is fully re-charged, a . . is used.

16. Inside a battery-charger using the a.c. mains, there must be: (i) a . . ; and (ii) a . .

17. Is a small truck in a railway station driven by an accumulator or a dry battery? Give *two* reasons for your answer.

18. The electrodes of a dry type Leclanché cell are made of: (*a*) zinc and lead; (*b*) carbon and lead; (*c*) copper and zinc; (*d*) carbon and zinc; (*e*) copper and lead. (*M.*)

19. When a simple cell is connected to a torch bulb, the bulb first lights, then quickly dims and goes out. (*a*) What causes the current to decrease quickly? (*b*) How may the current be caused to flow again? (*L.*)

20. What would be seen to be happening to the flow of electricity as indicated by the meter of the apparatus shown in Fig. 25A? What would be the effect of quickly lifting and replacing the copper plate in the acid? (*W.M.*)

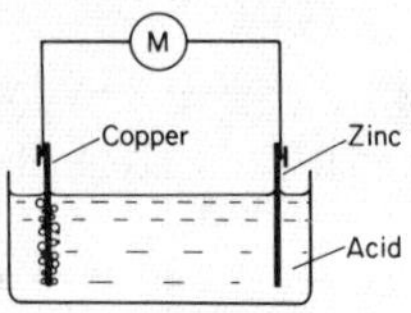

Fig. 25A

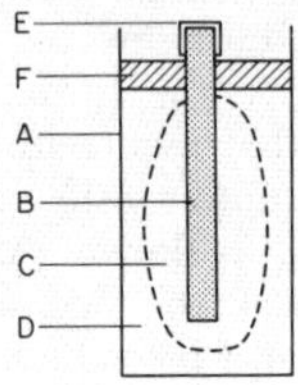

Fig. 25B

21. Complete the key of this diagram of a dry cell (Leclanché type) Fig. 25B): A . . can; B . . rod; C . . powder; D . . paste; E . . cap; F . . seal. (*Mx.*)

22. State *two* precautions which should be taken in the use of a lead accumulator. (*L.*)

23. Complete Fig. 25C by: (*a*) labelling the plates to show what they are composed of; (*b*) showing how hydrogen bubbles cause 'Polarization'. (*W.M.*)

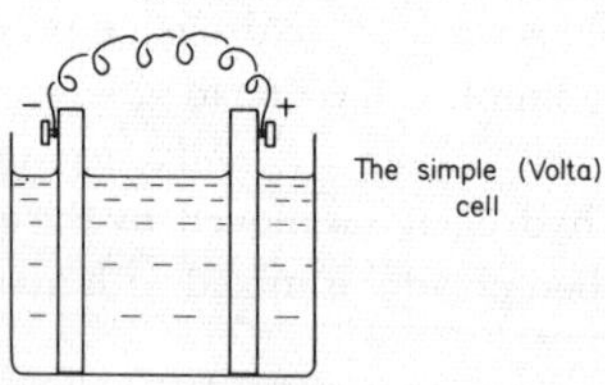

Fig. 25C

24. Name the substances used in a dry cell for: (*a*) the positive pole; (*b*) the negative pole; (*c*) the electrolyte; (*d*) the depolarizer. (*Mx.*)

25. (*a*) Draw a labelled diagram showing the construction of some form of electric cell. Indicate which is the positive and which the negative electrode.

(*b*) What is the main difference between primary and secondary cells? Give reasons why you would not use a 12-volt dry battery as a car battery. (*S.E.*)

26. Fig. 25D shows a battery hydrometer, used for measuring the relative density of the liquid in a motor car battery.

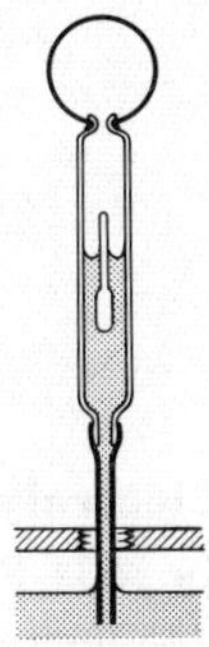

Fig. 25D

(*a*) If you tested the liquids in three batteries and found that the hydrometer readings were: (i) 1·110 (1110); (ii) 1·210 (1210); (iii) 1·250 (1250); what would the readings tell you about each battery?

(*b*) Explain carefully how you would test a battery with a hydrometer.

(*c*) Draw a large labelled diagram of the hydrometer float, and mark on it the readings 1·100 and 1·300.

(*d*) Draw the cross-section of one cell of a motor car battery. Label the active materials in the plates and the liquid in the cell. Show the positive and negative terminals of the cell.

(*e*) Draw and label a circuit to show how you would charge three 2-volt batteries using a 12-volt d.c. supply (*S*.)

27. The circuit diagram is of a battery charger suitable for charging a 12-volt car battery, Fig. 25E.

(*a*) What are the purposes of: (i) the transformer?; (ii) the rectifier?

(*b*) In which position would it be advisable to place the switch arm at the commencement of charging and why?

(*c*) The ammeter would show a reduction in the charging current shortly after connecting to a battery. What would be the cause of this?

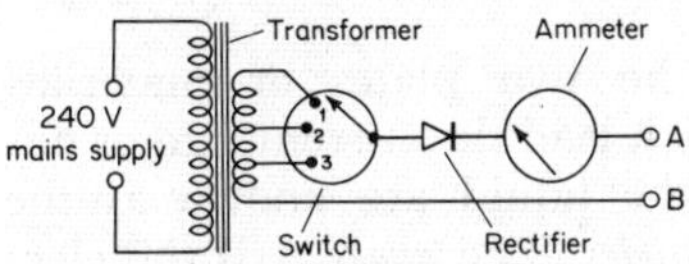

Fig. 25E

(*d*) An average current of $3\frac{1}{3}$ amperes flowing for 10 hours is required to charge a battery. If the terminal voltage between A and B is 15 volts, how much would it cost to charge the battery if the charger is 50% efficient and one kilowatt hour of electrical energy costs $1\frac{1}{2}$p? (*S*.) (See also p. 467.)

28. (*a*) Draw a labelled diagram to show the structure of a Leclanché dry cell.

(*b*) What is polarisation in an electric cell? Explain how the effect of polarisation is reduced in a Leclanché cell.

(*c*) State and explain the probable consequences of leaving exhausted batteries for a long time in a metal torch. (*E.A.*)

26

ELECTROLYSIS

Electrolytes · Voltameter

In 1834 Faraday began to investigate the behaviour of liquid conductors such as salt and acid solutions. A dilute solution of copper sulphate solution or common salt (sodium chloride), or a dilute solution of sulphuric acid, are good conductors. This can be shown in connecting a battery and a small light bulb to two wires or metals dipping into the solution (p. 409). The bulb lights up. Pure water is a very poor conductor of electricity. Tap water conducts better owing to the dissolved salts in it.

Liquids such as salt and acid solutions which are good conductors of electricity are called *electrolytes*. The study of the flow of electricity through them is called *electrolysis*.

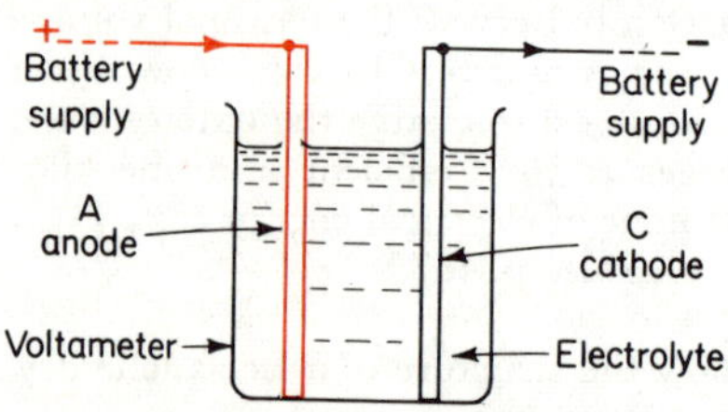

Fig. 26.1 A voltameter

The two plates or materials which lead the current into or out of the liquid are known as the *electrodes*. The *anode* A is the electrode on the positive side of the battery supply, so that the conventional current enters the solution by A. The *cathode* C is the electrode on the negative side of the supply, so that the current leaves the solution by C, Fig. 26.1. The whole vessel, containing electrolytes and electrodes, is known as a *voltameter*.

Typical Examples of Electrolysis

There are many examples of electrolysis, but to understand the principles concerned we shall consider two typical cases.

(1) *Electrolysis of Copper Sulphate Solution with Copper Electrodes*

If an electric current of about $\frac{1}{2}$ A is passed through a dilute solution of copper sulphate with copper electrodes for about 30 min, removal of the cathode shows that the part of it dipping into the solution is now covered with a bright fresh deposit of copper. When it is weighed the mass of the cathode is found to have increased by about 0·3 g. The anode, on the other hand, looks dull after removal from the solution, and when it is weighed it is found to have decreased by about 0·3 g. The density of the copper sulphate solution, determined by a hydrometer, is found to be unaffected by the electrolysis which has taken place.

(2) *Electrolysis of Acidulated Water*

Pure water is a poor conductor of electricity. If a little sulphuric acid is added it conducts much better. To investigate the electrolysis of water, the acidulated water can be poured into a *Hoffmann voltameter*. This is a glass apparatus consisting of inverted graduated burettes with a platinum electrode at the bottom, as shown in Fig. 26.2. When a battery is connected and the circuit switched on, gases are formed at the anode A and cathode C and are collected above the electrodes. On testing, oxygen is found above A and hydrogen above C, the ratio of the volumes being exactly 1:2. The solution is found to be slightly more concentrated, so that water has been lost by electrolysis and hydrogen and oxygen formed.

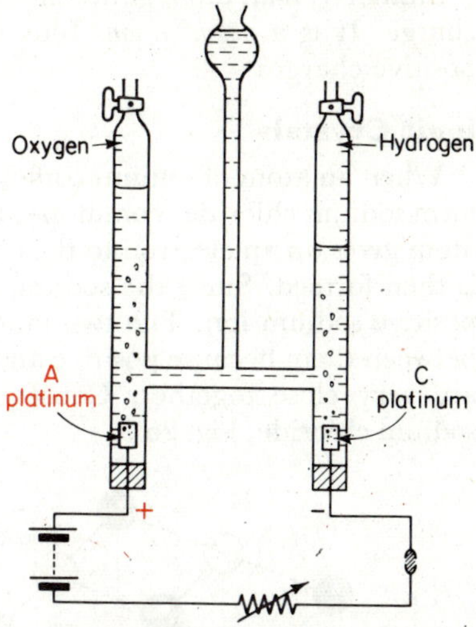

Fig. 26.2 Electrolysis of water

Conclusion. The electrolysis of copper sulphate solution and acidulated water both show that *the metal or hydrogen is always deposited at the cathode.*

This general rule applies to all cases of electrolysis and should be memorized. Thus if silver nitrate solution is electrolysed silver appears at the cathode. If dilute hydrochloric acid is electrolysed hydrogen appears at the cathode.

The nature of the electrode materials play an important part in determining the final products at the electrodes. Thus if copper sulphate solution is electrolysed using platinum electrodes copper is again deposited at the cathode, but oxygen is collected at the anode.

Ions

There are two kinds of electricity. They are called *negative* and *positive* electricity. These names were given because they behaved in an opposite way. For example, when a battery is connected to two separated plates, particles carrying negative electricity will move one way in the space between the plates and those carrying positive electricity will move the opposite way.

Atoms contain negative and positive electricity. For normal atoms, the amounts of each are equal. Thus a normal atom is electrically neutral. The negative electricity is carried by particles called *electrons*. They move round a central tiny stationary core or *nucleus* of the atom, creating a cloud of negative electricity. The nucleus contains all the positive electricity (see p. 411).

Electrons are extremely light particles—each has a mass about $\frac{1}{2000}$ of the mass of a hydrogen atom, which is the lightest atom. Thus when an atom loses one or two electrons, its mass is practically unaltered. It now carries a net quantity of positive electricity or 'charge' since the electrons lost carry negative electricity. We call this relatively heavy particle a *positive ion*.

Similarly, if an atom gains one or two electrons, it now has a negative charge. It is a *negative ion*. Ions may thus be carriers of negative or positive charges.

Ionic Crystals

When an atom of sodium comes together with an atom of chlorine to form sodium chloride (common salt) in a chemical reaction, the sodium atom gives up an electron to the chlorine atom. A negative chlorine ion is then formed. Since the sodium atom has lost an electron it forms a positive sodium ion. The two ions have a powerful force of attraction between them because positive and negative electricity attract and they are very close together. Consequently they form a solid crystal of sodium chloride, Fig. 26.3.

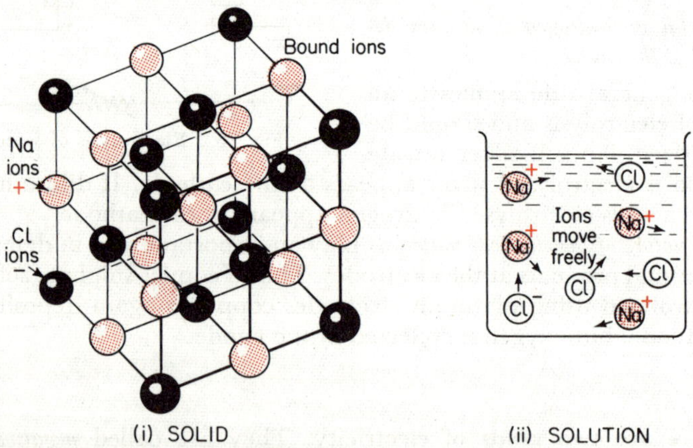

Fig. 26.3 Ions of sodium chloride

Water weakens considerably the force of attraction between the positive and negative ions. Thus when the crystal is placed in water, the ions fall away from each other and the solid structure disappears. A solution is now obtained which carries positive and negative ions. These move about haphazardly or randomly inside the liquid. But when a battery is applied to the electrodes, *the positive ions begin to drift in one direction, from the positive electrode (anode) to the other electrode (cathode).* When they reach the cathode, the positive ions become neutral atoms; they gain electrons which move along the wire. Thus sodium is deposited at the cathode. The chlorine ions carry a negative charge. Hence they drift the opposite way to the sodium ions. Consequently they move to the anode. *Thus ions are the current carriers in electrolytes.*

The movement of ions explains what happens during electrolysis. Since all metals and hydrogen carry positive electricity in solution, they are always deposited at the cathode, which is the electrode on the negative side of the battery.

Electroplating · Manufacture of metals

Electrolysis is used in a wide variety of practical applications.

Pure copper, which must be used in the manufacture of cables, is produced commercially by electrolysis of copper compounds, which are contained in large tanks. Cathode plates, dipping into the electrolyte, are raised after a time, and the pure copper deposited is stripped from the cathode. Sodium and aluminium are manufactured commercially by electrolysis.

Silver plating of objects such as spoons is carried out by making them the cathode of a voltameter containing silver compounds and passing a current through the solution. Steel objects, such as the bumpers of cars or the parts of a bicycle, are often protected by chromium-plating, which presents a bright appearance and prevents rusting. The handlebars of a bicycle, for example, are made the cathode of a voltameter containing a solution of acid and other additives, and a current is passed through the solution until a suitable deposit of chromium is obtained on the frame.

If plating is required for a rounded object, such as a spoon, a *circular anode* is used, Fig. 26.4 (i). If plating is needed on both sides of a flat object, for example, in silver-plating a medal, a *double anode* is used, Fig. 26.4 (ii).

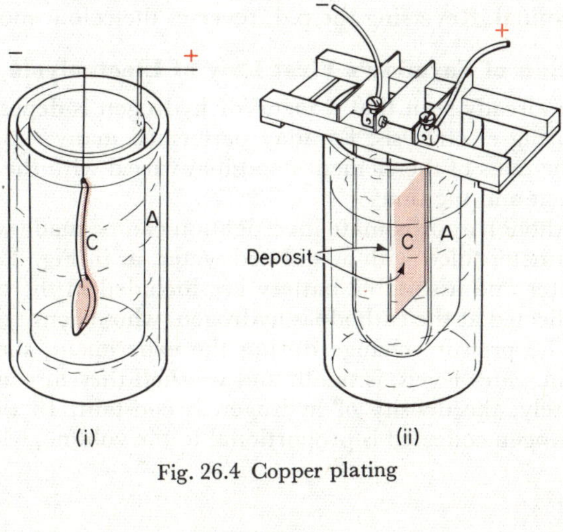

Fig. 26.4 Copper plating

Pole Finding by Electrolysis

If, for some reason, the negative and positive poles of a battery supply are not clearly marked or known, they can be identified by connecting the poles to a water voltameter, for example. Hydrogen appears at the cathode, so this electrode must be joined to the *negative* pole (see p. 453, Fig. 26.2).

Filter or blotting paper, dipped into a solution of sodium sulphate containing a few drops of phenolpthalein, can be used in a much simpler method of pole finding. The bare ends of two insulated wires

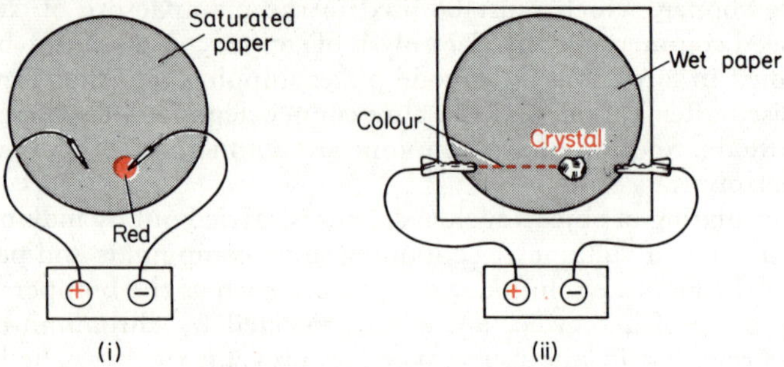

Fig. 26.5 Testing battery polarity

joined to the battery are pressed on the wet paper, a short distance apart, Fig. 26.5 (i). A red colour appears at the wire joined to the negative pole.

A colour experiment can also be carried out with a crystal of potassium permanganate on a wet filter paper, Fig. 26.5 (ii). The leads from a 100 V supply from a dry battery or Labpack are placed on either side of the crystal. After a time, colour spreads across the paper towards the positive terminal. Reversing the p.d. reverses the colour movement.

Investigation of Faraday's First Law of Electrolysis

We have already seen that a metal or hydrogen is deposited on the cathode during electrolysis. Faraday performed many experiments to find how the mass of the element deposited varied with the magnitude of the current and the time.

A quick though approximate investigation can be made with a Hoffmann voltameter filled with acidulated water, as in Fig. 26.2. A rheostat, ammeter and a suitable battery are included in the circuit. The element collected at the cathode is hydrogen, whose density varies with pressure. The pressure change during the experiment, shown by the difference in water levels, is small, and we shall therefore assume that, approximately, the density of hydrogen is constant. In this case the *mass* of hydrogen collected is proportional to the volume, which we can read off.

1. *Constant Current*

The current is kept constant at a convenient value such as 0·5 A by means of the rheostat and ammeter. The volume *v* of hydrogen produced is read at five consecutive equal intervals of time *t* with the aid of a stop-watch. Typical results are shown in the table below. The ratio volume/time is found to be practically constant, or if a graph of volume v. time is plotted, it is found to be a straight line which passes through the origin.

Conclusion. For a constant current in a voltameter,

Mass deposited ∝ Time.

Volume of hydrogen (v) (cm³)	*Time (t) (s)*	*Volume/Time (cm³/s)*
4·4	80	0·055
5·0	90	0·055
5·8	100	0·058
6·2	110	0·056
7·0	120	0·058
7·4	130	0·057
8·0	140	0·057

Current Constant

Volume of hydrogen (cm³)	*Current (A)*	*Volume/Current (cm³/A)*
8·0	0·6	13·3
9·4	0·7	13·4
12·1	0·9	13·4

Time Constant

2. *Constant Time*

This time several currents are passed into the voltameter for the same time on each occasion, such as 2 min. The results for three currents are shown in the table. The ratio volume/current is practically a constant.

Conclusion. Assuming the volume of hydrogen is practically proportional to its mass, then for a constant time,

Mass ∝ Current.

Faraday's First Law · Electrochemical Equivalent

The two results of the experiment can be combined into one general law. It is known as *Faraday's first law of electrolysis*, after the discoverer, who performed many careful experiments:

The mass of an element deposited by electrolysis in a given voltameter is directly proportional to the current and to the time.

Thus if m is the mass, I the current and t the time, then

$$m \propto It,$$

or

$$m = zIt \quad . \quad . \quad . \quad . \quad . \quad . \quad . \quad (1)$$

where z is a constant called the *electrochemical equivalent* of the element deposited.

The explanation of Faraday's law follows directly from our knowledge that ions carry the current through electrolytes (see p. 454). The product '$I \times t$' or 'current $\times$ time' is the *quantity* of electricity Q which has passed through the voltameter, since 1 *coulomb* is the quantity which has passed in 1 second when the current is 1 ampere (see p. 414). The expression in (1) is thus better stated as:

$$m = zQ \quad . \quad . \quad . \quad . \quad . \quad . \quad . \quad (2)$$

Now the ions which carry the current have both charge and mass, and the mass of an ion is practically the same as the mass of its atom (p. 454). Thus if 50 ions, for example, reach the cathode at the end of a given time, 50 atoms of copper are deposited and 50 units of charge have passed through the electrolyte. If 80 ions reach the cathode, then 80 atoms are deposited and 80 units of charge have passed through the electrolyte. It can thus be seen that Faraday's first law is due to the ionic structure of crystals (p. 454).

The mass of silver used during silverplating can be found from the formula $m = zIt$. From tables giving electrochemical values, z, that for silver is practically 0·0011 gramme per coulomb. Suppose a medal was silverplated using a current of 0·5 ampere for 30 min or 1800 s. Then

mass of silver deposited, $m = zIt = 0{\cdot}0011 \times 0{\cdot}5 \times 1800 = 0{\cdot}99$ g

SUMMARY

1. Electrolyte is a liquid which conducts electricity, e.g. acid or salt solutions.
2. Ions carry current through an electrolyte.
3. Metal or hydrogen is always deposited on cathode, which is the electrode on the negative side of battery.
4. Electrolysis of water—platinum electrodes in dilute sulphuric acid solution, hydrogen formed at cathode, oxygen at anode. Electrolysis of copper sulphate solution with copper electrodes—copper deposited at cathode, equal mass lost from anode.
5. Faraday's first law: The mass deposited is directly proportional to the current and to the time.

PRACTICAL

1. Electro-writing

Method. Soak filter paper A in a solution of sodium sulphate containing a little phenolphthalein. Place it on a copper plate B, Fig. 26.6. Connect the posi-

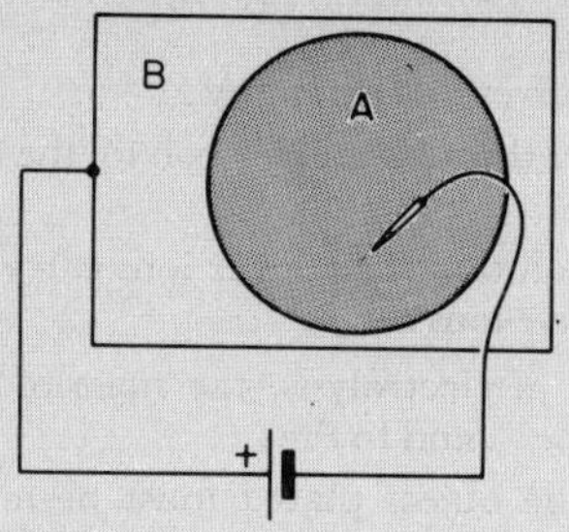

Fig. 26.6 Electro-writing

tive pole of a battery to the plate. Connect a banana-plug or metal 'probe' to the other pole. Press firmly on the wet paper and write or draw on it in the red colour obtained.

2. Electrolysis of salt solution

Method. (i) Fill a beaker with common salt solution.

(ii) Invert over the solution two small test-tubes X and Y filled with water, and support them vertically in clamps, Fig. 26.7.

(iii) Arrange a carbon electrode beneath each test tube—clean carbon electrodes from old dry batteries are suitable.

(iv) Connect a battery supply of a few volts and collect the gas obtained at each electrode. Test for hydrogen at the cathode C—the other gas above A is chlorine, which is distinguished by its pungent smell.

If the salt solution is initially coloured with neutral litmus, the products of electrolysis are shown by colour changes near the electrodes.

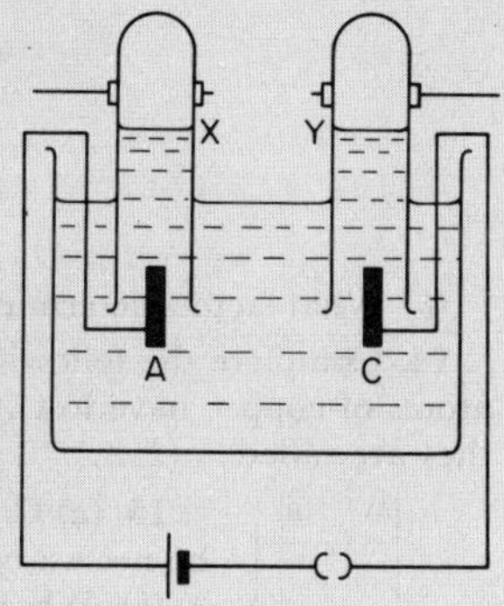

Fig. 26.7 Electrolysis of salt solution

3. Electrolysis of acidulated water (p. 453)

Method. Repeat **2**, but use nickel electrodes to obtain hydrogen and oxygen. Compare the volumes of the gases obtained after some time.

4. Copper plating (p. 452)

Method. Use a beaker of copper sulphate solution, a copper anode, a key or other metal article as the cathode for copper plating, and a battery. Why can you not plate plastic articles?

EXERCISE 26 · ANSWERS, p. 616

What are the missing words in the following statements 1–11?

1. The cathode in a voltameter is the plate on the . . side of the battery.

2. A solution which conducts electric current well is called an . .

3. In the electrolysis of acidulated water, the electrodes are usually . .

4. In the electrolysis of water, hydrogen forms at the . . and oxygen at the . .

5. In the electrolysis of copper sulphate solution, . . is deposited on the . .

6. In the electrolysis of copper sulphate with copper electrodes, copper is lost from the . .

7. In electrolytes, the current is carried by . .

8. When a current flows through an electrolyte, the . . ions move towards the cathode.

9. In copper sulphate solution the copper ions carry a . . charge; in the electrolysis of water, the positive ions are . .

10. From the first law of electrolysis, the mass of an element deposited is directly proportional to the . . and to the . .

11. In silver-plating, the object plated must be made the . . of the voltameter.

12. When acidulated water is electrolysed using platinum electrodes; (*a*) . . is produced at the anode; (*b*) . . is produced at the cathode. (*Mx.*)

13. (*a*) On which electrode is the copper deposited, Fig. 26A?

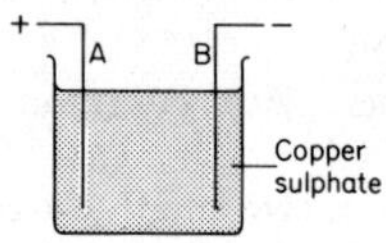

Fig. 26A

(*b*) What factors determine the weight of copper deposited? (*Mx.*)

14. Complete the following sentences: In a solution of copper sulphate the atoms of copper have lost . . and consequently have a . . charge. In this state they are called . . (*E.A.*)

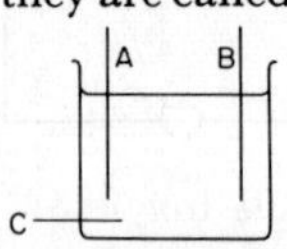

Fig. 26B

15. (*a*) Complete Fig. 26B to represent a circuit which would be necessary if B is to be copper-plated

(*b*) What material would A be?

(*c*) What would the liquid C be?

(*d*) Show clearly the positive of your supply. (*N.W.*)

16. (*a*) State what is meant by the following: (i) electrolysis; (ii) voltameter; (iii) electrolyte; (iv) electrode; (v) cathode; (vi) anode.

(*b*) Describe fully an experiment to show that the weight of a substance deposited during electrolysis is proportional to the quantity of electricity which has passed.

How much copper will be deposited in twenty minutes in a copper sulphate voltameter having copper electrodes when the steady current is 2 amperes? (1 coulomb deposits 0·000 33 g of copper.) (*Mx.*)

17. (*a*) Draw a simple diagram illustrating an atom. Label each of the three types of particle it contains.

(*b*) What is the difference between an ION and an ATOM?

(*c*) The electrochemical equivalent of silver is 0·001 118 gramme per coulomb.

What mass of silver would be deposited in $\frac{3}{4}$ hour, when a current of 2 amperes is passed through a solution of a silver salt? (*S.E.*)

27

ELECTRICAL ENERGY AND DOMESTIC APPLICATIONS

Electrical Energy

ELECTRICAL energy can be transformed into a wide variety of other useful forms of energy. In the electric motor, for example, most of the electrical energy supplied is changed into mechanical energy of rotation for driving machines of one kind or another. In the telephone earpiece, most of the electrical energy is transformed into sound energy.

One very useful transformation of electrical energy is into heat energy. This has special application in the home. Thus when a particular switch is pressed, electric lamps light up owing to the heat produced in the filament. Electric cookers, electric fires, electric irons or electric blankets all change electrical energy into heat energy.

Basically, the heat produced in a metal when a current flows is due to the 'collisions' of the moving electrons inside it with the atoms of the metal. The electrons give up energy to the atoms on collision, which then vibrate faster about their average fixed position in the metal structure. The increase in energy of the vibrating atoms is equal to the heat produced because heat is a form of energy (p. 212).

Electric Filament Lamp

The electric lamp converts most of the electrical energy supplied into heat. Only a very small percentage of the energy supplied is changed into *luminous energy*. This is the kind of energy which produces the sensation of vision.

Fig. 27.1 shows details of the *filament lamp*, which is most widely used.

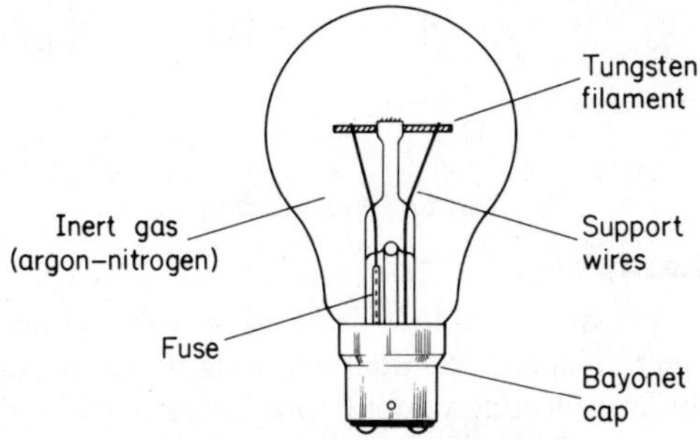

Fig. 27.1 Tungsten filament lamp

It has a tungsten filament or wire—tungsten has a very high melting point and can therefore become white hot without melting. A small amount of argon gas is added after the air is removed. This is a very inactive gas and prevents oxidation of the tungsten since no oxygen is present. It also prevents evaporation of the metal into the space outside.

In electrical wiring in houses and buildings, the lamps are arranged to be in *parallel* across the mains, Fig. 27.2. This means that each lamp

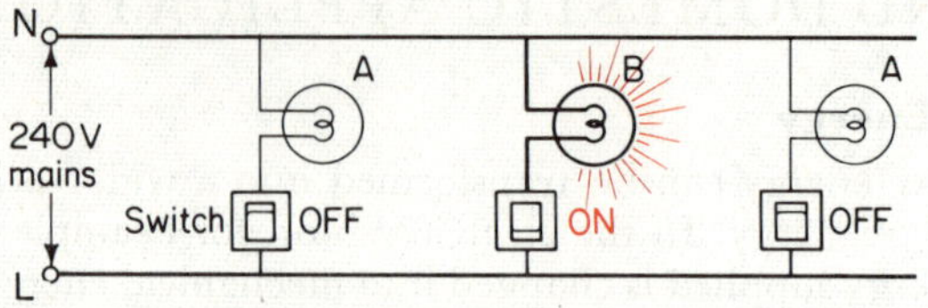

Fig. 27.2 Lamps in mains circuit

has a mains p.d. of say 240 V when it is switched on. By arranging the lamps in parallel, a lighted lamp B in one room of a house is not affected when a lamp A in another room is switched on or off. The lamp B continues to be on. If the lamps were arranged in series, however, switching off one lamp would switch off all the others. This is usually the case for small lamps on Christmas trees. The lamps are in series. If one lamp fails, the rest of the lamps go out, Fig. 27.3.

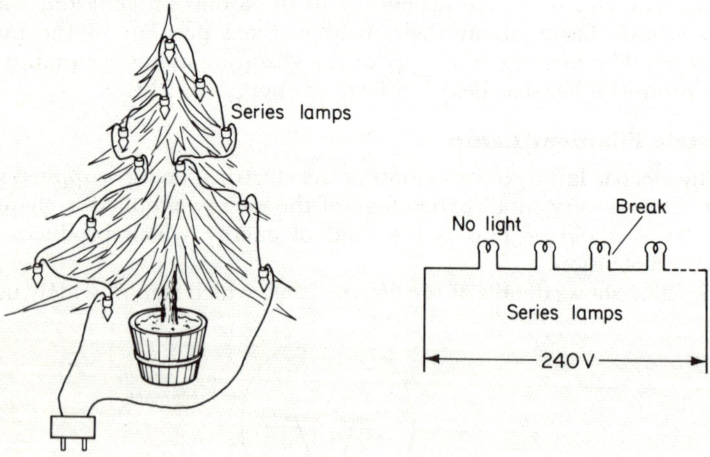

Fig. 27.3 Series lamps

Fluorescent Lamps

A gas at low pressure inside a long glass tube glows when a high voltage is connected across metal terminals at each end of the tube. Some gases, such as mercury vapour, produce invisible ultra-violet rays when they glow. This is the basis of the *fluorescent lamp*, now used in the home and in industry and in street lighting.

Fig. 27.4 shows a simplified circuit for a fluorescent tube. It has two filaments or cathodes C at each end. When the lamp is switched on, a current initially flows from the mains through both cathodes. The cathodes become hot and produce current carriers (electrons) inside the tube. Shortly after switching on, a high voltage is automatically produced across the cathodes by special circuitry. The tube then glows. A short wait is necessary after switching on a fluorescent lamp, so that both cathodes can become hot and start the action.

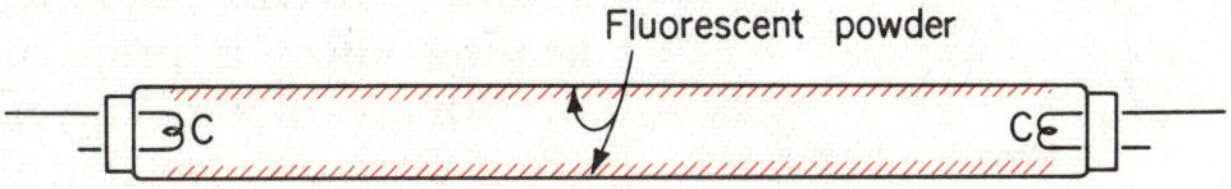

Fig. 27.4 Fluorescent lamp

Most of the light coming from the lamp is obtained from fluorescent powders coating the inside of the tube, which are exposed to the ultra-violet light. Different coloured light is obtained by using different powders. There is no glare from such lamps, and little shadow. They have the advantage of being more efficient than the filament type of lamp, as a higher percentage of the electrical energy supplied is converted to light energy. The cost of running them is therefore much less than the filament type.

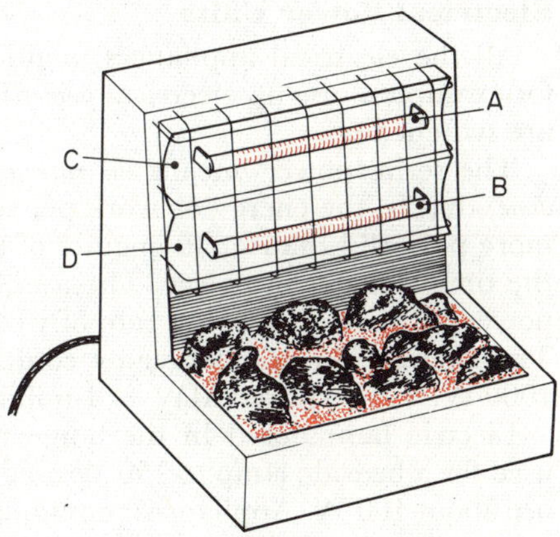

Fig. 27.5 Electric fire element

Electric Fires

The heating effect of the current is used in the electric fire. The heating elements A and B are made of Nichrome (p. 421), Fig. 27.5. This nickel-chrome alloy not only has a high electrical resistance but does not oxidize at high temperatures. Highly-polished chrome concave reflectors C and D are situated behind A and B. They reflect the radiant heat into the room (p. 297).

Hot-wire Ammeter

The heating effect of a current is used in the construction of an instrument known as a 'hot-wire' ammeter. Its main details are shown in Fig. 27.6. PQ is a length of resistance wire connected to fixed terminals at P and Q, and the current to be measured flows through the wire, which then becomes hot. The length of the wire now increases, so that it begins to sag slightly; the point M on the wire is thus lowered. A

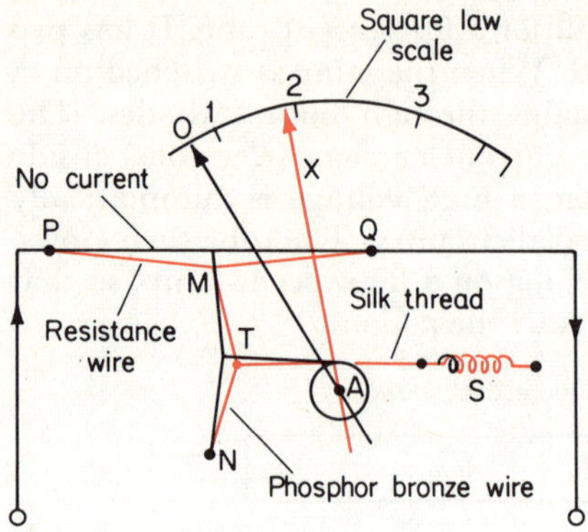

Fig. 27.6 Hot-wire ammeter

silk thread passing round a grooved wheel A has one end connected to T, a point on a wire MN, and the other end to a spring S. As the wire sags, A turns, and a pointer X connected to the axle moves over a scale. This is calibrated in amperes by passing known currents into PQ. The heating effect is proportional to the square of the current for a given resistance, so that the scale is not a uniform one; that is, equal steps along the divisions of the scale do not represent equal increases in current (see p. 523).

Heat is produced whichever direction the current flows. Hence the hot-wire ammeter can measure alternating current (a.c.), one which reverses in direction, as well as direct current (d.c.).

Electrical Power Units

All the electrical appliances mentioned—lamps, fires and cookers, for example—use up electrical *power* from the mains supply when they are switched on.

The term 'power' means *the rate at which energy is used up or work is done*, that is, the energy or work per second. Large engines are usually more powerful than small engines of the same kind. Observe carefully the time element in power. The *watt*, symbol W, is a practical unit of power; it is defined as the rate of working at 1 joule per sec (p. 150). The *kilowatt* kW is a larger or commercial unit of power; 1 kW = 1000 W. The *megawatt* MW = 1 million watts.

Electric lamps used in the home may range in power from 40 W used for a bedside lamp to 150 W used in a garage. A television set may use about 100 W. Appliances providing heat usually need much greater power. An electric iron may be 750 W. An electric kettle may be 2 kW (2000 W). An electric fire may be 1 or 2 kW. An immersion heater for a hot-water tank may be 3 kW. An electric cooker may have a total power of 10 kW.

The 'horse-power' (hp) is a unit of power used in connection with engines. About 750 W = 1 hp. An electric motor used in a small vacuum cleaner is rated as $\frac{1}{6}$ hp. The power is thus about $\frac{1}{6}$ of 750 W or 125 W.

Power Formula

Scientists define the volt, the unit of electrical p.d. in terms of energy. This was explained on p. 417. From the definition, if 1 coulomb of electricity moves between two points having a p.d. of 1 V, then 1 joule of energy is released. Now 1 coulomb of electricity is the quantity passing a section in a wire in 1 s when the current is 1 ampere. Thus:

Current	*P.D.*	*Time*	*Energy produced*
1 A	1 V	1 s	1 joule

or

Current	*P.D.*	*Energy per second or Power*
1 A	1 V	1 joule per second or 1 W

Hence if a current of 3 A flows between two points when the p.d. is 1 V, the power is 3 W, Fig. 27.7 (i). If a current of $\frac{1}{4}$ ampere flows in a lamp filament whose p.d. is 240 V, the power is $\frac{1}{4} \times 240$ or 60 W,

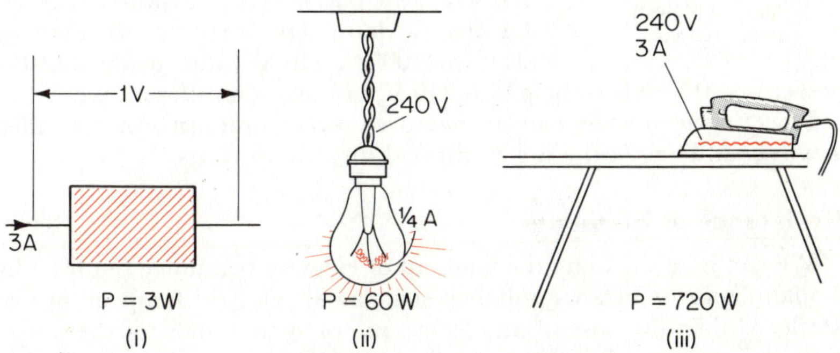

Fig. 27.7 Power ratings

Fig. 27.7 (ii). If the current of 3 A flows in an electric iron element when the p.d. is 240 V, the power is 3×240 or 720 W, Fig. 27.7 (iii).

From these figures, it follows that if I amperes flows between two points having a p.d. of V volts, the power P is given by

$$P = IV \text{ watts.}$$

It should be noted that the magnitude of the power depends on the magnitude of both the current and the p.d. An electric fire element may carry a current of $8\frac{1}{3}$ A on a 240 V mains. Then

$$P = IV = 8\tfrac{1}{3} \times 240 = 2000 \text{ W} = 2 \text{ kW}.$$

In the Grid system, used for distributing electrical power throughout the country, p.ds. of many tens of thousands of volts are used at power stations and elsewhere. Currents of tens of amperes flow along cables. Large quantities of electrical power are thus available for use in homes and industry.

Power Measurement

Since power $P = IV$, the power of an appliance in watts can be measured by measuring the current I flowing in it in amperes and the p.d. V across it in volts, and multiplying the two numerical values. Fig. 27.8 shows a motor headlamp or ray-box lamp L, with a 12 V battery B connected to it. An ammeter A is used for measuring the current flowing. A voltmeter V in parallel with the lamp is used to measure the p.d. If $I = 2$ A, then

$$\text{power} = IV = 2 \times 12 = 24 \text{ W}.$$

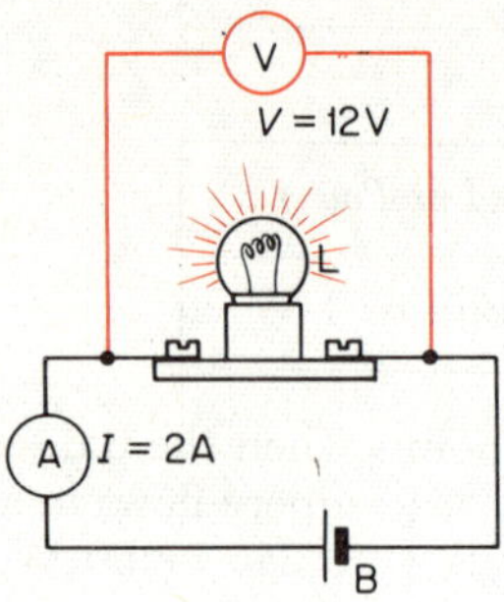

Fig. 27.8 Power measurement

If the battery supply is reduced to 10 V, the current flowing may be 1·8 A. The power is then 10 × 1·8 or 18 W. Thus in rating lamps for power, the p.d. must also be stated by the manufacturer. For example, the motor headlamp bulb is rated as 24 W, 12 V; this means that when the p.d. is 12 V, the power is 24 W. An electric lamp for domestic use may be rated as '100 W, 240 V'; this means that the power is 100 W when the p.d. is 240 V, but not at a different p.d.

Power in appliances can be measured directly on instruments called *watt-meters*. Their scales are calibrated directly in watts.

Resistance of Elements

We can now calculate the filament or element resistance required by a manufacturer of an appliance such as an electric lamp or fire or kettle. Unlike the case of an electric motor, where most of the power supplied is changed to mechanical energy of rotation, these appliances change *all* the energy supplied into heat. This means that if the resistance of the filament or element is R and the current supplied is I, then the p.d. across the resistance $V = IR$, from Ohm's law (p. 422).

Consider the case of an electric lamp rated as '60 W, 240 V'. This means that when the p.d. applied is 240 V the power consumed is 60 W. (It should be noted that when the p.d. applied is not 240 V, the filament resistance is altered because it depends on its temperature, p. 425.) The power consumed is then not 60 W.) From $P = IV$ it follows that the current I flowing in the lamp when used normally is given by

$$60 = I \times 240$$

$$\therefore\ I = \frac{60}{240} = \tfrac{1}{4}\text{ A}.$$

$$\therefore\ \text{Resistance of filament } R = \frac{V}{I} = \frac{240}{\frac{1}{4}} = 960\ \Omega.$$

Thus the lamp manufacturer needs a tungsten filament of 960 Ω resistance at the working temperature.

Suppose the resistance R of a 1 kW fire element is required. Then, from $P = IV$ watts,

$$1000 = I \times 240$$

$$\therefore\ I = \frac{1000}{240} = 4\tfrac{1}{6}\ \text{A}$$

$$\therefore\ R = \frac{V}{I} = \frac{240}{4\frac{1}{6}} = 57{\cdot}6\ \Omega.$$

The manufacturer therefore needs Nichrome wire of resistance 57·6 Ω at the working temperature of the element.

Commercial Units of Energy

When the Area Electricity Boards present their accounts for the cost of lighting and heating premises they are concerned with the amount of electrical *energy* consumed. Energy = Power × Time, from the definition of power (p. 150). Hence a unit of energy could be a unit of power multiplied by a unit of time. In industry a unit of energy known as the *watt-hour* is used. It is the energy consumed when the power of 1 W is used for 1 h. Thus the energy consumed by six 60 W lamps in a room, burning continuously for 8 h,

$$= 6 \times 60\ \text{W} \times 8\ \text{h} = 2880\ \text{watt-hours.}$$

A larger unit of energy, used commercially, is the *kilowatt-hour kWh* or Board of Trade unit. Thus 1 kWh = 1000 watt-hours = energy used in 1 hour when the power is 1000 W (1 kW).

Hence 2880 watt-hours = 2·88 kilowatt-hours or 2·88 units.

If the cost is 3p a unit, the total cost of using the lamps is therefore 8·64p.

EXAMPLE

A factory contains 30 100-W and 50 60-W lamps, which are used continuously for 20 h a week at a cost of 3p per (Board of Trade) unit. Calculate the total cost per week.

Power used by 30 100-W lamps = 30 × 100 W = 3000 W = 3 kW
Power used by 50 60-W lamps = 50 × 60 W = 3000 W = 3 kW

∴ total power used = 6 kW

∴ number of kilowatt-hours = no. of kilowatts × no. of hours

= 6 × 20 = 120

Cost of 1 kWh = 3p

∴ total cost = 120 × 3p = £3·60

Electricity Meter Bills

Meters which read kilowatt-hours (or Board of Trade units) directly are installed in homes and buildings by the Electricity Board. Plate

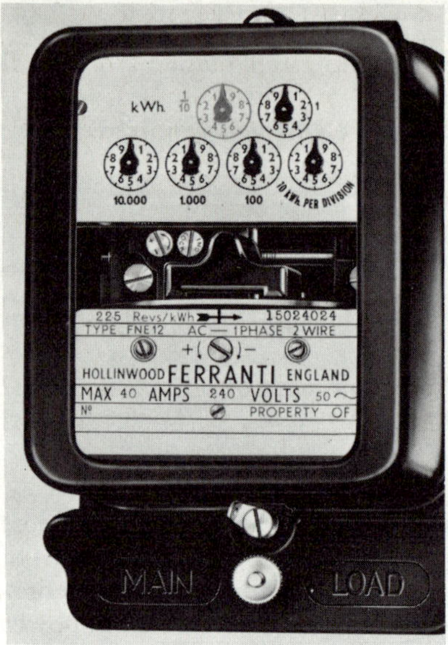

Plate 27 (A) Domestic electricity meter. Dials register kilowatt-hours or 'units'.

27A. Fig. 27.9 (i) shows a meter at the beginning of a period. The dials show a meter reading of 35172. After a period of ten weeks the dials show an increased reading of 37706, Fig. 27.9 (ii). Note carefully that the figure read is that which the pointer has just *passed*. The bill supplied to the consumer may be as follows:

Meter readings		*Units consumed*	*Units rate (Pence)*	*Amount*
Present	*Previous*			
37706	35172	2534	0·7	£17·74
Fixed charge				1·50
Consumer Number 51 2970 1690 20		Period ended 1. 3. 68		Total 19·24

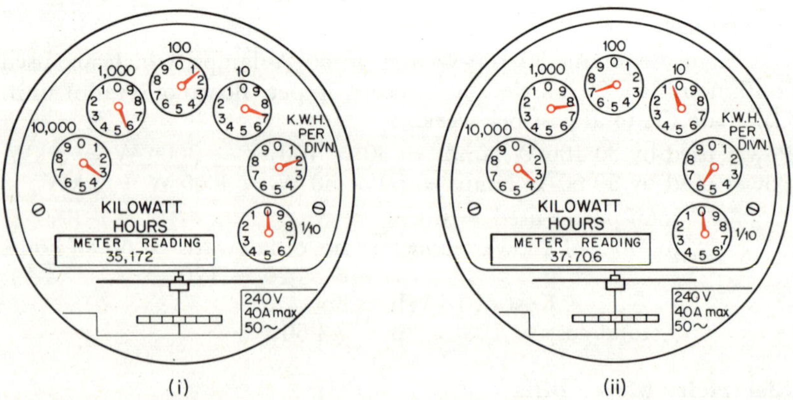

Fig. 27.9 Electricity (kilowatt-hour) meter

Electrical Energy Consumption

Some examples of power consumption in the home are approximately as follows:

Television and radio receivers	100 W (watts)
Small domestic vacuum cleaner	120 W
Electric kettle	750 W
Electric fire	2 kW (kilowatts)
Immersion heater	3 kW
Electric cooker	5 kW

A small house may use on the average in winter:

(*a*) Lighting 400 W
(*b*) Electric fires 2 kW
(*c*) Entertainment 100 W
(*d*) Refrigerator 100 W

Total power used = 2 600 W or 2·6 kW.
Assuming 5 hours use per day, total energy = 2·6 × 5 = 13 kWh (kilo-watts-hour)
∴ Total energy used in 10 weeks
=(10 × 7) × 13 = 910 kWh.

If 1 kWh, or Board of Trade unit, costs 3p, then charge
= 910 × 3p = £27·30.

ELECTRICAL INSTALLATIONS

Line (L), Neutral (N), Earth (E)

Electricity is an extremely convenient, cheap and clean source of power. Practically all buildings and homes in this country use electricity for lighting and many for heating. The electricity is distributed throughout the United Kingdom by a nationwide system of power stations, interconnected by cables and other necessary appliances such as transformers. This is called the *Grid system* and is discussed later (p. 540).

The domestic supply in this country is mainly 220/240 V a.c. This is supplied by two cables from a local sub-station. One cable is called the *live* or *line*, L (brown) and is 240 V a.c. relative to the other cable which is known as the *neutral*, N (blue). The neutral line is earthed originally at the power station.

In domestic supplies, a third cable is introduced for safety. This is called the *earth*, E (green-yellow) as it makes a good connection to the earth terminal provided by the electrical contractor. The potential of this earth may be called a 'zero' potential.

Most continental countries use the colour code stated above and this must be remembered in connecting appliances to the mains:

Brown (*live*), Light Blue (*neutral*), Green-Yellow stripes (*earth*).

As a safety precaution, the metal casings of all electrical appliances used in the home, such as electric fires, are connected by the earth cable E to earth when used (p. 471). If a fault occurs in the appliance and no earth were used, a dangerously high current from the 240 V live cable, now touching the casing by accident, would pass through the body of a person touching the appliance into the earth. With the casing earthed, however, the current passes directly to earth and a person touching the appliance is then safe from injury. Of course, the fuse is blown if the mains is 'shorted' to earth (p. 471) so that the mains is then cut off from the appliance.

Fuses

The mains power supply should be reliable. A large electrical failure or short circuit in a particular house, for example, should not affect the electricity supply to other users nearby. This is done by protecting domestic wiring with *fuses* or miniature circuit breakers. These are devices which automatically cut off the mains supply if too high a current flows by accident in a particular circuit.

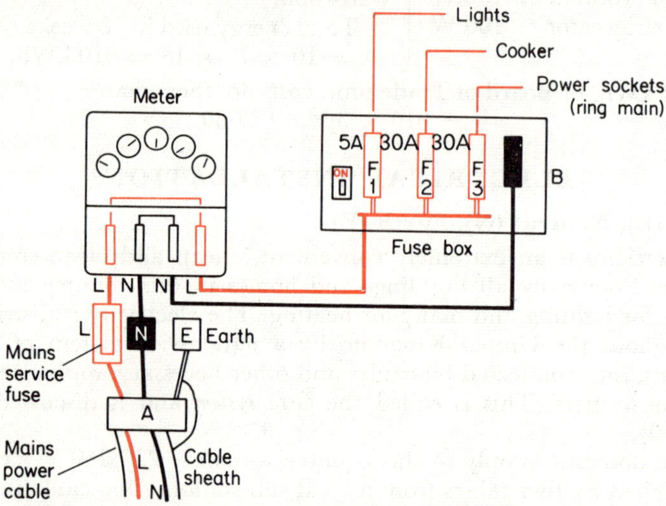

Fig. 27.10 Domestic wiring installation

A typical house wiring system is shown simplified in Fig. 27.10. The mains cables L and N enter at A. A mains service fuse in a box is placed in the live (L) lead. This mains cut-out operates at a high current value such as 60-100 A, and is sealed by the Electricity Board. It is the last in a series of measures to safeguard against dangerous high currents in the circuit.

A meter is connected into the supply. It measures the total amount of electrical energy used in the whole house. The supply is then joined to a *distribution box* B. This contains an on-off switch, and a set of fuses such as F_1, F_2, F_3, one for each circuit in the house. The switch is used to shut off the mains supply completely when the fuses are being cleaned or replaced. It should be noted that the fuses are always connected in the live or line (L) lead of a circuit. If they were placed in the neutral lead, and a fault occurred by accidental shorting of the live cable L to earth, no protection would be given by the fuse, Fig. 27.11.

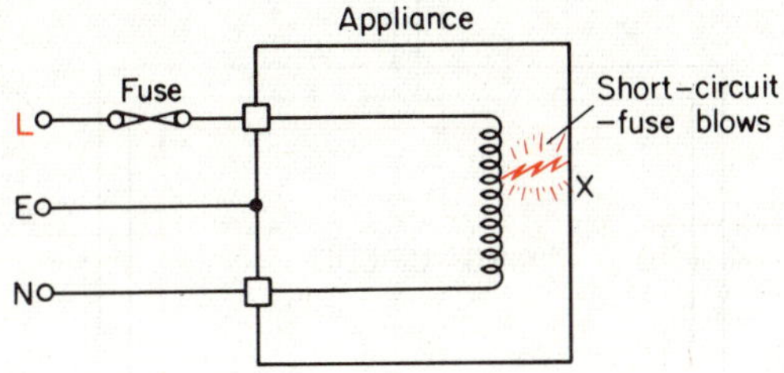

Fig. 27.11 Earthing for safety

Fuse Rating

The 'fuse rating' is the maximum safe current permitted to flow in it before the fuse breaks. For lighting rooms in a house, only small currents are required in the lamps. The connecting wires can thus be thin and inexpensive. The protective fuse wire is normally rated at 5 A. For heating purposes, large currents and hence thicker connecting wire are needed. Fuse wire of 30 A rating is used. The total current used in a house may be as much as 50 A or more and this current flows in the mains cable.

House Circuits · Ring Circuit

A typical domestic installation would have circuits for lighting, heating and cooking, and outlets for using television and vacuum cleaners for example. Normally, electric cookers, central heating units and immersion heaters, which use relatively high amounts of power, have their own separate permanent circuits, each with a separate fuse.

Television sets, vacuum cleaners and electric irons, however, are examples of domestic appliances which use relatively low power. They may therefore be connected at the same time in one circuit, using different socket outlets. This circuit is called a *ring main circuit*, Fig. 27.12. It consists essentially of a loop of cable C, both ends of which are joined to the supply at the distribution box B. As shown, the power needed for separate sockets or for lighting circuits can be taken off any part of the ring. The current carried by each cable section is thus only half of what it would be if the circuit were joined straight to the distribution box. The cable needed for a ring main is therefore of a lower rating than that required for direct connection to the mains and the cost is therefore less. Another advantage is that new sockets can be joined in the ring main circuit very easily. Fig. 27.12 shows a circuit with four outlets or points in the same room.

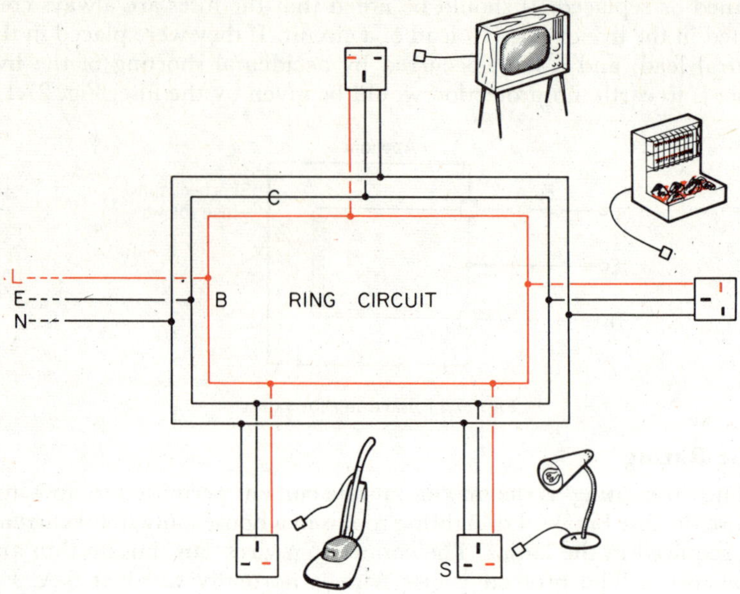

Fig. 27.12 Ring circuit

Fused Plugs

Since a greater number of appliances are used from a ring circuit compared to the older-type circuit, the fuse at the distribution box in the ring circuit has a very high rating. It follows that if a fault occurs, a very high current must flow before the distribution box blows and cuts off the supply. If the fault occurs in a particular appliance such as an electric iron, this high current may be many times greater than the maximum it can carry. The appliance may then be seriously damaged and beyond repair.

To safeguard appliances used on a ring circuit, each plug connected to it has its own fuse, that is, the appliance is separately fused. The plug, called a '13-amp plug' is shown in Fig. 27.13. It has three pins of rectangular cross-section and can only be inserted one way, the right way, into its particular socket. The latter has safety shutters over the live and neutral connections which only open when the plug is inserted. The shutters are a safeguard against mischievous small children. The plug has a plastic insulating case, terminals N and E which are set at the top of their respective pins, and a terminal A. The top of the live pin L does not have a terminal on it, but has a clip which holds one end of a cartridge fuse F. The other end of the fuse is joined to a clip on the top of the terminal A.

When the plug is connected to an appliance, the cable C is gripped on its outer insulation by the cable-grip. This ensures that the plug

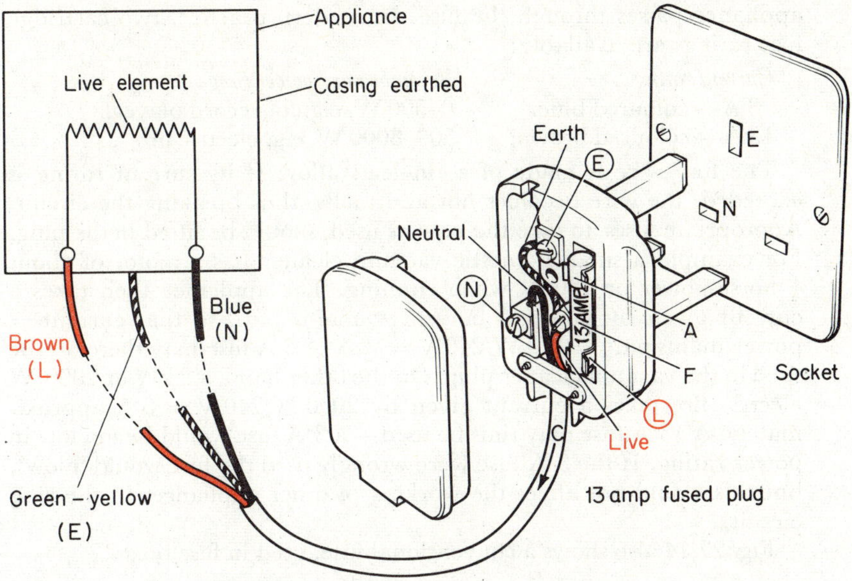

Fig. 27.13 Power socket and fused plug

connections are not easily broken. The three inner conductors of the cable are then connected as shown. The green-yellow striped or earth wire goes to pin E. The blue or neutral wire goes to pin N. The brown or live (line) wire goes to terminal A, and hence, through the fuse, to pin L. In connecting the wires to the plug, each is stripped of its rubber insulation only of sufficient length for a connection to be made, and then wound in a clockwise direction about the terminal post. Thus on tightening the terminal, the wire tends to be wrapped more firmly round the post.

Cartridge Fuses

The fuses used in the 13 A plug are *cartridge fuses*. Each consists of a length of fuse wire connected to metal caps on the end of a short tube. Fig. 27.14. The fuse is connected in the live cable which passes to the appliance, as shown in Fig. 27.11, so that all the current taken by the

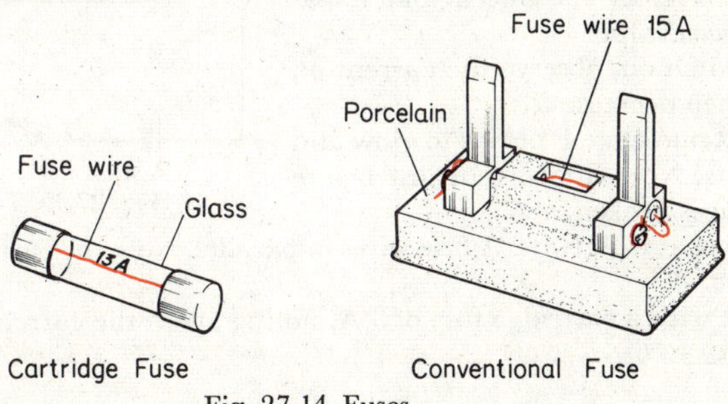

Fig. 27.14 Fuses

appliance passes through the fuse. In modern practice, two cartridge fuse ratings are available:

Current rating	*Recommended power range*
3 A—coloured blue.	0–500 W, e.g. for record player.
13 A—coloured brown.	500–3000 W, e.g. electric fire.

The fuse wire is made of a tin–lead alloy. If its current rating is exceeded, the wire becomes hot and melts, thus breaking the circuit. Appropriate fuses, to take the powers used, should be fitted in the plug. For example, a small domestic vacuum cleaner has a motor of about $\frac{1}{6}$ horse-power or 120 W when running. The appliance then takes a current given by power = current × mains p.d., so that current = power/mains p.d. = 120 W/240 V = $\frac{1}{2}$ A. A 3 A fuse may therefore be used in the vacuum cleaner plug. On the other hand, a 2 kW or 2000 W electric fire takes a current given by 2000 W/240 V = 8 A approximately. A 13 A fuse may thus be used—a 3 A fuse would be too low in power rating. If the 3 A fuse were wrongly used the fuse would 'blow', but this would not affect the working of other appliances in the ring circuit.

Fig. 27.14 also shows a conventional fuse, used in fuse boxes.

SUMMARY

1. Power = IV watts (I in amperes, V in volts).
2. Energy = IVt joules.
   Energy in kilowatt-hours (kWh) = kilowatts × hours.
3. Fused plugs have three terminals, L, N, E (earth connection to appliance casing for safety) and fuses of 3 A (lighting or low power) or 13 A (power).
4. Lighting circuits use relatively small currents and small fuses. Power circuits use relatively high currents and large fuses.

PRACTICAL (Notes for guidance, p. 26)

1. Testing fuses

Apparatus. 2 V accumulator B; rheostat R able to carry currents greater than 5 amp; 2 amp fuse wire F joined to two crocodile clips; switch S; connecting wire.

Method. (i) Connect the series circuit shown in Fig. 27.15. Check that R has the *maximum* value.

(ii) Switch on, observe the current on A, and then decrease R.

(iii) At one stage F begins to glow and then melts. Note the current just before the circuit is broken.

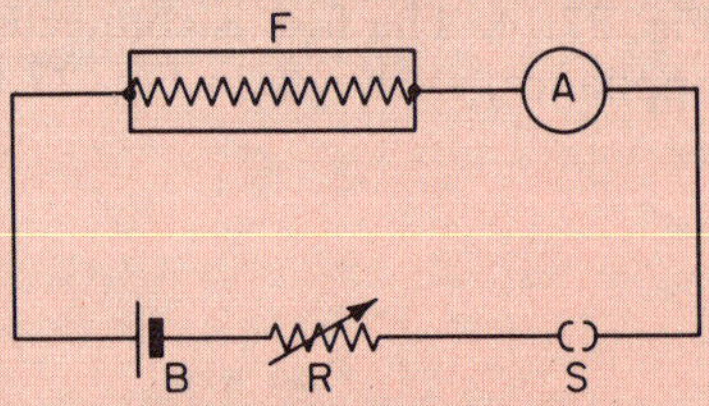

Fig. 27.15 Testing fuses

(iv) Repeat with two 2 A fuse wires in parallel. Note the current at which the fuse blows.

Repeat with a cartridge fuse of 3 A, noting again the current just before the fuse breaks.

Measurements.

Fuse rating	Current measured on breaking

2. Power of lamp

Apparatus. 6 – 2 V accumulators; 12 V – 24 W motor headlamp or ray-box lamp; ammeter 0–3 A, A; voltmeter 0–12 V, V; connecting wire. (Otherwise, use a 6 V – 12 W or 6 V – 24 W lamp, and suitable meters.)

Method. (i) Connect one 2 V accumulator to the lamp with the ammeter in series, starting from the positive pole and working round to the negative pole. Then connect the voltmeter across the lamp, Fig. 27.16.

(ii) Note the reading of current, I and p.d., V.

(iii) Repeat for 4 V (two accumulators), then 6 V, 8 V, 10 V, and 12 V. Enter the results and calculate the power each time from $P = IV$.

Measurements.

I (amp)	V (volt)	$P = IV$ (watt)

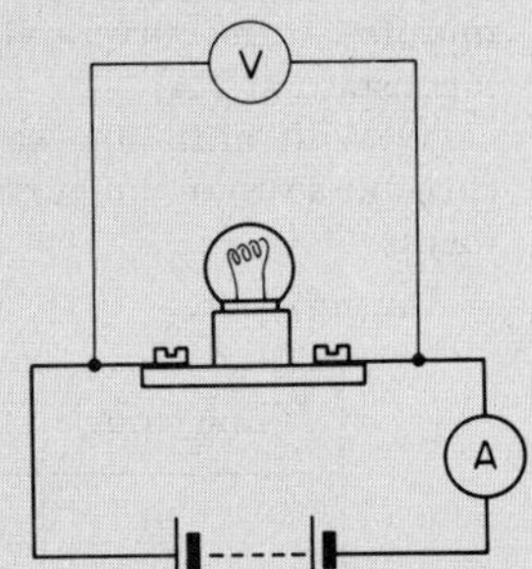

Fig. 27.16 Power of lamp

Graph. Plot P v. V. Draw a smooth curve through all the points.

(*a*) Do your results agree with the rating '12 V – 24 W'?

(*b*) Repeat with another light bulb, such as 2·5 V, 0·3 A. Use a rheostat in series with a 2 V or 4 V supply, or a dry battery supply, to obtain varying values of V up to 2·5 V maximum.

3. Heating effect (p. 461)

Apparatus. 6 V accumulator B; ammeter 0–5 A; rheostat R of a few ohms for currents 3 A or more; bare Nichrome wire C of about 1 ohm resistance; switch S; small calorimeter D and thermometer. Fig. 22.17

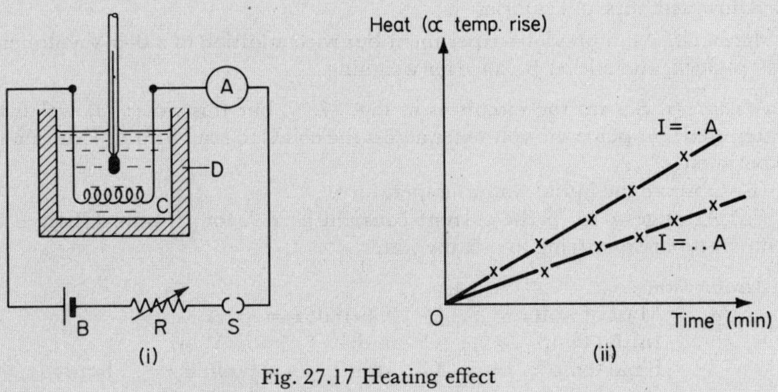

Fig. 27.17 Heating effect

Method. (i) Coil the Nichrome wire by winding it round a pencil. Push the turns close to each other after removing the coil but make sure they do not touch.

(ii) Connect the circuit shown in Fig. 27.17, using crocodile clips for attaching the ends of the Nichrome coil. Switch on. Adjust the rheostat for a reading of 2 A on the meter.

(iii) Switch off. Place the coil well into the calorimeter. Add sufficient water to cover the coil; about 80–100 cm^3 of water should be used. Note the water temperature.

(iv) Switch on. Adjust the rheostat for 2 A. Stirring gently to mix the water, note the temperature after four consecutive equal intervals of time such as 5 minutes. If the current alters during the experiment, adjust the rheostat to keep it constant at 2 A.

(v) Wait until the water cools down—do not empty the water. Alter the rheostat so that the current is 3 A and repeat the four temperature measurements.

Measurements.

Time (min)	Temperature (°C)	Temperature rise (deg C)
0	(initial) . .	

From the measurements, obtain the temperature rise from the initial temperature after 5, 10, 15 and 20 min respectively. This is a measure of the heat gained in these times. Plot a graph of temperature rise (heat gained) v. time. See if all the points lie on a straight line passing through the origin of the graph. Label each graph with the particular current used.

Conclusion. (i) From your graph, what can be deduced about the way the heat supplied by a constant current varies with the time?

(ii) Divide the temperature rise in 20 min produced by the larger current by the temperature rise in 20 min produced by the smaller current (one decimal place). Is this ratio roughly proportional to the ratio of the two currents *or* to the ratio of the *squares* of the currents?

4. Kilowatt-hours and calories

Apparatus. As in previous experiment but with addition of a 0–5 V voltmeter, a stop-clock, and a lever balance for weighing.

Method. (i) Set up the circuit as in Fig. 27.17, but this time: (*a*) weigh the water used; (*b*) place the voltmeter across the coil C to read its p.d. V during the experiment.

(ii) Observe the initial water temperature.

(iii) Arrange to keep the current constant at 2 A for 10 min. Observe the temperature rise, stirring to mix the water.

Measurements.

Mass of water	= . . g	Current I	= . . A
Initial temp	= . . °C	p.d. V	= . . V
Final temp	= . . °C	time t	= . . min = . . hours

Calculation.

Kilowatt-hours used = $I \times V \times t/1000$ = . . kWh.

Heat produced in calories = mass of water × temp rise.
= . . calories.

Conclusion. From your results, find the number of calories produced by 1 kilowatt hour.

Note. The result is approximate because the thermal capacity of the calorimeter has been neglected in the calculation.

EXERCISE 27 · ANSWERS, p. 616

1. Complete the table by writing in the correct units. The first answer has been inserted as an example.

To measure	The unit used is
Electric potential	the volt
,, current	
,, resistance	
,, power	
,, energy	

(*Mx.*)

2. A 13 A plug-cover is made of plastic or rubber, the pins coming from it are made of brass and inside there is a fuse.

(i) Why is the cover made of plastic?
(ii) Why are the pins made of brass?
(iii) What is the purpose of the fuse? (*S.E.*)

3. How long would it take for a 100 W electric light bulb to use 1 unit of electricity? How long would it take for a 2 kW fire to use 1 unit of electricity? (*S.E.*)

4. An electric lamp is marked 240 V 100 W. How much would it cost to use this lamp for 15 hours if electricity cost 1p per unit? (*E.A.*)

5. Complete the following: *Unit* *Measurement of*

Ampere . .
Volt . .
Ohm . .
Watt . . (*Mx.*)

6. You would not use a covered 'Resistance wire' to connect a table-lamp to an electrical point because the light would be . . and the resistance wire would become . .

In an electric kettle the 'earth-wire' connects the . . of the kettle to the earth.

A 5 amp fuse will . . and break if more than 5 amps of current flows through it. (*W.Md.*)

7. In a household electrical circuit a fuse may be placed in: (*a*) the live wire; (*b*) the neutral wire; (*c*) both wires.

State which of these is the safest and in each case give *one* reason for the others being less safe. (*E.A.*)

8. The following appliances are to be used on separate 240 V supplies. Calculate the current used by each and say which fuse, 2 amp, 5 amp, or 13 amp, should be incorporated with each: (i) a television set rated at 150 W; (ii) an electric iron rated at 750 W; (iii) an immersion heater rated at 3000 W; (iv) a hair dryer rated at 500 W.

How much will it cost to run the television set for 100 days for an average of 4 hours a day at 3p per B.O.T. unit? (*Mx.*)

9. Four 240 V – 100 W light bulbs are used for an average of 5 hours per day for a period of 60 days. What would be the electricity bill at the end of this time if the first 72 units are charged at 3p per unit and the remainder at 1p per unit? (*W.Md.*)

10. (*a*) What is the purpose of a fuse in an electrical circuit?

(*b*) If a circuit contains a 5-amp fuse and the voltage is 240 V, what is the maximum power (wattage) which may be taken from the circuit?

(*c*) What would be the danger involved in replacing a blown fuse with one which would carry a larger current?

(*d*) What is the purpose of earthing an electric kettle? (*M.W.*)

11. (*a*) What is a 'ring main' circuit? What are the advantages gained from installing this system in a new house? What special arrangements have to be made for equipment like cookers?

(*b*) Read the meters in Fig. 27A. Calculate the cost of the electricity used during the quarter. The cost of the first 54 units is 3p each and the remainder are charged at 1p each. (*W.Md.*)

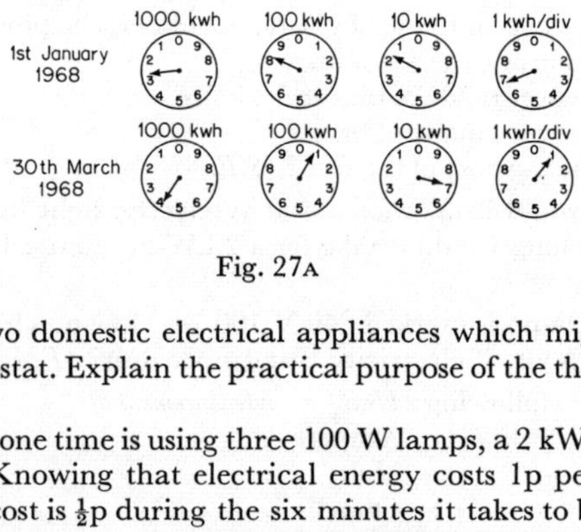

Fig. 27A

12. Name any two domestic electrical appliances which might normally be fitted with a thermostat. Explain the practical purpose of the thermostat in each case.

A householder at one time is using three 100 W lamps, a 2 kW electric fire and an electric kettle. Knowing that electrical energy costs 1p per unit he calculates that the total cost is $\frac{1}{2}$p during the six minutes it takes to boil the water in the kettle. What is the 'wattage' of the kettle? (*M.*)

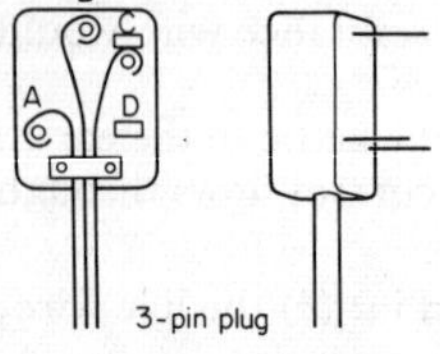

Fig. 27B

13. (i) What is the shape of the three pins, Fig. 27B?

(ii) Why is the direction of the wire about screw A wrong?

(iii) What are the colours of the wires attached to screws A, B, C?

(iv) What is placed in the gap CD?

(v) How should the value of the component placed between C and D vary with the rating of the appliance fixed to the plug?

(vi) What is the name of the circuit for which this sort of plug is designed. (*E.A.*)

14. Why are fuses necessary in a circuit?

In the circuit in Fig. 27C, reproduce on your paper sections where fuses should be placed and also the position of the main switch.

What determines the sizes of the fuses used in domestic circuits at different points? (*W.Md.*)

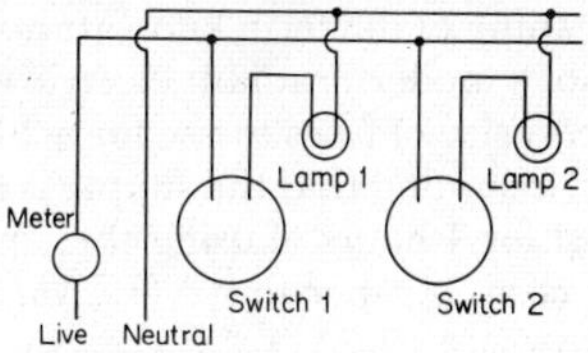

Fig. 27C

15. Assuming that electricity costs 2p per unit (kilowatt h) (*a*) what is the cost of using: (i) a 3 kW heater for 2 hours; (ii) a 100 W light bulb for 5 hours? (*b*) How long may they be used together for 31p? (*L.*)

16. (*a*) Apart from good insulation what two other safety precautions are applied in the electric wiring of buildings and what is their purpose?

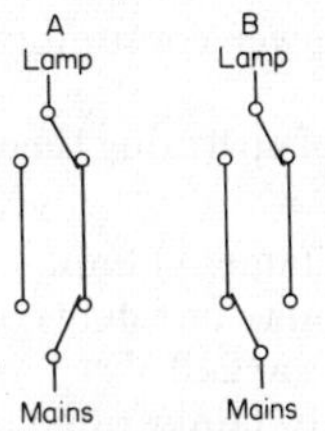

Fig. 27D

(*b*) Here are two diagrams, Fig. 27D. State what you can deduce from each one.

(*c*) Describe the construction of the modern electric filament lamp. (*W.Md.*)

17. (*a*) An electrician is required to fit a 2 kW immersion heater in a tank. (Mains voltage 240 V.) Draw a circuit diagram, showing a switch and fuses, of the installation. Calculate the current required and state the 'fuse value' you would employ.

(*b*) What would be the cost of running the heater for 8 hours per day for a week at 3p per unit?

(*c*) Draw a diagram of a popular type of *either* electric fire *or* iron *or* electric water heater and describe its construction. (*Mx.*)

18. (*a*) A resistor of 6 Ω is connected to the terminals of a 12 V supply. What current will flow through the resistor?

(*b*) A lamp bulb is marked 200 V 100 W.

(i) What current flows through the lamp bulb in normal use?

(ii) What is the resistance of this lamp bulb when in use?

(*c*) Three such bulbs are used in a long corridor using the circuit shown, Fig. 27E:

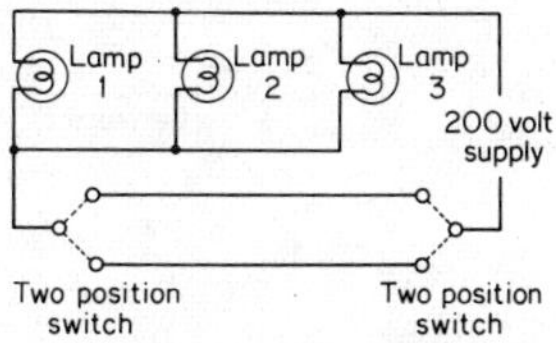

Fig. 27E

(i) What is the purpose of having two switches in the circuit?

(ii) Use your answer (*b*) above which gives the

current through one bulb used singly, to find the total current used by the three bulbs together.

(iii) What power will be used by the three bulbs being used together? (*M.*)

19. (*a*) Explain the meaning of the term kilowatt hour.

(*b*) Explain the action of a modern radiant electric fire.

(*c*) Determine the correct size of fuses to use for a 2 kW fire, a 750 W iron and a 3 kW immersion heater, assuming that the supply is rated at 240 V.

What would be the cost for 4 hours of using these pieces of equipment separately if electrical energy costs $1\frac{1}{2}$p per unit? (*W.Md.*)

20. (*a*) You have a 10 Ω and two 5 Ω resistors. Show by diagrams how you would connect to give resistances of 20 Ω and 12·5 Ω.

(*b*) What current is a 60 W bulb intended to carry if it is designed for the 240 V main?

(*c*) What would you notice if you connected the bulb referred to in (*b*) to the 200 V main? Give reasons for your answer.

(*d*) (i) Show by a diagram how you would connect twenty fairy light bulbs marked 24 V-10 W to work off a 240 V main.

(ii) What will be the total power consumption if all the lights are working correctly?

(iii) What would be the cost of operating them for 50 hours if 1 kWh costs 1p? (*S.E.*)

21. (*a*) Describe the electric filament lamp.

(*b*) How many 150 W lamps may be safely connected in a circuit which has a 5-amp fuse, if the mains supply is at 240 V?

(*c*) What is the cost of using 10 lamps rated at 150 W for 6 hours, if a unit of electricity costs 1p?

(*d*) State how the resistance of a filament lamp varies with its temperature. (*E.A.*)

22. (*a*) Fig. 27F represents the production of electricity by a generator.

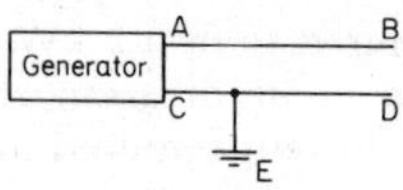

Fig. 27F

(i) What name is given to the wire AB?

(ii) What name is given to the wire CD?

(iii) What is the meaning of the symbol E?

(*b*) When current comes into a house, it goes through three things before being split up into different circuits. List the three things in the order in which the current passes through them.

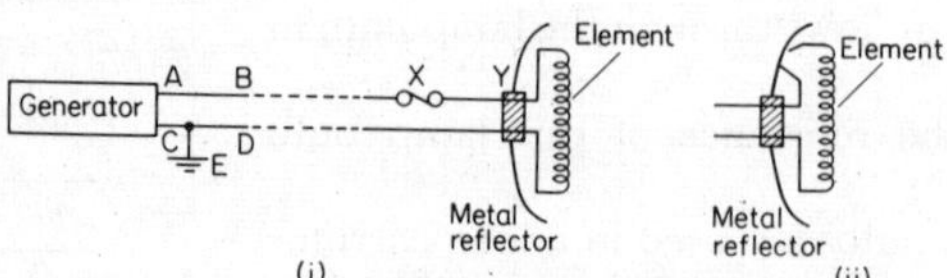

Fig. 27G

(*c*) Fig. 27G represents an unearthed electric fire and shows how it is connected to the generator.

(i) What is X?

(ii) What sort of material is Y?

(iii) What happens if: (*a*) the element breaks and touches the reflector when the fire is switched on, as in Fig. 27G (ii); (*b*) a person touches this reflector and so connects it to earth?

(iv) What would happen in (iii) (*a*) and (iii) (*b*) if the reflector was earthed?

(*d*) Draw a simple diagram to show how you can get a shock from an electric kettle even though the kettle is switched OFF (the switch having been put into the wrong wire). (*E.A.*)

23. (*a*) (i) Describe carefully how you would set up a circuit to determine the true wattage of the lamp from a car tail-light if the lamp is labelled 12 V 6 W.

(ii) Draw the circuit diagram and explain what readings you would take.

(iii) Show how you would calculate the result.

(*b*) An electric heater for use on 240 V mains has two elements of resistance 100 Ω arranged in parallel. Calculate: (i) the effective resistance of the heater; (ii) the total current flowing when the heater is used; (iii) the cost of using the heater for 10 hours at 3p per unit. (A unit is 1 Kilowatt-hour.) (*Mx.*)

24. A 250 V – 500 W electric lamp used in a film strip projector is found to burn out rather frequently because the initial current flowing is too high. It could be protected by using a resistor and thermostat as shown in the drawing, Fig. 27H.

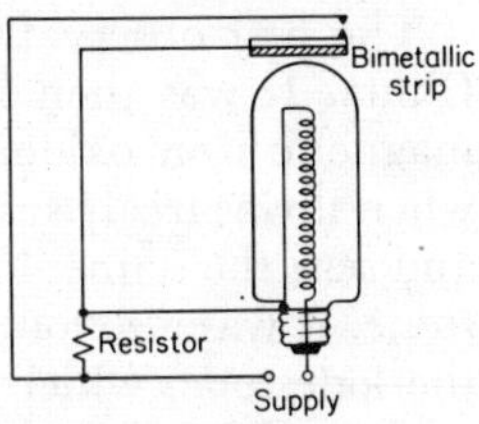

Fig. 27H

(*a*) Explain how the filament is protected.

(*b*) The bimetallic strip in the thermostat is made from brass and invar. Which alloy would be nearer the lamp?

(*c*) If the resistor were not present and the resistance of the filament were 50 Ω when cold, how much current would flow when it was connected to the 250 V mains supply?

(*d*) What is the working (hot) resistance of the lamp?

(*e*) What would be a suitable value for the safety resistor if the initial current were to be limited to 2 amperes? (*S.*)

25. (*a*) Draw a labelled diagram to show the structure of an electric filament lamp. List the materials used and state why they are suitable for their purpose.

(*b*) Explain why lamps in houses are normally connected in parallel.

(*c*) (i) Calculate the current which flows in normal use through a lamp marked '250 V 100 W'. Calculate the resistance of the lamp.

(ii) Draw a circuit diagram to show two lamps, each marked '250 V 100 W', connected in series to a 250 volt supply. Calculate the current and power of the circuit. Neglect any changes of resistance due to temperature changes. (*E.A.*)

28

MAGNETISM

MODERN technology relies to a great extent on efficient magnets, some permanent and others temporary, and on magnetic materials. They play an important part in the generation of electrical power, in communications and in computers, for example. The telephone earpiece, the microphones used in broadcasting stations and the loudspeaker in a radio receiver all depend on magnets and magnetic materials to function efficiently. A television cathode-ray tube has a shield made of magnetic material. Tapes in tape-recorders use a special type of magnetic material.

Lodestone

The first observations on magnetism began over 2000 years ago in China. It was then known that a mineral called *lodestone*, which is a magnetic iron oxide, always pointed approximately north and south when it was freely suspended. It was used for navigation across country and sea; the name 'lodestone' was given because it acted as a 'leading' stone. It was also found that iron and steel were attracted to the ends of the lodestone, which was a natural magnet. Little progress, however, was made in the study of the subject until 1603, when Dr Gilbert became interested in the phenomenon. He was a physician to Queen

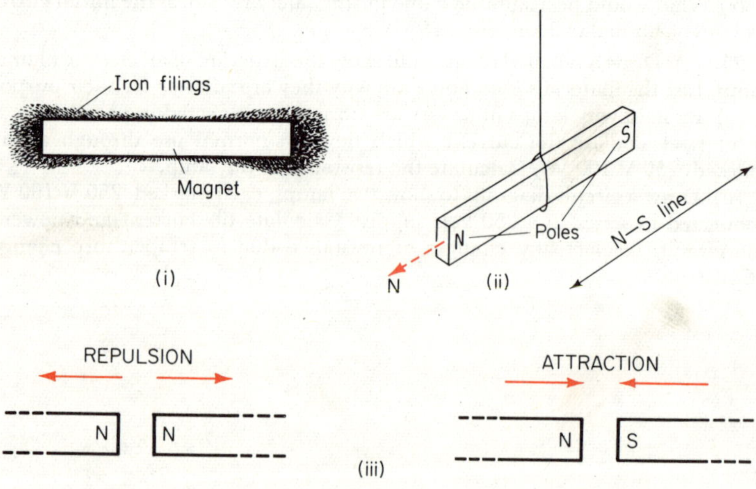

Fig. 28.1 Properties of magnet

Elizabeth, and his researches, published in a book called *De Magnete*, have led him to be regarded as the founder of the science of magnetism.

Fundamental Observations

Experiment shows that:

(i) iron filings cling mainly round the ends of a bar magnet, Fig. 28.1 (i);

(ii) the bar magnet, suspended so as to swing freely in a horizontal plane, always comes to rest with its axis pointing roughly north–south, Fig. 28.1 (ii).

The ends of the magnet, where the attracting power is greatest, are called its *poles*. The pole which points towards the north is called the 'north-seeking' or north (N) pole of the magnet; the other is called the south (S) pole.

(iii) If a N-pole of a magnet is brought near to the N-pole of a suspended magnet repulsion occurs. If the N-pole is brought near to the S-pole attraction occurs, Fig. 28.1 (iii).

Thus like or similar poles repel (i.e. two N- or two S-poles repel), and *unlike poles attract* (i.e. a N- and S-pole attract).

Methods of Making Magnets · Electrical Method

The best and quickest method, or industrial method, of making a magnet is to use the magnetic effect of an electric current (p. 408). A coil of insulated wire of many turns, called a *solenoid*, is used to carry a

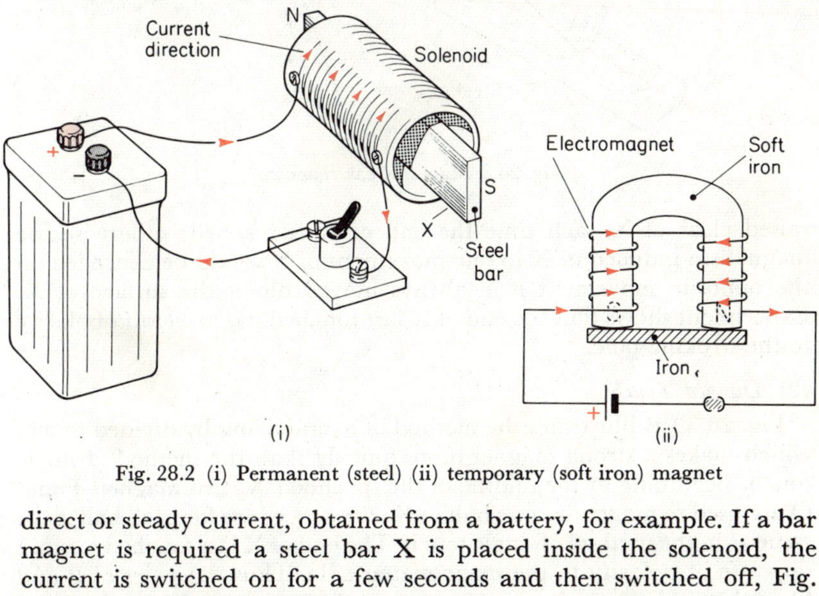

Fig. 28.2 (i) Permanent (steel) (ii) temporary (soft iron) magnet

direct or steady current, obtained from a battery, for example. If a bar magnet is required a steel bar X is placed inside the solenoid, the current is switched on for a few seconds and then switched off, Fig. 28.2 (i). On testing, X is found to be a magnet with N and S poles as shown. We shall see later that a rule for polarity can be stated as follows:

> If the current flows *clockwise* in the coil when one end of it is viewed, then X has a *south* (S) pole at this end. If the current flows anti-clockwise the end of X is north (N).

If a *ring* or *horse-shoe* magnet is required, an insulated solenoid is wound all round the material, and a steady current is switched on and then off, Fig. 28.2 (ii).

Other Methods of Making Magnets

(1) *Single Touch*

A simple method of making a steel knitting needle, or a piece of clock spring, into a magnet consists of laying the specimen X on a table, and stroking it repeatedly in one direction with a pole of a magnet Y, Fig. 28.3 (i). This is known as the method of single touch. Y must be

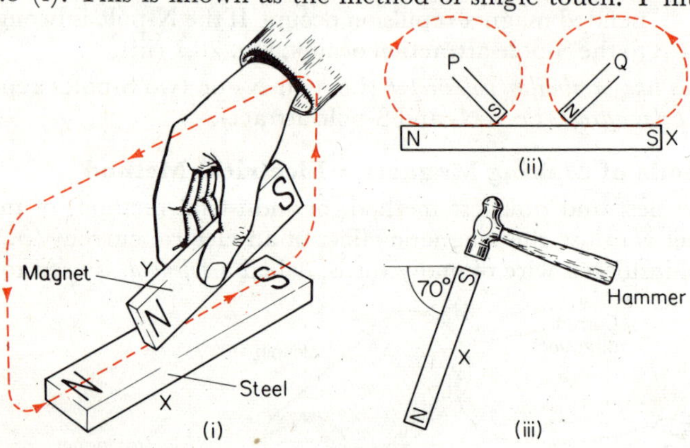

Fig. 28.3 Making weak magnets

raised clear of X each time the end of X is reached; otherwise the magnetism induced in X in one movement of Y would be cancelled on the opposite movement if Y always moved along the surface of X. Experiment shows that the end of X last touched has an *opposite* polarity to the stroking pole.

(2) *Divided Touch*

Fig. 28.3 (ii) illustrates the method of magnetizing by divided touch, which makes a strong magnet more quickly than the method of single touch. Beginning at the middle of the specimen X, two magnets P and Q are used to magnetize one half of X; the procedure for each half is the same as in the method of single touch. The end of X last touched is again opposite in polarity to the magnetizing pole. Thus the poles of P and Q used must be opposite in polarity to make X a normal magnet.

If the same poles of P and Q are used, a N-pole appears at each end of X and a S-pole in the middle. These are called *consequent poles*. X is not then a 'magnet' in the normal sense of the word. If it is suspended it will not settle in any particular direction, as its resultant magnetism is zero.

(3) *Hammering in the Earth's Field*

In the 17th century a weak magnet was made by hammering one end of the specimen X, held pointing north; the best position to hold X is about 70° inclined to the horizontal, Fig. 28.3 (iii). Instead of a magnet, such as Y in Fig. 28.3 (i), the magnetic influence of the earth is used in this case (see p. 492). In this country, the lower end of the specimen has a north polarity. This is the case for countries such as the United States or Russia, which are also in the northern hemisphere. In Australia or South America, which are in the southern hemisphere, the lower end has south magnetic polarity.

Demagnetization

Magnets can be partially demagnetized by hammering them hard when they are pointing east–west, that is, about 90° to the earth's magnetic field direction, or by heating them strongly.

The most effective method of demagnetization is to use an alternating current. A low mains voltage *V*, such as 12 V a.c., is connected in series with a suitable rheostat R and a solenoid X, Fig. 28.4. *The solenoid is placed with its axis pointing east–west.* The object to be demagnetized, a bar magnet or wrist-watch, for example, is then placed inside S and the alternating current is switched on. After a few seconds the object is slowly withdrawn from the solenoid to a long distance away. It will then be demagnetized.

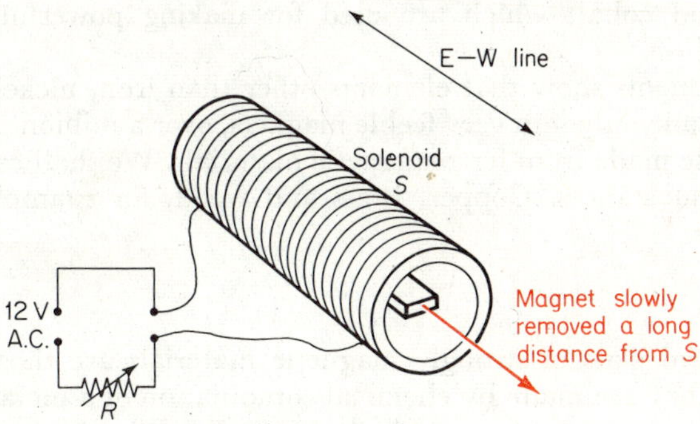

Fig. 28.4 Demagnetization

The alternating current used reverses every $\frac{1}{100}$ s, and hence reverses the magnetism in the material one hundred times per second.

This has the effect of making the material magnetically softer. The magnetism soon shrinks to a very small value and disappears.

Magnetic and Non-magnetic Materials

Iron, nickel, cobalt and certain alloys of these metals can be made into strong magnets. They are hence strongly magnetic and are called *ferromagnetic* materials.

If a bar of pure or soft iron is placed inside a solenoid and the current is switched on, the iron becomes a powerful magnet which can pick up heavy pieces of iron. When the current is switched off, however, the iron falls to the ground. *Temporary magnets are therefore made of soft iron.* Electromagnets, which are temporary magnets, hence use iron.

Steel is an alloy of iron, made by adding a small percentage of carbon to pure iron. It is generally a much harder metal than pure or soft iron. If a bar of steel is placed inside a solenoid and the current is switched on, the steel becomes a magnet and can pick up pieces of iron. When the current is switched off the iron remains attracted to the steel. Thus *permanent magnets are made of steel.* Steel is more difficult to magnetize than iron, but loses its magnetism much less easily than iron.

A vast amount of research has been spent in finding alloys which can be made into powerful magnets. Special alloys such as mu-metal have been developed for the electromagnet and the transformer, in which temporary magnets are used. Alni, alcomax and ticonal are alloys of nickel and cobalt which are used for making powerful permanent magnets.

Experiments show that elements other than iron, nickel and cobalt can be made only into very feeble magnets, over a million times weaker than those made from ferromagnetic materials. We shall call them *non-magnetic* substances. Copper, brass and wood, for example, are non-magnetic.

Ferrites

A special class of strongly magnetic materials are those known as *ferrites*. They are made by chemical combination of a metal oxide such as zinc oxide with ferric oxide (Fe_2O_3). Ferrites can be magnetized strongly and, even more important, they are not demagnetized easily once they are magnetized. Ferrite rods, which are black and hard, are used in aerials of transistor receivers. They are particularly useful for reception of microwaves, which are radio waves of very high frequency (p. 272). Usually there are considerable power losses in magnetic materials due to circulating electric currents inside them (see p. 539). Ferrites have a high electrical resistance. Hence the current and power loss are extremely small. A fine iron oxide power is used to coat the tapes used in magnetic tape-recorders (p. 391).

The Magnetic Filter

The attraction of a magnet for iron is used in industry for cleaning oil and for separating iron from non-ferrous materials mixed with it. Fig. 28.5 illustrates the essential features of a magnetic filter system. It is used for extracting small iron particles contaminating oil or any other liquid. M is a powerful magnet made of ticonal. C is an iron filter cage which is magnetized by M. The dirty oil is poured into the filter at A, and the iron particles mixed with it collect in the iron cage owing to the powerful attraction on them, as shown. The clean oil issues through B, the bottom of the filter cage.

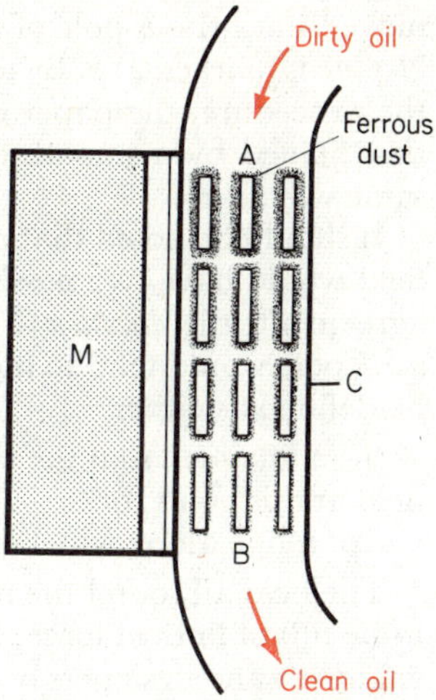

Fig. 28.5 Magnetic filter

Magnetic Fields · Lines of Force

If a small compass needle is placed at a point *a* near to the north pole N of a bar magnet, the needle or light magnet immediately swings round on its support and settles in a definite direction, Fig. 28.6. At other points near the magnet, such as *b*, *c* and *d*, the needle settles in a different direction. In the area or region round the magnet, then a magnetic force is obtained. We call this region a *magnetic field*. A compass needle is a sensitive method of finding the direction of the magnetic force at a point in the field.

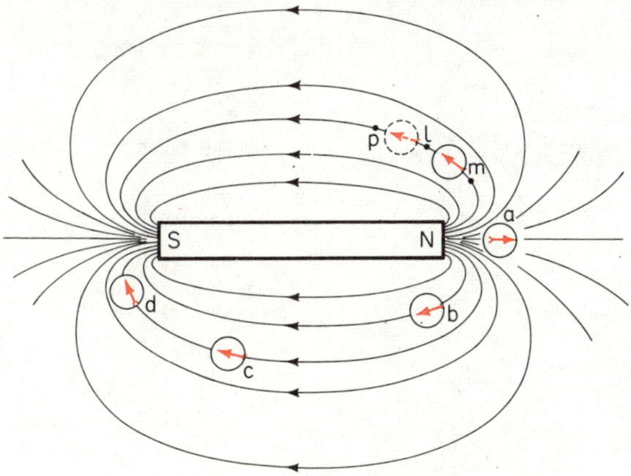

Fig. 28.6 Plotting magnetic field

The direction of the magnetic forces in an area of the field can be mapped out by marking the north and south ends of a compass needle with dots at *l* and *m*, say, on a sheet of paper. The compass is then moved until the S-pole of the needle is at l and the new position of the N-pole is marked at p. By moving the compass in this way and repeating the procedure, the paper can be covered by a series of dots. These are then joined by a smooth curve. Other lines of force are drawn in the same way.

It should be noted that no lines of force cross; otherwise the magnetic field would have two possible directions at the point of intersection. By agreement, the *direction* of the field at a point is the direction which a *north* pole would tend to move if placed at that point. A line of force can be defined as either:

(i) a line such that the tangent to it at any point is the direction of the field at this point; or

(ii) a line along which a free N-pole would tend to move.

The field all round the magnet, in three dimensions, can be imagined to be full of lines of force. Magnetic lines of force are used by electrical engineers and designers of electrical instruments. Astronomers use them in their theories of the origin of the universe.

Some Magnetic Fields

A vivid demonstration of magnetic fields can be obtained by sprinkling iron filings on a sheet of paper laid on magnets, and then tapping the paper lightly. The filings become tiny magnets by the process of induction (see p. 489). Tapping the paper gives them the necessary freedom to settle in the direction of the magnetic field, like miniature compass needles, and so they settle along the field lines.

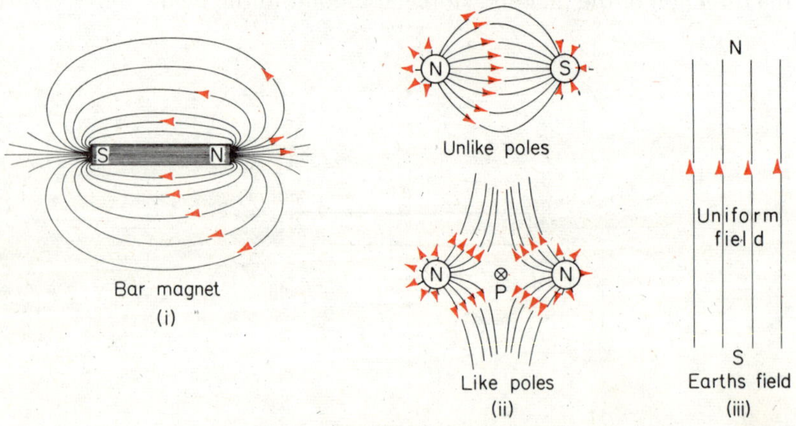

Fig. 28.7 Magnetic fields

Fig. 28.7 illustrates a few typical lines of force in some magnetic fields obtained with a compass needle. The lines exist in space, so that the sketches represent a section in a horizontal plane. Points worth noting are:

(i) *Bar Magnet.* The lines are oval in shape and come out of the N-pole into the air and enter the S-pole. The lines are continuous; one should imagine them inside the magnet passing from the south pole S to the north pole N in the magnetic material.

(ii) *Unlike and Like Poles.* The field between the N- and S-poles has many lines and is therefore strong. In contrast, there are no lines round P between the N- and N-poles facing each other, and hence there is no magnetic force or field here, Fig. 28.7 (ii).

(iii) *Earth's Field.* Locally, the field consists of parallel lines pointing northwards, Fig. 28.7 (iii). The density of the lines at any part of the field is hence constant. The earth's field is an example of a 'uniform field', one whose direction and strength is constant, whereas the field round a bar magnet is non-uniform.

(iv) *Bar Magnet, N-pole Pointing South.* Note the existence of *neutral points* at P_1 and P_2, Fig. 28.8. Here the strength of the earth's field exactly counter-balances that due to the magnet. Since there is no resultant field here, there are no lines of force and a compass does not settle in any particular direction at these points.

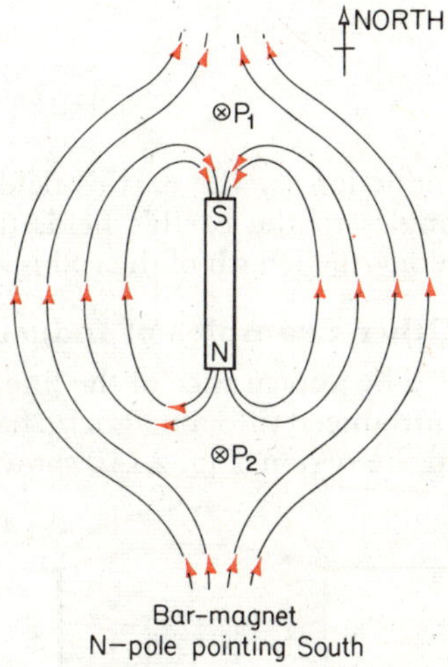

Fig. 28.8 Field round magnet

Magnetic Induction

Mu-metal is a magnetic alloy which can be magnetized strongly by very weak magnetic fields (p. 486).

If a long rod of mu-metal is held pointing downwards at an angle of about 70° to the horizontal the lower end A is observed to repel the N-pole of a suspended magnetic needle, Fig. 28.9 (i). The other end is observed to repel the S-pole of the needle. The rod is therefore a magnet.

A surprising change occurs when the rod is turned round so as to point in an east–west direction and held horizontal. This time the end A *attracts* both the N-pole of the magnetic needle and its S-pole, Fig. 28.9 (ii). Likewise, the other end attracts both the S-pole of the needle and its N-pole. The rod is hence unmagnetized. On turning the rod round to lie in the north–south direction, the rod becomes a magnet again.

Explanation. When it is placed in the direction of the earth's magnetic field that is, north–south, the magnetic field magnetizes the rod. Since the rod is not in contact with a magnet, as in the method of single touch, the magnetism in the rod is called *induced magnetism.* The phenomenon is called *magnetic induction*, and this is an example of magnetic

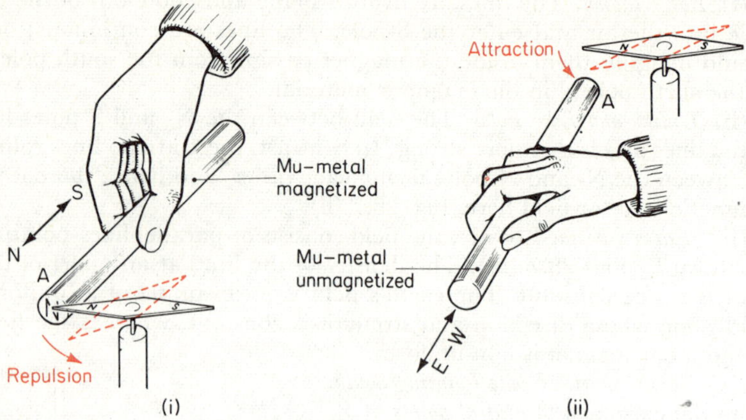

Fig. 28.9 Induced magnetism

induction by the earth's field. If the rod is placed east–west, at right angles to the earth's field, the induced magnetism due to the earth along the length of the rod is zero.

Other Examples of Induction

The appearance of the lines of force when mu-metal or soft iron X is introduced into a magnetic field can be shown by sprinkling iron filings in the region. Fig. 28.10 shows the lines of force when X is between the poles N and S of two strong magnets. Compared with the appearance when air is between the poles, the lines of force now crowd into the iron. The concentration of the lines may be increased many hundreds of times with soft iron alloys such as mu-metal. This is due to the strong induced magnetism in the metal.

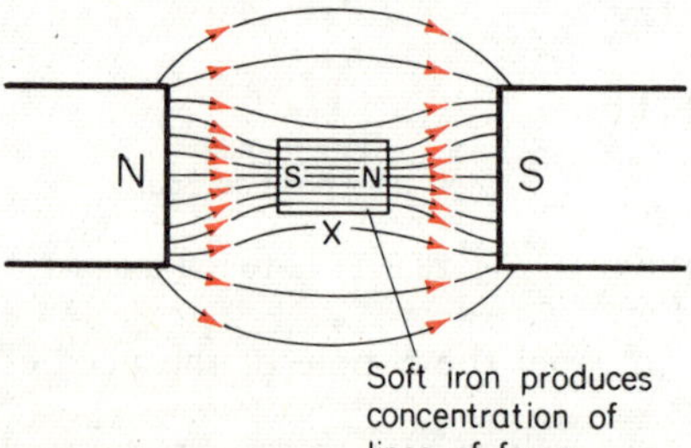

Fig. 28.10 Soft iron in magnetic field

When a magnet is placed near an unmagnetized steel pin, the pin first becomes magnetized by induction. It is then attracted to the magnet, Fig. 28.11 (i), (ii), (iii). *Induction thus precedes attraction.* This explains why unmagnetized iron and steel are attracted to magnets. Steel objects, such as pliers or railings or girders in buildings, are often found to be magnetized, Fig. 28.11 (iv). This is due to induction by the earth's magnetic field.

Magnetic Shield

The concentration of lines of force in soft iron can be used to shield

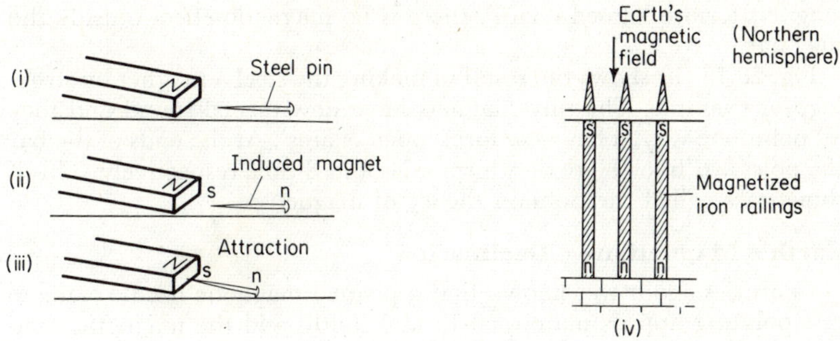

Fig. 28.11 Induction by magnet

objects from unwanted magnetic fields. Fig. 28.12 (i) shows an object X with a soft-iron ring round it and a powerful magnet Y outside. All the lines of force pass through the ring. None passes into the air inside the ring. Thus X is shielded from the magnet. The electron beam inside cathode-ray tubes in television receivers is shielded from external magnetic fields by placing a soft-iron cylinder round the neck of the tube. Fig. 28.12 (ii).

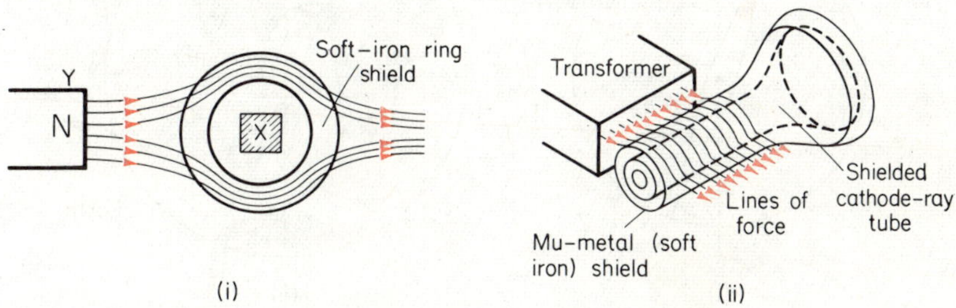

Fig. 28.12 Magnetic screening

Theory of Magnetism

Magnetism is due to moving electrons in atoms, which rotate and spin and set up tiny electric currents (p. 503). A completely satisfactory theory of magnetism has still not been made. Millions of tiny magnetized regions, called *domains*, appear to exist in iron and steel, even though the materials are not magnetized. The direction of the magnetism in the domains is shown by the arrows in Fig. 28.13 (i), which illustrates diagrammatically a bar of unmagnetized steel. Since the tiny

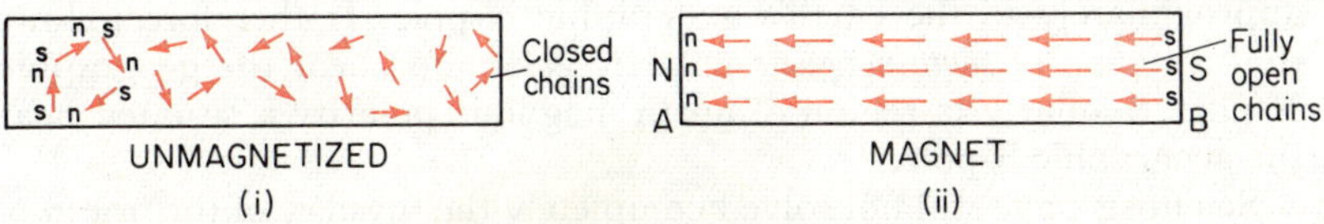

Fig. 28.13 Closed and open chains

magnets form a 'closed chain', there is no magnetic effect outside the steel bar.

Fig. 28.13 (ii) shows the result of making the steel a magnet by stroking, for example. The tiny magnets have now turned round and they all point one way. They now form 'open chains'. At the ends of the bar the poles are 'free'. Here they form a N- and S-pole respectively. This is sometimes called the domain theory of magnetism.

Earth's Magnetism · Declination

Centuries ago it was known that a pivoted magnetic needle came to rest pointing approximately north and south, and the magnetic compass needle is still used for navigation.

At a particular place on the earth, the magnetic north is not usually in the same direction as the geographic north there. The angle between the two directions is called the *declination* or *variation*, Fig. 28.14 (i). The

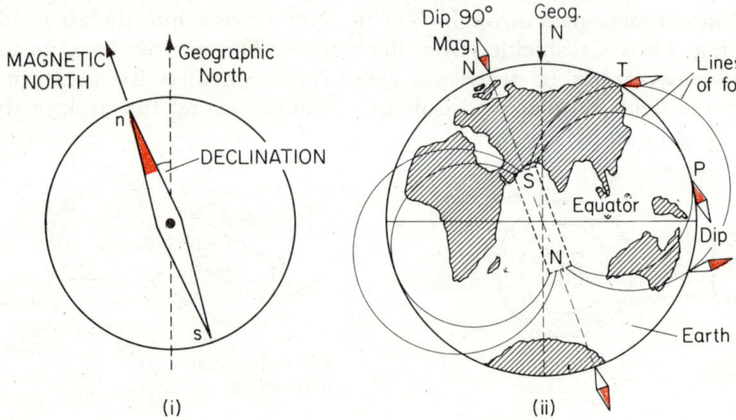

Fig. 28.14 Earth's magnetism

declination varies all over the world. Seamen need to know the declination to navigate by magnetic compass. Maps are therefore prepared periodically showing the declination at different parts of the world.

Magnetic Poles of Earth

Since unlike poles attract, a north magnetic pole is attracted by a south magnetic pole. Now the north magnetic pole of a compass points approximately to the earth's geographic N-pole. It therefore follows that a region of *south magnetic* polarity is situated near the geographic N-pole. Similarly, a region of north magnetic polarity is situated near the geographic S-pole.

Scientists have still not solved completely the mystery of the origin of the earth's magnetism. Some of the common observations can be explained by imagining a fictitious magnet at the middle of the earth, as shown in Fig. 28.14 (ii). No actual magnet could exist—the enormously high temperature inside the earth would destroy its magnetism.

Angle of Dip

If a non-magnetic uniform piece of metal, such as brass, is suspended at its centre of gravity M, the brass remains horizontally in equilibrium, Fig. 28.15 (i). If, however, a magnetic needle is suspended at its centre

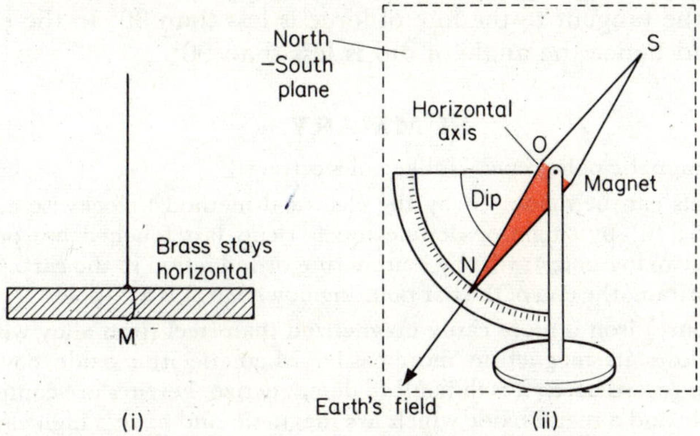

Fig. 28.15 Dip

of gravity O so that it is free to take up any position in a magnetic north–south plane, it 'dips' at an angle of about 65° to the horizontal in this country, Fig. 28.15 (ii). Now, in general, a freely-suspended magnetic needle points in the direction of the magnetic field in which it is situated. Consequently the earth's magnetic field in Great Britain acts at an angle of about 65° to the horizontal.

In this country, the north pole of the dip-needle points downwards. In Australia on the other side of the world, the south pole of the dip-needle points downwards.

Variation of Angle of Dip

If a freely suspended magnetic needle is taken to various places on the earth's surface, the needle 'dips' at different angles to the horizontal. Near the geographic N- and S-poles, for example, the needle dips vertically, and the angle of dip is then 90°. Near the equator the freely suspended needle is horizontal, and the angle of dip is then zero. In Great Britain the angle of dip was about 66° in 1968. The angle at a given place on the earth varies very slightly every hour and every day. At the end of each year there is a change of a small fraction of a degree.

Fig. 28.14 (ii) illustrates how a fictitious magnet in the middle of the earth can account for the variation of the angle of dip all over the world.

Some of the lines of force due to the magnet are shown. The tangent to the line of force passing through a place P is the direction of the magnetic field there (p. 488). Now at this place the tangent is parallel to the earth's surface. Thus the earth's field is horizontal at P, and the angle of dip is therefore zero. Near the geographic N-pole, a tangent to the line of force is vertical, and hence the angle of dip is 90° here. This region contains the magnetic N-pole of the earth. In a magnetic survey an aeroplane equipped with a specially designed magnetic dip-needle has located this pole about 1600 km from the geographic N-pole. At T on the globe the tangent to the line of force is less than 90° to the earth's surface, and hence the angle of dip is less than 90°.

SUMMARY

1. Like magnetic poles repel. Unlike poles attract.

2. Magnets can be made: (i) by the electrical method ('clockwise current-south pole'); (ii) by single or double touch ('end last touched has opposite polarity to stroking pole'); (iii) by hammering or induction in the earth's field. (In Great Britain, the end of the bar pointing downwards is a N-pole.)

3. Soft (pure) iron is more easily magnetized than steel (iron alloy with carbon), and loses its magnetism more easily. Magnetic iron oxide powder is used in tape-recorders, as it is difficult to demagnetize. Ferrites are compounds of iron oxide and a metal oxide which are magnetic and have a high electrical resistance, thus reducing energy losses in radio reception, for example.

4. A *magnetic field* is a region in which a magnetic force may be detected. A *line of force* is a line along which a N-pole would tend to move if it were free. Magnetic fields can be plotted with the aid of a compass needle. The appearance of the whole field can be seen by using iron filings.

5. Angle of dip = angle made with horizontal by earth's total magnetic field. It is 90° at the magnetic poles and zero at the magnetic equator.

6. Angle of declination = angle between magnetic north and geographic north directions at the place concerned.

PRACTICAL

1. Magnetic and non-magnetic materials

Method. (i) Obtain a mixture of many substances, copper, brass, aluminium, iron, steel, wood, paper, glass, crystals of copper sulphate, for example. Test each for attraction by a magnet. Tabulate your results.

Magnetic	Non-magnetic

(ii) Mix iron filings thoroughly with salt or sand. Using a magnet, extract all the iron filings from the mixture.

2. Testing magnets and non-magnets

Apparatus. Powerful (e.g. Ticonal) magnet; suspended magnetic needle or compass-needle; cork of about 5 cm diameter; large bowl or dish.

Method. (i) From some distance away, bring the N-pole of the magnet slowly towards the N-pole of the compass-needle. Observe the movement of the N-pole. Repeat with the S-pole of the magnet.

(ii) Repeat with an *unmagnetized* piece of iron or steel. What is the difference from (i)? What is the only sure test of magnetism?

(iii) Bring the N-pole of the magnet very quickly up to the N-pole of the compass. What do you observe? Why is the N-pole attracted?

(iv) Float a cork in water in a bowl and place the magnet on the cork. Observe the motion of the magnet. When it comes to rest, deflect it slightly with the finger and watch it settle again. What happens if the magnet is turned right round?

Replace the magnet by an unmagnetized piece of iron or steel and observe the motion of the metal. Repeat with wood or glass.

(v) With the aid of a compass-needle, test the radiators and other metal fittings such as pipes and taps in your room for magnetism. Make a list of them, stating which are: (*a*) unmagnetized; (*b*) weakly magnetized; (*c*) strongly magnetized.

3. Making magnets

Apparatus. Powerful (Ticonal) magnet; clock-spring or steel knitting-needle; compass-needle.

Method. (i) First test both ends of the clockspring or knitting-needle with the compass-needle. If magnetized, demagnetize by heating in a flame—or obtain new and unmagnetized material.

(ii) Make a magnet by the method of: (*a*) single touch, p. 484. (*b*) divided touch, p. 484. Each time test the polarity at the end *last* stroked. Is it opposite or the same polarity as the stroking pole?

4. Distinguishing three similar rods

Apparatus. Three similar rods, A, B, C, one a magnet, another unmagnetized soft-iron, and the third a non-magnetic material, and each painted the same colour.

Method. Find out which rod is a magnet, which is unmagnetized and which is non-magnetic. Remember that the magnetism of a rod or bar-magnet is strongest at the ends or poles and decreases towards the middle, and try to distinguish the rods by means of the attraction between them.

5. Iron and steel (p. 486)

Apparatus. Powerful (Ticonal) magnet; four steel pins or needles; four iron nails; compass-needle.

Method. (i) Attract the steel pins one after the other so they are all suspended as shown in Fig. 28.16. Test the polarity of the free end A by bringing it in turn near to the poles of a compass-needle. Gently remove the top pin B from the magnet. Observe if some pins are still attracted to B.

(ii) Repeat with the iron nails. After testing for magnetism, remove the top nail. Are some nails still attracted to the top nail?

Conclusion. State a conclusion about one magnetic property of steel compared with iron.

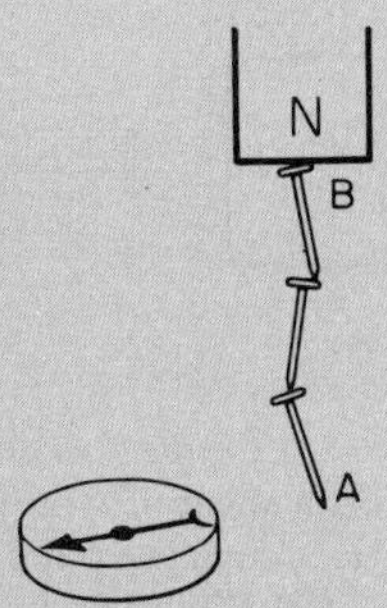

Fig. 28.16
Iron and steel

6. Induction (p. 489)

Apparatus. Powerful (Ticonal) magnet; iron nails; bar

of mu-metal (very soft iron); compass-needle; two bar-magnets; iron filings.

Method. (i) Hold an iron nail vertically with one end dipping into some iron filings on paper, Fig. 28.17. See if any filings cling to the nail when it is raised.

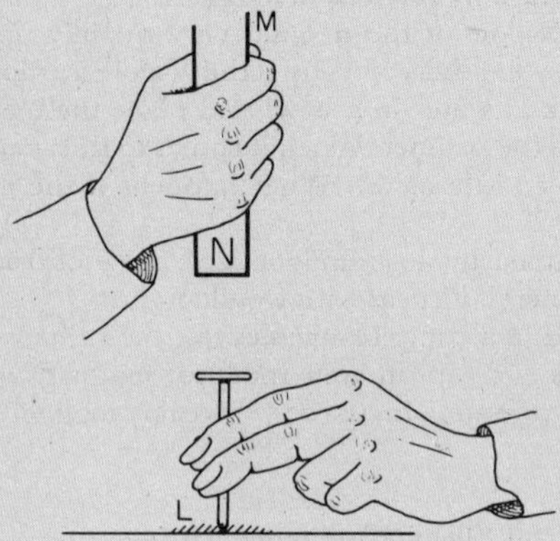

Fig. 28.17 Induction

Now hold a powerful magnet M above the vertical nail L but not touching it, and see if iron filings are attracted to the nail on raising it. Then remove M. Observe what happens to the filings and explain.

(ii) Repeat the experiment on p. 489 with the mu-metal bar. When does the mu-metal become magnetized in the earth's field?

7. Magnetic fields (p. 488)

Apparatus. Two bar-magnets; sheet of white paper; iron filings; compass-needle.

Method. (*a*) *Iron Filings.* (i) Bar-magnet: Place the bar-magnet below the paper. Sprinkle iron filings *lightly* on the paper above the magnet position. Tap the paper. Draw a sketch of the appearance of the field.

(ii) Bar-magnets in line, with N-poles facing near each other. Place the bar-magnets below the paper and repeat. Draw a sketch.

(iii) Place the N- and the S-pole ends of two bar-magnets on paper and facing each other. Move them apart until it can be seen that an iron nail can easily fit into the space between. (*a*) Sprinkle iron filings between the poles, tap the paper lightly. Observe the appearance of the magnetic field between the N- and S-poles and draw a sketch of it. (*b*) Now place the iron nail between the N- and S-poles, Fig. 28.18. Tap the paper lightly. Observe the new appearance of the field. Draw a sketch.

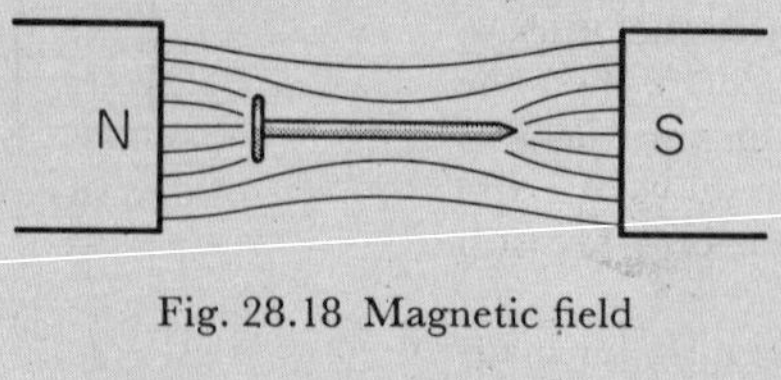

Fig. 28.18 Magnetic field

(*b*) *Compass-needle.* (i) With all magnets well removed, place a compass-needle on a sheet of white paper. When the needle has settled in a north–south direction, turn the paper until its longer edge is parallel to the needle.

(ii) Place one bar-magnet in the middle of the paper with its N-pole pointing southwards. By the method described on p. 487, plot with a compass-needle the lines of force round the magnet. Observe what happens when the compass-needle is moved away from the south-pole of the magnet towards the north. Draw a sketch of the lines round the magnet.

(*c*) *Moving pole.* (i) Magnetize a steel needle A by single touch so that the 'eye' is a north pole. Test it with a compass-needle.

(ii) Push the needle through a piece of cork so that the eye is just above the cork. Float the cork on water in a large glass bowl or trough. Now attach a bar-magnet M by Sellotape to the edge of the bowl, Fig. 28.19. Observe the movement of the 'eye' or N-pole of the needle—it moves along a line of force round the magnet. Repeat with a Ticonal magnet in place of the bar-magnet.

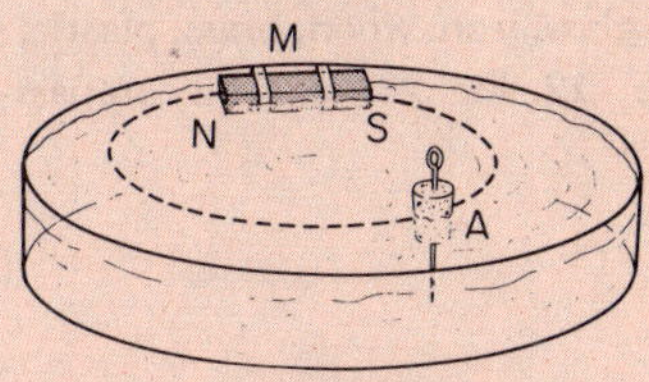

Fig. 28.19 Moving pole

8. Magnetizing filings

Apparatus. Thin test-tube; iron filings; powerful (Ticonal) magnet; compass-needle.

Method. Fill a thin test tube with iron filings. Insert a cork at the top. Place the tube on the table and stroke it several times lengthwise as in magnetizing by single touch, Fig. 28.20 (p. 484). Observe the movement of the filings during the stroking.

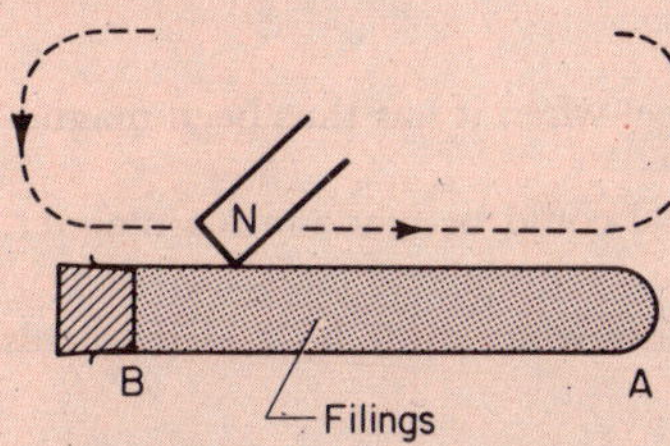

Fig. 28.20 Magnetizing filings

Bring the compass-needle to both ends A and B of the tube in turn. Is there evidence of polarity at the ends? Now shake the tube so that the filings are disturbed. Test the ends again. Has the magnetism disappeared?

Note. This experiment suggests that magnets may consist of millions of very tiny regions of magnetism inside them all pointing one way. When demagnetized, the regions all point in different directions, so their net effect is zero (p. 491).

EXERCISE 28 · ANSWERS, p. 617

What are the missing words in the following statements 1–10?

1. The N-pole of a magnet attracts a . . pole.

2. The S-pole of a magnet repels a . . pole.

3. The geographic north pole has a magnetic . . polarity.

4. To make a temporary magnet such as an electromagnet, . . should be used as the core.

5. To make a permanent magnet, . . should be used as the material.

6. Before a steel pin is attracted to a magnet, the pin becomes . .

7. When a S-pole of a magnet is used to magnetize a length of steel, the end last touched becomes a . . pole.

8. In the method of magnetizing by single touch, at the end of each stroke the magnet should be . .

9. The magnetic field strength outside a magnet is . . by the presence of soft iron there.

10. A television tube is usually surrounded by soft iron to . . the tube from magnetic influences outside.

11. *Underline* those of the following which are attracted by a strong magnet: glass, iron, wood, brass, plastic, steel, nickel, cardboard, zinc, cobalt. (*Mx.*)

12. Fig. 28A shows a compass-needle placed near to a bar-magnet on a bench.

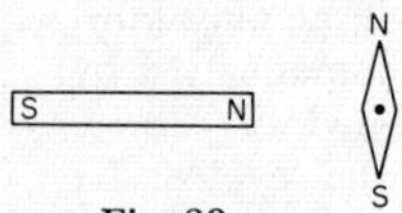

Fig. 28A

(*a*) Mark on the diagram the forces due to the bar-magnet which act on the needle.

(*b*) Will the needle rotate clockwise or anticlockwise? (*E.A.*)

13. A magnet is stroked along a piece of steel as indicated in Fig. 28B. Mark

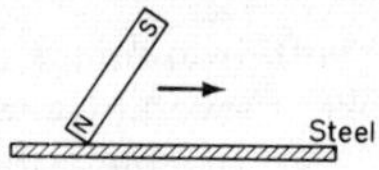

Fig. 28B

on the diagram the polarity of the piece of steel when it has thus been magnetized.

Give *two* other ways in which a piece of steel could be made into a magnet. (*S.E.*)

14. Complete the drawing Fig. 28C to show what must be added to this

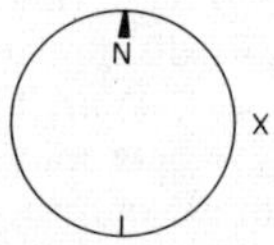

Fig. 28C

circular card to turn it into an instrument to find the direction of the N-pole. How would the instrument be affected by a piece of copper placed at X? (*W.M.*)

15. Complete Fig. 28D by drawing in the pattern of the lines of force you would expect to find around magnets positioned as shown. (*E.A.*)

Fig. 28D

16. Sketch the lines of force in the magnetic fields: (*a*) of the horseshoe magnet shown in Fig. 28E (i); (*b*) existing in the region of the magnetic poles and the soft iron ring shown in Fig. 28E (ii).

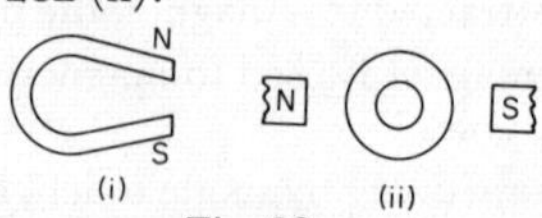

Fig. 28E

Indicate the direction of the fields with arrows on lines of force. Dotted lines must not be used to represent lines of force. (*E.A.*)

17. How would you test whether a piece of steel was magnetized: (i) if you had a magnet; (ii) if there was no magnet available? (*L.*)

18. (*a*) When the iron rod AB comes under the influence of the strong magnet NS, Fig. 28F the rod becomes a . . with a . . pole at A. Insert the missing words.

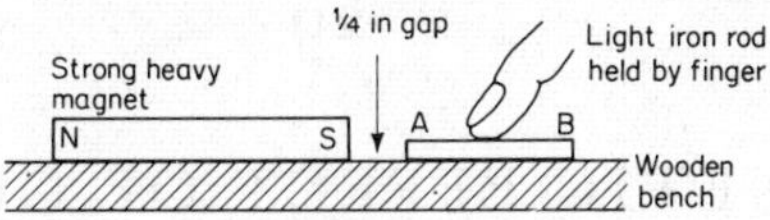

Fig. 28F

(*b*) What happens to AB when NS is removed?

(*c*) NS is replaced and the finger removed. What happens to AB now? (*Mx.*)

19. The ends of two bar magnets, both north seeking poles nearest together, are placed as shown, Fig. 28G (i). The magnetic field around these poles is shown also.

(*a*) What is the point X called?

(*b*) One of the magnets is now reversed as shown, Fig. 28G (ii). Sketch in the lines of magnetic force around these poles and between the poles.

(*c*) The two magnets are then used to pick up small steel ball-bearings with the result shown, Fig. 28G (iii); this result occurring each time the experiment is repeated. What conclusion can you draw from this?

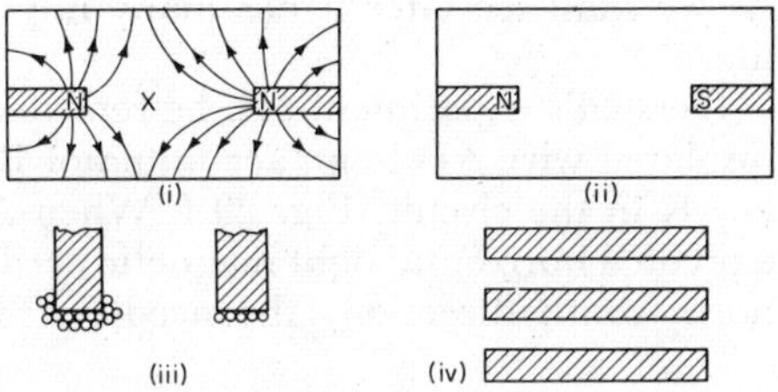

Fig. 28G

(*d*) The two magnets and an unmagnetized steel bar are placed on a table as shown, Fig. 28G (iv). All are unmarked and look identical. How could you find out which of the three is the unmagnetized bar? (*M.*)

20. In its simplest form the Earth's magnetic field can be likened to a large bar-magnet situated on the Earth's axis. Draw the Earth with the magnet in position and the lines of force it produces in and around the Earth. (*E.A.*)

21. Two rods AB and CD are brought near to the N-pole of a magnet. Both ends A and B of the first rod are attracted by the pole of the magnet. With the second rod end C is attracted but end D is repelled: (*a*) which rod is a magnet?; (*b*) which end of it is a S-pole? (*L.*)

22. Complete these diagrams of magnets, Fig. 28H to show the lines of force, with arrows indicating the direction of the lines. (*Mx.*)

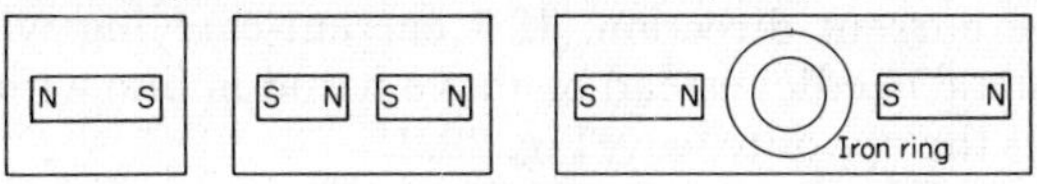

Fig. 28H

23. (*a*) Describe *two* methods of making magnets, using an electric current in one case. Give the materials used, polarities of magnets and direction of current.

(*b*) A soft iron bar is placed on a bench near a powerful bar-magnet. What effect does the magnet have on the bar? Briefly describe a theory to account for this effect. (*E.A.*)

29

MAGNETIC EFFECT OF CURRENT

Oersted's Discovery

An electric current has a heating effect and a chemical effect. The most important effect of an electric current, however, is its magnetic effect. It was discovered by Oersted in 1820 while he was lecturing to students. As we shall see later it has many important applications in everyday life.

Oersted's experiment can be repeated by connecting a long piece of insulated wire AD to an accumulator B, with a small rheostat R and a key K in the circuit, Fig. 29.1. When AD is held parallel to and over a pivoted horizontal light magnetic needle NS (i.e. the wire is placed in a north–south direction) the needle is deflected. When the current is

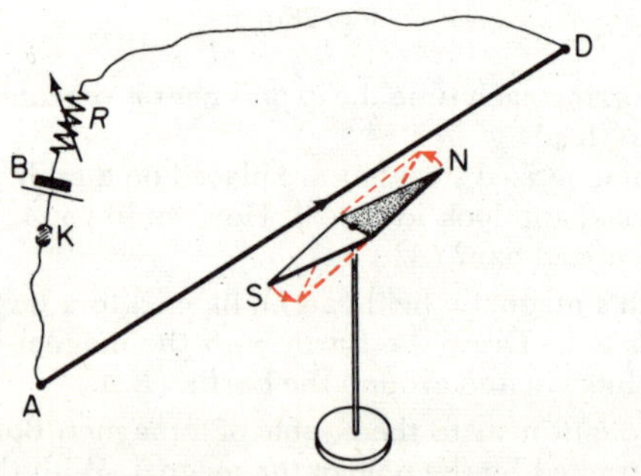

Fig. 29.1 Magnetic effect of current

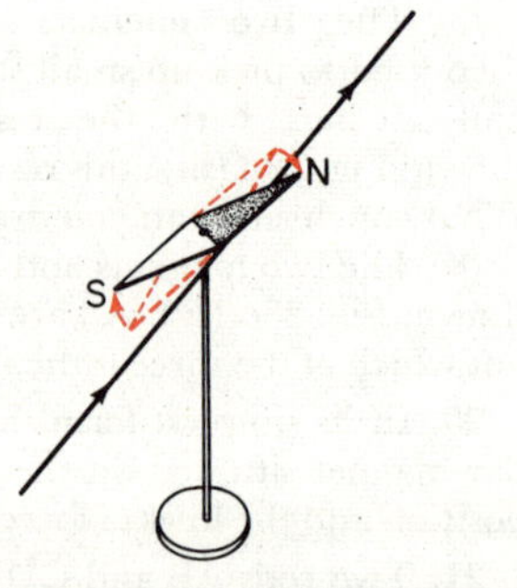

Fig. 29.2 Current below needle

increased by means of R the deflection increases. For large currents the deflection is nearly 90°, that is, the needle then points nearly perpendicular to the current direction. If a current-carrying wire is placed under a magnetic needle instead of above it and in line with its axis, the needle deflects the opposite way, Fig. 29.2.

From the way the needle turns when the current-carrying wire is held parallel to it, we can see that the forces on the poles are *perpendicular* to the current direction. This is illustrated in Fig. 29.1 and 2. We therefore conclude that:

(1) a current has a magnetic field all round it;
(2) the magnetic field is in a direction perpendicular to the current.

Forces due to Magnetic Field

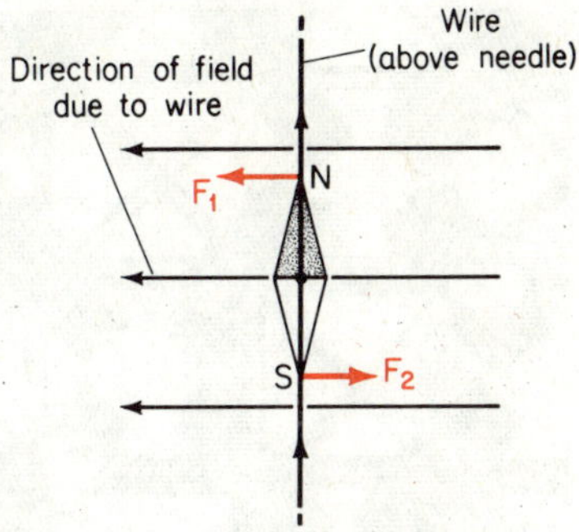

Fig. 29.3 Force due to current

The direction of a magnetic field is taken, by convention, to be the direction a *north* pole would tend to move if placed in the field. Fig. 29.3 shows the direction of the magnetic field when the current is parallel to the magnetic needle. The field is perpendicular to the current direction and the arrow shows the movement of a N-pole in the field. The N-pole of the needle is thus urged in the same direction by a force F_1, and the S-pole in the opposite direction by force F_2, so the needle NS turns.

Magnetic Field Round Straight Wire

The appearance of the magnetic field round a straight current-carrying wire can be investigated by using a large rectangle or square ABCD of side about 50 cm made with 10 turns of insulated copper wire, Fig. 29.4. The plane of the coil is placed vertically and a horizontal board X is positioned through its centre.

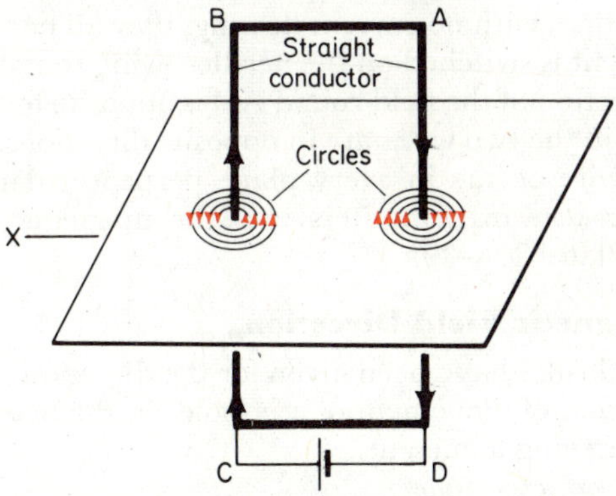

Fig. 29.4 Magnetic field round straight wire

A current of a few amperes is then passed into the coil, some iron filings are lightly sprinkled round and between the vertical sides AD and BC, and the board is tapped gently. Since AD and BC are reasonably far apart, each can be considered as a straight wire. AD carries a downward current, while BC carries an upward current.

The field pattern round a straight wire is seen to consist of *circles* with the wire as centre. This means that the field is symmetrical round the wire, as we may expect when there are no other magnetic influences.

Plate 29(A) Memory store of computer. Ferrite rings, magnified, linked by conductors carrying information.

Plate 29(B) Memory store undergoing final test before use.

The same effect is shown by placing compass needles all round and near to the wire. At first, with no current flowing, they all point north–south. When the current is switched on the needles swing round and settle in a circle. The direction of the field round AD is opposite to that round BC, as the currents in the two wires are in opposite directions. Of course, the field round a wire occurs in every plane perpendicular to itself. One form of *memory store* in computers uses the magnetic field due to a straight wire. Plates 29A–29B.

Rules for Magnetic Field Direction

Several useful rules have been given for the direction of the magnetic field (the direction of movement of a N-pole) in the magnetic field of a straight wire carrying a current.

(1) *Maxwell's Corkscrew Rule*

If a right-handed corkscrew is turned so that its point travels along the current direction, the direction of rotation of the corkscrew gives the direction of the magnetic field.

Fig. 29.5 (i) shows a straight current-carrying wire AB. At a point P above it a N-pole *n* moves from left to right, as shown, according to Maxwell's rule. At a point Q below it a *n*-pole moves from right to left in the opposite direction. If the corkscrew rule is applied to the wire AB, Fig. 29.5 (ii), the *n*-pole of the needle below it moves to the left as at Q in Fig. 29.5 (i). The S-pole needle moves in the opposite direction. If the magnetic needle is placed above the wire AB, Fig. 29.5 (iii), the

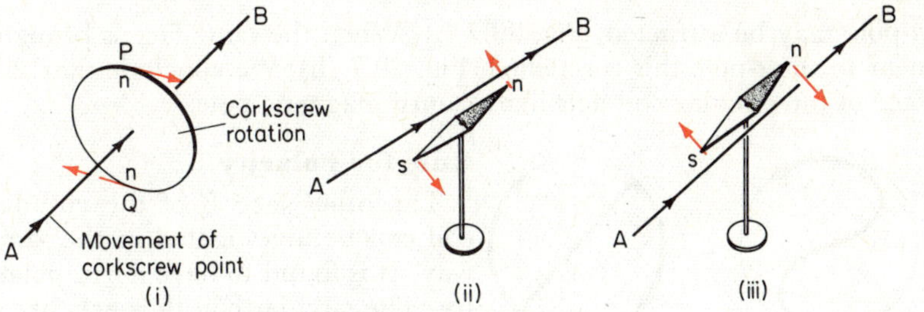

Fig. 29.5 Maxwell's corkscrew rule

n-pole moves to the right, as at P in Fig. 29.5 (i), and hence the *s*-pole moves to the left.

(2) *Clenched Fist Rule*

Grasp the wire with the right hand so that the thumb points in the current direction and clench the fist, Fig. 29.6. The direction of the curled fingers gives the direction of the field. It is left to the reader to show that this rule applies to the cases just considered.

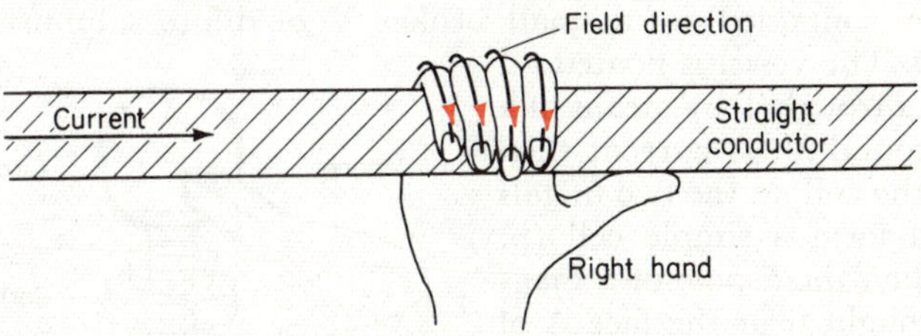

Fig. 29.6 Right hand rule

Circular Coil

The magnetic effect due to a wire can be increased by winding it into a narrow circular coil of many turns. All parts of the wire are now close to the area surrounded by the coil. The total magnetic effect in this region is thus increased.

A simple narrow circular coil can be made by winding thin insulated wire round the finger, and then removing the coil obtained. When one face of the coil AB is brought near to a suspended magnetic needle the

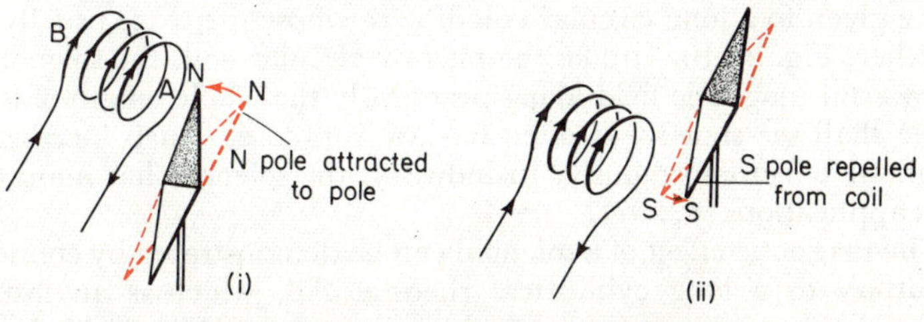

Fig. 29.7 Magnetic effect due to circular coil

n-pole may be attracted, Fig. 29.7 (i). When the same face is brought near to the *s*-pole this is repelled, Fig. 29.7 (ii). We conclude that this face of the circular coil acts like a south magnetic pole.

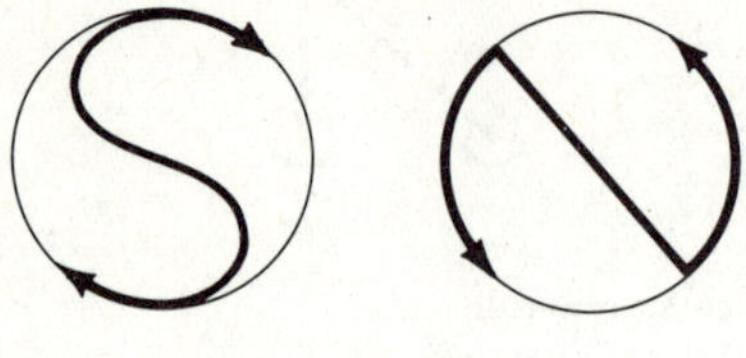

Fig. 29.8 Clock rule

Rule for Polarity

The other face B of the circular coil can be investigated in the same way. It is found to have north polarity. The circular coil thus acts like a *short magnet*, with one face north and the other face south. A simple 'clock' rule for polarity is as follows:

Clockwise current → South pole. Fig. 29.8.
Anti-clockwise current → North pole.

Demonstration of Polarity

The magnetic polarity of the faces of a narrow circular coil can be demonstrated by joining a small coil to the terminals of a piece of copper and zinc contained in a small beaker V of dilute sulphuric acid, Fig. 29.9. The vessel is floated on water in a trough T by means of a cork C round V. A current then flows in the coil, as the two metals and acid form a simple cell (p. 441). When the S-pole of a magnet is brought near the face A of the coil, the whole vessel drifts across the water away from the magnet. If the magnet is turned round and the N-pole held near A, the vessel drifts across the water towards the magnet. This simple experiment shows that the current in the coil has a magnetic effect which causes the face A to behave like a south magnetic pole.

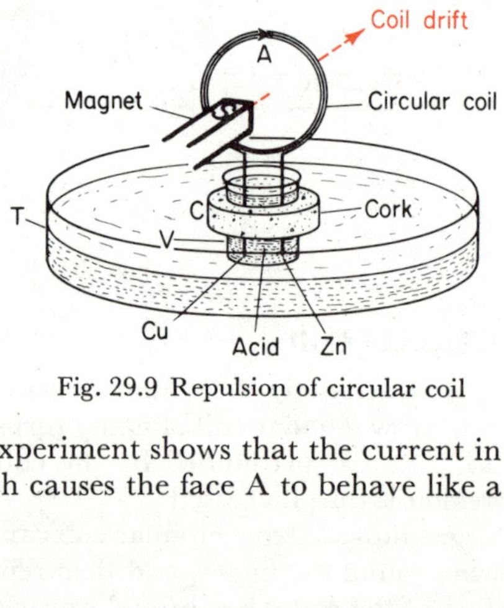

Fig. 29.9 Repulsion of circular coil

Solenoid or Long Coil

The most useful form of current-carrying wire is a *solenoid*. This is the name given to a long circular coil of wire whose turns are usually close together, Fig. 29.10. Unlike the narrow circular coil, the solenoid has a powerful magnetic field along practically the whole length of its axis as we shall see shortly. It often has an iron core, which increases the magnetic effect enormously. In industry, the solenoid has many practical applications (p. 507).

The magnetic effect of a solenoid can be demonstrated by connecting a battery to a long cylindrical rheostat AB, which is an insulated solenoid, or to a long circular coil of copper wire, Fig. 29.10. When a

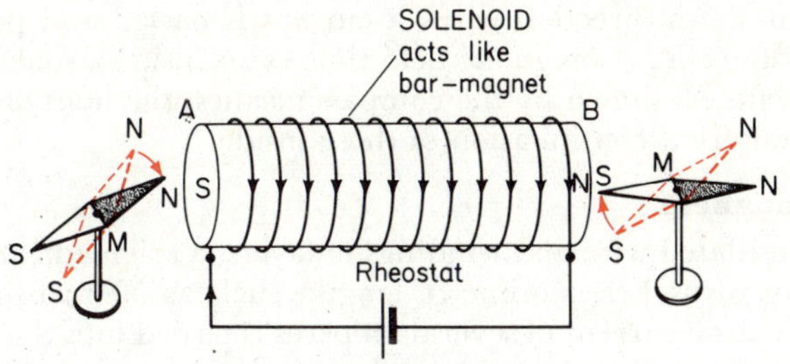

Fig. 29.10 Magnetic effect of solenoid

suspended magnetic needle M is placed near the end B, the S-pole of the needle is attracted towards it. When the needle is taken to the other end A the N-pole is attracted towards it.

The solenoid thus acts like a *bar magnet*. The rule for magnetic polarity is the same as for the narrow circular coil, that is, if the current flows clockwise when one end is viewed that end acts like a S-pole. If it flows anti-clockwise that end acts like a N-pole.

Magnetic Field Round Solenoid

The magnetic field round a solenoid can be demonstrated by using the long cylindrical rheostat as a solenoid, Fig. 29.11 (i); or by passing insulated wire through many holes in a perspex base and forming a coil, which has the advantage of allowing the field inside the solenoid to be seen, Fig. 29.11 (ii).

As the turns of the rheostat solenoid are usually vertical, a board B is placed horizontal, that is, in a plane perpendicular to the current-carrying turns. When iron filings are spread on B and the board is lightly tapped, the filings settle round the solenoid in a similar pattern to that round a bar magnet (p. 488), Fig. 29.11 (i). When magnetic compass needles are placed inside the solenoid A, Fig. 29.11 (ii), and the axis of S is turned to point east–west, all the needles swing round from

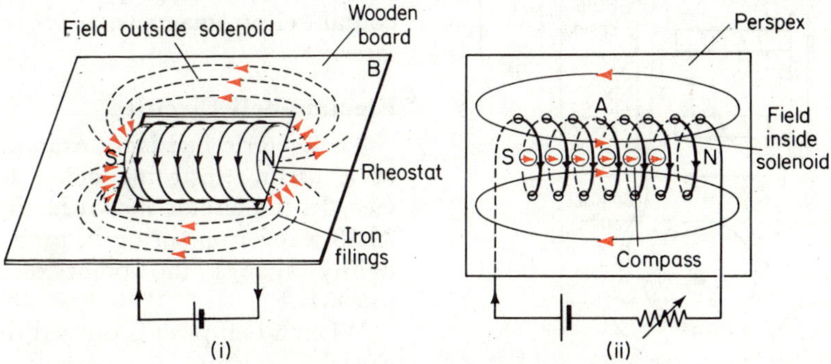

Fig. 29.11 Magnetic field of solenoid

their north–south direction when a current is passed and point along the axis of the coil. A magnetic field thus exists inside a solenoid carrying a current. As shown by the compass needles, the lines of force outside the coil are a continuation of those inside.

Electromagnets

Using insulated wire and windings in layers, a solenoid can be made with many turns per centimetre length, such as 50 turns per centimetre. If a large current of several amperes is passed into the solenoid a powerful magnetic field is obtained practically everywhere inside. A long solenoid can therefore be used for making *permanent magnets*, such as bar magnets. Fig. 29.12 (i).

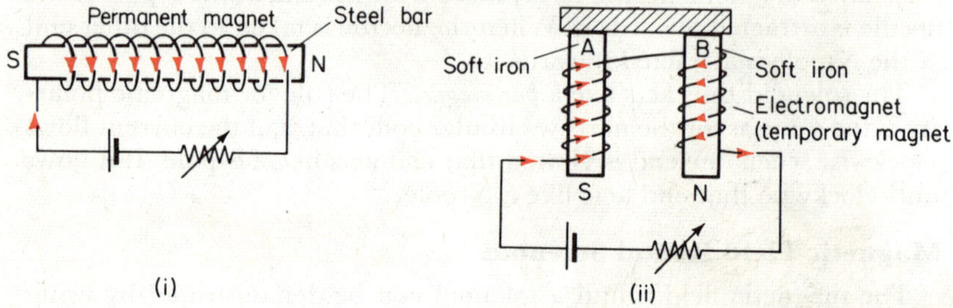

Fig. 29.12 Permanent magnet and electromagnet

An *electromagnet* or temporary magnet can be made by winding solenoids in opposite directions round two soft-iron cores A and B, Fig. 29.12 (ii). The lower end of A then acts as a S-pole and the lower end of B as a N-pole, as shown.

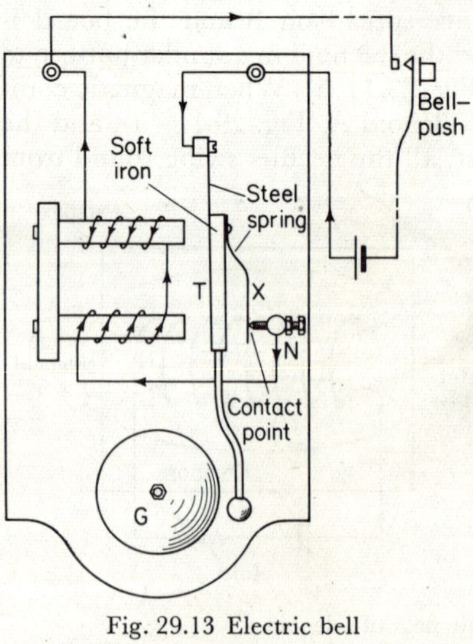

Fig. 29.13 Electric bell

Electromagnetic devices are used in a wide variety of applications in industry. In communications, for example, numerous magnetic relays and telephone receivers are employed which contain electromagnets, as we see later.

Electric-bell Circuit

The electric bell is an example of a useful electromagnetic device. In the circuit shown in Fig. 29.13 a soft-iron spring X presses lightly against the point of a screw N.

When a bell-push is pressed the electric circuit is completed through the contact between X and N. The iron bar T is now attracted to the electromagnet. The circuit is then broken so that T is released. It falls back again to make the contact between X and N once more. Thus the iron is attracted repeatedly by means of the 'make-and-break' contact. A clapper is attached to the iron T. This strikes a gong G repeatedly. The tip of the screw is therefore tungsten or other metal of high melting-point, which is unaffected by the heat.

Magnetic Relay

Magnetic relays help to pass messages from one part of an electric circuit to another. The principle of a magnetic relay is illustrated in Fig. 29.14. The relay consists of a solenoid with a projecting soft-iron

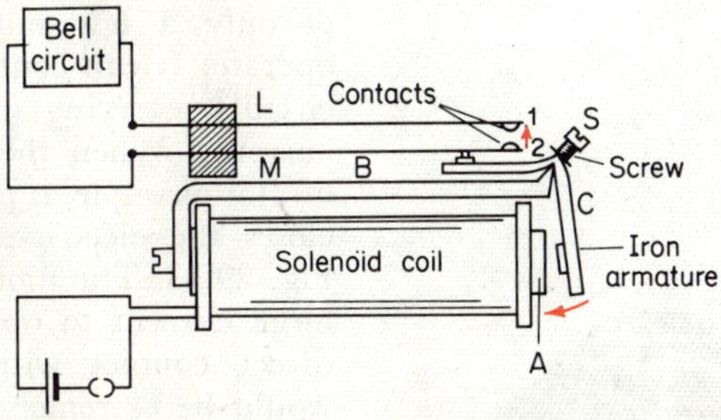

Fig. 29.14 Magnetic relay

core, A, inside it. A bar of soft iron B helps to complete an iron 'circuit'. At C a bent piece of soft iron called the armature (or moving part) can rock about an edge of B. A screw S controls the degree of armature movement.

When a telephone subscriber lifts the receiver a current flows along telephone wires to the solenoid of a relay. The magnetized iron core

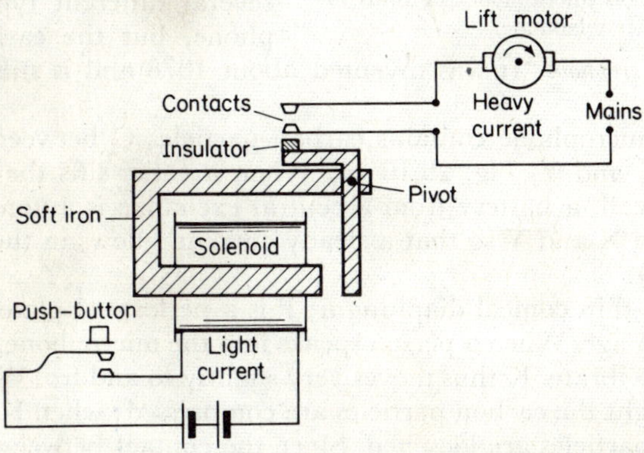

Fig. 29.15 Application of magnetic relay

Plate 29(c) Telephone earpiece (top) and carbon microphone (bottom) of Post Office telephone.

then attracts the armature and the contacts 1 and 2 close. The circuit connected to the light springs L and M is now made, and this in turn may operate a calling lamp on a switchboard at a distant exchange. The complex system of telephone circuits throughout the country requires millions of relays for passing on the information.

A relay is an electromagnetic switch, and may require a current of only a few milliamperes to operate. It can control, however, circuits carrying much higher currents. When the button in a lift, for example, is pressed a relay closes the electric-motor circuit, Fig. 29.15. The motor requires a large current to operate, and as direct contact with the circuit would be extremely dangerous if the insulation broke down, the relay helps to protect the operator.

Carbon Microphone

Communication by telephone requires a *microphone*, an apparatus which converts sound energy to electrical energy. There are several different types of microphone, but the earliest was the *carbon microphone*. It was invented about 1878 and is still used today. Plate 29c.

This microphone contains carbon particles G between two carbon blocks X and Y, Fig. 29.16 (i). When a caller lifts the telephone to make a call, a battery from a central exchange is automatically connected to X and Y so that a steady current I flows in the circuit, Fig. 29.16 (ii).

K is a thin conical diaphragm; P is a perforated plate protecting it from damage. When a person speaks into the microphone, sound waves make K vibrate. K thus moves very slightly to and fro. When K moves to the right the carbon particles are compressed; when K moves to the left the particles are loosened. Since the contact between the particles is better in the former case, the electrical resistance between X and Y is

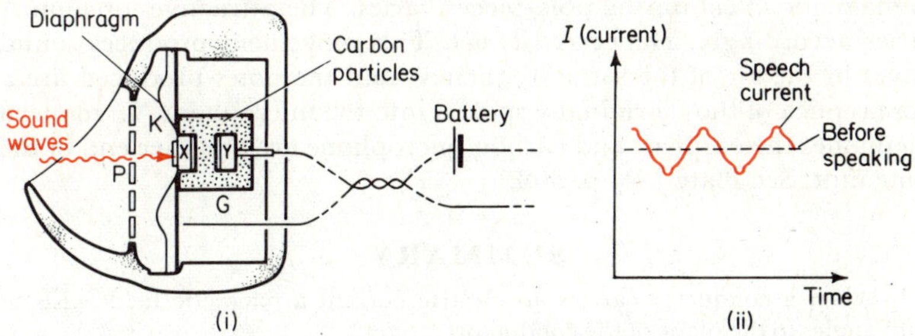

Fig. 29.16 Carbon microphone

decreased when the particles are compressed. A *varying current* thus flows in the circuit. The variations follow exactly the same frequency as the sound waves. This is illustrated in Fig. 29.16 (ii). The varying electric current travels along to a telephone earpiece at the receiver's end of the telephone line. Here, as we now explain, the electrical energy is changed back to sound energy.

Telephone Earpiece

After years of continued efforts, Alexander Graham Bell designed the first telephone in 1876. Nowadays we are so used to the existence of the telephone that we are apt to overlook Bell's service to society in enabling people to communicate easily with each other. If we think of how quickly a doctor can be called, we can appreciate the practical value of Bell's researches.

The telephone earpiece has the opposite function to that of the microphone. It changes electrical energy back into sound energy. In one form a permanent magnet X is bolted to pieces of soft iron, and coils of insulated wire, represented by B and D, are placed round the soft iron. A flexible soft-iron plate or diaphragm A, made of an alloy, called *stalloy*, is near the end of the iron pole-pieces, as shown, Fig. 29.17.

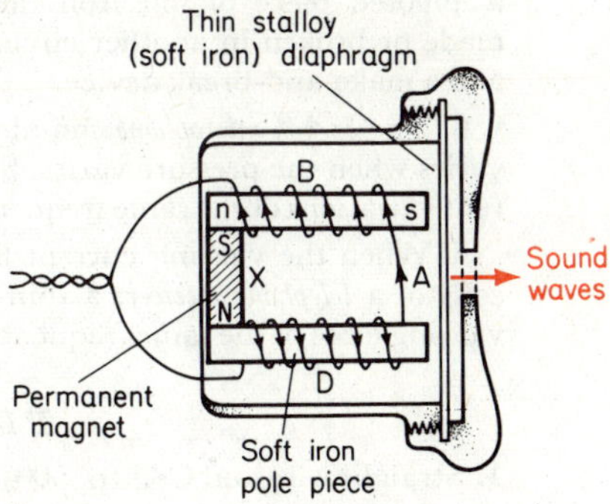

Fig. 29.17 Telephone earpiece

The magnet X induces magnetic *s*- and *n*-poles in the pole-pieces near A. The diaphragm is attracted by the *s*- and *n*-poles and is thus held in tension. When a person speaks into the microphone at the other end of the telephone line the sound energy is converted into electrical energy, as already explained. Electric currents, varying at the frequency of the sound, travel along and pass into the coils B and D, which are connected together. Since the current varies, the strength of its magnetic effect on the pole-pieces varies. The attractive force on A varies accordingly. Hence A *vibrates*. This movement produces sound waves in the air of the same frequency, and the notes produced are a close replica of those originally spoken into the microphone. In modern telephones the earpiece and carbon microphone are at either end of the same unit. See Plate 29c, p. 508.

SUMMARY

1. When a conductor carries an electric current a magnetic field exists at right angles to the plane of the conductor.

2. Maxwell's corkscrew rule states: If a right-handed corkscrew is turned so as to move in the direction of the current in a conductor, the direction of rotation of the corkscrew is the direction of the lines of force. In a coil, a clockwise current makes that face act like a S-pole; anticlockwise current makes the face act like a N-pole.

3. The lines of force round a *straight* current-carrying wire are circular. For a flat *circular coil* they are straight in the middle of the coil in a plane through its centre perpendicular to the coil, but circular near the edges. The lines of force pass through and round a *solenoid*, similarly to the lines round a bar magnet.

4. *Electromagnets* are usually solenoids wound round soft iron; when the current is switched off the magnetism in the iron practically disappears.

5. The *magnetic relay* has a solenoid and soft-iron core. When a current flows a pivoted piece of soft iron (armature) is attracted and contacts are then made or broken in another circuit. An *electric-bell circuit* has an electromagnet and a make-and-break device.

6. The *carbon microphone* contains carbon granules whose electrical resistance varies when the pressure varies. Sound-wave pressure is thus changed into current variations of the same frequency.

7. When the varying current from a microphone flows through the speech coils of a *telephone receiver*, a thin iron plate or diaphragm is attracted with a varying force of the same frequency. Sound waves are then produced.

PRACTICAL

1. Straight wire and Coil (p. 500)

Apparatus. 2 V accumulator; small rheostat; length of insulated copper wire or flex; compass-needle.

Method. Connect the accumulator, rheostat and copper wire in series.

(i) Hold the straight wire over the top of the compass and in line with the needle. Increase the current and observe the deflection. Place the wire below the compass and note the deflection. Draw a sketch in each case. Does the direction of deflection of the needle agree with Maxwell's rule (p. 502)?

(ii) Make a coil by winding the wire round your finger and then removing it carefully. With a current flowing in the coil, bring one face of it towards one pole of the compass-needle and then towards the other pole. Observe what happens in each case. Repeat with the other end of the coil. Draw a sketch of the results in each case. Does this verify the 'Clock' rule for polarity, p. 504?

2. Simple electromagnet (p. 506)

Apparatus. 2 V accumulator; small rheostat; connecting wire; long iron nail or bolt; steel knitting-needle; iron filings; compass-needle.

Method. (i) Connect the accumulator, rheostat, connecting wire in series, Fig. 29.18. Strip part of the insulation from the connecting wire to expose it and see if some iron filings are attracted to the bare wire A by dipping A in the filings.

(ii) Wind the insulated wire round the iron nail or bolt and observe the attraction of iron filings by the iron. Switch off the current and see if the filings drop off.

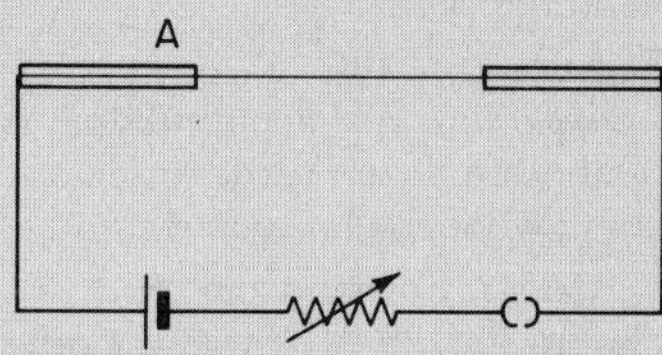

Fig. 29.18 Straight wire and coil

(iii) Wind wire round the steel needle and repeat. Do the filings stay on? What does this show about iron and steel? Does the polarity of the steel magnet agree with the 'clock' rule?

3. Polarity of solenoid (p. 504)

Apparatus. 2 V accumulator; small rheostat; thread; wooden clamp and stand; connecting wire; switch; compass-needle; magnet.

(i) Wind the connecting wire in a large loose coil. Suspend the coil A by a

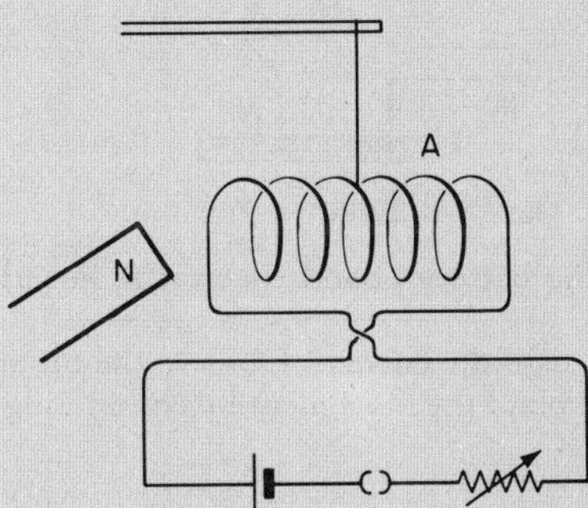

Fig. 29.19 Simple electromagnet

thread from the clamp so that it is horizontal, Fig. 29.19. Connect the coil by long leads in series with the accumulator, small rheostat and switch.

(ii) Switch on the current and increase it. Observe if the coil turns. By means of a compass-needle, see if the axis of the coil points north–south when it finally comes to rest.

(iii) Bring one pole of a magnet near to the end of the solenoid. Observe the polarity of this end. Obtain the polarity of the other end of the coil. Then reverse the current and repeat.

4. Electric bell (p. 506)

Apparatus. Electric bell; accumulator or battery supply; rheostat to vary the current in the bell coils; switch.

Method. Connect the supply B, the electric bell A, the rheostat R and switch S in series, Fig. 29.20. Make R zero resistance, switch on, and check that the

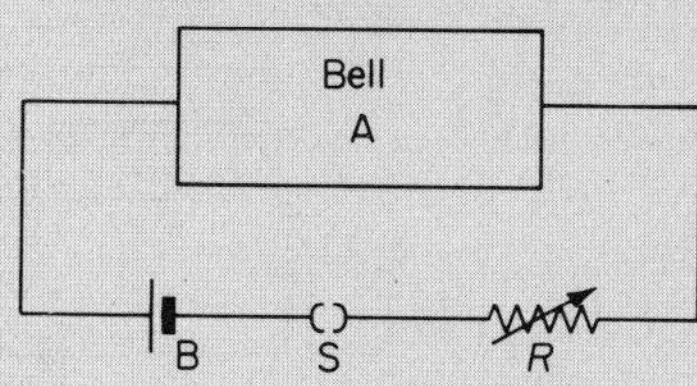

Fig. 29.20 Electric bell

bell is working. Investigate the effect on the working of the bell of: (i) varying the current—do small or large currents give better results? (ii) adjusting the make-and-break—when are best results obtained? (iii) shorting out the make-and-break by joining the two terminals across it with connecting wire—explain what happens.

5. Jumping Coil

Apparatus. 2 V accumulator; small rheostat; copper wire to make a loose coil of about a dozen turns round a mu-metal or soft-iron rod; small dish with mercury; wooden clamp and stand.

Method. Suspend one end A of the coil and the soft-iron rod D from the clamp, Fig. 29.21. Twist the other end B of the coil so that the wire *just* dips into

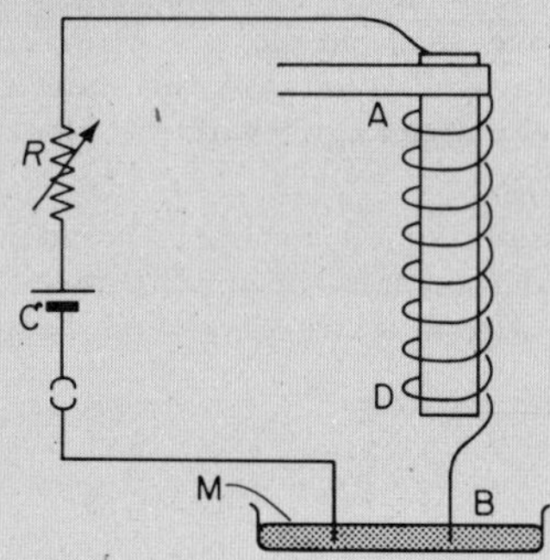

Fig. 29.21 Jumping coil

the mercury M. Connect the battery C and rheostat R in series, placing one lead inside the mercury.

Move the rheostat to increase the current. Observe the up-and-down movement of the coil. Can you explain the movement by considering the neighbouring turns?

6. Magnetic field

Apparatus. 2 V accumulator; long rheostat of a few ohms; switch; board B covered with white paper; iron filings; wooden clamp and stand.

Method. Connect the rheostat R, switch S and accumulator A in series. By means of the wooden clamp, support the board B and paper alongside and close to the middle of the rheostat, Fig. 29.22. Sprinkle iron filings lightly on the board. Switch on the current. Tap the board lightly and increase the current.

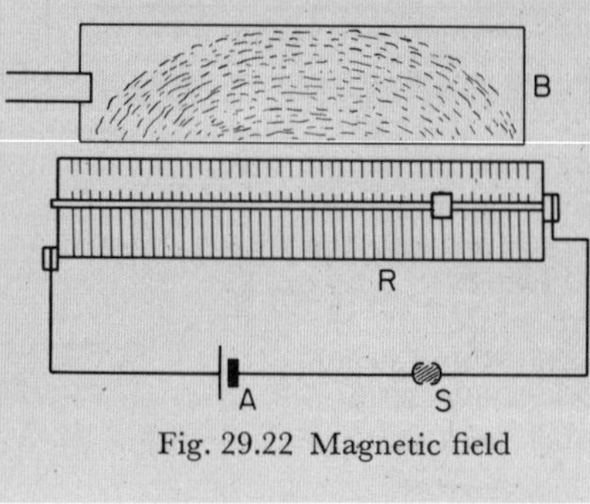

Fig. 29.22 Magnetic field

Observe and draw the appearance of the magnetic field. This is the field outside a rheostat coil or *solenoid*.

7. Simple buzzer

Method. Make a simple buzzer by using: (i) a solenoid C of many turns of enamelled or insulated thin copper wire wound round a mu-metal or soft-iron rod M;

(ii) springy steel P with a soft-iron head A attached;

(iii) metal strip Q with a small screw B in a hole at the top, just touching P;

(iv) dry batteries or accumulator X with a switch S, Fig. 29.23. If necessary

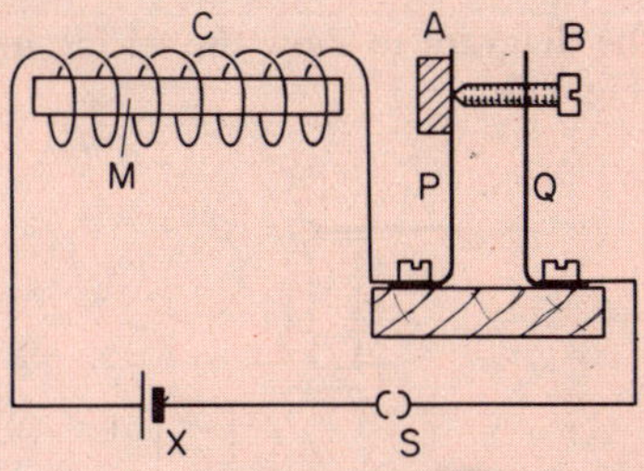

Fig. 29.23 Simple buzzer

use emery paper to clean the surface of P opposite the screw, as well as the point of the screw, to make better electrical contact. Also, try adjusting the screw-point against P.

EXERCISE 29 · ANSWERS, p. 617

What are the missing words in the following statements 1–10?

1. When a current flows clockwise round the end of a solenoid (long circular coil), this end acts like a . . magnetic pole.

2. When one end of a solenoid is repelled by a N-pole, the current flowing here is in a . . direction.

3. To increase the magnetic effect of a current in a coil, a . . core is used.

4. In an electromagnet with two cores, the coils must be wound in . . directions on the cores.

5. When an electric bell circuit is working, the circuit is . . repeatedly at the contacts.

6. In a telephone earpiece, the speech current produces a variation in . . in the pole pieces.

7. The sound vibrations are reproduced by the telephone earpiece by vibrations of the . .

8. When a magnetic relay is operated, a pivoted soft-iron is attracted by the . .

9. The magnetic field pattern outside a long current-carrying straight wire consists of . . lines.

10. The magnetic field pattern inside a long current-carrying solenoid consists of . . lines; the solenoid acts like a . . in its magnetic effect outside the coil.

11. The core of an electromagnet is made of . . (*M.*)

12. The diagram is of a wire coil wound round a cardboard former, Fig. 29A. Indicate the following: (*a*) the polarity of the cell; (*b*) the direction of the current flow; (*c*) if a piece of iron is placed inside the coil indicate the polarity of the resulting electro-magnet. (*Mx.*)

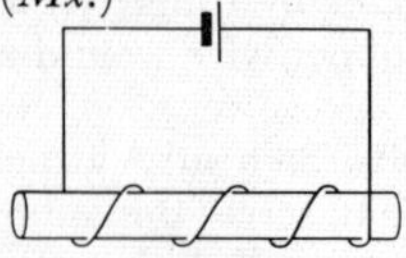

Fig. 29A

13. (*a*) Complete the diagram to show the wiring inside the electric bell to terminals T_1 and T_2, Fig. 29B.

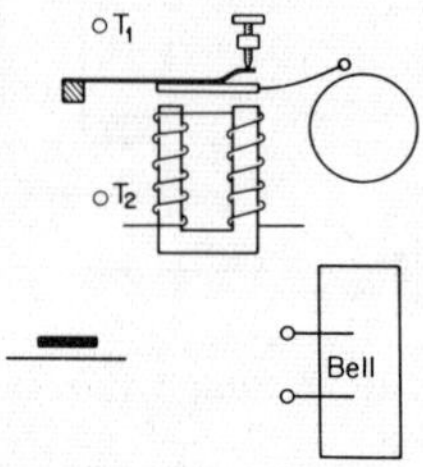

Fig. 29B

(*b*) Complete the lower circuit diagram showing how the electric bell may be rung from either of two switches. (*L.*)

14. Fig. 29C represents the inside parts of a telephone earpiece. Label the various parts of this and explain clearly how this earpiece is able to produce sounds. (*M.*)

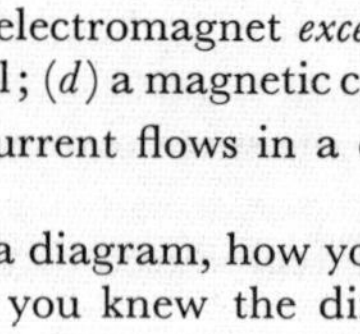

Fig. 29C

15. All the following use an electromagnet *except*: (*a*) a telephone earpiece; (*b*) a compass; (*c*) an electric bell; (*d*) a magnetic crane; (*e*) a loud-speaker. (*M.*)

16. When a direct electric current flows in a coil (a solenoid), a magnetic effect is produced.

(*a*) Describe, with the aid of a diagram, how you could predict which end of the coil would be a N-pole if you knew the direction of current, Fig. 29D.

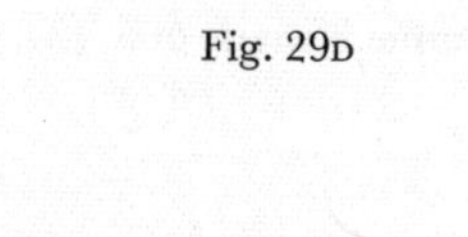

Fig. 29D

Mark the conventional current as —←— or the electron flow as $\underset{e}{—\rightarrow—}$.

(*b*) List *two* ways in which the magnetic effect of the coil can be increased.

(*c*) What would happen to the magnetic effect if a long piece of wire were doubled and then made into a solenoid as shown? (*E.A.*)

17. (*a*) Draw a straight wire carrying an electric current and the lines of magnetic force produced by the current.

(*b*) Draw a labelled diagram and explain the working of an electric bell. How would you change the bell to make it strike only once when the bell is pressed? (*E.A.*)

18. Outline *briefly* all the various stages involved by which one man speaks into a telephone and another, a long distance away, is able to hear what he says. (*S.E.*)

19. (*a*) How could you show that a magnetic effect is produced when an electric current flows through a wire?

(*b*) Draw a diagram to show what sort of field you would expect to find when a current flows in (i) a straight wire; and (ii) a long coil. Indicate in each case the direction of the current and magnetic field. Also, (iii) what would be the effect of inserting an iron core into the coil carrying a current? (*S.E.*)

20. (*a*) What is an electro-magnet, and how does it differ from a permanent magnet?

(*b*) Describe with the help of a detailed diagram how an electro-magnet is used in *either*: (i) an electric bell; *or* (ii) a telephone earpiece. (*Mx.*)

21. (*a*) Describe one way in which: (i) a piece of soft iron may be magnetized and then demagnetized; (ii) a piece of steel may be magnetized and then demagnetized. Name a material used to make strong permanent magnets.

(*b*) A single thick insulated wire running in a north–south direction passes through a room in which you are working. You believe that the wire is carrying a heavy current, but you are unable to see any other part of the circuit and you must not break the wire in any way. Describe simple tests you could perform which might check your belief. What would be the result of each test if in fact: (i) a large direct current flowed; (ii) a large alternating current flowed? (*S.E.*)

22. (*a*) You are given an iron bar and a steel bar of a similar size. Describe experiments you could perform to find out which is the better material to use when making: (i) a permanent magnet; (ii) an electro-magnet; Explain clearly how your experimental results justify your conclusions.

(*b*) Draw a circuit diagram showing how a low-power switch can be made to operate a relay which will automatically complete a high-power circuit. (*Mx.*)

23. (*a*) Give a labelled diagram of a horseshoe electro-magnet to show clearly the directions in which the coils are wound.

(*b*) Say what happens when the current in its coil is cut off.

(*c*) Draw a large labelled diagram of an electric bell connected to a switch and a cell, and explain its action. (*Mx.*)

24. (*a*) If you want to replace the resistance wire on an electric fire, state all the factors that you would take into consideration.

(*b*) Describe the construction of an electric bell and how it operates from a battery circuit. What alterations would you have to make in the circuit if you wired it to the mains? (*W.Md.*)

30

FORCE ON CONDUCTOR · THE MOTOR PRINCIPLE

SOON after Oersted's discovery of the magnetic effect of a current, Ampere showed in 1821 that, under certain conditions, a force was exerted on a current-carrying conductor situated in a magnetic field. From Ampere's fundamental work in the laboratory, useful instruments such as the electric motor, the moving-coil measuring instruments, and the moving-coil loudspeaker were all developed.

Demonstration of Force

The force on a current-carrying conductor in a magnetic field can be demonstrated with the apparatus shown in Fig. 30.1 (i). A smooth brass cylindrical rod AL is placed across two horizontal brass rails PQ and RT, and a battery C and a small rheostat D are connected in series

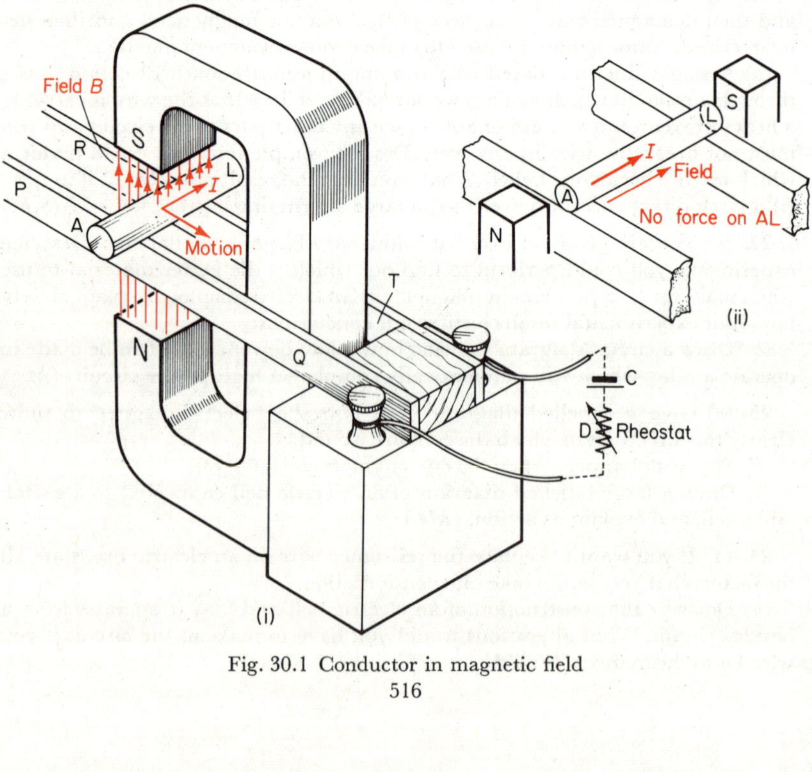

Fig. 30.1 Conductor in magnetic field

to the ends of the rail. A powerful horseshoe magnet is then positioned so that the rod AL is between its poles and the magnetic field is vertical. The magnetic field, denoted by B, is then *perpendicular* to the length of the rod.

1. When the circuit is made and a current I flows along AL the rod is observed to roll along the rails. A force thus acts *at right angles* to the field, and to the length AL of the conductor.

2. When the current is increased by altering the rheostat, the rod moves faster. The force on the rod thus increases when the current I increases.

3. When the magnet is moved slightly sideways so that the strength of the magnetic field at the rod AL is decreased, the rod moves less quickly. The force thus decreases when the magnetic field strength decreases. Likewise, the force increases when the field strength increases.

4. When the magnet is turned round so that the field is *parallel* to the length AL of the rod, and the circuit is switched on, the current-carrying rod remains practically still, Fig. 30.1 (ii). There is no force now on the rod.

Conclusions. A force acts on a current-carrying conductor when it is at right angles to a magnetic field. The direction of the field is perpendicular both to the current and to the field direction. The magnitude of the force increases when the current increases and when the field strength increases.

When the angle between the conductor and field decreases from 90° the force decreases. It becomes *zero* when the conductor is *parallel* to the field.

Direction of Force

The direction of the force when a current-carrying wire is situated in a perpendicular magnetic field is given by *Fleming's left-hand rule.* It states:

If the thumb and first two fingers of the left hand are held at right angles to each other, with the forefinger pointing in the direction of the magnetic field B and the middle finger pointing in the direction of the current I, then the thumb

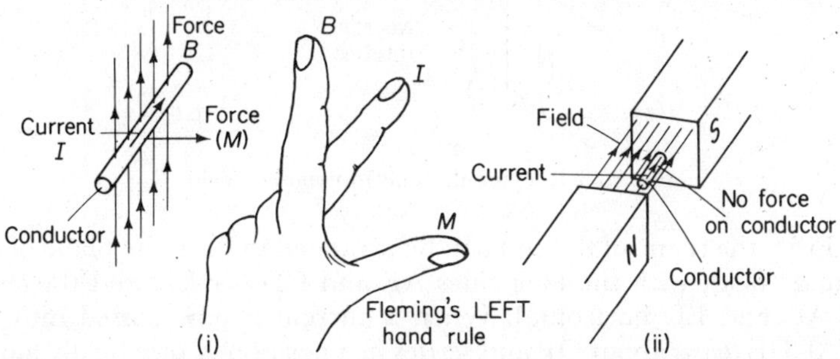

Fig. 30.2 Fleming's rule

points in the direction of Motion *of the conductor, i.e. in the direction of the force acting on it.*

The rule is illustrated in Fig. 30.2 (i). Note carefully that the rule applies only if the magnetic field and current are perpendicular, or inclined, to each other. In Fig. 30.2 (ii), the field and current are parallel to each other. No force acts on the conductor.

Forces on Rectangular Coil

So far we have investigated the force on a straight wire carrying a current. If the wire is bent so that it forms a *rectangular coil* it can be suspended between two points by flexible strips of foil in the magnetic field between two poles N and S of a powerful horse-shoe magnet, Fig. 30.3.

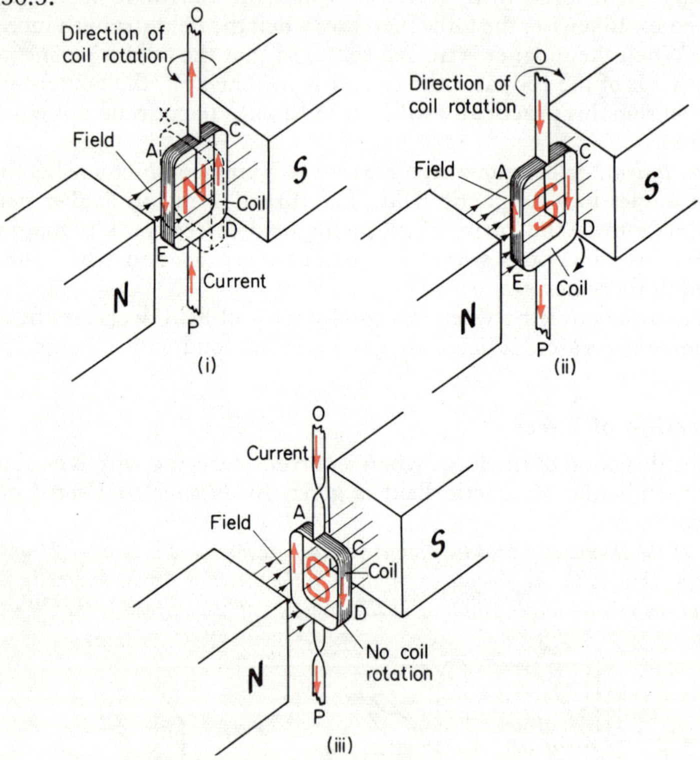

Fig. 30.3 Rectangular coil in magnetic field

1. First, the plane of the coil can be arranged to lie in the plane of the magnetic field, with the long sides AE and CD vertical and the short sides AC and ED horizontal. When a current is now passed into the coil, ACDE *twists* about OP and settles in a position X practically facing the poles, Fig. 30.3 (i).

2. If the circuit is broken and the battery terminals reversed, the current flows in the opposite direction in the coil. The rotation of the coil now reverses, Fig. 30.3 (ii).

3. If the coil is turned so that it faces the N- and S-poles of the magnet, that is, the plane of the coil is perpendicular to the field, and a current is now passed into the coil as shown, there is no movement. Fig. 30.3 (iii).

Explanation by Clock Rule

The results of the experiment can be explained from the clock rule for the polarity of a current-carrying coil, stated on page 504. In Fig. 30.3 (i), the current flows round the face of the coil viewed in the direction CAED. This is *an anti-clockwise* direction. Hence this face acts like a *north-N*-pole. The N-pole of the magnet repels this face and the S-pole of the magnet attracts this face. Hence the coil rotates as shown about its axis OP.

In Fig. 30.3 (ii), however, the current flows in the reverse direction, which is EACD. This is a *clockwise* direction. The coil face is thus S-polarity and hence turns towards the N-pole this time. The direction of rotation about the axis OP is thus in the reverse direction to Fig. 30.3 (i).

In Fig. 30.3 (iii), the current flows clockwise round the face ACDE. This face hence acts like a S-pole. The coil is already facing the N-pole. Thus the coil does not move this time.

Electric Motor

The electric motor is widely used for driving electric trains and many machines in industry. In its simplest or basic form it consists of:

1. a *coil of wire, abcd*, (*armature*), which can turn about a fixed axis O;
2. a powerful *magnetic field* in which the coil turns;
3. a *commutator*, which, in its simplest form, is a split copper ring whose two halves A and B are insulated from each other, Fig. 30.4.

The ends of the coil are each soldered to one half of the commutator, which rotates with the coil. As it turns, fixed brushes L and M press against the commutator, so that a current from a connected battery PQ always flows through the commutator metal into the coil.

Principle of Action

Suppose the coil *abcd* is horizontal and is situated between the poles N and S of a permanent magnet, Fig. 30.4 (i). When a current flows in the direction *dcba* this face of the coil appears to flow clockwise to an observer looking at it from above. Hence, from the clock rule on p. 504, this face of the coil acts like a south magnetic pole, see Fig. 29.8. Now like poles repel and unlike attract. The coil thus begins to rotate about the horizontal axis O in an anti-clockwise direction, as shown by the arrow X.

While the coil turns, the two halves of the commutator A and B

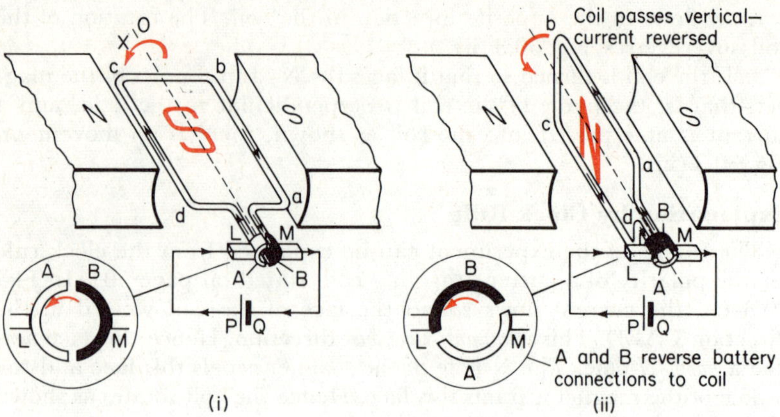

Fig. 30.4 Action of electric motor

rotate with it. A keeps in contact with the brush L and B with the brush M. When the coil just passes the vertical, however, A now makes contact with the brush M and B with the brush L, Fig. 30.4 (ii). The battery connections *to the coil* are thus reversed. The current therefore reverses in the coil. The side of the coil facing the N-pole of the magnet thus acts as a north-magnetic pole, and hence, by the action between

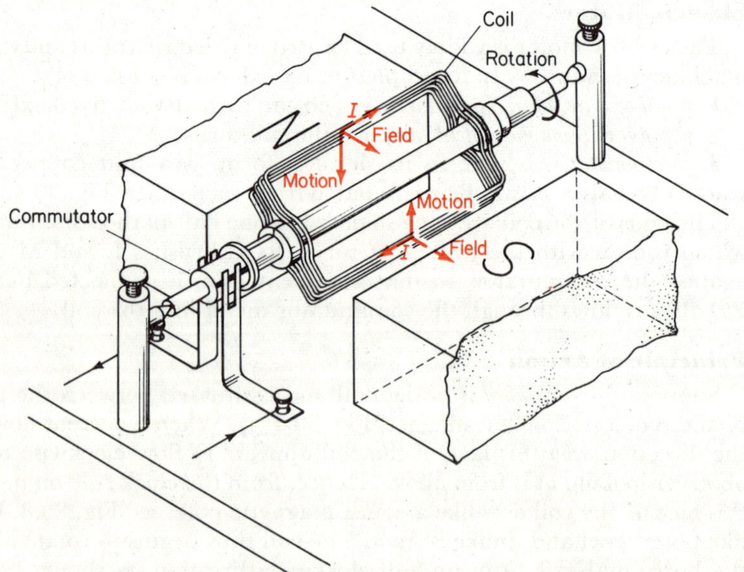

Fig. 30.5 Simple motor

the poles, the coil continues to spin round in the same direction about the axis O.

Fig. 30.5 shows a model motor, with current I flowing into the coil by means of two terminals at the base. Can you explain why the coil rotates about its horizontal axis as shown?

Commercial electric motors in industry, which may be used for driving lathes or heavy rollers as in printing presses, are very powerful. They have strong magnetic fields, carry high currents, and use many coils of wire. This produces a powerful rotation, and machines may be coupled by belts or gear wheels to the motor.

Moving-coil Instrument

Measurement of current and potential difference (voltage) is needed in all branches of electricity, such as sound radio, television, telecommunications and electrical machines. See Plate 30A. The most

Plate 30(A) British Airways VC10 flight deck, showing the numerous electrical instruments and automation devices.

accurate commercial instrument for measuring current and potential difference uses the movement of a rectangular current-carrying coil in a magnetic field. The essential features are: (i) an insulated rectangular coil ABCD; (ii) a powerful magnetic field produced by the curved poles N and S of a horse-shoe magnet; (iii) a soft-iron cylinder E to concentrate the magnetic lines of force towards its centre; (iv) two springs, oppositely wound, to control the rotation of the coil about a spindle moving in jewelled bearings at X and Y. Fig. 30.6 (i) illustrates a side view of the apparatus, while Fig. 30.6 (ii) is a view from above.

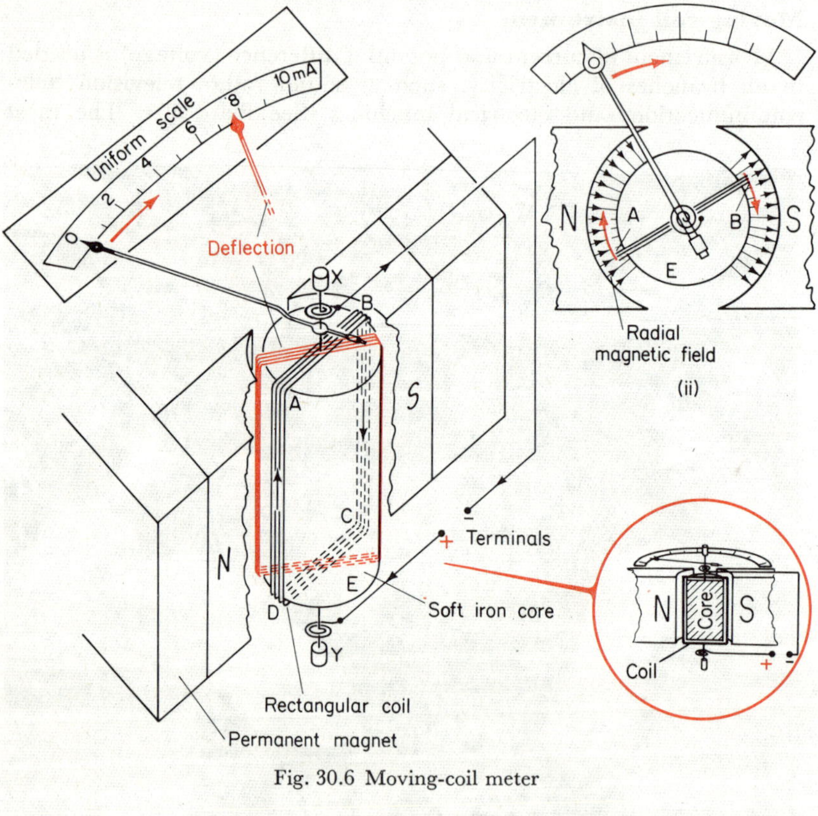

Fig. 30.6 Moving-coil meter

When the instrument is used as an ammeter or a voltmeter, the terminals of the instrument are connected to the electrical circuit. A current then flows through the coil via the springs, each spring being connected to one terminal, as shown. The face DABC of the coil acts like a S-pole, since the current flows clockwise. It is therefore repelled by the S-pole of the magnet and attacked by the N-pole of the magnet, that is, it rotates about the axis XY in a clockwise direction.

Unlike the coil in the electric motor, the rotation of the coil DABC is controlled by springs. The springs bring the coil to rest after it has turned through an angle. If the spring is strong, the coil rotates through a small angle when carrying a moderate current. If the spring is weak, the angle of rotation will be greater. When the current is switched off the spring untwists and restores the coil to its 'zero' position.

Advantages of Moving-coil Instrument

There are many advantages of this type of electrical instrument or meter.

Firstly, the scale is a regular or uniform one, that is, equal divisions represent equal steps of current or p.d. The scale can thus be subdivided into tenths of amperes or other units very accurately, and can then be read very accurately. Other instruments than the moving-coil type may have an irregular or non-uniform scale. Accurate readings between divisions are then difficult. The regular scale of the moving-coil instrument is basically due to the presence of the soft-iron cylinder E, which creates a radial magnetic field.

Secondly, by fitting on suitable resistances, the same instrument can read many different ranges of current or of potential difference. For example, the instrument could then read 0 to 0·15 A or 0 to 15 A as an ammeter. The same instrument could also be made to read 0 to 3 V or 0 to 150 V. The moving-coil instrument can also measure resistance (see p. 423).

Thirdly, stray magnetic fields in the neighbourhood of the instrument are usually very small compared with the magnetic field between the powerful magnet and the cylinder. Consequently they have negligible influence on the deflection of the pointer.

Multimeter Principle

Commercial instruments called *multimeters* provide different ranges of current and potential difference simply by turning a switch. This connects suitable resistors in parallel for current ranges or in series with the coil for p.d. ranges. See Plate 30B.

Plate 30(B) AVO meter, showing the rectangular coil in a magnetic field and scales reading amps, volts and ohms, as well as other electrical quantities.

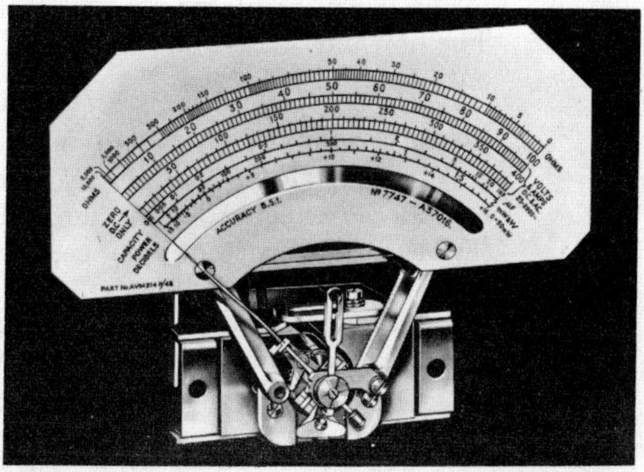

Fig. 30.7 shows the principle of changing from a small current range 0–10 mA (milliamp) to a larger current range, 0–1 A. A suitable resistor R is placed in *parallel* with the coil between the terminals A, B. Suppose the maximum current of 1·00 A flows towards A. The pointer must then be deflected full scale to the

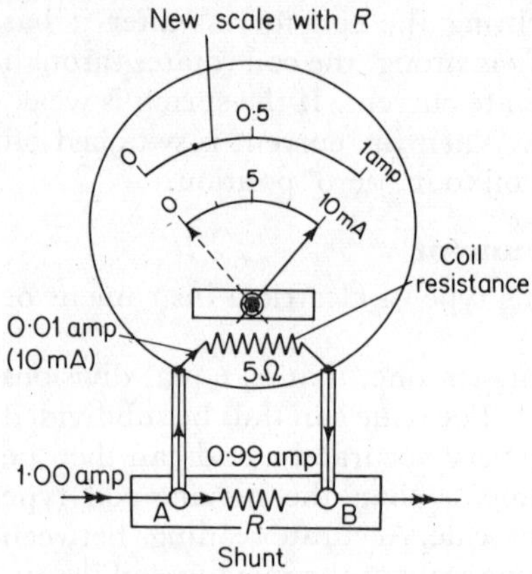

Fig. 30.7 Converting milliammeter to ammeter

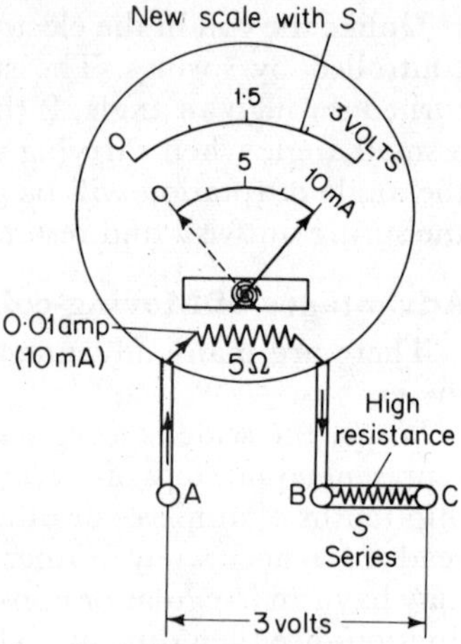

Fig. 30.8 Converting milliammeter to voltmeter

10 mA division. This means that a current of 10 mA or 0·01 A flows in the coil. R thus diverts or 'shunts' a current of 1–0·01 A or 0·99 A. The coil resistance, say 5 Ω, is shown. Hence the resistance R must be 0·01/0·99 or $\frac{1}{99}$ of 5 Ω, which is 0·0505 Ω. On switching to the 0–1 A range, then, a resistance of this value is connected in parallel. The new current scale with R is shown in Fig. 30.7. Other current ranges need different values of R.

Fig. 30.8 shows the principle of changing the same milliammeter to measure a potential difference of 0–3 V. This time a suitable resistor S is connected in *series* with the coil. Suppose the maximum p.d. of 3 V is joined to the new terminals, A and C, as shown. The pointer must then deflect full scale to the 10 mA division. This means that a current of 10 ma or 0·01 A flows in the coil or along ABC. The resistance between A and C, from Ohm's law,

$$= \frac{V}{I} = \frac{3\ \text{V}}{0{\cdot}01\ \text{A}} = 300\ \Omega.$$

The coil resistance provides 5 Ω. Hence S must be 295 Ω. On switching to the 0–3 V range, then, a resistance of 295 Ω is connected in series. The new p.d. scale is shown in Fig. 30.8. Other p.d. ranges need different values of R.

Simple Current Balance

An *ampere balance* at the National Physical Laboratory measures current very accurately by counterbalancing *the force between currents*. A simple form of current balance, which uses a magnet, can be made as follows, Fig. 30.9:

1. Attach a small (approx 1 cm) alcomax magnet M near the end of a straw with a small piece of Selotape.

2. Balance the straw on the needle N to find the centre of gravity. Then push the needle through the straw at O, about a millimetre away from the centre of gravity on the other side of the axis of the straw to the magnet.

3. Balance the straw and magnet by placing the needle in grooves D and E cut in the aluminium support B, and then put a rider R, made of a few centimetres of 26 s.w.g. bare copper wire, on the straw, as shown. The straw should balance when R is about 5 cm from O, and the rider may be moved with a piece of wire.

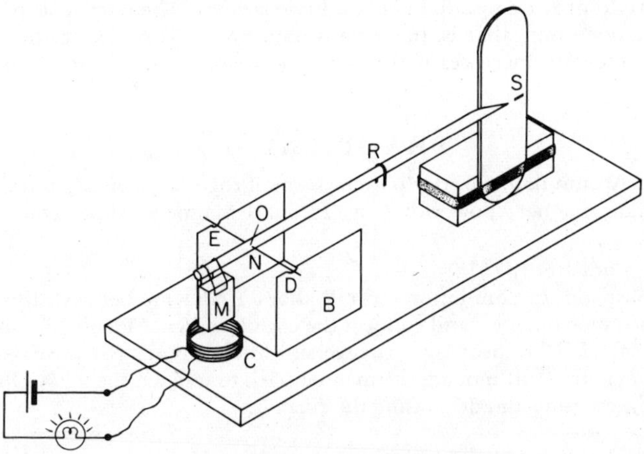

Fig. 30.9 Simple current balance

4. When the straw is horizontal, mark a reference line S on the wooden spatula near the end of the straw, as shown.

Make sure there are no draughts to upset the equilibrium of the straw. Connect a 2·5 V bulb and a 1·5 V dry cell, for example, in series with the coil C so that M is attracted by the current flowing in C. If necessary, reverse the battery terminals. Fig. 30.9. Move the rider R along the straw until the straw returns to the reference mark S. Mark the position of the rider on the straw or measure its distance from O. This is now a measure of the current, which may be called 'one unit' of current.

Add a second similar lamp in parallel with the first lamp, move R to restore equilibrium as before, observe the new position of R and estimate the current in terms of the 'unit current'. Repeat by placing three lamps in parallel. Make a table of your observations and your deductions.

SUMMARY

1. A force acts on a current-carrying conductor when it is perpendicular to a magnetic field or inclined to the field. The direction is perpendicular to both the

current and the field direction. No force acts on the conductor if it is parallel to the field.

2. Fleming's left-hand rule states: If the thumb and first two fingers of the left hand are held at right angles to each other, with the forefinger pointing in the direction of the field and the middle finger in the current direction, the thumb points in the direction of motion of the conductor.

3. The simple electric motor has: (i) a coil of insulated wire; (ii) a magnetic field; (iii) a commutator which reverses the current in the coil after half a revolution so that the coil keeps turning round.

4. The moving-coil instrument has a rectangular coil, a permanent magnet, a soft-iron core to provide a radial field and two springs. The current is proportional to the deflection, that is, the scale is uniform—this is due to the radial field. The sensitivity increases if the spring is weak or the magnetic field is strong.

PRACTICAL

Apparatus. Accumulators or dry batteries; small rheostat; switch; aluminium foil; horseshoe magnet; powerful (e.g. Ticonal) magnets; clips; connecting wire or flex.

1. Force on conductor (p. 516)

Method. Suspend an aluminium strip T about 1 cm wide between the poles N–S of a horseshoe magnet, and connect the circuit shown, Fig. 30.10. Observe the movement of T. Repeat by: (i) reversing the current; (ii) reversing the poles of the magnet; (iii) moving the magnet back to weaken the field. Observe the effect of increasing and decreasing the current.

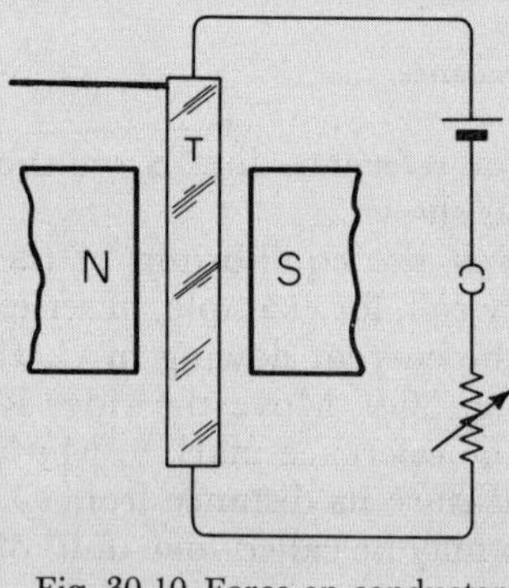

Fig. 30.10 Force on conductor

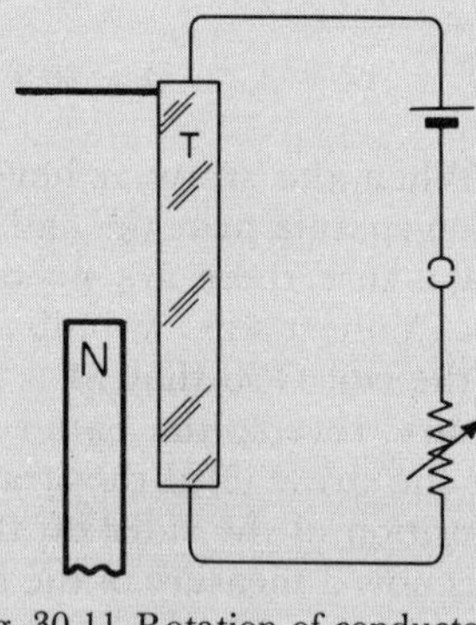

Fig. 30.11 Rotation of conductor

2. Rotation of conductor (p. 518)

Method. Place the N-pole of a powerful magnet alongside the lower end of an aluminium strip T and parallel to the strip, Fig. 30.11. Switch on the current. Observe the movement of T. Observe the effect of increasing the current.

3. Rotation of coil (p. 518)

Method. Make a small rectangular coil C of many turns of thin insulated copper wire by winding around one of the poles of a horseshoe magnet and then removing the coil. Attach one end of C to an aluminium strip T, Fig. 30.12. Place the coil between the poles of a horseshoe magnet, connect the current supply as shown, and switch on. Observe the movement of the coil. Switch off and observe the effect of: (i) reversing the current; (ii) reversing the magnet poles.

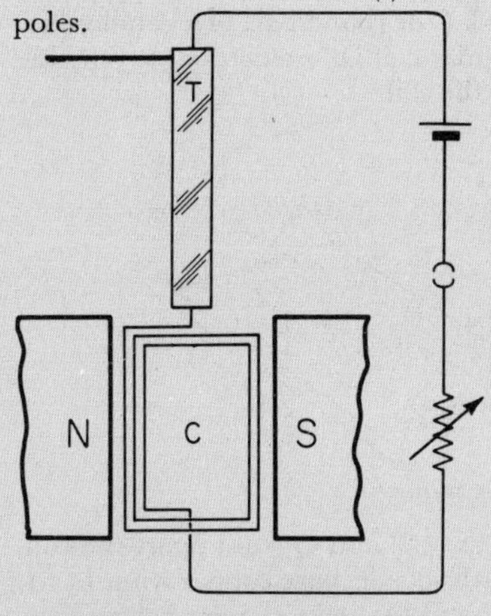

Fig. 30.12 Rotation of coil

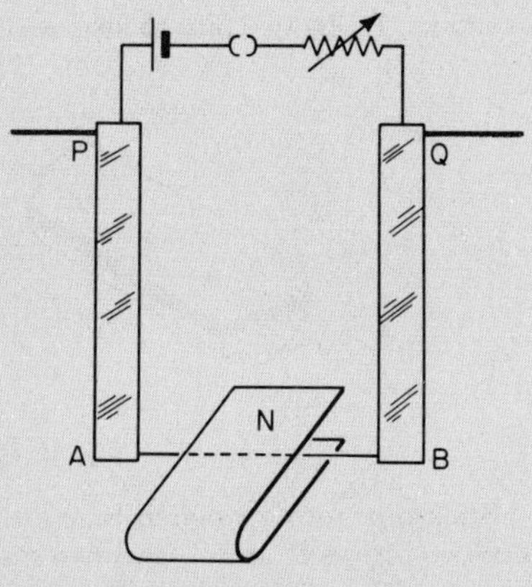

Fig. 30.13 Swinging wire

4. Swinging wire

Method. Suspend a length of wire AB horizontally from two aluminium strips PA, QB, as shown, Fig. 30.13. Place a horseshoe magnet M as shown. Connect the current supply. Switch on, increase the current and observe the movement of AB. If it swings into the magnet, reverse the battery connections. Observe the movement of AB.

5. Moving wire (p. 516)

Method. Support a bare piece of copper wire CD on two bare copper rectangular-shaped frames A and B, Fig. 30.14. Place the poles N–S of a horseshoe

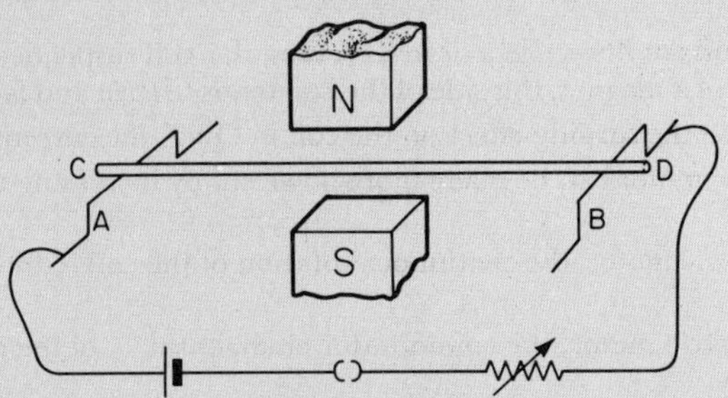

Fig. 30.14 Moving wire

magnet, or powerful magnets, to produce a vertical magnetic field. Connect the current supply. Switch on and increase the current . Observe the movement of CD. Reverse: (i) the current; (ii) the poles; and observe the change in movement of CD.

Now place the poles N–S so as to produce a horizontal magnetic field. Repeat your observations. What is the difference between this case and the previous one?

6. Simple motor (p. 520)

Method. Wind about thirty turns of thin (e.g. s.w.g. 32) insulated copper wire round a groove cut in opposite sides of a cork C or round part of a candle, Fig. 30.15. Bare the two ends A, B of the rectangular coil D, brought out to one side as shown. Insert two pins to form an axle for the coil.

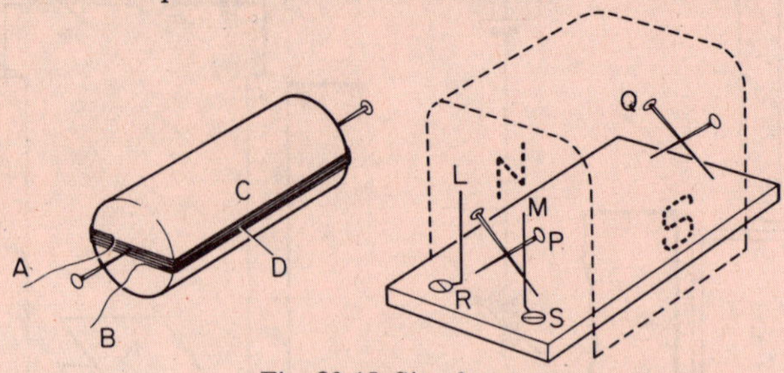

Fig. 30.15 Simple motor

Stick pins into a wooden base crosswise, as at P and Q, to support the coil. Fix two screws R and S, and two short lengths of stiff bare copper wire, L, M, bent as shown. Place the coil and axle on P and Q, make contact between the bare wires of the coil and L and M, and then place a horseshoe magnet round the coil. Connect the battery and increase the current. Give the coil a slight push to help rotation. Check that the bare wires of the coil are touching both L and M if no rotation is obtained.

7. Ampere-balance

Method. Make a simple ampere-balance as described on p. 525.

EXERCISE 30 · ANSWERS, p. 617

What are the missing words in the following statements 1–14?

1. When a current flows clockwise in a coil, this face acts as a . . magnetic pole.

2. When a current flows *clockwise* in a rectangular coil suspended between the N- and S-poles of a magnet, this side of the coil tends to turn and face the . . pole.

3. To increase the turning effect on the coil in Qn 2, the current should be . .

4. An electric motor can be made more powerful by increasing the current or the . . or the . .

5. In an electric motor, the continuous rotation of the coil is due to the action of the . .

6. In the electric motor, the commutator changes the . . of the current in the coil continually.

7. When the motor is working, the rotating commutator presses against fixed brushes permanently joined to the . .

8. In a moving-coil meter, the coil turns through an angle directly proportional to the . .

9. In a moving-coil meter, the rotation of the coil is controlled by . .

10. In a *sensitive* moving-coil meter, very . . springs are needed.

11. To change a moving-coil milliammeter into an ammeter, a . . resistance is added.

12. To change a moving-coil milliammeter into a voltmeter, a . . resistance is added.

13. The scale of the moving-coil meter is a . . one. This is due to the . . magnetic field in which the coil moves.

14. To change a moving-coil meter into a simple motor, remove the . . and add a . .

15. Read the following passage carefully and explain the meaning of the four terms underlined:

'A particular electric motor is supplied with *direct-current* which is led to and from a *split-ring commutator* by means of *carbon-brushes*. From this commutator the current flows through a coil which rotates between the *pole-pieces* of a magnet.' (*M.*)

16. Fig. 30A (i) and (ii) both represent the same sensitive moving-coil meter. Diagram (iii) shows three separate resistances.

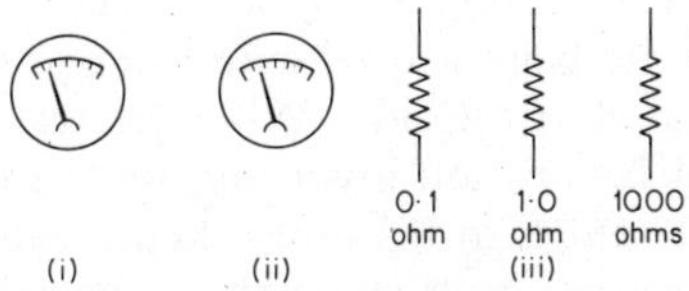

Fig. 30A

Complete diagram (i) to show *one* of the three resistances connected to the meter, to convert it to an *ammeter*. Label the value of the resistance used.

Complete diagram (ii) to show *one* of the three resistances connected to the meter, to convert it to a *voltmeter*. Label the value of the resistance used. (*S.*)

17. (*a*) Describe, and explain the action of, a simple two-pole electric motor. What is the purpose of the commutator?

(*b*) State *two* ways in which the simple motor may be improved. (*E.A.*)

18. (*a*) Explain with the help of a diagram, or diagrams, how a moving-coil galvanometer works.

(*b*) A galvanometer has a resistance of 5 Ω and gives a full scale deflection when 25 mA passes through it. Show by means of a diagram how you would convert this galvanometer into a voltmeter.

(*c*) Suppose the meter has to read 0–5 V. Calculate the value of the resistance which has to be used. (*S.E.*)

19. (*a*) Label the diagram of a simple d.c. electric motor. Explain how this motor works.

(*b*) Indicate on your diagram the direction of rotation of the coil, giving a reason for your answer. How may this direction be reversed?

(*c*) What is the effect on the current taken by the motor of its speed of rotation? What is the purpose of a starting resistance? (*L.*)

20. Describe, with the aid of a diagram, the construction and mode of action of a moving-coil ammeter. Explain carefully how the current causes the pointer to move and how the movement is controlled. How would you adapt an ammeter of resistance 15 Ω giving a full scale deflection of 20 mA into a voltmeter reading up to 10 V? (*W.Md.*)

21. The magnetic effect of a current is put to use in the d.c. motor. Describe, with the aid of diagrams, the action of this motor. (*W.Md.*)

31

ELECTROMAGNETIC INDUCTION
THE DYNAMO PRINCIPLE

THE year 1791 saw the birth of one of the greatest of English experimental scientists. Michael Faraday was the son of poor parents, who sent him to work at a bookshop at the age of 15; there, undeterred by his lack of education, he began to take an interest in the books around him especially on the scientific side. When he was 20 he attended the lectures at the Royal Institution given by Sir Humphry Davy, and at the end of the course sent him his notes, beautifully written and illustrated, and asked if there was a vacancy at the Institution. Davy was impressed by the work, and offered him the post of laboratory assistant. From this position he rose to be Davy's personal assistant and, at the age of 33, when his pre-eminence in science was already established, he was made Director of the Royal Institution on Davy's retirement. Faraday's pioneer work on the physical principles of electromagnetism, led the way to the dynamo and the generator, without which commercial electrical lighting and heating could never have been obtained.

Using Magnetism to Produce Electricity

It had been known since 1820 that an electric current gave rise to magnetic effects (p. 500). Faraday, like many experimental physicists at

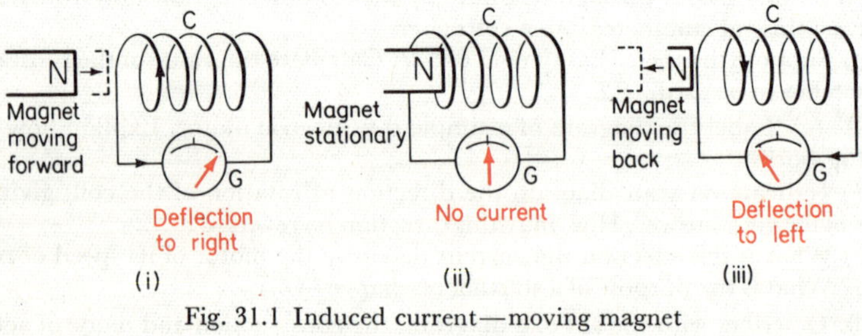

Fig. 31.1 Induced current—moving magnet

that time, began experiments to obtain the reverse effect. In 1832 he succeeded in 'using magnetism to obtain electricity'. Fig. 31.1 shows simple apparatus to investigate this phenomenon. C is a solenoid or coil with many turns connected to a centre-scale zero galvanometer G. Thus a current in either direction in C can be detected by G.

1. *Magnet Moving, Coil Still*

(i) When the N-pole of a powerful magnet such as a Ticonal one is pushed towards one end of C, the needle in G deflects to the right, Fig. 31.1 (i). An electric current is therefore obtained in the circuit. It is called an *induced current*, since there is no cell or battery in the circuit, and this is an example of *electromagnetic induction*.

(ii) When two and then three similar magnets are pushed into the coil greater induced effects are produced.

(iii) When a magnet is at rest, even though it may then be right inside the coil C, the induced current is zero, Fig. 31.1 (ii).

(iv) When the N-pole is removed quickly the needle is deflected to the left, Fig. 31.1 (iii). A current in the opposite direction to that in (i) is therefore obtained.

(v) When the magnet is moved faster to or from the end of the coil the induced current is increased.

(vi) When very soft iron, such as mu-metal, is placed inside the coil as a core, and the experiment is repeated, a much larger induced current is obtained.

Conclusions. An induced current flows only while the magnet is moving. The magnitude of the induced current increases when the strength of the magnet and the speed of the magnet are increased, and when a soft-iron core is inside the coil.

2. *Coil Moving, Magnet Still*

(i) Keeping the N-pole stationary, move the coil C quickly towards N. An induced current is obtained in C, Fig. 31.2 (i).

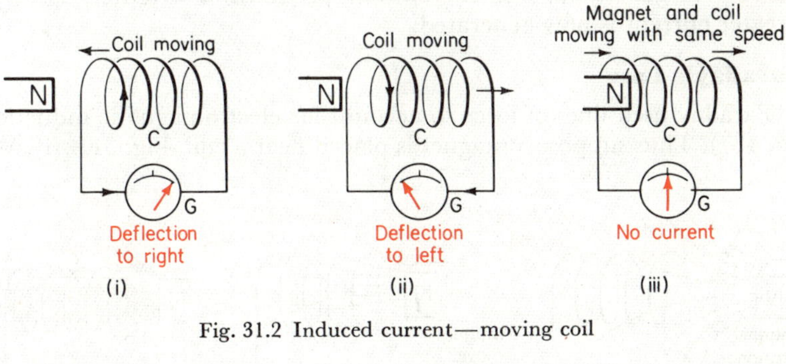

Fig. 31.2 Induced current—moving coil

(ii) Repeat, moving the coil C quickly back from N. An induced current is now obtained in the opposite direction, Fig. 31.2 (ii).

(iii) Move the coil and magnet together at the same speed. No induced current is obtained, Fig. 31.2 (iii).

Conclusion. Together with the conclusion in Experiment 1, it can now be stated that: an induced current flows when there is *relative motion* between the coil and magnet.

Bicycle Dynamo

A bicycle dynamo is a useful generator of current. A demonstration model is shown in Fig. 31.3. When the wheel A is turned, the disc magnet B is spun round fast by means of a gearing arrangement (p. 248). A stationary coil C in front of B, having a large number of

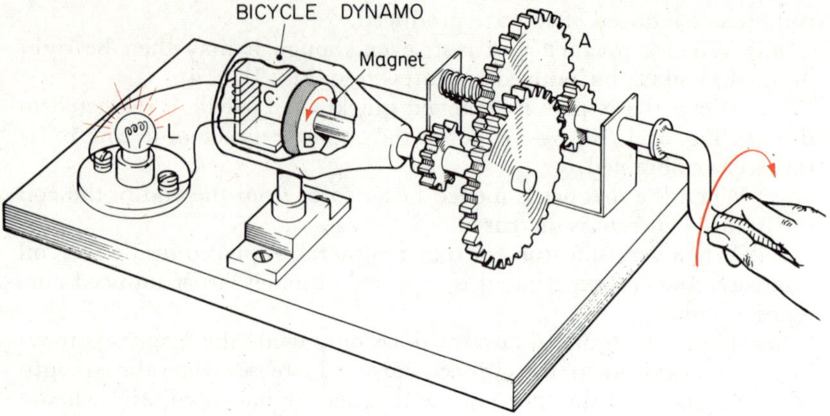

Fig. 31.3 Bicycle dynamo

turns and wound round soft iron, is connected to the terminals of a lamp filament L. The induced current in C makes the lamp glow. A slow rotation of the magnet produces a dim light, showing that only a small current is generated. Faster rotation produces a brighter light. A greater current is now generated.

Faraday's Law

Faraday used lines of force to account for electromagnetic induction (p. 487). Thus suppose a magnet is placed near a coil, Fig. 31.4 (i). We

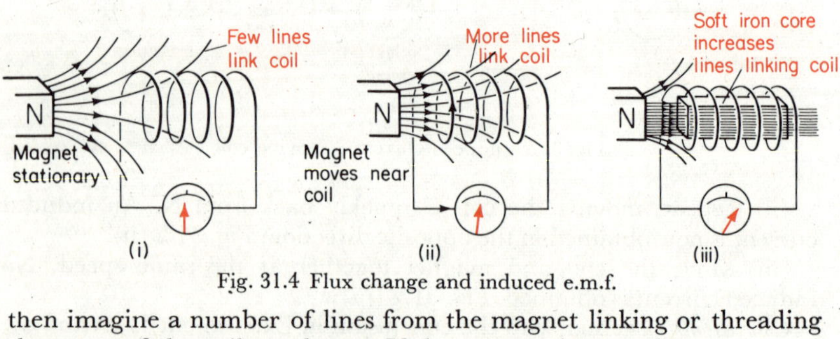

Fig. 31.4 Flux change and induced e.m.f.

then imagine a number of lines from the magnet linking or threading the turns of the coil, as shown. If the magnet is moved nearer, more lines link the turns, Fig. 31.4 (ii). Faraday thus said that an *induced e.m.f.*

is obtained when a *change* is made in the number of lines linking the coil. A slight magnet movement produces a small change; the induced e.m.f. is therefore small. A large magnet movement at the same speed produces a greater change and hence a greater e.m.f. The induced e.m.f., like the e.m.f. of a battery, produces an induced current in the coil when its ends are joined to a galvanometer, for example. A soft-iron core in a coil increases considerably the number of lines linking it, Fig. 31.4 (iii).

As we saw on p. 531, the induced current, and hence the e.m.f., increases when the speed of movement of the magnet increases. The magnitude of the e.m.f. thus depends not only on the magnitude of the change in the number of lines linking the coil, but also on how *fast* the change is made. The faster the change, the greater is the induced e.m.f. *Faraday's law* states that *the induced e.m.f. is proportional to the rate of change of the lines linking the coil.*

An induced e.m.f. can be detected by joining a coil with many turns and a soft-iron core to the signal or Y-plates of a cathode ray oscilloscope (p. 554). The plates are separated, so that no current can possibly flow. The trace on the oscilloscope screen only responds to a p.d. or e.m.f. connected to the plates. When a powerful magnet is pushed quickly to-and-from the coil, the trace on the screen moves up and then down. An e.m.f. which reverses in direction, or *alternating e.m.f.*, is therefore generated.

Direction of Induced e.m.f. and Current

The law for the *direction* of the induced current was given by Lenz. It states:

The induced current flows in such a direction as to *oppose* the motion or change producing it.

Suppose a N-pole of a magnet is pushed towards the face of a coil C as in Fig. 31.1 (i). The induced current then flows to make this face a N-pole, so as to repel the advancing magnet. The current hence flows anti-clockwise (p. 504).

If the N-pole of the magnet is moved back, as in Fig. 31.1 (iii), the current flows so as to stop the movement. It therefore creates a S-pole in the face of the coil. The current hence flows clockwise (p. 504).

For a similar reason, if a magnet is pushed towards and then right through a coil, the induced current flows one way first and then reverses. Demonstrations of Lenz's law are given under *Practical* on p. 541.

Lenz's law shows that when the magnet of a bicycle dynamo, for example, is rotated, energy is spent in overcoming the force of opposition to its movement. This energy is the source of the electrical energy produced in the bicycle lamp. In contrast, the source of the energy in a lamp when a torch battery is connected, is the chemical energy in the battery.

Car Speedometer

The speedometer in a car often works by an application of Lenz's law. The principle is illustrated in Fig. 31.5.

A magnet M, coupled to the gear-box, is rotated at a speed proportional to the car speed. Induced currents then circulate round an

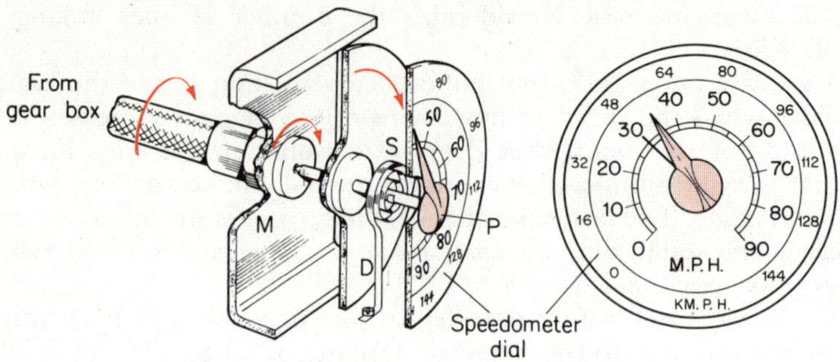

Fig. 31.5 Car speedometer

aluminium disc D pivoted in front of M. To 'oppose' the motion of M, D starts to rotate in the same direction. The degree of rotation is controlled by a spring S. When M turns faster, D turns through a larger angle. An attached pointer P can thus register the speed of the car on a dial, which is calibrated on runs at known speeds.

Principle of Simple Dynamo

In the bicycle dynamo, a magnet is turned and the coil is stationary. In the a.c. dynamo, a coil is rotated between the poles of a stationary magnet.

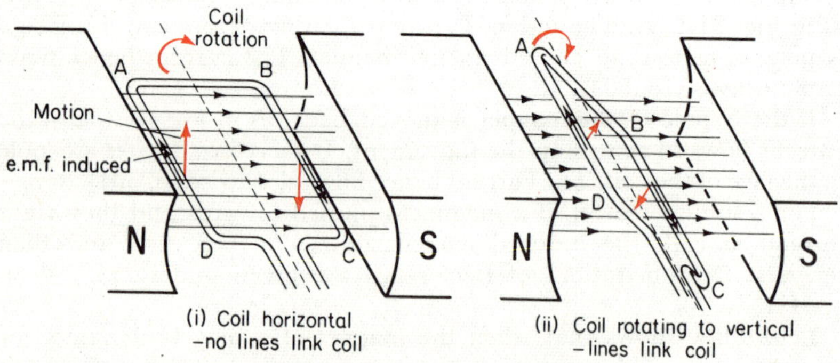

Fig. 31.6 Action of simple dynamo

Fig. 31.6 shows the coil of a simple dynamo in two positions. It illustrates how the number of lines of force through the coil change as it rotates, thus generating an induced e.m.f. in the coil.

Fig. 31.7 shows a section DC of the coil, and the magnitude and direction of the induced e.m.f. at four main positions. When the coil is horizontal, Fig. 31.7 (i), the conductors DA and CB sweep at right angles across the field lines. A maximum e.m.f. is then obtained. When

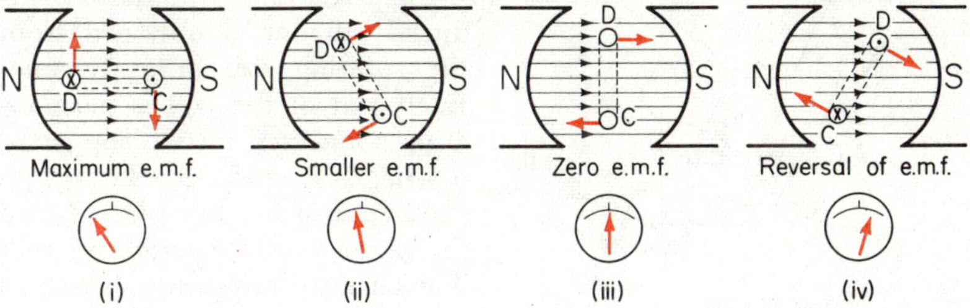

Fig. 31.7 Direction and magnitude of induced e.m.f.

the coil reaches the vertical, Fig. 31.7 (iii), the conductors DA and CB move parallel to the field lines. No induced e.m.f. is obtained at this instant because there is zero rate of change of the lines linking the coil. As the coil passes the vertical the conductors DA and CB move downward, Fig. 31.7 (iv). *Thus the e.m.f. now reverses.* The reversal of e.m.f. occurs twice in one complete revolution of the coil.

A.C. Voltage

The variation of e.m.f. or voltage is shown in Fig. 31.8. It is an *alternating* e.m.f. or a.c. voltage, that is, it reverses periodically. Generators at power stations work on a similar principle to dynamos and the mains voltage in this country is usually 240 V a.c. Alternating current

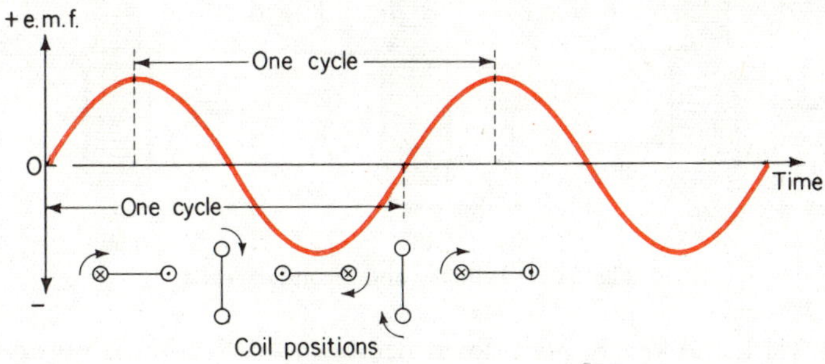

Fig. 31.8 A.C. voltage

thus flows through lamps and electric heaters. The frequency of the mains voltage in this country is 50 Hz (cycles per second), that is, the voltage goes through one complete cycle of changes in $\frac{1}{50}$ s, after which it begins all over again. In the United States of America, the frequency is 60 Hz. The generators in this country thus rotate at 50

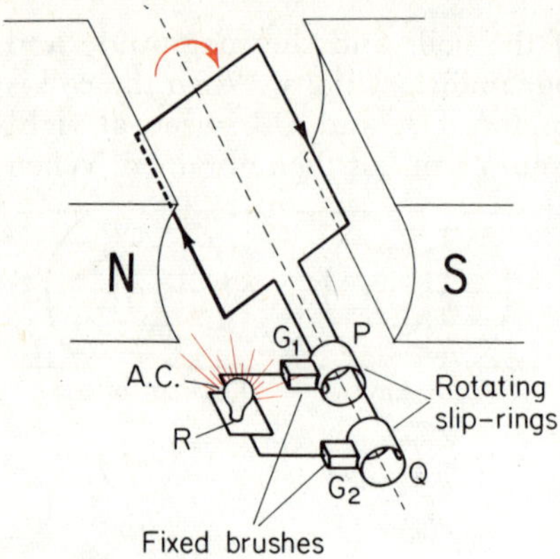

Fig. 31.9 Action of commutator

r.p.s., and in the United States at 60 r.p.s. The maximum value of the e.m.f. is called its *amplitude* or *peak value*.

Fig. 31.9 shows how the induced current is obtained from the rotating coil of a dynamo. Each end of the coil is permanently connected to two copper or *slip-rings*, P and Q. The rings press against fixed brushes G_1 and G_2 as they rotate with the coil. The current thus passes through a resistance R, such as a lamp, joined to G_1 and G_2.

Primary and Secondary Coils

Instead of using a magnet to produce an induced current, a solenoid can be used instead. It acts as a magnet when carrying a current (p. 505).

Fig. 31.10 shows a solenoid A in series with an accumulator L and a tapping key K, with another coil C near it.

(i) When A is close to C and K is depressed, a slight deflection is obtained in G, Fig. 31.10 (i). With a soft iron inside both A and C, as shown, a very much larger deflection is obtained, Fig. 31.10 (ii).

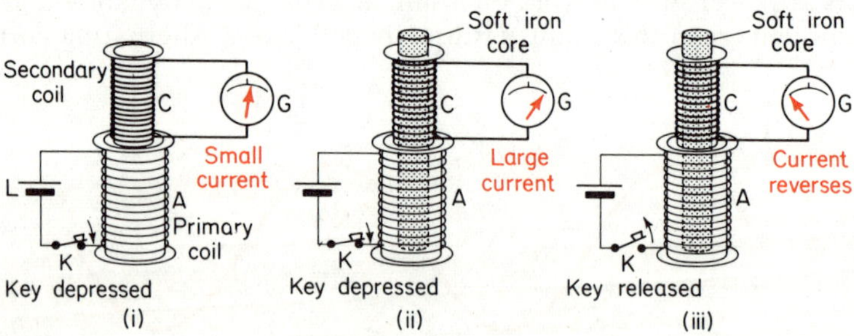

Fig. 31.10 Primary and secondary coils

(ii) With the key K held down firmly, no deflection is observed on G. The induced current thus flows only while a current *change* is made in the solenoid A.

(iii) When K is released so that the solenoid circuit is broken a deflection in G is obtained in the opposite direction to that in (i), Fig. 31.10 (iii). The deflection then dies down quickly to zero.

(iv) Repeat the above experiment using fewer turns in the coil C. A smaller deflection is then obtained in making and breaking the circuit.

Conclusion. An induced current is obtained in a coil C near another coil A connected to a battery only when the circuit of A is made or broken. A soft-iron core, and more turns of wire in C, increases the induced current. Coil A is known as the 'primary' coil and coil B as the 'secondary' coil.

Induction Coil

The *induction coil* uses a primary and secondary coil to produce an e.m.f. of several thousand volts from a battery supply of only 6 V for example. One form of apparatus is shown in Fig. 31.11. It consists of:

1. A primary coil P of a few hundred turns of thick insulated copper wire, to which a battery B with a switch K is connected.

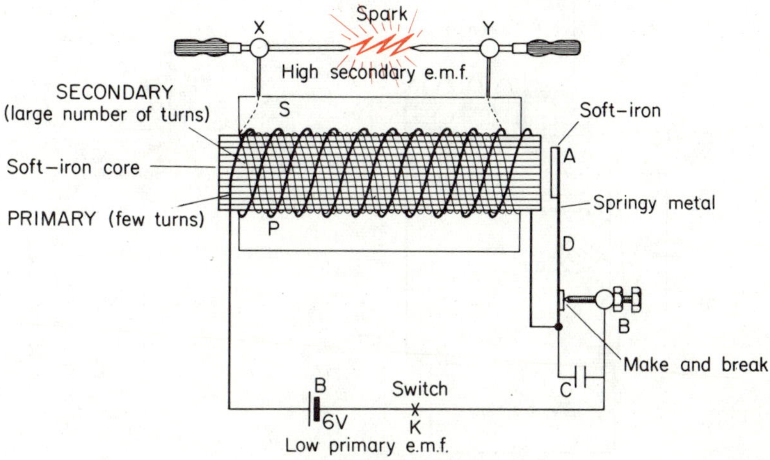

Fig. 31.11 Induction coil

2. A secondary coil S of several thousand turns of thin insulated copper wire wound round P, with terminals at X and Y.

3. A soft-iron core in the form of a bundle of soft-iron wires (see p. 539).

4. A make-and-break arrangement, as in the electric bell, consisting of a soft-iron head A at the end of a springy steel strip of metal D which makes light contact with the tungsten tip of a screw B. A capacitor C is placed across D and B to 'quench' the spark obtained at the tip of the screw when the machine is working.

Action. When the current is made by closing K a current flows in the coil P. Owing to the soft-iron core inside, it becomes a powerful magnet. The iron A is therefore attracted by P. This breaks the contact at the tip of the screw B. The current in the coil thus rapidly falls, the magnetism decreases, and so A is released. The springy metal D hence falls back and makes contact again with the tip of the screw. Thus A moves to-and-fro, making and breaking the primary circuit with P.

The current in P hence rises and falls repeatedly. At the break, it falls to zero in an extremely short time. A very fast change is therefore made in the large number of lines of force linking the secondary coil, S. This produces a very high average induced e.m.f., such as 30 000 V, at its terminals, X, Y. A spark several centimetres long can therefore be obtained between X and Y.

Ignition Coil

An induction coil is used to produce a spark for igniting the mixture of gases in the petrol engine (see p. 238). The secondary coil is joined to two electrodes in the *sparking plug*, Fig. 31.12. One electrode B is earthed

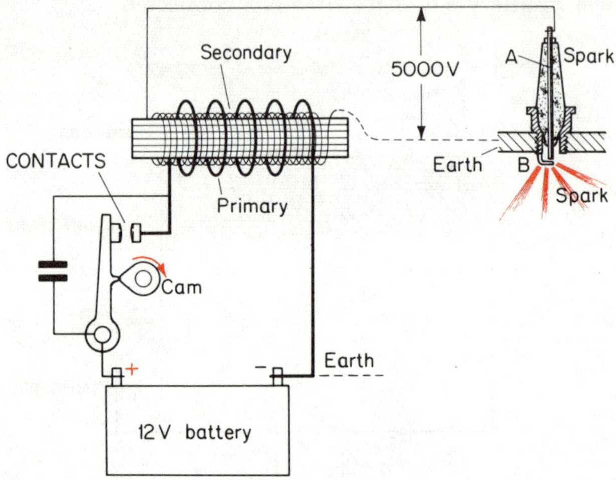

Fig. 31.12 Ignition coil

when the metal casing, to which it is connected, is screwed into the engine cylinder head—the chassis or car-frame is the earth for electrical supplies. The central or high-voltage electrode A is separated from B by a very small gap of the order of $\frac{1}{2}$ millimetre. It is protected by a ceramic insulator.

A cam, driven from the engine, is used to break the contacts in the primary coil circuit. The sudden drop in current in the primary circuit induces a very high voltage of some thousands of volts at the secondary terminals. A spark is then obtained across the small air-gap between A and B. The cam is arranged to turn at half the engine speed. The contacts are then broken once every four strokes, at the beginning of the power stroke (see p. 239).

The Transformer

As we shall see later, alternating e.m.f.s or a.c. voltages require to be changed from low to high values in order to transmit a.c. power economically over long distances. The voltage also needs to be changed from a high to a lower, and much less dangerous, value when brought into the home, for example.

A *transformer* changes the magnitude of an a.c. voltage. It consists simply of two insulated coils P and S, called primary and secondary coils, wound round a soft-iron core, Fig. 31.13. The core is made of

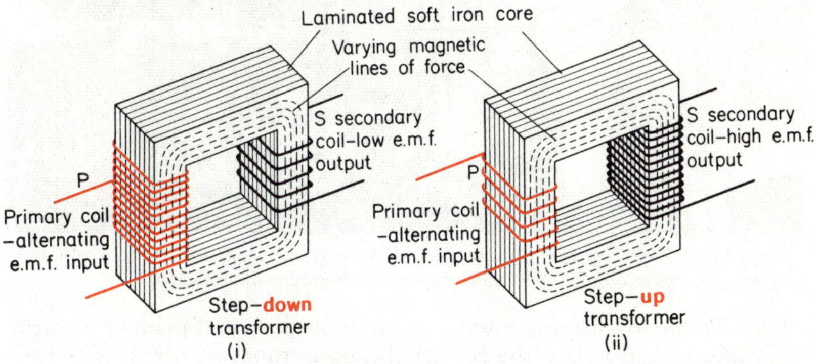

Fig. 31.13 Transformer

laminae or sheets of soft iron, insulated by varnish from each other. This reduces the heat losses of energy inside the iron, which would be considerable if a solid block of metal were used and induced currents circulated inside it.

One type of demonstration mains transformer has a large number of primary turns and about 60 times fewer secondary turns of thicker wire, Fig. 31.13 (i). When the 240 V a.c. mains is connected to the primary, a low voltage of about 4 V is rcorded on a high-resistance a.c. voltmeter such as an AVO-meter connected across the secondary.

The transformer thus has stepped down the a.c. voltage in the ratio 4 : 240 or 1 : 60. This is the same as the ratio of the number of secondary turns, n_s, to the number of primary turns, h_p. A ray-box transformer which produces 12 V a.c. from a 240 V a.c. mains supply is a step-down transformer, with 20 times fewer turns in the secondary compared with the primary.

When the number of secondary turns is greater than that of the primary turns, a correspondingly greater alternating e.m.f. is produced at the secondary terminals, Fig. 31.13. (ii) A step-up radio transformer may have ten times as many turns in the secondary compared with the primary, and steps-up the e.m.f. 10 times. Generally, a commercial transformer, which has a soft-iron core, obeys the following law for e.m.f.s.

$$\frac{E_s}{E_p} = \frac{n_s}{n_p}$$

Plate 31(A) High voltage transformers. The large oil tank, top right, circulates oil to cool the windings. Note also the high voltage insulators used.

where E_s and E_p are the e.m.f.s in the secondary and primary respectively and n_s and n_p are the corresponding number of turns. The ratio n_s/n_p is called the turns-ratio of the transformer. A step-up transformer has a turns-ratio greater than 1; a step-down transformer has a turns-ratio less than 1. Fig. 31.13 illustrates that the number of magnetic lines of force or flux linking the secondary coil, compared with that linking the primary coil, is always the ratio of their number of turns. Thus the induced e.m.f.s have the same ratio.

Plate 31(B) Main control room of Central Electricity Generating Board. All switching and distribution of electricity on the National Grid are made here.

Transmitting Electrical Power · Grid System

An electric lamp, which has a current of $\frac{1}{2}$ A when the mains voltage is 240 V, uses an amount of power given by

$$\text{power} = \tfrac{1}{2}\,\text{A} \times 240\,\text{V} = 120\,\text{W}.$$

Generally, the power in an appliance when the current is I amp and the voltage across it is V volts is given by IV watts, that is,

$$\text{power} = \text{current} \times \text{voltage}.$$

A given amount of power such as 2000 W can thus be supplied either by having a current of 1 A and a voltage of 2000 V or by having a current of 10 A and a voltage of 200 V. The heat or wastage of power in the cables from the generator is much more when it carries 10 A than 1 A. Further, heavy currents require thicker cables and hence more copper. It is therefore more economical to supply power at *high* voltages, when the current is less.

This is why the national system for distributing electrical power, called the National Grid System, uses high 'tension' or high voltage. The generators at national power stations produce 11 000 V. This is stepped up by huge transformers to nearly 400 000 V for distribution over large distances. Pylons and a network of cables are used to transmit the power. See Plates 31A, 31B.

SUMMARY

1. Magnet moving near a closed coil, or coil moving near magnet, produces an induced e.m.f. or current.

2. In a bicycle dynamo, a magnet rotates near a coil joined to a light bulb.

3. Current changes in a primary coil produces an e.m.f. in a secondary coil near it.

4. Induced e.m.f. is proportional to the rate of change of magnetic lines linking the coil (Faraday's law).

5. Induction coil (ignition coil)—high e.m.f. and spark produced at secondary terminals when primary circuit broken rapidly.

6. Dynamo—coil rotates steadily between the poles of a magnet. a.c. obtained. For d.c., a commutator is used.

7. Grid system—electrical power distributed over country at high voltage. Current then small and wastage of power in cables is reduced.

8. Transformers change alternating voltages. Secondary e.m.f./primary e.m.f. = number of secondary turns/number of primary turns, with commercial transformer (soft iron core).

PRACTICAL

1. Moving magnet and coil (p. 530)

Apparatus. Coil with large number of turns powerful (e.g. Ticonal) magnets; sensitive meter (e.g. 0–1 milliamp or microammeter) with centre zero or 'zero' adjusted for pointer deflections both ways; soft-iron or mu-metal rod.

Method. (i) Connect the coil, C, to the galvanometer. Observe and record the deflection in the following cases:

(*a*) N-pole of magnet moved towards C slowly. Repeat by moving N-pole quickly to C. Each time keep the magnet stationary inside C and observe the final deflection.

(*b*) Repeat with the S-pole.

(*c*) Repeat with two magnets of like poles together—Sellotape if magnets powerful.

(*d*) Repeat (*a*) and (*c*) after adding a soft-iron core to the coil. Move the magnets to-and-fro near the coil. What type of current is generated?

(*e*) With mu-metal in the coil, hold the coil with its axis in a N–S direction and pointing about 70° to the horizontal. Turn the coil sharply to point E–W. Is there a deflection? If so, explain it. Tabulate your observations, as in the table below, State a *Conclusion* or *Conclusions*, about the magnitude of induced e.m.f. and current.

Movement	Deflection (small or large)

2. Moving coil

Method. Fix a powerful magnet in a wooden clamp. With a soft-iron core inside the coil and the coil joined to a sensitive galvanometer or meter, move the coil: (*a*) towards the magnet; (*b*) away from it; (*c*) to-and-from the magnet (p. 531). Observe also the effect of turning the coil round in front of the magnet. Tabulate the results as in 1. State a *Conclusion* about the induced e.m.f. and current.

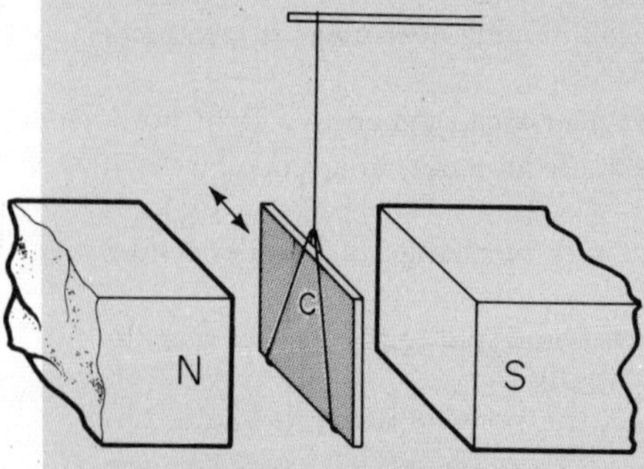

Fig. 31.14 Induced currents

3. Induced currents and opposition

Method. (i) Sellotape aluminium foil across both surfaces of a piece of cardboard C, Fig. 31.14.

(ii) Suspend the cardboard by thread from a wooden clamp and push it slightly so that it swings.

(iii) Now place a U-shaped powerful magnet so that C swings across the magnetic field between N–S—two powerful magnets positioned either side may be used in place of the U-magnet. Observe any change in the movement of C.

Repeat, (*a*) removing the magnet and then bringing it back, (*b*) using C *without* foil, (*c*) using other materials in place of C.

Note. Induced currents *oppose* the motion producing them—Lenz's law in electromagnetic induction.

4. Moving straight wire

Method. (i) Suspend a wire BC from supports at AD so that BC can swing freely about AD, Fig. 31.15.

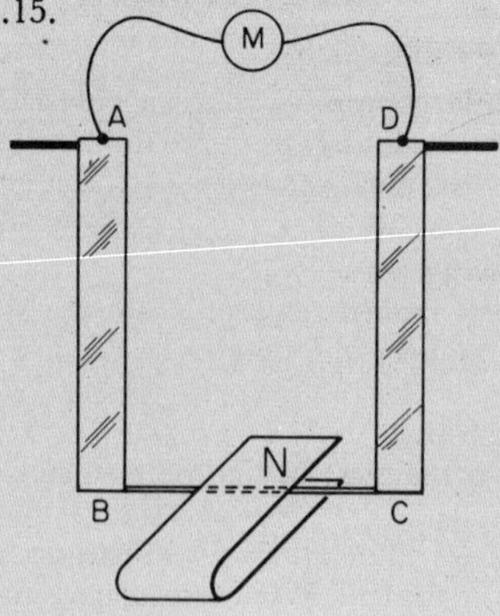

Fig. 31.15 Moving wire

(ii) Arrange the N- and S-poles of two powerful magnets or a U-shaped magnet so that BC cuts the field of the magnet when it swings.

(iii) Connect a sensitive centre-zero galvanometer or meter M across A and D. Observe the deflection obtained.

Turn the magnet poles round so that BC swings *parallel* to the field. Observe the deflection compared with before.

State a *conclusion*.

5. Motor in reverse

Method. (i) Connect a sensitive meter to the terminals of a small or toy electric motor.

(ii) Flick the armature or copper turns so as to make it turn one way, and observe the deflection in the meter. Reverse the rotation of the armature and observe the deflection again. Is a direct or alternating current obtained?

(iii) Connect a low-voltage bulb to the terminals. Arrange a 'drive' on the axle and see if the bulb will light when the motor is driven.

6. Coil (Choke) in a.c. circuit

Apparatus. 4 V d.c. battery and 4 V a.c. mains supply, two similar 2·5 V lamps X and Y, insulated coil of wire A of many turns in which a soft iron bar can be inserted, resistance B about the same resistance as the wire used for coil A, key K.

Method. (i) Connect the circuit shown in Fig. 31.16, using first the 4 V d.c. supply.

(ii) Press the key K and observe the brightness of the lamps X and Y. Is the brightness roughly the same or much different? Try the effect of pushing a bar of soft iron inside A.

(iii) Now replace the d.c. battery by the 4 V a.c. supply. Press the key K and observe the brightness of X and Y. Is this roughly the same or much different? Push a soft iron bar inside the coil A and observe the effect on the brightness of X and Y.

Conclusions. From your results, answer the following questions:

(*a*) In a d.c. circuit, has the coil A with a soft iron bar inside a similar effect on the current flowing as a *resistance* B of the same value as the coil?

(*b*) In an a.c. circuit, has the coil A with a soft iron bar inside a smaller or larger 'resistance' to the current flow than the resistance B? Why do you think engineers gave the name 'choke' to such a coil when it is used in an a.c. circuit?

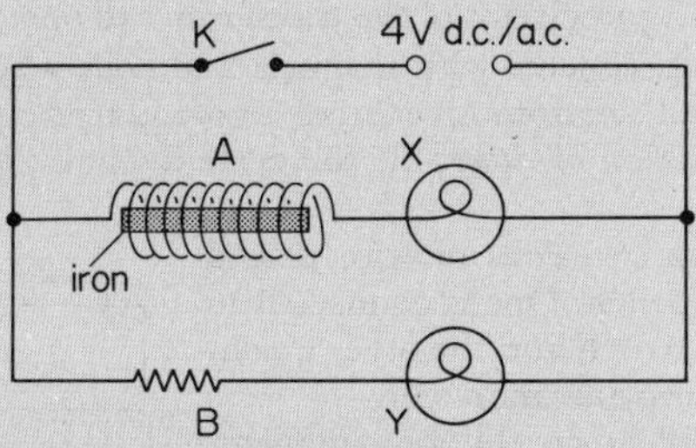

Fig. 31.16 Action of 'choke' in a.c. circuit

EXERCISE 31 · ANSWERS, p. 617

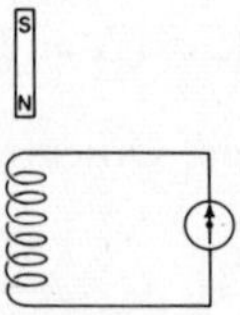

Fig. 31A

1. The diagram Fig. 31A shows a bar-magnet which may be moved into and out of a solenoid which is joined in series with a centre zero galvanometer. As the N-pole is pushed into the coil the galvanometer shows a deflection to the right.

(*a*) What is this effect called?

(*b*) What deflection, if any, occurs when: (i) the N-pole is removed; (ii) the S-pole is inserted; (iii) the magnet is at rest in the coil? (*L.*)

2. An electric current may be produced by moving a magnet in a coil of wire. The amount of current produced will *not* be altered by: (*a*) decreasing the number of turns on the coil; (*b*) moving the magnet more quickly; (*c*) increasing the number of turns on the coil; (*d*) using a stronger magnet; (*e*) using the opposite pole of the magnet. (*E.A.*)

3. (*a*) With the aid of a large labelled diagram, describe the action of a simple form of a.c. generator in which a single loop rotates between the poles of a magnet.

(*b*) How is the a.c. fed to the external circuit?

(*c*) Describe the use of the split-ring commutator for changing the output to uni-directional current d.c. (*Mx.*)

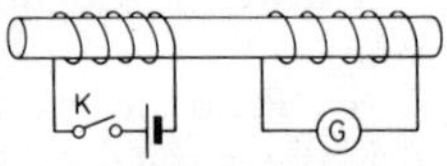

Fig. 31B

4. The circuit diagram Fig. 31B shows two coils of insulated copper wire wound on to a cardboard tube. G is a centre-zero galvanometer (i.e. it may be deflected to the left or right depending on the direction of the current). Describe what will happen when the switch K is closed for several seconds and then opened again. What will be the effect of repeating the experiment with an iron bar placed in the tube? (*S.E.*)

5. Write a short essay on 'induced currents'. Your essay should explain what is meant by an induced current, and what factors affect the size of such a current. You should mention any simple experiments you have seen to illustrate the facts you mention. (*M.*)

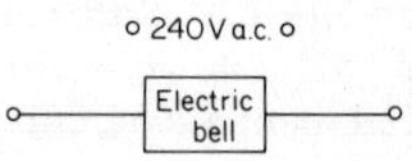

Fig. 31C

6. (*a*) Complete Fig. 31C to show how a transformer to transform the 'mains' voltage of 240 V to 6 V is needed to operate the bell.

(*b*) State the turns ratio required.

(*c*) Show how a switch (S) may be placed in the output circuit of the transformer to operate the bell. (*L.*)

7. (*a*) Describe experiments with magnets and coils which demonstrate the production of induced electromotive forces (or of induced currents).

(*b*) Explain the action of *either:* (i) the cycle dynamo; *or* (ii) the induction coil. (*Mx.*)

8. Fig. 31D shows two coils of wire placed close together on a bench. One is connected to a battery through a switch and the other is connected to a centre-zero galvanometer.

(*a*) Explain the effect on the galvanometer when the switch Sw is: (i) open; (ii) at the instant of closing; (iii) closed; (iv) at the instant of opening.

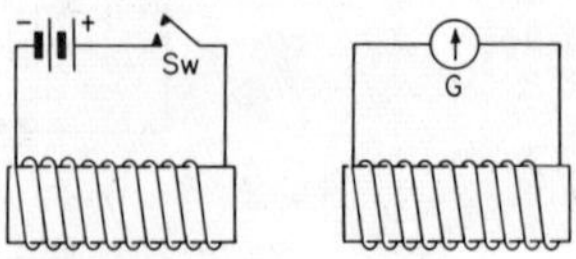

Fig. 31D

(*b*) How is this effect used in the ignition system of a car? (*E.A.*)

9. Fig. 31E (i) shows a very simple a.c. dynamo. The coil is driven round, and the current generated is supplied to a circuit by carbon brushes which touch

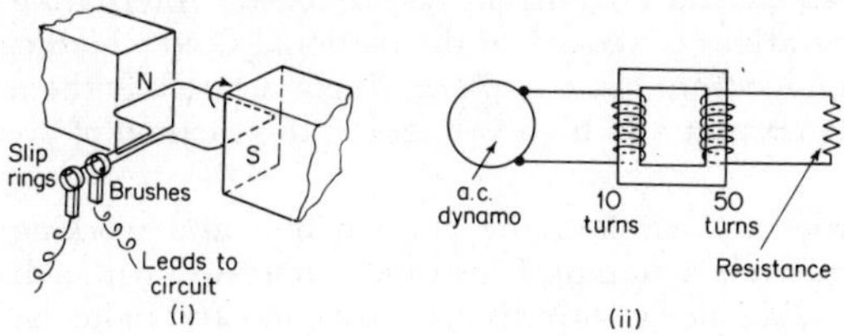

Fig. 31E

the slip rings shown. Draw a sketch graph to show how the current flowing will vary during one complete revolution of the coil, starting from the position shown in diagram (i).

What part of the dynamo would you modify in order to make it supply a direct current?

Draw a labelled sketch of the modified part of the dynamo.

The simple dynamo shown gives a 2 V output, and supplies a current of 4 A to the primary coil of the transformer shown in Fig. 31E (ii). What will be the voltage output of the transformer secondary coil?

What current will be flowing in the transformer secondary if the transformer is perfectly efficient (i.e. no energy losses in the transformer itself)?

Explain briefly how the transformer works. (*S.*)

10. (*a*) Calculate the current if 1 kW is transmitted at: (i) 3000 V, 132 000 V. (Leave the answers as simple fractions.) (ii) Now explain why electricity is transmitted through the National Grid System at 132 000 V instead of at the 3000 V at which it is produced.

(*b*) Describe briefly, or give a labelled diagram of the appliance used to convert electricity at 3000 V into electricity at 132 000 V. (*E.A.*)

11. (*a*) How would you show by experiment that an electric current can be produced by electromagnetic induction?

(*b*) Two coils of insulated wire are wound on a soft-iron core. The first coil is connected to a current supply and the second to a lamp. The lamp is seen to light up and remain alight as long as the current remains on. Give a full and careful explanation of what is happening.

(*c*) Give one advantage there is in transmitting alternating rather than direct current over long distances. (*S.E.*)

12. Electrical power is produced at power-stations by alternators and transmitted through the National Grid at 240 000 V.

(*a*) Why are the machines producing the electrical energy called 'alternators'?

(*b*) Why is the power transmitted at such a high and dangerous voltage? What would be the difficulties attached to transmitting the power required by the town through overhead wires at 240 V?

(*c*) Draw a simple diagram of the apparatus used to change the high voltage from the grid lines into the 240 V required for use in houses. What other change is made in the electrical energy at this point? (*W.Md.*)

13. Explain in detail with your own simple diagram, the construction of a step-down transformer. Give a scientific reason for the construction of, and choice of materials used in, each part of the transformer. (*M.*)

14. How can an alternating current be produced? Alternating current produced by power stations is 'fed-in' to the National Grid which carries electric power at high voltage from place to place. Explain carefully the reasons for the use of alternating current and high voltages in this method of power transmission. (*M.*)

15. (*a*) Describe and explain the construction and working of a simple dynamo (such as a cycle dynamo). Illustrate your answer with a diagram.

(*b*) A boy is cycling along with his cycle dynamo and lights on. He switches off the lights but leaves the dynamo so that the cycle continues to drive it. Will switching off the lights make the cycle any easier to pedal? Give reasons for your answer.

(*c*) It is possible for a cyclist by cycling rapidly downhill with the dynamo on to 'blow' his lamp bulbs. Explain why this should be so. If both lamps are worked off the dynamo and only one of them goes out, what does this suggest about the way in which the lamps are wired into the circuit? (*S.E.*)

16. In the National Grid System, a.c. is transmitted rather than d.c. because of a device which has no moving parts. Describe this device with the aid of a diagram and explain its action. What is the purpose of a sub-station in the Grid System? (*W.Md.*)

17. (*a*) Draw a wave form diagram for alternating current. Indicate a CYCLE and give the common a.c. mains frequency used in this country.

(*b*) Describe an experiment which would show that a force acts on a conductor which is carrying a current in a magnetic field. Illustrate your answer with a diagram showing clearly the direction of current, magnetic field and force.

(*c*) How could you tell by inspection whether a generator is designed to supply alternating or direct current? Give your reasons. (*S.E.*)

18. (*a*) Describe how an electromotive force may be induced in a coil.

(*b*) Explain the working of a transformer. Illustrate your answer by a diagram of a STEPDOWN transformer.

(*c*) A 12 V – 48 W bulb is connected to a transformer running off a 240 V mains. What current will the transformer take from the mains? (assume no energy losses.) (*S.E.*)

19. (*a*) How do you calculate the power in a circuit when you know the voltage and the current in amperes?

(*b*) Calculate the current flowing through a cable when 1 kW of power is transmitted at: (i) 3000 V; (ii) 132 000 V.

(*c*) Remembering the results obtained in part (*b*), explain why electrical energy is transmitted through the grid cables at 132 000 V.

(*d*) Describe the structure of a 'step-down' transformer. (*Mx.*)

32

ELECTRONICS

ELECTRONS · CATHODE-RAY TUBE · DIODE VALVE

Conduction in Gases

AT normal pressures air is a poor conductor of electricity. Bare wires and cables, supported high above the ground in the telephone and Grid system, do not therefore require insulation. Submarine cables, however, require careful insulation because sea-water is a good conductor.

With very high voltages, air at normal pressure does conduct electricity. This occurs at engineering works where columns of insulating material are tested. For this purpose, a voltage of several hundred thousand volts is connected between two metal electrodes at the top and bottom of the column. A long electric spark, and simultaneously a tiny current, is usually obtained through the air. This shows that the material in the columns was a better insulator than air.

A gas will conduct at much lower voltages, however, if only a little gas is used. A small neon lamp, used in a screwdriver by electricians to test mains voltages, for example, contains neon gas at a very low pressure. When the metal point of the screwdriver is pressed against a point at a voltage greater than about 100 V, the gas glows. It now conducts and a small current flows.

Discharge Tube

In order to study conduction in gases, the gas concerned is passed into a long glass tube called a *discharge tube*. This has metal electrodes C and A at either end, Fig. 32.1. A side tube enables the gas to be pumped out while the voltage is applied, as a smaller amount of gas will be a better conductor. (*Warning*. SAFETY regulations must be followed when using the discharge tube.)

Use air as the gas and set up the discharge tube in a dark room. The induction coil is a machine which can conveniently provide a high voltage of several thousand volts (p. 537). Connect the terminals of the machine across C(−) and A (+), and then switch on the voltage. Pump the air out slowly from the tube.

As most of the air is pumped out, long blue streamers or sparks flash between A and C—the air pressure is lowered to about 20 mm of mercury and the air conducts, Fig. 32.1 (i). When the air pressure is lowered further, the discharge widens and then breaks up into 'discs'.

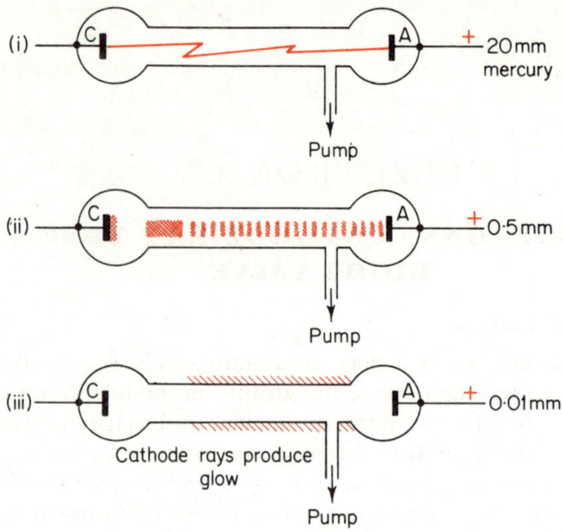

Fig. 32.1 Discharge tube effects

A glow now appears round the cathode C, Fig. 32.1 (ii). See also Plate 32A. The dark space now increases and at a very low pressure of about 0·01 mm mercury, when very little air is left in the tube, the glass glows with a green light, Fig. 32.1 (iii).

Cathode Rays · The Electron

The green glow is due to fluorescence of the glass. It is caused by invisible rays coming from the cathode which strike the glass. They were therefore called *cathode rays* about 1890, when the phenomenon was first

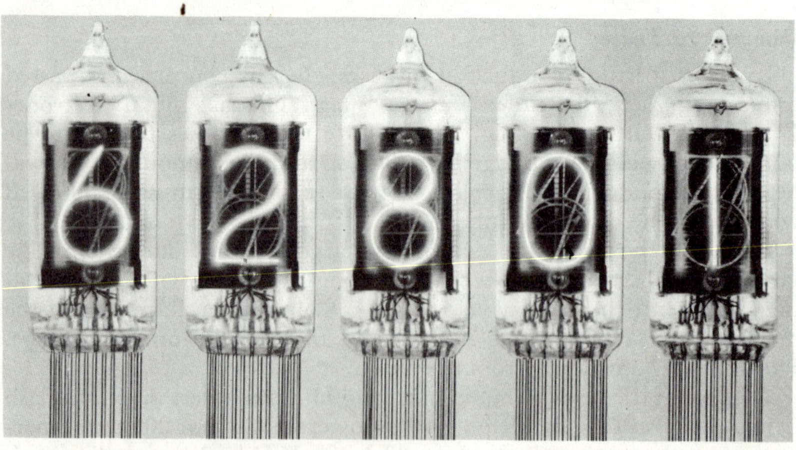

Plate 32(A) Electrical (cold cathode) tubes which display numbers. They are used in computers and in modern cash registers.

observed. For many years scientists were puzzled by the nature of cathode rays.

When the N-pole of a Ticonal (strong) magnet is brought very close and at right angles to the tube, the glow moves, Fig. 32.2. Thus the cathode rays are deflected by a magnet perpendicular to their direction.

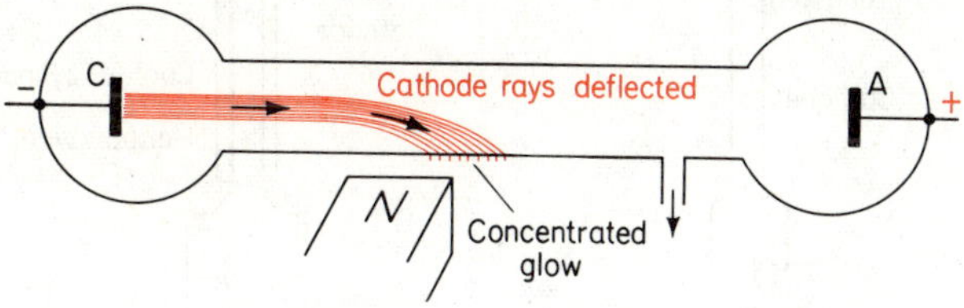

Fig. 32.2 Magnetic deflection of cathode rays (electrons)

If a S-pole is used, the glow deflects the other way.

Conclusions. 1. The cathode rays are therefore easily affected by a magnetic field. They are hence not electromagnetic waves, and are probably extremely light particles carrying a quantity of electricity or charge.

2. From the deflection of the glow in Fig. 32.2 it follows that the moving particles act like an electric current—we have seen on p. 516 that a metal conductor carrying an electric current is deflected when it is perpendicular to a magnetic field. Applying Fleming's left-hand rule to the deflection of the glow, we find the current flows from A to C. But the current direction in Fleming's left-hand rule represents the movement of positive electricity. This is equivalent to *negative* electricity moving from C to A. The particles which create the glow hence carry negative electricity, and they were later called *electrons*.

In 1896 Sir J. J. Thomson found that the electron had a mass far less than that of the hydrogen atom, which is the lightest atom. Experiments show that:

Mass of electron $= \frac{1}{2000}$ *of mass of hydrogen atom* (*approximately*).

Hot Cathodes

In 1902 Richardson found that electrons are readily obtained from hot metals. Metals contain many free electrons (p. 412). If a fine tungsten wire, for example, is heated to a high temperature by connecting a battery of a few volts, the extra energy given to the electrons enables them to break through the surface of the metal and exist outside as an electron 'cloud'. This is called *thermionic emission.* The effect is analogous to vaporization near the boiling point, where molecules break through a liquid surface and form vapour outside.

Later it was found that the oxides of barium and strontium emit electrons at much lower temperatures than tungsten wire. A tungsten wire glows white hot when it emits electrons. In contrast, the oxides of barium and strontium appear dull when they emit electrons—the temperature required for emission is much lower.

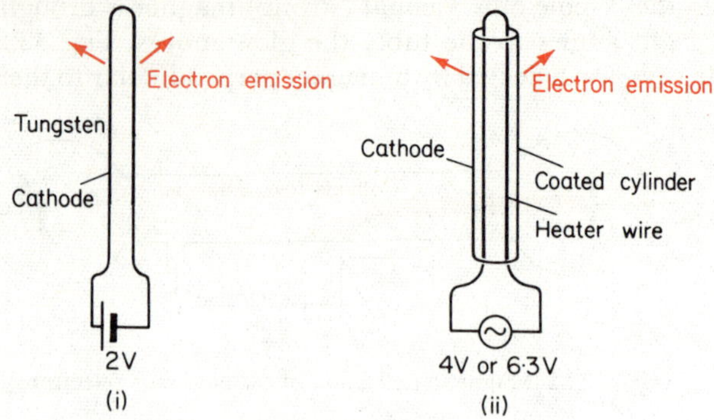

Fig. 32.3 Directly and indirectly heated cathodes

The emitter of electrons is generally called the *cathode*. In early radio valves (p. 556) the cathode was a hot fine tungsten wire, Fig. 32.3 (i). This is a *directly heated* valve. Modern valves, however, also contain a tungsten wire, but it is used only as a source of heat. It warms a cylinder near it whose surface is coated with a mixture of barium and strontium oxides, which readily emits electrons, Fig. 32.3 (ii). The cylinder is therefore the cathode in this case and the wire is the heater. This is consequently an *indirectly heated* cathode. The voltage required for the heater is low, such as 6·3 V or less, and it can be obtained from a d.c. supply such as accumulators, or an a.c. supply. In the latter case it is conveniently obtained from a step-down mains transformer (p. 539).

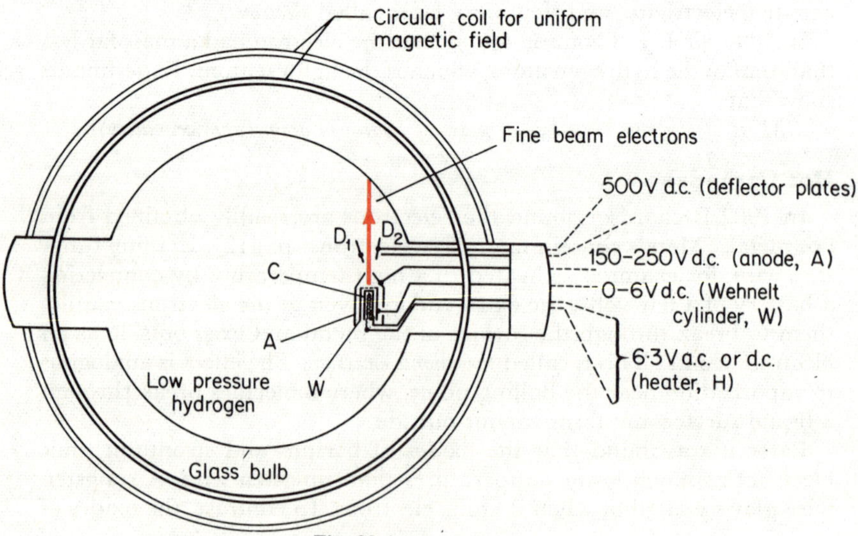

Fig. 32.4 Fine beam tube

Fine Beam Tube

Since electrons are easily produced by using a hot cathode, experiments on electrons can be very conveniently carried out using this as the source.

In a *fine beam tube* a conical metal anode A with a hole at the top is placed over the cathode C, and kept at a high positive potential of a few hundred volts relative to the cathode, Fig. 32.4. The glass tube containing the cathode and anode has a very small amount of hydrogen inside. In this case the fast-moving electrons which pass through the hole in the anode produce a fine beam of light as they ionize the gas molecules (compare p. 547). The beam thus shows the path of the electrons. Any movement of electrons inside the tube is clearly shown by the movement of the fine luminous beam. See Plate 32B, p. 552.

Effects of Magnetic Field

The LEYBOLD fine beam tube is designed for studying the movement of electron beams when magnetic and electric fields are applied. A uniform *magnetic field* is produced by passing a current through two large parallel circular coils on either side of the tube, Fig. 32.4. The coils act respectively like a north and a south magnetic pole which face each other (p. 504). The whole beam is situated in the field between the coils. The magnetic field strength can be altered if required by varying the strength of the current in the coils.

Connect the required voltages to the tube to produce a beam, as shown in Fig. 32.4.

Switch on the cathode heater first, then the Wehnelt cylinder and the anode voltage. A fine vertical luminous beam should be seen in the tube. Switch on the current in the coils, and examine the effect of increasing it from 0 to 2 A. Observe the *circular path* of the electrons and the change in radius as the magnetic field is varied in strength, Fig. 32.5. Turn the tube round so that the magnetic field is not

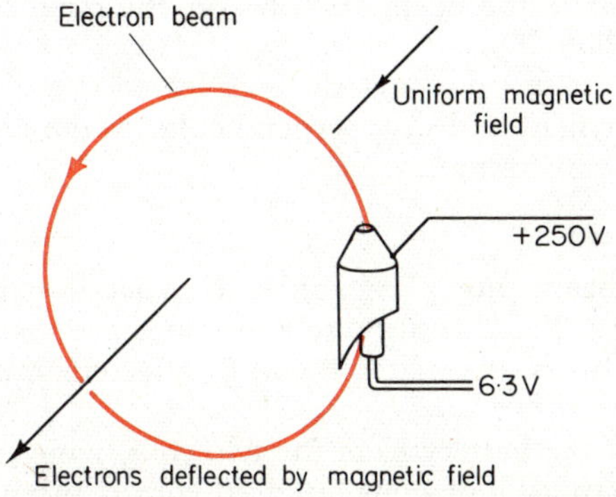

Fig. 32.5 Magnetic deflection of electrons

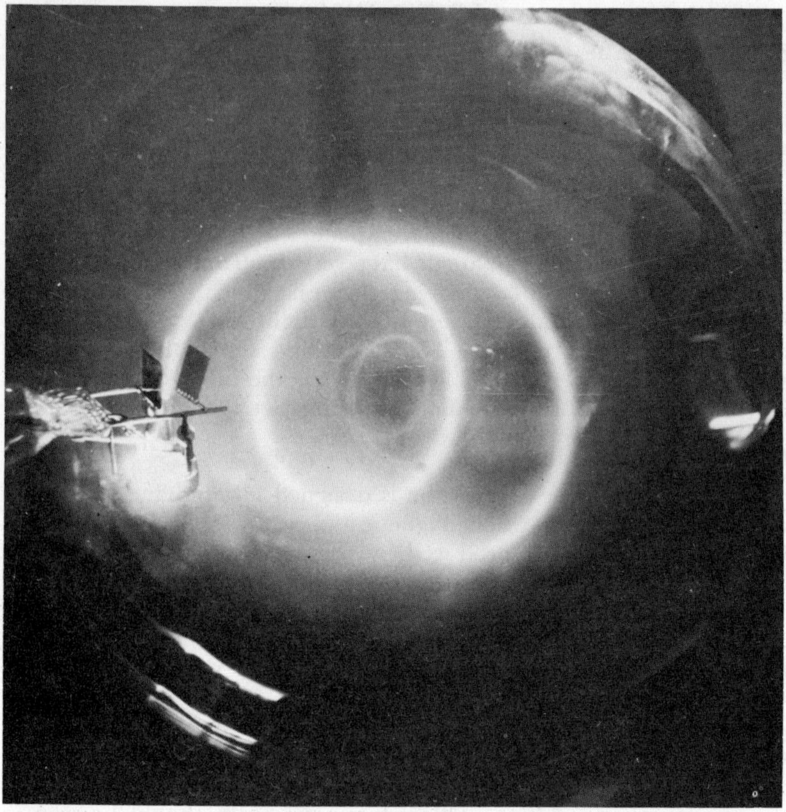

Plate 32(B) Spiral electron path in a *LEYBOLD* fine-beam tube, due to a magnetic field at a small angle to the electron beam. The beam passes initially through a conical anode and then through two plates which may be used to apply an electric field.

perpendicular to the beam and observe the *spiral path* of the luminous beam. See Plate 32B.

The beam (a gaseous current) is deflected in a circular path because the magnetic field is always perpendicular to the direction of the beam and constant in strength.

Electric Field

The fine beam tube also enables us to see the effect on electrons of an *electric field*. For this purpose two plates are used. The beam passes centrally between the plates P and Q after emerging from the anode, Fig. 32.6.

Switch off the battery from the two coils, which are no longer used. Connect a battery B of a few hundred volts between P and Q, and join the anode to the centre of the battery supply.

When P is made positive with respect to the anode and Q negative, the beam is deflected towards P. If the outside battery terminals are reversed, so that P is negative and Q is positive, the beam is deflected towards Q. An alternating p.d. applied to P and Q would thus make the beam move to-and-fro rapidly.

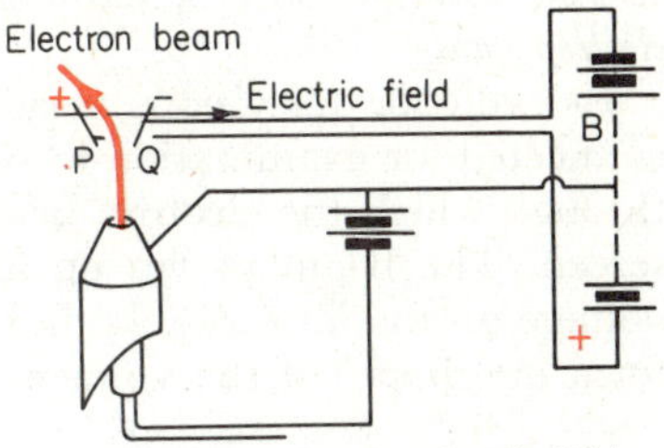

Fig. 32.6 Electric deflection of electrons

Cathode-ray Tube and Oscillograph

The discovery of cathode rays or electrons led to a vast field of practical applications grouped under the heading *Electronics*. Electrons are so light that they are highly sensitive to electrical or magnetic variations, as we have just seen.

The glow produced by fast-moving electrons on a fluorescent screen led to the important invention of the *cathode-ray tube*. This is used for television and in radar. See Plate 32c. In the form of the *cathode-ray oscillograph* (*C.R.O.*) it is used for measurements and demonstrations connected with radio, television and telecommunications.

Basically, the C.R.O. has: (1) a cathode C which emits electrons; (2) a plate G which is kept at a negative potential, so that the number of electrons per second reaching the screen, or *brightness* of the picture, can be controlled; (3) an *electron lens*, consisting of metal plates or cylinders, A_1, A_2 and A_3, all kept at a high potential relative to C of the order of a thousand volts, Fig. 32.7. The potential of A_2 varies the focal length of the lens, so that the electron beam can be *focused* on to the screen S. The high positive potentials of these metals, which are anodes, produce a fast-moving electron beam whose energy can be converted into light energy of fluorescence.

Plate 32(c) Radar screen, used in air traffic control. The dots indicate aircraft and this is superimposed on a map of the air lanes above the airport.

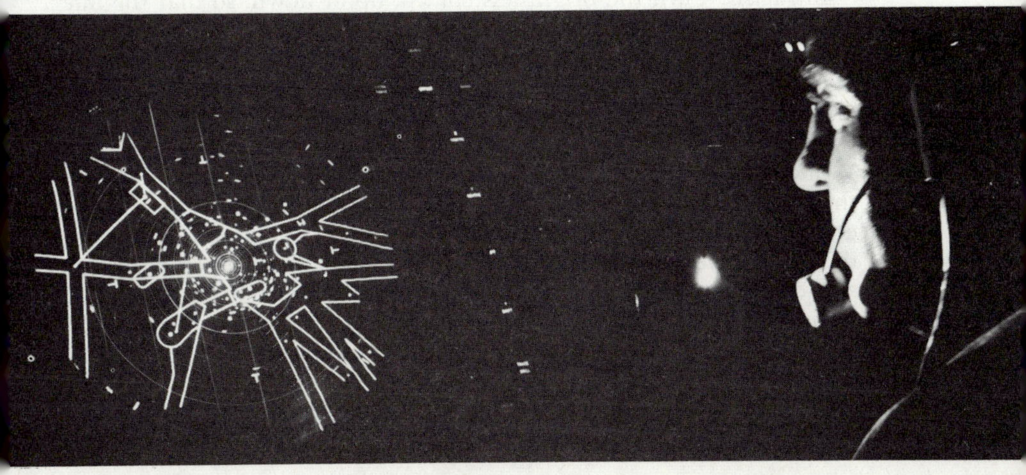

The arrangement of cathode and anodes is sometimes called an *electron gun.*

In radio or television, varying or alternating voltages are always connected for examination to two metal plates, Y_1, Y_2, called *Y-plates,* through which the electron beam passes before striking the fluorescent screen. The beam moves up and down in response to the changing voltage on the Y-plates. It thus traces a line on the screen. The waveform or 'shape' of the voltage can be seen when a *time-base* circuit is

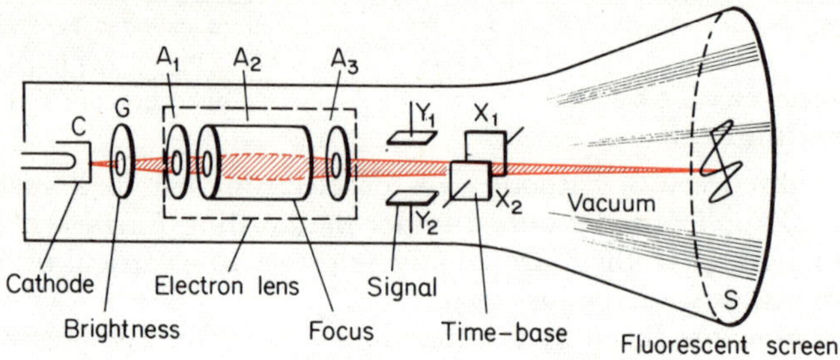

Fig. 32.7 Cathode ray tube

switched on. This special circuit provides a voltage connected to metal plates X_1, X_2 called *X-plates,* through which the beam also passes, so that the beam is deflected horizontally. Thus as the beam moves up and down in response to the voltage in the Y-plates, it is also swept horizontally. A waveform is now produced with a horizontal *time-axis.* In this way a faulty waveform can be traced in a radio receiver, and a radar operator can check that a radio signal reflected back from an aeroplane is the same as that sent out.

Using the C.R.O.

Make sure the time-base is connected to the X-plates, and *switch on* the instrument. Allow it to warm up, when a horizontal line appears on the screen.

Brightness. Turn the brightness control up or down, so that the line trace is clearly visible. The minimum brightness should be used to prolong the life of the screen—a very bright trace will 'burn' the screen.

Focus. Turn the focus control until the line trace is seen as sharply as possibly.

Signal or Y-plates. Connect a coil with a large number of turns to the Y-plates. Push a powerful magnet towards it and then back. Observe the up-and-down movement of the line due to the induced e.m.f. in the coil. Switch off the time-base so that a weak spot of light is obtained on the screen. Repeat the movement of the magnet and observe the up-and-down movement of the spot, and then switch on the time-base again.

Time-base. The spot moves from left to right across the screen with a uniform or constant velocity. When it reaches the end of its movement, it 'flies' back at very high speed to its original starting-point on the left of the screen.

Observe that the time-base control is calibrated in the times taken by the spot to travel 1 cm from left to right, such as 10 milliseconds ($\frac{1}{100}$ s) per cm. The fly-back time is negligibly small. Switch the time-base control to higher speeds and observe the continuous line. At higher speeds the velocity of the spot from left to right is still uniform and the rapid movement is seen as a continuous line.

Signal Waveforms

A signal on the Y-plates will make the spot of light move up-and-down in response. If the time-base makes the spot move to and fro horizontally in the same time, that is, the frequency of the time-base is exactly the same as that of the signal, then a stationary pattern is

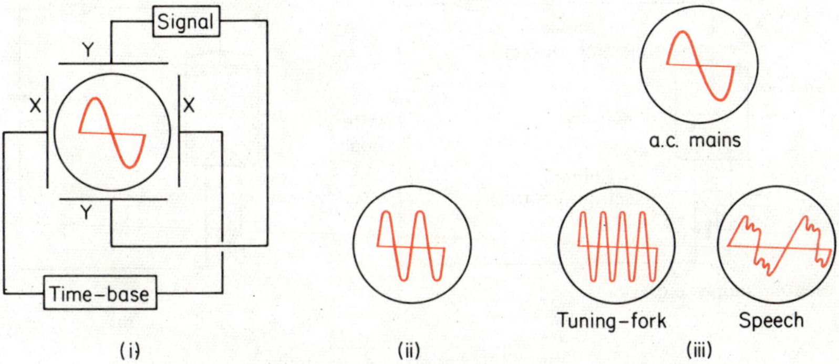

Fig. 32.8 Waveform on cathode ray tube screen

seen of one cycle of the signal, Fig. 32.8 (i). If the signal frequency is exactly twice that of the time-base, then two cycles of the signal are seen, Fig. 32.8 (ii). In this way, by varying the frequency or speed of the time-base, the waveform or pattern of a signal can be made stationary on the screen and then studied.

When a coil is connected to the signal plates and a magnet is moved rapidly to and fro, the a.c. pattern can be seen by using a low time-base speed. When a low a.c. voltage from the mains is connected, a slightly higher time-base speed may be required to see a stationary pattern. Waveforms produced by connecting a microphone and holding a sounding tuning fork in front of it, or by whistling or speaking into the microphone, all require a higher time-base speed than that for the a.c. mains, as their frequencies are higher, Fig. 32.8 (iii).

Electron beams are influenced by magnetic fields, as shown on

p. 551. When a powerful magnet is brought near to a wave-trace on the screen it is therefore affected.

Radio Valve

In 1902 Sir J. A. Fleming produced the first radio valve, for use in radio detection. (p. 560). It is called a *diode valve* because it has two separated metals C and A inside a vacuum in a thin glass 'bottle', Fig. 32.9. C, called the *cathode*, was a thin tungsten wire which was heated to a high temperature by a low-voltage battery D. This 'boiled off' some electrons which were inside the metal, that is, the heat gave some electrons extra energy to escape from the metal and exist outside. The metal A opposite C is called the *anode*.

If a high-voltage battery is joined with its positive pole to A and its negative pole to C, the electrons (negative charges) move towards A, Fig. 32.9 (i). They flow all round the circuit, that is, from A through

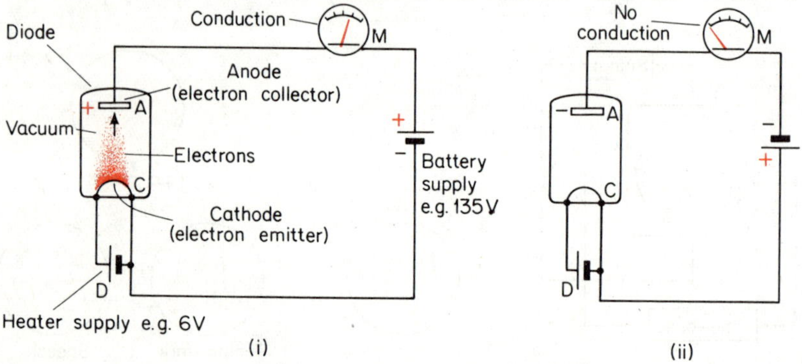

Fig. 32.9 Action of diode valve

the battery and back to C. Consequently a current flows in a meter M in the anode circuit. It is usually a few milliamps when the p.d. between A and C is about a hundred volts. The valve thus conducts in this case.

Suppose, however, that the battery terminals are turned round, and the negative pole is joined to A and the positive pole to C, Fig. 32.9 (ii). This time electrons are repelled back to C. None crosses the vacuum to A. The reading on the meter is now zero. The valve does not therefore conduct in this case.

Summarizing: A diode radio valve conducts when a battery is connected so that the anode is positive relative to the cathode. It does not conduct when the anode is negative relative to the cathode. C is the emitter of electrons (carriers of current) and A is the collector when the valve conducts.

As described on p. 571, commercial radio valves or cathode ray tubes

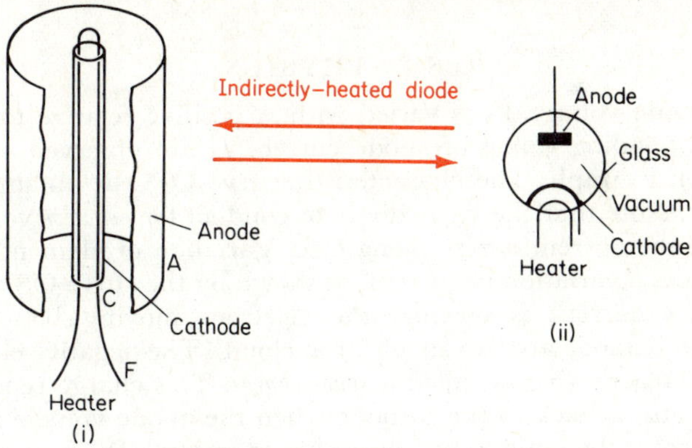

Fig. 32.10 Directly and indirectly heated diode

in television receivers have indirectly-heated cathodes, as in Fig. 32.10, and not directly heated cathodes.

Diode Characteristic

The characteristic action of a diode can be investigated with a TELTRON type diode and the circuit shown in Fig. 32.11 (i).

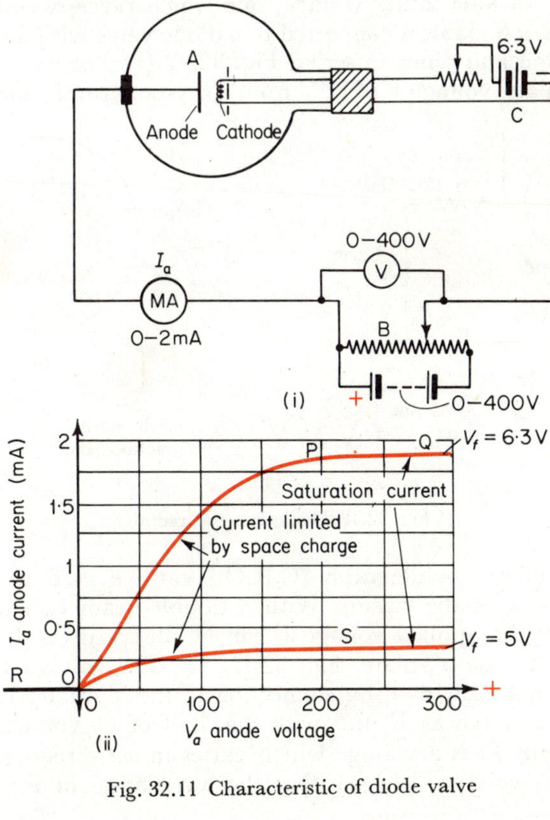

Fig. 32.11 Characteristic of diode valve

The anode voltage V_a is varied with A positive relative to C, and the corresponding values of anode current I_a are observed and then plotted on a graph. The characteristic curve OPQ is obtained, Fig. 32.11 (ii). Note that the valve does not conduct for *negative* voltages of V_a. Thus the current is zero along OR. Variation of filament voltage V_f produces a variation in current, as shown by the curve OS.

When a current is flowing, the electrons moving between the cathode and anode are like an 'electron cloud'. The negative electricity on them creates what is called a *space charge*. This charge repels some of the electrons back to the cathode when the anode voltage is small. The current is then said to be 'space charge limited'. When the positive anode voltage is sufficiently high, however, the attractive force exerted on electrons at the cathode overcomes completely the effect of the space charge. *All* the electrons emitted per second by the cathode now reach the anode. Thus the current reaches a constant or *saturation* value, as shown by the horizontal part of the characteristic curves in Fig. 32.11.

Diode as Rectifier

Suppose an alternating voltage, one which reverses continually in direction (see p. 535), is connected to a diode valve with a resistance R of a few thousand ohms in series, Fig. 32.12 (i). For convenience one may use an a.c. voltage V of 12 V from a ray-box transformer.

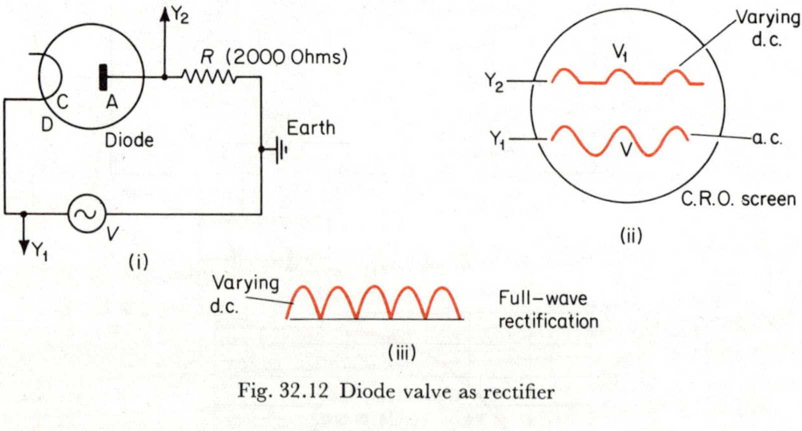

Fig. 32.12 Diode valve as rectifier

A cathode-ray oscillograph (C.R.O.) can be used to investigate what happens in the circuit. With a double-beam oscillograph, the variation of the applied voltage V can be observed on the screen by connection to the Y_1-plate. Fig. 32.12 (ii). The voltage V_1 across R can be compared with V by connection to the Y_2-plate. V_1 is seen to be the same wave as V, but with one half of its voltage waveform missing. Thus V_1 is a voltage which varies in *one* direction, that is, a varying d.c. voltage. We say that the alternating or a.c. voltage V

is 'rectified' by the diode valve. The result is called *half-wave rectification* because only one half of the wave appears.

The valve acts as a rectifier because it allows current to flow through it only when the anode is positive in potential relation to the cathode. Since the potential is negative on one half of a cycle, this half does not appear in the output.

To obtain *full-wave rectification*, which gives a smoother d.c. voltage, two diodes must be used. One diode then conducts on the positive half of the cycle and the other on the negative half of the same cycle. The output is shown in Fig. 32.12 (iii).

RADIO RECEIVERS · JUNCTION DIODE · TRANSISTOR

Modulated Wave and Detection

When a person speaks into a microphone, varying electric currents or oscillations are produced in a range of frequency from about 20 to 16 000 Hz. They are called audio-frequency (A.F.) oscillations. At the transmitting station, radio waves are used as carriers of the sound

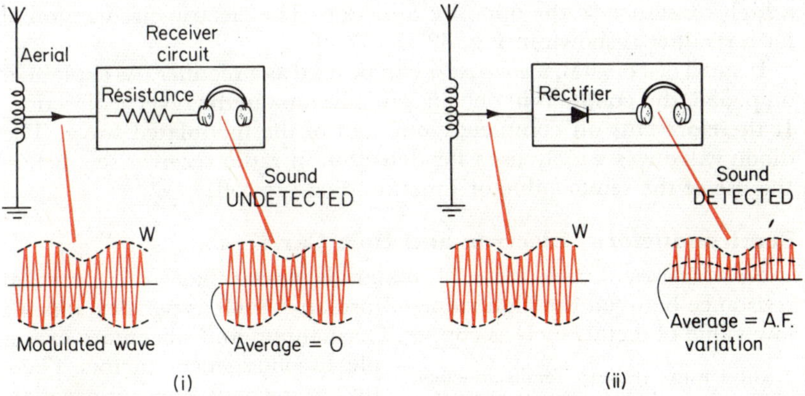

Fig. 32.13 Modulated wave and rectifier

wave. Radio waves have much higher frequencies than sound waves, such as 1 million Hz (1 MHz), and they are said to be 'modulated' by the audio-frequency. One form of modulated radio wave is shown by W in Fig. 32.13 (i). The amplitudes or *peaks* of the wave vary at the audio-frequency carried.

When the modulated R.F. wave arrives at the aerial of a radio receiver, a small voltage of exactly the same wave form is induced and passed to the electrical circuit of the receiver, as shown diagramatically.

If the circuit contained only a resistance, the varying current flowing would have exactly the same wave form as the induced voltage. This is due to the fact that a resistance wire conducts equally well in either direction. The average current is hence zero, Fig. 32.13 (i). The sound-intelligence or message carried by the modulated wave is then *not* detected by the circuit.

In the early days of radio reception the need for an efficient *rectifier* was recognized. A rectifier is a component which has a low resistance in one direction and a high resistance in the reverse direction. Thus when a modulated voltage is connected to a circuit containing a rectifier, current would flow when the voltage was in one direction, say corresponding to the upper half of the modulated curve, and hardly at all in the reverse direction. The resulting current is shown in Fig. 32.13 (ii). Its variations are now practically all in one direction. Thus the *average* value, as shown, follows the peaks of the modulated voltage. This is the audio-frequency (A.F.) variation carried by the wave. Hence earphones in the circuit can now detect the sound.

Crystal and Diode Valve

An early rectifier used for detection was a piece of carborundum crystal with a steel point pressing against it. The junction between the crystal and the point had a low resistance from the crystal to steel but a high resistance in the opposite direction. The electric circuit symbol for a rectifier is shown in Fig. 32.13 (ii).

Instead of a crystal, a *diode valve* can be used as a rectifier. As explained on p. 558, this conducts in one direction but not in the reverse direction. It therefore cuts off completely one half of the modulated wave. The diode valve was widely used for detection in radio receiver sets before the use of the semiconductor junction diode (p. 561).

Semiconductors · Electron and Hole Carriers

Semiconductors are a class of materials which have an electrical resistance between the high value of insulators such as perspex and the low value of metals such as copper. Germanium and silicon are examples of solid semiconductors. These two semiconductors are widely used in the semiconductor industry, which is so prominent today.

Plate 32(D) Light-sensitive resistors, semiconductors, falling from 10 megohms (dark) to 100 ohms (bright)—used to trigger electric circuits in computers.

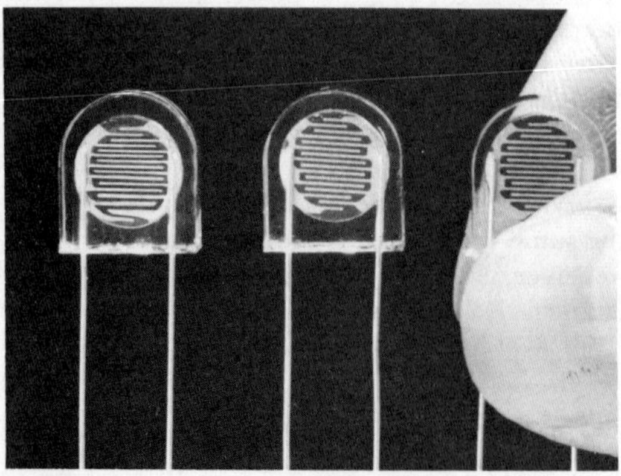

When a battery is connected to a pure semiconductor, a small current flows. The current is carried by two types of carriers, in the same way as current is carried by two types of carriers, negative and positive ions, in electrolytes (see p. 412). One carrier is a free electron, which, it will be remembered, carries negative electricity. In the case of a metal, the free electron leaves behind an atom which is positively charged, or a positive ion, and this ion has no effect on other ions or atoms round it. In the case of a semiconductor, however, the positive ion left behind attracts an electron from a neighbouring neutral atom X, Fig. 32.14 (i). This leaves X with a *positive* charge equal to that on the electron, as shown. X then attracts an electron from a neighbouring atom Y, leaving Y with a positive charge. And so on. *Thus a positive charge drifts through the semiconductor when a battery is connected to it.*

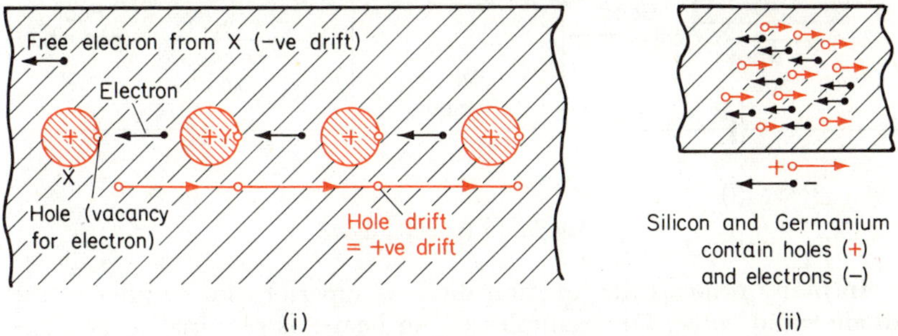

Fig. 32.14 Semiconductor—electron and hole charge carriers

Because the movement of an electron from an atom leaves a vacancy or 'hole' in its electronic structure, the movement of positive charge is described as the movement of a *hole*. Thus in a semiconductor, the carriers of current are *free electrons* (negative charges) *and holes* (positive electricity). Fig. 32.14 (ii). In metals the carriers of current are only free electrons. The resistance of a semiconductor is sensitive to light. See Plate 32D.

N- and P-type Semiconductors

Pure semiconductors have equal numbers of electrons and holes. These are relatively few in number. If a great majority of holes or positive charges are required, the element is 'doped'. A tiny amount of a particular different element is added. The impure semiconductor is now called a *p-type semiconductor* ('p' represents 'positive'). If a great majority of electrons or negative charges are required, a different impurity is added to the pure semiconductor. A *n-type semiconductor* is now obtained ('n' represents 'negative'). P- and n-semiconductors are widely used in industry.

Semiconductor Junction Diode

A special industrial melting process can produce an alloy with p- and n-semiconductors in contact. The result is represented diagrammatically in Fig. 32.15. Their junction is called a *p–n junction*. When a low-voltage battery B is joined with its positive pole to the p-terminal and its negative pole to the n-terminal, the p–n junction conducts well, Fig. 32.15 (i). When the battery terminals are reversed, so that its *negative* pole is joined to the p-terminal and the *positive* pole to the n-terminal, the p–n junction conducts only very slightly, Fig. 32.15 (ii). The *junction diode*, as it is known, is thus a *rectifier*.

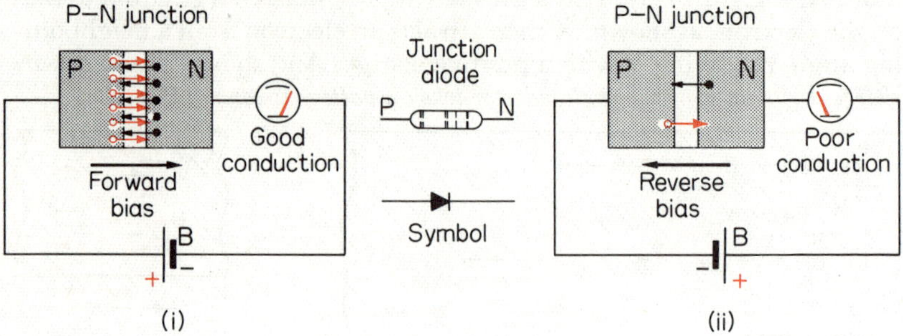

Fig. 32.15 Junction diode

In many respects the junction diode is superior as a rectifier to the diode radio valve. For example: (i) no heater is required to produce the current carriers—they are already there; (ii) it is more robust—it is less liable to break; (iii) it is much smaller; (iv) it is cheaper to manufacture in large numbers; (v) it only needs a battery of a few volts to operate it in a radio receiver, where it is used as a detector of the incoming modulated radio waves.

Fig. 32.16 shows a junction diode, type OA 60, with a low-voltage battery connected and a milliammeter in series. When the positive pole of the battery is joined to the p-side of the diode, the diode is said to be 'forward-biased'. It now conducts well, Fig. 32.16 (i). When the negative pole of the battery is joined to the p-side, the diode is said to be 'reverse-biased'. Now it conducts only slightly, Fig. 32.16 (ii).

Summarizing. The p–n junction diode is a semiconductor device which acts as a rectifier. It conducts well when a battery is connected with its positive pole to the p- and its negative pole to the n-semiconductor. This is because the battery now urges the large number of positive charges in the p-semiconductor and the large number of negative charges in the n-semiconductor across the p–n junction. This does not happen when the battery terminals are reversed.

Transistor

The junction diode can only rectify. In 1948 two American scientists, Bardeen and Brattain, found how to make a semiconductor *amplifier* of current. They called it a *transistor*.

Basically, a transistor has three semiconductor layers. Fig. 32.17 (ii) shows diagrammatically two outer p-semiconductors with an extremely thin n-semiconductor sandwiched between them. This is called a

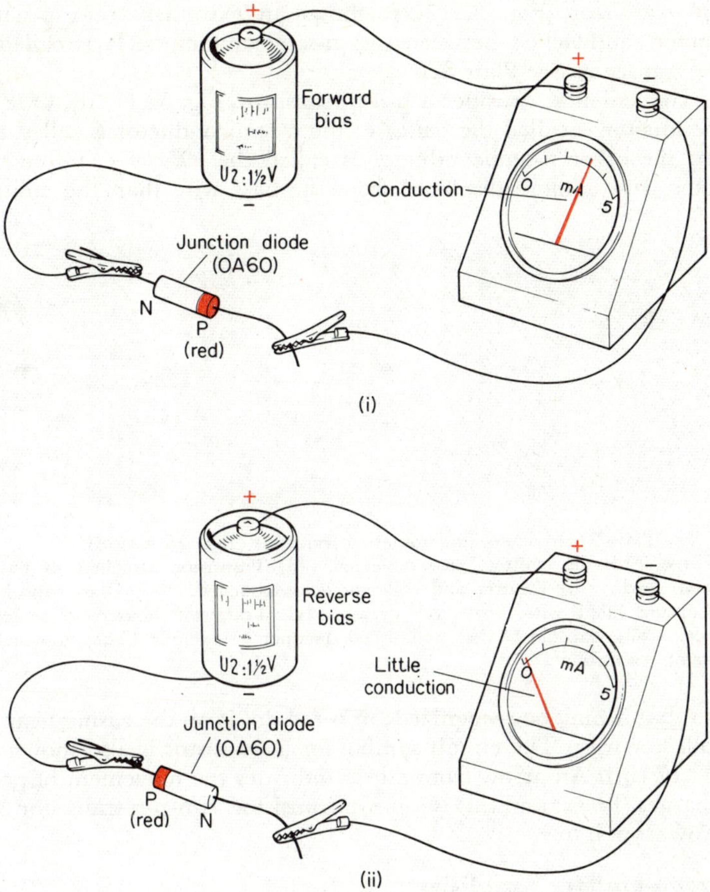

Fig. 32.16 Junction diode and battery

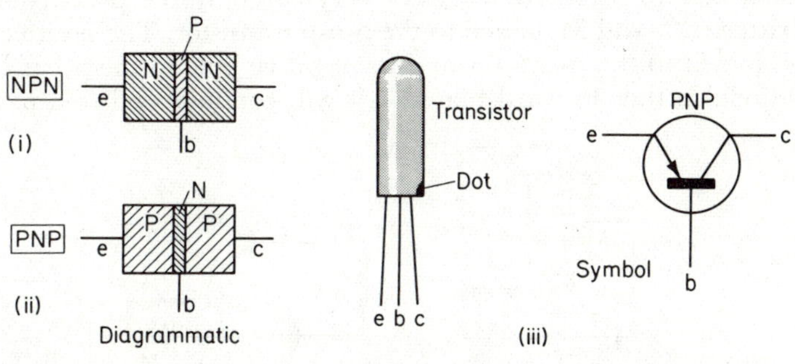

Fig. 32.17 Transistors

'p-n-p' transistor. Fig. 32.17 (i) shows an extremely thin p-semiconductor sandwiched between two n-semiconductors. It is called a 'n-p-n' transistor. See Plate 32E.

For convenience, consider a p-n-p transistor, Fig. 32.17 (ii). One p-semiconductor is called the *emitter* e; the n-semiconductor is called the *base* b; the other p-semiconductor is called the *collector* c. Often the collector wire is more displaced from the base wire than the emitter

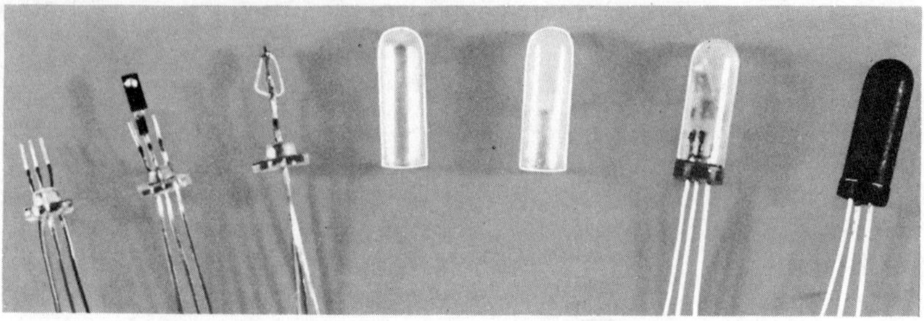

Plate 32(E) Stages in completing transistor (*from left to right*).
(i) Three leads for emitter, base collector. (ii) Transistor attached to base (central) lead. (iii) Emitter and collector leads attached. (iv) Glass capsule. (v) Capsule filled with protective grease. (vi) Transistor housed in sealed capsule. (vii) Capsule coated with black lacquer to exclude light, to which transistor is sensitive.

wire so that it may be recognized; or a red dot is on the casing near to the collector wire. The circuit symbol for a transistor is also shown in Fig. 32.17 (iii). An arrow from e to b indicates the movement of positive charges (holes) and this is a p-n-p transistor. A n-p-n transistor has an arrow from b to e.

Common-emitter Amplifier

The most common way of using a transistor as a current amplifier is shown in Fig. 32.18 (i). Observe very carefully the polarity of the two batteries, L and M, joined to the p-n-p transistor. The positive pole of L is joined to the p-emitter and its negative pole to the n-base. The p–n 'diode' is thus forward biased—it will conduct well (see p. 562).

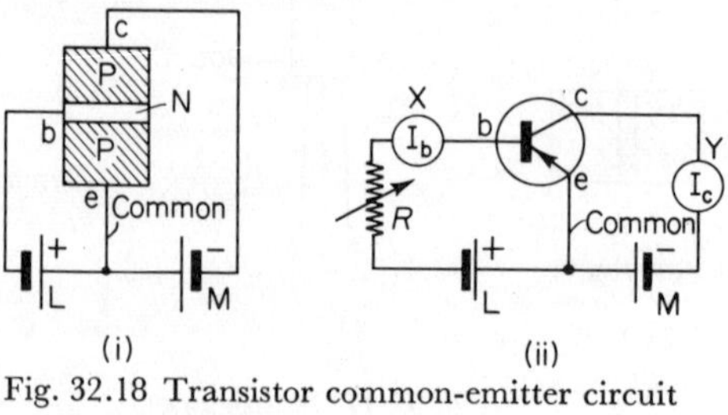

Fig. 32.18 Transistor common-emitter circuit

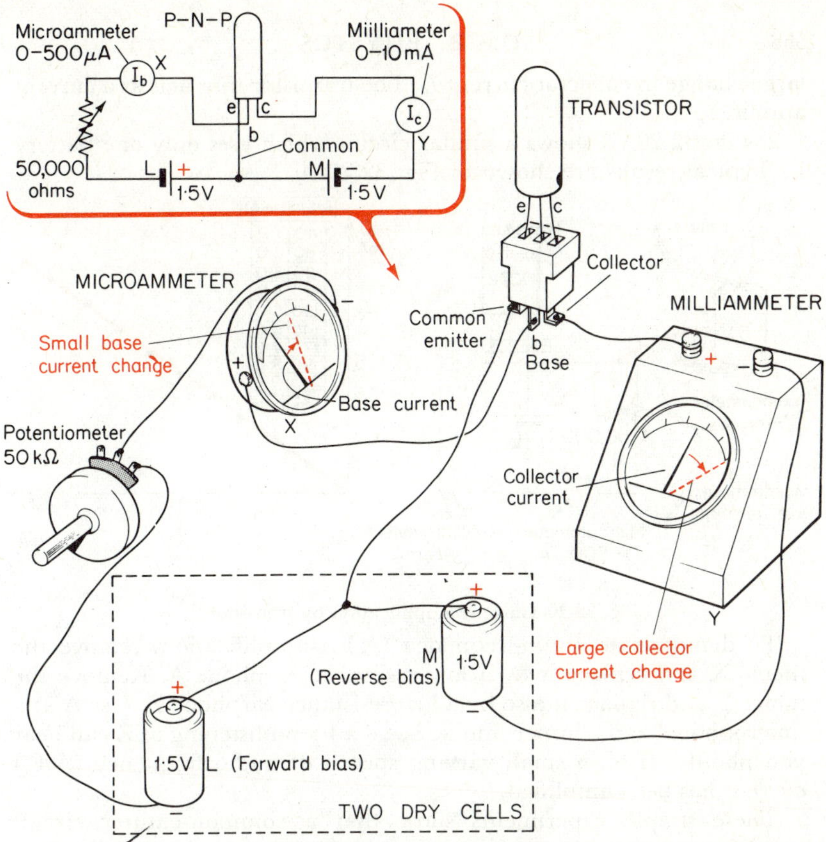

Fig. 32.19 Transistor circuit

On the other hand, the *negative* pole of the battery M is joined to the p-collector and its positive pole to the n-base. This p–n 'diode' is therefore *reverse-biased* (see p. 562). If, by accident, it is forward-biased, the transistor would be ruined. Always remember to reverse-bias the collector-base.

Fig. 32.18 (i) shows that the emitter lead is common to the base and collector circuits. The arrangement is therefore called a *common-emitter* amplifier. Fig. 32.18 (ii) shows the same circuit, this time with meters X and Y to record the base current I_b and the collector current I_c, and a rheostat R for varying the base current. Varying R will alter the base current I_b, as we shall see shortly, and we can then see what happens to the collector current I_c.

Current Amplification

1. Connect up the circuit shown in Fig. 32.19, using a p-n-p transistor. The base current I_b can be altered by changing the setting of the potentiometer. Note that a small change in base current produces a

large change in collector current I_c. The transistor thus acts as a current amplifier.

2. Fig. 32.20 (i) shows a similar circuit which uses only one battery L. Typical results are shown in Fig. 32.20 (ii).

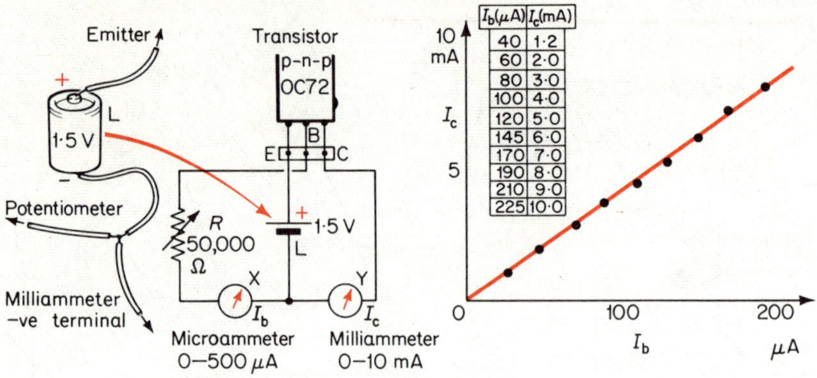

I_b(μA)	I_c(mA)
40	1·2
60	2·0
80	3·0
100	4·0
120	5·0
145	6·0
170	7·0
190	8·0
210	9·0
225	10·0

(i) (ii)

Fig. 32.20 Current amplification by transistor

To demonstrate audio-frequency (A.F.) amplification, remove the meter X and replace it by a low resistance earphone A. Remove the meter Y and replace it also by a low resistance earphone Z. Use A as a 'microphone' and whisper into it. See if a friend listening at Z can hear you plainly. If so, a small varying speech or audio frequency (A.F.) current has been amplified.

These simple experiments show that a common-emitter circuit amplifies current. On this account the common-emitter circuit is widely used as A.F. amplifiers in transistor radio receivers. The A.F. signal is always applied to the base circuit and the amplified signal is obtained in the collector circuit. If the latter signal is passed to the base circuit of another transistor with a common-emitter arrangement, more amplification is obtained. The strength of the signal thus increases further.

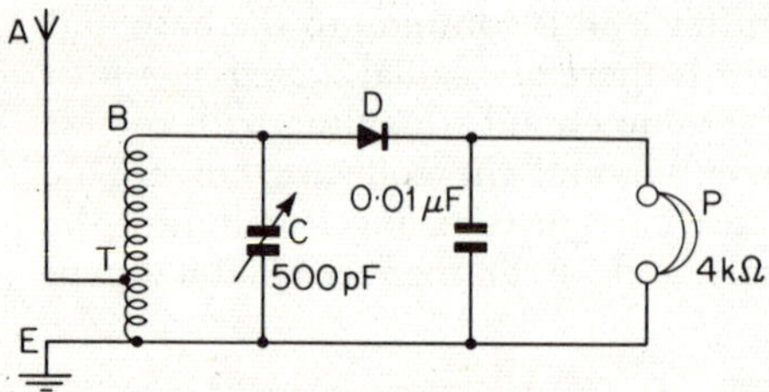

Fig. 32.21 Simple receiver

Simple Receiver

A very simple receiver is shown diagrammatically in Fig. 32.21. The layout on a board is shown in Fig. 32.22.

B is a small coil of about 100 insulated turns of very thin wire (e.g. standard wire gauge (s.w.g.) 34)—such a suitable receiver coil can be purchased. C is a variable tuning capacitor of maximum capacitance 0·0005 μF. D is a detector such as a junction diode OA 60 or a crystal. P are high resistance phones, such as 2000 Ω (2kΩ) per earpiece.

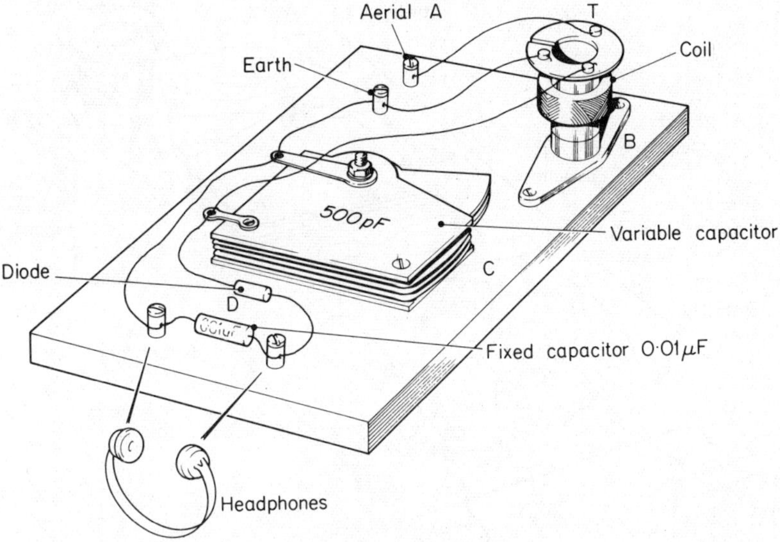

Fig. 32.22 Receiver circuit

The aerial wire A is as high as possible and is joined to the coil at T or at B. The lower end of the coil can be earthed, E, if required. By varying the tuning capacitor C, local broadcasting stations can be picked up.

One-transistor Receiver

As already explained, the transistor can be used as an amplifier to increase the strength of the audio-frequency signals detected.

Fig. 32.23 shows a common-emitter transistor amplifier, which can be connected to a simple junction diode receiver. The varying base

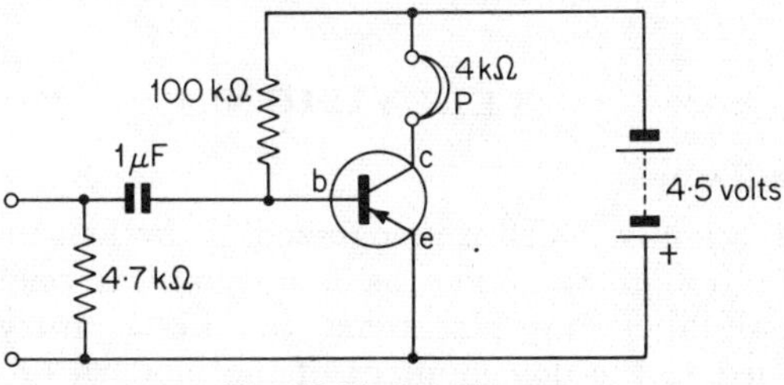

Fig. 32.23 Amplifier

currents (A.F. signal) are amplified and heard in earphones P in the collector circuit. Note carefully that with a p-n-p transistor, the positive pole of the battery is joined to e and the negative pole to the collector side c. The layout on a board is shown in Fig. 32.24.

The reader interested in electronic circuits using transistors is

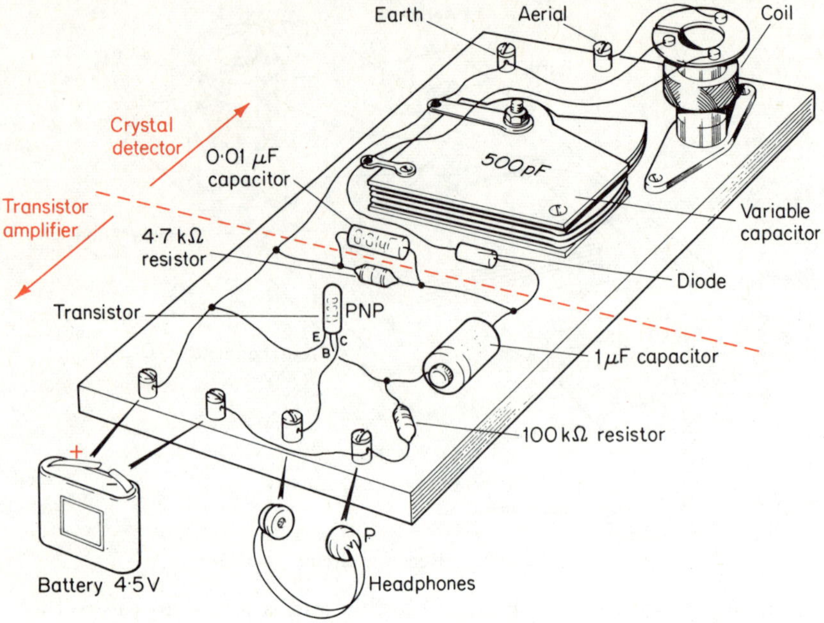

Fig. 32.24 Detector and amplifier

recommended to the RADIONIC range of electronic kits. Many different circuits are easily assembled from all the components supplied—transistors, diodes, resistors, capacitors, coils, for example—and no soldering iron or mains voltage are needed, only one or two 4·5 V batteries. Among numerous circuits are those for making transistor radio receivers and a burglar alarm. RADIONIC PRODUCTS LTD have many educational electronic and radio circuits which can be assembled by pupils.

TELEVISION

TV Camera Tube

The British scientist Baird is recognized as the first man to transmit pictures. The system he used was a mechanical one and had few practical possibilities but researches in this country, notably by Schoenberg, led to the development of the modern or electronic TV camera tube.

One form of a modern TV camera is shown in Fig. 32.25. It utilizes the *photo-electric effect*. This is the name given to the emission of electrons from a metal surface when it is illuminated by light, as in the photo-electric cell (p. 397). The surface is called 'photo-sensitive'. Some metals are sensitive to all the colours in the visible spectrum. Others are

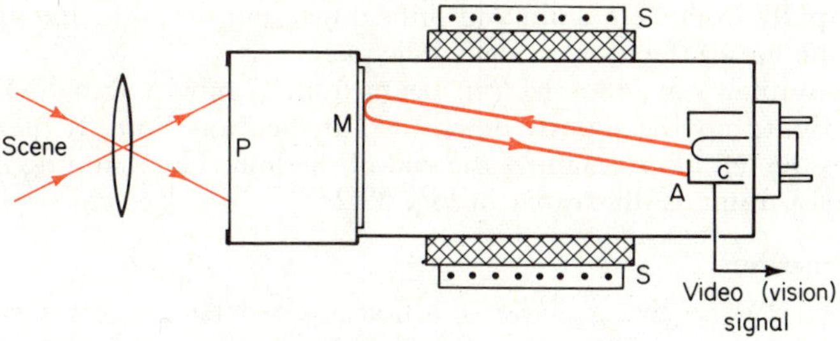

Fig. 32.25 Television camera

sensitive only to particular colours. And others may be sensitive only to ultra-violet (invisible) light.

When a TV camera tube is pointed at a particular scene on a stage, for example, the light is focused by the camera lens on a very thin layer of photo-sensitive material P, Fig. 32.25. If the light from a bright part of the scene, such as the light from a white dress, falls on the area in the middle of P, this part of P emits a large number of electrons. If the light from a dark suit on the stage falls on the area near the corner of P, this part of P emits a relatively few number of electrons. In this way, the whole surface of P emits electrons from every part in proportion to the light intensity of the scene televised. These electrons are incident on another photo-sensitive surface M in front of P. They produce on M an 'electrical image' of the scene televised. Plate 32F shows a TV camera tube.

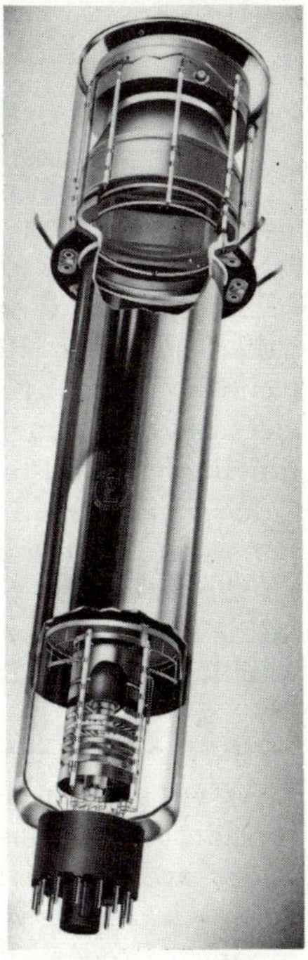

Plate 32(F) Television camera tube—image orthicon type.

Scanning

The vision signal, called the *video signal*, is picked up by means of an electron beam from a hot cathode C. This beam 'scans' the electrical image on M. Scanning is a process similar to the way one reads a page in a book. The eye scans a line on the page from left to right, then moves

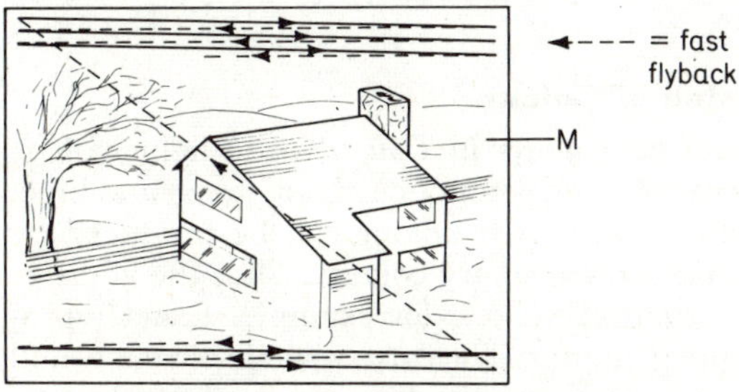

Fig. 32.26 Line scanning of picture

very rapidly to the left again and shifts down slightly to the line below, and so on for all the lines on the whole page.

In a similar way, the electron beam from C moves across M from left to right, moving slightly downward at the same time. It then flies back to the left after reaching the end of the line. The scanning movement of a frame is illustrated in Fig. 32.26.

TV Receiver

At the TV receiving aerial in a house, a reverse process occurs to what has previously been described. This is illustrated in Fig. 32.27. The electrical components inside the TV receiver have to amplify the weak video signal after extracting it. This is then passed to the electron beam inside, emitted by a hot cathode. The sound signal must also be amplified after extraction. Further, line and frame scanning must be provided together with synchronisation of sound and picture.

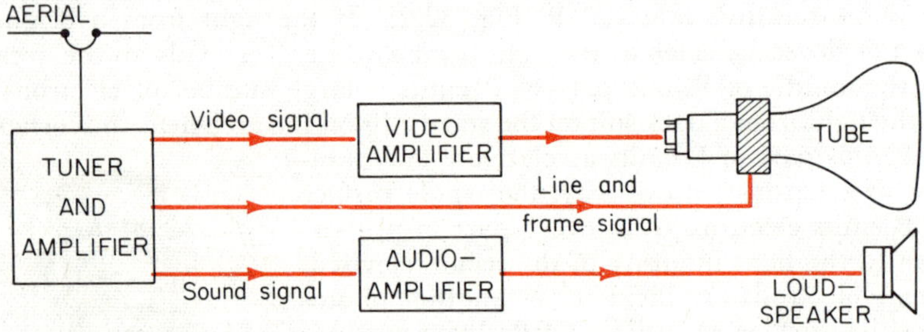

Fig. 32.27 Television receiver system

The interior face or screen of the TV tube is coated with materials called *phosphors*. Phosphors glow for a short time when high-energy electron beams are incident on them. As illustrated in Fig. 32.26, the electron beam in the tube scans the whole of the screen repeatedly, moving from left to right and then rapidly down and across again. The video signal passed to the beam controls the number of electrons emitted per second by the beam. Thus light and shade, or a picture, is built up on the screen by the moving beam. Plate 32G shows the components inside a TV receiver. TV programmes may now be beamed all over the world. See Plate 32H.

Colour TV · Transmission of Colour

As we saw in the section on colours in *Optics*, white light can be considered to consist of three coloured components, red, green and blue. These are called the *primary colours*. Any colour can be produced by adding in the right proportions the primary colours. Thus the additive mixing of red and green produces yellow, for example. Exact reproduction of a colour is a complex matter. The correct shade of yellow and its brightness, for instance, would be required in colour television.

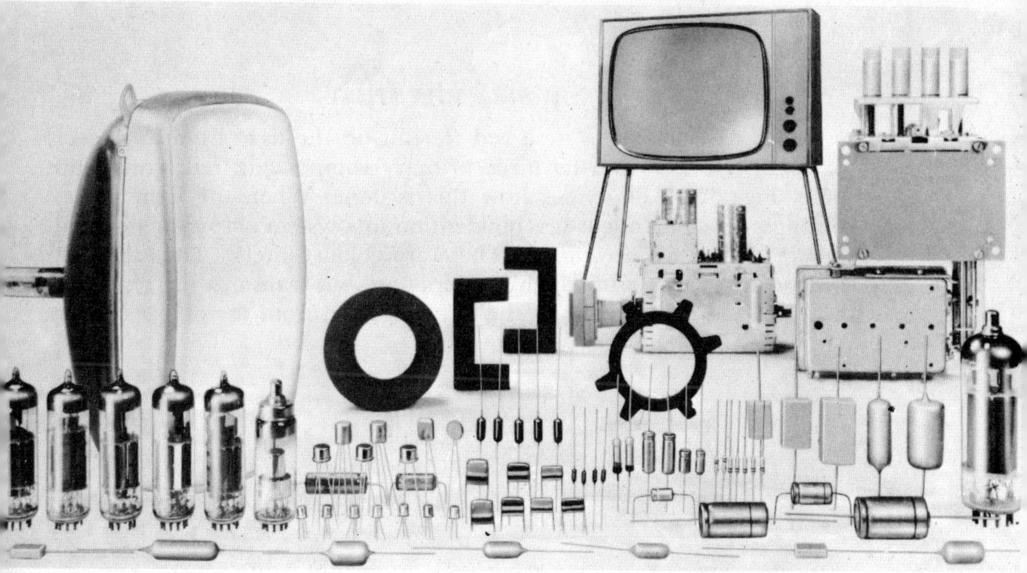

late 32(G) TV receiver components, showing cathode ray tube (left rear), valves (left front), transistors eft centre front), deflection magnets (centre rear), resistors, and other components.

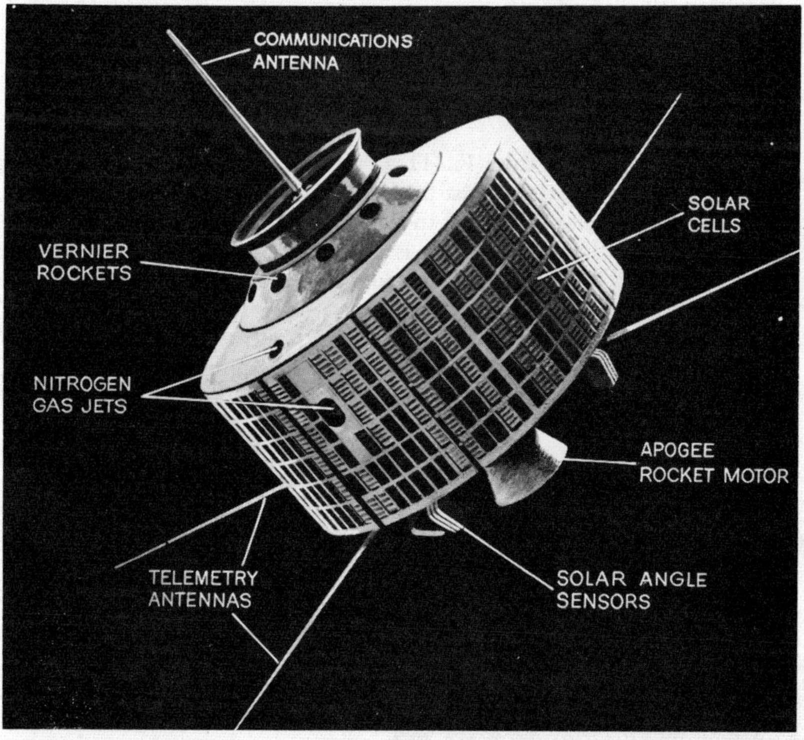

Plate 32(H) Communications satellite SYNCOM, for beaming television from one part of the world to another.

A *TV colour camera* is designed to split up the light from an object or scene televised into its three primary components, red, green and blue. Fig. 32.28 illustrates how this is done. When the light passes through the camera lens it is incident on to a system of specially-coated mirrors called *dichroic mirrors*. These are colour 'filters'. Thus the first mirror M reflects light which is mainly red but transmits the rest. The reflected red components of the light received from the object is then

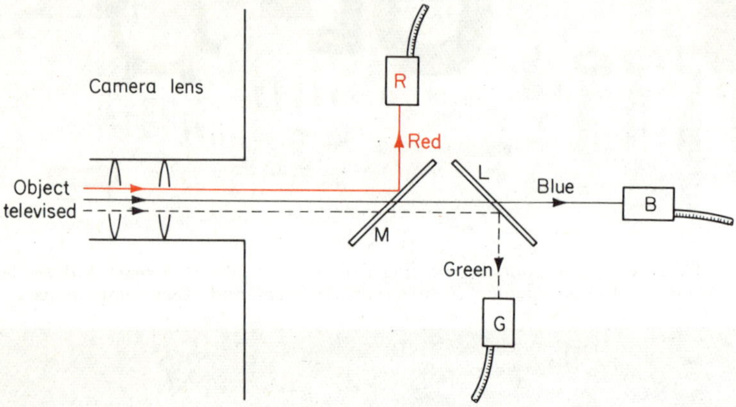

Fig. 32.28 Colour TV camera

detected by a camera tube R. This contains a plate whose surface is sensitive mainly to red, so that a 'red' video (vision) voltage or signal is obtained. The rest of the light incident on M falls on another dichroic mirror L. This reflects light which is predominantly green but transmits the remainder. Thus the green component is reflected and it is detected by a camera tube G. The blue component is transmitted and detected by the tube B. Thus a 'green' video signal and a 'blue' video signal are produced. The resulting three-colour video signal is then processed by complex electronic circuits and finally radiated from the TV transmitter aerial.

Plate 32(1) Shadow mask of colour TV receiver tube, showing inspection of holes highly magnified.

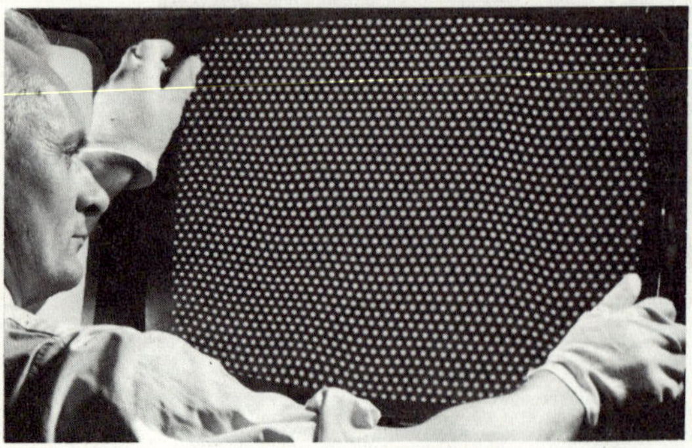

TV Colour Receiver

TV colour receivers detect and amplify the colour video signal sent out by the transmitter. Special electronic circuits inside them then separate out the three colour signals and they are passed to three electron 'guns' in the neck of the television tube, as discussed shortly.

The other end of the tube,

where the colour picture is seen, has its inner face covered with an array of phosphor dots, as illustrated in Fig. 32.29. One type of phosphor glows red when an electron beam is incident on it. Another type of phosphor glows green. A third type glows blue. Nearly half a million dots are used for each of the three colours. The phosphor dots are

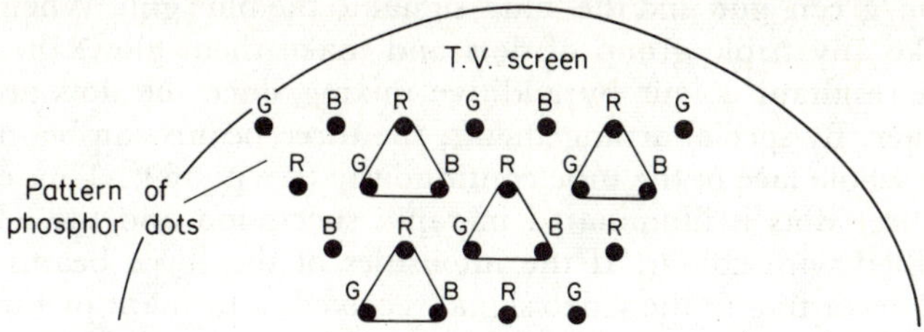

Fig. 32.29 Colour TV screen

arranged in triple groups, red, green and blue, R, G, B, as shown. A metal screen or *shadow mask* is placed a short distance from the phosphor array. This mask has very small holes at regular intervals, one hole opposite the centre of each triple group of dots. See Plate 32I.

When the receiver is in operation, any group of three dots can be made to glow by incident electron beams, obtained from three electron guns in the neck of the tube, Fig. 32.30. These are aimed very accur-

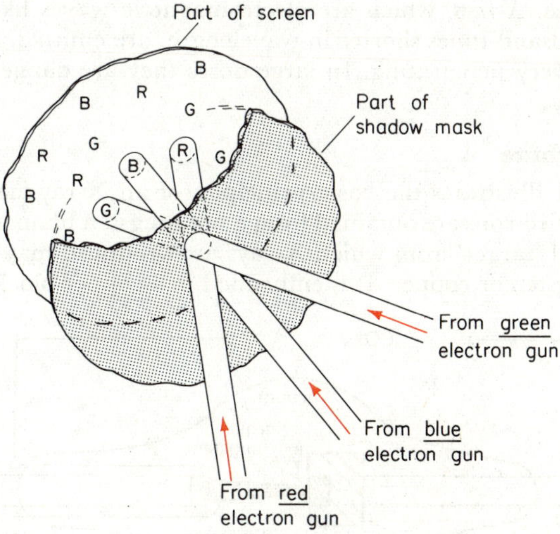

Fig. 32.30 Producing colours on screen

ately at the centre of a hole in the shadow mask as shown, so that one beam is incident on the red phosphor dot of a triple group, a second beam is incident on the green dot, and the third is incident on the blue dot. In this case the beam from each gun will always produce the same colour when incident on any hole of the shadow mask. Thus, in effect, we have a 'Red', 'Green' and 'Blue' gun.

The three colour video signals from the transmitter are passed to one of the three guns—the 'red' signal to the 'red' gun, the 'green' signal to the 'green' gun and the 'blue' signal to the blue gun. When the beams strike any triple group of dots and make them glow, the eye detects the resultant colour by additive mixing since the dots are so close together. By special arrangements, the three beams can be made to scan the whole face of the tube continuously (see p. 569). Thus each group of three dots is illuminated in rapid succession and the whole screen is filled with colour. If the intensities of the three beams are also varied according to the video signal received, a brilliant picture of the original object or scene televised can be faithfully produced.

X-RAYS

Nature of X-rays

The television camera utilizes the photo-electric effect. As explained previously, light falls on a photo-sensitive metal surface inside it and the energy in the light liberates some electrons from the atoms in the surface.

A reverse phenomenon occurs when high-speed electrons bombard a metal surface. *X-rays*, which are electromagnetic waves like light but about a thousand times shorter in wavelength, are emitted. See p. 273. X-rays are very penetrating. In large doses they are dangerous to the human body.

X-ray Machine

Fig. 32.31 illustrates the basic principles of an X-ray machine. The high-speed electrons are obtained from a hot tungsten filament F.

The metal 'target' from which X-rays are produced may be a metal such as tungsten or copper. It is embedded in a copper block A directly

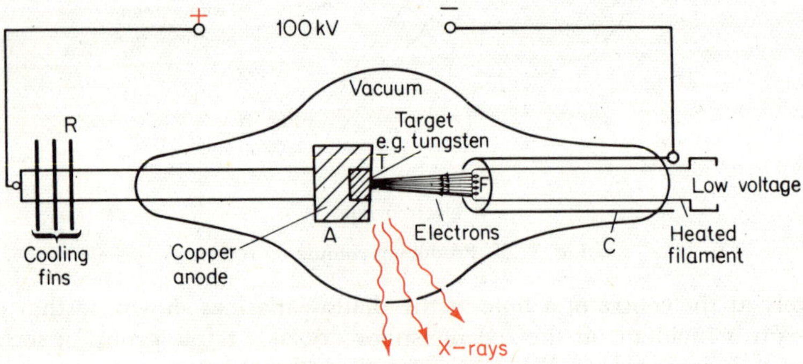

Fig. 32.31 X-ray tube

opposite F. All the apparatus is contained in a glass vessel from which the air is completely pumped out, leaving a vacuum, so that the electrons from F are not slowed down in their journey to the target. A metal cylinder C helps to focus the electrons on the target.

By stepping-up the voltage from the mains, the anode A can be kept at a high positive voltage such as 100 000 V (100 kV) or more relative to the filament. This accelerates the electrons to very high speeds. As explained previously, X-rays are produced from some target atoms after the highly-energetic electrons crash into them. A considerable amount of heat is also produced in the metal target and the surrounding metal A. Metal 'fins' R of large surface area help to cool the metal by passing heat to the surroundings. In X-ray tubes using higher voltages, water is used for cooling purposes.

With a high voltage across the X-ray tube, more penetrating or 'harder' X-rays are produced. A low voltage produces less-penetrating or 'soft' X-rays.

Nowadays, most hospitals are equipped with X-ray machines. A fracture of a bone can easily be detected from a radiograph of the limb concerned, the radiograph being the 'picture' obtained when X-rays are incident through the limb on to a photographic plate, Fig. 32.32.

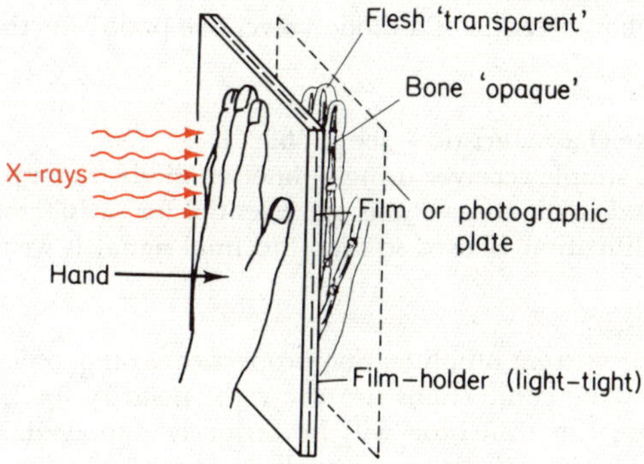

Fig. 32.32 X-ray photograph

X-ray machines are also used industrially for detecting flaws and defects in steel plates that are invisible to the eye; X-rays pass more easily through the flaws than through the rest of the material.

SUMMARY

1. Electrons (negative charges) are produced by hot cathodes. They may be deflected by magnetic and electric fields.

2. Cathode ray oscillograph—has a cathode ray tube with controls for brightness, focus, time-base (X-plates). Signal applied to Y-plates.

3. Radio diode valve—anode and cathode in vacuum in a glass bottle. Changes a.c. to d.c. (rectifies).

4. Radio waves (high frequencies) are modulated to carry sound (audio) frequencies.

5. Semiconductors, e.g. silicon or germanium, have current carriers of electrons (−) and holes (+). P-types have an excess of holes. N-types have an excess of electrons.

6. Junction diode—alloy of p- and n-type semiconductors whose junction acts as a rectifier.

7. Transistor—a p-n-p transistor has a p-emitter, n-base, p-collector. Acts as a current amplifier.

8. TV camera has a photosensitive surface—it emits electrons when illuminated. TV receiver produces light when electrons are incident on fluorescent screen.

9. Colour TV receiver—screen has phosphor 'dots' sensitive to red R, green G, blue B. Three electron beams receive R, G, and B signals from distant transmitter and scan the screen, producing colour.

10. X-rays are electromagnetic waves of very short wavelength such as 10^{-8} cm. They are emitted when fast-moving electrons are incident on tungsten or copper, for example. X-rays are penetrating rays.

PRACTICAL

1. Diode Valve

Investigate the characteristic of a diode valve. See p. 557 for the circuit and method.

2. Junction diode

(i) Investigate the characteristic—see p. 563.

(ii) Make up the simple receiver using a junction diode, as on p. 566. A long high aerial and good earth connections are essential for satisfactory reception. Note that no amplification is used so that the final signal is weak. Use high-resistance phones.

3. Transistor

(i) Investigate the current amplification properties as on p. 565. Take care to ensure that the battery connections are the right polarity for the particular transistor, otherwise the transistor will be seriously damaged. See whether speech can be amplified by placing a microphone in the base circuit and listening with an earpiece connected in the collector circuit. See p. 566.

4. Transistor receiver

Make up the receiver circuit shown on p. 567. Make sure that the battery poles are connected the right way round, that all the connections are firm, and that a good aerial and earth are used. High resistance phones are necessary.

EXERCISE 32 · ANSWERS, p. 617

1. What name is given to the kind of radio valve in the circuit shown in Fig. 32A? Name the parts of the valve: P, Q, R. (*Mx.*)

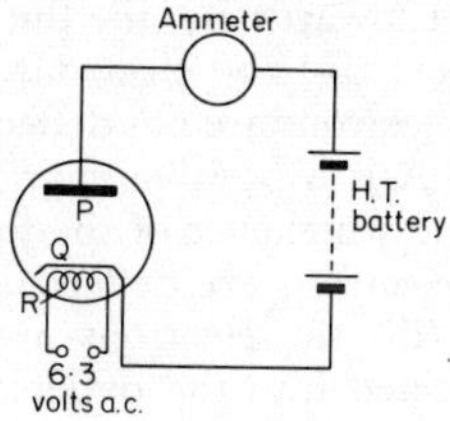

Fig. 32A

2. The tube shown in Fig. 32B is highly evacuated. When the high voltage is applied as shown. (*a*) what particles will carry electricity between A and B; (*b*) what, other than heat, is produced when these particles strike B? (*L.*)

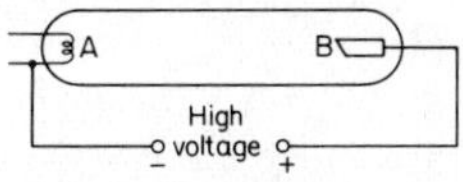

Fig. 32B

3. Fig. 32C shows a simple cathode ray tube. C is the cathode. A is the anode.

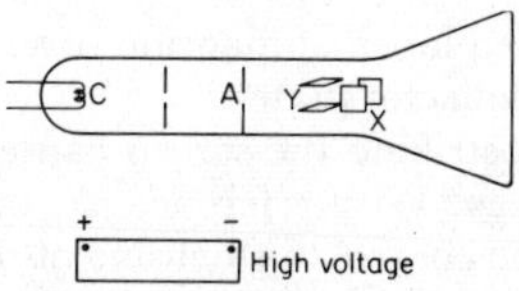

Fig. 32C

(*a*) Show how the high voltage source is connected to the tube.

(*b*) What is the purpose of the plates (i) X (ii) Y. (*L.*)

4. Fig. 32D represents a diode valve.

(*a*) What is represented by A?

(*b*) What is represented by B?

(*c*) Which way will the electrons flow through the valve? (*L.*)

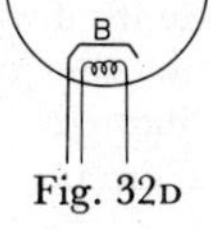

Fig. 32D

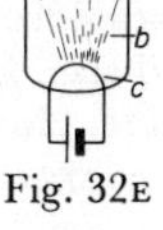

Fig. 32E

5. In Fig. 32E, what are (*a*) . ., (*b*) . ., (*c*) . .? (*Mx.*)

6. State the form of energy needed to free electrons from their atoms in: (i) the cathode of a thermiomic diode, (ii) the sensitive plate of a photo-electric cell. (*Mx.*)

7. (*a*) Name three particles found in the atom: (i) . . (ii) . . (iii) . .

(*b*) How can cathode rays be deflected? (*Mx.*)

8. Fig. 32F shows a beam of electrons passing between two metal plates A and B.

(*a*) If A is a N-pole and B a S-pole underline whichever of the following statements is correct: (i) the electrons are deflected towards A; (ii) the electrons are deflected towards B; (iii) the electrons are deflected out of the paper; (iv) the electrons are deflected into the paper; (v) the electrons are not deflected.

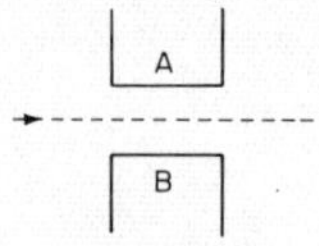

Fig. 32F

(*b*) If A is a positive charge and B is a negative charge underline whichever of the following statements is correct: (i) the electrons are deflected towards A; (ii) the electrons are deflected towards B; (iii) the electrons are deflected out of the paper; (iv) the electrons are deflected into the paper; (v) the electrons are not deflected. (*L.*)

9. How can electrons be made to stream across a space from one metal object to another? Describe the construction of the diode valve and show graphically, using the axes shown in Fig. 32G, how the anode current varies with the anode voltage. (*W.Md.*)

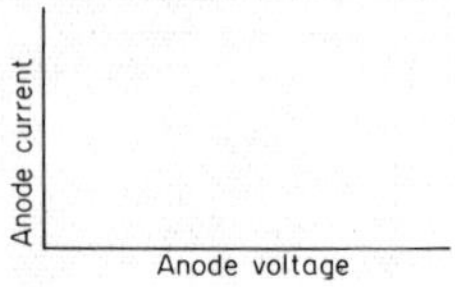

Fig. 32G

10. (*a*) Draw a simplified labelled diagram of a cathode-ray tube having two anodes and electrostatic deflector plates.

(*b*) The electron beam striking the screen causes the coating to fluoresce so that a patch of light is seen. With reference to your diagram where necessary explain: (i) how would you control the focusing of the beam; (ii) how you would control the brilliance of the light patch; (iii) why the application of the time base causes a line to be seen on the screen. (The control and time base circuits are not required.)

(*c*) Fig. 32H shows the screen of a simple radar oscilloscope when a pulse is emitted and its echo received. The time base runs at 16 kilocycles per second.

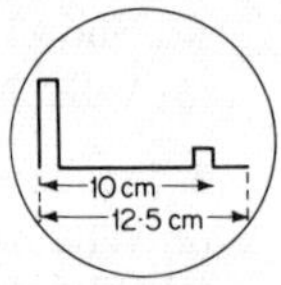

Fig. 32H

Assuming the flyback time is zero: (i) what time interval is represented by the whole time base line; (ii) what time interval separates the blips; (iii) how far away in kilometres is the object detected by the radar, assuming the velocity of radio waves to be 3×10^8 metres per second? (*E.A.*)

11. You are provided with two diode valves the filaments of which are identical in shape and size. One is made of tungsten and the other tungsten coated with barium oxide. How would you determine which filament gave the greater emission when connected to a 2 V supply? Draw a circuit diagram of the arrangement you would use. (*Mx.*)

12. A spot of light is formed on the screen of a cathode-ray tube when electrons strike it. Explain where these electrons come from and how the path of these electrons can be altered so that the spot of light will trace out a pattern or picture. (*M.*)

13. (*a*) Give a large, clearly labelled diagram to show the structure of the kind of cathode-ray tube used in oscilloscopes.

(*b*) Say what the cathode-ray beam consists of, and explain how it is produced.

(*c*) Explain: (i) how a visible spot appears on the screen at the end of the tube; (ii) how this is deflected horizontally and vertically. (*Mx.*)

14. (*a*) Draw a large diagram (not the circuit symbol) of a *thermionic* diode to show its *structure*. Label all the parts.

(*b*) Assuming that such a diode has its cathode correctly heated, explain what happens when: (i) its anode is raised to a higher positive potential than its cathode; (ii) its anode is made negative with respect to its cathode; (iii) an alternating potential is applied between anode and cathode. (*Mx.*)

15. Draw two diagrams of a thermionic diode: (i) a section to show its construction; (ii) a symbolic figure used to represent the diode in circuit drawings.

Explain, with the aid of diagrams, how the diode acts as an electron valve in the process known as *rectification*. (*Mx.*)

16. (*a*) (i) What are cathode rays?; (ii) how can they be produced? How does a hot filament assist the production of cathode rays?; (iii) draw diagrams to show two methods by which cathode rays may be deflected.

(*b*) Draw a diagram showing the main essentials of a modern cathode-ray tube explaining briefly the function of each part. What everyday object utilizes a cathode-ray tube? (*S.E.*)

17. Fig. 32I represents a type of radio valve. What type of valve is this? Label the various parts lettered A to E. Explain briefly how this valve could be used to amplify a signal? (*M.*)

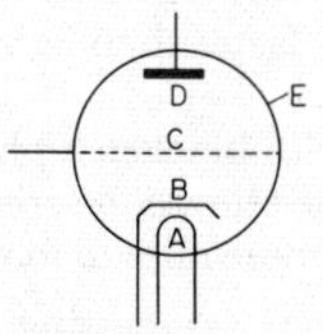

Fig. 32I

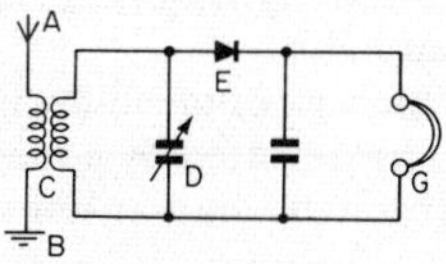

Fig. 32J

18. Complete the key to this crystal detector circuit diagram Fig. 32J: A . ., B . ., C . ., D . ., E . ., G . .(*Mx.*)

19. (*a*) Compare the valve and transistor from the following aspects: (i) the materials used in construction; (ii) the names given to the parts of a transistor corresponding to the cathode, grid and anode of a triode valve; (iii) the difference in their amplification property; (iv) the difference in the applied voltages in use; (v) the difference in power consumption; (vi) the difference in noise.

(*b*) Briefly describe the construction of a 'p-n-p' transistor. (*W.Md.*)

20. Fig. 32K represents a simple radio receiver including one transistor. Various parts are labelled. Explain briefly the particular purpose of each of these parts (*M.*)

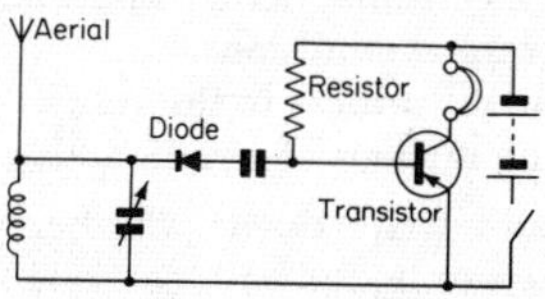

Fig. 32K

21. Explain simply the photo-electric effect and describe how it can be put to use; (i) as a burglar alarm; (ii) in the cinema. (*W.Md.*)

22. Compare the action of the photo-electric cell and the diode valve. (*W.Md.*)

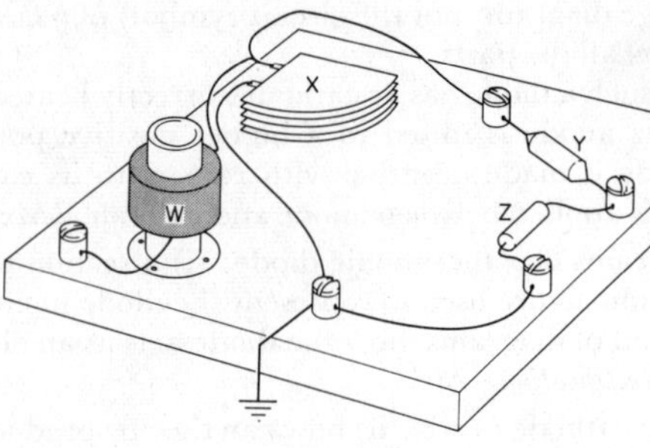

Fig. 32L

23. Fig. 32L shows a radio receiver.

(*a*) Draw a circuit diagram of the receiver. Label each part with the corresponding letter shown on Fig. 32L.

(*b*) Name and explain the function of each of the labelled parts.

(*c*) What else is required to complete this receiver. Where should this additional part be connected? (*E.A.*)

24. X-rays. (i) X-rays travel with a speed: (*a*) much slower than light; (*b*) slower than light; (*c*) the same as that of light; (*d*) faster than light; (*e*) much faster than light.

(ii) Which *one* of the following will X-rays *not* do? (*a*) blacken a photographic plate; (*b*) be deviated by a magnetic field; (*c*) cause a television screen to glow; (*d*) pass through a human hand; (*e*) cause atoms and molecules to ionise. (*N.W.*)

25. Select the best answer. X-rays are formed by: (*a*) passing an electric current through uranium; (*b*) bombarding uranium with mesons; (*c*) bombarding metal targets with high speed electrons; (*d*) radioactive decay of uranium; (*e*) a neuron hitting an electron. (*E.A.*)

26. What are X-rays? Explain the difference between hard and soft rays. What are the principle uses of X-rays in everyday life? (*W.Md.*)

27. Write a short essay on X-rays. Your answer might include some reference to their production, properties and uses. (*M.*)

28. This question is about cathode rays and X-rays. Below are several statements.

(i) They travel in straight lines.
(ii) They carry a negative electrical charge.
(iii) They are a form of electromagnetic radiation.
(iv) They affect photographic emulsions.
(v) They can cause some substances to fluoresce.
(vi) They originate in the nucleus of a radioactive isotope.

Read each one in turn and write down whether the statement is true for cathode rays only, for X-rays only, for both cathode and X-rays, or for neither. (*W.Md.*)

33

RADIOACTIVITY · ATOMIC STRUCTURE · NUCLEAR ENERGY

Becquerel · Rutherford

In the previous chapter we saw that electrons can be liberated from atoms in metals. Since these particles are obtained fairly easily, for example, from a hot cathode or in the photo-electric effect, the electrons are likely to be in the outermost parts of the atom.

The first clues on the heart or nucleus of the atom, and of atomic structure, were provided by a phenomenon discovered by Becquerel in 1896. He placed a uranium compound on a photographic plate covered with lightproof paper, and found to his surprise that, on developing, the plate was fogged. He traced this effect to some unknown radiation coming from the uranium compound. The phenomenon, called *radioactivity*, was investigated in 1897 by a New Zealand scientist, then Ernest Rutherford and later Lord Rutherford.

α- and β-particles and γ-rays

It was soon found that radioactive substances emitted one or more of three kinds of radiations. They were called α-particles, β-particles and γ-rays.

α-particles. These have a mass about the same as a helium atom. They carry a quantity of positive electricity or positive charge. They are shot out of the radioactive substance at high speed, but travel a distance of only several centimetres in air at normal pressure because they collide with many molecules of air. See Plate 33A. α-particles are absorbed by thin paper.

β-particles. These are usually electrons. Compared with α-particles, they are extremely light. They carry a negative charge (see p. 549). They are more penetrating than α-particles and can pass through thin sheets of aluminium.

γ-rays. These are electromagnetic waves of extremely short wavelength, shorter even than X-rays (see p. 273). They are much more penetrating than β-particles. They can pass through thick metal and are stopped only by very thick blocks of lead. γ-rays are dangerous and may cause injury or death if absorbed by the human body from an intense source. Under control, γ-rays are used in medical treatment. Plate 33B.

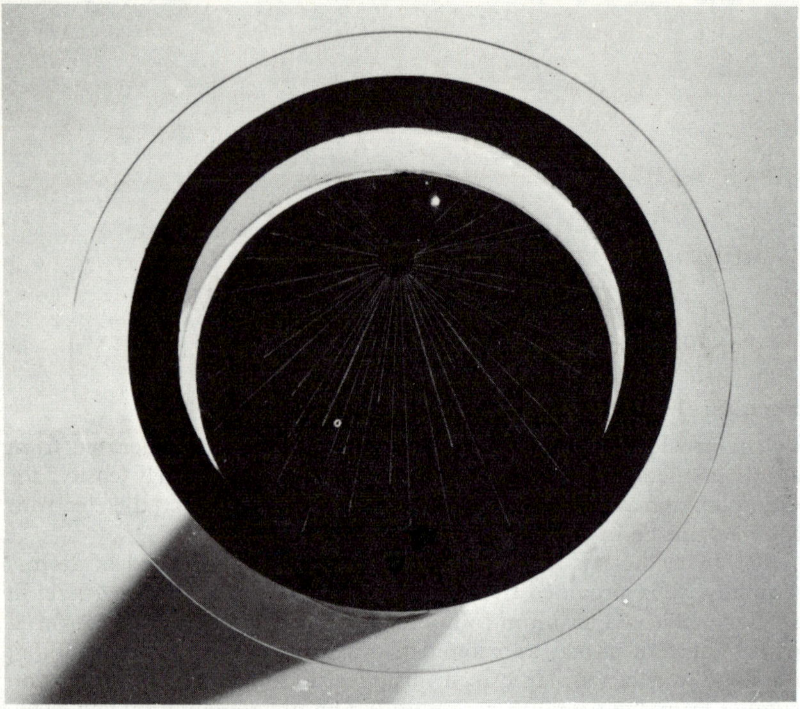

Plate 33(A) Alpha-particle streaks in a cloud chamber, showing long tracks (high energy particles) and short streaks (smaller energy particles).

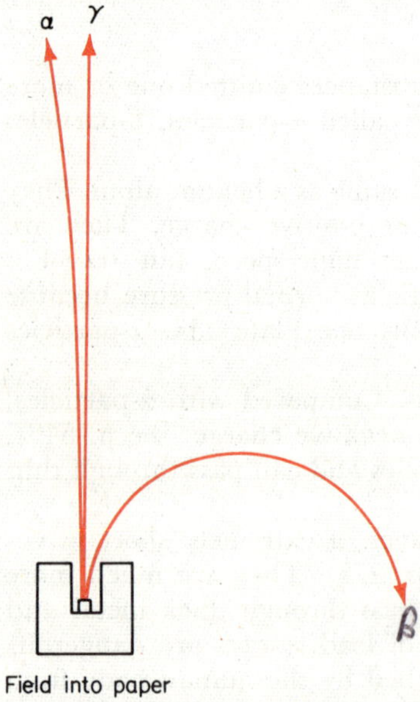

Fig. 33.1 Magnetic field effect on α-, β-particles and γ-rays

Fig. 33.1 shows diagrammatically how differently the α- and β-particles and γ-rays would behave in a powerful magnetic field. The α-particles (positively charged and heavy) would be deflected slightly. The β-particles (negatively charged and very light) would be considerably deflected. The γ-rays (electromagnetic waves) would be unaffected.

It is now known that these radiations come from the break-up of the central core or *nucleus* of the uranium atom. This is one of the heaviest atoms and its nucleus, like a top-heavy load, is unstable.

Detectors of Radiation

There are several types of detectors of radiation. One of the most widely used is the *Geiger-Müller*

(*GM*) *tube*. This is a small closed glass tube containing a little gas. A wire inside is connected to one electrode and the tube forms the other electrode. A voltage of several hundred volts is connected across one form of GM tube.

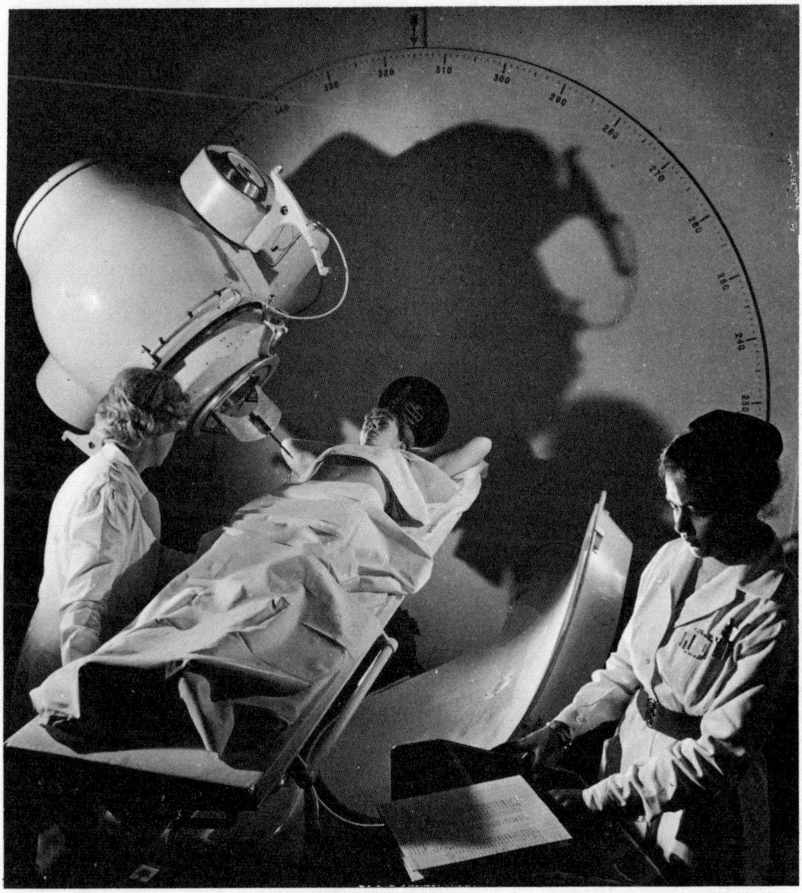

Plate 33(B) Cobalt unit in use at Royal Free Hospital, London. The cobalt source emits γ-radiation of high energy, which is concentrated on deep-seated tumours. Lead-lined sheets are used to cover the patient. The circular scale in the background is used to fix the direction of the γ-beam.

When a α-ray or β-particle enters the tube a tiny current flows between the electrodes. This can be amplified and passed to a loudspeaker, when a 'click' is heard. An intense source of radiation produces a rapid succession of 'clicks' and this can be used to give warning in a laboratory if a dangerous level of radiation is passed.

Alternatively, the amplified current from the GM tube can be made to move a spot of light round the face of an electronic tube. Fig. 33.2 shows a GM tube connected to a PANAX *scaler*. This instrument has two electronic tubes with numbers 0 to 9 on dials round their faces, as shown. One represents 'units', the other represents 'tens'. Each α- or β-particle or γ-ray passing into the GM tube produces a count of one unit. 'Hundreds' are passed to and registered by an electromagnetic counter. The scaler is thus a device for counting individual

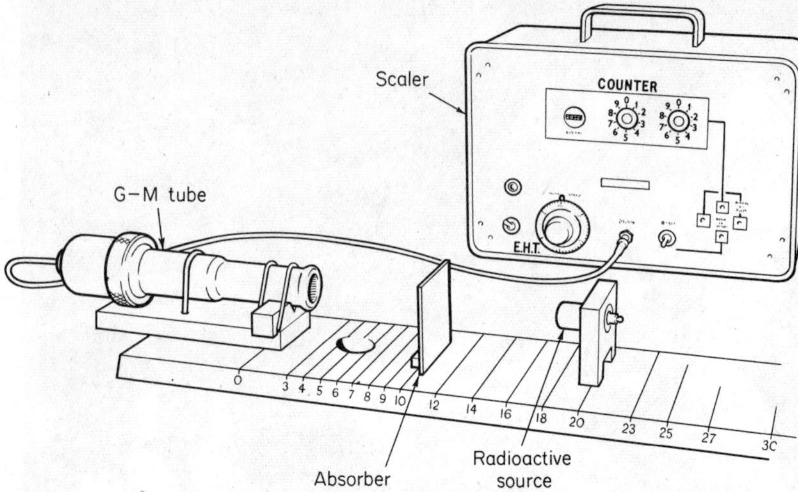

Fig. 33.2 Geiger–Müller (G–M) tube and scaler

radiations. The intensity of a radiation is proportional to the counts per minute. Thus a radiation of high intensity makes the spot of light move very fast round the dials. The high voltage needed to operate the GM tube is also provided by the scaler unit. It is varied by the dial marked 'E.H.T.' in Fig. 33.2. The diagram shows the arrangement in an experiment to investigate the absorption of radiation by a metal plate. See also Plate 33C.

α-particles can be readily detected by a *solid state detector*. This is basically a p–n junction (p. 561) which passes more current when exposed to α-particles. They can also be detected by GM tubes with specially-prepared thin windows.

As shown in Plate 33D, great care must be exercised in handling radioactive elements.

The Nucleus

At Rutherford's suggestion, two of his students fired α-particles at extremely thin gold foil and studied what happened. They found that most of the particles passed straight through, showing that there were empty spaces between the gold atoms, Fig. 33.3 (i).

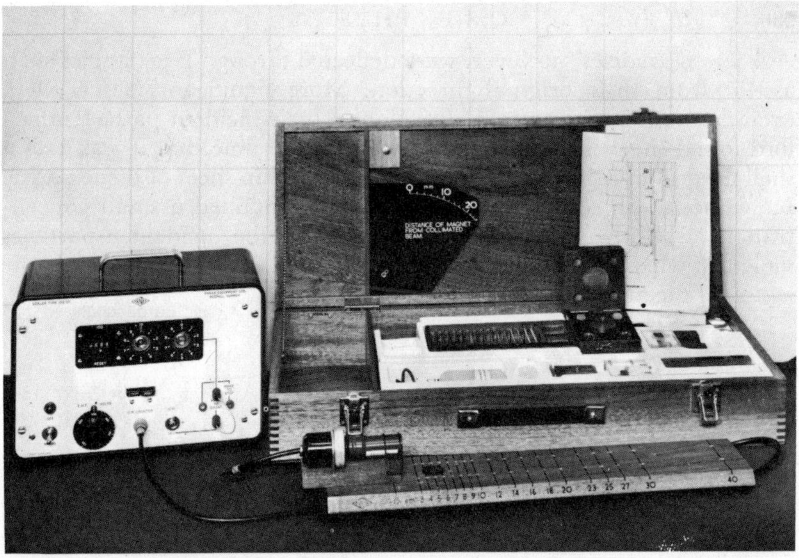

Plate 33(c) Scaler (left); Geiger–Müller tube (on graduated board); large case with long box containing aluminium and lead absorbers; wide open box containing weak sources of radiation; and a stronger source, in centre, covered with a lead disc.

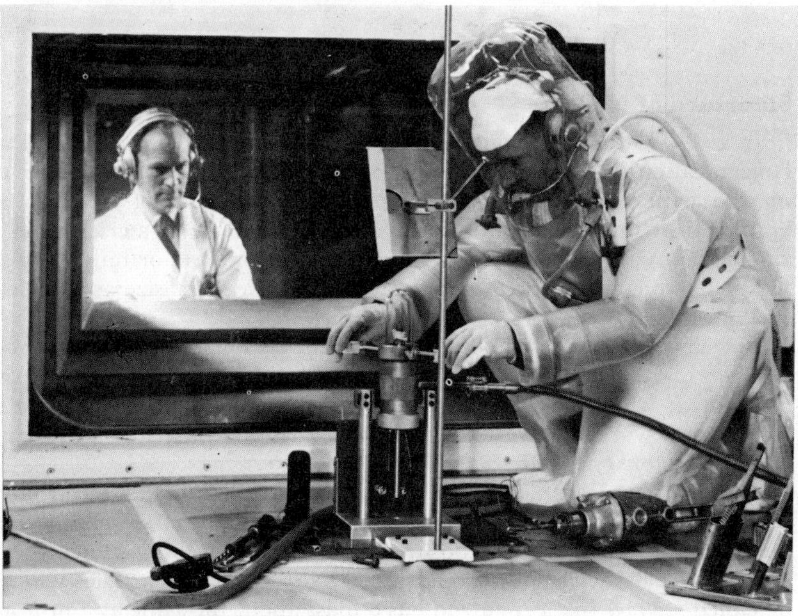

Plate 33(d) High-activity handling at Harwell. A maintenance mechanic in protective clothing adjusting equipment in a highly active cell, which has walls over 5ft thick. The work is directed from behind the glass shield, which is part of a tank also more than 5 ft thick containing zinc bromide solution.

A few α-particles, however, were deflected through large angles such as 45° from their original direction. More significant, a few were even detected in an opposite direction to their incident path. Rutherford found this very surprising. He said at the time that it was as if a shell fired from a gun had been repelled by a thin sheet of tissue paper. He came to the conclusion that the atom contained a small concentration of positive electricity, which repelled the incident α-particles violently when they came very close, Fig. 33.3 (ii). He called it the *nucleus* of the atom.

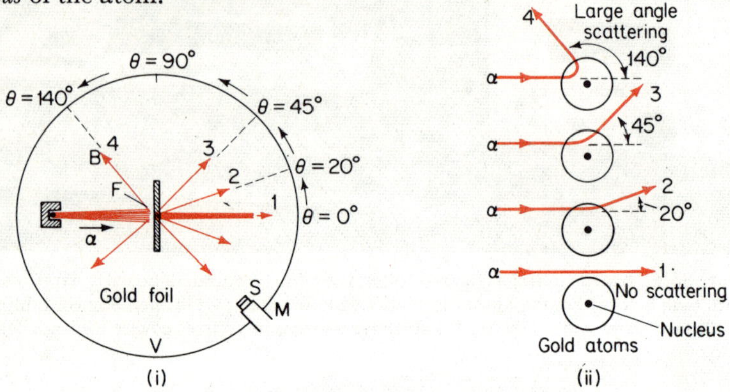

Fig. 33.3 Scattering of α-particles; discovery of nucleus

Structure of Nucleus

In 1911, Rutherford suggested that the 'structure' of the atom was a concentration of matter in the centre or nucleus, which carried a positive charge, with electrons moving round the nucleus. Most of the atom is empty. If we imagine the nucleus magnified to the size of a cricket ball, the farthest part of the atom would be some kilometres or miles away. Here electrons would be moving, each about the same size as the ball in the centre.

The simplest atom is the hydrogen atom. Its nucleus is called a *proton* (p); it carries a positive charge numerically equal to that on an electron, *e*, which moves round it in a circular path, Fig. 33.34 (*a*). Subsequent work by Rutherford showed that the nuclei of all atoms contain protons.

The charge on an electron is a basic unit of quantity of electricity and its *numerical* value is given the symbol *e*. The negative charge on an electron is thus $-e$. The positive charge on a proton is hence $+e$.

In 1932 Chadwick showed that nuclei also contains particles which he called *neutrons* (n). A neutron has a mass about the same as a proton but carries no charge. It is believed that protons and neutrons are the building blocks of all nuclei.

Fig. 33.4 shows diagrammatically the particles in some atoms.

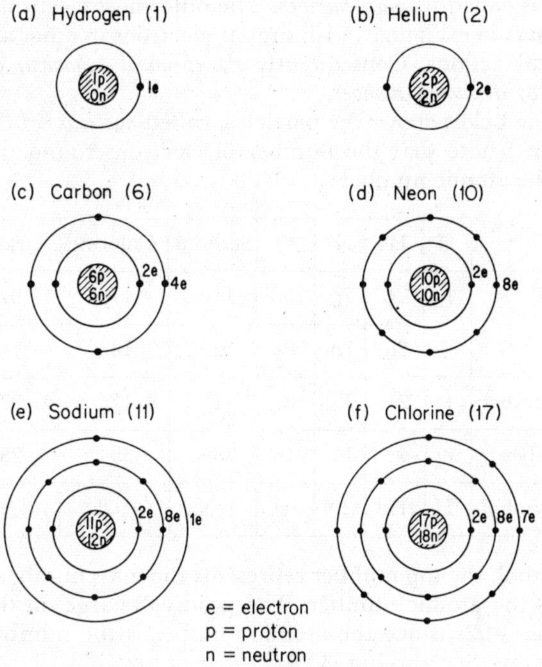

Fig. 33.4 Particles inside some atoms

Particles in Atoms

We can now discuss atoms more fully. As we have seen, electrons, which surround the nucleus, are so light that practically the whole mass of the atom is concentrated in the nucleus. A normal atom, however, is electrically neutral. Thus since helium, for example, has two electrons carrying two units of negative charge or $-2e$, the nucleus must have a positive charge of two units or $+2e$. Hence the nucleus contains two protons (positive charges). But the *mass* of a helium atom is *four* times the mass of a hydrogen atom, and we have only accounted for two particles (protons) of the same mass as the hydrogen atom. The helium nucleus must therefore contain two neutrons.

Summarizing: A helium atom with a mass of four has two protons and two neutrons. The positive charge on the nucleus is two units or $+2e$ and is carried by the protons. This balances the two units of negative charge or $-2e$ on the two electrons round the nucleus.

Atomic Number and Mass Number

The number of protons or electrons in an atom is called its *atomic number*. The number of particles in the nucleus, both protons and neutrons, is called its *mass number*. The outermost electrons in an atom can take part in exchanges with similar electrons in other atoms, that is, in chemical actions. Consequently *the chemical behaviour of an atom is determined by its atomic number.*

The table below shows the particles, called *nucleons*, in the nucleus of some atoms; note that the number of electrons round the nucleus is equal to the atomic number:

	H	He	N	O	Sodium	Chlorine	Uranium
Nucleons	1p	2p	7p	8p	11p	17p	92p
		2n	7n	8n	12n	18n	146n
Atomic number	1	2	7	8	11	17	92
Mass number	1	4	14	16	23	35	238
Nuclear symbol	${}^{1}_{1}H$	${}^{4}_{2}He$	${}^{14}_{7}N$	${}^{16}_{8}O$	${}^{23}_{11}Na$	${}^{35}_{17}Cl$	${}^{238}_{92}U$

In the symbol, the top number represents the mass number; the bottom number is the atomic number. The positive charge on the nucleus of uranium is $+92e$, since the atomic number is the number of protons in the nucleus. See also Fig. 33.4.

Isotopes

The atomic or chemical weight of an element is a measure of the average mass of all the atoms in a sample. Assuming the atomic weight of hydrogen is 1, that of chlorine is about 35·5. The appearance of a fraction or decimal in the atomic weight of an element was unexplained for some time. Experiments showed, however, that *all the atoms in a sample of an element did not have the same mass.* They all had the same atomic number so that they behaved the same chemically. A sample of chlorine, for example, contains about 80% of atoms of mass number 35 and atomic number 17 and 20% of atoms of mass number 37 and atomic number 17. Atoms of mass number 35 contained 17 protons and 18 neutrons. Atoms of mass number 37 contained 17 protons and 20 neutrons. Since the atomic number was 17 in each case, the chemical behaviour was the same for both types of atoms.

Atoms which have the same chemical properties but a different mass are called *isotopes*. All elements have isotopes. Hydrogen has an isotope of mass number 2 which is therefore twice as heavy as ordinary hydrogen. It is called *heavy hydrogen*. Another has a mass number 3 and is called *tritium*. Both isotopes have one proton in their nucleus, so the atomic number is one. Their chemical behaviour is thus the same as ordinary hydrogen.

Oxygen has an isotope of mass number 17. Most oxygen atoms in a sample have a mass number 16. Each has the same atomic number 8. Natural uranium contains less than one per cent in weight of an isotope of mass number 235, whereas most of the uranium atoms have mass number 238. Uranium-235 is the atom used in nuclear reactors (p. 592).

Radioactive Isotopes

Isotopes can be made artificially by firing neutrons or protons at elements. These istopes are unstable. Since they emit radiation such as β-particles or γ-rays, they are known as *radioactive isotopes.*

Plate 33(E) Gear-box inspection by gamma-rays from a radio-isotope, which is mixed with the oil before the car runs.

Radioactive isotopes are now widely used in medicine and industry. They are exported abroad. The passage of food through the human body, for example, can be studied by adding a little of a harmless radioactive substances to it and then tracing its progress by a Geiger-Müller tube from the radiations emitted. The carbon-14 isotope has been mixed with insecticides and used to trace their action on plants. Watermarks on printing paper may be made by exposing the paper to weak β-particles from the isotope sulphur-35. Gear boxes in cars have been examined for wear by mixing a small quantity of a radioactive isotope with oil and tracking the radiations after a run. Plate 33E.

Artificial Transmutation

The first example of a man-made isotope occurred in 1919, when Rutherford bombarded atoms of nitrogen $^{14}_{7}N$ with α-particles, $^{4}_{2}He$. He found that a proton, $^{1}_{1}H$, was obtained from a nitrogen nucleus.

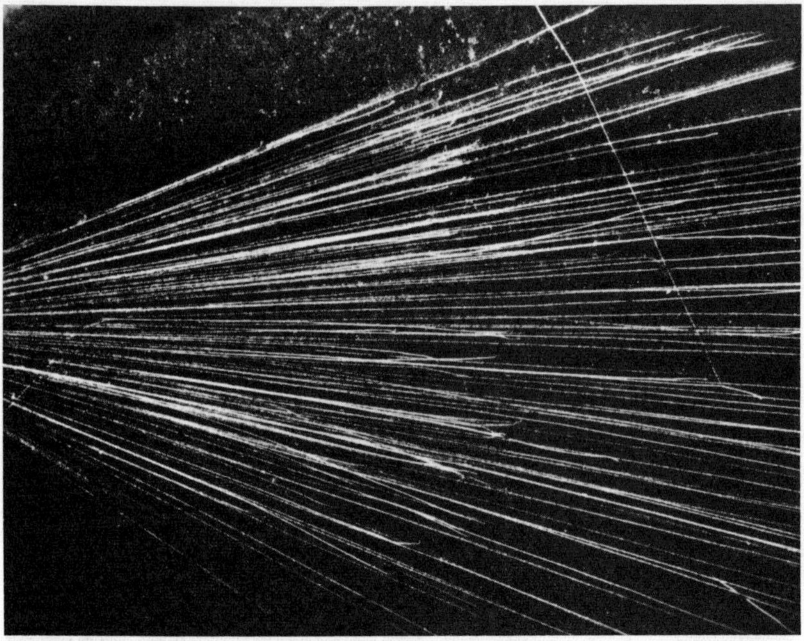

Plate 33(F) Nuclear collision by α-particle, which transmutes a nitrogen to an oxygen atom. The streaks show α-particles moving through nitrogen gas. One α-particle (*right centre*) has collided and merged with a nitrogen nucleus, and this has broken into an oxygen nucleus (*short track*) and a proton (*long thin track crossing others*). This historic photograph was taken by Lord Blackett, F.R.S., in 1925 using a Wilson cloud chamber.

See Plate 33F. This led to the discovery of protons in the nuclei of all elements.

If the nucleus of the atom left after the nuclear reaction is denoted by X, then the reaction can be written as follows:

$$^{4}_{2}He + {}^{14}_{7}N \longrightarrow {}^{1}_{1}H + {}^{17}_{8}X.$$

The total mass on the left side is 4 + 14 or 18, the same as the total mass on the right side. The total nuclear charge on the left side is 2 + 7 or 9 units, the same as on the right side. Now the atom X has an atomic number 8. This is the atomic number of *oxygen* (p. 588). Hence an atom of oxygen was produced from an atom of nitrogen. This is called *transmutation*. Only a very tiny percentage of nitrogen gas undergoes transmutation on bombardment with α-particles.

Nowadays, very powerful machines have been built for nuclear investigations by bombardments of elements. See Plate 33G.

Radioactive Transmutation

The emission of an α-particle from the nucleus of a radioactive element also produces transmutation. As an illustration, consider the case of uranium. This has a mass number of 238 and an atomic number 92. Thus its nucleus has a charge of $+92e$ (see p. 588). When an α-particle is emitted, its nuclear charge decreases by $+2e$ (the atomic number of the α-particle is 2). The nucleus left has thus a charge $+90e$, or an atomic number 90. It is therefore the nucleus of a new element, in this case the element thorium.

Suppose now that a β-particle is emitted from the thorium nucleus. The β-particle is an electron (p. 581). It therefore has a negative charge, $-e$. The charge on the thorium nucleus, which was $+90e$, now becomes $+91e$. The atomic number has thus increased from 90 to 91. A new element, palladium, is formed.

Plate 33(G) Van de Graaff electrostatic generator used at Aldermaston, producing 6 million volts for nuclear investigations.

Nuclear Energy

The electrons in a normal atom are bound to the atom by forces of attraction between them and the nucleus. Energy is therefore needed to take electrons away from the atom. In the photoelectric effect, this is provided by the energy in the incident light.

The particles in the nucleus, protons and neutrons, are called 'nucleons'. The nucleons are kept together in the very tiny volume of the nucleus by powerful forces whose nature is not yet fully known. To take all the nucleons apart requires an enormous amount of energy. It is called the *binding energy* of the nucleus. By comparison, the energy needed to remove electrons from an atom is about a million times smaller.

Nuclear Fission · Chain Reaction

When the nucleus of the heavy element uranium is split into two parts of roughly about the same mass, the nucleus is said to undergo *fission*. The mass of the two parts together is less than the mass of the uranium nucleus. *The difference in mass is a measure of the nuclear energy released*. Einstein's *mass-energy* relation shows how the energy can be calculated and is the key formula in all nuclear energy calculations. It states:

Energy released = *mass change* $\times$ 90 *million million* (9×10^{13}) joules,

where the mass change is in grammes. Calculation shows that if all the atoms in about 1 kg of uranium could undergo fission, the energy released would be as much, theoretically, as that obtained by burning about 1 million kg of coal.

Nuclear fission may be obtained by bombarding a uranium-235 atom with a neutron. The neutron has no charge (p. 586). It can therefore penetrate deeply into the nucleus. Fig. 33.5 illustrates the

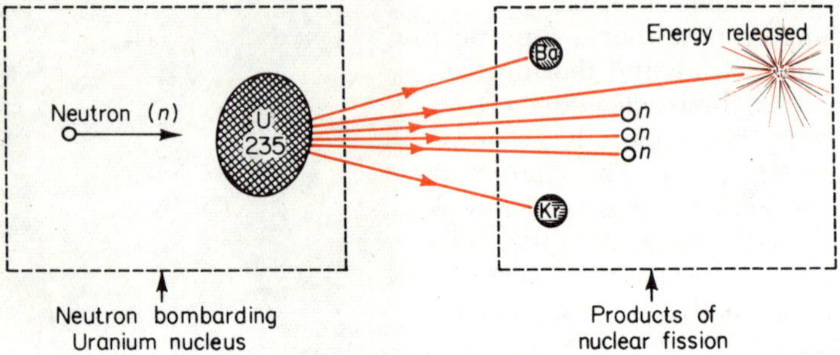

Fig. 33.5 Nuclear fission

reaction. Several neutrons are produced in addition to the two nuclei of barium (Ba) and krypton (Kr). If these neutrons in turn can be captured by other uranium nuclei, the number of atoms which undergo fission would multiply rapidly. Fig. 33.6 illustrates how one neutron in this way produces fission of 27 atoms (4th stage). This multiplying action is called a *chain reaction.*

Nuclear Reactor Principle

Natural uranium contains about 1 part by weight of atoms of atomic weight 235 and 139 parts by weight of atoms of atomic weight 238. Nuclear fission occurs with the atoms of atomic weight 235 when uranium is used in nuclear reactors. Plates 33H, 33I.

Fission takes place only if the bombarding neutron is slow. Graphite is therefore used round the uranium to moderate the speed of the neutron, so that the chain reaction is prevented from dying out. If there are too many neutrons the reaction will proceed too fast and get out of hand, and this is controlled by neutron-absorbing boron steel rods. These rods are moved in and out of the reactor from the control room by small electric motors, which raise them through the floor to a suitable position. In the event of an electrical failure the rods would fall and shut off the reactor automatically.

The reactor is started by a charge machine, which lowers uranium

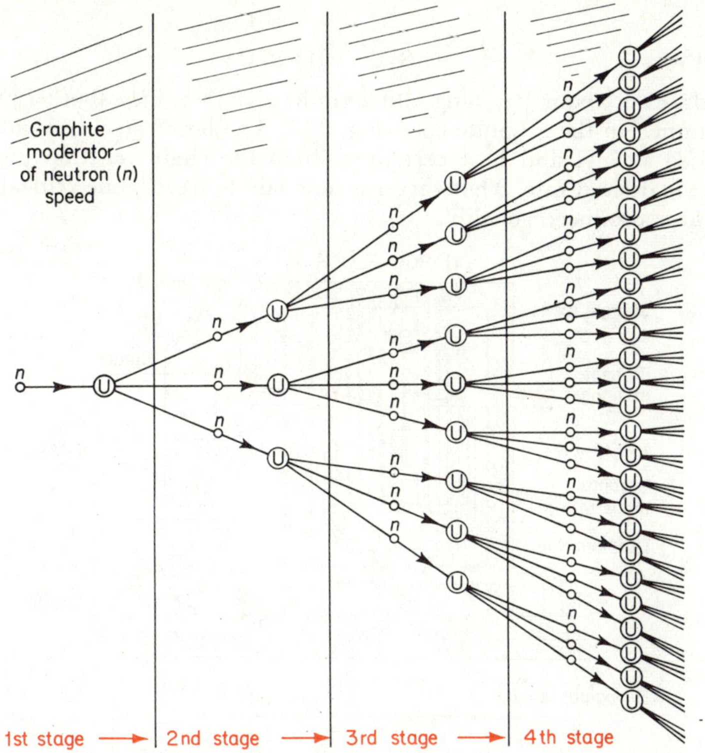

Fig. 33.6 A chain reaction

Plate 33(H) Interior of a reactor, showing the loading of fuel elements and the control rod channels.

rods, each about 1 m long and 2 cm in diameter, into about 1700 fuel channels in the graphite core, Fig. 33.7. The boron steel rods are then raised slowly, and in a certain position the chain reaction proceeds at the desired rate. The reactor is now said to have 'gone critical', and heat is produced steadily.

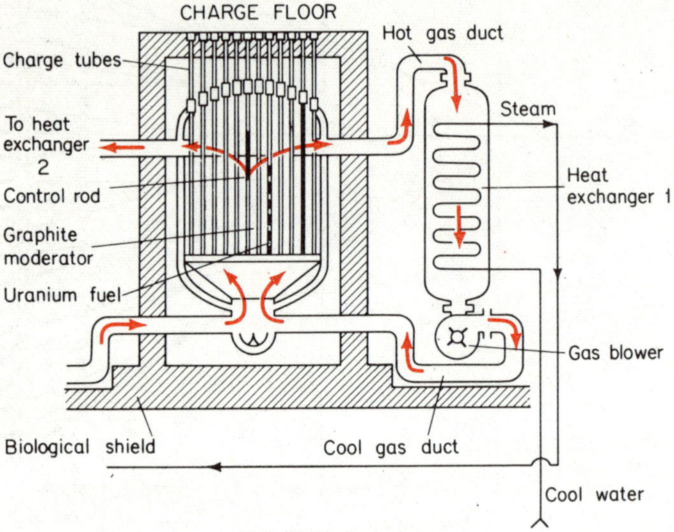

Fig. 33.7 A nuclear reactor

Carbon dioxide gas is blown through the fuel elements under pressure, and the hot gas is led into heat exchangers outside the reactor. Here it heats up water which flows through an independent pipe system in the exchanger, and this is converted into high-pressure and low-pressure steam. The steam is used to drive the turbines which turn electrical generators, and the electricity obtained is fed to the National Grid System to supplement the electrical energy produced by burning coal at conventional power stations. The nuclear reactor can operate day and night for a few years with the same uranium fuel. The reactor core is shielded by a welded-steel pressure vessel and a concrete biological shield, which protects operators outside from the intense radiation inside the core.

Nuclear Fusion

We have seen that a considerable amount of energy is released when a heavy nucleus such as uranium disintegrates into two large parts; this is nuclear fission. Experiments show that a considerable release of energy is also obtained when the nuclei of the lightest elements are *fused* to form a heavier nucleus, and this is known as *nuclear fusion*.

One transformation of matter into energy is the fusion of deuterons, $^{2}_{1}H$, the nuclei of heavy hydrogen, into helium nuclei. As the sun contains a considerable amount of hydrogen, it was suggested in 1939 that the energy of the sun was basically due to nuclear fusion. It has been

Plate 33(I) British Experiment Pile O, BEPO, at Harwell, a natural uranium-fuelled graphic-moderated reactor. For research purposes, scientists are loading a large tube containing materials into the reactor core.

estimated that, theoretically, the energy released from the fusion of all the atoms in 1 kg of deuterium gas, heavy hydrogen, is equivalent to that released by burning nearly 3 million kg of coal.

In order to obtain nuclear fusion, the nuclei must approach near enough to each other to overcome the repulsion of their like charges.

The lightest elements have the smallest nuclear charge, and hence the chance of nuclear fusion is greatest for such elements. The most practical way of achieving nuclear fusion is to raise the temperature of deuterium gas to millions of degrees, which is the temperature in the heart of the sun. At these very high temperatures deuterons fuse together, a process known as *thermonuclear fusion*. Very heavy electrical discharges are sent through the gas to heat it to such enormously high temperatures, and researches into methods of retaining the energy in the gas, and hence to promote fusion, are at present being made in Great Britain and abroad. If methods for nuclear fusion were successful a cheap source of power would be available. Heavy hydrogen forms about 1 part in 45 000 of water, and if heavy hydrogen were extracted from sea-water it could provide limitless power at a very economic price.

DEMONSTRATIONS

Demonstrations in radioactivity may be carried out with equipment designed for schools by PANAX EQUIPMENT LTD, Holmethorpe Estate, Redhill, Surrey. This comprises radioactive sources of α-, β-particles and γ-rays suitable for schools, and a GM tube and scaler (see p. 586). Safety regulations must be obtained from the Ministry of Education prior to use.

SUMMARY

1. α-particles are positively charged nuclei of helium (mass about four times that of the hydrogen atom and carrying a charge of $+2e$). They are stopped by thin paper. Owing to their heavy mass, they are not deflected appreciably in a magnetic field.

2. β-particles are usually electrons and negatively charged. They are stopped by aluminium plate several millimetres thick. They are easily deflected in a powerful magnetic field, as they are so light.

3. γ-rays are electromagnetic waves. They are stopped by very thick lead blocks. They are not deflected by magnetic fields.

4. The atom consists of a small central nucleus containing protons and neutrons; a proton is a hydrogen nucleus. The number of protons is called the *atomic number*; the total number of protons and neutrons is called the *mass number*. The number of electrons round the nucleus in the rest of the atom is normally equal to the number of protons, and determines the chemical nature of the atom.

5. An *isotope* is an atom which has the same atomic number and hence the same chemical properties as another atom with a different mass. A *radioactive isotope* is used in medicine and industry.

6. *Nuclear fission* is the 'splitting' of a heavy atom, such as uranium, into two heavy parts; it is produced when suitably moderated neutrons are fired into a mass of uranium-235, with the release of nuclear energy. *Nuclear fusion* occurs in the sun—hydrogen nuclei fuse to form helium nuclei, with the release of nuclear energy.

EXERCISE 33 · ANSWERS, p. 617

1. The lightest of the following is: (*a*) any atom; (*b*) a molecule; (*c*) a proton; (*d*) an electron; (*e*) a hydrogen atom. (*M.*)

2. Complete the following table:

particle	mass	charge
proton neutron electron		

Any standard convention will be accepted. (*Mx.*)

3. An atom consists of a nucleus made up of . . and . . around which revolve particles called . . (*W.Md.*)

4. (*a*) From which part of an atom do radioactive rays come from?

(*b*) If the radiations penetrate only a few centimetres of air, what type of radiations are they? (*L.*)

5. Fig. 33A represents an atom. (*a*) What is A?

(*b*) Name two particles which occur in A.

(*c*) What are the particles labelled B called? (*L.*)

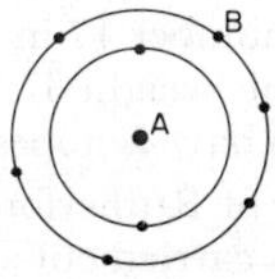

Fig. 33A

6. Of the three normally occurring radioactive radiations: (*a*) which has a positive charge; (*b*) which is the most penetrating; (*c*) which has no electric charge? (*L.*)

7. Which of the following statements are correct?

(i) *Electrons* have: (*a*) no mass; (*b*) a mass less than that of a proton; (*c*) a mass equal to that of a helium atom; (*d*) a mass greater than that of a neutron.

(ii) *Neutrons* have: (*a*) a double positive charge; (*b*) a single positive charge; (*c*) a negative charge; (*d*) no electric charge.

(iii) *Protons*: (*a*) wander from atom to atom; (*b*) are groups of atoms: (*c*) are found in the nucleus of atoms; (*d*) orbit the nucleus in atoms. (*S.E.*)

8. (*a*) Draw a diagram of a simple atom showing the nucleus and 2 electrons.

(*b*) In this atom: (i) what type of charge will there be on the nucleus? (ii) what is the value of this charge? (*L.*)

9. What are the names of the three types of rays given off by a radioactive substance? Define any properties you know they possess. Why is it that the largest atoms are radioactive? (*W.Md.*)

10. (*a*) What is an ion?

(*b*) Draw and label a simple picture of a helium atom that has an atomic number of 2 and an atomic weight of 4.

(*c*) Chlorine is made up of two types of atoms, both of atomic number 17, but one of atomic weight 35 and the other of atomic weight 37. These are called, . . of chlorine. What is the missing word? What are the similarities and differences between these atoms? (*E.A.*)

11. (*a*) Which of the following are parts of all atoms: neutron, meson, proton, hyperon, electron, α-particle? Is there any item in the list that is a part of certain atoms only? If so, name it, and its property.

(*b*) One of the list in (*a*) is shown to be a part of all atoms by experiments on electrical discharge through gases. Which is it and how can its presence in a discharge tube be shown to illustrate two properties you know it possesses? (*W.Md.*)

12. (*a*) In what way are electrons, protons, and neutrons alike, and in what ways do they differ?

(*b*) Draw a simple diagram of an atom which contains all of these particles. Give the mass number of your atom.

(*c*) Why is an atom electrically neutral?

(*d*) Account for the difference between a good conductor of electricity and an insulator in terms of atomic structure. (*S.E.*)

13. Radioactive substances were found to give off three types of rays. What are they called and how do they: (i) react to a magnetic field?; (ii) act when different thicknesses of lead sheeting are placed in their path?

What changes are brought about to an element in the process of radioactive decay? (*W.Md.*)

14. Chlorine has an atomic number 17 in the form of isotopes, one of atomic weight 35 and the other of atomic weight 37. Explain the terms underlined, and name two other elements which have isotopes. (*W.Md.*)

15. (*a*) What was the result of Rutherford's bombardment of the atoms of nitrogen? Explain how this was carried out and how it lead to the first transmutation process.

(*b*) What was the meaning of: (i) mass number; (ii) atomic number, and in what way are they related in the isotopes of an element? Explain a use to which an artificial isotope can be put. (*W.Md.*)

16. (*a*) What are α-particles?

(*b*) What are β-particles?

(*c*) List *four* different ways in which α and β particles can be detected and explain one of them in detail. (*E.A.*)

17. (i) Explain the terms: (*a*) isotope; (*b*) radioactive.

(ii) Name the *three* types of radiation normally associated with radioactivity.

Describe and explain *one* practical use of a radioisotope in medicine *or* industry *or* agriculture. Mention, if you can, the nature of the radiation and the name of the isotope. (*S.E.*)

18. (*a*) Fission means a splitting into parts. Explain how this word is used in atomic physics.

(*b*) Fusion means melting together. Explain how this word is used in atomic physics.

(*c*) What is a chain reaction? How is it controlled in an atomic pile? (*E.A.*)

34
STATIC ELECTRICITY

Charging by Rubbing

If you rub a plastic balloon on your jacket or dress, the rubbed balloon can attract small pieces of paper. The same power of attraction is shown by a plastic comb after it is rubbed by combing the hair vigorously.

More than 2000 years ago the Greeks found that wheat particles were attracted to amber necklaces worn by peasants in the field. The greek word for amber is 'elektron'. Any rubbed object which has a similar power of attraction is now said to be 'electrified' or *charged*, or to have a 'charge'.

Positive and Negative Charges

A simple experiment shows that there are *two* different kinds of charge.

In Fig. 34.1 (i), a *polythene* strip X, rubbed with a duster, is suspended in a stirrup by a thread. When a similar rubbed polythene strip A is brought near to one end of X, this end is repelled. If, however, a *cellulose acetate* strip B, previously rubbed with a duster, is brought near to X, then X is attracted, Fig. 34.1 (ii).

Fig. 34.1 Negative and positive charges

This experiment shows that the charge on the rubbed polythene is different from, or *unlike*, the charge on the rubbed acetate. Also, we see that

like (similar) charges repel, unlike charges attract.

This is a fundamental law of *electrostatics*, as the subject is known.

Early investigators decided to call the charge on ebonite rubbed with fur a *negative* (—ve) charge. The charge on rubbed polythene is also a

—ve charge. The charge on a glass rod rubbed with silk was found to act oppositely to that charge on a rubbed ebonite rod. It was therefore called a *positive* (+ve) charge. The charge on a rubbed acetate strip is also a +ve charge.

Since like charges repel, two +ve or two —ve charges repel each other. Since unlike charges attract, a —ve and a +ve charge attract each other.

Atomic Structure and Charges

The existence of —ve and +ve charges can be explained from the structure of the atom, which was discussed in detail on p. 587. There we showed that all atoms have (i) a central core or nucleus carrying a +ve charge, (ii) particles called *electrons*, carrying a —ve charge, which move round the nucleus like planets orbiting the sun. As the atoms become heavier, the charge on the nucleus and the number of orbiting electrons both increase. In all atoms, the total —ve charge on the electrons is equal to the +ve charge on the nucleus.

Insulators have atoms in which the electrons are firmly 'bound' to the nucleus, that is, they stay in orbit round the nucleus. This is the case for polythene, cellulose acetate, ebonite, glass and plastic materials.

Metals, however, have atoms in which one or more electrons are 'free', that is, they are no longer bound to the nucleus of a particular atom but drift from one atom to another through the metal structure. This drift of free electrons is irregular or haphazard—it occurs in all different directions. Solid electrical *conductors* have free electrons.

Explanation of Charging by Rubbing

We can now explain why polythene and cellulose acetate become charged on rubbing.

When polythene is rubbed with a duster, some of the electrons in the outer parts of the atoms on the duster are transferred to the polythene. Now electrons carry —ve charges. So the polythene has a —ve charge after rubbing. Suppose the —ve charge is —100 units. Then the duster, which has lost this charge, has a surplus +ve charge equal to +100 units.

When a cellulose acetate strip is rubbed with a duster, this time some electrons (—ve charges) are transferred from the strip to the duster. So the duster has a —ve charge. The acetate has an equal +ve charge.

You should see that charging by rubbing does not *create* charges. The charges are there all the time. Rubbing simply re-distributes the charges, say from the duster to the polythene or from the acetate to the duster. Note carefully that the total charge on the duster and polythene or acetate is *zero* before and after the rubbing.

Charges in Motion. Current and Static Electricity

If a metal rod is held in the hand and rubbed with a duster, no charge is obtained on the metal. The metal and the human body are conductors. Any electrons produced by rubbing can move along the metal and pass through the body to the earth, because these are conductors. The one-way drift of electrons is called an 'electric current', Fig. 34.2 (i). See page 412, where electric current is discussed in detail.

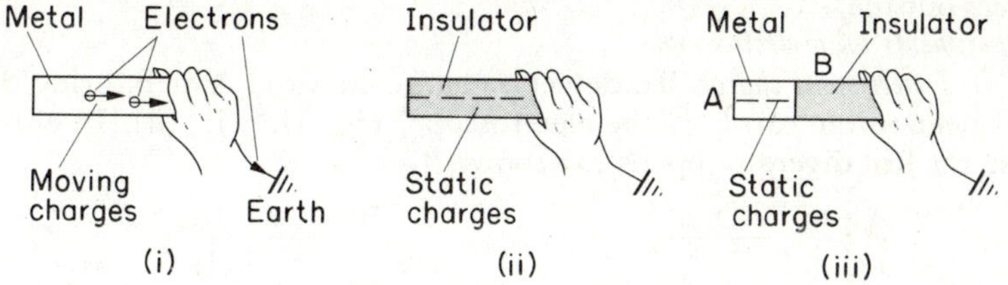

Fig. 34.2 Conductor and insulator

On the other hand, the charge produced by rubbing polythene does not flow away. This is because polythene is an insulator. For the same reason, charges remain on cellulose acetate, glass or ebonite when rubbed. These charges are called *static* charges because they do not move, Fig. 34.2 (ii). In this chapter we shall discuss mainly static charges.

If a metal rod A is attached to an insulator B, Fig. 34.2 (iii), B can be held in the hand while A is rubbed. In this case a static charge can be detected on the metal because the charge can not leak away through the insulator to the earth.

Gold Leaf Electroscope

A simple instrument for investigating electric charges is the *gold leaf electroscope*, Fig. 34.3. This has a metal cap C at the top of a vertical

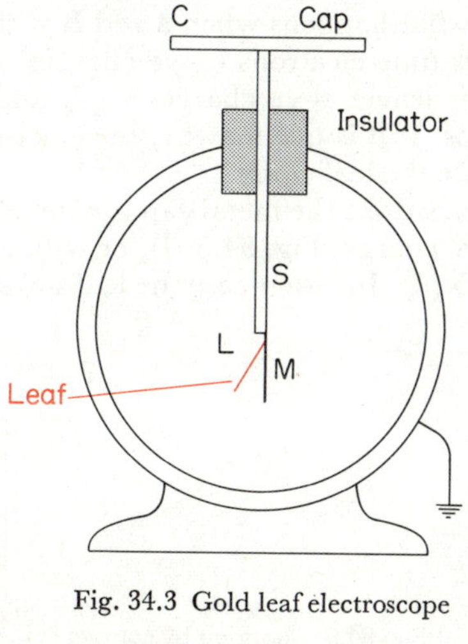

Fig. 34.3 Gold leaf electroscope

metal stem S, and a gold leaf L is attached to the bottom M. The leaf is the sensitive moving part of the electroscope. The metal S and attachments are carefully insulated by plastic material from the surrounding metal case. The case is draught-proof and has plane glass sides. It is usually earthed to protect the leaf from electrical disturbances outside.

Experiments with electroscope

(i) *Detection of charge.* To detect a charge on a rod A or B, bring the rod near to the cap C of the electroscope, Fig. 34.4 (i), (ii). In either case the leaf diverges (opens), as shown.

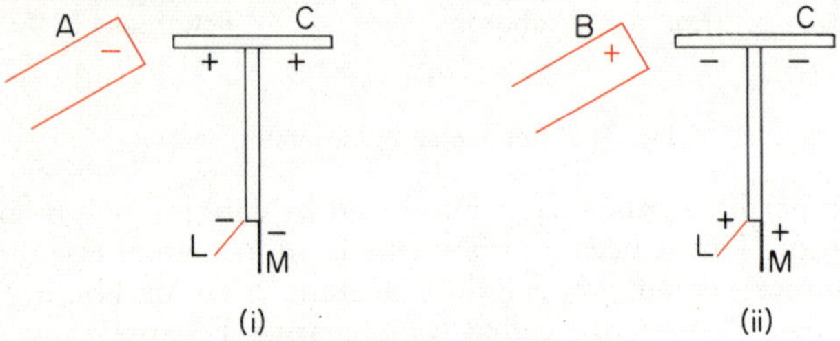

Fig. 34.4 Detection of charge

Explanation: Suppose the charge on A is —ve. When it is near C, Fig. 34.4 (i), the free electrons in the metal are repelled, since electrons carry —ve charges and like charges repel. Thus electrons move away from C and reach the leaf L and M, where they can go no further. Since L and M both have —ve charges, L is repelled by M and so the leaf opens.

The movement of electrons from C leaves the cap with an equal +ve charge, as shown. If the charge on A is taken away, the electrons return to C from L and M and so the leaf closes.

Fig. 34.4 (ii) shows what happens when a rod B with a +ve charge is brought near B. This time electrons (—ve charges) are attracted to C from L and M. This leaves +ve charges on L and M. Repulsion occurs, so the leaf opens. If B is taken away, the electrons return from C to L and M and hence the leaf closes.

(ii) *Charging by contact.* Stroke the metal cap C of an electroscope with a rod A carrying a —ve charge, Fig. 34.5 (i), or with a rod B carrying a +ve charge, Fig. 34.5 (ii). In either case the leaf stays open.

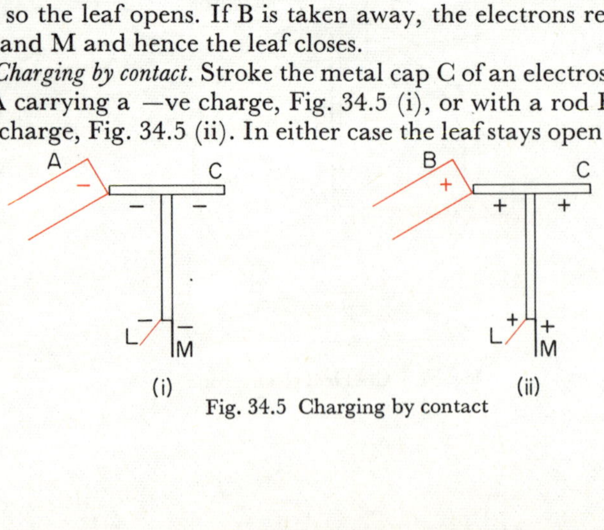

Fig. 34.5 Charging by contact

Explanation: Some of the charge on the rod is transferred by contact to C. The charge spreads along the metal, a conductor, to L and M at the bottom and so the leaf opens. Note that the sign of the charge on the leaf is the same as that on the rod.

(iii) *Finding the sign of a charge.* To find out if the charge on a rod X is −ve or +ve, first charge the electroscope −ve by stroking with a polythene strip, Fig. 34.6 (i). Now bring X *slowly* towards the cap C, Fig. 34.6 (ii). If the leaf opens more, as shown, then the charge on X must be −ve.

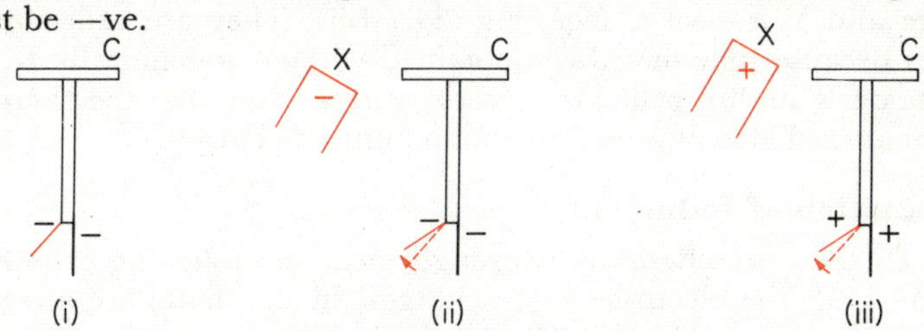

Fig. 34.6 Finding sign of charge

Suppose, however, that the leaf closes a little when X is brought near C. Then X may have a +ve charge *or* it may be uncharged. The only sure way to find if X has a +ve charge is to bring it near the cap of an electroscope with a +ve charge. If the leaf opens more, then X must have a +ve charge, Fig. 34.6 (iii).

Charging by Induction

On p. 489, we saw that magnetism could be induced in soft iron without actually touching the iron. Electric charges can also be induced in objects without actually touching them.

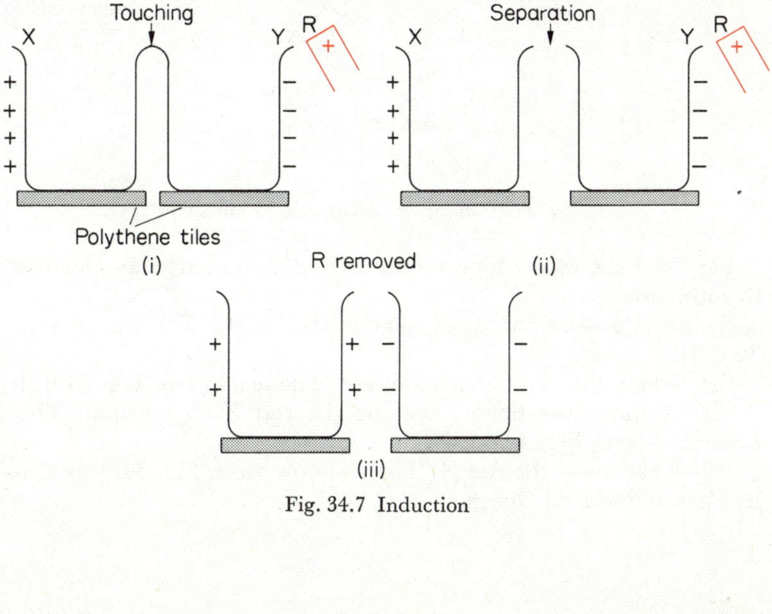

Fig. 34.7 Induction

Fig. 34.7 shows how this can be done. X and Y are two metal cans standing on polythene insulating tiles. They are brought near each other so that the metals touch, Fig. 34.7 (i).

A rod R with a +ve charge is now brought near to one side of Y say. Keeping R in position, X is separated from Y by moving the tile below X, taking care not to touch the can, Fig. 34.7 (ii). Then R is removed completely, Fig. 34.7 (iii).

By testing with an electroscope, X will be found to have a +ve charge and Y a −ve charge, Fig. 34.7 (iii). They are called *induced charges* because they have been obtained without touching by R. The charge on R itself is called the *inducing charge*. Note that the charge on R is unaltered after it is used to obtain induced charges.

Explanation of Induction

When the +ve charge R is brought near the touching cans X, Y, Fig. 34.7 (i), the electrons (−ve charges) in the metal are attracted. So they move from X to Y, the side of the can nearest to R. The can X which has lost the −ve charge is left with an equal +ve charge.

When the cans are separated, Fig. 34.7 (ii), the +ve and −ve charges remain on X and Y respectively. It is important to keep R in position while the cans are separated, otherwise the −ve charge (electrons) would flow back to X.

When R is now taken away, Fig. 34.7 (iii), the charge on X and Y spread over the surfaces. So X has an induced +ve charge and Y an equal induced −ve charge.

Charging Electroscope by Induction

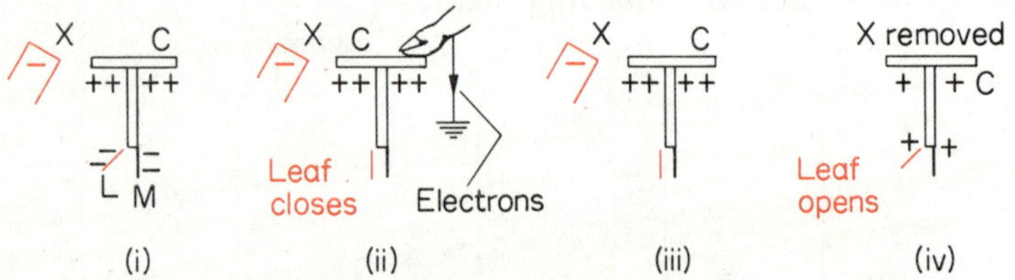

Fig. 34.8 Charging electroscope by induction

Fig. 34.8 shows the four stages necessary to charge an electroscope by induction.

(i) Bring a −ve charge X near to the cap C. The leaf opens, Fig. 34.8 (i).

(ii) Touch the cap C with a finger. The leaf closes, Fig. 34.8 (ii).

(iii) Remove the finger, keeping the rod X in position. The leaf remains closed, Fig. 34.8 (iii).

(iv) Take away the rod X. The leaf now *opens*, Fig. 34.8 (iv). So the leaf has an induced charge.

Explanation: When X is brought near to C, Fig. 34·8 (i), its −ve charge repels electrons (−ve charges) from C to L and M. The leaf opens due to repulsion between the like charges at L and M.

When the cap C is touched, the electrons escape through the metal and body to earth. So the leaf closes. The +ve charge remains, however, at C. When the finger is removed, the leaf remains closed. But when X is taken away, the +ve charge at C spreads over the metal. The +ve charges at L and M repel each other and so the leaf opens.

Note that the induced charge on the electroscope is +ve, whereas the inducing charge is −ve. Is the induced charge *always* opposite in sign to the inducing charge?

Distribution of Charge over Surfaces

Since like charges repel, the charge on a hollow or solid metal sphere will move away from the centre as far as it will go. The charge on a conductor of any shape is always found on the surface and never inside the conductor.

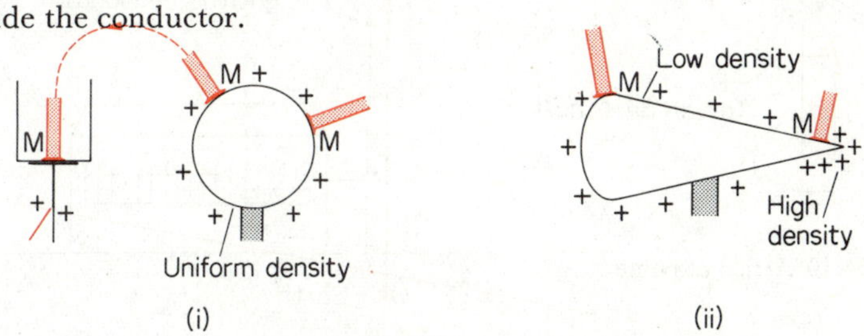

Fig. 34.9 Surface density of charge

The *density* of the charge at different parts of the surface can be investigated by using a 'proof plane', a small piece of metal M attached to one end of an insulating rod. As illustrated in Fig. 34.9 (i), when M is placed in contact with any part of a charged surface, it collects some charge by contact. The amount collected depends on the density of the charge at the particular place—the greater the density, the larger will be the charge on M. The amount of charge collected can be estimated roughly by placing the metal M inside an insulated can joined to an electroscope. See Fig. 34.9 (i). M then gives up all its charge to the can and electroscope. So a large divergence of the leaf shows a high surface density; a small divergence shows a small surface density.

Results are shown roughly in Fig. 34.9 (i). A charged metal sphere has a uniform (constant) surface density all over, Fig. 34.9 (i). A pear-shaped conductor, however, has a *high density at the pointed part of the surface*, Fig. 34.9 (ii).

Action at Points

Fig. 34.10 shows a demonstration of the effect produced by the high density of charge at a pointed conductor. A metal 'windmill' A, with sharp points, is balanced on a pivot O on an insulating stand, Fig. 34.10. A wire OB is then joined to the terminal of a van de Graaff generator, which can build up the charge on the metal to a high value (p. 607). When the generator is started A becomes charged, and soon it begins to spin round O. The direction of rotation is opposite to that of the points, as shown. In a darkened room, a circular glow can be seen as A rotates.

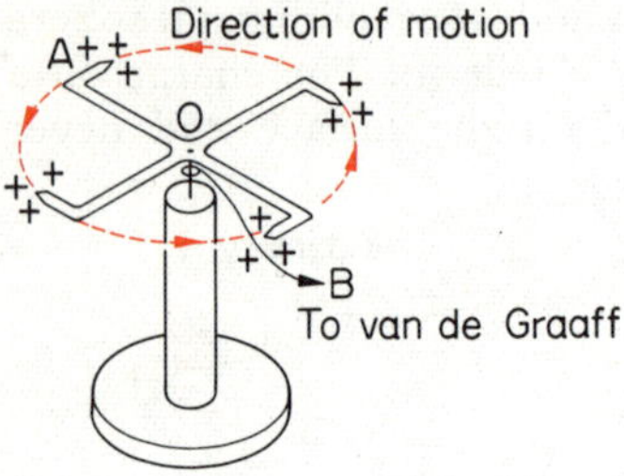

Fig. 34.10 Action at points

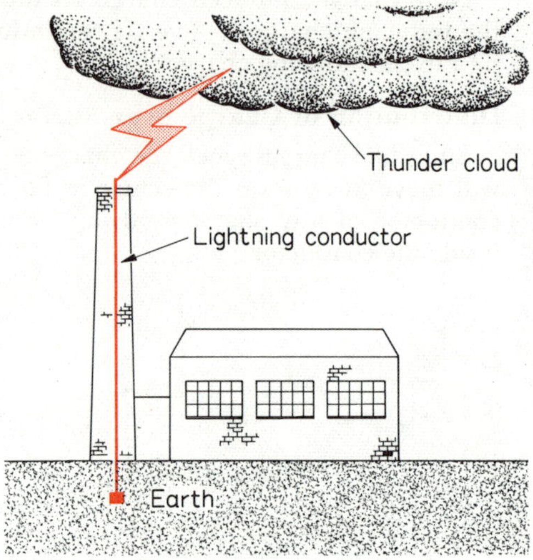

Fig. 34.11 Lightning conductor

Explanation: Suppose A has a +ve charge. The high density of charge at a point produces a powerful attractive force which tears off electrons (−ve charges) from the air molecules round the point. The remaining charge on the molecules is +ve and they are therefore repelled away from the point. This produces a *reaction* on the point, which makes the windmill turn in the opposite direction.

A *lightning conductor* is a very long metal rod, with a sharp point at the end above the building it is required to protect. The other end is buried deep in the earth below the building, Fig. 34.11. During a storm, a thundercloud with a large −ve charge may build up above the conductor, as shown. A +ve charge is then induced at the point (see p. 604). By the same process just described for the metal windmill, +ve charge streams away from the point in an upward direction towards the −ve charge in the cloud. This helps to neutralise the −ve charge, thus protecting the building from any violent discharges from the cloud. The tall Post Office Tower in London has a lightning conductor for protection in electric storms.

Van de Graaff Electrostatic Generator

Van de Graaff designed a generator which can quickly build up a very large charge on a conductor.

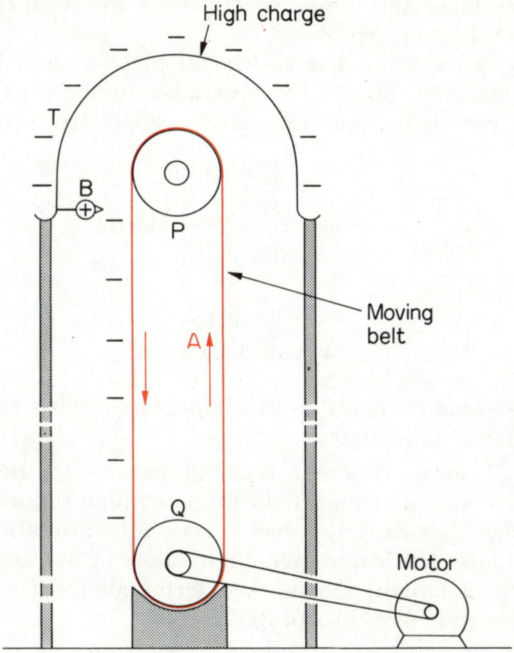

Fig. 34.12 Van de Graaff generator

In a school laboratory model, a rubber or silk belt A moves round two insulated rollers P and Q. The drive is provided by a small electric motor. Suppose A obtains a —ve charge by rubbing against Q, Fig. 34.12. The charge is carried upward past a pointed conductor B. As the —ve charge passes B, it induces a +ve charge on the point and a —ve charge on a large metal hemisphere T to which B is joined.

By the action at points, +ve charge on air molecules then streams away from the point at B towards the —ve charge on the belt in front of it. The —ve charge is thus neutralised, leaving only the induced —ve charge on T. When the belt passes round to the bottom it again collects some —ve charge, so once again T obtains another —ve charge. In this way the charge on the metal hemisphere quickly grows to a large value. Van de Graaff generators are used in nuclear research. See Plate 33 (G), p. 591.

Capacitors

A *capacitor* is a device which can store charge. Small and large capacitors are widely used in electronic circuits, for example in transistor radios and television sets. They are also used in telecommunication circuits, which transmit and receive messages by wire and radio. Some small and large capacitors are shown in the simple radio receiver circuits on pages 566–8.

Basically, a capacitor has two metal plates A and B separated by insulating material, Fig. 34.13. A variable tuning capacitor, shown in Fig. 32.22, has air between the plates. Capacitors of fixed values may

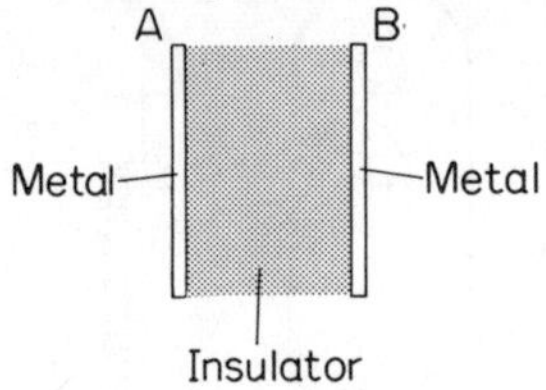

Fig. 34.13 Capacitor

have polystyrene or paraffin-waxed paper or mica as the insulating material between the plates.

Fig. 32.24 shows different types of capacitors. In each case the terminals are already connected to the two plates inside the capacitor. The *electrolytic-type* capacitor has a very thin insulating material between the plates inside and gives high values of 'storage' ability. When it is used in a circuit, the marked terminals must be joined to the correct +ve and −ve sides of the circuit.

Charging and Discharging Capacitors

A capacitor C can be *charged* simply by connecting a battery D to it, Fig. 34.14 (i). Electrons are then driven by the battery from one plate A to the other B. The −ve charge on B repels electrons moving towards it and so the electron flow stops at one stage. The capacitor C is then full charged by the battery. The plate B now has a −ve charge Q and the plate A has an equal +ve charge Q.

The capacitor can be *discharged* by removing the battery and connecting the plates together, Fig. 34.14 (ii). The electrons then return from B to A, leaving both plates uncharged.

If a high resistance of the order of a million ohms is included in the circuits, the electron flow or current can be slowed down and observed in a suitable current meter. See 'Experiments', p. 612.

The capacitor stores more charge when a higher potential difference is connected across it, for example, when two batteries in series are used in place of the one shown in Fig. 34.14 (i). This is because the two batteries can drive more electrons on to the capacitor plates than one battery.

Capacitance

Experiment shows that capacitors can store more charge if the area of their plates are increased, if the plates are closer together, or if they have special insulating material between them. When the same battery is used, those capacitors which store large charges are said to have larger *capacitance*.

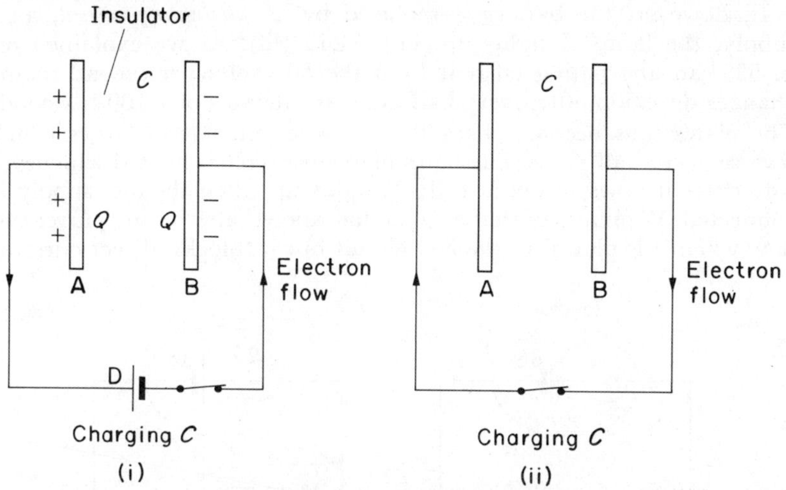

Fig. 34.14 Charging and discharging capacitor

Capacitance is measured in units of a *farad*, symbol F. Practical capacitors usually have values of the order of a *microfarad*, one millionth of a farad, symbol μF. The radio receiver circuits on pages 566–8 show capacitors of different values. A *picofarad*, symbol pF, is a small capacitance equal to one millionth of 1 μF.

Capacitors in d.c. and a.c. Circuits

As we shall see, a capacitor has a different effect when used in a direct current, d.c., and then in an alternating current, a.c., circuit.

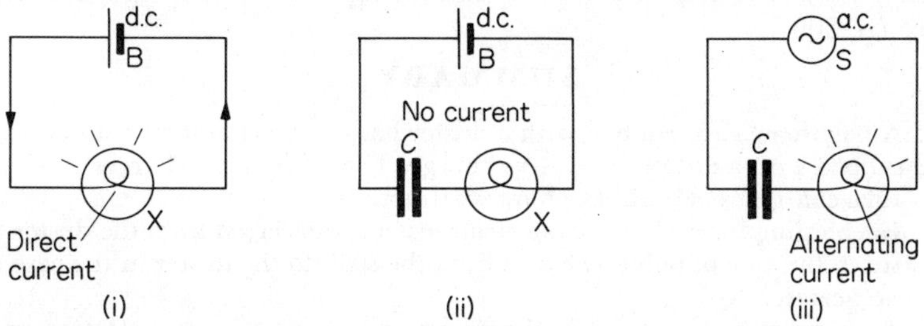

Fig. 34.15 Capacitor in d.c. and a.c. circuits

A lamp X glows when a suitable battery B is connected to it, Fig. 34.15 (i). The battery produces a current always flowing in the same direction—it is a d.c. supply.

If a capacitor C is now included in the circuit, the lamp does not light up, Fig. 34.15 (ii). No current now flows because there is an insulator between the plates of C.

If, however, the battery is replaced by an *alternating current*, a.c., supply, the lamp X lights up. Fig. 34.15 (iii). As we explained on p. 535, an alternating current from the 50 cycles per second mains changes direction after every half-cycle at intervals of 1/100th second. The plates thus become charged with +ve and −ve charges which reverse every half cycle. The lamp filament becomes heated whichever way current flows through it. So X lights up when the a.c. supply is connected. We may say that a capacitor 'allows' alternating current to flow when it is placed in the a.c. circuit but it 'blocks' direct current.

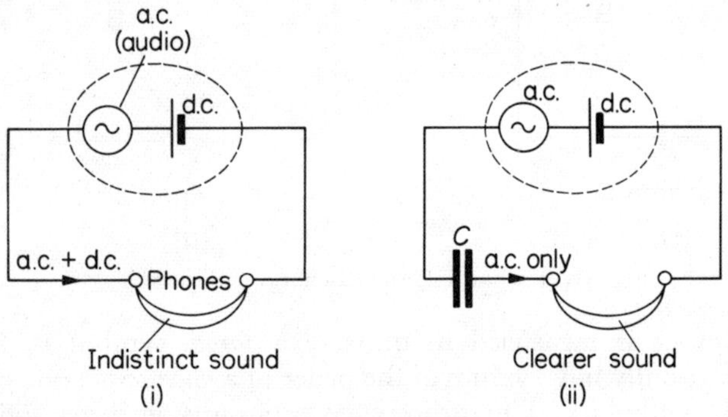

Fig. 34.16 Use of capacitor

Telephones, used to detect the audio (speech) currents in a 'mixture' of the audio currents (a.c.) and direct currents (d.c.), will give a clearer sound when a suitable capacitor is included in series with it, Fig. 34.16. The capacitor will 'block' the direct currents but allow the audio (a.c.) currents to flow through the speech coils inside the earpiece (p. 509).

SUMMARY

1. A polythene strip rubbed with a duster has a −ve charge; a lead acetate strip rubbed with a duster has a +ve charge. These are static charges.

2. Like charges repel; unlike charges attract.

3. In charging by rubbing, some electrons are transferred from the duster to the strip in the case of polythene and from the strip to the duster in the case of the lead acetate.

4. The sign of a charge can be found by using a charged leaf electroscope. An increased divergence of the leaf is the only sure test of the sign.

5. When an electroscope is charged by induction, (i) a charged rod is

brought near the cap, (ii) the cap is then touched, (iii) the finger is taken away while keeping the rod near the cap, (iv) the rod is finally taken away. The leaf then opens and has a charge *opposite* to the inducing charge, the charge on the rod.

6. A pointed conductor has a high density of charge at the points. The air molecules round the point have electrons torn off by the powerful electric force on them, leaving the air molecules with a +ve charge. If the pointed conductor has a +ve charge, the charged air molecules are repelled away from the point. This 'action at points' is used in the lightning conductor and in the van de Graaff generator.

7. A capacitor is a device which stores charge. It has two plates separated by an insulator. It allows alternating current but not direct current to flow in a circuit in which it is present.

PRACTICAL

1. Investigating charges

Apparatus. Small light conducting sphere, nylon thread, wire stirrup, clamp and stand, polythene and lead acetate strips, duster.

Method. (i) Suspend a small conducting sphere by nylon (insulating) thread from one end of a clamp. Rub a polythene strip hard with a duster and then transfer some charge from the strip to the sphere by rubbing the strip on the sphere. After some charge is transferred to it, what happens to the sphere when the polythene strip is brought slowly towards it?

(ii) Rub the acetate strip hard with the duster and then bring it towards the charged sphere. What happens now? Why?

(iii) Put a −ve or a +ve charge on the sphere with the rubbed polythene or acetate strip. Then, observing the attraction or repulsion of the sphere, find the *sign* of the charge on (*a*) a plastic balloon rubbed on the sleeve, (*b*) a rubbed plastic penholder, (*c*) a rubbed plastic ruler.

Find out by experiment if the sign of the charge on a rubbed object depends on the nature of the material used for rubbing it, for example, on the material of a jacket or a dress or a duster.

Conclusions. Write an account of your results in part (iii).

2. Conducting properties of materials

Apparatus. Gold leaf electroscope, polythene strip and duster. Metal wire, cotton, nylon thread, perspex ruler, wooden ruler, dry paper, moistened paper, pencil lead, metal rod, coin.

Method. (i) Rub the polythene strip hard with the duster and charge the electroscope by contact so that the leaf opens wide.

(ii) Holding one end of the different materials in turn, touch the cap of the electroscope with the other end. Observe whether the leaf falls quickly or slowly, recharging the electroscope when necessary.

Conclusions. Make a list of the good and poor conductors, putting them in an order if you can.

3. Charging by induction

Apparatus. Gold leaf electroscope, small light conducting sphere, nylon thread, clamp and stand, polythene and lead acetate strips, duster.

Method. (i) Using the method shown on p. 604, charge the electroscope by induction with the rubbed polythene strip.

Observe the effect on the open leaf when (*a*) the rubbed polythene strip, (*b*) the rubbed acetate strip are brought in turn *slowly* towards the electroscope cap.

(ii) Charge the electroscope by induction using the rubbed acetate strip. Find the *sign* of the induced charge.

(iii) Suspend the conducting sphere by nylon thread from a clamp. Charge the sphere by induction in the same way as the electroscope was charged, using the rubbed polythene strip. Find the sign of the induced charge.

Now discharge the sphere by touching it. Recharge it by induction using the rubbed acetate strip. Find the sign of the induced charge.

4. Capacitors

Apparatus. Battery B, 0–9 V; capacitors C of various values, 100 to 500 μF electrolytic; large resistance R, 1000 to 5000 ohms; centre-scale meter G, 2·5 mA–0–2·5 mA; keys K_1, K_2.

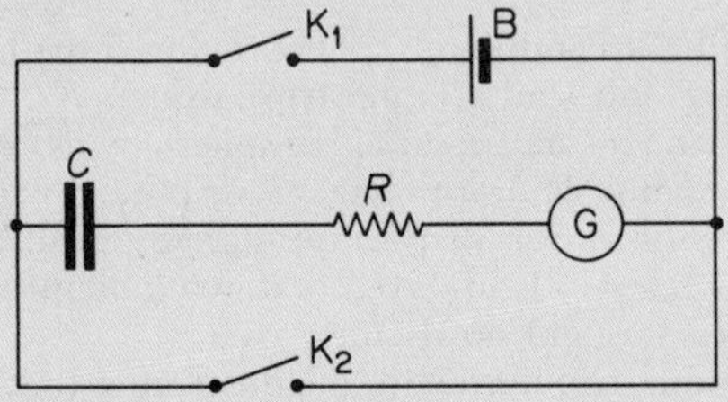

Fig. 34.17 Experiment on charging and discharging capacitor

Method.

(i) Connect the circuit shown in Fig. 34.17; use a capacitor C of low value, a resistor R of high value, and a low battery supply B such as 1·5 V.

(ii) Press K_1 to charge C and observe G. If the meter reading is too small, or reached too quickly, try varying the values of B, C or R to get readings you can observe.

(iii) Release K_1 *first* and *then* press K_2 to discharge C. Observe the readings in G. What difference do you notice about the current when the capacitor is discharging?

(iv) Repeat the charging and discharging of C with (*a*) a larger battery supply, and (*b*), a larger capacitor.

Conclusions. State your conclusions in (iv) (*a*) and (*b*).

5. Capacitor in a.c. circuit

Apparatus. Components C, R and meter G as in Experiment 4, but hand driven bicycle dynamo to provide a.c. in place of the d.c. battery B.

Method. (i) By turning the bicycle dynamo slowly, a slow alternating voltage can be obtained. Use this a.c. supply in place of the d.c. battery B and connect up the circuit of Fig. 34.17. Observe the effect on the reading of G when K_1 is closed and the slow a.c. is applied.

(ii) Release K_1. What happens in G when the key K_2 is now closed? Explain your observations.

EXERCISE 34

1. Fig. 34A (i) and (ii) show two small charges near each other. Copy the sketches and show on them the force (*a*) on A due to B; (*b*) on C due to D.

If A is discharged by touching, is A now repelled by B? Is A now attracted by B?

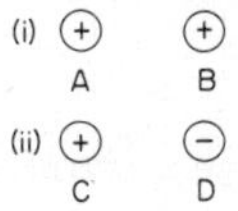

Fig. 34A

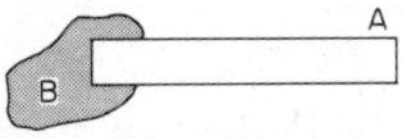

Fig. 34B

2. A polythene strip A is rubbed hard with a duster B. Fig. 34B. (*a*) What charge is on A and B? (*b*) Where did the charges come from? (*c*) How would you test the *sign* of the charges on A and on B?

3. A rubbed polythene strip is held over some small pieces of paper on a table. Explain why the pieces jump up and down below the strip and the table.

4. A rubbed acetate strip A has a +ve charge and is held near two spherical conductors B and C which touch each other, Fig. 34C.

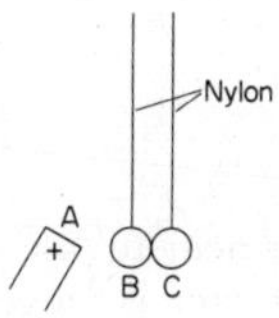

Fig. 34C

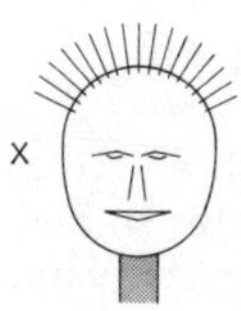

Fig. 34D

What charges are obtained on B and C when they are separated by means of the nylon thread? Why do B and C have these charges?

5. In Fig. 34D, X is a conductor representing a model 'head' with nylon threads as 'hair' on top. When X is given a high charge, the threads spread outwards as shown.

Explain the appearance of the threads. Why does X lose some of its charge although it is on an insulating support?

6. A glass rod is rubbed vigorously with a piece of dry silk. A positive electrical charge is produced on the glass.

(i) Why is the glass so charged? (ii) What effect does this have on the silk? (iii) Given a negatively charged gold leaf electroscope, how could you prove that the charge on the glass is positive? Say what you would do and what you would expect to see happen. (*W.Md.*)

7. Explain the following:

(i) It is difficult to do electrostatic experiments effectively in damp weather.

(ii) A charge can be obtained on a rubbed polythene strip held in the hand but not on a rubbed metal rod held in the hand.

(iii) A 'crackling' noise may be heard on removing a nylon shirt or blouse or stockings.

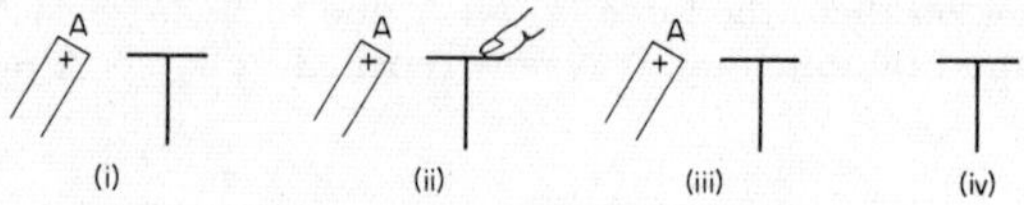

Fig. 34E

8. Fig. 34E shows the four stages of charging an electroscope by induction. The leaf is deliberately omitted from the diagrams.

Copy the four sketches and shown on them (*a*) the leaf position; (*b*) the charges on the electroscope. *Explain* what happens in each case.

9. Fig. 34F shows (i) a rod A with a +ve charge; (ii) a rod B with a −ve charge; (iii) a metal plate C held in the hand. In turn, each is brought slowly towards the cap of an electroscope having a +ve charge.

In each case, state whether the divergence of the leaf increases or decreases or stays the same. Give a reason for your answers.

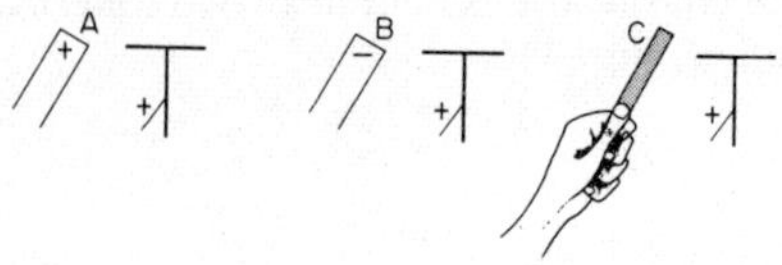

Fig. 34F

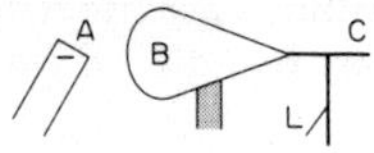

Fig. 34G

10. A strip A with a −ve charge is brought near to one side of an insulated pear-shaped conductor B, Fig. 34G. The conductor is moved to touch the cap C of an electroscope. Explain, showing the charge on a sketch, why the leaf opens.

Keeping A present, the conductor B is touched. What happens to the leaf? If the finger is taken away, what happens now to the leaf? Explain your answers.

11. A lightning conductor has a sharp point at one end and the other is buried deep in the earth.

Explain what happens when a thundercloud is over a building protected by the lightning conductor.

12. A model of a van de Graaff generator has a *rubber* belt, an *electric motor*, a large *metal hemisphere* at the top, and a *pointed conductor* joined to the hemisphere at the top.

Explain the purpose of each of the items in italics.

13. What is a *capacitor*? Draw diagrams showing how you would (i) charge and (ii) then discharge a capacitor. Explain briefly what happens in each case.

Draw a sketch of a variable capacitor such as a tuning capacitor.

14. Two metal cans A and B of different sizes rest on two identical gold leaf electroscopes as shown in Fig. 34H. Each can is given exactly the same quantity of negative charge.

(i) Show in a diagram the divergence of the leaf on each electroscope.

(ii) Which of the two arrangements has the greater capacitance, A or B?

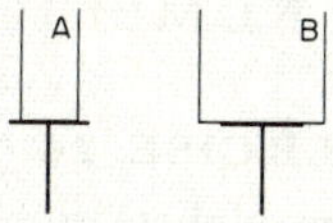

Fig. 34H

(iii) Which will have been charged to the greater potential?

(iv) If the two cans are now carefully connected, without either being earthed, which way will electrons flow?

(v) Give a reason for your answer to part (iv). (*Mx.*)

(*Hint.* The divergence of the leaf is a measure of the potential of the capacitor, assuming the surrounding case of the electroscope has zero potential.)

15. A lamp with a capacitor in series does not light up when a d.c. battery is connected but lights up when an a.c. supply from the mains is connected. Explain.

ANSWERS TO NUMERICAL EXERCISES

EXERCISE 24 (p. 436)

1. *d* **2.** copper, lead, copper sulphate, sulphuric acid **3.** chemical
4. (*a*) 120 Ω (*b*) 1 A **5.** rubber, polythene; silver, copper **6.** *e*
9. A–battery, B–switch, C–voltmeter, D–ammeter, E–rheostat
10. (*a*) 8Ω (*b*) 2A (*c*) 10 V **11.** 2Ω **12.** 5·0 Ω **13.** (*a*) 1·5 (*b*) 2 A
14. (*b*) (i) 36 Ω (ii) 9 Ω (iii) (*c*) one 10 Ω in series with two 50 Ω in parallel
15. (*b*) 0·1 A (*c*) (i) $1\frac{1}{3}$ Ω (ii) $4\frac{1}{3}$ Ω (iii) 6/13 A (iv) $1\frac{5}{13}$ V (v) 8/13 V (vi) 4/13, 2/13 A
17. (ii) 8 V (iii) 2 Ω (iv) $1\frac{1}{3}$ A (v) $\frac{1}{2}$ Ω (vi) 600 C (vii) 16 W **18.** 5 Ω
19. (*a*) $\frac{1}{4}$ A (*b*) 1 A (*c*) $\frac{1}{2}$ A

EXERCISE 25 (p. 449)

1. copper, zinc **2.** hydrogen **3.** copper **4.** hydrogen **5.** carbon, zinc
6. manganese dioxide **7.** conductor
8. sal-ammoniac soln; manganese dioxide **9.** accumulator
10. accumulator **11.** lead peroxide, lead **12.** sulphuric acid
13. relative density, hydrometer **14.** positive, negative **15.** hydrometer
16. (i) transformer (ii) rectifier **18.** *d* **20.** decreasing, increasing
21. A–zinc, B–carbon, C–carbon, D–sal-ammoniac, E–brass, F–pitch
24. (*a*) carbon (*b*) zinc (*c*) sal-ammoniac (*d*) manganese dioxide
26. (*a*) i–poor, ii–needs re-charge, iii–good **27.** $1\frac{1}{2}$p

EXERCISE 26 (p. 459)

1. positive **2.** electrolyte **3.** platinum **4.** cathode, anode
5. copper, cathode **6.** anode **7.** ions **8.** positive **9.** positive, hydrogen
10. current, time **11.** cathode **12.** (*a*) oxygen (*b*) hydrogen **13** (*a*) B
14. electrons, positive, ions **15.** (*a*) copper (*b*) copper sulphate **16.** 0·792 g
17. 6·037 g

EXERCISE 27 (p. 477)

1. ampere, ohm, watt, joule **3.** 10, $\frac{1}{2}$ hr **4.** 1·5p
5. current, p.d. resistance, power **6.** dim, hot, casing, melt **7.** live
8. (i) 2 (ii) 5 (iii) 13 (iv) 5 A; £1·80 **9.** £2·64 **10.** 1200 W
11. 2817; 4071; £10·62 **12.** 2700 W
13. (iii) A–blue, B–green-yellow, C–brown (iv) fuse **15.** (i) 12p (ii) 1p (iii) 5h **17.** (*a*) $8\frac{1}{3}$ A, 13 A fuse (*b*) £3·36
18. (*a*) 2 A (*b*) (i) $\frac{1}{2}$ A (ii) 400 Ω (*c*) (ii) $1\frac{1}{2}$ A (iii) 300 W
19. 13, 5, 13 A; 12p, $4\frac{1}{2}$p, 18p
20. (*a*) series 10 Ω; series, 10Ω with two 5Ω in parallel (*b*) $\frac{1}{4}$ A (*d*) (ii) 200 W (iii) 20 d
21. (*b*) 8 (*c*) 9p (*d*) increases
22. (*a*) (i) live (ii) neutral (iii) earth (*c*) (i) fuse (ii) tinned copper
23. (*b*) (i) 50 Ω (ii) 4·8 A (iii) 35p
24. (*b*) brass (*c*) 5 A (*d*) 125 Ω (*e*) 75 Ω
25. (*c*) (i) 0·4 A, 625 Ω (ii) 0·2 A, 50 W

EXERCISE 28 (p. 497)

1. south **2.** south **3.** south **4.** soft iron **5.** steel **6.** magnetized **7.** north **8.** raised **9.** increased **10.** shield **11.** iron, steel, nickel, cobalt. **12.** clockwise **14.** unaffected **18.** magnet, north **21.** (*a*) CD (*b*) C

EXERCISE 29 (p. 513)

1. south **2.** anticlockwise **3.** soft iron **4.** opposite **5.** broken and made **6.** magnetism **7.** diaphragm **8.** iron core **9.** circular **10.** straight, magnet **11.** soft iron **15.** *b*

EXERCISE 30 (p. 528)

1. south **2.** north **3.** increased
4. number of turns/area/magnetic field strength **5.** commutator
6. direction **7.** battery **8.** current **9.** springs **10.** weak **11.** parallel
12. series **13.** uniform (linear), radial **14.** springs, commutator
16. ammeter—0·1 Ω shunt, voltmeter—1000 Ω series **18.** (*c*) series 195 Ω
20. series 485 Ω

EXERCISE 31 (p. 544)

2. *e* **6.** 1:40 **9.** 10 V, 0·8 A **10.** (*a*) $\frac{1}{3}$ (*b*) $\frac{1}{132}$ A **18.** 0·2 A
19. (*b*) (i) $\frac{1}{3}$ (ii) $\frac{1}{132}$ A

EXERCISE 32 (p. 577)

1. P = anode, Q = cathode, R = heater **2.** (*a*) electrons (*b*) X-rays
4. (*a*) anode (*b*) cathode (*c*) B to A **5.** (*a*) anode (*b*) electrons (*c*) cathode
6. (i) heat (ii) light **7.** electrons, protons, neutrons **8.** (*a*) iii (*b*) i
10. (i) 1/16 000 s (ii) 1/20 000 s (iii) 7500 metres
17. triode; A–heater, B–cathode, C–grid, D–anode, E–glass envelope
18. A–aerial coil, B–earth, C–receiver coil, D–tuning capacitor, E–diode, G–telephone earpiece **23.** (i) *c* (ii) *b* **24.** *c*

EXERCISE 33 (p. 597)

1. electron **2.** proton —mass 1, charge $+e$; neutron —mass 1, charge 0; electron —mass 1/2000 (approx), charge $-e$
3. protons, neutrons, electrons **4.** (*a*) nucleus (*b*) α-particles
5. (*a*) nucleus (*b*) protons, neutrons (*c*) electrons
6. (*a*) α-particles (*b*) γ-rays (*c*) γ-rays **7.** (i) *b* (ii) *d* (iii) *c*
8. (i) positive (ii) $+2e$ **10.** isotopes
11. (*a*) neutron, proton, electrons (*b*) electrons

Revision Questions · ANSWERS, p. 625

The following questions are on basic points of the syllabus. Generally only short answers are required.

Mechanics

1. *metre/second, metre, newton, kilogramme/metre*^{3}, *newton/metre*^{2}, *watt, joule, hertz.* From the above list of units, choose *one* unit in which each of the following quantities can be measured: (*a*) power; (*b*) pressure; (*c*) density; (*d*) wavelength; (*e*) force. (*Mx.*)

2. From the graph we see that the body
(*a*) starts from rest
(*b*) has uniform acceleration for 5 seconds.
(*c*) slows down after 5 seconds.
Which statements are correct? (*L.*)

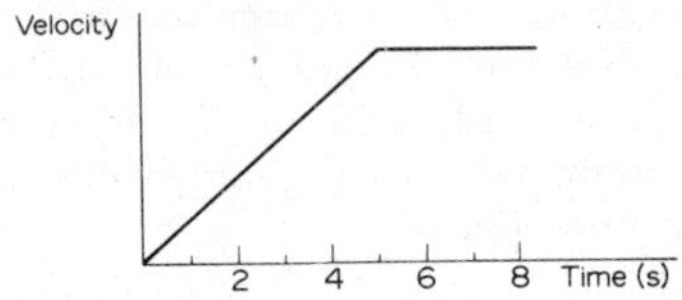

3. In the following, select from the alternatives given the one which *best* completes the statement.
A spring balance is extended 20 mm by a force of 30 N. The extension produced by a force of 75 N will be
A 4 mm, *B* 30 mm, *C* 2 mm, *D* 50 mm, *E* 25 mm. (*N.W.*)

4. (*a*) Name the form of energy possessed by (i) a body due to its motion; (ii) a body due to its high position; (iii) a spring under tension.
(*b*) Name the forms of energy given out by the filament of a car headlamp when in use. (*E.A.*)

5. ABCDE is a uniform metre rule pivoted at its midpoint C. Weights of 40 N and 30 N are attached at A and E respectively. The rule may be balanced by (*a*) placing a 20 N force at D; (*b*) adding an extra 10 N force at E; (*c*) reducing the weight at A by 10 N force. Which statements are correct? (*L.*)

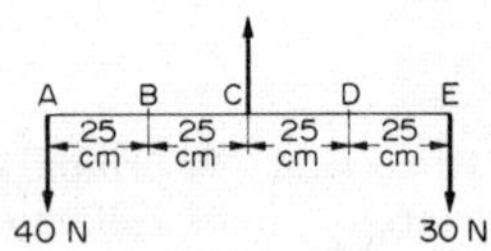

6. Complete the following definition of a newton:
A newton is the force needed to give a mass of . . . an acceleration of . . . (*Mx.*)

7.

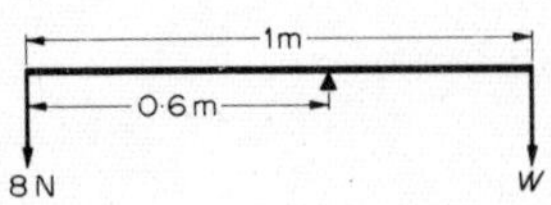

A rod is pivoted as shown in the diagram. Calculate the weight *W* required to keep the rod in a horizontal position. (Neglect the weight of the rod.) (*Mx.*)

Fluids. Matter

8. Three diagrams of the same block of metal, 10 cm × 5 cm × 2 cm, are shown, standing on a bench on different faces.

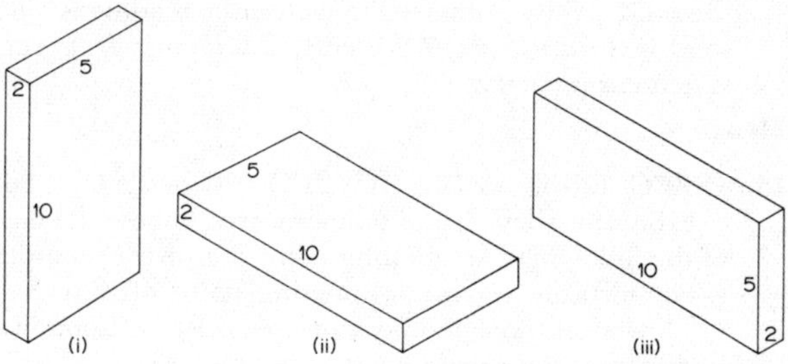

(*a*) What is the volume of the block?
(*b*) If the block has a mass of 300 g what is its density?
(*c*) In which case is the pressure on the bench greatest? Give a reason.
(*d*) Calculate this pressure. (*E.A.*)

9. Mercury is used in a barometer because it (*a*) has a high boiling point; (*b*) has a large relative density; (*c*) is a good conductor of heat. Which statement is correct? (*L.*)

10. A boy is given a length of copper wire which stretches fairly easily and he decides to do an experiment to test whether Hooke's law is true for the wire for loads of up to 20 N.

(*a*) State Hooke's law. (*b*) Draw a diagram to show the arrangement of the apparatus which would enable him to do the experiment. (Your diagram should show clearly how the measurements are taken.) (*c*) State exactly what measurements would be taken. (*d*) Name the precautions which he should take. (*e*) The results show that Hooke's law is true for loads up to 9 N and that a load of 18 N breaks the wire. Sketch a graph to show the results. (*Mx.*)

11. Select from the alternatives given the one which *best* completes the following statement:

The important physical principle on which the hydraulic braking system of a car depends is that: *A* pressure is increased when applied by fluids; *B* hydraulic brakes do not wear out; *C* pressure in fluids is transmitted equally in all directions; *D* these brakes act more quickly than other types; *E* only a small force has to be applied to stop the car. (*N.W.*)

12.

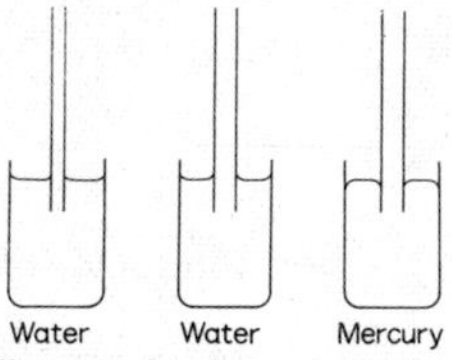

The diagrams show clean glass tubes partly immersed in liquids. Copy them and show clearly where you would expect the liquid levels to be in each tube. (*L.*)

13. When a hydrometer is placed in a liquid and settles in its equilibrium position, *A* the density of the liquid is equal to that of the hydrometer; *B* the density of the liquid is proportional to the length of the hydrometer outside the liquid; *C* the weight of the hydrometer is proportional to the density of the liquid; *D* the weight of the hydrometer is equal to the weight of liquid displaced; *E* the upthrust on the hydrometer is equal to the weight of the hydrometer outside the liquid. Which statement is correct?

14. A solid is suspended from a spring balance, which then reads 2·0 N. When the solid is fully immersed in water, the reading is 1·8 N. The density of the solid is *A* 10 g/cm³; *B* 8 g/cm³; *C* 6 g/cm³; *D* 4 g/cm³; *E* 2 g/cm³. Which statement is correct?

Heat

15. 1530°C, 120°C, 55°C, 37°C, 19°C, 0°C, −12°C, −50°C.

From the above list of temperatures, choose the most likely value for *each* of the following: (*a*) melting point of iron; (*b*) temperature of a room that is comfortably warm; (*c*) melting point of pure ice at normal pressure; (*d*) lowest outdoor temperature recorded in London in winter; (*e*) normal body temperature of a healthy person. (*Mx.*)

16. In the following, select from the alternatives given the one which *best* completes the statement.

A maximum thermometer records its reading by having *A* an index within the surface of alcohol; *B* a constriction in a tube containing alcohol; *C* an index outside the surface of alcohol; *D* an index outside the surface of mercury; *E* a constriction in a tube containing mercury. (*N.W.*)

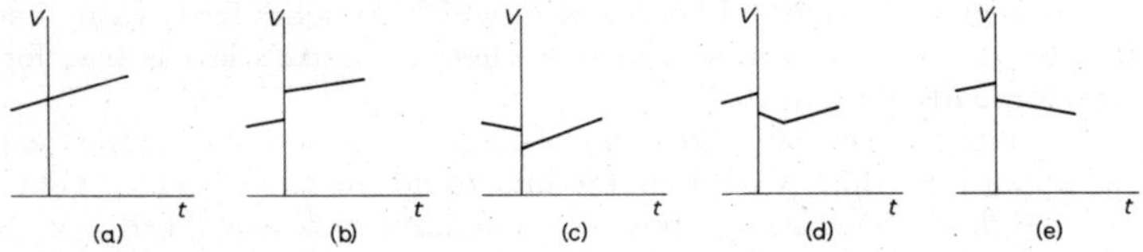

17. Which graph above shows the volume (*V*) —temperature (*t*) relationship for a fixed mass of water between −3°C and +10°C? (*L.*)

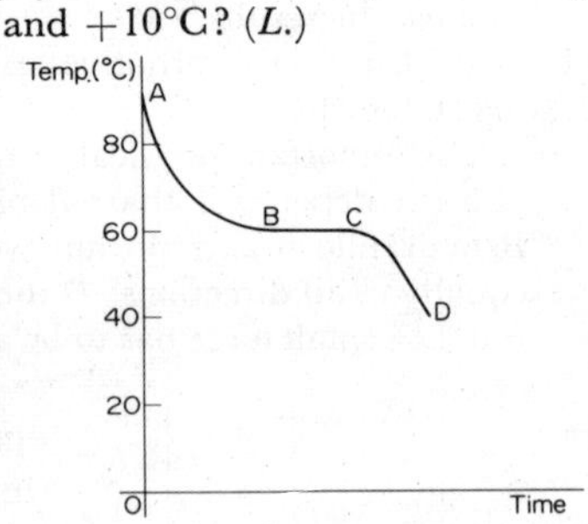

18. The diagram shows the change of temperature with time as a substance cools. This substance is in its liquid state at 100°C. (*a*) What are the states of the substance (i) between A and B; (ii) between B and C; (iii) between C and D? (*b*) What is the significance of the temperature 60°C on the graph? (*N.W.*)

19. Copper, lead, glass, air, water.

(*a*) Of the above list of substances, (i) which is the best conductor of heat? (ii) which is the worst conductor of heat?

(*b*) If equal volumes of all the above were heated from 10°C to 60°C, (i) which substance would expand most? (ii) which substance would expand the next most?

(*c*) In which of the above substances are the molecules furthest apart at 60°C? (*Mx.*)

20. What effect does an increase in pressure have on (*a*) the freezing point; (*b*) the boiling point of water? (*L.*)

Optics

21. In the following, select from the alternatives given the one which *best* completes the statement.

A magnifying glass is *A* a converging lens used to produce a real magnified image; *B* a diverging lens used to produce a virtual erect image; *C* a converging lens used to produce a magnified erect image; *D* a combination of a converging and a diverging lens; *E* a diverging lens used to produce a real erect image. (*N.W.*)

22. 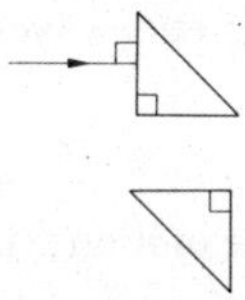

(*a*) Complete the diagram to show how a prism periscope works.

(*b*) Draw a diagram showing how two plane mirrors can be used as a periscope. Show the path of the rays. (*Mx.*)

23. Which of the following will cause an image to be formed which is the same size as the object for all object distances? (*a*) plane mirror; (*b*) concave mirror; (*c*) convex mirror; (*d*) diverging lens; (*e*) converging lens. (*L.*)

24. Describe, with the aid of a labelled diagram, how a pure spectrum from white light may be cast on a screen. Explain the function of each part of the apparatus. (*E.A.*)

25. In the following, select from the alternatives given the one which *best* completes the statement:

The critical angle is: *A* only involved when light passes into a more dense medium; *B* the largest angle a prism can have; *C* the angle of reflection when light is reflected back into the more dense medium; *D* the angle of incidence in the more dense medium which gives an angle of refraction of 90° in the less dense medium; *E* the angle between the red and the violet end of the spectrum when white light is dispersed by a prism. (*N.W.*)

26. Red, yellow, blue, violet, orange.

From the above list, choose (*a*) two primary coloured lights; (*b*) one secondary coloured light; (*c*) two coloured lights which when added together would give white light; (*d*) the coloured light which would be deviated *least* by a prism for a given angle of incidence; (*e*) the coloured light which has the shortest wavelength. (*Mx.*)

27. Complete the ray diagram to show the converging (convex) lens being used as a magnifying glass. Show clearly the positions of the object and image, and draw sufficient construction lines to show how the image is formed. (*L.*)

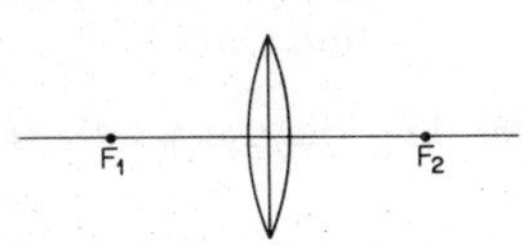

Waves . Sound

28. In the following, select from the alternatives given the one which *best* completes the statement.

The pitch of a note is dependent on: *A* the velocity of sound in air; *B* the temperature of the air; *C* the frequency of the sound source; *D* the wavelength of the sound waves; *E* the presence of harmonics. (*N.W.*)

29. Which has the longest wavelength? (*a*) radio wave; (*b*) ultra-violet light; (*c*) gamma rays; (*d*) visible light; (*e*) X-rays. (*L.*)

30. The velocity of sound in air is 340 m/s. The wavelength of a piano note is 0·8 m. Which of the following statements is correct.

The frequency of the note is: *A* 340·8 Hz; *B* 425 Hz; *C* 688 Hz; *D* 1360·8 Hz; *E* 13 608 Hz.

31. What are the missing words:

(*a*) Waves incident on a wall are . . .; (*b*) Waves incident on a narrow opening which spread out after passing through are said to be . . .; (*c*) Light, radio waves and X-rays are all examples of . . . waves; (*d*) Infra-red rays have . . . wavelengths than visible rays; (*e*) Rays which have the shortest wavelength among all the electromagnetic waves are called . . . rays.

32. (*a*) The following are examples of wave motion:

radio waves, sound waves, light waves, water waves.

Select from this list: (i) an example of a transverse wave motion; (ii) an example of a longitudinal wave motion.

(*b*) What is the velocity of sound in air if a wave of frequency 1320 Hz has a wavelength of 0·25 m? (*N.W.*)

33. What are the missing words:

(*a*) When the amplitude of a sound wave is larger, the sound becomes . .
(*b*) The quality or timbre of a note is due to the accompanying . .
(*c*) The velocity of sound in air depends on the . . of the air.
(*d*) Sound waves can not travel through a . .

Magnetism

34. In the following statement, which answers are correct:

Soft iron is used for the core of a transformer because it (*a*) is easily magnetised; (*b*) may be strongly magnetised; (*c*) keeps its magnetism well. (*L.*)

35. (*a*) Draw a diagram of the pattern of lines of force in the space between the two magnets shown. Show the direction of the lines of force.

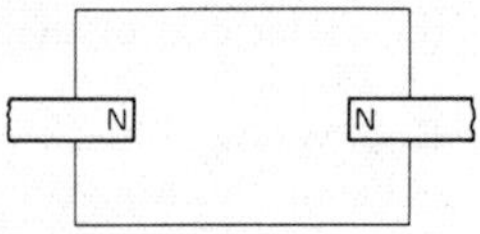

(*b*) A vertical wire carrying a current passes down through a piece of card as shown. Show in a diagram the pattern of the lines of force on the card and show their direction. (*Mx.*)

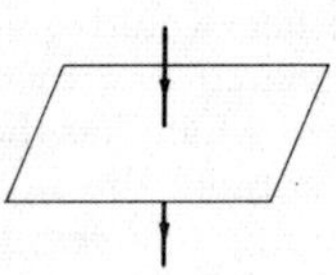

36. The diagrams (*a*), (*b*) and (*c*) show three ways of making magnets in

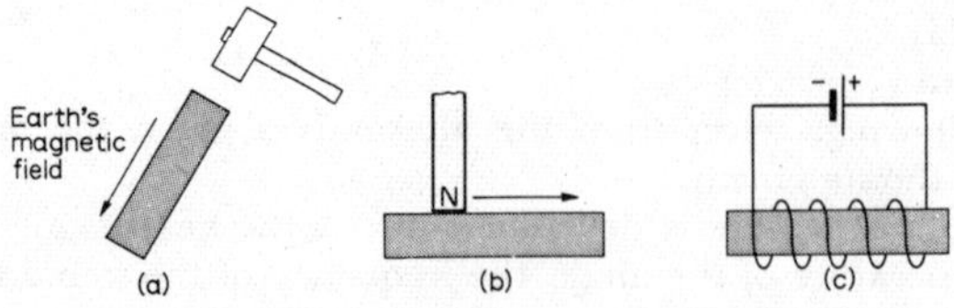

England. Mark in diagrams the polarity of the magnets being produced in each case. (*E.A.*)

37. In the following statements, which are correct:
(*a*) Steel is used in electromagnets. (*b*) There is a limit to the amount of magnetism which can be produced in a steel bar. (*c*) When a needle is attracted to a magnet the needle becomes magnetised. (*d*) The north geographic pole of the Earth is a south *magnetic* pole.

Electricity

38. In the following, select from the alternatives given the one which *best* completes the statement:
The current taken by a 2 kW electric fire when used on a 250 V mains is: *A* 125 A; *B* 4 A; *C* 1 A; *D* 20 A; *E* 8 A. (*N.W.*)

39. The diagram shows two platinum electrodes dipping into dilute sulphuric acid.

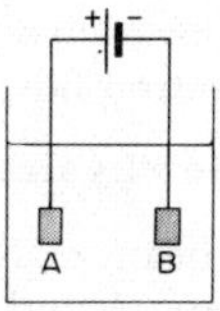

(*a*) Electrode A is called . .
(*b*) Electrode B is called the . .
(*c*) The current is carried through the electrolyte by neutrons, molecules, electrons, ions, protons. Which is the correct answer?
(*d*) What gas appears at electrode A?
(*e*) What gas appears at electrode B? (*Mx.*)

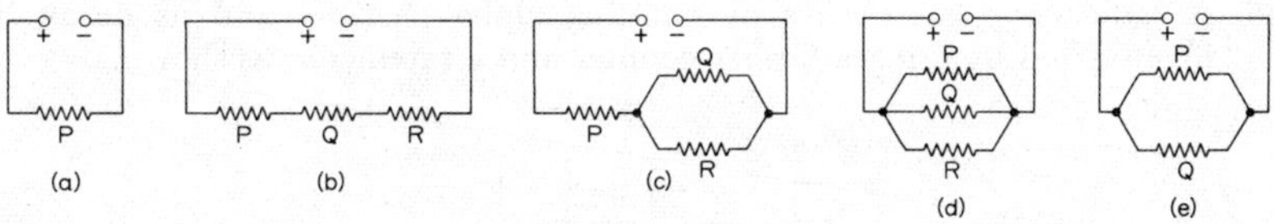

40.
In the diagram, P, Q and R are equal resistors. The same voltage is applied to each circuit. In which case is the voltage across P least? (*L.*)

41. A boy is given a 12-volt lamp and decides to measure the resistance of the lamp filament using the ammeter–voltmeter method. He decides to apply various voltages to the lamp and to measure the current in each case.
(i) Draw the full circuit diagram showing clearly where the voltmeter and ammeter are placed in the circuit.
(ii) Two of the boy's results are given below.

voltmeter reading	2·0 V	12 V
ammeter reading	1·0 A	2·0 A

Calculate the resistance of the lamp filament in each case and also the power used by the lamp in each case.
(iii) Explain why the resistance of the lamp filament is different in the two cases. (*Mx.*)

42. In the following, select from the alternatives given the one which *best* completes the statement.
One advantage of a lead acid accumulator which makes it suitable for use as a car battery is that it: *A* never runs down; *B* can easily be recharged; *C* provides the high voltage for the spark plug; *D* can only produce small currents; *E* is very light in weight. (*N.W.*)

43. When the switch S is closed: (*a*) the ammeter reading in A increases; (*b*) the current through Q increases; (*c*) the voltmeter reading in V increases.

Which statements are correct? (*L.*)

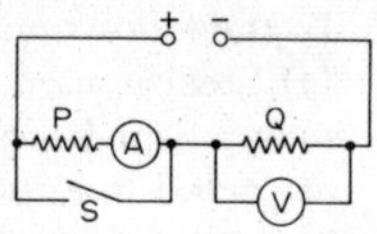

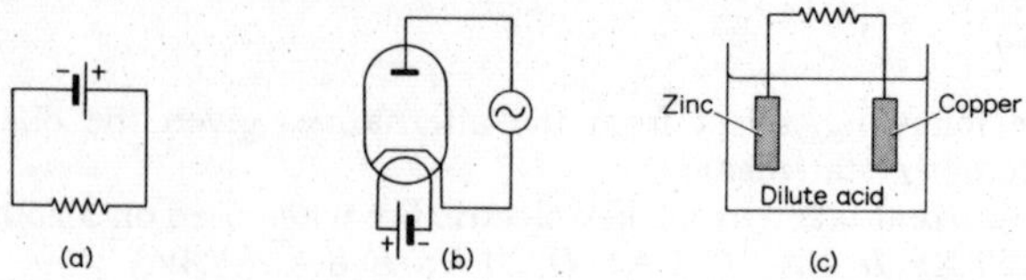

44.

Copy each of the circuits shown above and mark in each the direction of the electron flow with an arrow by the side of the wire. (*E.A.*)

Atomic Physics

45. A beam of X-rays is fired between the two parallel plates A and B. When A is positively charged and B negatively charged, the beam is: (*a*) unaffected; (*b*) deflected towards A; (*c*) accelerated.

Which statements are correct? (*L.*)

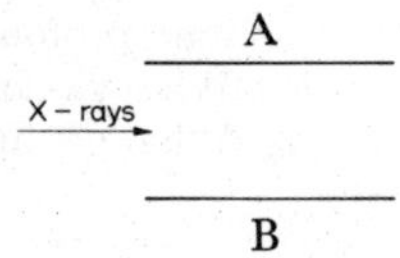

46. A radioactive gas decays by emitting alpha particles and its decay is investigated by using a Geiger counter and a ratemeter, as shown.

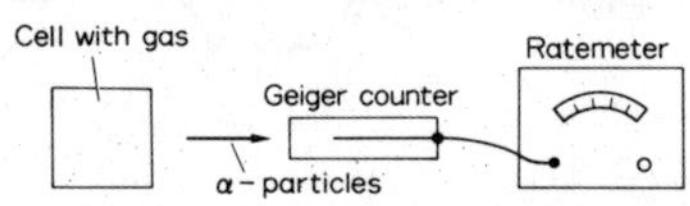

The cell and Geiger counter have very thin windows and the counter is placed very close to the cell. (i) Explain why this is so. (ii) Why would this not be necessary if gamma rays were being investigated? (*Mx.*)

47. When an object is being electrically charged: (*a*) the charge on an electron changes; (*b*) protons change into electrons; (*c*) neutrons are being removed or added; (*d*) the charge on a proton changes; (*e*) electrons are being removed or added.

Which answer is correct? (*L.*)

48. (*a*) (i) Name the particles to be found in the nucleus of an atom. (ii) What charges do these particles carry?

(*b*) What other particle exists in an atom outside its nucleus?

(*c*) If an atom is to be electrically neutral which particles must exist in equal numbers? (*N.W.*)

49. If gas atoms have 86 protons and 134 neutrons in their nuclei and one of the atoms gives off an alpha particle: (i) how many protons will be left in the nucleus; (ii) how many neutrons will be left in the nucleus? (*Mx.*)

50. Radioactive sources may emit alpha, beta and gamma emissions. Which of these: (*a*) consists of helium nuclei; (*b*) consists of electrons; (*c*) is an electromagnetic radiation; (*d*) has the greatest penetrating power; (*e*) will be absorbed by thin paper; (*f*) is not deflected by a magnetic field? (*E.A.*)

ANSWERS TO REVISION QUESTIONS

1. (*a*) watt (*b*) N/m^2 (*c*) kg/m^3 (*d*) metre (*e*) N **2.** (*a*), (*b*) **3.** *D*
4. (*a*) (i) kinetic energy; (ii) potential energy; (iii) potential energy (*b*) light, heat
5. (*a*), (*b*), (*c*) **6.** 1 kilogramme, 1 m/s^2 **7.** 12 N
8. (*a*) 100 cm^3 (*b*) 3 g/cm^3 (*c*) (iii) (*d*) 0·3 N/cm^2 (3000 N/m^2)
9. (*b*) **11.** *C* **13.** *D* **14.** A
15. (*a*) 1530 (*b*) 19 (*c*) 0 (*d*) −12 (*e*) 37°C
16. *D* **17.** (*d*) **18.** (i) liquid; (ii) liquid and solid; (iii) solid
19. (*a*) (i) copper; (ii) air (*b*) (i) air; (ii) water (*c*) air
20. (*a*) lowers f.p. (*b*) raises b.p. **21.** *C* **23.** (*a*) **25.** *D*
26. (*a*) red, blue (*b*) yellow (*c*) blue, yellow (*d*) red (*e*) violet
28. *C* **29.** (*a*) **30.** *B* **31.** (*a*) reflected (*b*) diffracted (*c*) electromagnetic (*d*) longer (*e*) gamma
32. (*a*) (i) water (or radio or light) waves; (ii) sound waves (*b*) 330 m/s
33. (*a*) louder (*b*) overtones (*c*) temperature (*d*) vacuum
34. (*a*), (*b*) **37.** (*b*), (*c*), (*d*) **38.** *E*
39. (*a*) anode (*b*) cathode (*c*) ions (*d*) oxygen (*e*) hydrogen **40.** (*b*)
41. (ii) 2 Ω, 2 W (iii) 6 Ω, 24 W **42.** *B* **43.** (*b*), (*c*) **45.** (*a*) **47.** (*e*)
48. (*a*) (i) protons, neutrons; (ii) +ve, none (*b*) electrons (*c*) protons, electrons
49. (i) 84 (ii) 132 **50.** (*a*) α (*b*) β (*c*) γ (*d*) γ (*e*) α (*f*) γ

Revision Paper 1 · ANSWERS, p. 632

1. Complete this table to show which units are used to measure the quantities indicated:

Quantity	One metric unit
Weight	
Density	
Work	
Power	

(*Mx.*)

2. (*a*) Fig. P1.A (i) represents a loaded lever balanced at its centre of gravity. Find the distance marked x.

(*b*) Fig. P1.A (ii) represents a uniform beam 30 cm long. A force acts on this beam as shown to keep it in a fixed position. Find the weight of the beam.

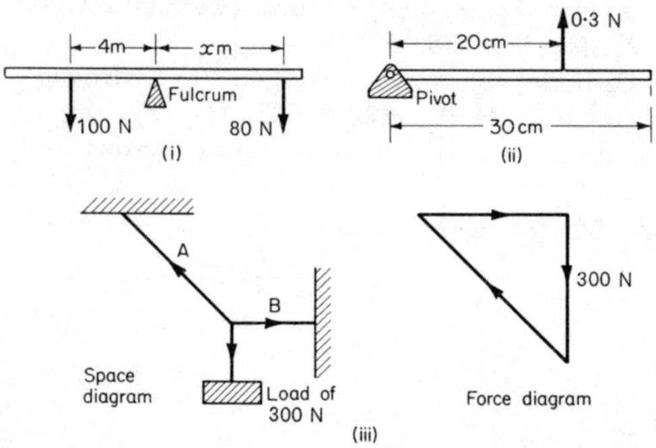

Fig. P1.A

(*c*) A load is supported by two wires, one from the ceiling and one from a wall as shown in Fig. P1.A (iii). A force diagram is also drawn to scale. Use this force diagram to find the tensions in the wires A and B. (*M.*)

3. (*a*) What is the difference between heat and temperature?

(*b*) What is a thermostat?

Give a detailed description of the structure and action of a thermostat which can be set to control the room temperature.

(*c*) What makes a clinical thermometer: (i) sensitive; (ii) quick acting, (iii) self registering?

In the clinical thermometer the bulb is not quite full at room temperature. Why is this? If it registered 104·4°F, what would the reading be on: (i) the Celsius Scale; (ii) the Absolute Scale? (*W.Md.*)

4. (*a*) Copy Fig. P1.B and show on it how the image of the object, seen by the observer, is formed. Indicate as precisely as you can the position of the image. The object is 3 cm from the mirror.

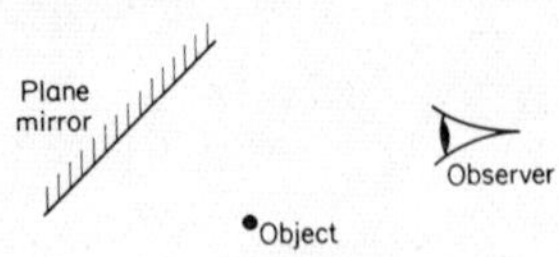

Fig. P1.B

(*b*) During the course of training for a life-saving certificate a boy is required to dive into the water and recover a brick from the bottom of the pool. At his first attempt he 'overshoots' and misses the brick. Suggest why this happens. Illustrate your answer with a diagram.

(*c*) Draw a labelled diagram to show what happens when a narrow beam of white light is passed into a 60° glass prism. (*S.E.*)

5. (*a*) Select from the following list the material you would use for: (i) the core of an electromagnet; (ii) a strong permanent magnet;

LEAD ZINC IRON COPPER MAGNESIUM STEEL.

(*b*) When the molecular structure of certain metals is distributed by hammering or by heating, they may become magnets. How would you explain this?

(*c*) Copy Fig. P1.C and indicate the type of magnetic field that exists.

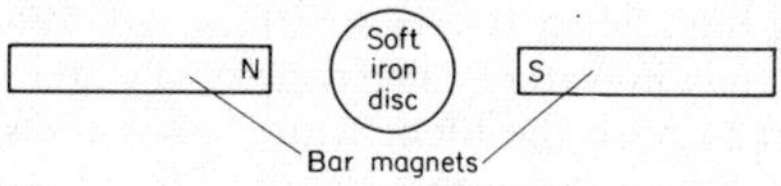

Fig. P1.C

Draw a similar diagram to show what changes, if any, would be produced on the field, by replacing the soft-iron disc by a brass disc. (*S.E.*)

6. Fig. P1.D is a diagram of a typical house wiring circuit. The light bulbs are all rated at 240 V 100 W and the power sockets are all 'shuttered' and designed for 13 amp fused-plugs.

(*a*) Which circuits contain faults and what are these faults?

(*b*) What fuses would be correct at A and B for maximum circuit safety?

(*c*) Draw a simple diagram of a circuit used to provide two-way switching for a single bulb on a staircase. (One switch at the bottom and the other at the top.) (*W.Md.*)

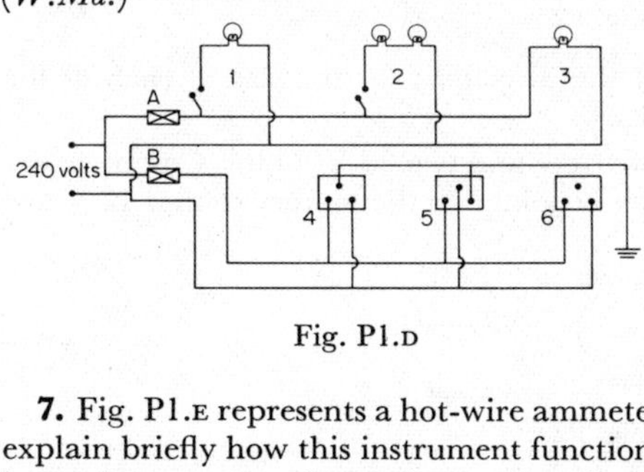

Fig. P1.D

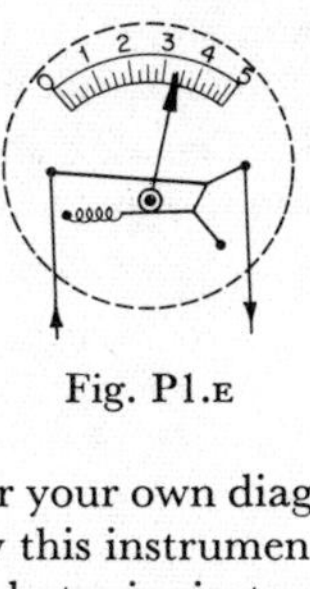

Fig. P1.E

7. Fig. P1.E represents a hot-wire ammeter. Using this, or your own diagram, explain briefly how this instrument functions. Explain why this instrument can be used to measure alternating current. In what ways is the hot-wire instrument inferior to a moving coil ammeter? (*M.*)

Revision Paper 2 · ANSWERS, p. 632

1. A beaker was found to have 60 g mass. Some liquid was poured in and the whole then had 112 g mass. What mass of liquid was poured in?

This was then poured into a measuring jar which already contained some of the liquid standing with its surface at the 35 cm³ mark. The surface rose to the

85 cm³ mark. What was the volume of the added liquid? Calculate the density of the liquid. (*Mx.*)

2. Complete the ray diagrams in Fig. P2.A (*Mx.*)

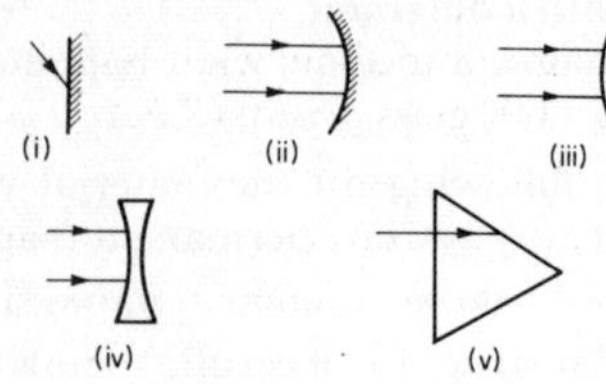

Fig. P2.A

3. A small inflatable rubber lifebelt has a volume of 10 000 cm³ when inflated. The weight of the lifebelt is very small indeed. What force is necessary to submerge it completely in water? (The density of water is 1 g/cm³.)

Is the force needed to push the lifebelt just below the surface any different from that required to take it down to a depth of 6 m? Give a reason for your answer.

Explain why a small lifebelt like the one mentioned above is able to support in the water, a man of weight 700 N.

A larger lifebelt is made of cork, whose relative density is 0·35, and the volume of the belt is 13 000 cm³. What volume of the lifebelt is *below* the waterline, when it floats in water? (*S.*)

4. Fig. P2.B shows a uniform steel rod, of length 20 cm and mass 2 kg, balanced at a point 4 cm from the end where a weight is attached. On the

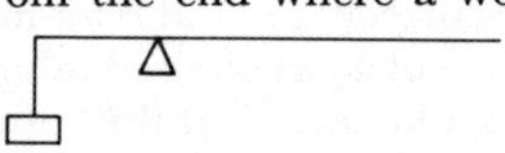

Fig. P2.B

diagram, show (*a*) the position; (*b*) the direction; (*c*) the size of each of the three forces acting on the rod. (*E.A.*)

5. (*a*) Fig. P2.C shows a 12 V car battery and two 36 W bulbs. Complete the diagram to show how both bulbs may be joined to the battery so that 12 V are

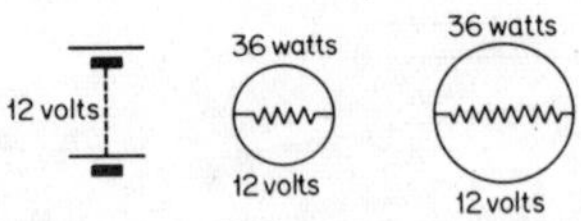

Fig. P2.C

applied to each. Include in your diagram a switch which will operate both bulbs at the same time: (*b*) when both bulbs are lit, what current is the battery supplying? (*L.*)

6. A water-heating system consists of a boiler, a hot-water storage cylinder, a cold-water cistern and connecting pipes. The water is heated either by a fire under the boiler or by an electric immersion heater in the cylinder.

(*a*) Make a diagram of the system showing how the hot water circulates and how hot water which has been drawn off can be replaced by cold water. Include in your drawing a pipe from which the hottest water in the system could be drawn.

(*b*) Which of the alternative methods of heating the water is the most efficient? Explain why.

(*c*) The storage cylinder is usually made of copper and is covered with a fibre glass jacket. Why are these two materials used?

(*d*) How much heat in megajoules (MJ) would be required to raise the temperature of the water in the cylinder from 15°C to 65°C if it holds 130 litres? (Specific heat capacity of water = 4200 J/kg °C. 1 MJ = 10^6 J.) (*S.*)

7. (*a*) If you want to replace the resistance wire on an electric fire, state all the factors that you would take into consideration.

(*b*) Describe the construction of an electric bell and how it operates from a battery circuit. What alterations would you have to make in the circuit if you wired it to the mains? (*W.Md.*)

8. (*a*) What is *alternating current*?

(*b*) With the aid of a diagram describe a simple A.C. generator. Explain how it produces A.C.

(*c*) Give sketches of the trace you see on a cathode-ray oscilloscope when the voltage applied to the deflector plates is: (i) A.C.; (ii) half-wave rectified A.C.; (iii) full -wave rectified A.C. (*Mx.*)

Revision Paper 3 · ANSWERS, p. 632

1. An object weighs more at the poles than at the equator because: (*a*) the earth is not truly shaped like a ball; (*b*) air rises at the equator; (*c*) the earth revolves round the sun; (*d*) the axis of the earth is inclined; (*e*) greater land masses exist at the poles. (*S.E.*)

2. Fig. P3.A shows the same bottle being used throughout the *four* weighings. Calculate the relative densities of the liquids 1 and 2. (*Mx.*)

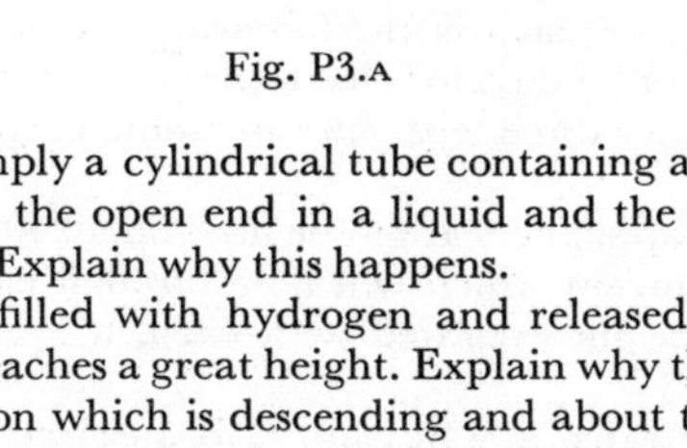

Fig. P3.A

3. (*a*) A syringe is simply a cylindrical tube containing a tight fitting piston. When it is placed with the open end in a liquid and the piston is drawn up, liquid rises in the tube. Explain why this happens.

(*b*) A small balloon filled with hydrogen and released in the atmosphere usually bursts when it reaches a great height. Explain why this is so.

(*c*) A man in a balloon which is descending and about to land, trails a very long rope. One end is firmly attached to the basket of the balloon. As more and more of the rope comes in contact with the ground the rate of descent is checked. Explain why this happens. (*S.E.*)

4. You are required to complete the table on p. 605. In defining size use, magnified, same size, or diminished. In defining nature, state whether real or virtual, erect or inverted, if possible. Only one practical use need be given in each case. (*W.M.*)

	Position of Object	*Image*			*Practical Use*
		Posn.	*Size*	*Nature*	
A. Concave Mirror	Between centre of curvature and focus				
	At the focus ..				
	Between focus and pole of mirror ..				
B. Convex Lens	Outside twice the focal length .				
	Between twice the focal length and the focus				
	Inside the focal length				

5. Consider the three statements given below and give a scientific reason for each of them:

(*a*) A voltmeter must never be put into an electrical circuit in such a way that the whole of the circuit current is expected to flow through it.

(*b*) Care must be taken when putting a moving-coil ammeter into a circuit to make certain that the current flows through it in the proper direction.

(*c*) A hot-wire ammeter can be used to measure both direct and alternating currents. (*M*)

6. (*a*) Name and describe the *four* methods by which heat can escape from a beaker of hot drink standing on a metal tray.

(*b*) Describe the construction of the vacuum (thermos) flask and explain how it reduces the escape of heat from the contents.

(*c*) 100 g of hot water was poured into a thermos flask and its temperature was found to be 80°C. To this was added some cold water at 20°C. The mixture was stirred and its final temperature was 40°C. Assuming that no heat escapes, find how much cold water was added. (*Mx.*)

7. (*a*) Give reasons for each of the following statements: (i) an alternating electric current cannot be used for electroplating; (ii) a plug carrying a mains lead should always have three pins; (iii) an ammeter should always have a low electrical resistance.

(*b*) The following appliances are to be used on a 240 V mains electrical supply. Calculate the current which will flow through each appliance and state which fuse should be incorporated with each, a 2 amp fuse, a 5 amp fuse or a 13 amp fuse.

(i) a television set rated at 140 watts; (ii) an electric iron rated at 750 W. (iii) an immersion heater of resistance 20Ω. (*M.*)

8. Fig. P3.B shows a simplified cathode-ray tube.

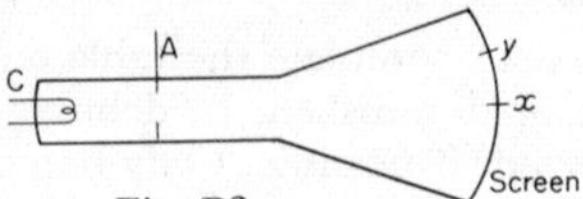

Fig. P3.B

(*a*) What will you do to make C produce electrons?

(*b*) What will you do to accelerate these electrons through A?

(*c*) These electrons will strike the screen at x. How would you deflect the electrons so that they strike the point y: (i) by an electric field; (ii) by a magnetic field? (To answer these, re-draw the diagram in your answer paper and add what you think is required.)

(*d*) With what is the screen coated? What happens when the electrons strike it? (*E.A.*)

Revision Paper 4 · ANSWERS, p. 632

1. Complete the table to show which units are used to measure the quantities indicated. If there are no units write *none*.

Quantity	One metric unit
Force	
Density	
Work	
Relative Density	

(*Mx.*)

2. If an empty bottle has 50 g mass and when filled with water 100 g mass, what is the mass when filled with a liquid of relative density 0·8? (*L.*)

3. Two tugs pull a ship into harbour. One pulls due north with a force of 40,000 newtons, the other due west with 50,000 newtons.

(*a*) By drawing a parallelogram find the magnitude and direction of the resultant force on the ship.

(*b*) If the ship accelerates from rest at a rate of 0·6 m/s^2, what is the speed of the ship after half a minute?

(*c*) The ship continues to move with this speed for 2 minutes and then comes to rest after a further minute. Draw a speed/time graph of the ship's motion for the whole $3\frac{1}{2}$ minutes. (*E.A.*)

4. Name the substances used in a dry cell for: (*a*) the positive pole; (*b*) the negative pole; (*c*) the electrolyte; (*d*) the depolarizer. (*Mx.*)

5. (*a*) What does Fig. P4.A illustrate?

(*b*) What form of energy is present: (i) at the point P; (ii) in the water droplets at Q; (iii) in the running water at R; (iv) in the water vapour at S.

(*c*) A lidless saucepan of hot water loses heat in four ways. What are the names of these?

(*d*) A copper can weighing 150 g, and containing 200 g of water, cools from 90°C

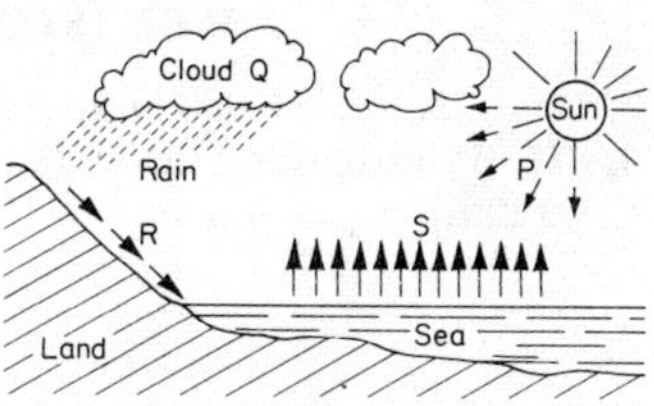

Fig. P4.A

to 70°C. If the specific heat capacity of water and copper is respectively 4·2 J and 0·4 J per g per deg C; (i) calculate the heat lost by the water; (ii) calculate the heat lost by the can; (iii) suggest *one* way in which the rate of cooling could be slowed down; (iv) suggest *one* way in which the rate of cooling could be increased. (*M.*)

6. (*a*) Draw a ray-diagram showing a converging lens forming a real image of an object.

(*b*) Draw a ray-diagram showing a diverging lens forming a virtual image of an object.

(*c*) Draw two ray-diagrams of an eye of a long sighted person looking at a point object a short distance from the eye, first without and then with a correcting lens.

(*d*) A camera has a variable aperture and a variable speed. What adjustments of these would you make to take a photograph of: (i) an athlete on a bright summer day; (ii) a cathedral? (*E.A.*)

7. (*a*) Give three sizes of plugs, stating the value of fuse available and name an appliance for which each would be suitable.

(*b*) Name the possible reasons for a fuse blowing and what steps you would take to check and repair the fault.

(*c*) Describe the construction and mode of action of the transformer in a model electric train circuit. What is its purpose? (*W.Md.*)

8. Describe, and explain in detail, the working of *one* of the following: (i) a microphone; (ii) a telephone earpiece; (iii) a loudspeaker. (*S.E.*)

ANSWERS TO REVISION PAPERS

REVISION PAPER 1 (p. 626)

2. (*a*) $x = 5$ m (*b*) 0·4 N (*c*) A–420 N, B–300 N **3.** (i) 40·2°C (ii) 313·2 K
5. (i) iron (ii) steel **6.** (*a*) 2, 5, 6 (*b*) 5 A, 30 A

REVISION PAPER 2 (p. 627)

1. 52 g; 50 cm³, 1·04 g/cm³ **3.** 100 N, 4550 cm³
4. (*c*) 30 N, 20 N, 50 N **5.** 6 A **6.** 27·3 MJ

REVISION PAPER 3 (p. 629)

1. *a* **2.** 0·8, 1·1 **6.** 200 g
7. (i) 7/12 A, 2 A fuse (ii) $3\frac{1}{8}$ A, 5 A fuse (iii) 12 A, 13 A fuse

REVISION PAPER 4 (p. 631)

2. 90 g **3.** (*a*) 64 000 N at N 51° W (*b*) 18 m/s
5. (*b*) (i) radiation (ii) potential (iii) kinetic (iv) heat (*d*) (i) 16 800 J (ii) 1200 J

INDEX